# PORTFOLIO
# AND
# INVESTMENT
# SELECTION:
# THEORY AND PRACTICE

# PORTFOLIO AND INVESTMENT SELECTION: THEORY AND PRACTICE

**Haim Levy**
*Hebrew University of Jerusalem and University of Florida, Gainesville*

**Marshall Sarnat**
*Hebrew University of Jerusalem*

**Prentice/Hall** PHI **International**

ENGLEWOOD CLIFFS, NEW JERSEY   LONDON   NEW DELHI   RIO DE JANEIRO
SINGAPORE   SYDNEY   TOKYO   TORONTO   WELLINGTON

*Library of Congress Cataloging in Publication Data*
Levy, Haim.
    Portfolio and investment selection.
    Bibliography: p.
    Includes index.
    1. Investment analysis.  2. Portfolio management.
I. Sarnat, Marshall.  II. Title.
HG4529.L48    1983    332.6    83-9727
ISBN 0-13-687558-0

*British Library Cataloging in Publication Data*
Levy, Haim
    Portfolio and investment selection
    1. Investment—Decision making.
    I. Title    II. Sarnat, Marshall
    332.6    HG4527

    ISBN 0-13-687558-0

ISBN 0-13-687558-0

PRENTICE-HALL INTERNATIONAL, INC., London
PRENTICE-HALL OF AUSTRALIA PTY., LTD., Sydney
PRENTICE-HALL CANADA, INC., Toronto
PRENTICE-HALL OF INDIA PRIVATE LIMITED, New Delhi
PRENTICE-HALL OF JAPAN, INC., Tokyo
PRENTICE-HALL OF SOUTHEAST ASIA PTE., LTD., Singapore
PRENTICE-HALL, INC., Englewood Cliffs, New Jersey
PRENTICE-HALL DO BRASIL LTDA., Rio de Janeiro
WHITEHALL BOOKS LIMITED, Wellington, New Zealand

Printed in the United States of America

10 9 8 7 6 5 4 3

# Contents

# PART II

# THE FOUNDATIONS OF INVESTMENT DECISION-MAKING    75

# PART IV
# EQUILIBRIUM MODELS: THEORY AND EMPIRICAL TESTS    393

# Preface

In less than a generation the field of finance has undergone a major revolution. Traditional decision-making methods and rules of thumb for the selection of risk assets have given way to more sophisticated tools, which have evolved from the relatively recent theories of risk diversification and portfolio balance. Today many institutional investors provide a "beta service", a concept unheard of among the Wall Street practitioners less than a generation ago.

This book incorporates recent advances in efficiency analysis which permit the derivation of decision rules from easily understood assumptions regarding investors' underlying attitudes toward risk. A great deal of effort has been expended (with some success, we hope) to make the innovations in efficiency analysis which have shaped the "New Finance" accessible to the nonmathematical reader. The text emphasizes diagrammatic presentation which can readily be followed without formal mathematical training. Technical appendices have been added for those readers who desire more rigorous proofs of the verbal and geometric arguments of the text. It should be emphasized, however, that although the text can be read independently of the appendices, some familiarity with the text is necessary if the appendices are to be placed in their proper perspective. More specifically, we have had in mind the requirements of that, by now proverbial, student of business and economics "who knows only high school algebra", but since we are "risk averters", two brief elementary Mathematical and Statistical Supplements have been included just in case.

Some of the theoretical models which characterize the "New Finance" are presented in this book. To make the theoretical models more digestible, we apply the theoretical formulas to actual data, and whenever possible computer outputs are reviewed in the text, which illustrates the ever growing role of computers in modern portfolio selection and decision-making. Moreover, some short computer programs are reproduced in full in the appendices of the appropriate chapters, in the hope that some students at least will try to run them on the installations in their universities.

We believe that the end-of-chapter problems and the data case problems constitute one of the strongest points of this text. Many of these problems are based on real data, in an attempt to bring the student closer to the desired goal of bridging between theory and practice. Also, the Data Set supplement at the end of the book includes actual data which are used in the many case problems accompanying every chapter. Some of the data set problems actually force the student to use the computer, as they cannot be solved by manual calculations. Some relatively difficult "extra-credit" problems have been included for the benefit of the more advanced students. They are identified by an asterisk (*).

The book provides a flexible teaching instrument and has been used as the basis for both one- and two-semester courses in investment analysis and portfolio selection at several universities. Both the students and their teachers survived, and with no apparent ill effects.

We also hope that the book will prove of more than passing interest to professional investment analysts and portfolio managers, thereby helping to bridge at least partly over the gap which has emerged between the more experienced practitioners of the art of decision-making under risk and uncertainty and some of their academic colleagues.

This book is an outgrowth of an earlier text entitled *Investment and Portfolio Analysis*, published in 1972. However a quick comparison of the two tables of contents will be more than enough to convince the reader that the differences between the two texts far outweigh the commonalities. The present volume actually constitutes an entirely new textbook rather than a revision of the 1972 book. To be more specific, chapters 3, 9, 10, 12, 13, 14, 16, 17 and 19 present new material which does not exist at all in the previous edition. Those chapters that do appear in the 1972 book have been updated and thoroughly revised, and, we hope, greatly improved in the process.

We would like to thank our students at the University of Florida, University of California, Berkely and Los Angeles, University of Pennsylvania, University of Toronto and the Hebrew University of Jerusalem for their roles as "guinea-pigs" in the development of this text. We used the material in the book in various combinations in graduate courses at these universities and we believe the presentation greatly benefited from the actual teaching experience and from the many critical comments of our students.

We would like to acknowledge the help of the many people whose valuable suggestions and assistance greatly improved both the 1972 edition and the present revision:

| | | |
|---|---|---|
| Johan Ankerstjerne | Jeffrey Callen | Yoram Landskroner |
| Fred D. Arditti | Julian Franks | Azriel Levy |
| M. J. Arlington | Dan Galai | Moshe Levy |
| Rinat Bahat | Mira Gelbshtein | Tal Mundlak |
| Moshe Ben-Horim | Myron J. Gordon | Alexander Robichek |
| Simon Beninga | Giora Hanoch | Latha Shenkar |
| Avi Bick | Nancy L. Jacob | Esther Tuval |
| Hilda Bin-Nun | Yehuda Kahane | Julie Westberry |
| Robert Brooks | Yoram Kroll | Mordechai Yalovsky |
| Mary Broske | Menachem Landau | Adel Zarmati |

We owe special thanks to Zvi Lerman who for two years provided assistance far beyond the call of duty.

We will welcome any comments and suggestions for further improvement of the text from all the future users.

HAIM LEVY
MARSHALL SARNAT

# Introduction

Man should always divide his wealth into three parts: one-third in land, one-third in commerce and one-third retained in his own hands.

*Babylonian Talmud*

The sages of the Talmud suggested what is perhaps the world's first diversified investment portfolio, and despite the vicissitudes of fifteen hundred years their device is not without merit even today. A formal statement of the theory of risk diversification and portfolio selection, however, did not become available until the 1950s when Harry Markowitz and James Tobin published their pioneering studies.[1] This book is nothing more than an attempt to explain, in a systematic manner, why for almost two millennia most investors (but not necessarily economists) have been following the advice implied in the Talmudic dictum.

## 1    Positive and Normative Aspects

Diversification of investment, following Markowitz, is usually classified as the subject of the theory of portfolio selection. Portfolio theory, like most economic theories, has two distinct aspects: (a) viewed as a *positive* theory, it attempts to explain and predict phenomena in capital markets, (b) viewed as a *normative* theory, it sets out criteria concerning the ways in which investment decisions *should* be made and stipulates the rules for attaining desired ends. We owe this distinction to John Neville Keynes, the distinguished Victorian logician and political economist, and the father of a very famous son who made his mark not only in economics but in the art of finance as well.[2]

The distinction of positive from normative theory can also provide a long overdue funeral for that old chestnut, "Well, that may be all right in theory but it is no good in

---

[1] H. M. Markowitz, "Portfolio Selection", *Journal of Finance* VII (March 1952), and *Portfolio Selection*, New York: Wiley, 1959; J. Tobin, "Liquidity Preference As Behavior Towards Risk", *Review of Economic Studies* XXVI (February 1958).

[2] The significance of the elder Keynes' distinction was rediscovered and analyzed in detail by Milton Friedman in his essay, "The Methodology of Positive Economics", in *Essays in Positive Economics*, Chicago and London: University of Chicago Press, 1953.

practice." From the positive standpoint, a theory whose explanations and predictions do not hold true for the class of phenomena to which it applies is simply a "bad" theory and should be replaced. This also follows from more general considerations of the philosophy of science which suggest that an infinity of theories exist to explain the necessarily finite number of observed facts.[3] Thus to be acceptable a theory must provide the best available explanation (prediction) of the phenomena being studied.

In the above sense we seek a realistic explanation of investment behavior and of security markets. But it should be noted that to be useful, a theory must be abstract; we seek a map which can guide us through the complex maze of decision-making under uncertainty rather than a detailed photograph which only reproduces the complexities of the maze itself.

Throughout the book we present and discuss several theories. In all cases we first stipulate the set of assumptions underlying the specific theoretical model. Then we present, whenever possible, empirical evidence which tests the predictive power of the theoretical model. In some cases, even though the assumptions used to derive a theoretical model are unrealistic (e.g., the no-tax assumption), still the model is found to have high predictive power and is therefore considered a "good" model.

Remember that if we make no assumptions whatsoever in deriving a theoretical model, we end up with a detailed photograph of the maze (namely the stock market) which is too complex to comprehend. Thus, we must make simplifying assumptions (e.g. no taxes, no transaction costs, etc.) in order to replace the complicated real-life photograph with a simpler map which can guide us through the maze.

Since the quality of a theoretical model can be judged either by the logic of the underlying assumptions or by its predictive power, we make an effort to weave empirical evidence with the theoretical models almost in every chapter. Some models are initially derived under highly restrictive (and possibly unacceptable) assumptions. Once the main results of the model emerge and are understood, some of the initial assumptions are gradually relaxed to obtain a model based on more sound and realistic assumptions. As an analogy, we start with a rough map of the maze rather than with a full photograph. But once we have looked at the map and know which direction to take, we build in additional detail (e.g., relax some assumptions), which refine our walk through the maze, and hopefully also our decision-making in the face of uncertainty.

## 2     Plan of the Book

This book is divided into five parts. Part I, in essence, is an introduction to the book. Chapter 1 outlines the structure of the capital markets, the various existing financial instruments, and in particular the relative importance of stocks, bonds, and options in the securities markets. The relative importance of stocks and bonds in the US, Canada, the major European countries and Japan is presented and analyzed. Chapter 2 sets out the

---

[3] *Ibid.*, p. 9. It also follows that although a theory can be rejected, we cannot establish the "truth" of a particular theory since there always exists the possibility of finding an alternative hypothesis which can account for the same phenomena.

fundamentals underlying the measurement of profitability to investors in securities. We also present the historical records of rates of return from which we can learn about the basic characteristics of the rates of return distributions of various securities, an essential input for constructing investment portfolios.

Part II is devoted to two major topics. The first is a general framework for decision-making under *certainty* (Chapter 3). The second topic focuses on foundations of decision-making under *uncertainty*. It is covered in three chapters: Chapter 4 presents and analyzes various approaches to choice among risky assets and lays the foundations for the expected utility criterion. Chapter 5 analyzes alternative preference structures, while Chapter 6 presents the stochastic dominance rules which require only limited partial information about the decision-maker's preferences.

Part III is devoted to the mean–variance (MV) analysis of portfolio selection. Chapter 7 presents the foundations of the mean–variance criterion. Chapter 8 applies the mean–variance criterion to portfolio selection. Chapter 9 describes in detail the actual technique used to trace the MV efficient frontier. Chapter 10 deals with the Single Index Model (SIM)—a method which attempts to determine the MV efficient portfolios in a relatively simple manner.

In Part IV we develop equilibrium models for the pricing of risky assets. We first derive the well-known Capital Asset Pricing Model (CAPM—Chapter 11) and define the risk index, beta. Chapter 12 is devoted to measuring the risk index (beta) in practice. Chapter 13 relaxes some of the original CAPM assumption and provides alternative theoretical models, with an emphasis on the recent Arbitrage Pricing Theory (APT). In Chapter 14 the empirical evidence relating to the equilibrium models is presented and discussed. Finally, Chapter 15 focuses on investment performance measures, based mainly on the CAPM framework. In this chapter, the empirical evidence and the theoretical models are given side by side.

Part V is devoted to issues which recently aroused considerable interest among academicians and practitioners alike. Chapter 16 provides a background survey of the options market and analyzes the basic features of the various types of options. The equilibrium models of option valuation and the empirical evidence testing these models are given in Chapter 17. Chapter 18 is an application of the portfolio model to problems of international finance, where we examine the potential of risk reduction by means of holding an internationally diversified portfolio. Chapter 19 concludes the book with a discussion of market efficiency. We first present the various definitions of market efficiency and then survey the empirical tests which challenge the efficiency hypothesis.

# PART I

## The Capital Markets:
## Survey and the Historical Record

# 1

# The Capital Market

Investment and portfolio decisions are taken within the framework provided by a complex of financial institutions and intermediaries which together comprise the capital market. It is this market which provides the mechanism for channeling current savings into investment in productive facilities, that is, for allocating the country's capital resources among alternative uses. In effect, the capital market provides an economy's link with the future, since current decisions regarding the allocation of capital resources are a major determining factor of tomorrow's output. The crucial role played by the capital market in shaping the pattern and growth of real output imparts a social significance to individual investment and portfolio decisions.

## 1.1    The Primary Securities Market

To place the capital market in proper perspective it is useful to distinguish between the "primary" and "secondary" securities markets. The primary market for securities is the *new issues* market which brings together the "supply and demand" or "sources and uses" for new capital funds. In this market the principal source of funds is the domestic savings of consumers and businesses; other suppliers include foreign investors and state and local governments. The principal uses of funds are: the long-term financing of the investment in housing (mortgages), the long-term investment of corporations and other businesses, and the long-term borrowing of federal, state, and local government. The ultimate suppliers of funds are those sectors with a surplus of current income over expenditure (savings); and these funds flow to their ultimate users, namely, economic units which issue securities to finance a surplus of expenditures over their current incomes.

In a highly developed capital market by far the largest proportion of individuals' savings reaches the new issues market *indirectly* via a financial intermediary. For example, the savings of most individuals are channeled to an ultimate user, say a corporation desiring to finance an expansion of its productive facilities, via a pension

3

fund, an insurance company, an investment company, or a similar institution. More-over, most individual investors are unfamiliar with the new issues market and its institu-tions, such as underwriters and selling syndicates which serve as middlemen between the corporate demanders of funds and the individual investors and financial institutions which supply the funds. To most investors the term *securities market* is synonymous with the "stock exchange".

## 1.2  The Secondary Securities Market

The purpose of a stock exchange or *secondary* securities market, like any other organized market, is to enable buyers and sellers to effect their transactions more quickly and cheaply than they could otherwise. However, since a stock exchange typically deals in *existing* securities rather than in new issues, its economic significance may be misunderstood.

As we noted above, the primary function of the capital market relates to the chan-neling of savings into capital formation; hence the capital market's economic sig-nificance stems from its impact on the allocation of capital resources among alternative uses. But an increase in the volume of securities trading in the stock market does *not* represent an increase in the economy's aggregate savings, every purchase of an *existing* security being exactly offset by the sale of the same security. For the economy as a whole, an increase in savings in the form of securities ownership is measured by the volume of net new issues of securities, while transactions in existing securities represent shifts among owners, which always cancel out in the aggregate. Similarly, transactions in existing securities do not provide additional funds to finance capital formation; here again it is the volume of net new issues which provides additional financing to business enterprises. An analogy can readily be drawn from the automobile market. The sales of new Ford cars (new issues) by the Ford Motor Company (issuing firm) provide revenue (investment funds) to the company; transactions in older models of Ford cars (existing securities) in the used car market (stock exchange) do not. But just as the existence of a resale market for cars affects the willingness of consumers to purchase new Fords, the availability of an efficient secondary market for securities is one of the more important factors inducing investors to acquire new issues of securities. And the connection between the primary and secondary markets is even stronger in the case of the securities market, since new issues are often close, or even perfect, substitutes for outstanding securities.

The basic economic function of a stock exchange is to provide marketability for long-term investments, thereby reducing the personal risk incurred by investors and broadening the supply of equity and long-term debt capital for the financing of business enterprise. For example, even though the investment in a common stock is fixed for the life of the firm, the ability to shift ownership to others during the course of this period permits more individuals to participate in the long-term financing of companies. In an economy with a well developed secondary securities market, the fixed investment of firms is provided by a changing group of individuals, none of whom may have been willing to commit his personal resources for the entire or even a substantial part of the life of the enterprise. Thus in an efficient stock exchange the supply of credit, which from the private investor's viewpoint is often inherently short-term, is transformed into a supply of long-term investment funds for the financing of capital formation. The ability to transfer the risks of investment forges a link between the stock exchange and the new issues market, and this greatly enhances the ability of business enterprises to mobilize additional long-term capital to finance the creation of new, or the expansion of existing, production facilities.

To effectively fulfill its functions as an allocator of capital, the securities market should be influenced solely by economic considerations; the prices of the various securities should reflect their expected returns and risk characteristics. In an efficient market current prices for a company's securities will reflect the investors' best estimates of the firm's anticipated profitability and of the risks attaching to these profits. And since—other things being equal—rising stock prices attract investors, the allocation of capital will be *biased* in favor of firms with relatively high levels of risk-adjusted profits. On the other hand, firms with low profitability or excessive riskiness will find it difficult, expensive, or on occasion even impossible to raise additional capital for expansion.

The prerequisites for such an efficient securities market are roughly the same as those of any "perfect" or purely competitive market:

(a)  the products traded in the market must be homogeneous;
(b)  the market must be comprised of many relatively small buyers and sellers;
(c)  there must be free entry and exit into and out of the market.

Although a securities market is made up of many types of securities (common stocks, preferred stocks, and bonds) of a large number of companies, each class of securities is homogeneous in the sense that the risk-adjusted rates of return of the various classes of securities comprise homogeneous commodities. One share of a given risk class is as good as any other and therefore they must sell at the same price. In addition, a modern securities market is made up of a large number of relatively small buyers and sellers so that it is difficult for any individual to influence prices. For example, there are over three million shareholders on record of American Telephone and Telegraph stock, no one of whom owns as much as 1% of the outstanding shares. On the other hand, although anyone who owns a security can always sell it to anyone willing to buy it, entry into the market proper, for example acquiring a seat on the stock exchange, is not free. But even when such deviations are taken into account, it is to the stock exchange that we often point when in need of a real life model which approximates the "perfect" market of economic theory.[1] The last chapter of this book (Chapter 19) deals with these aspects within a modern formal framework known as "market efficiency".

This rather sanguine view of the stock market and its impact on the allocation of capital is not universally held. To some the New York Stock Exchange is a den of iniquity; to other, more sophisticated, observers stock market prices reflect mass

---

[1] See William J. Baumol, *The Stock Market and Economic Efficiency*, New York: Fordham University Press, 1965.

psychology with little if any connection to underlying economic values. The case against the stock exchange was most forcibly expressed during the 1930s by the most famous economist of the time, John Maynard Keynes. In a characteristically brilliant passage which goes a long way towards explaining his own success as an investor, Keynes described the stock exchange as a place where most investors attempt to guess what average opinion thinks average opinion will be like one month hence, while others practice the "fourth, fifth and higher degrees" of this art.[2]

It should be recalled that Keynes was writing at a time when a worldwide financial crisis had so undermined public confidence that stock prices did often appear to be unconnected with any underlying economic values. Taking a somewhat longer view, however, there is really no inherent contradiction between the kind of speculative behavior which Keynes described and the thesis that stock prices, in the long run, reflect economic values. For this purpose it is sufficient that some investors become conditioned to the fact that stock prices rise when profits and dividends increase, so that it "pays" to exploit all available information in an attempt to anticipate such possibilities. The available statistical evidence suggests that Keynes notwithstanding, the pure speculator does *not* rule the roost, and therefore the quest for quick capital gains has not divorced the trend in the price of a company's stock from the expectation of future profits.

## 1.3    The Securities Exchanges

Although regional stock exchanges exist in a dozen cities all over the USA, the two largest US markets are located a stone's throw from one another in the heart of the New York financial district. These are the so-called "Big and Little Big Boards", the New York and American Stock Exchanges. Taken together these two national exchanges dominate the US capital market.

As we can see from Table 1.1, the NYSE is by far the biggest exchange. This table illustrates the dollar volume of equity securities on the various US exchanges (excluding options). The NYSE accounts for more than 80% of the total volume. Changing over from dollar volume to share volume does not alter materially the figures of Table 1.1. Thus, the NYSE, which is the oldest exchange (founded in 1792), is also the biggest and the most important.

A breakdown of the volume of sales by type of security reveals that sales of stocks account for about 93% of the total market value of sales on US exchanges in 1979 while options account for about 7% of the total volume (see Table 1.2). However, note the increasing role of options in recent years. Table 1.2 reveals that not only academics show increased interest in options, but also investors who regard the options market and its wide range of colorful combinations as highly attractive.

Thus, we see an overall tendency for growth in the activity of the US exchanges,

[2] John Maynard Keynes, *The General Theory of Employment Interest and Money*, New York: Harcourt Brace, 1936, p. 156.

**Table 1.1**
**Dollar Volume by Exchanges\* (in percentages)**

| Year | Total Dollar Volume ($ '000) | NYSE | AMEX | MIDW | PSE | PHLE | BOSE | CNSE | Other‡ |
|------|------------------------------|-------|-------|------|------|------|------|------|--------|
| 1935 | 15,396,139 | 86.64 | 7.83 | 1.32 | 1.39 | 0.88 | 1.34 | 0.04 | 0.56 |
| 1940 | 8,419,772 | 85.17 | 7.68 | 2.07 | 1.52 | 1.11 | 1.91 | 0.09 | 0.45 |
| 1945 | 16,284,552 | 82.75 | 10.81 | 2.00 | 1.78 | 0.96 | 1.16 | 0.06 | 0.48 |
| 1950 | 21,808,284 | 85.91 | 6.85 | 2.35 | 2.19 | 1.03 | 1.12 | 0.11 | 0.44 |
| 1955 | 38,039,107 | 86.31 | 6.98 | 2.44 | 1.90 | 1.03 | 0.78 | 0.09 | 0.47 |
| 1960 | 45,309,825 | 83.80 | 9.35 | 2.72 | 1.94 | 1.03 | 0.60 | 0.07 | 0.49 |
| 1961 | 64,071,623 | 82.43 | 10.71 | 2.75 | 1.99 | 1.03 | 0.49 | 0.07 | 0.53 |
| 1962 | 54,855,293 | 86.32 | 6.81 | 2.75 | 2.00 | 1.05 | 0.46 | 0.07 | 0.54 |
| 1963 | 64,437,900 | 85.19 | 7.51 | 2.72 | 2.39 | 1.06 | 0.41 | 0.06 | 0.66 |
| 1964 | 72,461,584 | 83.49 | 8.45 | 3.15 | 2.48 | 1.14 | 0.42 | 0.06 | 0.81 |
| 1965 | 89,549,093 | 81.78 | 9.91 | 3.44 | 2.43 | 1.12 | 0.42 | 0.08 | 0.82 |
| 1966 | 123,697,737 | 79.77 | 11.84 | 3.14 | 2.84 | 1.10 | 0.56 | 0.07 | 0.68 |
| 1967 | 162,189,211 | 77.29 | 14.48 | 3.08 | 2.79 | 1.13 | 0.66 | 0.03 | 0.54 |
| 1968 | 197,116,367 | 73.55 | 17.99 | 3.12 | 2.65 | 1.13 | 1.04 | 0.01 | 0.51 |
| 1969 | 176,389,759 | 73.48 | 17.59 | 3.39 | 3.12 | 1.43 | 0.67 | 0.01 | 0.31 |
| 1970 | 131,707,946 | 78.44 | 11.11 | 3.76 | 3.81 | 1.99 | 0.67 | 0.03 | 0.19 |
| 1971 | 186,375,130 | 79.07 | 9.98 | 4.00 | 3.79 | 2.29 | 0.58 | 0.05 | 0.24 |
| 1972 | 205,956,263 | 77.77 | 10.37 | 4.29 | 3.94 | 2.56 | 0.75 | 0.05 | 0.27 |
| 1973 | 178,863,622 | 82.07 | 6.06 | 4.54 | 3.55 | 2.45 | 1.00 | 0.06 | 0.27 |
| 1974 | 118,828,272 | 83.62 | 4.39 | 4.89 | 3.50 | 2.02 | 1.23 | 0.06 | 0.29 |
| 1975 | 157,555,469 | 85.04 | 3.66 | 4.82 | 3.25 | 1.72 | 1.18 | 0.17 | 0.16 |
| 1976 | 195,224,815 | 84.35 | 3.87 | 4.75 | 3.82 | 1.68 | 0.93 | 0.53 | 0.07 |
| 1977 | 187,393,082 | 83.96 | 4.60 | 4.79 | 3.53 | 1.62 | 0.73 | 0.74 | 0.03 |
| 1978 | 249,603,319 | 84.35 | 6.17 | 4.19 | 2.84 | 1.63 | 0.61 | 0.17 | 0.04 |
| 1979 | 300,728,389 | 83.65 | 6.93 | 3.82 | 2.85 | 1.80 | 0.56 | 0.35 | 0.04 |

\* Dollar volume for exchanges includes stocks, rights and warrants.
‡ Others include all exchanges not listed above.

*Source:* SEC 46th Annual Report, 1980.

**Table 1.2**
**Dollar Volume of Equity Securities on US Exchanges ($ '000)**

| Year | Total Volume at Market Value | Stocks | Options | Warrants | Rights |
|------|------|------|------|------|------|
| 1974 | 120,488,495 | 118,434,000 | 1,660,220 | 389,251 | 4,301 |
| 1975 | 163,978,938 | 157,260,586 | 6,423,469 | 285,859 | 9,024 |
| 1976 | 206,959,037 | 194,969,057 | 11,734,222 | 248,124 | 7,634 |
| 1977 | 198,292,217 | 187,202,855 | 10,399,135 | 184,435 | 5,792 |
| 1978 | 268,508,724 | 249,257,272 | 18,953,204 | 343,723 | 2,323 |
| 1979 | 323,899,993 | 299,973,110 | 22,725,724 | 748,361 | 6,918 |

*Source*: SEC 46th Annual Report, 1980.

with the options market registering a truly outstanding growth in recent years. Some indication of the growth of the securities market can be gleaned from the fact that on March 16, 1830, the dullest day in the history of the New York Stock Exchange, only 31 shares were traded; 138 years later, on April 10, 1968, NYSE recorded its first 20 million share trading day, and just 10 years later, April 17, 1978, became the first 60 million share day in history.

### 1.3.1   Stocks Versus Bonds on Various US Exchanges

Traded securities are not limited to equities (stocks, warrants, rights, and options): another important component of the securities market are bonds—debt instruments issued by corporations, central governments, and local municipal and state authorities in order to borrow money from the public. Bonds promise the investors periodic interest payments in the form of so-called coupons (usually paid every six or twelve months) and repayment of principal on maturity date.

Table 1.3 presents the market value of all stocks and bonds listed on all the US securities markets for the period 1965–1981. The proportion of bonds in the total market value of listed securities increased from around 35% in the 1960s and the early 1970s to over 50% in the second half of the 1970s and in the early 1980s. This represents an overall increase in debt financing in the US during the last decade. Since equity securities are only issued by business corporations, whereas bonds are issued also by the Federal government, by state and local governments, and even by some Federal agencies, it is appropriate to examine the proportion of corporate bonds out of the total securities issued by US corporations. These data are also set out in Table 1.3, which shows that the proportion of corporate bonds out of all corporate securities nearly doubled from 15% in 1965 to 27% in 1981. This pattern points to a significant shift from predominantly equity financing of US corporations to a financing mix with a much higher debt component.

Table 1.4 gives the composition of all listed bonds in the US by main issuing categories. We see from the table that the corporate bonds steadily account for around

## Table 1.3
### Market Value of Listed Stocks and Bonds in the USA
### ($ Billions)

| Year | Stocks (1) | Bonds Total (2) | Bonds Corporate (3) | Proportion of All Bonds out of Total Market Value of All Securities (%) (2)/[(1) + (2)] | Proportion of Corporate Bonds out of Corporate Securities (%) (3)/[(1) + (3)] |
|------|-----------|-------|-----------|-----|-----|
| 1965 | 714   | 382   | 123 | 35 | 15 |
| 1970 | 864   | 541   | 206 | 39 | 19 |
| 1971 | 1,030 | 594   | 231 | 37 | 18 |
| 1972 | 1,169 | 634   | 252 | 35 | 18 |
| 1973 | 921   | 680   | 264 | 42 | 22 |
| 1974 | 662   | 742   | 287 | 53 | 30 |
| 1975 | 812   | 855   | 317 | 51 | 28 |
| 1976 | 943   | 973   | 354 | 51 | 27 |
| 1977 | 997   | 1,113 | 391 | 53 | 28 |
| 1978 | 1,044 | 1,233 | 422 | 54 | 29 |
| 1979 | 1,183 | 1,374 | 454 | 54 | 28 |
| 1980 | 1,516 | 1,520 | 504 | 50 | 25 |
| 1981 | 1,432 | 1,682 | 533 | 54 | 27 |

*Source*: OECD Financial Statistics, various issues.

## Table 1.4
### Breakdown of the Market Value of Listed US Bonds by Issuer (in percent)

| Year | Corporations | Federal Government | Federal Agencies | State and Local Governments | Total |
|------|-------------|--------------------|------------------|------------------------------|-------|
| 1965 | 32.2 | 37.2 | 4.4  | 26.2 | 100.0 |
| 1970 | 38.1 | 26.5 | 8.9  | 26.5 | 100.0 |
| 1971 | 38.9 | 24.4 | 8.7  | 28.0 | 100.0 |
| 1972 | 39.8 | 23.2 | 9.8  | 27.2 | 100.0 |
| 1973 | 38.8 | 20.9 | 12.3 | 28.0 | 100.0 |
| 1974 | 38.7 | 19.2 | 14.1 | 28.0 | 100.0 |
| 1975 | 37.1 | 21.8 | 14.1 | 27.0 | 100.0 |
| 1976 | 36.4 | 24.8 | 14.4 | 24.4 | 100.0 |
| 1977 | 35.1 | 25.6 | 14.9 | 24.4 | 100.0 |
| 1978 | 34.3 | 25.4 | 16.7 | 23.6 | 100.0 |
| 1979 | 33.0 | 25.3 | 18.9 | 22.8 | 100.0 |
| 1980 | 33.2 | 26.2 | 18.4 | 22.2 | 100.0 |
| 1981 | 31.7 | 27.7 | 19.1 | 21.5 | 100.0 |

*Source*: OECD Financial Statistics, various issues.

30–40% of the total listed debt financing over the years. Although the share of the Federal government shrank from 37% in 1965 to 28% in 1981, the share of the Federal agencies increased dramatically from 4% in 1965 to 19% in 1981, so that the total proportion of Federal-backed bonds remained fairly steady at around 40–45% over the years. State and local governments account for the remaining 20–30% of all listed bonds over the years.

There is a significant difference in the listing pattern of stocks and bonds on the different US exchanges. While around 75–80% of the total equity is listed on the New York Stock Exchange, NYSE accounts for only 35–40% of the total bonds (in market value). This is due to the fact that NYSE lists only corporate bonds, US government bonds, and New York City bonds, while the rest of state and municipal bonds are listed on other exchanges.

### 1.3.2   Security Exchanges Outside the USA

Stocks and bonds are issued by corporations and governments in all the developed countries, where they are traded domestically on the national exchanges. Table 1.5 lists data on the market value of listed securities on some exchanges around the world. Although the figures are given in the domestic currency of each country, which complicates comparison across exchanges, even so it is easily seen that the US security market is by far the largest in the world (allowing for the exchange rates of the various currencies to the dollar). Indeed, the pie chart in Figure 1.1 shows that the US securities market represented nearly 50% of the world equity and bond market at the end of 1980. In other words, the US security exchanges match all the exchanges in Europe, Asia, Canada, and Australia combined.

Another interesting factor is the proportion of bonds versus stocks in different countries. On the whole, bonds have a higher weight in the securities markets outside the United States. While US equities represent more than half the world equity markets, it is the non-US bonds that predominate in the world bond markets (accounting for over 60% of the bond market—see Figure 1.1). In countries such as Austria, Germany, and Japan, bonds account for more than 80% of the total value of all outstanding securities, compared to about 50% in the US (see Table 1.5). This means that financing by debt is much more prevalent among businesses outside the US, whereas American corporations, despite the clear increase in debt financing in recent years, still finance the major part of their investments by equity.

Figure 1.2 demonstrates the relative weights of various non-US equity markets at the end of 1980. Japan is by far the largest market outside the US, accounting for 34% of non-US equity in the world. Second on the list is the United Kingdom with 18.1%, followed by Canada with nearly 11% and Germany with less than 7%. The leaders in non-US bond markets (Figure 1.3) are also Japan (with 31.2%), Germany (16%), and the United Kingdom (12%). Thus, while the US securities market is the largest in the world, Japan has the largest securities market outside the US, while the biggest securities exchanges in Europe are Germany and the United Kingdom. It is also worth

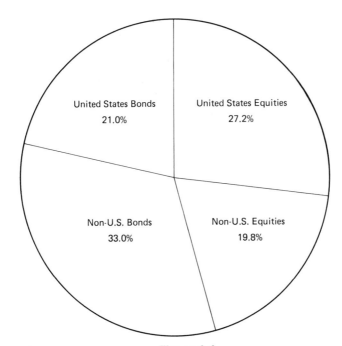

**Figure 1.1**
**Size of World Equity and Bond Markets at the End of 1980 in Billions of US Dollars**
**(World Total = $5,289.9 Billion)**

*Source:* R. Ibbotson, C. R. Carr, and A. W. Robinson, "International Equity and Bond Returns",
*Financial Analysts Journal,* July–Aug. 1982.

**Table 1.5**
**Market Value of Listed Stocks and Bonds on Various Exchanges Around the**
**World (in millions of domestic currency)***

| Country | Stocks | Bonds | Proportion of Bonds out of Total Listed Securities (percent) |
|---------|--------|-------|:---:|
| Austria | OS 68,708 | OS 376,336 | 85 |
| Finland | FM 39,343 | FM 32,853 | 45 |
| France | FF 232,260 | FF 580,500 | 71 |
| Germany | DM 91,420 | DM 616,517 | 87 |
| Israel | IS 98,947 | IS 61,889 | 38 |
| Italy | Lit 7,185,500 | Lit 15,638,900 | 69 |
| Japan | Y 21,551,500 | Y 174,603,600 | 89 |
| United Kingdom | £90,119 | £70,676 | 44 |
| USA | $1,432,396 | $1,682,358 | 54 |

* All data for end of 1981, except Finland and United Kingdom (1980).

*Source: OECD Financial Statistics,* 1982; Israel Statistical Abstract, 1982.

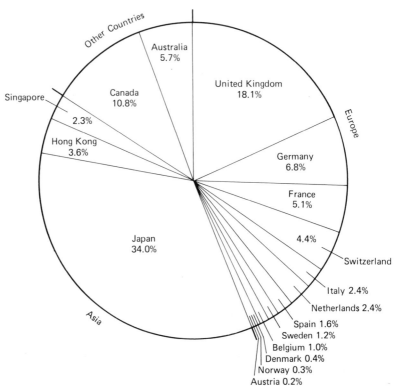

**Figure 1.2**
**Market Values of Non-US Equities at the End of 1980 in Billions of US Dollars**
**(Non-US Equity Total = $1,049.3 Billion)**

*Source:* R. Ibbotson, C. R. Carr, and A. W. Robinson, "International Equity and Bond Returns", *Financial Analysts Journal*, July–Aug. 1982.

mentioning that US crossborder bonds, traded in dollars in the Euromarket, account for as much as 6.3% of the world bond market.

The bond market, while certainly less colorful than the stock market, definitely cannot be ignored on the world scene. In most chapters of this book we analyze decision-making under uncertainty, which includes decisions about investment in stocks and bonds alike.

## 1.4    Placing an Order

The New York Stock Exchange provides a continuous auction market in listed securities, but as active trading on the floor of the Exchange is limited to members, the

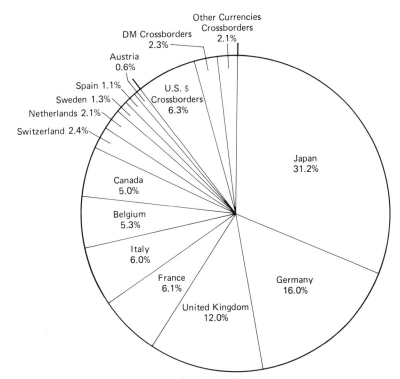

**Figure 1.3**
**Market Values of Non-US Bonds at the End of 1980 in Billions of US Dollars**
**(Non-US Equity Total = $1,748.3 Billon)**

*Source:* R. Ibbotson, C. R. Carr, and A. W. Robinson, "International Equity and Bond Return", *Financial Analysts Journal*, July–Aug. 1982.

typical investor desiring to buy or sell a listed security must first contact a brokerage firm which handles such orders. The broker acts as the customer's agent, and for simplicity we shall assume that the investor has selected a member firm of the New York Stock Exchange. The initial step is to open an account which typically can be of two types:

*Cash Account*

A cash account is limited to purchases and sales for cash; that is, the securities must be paid for in cash upon delivery.

*General Account*

A general account is opened for an investor who in addition to cash transactions may also wish to purchase securities on credit or to sell them short.

For the moment let us assume that a cash account is opened, and that our hypothetical investor wants to buy the stock of the Ford Motor Company. However, simply stipulating the stock one wants to buy does not provide the broker with sufficient information. The customer must also indicate the number of shares to be purchased and the type of order. The number of shares to be acquired has special significance in the securities business since lower commissions are payable on shares purchased in *round lots*, that is, in multiples of 100 shares (or 10 for stocks with relatively high share price). Any fractional purchases or sales are considered *odd lots* and an additional commission is charged on such transactions. Similarly the customer must indicate the type of order, usually a "market" or "limit" order, which he desires to place. The market order instructs the broker to buy (sell) the securities in question at the best obtainable price. The limit order, as its name implies, instructs the broker to buy (sell) the security at the stipulated limit price or better. In the case of a purchase, this means to buy at the limit price or below; in the case of a sale, to sell at the limit price or above. The customer must also indicate the length of time he wishes the limit order to remain in effect, should the broker be unable immediately to obtain the stipulated price in the market.

A special type of limit order, the so-called *stop-loss* order, has gained considerable notoriety. For example, an investor who is holding a particular stock in the hope that its price may rise might give his broker a limit order to sell the stock should the price fall ten points below the current market price of, say, 92. Thus, if the price should fall to 82, the limit order becomes a market order to sell. If a customer is short in the stock, he might try to limit his losses should the price rise. In such cases the procedure is reversed and he orders the broker to buy the shares, in order to cover his short position, should the price rise above a given limit. Note, however, that the placing of stop-loss orders does *not* guarantee that the stock will be sold at the limit price. If the market drops sharply, the broker may be unable to sell the customer's shares until they have fallen considerably below the stop-loss price. Since a backlog of stop-loss orders could conceivably set off a chain reaction of automatic selling, should the price of the stock fall, the Exchange on occasion has suspended the placing of such orders for certain stocks.

Now let us return to our hypothetical investor at the broker's office. At most local offices a remote terminal hooked to a computer-fed information system provides up-to-date information on the last recorded sale and current bid and asked prices for listed stocks. After checking on the prices, our investor puts in a market order to buy a round lot of 100 shares of Ford common. This order is relayed to the broker's partner on the floor of the Exchange, who takes it to the area or "post" at which Ford stock is traded.

## 1.5    The Specialist

The actual transaction is effected by approaching a member of the Exchange who specializes in the trading of Ford stock and who, by his readiness to buy and sell Ford stock, creates a continuous market for the stock. The *specialist*, as he is called, keeps a "book" in which he records limit orders from all over the country to buy and sell Ford stock. In our example, when the broker's representative approaches the specialist he will ask for the current quotation. The specialist consults his book and answers, say, 62 to $62\frac{1}{2}$, which means that the highest bid price in his book is $62 and the lowest price at which he has an offer to sell is $62.50. Our broker's floor partner might bid $62\frac{1}{4}$ in the hope that one of the traders standing around the specialist might have received a sale order at that price. If not, he raises his bid to $62\frac{1}{2}$ and the transaction is effected when the specialist calls out "sold." The broker and specialist record this transaction, and a report of the transaction is transmitted by an Exchange employee to the Exchange's computer center. Within seconds the report is flashed by ticker to subscribers all over the country. If our investor waits at his broker's office, he can watch the ticker report of his transaction which the broker usually projects electronically on a wall display panel.

The role of the specialist is crucial to the functioning of the market. He is in possession of very valuable information. In effect the specialist is the only person on the floor of the Exchange with up-to-date, albeit partial, knowledge of the supply and demand for the security in question.[3] His book, at any moment of time, summarizes investors' offers to buy and sell the stock at varying prices. The specialist does not share this information with other traders; that is, he is a "monopolist" with respect to this information. This fact is very important since the specialist not only serves as an intermediary, but can also trade on his own account and could conceivably exploit his knowledge by buying and selling selectively to maximize his own profits.

It should be noted that the specialist is not free to act solely on his own behalf. His primary function is to help maintain a "fair and orderly" market by buying and selling on his own account. Thus he is constrained in his own trading to transactions which narrow the price changes between sales, thereby achieving greater price continuity than would otherwise be the case. The Exchange regularly checks the activities of the specialists, verifying that their transactions are "stabilizing", in the sense that they represent purchases at prices below, or sales at prices above, the previous different price. Thus by buying and selling *against* the market the specialist dampens price fluctuations. Some measure of the effectiveness of the specialist system can be gleaned from the results of an examination carried out by the Exchange of six million transactions. The examination showed that 94% of the transactions took place at the same price as the preceding transaction, or within a spread of not more than $\frac{1}{4}$ point.

## 1.6    Margin Trading

The extension of credit to finance the purchase of securities, or "trading on margin" as such transactions are usually called, has been subject to federal regulation since 1934. The Securities Act of 1934 empowers the Board of Governors of the Federal Reserve System to regulate the extension of credit by banks and brokers to customers for the purchase of stocks or bonds. The regulation stipulates the *margin*, that is, the cash

---

[3] The information is only partial, since the specialist's book includes only limit orders which have been placed in advance of anticipated changes in market price. Should the price change, other investors may also be induced to buy or sell at that price, and will do so by means of market orders.

amount a credit customer must pay when purchasing a security, the balance being advanced by the broker. Thus an 80% margin requirement essentially means that the customer's initial equity in the purchase of, say, $10,000 of common stocks must be at least $8,000. Credit can be extended by the broker only up to $2,000.

In addition to the Federal Reserve System's *initial* margin requirement, the Exchange also sets requirements for *maintenance* margins, that is, the minimum equity requirements which apply to the account after the day of the transaction. In general, a customer's equity must be at least 25% of the market value of the securities carried in the margin account, and therefore serving as collateral for the broker's loan. This is the *minimum* requirement; individual brokers may, and often do, set maintenance margins at higher levels. In addition, the Exchange imposes higher margins on especially volatile issues. Continuing margin control is necessary if the broker's loan is to be safeguarded. When falling stock prices reduce the collateral value of the stock held in the margin account, the maintenance margin requirement ensures that the value of the collateral will always exceed the customer's debit balance with the broker. Should the value of the stock fall below the maintenance margin requirement, a call goes out to the customer "for more margin", that is, to deposit additional cash in the account. If the customer fails to do this, the broker can restore the minimum margin by selling off a sufficient quantity of the stock held in the margin account.

Since the maintenance margin (25%) is considerably below the Federal Reserve System's initial margin (70–80% in recent years), the price of a stock must decline drastically before any distress selling will occur owing to lack of margin.

## 1.7    Short Selling

When an investor feels confident about a stock's chances he can purchase that stock. If he is particularly "bullish" about the stock, he will borrow money to finance further purchases; that is, he will acquire the stock on margin. But what about the proverbial "bear" who thinks that the price of a particular stock is going to fall significantly in the near future? If he owns the stock he can sell it, but what can the bearish investor do if he doesn't own the stock in question, or after he has sold off his holdings? The answer to this dilemma is to sell the stock short, a short sale being defined as the sale of stock which an investor does not own. Thus the investor can borrow the stock and sell it on the market at the current price in anticipation of buying it back at reduced prices, thereby profiting from the decline.[4]

Although the very term *short sale* smacks of speculation, short sales are made for a variety of reasons, not all of them speculative. For example, an investor may "sell short against the box"; that is, borrow a stock and sell it even though he owns the stock himself. The "box" in this case refers to the safe deposit box of the short seller. The

---

[4] The lender of the stock is compensated for the loan of the stock since the proceeds of the short sale can be invested by the lender; the lender is also entitled to any dividends declared during the time the stock is out on loan.

motives for such a short sale are usually not speculative. For example, having made a profit in a particular stock in December, the owner may sell the stock short and then deliver his own stock to the lender to cover the short sale in January, thereby carrying his profit over to the next tax year. Similarly short sales are used for a variety of hedging purposes, e.g., holding some stocks "long" and some "short" may prove a good prescription for portfolio stabilization.[5] However, the specialists and professional traders on the floor of the Exchange account for the majority of short sales, most of which are technical in nature. Thus a heavy wave of buying orders may be met by the specialist partially out of his own inventory and partially by short selling the stock.

## 1.8    Stock Price Indexes

Almost all investors are concerned with general market conditions as well as with the particular securities comprising their portfolios. In 1965 the New York Stock Exchange introduced a comprehensive measure of the market trend. The composite index covers all listed stock; changes in the index are printed every half hour on the ticker tape. Four subgroup indexes—Industrial, Transportation, Utility, and Finance—and their net changes also appear on the tape every hour. The indexes are adjusted to eliminate the effects of changes in capitalization (splits and stock dividends) and of new listings and delistings.[6] The prices of each stock are weighted by the number of shares listed, and the aggregate market value is expressed relative to the base period (December 1955 equals 50). But despite the fact that the New York Stock Exchange is the nation's paramount securities market, this index is a relative newcomer to the financial scene; most investors, and the general public as well, turn to a much better known indicator of market trends, which is not strictly speaking an index: the Dow-Jones Average.

If the NYSE Index is the newest of the major market indicators, the Dow-Jones is the oldest. In 1884, Dow, Jones and Company began publishing stock price averages in a daily newsletter which was the precursor of the *Wall Street Journal*. Today the company publishes four averages of prices for selected stocks listed on the New York Stock Exchange: 30 industrials, 20 railroad stocks, 15 utilities, and the composite average for the 65 stocks. The averages are reported regularly during days of trading on the Exchange, and are sent out at half-hour intervals over the Dow-Jones news ticker service. The Dow-Jones averages appear in the *Wall Street Journal* and in the financial pages of leading newspapers all over the world.

The 30 industrials constitute the best known of the four averages, and when the financial press reports new highs or lows for the D-J average, the reference is invariably to the industrials. As the name implies, the D-J indicators are actual *averages* of stock prices; the denominator, however, is adjusted for stock splits in order not to disturb the average. Figure 1.4 charts the Dow-Jones industrial average for the period 1929–80. The industrial average is a "blue chip" average, since the 30 stocks included

---

[5] For more details, see Chapter 9.
[6] These alterations are handled by adjusting the base value to eliminate their impact on the index.

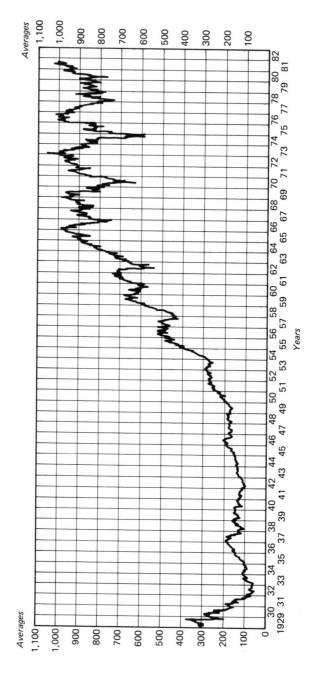

**Figure 1.4**
**The Dow–Jones Industrial Index 1929–1981**

*Source:* Moody's Industrial Manual (Vol. 1), 1981.

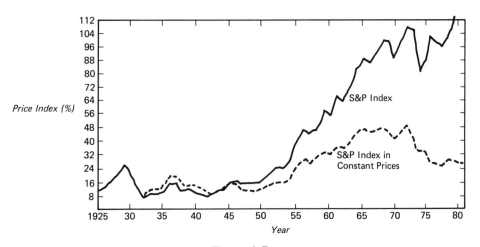

**Figure 1.5**
**S & P Composite Stock Index in Nominal and Constant Prices, 1925–1980.**

*Source* (also for CPI): *Business Condition's Digest*, US Department of Commerce, Bureau of Economic Analysis, various issues.

represent a cross-section of the best known and largest companies listed on the Exchange. These include AT&T, American Tobacco, DuPont, General Electric, General Motors, Sears Roebuck, and US Steel. From time to time substitutions have taken place in the list; perhaps the best known substitution was the removal of IBM from the list in 1939. Had this not occurred, the D-J industrials would have "broken 1,000" at the beginning of the 1960s, instead of following the curve shown in Figure 1.4. This suggests that some care should be exercised when interpreting the averages. In particular, no significance attaches to the absolute *level* of the average and attention should be directed to the change (preferably the *percentage* change) in the average over time. Thus when the average stands at, say, 800 points, a fall of 16 points to 784 does not necessarily indicate a national disaster, but rather that the prices of the 30 D-J industrial stocks have declined by 2% on the average.

Standard & Poor's Corporation publishes another well-known series of stock price indexes:

> 500 stocks, composite index
> 425 industrials
> 25 railroads
> 50 utilities

All of these indexes are reported regularly during the day by the various news services.[7] Unlike the D-J averages, the S&P indexes are "indexes" in the full sense of the term, that is, current market value (price times number of shares) is expressed as a percentage

[7] Standard & Poor's publishes indexes for many industry subgroups, as does Moody's.

*relative* to the market value of a common base period. In the case of the S&P indexes, a base of 10 is given to the average stock prices during the years 1941–1943. A base of 10 rather than the more common 100 was chosen so that the resulting index number would more closely approximate the actual average of prices on the NYSE. The new index was chained to the older S&P 90 stock composite index, so that the indexes are available for earlier years as well.

Figure 1.5 sets out the Standard & Poor's Composite Index for the period 1925–1980 in nominal terms and in constant prices (deflated by the consumer price index). Inflation accounts for a significant part of the rise in stock prices over the period. An examination of Figure 1.5 also indicates the crucial importance of the timing of investments. For the unlucky individual who invested in a representative cross-section of common stocks in 1929, on the eve of the Great Depression, stock prices did not regain their initial levels until 1954 in nominal terms, and not until 1956 in constant real terms. On the other hand, investments made at the trough of the depression in 1931 fared much better; by 1936, the S&P index had doubled both in nominal and real terms and by 1954 the nominal index was more than four times its 1931 level, while in real terms stock prices more than doubled between 1931 and 1954. Since 1970 the S&P index has dropped in constant prices, and investors have lost a significant percentage of their investments (in real terms) in the last decade.

### 1.8.1  Stock Price Indexes Outside the USA

Stock price indexes are of course also calculated and published regularly for stock exchanges outside the USA. Some of the well-known indexes are the following:

| | |
|---|---|
| Belgium | – Indice de la Bourse 'de Bruxelles |
| France | – INSEE |
| Germany | – Herstatt Index |
| Israel | – Central Bureau of Statistics Stock Index |
| Netherlands | – ANP/CBS |
| Switzerland | – Schweizerische Kreditanstalt |
| United Kingdom | – Financial Times Industrial Ordinary |

Stock indexes for exchanges outside the USA can be looked up easily in *International Financial Statistics* published monthly by the International Monetary Fund. These published data are usually based on the most reliable domestic stock index available for each country.

The various indexes reveal the trend of prices in the stock markets. The profit on each security (stocks, bonds, etc.) is calculated by the rate of return for the appropriate holding period. The method to calculate rates of return and the historical records of rates of return are covered in the next chapter.

### 1.8.2  Commodity Indexes: Spot and Futures

There are many other price indexes that the reader can find in the financial news media (e.g., *Wall Street Journal, Barron's,* and others). A relatively new important index is the commodity price index. This index represents the prices of contracts to buy and sell 12 commodities at a specified date: the commodities covered are cattle, coffee, copper, corn, cotton, gold, hogs, lumber, silver, soybeans, sugar, and wheat. The commodity index enables traders to compare the performance of their own holdings of commodity contracts to the general trend. It also provides an indication of raw material prices. There are two main commodity indexes, the spot (or cash) index and the futures index.

The *spot index* (cash index) represents the average price of the 12 commodities on a given day, divided by the average price on the previous day. *Futures* are contracts to deliver (or buy) a given commodity at a fixed price on a specified day in the future. The *futures index* represents the average price of the contracts to deliver the 12 commodities five months into the future. Table 1.6 and Figure 1.6 illustrate the two commodity indexes for the period 1975–1981. The futures index is generally regarded as indicating the future trend of commodity prices.

Futures contracts provide important hedging instruments. A firm which, say, needs soybean for delivery in five months' time can buy a futures contract hedging

**Table 1.6**

**A Seven-year History of the Dow-Jones Commodity Price Indexes: Spot (Cash) and Futures**

| Month (last trading day) | Futures Index | Cash Index | Month (last trading day) | Futures Index | Cash Index | Month (last trading day) | Futures Index | Cash Index |
|---|---|---|---|---|---|---|---|---|
| Dec 1974 | 100.00 | 100.00 | May | 125.84 | 123.85 | Sept | 172.40 | 165.32 |
| | | | June | 115.51 | 116.61 | Oct | 166.11 | 157.52 |
| Jan 1975 | 94.15 | 94.06 | July | 105.97 | 107.57 | Nov | 177.81 | 166.00 |
| Feb | 90.47 | 89.99 | Aug | 103.15 | 105.77 | Dec | 200.39 | 188.58 |
| March | 95.70 | 94.78 | Sept | 101.72 | 101.53 | | | |
| Apr | 91.52 | 96.30 | Oct | 102.14 | 101.77 | Jan 1980 | 228.17 | 213.61 |
| May | 89.26 | 95.35 | Nov | 106.64 | 105.71 | Feb | 227.21 | 211.79 |
| June | 90.75 | 98.10 | Dec | 111.58 | 110.67 | Mar | 176.46 | 153.60 |
| July | 98.99 | 102.39 | | | | Apr | 164.08 | 153.27 |
| Aug | 102.04 | 105.11 | Jan 1978 | 111.55 | 112.57 | May | 172.12 | 157.61 |
| Sept | 100.57 | 105.46 | Feb | 109.63 | 112.17 | June | 182.66 | 172.91 |
| Oct | 95.05 | 97.22 | Mar | 113.70 | 115.30 | July | 180.88 | 176.02 |
| Nov | 95.18 | 99.51 | Apr | 111.40 | 114.00 | Aug | 183.11 | 174.47 |
| Dec | 96.83 | 98.06 | May | 120.26 | 119.71 | Sept | 196.15 | 182.18 |
| | | | June | 111.85 | 114.27 | Oct | 194.81 | 187.09 |
| Jan 1976 | 97.64 | 95.65 | July | 112.98 | 113.34 | Nov | 195.00 | 178.84 |
| Feb | 101.46 | 98.91 | Aug | 117.35 | 116.28 | Dec | 181.54 | 165.63 |
| Mar | 100.29 | 95.55 | Sept | 120.82 | 118.69 | | | |
| Apr | 106.08 | 102.44 | Oct | 125.75 | 123.72 | Jan 1981 | 169.50 | 153.79 |
| May | 110.05 | 106.28 | Nov | 121.17 | 118.93 | Feb | 162.90 | 150.09 |
| June | 117.63 | 112.42 | Dec | 122.98 | 119.00 | Mar | 164.49 | 150.40 |
| July | 109.23 | 106.02 | | | | Apr | 158.92 | 141.22 |
| Aug | 107.88 | 104.98 | Jan 1979 | 126.90 | 123.18 | May | 155.48 | 147.72 |
| Sept | 108.71 | 103.26 | Feb | 133.46 | 130.58 | June | 140.10 | 137.68 |
| Oct | 110.75 | 103.74 | Mar | 131.54 | 128.78 | July | 145.82 | 141.25 |
| Nov | 113.12 | 107.63 | Apr | 136.87 | 132.48 | Aug | 139.75 | 132.96 |
| Dec | 121.25 | 112.91 | May | 134.91 | 133.52 | Sept | 139.85 | 131.67 |
| | | | June | 145.62 | 141.90 | Oct | 142.01 | 130.34 |
| Jan 1977 | 120.77 | 112.74 | July | 140.52 | 138.86 | Nov | 135.88 | 128.87 |
| Feb | 130.65 | 122.38 | Aug | 154.07 | 150.20 | Dec | 133.79 | 125.46 |
| Mar | 138.91 | 129.11 | | | | | | |
| Apr | 134.97 | 130.09 | | | | | | |

*Source: The Wall Street Journal,* January 4, 1982. Reprinted by permission of The Wall Street Journal, © Dow Jones and Company, Inc., 1982. All rights reserved.

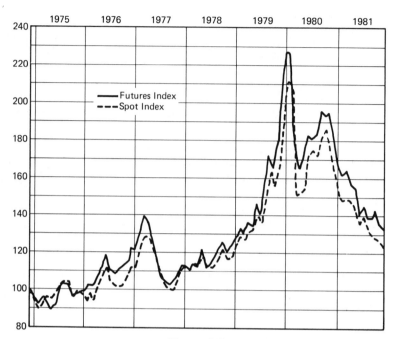

**Figure 1.6**
**Dow-Jones Commodity Price Indexes (Spot and Futures)**

against a possible increase in the soybean prices in the future. There are also futures contracts for foreign currencies and for interest rates (these are generally called forward transactions). In principle, we can look at futures as another investment medium and a portfolio of futures contracts can be constructed according to the same principles as a stock portfolio.

## 1.9    Shareholder Characteristics

The NYSE 1980 survey disclosed some important information regarding the shareholders, which is summarized in Tables 1.7 and 1.8. The number of individual shareholders increased from about six million in 1952 to approximately 30 million in 1980 (see Table 1.7). About 85% of the shareholders in 1980 had incomes of $10,000 or more. Also it is interesting to note that the proportion of women among the adult shareholders is about 50%, and the median age of all investors is 46 years.

Table 1.8 illustrates the breakdown of shareholders by age, education, occupation, income and size of portfolio. About 67% of all investors in 1980 held a relatively small portfolio of under $10,000. Only 25% held portfolios of $25,000 or larger. This finding

Table 1.7
**Highlights of NYSE Shareowner Surveys**

| | 1952 | 1956 | 1959 | 1962 | 1965 | 1970 | 1975 | 1980 |
|---|---|---|---|---|---|---|---|---|
| No. of Individual Shareowners (thousands) | 6,490 | 8,630 | 12,490 | 17,010 | 20,120 | 30,850 | 25,720 | 29,840 |
| No. Owning Shares Listed on NYSE (thousands) | n/a | 6,880 | 8,510 | 11,020 | 12,430 | 18,290 | 17,950 | 23,520 |
| Adult Shareowner Incidence in Population | 1 in 16 | 1 in 12 | 1 in 8 | 1 in 6 | 1 in 6 | 1 in 4 | 1 in 6 | 1 in 5 |
| Median Household Income | $7,100 | $6,200 | $7,000 | $8,600 | $9,500 | $13,500 | $19,000 | $27,750 |
| No. of Adult Shareowners with Household Income: | | | | | | | | |
| Under $10,000 (thousands) | n/a | n/a | 9,340 | 10,340 | 10,080 | 8,170 | 3,420 | 1,720 |
| $10,000 & Over (thousands) | n/a | n/a | 2,740 | 5,920 | 8,410 | 20,130 | 19,970 | 25,410 |
| No. of Adult Female Shareowners (thousands) | 3,140 | 4,260 | 6,350 | 8,290 | 9,430 | 14,290 | 11,750 | 13,530 |
| No. of Adult Male Shareowners (thousands) | 3,210 | 4,020 | 5,740 | 7,970 | 9,060 | 14,340 | 11,630 | 14,030 |
| Median Age | 51 | 48 | 49 | 48 | 49 | 48 | 53 | 46 |

n/a: not available.
*Source: NYSE Fact Book 1981.*

**Table 1.8**
**Selected Characteristics of Individual Shareowners in Public Corporations**
(thousands)

|  | 1956 | 1959 | 1962 | 1965 | 1970 | 1975 | 1980 |
|---|---|---|---|---|---|---|---|
| *Age* | | | | | | | |
| Under 21 | n/a | 197 | 450 | 1,280 | 2,221 | 1,818 | 2,280 |
| 21–34 | 2,230 | 2,444 | 2,390 | 2,626 | 4,500 | 2,838 | 6,331 |
| 35–44 | 1,240 | 2,064 | 3,528 | 4,216 | 5,801 | 3,976 | 5,854 |
| 45–54 | 1,700 | 2,800 | 4,519 | 4,752 | 7,556 | 5,675 | 5,391 |
| 55–64 | 2,020 | 2,666 | 3,202 | 3,549 | 6,084 | 5,099 | 5,083 |
| 65 and Over | 1,090 | 2,133 | 2,617 | 3,347 | 4,330 | 5,800 | 4,534 |
| *Education* | | | | | | | |
| 3 Years High School or less | 1,570 | 2,804 | 3,007 | 3,106 | 3,566 | 1,621 | 1,725 |
| 4 Years High School | 2,750 | 3,130 | 4,828 | 5,344 | 8,697 | 6,580 | 5,669 |
| 1–3 Years College | 1,540 | 2,587 | 3,284 | 4,012 | 5,867 | 5,301 | 9,243 |
| 4 Years College or More | 2,420 | 3,566 | 5,137 | 6,028 | 9,999 | 9,886 | 10,486 |
| *Occupation* | | | | | | | |
| Professional & Technical | 1,010 | 1,934 | 2,682 | 3,136 | 6,320 | 4,273 | 6,024 |
| Clerical & Sales | 1,490 | 1,801 | 2,959 | 2,903 | 4,415 | 3,399 | 3,881 |
| Managers & Proprietors | 1,140 | 1,982 | 2,276 | 2,330 | 3,981 | 3,726 | 5,259 |
| Craftsmen & Foremen | 520 | 580 | 927 | 924 | 1,377 | 1,154 | 1,530 |
| Operatives & Laborers | 140 | 411 | 439 | 647 | 849 | 748 | 1,305 |
| Service Workers | 430 | 326 | 423 | 414 | 622 | 452 | 233 |
| Farmers & Farm Laborers | 230 | 73 | 65 | 64 | 170 | 234 | 145 |
| Housewives, Retired Persons, & Nonemployed Adults | 3,320 | 4,000 | 5,462 | 8,072 | 10,320 | 9,402 | 8,011 |
| *Income* | | | | | | | |
| Under $5,000 | 3,195 | 3,518 | 2,991 | 2,977 | 2,389 | 780 | 241 |
| $5,000–$9,999 | | 5,826 | 7,348 | 7,100 | 5,779 | 2,636 | 1,480 |
| $10,000–$14,999 | 5,285 | 1,741 | 3,170 | 4,862 | 8,346 | 4,552 | 3,142 |
| $15,000–$24,999 | | 689 | 1,967 | 2,477 | 7,670 | 8,778 | 6,848 |
| $25,000 & Over | | 314 | 780 | 1,073 | 4,114 | 6,642 | 15,419 |
| *Portfolio* | | | | | | | |
| Under $10,000 | n/a | n/a | n/a | n/a | 8,810 | 11,647 | 17,699 |
| $10,000–$14,999 | n/a | n/a | n/a | n/a | 9,001 | 3,072 | 2,263 |
| $15,000–$24,999 | n/a | n/a | n/a | n/a | 8,272 | 2,760 | 1,805 |
| $25,000 & Over | n/a | n/a | n/a | n/a | 4,437 | 5,909 | 4,436 |

*Note:* Except for age, selected characteristics are those of adult shareowners only.
*n/a:* not available.
*Source: NYSE Fact Book 1981.*

is important for the theory of diversification. Since one cannot diversify $10,000 in a very large number of stocks, it implies that 67% of the shareholders hold portfolios with limited diversification (for the implication of this finding to portfolio theory, see Chapters 13 and 14).

The information in these two tables is important for understanding investors' behavior and the changes of the typical investor characteristics over time. This information is of particular interest to the investment analyst and consultant. Brokerage houses try to attract investors. Thus, the advertising of the various brokerage houses should be "tailored" to the potential investors and match their characteristics (age, education, sex, etc.).

## Summary

In this chapter we have briefly described the various stock exchanges and the role of the primary and secondary securities markets. It is explained how an order is placed and the role of short sales and margin trading is discussed. Finally we considered the various stock indexes and the characteristics of the shareholders in the USA. This background information is important for the development of portfolio selection models which we present in the following chapters.

## Questions and Problems

1.1 Distinguish between the primary and secondary securities markets.

1.2 What are the principal economic functions of a stock exchange?

1.3 How do stock market prices affect the allocation of capital resources in the economy?

1.4 What is the function of the specialist on the NYSE? Can you think of a feasible alternative for the "specialist system of trading"?

1.5 Calculate the growth rate in the market value of stocks and of options. Which has a higher growth rate in 1979? Which has a higher growth rate in 1974–1979? Use the data in Table 1.2.

1.6 Prepare a table which shows the percentage of investors, by size of portfolio held, for the year 1980. (Use the data in Table 1.8.)

1.7 Use the data in Tables 1.3 and 1.4 to calculate the annual average growth rate in the market value of different categories of listed bonds between the years 1965 and 1981.

1.8 An investor purchased $8,000 worth of stock on margin account, taking a $2,000 loan from the broker.
(a) What is the initial margin requirement?
(b) If the maintenance margin is 25%, how far can the market value of the stock drop before the investor is called upon to advance more equity?

(c) If the market value of the stock drops to $2,500, how much of the stock should be liquidated to restore the maintenance margin?

(d) If the market value of the stock rises to $10,000, what is the margin position? Wha can the investor do?

1.9 · An investor purchased stock worth $10,000 on a margin account with 70% margin requirement. How much can he borrow from his broker? What is the equity in this invest ment?

Now suppose that the value of his stock dropped to $2,000. Does the broker have collateral to secure his loan? What would you recommend the broker to do?

1.10 (a) An investor sells short a share of stock with current price of $100. The price subse quently rises to $120. Calculate the investor's profit or loss from the transaction

(b) An investor holds shares of a stock with price of $100 per share in December 1983 The shares were bought in October 1983 at a price of $50 per share. The investor needs cash badly now. If he sells the stock, he will have to pay capital gains tax for 1983. What would you recommend to the investor in order to defer the tax obligation to 1984? Explain.

1.11 Use the data of Table 1.6 to calculate the profit (the change in index) for an investor who purchased the spot index in January 1975 and held it through to January 1977. Repeat the same calculation for an investor who purchased the futures index. Which investment proved more profitable?

## Selected References

Asay, M. R., "Implied Margin Requirements on Options and Stocks", *Journal of Portfolio Management*, Spring 1981.

Baumol, W. J., *The Stock Market and Economic Efficiency*, New York: Fordham University Press, 1965.

Brown, J. M., "Post-Offering Experience of Companies Going Public", *Journal of Business*, January 1970.

Cohen, J. B., and Zinbarg, E. D., *Investment Analysis and Portfolio Management*, Homewood, Ill.: Irwin, 1967.

Eiteman, W. J., Dice, C. A., and Eiteman, D. K., *The Stock Market*, 4th ed., New York: McGraw-Hill, 1966.

Furst, R. W., "Does Listing Increase the Market Price of Common Stocks?" *Journal of Business*, April 1970.

Ibbotson, R. G., Carr, R. C., and Robinson, A. W., "International Equity and Bond Returns", *Financial Analysts Journal*, July–August 1982.

Leffler, G. L., and Farwell, L. C., *The Stock Market*, 3rd ed., New York: Ronald Press, 1963.

Miller, D. E., "New York Stock Exchange", *Financial Executive*, April 1977.

Renshaw, E. F., "Estimating the Return on S&P's Industrial Price Index", *Financial Analysts Journal*, January–February 1969.

Sharpe, W. F., *Investments*, 2nd ed., Englewood Cliffs, N.J.: Prentice-Hall, 1981.

*The New York Stock Exchange Fact Book*, New York: NYSE, annual issues.

Van Horne, J. C., "New Listings and Their Price Behavior", *Journal of Finance*, September 1970.

Weinstein, S., "Hot New Indicator: A Simple Index Has Been Right on the Money Calling Market Trends [last hour index]", *Barron's*, June 15, 1981.

West, S., and Miller, N., "Why the New NYSE Common Stock Indexes?" *Financial Analysts Journal*, May–June 1967.

# 2

# Rates of Return

The area of portfolio selection has two facets, theory and practice. For theoretical purposes, we can make certain assumptions regarding the profitability of the various assets and then proceed to derive the corresponding conclusions, such as the relationship between the assets' average rate of return and risk. However, in order to apply the portfolio selection tools in practice, we need to have some idea of the actual rates of return on the relevant assets and to learn how these rates of return are measured.

Rates of return and their probability distributions are essential ingredients for the construction of investment portfolios, and no applications are possible without this information. We therefore devote this chapter to the techniques of measuring the rates of return, or the profitability, of various securities and reproduce the historical record of the rates of return on various assets.

## 2.1    Alternative Measures of Profitability

The net present value (NPV) method, widely discussed in basic finance texts, was developed to solve the capital budgeting problem of the business firm. But the investment in financial securities, by its very nature, differs from the investment in physical assets: financial assets tend to be highly divisible—you cannot build two-thirds of a bridge but you can buy one-millionth of a share in the ownership of AT&T. Thus for all practical purposes, scale problems can usually be ignored when analyzing securities.

The investment in capital goods usually involves a long-term commitment of resources over a fixed number of years (that is, disinvestment is costly and often uneconomic); most securities, independent of their date of maturity (if any),[1] can be held for as short or as long a period as is desired; in other words, investments in

---

[1] Common stock or preferred stock as well as perpetual bonds have no formal redemption dates.

securities are highly reversible. Finally, while the firm is often faced with mutually exclusive alternatives, the decision to purchase a share of AT&T does not generally preclude the purchase of GM stock.

Thus, when analyzing investments in securities, differences in scale and duration among alternative investments can safely be ignored. This property of financial investments is of considerable importance since we seek a measure of return which can rank the alternative investments for all investors without determining their individual discount rates (needed in capital budgeting for NPV calculations). What is required is a measure of return which provides a ranking of the financial investments. This ranking must be objective, relying on data available to *all* investors and independent of individual investor preferences.

### 2.1.1   The Rate of Return on Common Stocks

Two alternative formulations of a time-adjusted rate of return[2] on common stocks have been advocated in financial literature. Both of these measures are based on the total cash flow, dividends and capital gains (losses), emanating from the ownership of common stock. The first method simply applies the familiar formula for the internal rate of return (IRR) to the problem of determining the rate of return on investments in common stock:

$$P_0 = \frac{D_1}{(1 + R)} + \frac{D_2}{(1 + R)^2} + \cdots + \frac{D_{n-1}}{(1 + R)^{n-1}} + \frac{D_n + P_n}{(1 + R)^n}$$

$$= \sum_{t=1}^{n} \frac{D_t}{(1 + R)^t} + \frac{P_n}{(1 + R)^n} \tag{2.1}$$

where:

$R$ = the internal rate of return (a measure of the rate of profitability)
$D_t$ = the cash dividend received in period $t$ ($t = 1, 2, \ldots, n$)
$P_n$ = the market price of a share at the close of period $n$
$P_0$ = the initial market price of a share of common stock.

This formula is perfectly general and can be adapted to any holding period. It views the cashflow to the investor as the stream of dividends plus the share's terminal market value.

The alternative formulation views the return on a common stock as the geometric

---

[2] Since we require a measure for multi-period investment, undiscounted measures of return such as the dividend yield $D/P$, are unsatisfactory for our purposes. The dividend yield also includes only part of the benefits accruing to the shareholder since it ignores capital gains.

mean of a series of annual rates of return, and hence we shall refer to it as the "geometric mean rate of return." This formulation defines the rate of return in any period $t$ as

$$R_t = \frac{D_t + (P_t - P_{t-1})}{P_{t-1}}$$

$$= \frac{D_t + P_t}{P_{t-1}} - 1 \qquad (2.2)$$

where:

$R_t =$ the rate of return in period $t$
$P_t =$ the share's market price at the end of period $t$.

For multi-period investments the geometric mean of one-period rates of return is taken:[3]

$$1 + \bar{R} = \sqrt[n]{\prod_{t=1}^{n} \frac{D_t + P_t}{P_{t-1}}}$$

$$= \sqrt[n]{\prod_{t=1}^{n} (1 + R_t)} = \left[\prod_{t=1}^{n} (1 + R_t)\right]^{1/n} \qquad (2.3)$$

where $\bar{R}$ is the geometric mean rate of return; the exponent $1/n$ is the usual notation for extracting the $n$th root.

A comparison of the two formulas shows that they provide identical measures of return for single-period investments. Setting $t$ equal to one in Equation (2.1) and multiplying both sides by $(1 + R)/P_0$ gives

$$1 + R = \frac{D_1 + P_1}{P_0}$$

or

$$R = \frac{D_1 + P_1}{P_0} - 1 \qquad (2.4)$$

which is the same as (2.2). In the general case where shares are held for more than one

[3] The symbol $\Pi$ indicates multiplication, just as the symbol $\Sigma$ indicates summation. For example

$$\prod_{t=1}^{3} (1 + R_t) = (1 + R_1)(1 + R_2)(1 + R_3)$$

period, both formulations implicitly assume reinvestment of the interim cash dividends. It should be recalled in this context that "reinvestment" is the obverse side of "compounding", and as such it is an inherent property of any time-discounted formula. It is *not* a behavioral assumption regarding the investment habits of individuals. However, it does raise the problem of the implicit rates at which the interim receipts are assumed to be reinvested (compounded).

To make these rates explicit we multiply both sides of the IRR formula (2.1) by $(1 + R)^n$, to obtain the future value of the shares after $n$ reinvestment periods,

$$
\begin{aligned}
P_0(1 + R)^n &= \left[ \sum_{t=1}^{n} D_t(1 + R)^{n-t} + P_n \right] \\
&= \left[ \sum_{t=1}^{n-1} D_t(1 + R)^{n-t} + D_n + P_n \right]
\end{aligned}
\tag{2.5}
$$

The geometric mean formula presents a somewhat more difficult problem. Let us start with the case where $n = 2$. Squaring both sides of (2.3) and setting $n = 2$, we have

$$
\begin{aligned}
(1 + \bar{R})^2 &= \prod_{t=1}^{2} \frac{D_t + P_t}{P_{t-1}} = \frac{D_1 + P_1}{P_0} \cdot \frac{D_2 + P_2}{P_1} \\
&= \frac{D_1}{P_0} \cdot \frac{D_2 + P_2}{P_1} + \frac{P_1}{P_0} \cdot \frac{D_2 + P_2}{P_1} \\
&= \frac{1}{P_0} \left[ D_1 \cdot \frac{D_2 + P_2}{P_1} + D_2 + P_2 \right]
\end{aligned}
\tag{2.6}
$$

But since $(D_2 + P_2)/P_1 \equiv (1 + R_2)$, this can be written as

$$
(1 + \bar{R})^2 = \frac{1}{P_0} [D_1(1 + R_2) + D_2 + P_2]
\tag{2.7}
$$

Generalizing this result for $n$ investment periods and multiplying both sides by $P_0$, we get

$$
\begin{aligned}
P_0(1 + \bar{R})^n &= D_1(1 + R_2)(1 + R_3) \ldots (1 + R_n) + D_2(1 + R_3)(1 + R_4) \ldots (1 + R_n) \\
&\quad + D_3(1 + R_4)(1 + R_5) \ldots (1 + R_n) + \cdots + D_{n-1}(1 + R_n) + D_n + P_n
\end{aligned}
$$

or in more compact notation

$$
P_0(1 + \bar{R})^n = \left[ \sum_{t=1}^{n-1} D_t \prod_{j=t}^{n-1} (1 + R_{j+1}) + D_n + P_n \right]
\tag{2.8}
$$

which is again the future value of the investment after $n$ compounding periods.

A comparison of Equations (2.8) and (2.5) shows that the two alternative formulations do not provide identical measures of return in the multiperiod case if dividends are paid,[4] and that the only difference between them stems from differing assumptions regarding the reinvestment rate. Thus the IRR implicitly assumes reinvestment at the constant long-run average rate $R$, while the geometric mean rate, despite its name, implicitly assumes reinvestment at the varying *short-term rates of return* which are actually available in the market during the periods subsequent to the receipt of the dividend. The use of short-term rates rather than a constant average rate has important theoretical advantages: the vector of short-term rates more accurately reflects the opportunity cost of the dividend in the market.[5] Since the initial investment outlay can be considered free of size constraints, and the cash flows are brought to common terminal dates, a ranking of common stocks using the geometric mean rate of return is consistent with an NPV ranking, independent of the discount rate. Thus this measure of return is appropriate for all investors.[6]

### EXAMPLE

Consider a stock currently trading at the price $P_0 = \$100$ per share. We will analyze a two-year investment, with the shareholder receiving cash dividend $D_1 = \$10$ at the end of the first year and $D_2 = \$10$ at the end of the second year. The share price after the distribution of the cash dividend was $P_1 = \$50$ at the end of the first year and $P_2 = \$100$ at the end of the second year. Our objective is to determine the *annual* rate of return or profitability on this two-year investment.

Using the internal rate of return approach, the annual profitability is given by the IRR $R$ which solves the defining equation

$$P_0 = \frac{D_1}{1 + R} + \frac{D_2 + P_2}{(1 + R)^2}$$

or plugging in the numerical values

$$100 = 10/(1 + R) + (10 + 100)/(1 + R)^2$$

This is a quadratic equation in the unknown $x = 1/(1 + R)$, and solving it we easily find $R = 0.10$ or 10%.

By the same approach, assuming reinvestment of the cash dividends at the rate of $R = 10\%$, we obtain for the investor's terminal wealth after two years,

$$P_0(1 + R)^2 = 100 \times (1.1)^2 = \$121$$

[4] If no dividends are paid ($D_t = 0$) both the internal and geometric mean rates of return are equal to $\sqrt[n]{P_n/P_0} - 1$ or $(P_n/P_0)^{1/n} - 1$.

[5] Optimum solutions to investment problems require the use of short-term rates. The use of a long-term average is not permissible, since an infinity of short-term combinations can be defined which are compatible with any given long-term average rate. See M. J. Bailey, "Formal Criteria for Investment Decisions", *The Journal of Political Economy* LXVII (October 1959).

[6] Since common stocks represent risky investments, an investment decision requires a measure of risk as well as a measure of return. Here we consider only the question of return; the problem of risk is taken up in subsequent chapters.

Let us now turn to the geometric mean approach. The rate of return on the first year's investment is given by

$$R_1 = \frac{D_1 + P_1}{P_0} - 1 = \frac{10 + 50}{100} - 1 = -0.40 \text{ or a } loss \text{ of 40\% of the investment.}$$

For the second year, we have

$$R_2 = \frac{D_2 + P_2}{P_1} - 1 = \frac{10 + 100}{50} - 1 = 1.2 \text{ or a } profit \text{ of 120\%.}$$

The geometric mean annual rate of return $\bar{R}$ is given by

$$\bar{R} = \sqrt{(1 + R_1)(1 + R_2)} - 1 = \sqrt{(1 - 0.40)(1 + 1.20)} - 1 = \sqrt{1.32} - 1 \approx 0.15.$$

The geometric mean annual rate of return is thus $\bar{R} \approx 15\%$. Which of the two different results, $R = 10\%$ and $\bar{R} = 15\%$, is the correct measure of the investment's annual profitability over the two-year holding period? The answer is obviously dependent on the assumptions that we are willing to make regarding the reinvestment of the $10 cash dividend at the end of each year. If we are looking for an *objective* profitability measure, then only the geometric mean annual rate of return $\bar{R} = 15\%$ is the correct figure, since in this calculation we assume reinvestment of the first-year $10 cash dividend in the same stock at the actual rate of return *available in the market* in the second year. To see this from a different angle, let us evaluate the future value of the investment under the two alternative approaches.

By the internal rate of return method, $R = 10\%$, and we get the future value

$$\$100 \times (1.1)^2 = \$121$$

whereas by the geometric mean method, $\bar{R} = 15\%$, and we get the future value

$$\$100 \times (1.15)^2 = \$132$$

To convince ourselves that $\bar{R} = 15\%$ is the appropriate profitability measure, let us determine the market value of the investment at the end of the second year. Initially we invest $P_0 = \$100$ in one share of common stock. At the end of year 1 we receive $10 cash dividend and we buy more shares at the current share price $P_1 = \$50$. We thus increase our holdings by $10/\$50 = 0.2$ shares of the same stock. In year 2 our portfolio thus consists of 1.2 shares of the stock, but this did not involve any increase in our initial investment of $100: we simply reinvested the dividends in the same stock. At the end of year 2, when the stock pays a $10 cash dividend per share, we get $10 \times 1.2 = \$12$ in cash for our 1.2 shares. Moreover, at the end of year 2, when the stock price is $P_2 = \$100$, our 1.2 shares are worth $100 \times 1.2 = \$120$. The terminal wealth at the end of the second year is thus given by

$$\$100 \times 1.2 + \$10 \times 1.2 = \$120 + \$12 = \$132$$

This is exactly the result that we obtained by applying the geometric mean rate of return $\bar{R} = 15\%$ in future value calculations.

To sum up, the geometric mean annual rate of return provides an objective profitability measure, since it assumes reinvestment of all cash dividend streams in the same security at the actual rates of return available in the market at the relevant time.

### 2.1.2   Adjusting the Rate of Return

The empirical application of the geometric mean formula requires a number of adjustments. More specifically, procedures must be defined for handling the following problems:

(a)   Current dividends plus the change in share prices do not always accurately represent the total return to shareholders, owing to a wide variety of splits, stock dividends, and rights offerings.

(b)   Cash dividends are typically received at varying dates during the year and not necessarily on the last day of the year, as might seem to be implied by Equation (2.8).[7]

An operational solution to these problems can be found by redefining the geometric mean rate of return in a manner which consistently reinvests upon receipt all cash dividends, stock dividends, and the market value of rights.[8] An index of shares is introduced representing the value of the initial investment. It is set equal to 100 in the base year and shares received via subsequent splits or stock dividends are added to the index at the time they are allocated. We assume that rights are sold in the market[9] on the first day of trading and the proceeds of the "sale" (that is, the market value of the rights) are used to "purchase" additional shares. These shares are then added to the index.[10]

Since a lag exists between the date a share is listed ex-dividend and the time the company's check becomes available, the reinvestment of the cash dividends should be lagged as well. For simplicity, we use the proceeds of cash dividends to purchase additional shares on the fifteenth of the month following the ex-dividend date, and the shares so acquired are also added to the index of shares on that date.

The reinvestment of stock dividends (splits) and the value of rights is designed to keep the initial investment intact throughout the investment period. Failure to do this

---

[7] Problems of intra-year timing arise owing to the convention of calculating *annual* rates of return. If investment periods are defined to coincide with the ex-dividend dates, this problem disappears.

[8] The reader who is interested in the detailed procedures, including programming instructions, is directed to L. Fisher and J. Lorie, "Rates of Return on Investments in Common Stocks", *Journal of Business* XXXVII (January 1964).

[9] These reinvestment "transactions" are theoretical, and therefore commissions and taxes should not be charged.

[10] An equivalent procedure would be to exercise the rights and immediately sell enough of the shares to cover the subscription price of the shares previously acquired via the exercise of the rights.

implies the sale of part of the shareholder's ownership interest in the firm. The reinvestment of cash dividends, as we have shown, is an inherent theoretical property of the geometric mean rate of return, or for that matter of any compounded rate of return. It should also be emphasized that the reinvestment of the interim cash dividends is necessary to ensure comparability among the shares of different companies. This procedure preserves the equivalence between current income and capital appreciation.[11] Investors can be assumed to remain indifferent to a 10% per annum increase in stock prices or to an annual 10% cash dividend (with no price appreciation) if and only if they are permitted to reinvest the cash dividends in the original shares.

The adjusted rate of return for any given year[12] is derived using the following formula:

$$R_t^* = \frac{V_t - V_{t-1}}{V_{t-1}} = \frac{V_t}{V_{t-1}} - 1 \tag{2.9}$$

where:

$R_t^*$ = the adjusted rate of return in year $t$
$V_t$ = the market value of the investment at the end of year $t$
$V_{t-1}$ = the market value of the investment at the end of the previous year, $t - 1$.

The market value of the investment is calculated by multiplying the index of shares (reflecting the reinvestment of stock dividends, splits, value of rights, and cash dividends) by the market price of a share at the end of the year. For multi-period investments the formula becomes

$$1 + R^* = \sqrt[n]{\prod_{t=1}^{n} \frac{V_t}{V_{t-1}}} = \left[ \frac{V_1}{V_0} \cdot \frac{V_2}{V_1} \cdot \ldots \cdot \frac{V_n}{V_{n-1}} \right]^{1/n} = \left( \frac{V_n}{V_0} \right)^{1/n} \tag{2.10}$$

### 2.1.3   The Effect of Inflation on Rates of Return

We have so far dealt in *nominal* market values, ignoring the effects of inflation. As a result, formulas (2.9) and (2.10) yield the *nominal* annual rate of return on investment. The same formulas can be used to compute the *real* rates of return if we plug in the real, inflation-adjusted market value for $V_n$, expressed in money units with the same purchasing power as the initial market value $V_0$. Thus, assume that during the $n$-year period the mean annual inflation rate was $\bar{h}$ percent. Then the nominal market value $V_n$ based on the market prices at the end of year $n$ can be reduced to base year terms in which the

[11] Abstracting from differences which may properly exist owing to the differential taxation of current income and capital gains.
[12] The rate of return is calculated from January 15 to January 14 of the following year to avoid any possible bias due to the use of the calendar year.

· initial market value $V_0$ is measured: to this end, divide $V_n$ by the cumulative $n$-year inflation adjustment factor $(1 + \bar{h})^n$ to obtain the end-of-period market value in base year terms, $V_n/(1 + \bar{h})^n$. Plugging this *real* terminal market value in formula (2.10), we obtain for the real, inflation-adjusted annual rate of return $R_r^*$,

$$1 + R_r^* = \left( \frac{V_n/(1 + \bar{h})^n}{V_0} \right)^{1/n} = \left( \frac{V_n}{V_0} \right)^{1/n} \bigg/ (1 + \bar{h}) = \frac{1 + R^*}{1 + \bar{h}} \qquad (2.11)$$

Thus, the *real* annual return $1 + R_r^*$ is obtained by dividing the *nominal* annual return $1 + R^*$ by the annual mean inflation adjustment factor $(1 + \bar{h})$.

Table 2.1 sets out the nominal rates of return on DuPont common stock for the five-year period 1976–1980. The annual inflation rates are usually calculated from the annual change in the Consumer Price Index (CPI). Thus, the CPI for 1979 was 138.25 (base year 1975 = 100) and for 1980 it was 155.39, so that the inflation rate in 1980 is calculated as $h = CPI_{1980}/CPI_{1979} - 1 = 155.39/138.25 - 1 = 0.1240$, or 12.40%, as shown in Table 2.1. The nominal rate of return in 1980, $R^* = 11.17\%$, can be adjusted for inflation using formula (2.11),

$$1 + R_r^* = \frac{1 + 0.1117}{1 + 0.1240} = 0.9891$$

so that the *real* rate of return in 1980 was $R_r^* = 0.9891 - 1 = -0.0109$, or $-1.09\%$. Thus a respectable rate of return of over 11% is actually a negative rate of return of *minus* 1% in real terms, when adjusted for the inflation in 1980. Similarly in 1979, a positive (though admittedly low) nominal rate of return $R^* = 2.65\%$ is transformed into a negative real rate of return $R_r^* = -9.41\%$ by adjustment for the annual inflation.

How does the inflation affect multiyear performance? The geometric mean annual rate of return of DuPont over the five-year period 1976–1980 is calculated from Table 2.1 as

$$1 + \bar{R}^* = [(1 + R_1)(1 + R_2)(1 + R_3)(1 + R_4)(1 + R_5)]^{1/5} =$$
$$= [1.1102 \times 0.9348 \times 1.1133 \times 1.0265 \times 1.1117]^{1/5} = (1.3185)^{1/5} = 1.0569$$

**Table 2.1**
**Rates of Return on DuPont Common Stock, 1976–1980**

| Year | Nominal Return $R^*$ | Inflation Rate $h$ | Real Rate of Return $R_r^*$ |
|---|---|---|---|
| 1976 | 11.02% | 4.81% | 5.93% |
| 1977 | −6.52 | 6.77 | −12.45 |
| 1978 | 11.33 | 9.03 | 2.11 |
| 1979 | 2.65 | 13.31 | −9.41 |
| 1980 | 11.17 | 12.40 | −1.09 |

*Source*: The CRSP Return File for nominal rates of return. US CPI data for inflation rate.

or $\bar{R}^* = 5.69\%$. The average inflation rate for the period is similarly calculated as

$$1 + \bar{h} = (1.0481 \times 1.0677 \times 1.0903 \times 1.1331 \times 1.1240)^{1/5} = (1.5539)^{1/5} = 1.0922$$

or $\bar{h} = 9.22\%$.[13]

The real average annual rate of return on DuPont common over the period 1976–1980 is thus given from (2.11) by

$$1 + \bar{R}_r^* = \frac{1 + \bar{R}^*}{1 + \bar{h}} = \frac{1.0569}{1.0922} = 0.9677$$

Hence $\bar{R}_r^* = 0.9677 - 1 = -0.0323$ or $-3.23\%$. Thus, over the five-year period 1976–1980, a fairly respectable annual rate of return of nearly 6% actually represents a negative rate of return of below *minus* 3% in real, inflation-adjusted terms. The profitability of DuPont common stock in this period simply did not catch up with inflation: anyone who invested $100 in DuPont stock at the beginning of 1976 had only $97 of *equivalent purchasing power* at the end of 1980. Stocks are thus not necessarily a hedge for inflation.

## 2.2    Calculating the Rate of Return in Practice

To illustrate the calculation of the rate of return in practice, we will consider a number of real-life examples drawn from companies that distribute cash and stock dividends, split their stock, and float rights issues. The effect of differential income and capital tax rates will also be examined.

### 2.2.1    Adjustment of Rate of Return for Cash and Stock Dividends

Let us consider the stock of Cannon Mills during the year 1980. Table 2.2 sets out the necessary data for adjusting the number of shares held as a result of various distributions. The year began with a 10% stock dividend, which was followed by four quarterly cash dividends of $0.30 per share. Suppose that the investor purchased 100 shares of Cannon Mills stocks at the beginning of 1980: the price on January 2, 1980, was $24\frac{6}{8}$, so that the total initial investment was $2,475 for 100 shares. The year opened with a 10% stock dividend declared by the company: as a result the investor's holdings automatically increased to $100 \times 1.10 = 110$ shares even before the first-quarter cash dividend was declared. Thus, when the first-quarter cash dividend of $0.30

---

[13] The mean annual inflation rate also may be calculated as the geometric mean of the CPI, thus
$$1 + \bar{h} = (CPI_{1980}/CPI_{1975})^{1/5} = (155.39/100)^{1/5} = (1.5539)^{1/5} = 1.0922$$
or $\bar{h} = 9.22\%$, which coincides with the above figure.

**Table 2.2**
**Calculation of Index of Shares for Cannon Mills Common, 1980***

| Cash Dividends ($ per share) | Stock Dividends† | Share Price on 15th of Following Month | Additional Shares Acquired | Index of Number of Shares |
|---|---|---|---|---|
| | | | | 100.00 |
| | 10% | | 10 | 110.00 |
| 0.30 | | $22\frac{3}{8}$ | 1.47 | 111.47 |
| 0.30 | | $21\frac{7}{8}$ | 1.53 | 113.00 |
| 0.30 | | $23$ | 1.47 | 114.47 |
| 0.30 | | $22\frac{4}{8}$ | 1.53 | 116.00 |

* All transactions within the year are given in strict chronological order.
† A 10% stock dividend means that each investor receives additional shares in an amount equal to 10% of his original holding.

per share was declared, the investor received a total of $0.30 \times 110 = \$33$ in cash. It usually takes some time (up to a fortnight) until the dividend check reaches us in the mail, so that the cash is usually assumed to be reinvested at the prices prevailing on the 15th of the month following the declaration of the dividend. The price of Cannon Mills common on the 15th of the following month was $22\frac{3}{8}$, and by reinvesting the $33 received in cash dividend the investor increased his holdings by $33/$22.375 = 1.47$ shares. The index of shares after the reinvestment of the first-quarter dividend is thus set at $110 + 1.47 = 111.47$. The second-quarter dividend is correspondingly paid on 111.47 shares, and the investor receives $0.30 \times 111.47 = \$33.44$ in cash. The price of a share on the 15th of the following month is $21\frac{7}{8}$, and by reinvesting the cash dividend the investor adds to his holdings $33.44/$21.875 = 1.53$ shares. The index of the number of shares at the end of the second quarter thus grows to $111.47 + 1.53 = 113.00$. Similar calculations are made for the dividend payments received at the end of the following two quarters. If the proceeds of all cash dividends are consistently reinvested on the 15th of the month following the ex-dividend date, the index of shares rises from 100 at the beginning of the year to 116.00 at the end of the year. It should be noted that failure to reinvest the interim dividends would be tantamount to ignoring the need for time discounting *within* the year, and since dividend payment dates of various firms do not always coincide, the comparability of the rates of return would be impaired.

In order to complete the rate of return calculations, we need the share market price at the beginning of the year and at the end of the year: these market prices will enable us to evaluate the initial and the terminal value of the investment. For Cannon Mills common, we have the following data:

Share price on January 2, 1980      $P_0 = \$24\frac{6}{8}$
Share price on December 31, 1980    $P_1 = \$25\frac{7}{8}$

Applying formula (2.9), we obtain for the nominal annual rate of return

$$R^*_{1980} = \frac{V_1}{V_0} - 1 = \frac{\$25.875 \times 116.00}{\$24.750 \times 100.00} - 1 = \frac{\$3,001.50}{\$2,475.00} - 1 = 0.2127$$

that is, the pre-tax rate of return to investors in Cannon Mills common stock in 1980 was 21.3%.

### 2.2.2  Adjustment of Rate of Return for Cash Dividends and Splits

Table 2.3 sets out the share index for Mary Kay Cosmetics in 1980. Here, in addition to the quarterly dividend payments, the company split its stock 2-to-1 in the last quarter, so that each shareholder received *two* new shares for each old share held. Here, as in the previous examples, each transaction must be considered in its proper chronological order. For example, an investor who started the year with 100 shares had a total of 101.38 shares (due to reinvestment of the quarterly cash dividends) when the split was declared. These extra shares are naturally eligible for the split, just as the 10 extra shares added by the stock dividend in the Cannon Mills example were eligible for the first-quarter cash dividend (see Table 2.2). By the end of the year, an investor who started with 100 shares, reinvested the cash dividends, and kept the split shares had 203.40 shares in his closing portfolio.

The beginning- and end-of-year share market prices were as follows:

Share price on January 2, 1980     $P_0 = \$28\frac{6}{8}$
Share price on December 31, 1980   $P_1 = \$26\frac{4}{8}$

The rate of return on Mary Kay Cosmetics common is calculated as follows:

$$R^*_{1980} = \frac{V_1}{V_0} - 1 = \frac{\$26.500 \times 203.40}{\$28.750 \times 100.00} - 1 = \frac{\$5,390.10}{\$2,875.00} - 1 = 0.875$$

**Table 2.3**
**Calculation of Index of Shares for Mary Kay Cosmetics, 1980\***

| Cash Dividends ($ per share) | Split† | Share Price on 15th of Following Month | Additional Shares Acquired | Index of Number of Shares |
|---|---|---|---|---|
| | | | | 100.00 |
| 0.15 | | $27\frac{3}{8}$ | 0.55 | 100.55 |
| 0.15 | | $35\frac{3}{8}$ | 0.43 | 100.98 |
| 0.20 | | $50 | 0.40 | 101.38 |
| | 2-for-1 | | 101.38 | 202.76 |
| 0.10 | | $31\frac{7}{8}$ | 0.64 | 203.40 |

\* All transactions within the year are given in strict chronological order.
† A 2-for-1 split means that each shareholder gets 2 new shares for each old (pre-split) share held, and the old shares are withdrawn. This is numerically equivalent to a 100% stock dividend.

Thus the rate of return on Mary Kay Cosmetics common stock was 87.5% in 1980. The importance of making the adjustments can readily be seen if we calculate the *meaningless* unadjusted rate of return based on the total annual cash dividend and the end-of-year share price:

$$\frac{D + P_1}{P_0} - 1 = \frac{\$0.60 + \$26\frac{4}{8}}{\$28\frac{6}{8}} - 1 = -0.0574$$

or −5.74%. Thus failure to adjust the calculations for reinvestment of dividends and mainly for the split results in a negative rate of return. It should be clear from this example that care must be exercised when making rough rule-of-thumb calculations of rates of return from stock prices published, for example, in the financial pages of the local newspaper.

### 2.2.3  Adjustment for Cash Dividends, Splits, and Rights

The final example considered is that of IBM. Table 2.4 sets out the index of the number of shares for IBM common stock in 1966. This particular year was chosen since IBM paid cash dividends, split its stock, and also floated a rights issue. Once again, it should be noted that all of the above benefits must be listed in exact chronological order. An investor who held 100 shares of IBM at the beginning of the

**Table 2.4**
**Calculation of Index of Shares for IBM,1966\***

| Cash Dividends ($ per share) | Split and Rights | Share Price on 15th of Following Month | Additional Shares Acquired | Index of Number of Shares |
|---|---|---|---|---|
| | | | | 100.00 |
| 1.50 | | $513\frac{4}{8}$ | 0.29 | 100.29 |
| | 3 for 2 | | 50.15 | 150.44 |
| 1.10 | | $342\frac{4}{8}$ | 0.48 | 150.92 |
| | 1 for 40 $P_s = 285$† | 355 | 0.74 | 151.66 |
| 1.10 | | 348 | 0.48 | 152.14 |
| 1.10 | | $352\frac{4}{8}$ | 0.47 | 152.61 |

\* All transactions within the year are given in strict chronological order.
† This means that one "new" share is offered to a holder of 40 "old" shares at a below-market subscription price of $285 (while the market price is $355). For rights no time lag is necessary and the relevant calculation is:

$$\frac{150.92 \cdot \$1.75}{\$355} = 0.74 \text{ shares}$$

where   150.92 = number of shares eligible for rights offering
$1.75 = market value of the rights attaching to one share
$355 = market price of shares on first day of trading after rights issue.

year and reinvested the cash dividends, held the split stock, and used the proceeds from the sale of the rights to purchase additional shares had 152.61 shares at the end of the year. The rate of return on IBM common for 1966 was:

$$R^*_{1966} = \frac{152.61 \cdot 384\frac{4}{8}}{100 \cdot 492\frac{4}{8}} - 1 = 19.14\%$$

where:

$384\frac{4}{8}$ = the price of a share at the end of the year
$492\frac{4}{8}$ = the price of a share at the beginning of the year.

Thus the rate of return on IBM Common stock was about 19% in 1966. Once again care has to be taken to adjust the calculation; a rough rule-of-thumb calculation, based on beginning- and end-of-year prices and the cash dividend, results in a meaningless negative rate of return.

### 2.2.4 After-tax Rates of Return

To this point we have ignored taxes on dividend income and capital appreciation. Clearly, we can have as many rates of return as there are income tax brackets. The rates of return on common stock held by a pension fund would presumably be calculated on a pre-tax basis if the fund is exempt from both income and capital gains taxes. The appropriate calculation for individuals would have to reflect their marginal tax rates, and, of course, these rates vary from individual to individual.

Consider the investment in AT&T stock, which in 1980 paid a regular quarterly dividend of $1.25 per share. The data set out in Table 2.5 show that, with all dividends

**Table 2.5**
**Pre-tax Rate of Return on AT&T Common Stock, 1980**

| Cash Dividends ($ per share) | Share Price on 15th of Following Month | Additional Shares Acquired | Index of Number of Shares |
|---|---|---|---|
| | | | 100.00 |
| 1.25 | $47\frac{1}{8}$ | 2.65 | 102.65 |
| 1.25 | $53\frac{7}{8}$ | 2.38 | 105.03 |
| 1.25 | $53\frac{2}{8}$ | 2.47 | 107.50 |
| 1.25 | $45$ | 2.99 | 110.49 |

Share price January 4, 1980    $P_0 = \$52$
Share price December 31, 1980    $P_1 = \$47\frac{7}{8}$

Pre-tax rate of return $= \dfrac{\$47\frac{7}{8} \times 110.49}{\$52 \times 100.00} - 1 = 0.0173$, or 1.73%.

reinvested, the index of the number of shares increased from 100 to 110.49 during the year 1980. On this basis, the rate of return on AT&T common in 1980 was 1.73%. The same rate of return could have been earned by skipping all dividend payments and declaring a 10% stock dividend (more precisely, a stock dividend of 10.49%) during 1980: this would bring the end-of-year index of number of shares to the same level and ensure the same rate of return.

This argument assumes, however, that investors pay no taxes and that the entire cash dividend is available for reinvestment. The rate of return calculated in this way is accordingly called the *pre-tax* rate of return. In reality, dividend income is taxed according to the individual investor's income tax bracket, and it is quite possible that some investors are left with only $0.625 per share after paying 50% tax on AT&T cash dividend, while others (such as tax-exempt pension funds or senior citizens) get to keep the entire amount. The amount available for reinvestment thus varies from one investor to another, depending on the tax bracket, and the *after-tax* rate of return changes accordingly.

Stock dividend, on the other hand, is not considered income: it is treated as capital appreciation and is therefore taxed at the capital gains rates, which are generally lower than income tax rates.

Consider an individual in the 50% income tax bracket, while the capital gains rate is only 20%. This individual is left with $1.25 \times 0.50 = \$0.625$ for reinvestment out of

**Table 2.6**
**After-tax Rate of Return on AT&T Common Stock, 1980, Assuming 50% Income Tax Rate**

| Cash Dividend ($ per share) | | Price on 15th of Following Month | Additional Shares Acquired | Index of Number of Shares |
|---|---|---|---|---|
| Before Tax | After 50% Tax | | | |
| | | | | 100.00 |
| 1.25 | 0.625 | $47\frac{1}{8}$ | 1.33 | 101.33 |
| 1.25 | 0.625 | $53\frac{7}{8}$ | 1.18 | 102.51 |
| 1.25 | 0.625 | $53\frac{2}{8}$ | 1.20 | 103.71 |
| 1.25 | 0.625 | $45 | 1.44 | 105.15 |

Share price January 4, 1980    $P_0 = \$52$
Share price December 31, 1980    $P_1 = \$47\frac{7}{8}$

$A$: After-tax rate of return $= \dfrac{\$47\frac{7}{8} \times 105.15}{\$52 \times 100.00} - 1 = -0.0319$ or $-3.19\%$.

$B$: *Capital loss adjustment*
    Capital loss component $= \$47\frac{7}{8} \times 100 - \$52 \times 100 = -412.50$
    Capital gains tax rebate $= 0.20 \times \$412.50 = 82.50$
    After-tax rate of return adjusted for capital loss tax rebate $=$

$$\frac{\$47\frac{7}{8} \times 105.15 + \$82.50}{\$52 \times 100.00} - 1 = -0.0160 \text{ or } -1.60\%$$

Strictly speaking capital loss is also possible on the additional shares purchased through reinvestment of dividends, but this component is small as only 5.15 new shares were purchased after the original 100 shares.

AT&T's quarterly cash dividend. His index of the number of shares will increase to only 105.15, as shown in Table 2.6, and his rate of return will be negative, $-3.19$.[14]

Now, if the cash dividend is skipped and a 10.49% stock dividend is substituted the end-of-year value of the investment will be

$$\$47\tfrac{7}{8} \times 110.49 = \$5,289.71$$

Assuming that the investor purchased 100 AT&T shares a year earlier at $52 per share, his capital gain is

$$\$5,289.71 - \$5,200 = \$89.71$$

After paying 20% of this amount in capital gains tax, the investor is left with

$$\$5,289.71 - \$89.71 \times 0.20 = \$5,271.77$$

The *after-tax rate of return* in this case is thus

$$\frac{\$5,271.77}{\$5,200} - 1 = 0.0138$$

i.e., a positive return of 1.38% compared with a *loss* of 3.19% in case of cash dividend. Thus, cash dividend and stock dividend (or split) are equivalent only for tax-exempt investors. When dividend income and capital gains are taxed at differential rates, individuals in different tax brackets will differ in their preferences for these cash and non-cash distributions.

## 2.3 Rates of Return of Bonds and Preferred Stocks

We turn now to the examination of the principles underlying the measurement of profitability of fixed-income-bearing securities, such as bonds and preferred stocks. We shall first generalize the rate of return concept developed in previous sections for common stocks to cover bonds and preferred stocks.

### 2.3.1 The Holding-period Rate of Return

Formula (2.2) for computing the rate of return on common stock presented in

[14] Since the stock price dropped from $52 to $47\tfrac{7}{8}$ during the year, the investor can show a capital loss of $412.50 on his original investment in 100 shares. This capital loss can be offset against his capital gains, resulting in a tax saving of $82.50. If added to the value of the investment, the tax saving slightly increases the rate of return, which however remains negative, $-1.6\%$ (see Table 2.6 for details).

Section 2.1.1 can readily be generalized to cover fixed-income-bearing securities, and for that matter other financial assets as well. The application of the geometric mean rate of return to preferred stock requires no special treatment. As is true of a common stock, the rate of return on a preferred share in any particular period is given by the formula

$$R_t = \frac{D_t + (P_t - P_{t-1})}{P_{t-1}}$$

$$= \frac{D_t + P_t}{P_{t-1}} - 1$$

where:

$R_t$ = the rate of return in period $t$
$P_t$ = the share's market price at the end of period $t$
$D_t$ = the cash dividend received in period $t$.

Since stock dividends, and rights, are usually not offered to preferred shareholders, no further adjustments are necessary and the rate of return on a preferred stock held over $n$ years can be found by taking the geometric mean.

$$\bar{R} = \left[ \prod_{t=1}^{n} (1 + R_t) \right]^{1/n} - 1$$

where $\bar{R}$ is the geometric mean rate of return (compare formula (2.3)).

The rate of return on a bond in any given period can be calculated as a straight-forward extension of the formula for a preferred share:

$$R_t = \frac{C_t + P_t}{P_{t-1}} - 1 \tag{2.12}$$

where:

$R_t$ = the rate of return to an investor in a bond in period $t$
$C_t$ = the interest coupon received in period $t$ (the equivalent of dividends for bonds)
$P_t$ = the market price of the bond at the end of period $t$.

If the investment period spans several years, the geometric mean formula is again applied:

$$\bar{R} = \left[ \prod_{t=1}^{n} (1 + R_t) \right]^{1/n} - 1 \tag{2.13}$$

The rate of return on a bond calculated from formula (2.12) or the corresponding geometric mean (2.13) is called the *holding-period* rate of return, to distinguish it from the yield to maturity—a different measure of bond profitability considered in the next section.

Thus the geometric mean rate of return can be applied to preferred stock and bonds as well as to common stock. It should be emphasized that when comparing the *historical* rates of return on bonds and stocks, the same formula, that is, the geometric mean, should be used for both. This cautionary note is introduced since we now turn our attention to an alternative, and much better known, formula for calculating the yield to maturity of a bond. The two should not be confused.

### 2.3.2 Bond Yields

The investor contemplating the purchase of a bond is often concerned with the rate of return which the bond offers if held to maturity, independent of fluctuations in the bond's price during the interim period. An insurance company, for example, is concerned with the *long-term* return which can be earned on bonds currently purchased, since this is an important factor influencing the terms which the company is able to offer new policyholders; similarly, many investors contemplating the purchase of a bond are concerned with the yield such a bond affords if held to maturity. The rate of return, when a bond is held until redemption, is called its "yield to maturity" or "redemption yield", and is given by a simple application of the familiar formula for the internal rate of return (compare Equation (2.1))

$$P_0 = \frac{C_1}{1 + R} + \frac{C_2}{(1 + R)^2} + \cdots + \frac{C_n}{(1 + R)^n} + \frac{P_n}{(1 + R)^n}$$

$$P_0 = \sum_{t=1}^{n} \frac{C_t}{(1 + R)^t} + \frac{P_n}{(1 + R)^n}$$

where:

$C_t$ = the interest coupon in period $t$
$P_0$ = the current market price of the bond
$P_n$ = the redemption value of the bond at maturity
$R$ = the yield to maturity of the bond.

In practice the calculation of yields to maturity is a relatively simple matter since detailed bond tables are available which eliminate all of the tedious arithmetic necessary to calculate the yield. Using the sample bond table pages given in Table 2.7 we can easily "calculate" the yield to maturity of a bond with, say, a 5% coupon and 20 years remaining to maturity. If the offering or market price is $1,000 (that is, 100% of face value) the yield is 5%. If the market price is above the face value of the bond, for example, $1,110 or 110%, the yield can be found by running down the 20-year column

## Table 2.7
## Sample Bond Table for 5% Coupon Bond

| Yield | Years and months | | | | | | | |
|---|---|---|---|---|---|---|---|---|
| | *19–5* | *19–6* | *19–7* | *19–8* | *19–9* | *19–10* | *19–11* | *20–0* |
| 0.00 | 197.08 | 197.50 | 197.92 | 198.33 | 198.75 | 199.17 | 199.58 | 200.00 |
| 0.25 | 189.97 | 190.35 | 190.72 | 191.10 | 191.48 | 191.85 | 192.23 | 192.61 |
| 0.35 | 187.21 | 187.58 | 187.94 | 188.30 | 188.66 | 189.02 | 189.38 | 189.74 |
| 0.40 | 185.85 | 186.21 | 186.56 | 186.92 | 187.27 | 187.62 | 187.98 | 188.33 |
| 0.45 | 184.50 | 184.85 | 185.20 | 185.55 | 185.89 | 186.24 | 186.59 | 186.93 |
| 0.50 | 183.17 | 183.51 | 183.85 | 184.19 | 184.53 | 184.87 | 185.21 | 185.54 |
| 0.55 | 181.84 | 182.18 | 182.51 | 182.84 | 183.17 | 183.51 | 183.84 | 184.17 |
| 0.60 | 180.53 | 180.86 | 181.18 | 181.51 | 181.83 | 182.16 | 182.48 | 182.81 |
| 0.65 | 179.23 | 179.55 | 179.87 | 180.18 | 180.50 | 180.82 | 181.14 | 181.46 |
| 0.70 | 177.94 | 178.25 | 178.56 | 178.87 | 179.19 | 179.50 | 179.81 | 180.12 |
| 0.75 | 176.66 | 176.97 | 177.27 | 177.58 | 177.88 | 178.19 | 178.49 | 178.80 |
| 0.80 | 175.39 | 175.69 | 175.99 | 176.29 | 176.59 | 176.88 | 177.18 | 177.48 |
| 0.85 | 174.14 | 174.43 | 174.72 | 175.01 | 175.30 | 175.60 | 175.89 | 176.18 |
| 0.90 | 172.89 | 173.18 | 173.46 | 173.75 | 174.03 | 174.32 | 174.60 | 174.89 |
| 0.95 | 171.66 | 171.94 | 172.22 | 172.49 | 172.77 | 173.05 | 173.33 | 173.61 |
| 1.00 | 170.43 | 170.71 | 170.98 | 171.25 | 171.52 | 171.80 | 172.07 | 172.34 |
| 1.05 | 169.22 | 169.49 | 169.75 | 170.02 | 170.29 | 170.55 | 170.82 | 171.09 |
| 1.10 | 168.02 | 168.28 | 168.54 | 168.80 | 169.06 | 169.32 | 169.58 | 169.84 |
| 1.15 | 166.82 | 167.08 | 167.34 | 167.59 | 167.85 | 168.10 | 168.36 | 168.61 |
| 1.20 | 165.64 | 165.89 | 166.14 | 166.39 | 166.64 | 166.89 | 167.14 | 167.39 |
| 1.25 | 164.47 | 164.72 | 164.96 | 165.20 | 165.45 | 165.69 | 165.93 | 166.18 |
| 1.30 | 163.31 | 163.55 | 163.79 | 164.02 | 164.26 | 164.50 | 164.74 | 164.98 |
| 1.35 | 162.16 | 162.39 | 162.63 | 162.86 | 163.09 | 163.32 | 163.55 | 163.79 |
| 1.40 | 161.02 | 161.25 | 161.47 | 161.70 | 161.93 | 162.15 | 162.38 | 162.61 |
| 1.45 | 159.89 | 160.11 | 160.33 | 160.55 | 160.77 | 161.00 | 161.22 | 161.44 |
| 1.50 | 158.77 | 158.98 | 159.20 | 159.42 | 159.63 | 159.85 | 160.07 | 160.28 |
| 1.55 | 157.65 | 157.87 | 158.08 | 158.29 | 158.50 | 158.71 | 158.92 | 159.13 |
| 1.60 | 156.55 | 156.76 | 156.97 | 157.17 | 157.38 | 157.58 | 157.79 | 158.00 |
| 1.65 | 155.46 | 155.66 | 155.86 | 156.06 | 156.27 | 156.77 | 156.67 | 156.87 |
| 1.70 | 154.38 | 154.58 | 154.77 | 154.97 | 155.16 | 155.36 | 155.56 | 155.75 |
| 1.75 | 153.30 | 153.50 | 153.69 | 153.88 | 154.07 | 154.26 | 154.45 | 154.64 |
| 1.80 | 152.24 | 152.43 | 152.61 | 152.80 | 152.99 | 153.17 | 153.36 | 153.55 |
| 1.85 | 151.18 | 151.37 | 151.55 | 151.73 | 151.91 | 152.09 | 152.28 | 152.46 |
| 1.90 | 150.14 | 150.32 | 150.49 | 150.67 | 150.85 | 151.02 | 151.20 | 151.38 |
| 1.95 | 149.10 | 149.28 | 149.45 | 149.62 | 149.79 | 149.96 | 150.14 | 150.31 |
| 2.00 | 148.07 | 148.24 | 148.41 | 148.58 | 148.75 | 148.91 | 149.08 | 149.25 |
| 2.05 | 147.05 | 147.22 | 147.38 | 147.55 | 147.71 | 147.87 | 148.04 | 148.20 |
| 2.10 | 146.04 | 146.21 | 146.36 | 146.52 | 146.68 | 146.84 | 147.00 | 147.16 |
| 2.15 | 145.04 | 145.20 | 145.35 | 145.51 | 145.66 | 145.82 | 145.97 | 146.13 |
| 2.20 | 144.05 | 144.20 | 144.35 | 144.50 | 144.65 | 144.80 | 144.96 | 145.11 |

**Table 2.7 continued**

*Years and months*

| Yield | 19–5 | 19–6 | 19–7 | 19–8 | 19–9 | 19–10 | 19–11 | 20–0 |
|---|---|---|---|---|---|---|---|---|
| 2.25 | 143.07 | 143.21 | 143.36 | 143.51 | 143.65 | 143.80 | 143.95 | 144.09 |
| 2.30 | 142.09 | 142.23 | 142.38 | 142.52 | 143.66 | 142.80 | 142.95 | 143.09 |
| 2.35 | 141.12 | 141.26 | 141.40 | 141.54 | 141.68 | 141.81 | 141.95 | 142.09 |
| 2.40 | 140.16 | 140.30 | 140.43 | 140.57 | 140.77 | 140.84 | 140.97 | 141.11 |
| 2.45 | 139.21 | 139.34 | 139.47 | 139.60 | 139.73 | 139.86 | 140.00 | 140.13 |
| 2.50 | 138.27 | 138.40 | 138.52 | 138.65 | 138.75 | 138.90 | 139.03 | 139.16 |
| 2.55 | 137.33 | 137.46 | 137.58 | 137.70 | 137.83 | 137.95 | 138.07 | 138.20 |
| 2.60 | 136.41 | 136.53 | 136.65 | 136.76 | 136.88 | 137.00 | 137.12 | 137.24 |
| 2.65 | 135.49 | 135.61 | 135.72 | 135.83 | 135.95 | 136.07 | 136.18 | 136.30 |
| 2.70 | 134.58 | 134.69 | 134.80 | 134.91 | 135.02 | 135.14 | 135.25 | 135.36 |
| 2.75 | 133.67 | 133.78 | 133.89 | 134.00 | 134.11 | 134.22 | 134.33 | 134.44 |
| 2.80 | 132.78 | 132.89 | 132.99 | 133.09 | 133.20 | 133.30 | 133.41 | 133.52 |
| 2.85 | 131.89 | 131.99 | 132.09 | 132.19 | 132.30 | 132.40 | 132.50 | 132.60 |
| 2.90 | 131.01 | 131.11 | 131.21 | 131.30 | 131.40 | 131.50 | 131.60 | 131.70 |
| 2.95 | 130.14 | 130.23 | 130.33 | 130.42 | 130.52 | 130.61 | 130.71 | 130.80 |
| 3.00 | 129.27 | 129.36 | 129.45 | 129.55 | 129.64 | 129.73 | 129.82 | 129.92 |
| 3.05 | 128.41 | 128.50 | 128.59 | 128.68 | 128.77 | 128.85 | 128.94 | 129.04 |
| 3.10 | 127.56 | 127.65 | 127.73 | 127.82 | 127.90 | 127.99 | 128.07 | 128.16 |
| 3.15 | 126.72 | 126.80 | 126.88 | 126.96 | 127.05 | 127.13 | 127.21 | 127.30 |
| 3.20 | 125.88 | 125.96 | 126.04 | 126.12 | 126.20 | 126.28 | 126.36 | 126.44 |
| 3.25 | 125.05 | 125.13 | 125.20 | 125.28 | 125.36 | 125.43 | 125.51 | 125.59 |
| 3.30 | 124.23 | 124.30 | 124.38 | 124.45 | 124.52 | 124.59 | 124.67 | 124.75 |
| 3.35 | 123.41 | 123.49 | 123.55 | 123.62 | 123.69 | 123.76 | 123.84 | 123.91 |
| 3.40 | 122.60 | 122.67 | 122.74 | 122.81 | 122.87 | 122.94 | 123.01 | 123.08 |
| 3.45 | 121.80 | 121.87 | 121.93 | 122.00 | 122.06 | 122.13 | 122.19 | 122.26 |
| 3.50 | 121.00 | 121.07 | 121.13 | 121.19 | 121.25 | 121.32 | 121.38 | 121.45 |
| 3.55 | 120.22 | 120.28 | 120.34 | 120.40 | 120.45 | 120.51 | 120.58 | 120.64 |
| 3.60 | 119.43 | 119.50 | 119.55 | 119.61 | 119.66 | 119.72 | 119.78 | 119.84 |
| 3.65 | 118.66 | 118.72 | 118.77 | 118.82 | 118.88 | 118.93 | 118.99 | 119.04 |
| 3.70 | 117.89 | 117.95 | 117.99 | 118.05 | 118.10 | 118.15 | 118.20 | 118.26 |
| 3.75 | 117.13 | 117.18 | 117.23 | 117.28 | 117.32 | 117.37 | 117.43 | 117.48 |
| 3.80 | 116.37 | 116.42 | 116.47 | 116.51 | 116.56 | 116.61 | 116.65 | 116.70 |
| 3.85 | 115.62 | 115.67 | 115.71 | 115.75 | 115.80 | 115.84 | 115.89 | 115.94 |
| 3.90 | 114.88 | 114.92 | 114.96 | 115.00 | 115.05 | 115.09 | 115.13 | 115.18 |
| 3.95 | 114.14 | 114.18 | 114.22 | 114.26 | 114.30 | 114.34 | 114.38 | 114.42 |
| 4.00 | 113.41 | 113.45 | 113.49 | 113.52 | 113.56 | 113.60 | 113.64 | 113.78 |
| 4.05 | 112.68 | 112.72 | 112.76 | 112.79 | 112.82 | 112.86 | 112.90 | 112.94 |
| 4.10 | 111.97 | 112.00 | 112.03 | 112.06 | 112.10 | 112.13 | 112.17 | 112.20 |
| 4.15 | 111.25 | 111.29 | 111.32 | 111.34 | 111.38 | 111.41 | 111.44 | 111.47 |
| 4.20 | 110.55 | 110.58 | 110.60 | 110.63 | 110.66 | 110.69 | 110.72 | 110.75 |

**Table 2.7 continued**

| | Years and months | | | | | | | |
|---|---|---|---|---|---|---|---|---|
| Yield | 19–5 | 19–6 | 19–7 | 19–8 | 19–9 | 19–10 | 19–11 | 20–0 |
| **4.25** | 109.84 | 109.88 | 109.90 | 109.92 | 109.95 | 109.98 | 110.01 | **110.04** |
| 4.30 | 109.15 | 109.18 | 109.20 | 109.22 | 109.25 | 109.27 | 109.30 | 109.33 |
| 4.35 | 108.46 | 108.49 | 108.51 | 108.53 | 108.55 | 108.57 | 108.60 | 108.62 |
| 4.40 | 107.78 | 107.80 | 107.82 | 107.84 | 107.86 | 107.88 | 107.90 | 107.93 |
| 4.45 | 107.10 | 107.12 | 107.14 | 107.15 | 107.17 | 107.19 | 107.21 | 107.23 |
| 4.50 | 106.42 | 106.45 | 106.46 | 106.47 | 106.49 | 106.51 | 106.53 | 106.55 |
| 4.55 | 105.76 | 105.78 | 105.79 | 105.80 | 105.82 | 105.83 | 105.85 | 105.87 |
| 4.60 | 105.10 | 105.11 | 105.12 | 105.13 | 105.15 | 105.16 | 105.18 | 105.19 |
| 4.65 | 104.44 | 104.46 | 104.46 | 104.47 | 104.48 | 104.50 | 104.51 | 104.57 |
| 4.70 | 103.79 | 103.80 | 103.81 | 103.82 | 103.83 | 103.84 | 103.85 | 103.86 |
| 4.75 | 103.14 | 103.16 | 103.16 | 103.17 | 103.17 | 103.18 | 103.19 | 103.20 |
| 4.80 | 102.50 | 102.51 | 102.52 | 102.52 | 102.53 | 102.53 | 102.54 | 102.55 |
| 4.85 | 101.87 | 101.88 | 101.88 | 101.88 | 101.88 | 101.89 | 101.90 | 101.91 |
| 4.90 | 101.24 | 101.25 | 101.25 | 101.25 | 101.25 | 101.25 | 101.26 | 101.27 |
| 4.95 | 100.61 | 100.62 | 100.62 | 100.62 | 100.62 | 100.62 | 100.62 | 100.63 |
| **5.00** | 100.00 | 100.00 | 100.00 | 99.99 | 99.99 | 99.99 | 100.00 | **100.00** |
| 5.05 | 99.38 | 99.38 | 99.38 | 99.37 | 99.37 | 99.37 | 99.37 | 99.38 |
| 5.10 | 98.77 | 98.77 | 98.77 | 98.76 | 98.76 | 98.75 | 98.75 | 98.76 |
| 5.15 | 98.17 | 98.17 | 98.16 | 98.15 | 98.15 | 98.14 | 98.14 | 98.14 |
| 5.20 | 97.57 | 97.57 | 97.56 | 97.55 | 97.54 | 97.54 | 97.53 | 97.53 |
| **5.25** | 96.97 | 96.97 | 96.96 | 96.95 | 96.94 | 96.93 | 96.93 | **96.93** |
| 5.30 | 96.39 | 96.38 | 96.37 | 96.36 | 96.35 | 96.34 | 96.33 | 96.33 |
| 5.40 | 95.22 | 95.21 | 95.20 | 95.18 | 95.17 | 95.16 | 95.15 | 95.14 |
| 5.50 | 94.07 | 94.06 | 94.05 | 94.03 | 94.01 | 94.00 | 93.99 | 93.98 |
| 5.60 | 92.95 | 92.94 | 92.91 | 92.89 | 92.88 | 92.86 | 92.85 | 92.84 |
| 5.70 | 91.84 | 91.82 | 91.80 | 91.78 | 91.76 | 91.74 | 91.72 | 91.71 |
| 5.75 | 91.29 | 91.27 | 91.25 | 91.23 | 91.21 | 91.19 | 91.17 | 91.15 |
| 6.00 | 88.62 | 88.60 | 88.56 | 88.54 | 88.51 | 88.49 | 88.46 | 88.44 |
| 6.50 | 83.58 | 83.55 | 83.51 | 83.47 | 83.44 | 83.40 | 83.37 | 83.34 |
| 7.00 | 78.93 | 78.90 | 78.85 | 78.80 | 78.76 | 78.72 | 78.68 | 78.64 |

of the appropriate page of the bond table until 110 is found and then glancing across to the left-hand column to find the yield. In this particular case the yield to maturity is approximately 4.25%.[15] Similarly, should the same bond be selling at a discount from face value, for example, $969.30 (96.93% of face value) the yield to maturity will be greater than the coupon yield, in this instance 5.25%. Currently the use of bond tables

[15] The bond tables themselves are simply very elaborate present value tables which reflect the payment of interim interest and permit a very accurate calculation of the yield. If the exact bond price does not appear in the table, the correct yield can be found by interpolation.

has been largely superseded by financial hand calculators, all of which are prepro-grammed for fast and easy yield-to-maturity calculations.

A word of caution before we turn to the description of the yield curves. The yield to maturity, despite its widespread use, is not the true long-term profitability of the bonds held to maturity. The reason is that the bonds pay the interest coupons every six months, and the investor may be unable to reinvest the interim cash receipts at the same rate of return $R$. For example, suppose that the yield to maturity of a bond is $R = 10\%$. At the end of the first year, interest rates drop from 10% to 5%. The cash receipts in this case will be reinvested only at 5%, and the 10% yield to maturity which emerges from the calculations is thus not the true long-term profitability: it suffers from the usual reinvestment rate difficulty of internal rate of return calculations (see Section 2.1). However, the yield to maturity gives a convenient proxy for the long-term profitability of bonds and is widely used in practice. Moreover, in case of accrual bonds which pay no interim interest coupons, the yield to maturity measures precisely the long-term profitability of the bonds, as no reinvestment of interim cash payments is involved.

### 2.3.3  The Time Pattern of Yields: The Yield Curve

At any point in time the yields on bonds will differ chiefly for two reasons:

(a)   differences in time to maturity, and
(b)   differences in the risk of default.

Abstracting from the latter we can concentrate on the yield vs. maturity relationship by considering bonds which are identical in every respect but maturity. The family of out-standing US Treasury issues provides such a population for studying the time patterns of yields.[16]

At first glance it would appear that liquidity considerations alone should be suf-ficient to determine the yield–maturity relationship. Such an approach suggests that a "premium" will exist for giving up liquidity so that the yield on long-term bonds will be above the yield of shorter-term bonds. This "liquidity preference" explanation is often identified with the work of Keynes, who viewed the rate of interest as the "reward for parting with liquidity".[17] Equivalently, such an approach suggests that a graphic portrayal of the yield vs. maturity relationship for otherwise identical securities, at any given point of time, will result in a monotonically rising "yield curve". Such a curve is illustrated in Figure 2.1, and represents the hypothetical time structure of bond yields

---

[16] Strictly speaking, the yields on government securities of a given maturity provide a homogeneous population only when all the bonds are selling at par. Owing to the differential taxation of interest income and capital gains, the pre-tax yields of two bonds with the *same* post-tax yield will tend to differ where one of the bonds is selling at a discount from par. For an analysis of this tax effect and the bias which it introduces into the observed yield curve, see A. A. Robichek and W. D. Niebuhr, "Tax-Induced Bias in Reported Treasury Yields", *Journal of Finance* XXV (December 1970).

[17] J. M. Keynes, *The General Theory of Employment, Interest and Money*, New York: Harcourt, Brace, 1936, Chapter 13.

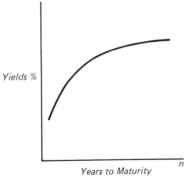

Yields %

Years to Maturity $n$

**Figure 2.1**

for a given class of bonds on a particular date. Years to maturity are measured along
the horizontal axis and yield to maturity is measured in percentage along the vertical
axis.

The simplified liquidity considerations which we have sketched above are,
however, not sufficient in themselves to account for the time pattern of interest rates.
Historically, three additional types of yield curves have been observed in the capital
market. At various times during the past 70 years, the yield curve has been (a)
monotonically decreasing—the yields on long-term maturities were *below* those of
short-term maturities; (b) "humped"—the yield curve rises between short- and
intermediate-term bonds and then declines for longer-term maturities; (c) stable—the
yield curve remains flat as the yields on short- and long-term securities are the same.
These three additional varieties of yield curve, decreasing, humped, and flat, are
illustrated in Figure 2.2.

The yield curve is a simplified graphical representation of the yields of a given risk
class of securities on a particular day. From time to time the yield curve may change,
and in fact all of the types of yield curves illustrated in Figures 2.1 and 2.2 have been
observed at one time or another. Figure 2.3 sets out the yield curves for corporate bonds

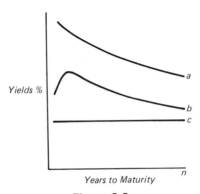

Yields %

Years to Maturity $n$

**Figure 2.2**

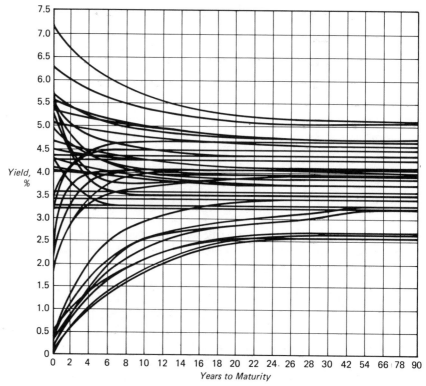

**Figure 2.3**
**Superimposed Basic Corporate Yield Curve, 1900–1942**

*Source:* David Durand, *Basic Yields of Corporate Bonds 1900–1942*, National Bureau of Economic Research, Technical Paper no. 3, June 1942.

which were calculated by David Durand for the first four decades of this century.[18] It is apparent from the diagram that the upward sloping yield curve, which represents a situation in which long-term yields exceed short-term yields, cannot be considered to constitute the "normal" relationship, at least from the statistical point of view; while it is true that for the period 1900–1960, for which data were analyzed, yield curves were on the average positively sloped, negatively sloped or humped curves were not uncommon.[19] In general, short-term rates tended to be high relative to long-term rates at the peaks of the business cycle, while the opposite relationship, that is, low short-term rates relative to long-term rates, existed at cyclical troughs.[20] Theory can be reconciled with these empirical findings, even within the framework

[18] See D. Durand, *Basic Yields of Corporate Bonds 1900–1942*, Technical Paper no. 3, New York: National Bureau of Economic Research, June 1942.
[19] See R. A. Kessel, *The Cyclical Behavior of the Term Structure of Interest Rates*, Occasional Paper No. 91, New York: National Bureau of Economic Research, 1965.
[20] *Ibid.*, p. 4.

of liquidity preference, by explicitly introducing expectations regarding the future level of interest rates, The so-called expectations hypothesis is especially popular among economists; well known variants have been expounded by Fisher, Keynes, Hicks, and Lutz.[21] In what follows we shall set out a highly simplified alternative view of expectations which can be used to reconcile the empirical evidence regarding the slope of the yield curve.[22]

To bring out the crucial role played by expectations let us make the following simplifying assumptions:

(a)  future short-term rates are known with certainty;
(b)  there are no transaction costs on borrowing or lending;
(c)  lenders and borrowers enjoy complete shiftability among bonds of different maturities; that is, an investor is indifferent between the purchase of a ten-year bond or ten purchases of one-year bonds.

Under these assumptions the yield on all investments taken for a given period will be equalized, independent of whether we deal with an investment for the entire duration of the period or a series of short-term investments repeated several times over the period in question. Competition in the market will ensure that under these assumptions the sum to which a dollar accumulates over $n$ years at the long-term rate $R_n$ must be equal to the future value which accumulates over $n$ years using the short-term rates $r_1, r_2, \ldots, r_n$:

$$1 + R_1 = 1 + r_1$$
$$(1 + R_2)^2 = (1 + r_1)(1 + r_2)$$
$$\cdots\cdots\cdots\cdots\cdots\cdots$$
$$(1 + R_n)^n = (1 + r_1)(1 + r_2) \cdots (1 + r_n)$$

From these relationships we can derive the appropriate formula for the long-term rate.

Since investors must receive the same capital sum by accumulating two periods at the rate $R_2$ or one period at $r_1$ and a second period at the *forward* rate $r_2$, the long-term rate is the geometric average of the relevant forward short rates:

$$R_1 = (1 + r_1) - 1$$
$$R_2 = [(1 + r_1)(1 + r_2)]^{1/2} - 1$$
$$R_3 = [(1 + r_1)(1 + r_2)(1 + r_3)]^{1/3} - 1$$
$$\cdots\cdots\cdots\cdots\cdots\cdots\cdots\cdots\cdots\cdots$$
$$R_n = [(1 + r_1)(1 + r_2)(1 + r_3) \cdots (1 + r_n)]^{1/n} - 1$$

[21] A convenient summary of the expectations hypothesis can be found in F. A. Lutz, *The Theory of Interest*, Dordrecht, Holland: D. Reidel Publishing Co., 1967, Chapter 17.

[22] For more detailed discussions of the expectations hypothesis see J. R. Hicks' classic analysis in his *Value and Capital*, 2nd ed., Oxford: Oxford University Press, 1953, Chapter 11; and B. G. Malkiel, "Expectations, Bond Prices, and the Term Structure of Interest Rates", *Quarterly Journal of Economics*, Vol. 76 (May 1962).

Using this formula we can also infer the expected forward short-term rates from the existing long-term rates. For example, the forward short-term rate $r_3$ (expected to prevail during the third year in the future) is derived as follows:

$$1 + r_3 = \frac{(1 + R_3)^3}{(1 + R_2)^2}$$

Viewing the long-term rate as an average of the expected short-term rates yields the following conclusions, which can help to reconcile the existence of the differing shapes of the yield curve discussed above.

(1)    If the short-term rates are expected to remain unchanged, all long-term rates will equal the short-term rates.

(2)    If at a given point in time the (geometric) average of the expected short-term rates up to the maturity date of the long-term bond is above the current short-term rate, the long rate will be above the short rate.

(3)    If the (geometric) average of short rates increases as additional time periods are considered (that is, $r_2 > r_1, r_3 >$ average of $r_1$ and $r_2$, and so on) the yield curve will be monotonically increasing. If after a given period the future short rates remain unchanged, the yield curve will eventually flatten out.

(4)    Conversely, if at a given moment, the (geometric) average of the expected short-term rates is below the current short-term rate, the long-term rate will be *below* the short-term rate, and by using a line of reasoning similar to that used in (3) above, the yield curve will be downward sloping, if the expected short-term rates are expected to fall.

Thus by introducing "expectations" all types of yield curve—upward sloping, stable, downward sloping, or for that matter any combination of the three, can be rationalized.[23]


## 2.3.4 Duration of Bonds

The years to maturity of a bond indicate how long the investor should wait before receiving the face value of the bond on redemption. It is common to think that bonds with similar maturity have common characteristics, e.g., the same risk of price volatility. In practice, however, this is not the case, since bonds with identical years to maturity may differ with regard to the pattern of interest payments over time. It is clear that a bond which pays high interest in relatively early years has a shorter "true length", since investors receive a relatively large part of the total cash flow before the "formal" maturity of the bond.

---

[23] For a more detailed and critical evaluation of the expectations hypothesis see Lutz, *op. cit.*

The notion of *duration* was introduced by Macaulay[24] to describe the true length of a bond. The duration of any loan is simply the weighted average of the maturities of the individual loans that correspond to each future payment. The present values of the individual payments are used as weights. Duration $D$ is defined as

$$D = \left[ \frac{C_1}{(1+r)} \cdot 1 + \frac{C_2}{(1+r)^2} \cdot 2 + \cdots \right.$$
$$\left. + \frac{C_n}{(1+r)^n} \cdot n + \frac{P_n}{(1+r)^n} \cdot n \right] \Big/ \left[ \sum_{t=1}^{n} \frac{C_t}{(1+r)^t} + \frac{P_n}{(1+r)^n} \right]$$

Here $r$ is the applicable discount rate for present-value calculation. In this definition of duration, the present value of the coupon received at the end of year $1 [C_1/(1+r)]$ is multiplied by 1, the present value of the payment received at the end of year 2 $[C_2/(1+r)^2]$ is multiplied by 2, and so on. Defining the weights in this weighted average as

$$a_1 = C_1/(1+r), \, a_2 = C_2/(1+r)^2, \ldots, a_i = C_i/(1+r)^i, \ldots,$$

and for the last term

$$a_n = (C_n + P_n)/(1+r)^n$$

we can express the duration of a bond by the formula

$$D = \frac{\sum\limits_{t=1}^{n} t a_t}{\sum\limits_{t=1}^{n} a_t}$$

Duration is thus an index which measures the average number of years an investor has to wait until he recoups his investment. Two bonds with identical duration but different years to maturity have more in common than two bonds with the same maturity but different duration. As bonds lengthen in time to maturity, the true length or duration increases at a decreasing rate, because of the effect of discounting. A 25-year bond is surprisingly little different from a 50-year bond, but a 6-year bond is approximately twice as long as a 3-year bond. Duration is thus a concept which characterizes the risk dimension of bonds better than years to maturity.

[24] F. Macaulay, *The Movements of Interest Rates, Bond Yields, and Stock Prices in the United States Since 1856*, New York: National Bureau of Economic Research, 1938.

### 2.3.5   Inflation and the Yield Curve

Inflation is clearly one of the major mechanisms that determine the formation of interest-rate expectations. It seems that in periods of no inflation or in periods characterized by steady long-run inflation rates, the yield curve has the typical upward sloping shape of Figure 2.1, with short-term rates lower than the long-term rates. If the rate of inflation changes upward from the established long-run level, the yield curve may develop a hump (see Figure 2.2, curve *b*) whose peak will be located at maturities approximating the length of time that the "abnormally high" inflation is expected to persist. Since short-term interest rates are expected to compensate the investor for the effect of inflation they will be higher than long-term rates (relevant after the abnormal inflation has subsided) and the humped curve will have a long descending tail. In real life, it seems that high inflation rates above normal or above average apparently are not expected to continue very long, and a prominent hump correspondingly develops at early maturities, around 1 year. Given a very abrupt jump in inflation rates, which is not expected to persist beyond a couple of months, the hump will shift to very low maturities and the entire yield curve may have a generally downward sloping appearance (see Figure 2.2, curve *c*), but this is a relatively rare occurrence.[25]

Figure 2.4 illustrates schematically the yield curve patterns observed in different years characterized by sudden changes in inflation rates. The 1960–1965 period was characterized by persistently low inflation rates (1.4% annual average). The yield curve adjusted to this level of expected long-run inflation, developing the "normal" upward-sloping shape. In 1966 the inflation increased to 3.4% annually, i.e., about 2% above the previous long-run figure. The yield curve developed a hump around maturities of one year. The inflation in 1969 reached a still higher level, 6.1% annually or 4.7% above the long-run inflation represented by the "calm" 1960–1965 period: the hump became more prominent. In 1971–1972 the inflation settled back to around 3%: the market apparently interpreted this as a new level of long-run inflation and the yield curve again resumed its "normal" upward sloping shape (though at a generally higher level). A jump to 12% inflation in 1974 again resulted in a prominent hump at around one-year maturities. A similar interpretation applies to the upward sloping curve in 1976 (long-run annual inflation assumed to stabilize at 5%), followed by a distinct hump in late 1979–early 1980, when inflation rates hit an abnormal high at an annualized 20% level. In the last quarter of 1979 and the first quarter of 1980 the hump shifted to six-month maturities or did not appear at all: the investors apparently did not expect the abnormally high inflation to persist for any significant length of time (how wrong they proved to be!). Humps at longer maturities, indicative of longer inflationary expectations, are observed more seldom. Thus the yield curves in 1968–1970 showed a very gentle hump at maturities around four–five years, possibly indicating expectations of long-term abnormally high inflation rates.

The yield curve is a subject of considerable theoretical appeal, but it is not without significance for the intelligent investor. An understanding of the forces which determine the term structure of interest rates goes a long way toward dispelling the popular belief

---

[25] Z. Lerman, "Inflation and the Structure of Interest Rates", *Research in Finance*, Vol. 4, 1983.

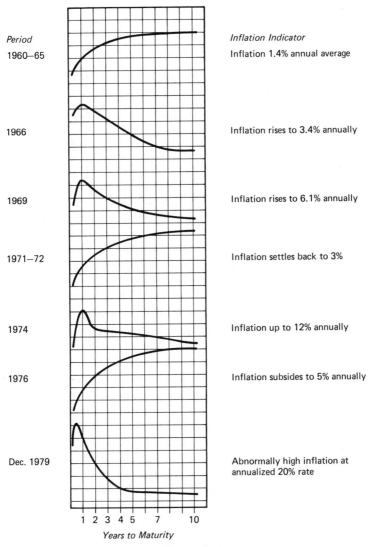

**Figure 2.4**
**Inflation and the Yield Curve**

*Source:* Z. Lerman, "Inflation and the Structure of Interest Rates", *Research in Finance*, Vol. 4, 1983.

that the investment in bonds is less risky than the investment in other securities. At a time of volatile changes in expectations, the magnitude of the changes in long-term bond prices can be (and has been) dramatic. Moreover, it is difficult to conjure up a field in which the professional analyst has a greater comparative advantage over his untutored counterpart. Intuition is simply not enough to explain what often appear to be bewildering changes in bond prices and yields.

## 2.4 The Historical Record

The investment spectrum available to the investor is quite broad: it covers securities (like stocks and bonds), real estate (land, buildings, etc.), commodities (pork bellies and wheat), gold, silver, and other precious metals, as well as stamps, coins, art, and so on. Any investor, before making an investment decision, is naturally interested in looking at the *ex-post*, or historical performance of the various investment instruments. In particular, we would like to have information about the past rates of return of the various investment channels and their variability over time. What investment medium provided the highest rate of return? Which was a good hedge against inflation? Although no one can guarantee that past performance will be replicated in the future, the historical information is frequently used for future prediction, and especially for studying the general properties of the rates of return distribution (such as variability) of the various assets.

Figure 2.5 shows the total wealth accumulated up to any given year by investing $1 at the end of 1925 in four different investment instruments: common stocks, small capitalization stocks, long-term US Government bonds, US Treasury Bills. In all cases, the interim cash receipts are assumed to have been reinvested in the same securities, as explained in the previous sections. A separate curve plots the course of inflation (as represented by the consumer price index, CPI), so that we can easily see what instruments beat the inflation and what failed to do so. For example, the $1 investment in common stocks made at the end of 1925 grew to about $5 in 1950, to $30 in 1960, and to $133.62 by year-end 1981. The $1 investment in small stocks grew to a phenomenal $597.10 in this period. The $1 investment in long-term bonds grew to $5.16 by the end of 1981, and the investment in Treasury Bills increased to $5.25 in the same period. Since the inflation index increased from 1.00 to 5.24 in the period 1925–1981, we see that the accumulated value of the investment in Treasury Bills for many years tracked the inflation index, whereas the investment in stocks and even in long-term bonds (except for the last 5 years) on the whole managed to beat inflation. In *real, inflation-adjusted terms*, investors who held Treasury Bills in fact lost money all through the period 1946–1964, when the Treasury Bills curve in Figure 2.5 is below the inflation curve. In the 1970s, the Treasury Bills investment index and the inflation index almost coincide, and over the entire period from 1925 through 1981 the investment in Treasury Bills yielded a minute real rate of return which can be calculated as $5.25/5.24 - 1 = 0.00191$, or 0.2% over 51 years! Thus the real annual rate of return on Treasury Bills was virtually zero.

The investment in common stocks, and especially in small stocks, held over the entire 51-year period was the most profitable. This is true, however, for an investor who stayed with common stocks for a long period, from 1925 to 1981. For investors with a shorter holding period of, say, one year, we cannot assert that investment in common stock was always more profitable than investment in long-term bonds for each of the years studied. The reason is that the rates of return on common stock were more volatile or more variable than the rates of return on other assets. Figure 2.6 demonstrates the variability of the returns on common stocks and on bonds. It is clear that

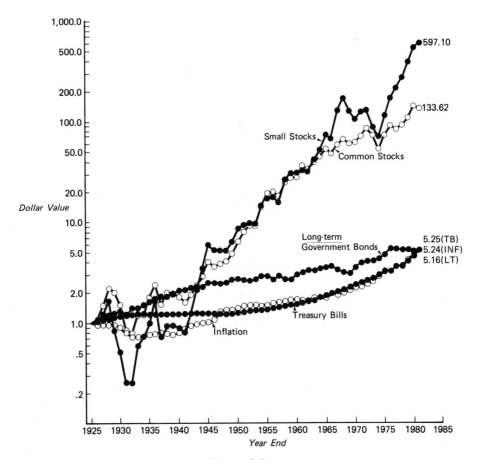

**Figure 2.5**
**Wealth Indices of Investments in the US Capital Markets, 1926–1981**

*Source:* R. Ibbotson and R. Sinquefield, *Stocks, Bonds, Bills and Inflation*, The Financial Analysts
Research Foundation (1982).

common stocks in the past were more risky, or volatile, than long-term Government
bonds. For example, in the 1930s the stock prices, and particularly the prices of small
stocks, went down more sharply than the bond prices.

Table 2.8 provides a historical record of the annual rates of return on various
investment instruments for each of the years in the period 1926–1981. The last column
of the table gives the annual inflation rate, which can be used to compute the real rates
of return in each of the years. Some statistical characteristics of the rate of return
distributions are given in Table 2.9. We see from Table 2.9 that the mean rate of return
on long-term government bonds and on US Treasury Bills was virtually equal to the
mean inflation rate, which implies a zero rate of return in real, inflation-adjusted terms
over the period 1926–1981. The mean rate of return on the other securities, especially

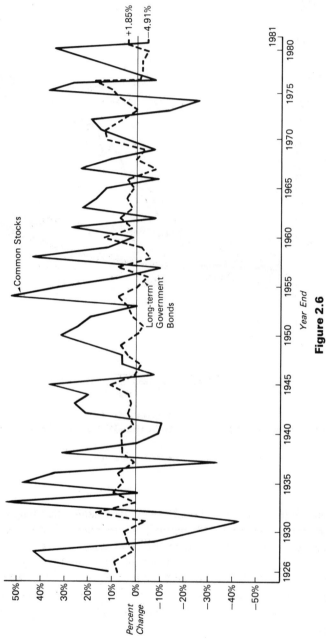

**Figure 2.6**

**Volatility of Annual Returns from the US Capital Markets 1926–1981: Common Stocks versus Long–Term Government Bonds.**

*Source:* R. Ibbotson and R. Sinquefield, *Stocks, Bonds, Bills and Inflation,* The Financial Analysts Research Foundation (1982).

# Table 2.8
## Year-by-Year Total Returns 1926–1981 (Including Reinvestment Income)

| | | | | Rates of Return | | | |
|---|---|---|---|---|---|---|---|
| Year | Common Stocks | Small Stocks | Long-term Corporate Bonds | Long-term Government Bonds | US Treasury Bills | Changes in Consumer Price Index |
| 1926 | 0.1162 | 0.0028 | 0.0737 | 0.0777 | 0.0327 | 0.0149 |
| 1927 | 0.3749 | 0.2210 | 0.0744 | 0.0893 | 0.0312 | −0.0208 |
| 1928 | 0.4361 | 0.3969 | 0.0284 | 0.0010 | 0.0324 | −0.0097 |
| 1929 | −0.0842 | −0.5136 | 0.0327 | 0.0342 | 0.0475 | 0.0019 |
| 1930 | −0.2490 | −0.3815 | 0.0798 | 0.0466 | 0.0241 | −0.0603 |
| 1931 | −0.4334 | −0.4975 | −0.0185 | −0.0531 | 0.0107 | −0.0952 |
| 1932 | −0.0819 | −0.0539 | 0.1082 | 0.1684 | 0.0096 | −0.1030 |
| 1933 | 0.5399 | 1.4287 | 0.1038 | −0.0008 | 0.0030 | 0.0051 |
| 1934 | −0.0144 | 0.2422 | 0.1384 | 0.1002 | 0.0016 | 0.0203 |
| 1935 | 0.4767 | 0.4019 | 0.0961 | 0.0498 | 0.0017 | 0.0299 |
| 1936 | 0.3392 | 0.6480 | 0.0674 | 0.0751 | 0.0018 | 0.0121 |
| 1937 | −0.3503 | −0.5801 | 0.0275 | 0.0023 | 0.0031 | 0.0310 |
| 1938 | 0.3112 | 0.3280 | 0.0613 | 0.0553 | −0.0002 | −0.0278 |
| 1939 | −0.0041 | 0.0035 | 0.0397 | 0.0594 | 0.0002 | −0.0048 |
| 1940 | −0.0978 | −0.0516 | 0.0339 | 0.0609 | 0.0000 | 0.0096 |
| 1941 | −0.1159 | −0.0900 | 0.0273 | 0.0093 | 0.0006 | 0.0972 |
| 1942 | 0.2034 | 0.4451 | 0.0260 | 0.0322 | 0.0027 | 0.0929 |
| 1943 | 0.2590 | 0.8837 | 0.0283 | 0.0208 | 0.0035 | 0.0316 |
| 1944 | 0.1975 | 0.5372 | 0.0473 | 0.0281 | 0.0033 | 0.0211 |
| 1945 | 0.3644 | 0.7361 | 0.0408 | 0.1073 | 0.0033 | 0.0225 |
| 1946 | −0.0807 | −0.1163 | 0.09172 | 0.0010 | 0.0035 | 0.1817 |
| 1947 | 0.0571 | 0.0092 | −0.0234 | −0.0263 | 0.0050 | 0.0901 |
| 1948 | 0.0550 | −0.0211 | 0.0414 | 0.0340 | 0.0081 | 0.0271 |
| 1949 | 0.1879 | 0.1975 | 0.0331 | 0.0645 | 0.0110 | −0.0180 |
| 1950 | 0.3171 | 0.3875 | 0.0212 | 0.0006 | 0.0120 | 0.0579 |
| 1951 | 0.2402 | 0.0780 | −0.0269 | −0.0394 | 0.0149 | 0.0587 |
| 1952 | 0.1837 | 0.0303 | 0.0352 | 0.0116 | 0.0166 | 0.0088 |
| 1953 | −0.0099 | −0.0649 | 0.0341 | 0.0363 | 0.0182 | 0.0062 |
| 1954 | 0.5262 | 0.6058 | 0.0539 | 0.0719 | 0.0086 | −0.0050 |
| 1955 | 0.3156 | 0.2044 | 0.0048 | −0.0130 | 0.0157 | 0.0037 |
| 1956 | 0.0656 | 0.0428 | −0.0681 | −0.0559 | 0.0246 | 0.0286 |
| 1957 | −0.1078 | −0.1457 | 0.0871 | 0.0745 | 0.0314 | 0.0302 |
| 1958 | 0.4336 | 0.6489 | −0.0222 | −0.0610 | 0.0154 | 0.0176 |
| 1959 | 0.1195 | 0.1640 | −0.0097 | −0.0226 | 0.0295 | 0.0150 |
| 1960 | 0.0047 | −0.0329 | 0.0907 | 0.1378 | 0.0266 | 0.0148 |
| 1961 | 0.2689 | 0.3209 | 0.0482 | 0.0097 | 0.0213 | 0.0067 |

**Table 2.8    continued**

*Rates of Return*

| Year | Common Stocks | Small Stocks | Long-term Corporate Bonds | Long-term Government Bonds | US Treasury Bills | Changes in Consumer Price Index |
|------|------|------|------|------|------|------|
| 1962 | −0.0873 | −0.1190 | 0.0795 | 0.0689 | 0.0273 | 0.0122 |
| 1963 | 0.2280 | 0.2357 | 0.0219 | 0.0121 | 0.0312 | 0.0165 |
| 1964 | 0.1648 | 0.2352 | 0.0477 | 0.0351 | 0.0354 | 0.0119 |
| 1965 | 0.1245 | 0.4175 | −0.0046 | 0.0071 | 0.0393 | 0.0192 |
| 1966 | −0.1006 | −0.0701 | 0.0020 | 0.0365 | 0.0476 | 0.0335 |
| 1967 | 0.2398 | 0.8357 | −0.0495 | −0.0919 | 0.0421 | 0.0304 |
| 1968 | 0.1106 | 0.3597 | 0.0257 | −0.0026 | 0.0521 | 0.0472 |
| 1969 | −0.0850 | −0.2505 | −0.0809 | −0.0508 | 0.0658 | 0.0611 |
| 1970 | 0.0401 | −0.1743 | 0.1837 | 0.1210 | 0.0653 | 0.0549 |
| 1971 | 0.1431 | 0.1650 | 0.1101 | 0.1323 | 0.0439 | 0.0336 |
| 1972 | 0.1898 | 0.0443 | 0.0726 | 0.0568 | 0.0384 | 0.0341 |
| 1973 | −0.1466 | −0.3090 | 0.0114 | −0.0111 | 0.0693 | 0.0880 |
| 1974 | −0.2647 | −0.1995 | −0.0306 | 0.0435 | 0.0800 | 0.1220 |
| 1975 | 0.3720 | 0.5282 | 0.1464 | 0.0919 | 0.0580 | 0.0701 |
| 1976 | 0.2384 | 0.5738 | 0.1865 | 0.1675 | 0.0508 | 0.0481 |
| 1977 | −0.0718 | 0.2538 | 0.0171 | −0.0067 | 0.0512 | 0.0677 |
| 1978 | 0.0656 | 0.2346 | −0.0007 | −0.0116 | 0.0718 | 0.0903 |
| 1979 | 0.1844 | 0.4346 | −0.0418 | −0.0122 | 0.1038 | 0.1331 |
| 1980 | 0.3242 | 0.3988 | −0.0262 | −0.0395 | 0.1124 | 0.1240 |
| 1981 | −0.0491 | 0.1395 | −0.0096 | 0.0185 | 0.1471 | 0.0894 |

*Source*: R. Ibbotson and R. Sinquefield, *Stocks, Bonds, Bills and Inflation*, The Financial Analys Research Foundation (1982).

on stocks, was higher than the mean inflation rate. However, the higher the mean rate c return, the higher is the standard deviation of the distribution. This means that th distribution of rates of return on common stocks and small stocks is more widel spread, and there is a higher probability of having large deviations from the mean (bot positive and negative) in any given year.

Evaluating the tradeoff between the higher mean profitability of stocks and th higher variability of their rates of return is the heart of this book, and the relevant con cepts and techniques will be studied in the following chapters. At this stage, it suffices present the objective data as they emerge from the historical record.

### 2.4.1   International Equity Returns

How did the securities markets in Asia and in Europe fare compared with the U stocks? Table 2.10 presents some indicators of mean rates of return and of termin

**Table 2.9**
**Statistical Distribution Parameters of Investment Total Annual Returns**
**1926–1981**

| Series | Geometric Mean | Arithmetic Mean | Standard Deviation | Distribution |
|--------|----------------|-----------------|--------------------|--------------|
| Common Stocks | 9.1% | 11.4% | 21.9% | |
| Small Stocks | 12.1 | 18.1 | 37.3 | |
| Long-term Corporate Bonds | 3.6 | 3.7 | 5.6 | |
| Long-term Government Bonds | 3.0 | 3.1 | 5.7 | |
| US Treasury Bills | 3.0 | 3.1 | 3.1 | |
| Inflation | 3.0 | 3.1 | 5.1 | |

+90x        0x        −90x

*Definitions:*  Geometric mean $\bar{R}_g = \left[ \prod_{t=1}^{n} (1 + R_t) \right]^{1/n} - 1$

Arithmetic mean $\bar{R}_a = \dfrac{1}{n} \sum_{t=1}^{n} R_t$

Standard deviation $\sigma = \sqrt{\dfrac{1}{n-1} \sum_{t=1}^{n} (R_t - \bar{R}_a)^2}$

where $R_t$ is the annual rate of return in year $t$.

*Source:* R. Ibbotson and R. Sinquefield, *Stocks, Bonds, Bills, and Inflation,* The Financial Analysts Research Foundation (1982).

wealth of investors in 17 different countries outside the US, measured over the period 1960–1980. A \$1 investment in equities made in 1960 grew by year-end 1980 to a striking \$20.86 in Japan and to \$22.29 for all Asian exchanges on average, compared with only \$5.78 in the US. Canada, the next-door neighbor of the USA, also attained a substantially higher return on equity, the \$1 investment made in 1960 growing to \$8.47 in 1980. The rates of return on European equities were much lower, with terminal wealth indexes ranging from a high of over \$7.00 for Norway, Switzerland, and the United Kingdom to a low of \$1.63 for Italy.

Figure 2.7 presents in graphical form the cumulative wealth indexes of Asian, European, and other non-US equities compared with US stocks over the period 1960–1980. The Asian equities outstripped by a long shot the investment in stocks in all

**Table 2.10**
**World Equities: Summary Statistics, 1960–1980**

| Asset | Annual Returns in US Dollars | | Year-End Wealth Index 1959 = 1.00 |
|---|---|---|---|
| | Compound Return (%) | Standard Deviation (%) | |
| Non-US Equities: | | | |
| Europe | | | |
| Austria | 9.1 | 16.9 | 6.23 |
| Belgium | 9.2 | 13.8 | 6.39 |
| Denmark | 9.5 | 24.2 | 6.72 |
| France | 6.2 | 21.4 | 3.56 |
| Germany | 8.3 | 19.9 | 5.32 |
| Italy | 2.4 | 27.2 | 1.63 |
| Netherlands | 9.3 | 17.8 | 6.45 |
| Norway | 10.3 | 49.0 | 7.81 |
| Spain | 8.4 | 19.8 | 5.49 |
| Sweden | 8.4 | 16.7 | 5.40 |
| Switzerland | 10.2 | 22.9 | 7.74 |
| United Kingdom | 10.0 | 33.6 | 7.39 |
| Europe Total | 8.4 | 16.2 | 5.47 |
| Asia | | | |
| Hong Kong* | 24.6 | 61.3 | 11.24 |
| Japan | 15.6 | 31.4 | 20.86 |
| Singapore* | 23.2 | 66.1 | 9.96 |
| Asia Total | 15.9 | 33.0 | 22.29 |
| Other | | | |
| Australia | 9.8 | 22.8 | 7.12 |
| Canada | 10.7 | 17.5 | 8.47 |
| Other Total | 10.6 | 17.1 | 8.24 |
| Non-US Total Equities | 10.6 | 16.3 | 8.23 |
| US Total Equities | 8.7 | 17.7 | 5.78 |
| World Total Equities | 9.3 | 15.8 | 6.47 |

* 1970–1980.
*Source*: R. Ibbotson, C. R. Carr, and A. W. Robinson, "International Equity and Bond Returns", *Financial Analysts Journal* (July–August 1982).

the other countries, with the period since 1970 characterized by particularly striking growth. It seems that while the US, Europe, and other Western countries succumbed to the oil crisis of the 1970s, the Asian economies proved to be much more adaptive and resilient in the face of unexpected shocks.

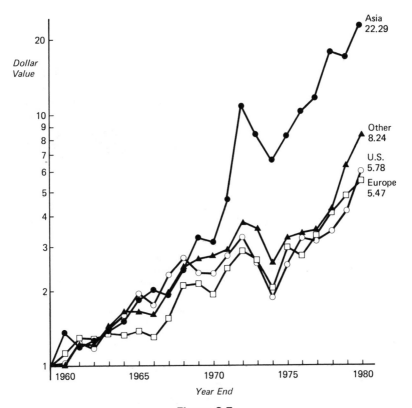

**Figure 2.7**
**US-dollar-adjusted Cumulative Wealth Indexes of World Equities, 1960–1980**
**(Year-end 1959 = 1.00)**

*Source:* R. Ibbotson, C. R. Carr, and A. W. Robinson, "International Equity and Bond Returns," *Financial Analysts Journal* (July–Aug. 1982).

### 2.4.2 Rates of Return on Other Investment Media

Most investors hold portfolios of securities (stocks, bonds, warrants, and options), and textbooks on portfolio selection naturally concentrate on these investment instruments. However, investment in other assets, such as commodities, real estate, art, etc., should not be ignored. Before taking up the main subject matter of this book, namely analysis and selection of securities portfolios, we would like to present briefly the past rates of return on alternative assets, other than stocks and bonds.

Gold has perennial, almost mystical attraction for most investors. The historical record indicates that over ten years rates of return on gold were superior to rates of return on stocks. This phenomenon is not restricted to US securities, and actually

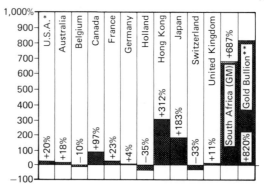

*Standard and Poor's 500
**1971 gold price is average for year as reported by IMF
Source: Andre Sharon, First Vice-President and Dir. of International Research,
Drexel Burnham Lambert, Incorporated

**Figure 2.8**
**Performance of International Equity Markets (in Local Currency) Year-end 1971
to Year-end 1981.**

Reproduced from: E. Sherman, "Gold: A Conservative, Prudent Diversifier", Journal of Portfolio
Management, Spring 1982.

characterizes many other Western exchanges. Figure 2.8 shows that in the period
1971–1981 the total return on gold was over 800%, so that gold outperformed by a
very substantial margin all the Western stock markets, despite the steep decline in gold
prices since September 1980. A close second on the profitability scale for 1971–1981 is
the South African stock market, with slightly less than 700% total return. This is not
surprising, since many of the South African stocks represent gold mines and gold-
related industries.

Table 2.11 shows the geometric average annual rate of return on some conventional
and unconventional investments over the ten- and five-year periods ending in May
1981. In both these periods, the best, most profitable investments proved to be oil, gold,
and US coins. The rates of return on most investment instruments covered in this table
were higher than the annual increase in the consumer price index (CPI), so that they
generally yielded a positive real, inflation-adjusted return. The rate of return on the US
common stock index, on the other hand, yielded a *negative* real return over the last ten
years, and a very small positive (almost zero) real return over the last five years.

In what follows, we will focus on securities portfolios, but the investor should keep
in mind that in practice a much wider investment spectrum is available and that the
standard tools of portfolio selection and analysis are equally applicable to all investment
media.

**Table 2.11**
**Compound Annual Rates of Return (%) for Periods Ending May 1981**

|  | 10 Years | Rank | 5 Years | Rank |
|---|---|---|---|---|
| Oil (Saudi Arabian Light) | 30.8% | 1 | 20.9% | 3 |
| Gold | 28.0 | 2 | 30.7 | 1 |
| US Coins | 27.1 | 3 | 29.7 | 2 |
| Silver | 21.5 | 4 | 20.1 | 4 |
| Farmland | 14.6 | 5 | 14.8 | 6 |
| Diamonds | 14.5 | 6 | 16.9 | 5 |
| Housing | 10.3 | 7 | 11.6 | 7 |
| CPI | 8.3 | 8 | 9.7 | 9 |
| Stocks (S&P 500) | 5.8 | 9 | 9.8 | 8 |
| Foreign Exchange (Index of Several Currencies) | 5.3 | 10 | 3.1 | 10 |
| Bonds (Salomon Brothers Index) | 3.8 | 11 | 1.1 | 11 |

*Source*: E. Sherman, "Gold: A Conservative, Prudent Diversifier", *Journal of Portfolio Management*, Spring 1982.

## Summary

When analyzing the *ex-post* profitability of investments in various assets, we seek a measure of return which provides an appropriate ranking of investments for all investors, independent of their individual preferences. Two alternative formulations based on the total cash flow have been advocated. The first applies the internal rate of return formula to the stream of dividends and the asset's terminal market value; the second is defined as the geometric mean of the annual rates of return (with reinvestment of dividends, interest coupons, and all other interim cash payments and distributions). The only difference between the two measures of return reflects differing implicit assumptions regarding the reinvestment rate. The geometric mean assumes reinvestment at the short-term rates actually available in the market. This is conceptually more appropriate than the internal rate of return's implicit assumption of reinvestment at the constant long-term average rate of return. The empirical application of the geometric mean formula is straightforward, and a method for systematically "reinvesting" all cash dividends, stock dividends, and the market value of rights is described.

While conceptually the geometric mean is the appropriate measure of *ex-post* profitability on all assets, the internal rate of return is commonly used as a measure of *ex-ante* bond profitability. In the specific case of bonds, this measure is called "yield to maturity".

The historical rates of return and their distributions for various assets are presented at the end of the chapter. We can use this historical record as a basis for future investment decisions. In general, the past does not repeat itself in the future, but some general features of the rates of return distribution (e.g., the variability of the rates of return) do not change significantly over time and can be used by portfolio managers for investment decision-making.

## Summary Table

1. The internal rate of return on an investment, $R$, is given by solving the equation

$$P_0 = \sum_{t=1}^{n} \frac{D_t}{(1+R)^t} + \frac{P_n}{(1+R)^n}$$

   where $D_t$ is the cash dividend received in year $t$, $P_0$ and $P_n$ are the asset prices at $t = 0$ and $t = n$, respectively.

2. The geometric mean rate of return, $\bar{R}$, is given by

$$1 + \bar{R} = \left[ \prod_{t=1}^{n} (1 + R_t) \right]^{1/n}$$

   where $R_t$ is the rate of return in year $t$, and $n$ is the number of years.

3. $\bar{R}$ is superior to $R$ for ranking investments since it implies reinvestment of interim cash dividends at the marginal rate of return actually available in the market at reinvestment time.

4. In calculating the *ex-post* rates of return, adjustments should be made for stock dividends, splits, and rights issues.

5. The adjusted (or total) mean rate of return $R^*$ is given by

$$1 + R^* = (V_n/V_0)^{1/n}$$

   where $V_0$ and $V_n$ stand for the (adjusted) value of the investment in period $t = 0$ and period $t = n$, respectively.

6. The *real* adjusted rate of return $R_r^*$ is given by

$$1 + R_r^* = \frac{1 + R^*}{1 + \bar{h}}$$

   where $\bar{h}$ is the (geometric) mean inflation rate over the period.

7. The yield to maturity of a bond is given by $R$ which solves the equation

$$P_0 = \sum_{t=1}^{n} \frac{C_t}{(1+R)^t} + \frac{P_n}{(1+R)^n}$$

   where $C_t$ is the coupon, or interest paid in period $t$, $P_0$ is the current market price of the bond, and $P_n$ is the redemption value of the bond at maturity. The yield-to-maturity of a bond is an *ex-ante* index of profitability, while the usual internal rate of return is an *ex-post* index.

8. The duration of a bond, $D$, is defined as

$$D = \sum_{t=1}^{n} t a_t \bigg/ \sum_{t=1}^{n} a_t$$

   where $a_t$ are weights and $t$ are the years in which the cashflows are received. The weights $a_t$ are the present value coefficients of the cashflows received in year $t$.

## Questions and Problems

2.1 A stock that you bought for $100 in January 1981 paid a $8 dividend in December 1981, when its price was $120.
(a) Calculate the rate of return on your investment.
(b) The 1981 inflation rate was around 9%. What was the real rate of return in this case?

2.2 Suppose that you invested $100 in a diversified portfolio of common stocks in the beginning of 1971, while your friend chose a portfolio of small stocks.
(a) Using the rates of return in Table 2.8, calculate the terminal wealth of each portfolio at the end of 1980 (after 10 years).
(b) What was the geometric mean annual rate of return of each of the two portfolios?
(c) Using the inflation rates from the last column in Table 2.8, find the real terminal wealth in dollars of 1971 purchasing power and calculate the corresponding real, inflation-adjusted annual rate of return.

2.3 Using the data of Table 2.8 calculate the cumulative value of the investment of $100 made at the end of 1971 in long-term corporate bonds and long-term Government bonds and held through 1981. Find the geometric mean annual rate of return of both investments. Which performed better over the 10-year period 1972–81?

2.4 The following table lists the price of Texas Instruments stock and the cash dividends paid between 1972 and 1981. Calculate the pretax rate of return on Texas Instruments stock by
1) the internal rate of return method;
2) the geometric mean rate of return method.
Repeat the above calculation assuming 25% tax rate on cash dividends.

| Year | Price of Stock* ($) | Dividends Paid ($) |
|------|---------------------|--------------------|
| 1972 | 95 | 0.415 |
| 1973 | $138\frac{7}{8}$ | 0.725 |
| 1974 | $115\frac{3}{4}$ | 1.000 |
| 1975 | $119\frac{3}{8}$ | 1.000 |
| 1976 | $129\frac{3}{4}$ | 1.080 |
| 1977 | $102\frac{1}{4}$ | 1.410 |
| 1978 | $92\frac{1}{2}$ | 1.760 |
| 1979 | 101 | 2.000 |
| 1980 | $150\frac{3}{4}$ | 2.000 |
| 1981 | $126\frac{1}{4}$ | 2.000 |

*Note: Price of stock is represented by the high price of the stock for that year.

Data from Standard and Poor's Corp. *Standard NYSE Stock Reports*, Volume 49/Number 231/Section 24.

2.5    The following table gives the annual inflation rate in the Consumer Price Index for the period 1972 through 1981. Using the data given in problem 2.1, calculate the real rate of return on the stock of Texas Instruments (pre-tax and post-tax).

| Year | Inflation Rate (%) |
|------|--------------------|
| 1972 | 3.42 |
| 1973 | 8.88 |
| 1974 | 12.20 |
| 1975 | 7.01 |
| 1976 | 5.25 |
| 1977 | 6.77 |
| 1978 | 9.03 |
| 1979 | 13.32 |
| 1980 | 12.41 |
| 1981 | 8.93 |

Source: U.S. Department of Labor, Bureau of Labor
Statistics, Consumer Price Index.

2.6    Calculate the rate of return on IBM stock for 1982 given the following information on dividends and stock prices.

| Dividends Paid ($) | Date |
|--------------------|------|
| 0.86 | January 25, 1982 |
| 0.86 | April 26, 1982 |
| 0.86 | July 27, 1982 |
| 0.86 | October 26, 1982 |

Data from Moody's Investors Annual Service,
Dividends through December 31, 1982.

| Price of Stock ($) | Date |
|--------------------|------|
| $58\frac{2}{8}$ | January 4, 1982 |
| $62\frac{2}{8}$ | February 16, 1982 |
| $62\frac{7}{8}$ | May 17, 1982 |
| $62\frac{7}{8}$ | August 16, 1982 |
| 51 | November 16, 1982 |
| $56\frac{7}{8}$ | December 31, 1982 |

Data from Standard and Poor's Corporation, *Daily Stock Price Record, NYSE*, various issues.

2.7 Calculate the rate of return on First National Boston Corp stock given the following information on dividends and stock prices. The stock underwent a 3 for 2 split on March 26, 1982.

| Dividends Paid ($) | Date |
|---|---|
| 0.72 | February 25, 1982 |
| 0.48 | May 27, 1982 |
| 0.48 | August 26, 1982 |
| 0.53 | November 24, 1982 |

Data from Moody's Investors Annual Service, Dividends through December 31, 1982.

| Price of Stock ($) | Date |
|---|---|
| $45\frac{5}{8}$ | January 4, 1982 |
| $40\frac{7}{8}$ | March 15, 1982 |
| $23\frac{2}{8}$ | June 15, 1982 |
| $24\frac{1}{8}$ | September 15, 1982 |
| $46\frac{1}{8}$ | December 15, 1982 |
| $45\frac{5}{8}$ | December 31, 1982 |

Data from Standard and Poors' Corporation, *Daily Stock Price Record*, NYSE, various issues.

2.8 Calculate the return on Emerson Radio Corp. stock given the following information.

| Date | Event |
|---|---|
| March 27, 1982 | 5 for 3 split |
| November 30, 1982 | 1 right for each 6 shares |
|  | No dividends paid during the year. |

Data from Moody's Investors Annual Service, Dividends through December 31, 1982.

| Price of Stock ($) | Date |
|---|---|
| $12\frac{3}{8}$ | January 4, 1982 |
| $14\frac{6}{8}$ | November 30, 1982 |
| $13\frac{7}{8}$ | December 15, 1982 |
| $12\frac{2}{8}$ | December 31, 1982 |

Data from Standard and Poor's Corporation, *Daily Stock Price Record, NYSE*, various issues.

The rights were traded on December 15, 1982, at a market price of $1.06 per right.

2.9  The following two tables give some basic information about the price and the distributions to shareholders of Texas Instruments and Onieda stock in 1980.
(a) Calculate the annual rate of return on the stock, assuming reinvestment of all interim distributions.
(b) What was the real, inflation-adjusted rate of return on these stocks? The inflation rate in 1980 was 12.4%.

**Texas Instruments**

| | | | | | | |
|---|---|---|---|---|---|---|
| Price Jan. 4, 1980 | $22\frac{6}{8}$ | | | | | |
| Price Dec. 31, 1980 | $20\frac{4}{8}$ | | | | | |
| Dividends | | $0.15 | · 4% stock div. | $0.20 | $0.20 | $0.15 |
| (in chronological order) | | | | | | |
| Price on 15th of following month, $ | | $29\frac{7}{8}$ | | 22 | $34\frac{2}{8}$ | $23\frac{7}{8}$ |

**Onieda**

| | | | | | | | | |
|---|---|---|---|---|---|---|---|---|
| Price Jan. 4, 1980 | $24\frac{3}{8}$ | | | | | | | |
| Price Dec. 31, 1980 | $21\frac{7}{8}$ | | | | | | | |
| Dividends | | $0.15 | Split 2/1 | $0.15 | $0.15 | $0.14 | Split 5/4 | |
| (in chronological order) | | | | | | | | |
| Price on 15th of following month, $ | | $29\frac{7}{8}$ | | $14\frac{2}{8}$ | $23\frac{7}{8}$ | 26 | | |

2.10  Columbia Pictures distributed only cash dividends in 1980 (see following table for data). Calculate the rate of return on Columbia Pictures stock for a tax-exempt pension fund and for an individual in the 60% tax bracket. Assume 20% capital gains tax rate.

**Columbia Pictures**

| | | | | | |
|---|---|---|---|---|---|
| Price Jan. 4, 1980 | $33 | | | | |
| Price Dec. 31, 1980 | $43\frac{3}{8}$ | | | | |
| Dividends | | | | | |
| (in chronological order) | | $0.125 | $0.125 | $0.125 | $0.125 |
| Price on 15th of following month, $ | | $36\frac{2}{8}$ | $29\frac{6}{8}$ | $32\frac{1}{8}$ | $36\frac{3}{8}$ |

2.11  You have bought a deep discount 6% bond for $85. The bond matures in five years, when you will get $100 (the bond's face value or par). Assuming that the interest coupon is paid annually (the first coupon one year from today), find the yield-to-maturity of your investment.

2.12  A $100, 8% bond with 10-year maturity and annual coupon was issued at par (i.e., sold at $100 to the public). After three years, the prevailing interest rates jumped to 15%.
(a) What happened to the market price of the bond?
(b) If for liquidity reasons you were forced to sell the bond at that point in time, what would your return on investment be? Was this a risky or a riskless investment? Why?

2.13  "Government bonds are a virtually riskless investment." Appraise this statement critically by considering the following alternative scenarios:
An individual purchases a $100 par bond bearing 10% interest annually. The bond has $n = 1, 2, 5, 10$ or $20$ years to maturity. The individual then sells the bond after holding it for one year. Calculate the individual's total holding rate of return on the investment assuming that:
(a) The market interest rate after a year is 10% as before.

(b) The market interest rate dropped to 5%.

(c) The market interest rate increased to 15%.

2.14  Consider two $100 bonds, an 8%, 20-year bond and a 6%, five-year bond, both with annual coupon.

Find the duration of the two bonds, assuming 10% discount rate. Compare your results.

2.15  In a long period without inflation, the interest rates stabilized at around 6% for all horizons. A sudden burst of inflation drove the one-year market rates to 15%, while the two-year rates rose only to 12%.

(a) Estimate the inflationary expectations for the coming two years (assuming that the *real* interest rate did not change).

(b) Assuming that after the second year the inflation will drop back to zero, estimate the five-year and the ten-year interest rates.

2.16  The year 1976 was characterized by relatively stable long-run inflation and the yield curve of government bonds in that year was normally upward sloping, as we can see from the following data:

| Maturity | Yield |
|----------|-------|
| 1 year   | 5.92% |
| 2 years  | 6.50% |
| 3 years  | 6.52% |
| 5 years  | 7.20% |
| 7 years  | 7.46% |
| 10 years | 7.54% |
| 20 years | 7.86% |
| 30 years | 7.94% |

*Source*: Salomon Brothers, *Analytical Record of Yields and Spreads*.

(a) Draw the initial yield curve.

(b) Assume now that the inflation rate suddenly flared up, increasing by 15% per annum above the previous stable level, but this abnormal inflation level persisted only for two years, after which the inflation dropped back to normal.

Assuming that the pre-inflation 1976 yield curve fully adjusts for inflation, calculate the effect of inflation on the interest rates represented by the above yield curve and construct the yield curve corresponding to the new state of nature. *Hint:* Assume a $1 par bond (i.e., $P_0 = P_n = \$1$ in the yield-to-maturity formula), so that the coupon is equal to the yield. Calculate the nominal coupon (yield-to-maturity) for bonds of various $n$ treating the empirical data as the real yields to maturity which do not change.

2.17  The following table lists the value of rare U.S. coins over a period of time.

(a) Determine the geometric mean rate of return on each coin over the entire period 1955–1980 (assuming that the coins are purchased at the end of 1955 for the price given in the table).

(b) Use the changes in consumer price index from Table 2.8 to determine the average annual inflation rate during 1955–1980 and find the real (inflation-adjusted) annual geometric mean growth rate of the investment in rare coins.

(c) How did the investment in rare coins perform relative to the investment in common stocks during 1955–1980? (See Table 2.8 for data.)

*Value of U.S. Coins (in $)*

|               | 1955 | 1960 | 1965 | 1970 | 1975 | 1978  | 1980  |
|---------------|------|------|------|------|------|-------|-------|
| 1835 gold $5  | 27   | 34   | 90   | 157  | 336  | 448   | 583   |
| 1853 gold $1  | 7    | 13   | 22   | 56   | 134  | 157   | 336   |
| 1795 silver $1| 67   | 134  | 224  | 403  | 941  | 1,009 | 1,345 |
| 1870S dime    | 13   | 34   | 134  | 269  | 897  | 1,233 | 1,457 |
| 1794 penny    | 22   | 34   | 112  | 224  | 336  | 359   | 448   |

*Source:* Christie's London. Reproduced from A. Zeikel, "Portfolio Management", *Journal of Accounting Auditing and Finance* (Spring 1981).

2.18   The following table lists the value of rare U.S. stamps over the 40-year period 1940–1979.
(a) Determine the geometric mean rate of return on each stamp over the entire period 1940–1979 (assuming that the stamps are purchased at the end of 1940 at the price given in the table).
(b) Use the changes in consumer price index from Table 2.8 to determine the average annual inflation rate during 1940–1979 and find the annual geometric mean growth rate in real terms.
(c) How did the investment in rare stamps perform relative to the investment in common stocks? Relative to the investment in rare coins (see Problem 2.17)?
(d) What are the relative advantages and shortcomings of investment in rare stamps and coins compared with investment in financial instruments?

*Value of Selected U.S. Stamps (in $)*

|                              | 1940 | 1964 | 1972  | 1974  | 1979  |
|------------------------------|------|------|-------|-------|-------|
| 1847 red brown               | 40   | 124  | 400   | 450   | 1,200 |
| 1847 black                   | 150  | 375  | 1,850 | 2,750 | 8,500 |
| 1875 reprint of red brown    | 10   | 85   | 235   | 250   | 750   |
| 1875 reprint of black        | 12   | 115  | 325   | 375   | 900   |
| 1969 pictorials              | 420  | 879  | 2,708 | 3,460 | 7,505 |
| Columbian issues             | 240  | 674  | 2,486 | 2,963 | 7,588 |
| Trans-Mississippi issues     | 121  | 360  | 1,099 | 1,421 | 3,164 |
| Pan-American issues          | 13   | 43   | 102   | 142   | 366   |
| 1902–1903 regular issues     | 128  | 358  | 810   | 980   | 2,714 |
| Panama–Pacific (Perf. 10)    | 56   | 140  | 373   | 446   | 1,000 |
| 1914–15 Single line wmk.     | 67   | 158  | 314   | 353   | 986   |
| 1918 $2 and $5 Franklins     | 35   | 100  | 180   | 205   | 800   |
| 1922–25 regular issues       | 24   | 64   | 134   | 189   | 579   |
| White Plains Souve. Sheet    | 7    | 72   | 125   | 160   | 450   |
| First Airmails               | 7    | 34   | 92    | 140   | 310   |
| Second Airmails              | 6    | 30   | 76    | 119   | 267   |
| Graf Zeppelin Issues         | 47   | 316  | 700   | 835   | 3,050 |

*Source: Trusts and Estates,* January 1980. Reproduced from A. Zeikel, "Portfolio Management", *Journal of Accounting Auditing and Finance* (Spring 1981).

## Data Set Problems

1. Use the Data Set at the end of the book to calculate the geometric mean annual rate of return of Alpha Fund (No. 2) and Amcap Growth Fund (No. 21).

2. Calculate the terminal value of $100 invested in each of these funds in 1971 assuming that the investment is held through 1980. What is the relationship between terminal value and geometric mean annual rate of return?

3. Calculate the geometric mean annual rate of return and the terminal value of the investment for both funds in real, inflation adjusted terms. Compare the results with those obtained in problems 1 and 2 above and analyze the difference.

4. Draw on the same diagram the value of your investment in year $t$ ($t = 1971, 1972, \ldots, 1980$) for Alpha Fund (No. 2) and for Transamerica Income Fund (No. 84). Calculate the geometric mean annual rate of return of the two funds and analyze your results.

## Selected References

Bailey, M. J., "Formal Criteria for Investment Decisions", *Journal of Political Economy*, vol. 57 (Oct. 1959).

Black, F., "The Dividend Puzzle", *Journal of Portfolio Management* (Winter 1976).

Black, F. and Scholes, M., "The Effects of Dividend Yield and Dividend Policy on Common Stock Prices and Returns", *Journal of Financial Economics* (May 1974).

Brigham, E. F. and Pappas, J. L., "Rates of Return on Common Stock", *Journal of Business* (July 1969).

Caks, J. "The Coupon Effect on Yield to Maturity", *Journal of Finance* (March 1977).

Carr, J. L., Halpern, P. J., and McCallum, J. S., "Correcting the Yield Curve: A Reinterpretation of the Duration Problem," *Journal of Finance* (September 1974).

Durand, D., *Basic Yields of Corporate Bonds 1900–1942*, Technical Paper No. 3, New York: National Bureau of Economic Research (June 1942).

Elton, E. J. and Gruber, M. J., "Marginal Stockholder Tax Rates and the Clientele Effect", *Review of Economics and Statistics* (Feb. 1970).

Fama, E. G. and Miller, M. H., *The Theory of Finance*, New York: Holt, Rinehart and Winston (1972).

Fisher, I., *The Theory of Interest*, New York: Macmillan (1930).

Fisher, L., "Determinants of Risk Premiums on Corporate Bonds", *Journal of Political Economy*, vol. 57 (June 1959).

Fisher, L. and Lorie, J. H., "Rates of Return on Investments in Common Stocks", *Journal of Business* (Jan. 1964).

Gordon, M. J., *The Investment, Financing, and Valuation of the Corporation*, Homeland, Ill.: Irwin (1962).

Haugen, R. A. and Ubell, J. G., "Rates of Return to Stockholders of Acquired Companies", *Journal of Financial and Quantitative Analysis* (Jan. 1972).

Hicks, J. R., *Value and Capital*, 2nd ed., Oxford: Oxford Univ. Press (1953).

Ibbotson, R. G., Carr, R. C., and Robinson, A. W., "International Equity and Bond Returns", *Financial Analysts Journal* (July–Aug. 1982).

Ibbotson, R. G. and Sinquefield, R. A., *Stocks, Bonds, Bills and Inflation: The Past and the Future*, Charlottesville, Va.: The Financial Analysts Research Foundation (1982).

Keef, S. P., "Rights Issues: A Plea for the Private Shareholder", *Accountancy* (1981).

Kessel, R. A., *The Cyclical Behavior of the Term Structure of Interest Rates*, Occasional Paper No. 91, New York: National Bureau of Economic Research (1965).

Kirshner, D. and Udinsky, J. H., "A Comparison of the Relative Predictive Power for Financial Models of Rates of Return", *Journal of Financial and Quantitative Analysis* (June 1979).

Kraft, J. and Kraft, A., "Determinants of Common Stock Prices: Time Series Analysis", *Journal of Finance* (May 1977).

Lerman, Z., "Inflation and the Structure of Interest Rates", *Research in Finance*, vol. 4 (1983).

Levy, H. and Sarnat, M., *Capital Investment and Financial Decisions*, 2nd ed., London, Prentice-Hall International (1982).

Livingston, M., "Bond Taxation and the Shape of the Yield-to-Maturity Curve", *Journal of Finance* (March 1979).

Livingston, M., "The Pricing of Premium Bonds", *Journal of Financial and Quantitative Analysis* (September 1979).

Livingston, M. and Caks, J., "A 'Duration' Fallacy", *Journal of Finance* (March 1977).

Lutz, F. A., *The Theory of Interest*, Dordrecht, Holland: D. Reidel Publ. Co. (1967).

Macaulay, F., *The Movements of Interest Rates, Bond Yields, and Stock Prices in the United States Since 1856*, New York: National Bureau of Economic Research (1938).

McConnell, J. J. and Schlarbaum, G. G., "Returns, Risks and Pricing of Income Bonds 1956–76 (Does Money Have an Odor?)", *Journal of Business* (Jan. 1981).

Malkiel, B. G., "Expectations, Bond Prices, and the Term Structure of Interest Rates", *Quarterly Journal of Economics* (May 1962).

Malkiel, B. G., *The Term Structure of Interest Rates: Expectations and Behavior Patterns*, Princeton, N.J.: Princeton Univ. Press (1966).

Millar, J. A., "Split or Dividend: Do the Words Really Matter?" *Accounting Review* (Jan. 1977).

Robichek, A. A. and Niebuhr, W. D., "Tax-induced Bias in Reported Treasury Yields", *Journal of Finance* (Dec. 1970).

Roll, R., *The Behavior of Interest Rates*, New York: Basic Books (1970).

Sharpe, W. F., *Investments*, 2nd ed., Englewood Cliffs, N.J.: Prentice/Hall (1982).

Sharpe, W. F. "Factors in NYSE Security Returns, 1931–1971", *Journal of Portfolio Management* (Summer 1982).

Sherman, E., "Gold: a Conservative, Prudent Diversifier", *Journal of Portfolio Management* (Spring 1982).

# PART II
# The Foundations of Investment Decision-Making

# 3

# Investment Decisions Under Certainty

Certainty refers to situations when the investor knows with probability 1 what the return on his investment is going to be in the future. Such investments almost do not exist outside the realm of textbooks. Treasury Bills or Government bonds are sometimes mentioned as an example of certain investments. The Government (which by definition cannot go bankrupt) guarantees repayment of principal plus, say, 5% interest on the investment, so that each $1 invested in Treasury Bills is worth $1.05 at the end of the investment period. This corresponds to a certain rate of return of 5%. However, even this investment is not certain in *real* terms. If an inflation of $h\%$ is observed during the investment period, then the real rate of return on a 5% Treasury Bill is $1.05/(1 + h) - 1$, which is less than 5%. However, since the inflation rate $h$ is a random variable, unknown in advance, the real rate of return is not certain anymore.

This example indicates that certain or riskless investments are rare and in most countries are simply unavailable. Nevertheless we devote this chapter to the investment-consumption decision under certainty, and most of the concepts introduced in this chapter will be extended to the conditions of uncertainty throughout the rest of the book. In particular, concepts like the opportunity set (or the efficient frontier), investor preferences, borrowing and lending, all will be used in a very similar fashion in application to uncertain investments.

## 3.1    The Investment Schedule

We start with an investor who faces investment in physical assets (e.g. machinery, buildings, etc.) and then analyze the implications for investors investing in securities.

Consider an investor with an initial endowment equal to $W_0$, who must decide how to divide his wealth between current consumption and investment in productive assets. As a first step let us assume that he arrays all of his potential investment opportunities in descending order of profitability, that is by their rates of return (see Table 3.1).

In a one-year investment, in which the investment outlay takes place at the begin-

**Table 3.1**

| Project | Required Investment Outlay | Net Cash Receipts at End of Year | Rate of Return |
|---------|----------------------------|----------------------------------|----------------|
| A | 100 | 200 | 100% |
| B | 100 | 150 | 50% |
| C | 500 | 600 | 20% |
| D | 300 | 315 | 5% |

ning of the year and the net cash receipt is received at the end of the year, the rate of return on investment is readily calculated by dividing the net receipts by the initial outlay, and then reducing the quotient by one. Assuming an initial endowment of $1,000 such an investment schedule (which is also called the transformation curve or investment opportunity curve) is illustrated graphically in Figure 3.1.

Points $W_0$, $a$, $b$, $c$ and $d$ represent the attainable combinations of current and future consumption, given the investor's initial endowment of $1,000 and the four investment opportunities $A$, $B$, $C$ and $D$. For example he can consume $W_0$ this year and nothing next year, but even though this alternative is physically available it cannot be recommended to an individual who desires to survive next year. On the other hand, if investment $A$ is executed, he can reach point $a$ which denotes current consumption of $900 ($W_0$ less the required investment outlay of project $A$) and consumption of $200 next year, which is the cashflow that project $A$ produces in the second period. Similarly by executing the other investment alternatives the individual can reach points $b$, $c$ and $d$.

To simplify the presentation, the discrete attainable points of Figure 3.1 are connected to form the investment opportunities curve $W_0 d$. This is tantamount to assuming that the investment projects are infinitely divisible, that is they can be broken down into

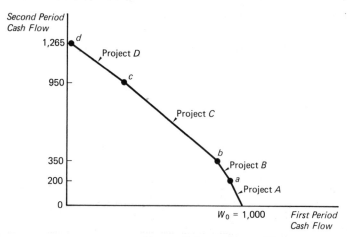

**Figure 3.1**

very small components so that the investment alternatives can be represented by a continuous curve instead of by a series of discrete points. The reader should also note that when moving from $W_0$ to $d$, the slope of the opportunity curve declines, which reflects the fact that the projects have been arrayed in descending order of profitability from point $W_0$ to point $d$. Which projects should be accepted, or in other words which point on the investment opportunity curve is optimal? Before we can answer this question, a way must be found to represent investors' tastes or preferences. This can be done by introducing another important tool of analysis, the *indifference curve*.

## 3.2    The Meaning of Indifference Curves

Consider a rational[1] individual who is faced with the problem of choosing that combination of current and future consumption $(c_0, c_1)$ which will maximize his satisfaction, where $c_0$ and $c_1$ denote cashflows (consumption) in the first and second periods respectively. One possible combination is represented by point $M$ in Figure 3.2. Whenever a combination such as $M$ is replaced by an alternative located in the direction of the arrow marked $a$ the satisfaction derived from the cashflow combination is increased; every movement along the line $Ma$ increases current consumption without altering future consumption. Conversely, any movement in the direction of arrow $b$ is undesirable, because consumption in the second period is reduced without any compensating increase in first-period consumption, which is clearly to the individual's disadvantage. Since any movement in the direction of arrow $b$ reduces the investor's satisfaction while any movement in the direction of arrow $a$ increases it, a point can be found between $a$ and $b$ (for example $N$) at which the individual's satisfaction is neither increased nor decreased. If we substitute combination $N$ for combination $M$, the first-period cashflow $c_0$ increases and the second-period cashflow $c_1$ decreases, but as we have assumed that the individual's satisfaction remains unchanged, the impact of the

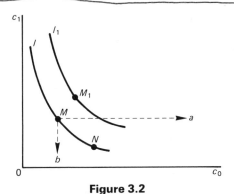

**Figure 3.2**

[1] By "rational" we simply mean that, other things being equal, such an individual prefers *more* to *less* consumption.

increase in $c_0$ on the individual's satisfaction is exactly offset by the decrease in $c_1$.
Hence the investor is indifferent to the choice between the two consumption combinations represented by points $M$ and $N$.[2] Other combinations of $(c_0, c_1)$ can also be found which leave the individual indifferent, that is, with the same level of satisfaction which he derived from combination $M$. In principle all such combinations can be plotted along an "indifference curve" such as $I$ of Figure 3.2. If we start with a point such as $M_1$, we can repeat the process and generate yet another indifference curve such as $I_1$, and so on until an entire indifference map is constructed which represents an investor's tastes with respect to current and future cashflows (consumption).

The indifference curves of Figure 3.2 decline from left to right which indicates that the rational investor must be compensated by an increase in future consumption when his current consumption is reduced. The curves also have been drawn convex to the origin on the assumption that each additional decrease in current consumption requires increasingly larger increments of future consumption if the individual is to remain indifferent to the change.

Another important property of the indifference map is that the indifference curves of a single individual *cannot* intersect. This can be proved by examining Figure 3.3 in which two indifference curves $I$ and $I_1$ of the *same* individual intersect at point $R$. Since $R$ and $R_1$ are located on the same indifference curve ($I$), the individual, by definition, must be indifferent between them. $R_2$ and $R$ also lie on a single indifference curve ($I_1$) so that the individual is also indifferent between these two alternatives. It follows that the individual must also be indifferent between $R_1$ and $R_2$, but this contradicts the assumption that the investor is rational, because $R_2$ represents larger cashflows in both periods.

An investor's final choice out of all available cashflow combinations depends on his tastes. He will choose that combination which allows him to reach the highest indifference curve, for the higher the curve, the greater his satisfaction or what is called

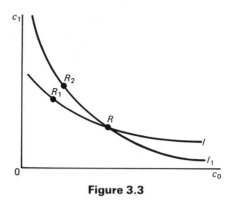

**Figure 3.3**

---

[2] To facilitate the graphical representation the indifference curves of Figure 3.2 have been drawn as continuous curves, that is independent of the actual available alternatives. Clearly, no potential investment option may exist which permits an individual to achieve the consumption pattern represented by a point such as $M$ or $N$. However, from the fact that both these points lie on the same indifference curve we can conclude that had such alternatives been available, the individual would have been indifferent between them.

.in the economist's jargon "utility". Figure 3.4 superimposes an individual's indifference map on an opportunity set of alternative cashflow combinations denoted by points $a$, $b$, $d$, $e$ and $f$.

The individual would prefer a combination which would allow him to reach indifference curve $I_5$, but such a combination is not attainable (indifference curve $I_5$ does not touch any of the attainable points). The best that he can do, given the opportunity set, is to choose combination $a$, the option which lies on indifference curve $I_3$. As no other existing choice will permit him to reach a higher level of satisfaction (utility), the cashflow pattern represented by point $a$ constitutes his *optimal choice*. Should he choose another alternative out of the available set, say point $f$, his satisfaction will fall since this option only permits him to reach indifference curve $I_2$, which represents a lower level of utility.

Can we infer from this analysis that no individual will ever prefer option $f$; or alternatively, does option $a$ represent the optimal choice for *all* individuals? Because the shape of the indifference curves varies from one individual to another it is conceivable that a second individual may have an indifference map, representing his individual preferences, in which the highest indifference curve touches point $f$ rather than point $a$. In fact, depending on the shape of the curves some other alternative may constitute the optimal choice for a particular individual. This is illustrated in Figure 3.5 which sets out the indifference curves of two *different* individuals.[3] From the shape of their indifference curves we can see that the individual whose tastes are represented by curve $I_A$ would choose point $a$ while the other individual with indifference curve $I_B$ would prefer point $f$.

The reader should note that the indifference curve $I_A$ is steeper than $I_B$. This means that when the current consumption ($c_0$) is decreased by one unit, individual $A$ requires a greater compensatory increase in future consumption ($c_1$). For individual $B$, on the

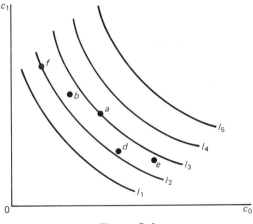

**Figure 3.4**

[3] The reader should note that the intersection of the indifference curves of two *different* individuals does not contradict our previous proof that the indifference curves of the *same* individual cannot intersect.

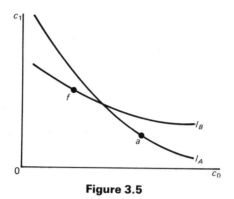

**Figure 3.5**

other hand, a lower current consumption represents a lesser drawback and therefore this individual requires a smaller compensating increase in future consumption in order to leave his level of satisfaction unchanged.

## 3.3    Optimal Investment–Consumption Decisions

Now we are in a position to combine the concepts of an investment opportunity curve and an indifference map in order to determine the investor's optimal investment policy. Figure 3.6 superimposes the indifference curves of a hypothetical individual confronted by the investment opportunities which are summarized in the curve $W_0 d$. Note that the initial endowment equals $W_0$. From Figure 3.6 it is clear that the cashflow pattern $(c_0^*, c_1^*)$ denoted by $c^*$ permits the individual to reach his highest indifference curve $(I_2)$. This occurs at the point of tangency between the opportunity curve and an indifference

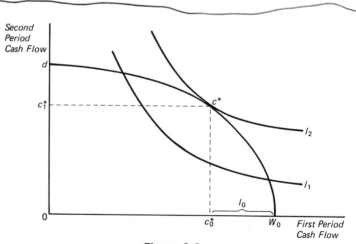

**Figure 3.6**

curve. The *optimal* consumption combination also dictates the optimal investment policy: point $c^*$ can be attained by consuming $c_0^*$ in the current period and investing the amount $W_0 - c_0^* = I_0$ in order to provide a cashflow in the second period which is sufficient to support a consumption of $c_1^*$.

It is obvious from this analysis that two investors with different indifference curves will choose *different* investment–consumption combinations in spite of the fact that both have the same initial endowment $W_0$ and face the same opportunity set. We turn now to see how this analysis and conclusions are changed when investors are allowed to borrow and lend at the riskless interest rate $r$.

## 3.4    The Money Market Line

Consider an individual confronted by the net cashflows $c_0$ in period one and $c_1$ in the second period. Assuming that the investor can borrow and lend at interest rate $r$, he may borrow $c_1/(1 + r)$ in this period and increase his current consumption to $c_0 + c_1/(1 + r)$. In the second period he has to repay the loan plus interest, $[c_1/(1 + r)](1 + r) = c_1$, which is exactly the amount available to him, and his consumption in the second period will be zero. The present value (PV) of his consumption mix in this case is given by $PV = c_0 + c_1/(1 + r)$, where PV is the present value of consumption, or the maximum that the investor can consume in the first period. This equation can be rewritten as

$$c_1 = PV(1 + r) - c_0(1 + r)$$

which is a straight line, indicating that for a given PV of consumption (say PV = $1) infinitely many combinations of consumption bundles $(c_0, c_1)$ exist, all lying on the same straight line characterized by this PV. By borrowing and lending at the rate $r$, the investor can move along this straight line as he wishes, adjusting the consumption bundle without changing the PV level; hence the name money market line.

For example, suppose that the investor has at the optimal point $c_0 = \$1, c_1 = \$1.1$, while the borrowing and lending interest rate is $r = 10\%$. His PV of consumption is $PV = 1 + 1.1/1.1 = \$2$. Suppose that line $PV_2$ of Figure 3.7 represents this situation. The investor can move to $c_0 = \$2$ and $c_1 = 0$ simply by borrowing $1 in the first period and repaying $1.1 in the second period. He can also choose the point $c_0 = 0, c_1 = \$2.2$ simply by lending $1 and receiving in the second period $1 \cdot (1 + r) = \$1.1$ *plus* his second period cashflow from investment $c_1 = \$1.1$, a total of $2.2. By changing the amount that he borrows or lends, he can move to any point on the money market line denoted by $PV_2$.

Let us turn to the first line in Figure 3.7 denoted by $PV_1$. The equation of this line is $c_1 = PV_1(1 + r) - c_0(1 + r)$. Since the $r$ which appears in the line formula is a constant, the intercept of this line with the vertical axis is the constant $PV_1(1 + r)$ and the slope of the line is given by $-(1 + r)$. All the combinations of cashflows $(c_0, c_1)$

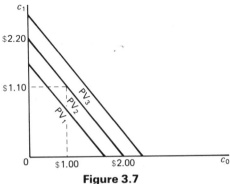

**Figure 3.7**

which lie on this line yield the same present value of consumption, which in this particular case is equal to $PV_1$. Now, suppose that we wish to find all the combinations $(c_0, c_1)$ which yield a higher PV, say $PV_2$. In this case we substitute $PV_2$ for $PV_1$ in the above equation, thereby generating another line *with the same* slope $-(1 + r)$, but with a higher intercept on the vertical axis. Therefore if the investor has a higher initial consumption bundle, he can move on a money market line $PV_2$ which is higher than $PV_1$. The equation of line $PV_2$ will be

$$c_1 = PV_2(1 + r) - c_0(1 + r)$$

which also describes a linear relationship between current consumption $c_0$ and future consumption $c_1$. By considering alternative values of PV we derive a family of parallel straight lines each with the property that all consumption combinations on a given line represent the same PV; hence the name iso-PV lines or equal-PV lines.

Let us examine the set of typical iso-PV lines drawn in Figure 3.7. Which PV line will the investor desire to reach? Obviously, he would prefer the highest line $PV_3$ since this line includes the combinations of $c_0$ and $c_1$ with the highest PV. But not all of these lines represent attainable cashflow combinations; the feasibility of an iso-PV line depends on the individual's initial endowment, $W_0$, as well as the available investment opportunities (the investment curve).

Figure 3.8 superimposes the investment opportunity curve on a family of iso-PV lines. The initial endowment is denoted by point $W_0$ on the horizontal axis. The individual would prefer to reach the line $PV_4$; however, none of the combinations $(c_0, c_1)$ which lie on this line are attainable because this line lies to the right of the investment curve. Point $a$ is attainable as he can invest part of his initial endowment and "move" along the investment curve to this point. But will be choose this point? The answer is unequivocally negative, because point $c^*$ which is also attainable (by investing $I_0$) represents a higher level of PV ($PV_3 > PV_1$). Given the investment opportunities and his initial endowment, the combination of net cashflows ($c_0^*, c_1^*$) denoted by point $c^*$, and the current investment outlay $I_0$ required to achieve this combination, are the best possible alternatives in the sense that they maximize the net present value of the cashflows. The point $c^*$, denoted by a single superior asterisk, is thus the optimum point in case of investment in physical production opportunities.

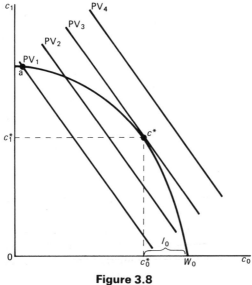

**Figure 3.8**

Will an individual who can borrow and lend at interest rate $r$ necessarily choose the cashflow (consumption) combination denoted by point $c^*$? To answer this question the individual's tastes (indifference map) must be taken into account and, moreover, the analysis must incorporate the fact that the individual is confronted by financial as well as physical investment opportunities. This is done in Figure 3.9 which superimposes the individual's indifference curves on the investment opportunity curve and the iso-PV line of Figure 3.8.

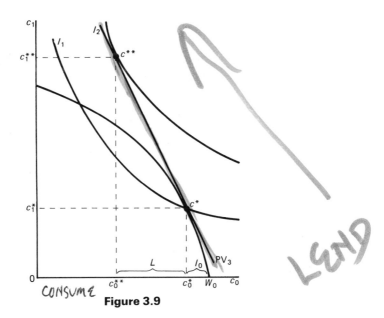

**Figure 3.9**

As before, the individual invests the amount $I_0$ thereby reaching point $c^*$, the point of tangency between the highest attainable iso-PV line and the opportunity curve. But the indifference curve which passes through point $c^*(I_1)$ lies below $I_2$, which is also attainable if financial alternatives are taken into account. Given his tastes (the shape of his indifference curves), the individual can reach a higher level of satisfaction by lending the amount $L$ at the interest rate $r$. This is indicated by a movement along the iso-PV line to $c^{**}$ at which point the iso-PV line is tangent to indifference curve $I_2$. The individual prefers lending to investing beyond point $c^*$ because he will receive $L(1 + r)$ in period 2 in return for the loan; the effective rate of interest on the financial transaction $r$ is greater than the rate of return on productive investment beyond this point, as a comparison of the slopes of the investment curve and the PV line clearly shows.

Should the point of tangency with the indifference curve $c^{**}$ lie to the right of point $c^*$, the individual would again invest up to point $c^*$ as before, but would borrow the amount $B$ in order to increase his current consumption (see Figure 3.10).

Note that the indifference curves of Figure 3.10 are quite steep, which indicates that this individual gives high priority to current relative to future cashflows (consumption). However, despite this strong preference for current consumption, the individual in this case first takes advantage of his productive opportunities and invests $I_0$, that is up to the point $c^*$; the preferred consumption pattern $c^{**}$ is achieved by a financial transaction, in this instance borrowing. Finally if an indifference curve is tangent to the investment productivity curve at point $c^*$ itself, the individual neither borrows nor lends, and point $c^*$ represents the optimum combination of cashflows (consumption). Thus while $c^*$ is the optimum point when only production opportunities are considered, $c^{**}$ is the optimum attainable by employing investment in production together with capital market transactions.

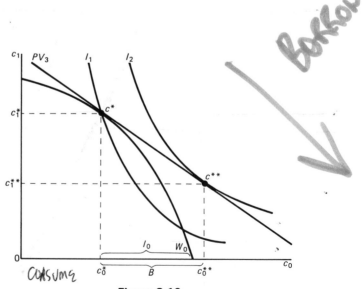

**Figure 3.10**

## 3.5    Separation of Investment and Financing Decisions

The slope of the investment opportunity curve at any point measures the marginal rate of productivity or the rate of return on the marginal $1 invested. The slope of the indifference curve at each point measures the subjective rate of substitution between present and future consumption. In other words when the investor gives up $1 of consumption in the first period, it tells us how much he requires in the second period in order exactly to compensate him, or to leave him indifferent in terms of utility. It is called "subjective" since it differs from one investor to another. Finally, the slope of the PV lines measures the "price of money", i.e. the interest rate.

Equating the slope of the investment opportunity curve to the slope of the money market lines we find the optimal investment. Then, equating the slope of the indifference curves to the slope of the money market line through the optimal investment point, we find the optimal amount of borrowing or lending, i.e., the optimum financial decision.

The striking feature of the analysis is that the optimal investment decision denoted by point $c^*$ does *not* depend on the shape of the indifference curves. Whether the individual desires to redistribute his consumption over time by either borrowing or lending, the investment decision, as we have just seen, remains the same. The projects represented by the segment $W_0 c^*$ of the investment curve are accepted. Thus, as long as the individual chooses investments so as to maximize PV of consumption, that is to reach the highest attainable iso-PV line, he also ensures that he will be able to maximize his satisfaction (utility) by redistributing (if necessary) his consumption over time by means of borrowing or lending.

The independence of investment and financing (i.e. borrowing or lending) decisions is called "separation" and lies at the very heart of the modern theory of finance. It is the existence of an efficient capital market which permits the individual to reach physical investment decisions without *explicitly* considering the financing decisions, as long as the opportunity cost of using the capital resources is fully reflected in the evaluation of the economic investment opportunities.

## 3.6    Finding the Optimal Investment: A Formal Solution

From the intuitive graphical illustration in the previous sections, it is clear that we have to follow two steps in order to find the optimal investment–consumption decision:

Step 1:   Equate the slope on the investment opportunity curve to the slope of the money market line $-(1 + r)$. The solution of this equation yields the optimal investment in physical assets.

Step 2:   Equate the slope of the money market line through the optimal investment point from step 1 to the slope of the indifference curve. The solution yields the optimal financial activity, namely the optimal borrowing or lending, and leads to the optimal consumption bundle reached by combining investment in physical assets and financial activity.

We now analyze the two steps in detail.

*Step 1*

Suppose that the investment schedule is given in the functional form by some function $g$ relating the future consumption to investment,

$$c_1 = g(W_0 - c_0) = g(I)$$

where

$c_0$ is the consumption in the first period

$W_0$ is the initial endowment

$W_0 - c_0$ is the investment in physical assets, so that $W_0 - c_0 = I$, where $I$ denotes the investment

$c_1$ is the future cashflow which results from investment $I$ in the current period, namely the second period consumption.

To find the optimal investment $I^*$, equate the slope of the investment opportunity curve to the slope of the money market line $-(1 + r)$:

$$\frac{dc_1}{dc_0} = g'(I) = -(1 + r)$$

where $g'(I)$ is the slope of the investment schedule (the first derivative of the corresponding function with respect to $c_0$). Given a specific investment opportunity function, we can solve the above equation which yields the optimal investment in physical assets, $I^*$.

*Step 2*

The investor's utility $U$ from any consumption bundle $(c_0, c_1)$ is given by $U = f(c_0, c_1)$, where $U$ denotes utility and $f$ is the functional form of the indifference curve. We seek the tangency point between the money market line through the optimal consumption point from Step 1 and one of the individual's indifference or utility curves.

Take a total differential of $U$ to obtain:

$$dU = \frac{\partial f}{\partial c_0} dc_0 + \frac{\partial f}{\partial c_1} dc_1$$

which can be rewritten also as $dU = f_0 dc_0 + f_1 dc_1$, where $f_0$ and $f_1$ are the partial derivatives with respect to $c_0$ and $c_1$, respectively.

Since on a *given indifference curve* (the one that is tangent to the highest money market line) there is no change in the level of the utility between different consumption bundles, $dU$ must be equal to zero, which implies that on a *given indifference curve* we must have,

$$f_0 dc_0 + f_1 dc_1 = 0$$

or

$$\frac{dc_1}{dc_0} = -\frac{f_0}{f_1}$$

But $dc_1/dc_0$ is the slope of the given indifference curve. The slope is along a *given* indifference curve $U$, since we measure the required change in $c_1$ ($dc_1$) when we decrease $c_0$ by $dc_0$ such that the investor's utility does not change (recall that $dU = 0$). This fact can be denoted by adding a subscript to the derivative, $(dc_1/dc_0)_U$. Thus, to solve for the optimal amount of borrowing or lending, equate

$$\left( \frac{dc_1}{dc_0} \right)_U = -(1 + r)$$

and the solution indicates whether the investor is a borrower or a lender. We turn to illustrate this solution by means of a numerical example.

EXAMPLE

Consider an investor with initial endowment $W_0 = \$16,000$ and utility function $U = c_0 \cdot c_1$ facing an investment opportunity set described by the function

$$c_1 = 240(16,000 - c_0)^{1/2}$$

The interest rate for lending and borrowing is $r = 20\%$. The corresponding investment opportunity curve and the money market line are drawn in Figure 3.11. If the investor consumes all the available funds in the current period ($c_0 = \$16,000$), there will be nothing left to consume in the next period ($c_1 = 0$). Conversely, if he consumes nothing in the first period ($c_0 = 0$), investing the entire amount available ($W_0 = \$16,000$) he will receive a return $c_1 = 240(16,000)^{1/2} = 240 \times 126.5 = \$30,360$ for consumption in the next period. The opportunity curve thus rises from the point $c_0^{max} = W_0 = \$16,000$ on the horizontal axis to the point $c_1^{max} = \$30,360$ on the vertical axis.

*Step 1.* To obtain the optimal investment decision, differentiate the investment opportunity curve

$$\frac{dc_1}{dc_0} = -\frac{120}{(16,000 - c_0)^{1/2}}$$

and set the slope equal to the slope of the money market line,

$$-\frac{120}{(16,000 - c_0)^{1/2}} = -1.20$$

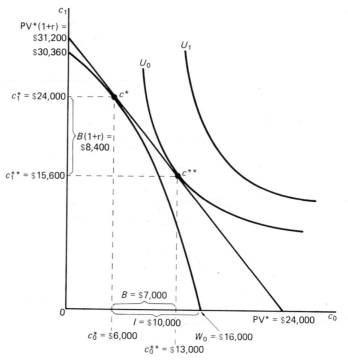

**Figure 3.11**

Solving for $c_0$, we obtain the optimal current consumption

$$c_0^* = \$6,000$$

Substituting this result in the equation of the investment opportunity set, we get for optimal second period consumption

$$c_1^* = 240 \times (10,000)^{1/2} = \$24,000$$

By consuming $c_0^* = \$6,000$ from the initial endowment $W_0 = \$16,000$, the investor leaves $I^* = W_0 - c_0^* = \$10,000$ for investment in physical assets. This investment yields a return $c_1^* = \$24,000$ in the next period. In deriving this result, we did not make use of individual investor's preferences and only exploited the information about the investment opportunities and the money market line open to all investors. The investment strategy $I^* = \$10,000$ with next-period return $c_1^* = \$24,000$ is thus optimal for *all* investors, when they face borrowing and lending opportunities at interest rate $r = 20\%$.

*Step 2.* To determine the investor's optimal financial decision, we need to find the tangency point between the market line through the optimal point in Step 1, $c_0^* = \$6,000$, $c_1^* = \$24,000$, and the investor's indifference map. First find the money market line through $(c_0^*, c_1^*)$. We know that the equation of the money market line is

$$c_1 = PV^*(1 + r) - c_0(1 + r)$$

where PV* is the present value of the optimal consumption point $(c_0^*, c_1^*)$. Thus

$$PV^*(1 + r) = c_0^*(1 + r) + c_1^*$$

Substituting $c_0^* = \$6,000$, $c_1^* = \$24,000$, $1 + r = 1.20$, we obtain

$$PV^*(1 + r) = \$31,200$$

and the market line equation is thus

$$c_1 = 31,200 - 1.2c_0$$

This is a straight line with slope of $-1.20$ and vertical intercept $PV^*(1 + r) = \$31,200$ (see Figure 3.11).

Now take the total differential of the utility curves $U = c_0 \cdot c_1$,

$$dU = \frac{\partial U}{\partial c_0} dc_0 + \frac{\partial U}{\partial c_1} dc_1 = c_1 dc_0 + c_0 dc_1$$

and since along the particular indifference curve tangent to the given market line there is no change in utility $dU = 0$, we have for the slope of the indifference curve

$$\left( \frac{dc_1}{dc_0} \right)_U = -\frac{c_1}{c_0}$$

Equating this slope to the slope of the money market line, we obtain

$$-\frac{c_1}{c_0} = -1.20$$

This is an equation in two unknowns, $c_0$ and $c_1$. Since the tangency point also lies on the money market line, we can substitute $c_1$ from the money-market expression $c_1 = 31,200 - 1.2c_0$ to obtain

$$\frac{31,200 - 1.2c_0}{c_0} = 1.2$$

Solving this we obtain

$$c_0^{**} = \frac{31,200}{2.4} = 13,000$$

and similarly

$$c_1^{**} = 31{,}200 - 1.2 \times 13{,}000 = 15{,}600$$

The double asterisk denotes the optimum point when physical investment opportunities and financial transactions are considered.

By combining the investment in physical assets with financial activities, the individual investor with the utility function $U = c_0 \cdot c_1$ reached the optimal consumption bundle

$$c_0^{**} = \$13{,}000$$

$$c_1^{**} = \$15{,}600$$

Since the optimal investment decision $I = \$10{,}000$ only left $c_0^* = \$6{,}000$ available for consumption in the first period, he obviously had to *borrow* the amount $B$ given by,

$$B = c_0^{**} - c_0^* = \$13{,}000 - \$6{,}000 = \$7{,}000$$

in order to augment his funds and to reach the current period consumption $c_0^{**} = \$13{,}000$ (see Figure 3.11). This loan plus interest at $r = 20\%$ will have to be repaid in the next period:

$$B(1 + r) = 7{,}000 \times 1.2 = \$8{,}400$$

The loan will be repaid from the future return on investment, $c_1^* = \$24{,}000$, so that the investor will effectively be left with:

$$c_1^{**} = c_1^* - B(1 + r) = 24{,}000 - 8{,}400 = \$15{,}600$$

for second-period consumption, which is of course identical to the above solution for $c_1^{**}$.

## 3.7    Investment in Securities Under Certainty

Suppose now that investors do not consider investment in physical assets but concentrate only in securities. Moreover suppose that we have full certainty and the rates of return on the following three securities are known in advance

$$
\begin{array}{ll}
\text{IBM} & = 20\% \\
\text{Xerox} & = 15\% \\
\text{AT\&T} & = 10\%
\end{array}
$$

The investor is small relative to the market and he can buy any amount that he wants of each of these securities without affecting the market prices and the rates of return. Suppose that the investor's initial endowment is $W_0 = \$1,000$. What is his investment schedule like?

Figure 3.12 illustrates the investment opportunity set. The slope of the IBM line is $-1.2$, which implies that the investor can invest any amount that he wishes in this stock and get 20% return on investment. The slope of the Xerox line is only $-1.15$ and that of AT&T is $-1.10$.

If we superimpose the investor's indifference curves on this opportunity set we get the optimum point $M$ which in this particular case shows current consumption $c_0 = \$500$ and investment $I = \$500$ in IBM stock. The investment yields a return of $\$500(1.2) = \$600$ in the second period, which constitutes the second-period consumption. How much is invested in Xerox and AT&T? The answer is clearly zero. The investor will not invest in securities which yield 15% or 10% when he can get for certain a higher 20% rate of return.

Thus, in case of certainty, when all investors agree on future rates of return, no one will hold AT&T and Xerox shares. This is of course impossible, and in equilibrium some investors must hold these stocks since they are traded in the market. How can we

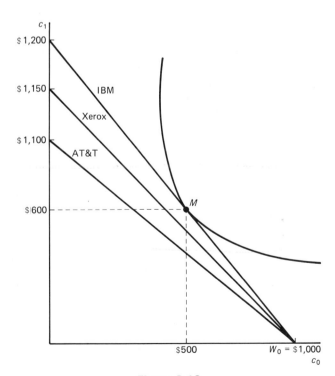

**Figure 3.12**

resolve this paradox? We have two possibilities:

(a)   Under condition of certainty, the price of the stock of Xerox and AT&T must fall until the certain rate of return to future investors on these assets will be 20%. More generally, under certainty all financial assets must yield the same rate of return,[4] which is equal to the market interest rate $r$. In this case all financial assets may be considered as a single asset, since we cannot distinguish one from another. This is of course unrealistic and here we turn to the second explanation, which is the heart of this book.

(b)   In real life we never have full certainty. No stock provides a known rate of return with certainty. In this case the investor also faces risk, and he has a motive for diversification of his investment in the various financial assets. Thus, he will hold a portfolio of various assets which may include in our example IBM, Xerox, AT&T, and also the riskless asset.

Thus, decision-making under conditions of uncertainty is more difficult. The investor can choose the first period consumption $c_0$, and the investment $I = W_0 - c_0$. However, the second-period consumption is not certain any more. If the stock price goes up rapidly after the investor purchases it, the rate of return will be high and the second-period consumption will be high. But if the stock price falls, the investor may face a negative rate of return and hence a low consumption in the second period. Since the future is uncertain, this may also affect the investor's behavior in the financial market. For example, he may be reluctant to borrow a large amount of money in the first period, lest the return on his investment will be negative and he will be unable to repay the loan. The rest of this book is devoted to decision-making under conditions of uncertainty. However, before we turn to describe the theory of decision-making under uncertainty, we would like to summarize our results of the certainty case and indicate the parallel results under uncertainty, which we will develop in detail in the coming chapters.

(a)   "Separation"—All investors, independently of their preferences, choose the same investment bundle, and only the second decision, namely how much to borrow (or lend) in order to finance this investment, is a function of the investor's preferences. Thus we separate the decision on the investment in physical assets from the decision of investment in the money market. *The parallel under uncertainty:* we have a separation between the decision to invest in risky securities and the decision to invest in the money market. All investors, independently of their preferences, will choose the same

---

[4] In a perfect market under conditions of certainty all physical assets also must yield the same rate of return. However, unlike investment in securities which are available to all investors, it may be that investments in physical assets may yield different rates of return, at least in the short run. In the long run, physical assets which are very profitable may attract more investors, and their profitability in the long run must decline. However, in the short run, until more entrepreneurs invest in the attractive projects, we may observe various projects with various rates of return.

         bundle of risky assets (see Chapter 11). They differ only with respect to the amount of money borrowed or lent.

(b)    The optimal investment–consumption decision under certainty is achieved when the marginal rate of substitution on a given indifference curve $(dc_1/dc_0)_U$ is equal to the interest factor $-(1 + r)$, where $r$ represents the price of money.

         *The parallel under uncertainty:* the marginal rate of substitution between profit and risk, at the optimum, is equal to the market price of risk (see Chapter 8).

(c)    The slope of the money market line measures the interest rate or the price of money.

         *The parallel under uncertainty:* The slope of the market line, on which investors can move by borrowing and lending, measures the price of the unit of risk (see Chapter 11).

Thus, in the rest of the book we will develop and apply similar concepts which are appropriate to the uncertainty case; the theory of decision-making under uncertainty will lead us to optimal borrowing (or lending) and optimal investment in risky assets on the one hand, and will rule out unrealistic situations, like those in Figure 3.12, when the entire investment is concentrated in one stock, on the other.

## Summary

Investors face two main decisions: how much of their wealth to invest in production (physical assets) and how much to invest in the capital markets (either lend or borrow money in order to finance the investment in production).

    Under conditions of certainty, investors can separate the two decisions. The production decision is objective in the sense that it does not depend on the investor's preferences. The decision of how to finance the investment, on the other hand, is subjective, since it is a function of the individual investor's preferences, i.e., his indifference curves or his marginal rate of substitution of consumption between the different periods.

    Applying the certainty model to investment in securities rather than to investment in physical assets, we discover a contradiction. If two securities have different rates of return, all investors will invest in the security with the higher rate of return (since the investment opportunity curve in this case is linear) and no one will invest in the other, lower-return security. As a result, the price of the higher-return security will go up, the price of the lower-return security will go down, and an equilibrium will be reached only when both securities yield the same return. In reality, we do observe securities with different rates of return, which only indicates that the certainty assumption cannot be used to explain stock price behavior. Thus, incorporating the risk dimension in the analysis may explain the demand for stocks with various rates of return. This is the main thrust of the rest of the book.

### Summary Table

*Optimal Investment–Consumption Decision Under Certainty*

1. **No borrowing or lending allowed**

   The optimum investment decision is found by equating:

   $$g'(I) = (dc_1/dc_0)_U$$

   where $g'(I)$ is the (objective) marginal rate of return on investment in production, $(dc_1/dc_0)_U$ is the (subjective) marginal rate of substitution between consumption in period $t = 0$ and in period $t = 1$, i.e., the slope of the individual investor's indifference curve.

2. **Borrowing and lending allowed at constant riskless interest rate $r$**

   (a) The optimum investment in physical assets is obtained by equating:

   $$g'(I) = -(1 + r)$$

   i.e., the slope of the money market line is equal to the marginal rate of return in production.

   (b) The optimum investment in financial markets (lending or borrowing) is obtained by equating:

   $$(dc_1/dc_0)_U = -(1 + r)$$

   i.e., the subjective rate of substitution equals the objective rate of substitution in the capital market.

   (c) The optimum consumption in period 0 (the present) is equal to the initial wealth less investment in physical assets, adjusted for investment in the capital markets (plus the amount borrowed in case of borrowing or minus the amount lent in case of lending).

   (d) *Separation property:* Management can separate the investment decision into steps 1 and 2: step 1 chooses the investment in production and step 2 decides on the financing. A correct decision in step 1 is crucial. Step 2 is not so crucial, since stockholders can move on their own along the capital market line by borrowing or lending in accordance with their preferences. Thus, the corporation can separate the production investment decision from the financing decision.

## Questions and Problems

3.1 The Eastern Metals Company is confronted with the following two-period independent projects:

| Project | Required Investment Outlay ($) | Net Cash Receipts at the End of the Year ($) |
|---|---|---|
| A | 750,000 | 900,000 |
| B | 400,000 | 420,000 |
| C | 200,000 | 260,000 |
| D | 300,000 | 330,000 |
| E | 250,000 | 400,000 |
| F | 100,000 | 140,000 |

The firm has initial available resources of $2 million.
(a) Plot the productivity schedule of the firm.
(b) Calculate, and show on the graph, how much the firm can "consume" next year if it "consumes":
(i) $350,000 this year?
(ii) $1,300,000 this year?
Which projects would it execute in each case?

3.2 Define the following terms:
(a) rational individual
(b) indifference curve
(c) optimal choice.

3.3 An individual is indifferent between the following consumption combinations:

| This Year ($) | Next Year ($) |
|---|---|
| 4,000 | 3,200 |
| 3,700 | 3,500 |
| 3,200 | 4,000 |
| 2,900 | 4,400 |

(a) Plot the indifference curve that represents the individual's tastes with respect to current and future consumption.
(b) What is the meaning of a *convex* indifference curve? Is the curve which you plotted in part (a) convex? Prove your answer.

3.4 (1) "I am indifferent between the consumption combinations ($2,200 this year; $2,500 next year) and ($2,600 this year; $2,000 next year)".
(2) "Consumption of $2,800 this year and $2,100 next year gives me the same satisfaction as consumption of $2,200 this year and $2,500 next year."
Regarding the above two quotations:
(a) Is it possible that both statements were made by the same individual?
(b) Is it possible that the statements were made by two different individuals?
Prove your answers.

3.5    Illustrate graphically the two-period consumption-investment model for the case of independent projects.
       (a) What are the equilibrium conditions when the only possibilities are investment and consumption?
       (b) What are the equlibrium conditions when it is also possible to lend or borrow?

3.6    An investor with an initial endowment of $2,500 is confronted with the following two-period independent investment options:

| Project | Required Investment ($) | First-year Receipts ($) |
|---------|-------------------------|-------------------------|
| A       | 200                     | 260                     |
| B       | 300                     | 450                     |
| C       | 100                     | 175                     |
| D       | 500                     | 525                     |
| E       | 200                     | 310                     |
| F       | 100                     | 110                     |
| G       | 200                     | 250                     |
| H       | 300                     | 300                     |
| I       | 400                     | 460                     |
| J       | 200                     | 360                     |

Assume that the investor's indifference curve is defined in the following manner: he requires compensation of 1.35 units of future consumption when his current comsumption is decreased by one unit. Answer the following questions, assuming that there is no possibility to borrow or lend money.
       (a) Plot the investor's productivity schedule.
       (b) How much will the investor invest in production?
       (c) What is the optimal consumption combination?
       (d) Is it possible that the investor will choose to consume $1,300 this year? Explain.

3.7    Assume that the investor is allowed to lend and borrow at an interest rate of 20%. Answer the following questions with regard to the data in Problem 3.6.
       (a) How much will the investor invest in production?
       (b) What is the net present value of the investment chosen by the investor?
       (c) What is the present value of the investor's total consumption in both periods?
       (d) What is the future value of the investor's total consumption in both periods?

3.8    An investor with initial endowment of $2,000 is confronted with the same ten investment options that appeared in Problem 3.6. Assume that projects A, C and G exclude projects H and J, that is if the investor decides to execute A, C or G, he cannot execute H or J, and likewise, if he chooses H or J he cannot choose A, C or G. Assume also that the interest rate is 20%, and answer the following questions:
       (a) Illustrate graphically the two mutually exclusive investment (productivity) curves.
       (b) Show and prove that the NPV rule gives the optimal investment decision in this case.
       (c) How much will the investor invest in production? Which projects will he carry out?
       (d) What is the present value of the total consumption in both periods?

3.9    "The two-period investment–consumption model gives a unique solution for the investment problem even when all the projects confronting the firm have the same IRR."

Appraise, for both the case of independent projects and the case of mutually exclusive projects.

3.10 "One who is not concerned about future consumption need not bother investing in production."
Appraise and prove your answer.

3.11 An investor with an initial endowment of $32,000 is confronted with the productivity curve defined as follows:

$$c_1 = 36(32,000 - c_0)^{1/2}$$

where $c_0$ indicates consumption at present and $c_1$ is the consumption in the future. Assume that the interest rate (for borrowing and lending) is equal to 20%. The investor's utility function, from which it is possible to derive his indifference curves, is defined as:

$$U(c_0, c_1) = 12c_0^2 + 10c_0c_1$$

Answer the following questions, using the two-period investment–consumption model:
(a) How much will the investor invest in production?
(b) What is the NPV of the investment chosen by the investor?
(c) What is the present value of his total consumption in both periods?
(d) Does the investor borrow or lend in the capital market? Give a numerical answer.
(e) What is the optimal allocation of consumption for the two periods?
Illustrate your answer graphically.

3.12 Consider an investment in physical assets when the initial wealth $W_0$ is $100. The investment transformation curve between current consumption $(c_0)$ and future consumption $(c_1)$ is such that the marginal return on successive investments of $10 is as follows:

| Marginal Investment ($) | Total Return ($) | Marginal Net Return ($) |
|:---:|:---:|:---:|
| 10 | 67.0 | 57.0 |
| 10 | 83.0 | 6.0 |
| 10 | 98.0 | 5.0 |
| 10 | 112.0 | 4.0 |
| 10 | 125.0 | 3.0 |
| 10 | 137.0 | 2.0 |
| 10 | 148.5 | 1.5 |
| 10 | 159.5 | 1.0 |
| 10 | 170.0 | 0.5 |
| 10 | 180.0 | 0.0 |

Assume that the borrowing and lending rate is 35% (i.e., $r = 0.35$).
(a) What is the optimal investment at time $t_0$? Show your solution on a diagram.
(b) Assume now that an individual has the following indifference curves between current and future consumption:

$$c_1 = a + \tfrac{1}{20} \cdot (c_0 - 100)^2 \qquad 0 \leqslant c_0 \leqslant 100$$

where $a$ is a constant along any indifference curve. Determine the optimal amount to be borrowed or lent by the individual at time $t_0$ as well as his total consumption at $t_0$ and at $t_1$.

(c) Work out parts (a) and (b) once again, this time assuming the following indifference curve:

$$c_1 = a + \tfrac{1}{20} \cdot (c_0 - 60)^2 \qquad 0 \leqslant c_0 \leqslant 60$$

Is there any change in the investment decision compared to parts (a) and (b)? Why?

3.13 (1) Consider a two-period investment productivity curve defined by the equation:

$$c_1 = 300(12{,}000 - c_0)^{1/2}$$

where $c_0$ is the current period consumption and $c_1$ is the next period consumption. The investor's initial endowment is $W_0 = \$12{,}000$.

(a) Draw the investment productivity curve in the $(c_0, c_1)$ plane by calculating several points of the curve.

(b) What is the maximum attainable current consumption? What is the corresponding future consumption?

(c) What is the maximum investment that can be made in the current period? What are the corresponding consumption levels $c_0$ and $c_1$? What is the average return on investment?

(d) Suppose the investor with total endowment $W_0 = \$12{,}000$ decides to invest $\$4{,}900$ in production. What are his consumption levels in the two periods, $c_0$ and $c_1$? Show the resulting two-period consumption strategy on your graph and indicate the production projects in which the individual invested his capital. What is his *average* return on investment? What is the marginal rate of return on investment?

(2) Now consider three investors whose indifference maps are described by the following two-period utility functions:

$$\text{Investor } A: \quad U(c_0, c_1) = c_0 + c_1$$
$$\text{Investor } B: \quad U(c_0, c_1) = 3c_0 + c_1$$
$$\text{Investor } C: \quad U(c_0, c_1) = c_0 \cdot c_1$$

(Each indifference curve corresponds to some constant value of the utility function, $U(c_0, c_1) = $ constant.)

(a) Show graphically the optimum consumption combination that each investor will choose.

(b) Find the corresponding optimum consumption combination analytically.

(c) How much will each individual invest in production?

(d) What is the marginal rate of return on investment at the optimum point for each investor? What is the average rate of return on total investment?

(3) Now suppose that in addition to the investment productivity curve there is a perfect capital market in which all investors can borrow and lend at a constant rate of 50%. Hence, 50% is in this case the cost of capital for all investors.

(a) Find analytically the optimum *production* policies of the three investors. Show your results graphically.

(b) What is the total amount invested by each investor in production?

(c) What is the marginal rate of return on production investments for each investor?

(d) What is the present value of the optimum production strategy of each investor? What is the future value? What is the equation of the money market line through the optimum production point?

(e) Find analytically the optimum consumption combination of investor $C$. Indicate whether investor $C$ acts as a borrower or a lender in the money market. What is the amount of borrowing or lending?

(f) Is investor $C$ better off with or without the money market?

3.14   In the Bible we find the following quotation:

> The Lord shall open unto thee his good treasure, the heaven to give the rain unto thy land in his season, and to bless all the work of thine hand: and thou shalt lend unto many nations, and thou shalt not borrow.
> (*Deuteronomy 28:12*)

Suppose that God opens his treasures to an investor whose initial wealth grows from $W_0$ to, say, $5W_0$. There is no change in the projects available and in the market interest rate. Show graphically a case where the investor changes, as a result of the increase in his wealth, from a borrower to a lender.

3.15   Consider an imaginary world of certainty with a securities market in which a single stock is traded at a price of $100 per share. Investors in this stock can earn a (certain) rate of return of 15%.

(a) Draw the investment opportunities curve facing an investor with initial wealth of $10,000. What is the analytical expression of this curve? Assuming that his utility curve is given by $U(c_0, c_1) = c_0 \cdot c_1$, how much will be invested in the stock?

(b) Now suppose that all investors can borrow and lend unlimited amounts of cash at a riskless interest rate of 20% ($r = 0.20$). Add the market line to your drawing of the investment opportunities curve. How much will the investor from (a) invest in the stock? How much will any other investor invest in the stock? What will happen to the stock price and to the rate of return on the stock in this case?

3.16   Again consider an imaginary world of certainty in which two stocks are traded at $1 share price, one promising a 25% rate of return and the other 10%.

(a) Draw the investment opportunities curves of the two stocks for an investor with $10,000 initial wealth.

(b) What will be the investment strategy of an investor with indifference curves of the form $U(c_0, c_1) = 20c_0^2 + 100c_0 \cdot c_1$? How will this strategy be affected by a change in the investor's preferences?

(c) Can this price and return structure persist or will it have to change? Can you tell what changes in the share prices and in the rates of return will occur to reach an equilibrium?

## Data Set Problems

1.   Calculate the average rate of return of each of the first five mutual funds in the Maximum Capital Gain category for the period 1971–1980. On the assumption that an investor with initial wealth of $10,000 can invest as much as he wishes in each of the funds (without affecting the price) and that he will earn with certainty the average rate of return on the investment, draw the production function consisting of these five funds. Assume that each fund is a "project" in the sense of a productive opportunity set discussed in the body of the text.

2.   Let the risk-free interest rate be $r = 5\%$. Find the optimum investment in the five funds you

used in Problem 1. Does it depend on the investor's preferences? Does it represent equilibrium in the securities market? Discuss.

3. Now assume that the initial price of a share in each of the five funds from Problems 1 and 2 is $100. Determine how the share prices will change when an equilibrium is established in the securities market. Plot the "production curve" before and after the change in the share prices. Assume as before that $r = 5\%$.

4. Now assume that due to some constraint, investors cannot invest more than 40% of the total funds in each of the five securities under consideration in the previous problems. Draw the "production curve" for this case, again assuming full certainty. What is the optimum investment in the five securities when the risk-free interest rate is 10%?

## Selected References

Alchian, A. A., "The Rate of Interest, Fisher's Rate of Return over Cost, and Keynes' Internal Rate of Return", *American Economic Review*, December 1955.

Bailey, M. J., "Formal Criteria for Investment Decisions", *Journal of Political Economy*, October 1959.

Beranek, W., "Some New Capital Budgeting Theorems", *Journal of Financial and Quantitative Analysis*, December 1977.

Beranek, W., "The AB Procedure and Capital Budgeting", *Journal of Financial and Quantitative Analysis*, June 1980.

Bernardo, J. J. and Lanser, H. P., "A Capital Budgeting Decision Model with Subjective Criteria", *Journal of Financial and Quantitative Analysis*, June 1977.

Bernhard, R. H., "Discount Methods for Expenditure Evaluation—A Clarification of Their Assumptions", *Journal of Industrial Engineering*, January–February 1962.

Bernhard, R. H. and Norstrom, Carl J., "A Further Note on Unrecovered Investment, Uniqueness of the Internal Rate, and the Question of Project Acceptability", *Journal of Financial and Quantitative Analysis*, June 1980.

Brick, J. R. and Thompson, H. E., "The Economic Life of an Investment and the Appropriate Discount Rate", *Journal of Financial and Quantitative Analysis*, December 1978.

Carlson, C. Robert, Lawrence, Michael and Wort, Donald H., "Clarification of the Reinvestment Assumption in Capital Analysis", *Journal of Business Research*, April 1974.

Chateau, Jean-Pierre, D., "The Capital Budgeting Problem Under Conflicting Financial Policies", *Journal of Business Finance & Accounting*, Winter 1975.

Greer, Willis R. Jr., "Capital Budgeting Analysis with the Timing of Events Uncertain", *Accounting Review*, January 1970.

Haskins, C. G., "Benefit–Cost Ratios vs. Net Present Value: Revisited", *Journal of Business Finance & Accounting*, Summer 1974.

Hirshleifer, J. H., "On the Theory of Optimal Investment Decision", *Journal of Political Economy*, August 1958.

Hoskins, Colin G., "Benefit–Cost Ratio Ranking for Size Disparity Problems", *Journal of Business Finance & Accounting*, 1977.

Jeynes, Paul H., "The Significance of Reinvestment Rate", *Engineering Economist*, Fall 1965.

Lere, John C., "Deterministic Net Present Value as an Approximation of Expected Net Present Value", *Journal of Business Finance & Accounting*, Summer 1980.

Lerner, Eugene M. and Rappaport, Alfred, "Limit DCF in Capital Budgeting", *Harvard Business Review*, September–October 1968.

Lin, S. A. Y., "The Modified Internal Rate of Return and Investment Criterion", *Engineering Economist*, Summer 1976.

Litzenberger, R. H. and Joy, O. M., "Decentralized Capital Budgeting Decisions and Shareholder Wealth Maximization", *Journal of Finance*, September 1975.

Longbottom, D. A. and Wiper, L., "Capital Appraisal and the Case for Average Rate of Return", *Journal of Business Finance & Accounting*, 1977.

Lopez Leautaud, J. I. and Swalm, R., "On the Internal Rate of Return Criterion: A Note on the Notes and Replies", *Engineering Economist*, Summer 1976.

Mao, James C. T., "The Internal Rate of Return as a Ranking Criterion", *Engineering Economist*, Winter 1966.

Oakford, R. V., Bhimjee, S. A. and Jucker, J. V., "The Internal Rate of Return, the Pseudo Internal Rate of Return, and the *NPV* and their Use in Financial Decision Making", *Engineering Economist*, Spring 1977.

Peasnell, K. V., "Capital Budgeting and Discounted Cash Equivalents: Some Clarifying Comments", *Abacus*, December 1979.

Rapp, Birger, "The Internal Rate of Return Method—A Critical Study", *Engineering Costs and Production Economics*, 1980.

Robichek, Alexander A. and Van Horne, James C., "Abandonment Value and Capital Budgeting", *Journal of Finance*, December 1967.

Ross, Stephen A., Spatt, Chester S. and Dybvig, Philip H., "Present Values and Internal Rates of Return", *Journal of Economic Theory*, August 1980.

Schwab, Bernhard and Lusztig, Peter, "A Comparative Analysis of the Net Present Value and the Benefit–Cost Ratios as Measures of the Economic Desirability of Investments", *Journal of Finance*, June 1969.

Scott, David F. Jr., Gray, Otha L. and Bird, Monroe M., "Investing and Financing Behavior of Small Manufacturing Firms", *MSU Business Topics*, Summer 1972.

Stapleton, R. C., "The Acquisition Decision as a Capital Budgeting Problem", *Journal of Business Finance & Accounting*, Summer 1975.

Sundem, G. L., "Evaluating Capital Budgeting Models in Simulated Environments", *Journal of Finance*, September 1975.

# 4

# Investment Decisions Under Uncertainty

In Chapter 3 we analyzed the investment decision when the return on investment was assumed to be certain. As we have seen in Chapter 2, in real life the return on securities is far from certain. The expectations of possible future gains must be based in part on historical data of past performance and in part on forecasts of future events, which can usually be made only on a highly tentative basis. As a result, investors can rarely be thought of as having very precise expectations regarding the future returns to be derived from a particular investment option. In fact, if we abstract for the moment from the investment in short-term government and other low-risk debt instruments, the best that an investor can reasonably be expected to do is to make some estimate of the *range* of possible returns and of the relative chances of earning high or low returns on the investment. In this chapter we discuss the nature of risk involved in investment decision-making.

## 4.1 The Nature of Risk

Formally, we can distinguish three states of investors' expectations:[1] (a) certainty, (b) risk, and (c) uncertainty.

### 4.1.1 Certainty

Strictly speaking, perfect certainty refers to cases where investors' expectations are *single-valued*; that is, the individual views prospective profits in terms of a particular outcome, and not in terms of a range of alternative possible returns. We shall also use the term *certainty* to describe those situations in which investors' expectations regarding

---

[1] This tripartite distinction is associated with Professor Frank Knight; see his *Risk, Uncertainty and Profit*, Boston and New York: Houghton Mifflin Company, 1921, Chap. VII.

future returns are bounded within a very narrow range. But do such investments exist in actual securities markets, outside of the realm of textbooks? At first glance it may appear that no security yields a perfectly certain income stream, but on reflection several illustrations can be found. For example, short-term Treasury bills permit the investor to calculate the exact return which he will receive upon redemption with what amounts to absolute certainty; we simply ignore the insignificant probability of a revolution or of a war which might destroy the existing monetary system. For the time being we also ignore the important question of inflation and its impact on the real return from investment, that is, on the return in terms of purchasing power. Similarly if we are willing to ignore the remote possibility of bankruptcy or financial default in such giants as General Motors and AT&T, the short-term notes of these companies can also be considered for all practical purposes as investments yielding safe returns.[2]

### 4.1.2  Risk

The term *risk* will be used to describe an option whose return is not known with absolute certainty, but for which an array of alternative returns and their probabilities are known; in other words, for which the distribution of returns is known. The distribution may have been estimated on the basis of *objective* (either *a priori* or *a posteriori*) probabilities, or on the basis of purely *subjective* probabilities.

An example of such a frequency distribution is given in Table 4.1, which sets out the historical record of rates of return for a hypothetical investment over the past 40

### Table 4.1
### An Example of a Frequency
### Distribution of Rates of Return

| Rates of Return (%) | Frequency (number of years) |
|---|---|
| −30.00 to −20.01 | 2 |
| −20.00 to −10.01 | 3 |
| −10.00 to  −0.01 | 5 |
|   0.00 to   9.99 | 10 |
|  10.00 to  19.99 | 9 |
|  20.00 to  29.99 | 6 |
|  30.00 to  39.99 | 3 |
|  40.00 to  49.99 | 2 |
| TOTAL | 40 |

[2] We limit the discussion to short-term (less than one year to maturity) bonds since in the longer run, fluctuations in interest rates may induce capital gains or losses, thereby changing the annual rates of return on such bonds. Needless to add, investors' expectations regarding future movements of interest rates are *rarely* single-valued.

years. The data of Table 4.1 were then used to prepare the familiar histogram, shown in Figure 4.1. Historical data of this sort are often available for financial investments, and can be used to facilitate current investment decisions. But even where a long series of past rates of return is available the decision to invest remains complex. There often may be no reason why the future distribution of returns should resemble their distribution in the past, and before arriving at a decision all of the factors that might indicate future changes in the distribution must be carefully examined.

Even if the distribution can be expected to remain unchanged, realizing high returns (the right-hand side of the histogram) or negative returns (the left-hand side) in any particular year is largely a matter of luck. In other words, even if we knew that the past will be reproduced in the future, investing for one year is like drawing one observation from the distribution of a random variable. A positive probability of drawing an observation from the groups "−30 to −0.01" clearly exists, in which case we shall suffer a loss; nevertheless, if the distribution is expected to remain unchanged, we can be reasonably certain that losses will never exceed 30%, nor will profits exceed 50%, in any given year.

### 4.1.3  Uncertainty

In this extreme case the possible range of returns is known but the probability of occurrence for each alternative is not. Of course, the borderline between uncertainty and risk is rather elusive; it is always possible to convert uncertainties into risks by introducing subjective probabilities. In the case of financial investment, probability beliefs are almost invariably subjective; therefore for the remainder of this book we shall use the terms *risk* and *uncertainty* interchangeably.

### 4.2    The Maximum Return Criterion

Let us initially assume a constant investment period, for example, one year, and assume that the decision maker can choose only a single investment option.[3] What decision rule

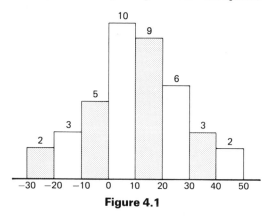

**Figure 4.1**

[3] We defer discussion of the important portfolio problem to Chapters 6 and 8 below.

**Table 4.2**
**Distribution of Possible Returns of Five Alternative Investments***

| A | | B | | C | | D | | E | |
|---|---|---|---|---|---|---|---|---|---|
| Return | Prob-ability | Return | Prob-ability | Return | Prob-ability | Return | Prob-ability | Return | Prob-ability |
| 8 | 1 | 10 | 1 | −8 | 1/4 | −4 | 1/4 | −20 | 1/10 |
| | | | | 16 | 1/2 | 8 | 1/2 | 0 | 6/10 |
| | | | | 24 | 1/4 | 12 | 1/4 | 50 | 3/10 |

* To facilitate comparison, the returns are given in percentages.

should the investor apply to choose the best alternative? To define the problem more precisely we shall assume that he is confronted with the five alternatives given in Table 4.2, that he has full information on all possible returns, and that their (objective or subjective) probabilities are also known. Two of the options (*A* and *B*) represent perfectly certain investments, while the other three alternatives (*C*, *D*, and *E*) entail varying degrees of risk. Such a situation is quite realistic: an investor can typically buy riskless short-term government bonds or deposit his money in a savings bank; alternatively, he can buy common stocks whose returns must be considered as highly uncertain random variables.

If the investor restricts himself to "safe" investments (options *A* and *B*), his choice is very simple. The only criterion required in this case is that of maximum return, and he will choose the alternative that offers the highest return at the end of the investment period. In our example he will choose option *B*, since *B* promises a 10% return as compared with the 8% offered by option *A*.

Such simple choice situations are hardly representative of a modern securities market; reality is much more complicated and for that matter much more interesting as well. Investors do not usually restrict themselves solely to safe prospects. A more realistic problem, therefore, is how to select the best option out of the five alternative choices *A*, *B*, *C*, *D*, and *E*. Can we still apply the maximum return criterion? Clearly we cannot do so without major qualifications. Whereas in the previous example of comparing only options *A* and *B* the returns were known with certainty (8% and 10% respectively), we have no such knowledge regarding the other three options. Suppose we try to compare options *B* and *C*: the return on *B* is 10%, but what return can we attribute to *C*? If we assume a negative return of −8%, *B* is clearly preferable; however, if we assume the return on *C* will be 16% or 24%, then it is equally clear that option *C* represents the better alternative. Since there is no *a priori* reason to single out any one of the three possible returns of option *C*, the maximum return criterion breaks down unless we restrict ourselves to the unrealistic (and trivial) problem of selecting investments under conditions of perfect certainty.

## 4.3    The Maximum Expected Return Criterion

To compare the desirability of alternative investments under conditions of uncertainty we must first devise a synthetic index which reflects the entire distribution of returns.

One of the most popular solutions to this problem stipulates that decisions should be reached on the basis of an investment's *expected return*, where expected return is defined as the mean of the random variable distribution (in this case the returns) weighted by the probabilities of occurrence.[4] For example, if we consider option *C* in Table 4.2 the expected return can be calculated as follows:

$$\tfrac{1}{4} \cdot (-8) + \tfrac{1}{2} \cdot 16 + \tfrac{1}{4} \cdot 24 = 12$$

Similarly we can readily calculate the expected returns[5] for the other alternatives:

| Option | Expected Return |
|--------|-----------------|
| A | 8 |
| B | 10 |
| C | 12 |
| D | 6 |
| E | 13 |

Having calculated the expected returns for each of the five alternatives we can then choose the option with the highest expected return, in our example option *E*, whose expected return is 13%.

The principle of maximum expected return is deceptively simple. But is such a criterion appropriate for *all* types of investors? For example, can we expect all individuals, independent of their particular tastes, to prefer uncertain options such as *C* and *E* to an option such as *B* which offers a smaller, but certain, return merely because the former have higher expected returns? Even if we restrict ourselves to a comparison of two uncertain alternatives, for example, *C* and *E*, similar problems arise. The maximum expected return criterion suggests that an option such as *E* should always be preferred to *C* since the former has a higher expected value. But option *E* does not dominate option *C* in every respect; the maximum loss that can be incurred if we choose *C* is 8%, while in option *E* we run the risk of losing as much as 20% of the investment.

### 4.3.1 The St. Petersburg Paradox[6]

The shortcomings of the expected return criterion can perhaps be illustrated best by considering the classic problem known as the "St. Petersburg Paradox", which was

---

[4] Since we shall be calculating expected values quite often, a more formal definition may prove helpful. Let $x$ be a discrete random variable with the probabilities $p(x)$. The expected value $E(x)$ is defined as follows:

$$E(x) = \sum_{x=-\infty}^{+\infty} x \cdot p(x).$$

For a more detailed discussion see the Statistical Supplement at the end of this book.

[5] In the special case of perfect certainty (options *A* and *B*) the expected return equals the actual return, since $E(x) = x \cdot 1$.

[6] For a short history of the St. Petersburg Paradox, or the St. Petersburg Game as it is often called, see W. Fellner, *Probability and Profit*, Homewood, Ill.: Irwin, 1965.

first formulated in the eighteenth century by the Swiss mathematician Nikolaus Bernoulli:[7]

> Peter tosses a coin and continues to do so until it should land "heads" when it comes to ground. He agrees to give Paul one ducat if he gets "heads" on the very first throw, two ducats if he gets it on the second, four if on the third, eight if on the fourth, and so on, so that with each additional throw the number of ducats he must pay is doubled. Suppose we seek to determine the value of Paul's expec-- tation.[8]

In general, if "heads" first appears on the $n$th toss, the player is awarded a prize equal to $2^{n-1}$. The size of the prize is uncertain, and depends on the results of each experiment, but when the coin lands "heads" for the first time the game is over, so that only one prize is awarded per game. Naturally, the player would like "heads" to appear only after a long series of "tails", since this increases his prize.

What would be a fair price for Paul to pay for the opportunity to play such a game? If "heads" comes up on the first toss, the prize is one ducat; the probability of this outcome is 1/2 since there is an equal probability of obtaining either "heads" or "tails" when an unbiased coin is tossed. What is the probability of winning two ducats? This prize results should the coin land "heads" for the first time on the second toss. The probability of getting "tails" on the first toss is 1/2, and since the two tosses are independent events, the probability of getting "heads" on the second toss is also 1/2. The joint probability of obtaining "tails" on the first toss and "heads" on the second (the event TH) is given by the product of the two probabilities:[9] $1/2 \cdot 1/2 = 1/4$. Theoretically the game can continue for a long time until the coin lands "heads" for the first time, but the probability of the game lasting for a great number of tosses is, of course, very small.

The principle of maximum expected return suggests that the game's expected value constitutes the maximum price for Paul to pay for this fair gamble. To facilitate the calculation of the expected value, we have set out the possible results of the coin tossing game in Table 4.3. If we denote the possible prize by $x$, the expected value (return) of the St. Petersburg game can be calculated as follows:[10]

$$E(x) = 1/2 \cdot 1 + 1/4 \cdot 2 + 1/8 \cdot 4 + 1/16 \cdot 8 + \cdots + 1/2^n \cdot 2^{n-1} + \cdots$$
$$= 1/2 + 1/2 + 1/2 + 1/2 + \cdots + 1/2 + \cdots = \infty$$

[7] The first published analysis of the problem was written by Daniel Bernoulli (a younger cousin) during his stay in St. Petersburg as a visiting scholar (1725–1733), hence the name "St. Petersburg".

[8] The problem as formulated by Nikolaus Bernoulli is quoted by Daniel Bernoulli in "Specimen Theoriae Novae de Mensura Sortis", *Papers of the Imperial Academy of Sciences in Petersburg*, Vol. V, 1738. An English translation, "Exposition of a New Theory on the Measurement of Risk", appears in *Econometrica* 22, No. 1, Jan. 1954, pp. 23–36.

[9] Since the outcome of each toss is independent of the outcomes of the other tosses, $p(H \cap T) = p(H) \cdot p(T) = 1/2 \cdot 1/2 = 1/4$. See A. M. Mood and F. A. Graybill, *Introduction to the Theory of Statistics*, 2nd ed., New York: McGraw-Hill, 1963, p. 43, and the Statistical Supplement.

[10] The expected return is calculated by first multiplying columns (3) and (4) of Table 4.3 and then summing the resulting products. It should also be noted that the probabilities of Table 4.3 add to 1; see note 13 below.

**Table 4.3**
**Summary of Possible Results of Coin Tossing Experiment**

| Toss on which "Heads" First Appears (1) | Description of the Result* (2) | Probability of the Result (3) | Prize (4) |
|---|---|---|---|
| 1 | H | 1/2 | 1 |
| 2 | TH | 1/4 | 2 |
| 3 | TTH | 1/8 | 4 |
| 4 | TTTH | 1/16 | 8 |
| ⋮ | ⋮ | ⋮ | ⋮ |
| $n$ | $[(n-1)T]H$ | $1/2^n$ | $2^{n-1}$ |

\* H signifies "heads"; T signifies "tails".

Since there is no theoretical limit to the number of tosses, the mathematical expectation of the game is infinite; that is, invoking the principle of maximum return, Paul should be prepared to pay any sum, however large, for the opportunity to play the game! Now assume that you are offered the opportunity to play such a game, of course in dollars rather than ducats. How much would you pay for the opportunity? An experiment conducted with a group of students revealed that most were prepared to pay only two or three dollars for a chance to play. A few were willing to pay as much as eight dollars but no one offered more than that. This contradiction between the amount that reasonable people are willing to pay for an opportunity to play the game and its infinite mathematical expectation constitutes the so-called "St. Petersburg Paradox", which troubled, and perhaps also entertained, some of the best mathematical minds of the eighteenth century.

Obviously, no one has an infinite amount of money and in practice will not be able to pay such a price for playing the game. Also, at least in theory, such a game may go on forever, and no one will be prepared to wait so long before receiving the prize, however large. Nevertheless, most people will not pay even a relatively small sum for this game (say, $100), which indicates that the maximum expected return, in general, cannot serve as a decision rule for decision making under uncertainty.

Special interest attaches to the solutions proposed independently by the mathematician Daniel Bernoulli and by his contemporary Gabriel Cramer, who sought to resolve the problem by rejecting the principle of maximum expected return and substituting expected utility in its place. Their efforts constitute an important intellectual milestone leading to the modern theory of choice under conditions of uncertainty.

### 4.3.2  Bernoulli's Solution

Bernoulli's solution rests on the idea that individuals are concerned with the utility, rather than the money value, of the alternative prizes, and that the additional utility afforded by the additional money increments decreases as the money value of the prize is increased. The latter assumption is usually referred to by economists as the principle of diminishing marginal utility of money; it reflects the notion that initial sums of money are used to provide more basic needs. Thus while total utility is increased by successive increments to an individual's wealth, it increases at a diminishing rate.[11] The particular assumptions made by Bernoulli were that the utility of money is a *logarithmic* function of the size of the money prize and that the function is of the following form:[12]

$$U(x) = b \log \frac{x}{a} \qquad (4.1)$$

where $U(x)$ is the utility derived from an amount of money $x$, and $a$ and $b$ are positive coefficients.

The logarithmic function embodies the notion that *equal proportionate* increases in wealth impart *equal absolute* additions to utility. This can be seen by considering two individuals with an initial wealth of $10 and $100 respectively. Let us assume that both investors have "Bernoulli" utility functions of the form $U(x) = b \log (x/a)$, and that we wish to increase their utilities by equal amounts. By how much must we increase each individual's wealth?

We first rewrite the utility function as follows:

$$U(x) = b \log \frac{x}{a} = b (\log x - \log a)$$

$$= b \log x - b \log a \qquad (4.2)$$

---

[11] Mathematically diminishing marginal utility means that the second derivative of the utility function is negative.

[12] Bernoulli's function clearly incorporates the assumption of diminishing marginal utility. Since both $a$ and $b$ are assumed to be positive, and the amount of money or wealth $x$ is greater than zero, from

$$U(x) = b \log \frac{x}{a} = b \log x - b \log a$$

we obtain for the first derivative

$$U'(x) = \frac{b}{x} > 0$$

That is, the function is monotone increasing. This function's second derivative is negative, that is, the marginal utility of money *decreases* as wealth is increased:

$$U''(x) = -\frac{b}{x^2} < 0.$$

It is worth mentioning that one can use the function $U(x) = \log x$ and obtain the same results (see Figure 4.2) as the function (4.1) is a positive linear transformation of this function—see Section 4.4.2.

For a discussion of derivatives and their use in financial analysis, see the Mathematical Supplement at the end of this book.

Table 4.4 sets out the answer to our problem using this utility function. Since log 10 = 1 the utility of the first individual's initial wealth of $10 equals

$$U(10) = b \log 10 - b \log a$$
$$= b - b \log a \qquad (4.3)$$

Similarly, the utility of the second individual's initial wealth of $100 is given by

$$U(100) = b \log 100 - b \log a$$
$$= 2b - b \log a \qquad (4.4)$$

A comparison of Equations (4.3) and (4.4) shows that if we increase the wealth of the poorer individual by $90, that is, from $10 to $100, his total utility will increase by $b$ units (simply subtract Equation (4.3) from Equation (4.4)). Now if we wish to increase the second individual's utility by an equal absolute amount, we must increase his wealth *in equal proportion*, that is, by $900 and not by $90. His new total wealth will then equal $1,000, with the following total utility:

$$U(1,000) = b \log 1,000 - b \log a$$
$$= 3b - b \log a \qquad (4.5)$$

Subtracting Equation (4.4) from Equation (4.5), we can verify that the wealthier individual's utility also increased by $b$ units. In other words, the utility of an additional $900 to the wealthier individual equals the utility of the $90 added to the wealth of his poorer friend. This reflects the idea that the poorer individual has not yet fulfilled various basic requirements so that the marginal value to him of each incremental dollar is relatively higher.

Using this logarithmic function, Bernoulli argued that in determining the value of the St. Petersburg Game an individual would consider the *utility* afforded by the alternative prizes rather than their dollar amounts, and therefore the amount of money he would be prepared to pay for the opportunity to play the game depends on the game's *expected utility* and not on its expected money return. Let us denote the number of the toss when "heads" first appears by $n$ (where $n = 1, 2, 3, \ldots$), and the utility derived

**Table 4.4**

|  | Individual A | Individual B |
|---|---|---|
| Initial Wealth | 10 | 100 |
| Total Utility* | $b - b \log a$ | $2b - b \log a$ |
| Addition to Wealth | 90 | 900 |
| New Total Wealth | 100 | 1,000 |
| New Total Utility | $2b - b \log a$ | $3b - b \log a$ |
| Addition to Utility Resulting from Increased Wealth | $b$ | $b$ |

* $b \log \dfrac{x}{a} = b(\log x - \log a) = b \log x - b \log a$.

from the prize $x$ awarded after $n$ tosses by $U(x)$. Thus if "heads" appears after $n$ tosses the money prize will be $x = 2^{n-1}$. The utility of this prize is given by

$$U(x) = b \log \frac{2^{n-1}}{a} = b \log 2^{n-1} - b \log a$$

$$= b[(n-1) \log 2 - \log a] \tag{4.6}$$

According to the principle of expected utility the individual will be willing to pay for the participation in the game at most an amount $x_0$ such that the utility $U(x_0)$ derived from this amount is equal to the game's expected utility $EU(x)$. For the expected utility of the game we write,

$$EU(x) = \sum_{x=1}^{\infty} p(x)U(x) \tag{4.7}$$

Substituting the utility from (4.6) and recalling that the probability of the game lasting for $n$ tosses is $1/2^n$, we obtain

$$EU(x) = \sum_{n=1}^{\infty} \frac{1}{2^n} b[(n-1) \log 2 - \log a]$$

$$= b \sum_{n=1}^{\infty} \frac{n-1}{2^n} \log 2 - b \sum_{n=1}^{\infty} \frac{1}{2^n} \log a \tag{4.8}$$

However, since $\sum_{n=1}^{\infty}(1/2^n) = 1$, and $\sum_{n=1}^{\infty}[(n-1)/2^n] = 1$ as well,[13] we find that the

---

[13] The expression

$$\sum_{n=1}^{\infty} \frac{1}{2^n} = \frac{1}{2} + \frac{1}{4} + \frac{1}{8} + \cdots = \frac{\frac{1}{2}}{1 - \frac{1}{2}} = 1$$

Omitting the term $n = 1$ whose value is zero, the sum $\sum_{n=1}^{\infty}(n-1)/2^n$ can be expanded as follows:

$$\sum_{n=2}^{\infty} \frac{n-1}{2^n} = \frac{1}{4} + \frac{2}{8} + \frac{3}{16} + \frac{4}{32} + \cdots$$

which can be broken down into the sum of the following components:

$$\frac{1}{4} + \frac{1}{8} + \frac{1}{16} + \frac{1}{32} + \cdots = \frac{1}{2}$$

$$\frac{1}{8} + \frac{1}{16} + \frac{1}{32} + \cdots = \frac{1}{4}$$

$$\frac{1}{16} + \frac{1}{32} + \cdots = \frac{1}{8}$$

$$\frac{1}{32} + \cdots = \frac{1}{16}$$

Hence,

$$\sum_{n=1}^{\infty} \frac{n-1}{2^n} = \frac{1}{2} + \frac{1}{4} + \frac{1}{8} + \frac{1}{16} + \cdots = 1$$

expected utility of the game equals

$$EU(x) = b \log 2 - b \log a = b \log \frac{2}{a} \qquad (4.9)$$

But as Equation (4.1) above clearly shows, $b \log (2/a)$ is also equal to the utility of \$2 or $EU(x) = U(2)$. It follows that an individual whose tastes are characterized by the Bernoulli utility function will pay \$2 at most to take part in the game. Alternatively, we can say that such an individual is indifferent between a perfectly certain promise of a gain of \$2 and the chance to play the game. Of course, if the individual is faced with a choice between playing the St. Petersburg Game or obtaining a perfectly certain income exceeding \$2 (say, \$3) he will prefer the second alternative even though the expected money return from the game is infinite! Thus by introducing the concept of expected utility and a logarithmic utility function Bernoulli resolved the paradox.

### 4.3.3  Cramer's Solution

Gabriel Cramer, an equally famous eighteenth century mathematician, independently provided a somewhat similar solution to the paradox.[14] Like Bernoulli, Cramer resolved the paradox by introducing the mathematical expectation of utility in place of the expected money return. However, Cramer chose the following type of utility function to illustrate the principle of diminishing marginal utility of money:[15]

$$U(x) = \sqrt{x}$$

In other words, Cramer represented the utility as being equal to the square root of the money gain. Using this utility function, the expected utility of the St. Petersburg Game becomes

$$EU(x) = \sum_{x=1}^{\infty} p(x)U(x) = \sum_{n=1}^{\infty} \frac{1}{2^n} \cdot \sqrt{2^{n-1}}$$

$$= \frac{1}{2} + \frac{\sqrt{2}}{4} + \frac{\sqrt{2} \cdot \sqrt{2}}{8} + \frac{\sqrt{2} \cdot \sqrt{2} \cdot \sqrt{2}}{16} + \cdots$$

[14] Cramer's solution was originally given in a letter which he wrote to Nikolaus Bernoulli, and is quoted by Daniel Bernoulli in his celebrated paper.
[15] Like Bernoulli's, Cramer's utility function, $U(x) = \sqrt{x} = x^{1/2}$, is also monotone increasing in terms of $x$; that is, its first derivative is positive (for $x > 0$):

$$U'(x) = \tfrac{1}{2} x^{-1/2} > 0$$

The second derivative is negative:

$$U''(x) = \tfrac{1}{2}(-\tfrac{1}{2})x^{-3/2} = -\tfrac{1}{4}x^{-3/2} < 0$$

Therefore this function also incorporates the assumption of diminishing marginal utility.

$$= \frac{1}{2} \cdot \frac{1}{1 - \dfrac{\sqrt{2}}{2}} = \frac{1}{2 - \sqrt{2}}$$

Thus the maximum price $x_0$ that such an individual will be ready to pay in order to participate in the game, obtained by equating

$$EU(x) = U(x_0) \text{ or } EU(x) = \sqrt{x_0}$$

is given by

$$x_0 = [EU(x)]^2$$

or

$$x_0 = \left( \frac{1}{2 - \sqrt{2}} \right)^2 = (1.707)^2 = \$2.914$$

The utility derived from \$2.914 is $U(2.914) = \sqrt{2.914} = 1.707$, which is exactly equal to the expected utility derived from the game.

### 4.3.4  An Alternative Solution

The utility functions proposed by Bernoulli and Cramer are not the only ones that solve the St. Petersburg Paradox. Thus consider the utility function $U_l$ shown in Figure 4.2. It consists of two linear sections: a rising section ($U(x) = x$) up to some prize value $x_k = 2^{k-1}$ (where $k$ is an integer number, say the number of tosses of the coin in the game) followed by a level section of constant utility value $U(x) = 2^{k-1}$ for all $x$ greater than $x_k = 2^{k-1}$. Mathematically, this function can be defined as follows:

$$U(x) = \begin{cases} x \ (= 2^{n-1}) & \text{for } 1 \leqslant n \leqslant k \\ 2^{k-1} & \text{for } n > k \end{cases}$$

where $n$ is the number of tosses until the first head shows.

Let us verify that this function also solves the St. Petersburg Paradox. Indeed, the expected utility of the game now is

$$EU(x) = \sum_{x=1}^{\infty} p(x)U(x) = \sum_{n=1}^{k} \frac{1}{2^n} 2^{n-1} + \sum_{n=k+1}^{\infty} \frac{2^{k-1}}{2^n}$$

Since $2^{n-1}/2^n = 1/2$ for every $n$, the first sum on the right is simply a sum of $k$ terms each equal to $1/2$. The first sum is thus equal to $k/2$. The second sum is a geometric progression. Factoring out the constant numerator, we obtain

$$\sum_{n=k+1}^{\infty} \frac{2^{k-1}}{2^n} = 2^{k-1}\left(\frac{1}{2^{k+1}} + \frac{1}{2^{k+2}} + \frac{1}{2^{k+3}} + \cdots\right)$$

Now factoring out the first $1/2^{k+1}$ of the series in parentheses, we obtain

$$\sum_{n=k+1}^{\infty} \frac{2^{k-1}}{2^n} = \frac{2^{k-1}}{2^{k+1}}\left(1 + \frac{1}{2} + \frac{1}{2^2} + \cdots\right) = \frac{1}{2^2}\cdot\frac{1}{1/2} = \frac{1}{2}$$

Summing the above results, we obtain for the expected utility of the St. Petersburg Game

$$EU(x) = \frac{k}{2} + \frac{1}{2} = \frac{k+1}{2}$$

If, say, $k = 24$ (i.e., the utility function increases linearly with $x$ up to $x = 2^{23}$ and then remains level), the expected utility of the game is

$$EU(x) = \frac{24 + 1}{2} = 12.5$$

and since it falls in the linearly rising range of the utility function, $U(x) = x$, this is also the amount that an individual with this utility function will be prepared to pay for the game.

Figure 4.2 plots Bernoulli's function $[U(x) = \log x]$ and Cramer's function

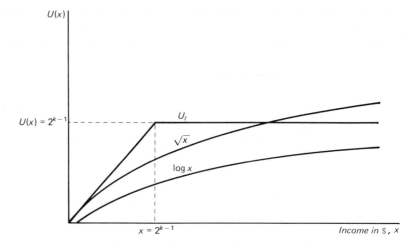

**Figure 4.2**

$[U(x) = \sqrt{x}]$ for comparison with the new function $U_l$ that we introduced here. All the three functions have the same general appearance, in the sense that initially they rise fairly steeply and then level off. The main difference between the three functions is that the Bernoulli and Cramer functions are not bounded at infinity (both $\log x$ and $\sqrt{x}$ increase to $\infty$ as $x$ goes to infinity), whereas the new function that we introduced is bounded by the constant value $2^{k-1}$.

## 4.4    The Modern Theory of Utility

Although the expected utility hypothesis was first formulated over 200 years ago, only comparatively recently was the deeper significance of this approach for decision making recognized. Bernoulli and Cramer were primarily interested in demonstrating the superiority of expected utility over expected monetary value. In particular, they showed that given the assumption of risk aversion (declining marginal utility of money), the expected utility approach can be used to resolve the St. Petersburg Paradox as well as to account for the willingness of people to purchase insurance policies with negative expected monetary values.

Not until the 1930s was the Bernoulli–Cramer analysis extended to the analysis of the general problem of choice under conditions of risk. In 1934 the German mathematician Karl Menger demonstrated that unless the utility function is bounded, new paradoxes can be constructed which cannot be resolved by the use of expected utility.[16] For example, the Bernoulli solution breaks down[17] if we assume that the prize to be awarded when "heads" comes up on the $n$th toss is equal to $e^{2^n}$. Today, the modern theory of expected utility resolves this difficulty by assuming that the utility function is bounded.[18] However, what was to prove a more far-reaching breakthrough was made by a brilliant young British logician, Frank Ramsey, in a paper published posthumously in 1931,[19] and later in 1944 by John von Neumann and Oskar Morgenstern in their monumental work on the theory of games.[20] Ramsey, and then von Neumann and Morgenstern, were concerned to demonstrate the superiority of the expected utility hypothesis not only vis-à-vis expected monetary value but also with respect to other possible theories of behavior. They achieved this by providing a rigorous axiomatic justification for the use of expected utility to explain choices under conditions of uncertainty.

[16] Karl Menger, "Das Unsicherheitsmoment in der Wertlehre", *Zeitschrift fur Nationalökonomie* 51, 1934.

[17] In this case the expected utility is given by $EU(x) = \Sigma_{n=1}^{\infty} (1/2^n) \log (e^{2^n}) = \Sigma_{n=1}^{\infty} (1/2^n) \cdot 2^n \log e = \log e \, \Sigma_{n=1}^{\infty} 1 = \infty$.

[18] See K. J. Arrow, *Aspects of the Theory of Risk-Bearing*, Helsinki, Yrjö Jahnssonin Säätiö, 1965.

[19] F. P. Ramsey, "Truth and Probability", in *The Foundations of Mathematics and Other Logical Essays*, London: K. Paul, Trench, Trusner and Co., 1931. For a sensitive appreciation of Ramsey, who died at the age of 26, see J. M. Keynes, *Essays in Biography*, London: Rupert Hart-Davis, 1951.

[20] See J. von Neumann and O. Morgenstern, *Theory of Games and Economic Behavior*, Princeton, N.J.: Princeton University Press, 3rd ed., 1953.

### 4.4.1   The Axiomatic Basis for Expected Utility

Von Neumann and Morgenstern demonstrated that if a decision maker fulfills a number of reasonable consistency requirements, the expected utility hypothesis leads to optimal results under conditions of uncertainty. More specifically, they showed that utility can be introduced into decision problems in such a way that an individual who acts solely on the basis of expected utility is also acting in accordance with his true tastes. In this section we shall sketch the axiomatic foundations of the expected utility hypothesis.[21] A more rigorous presentation of the axioms and a proof that their fulfillment implies the optimality of the expected utility hypothesis is presented in Appendix 4.1.

Let us assume that an individual is faced with three alternative risky options (or alternative lotteries) A, B, and C, from which he has to choose one. If the following six axioms hold, his optimal choice will be given by that option which maximizes his expected utility:

AXIOM 1
Any two alternatives are comparable, that is, the individual either prefers one to the other, or he is indifferent between them.

AXIOM 2
Both the indifference and the preference relations are transitive. That is, if the individual prefers option $A$ to option $B$ and $B$ to $C$ then he also prefers $A$ to $C$.

AXIOM 3
Where a risky option has as one of its prizes another risky option, the first option is decomposable into its more basic alternatives. This can be clarified by considering the following example: Let $Q$ be a lottery which includes two other lotteries $L_1$ and $L_2$ as prizes. (For example, $Q$ is a roulette wheel whose prizes are national lottery tickets.) Thus,

$$Q = [qL_1, (1 - q)L_2]$$

and

$$L_1 = [p_1A_1, (1 - p_1)A_2]$$

$$L_2 = [p_2A_1, (1 - p_2)A_2]$$

where $q$ is the probability of winning prize $L_1$, which is itself a lottery with a probability $p_1$ of winning prize $A_1$ and a probability $(1 - p_1)$ to win prize $A_2$. Similarly we define a second lottery, $L_2$. Now Axiom 3 asserts that lottery $Q$ can be reduced to the more

---

[21] Several axiomatic systems have been given; our presentation closely follows that of R. D. Luce and H. Raiffa, *Games and Decisions*, New York: Wiley, 1957.

basic form

$$Q = [qL_1, (1 - q)L_2] \sim \{q[p_1A_1, (1 - p_1)A_2], (1 - q)[(p_2A_1, (1 - p_2)A_2]\}$$

or

$$[qL_1, (1 - q)L_2] \sim [p^*A_1, (1 - p^*)A_2]$$

where

$$p^* = qp_1 + (1 - q)p_2$$

and the sign $\sim$ means "equivalent" indicating that the individual is indifferent between the two lotteries. That is, lottery $Q$ can be reduced to a simple lottery, which includes as its prizes the possible outcomes $A_1$ and $A_2$ with certain adjusted probabilities.

AXIOM 4

If an individual is indifferent between two risky options, they are interchangeable as alternatives in any compound option. For example, assume the following lottery $Q$ with three outcomes,

$$Q = (p_1 \cdot 1, p_2 \cdot 5, p_3 \cdot 10)$$

If the following relationship holds:

$$5 \sim (1/4 \cdot 1, 3/4 \cdot 6) = B$$

then

$$Q = (p_1 \cdot 1, p_2 \cdot 5, p_3 \cdot 10) \sim (p_1 \cdot 1, p_2[1/4 \cdot 1, 3/4 \cdot 6], p_3 \cdot 10) = Q_1$$

Thus the fourth axiom asserts that one can substitute $B$ in lottery $Q$ for 5, and so long as the individual is indifferent between the certainty of receiving 5 and the risky option represented by $B$, he will also be indifferent between $Q$ and $Q_1$.

AXIOM 5

If two risky options involve the same two alternatives, then the option in which the more preferred outcome has a higher probability of occurring is itself preferred. For example, if $Q = (1/4 \cdot 5, 3/4 \cdot 10)$ and $Q_1 = (1/2 \cdot 5, 1/2 \cdot 10)$, and if we assume that the individual prefers 10 to 5, then by Axiom 5 he also prefers $Q$ to $Q_1$, since the probability of getting 10 in option $Q$ is greater than in option $Q_1$. This assumption is usually referred to as the *monotonicity* axiom.

AXIOM 6

If $A$ is preferred to $B$ and $B$ to $C$ then a lottery can be defined involving $A$ and $C$ which is indifferent to $B$. This is known in the literature as the *continuity* axiom. An example may help to clarify its meaning. Let us assume that an individual prefers $10 to $8 and $8 to $1. The continuity axiom asserts that there exists a probability $p$ so that

$$(p \cdot 10 + (1 - p) \cdot 1) \sim 8$$

where the sign $\sim$ again means equivalent.

If one is willing to accept the above six axioms then it can be shown that the optimal investment under conditions of uncertainty is that which affords the *maximum expected utility* (see Appendix 4.1). However, some criticisms have been raised: It can be argued (and often is) that in certain cases one or more of the axioms do not hold, and therefore the expected utility approach is not applicable. But despite the admitted fact that in certain choice situations the analysis may not be appropriate, we shall apply the expected utility hypothesis throughout the remainder of the book when analyzing investment decisions in securities markets. This, in turn, implies our acceptance of the consistency relationships set out in the above six axioms.[22]

### 4.4.2   The Meaning of Utility

Care must be exercised when interpreting the modern theory of utility. Although the von Neumann–Morgenstern analysis provides a logically consistent rationale for the use of expected utility as a guide for decision making under conditions of uncertainty, it should be noted that the meaning of the utility concept which is used to explain (or guide) choices under risk is limited. In the modern theory of utility, the preference axioms logically *precede* utilities, not the other way around. As a result there is no need to discuss the meaning of "underlying subjective utilities" since utilities are attached to alternative options to reflect the underlying preferences, not to account for them in any philosophical or psychological sense. Similarly, the numerical properties of the von Neumann–Morgenstern utility function are also limited. The relevant class of utility functions are those which provide the same ranking of risky alternatives. Beyond this, no significance whatsoever can be attributed to the absolute magnitude of the utilities. The class of utility functions which have the desired property of preserving the ranking of alternatives is composed of utility functions which are increasing linear functions of one another. Consider the three utility functions presented in Table 4.5:

$$U_1(x) = \sqrt{x}$$

$$U_2(x) = -10 + 100\sqrt{x}$$

$$U_3(x) = -100 + \sqrt{x}$$

---

[22] Needless to add, the acceptance of the axioms should not be interpreted in a normative sense. In particular we do not mean to imply that decisions *should* be consistent, but rather that investors' decisions can fruitfully be analyzed and explained on the assumption that investors act as if to maximize expected utility. We shall also present empirical evidence on the explanatory power of this assumption when applied to securities markets in Chapter 5.

**Table 4.5**

|  | Option A | | | Option B | | | Option C | | Option D | |
|---|---|---|---|---|---|---|---|---|---|---|
| Probability | 1/4 | 1/4 | 1/2 | 1/4 | 1/4 | 1/2 | 1/2 | 1/2 | 2/3 | 1/3 |
| Return | 9 | 25 | 36 | 4 | 9 | 16 | 4 | 9 | 4 | 9 |
| $U_1(x)$* | 3 | 5 | 6 | 2 | 3 | 4 | 2 | 3 | 2 | 3 |
| $U_2(x)$† | 290 | 490 | 590 | 190 | 290 | 390 | 190 | 290 | 190 | 290 |
| $U_3(x)$‡ | −97 | −95 | −94 | −98 | −97 | −96 | −98 | −97 | −98 | −97 |
| $EU_1(x)$ | 5.00 | | | 3.25 | | | 2.50 | | 2.33 | |
| $EU_2(x)$ | 490.00 | | | 315.00 | | | 240.00 | | 223.33 | |
| $EU_3(x)$ | −95.00 | | | −96.75 | | | −97.50 | | −97.67 | |

* $U_1(x) = \sqrt{x}$
† $U_2(x) = -10 + 100\sqrt{x}$
‡ $U_3(x) = -100 + \sqrt{x}$

As can be clearly seen from Table 4.5, the *absolute* magnitudes of the expected utilities of the four alternative investment options $A$, $B$, $C$, and $D$ differ markedly depending on the utility function assumed. For example, using the first utility function, $U_1$, alternative $A$ has an expected utility of 5, while using $U_2$ and $U_3$ results in expected utilities of 490 and −95, respectively, for the same investment option. However, Table 4.5 also clearly shows that the *ranking* of the four options remains invariant independent of the utility function assumed; thus option $A$ is preferred to $B$, $B$ to $C$, and $C$ to $D$ in all three cases, that is, for each of the utility functions $U_1$, $U_2$, and $U_3$.

These three functions differ only in origin and in the (positive)[23] unit of measure; the invariance of the preference ranking in our example is a special case of the following general proposition:

A von Neumann–Morgenstern utility function is defined up to a positive linear transformation.

This theorem states that the ranking of a group of alternative options will remain constant using the utility functions $U(x)$ or $U^*(x) = a + bU(x)$, independent of the value of $x$, so long as $b$ is positive.[24]

---

[23] Where utility is a decreasing function of income ($b < 0$), the preference ordering does *not* necessarily remain the same, see below.

[24] Thus despite the fact that numerical values are assigned to alternative outcomes, utilities are not cardinal utilities in the usual sense of the term.

The proof of this theorem is straightforward. Assume the following two alternatives:

| | Option A | | Option B | |
|---|---|---|---|---|
| $x$ | $p(x)$ | | $y$ | $q(y)$ |
| *(return)* | *(probability)* | | *(return)* | *(probability)* |
| $x_1$ | $p_1$ | | $y_1$ | $q_1$ |
| $\vdots$ | $\vdots$ | | $\vdots$ | $\vdots$ |
| $x_n$ | $p_n$ | | $y_m$ | $q_m$ |

Now assume that for any general utility function $U$ we also have $EU(x) > EU(y)$; that is, option $A$ is preferred to $B$. Let us now prove that if a utility function of the form $U^*(x)$, where $U^*(x) = a + bU(x)$ (and where $b > 0$), is used, we will necessarily also have $EU^*(x) > EU^*(y)$. In other words, substituting such a function does not change the preference ordering of the two options.

First we compute $EU^*(x)$:

$$EU^*(x) = \sum_{i=1}^{n} p_i U^*(x_i) = \sum_{i=1}^{n} p_i[a + bU(x_i)] = a \sum_{i=1}^{n} p_i + b \sum_{i=1}^{n} p_i U(x_i)$$

and since

$$\sum_{i=1}^{n} p_i U(x_i) = EU(x) \quad \text{and} \quad \sum_{i=1}^{n} p_i = 1$$

we obtain

$$EU^*(x) = a + bEU(x)$$

Similarly, for $y$

$$EU^*(y) = a + bEU(y)$$

As $b > 0$, it clearly follows that if $EU(x) > EU(y)$, then also $EU^*(x) > EU^*(y)$. Thus any positive linear transformation of a given utility function preserves the ranking of the different options.

## 4.5    Alternative Attitudes Toward Risk

It will be convenient for the purposes of our analysis to be able to distinguish between two classes of investors: those who dislike risk, whom we shall call "risk averters"; and those who prefer risky prospects, whom we shall call "risk lovers". Suppose an individual is offered the opportunity of purchasing for $10 the following investment option:

| End-of-Period Value | Probability |
|:---:|:---:|
| 9 | 1/2 |
| 11 | 1/2 |

The expected end-of-period value of such an investment is $1/2 \cdot 9 + 1/2 \cdot 11 = 10$; that is, the expected value equals the initial purchase price. In other words, the net expected monetary return from this investment is zero.[25] Can an individual be expected to purchase such an option? Since we have rejected the principle of expected return and replaced it with the principle of expected utility, our answer depends on the individual's attitude toward risk, that is, on the degree to which he "likes" or "dislikes" to trade a safe prospect for an uncertain one.

DEFINITION
An individual whose utility function is concave will be called a risk averter.[26] The marginal utility of a risk averter declines with an increase in his wealth.

Thus every risk averter will prefer a perfectly certain return to an uncertain one with equal expected value. Taking our example, a risk-averse individual will not purchase the option, because in terms of utility the possible loss of one dollar *more than offsets* the equal possible gain of one dollar. It follows that a risk averter is not a gambler, and in fact will never voluntarily enter a "fair" game of chance, that is one in which the expected prize equals the price of participation.[27]

This conclusion can be clarified by using a simple graphical device. Figure 4.3 sets out the same investment problem: the purchase for $10 of an investment option whose end-of-period value has an equal probability of being $9 or $11. The possible end-of-period values are set out along the horizontal axis and utility is measured along the vertical axis. The individual's utility function $U(x)$ is drawn in Figure 4.3 as a *concave* curve rising from the origin; this is tantamount to assuming that he is risk-averse.

---

[25] We ignore the discount factor, which is tantamount to assuming a very short investment period.
[26] A utility function is concave when for every two possible values $x_1$ and $x_2$ and for all $0 < \alpha < 1$ we have

$$U[\alpha x_1 + (1 - \alpha)x_2] \geqslant \alpha U(x_1) + (1 - \alpha)U(x_2)$$

Graphically this means that a chord connecting points $x_1$ and $x_2$ will lie *below* the utility curve. An alternative definition of risk aversion is $U'(x) > 0$ and $U''(x) \leqslant 0$, where $U''(x) < 0$ at least for some range of $x$ (to avoid the case of a linear utility function throughout the range). In the rest of the book we use $U''(x) \leqslant 0$ (without stipulating $U''(x) < 0$ in some range) or $U''(x) < 0$ interchangeably. With either notation, risk aversion as defined here is implied.
[27] Our zero net return investment option serves as a good proxy for such a gamble.

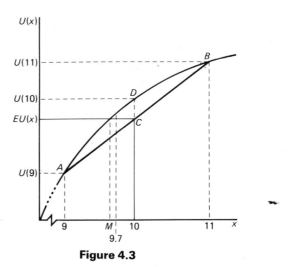

**Figure 4.3**

The expected utility of the assumed investment option is

$$EU(x) = \tfrac{1}{2}U(9) + \tfrac{1}{2}U(11)$$

The expected utility is represented graphically by point $C$ of Figure 4.3, the point at which a perpendicular rising from the mean value point 10 on the horizontal axis intersects the chord connecting the utilities of the outcomes $A$ and $B$.[28] A glance at Figure 4.3 shows that the utility of the certain purchase price, $U(10)$, which corresponds to point $D$ on the utility curve, is greater than the expected utility $EU(x)$ of the investment option, which corresponds to point $C$. Thus a risk-averse individual will not purchase an uncertain option whose expected value is equal to its purchase price, since the concavity of his utility function translates the *zero* monetary gain into a utility *loss*.

Now let us assume that the same individual is offered the same investment option, but at a lower price, say $9.70. The expected end-of-period value remains $10 so that the option has a positive expected return ($10 − 9.70). Will the individual purchase the option? Despite the lower price, Figure 4.3 clearly shows that he will *not* be willing to purchase the option since the utility of a perfectly certain sum of $9.70 exceeds the expected utility of the option (point $C$). How far must the price of the option fall before our risk-averse investor will be willing to acquire it? Again the answer can be readily inferred from Figure 4.3. The maximum price that he will be willing to pay is represented by point $M$ on the horizontal axis.[29] At this price $U(M) = EU(x)$; the difference between 10 and $M$ measures the "risk premium" required to induce the risk-averse individual to enter a fair gamble. At prices lower than $M$ (points to the left of $M$

---

[28] For a general proof that point $C$ represents the expected utility of such an option, see Appendix 4.2 at the end of this chapter.

[29] Strictly speaking, the prizes in all of the examples given in the text should be added to the individual's initial wealth; similarly, the price of the option should be deducted from his initial wealth.

on the horizontal axis) the investment option is attractive since it represents a gain in utility; conversely, at prices above $M$, as we have already seen, the option represents a loss of utility for the risk-averse investor.

Now let us turn our attention to a different class of possible investors—those optimistic fellows who have a preference, rather than an aversion, for risk. More formally, we shall define a risk lover as follows:

DEFINITION

An individual whose utility function is convex[30] will be called a risk lover. The marginal utility increases with an increase in the risk lover's wealth.

Unlike the previous case of risk aversion, a risk lover is by nature a gambler and will always prefer to enter a fair game of chance. It follows that such an individual will be willing to pay $10 (or perhaps even more) for the above mentioned option since it is equivalent to a fair gamble.

This result is illustrated in Figure 4.4, which sets out the relevant data for the same investment option along with a (convex) utility curve for a risk lover. As before, point $C$ on the chord connecting the utilities of the outcomes $A$ and $B$ represents the expected utility $EU(x)$ of the risky investment option. In this case, however, $EU(x)$ is clearly greater than $U(10)$, which is represented by point $D$, and the risk lover will willingly purchase such an option for a price of $10. He will also gladly pay a lower price, but what is the *maximum* price that he will be willing to pay to acquire such an option? This

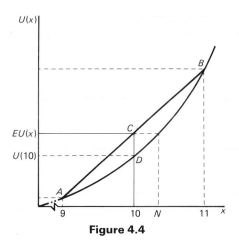

**Figure 4.4**

[30] A utility function is convex when for every pair of possible values $x_1$ and $x_2$, and for all $0 < \alpha < 1$, we have

$$U[\alpha x_1 + (1 - \alpha)x_2] \leqslant \alpha U(x_1) + (1 - \alpha)U(x_2)$$

An alternative definition of a risk lover's utility function is $U'(x) > 0$ and $U''(x) \geqslant 0$, with $U''(x) > 0$ in some range of $x$.

price is represented by point $N$ of Figure 4.4 since the utility of $N$ dollars is equal to the expected utility of the investment option. Since $N > 10$, it also follows that a risk lover will not only accept a fair gamble, but will also accept (within limits) an "unfair" gamble; that is, he will be willing to pay more than the expected value for a chance of winning.

We shall now illustrate these same relationships by a numerical example. Table 4.6 sets out the end-of-period values and probabilities for another hypothetical investment option whose price is again $10. Clearly this option is equivalent to a fair game of chance since its expected value equals its price:

$$E(x) = 7 \cdot 0.1 + 8 \cdot 0.2 + 9 \cdot 0.1 + 11 \cdot 0.5 + 13 \cdot 0.1$$

$$= \quad 0.7 \quad + \quad 1.6 \quad + \quad 0.9 \quad + \quad 5.5 \quad + \quad 1.3 \quad = 10$$

Table 4.6 also presents hypothetical utility schedules for two individuals, one of whom is assumed to be risk-averse while the second is assumed to have a preference for risk. As can be seen from the data of Table 4.6, higher end-of-period values are accompanied by increases in total utility in both cases; that is, the utility functions' first derivatives are positive for both the risk averter and the risk lover. Note, however, that the "marginal" utility (the change in utility per unit increase in end-of-period values) *decreases* for the risk averter and *increases* for the risk lover. Thus an increase in value from 7 to 8 increases the risk averter's utility by one unit $(6 - 5 = 1)$, an increase from 8 to 9 raises the utility by only 0.9 units, and so on. Conversely, an increase in value from 7 to 8 raises the risk lover's utility by 1.1 units $(6.1 - 5.0 = 1.1)$, an increase from 8 to 9 raises utility by 1.2 units, and so on.

Now let us compute the expected utility of the option for the risk lover by multiplying the alternative end-of-period utilities by their respective probabilities[31] and summing

**Table 4.6**
**Hypothetical Utility Schedules for a "Risk Lover" and a "Risk Averter"**

| Probability $p(x)$ | End-of-period Value $(x)$ | Utility Schedule of Risk Lover $U(x)$ | Utility Schedule of Risk Averter $U(x)$ |
|---|---|---|---|
| 0.1 | 7 | 5 | 5 |
| 0.2 | 8 | 6.1 | 6 |
| 0.1 | 9 | 7.3 | 6.9 |
| 0.0 | 10 | 8.6 | 7.7 |
| 0.5 | 11 | 10.0 | 8.3 |
| 0.0 | 12 | 13.0 | 8.8 |
| 0.1 | 13 | 18.0 | 9.0 |

[31] Note that the end-of-period values 10 and 12 both have zero probabilities.

the products:

| $x_i$ | 7 | 8 | 9 | 11 | 13 |
|-------|------|------|------|------|------|
| $U(x_i)$ | 5.0 | 6.1 | 7.3 | 10.0 | 18.0 |
| $p(x_i)$ | 0.1 | 0.2 | 0.1 | 0.5 | 0.1 |
| $U(x_i)p(x_i)$ | 0.50 | 1.22 | 0.73 | 5.00 | 1.80 |

$$EU(x) = \Sigma\ U(x_i)p(x_i) = 9.25$$

Since the expected utility of the option is greater than the utility of its price

$$EU(x) = 9.25 > U(10) = 8.6$$

the risk lover will purchase such an option.

With respect to the risk averter, the calculation of expected utility is as follows:

| $x_i$ | 7 | 8 | 9 | 11 | 13 |
|-------|------|------|------|------|------|
| $U(x_i)$ | 5.0 | 6.0 | 6.9 | 8.3 | 9.0 |
| $p(x_i)$ | 0.1 | 0.2 | 0.1 | 0.5 | 0.1 |
| $U(x_i)p(x_i)$ | 0.50 | 1.20 | 0.69 | 4.15 | 0.90 |

$$EU(x) = \Sigma U(x_i)p(x_i) = 7.44$$

In this case the utility of the price *exceeds* the expected utility of the investment option:

$$EU(x) = 7.44 < U(10) = 7.7$$

Therefore, the risk averter will not consider the option attractive.

## 4.6 The Special Case of a Linear Utility Function

We have used the two hundred year old St. Petersburg Paradox and the modern theory of expected utility developed by von Neumann and Morgenstern to show that rational individuals select investments which maximize their expected utility rather than the expected monetary return. Despite this it appears that some individuals and investment companies follow a policy of maximizing expected income. The question arises whether such behavior is inherently "irrational"; more specifically, does such behavior *necessarily* constitute a contradiction of the von Neumann–Morgenstern dictum that a rational individual will reach his investment decision in accordance with the principle of maximum expected utility? With a little effort we can demonstrate that the maximization of expected return does not necessarily contradict the expected utility principle, and that such behavior can be explained as a *special* case of the utility hypothesis, one in which the decision maker's utility function is assumed to be linear. This property is stated as follows:

> When an individual's utility function is linear, that is, of the form $U(x) = a + bx$ ($b > 0$), he will choose the investment that maximizes his expected return.

In order to prove this theorem, let us consider an individual confronted by the following alternatives:

| Alternative A | | Alternative B | |
|:---:|:---:|:---:|:---:|
| Return (x) | Probability p(x) | Return (y) | Probability q(y) |
| $x_1$ | $p_1$ | $y_1$ | $q_1$ |
| ⋮ | ⋮ | ⋮ | ⋮ |
| $x_m$ | $p_m$ | $y_n$ | $q_n$ |

where $A$ and $B$ represent two alternative options; $(x_1, \cdots, x_m)$ and $(p_1, \cdots, p_m)$ respectively denote the possible returns and probabilities of alternative $A$ and $(y_1, \cdots, y_n)$ and $(q_1, \cdots, q_n)$ denote the returns and probabilities of alternative $B$. We also know that the following relationship must hold:

$$\sum_{i=1}^{m} p_i = \sum_{i=1}^{n} q_i = 1$$

Let the individual's utility function be linear, that is, of the form $U(x) = a + bx$ (subject to the constraint that $b > 0$). We shall now show that such an individual's decision will be the same whether he chooses the option which maximizes his expected utility or the alternative which maximizes his expected monetary return. To do this we must prove that if

$$EU(x) > EU(y)$$

then it also necessarily follows that

$$E(x) > E(y)$$

The expected utility of option $A$ is defined as follows:

$$EU(x) = \sum_{i=1}^{m} p_i U(x_i)$$

Substituting the assumed *linear* utility function, this formula can be rewritten as

$$EU(x) = \sum_{i=1}^{m} p_i[a + bx_i]$$

$$= a \sum_{i=1}^{m} p_i + b \sum_{i=1}^{m} p_i x_i$$

However, since $\sum_{i=1}^{m} p_i = 1$ and $\sum p_i x_i = E(x)$ by definition, the following equation results:

$$EU(x) = a + bE(x)$$

Similarly we obtain for alternative $B$:

$$EU(y) = a + bE(y)$$

It is clear from these two equations that if the expected return of $A$ exceeds that of $B$ this implies that the expected utility of $A$ also exceeds that of $B$, and vice versa, which is what we set out to prove.

This equivalence between the principle of maximum expected return and the assumption of a linear utility function can also be seen in Figure 4.5, which sets out a linear utility function for a hypothetical investor. Once again assume that the investor is offered the opportunity to purchase for \$10 an option whose end-of-period value is expected to be \$11 with a probability of 1/2, or \$9 with a probability of 1/2; that is, there is an equal probability of gaining a net return of \$1 or suffering a net loss of \$1.

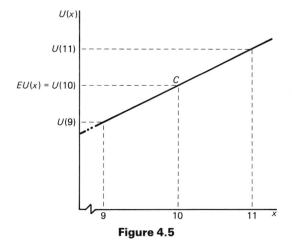

**Figure 4.5**

The expected utility of the option is

$$EU(x) = \tfrac{1}{2}U(9) + \tfrac{1}{2}U(11)$$

and as we have already shown, this value is given by point $C$ of Figure 4.5. In this case

$$EU(x) = U(10)$$

and, given a price of $10, the investor is indifferent with respect to the option. The investor can be induced to acquire the option only if we assume a price lower than $10; conversely, he definitely will not purchase the option if we assume a price higher than $10. Since as we have already seen the net expected monetary value of this option is exactly zero at a purchase price of $10 (that is, it represents a fair gamble), we can state alternatively that such an individual will purchase a risky option *if and only if* its net expected return is positive.

Thus a linear utility function is appropriate for neither a risk lover nor a risk averter, but represents, so to speak, a borderline case between the two. A risk lover (with a convex utility function) will always be willing to enter a risky venture which is equivalent to a fair gamble, that is, whose net expected value is zero; a risk averter, on the other hand, will never accept such a risk. The investor with a linear utility function is *indifferent* to risk. He does not take the dispersion of outcomes into account when reaching his decision. Thus, unlike the risk lover, he is unwilling to pay a premium to enter a fair game of chance; unlike the risk averter, he does not require a risk premium to induce him to enter such a game.

## 4.7    State-preference Theory

Typically the investment decision is characterized by the *certain* sacrifice of present resources for future *uncertain* benefits. In the rest of the book, we shall spell out a theory of investment choice under uncertainty in terms of returns and of the probability attached to these returns. In this section we shall present a brief review of an alternative approach which analyzes the investment decision under uncertainty in terms of the choice between consumption alternatives in different possible future "states of the world." Such a theory is usually referred to as the "time–state preference" or simply the "state-preference" approach to decision making problems.[32] Essentially this approach assumes that the evaluation of alternative investment options depends on the consumption opportunities in alternative possible states of the world. Thus a dollar's worth of

---

[32] State-preference theory has evolved from the pioneering work of K. J. Arrow, "The Role of Securities in the Optimal Allocation of Risk-bearing", *Review of Economic Studies* (Apr. 1964); G. Debreu, *Theory of Value*, New York; Wiley, 1959; and J. Hirshleifer, "Investment Decision Under Uncertainty: Choice-Theoretic Approaches", *Quarterly Journal of Economics* (Nov. 1965). A convenient review of much of the theory is given in A. A. Robichek, "Risk and the Value of Securities", *Journal of Financial and Quantitative Analysis* (Dec. 1969).

return in one state (for example, prosperity) may not be equivalent in terms of utility to an equal monetary return in a different state (depression).

Introducing the possibility that the utility of money differs in different states has some interesting implications for the analysis of investments in general and for the definition of risk in particular. To make the discussion manageable we shall consider a very restrictive case in which there exists only one present state (that is, the present is known with certainty); the future is represented by a single point in time (that is, we postulate a one-period model); and there are two *mutually exclusive* alternative states of the world, for example, war or peace, or economic depression and economic prosperity. Table 4.7 presents a very simplified numerical example of this approach.[33] The individual is assumed to hold probability beliefs regarding the alternative states of the world (column 2). Applying these probabilities to an option which yields $1, independent of which state occurs, yields the familiar result for a "riskless" security, namely, the expected return of such an option is also $1 (column 3). The state-preference approach is reflected in column 4, which sets out the value of $1 of return to the investor in each of the two possible states. Note that $1 of return is valued more in state 2 than in state 1, which might reflect the fact that the utility of real purchasing power in a depression, for example, is worth more to the individual than a corresponding unit of command over commodities during prosperity.[34] Applying this to our example of the "riskless" option gives a *subjective* value of 0.896 for the option which yields a return of $1 independent of the state of the world.

In the previous example we illustrated the valuation of a riskless option, that is, one that yields a given return with certainty. Table 4.8 sets out the relevant data for a "risky" option, the return on which is a random variable dependent on the state of nature that occurs. Again the expected value of this option is $1, but its subjective value to the investor is higher than in the previous case (0.913 as compared with 0.896),

#### Table 4.7
#### Value of a Riskless Option

| State | Return $x_i$ (1) | Probability of State $p_i$ (2) | $x_i \cdot p_i$ (3) | Value of One Dollar in Alternative States $u_i$ (4) | $x_i \cdot p_i \cdot u_i$ (5) |
|---|---|---|---|---|---|
| 1 (Prosperity) | 1.00 | 0.3 | 0.30 | 0.70 | 0.21 |
| 2 (Depression) | 1.00 | 0.7 | 0.70 | 0.98 | 0.686 |
|  |  |  | 1.00 |  | 0.896 |

[33] The numerical examples of Tables 4.7 and 4.8 and the textual discussion have been adapted from Robichek, *op. cit.*

[34] Alternatively it might reflect the correlation of the returns with the prices of the specific commodities which this particular investor desires to consume. See Y. Peles, "A Note on Risk and the Theory of Asset Value", *Journal of Financial and Quantitative Analysis* (Jan. 1971).

**Table 4.8**
**Value of a Risky Option**

| State | Return $x_i$ | Probability of State $p_i$ | $x_i \cdot p_i$ | Value of One Dollar in Alternative States $u_i$ | $x_i \cdot p_i \cdot u_i$ |
|---|---|---|---|---|---|
| 1 (Prosperity) | 0.80 | 0.3 | 0.24 | 0.70 | 0.168 |
| 2 (Depression) | 1.086 | 0.7 | 0.76 | 0.98 | 0.745 |
|  |  |  | 1.00 |  | 0.913 |

reflecting the fact that the second option offers the possibility of higher returns in state 2 when they are of most value to the investor.

Even this brief glimpse of the state-preference approach raises some very perplexing questions regarding the concept of risk, since the same option may be much more "risky" for one investor than for another when the utility of wealth in alternative states is taken into account (even if both have utility functions of the same general shape). In the extreme, this approach suggests that investment risk is unique to the individual; great care must be exercised when generalizing the analysis of risk options which was set out in the earlier sections of this chapter. Essentially, the previous approach is a special (degenerate) case of the state-preference approach—one in which a unique future state is postulated. Thus the utility of a given return at a given point of time may differ among investors depending on the shapes of their utility functions, but its utility for any *given* individual is assumed to be constant, independent of his consumption opportunities. The degree to which this admitted oversimplification of decision making behavior can provide a useful model for the analysis of investment decisions in security markets raises what is essentially an empirical question, which will be examined in the following chapter.

## Summary

The purpose of this chapter has been to set out the utility foundations of the theory of investment choice under conditions of risk or uncertainty. A risky (or uncertain) investment is defined as an option whose return is not known with absolute certainty, but for which an array of alternative returns and their (objective or subjective) probabilities are known. After a demonstration of the inappropriateness of the maximum return criterion for choices involving risk, the concept of expected value and its maximization was introduced. The shortcomings of the expected return criterion were then analyzed by considering the two hundred year old "St. Petersburg Paradox" and the solutions proposed by the eighteenth century mathematicians Daniel Bernoulli and Gabriel Cramer, both of whom attempted to resolve the paradox by substituting the principle of utility maximization for the principle of maximum money returns. Both the Bernoulli and Cramer solutions assume *concave* utility functions, that is, functions that incorporate the assumption of diminishing marginal utility of money.

Next, the modern theory of expected utility and its axiomatic basis, primarily associated with the work of von Neumann and Morgenstern, were introduced. The six axioms underlying the theory of expected utility were explained. A proof that their fulfillment implies the maximization of expected utility is given in Appendix 4.1. Some of the properties of the modern utility approach were then discussed. In particular it should be emphasized that a von Neumann–Morgenstern utility function is a tool of logical analysis far different from the concept of hedonistic utility of classical economics. In the modern theory of utility, an option has a high utility *because* individuals prefer that option, and *not* the other way around. Similarly, the numerical properties of the utility function are limited. Although von Neumann and Morgenstern postulate a cardinal utility function, that is, one in which absolute numbers are assigned to alternative levels of utility, the utility function is defined only up to a positive linear transformation.

We next defined several alternative risk attitudes and a simple geometric apparatus for portraying them. We distinguished between three basic types of investors:

(a)  risk averters—individuals with *concave* utility functions;
(b)  risk lovers—individuals with *convex* utility functions; and
(c)  risk-neutral individuals—individuals with linear utility functions.

The concept of utility frequently appears too theoretical, too complex, and perhaps too mathematical to help the average investor or the proverbial widow of financial lore. However, this concept is nothing more than a generalization of the principle of expected return or of expected profits. The major difference is that the use of utility permits us to place differential weights on different money outcomes. According to the expected return principle, a loss of $100 with a probability of 1/10 is equivalent to a possible loss of $1,000 with a probability of 1/100. By introducing the concept of utility, we allow for those cases in which because of the size of the loss involved an investor may impute a much larger penalty to the chance of losing $1,000. In the special case of a linear utility function, we revert to the principle of expected return.

The chapter concluded with a brief digression on state-preference theory, which introduces yet another dimension to risk analysis: the differential value of a given return to an investor in different alternative states of the world.

A final *caveat* may be in order. The modern theory of utility does *not* imply that investors assign utilities to alternative choices, but rather that they act *as if* such assignments have been made. The abstract theory is designed to explain and predict complex behavior patterns, and with the advent of the electronic computer, to simulate choice situations. Gathering reliable information regarding investors' tastes and forecasting an uncertain future are likely to remain the central problems of investment analysis for some time to come. With this in mind, we turn in the next chapter to the problem of determining investors' attitudes toward risk in actual securities markets.

# Summary Table

## 1. Certainty
*Definition:* The return $x$ is known with certainty, i.e., with probability $p(x) = 1$.
*Decision rule:*
    MRC (Maximum Return Criterion)—choose the option with the highest return $x$.

## 2. Uncertainty (or risk)
*Definition:* The return $x$ is a random variable with a probability distribution $p(x)$ (objective or subjective), where $0 \leqslant p(x) < 1$.
*Decision rules:*
    MRC   (Maximum Return Criterion)—not applicable, since each option is represented by a whole distribution of returns, and not by a single value.
    MERC  (Maximum Expected Return Criterion)—choose the option with the highest expected return $E(x)$. The rule is technically applicable, but may lead to paradoxical conclusions (e.g., the St. Petersburg Paradox).
    MEUC  (Maximum Expected Utility Criterion)—choose the option with the highest expected utility $EU(x)$. Under a certain set of axioms, MEUC is the optimal rule.

## 3. Relationship between the three rules
(a) *Under certainty:* MRC, MERC, and MEUC lead to the same decisions (as long as $U$ is nondecreasing):
*Equivalence of MRC and MERC:*
since $E(x) = \Sigma\, p(x)x = 1 \cdot x = x$,

$$x > y \text{ implies } E(x) > E(y) \text{ and vice versa}$$

*Equivalence of MRC and MEUC (for nondecreasing $U$):*
since $EU(x) = \Sigma\, p(x)U(x) = 1 \cdot U(x) = U(x)$

$$x > y \text{ and } U(x) > U(y) \text{ imply } EU(x) > EU(y) \text{ and vice versa}$$

(b) *Under uncertainty:* MERC leads to the same decisions as MEUC whenever the utility function is linear.

## 4. Alternative attitudes toward risk
*Risk averters:*    Nondecreasing downward-concave utility function, $U' \geqslant 0$, $U'' \leqslant 0$.
*Risk lovers:*     Nondecreasing downward-convex utility function, $U' \geqslant 0$, $U'' \geqslant 0$.
*Risk-neutrals:*   Nondecreasing linear utility function, $U' \geqslant 0$, $U'' = 0$.

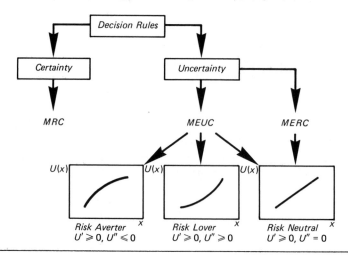

## APPENDIX 4.1

### Proof that the Expected Utility Principle Follows from the von Neumann–Morgenstern Axioms

The purpose of this appendix is to show that if an investor fulfills certain consistency requirements (given in Sec. 4.4.1), he will make his decisions according to the expected utility rule. To prove this statement, let us assume that the investor is faced with the following two lotteries:

$$L_1 = (p_1 A_1, p_2 A_2, \ldots, p_n A_n)$$

$$L_2 = (q_1 A_1, q_2 A_2, \ldots, q_n A_n)$$

(4.1.1)

where:

$A_i =$ a possible prize
$p_i =$ the probability of getting $A_i$ under lottery $L_1$
$q_i =$ the probability of getting $A_i$ under lottery $L_2$.

Obviously, $p_i \geqslant 0$, $q_i \geqslant 0$, and $\Sigma_{i=1}^n p_i = \Sigma_{i=1}^n q_i = 1$.
Without loss of generality, let us assume that[35]

$$A_1 \succ A_2 \succ A_3 \succ \cdots \succ A_n$$

where $\succ$ means preferable.
Using Axiom 6, we can find for each prize $A_i$ a lottery $A_i^*$ such that the investor will be indifferent between $A_i$ and $A_i^*$, that is,

$$A_i \sim [u_i A_1, (1 - u_i) A_n] \equiv A_i^*$$

where $\sim$ means "equivalent" and $u_i$ is some number. By Axiom 5, if

$$A_i \succ A_j$$

we expect that $u_i > u_j$, since we have to give higher weight to the best outcome $A_1$ under lottery $A_i^*$ than we expect under lottery $A_j^*$.[36]

---

[35] If this is not the case, we can always rearrange the prizes in such an order. See Axiom 1.
[36] We can assign the following values expressing $A_i^*$ in probabilistic terms:

$$u(A_1) = u_1 = 1$$
$$u(A_i) = u_i \qquad \text{where } 0 < u_i < 1 \text{ for } i = 2, \ldots, n - 1$$
$$u(A_n) = u_n = 0$$

There is no loss of generality since the utility function is determined up to a positive linear transformation (see Sec. 4.4.2). We can multiply each $u_i$ by a positive number and add a constant number to each $u_i$ without changing the preference order.

By Axiom 4 we can substitute $A_i^*$ for some $A_i$ in $L_1$ and in $L_2$. Since the preference and indifference relations are transitive (Axiom 2), we can continue this process serially till we get

$$L_1 = (p_1 A_1^*, p_2 A_2^*, \ldots, p_n A_n^*)$$

$$L_2 = (q_1 A_1^*, q_2 A_2^*, \ldots, q_n A_n^*)$$

(4.1.2)

Hence we move from a set of lotteries given by (4.1.1) to a set of composite lotteries given by (4.1.2). Using Axiom 3, we can simplify (4.1.2) and express these lotteries by the following simple form:

$$L_1 = [\bar{p}A_1, (1 - \bar{p})A_n]$$

$$L_2 = [\bar{q}A_1, (1 - \bar{q})A_n]$$

(4.1.3)

where:[37]

$$\bar{p} = p_1 u_1 + p_2 u_1 + \cdots + p_n u_n \quad \text{(Expected value of } u \text{ under } L_1)$$

$$\bar{q} = q_1 u_1 + q_2 u_2 + \cdots + q_n u_n \quad \text{(Expected value of } u \text{ under } L_2)$$

(4.1.4)

As $A_1 \succ A_n$, by Axiom 5 (monotonicity)

$$L_1 \succ L_2 \quad \text{if and only if } \bar{p} > \bar{q}$$

In conclusion, if Axioms 1 through 6 hold, then there are numbers (which we call utilities) $u_i$, associated with the prizes $A_i$, such that the lottery with the higher *expected value* of this number is preferred. That is to say, if $L_1 \succ L_2$, then we can assign a (numerical) utility function $u$ to this lottery such that

$$Eu(L_1) > Eu(L_2)$$

[37] Lottery $L_1$ can be written as follows:

$$L_1 = \{p_1[u_1 A_1, (1 - u_1)A_n], \ldots, p_n[(u_n A_1, (1 - u_n)A_n]\}$$

Hence

$$L_1 = \left[ \left( \sum_{i=1}^{n} p_i u_i \right) A_1, \left( 1 - \sum_{i=1}^{n} p_i u_i \right) A_n \right] = [\bar{p}A_1, (1 - \bar{p})A_n]$$

Similarly, by writing $q$ for $p$, $L_2$ is obtained.

## APPENDIX 4.2
### Graphical Representation of Expected Utility

Consider a distribution $x$ with two uncertain outcomes, $x_1$ with probability $(1-p)$ and $x_2$ with probability $p$. We will prove that the expected utility of this distribution is represented by the point $C$ (see Figure 4.6) where the perpendicular erected on the horizontal axis at the mean $E(x)$ of the distribution $[E(x) = (1-p)x_1 + px_2]$ meets the chord connecting the utilities of the two uncertain outcomes $U(x_1)$ and $U(x_2)$ (points $A$ and $B$ on the utility curve).

We thus have to prove that the height $h$ of the point $C$ from the horizontal axis is equal to the expected utility, i.e.,

$$h = EU(x) = (1-p)U(x_1) + pU(x_2) \tag{4.2.1}$$

To prove this, consider the two similar triangles $ACD$ and $ABE$ in Figure 4.6. The ratios of the corresponding sides in similar triangles are equal, and we may thus write for two pairs of corresponding sides:

$$\frac{AD}{AE} = \frac{CD}{BE} \tag{4.2.2}$$

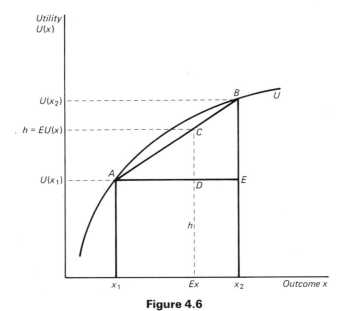

**Figure 4.6**

But clearly:

$$BE = U(x_2) - U(x_1)$$

$$CD = h - U(x_1)$$

$$AD = E(x) - x_1 = (1 - p)x_1 + px_2 - x_1 = p(x_2 - x_1)$$

$$AE = x_2 - x_1$$

Substituting these values in the two ratios in (4.2.2), we obtain:

$$\frac{p(x_2 - x_1)}{x_2 - x_1} = \frac{h - U(x_1)}{U(x_2) - U(x_1)} \qquad (4.2.3)$$

Reducing by $(x_2 - x_1)$ in the left-hand side of (4.2.3) and solving for $h$, we obtain:

$$h = p[U(x_2) - U(x_1)] + U(x_1)$$

or rearranging:

$$h = (1 - p)U(x_1) + pU(x_2) = EU(x)$$

We have thus proved (4.2.1), namely that $h$ is equal to the expected utility of the distribution $x$. Therefore, the point $C$, located at the height $h$ from the horizontal axis, indeed represents the expected utility of the two-outcome distribution, as claimed.

## Questions and Problems

4.1   Define the maximum expected return criterion. What is the major shortcoming of this criterion for decision making under conditions of risk?

4.2   Compare the Bernoulli and Cramer solutions to the St. Petersburg Paradox.

4.3   Resolve the St. Petersburg Paradox using a utility function other than the ones proposed by Bernoulli and Cramer. What property should the utility function have in order to resolve the Paradox?

4.4   In what sense do the von Neumann–Morgenstern Axioms "logically *precede*" the assignment of utilities?

4.5   Explain what is meant by a utility function which is defined up to a linear transformation. What is the significance of such a function for decision making? Analyze the impact of such a transformation on the origin and the scale of the utility function.

4.6    Define the following terms:
       (a) *risk averter*
       (b) *risk lover*
       (c) *risk neutrality*

4.7    "A risk averter will never enter a fair game of chance." Prove this statement graphically.
       In your answer indicate the "risk premium" necessary to induce him to agree to play.

4.8    "A risk-neutral investor, that is, one who has a linear utility function, makes his invest-
       ment decisions in accordance with the principle of maximum expected return, *rather than
       that of maximum expected utility*." Is this statement correct? Demonstrate your answer
       with a numerical example.

4.9    Assume that an individual is confronted with the problem of choosing *one* of the following
       investment options:

| Option A | | Option B | | Option C | | Option D | |
|---|---|---|---|---|---|---|---|
| Probability | Return | Probability | Return | Probability | Return | Probability | Return |
| 1/2 | −10 | 1/8 | −10 | 1/2 | 0 | 1/4 | −10 |
| 1/4 | 20 | 1/2 | 20 | 3/8 | 10 | 1/8 | 0 |
| 1/4 | 30 | 3/8 | 40 | 1/8 | 20 | 5/8 | 40 |

The return is in $ per $100 invested.
(a) Which option will be chosen according to the principle of maximum expected return?
(b) Which option will be chosen according to the maximum expected utility principle,
    using the following two alternative utility functions, $U_1(x)$ and $U_2(x)$:

| Return (x) | $U_1(x)$ | $U_2(x)$ |
|---|---|---|
| −10 | −100 | −100 |
| 0 | 0 | 0 |
| 10 | 86 | 120 |
| 20 | 150 | 260 |
| 30 | 200 | 440 |
| 40 | 232 | 660 |

(c) How does your answer to part (b) change if you assume that the individual has the
    following utility function:

$$U_3(x) = a + \frac{U_2(x)}{b} \quad \text{(where } b > 0)$$

Solve the problem numerically for the special case where $a = -10$ and $b = +10$, and
explain your results.
(d) Graph the above mentioned alternative utility functions, $U_1, U_2, U_3$, over the domain
    $(40 > x > -10)$ and indicate which of the functions represents a "risk averter" and
    which represents a "risk lover."
(e) Why is it impossible for $U_2$ and $U_3$ to represent *different* risk attitudes?
(f) Calculate the marginal utilities of money implied by $U_1$ and $U_2$. Show your calcula-
    tions. Are these results consistent with your answer to part (d)?

4.10 Assume the following two investment options:

| Option A | | Option B | |
|---|---|---|---|
| Probability | Return | Probability | Return |
| 1/2 | 2 | 1/2 | 8 |
| 1/2 | 10 | 1/2 | 20 |

(a) Show numerically and graphically which of the two options will be chosen by an investor whose utility function is given by:

$$U(x) = 1{,}000 + (x - 10)^3$$

(b) What is the maximum price that such an individual will be willing to pay for each option?

4.11 Consider three options:

| Option A | | Option B | | Option C | |
|---|---|---|---|---|---|
| Probability | Return | Probability | Return | Probability | Return |
| 1/2 | 1 | 1/4 | 1 | 1/4 | 1 |
| 1/2 | 4 | 1/2 | 3 | 1/2 | 2 |
| | | 1/4 | 4 | 1/4 | 4 |

An individual is considering the choice between $A$ and $B$ or between $A$ and $C$ only. In each of the two choices, assuming initial wealth $W_0 = \$100$ for all:

(a) Which option will be chosen by an individual making his choice by the principle of maximum expected return?
(b) Which option will be chosen by a risk-neutral individual with utility function $U(W) = W$?
(c) Which option will be chosen by a risk lover with $U(W) = W^2$?
(d) Which option will be chosen by a risk averter with $U(W) = \sqrt{W}$?
(e) What should be the middle outcome in Option $C$ (instead of 2) so that each individual will be indifferent between $A$ and $C$? Solve separately for each of the four individuals above.

4.12 This is a generalization of the previous problem. An individual is offered a chance to choose between two alternative options:

| Option A* | | Option B† | |
|---|---|---|---|
| Probability | Return | Probability | Return |
| $p$ | $X_0$ | $p - q$ | $X_0$ |
| $1 - p$ | $X_0 + \delta$ | $2q$ | $X_0 + \gamma$ |
| | | $1 - p - q$ | $X_0 + \delta$ |

\* $0 < p < 1$, $\delta > 0$
† $0 < q < 1$, $q < p$, $q < 1 - p$, $0 < \gamma < \delta$

(a) Discuss the constraints on $p$, $q$, $\gamma$, and $\delta$. How do these general parameters relate to the numerical values in the previous problem?

(b) Express in general terms the expected return on the two options. What is the relation between $\gamma$ and $\delta$ when the two options have equal expected returns?

(c) Express in general terms the difference between the expected utility of options $A$ and $B$. How can you determine from the expression for the difference in expected utilities which of the two options is preferred?

(d) Draw schematic utility functions of three individuals: risk neutral, risk lover and risk averter. On each of the three functions mark the outcomes of options $A$ and $B$ and by varying the middle-outcome parameter $\gamma$ (relative to $\delta$) determine when each of the individuals prefers option $A$ to $B$ and when option $B$ to $A$ (use the expression for the difference in expected utilities you obtained in part (c) above).

4.13   A risk averter with the utility function $U(W) = \sqrt{W}$ and initial wealth $W_0 = \$100$ has found a lottery ticket with the following prize distribution:

| Probability | Prize |
|:---:|:---:|
| $\alpha$ | $\$ 0$ |
| $1 - \alpha$ | $\$96$ |

(a) Find $\alpha$ if we know that he is willing to sell the lottery ticket for no less than $\$10.25$.

(b) Does $\alpha$ change when the initial wealth changes say to $W_0 = \$10,000$?

4.14   An individual with the utility function $U(X) = X - \frac{1}{8}X^2$ is allowed to choose between a certain income $X_A = \$2,000$ and an uncertain stream with five different outcomes with equal probabilities:

| Probability | 0.2 | 0.2 | 0.2 | 0.2 | 0.2 |
|:---:|:---:|:---:|:---:|:---:|:---:|
| Outcome (in '000 $) | 0 | 1 | 2 | 3 | 4 |

The utility function is defined for outcomes not exceeding $X_B = 4$.

(a) Which of the two options will the individual prefer?

(b) What is the minimal certain income that he will accept for "selling" the uncertain option?

In your answer discuss the constraint on the utility function. What happens if we also have an outcome $X_B = 5$?

4.15   An individual with the utility function $U(W) = W^2$ is known to be indifferent between the following two uncertain options:

| Option A | | Option B | |
|:---:|:---:|:---:|:---:|
| Probability | Terminal Wealth | Probability | Terminal Wealth |
| 1/2 | $\$ 96$ | $p$ | $\$ 90$ |
| 1/2 | $\$102$ | $1 - p$ | $\$105$ |

Calculate the unknown probability $p$ of option $B$.

4.16 A risk lover with the utility function $U(W) = (W/10)^2$ is indifferent between the following two options:

| Option A | | Option B | |
|---|---|---|---|
| Probability | Terminal Wealth | Probability | Terminal Wealth |
| 3/4 | 100 | 4/5 | 95 |
| 1/4 | 120 | 1/5 | x |

Find the unknown outcome $x$.

4.17 The following table lists the annual returns on stocks of Dow Chemical and DuPont. Assume that each year's return occurs with equal probability.
   (a) Which stock would an investor choose by the maximum expected return criterion?
   (b) An investor with utility function given by $U = \ln W$, where $W$ is the investor's terminal wealth, is willing to invest $100 in one of the stocks. Which stock would the investor choose by the maximum expected utility criterion? What is the maximum that the investor would be willing to pay for each stock?

| | Annual Return (%) | |
|---|---|---|
| Year | Dow Chemical | DuPont |
| 1972 | 31.19 | 26.33 |
| 1973 | 15.32 | −7.21 |
| 1974 | −2.32 | −39.32 |
| 1975 | 69.55 | 42.21 |
| 1976 | −3.39 | 11.02 |
| 1977 | −36.06 | −6.52 |
| 1978 | −2.14 | 11.33 |
| 1979 | 35.82 | 2.65 |
| 1980 | 5.13 | 11.17 |
| 1981 | −13.19 | −5.60 |

*Source:* CRSP monthly returns data tape.

## Data Set Problems

1. Using class intervals of 5% from −50% to +70%, draw a frequency distribution (i.e. a histogram like that in Figure 4.1) of the rates of return of the first three funds (combined) from the Maximum Capital Gain category. On a separate sheet, draw a histogram of the first three funds (combined) in the Senior Securities Policy category. Which category is characterized by higher uncertainty? Explain your results.

2. For the purpose of this problem assume that the entire population consists of the *first* fund in each category. Also assume that each annual observation gets the same probability (1/10).
   Investors with different utility functions consider investment in *one* of the funds from this population. Which fund will be selected by each of the following investors:
   (a) Linear utility function

(b) $U(R) = \log(100 + R)$, where $R$ is the rate of return as reported in percent in the Data Set and $100 + R$ is thus the investor's total terminal wealth on an initial investment of $100;

(c) $U(R) = -10 + 10 \log(100 + R)$

(d) $U(R) = (1 + R/100)^2$, where $1 + R/100$ is the investor's terminal wealth on an initial investment of $1.

Compare the ranking of the funds by investors with utility functions (b) and (c) above. Explain the result.

Compare the ranking of the funds by investors with utility functions (b) and (d) above. How do you account for the difference in ranking?

3. What is the certain income $R_0$ that you will be prepared to give up for $1 value of shares of Alpha Fund (No. 2) if

   (a) your utility function is of Bernoulli type,

$$U(R) = \log(1 + R/100),$$

   (b) your utility function is of Cramer type

$$U(R) = (1 + R/100)^{1/2}$$

Note that $R$ is the *rate* of return as reported in the data set, and $1 + R/100$ is the total return or terminal wealth on initial investment of $1. Assign probability of $1/10$ to each observation.

## Selected References

See Chapter 5.

# 5

# Alternative Shapes of the Utility Function

In the previous chapter we saw that investment decisions under conditions of uncertainty can be explained by invoking the principle of expected utility. While it is true that in some cases rational investors will apply the principle of expected return, this is a special case of the expected utility principle, in which the investor's utility function is linear. Although the expected utility hypothesis provides a powerful tool for rationalizing investors' behavior, it does not, by itself, provide a divining rod for choosing the "best" option out of a group of alternative investments. Investment choice remains a very difficult problem in the absence of more precise knowledge regarding the shape of the investor's utility function (that is, of his tastes). In this chapter we demonstrate how partial information on the investor's preferences can be useful in decision making and analyze the alternative sets of partial knowledge on preferences which are sound from an economic point of view.

## 5.1    Partial Information on Preferences and Decision Making

The need for additional information on the investor's preferences can be illustrated by means of the example in Table 5.1, which sets out the end-of-period values of three

**Table 5.1**

| Option A | | Option B | | Option C | |
|---|---|---|---|---|---|
| End-of-Period Value, $x_A$ | Probability | End-of-Period Value, $x_B$ | Probability | End-of-Period Value, $x_C$ | Probability |
| 95 | 1/2 | 85 | 1/2 | 70 | 1/2 |
| 105 | 1/2 | 100 | 1/4 | 130 | 1/2 |
| | | 140 | 1/4 | | |
| $E(x_A) = 100$ | | $E(x_B) = 102.5$ | | $E(x_C) = 100$ | |

alternative investments; for the sake of simplicity, we assume that all three have the same initial purchase price of $100. Let us suppose that an investor wishes to purchase one of these investment options, and we are given the task of recommending the "best" alternative. Let us further assume that the individual's utility function is known and is given by[1]

$$U(x) = 100 + 2\sqrt{x}$$

That is, we have complete information regarding his tastes. In this case all we have to do is to calculate the expected utility of each of the alternatives, which has been done in Table 5.2. Option B has the highest expected utility, therefore the investor should choose this alternative. Thus, given *full* information regarding an investor's utility function, one can readily determine the most preferable alternative.

Unfortunately, an investment consultant is rarely in possession of such detailed information regarding an investor's tastes. Moreover, even the investor himself is often unable to articulate the rules that guide his own behavior, and thus he cannot provide reliable information as to his preferences. In cases where investors' tastes are not known with any degree of accuracy—and these represent the vast majority of cases—the investment analysis becomes more difficult since it must be made on the basis of *partial* information only.

To illustrate how partial information can be used to reach an investment decision, let us assume a case in which our knowledge is limited to the fact that the investor is risk

### Table 5.2

| Option A | | | Option B | | | Option C | | |
|---|---|---|---|---|---|---|---|---|
| $x_A$ | $U(x_A)^*$ | $p(x_A)$ | $x_B$ | $U(x_B)^*$ | $p(x_B)$ | $x_C$ | $U(x_C)^*$ | $p(x_C)$ |
| 95 | 119.49 | 1/2 | 85 | 118.44 | 1/2 | 70 | 116.73 | 1/2 |
| 105 | 120.49 | 1/2 | 100 | 120.00 | 1/4 | | | |
| | | | 140 | 123.66 | 1/4 | 130 | 122.80 | 1/2 |
| | $EU(x_A) = 120.0^*$ | | | $EU(x_B) = 120.1^*$ | | | $EU(x_C) = 119.8^*$ | |

* Utility and expected utility are calculated using the following function: $U(x) = 100 + 2\sqrt{x}$.

[1] This utility function is appropriate for a risk averter, since

$$U'(x) = x^{-\frac{1}{2}} \geqslant 0 \qquad \text{(for all } x \geqslant 0\text{),}$$

and

$$U''(x) = -\tfrac{1}{2}x^{-\frac{3}{2}} \leqslant 0 \qquad \text{(for all } x \geqslant 0\text{).}$$

The restriction of the analysis to $x \geqslant 0$ reflects the fundamental fact that the value of the option (for example, the price of a security) or, in general, the investor's terminal wealth cannot fall below zero.

averse. Thus all we know about the shape of his utility function is that the first derivative is non-negative, $U'(x) \geqslant 0$, and that the second derivative is negative, $U''(x) < 0$. The second condition indicates that the investor is a risk averter, because the marginal utility of money declines, that is, the value to him of each additional dollar decreases, as his wealth increases. Such information is clearly partial since it does *not* permit us to find the exact shape of the individual's utility function. The function might, for example, be $U(x) = \sqrt{x}$, or $U(x) = \log x$, or any other function that meets the above mentioned requirements regarding the first two derivatives. In effect, *any* concave utility function will do.

Is the partial information that the utility function is concave sufficient to determine which of the three options given in Table 5.1 should be preferred? One thing is certain: option $A$ is clearly preferable to option $C$ since both have the same expected return while option $C$ has a larger dispersion of outcomes. A risk averter, other things being equal, dislikes dispersion, and he will prefer the option with the more stable income flow. Graphically this is illustrated in Figure 5.1, which shows clearly that if $U(x)$ is a concave function then

$$EU(x_A) > EU(x_C)$$

and the investor will always prefer option $A$ to option $C$. Thus his choice can be restricted to alternatives $A$ and $B$. But which of these two alternatives is preferable for our risk-averse investor? The partial information we have on the shape of the utility functions is not sufficient to answer this question. True, option $B$ has a greater dispersion of outcomes, but its expected return is also higher than that of $A$. In this instance it is impossible to tell which of the two options is preferable, since some risk-averse investors might prefer option $A$, while other risk averters might conceivably prefer option $B$. For example, if an investor has a concave utility function of the form

$$U(x) = 100 + 2\sqrt{x}$$

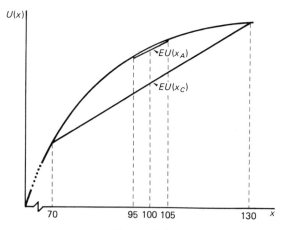

**Figure 5.1**

he would prefer option $B$ to option $A$, since the former has the higher expected utility (see Table 5.2). If, however, his utility function is concave, but of the form[2]

$$U(x) = 100 + 300x - x^2 \quad \text{(for } x \leqslant 150)$$

then option $A$ has the higher expected utility,[3] as may again be seen in Table 5.3.

The conclusion to be drawn from this simplified example is that if we have a complete specification of the investor's utility function we can choose a single option unequivocally; but if we have only partial information (for example, on the general shape of the utility function) we can only reduce the opportunity set by eliminating those options which are inferior for the entire class of functions.[4] Thus partial information on an individual's utility function permits us to reduce the number of feasible options but typically does not permit an unequivocal recommendation of a particular alternative.

Of course, the above example has been oversimplified. We dealt with only three alternatives in order to illustrate how partial information on individuals' tastes can be used to facilitate investment analysis. Our numerical example shows that with partial information on an investor's tastes we can divide all potential investments into two groups: one composed of those options which do not interest him, the second composed of all the options that he is likely to find profitable. We know that the rational investor will make his final choice from the second group, but we cannot specify what his exact

**Table 5.3**

| Option A | | | Option B | | | Option C | | |
|---|---|---|---|---|---|---|---|---|
| $x_A$ | $U(x_A)^*$ | $p(x_A)$ | $x_B$ | $U(x_B)^*$ | $p(x_B)$ | $x_C$ | $U(x_C)^*$ | $p(x_C)$ |
| 95 | 19.58 | 1/2 | 85 | 18.38 | 1/2 | 70 | 16.20 | 1/2 |
| 105 | 20.58 | 1/2 | 100 | 20.10 | 1/4 | 130 | 22.20 | 1/2 |
| | | | 140 | 22.50 | 1/4 | | | |
| $EU(x_A) = 20.1^*$ | | | $EU(x_B) = 19.8^*$ | | | $EU(x_C) = 19.2^*$ | | |

* Utility and expected utility are calculated using the following function: $U(x) = 100 + 300x - x^2$ (for $x \leqslant 150$). The numerical results are presented in thousands.

[2] The utility function $U(x) = 100 + 300x - x^2$ meets the requirements that $U'(x) \geqslant 0$ and that $U''(x) < 0$:

$$U'(x) = 300 - 2x \geqslant 0 \quad \text{(only for } x \leqslant 150)$$

$$U''(x) = -2 < 0$$

[3] Note that as we have already indicated, option $C$ is not preferred in either case.
[4] Rules for reducing the opportunity set are set out in Chapter 6.

choice will be. The ability to use partial information is not without economic significance. It should be emphasized that "search costs" can be minimized by an early
elimination of undesirable options, thereby enabling a proportionately larger
expenditure on the analysis of the remaining smaller subset.

As we have seen, the initial division into two groups depends on partial information
regarding the general shape of investors' utility functions. This immediately raises the
question of the assumptions that can reasonably be made regarding the tastes of the
investing public. Clearly, stronger assumptions regarding the shape of the utility function will enhance the selection process, that is, will reduce the size of the relevant
subset.[5]

In a somewhat different context this question has received considerable attention
from economic theorists who have attempted to rationalize individual behavior under
conditions of uncertainty. We now turn our attention to different approaches to the
problem of inferring the shape of investors' utility functions under conditions of
uncertainty. In the next chapters we use this partial information to construct
investment-decision rules.


## 5.2    The Friedman–Savage Hypothesis


Perhaps the best known attempt to use utility analysis to explain individuals' choices
under uncertainty was made by Friedman and Savage in their classic 1948 article.[6]
Friedman and Savage were troubled by an apparent inconsistency in people's behavior:
many people purchase insurance and also gamble, which would seem to imply a willingness to pay premiums for the opportunity to avoid risk, in the first instance, and to
undertake risk, in the second case. To remove the contradiction Friedman and Savage
attempted to infer the shape of the utility function implied by the following simplified
empirical evidence:[7]

1. Individuals always prefer higher to lower riskless income streams.
2. Many people in low income groups are willing to buy insurance.
3. Many people in low income groups are willing to buy lottery tickets.
4. Many people in low income groups purchase both insurance policies and
   lottery tickets.
5. Lotteries or raffles typically offer more than one prize.

What are the utility implications of the willingness to buy insurance? Consider an
individual who is weighing the purchase of an insurance policy against fire loss. Assume
that there exists a probability $\alpha$ that a fire will break out; if the individual fails to insure

[5] See Chapter 6.
[6] See Milton Friedman and Leonard J. Savage, "The Utility Analysis of Choices Involving Risk",
*The Journal of Political Economy* LVI, No. 4, Aug. 1948.
[7] The following paraphrases Friedman and Savage, *op. cit.*

the property he will be left with a salvage value equal to $I_1$ in Figure 5.2. However, there is also a probability $(1 - \alpha)$ that no fire will break out, in which case the individual's property will be worth $I_2$ $(I_2 > I_1)$. If the individual does *not* purchase the insurance policy his expected wealth will be $\bar{I}$, where

$$\bar{I} = \alpha I_1 + (1 - \alpha) I_2$$

Let us further assume that this individual is a risk lover, that is, he has a convex utility function. Will he be willing to take out fire insurance? The answer can be inferred from Figure 5.2, which sets out the relevant graphical analysis. If he does not take out insurance, his expected utility is

$$EU(I) = \alpha U(I_1) + (1 - \alpha) U(I_2)$$

which is represented in Figure 5.2 by point $C$, the intersection of the perpendicular originating from point $\bar{I}$ on the horizontal axis with the chord $AB$.[8] Suppose now that the individual insures his property. The average value of the individual's property $\bar{I}$, known among the insurers as the *actuarial value*, is actually the maximum value that the insurance company can guarantee to the policy holder, regardless of whether a fire breaks out or not. In fact, since insurance companies must charge a commission to cover expenses and to earn a profit, the maximum *net* certain property value they can offer is actually lower than $\bar{I}$, say $I^*$. Since $I^* < \bar{I}$, clearly $U(I^*) < U(\bar{I})$ so that $EU(I) > EU(I^*)$; therefore an individual who is a risk lover will *not* purchase an insurance policy (see Figure 5.2).

Can the purchase of insurance be rationalized by assuming risk aversion, that is, by assuming that the individual has a *concave* utility function? Figure 5.3 sets out such

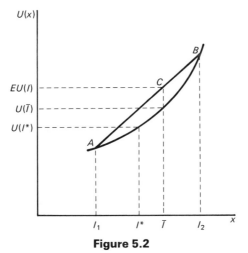

**Figure 5.2**

[8] For a formal proof that point $C$ represents $EU(I)$, see Appendix 4.2.

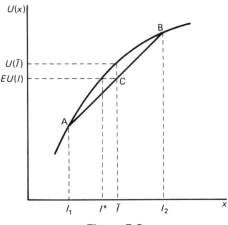

**Figure 5.3**

a function for our hypothetical property owner. As in the previous case, the expected property value without insurance is $\bar{I}$ where

$$\bar{I} = \alpha I_1 + (1 - \alpha)I_2$$

The expected utility without purchasing the policy is again given by

$$EU(I) = \alpha U(I_1) + (1 - \alpha)U(I_2)$$

that is, by point $C$ in Figure 5.3. From the diagram we can see that if $U(x)$ is concave, that is, if the individual is a risk averter, he will prefer a perfectly certain property value, even if it is somewhat lower than $\bar{I}$.

Without insurance the property owner faces either an outcome of $I_2$ (with a probability of $1 - \alpha$) or of $I_1$ (with a probability of $\alpha$). However since $U(\bar{I}) > EU(I)$, an individual with a concave utility function is vulnerable to risk, and therefore will prefer to "sell" this risk to the insurance company in return for a perfectly certain property value. Moreover, he will be willing to convert the risk option $[\alpha I_1, (1 - \alpha)I_2]$ into a perfectly certain value *lower* than $\bar{I}$; in other words, he will be prepared to pay a *premium* to reduce his risk. The maximum risk premium that he will be willing to pay is given by $\bar{I} - I^*$ because the utility of the certain amount $I^*$ is precisely equal to the expected utility of the risk option,

$$EU(I) \equiv \alpha U(I_1) + (1 - \alpha)U(I_2) = U(I^*)$$

If a higher premium is charged, thereby reducing the net property value below $I^*$, the individual will prefer the risk situation without insurance. Since members of low and medium income groups tend to purchase insurance, Friedman and Savage inferred that such individuals must have concave utility functions, that is,

$$U'(x) \geqslant 0; \quad U''(x) < 0$$

We must be careful not to confuse the notion of risk premium introduced here with the notion of the insurance premium that policy holders pay to the insurance companies. Referring back to the diagram in Figure 5.3, suppose that the individual agrees to convert his risky option to a certain guaranteed amount $I^*$. Then $\bar{I} - I^*$ is the *risk premium*, namely the amount that the individual is willing to lose "on average" by purchasing an insurance policy. The period insurance premium that the individual pays to the insurance company is greater, $I_2 - I^*$. If there is no fire and the policy holder does not claim against the policy, the insurers make a profit of $I_2 - I^*$. If there is a claim against the fire insurance policy, the insurance company loses $I^* - I_1$, the amount it pays to the policy holder $(I_2 - I_1)$ less the premium. Thus, the average profit of the insurance company is:

$$(1 - \alpha)(I_2 - I^*) - \alpha(I^* - I_1) = (1 - \alpha)I_2 + \alpha I_1 - I^* = \bar{I} - I^*$$

which is exactly the risk premium. To sum up, on average, the individual pays a risk premium of $\bar{I} - I^*$ to the insurance company, and this constitutes the average profit of the company.

Let us see if we can use the same line of reasoning to account for the observed empirical fact that people in the low and medium income groups buy lottery tickets even though the expected prize (income) is lower than the price of the ticket. A risk averter will not enter a "fair" gamble, let alone a lottery which represents an "unfair" gamble (see Chapter 4). From this evidence, Friedman and Savage concluded that the utility function must have a convex segment in addition to its concave segment. In other words, to reconcile gambling and insurance an individual's utility function must have *both* a convex and a concave segment, as is shown in Figure 5.4.

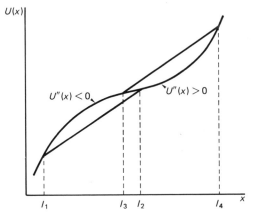

**Figure 5.4**

Individuals located in the convex section, where $U''(x) > 0$, might purchase a lottery ticket even if the expectation of the prize is lower than the price of the ticket. An individual whose wealth places him on the intermediate section of the utility function would be willing to take out insurance *and* buy a lottery ticket simultaneously. If such an individual is confronted by the choice between the outcomes $I_1$ and $I_2$ he might conceivably desire to insure his property; if, however, he must choose between losing the price of a lottery ticket (reducing his wealth to $I_3$) with a probability of $(1 - \beta)$, or winning a very large prize with a probability of $\beta$, thereby raising his wealth to $I_4$, the *same* individual will also be ready to purchase the lottery ticket. Since the modern theory of utility suggests that the behavior of individuals in choice situations dictates the form of the utility function, and not the other way around, Friedman and Savage concluded that the utility function must be wavelike, that is, it has both a concave and a convex segment.[9]

From the standpoint of investment analysis the Friedman and Savage results are rather negative, since apart from the trivial statement that $U'(x) \geqslant 0$, that is, that people prefer more to less wealth, no additional information can be gleaned regarding the shape of investors' utility functions. In particular we have no grounds for determining whether the investor is a risk averter or a risk lover; therefore we cannot specify whether investors' utility functions are concave or convex, because the Friedman–Savage analysis suggests that these functions will have both concave and convex segments.

## 5.3    The Subjective Utility Approach

In sharp contrast to Friedman and Savage, a number of economists have argued that concave utility functions comprise the only form of function appropriate for economic theory.[10] These writers contend that in addition to the requirement that the first derivative be positive or zero (that is, that utility does not decrease with wealth) the second derivative of the utility function *must* be negative. Essentially, as we have already seen, such a function is appropriate for risk averters and can be rationalized by assuming that the marginal utility of money (like that of any other good) declines as wealth increases. But how can this hypothesis be reconciled with the empirical fact that in the real world many individuals purchase lottery tickets, that is, enter "unfair" gambles? On the surface such behavior would seem to contradict the concave utility assumption since, as we have seen, a risk averter is not even prepared to accept a fair gamble.

---

[9] From the additional empirical observation that lotteries typically offer more than one prize Friedman and Savage also showed that the convex segment would be truncated and followed by a second concave segment.

[10] "If one draws the indifference curves which correspond to the Friedman and Savage hypothesis . . . one finds that in certain regions these indifference curves have 'wrong' curvatures. This fact is, of course, a cause for concern to the ordinalist just as it is to the cardinalist." M. Yaari, "Convexity in the Theory of Choice Under Risk," *Quarterly Journal of Economics* 75, No. 4, 1965, p. 281. See also J. Hirshleifer, "Investment Decision Under Uncertainty: Choice-Theoretic Approaches", *Quarterly Journal of Economics* 75, No. 4, 1965.

Friedman and Savage reconciled the coexistence of gambling and insurance by postulating that over some range the marginal utility of wealth increases, namely that individuals' utility functions contain both concave and convex segments. An alternative explanation of such behavior is obtained if one assumes a difference between the *objective* and *subjective* probabilities[11] which an individual attaches to the prizes. Yaari, for example, has hypothesized that subjective probabilities tend to be higher than objective probabilities when the latter are low, while they tend to be lower than high objective probabilities. Such an assumption is sufficient to resolve the apparent contradiction in the observed behavior of individuals *without* recourse to the concept of increasing marginal utility of wealth, that is, without postulating the existence of a convex segment of the utility function.

To clarify this point, consider the following example. An individual is offered a lottery ticket for $10. One hundred tickets are to be sold so that the gross return from this lottery is $1,000. Assume that a single prize of $800 is offered on the winning ticket (that is, the sponsors of the lottery intend to earn a profit of $200). Since the probability of winning is 1/100, the expected value of the prize is $1/100 \cdot \$800 = \$8$. Let us further assume that our individual has an initial wealth of $110. When weighing the purchase of the lottery ticket he is in essence choosing between a perfectly certain income of $110 if he does not buy a lottery ticket, and the following distribution: $100, with a probability of 99/100, if he buys a losing ticket, and $900, with a probability of 1/100, should he buy the winning ticket (see Table 5.4). We now assume that the individual has a concave utility function, for example, $U(x) = \sqrt{x}$.[12] The expected utility of the perfectly certain income of $110 (alternative $A$ in Table 5.4) is

$$EU(x) = p(110) \cdot U(110) = 1 \cdot \sqrt{110} = 10.49$$

since the probability of a certain outcome is always 1. His expected utility should he decide to buy the lottery ticket (alternative $B$ in Table 5.4) is

$$EU(x) = 99/100 \cdot \sqrt{100} + 1/100 \cdot \sqrt{900} = 99/10 + 3/10 = 102/10 = 10.20$$

---

[11] For example, the probability of a dice falling on any side is 1/6; this is the objective probability, since the die has six facets and is assumed to be balanced. When an individual bets on the fall of the dice, however, he can attribute subjective probabilities to the results of different throws, such as:

| Result of Throw | Objective Probability | Subjective Probability |
|-----------------|-----------------------|------------------------|
| 1 | 1/6 | 1/12 |
| 2 | 1/6 | 1/12 |
| 3 | 1/6 | 4/12 |
| 4 | 1/6 | 1/12 |
| 5 | 1/6 | 1/12 |
| 6 | 1/6 | 4/12 |

[12] Assuming positive wealth ($x > 0$), we see that $U'(x) = \frac{1}{2}x^{-1/2} > 0$ and $U''(x) = -\frac{1}{4}x^{-3/2} < 0$, as required.

**Table 5.4**

| Alternative A Not to buy lottery ticket | | Alternative B To buy lottery ticket | |
|---|---|---|---|
| Income | Probability | Income | Probability |
| 110 | 1 | 100 | 99/100 |
| | | 900 | 1/100 |
| EU(x) = 10.49* | | EU(x) = 10.20* | |

* Expected utility has been calculated using the following function: $U(x) = \sqrt{x}$.

Since the expected utility of forgoing the lottery ticket exceeds that of its purchase (10.49 > 10.20), the risk-averse individual will not purchase the ticket. Although our example assumes a particular utility function, $U(x) = \sqrt{x}$, this conclusion is perfectly general and holds for all concave utility functions. In other words, if an individual is risk-averse and computes the expected utility using the *objective* probabilities (that is, the correct probabilities for a game of chance), he will never accept a gamble. If, however, the individual is an "optimist", when weighing the purchase of the lottery ticket he may estimate his chances of winning at more than 1/100 (say 5/100). Thus his *subjective* probability of winning is 5/100, while the true, *objective* probability is only 1/100. In such a case he might well buy a lottery ticket even though he is a risk averter.

Table 5.5 calculates the expected utility of the lottery using the individual's *subjective* probabilities. The expected utility of alternative $A$ (not purchasing the ticket) remains 10.49, but the expected utility of alternative $B$ (buying the lottery ticket) becomes

$$95/100 \cdot \sqrt{100} + 5/100 \cdot \sqrt{900} = 95/10 + 15/10 = 9.5 + 1.5 = 11.0$$

Since 11.0 > 10.49, our risk-averse individual using subjective probability will purchase the lottery ticket. Many other examples can be found in which a relatively small

**Table 5.5**

| Alternative A Not to buy lottery ticket | | Alternative B To buy lottery ticket | |
|---|---|---|---|
| Income | Subjective Probability | Income | Subjective Probability |
| 110 | 1 | 100 | 95/100 |
| | | 900 | 5/100 |
| EU(x) = 10.49* | | EU(x) = 11.00* | |

* Expected utility has been calculated using the following function: $U(x) = \sqrt{x}$.

difference between the subjective and the objective probabilities convinces a risk averter to buy a lottery ticket which represents an "unfair" gamble using the objective probabilities.

We have illustrated the subjective utility approach using a specific utility function $U(x) = \sqrt{x}$. Figure 5.5 presents the same analysis in a more general form. Assume that an individual is choosing between a perfectly certain income $\bar{I}$ if he forgoes the lottery and the distribution $I_1$ with a probability of $\alpha$ and $I_2$ with a probability of $(1 - \alpha)$, if he purchases the lottery ticket. Let us further assume that the lottery represents a "fair" gamble so that

$$\bar{I} = \alpha I_1 + (1 - \alpha)I_2$$

As is clear from Figure 5.5, a risk averter will always prefer $\bar{I}$ to the lottery option since the utility of $\bar{I}$, point $D$, is greater than the expected utility of the risk option following the purchase of the lottery ticket, point $C$.[13]

Let us now assume that the individual is an optimist, or else that for lack of accurate information he estimates his chances of winning the lottery at $(1 - \beta)$, where $(1 - \beta) > (1 - \alpha)$. Using the higher subjective probability, his expected utility after buying the ticket will be represented by a point higher than $C$ on line $AB$ of Figure 5.5, for example, point $E$; since $E$ is higher than point $D$, purchasing the lottery ticket represents a higher level of expected utility than that associated with the certain income $\bar{I}$. As a result, the risk-averse individual will prefer the gamble, using the above mentioned subjective probabilities. Thus the existence of gambling can be rationalized *within* the framework of concave utility, or risk aversion.[14] We should hasten to add

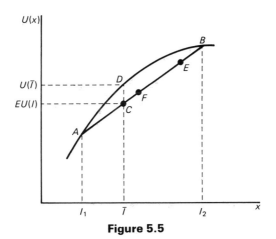

**Figure 5.5**

[13] The individual's expected utility is given by $EU(x) = \alpha U(I_1) + (1 - \alpha)U(I_2)$, which corresponds to point $C$ in Figure 5.5.

[14] Nils Hakansson has shown that risk aversion might be consistent with a Friedman–Savage utility function even without introducing subjective probabilities. According to this approach the convex segment of the utility function is attributable to the convexity of the borrowing constraint. For more details on this approach see Nils Hakansson, "Friedman–Savage Utility Functions Consistent with Risk Aversion", *Quarterly Journal of Economics* (Aug. 1970).

that assuming that the subjective probability of winning is higher than the objective probability is not a *sufficient* condition to induce a risk-averse individual to purchase a lottery ticket. For example, should the subjective expected utility be represented by a point such as $F$, which while higher than $C$ is lower than $D$, the individual will still prefer the perfectly certain alternative income $\bar{I}$, and therefore will not buy the lottery ticket despite his optimistic subjective estimate of the probability of winning.

### 5.3.1  The Pleasure of Gambling

In addition to the above explanation of gambling in terms of subjective probabilities, we can explain this behavioral feature solely on the basis of the pleasure derived from gambling, without the need to introduce subjective probabilities. We can look at the pleasure derived from gambling as a sort of psychic income. This is very similar to the explanation why people go fishing instead of buying fish in the supermarket.[15]

The utility function is thus regarded as depending on *two* variables: wealth *and* pleasure. It is therefore represented by a surface in space, and the utility $U$ is measured by the height of the points on this surface above the wealth–pleasure plane. The

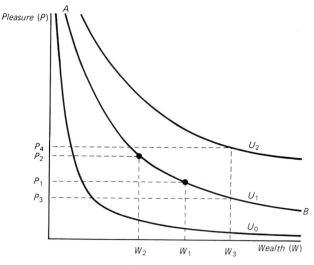

**Figure 5.6**

[15] In a recent article, Bailey *et al.* note that the actual structure of lotteries does not lead to the concave-upward section of the Friedman–Savage utility function. The fact that lotteries offer a very large number of small prices of $2 to $5 (in addition to a few very large prices of $10,000 and higher) seems to indicate that lotteries are adventurous entertainment or else designed to mislead participants about the true odds. In any event, these findings also explain gambling on the basis of non-income factors. For more details, see M. Bailey, M. Olson, and P. Wonnacott, "The Marginal Utility of Incomes Does Not Increase: Borrowing, Lending, and Friedman–Savage Gambles", *American Economic Review*, 1980, pp. 372–379.

individual's behavior in such a case is characterized by lines of equal utility on this surface (similar to isohypses or lines connecting points of equal height on a topographic map). Figure 5.6 shows a projection of such hypothetical iso-utility lines on the wealth–pleasure plane. By moving along a fixed iso-utility line (such as $AB$ in Figure 5.6) the individual will give up some wealth (from $W_1$ down to $W_2$) while increasing his pleasure (from $P_1$ up to $P_2$) without reducing his utility level. Similarly, the level of utility can be increased from $U_1$ to $U_2$ without any change in wealth (which remains constant at $W_3$) by increasing the pleasure variable from $P_3$ to $P_4$. The model of course can be extended beyond two variables and utility can be considered as a function of many variables (adding, for example, social status, peer appreciation, etc.), but as the number of variables increases we lose the sharp graphical presentation of utility. Thus investors may be risk averters and nevertheless participate in an *unfair* game as long as they derive enough pleasure from gambling.

## 5.4    Decreasing Absolute Risk Aversion

Economists who contend that it is plausible to assume risk aversion also maintain that the risk premium that an investor is willing to pay in order to get rid of a given risk decreases as the investor's wealth increases.

The risk premium is defined as that value $\pi$ which solves the following equation,

$$EU(W + x) = U(W + Ex - \pi)$$

where

$W$ is the investor's wealth (a certain quantity, not a random variable),

$x$ is the return on a risky asset held by the investor (a random variable with expected value $Ex$);

$\pi$ is the risk premium.

In other words $(W + Ex - \pi)$ is the certainty equivalent of the uncertain outcome $(W + x)$. (In the notation of Figure 5.3, $\bar{I}$ stands for the expected outcome $Ex$, $I^*$ is the certainty equivalent, and $\bar{I} - I^*$ is the risk premium $\pi$). If $x$ represents a random variable with small deviations around $W$, then Pratt[16] shows that $\pi$ is (approximately) given by

$$\pi \simeq -\frac{\sigma^2}{2} \frac{U''(W)}{U'(W)}$$

where $\sigma^2$ is the variance of $x$ (a measure of its deviation from $W$), and moments of

[16] J. W. Pratt, "Risk Aversion in the Small and in the Large", *Econometrica*, Jan.–Apr. 1964.

higher order than the variance are ignored (we leave the proof of this relationship as an end-of-chapter exercise).

Arrow,[17] using a different framework, obtains almost the same result for the risk premium $\pi$

$$\pi \simeq -\frac{h}{4}\frac{U''(W)}{U'(W)}$$

where $h$ is the symmetric deviation of the random return from $W$ (thus for a lottery with returns of $-1$ and $+1$, $h = 1$). We demonstrate below the proof suggested by Arrow.

Suppose that an investor whose initial wealth is $W_0$ is offered an amount of $+h$ and $-h$ dollars with even probability $\frac{1}{2}$ for each event. Thus, the random variable $x$ has the following form

$$x = \begin{cases} +h \text{ with probability } \frac{1}{2} \\ -h \text{ with probability } \frac{1}{2} \end{cases}$$

If the investor is risk-neutral, he will be indifferent to such a fair game. However, if the investor is risk-averse, he will reject this game. In order to induce a risk averter to accept the game, Arrow tries to make it more attractive by gradually increasing the probability of getting the favorable result ($+h$) from $\frac{1}{2}$ to some $p$, where $p > \frac{1}{2}$. This process of increasing $p$ continues until the risk averter becomes indifferent to the new random variable. The amount $(p - \frac{1}{2})$ by which the probability has to be increased above $\frac{1}{2}$ to reach the indifference point measures by how much one should increase the probability of the event $+h$ in order to induce the risk averter not to reject this game. The more risk-averse the decision maker is, the greater will be the gap $(p - \frac{1}{2})$. This probability spread may be used as an indicator of the risk premium that a risk averter is willing to pay to get rid of a given risk.

In order to determine the risk premium $(p - \frac{1}{2})$, let us represent the two possible events in terms of the utility which they provide, $U(W_0 + h)$ and $U(W_0 - h)$ for the events $+h$ and $-h$, respectively. We expand $U(W_0 + h)$ and $U(W_0 - h)$ in a Taylor series around the fixed point $W_0$ to obtain:[18]

$$U(W_0 + h) = U(W_0) + U'(W_0)h + \frac{U''(W_0)h^2}{2!} + \frac{U'''(W_0)h^3}{3!} + \cdots$$

$$U(W_0 - h) = U(W_0) - U'(W_0)h + \frac{U''(W_0)h^2}{2!} - \frac{U'''(W_0)h^3}{3!} + \cdots$$

---

[17] K. J. Arrow, *Aspects of the Theory of Risk Bearing*, Helsinki, Yrjö Jahnssonin, Säätiö, 1965.
[18] In certain circumstances the value of the function $f(t)$ can be expanded in a Taylor series around the fixed point $a$ and be written as the following series of terms:

$$f(t) = f(a) + f'(a)(t - a) + f''(a)(t - a)^2/2! + f'''(a)(t - a)^3/3! + \cdots$$
$$+ f^n(a)(t - a)^n/n! + \cdots$$

For further details see the Mathematical Supplement at the end of the book.

Since $h$ is assumed to be a small number, $h^3$ and higher orders of this deviation can be ignored (these terms approach zero). Ignoring higher-order terms with $h^i$ ($i \geqslant 3$) and multiplying the two expressions by the respective probabilities of the two outcomes $+h$ and $-h$ ($p$ and $(1-p)$, respectively), we obtain:

$$p \, U(W_0 + h) = p \, U(W_0) + p \, U'(W_0)h + p \, \frac{U''(W_0)h^2}{2!}$$

$$(1-p) \, U(W_0 - h) = (1-p) \, U(W_0) - (1-p)U'(W_0)h + (1-p) \, \frac{U''(W_0)h^2}{2!}$$

Adding the two equations, we have:

$$p \, U(W_0 + h) + (1-p) \, U(W_0 - h) = U(W_0) + U'(W_0)h(2p-1) + \frac{U''(W_0)h^2}{2!}$$

The left hand side is simply the expected utility of the random outcome. According to Arrow, $p$ has been increased until the investor is indifferent to the game. Hence the expected utility with the game (left hand side) is equal to the utility derived from the initial wealth, $U(W_0)$. This implies that:

$$U'(W_0)h(2p-1) + \frac{U''(W_0)}{2!} h^2 = 0$$

or, dividing through by $U'(W_0) \cdot 2h$ and rearranging,

$$(p - \tfrac{1}{2}) = -\frac{U''(W_0)}{U'(W_0)} \cdot \frac{h}{4}$$

Since $(p - \tfrac{1}{2})$ is the risk premium measure we obtain:

$$\pi \simeq -\frac{h}{4} \frac{U''(W_0)}{U'(W_0)}$$

The equality is approximate ($\simeq$) since this result has been obtained by omitting high order terms: hence, Arrow's expression for $\pi$ is an approximation, and not precise.

Both Arrow and Pratt assume that the random variable has very small deviations, so that third and higher powers can be ignored. Since $\sigma^2/2 > 0$ and $h/4 > 0$ are positive constants, the two risk premium measures are solely a function of the term $-U''(W_0)/U'(W_0)$ which appears in both Pratt's and Arrow's expressions. Figure 5.7 demonstrates the difference in the two approaches of Arrow and Pratt. Pratt employs the usual certainty equivalent approach to define $\pi$ as:

$$EU(W_0 + x) = U(W_0 + Ex - \pi)$$

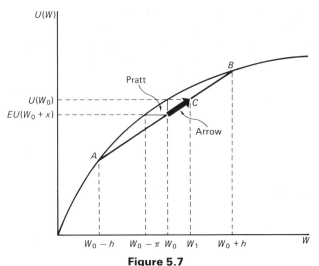

**Figure 5.7**

Thus, $\pi$ according to Pratt is the regular risk premium which is defined and explained in Sections 4.5 and 5.2 (note that in Figure 5.7 $Ex = 0$).

In Arrow's framework $x$ is a random variable which initially takes the values $+h$ and $-h$ with equal probabilities and has zero expected value. Arrow increases the probability of the favorable outcome $W_0 + h$ to $p(p > \frac{1}{2})$ until:

$$U(W_0) = EU(W_0 + x) = pU(W_0 + h) + (1 - p)U(W_0 - h)$$

Thus he moves along the chord $AB$ in the direction of the arrow up to point $C$. At this point we have a new game with outcomes $W_0 + h$ with probability $p > \frac{1}{2}$ and $W_0 - h$ with probability $(1 - p) < \frac{1}{2}$. The expected terminal wealth now is $W_1 = p(W_0 + h) + (1 - p)(W_0 - h)$.

At the indifference point we have:

$$EU(W_0 + x) = U(W_0)$$

which implies that the investor is indifferent to this risk with the new set of probabilities $p$ and $(1 - p)$. Thus, although we have two approaches to measure the risk-premium we obtain almost the same results:

$$\pi_A = -\frac{h}{4} \frac{U''(W_0)}{U'(W_0)}$$

$$\pi_P = -\frac{\sigma^2}{2} \frac{U''(W_0)}{U'(W_0)}$$

where the subscripts A and P denote the Arrow and the Pratt measures respectively. It is the common term of both indexes, $-U'''(W_0)/U'(W_0)$, that determines the *sign* of the risk premium.

### 5.4.1  Decreasing Absolute Risk Aversion and the Investors' Preferences

If the risk premium that the investor is willing to pay in order to get rid of a given risk decreases as his wealth increases, we say that his preferences show a *decreasing absolute risk aversion*. This implies that he becomes less risk averse at higher levels of wealth and hence will tend to increase his investment in risky assets. For example, suppose that there are only two assets, one risky and one riskless, and an investor with decreasing absolute risk aversion, whose initial wealth is $W_0 = \$1,000$, decides to invest $500 in the risky asset and $500 in the riskless asset. If the investor's wealth increases say, to $1,100, we expect his investment in the risky asset to increase, say, to $510.

Note that decreasing absolute risk aversion implies an increase in the absolute amount invested in the risky asset (from $500 to $510), but not necessarily an increase in the proportion invested in the risky asset. If the *proportion* of wealth invested in the risky asset increases, we say that the utility function shows decreasing *relative* risk aversion. There is almost complete agreement among economists that investors increase the *absolute* amount that they invest in the risky asset as their wealth increases, while the empirical evidence regarding the proportion invested in the risky assets is inconclusive. We therefore concentrate below only on the implication of decreasing *absolute* risk aversion on the investor's utility function.

The risk premium (using Pratt's treatment) is given by:

$$\pi \simeq -\frac{\sigma^2}{2} \frac{U''(W)}{U'(W)}$$

Decreasing absolute risk aversion implies that:

$$\frac{\partial \pi}{\partial W} < 0$$

or:

$$\frac{\partial}{\partial W}\left[-\frac{\sigma^2}{2}\frac{U''(W)}{U'(W)}\right] = -\frac{\sigma^2}{2}\frac{U'(W)U'''(W)-[U''(W)]^2}{[U'(W)]^2} < 0$$

Since $\sigma^2/2$ and the denominator are positive, $\partial\pi/\partial W$ can be negative only if the rest of the numerator is positive, or if $[(U''(W)]^2 - U'(W)U'''(W) < 0$. But both $|U''(W)|^2 > 0$ and $U'(W) > 0$, so that $\partial\pi/\partial W$ *cannot* be negative if $U'''(W) \leqslant 0$. Thus, a *necessary condition* for decreasing absolute risk aversion is $U'''(W) > 0$. We shall use this information in deriving investment criteria in Chapter 6.

**Table 5.6**

|  | Utility Function | |
|---|---|---|
|  | ln $W$ | $W - aW^2$ $(a > 0)$ |
| First derivative $U'(W)$ | $\dfrac{1}{W} > 0$ | $1 - 2aW > 0$ |
| Second derivative $U''(W)$ | $-\dfrac{1}{W^2} < 0$ | $-2a < 0$ |
| Risk premium $\quad \pi = -\dfrac{\sigma^2}{2}\dfrac{U''(W)}{U'(W)}$ | $\dfrac{\sigma^2}{2}\dfrac{1}{W} > 0$ | $\dfrac{\sigma^2}{2}\dfrac{2a}{1 - 2aW} > 0$ |
| Derivative of risk premium with respect to wealth $\partial\pi/\partial W$ | $-\dfrac{\sigma^2}{2}\dfrac{1}{W^2} < 0$ | $\dfrac{\sigma^2}{2}\dfrac{4a^2}{(1 - 2aW)^2} > 0$ |

EXAMPLE

Let us take two utility functions, one of which shows decreasing absolute risk aversion and one with increasing absolute risk aversion (see Table 5.6).

The function ln $W$, with decreasing absolute risk aversion ($\partial\pi/\partial W < 0$), is consistent with investor behavior as observed empirically, while the function $W - aW^2$ is contrary to the empirical evidence. In other words, if investors were to have the utility function $W - aW^2$, we would expect them to *decrease* the absolute amounts invested in the risky asset as their wealth $W$ increased. Note that with the function $U(W) = \ln W$ we actually have $U'''(W) = 1/W^3 > 0$, which is a necessary condition for decreasing absolute risk aversion. With the function $U(W) = W - aW^2$, on the other hand, we have $U'''(W) = 0$, and it is obvious that $\partial\pi/\partial W$ cannot be negative with such a function.

## 5.5    Risk Attitudes in the Stock Market: Some Empirical Evidence

This section will be devoted to an empirical study of investors' behavior based on mutual fund returns. Before presenting our empirical findings and analyzing their implications regarding the shape of investors' utility functions, it may help to clarify the theoretical considerations underlying the regression analysis. For this purpose we shall assume the most general form of utility function, that is, we place no restrictions whatever on its shape beyond the usual stipulation that its first derivative be positive. Such a function can of course be concave or convex, or composed of any number of concave and convex segments.

Despite the almost complete lack of specific information regarding investors' tastes we can still apply utility analysis. When making his investment decision, the investor in risk assets is confronted by a probability distribution of possible returns and a market price for each alternative investment. His decision, strictly speaking, depends on all the observations and the appropriate probabilities for each alternative distribution. Equivalently we can state that the investment decision will depend on *all* the moments of the probability distribution, for if the investor knows all the moments, he will generally know the exact features of the probability distribution.

To illustrate this claim, let us assume a general von Neumann–Morgenstern utility function $U(W + x)$, where $x$ denotes a random variable, the return on investment; $W$ is the investor's initial wealth; and $U$ is a general function about which we know nothing except that its first derivative is positive.

Expanding this utility function in a Taylor series around the fixed point $(W + Ex)$ gives

$$U(W + x) = U(W + Ex) + U'(W + Ex) \cdot [W + x - (W + Ex)]$$

$$+ \frac{U''(W + Ex)}{2!} \cdot [W + x - (W + Ex)]^2$$

$$+ \frac{U'''(W + Ex)}{3!} \cdot [W + x - (W + Ex)]^3$$

$$+ \frac{U''''(W + Ex)}{4!} \cdot [W + x - (W + Ex)]^4 + \cdots$$

where $Ex$ is the expected value of the random variable distribution, and the expression $U'(W + Ex)$ denotes the value of the first derivative of the utility function at point $(W + Ex)$, $U''(W + Ex)$ denotes the value of the second derivative at point $(W + Ex)$, and so on. Each of the factors $[W + x - (W + Ex)]$ simply reduces to the deviation from the mean $(x - Ex)$.

Since we have shown that a rational investor will select the investment option which maximizes his expected utility, we can write $EU(W + x)$ as follows (recalling that the expectation of a sum of random variables is equal to the sum of the expectations of the random variables)

$$EU(W + x) = U(W + Ex) + \frac{U''(W + Ex)}{2!} \cdot \sigma^2$$

$$+ \frac{U'''(W + Ex)}{3!} \cdot \mu_3 + \frac{U''''(W + Ex)}{4!} \cdot \mu_4 + \cdots$$

where $\sigma^2$ is the variance of the distribution defined as $E(x - Ex)^2$; $\mu_3$ is the third central moment of the distribution defined as $E(x - Ex)^3$, that is, an index of the distribution's asymmetry; and $\mu_k$ is similarly defined as the central moment of the $k$th order, $\mu_k = E(x - Ex)^k$. In general, the expected utility depends on all the moments of the probability distribution,[19] and to know if a particular moment is desirable or not one has to know the coefficient of this moment, that is, the appropriate derivative of the utility function at point $(W + Ex)$.

Assuming that an individual is rational and always prefers more money to less, an increase in the expected return $Ex$, other things being equal, should also increase his expected utility. With respect to the other moments, no *a priori* determination can be made. For example, we do not know whether raising the variance (or some other higher order moment), while keeping the rest of the moments unchanged, is desirable to investors. Precise theoretical answers cannot be given to questions such as these, but we can test empirically the degree to which investments with greater variance afford higher average returns. Should this be the case the following interpretation may be given: investors are averse to variance, and therefore the higher an investment's variance the higher the return needed to compensate investors for the greater variance (risk).

To determine the impact of the distribution moments on expected utility a regression analysis was carried out for a sample of US mutual funds. Data on rates of return were collected for 86 US mutual funds during a 25-year period.[20] The empirical study consists of two steps: (a) first, time-series data are used to calculate for each mutual fund $j$ the mean return $\bar{R}_j$ and the other *ex-post* distribution moments; (b) using these time-series estimates, a regression analysis is carried out using the following regression equation:

$$\bar{R}_j = a + \sum_{i=2}^{n} b_i \mu_{ij}$$

where $\bar{R}_j$ is the mean rate of return to investors in the $j$th mutual fund; $\mu_{ij}$ denotes the $i$th moment of the distribution for the same fund. For example, $\mu_{22}$ denotes the variance of the mutual fund indexed as number 2 and $\mu_{32}$ denotes the asymmetry measure for the same fund. We examined the first 20 moments only $(n = 20)$ because it appeared highly unlikely that any of the higher moments would prove significant.

The mean rate of return during the period, as well as the variance and the remaining 18 higher moments of the distribution of returns, were calculated for each mutual fund included in the regression. Of course the regression includes the *estimated* distribution moments, rather than the true moments, as explanatory variables.

The relationship of the distribution moments to investors' utility is derived from the regression analysis itself. Thus if a particular moment, for example the variance, is undesirable to most investors in mutual funds, we expect the coefficient of variance $b_2$

---

[19] Requiring information regarding the distribution moments is equivalent to requiring detailed information on the distribution itself. See, for example, A. M. Mood and F. A. Graybill, *Introduction to the Theory of Statistics*, New York: McGraw-Hill, p. 117.

[20] All of the data were obtained from the relevant annual editions of Arthur Wiesenberger and Company, *Investment Companies*.

to be positive, that is, any increase in variance must be accompanied by a compensating increase in the average rate of return $\bar{R}$.[21]

The results of the analysis for the entire 25-year period are summarized in Table 5.7. Although the regression equations include 21 variables (that is, a constant and the first 20 moments of the distributions), only the variance and the third moment are significant (the significance coefficient is greater in magnitude than the 99% critical $t$-value, $t_{0.99} = 2.40$. See Table 5.7).

The percentage of the variance explained by the regression ($R^2$) is very high ($R^2 = 0.86$) and most of the "explained" variance stems from the first three moments; the addition of higher moments increases $R^2$ only slightly. This would seem to indicate that the first three moments are the main factors which determine investors' decisions.

The coefficient of the variance ($b_2$) was found to be positive, and consequently we can conclude that investors are typically averse to variance. The magnitude of this coefficient is around 0.02, which means that a 1% increase in the variance must be accompanied by an increase of 0.02% in the average rate of return in order to compensate the investor for the added variance.

**Table 5.7**
**Analysis of Regression Results for the 25-year Period**

| Source of Variance | Sum of Squares | Degrees of Freedom | Mean Squares | $F^*$ | Critical Value (99%) | $R^2$ |
|---|---|---|---|---|---|---|
| Due to Regression | 544.3 | 2 | 272.2 | 162.3 | $F_{0.99} = 5.01$ | 0.86 |
| Deviation from the Regression | 92.2 | 55 | 1.7 | | | |

\* Due to tolerance limit only two moments remain in the regression; that is, the contribution of the other 18 moments to the $F$ value is negligible.

| Variable | Coefficient | t Value | Critical Value (99%) |
|---|---|---|---|
| Constant | 7.205 | 16.2 | $t_{0.99} = 2.40$ |
| Variance | 0.019 | 9.9 | |
| Skewness | −0.000064 | −8.4 | |

[21] In an unpublished paper on the relation between risk and return, M. H. Miller has pointed out that in cases where the random variables are identically distributed, this type of regression analysis can artificially produce significant statistical relationships between the first two moments of the distribution. Although the time distribution of mutual fund returns is not the same, we have (following a suggestion by Miller) carried out the regression analysis a second time using the geometric, rather than the arithmetic, mean. The results of this analysis are not materially different and fully corroborate the findings given in the text.

The regression coefficient of the third moment (skewness) is negative. This result suggests that the average investor in mutual funds likes *positive* asymmetry and avoids *negative* asymmetry. Thus increasing the skewness of the distribution *reduces* the required average return, since the investor feels compensated by the increased positive skewness, that is, by the small chance of obtaining a relatively high return.[22]

This empirical result has some theoretical support. Although expected utility is determined by the exact configuration of the distribution function, generally the first three or four distribution moments give most of the required information about the form of the distribution. In fact there exists a wide range of distributions for which the first four (or fewer) moments provide a complete specification of the shape of the probability function. Moreover, even experienced statisticians often find it difficult to interpret the meaning of higher moments. The first three moments represent a distribution's "location", its dispersion, and asymmetry, respectively; the additional information provided by the fourth, and higher, moments is not very clear[23] to the professional statistician, let alone to the uninitiated investor.

### 5.5.1    Implications for Utility Functions

Although decision making under uncertainty depends, in general, on all the moments of the distribution function, assuming a specific utility function allows us to concentrate on a subset of the distribution moments. For example, if we are willing to assume a quadratic utility function, investment decisions become a function of only the first two moments. The empirical analysis of mutual fund returns suggests that investors' decisions depend chiefly on the first three moments of the distribution of returns. Thus some of the empirical results appear to approximate those which we would expect from a cubic utility function, so it may be instructive to examine the implications of such an assumption.[24] A utility function which depends only on the first three moments *must* be of the following form:[25]

$$U(W + x) = a(W + x) + b(W + x)^2 + c(W + x)^3 + d$$

---

[22] This result can serve as a partial explanation of the behavior of people who participate in lotteries which typically have negative expected values but are characterized by high positive skewness. The preference for positive asymmetry was previously noted by F. D. Arditti, "Risk and the Required Return on Equity", *Journal of Finance* (Mar. 1967).

[23] See I. Kaplansky, "A Common Error Concerning Kurtosis", *Journal of the American Statistical Association* 40 (June 1945), p. 259.

[24] Of course this does not mean that all investors have cubic utility functions; although the percentage of explained variance is relatively high, it is *not* 100%. We are indebted to Nancy Jacob, who helped to clarify our thinking on this point. Moreover, the cubic utility function is not bounded, so that in order to avoid the reintroduction of a variant of the St. Petersburg Paradox, we must assume that beyond a certain point $(W_0)$ increments to wealth do not increase utility, that is, $U(W) = U(W_0)$ for all $W \geqslant W_0$.

[25] If we expand any utility function in a Taylor series it will always be dependent on *all* of the moments. However if the function is cubic, all of the derivatives of a higher order than three vanish, leaving only the first three moments.

Expanding this function in a Taylor series about the point $W$, we get

$$U(W + x) = U(W) + U'(W)x + \tfrac{1}{2}U''(W)x^2 + \tfrac{1}{6}U'''(W)x^3$$

After calculating the first three derivatives of $U$ at the point $W$, and substituting these derivatives in the above equation, we get[26]

$$U(W + x) = a_1 x + b_1 x^2 + c_1 x^3 + d_1$$

This function must have *both* concave and convex segments. Such a function is illustrated in Figure 5.8. From Figure 5.8 we can see that for low values of $x$ the investor is a risk averter and therefore dislikes variance, but for relatively high values of $x$ the investor becomes a risk lover, and consequently desires variance. This form of utility function is similar in many important respects to the one presented by Friedman and Savage (see Figure 5.4); both of these utility functions have the property that they can reconcile the purchase of insurance contracts with gambling, without recourse to subjective utility since in both cases investors prefer positive asymmetrical distributions (like a lottery's) but dislike negative asymmetry, and therefore buy insurance policies.

Although a cubic utility function is appropriate for both risk lovers and risk averters, we can conclude from the empirical evidence that the influence of risk averters

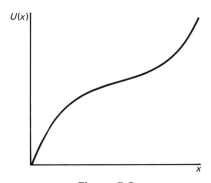

**Figure 5.8**

[26] The parameters of this equation, $a_1$, $b_1$, $c_1$, and $d_1$, are given by the following relations:

$$a_1 = a + 2bW + 3cW^2$$

$$b_1 = b + 3cW$$

$$c_1 = c$$

$$d_1 = aW + bW^2 + cW^3 + d$$

in the market for mutual funds shares is dominant. This conclusion stems from the fact that the coefficient of the variance in the empirical regressions is positive, that is, the average investor dislikes variance so that increasing the variance increases the required rate of return. Of course, this conclusion relates to the *average* investor and does not obviate the possibility that there are individual investors in this market who, in the relevant range, prefer a large variance.

### Summary

The primary purpose of this chapter has been to point out the crucial importance of the shape of the utility function for investment decisions. Various hypotheses regarding the probable shape of an investor's utility function were discussed, and the results of an empirical investigation into investors' risk attitudes were presented.

The first hypothesis discussed was that associated with Friedman and Savage. These two writers attempt to reconcile the observed phenomenon that many individuals simultaneously purchase lottery tickets (or gamble) and take out insurance. The former action indicates that the individual is not risk-averse, since such an individual would never purchase a lottery ticket (or gamble). Taking out insurance, on the other hand, indicates that the individual *is* risk-averse; a risk lover would never agree to purchase an insurance contract to avoid risk.

It follows, according to Friedman and Savage, that to avoid contradiction the utility function can be neither strictly concave nor strictly convex. They have shown that if the utility function has both a concave and a convex segment in the relevant range the apparent contradiction can be resolved. In the concave range the individual willingly pays a risk premium (takes out insurance), while in the convex range the *same* individual buys lottery tickets (or gambles).

An alternative approach to the same problem suggests that individuals' utility functions are always concave, that is, universal risk aversion prevails. Whereas Friedman and Savage hypothesized that over some range the marginal utility of wealth increases, the alternative approach assumes diminishing marginal utility of wealth over the entire range. The undisputed empirical observations that many individuals simultaneously gamble and take out insurance are reconciled, in this alternative approach, by assuming that subjective and objective probabilities diverge. In particular it has been assumed that subjective probabilities exceed their objective counterparts when the latter are low. This assumption is sufficient to show that a risk-averse individual will also be willing, on occasion, to gamble or to purchase lottery tickets, without recourse to a convex segment of the utility function.

We next presented some empirical evidence on risk attitudes in the stock market. A regression analysis of mutual funds returns over a 25-year period gave the following results:

(1)   Investors in mutual funds are, on the average, averse to variance: other things being equal, an increase in the variance of returns is accompanied by an increase in the average annual returns to investors.

(2)  The average mutual fund investor likes positive, and dislikes negative, asymmetry: he has a preference for even a small chance of obtaining an unusually high return.

(3)  Mutual fund returns can be "explained", to a large extent, in terms of three moments, since moments higher than the third order are not significant.

The dependence on the first three moments only suggests a cubic utility function. Since a cubic utility function has both concave and convex segments, these results appear to lend some support to the Friedman–Savage hypothesis. On the other hand,

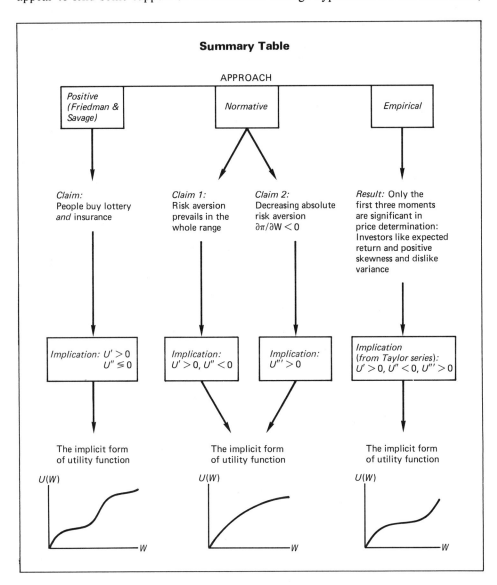

the empirical analysis also shows that the influence of risk averters is dominant since increases in the variance are always accompanied by increases in the average rate of return. These results refer to mutual funds only, so that one cannot be certain that they hold true for all choice situations.

Empirical findings as well as the claim of decreasing absolute risk aversion imply that $U''' > 0$. Namely investors like positive skewness and dislike negative skewness. This property by itself can explain insurance (getting rid of negative skewness) and gambling (buying positive skewness).

With this in mind, we shall develop in the next chapter three different criteria for the analysis of choices involving risk—a general criterion which is appropriate for all types of utility functions (concave, convex, or both); a risk aversion criterion which assumes that all utility functions are concave, and a third criterion which uses the additional information that $U''' > 0$.

## Questions and Problems

5.1    "The simultaneous existence of insurance companies and gambling dens indicates that many individuals do *not* have linear utility functions."
(a) Appraise the above quotation.
(b) How do Friedman and Savage account for this phenomenon?

5.2    Define the terms *subjective* and *objective* probability. How can these two concepts be used to rationalize the coexistence of risk aversion and gambling?

5.3    An individual with the utility function $U(x) = x^2$ and with initial wealth of $60 is known to be indifferent between two lotteries $A$ and $B$. Each option costs $5 and offers the following prizes:

| Option A | | Option B | |
|---|---|---|---|
| Probability | Prize | Probability | Prize |
| 1/2 | $35 | 1/2 | $10 |
| 1/2 | $45 | 1/2 | Y |

Given the above information, find the value of Y.

5.4    Mr. Horn, whose utility function is given by $U(x) = 100 + x^2$ and whose initial wealth is $100, is confronted with the following investments, $A$ and $B$:

| Investment A | | Investment B | |
|---|---|---|---|
| Probability | Return | Probability | Return |
| 1/2 | $ 0 | 1/2 | $ 0 |
| 1/2 | $20 | 1/2 | $40 |

Assuming that the price of $A$ is $10 and the price of $B$ is $20, will he purchase $A$? Will he be willing to purchase $B$? Prove your answer.

5.5    Prove that the risk premium, according to Pratt, is:

$$\pi \simeq -\frac{\sigma^2}{2}\frac{U''(W)}{U'(W)}$$

*Hint*: Use the defining equation for $\pi$ from Section 5.4 and expand both sides in a Taylor series (see Pratt, J. W., "Risk Aversion in the Small and in the Large", *Econometrica*, Vol. 32 (1964), 122–136).

5.6    Is Pratt's approximation of the risk premium true only for risk averters? Prove your answer.

5.7    "The risk premium decreases with increasing wealth". Verify this statement by calculating the risk premium of the following option

| Probability $p(x)$ | Return $x$ |
| --- | --- |
| 1/3 | 1 |
| 1/3 | 10 |
| 1/3 | 100 |

for two utility functions $U_1 = \log(W_0 + x)$ and $U_2 = \sqrt{W_0 + x}$, once for initial wealth $W_0 = 0$ and then again for $W_0 = 1,000$.
*Hint*: The risk premium $\pi$ is obtained by solving the following equation $EU(W_0 + x) = U(W_0 + Ex - \pi)$, where $W_0 + Ex - \pi$ is the certainty equivalent of the uncertain terminal wealth, see Section 5.4.

5.8    "Security appraisal can be limited to the analysis of the first three moments of the probability distribution of returns."
(a) Define the first three moments and explain what information each conveys regarding the distribution.
(b) What empirical evidence can support the above quotation?
(c) What are the limitations of the available empirical evidence?

5.9    Is there any similarity between a cubic utility function and a Friedman–Savage utility function?
       Prove your answer by analyzing the general cubic utility function,

$$U(y) = a_1 y + a_2 y^2 + a_3 y^3 + e$$

(with $a_1 > 0$) and compare the results with the Friedman–Savage function.

5.10   Give both empirical and theoretical justification to the assumption that $U'''(W) \geqslant 0$ (nonnegative third derivative of the utility function).

5.11   The Maxi Bus Company, which owns a fleet of 5,000 buses, does *not* insure its buses against theft, while the Mini Bus Company, which owns only 10 buses, does. Do these facts support the conclusion that the Maxi Bus Company is managed by risk lovers and the Mini Bus Company is run by risk averters? Prove your answer diagrammatically.

5.12   "An insurance company is a 'risk lover' by definition since it is always willing to undertake the 'risks' which risk averters refuse to accept." What is your opinion of this statement?

5.13  A German lottery, internationally advertised in *Business Week, Newsweek, Time Magazine* and other journals, uses the following sales pitch: "Do you want to become a millionaire? You can. Now we offer this opportunity, 21 times DM 1 MILLION ... 300,000 ticket numbers in the game, 113,306 winning numbers, 38 out of 100 numbers are winners." The price of a ticket to this lottery is DM738 and the prize schedule is as follows:

$$
\begin{array}{rl}
21 \times & \text{DM } 1,000,000 \\
35 \times & \text{DM } 100,000 \\
15 \times & \text{DM } 50,000 \\
33 \times & \text{DM } 25,000 \\
48 \times & \text{DM } 15,000 \\
96 \times & \text{DM } 10,000 \\
135 \times & \text{DM } 5,000 \\
198 \times & \text{DM } 3,000 \\
495 \times & \text{DM } 2,000 \\
3,030 \times & \text{DM } 1,000 \\
78,600 \times & \text{DM } 720 \\
9,000 \times & \text{DM } 600 \\
8,100 \times & \text{DM } 480 \\
7,200 \times & \text{DM } 360 \\
6,300 \times & \text{DM } 240 \\
\end{array}
$$

(a) How do you react to the claim that "38 out of 100 numbers are winners"?

(b) Calculate the premium that participants are willing to pay for the privilege of taking part in the lottery.

(c) Use a Friedman and Savage type utility function to demonstrate your results graphically. Show two individuals: one who buys a ticket and a non-buyer.
*Hint*: For purposes of graphical representation, assume a two-outcome lottery, DM 0 and DM 1 million.

5.14  An individual is faced with the following uncertain option:

| Probability | Return |
|:-----------:|:------:|
| 0.9 | -2 |
| 0.1 | 30 |

(a) Is it possible to explain the individual's attitude toward this option in terms of either of the following quadratic utility functions?

(i)  $U(x) = x - \dfrac{1}{20} x^2$

(ii)  $U(x) = x + 2x^2$

(b) Suggest a quadratic utility function of the general form $U(x) = x + \beta x^2$ that is appropriate for judging the attitude toward this option.
*Hint*: Investigate the general behavior of the function for various $\beta$ and establish the relevant range of $\beta$-values for risk lovers and risk averters.

5.15 Use the financial statements of property and liability insurance of the American General Insurance Company to estimate the risk premium that individuals in aggregate are willing to pay to the insurers.

**American General Insurance Company**
**Property and Liability Companies Consolidated Statement of Earnings**
**($000)**

|  | *1979* | *1978* | *1977* |
|---|---|---|---|
| Net Premiums Written | 696,206 | 658,513 | 608,063 |
| Investment Income | 117,369 | 99,852 | 92,230 |
| **Total Income** | **813,575** | **758,365** | **700,293** |
| Losses Incurred | 460,929 | 435,680 | 399,992 |
| Commissions | 230,501 | 206,426 | 199,627 |
| Other Expenses | 26,699 | 16,875 | 16,412 |
| Dividends to Policy Holders | 3,994 | 4,520 | 3,253 |
| **Total Expenses** | **722,123** | **663,501** | **619,284** |

*Source:* Annual financial statements of the American General Insurance Company.

5.16 An investor with utility function $U(W) = \sqrt{W}$ considers investing $1,000 in the stock of General Electric Co. or the stock of McGraw Edison Co. The annual returns on each of these stocks are given below. Assume that each return is equally probable and that the price of General Electric Co. stock is $99\frac{1}{8}$, and that of McGraw Edison Co. stock is $40\frac{3}{4}$, as given by the *Wall Street Journal* dated January 1, 1983. Which stock will the investor choose? If he did not have to make a choice between the two, would he be prepared to invest in both?

|  | *Return on Stock* (%) | |
|---|---|---|
| *Year* | *General Electric Co.* | *McGraw Edison Co.* |
| 1972 | 18.85 | 22.08 |
| 1973 | −11.46 | −48.65 |
| 1974 | −44.88 | −36.42 |
| 1975 | 43.02 | 113.64 |
| 1976 | 24.38 | 46.48 |
| 1977 | −6.64 | −7.22 |
| 1978 | −0.63 | −3.83 |
| 1979 | 13.72 | 12.95 |
| 1980 | 27.85 | 46.22 |
| 1981 | −1.30 | 4.52 |

*Source:* CRSP monthly returns data tape.

5.17 Utility functions of individuals are constructed empirically on the basis of extensive question-and-answer sessions intended to elucidate the individuals' preferences. (See Swalm, R., "Utility Theory—Insights into Risk Taking", *Harvard Business Review*, December 1966.) In order to convert the respondent's "yes-no" or "better-worse" answers into numerical utility schedules or graphs, it is necessary to fix *arbitrarily* the utility values for two values of the independent variable, $U(a)$ and $U(b)$ for some $x = a$

and $x = b$ (these are usually the endpoints of the range over which the utility function is investigated). This procedure is called *normalization* of the utility function.

(a) Suppose that one researcher used the normalization $U(0) = 0$, $U(1) = 1$, while the other researcher took $U(0) = -100$ and $U(1) = 100$. Show that both normalizations produce utility functions which are a positive linear transformation of one another.

(b) Prove in general that by arbitrarily fixing the value of the utility function at two points $a$ and $b$, we obtain a utility function which is a linear transformation of the "true" utility function $U^*(x)$.

(c) A quadratic utility function of a risk averter may be represented as $U_1(x) = x - bx^2$ or alternatively as $U_2(x) = (1 + a)x - ax^2$, where $a$ and $b$ are both positive. Show that the two functions differ in their normalization and represent one as a positive linear transformation of the other.

5.18  You are trying to construct an empirical utility function over the range of terminal wealth values from $a = \$0$ to $b = \$1000$. Fix arbitrarily $U(a) = U(0) = -100$ and $U(b) = U(1000) = 100$.

Now ask yourself what is the certain amount $c$ at which you are indifferent between $c$ and the chance of ending up with 0 or 1,000 with equal probabilities, i.e., the gamble $(1/2 \cdot a,\ 1/2 \cdot b) = (1/2 \cdot 0,\ 1/2 \cdot 1000)$. Calculate the utility value for this certainty equivalent, using the normalization you fixed above.

Then construct two partial gambles $(1/2 \cdot 0,\ 1/2 \cdot c)$ and $(1/2 \cdot c,\ 1/2 \cdot 1000)$ and repeat the procedure for each partial gamble, and so on.

In this way generate a schedule of utility values $U(x)$ for various $x$. Plot the result. If you have been truthful, this is your personal utility function. Are you a risk averter or a risk lover? (For more details, see the article by R. Swalm cited in Problem 5.17.)

5.19  A risk averter, who is an expected utility maximizer, is known to be indifferent between a certain income of $\$120$ and a risky investment yielding a return of $\$60$ with probability of $1/2$ or $\$240$ with probability of $1/2$.

(a) Given the normalization $U(60) = 60$ and $U(240) = 240$, estimate $U(R)$ (by calculating appropriate upper and lower bounds) for $R = \$120, \$100, \$200, 0, \$70, \$320$.

(b) The same individual as in part (a) is indifferent between a certain income of $\$200$ and a risky investment yielding a return of $\$120$ with probability of $p$ and $\$240$ with probability of $(1 - p)$. What are the maximum and the minimum possible values of $p$?

(c) What is the minimal income that the same individual will accept in order to give up a risky investment yielding a return of $\$60$ with probability of $1/3$ or $\$120$ with probability of $2/3$?

(d) Which of the following two options will be preferred by our individual?

| Option A | | Option B | |
|---|---|---|---|
| Return R | Probability p | Return R | Probability p |
| $\$ 60$ | 0.1 | $\$ 60$ | 0.3 |
| $\$120$ | 0.4 | $\$120$ | 0.0 |
| $\$240$ | 0.3 | $\$240$ | 0.6 |
| $\$360$ | 0.2 | $\$360$ | 0.0 |
| $\$480$ | 0.0 | $\$480$ | 0.1 |

## Data Set Problems

1. Calculate the mean, the variance, the third moment, and the skewness of the first mutual fund from each category in the Data Set. Assign probability of $1/10$ to each observation.

2. Assume that it is known that the investor's utility function is such that

$$U(W_0 + Ex) = 1$$
$$U''(W_0 + Ex) = -1$$
$$U'''(W_0 + Ex) = 1/10$$

and all the higher derivatives are zero. Which of the mutual funds considered in Problem 1 above is the optimal one for the particular investor? Explain.

3. Suppose that all the funds selected in Problem 1 have the same means and variances, but the skewness is different, as actually calculated in Problem 1. Which fund constitutes the optimum investment if we have partial information about the investor's utility function indicating that $U''' > 0$ and all the higher derivatives are zero?

## Selected References

Alchian, A. A., "The Meaning of Utility Measurement", *American Economic Review* (March 1953).

Amihud, Y., "A Note on Risk Aversion and Indifference Curves", *Journal of Financial and Quantitative Analysis* (September 1977).

Amihud, Y., "General Risk Aversion and an Attitude Toward Risk", *Journal of Finance* (June 1980).

Arditti, F. D., "Risk and the Required Return on Equity", *Journal of Finance* (March 1967).

Arrow, K. J., "Alternative Approaches to the Theory of Choice in Risk-taking Situations", *Econometrica* (October 1951).

Arrow, K. J., "*Aspects of the Theory of Risk-bearing*", Helsinki: Yrjö Jahnssonin Säätiö (1965).

Arrow, K. J., "The Role of Securities in the Optimal Allocation of Risk-bearing", *Review of Economic Studies* (April 1964).

Bailey, M., Olson, M., and Wonnacot, P., "The Marginal Utility of Income Does Not Increase: Borrowing, Lending, and Friedman–Savage Gambles", *American Economic Review* (1980), pp. 372–379.

Bernoulli, D., "Exposition of a New Theory on the Measurement of Risk", *Econometrica* (January 1954).

Borch, K., *The Economics of Uncertainty*, Princeton, N.J.: Princeton University Press (1968).

Borch, K., "A Note on Utility and Attitudes to Risk", *Management Science* (July 1964).

Borch, K., and Mossin, J., *Risk and Uncertainty*, Proceedings of the Conference on Risk and Uncertainty of the International Economic Association, London: Macmillan (1968).

Briscoe, G., Samuels, J. M., and Smyth, D. J., "The Treatment of Risk in the Stock Market", *Journal of Finance* (September 1969).

Cohn, R. A., Lewellen, W. G., Lease, R. C., and Schlarbaum, G. G., "Individual Investor Risk Aversion and Investment Portfolio Composition", *Journal of Finance* (May 1975).

Debreu, G., *Theory of Value: An Axiomatic Analysis of Economic Equilibrium*, New York: Wiley (1959).

Diamond, P., and Stiglitz, J., "Increases in Risk and in Risk Aversion", *Journal of Economic Theory* (July 1967).

Durand, D., "Growth Stocks and the Petersburg Paradox", *Journal of Finance* (September 1957).

Edwards, W., and Tversky, A., *Decision Making*, Harmondsworth, England: Penguin Books (1967).

Ellsburg, D., "Classic and Current Notions of 'Measurable Utility'", *Economic Journal* (September 1954).

Ellsburg, D., "Risk, Ambiguity and the Savage Axioms", *Quarterly Journal of Economics* (November 1961).

Engelbrecht, R., "A Note on Multivariate Risk and Separable Utility Functions", *Management Science* (June 1977).

Fellner, W. J., *Probability and Profit*, Homewood, Illinois: Irwin (1965).

Friedman, M., and Savage, L. J., "The Expected Utility Hypothesis and the Measurability of Utility", *Journal of Political Economy* (December 1952).

Friedman, M., and Savage, L. J., "The Utility Analysis of Choices Involving Risk", *Journal of Political Economy* (August 1948).

Graves, P. E., "Relative Risk Aversion: Increasing or Decreasing?" *Journal of Financial and Quantitative Analysis* (June 1979).

Hakansson, N., "Friedman–Savage Utility Functions Consistent with Risk Aversion", *Quarterly Journal of Economics* (August 1970).

Hirshleifer, J., "Investment Decisions Under Uncertainty: Applications of the State-Preference Approach", *Quarterly Journal of Economics* (May 1966).

Hirshleifer, J., "Investment Decision Under Uncertainty: Choice-Theoretic Approaches", *Quarterly Journal of Economics* (November 1965).

Hirshleifer, J., *Investment, Interest and Capital*, Englewood Cliffs, N.J.: Prentice-Hall (1969).

Kaplansky, I., "A Common Error Concerning Kurtosis", *Journal of the American Statistical Association* (June 1945).

Keynes, J. M., *Essays in Biography* (new edition with three additional essays), edited by Geoffrey Keynes. New York: Horizon Press (1951).

Kihlstrom, R. E., and Laffont, J. J., "A General Equilibrium Entrepreneurial Theory of Firm Formation Based on Risk Aversion", *Journal of Political Economy* (August 1979).

Knight, F. H., *Risk, Uncertainty and Profit*, Boston and New York: Houghton Mifflin (1921).

Lease, R. C., Lewellen, W. G., and Schlarbaum, G. G., "The Individual Investor: Attributes and Attitudes", *Journal of Finance* (May 1974).

Levy, H., "A Utility Function Depending on the First Three Moments", *Journal of Finance* (September 1969).

Luce, R. D., and Raiffa, H., *Games and Decisions*, New York: Wiley (1957).

Markowitz, H. M., *Portfolio Selection*, New York: Wiley (1959).

Markowitz, H. M., "The Utility of Wealth", *Journal of Political Economy* (1952).

Menger, K., "Das Unsicherheitsmoment in Der Wertlehre", *Zeitschrift für Nationalökonomie* (1934). An English translation, "The Role of Uncertainty in Economics", appears in M. Shubik (editor), *Essays in Mathematical Economics in Honor of Oskar Morgenstern*, Princeton, N.J.: Princeton University Press (1967).

Meyer, J., "Mean Variance Efficient Sets and Expected Utility", *Journal of Finance* (December 1979).

Miller, S. M., "Measures of Risk Aversion: Some Clarifying Comments", *Journal of Financial and Quantitative Analysis* (June 1975).

Moore, P. G., and Thomas, H., "Measuring Uncertainty", *Omega* (December 1975).

Mossin, J., *Theory of Financial Markets*, Englewood Cliffs, N.J.: Prentice-Hall (1973).

Mosteller, F., and Nogee, P., "An Experimental Measurement of Utility", *Journal of Political Economy* (October 1951).

Myers, S. C., "A Time-State-Preference Model of Security Valuation", *Journal of Financial and Quantitative Analysis* (March 1968).

Peles, Y., "A Note on Risk and the Theory of Asset Value", *Journal of Financial and Quantitative Analysis* (January 1971).

Pratt, J. W., "Risk Aversion in the Small and in the Large", *Econometrica* (January–April 1964).

Raiffa, H., *Decision Analysis*, Reading, Mass.: Addison-Wesley (1968).

Ramsey, F. P., "Truth and Probability", in *The Foundations of Mathematics and Other Logical Essays*, London: K. Paul, Trench, Trubner & Co. (1931).

Richard, S. E., "Multivariate Risk Aversion, Utility Independence and Separable Utility Functions", *Management Science* (September 1975).

Robichek, A. A., "Risk and the Value of Securities", *Journal of Financial and Quantitative Analysis* (December 1969).

Rosett, R. N., "Measuring the Perception of Risk", in *Risk and Uncertainty*, edited by Karl Borch and Jan Mossin, London: Macmillan (1968).

Savage, L. J., *The Foundations of Statistics*, New York: Wiley (1954).

Senneti, J. J., "Bernoulli, Sharpe, Financial Risk and the Petersburg Paradox", *Journal of Finance* (June 1976).

Sharpe, W. F., "Risk Aversion in the Stock Market: Some Empirical Evidence", *Journal of Finance* (September 1965).

Swalm, R. O., "Utility Theory—Insights into Risk Taking", *Harvard Business Review* (December 1966).

von Neumann, J., and Morgenstern, O., *Theory of Games and Economic Behavior*, 2nd ed., Princeton, N.J.: Princeton University Press (1947).

Williams, J. T., "A Note on Indifference Curves in the Mean-variance Model", *Journal of Financial and Quantitative Analysis* (March 1977).

Wippern, R., "Utility Implications of Portfolio Selections and Performance Appraisal Models", *Journal of Financial and Quantitative Analysis* (June 1971).

Yaari, M. E., "Convexity in the Theory of Choice Under Risk", *Quarterly Journal of Economics* (May 1965).

Zeckhauser, R., and Keeler, E., "Another Type of Risk Aversion", *Econometrica* (September 1970).

# 6

# The Efficiency Analysis of Investments Under Uncertainty: Stochastic Dominance Rules

In this chapter we develop appropriate investment criteria for the three alternative risk-choice situations noted at the end of the previous chapter. We initially assume that no information whatsoever is available on the shape of the utility function, apart from the fact that it is non-decreasing: $U(R)$ may be concave everywhere, or it may include both concave and convex sections. Within this entirely general framework we define an appropriate efficiency criterion which can be used to effect a preliminary screening of alternative investments by all investors. Next we assume the availability of additional information and develop an appropriate criterion for risk averters, that is, for the case in which utility functions are assumed to be concave throughout the relevant range. Intuitively it is almost obvious that the second criterion will permit us to make a more sensitive, but less general, selection of investments compared to the first rule. Finally, we add the assumption that the third derivative of the utility function is positive. In this way we obtain a third criterion which is appropriate to all risk averters with a decreasing absolute risk aversion.

## 6.1    The Concept of an Efficiency Criterion

Before beginning the analysis, let us define a number of basic concepts which we shall be using throughout this and the next few chapters. An *efficiency criterion* is a decision rule for dividing all potential investment options into two mutually exclusive sets: an *efficient* set or group and an *inefficient* set or group. The former set contains all of the desirable alternatives for a particular class of investors. Using an efficiency criterion, we can be certain that all individuals belonging to the class being analyzed will make their final choice from the efficient group. Conversely, we can be equally certain that no individual having the assumed type of utility function will choose an option from the inefficient set. Thus an efficiency criterion is a rule for effecting a preliminary screening of investments, whereby we are able to reduce the number of relevant alternatives facing the particular class of investors by an initial elimination of all undesirable (or inefficient) options.

The concept of an efficiency criterion is sufficiently important (and perhaps sufficiently vague as well) to warrant some clarification. Let us consider the following very unrealistic and very untypical criterion. Assume a class of investors ("the Plus Fivers") who prefer a risky option $F$ to a risky option $G$ if and only if

$$E_F(R) \geqslant E_G(R) + 5$$

Here $R$ is the return on the option (a random variable), $E_F(R)$ is option $F$'s expected return and $E_G(R)$ is option $G$'s expected return. Let us further assume that no additional information regarding investors' tastes (utility functions) is available, so that this is the sole criterion available to effect our initial screening. We shall now illustrate the use of this efficiency criterion on the following alternative investment options:

| Option | Expected Return |
|--------|-----------------|
| A | 9 |
| B | 10 |
| C | 3 |
| D | 6 |
| E | 11 |

Recall that our problem is to use the efficiency criterion to identify the efficient and non-efficient groups for our assumed "Plus Fiver" class of investors.

We start by comparing options $A$ and $B$. Since the expected return of the former, 9, is less than that of the latter, 10, $A$ is clearly *not* preferable to $B$. What about the reverse: perhaps $B$ is preferable to $A$, since it has the larger expected return? However, since our efficiency criterion requires a five-point spread between expected returns, a clear-cut preference cannot be established in this case either, and therefore we go on to compare $A$ and $C$:

$$E_A(R) > E_C(R) + 5$$

that is,

$$9 > 3 + 5$$

In this case option $A$ with an expected return of 9 is clearly preferable to option $C$ whose expected return is only 3. Therefore option $C$ is relegated to the inefficient group since we can be absolutely certain that no "Plus Fiver" will ever choose such an option as long as he has the alternative of choosing option $A$.

We go on to compare $A$ and $D$, but once again the required five-point spread between the expected returns does not obtain so neither $A$ nor $D$ is eliminated. This is also true for the comparison of $A$ and $E$ since the spread is only two points.

This does not complete the efficiency analysis. Since we must compare *all possible pairs* of investments, we go on to consider $B$. We have already compared $B$ with $A$, and since $C$ has already been eliminated from the efficient set[1] there is no need to compare $B$ and $C$. We go on to compare $B$ with $D$ and $E$, and the reader can verify that no elimination takes place. There now remains only one more comparison, that between $D$ and $E$. In this case the respective expected returns are 6 and 11, and

$$E_E(R) = E_D(R) + 5$$

Since our efficiency criterion is defined in terms of a five-point spread, option $D$ is eliminated from the efficient set.

Thus our hypothetical example results in the following partition: (a) an efficient set comprised of options $A$, $B$, and $E$; and (b) an inefficient set comprised of options $C$ and $D$. Without further information regarding their tastes we cannot be certain which alternative option a "Plus Fiver" will choose, but we may be absolutely certain that it will not be $C$ or $D$. Of course this particular division into efficient and inefficient groups is appropriate only for our "Plus Fiver" class of investors, but it does illustrate the general logic which underlies the efficiency analysis of investment choice.

In principle we can devise efficiency criteria for many other more meaningful classes of investors, for example risk averters, and by using such criteria identify the efficient subset of options out of which *all* risk averters will make their final choice. However, unless further information is available we cannot tell which of the options included in the efficient group will be selected. Moreover, there is no reason why all risk averters should necessarily select the same option from the group. It is possible (and in fact quite likely) that different individuals will choose different options, according to their individual preferences. Thus, even though we know that all of these investors have concave utility functions, the particular form of function may vary from individual to individual.

For example, consider the following forms, all of which, as we saw in previous chapters, meet the risk aversion requirements (they are all concave if we assume $a > 0$ and $b < 0$):[2]

$$U(R) = a\sqrt{R}; \quad U(R) = aR + bR^2; \quad U(R) = a \log R$$

Since the final choice among the efficient options will be made in accordance with the expected utility of the alternatives, it is possible, and in fact quite probable, that the option which maximizes the expected utility for an investor with a quadratic utility function may differ from that option which maximizes the expected utility of a risk-averse individual with a logarithmic utility function.

An individual investor's final selection from the efficient group will be referred to as the *optimal investment*, that is, the option which maximizes that individual's expected utility. From this definition it is obvious that the optimal investment may vary from one investor to another depending on individual tastes. However it is also possible for several investors to choose the same optimal option.

---

[1] It is a matter of indifference whether a particular option is eliminated by more than one alternative.
[2] In this chapter and throughout the rest of the book the argument of the utility function is specifically the (gross) return $R$, rather than the general terminal wealth variable $x$ used in Chapters 4 and 5.

To summarize, the investment decision among risky alternatives can be dichotomized into two steps: First, we reduce the number of investment alternatives by constructing an efficient set of options using an efficiency criterion appropriate for a given class of investors. Second, the individual makes his final choice in accordance with his own particular preferences. For the remainder of this chapter we shall be concerned with the first step, the construction of efficiency criteria for different classes of individual investors.

## 6.2    First Degree Stochastic Dominance (FSD): A General Criterion

The degree to which an efficiency criterion can reduce the size of the efficient group depends on the amount of available information regarding the investors to be studied. Frequently, however, very little information is available regarding investors' tastes, and as a result, we must construct our efficiency criteria on the basis of investors' presumed, rather than observed, preferences. For example, a group of efficient options might be constructed on the assumption that investors have logarithmic utility functions. Obviously, in this instance, our conclusions will be relevant only for those investors for which this assumption holds true. But when an efficiency criterion is based on the investors' assumed preferences, it is possible that only few investors will fulfill the particular assumption that has been made. It is even possible that no investors have logarithmic utility functions. In this extreme case the whole exercise is pointless, for we have constructed a group of efficient portfolios based on an assumption which does not reflect real investors' tastes, and therefore cannot be expected to explain their behavior. Clearly, the general validity and applicability of a criterion depend on the appropriateness of the underlying assumptions regarding investors' tastes.

In this section we shall try to devise an efficiency criterion of very broad applicability. We shall consider the most general case when investors are assumed to have no systematic preferences with respect to risk; no restrictions are placed on investors' utility functions beyond the reasonable assumption that they be nondecreasing with respect to the returns $R$. This means that the utility functions' first derivatives cannot be negative. This assumption, as we have already seen, is appropriate for risk lovers as well as for risk averters since the utility function can be either convex or concave. Moreover, in keeping with the Friedman–Savage hypothesis, an individual investor's utility function can have both convex and concave segments and still be included in this set. Our sole restriction is that investors behave consistently in the sense that, other things being equal, they must always prefer more money to less.

Now consider two investment options $F$ and $G$ represented by distributions of the net return $R$ (a random variable). Option $F$ is clearly preferable to option $G$ if and only if

$$E_F U(R) > E_G U(R)$$

for every utility function belonging to the set of nondecreasing functions. If the expected utility of option $F$ is greater than that of option $G$ for all investors independent of their attitudes towards risk, we can also conclude that no investor whose utility function is included in the set of all nondecreasing functions will ever choose option $G$, that is, option $G$ can safely be relegated to the inefficient group. When option $F$ eliminates another option $G$, using an efficiency criterion appropriate for a given class of investors, we shall say that $F$ *dominates* $G$.

In our example, $F$ dominates $G$ if and only if $E_F U(R) > E_G U(R)$. This result can be generalized by the following First Degree Stochastic Dominance (FSD) rule:

> **FSD Rule:** Given two cumulative probability distributions[3] $F$ and $G$, an option $F$ will be preferred over a second option $G$ by FSD, independent of the concavity or convexity of the utility function, if $F(R) \leqslant G(R)$ for all returns $R$, on the condition that for at least one value of $R$ $(R = R_0)$ the strong inequality holds, $F(R_0) < G(R_0)$.

The stipulation that the strong inequality must hold for at least one value of $R$ is tantamount to the requirement that the two distributions are *not* identical. Without this restriction, it is conceivable that $F(R) = G(R)$ for every value of $R$, in which case the rational investor would be indifferent between the two options, since they have identical probability distributions.

The rule is called *First Degree Stochastic Dominance* since we make only an assumption of first order on investors' preferences (namely that $U'(R) \geqslant 0$, or the first derivative of the utility function is non-negative).

A formal mathematical proof that the FSD criterion constitutes the appropriate efficiency criterion for all rational investors independent of their attitude toward risk is given in Appendix 6.1. But the meaning of FSD can best be brought out by means of a simple graphical analysis. FSD is equivalent to the requirement that the two cumulative probability distributions do not intersect; a necessary and sufficient condition for one option to dominate another option, therefore, is that the cumulative probability distributions do not intersect. Thus the entire cumulative distribution of one option must lie to the right of the distribution of the second option.

Figure 6.1 presents the cumulative distributions of four potential investment options: $a$, $b$, $c$, and $d$. Clearly option $a$ dominates option $b$, since the *entire* cumulative distribution of investment $a$ lies to the right of that of $b$, which means that FSD is fulfilled. If we denote the cumulative distribution of option $a$ as $F_a(R)$ and that of $b$ as $F_b(R)$, we can readily see from the diagram that for all values of $R$ the relationship $F_a(R) \leqslant F_b(R)$ always holds. Similarly, options $c$ and $d$ are also preferable to option $b$ since $F_c(R) \leqslant F_b(R)$ and $F_d(R) \leqslant F_b(R)$ for all values of $R$.[4] By the same token, we can see that option $c$ is also preferable to option $a$. Although the two cumulative distributions have one section in common, they do not intersect and there are other values of $R$

---

[3] The cumulative distribution $F(R)$ is the probability to obtain values of a random variable $R$ not exceeding some specific value $R_0$, i.e., $F(R) = \Pr(R \leqslant R_0)$. For more details, see the Statistical Supplement at the end of the book and also the numerical examples throughout this chapter.

[4] To simplify the discussion in the text, we shall take for granted the stipulation that for at least one value of $R$ the strong inequality must hold.

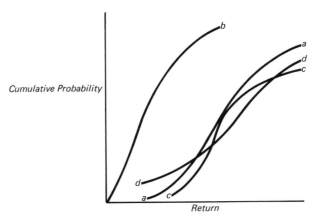

**Figure 6.1**

(one would be sufficient) where the distribution $c$ lies to the right of the distribution $a$. Thus, over the entire range of $R$, FSD holds: $F_c(R) \leqslant F_a(R)$, and option $c$ dominates option $a$. Distribution $d$, on the other hand, intersects both $c$ and $a$, so that FSD does not hold between either $d$ and $c$ or $d$ and $a$.

This presentation of FSD can also help to clarify some of the general concepts defined in the previous section of this chapter. We have used the FSD rule, as formulated above, in order to divide all potential options into two mutually exclusive groups: an efficient set comprising investments $c$ and $d$ and an inefficient set comprising investments $a$ and $b$. Not all the investment options of the efficient group are necessarily preferable to a given inefficient investment, but it should be emphasized that every option included in the inefficient group is dominated by at least one investment in the efficient group. From Figure 6.1 we can readily verify that while option $c$ dominates both of the inefficient options $a$ and $b$, option $d$, which is also included in the efficient set, does *not* dominate option $a$. Similarly we can also verify from Figure 6.1 that with respect to each of the options included in the efficient set, no preferred investment can be found in either the efficient or inefficient groups.

### 6.2.1  An Intuitive Interpretation of the FSD Criterion

We have defined FSD in terms of cumulative probability distributions and have stipulated that an option $F$ dominates an option $G$ if $F(R) \leqslant G(R)$. But this condition is equivalent to the requirement that the probability of receiving a return lower than some given amount, for example $k$, will always be *smaller* for option $F$ than for option $G$. Thus since $F(k) \leqslant G(k)$, it follows that

$$\text{Pr}_F(R \leqslant k) \leqslant \text{Pr}_G(R \leqslant k)$$

where Pr denotes probability. We can also rewrite FSD as follows: For an option $F$ to be preferred to an option $G$ the following relationship must hold for all values of $R$:[5]

$$1 - F(R) \geqslant 1 - G(R)$$

The expression $1 - F(R)$ is equivalent to the probability of receiving a return which is *greater* than or equal to a given $R$. Thus for option $F$ to dominate option $G$, the probability of receiving a return greater than or equal to some level $k$ must always be higher in option $F$ than in option $G$. Since the chances of earning a higher return are *always* greater, option $F$ will be preferred by risk averters and risk lovers alike.

### 6.2.2   The Concept of an Optimal Efficiency Criterion

Now that we have clarified the meaning of an efficiency criterion and an efficient set, let us define the concept of an *optimal* efficiency criterion.[6]

An optimal efficiency criterion is one which, given specific assumptions regarding investors' tastes, ensures a minimal efficient set.

In the previous section we developed a general efficiency criterion, $F(R) \leqslant G(R)$, which is appropriate for risk averters and risk lovers alike. Now let us assume that we are given another (arbitrary) efficiency criterion according to which an option $F$ is preferable to an option $G$ if and only if $F(R) + k \leqslant G(R)$ for all values of $R$ not exceeding some arbitrary finite value $M$ and $F(R) \leqslant G(R)$ for $R > M$;[7] here $k$ denotes any positive number, however small. This arbitrary criterion will be referred to as the "$k$ criterion" and it is illustrated graphically in Figure 6.2, which sets out the cumulative probability distributions of four investment options, $a$, $b$, $c$, and $d$. Invoking the FSD rule, it is clear that investments $c$ and $d$ comprise the efficient set while options $a$ and $b$ are relegated to the inefficient group. (Both $c$ and $d$ dominate options $a$ and $b$.) Let us now examine the composition of the efficient group using the arbitrary "$k$ criterion". Since options $c$ and $d$ intersect there can be no doubt that they must be included in the efficient group; there exists a value of $R(R < M)$ for which the cumulative probabilities of these two options are equal so that the "$k$ criterion" cannot hold. If we let $R_0$ denote the point of intersection of the two probability distributions, then

$$F_c(R_0) = F_d(R_0)$$

which also implies that

$$F_c(R_0) + k > F_d(R_0)$$

---

[5] We defined FSD as $F(R) \leqslant G(R)$. If we multiply both sides of the inequality by $-1$ and add 1, we obtain $1 - F(R) \geqslant 1 - G(R)$.

[6] Care should be taken not to confuse the *optimal efficiency criterion*, that is, the criterion which minimizes the efficient set for a given class of investors, with the *optimal investment option*, that is, the option which maximizes the expected utility of a particular investor.

[7] We limit the range to $R \leqslant M$ since for $R = \infty$ we always have $F(R) = G(R) = 1$ so that for $R = \infty$ the inequality $F(R) + k \leqslant G(R)$ cannot hold for a positive $k$ $(k > 0)$.

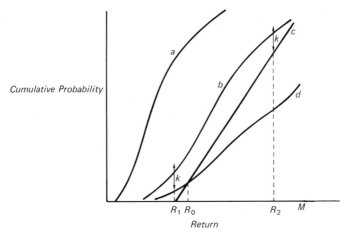

**Figure 6.2**

so that option $c$ is *not* preferable to $d$. In similar fashion it can be shown that option $d$ does not dominate option $c$ by the "$k$ criterion". At the same time a brief glance at Figure 6.2 shows that by the "$k$ criterion" option $b$ is also included in the efficient group, since it is dominated neither by option $d$ nor by option $c$. The required inequality between $b$ and $d$ does not hold at point $R_1$, while the required inequality between option $b$ and $c$ does not hold at point $R_2$:

$$F_d(R_1) + k > F_b(R_1)$$

and

$$F_c(R_2) + k > F_b(R_2)$$

From the above we can conclude that while the FSD efficient set comprises two investments, $c$ and $d$, the "$k$ criterion" efficient set includes three investments, $d$, $b$, and $c$. Option $a$ is not included in the efficient sets of either criterion.

What is the significant difference between the two criteria? Both are legitimate criteria for determining an efficient investment group. Moreover, if the "$k$ criterion" holds for any two investment options, $F$ and $G$, then FSD must also hold, since for all values of $R$, recalling that $k > 0$,

$$F(R) + k \leqslant G(R) \text{ implies } F(R) \leqslant G(R).$$

This means that any investment included in the FSD efficient group is necessarily also included in the "$k$ criterion" efficient set. Hence there is no danger that FSD efficient investments may be excluded. The converse, however, does not necessarily hold: it is quite conceivable that the "$k$ criterion" efficient set may include "superfluous" investments, which from the given information on investors' preferences might have been eliminated. Thus in our example option $b$ is included in the efficient group by the "$k$ criterion", but is eliminated by FSD. Accordingly the FSD criterion is to be preferred over the arbitrary "$k$ criterion", since given the single assumption that investors prefer more to less wealth ($U'(R) \geqslant 0$) the FSD rule reduces the efficient group of investments to the minimum.

This result can be generalized, and in Appendix 6.1, at the end of this chapter, a formal proof is presented of the *optimality* of the FSD rule. Any alternative criterion (for example, the "$k$ criterion") will be either too "poor" or too "rich" in efficient options. In the former case, a criterion may exclude options which are efficient, given the available information on investors' utility functions; in the latter instance, the criterion may include investments which should have been eliminated. The optimality of the FSD rule can be clarified by considering a number of specific examples.

EXAMPLE 1

Let us consider the two alternative investment options, $A$ and $B$, presented in Table 6.1.

A comparison of investments $A$ and $B$ clearly shows that option $A$ is preferable, since option $A$ offers an equal probability of double the returns from option $B$. This is equivalent to confronting an individual with the choice of betting on either of two unbiased roulette wheels, one of which pays the winner double the amount of the other for the same wager. Clearly all rational people would choose to play on the roulette wheel having the equal probability of larger payoffs, represented by alternative $A$, since common sense alone suffices to tell us that this option is preferable.

Let us check to see if the FSD rule reflects this common sense result, that is, if

$$F_A(R) \leqslant F_B(R)$$

for all values of $R$. The cumulative probability distributions appear in Table 6.1, and these data are used to construct Table 6.2, which sets out the relevant data for comparing the cumulative probability functions of the two options. The left-hand column of Table 6.2 includes all attainable returns from options $A$ and $B$ as well as several values of returns which are *not* attainable in either of the options. The reader can verify that the cumulative probability distributions are not affected by considering the unattainable levels of returns. In other words, the cumulative probability distribution of a *discrete* random variable is a step function, remaining constant for those values of $R$ which have a zero probability and rising in jump fashion at those values of $R$ for which the probability is positive.

**Table 6.1**

| | Option A | | | | Option B | |
|---|---|---|---|---|---|---|
| Probability | Cumulative Probability $F_A$ | Return (R) | | Probability | Cumulative Probability $F_B$ | Return (R) |
| 1/3 | 1/3 | 10 | | 1/3 | 1/3 | 5 |
| 1/3 | 2/3 | 20 | | 1/3 | 2/3 | 10 |
| 1/3 | 1 | 30 | | 1/3 | 1 | 15 |

**Table 6.2**

| Return (R) | Cumulative Probability of Option B $F_B$ | Cumulative Probability of Option A $F_A$ | $F_B$ Minus $F_A$ |
|---|---|---|---|
| −5 | 0 | 0 | 0 |
| 0 | 0 | 0 | 0 |
| 5 | 1/3 | 0 | 1/3 |
| 7 | 1/3 | 0 | 1/3 |
| 10 | 2/3 | 1/3 | 1/3 |
| 12 | 2/3 | 1/3 | 1/3 |
| 15 | 1 | 1/3 | 2/3 |
| 17 | 1 | 1/3 | 2/3 |
| 20 | 1 | 2/3 | 1/3 |
| 22 | 1 | 2/3 | 1/3 |
| 25 | 1 | 2/3 | 1/3 |
| 28 | 1 | 2/3 | 1/3 |
| 30 | 1 | 1 | 0 |
| 35 | 1 | 1 | 0 |

From the right-hand column of Table 6.2, we can see that for all levels of $R$, $F_A(R) \leqslant F_B(R)$. This can also be seen in Figure 6.3, which plots the cumulative probability distribution functions for the two options. The roulette wheel with the smaller returns is denoted by $B$ and the other alternative by $A$. Since $A$ lies to the right of $B$, the FSD rule is fulfilled, and option $A$ (the roulette wheel with the larger returns) is preferable to $B$, independent of the shape of the utility function, which is as it should be.

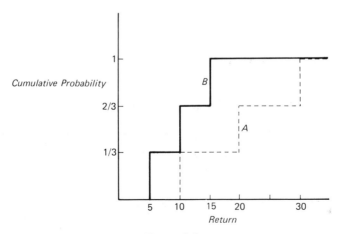

**Figure 6.3**

EXAMPLE 2

Since the roulette wheel example appears not only contrived but perhaps trivial as well, it might be argued that the FSD rule is superfluous and that common sense alone will suffice. While this may be true for the roulette wheel, Table 6.3 presents a less transparent example. In this example it is no longer intuitively obvious that one of the options should be preferred to the other. But as Figure 6.4 clearly shows, option *A* fulfills the FSD criterion and represents the preferable alternative for all investors, independent of their attitudes toward risk.

EXAMPLE 3

Let us assume a third example which is much closer to reality. Table 6.4 presents the annual *gross* returns to investors (per $100 of investment) for eight alternative investment options during the past eight years. These data were used to calculate the expected net return for each option.[8]

The data are set out in terms of dollar returns rather than in percentages, since

**Table 6.3**

| Option A | | | Option B | |
|---|---|---|---|---|
| Probability | Return (R) | | Probability | Return (R) |
| 1/4 | 5 | | 1/2 | 5 |
| 1/4 | 6 | | 1/4 | 12 |
| 1/2 | 20 | | 1/4 | 20 |

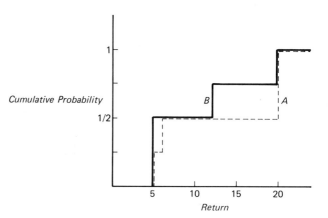

**Figure 6.4**

---

[8] For simplicity we use unadjusted historical data on the returns to investors to estimate the expected return. Clearly, an investment analyst might desire to change this expectation in keeping with his analysis of the company's prospects. Similarly a time period of eight years was chosen arbitrarily in order to illustrate the efficiency analysis.

**Table 6.4**
**Gross Annual Returns\* for Eight Hypothetical Investment Options (in dollars)**

| Year | Option | | | | | | | |
|------|------|------|------|------|------|------|------|------|
|      | 1 | 2 | 3 | 4 | 5 | 6 | 7 | 8 |
| 1976 | 90 | 70 | 160 | 145 | 60 | 30 | 150 | 110 |
| 1977 | 110 | 90 | 170 | 145 | 60 | 80 | 170 | 140 |
| 1978 | 110 | 70 | 170 | 120 | 20 | 80 | 170 | 140 |
| 1979 | 110 | 90 | 170 | 190 | 40 | 30 | 160 | 160 |
| 1980 | 110 | 130 | 170 | 120 | 60 | 80 | 170 | 160 |
| 1981 | 90 | 70 | 170 | 145 | 70 | 140 | 170 | 160 |
| 1982 | 110 | 130 | 160 | 190 | 120 | 80 | 180 | 160 |
| 1983 | 110 | 70 | 170 | 145 | 70 | 30 | 170 | 160 |
| Expected Net Return | 5.00 | −10.00 | 67.50 | 50.00 | −37.50 | −31.25 | 67.50 | 48.75 |

\* The annual returns were calculated per $100 of investment.

utility functions are defined in terms of absolute returns. In order to ensure comparability we calculate the return per $100 of investment.[9] Thus a return of 10% in a given year is entered in Table 6.4 as a gross return of $110; a negative rate of return of −20% is entered as a gross return of $80.

In the absence of any additional information we shall assume that the investor attributes a probability of 1/8 to each of the past outcomes, which enables us to set out the cumulative probability distributions for each of the eight alternatives (see Table 6.5). These distributions are plotted in Figure 6.5. Applying the FSD rule to the diagram we find that investment options 3, 4, and 7 comprise the efficient set. All the other options do not fulfill the FSD rule and can be relegated to the inefficient group. For example, option 8 is eliminated by option 7, which dominates it.

Given the assumption that investors prefer more to less wealth, and without stipulating whether they are risk averters or risk lovers, we have reduced the feasible set to the above three efficient options. In other words, all investors, irrespective of the shape of their utility functions, will make one of these efficient alternatives their final, or optimal, choice. The particular option chosen depends on an investor's tastes (utility function). In Table 6.6 we calculated the expected utility for each of the three efficient investments[10] using the following utility function:

$$U(R) = 100 + 100 \log R,$$

where $R$ is the gross return. The maximum expectation is that of option 3 (expected

[9] It should be recalled that we assume an efficient market in which an individual investor is small relative to the market as a whole. As a result his sell and buy orders do not affect securities' prices so that it makes no difference, institutional considerations aside, if we assume an investment of $100 or of $1,000.

[10] There is no need to calculate the expected utility of the inefficient options since each of their expectations is, by definition, below the expectation of at least one of the efficient options.

**Table 6.5**
**Cumulative Probability Distributions for Eight Hypothetical Investment Options \***

| Gross Return | $F_1$ | $F_2$ | $F_3$ | $F_4$ | $F_5$ | $F_6$ | $F_7$ | $F_8$ |
|---|---|---|---|---|---|---|---|---|
| 20 | 0 | 0 | 0 | 0 | 1/8 | 0 | 0 | 0 |
| 30 | 0 | 0 | 0 | 0 | 1/8 | 3/8 | 0 | 0 |
| 40 | 0 | 0 | 0 | 0 | 2/8 | 3/8 | 0 | 0 |
| 60 | 0 | 0 | 0 | 0 | 5/8 | 3/8 | 0 | 0 |
| 70 | 0 | 4/8 | 0 | 0 | 7/8 | 3/8 | 0 | 0 |
| 80 | 0 | 4/8 | 0 | 0 | 7/8 | 7/8 | 0 | 0 |
| 90 | 2/8 | 6/8 | 0 | 0 | 7/8 | 7/8 | 0 | 0 |
| 110 | 1 | 6/8 | 0 | 0 | 7/8 | 7/8 | 0 | 1/8 |
| 120 | 1 | 6/8 | 0 | 2/8 | 1 | 7/8 | 0 | 1/8 |
| 130 | 1 | 1 | 0 | 2/8 | 1 | 7/8 | 0 | 1/8 |
| 140 | 1 | 1 | 0 | 2/8 | 1 | 1 | 0 | 3/8 |
| 145 | 1 | 1 | 0 | 6/8 | 1 | 1 | 0 | 3/8 |
| 150 | 1 | 1 | 0 | 6/8 | 1 | 1 | 1/8 | 3/8 |
| 160 | 1 | 1 | 2/8 | 6/8 | 1 | 1 | 2/8 | 1 |
| 170 | 1 | 1 | 1 | 6/8 | 1 | 1 | 7/8 | 1 |
| 180 | 1 | 1 | 1 | 6/8 | 1 | 1 | 1 | 1 |
| 190 | 1 | 1 | 1 | 1 | 1 | 1 | 1 | 1 |

\* The symbol $F_i(i = 1, 2, \ldots, 8)$ denotes the cumulative probability distribution of the $i$th investment option.

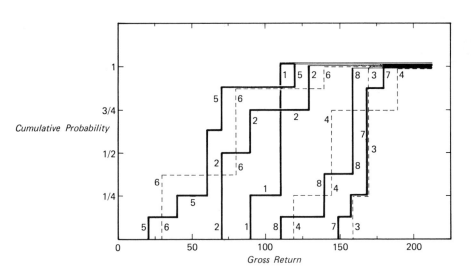

**Figure 6.5**

**Table 6.6**
**Annual Gross Returns, Utilities, and Expected Utilities of Three Efficient Options***

| Option 3 | | Option 4 | | Option 7 | |
|---|---|---|---|---|---|
| Utility | Return R | Utility | Return R | Utility | Return R |
| 320.41 | 160 | 316.14 | 145 | 317.61 | 150 |
| 323.04 | 170 | 316.14 | 145 | 323.04 | 170 |
| 323.04 | 170 | 307.92 | 120 | 323.04 | 170 |
| 323.04 | 170 | 327.88 | 190 | 320.41 | 160 |
| 323.04 | 170 | 307.92 | 120 | 323.04 | 170 |
| 323.04 | 170 | 316.14 | 145 | 323.04 | 170 |
| 320.41 | 160 | 327.88 | 190 | 325.53 | 180 |
| 323.04 | 170 | 316.14 | 145 | 323.04 | 170 |
| $E_3U(R) = 322.38$ | | $E_4U(R) = 317.02$ | | $E_7U(R) = 322.34$ | |

* Utilities were calculated using the following utility function: $U(R) = 100 + 100 \log R$

utility $= 322.38$), which is the optimal investment for all investors having the specified utility function.

To demonstrate the dependence of the *optimal* investment choice on the particular utility function, we recalculated the expected utilities of the three efficient options using a different utility function:

$$U(R) = 10 + \frac{1}{100} R^2$$

**Table 6.7**
**Annual Gross Return, Utilities, and Expected Utilities of Three Efficient Options***

| Option 3 | | Option 4 | | Option 7 | |
|---|---|---|---|---|---|
| Utility | Return R | Utility | Return R | Utility | Return R |
| 266 | 160 | 220.25 | 145 | 235 | 150 |
| 299 | 170 | 220.25 | 145 | 299 | 170 |
| 299 | 170 | 154.00 | 120 | 299 | 170 |
| 299 | 170 | 371.00 | 190 | 266 | 160 |
| 299 | 170 | 154.00 | 120 | 299 | 170 |
| 229 | 170 | 220.25 | 145 | 299 | 170 |
| 266 | 160 | 371.00 | 190 | 334 | 180 |
| 299 | 170 | 220.25 | 145 | 299 | 170 |
| $E_3U(R) = 290.75$ | | $E_4U(R) = 241.38$ | | $E_7U(R) = 291.25$ | |

* Utilities were calculated using the following utility function: $U(R) = 10 + \frac{1}{100} R^2$

Table 6.7 sets out the relevant data using this utility function. In this case option 7 is the optimal investment, that is, the alternative which maximizes expected utility.

We see from Example 3 that as the number of options increases, the screening for efficient options becomes more complicated. The job is best left to the computer. A useful computer program that constructs Stochastic Dominance efficient sets is given in Appendix 6.3. This program is based on a very simple algorithm (also described in Appendix 6.3) that can be "run manually", simulating the computer, to construct SD efficient sets when the number of options is still manageable.

### 6.2.3 The Relationship of the FSD Criterion to the First Two Distribution Moments

One of the most important characteristics of the probability distributions of all investment options is the expected return, or the first central moment of the distribution. When we refer to an investment's "profitability", we almost invariably have the expected return in mind. We turn now to the relationship of FSD to the expected return.

As we have already proved, an investment option $F$ dominates an alternative option $G$ by FSD *if and only if* the following relationship holds between the cumulative probability distributions:

$$F(R) \leqslant G(R)$$

The economic interpretation of this theorem is straightforward: for the family of all monotone *nondecreasing* utility functions, fulfillment of this criterion implies the following as well:

$$E_F U(R) \geqslant E_G U(R)$$

Thus if an option dominates another option by FSD, the expected utility of the former is no less than that of the latter for *all* investors, irrespective of their attitudes toward risk. The emphasis here is on *all* investors; the relationship *must* hold for all nondecreasing utility functions, independent of their shape. Thus, if we recall that the linear utility function $U(R) = R$ is also monotone nondecreasing, the above mentioned relationship between FSD and expected utility holds for the relationship between their expected returns as well:

$$E_F(R) \geqslant E_G(R)$$

that is, the expected return of $F$ must be no less than that of $G$.

A necessary condition for one option to be preferred to a second option by FSD is that the expected return of the preferred option be no less than the expected return of the second. This can be confirmed by looking at Table 6.4. For every inefficient option (investments 1, 2, 5, 6, and 8) there is at least one efficient option (investments 3, 4 and 7) which has a higher expected return.

The question which arises almost immediately is whether a similar systematic relationship can be found between the variances of the returns. Consider the three investment options given in Table 6.8; their cumulative probability distributions are drawn in Figure 6.6. From the diagram it is clear that, by FSD, investment $B$ dominates investment $C$, and option $A$ also is preferable to option $C$. The expected return of $C$ is lower than the expected returns of both $A$ and $B$, as required. With respect to the variance, however, no systematic relationship can be found: the variance of option $A$ is smaller than that of option $C$, while the variance of $B$ is greater than that of $C$. Thus, unlike the expected return, no necessary condition for dominance can be found regarding the second central moment, the variance. It follows that investments' expected returns, and not their variance, play the crucial role in determining efficiency by FSD.

An intuitive explanation for this phenomenon is not difficult to find. When defining FSD, we assumed that investors prefer more to less wealth, and therefore that they prefer higher expected returns. On the other hand we did *not* specify the investors' attitudes toward risk. The variance is an indicator of dispersion, and therefore an investor, other things being equal, will prefer a high variance if he is a risk lover, while a risk averter will prefer investments with a lower variance. Since FSD was designed to find the efficient set for risk lovers and risk averters alike, the variance does not play a clear-cut role in determining the preference order in this most general case.[11]

**Table 6.8**

| Option A | | Option B | | Option C | |
|---|---|---|---|---|---|
| Probability | Return | Probability | Return | Probability | Return |
| 1 | 10 | 1/2 | 6 | 1/2 | 3 |
| | | 1/2 | 18 | 1/2 | 9 |
| $E_A(R) = 10$ | | $E_B(R) = 12$ | | $E_C(R) = 6$ | |
| $Var_A(R) = 0$ | | $Var_B(R) = 36$ | | $Var_C(R) = 9$ | |

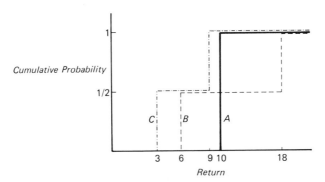

**Figure 6.6**

[11] We shall see that even if all investors are risk averters the variance still plays only a limited role in determining dominance.

### 6.3    Second Degree Stochastic Dominance (SSD): A Risk Aversion Criterion

As we pointed out in Chapter 5, there are two somewhat conflicting views regarding the shape of investors' utility functions. According to many economists an individual's utility function is necessarily concave, while according to others (in particular Friedman and Savage) it may contain convex as well as concave segments. In the preceding section we have presented a general efficiency criterion which corresponds to the Friedman–Savage view that the utility function may take any form provided only that the first derivative be non-negative. In this section we shall present an optimal efficiency criterion for those cases where investors are known to be risk averters.

Even if we had decisive theoretical and empirical evidence in support of the claim that utility functions generally contain convex sections with positive second derivatives, it would still pay to develop additional efficiency criteria for specific subgroups of investors. This point will become clear if we consider the following simple example. Let us assume that there are a million investors in the securities market; let us further assume that there is unequivocal proof that among them are risk lovers as well as risk averters, so that it cannot be presumed that an efficiency criterion which assumes concave utility functions will be appropriate for all investors. Clearly, it is the FSD rule which provides an optimal universally applicable criterion. But should a significant percentage of the investors, for example 70%, be risk averters, an additional screening using the SSD or risk aversion criterion can further reduce the relevant subset of efficient options, if not for all investors at least for a significant subgroup (700,000 in our hypothetical example).

Two things should be emphasized:

(a)    In developing additional criteria we do not mean to imply that the FSD rule should be replaced. On the contrary, it almost invariably pays to make an initial screening using FSD to eliminate options which are inefficient for *all* investors.

(b)    The stronger assumptions which underlie the risk aversion criterion will enable us to make a more sensitive preselection of investment options so that the efficient subset for risk averters can be expected to be smaller, and in most cases substantially smaller, than the efficient set derived using the FSD rule.[12]

If we again denote the cumulative probability distributions of two *different* investment options by $F$ and $G$, we obtain the following criterion for all risk averters, which is called the Second Degree Stochastic Dominance (SSD) rule.

**SSD Rule:** A necessary and sufficient condition for an option $F$ to be preferred over a second option $G$ by all risk averters is that the following relationship should

---

[12] The relative ability of these and other criteria to reduce the efficient set is tested empirically below.

hold for all $R$

$$\int_{-\infty}^{R} F(t)\,dt \leqslant \int_{-\infty}^{R} G(t)\,dt$$

or equivalently

$$\int_{-\infty}^{R} [G(t) - F(t)]\,dt \geqslant 0$$

with a strong inequality holding at least for some $R_0$.[13]

In this integral formulation of the SSD rule, it is assumed that the two options $F$ and $G$ are represented by continuous distributions. In case of discrete distributions $F$ and $G$, the integrals are replaced with sums, as will be demonstrated in the following examples.

This rule is called Second Degree Stochastic Dominance because the risk-aversion assumption is a second-order assumption on the investor preferences, using both the first and the second derivatives of the utility function ($U'' < 0$, in addition to $U' > 0$ assumed by FSD).

The integral over $F$ in the above formulation of the SSD rule represents the area *under* the cumulative distribution $F$ from $-\infty$ to some return $R$, and similarly for the integral over $G$. The integral over the difference $G - F$ represents the area from $-\infty$ to $R$ enclosed *between* the two cumulative distributions of $F$ and $G$ (taken with a + sign over the intervals where $F$ lies to the right of $G$, i.e., when $F(R) < G(R)$, and with a − sign over the intervals where $F$ lies to the left of $G$, i.e., when $F(R) > G(R)$). The SSD rule thus can be restated somewhat informally in the following terms:

**SSD Rule:** Option $F$ dominates option $G$ for all risk averters if and only if the area under the cumulative distribution of $F$ exceeds the area under the cumulative distribution of $G$ for all values of $R$ (equality of the areas for some $R$ is permissible), or equivalently if the cumulative area between the two distributions $F$ and $G$ remains non-negative for all values of $R$.

The meaning of SSD can readily be illustrated if we consider the two investment options $F$ and $G$ whose (continuous) cumulative probability distributions are drawn in Figure 6.7. According to the SSD rule, the cumulative probability distributions may intersect, but the *cumulative difference* between $G$ and $F$ must remain non-negative over

---

[13] A formal mathematical proof of the optimality of the Risk Aversion Criterion is given in Appendix 6.1. Thus, given the information that $U'(R) \geqslant 0$ and $U''(R) \leqslant 0$, no criterion can be developed to further reduce the subset of efficient investments resulting from a screening by the SSD rule without making additional assumptions regarding investors' utility functions and/or the probability distributions of returns.

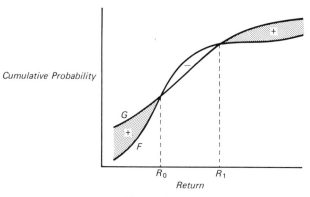

**Figure 6.7**

the entire domain of $R$. In Figure 6.7 the differences between the two distributions are marked with a plus sign where $F < G$, since the contribution to the integral is positive; and with a minus sign where $F > G$, since over this range the contribution to the integral is negative. A glance at the diagram shows that over the entire range of returns the *cumulative* area between the two distributions always remains positive, so that the SSD rule is fulfilled and option $F$ dominates option $G$ for all risk averters. This is true since up to the intersection point $R_0$ the distribution of $G$ lies above that of $F$ and therefore the area under $G$ exceeds the area under $F$. And while it is true that for the range between the two intersection points $R_0 < R < R_1$, $F$ lies above $G$, the preceding shaded area marked with a plus sign is greater than the area marked with a minus sign. Since beyond $R_1$, $G$ again exceeds $F$, the cumulative shaded areas *always* exceed the areas marked with a minus sign over the entire domain of $R$.

EXAMPLE 4
    Before we examine the general characteristics of SSD, let us apply it to the specific numerical example given in Table 6.9. From the data of this table we have computed the cumulative probability distributions for the two alternatives; these distributions are plotted in Figure 6.8. Since the two distributions intersect, both $F$ and $G$ are included in the FSD efficient set. But if we invoke the SSD rule, option $F$ is clearly preferable to

**Table 6.9**

| | Option F | | | Option G | |
| Return | Probability | Cumulative Probability | Return | Probability | Cumulative Probability |
|---|---|---|---|---|---|
| 1 | 1/4 | 1/4 | 1/2 | 3/16 | 3/16 |
| 2 | 1/4 | 1/2 | 3/2 | 3/16 | 6/16 |
| 9 | 1/4 | 3/4 | 5/2 | 4/16 | 10/16 |
| 10 | 1/4 | 1 | 7/2 | 3/16 | 13/16 |
| | | | 9/2 | 3/16 | 1 |

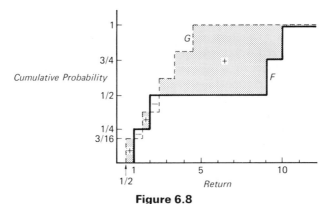

**Figure 6.8**

option $G$ since the cumulative difference between the two distributions is always non-negative. It is clear by inspection that the cumulative shaded area for which $F(R) < G(R)$ always exceeds the cumulative area for which $F(R) > G(R)$ over the entire domain of $R$. In other words, the cumulative area under $G$ is always greater than the cumulative area under $F$.

Of course it may not always be an easy matter to verify the dominance of one option over another by inspection, especially in cases where the probability distributions intersect a number of times. In such instances the area under the cumulative probability distributions can be calculated, as was done in Table 6.10. Up to a return of $\frac{1}{2}$, the area

**Table 6.10**
**Cumulative Area under $F$ and $G$ of Figure 6.8**

| Return | Cumulative Area under G | Cumulative Area under F | Cumulative Area under G − F |
|--------|-------------------------|-------------------------|------------------------------|
| 0 | 0 | 0 | 0 |
| 1/2 | 0 | 0 | 0 |
| 1 | 3/32 | 0 | 3/32 |
| 1 1/2 | 6/32 | 4/32 | 2/32 |
| 2 | 12/32 | 8/32 | 4/32 |
| 2 1/2 | 18/32 | 16/32 | 2/32 |
| 3 | 28/32 | 24/32 | 4/32 |
| 3 1/2 | 38/32 | 32/32 | 6/32 |
| 4 | 51/32 | 40/32 | 11/32 |
| 4 1/2 | 64/32 | 48/32 | 16/32 |
| 5 | 80/32 | 56/32 | 24/32 |
| 5 1/2 | 96/32 | 64/32 | 32/32 |
| 6 | 118/32 | 72/32 | 46/32 |
| 7 | 150/32 | 88/32 | 62/32 |
| 8 | 182/32 | 104/32 | 78/32 |
| 9 | 214/32 | 120/32 | 94/32 |
| 10 | 246/32 | 144/32 | 102/32 |
| 11 | 278/32 | 176/32 | 102/32 |

under both distributions (value of the integrals) is zero, as can readily be verified from Figure 6.8. Up to a return of 1, the cumulative area under $G$ is given by the first shaded rectangle marked with a plus sign. This rectangle has a base equal to 1/2 and a height (probability) equal to 3/16; therefore the area of the rectangle equals 3/32. The area under $F$ up to the same point is still zero. Up to a return of $1\frac{1}{2}$, an identical rectangle is added under $G$, so that the cumulative area becomes 6/32. The cumulative area under $F$ up to a return of $1\frac{1}{2}$ is given by a rectangle with a base of 1/2 and a height (probability) of 1/4; its area equals $1/8 = 4/32$. Thus the *difference* between the cumulative areas under $G$ and $F$ up to a return of 1 is equal to 3/32; up to a return of $1\frac{1}{2}$ the area under $G$ exceeds that under $F$ by 2/32, and so on for all possible values of return. A glance down the right-hand column of Table 6.10 verifies that the cumulative area under $G$ always exceeds that under $F$ at all possible levels of return, and therefore $F$ dominates $G$ by SSD.

The computer program and the algorithm described in Appendix 6.3 can be used to construct the SSD efficient set from any number of feasible options.

### 6.3.1   Some Basic Properties of the SSD Criterion

As was true for FSD, a necessary condition for the dominance of an option $F$ over an option $G$ by SSD is that the expected return of $F$ be greater than, or equal to, the expected return of $G$.[14] We have shown that $F$ dominates $G$ implies that

$$E_F U(R) \geqslant E_G U(R)$$

for *all* nondecreasing and in particular for all nondecreasing concave utility functions. However, since the linear utility function $U(R) = R$ is also concave, in the weak sense (recall that we require $U'' \leqslant 0$), it follows that

$$E_F(R) \geqslant E_G(R)$$

is a necessary condition for dominance by SSD.

Here again, the mean profitability plays a crucial role in determining the preference order. But despite the underlying assumption of risk aversion, a similar systematic preference for a smaller variance *cannot* be established. This contention can be illustrated by the example of the two options whose cumulative probability distributions are plotted in Figure 6.9. $F$ represents an option having some dispersion, while $G$ represents an option offering a perfectly certain return (return $R_0$ with a probability of 1). The latter's variance, of course, is zero by definition. However, it is clear from Figure 6.9 that the option having the larger variance (option $F$) dominates option $G$ by SSD since the cumulative area under $G$ exceeds the cumulative area under $F$ at all levels of return. Thus, despite the assumption of risk aversion, the SSD efficient set does not necessarily exclude investments having a relatively high variance.

---

[14] For a proof of the special case in which the cumulative distributions intersect only once, see Appendix 6.2.

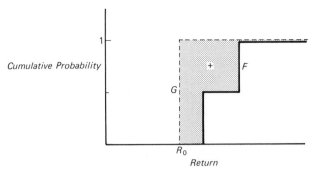

**Figure 6.9**

Another important property to be determined is the relationship between the FSD and SSD efficient sets:

The SSD efficient set is of necessity a subset of the FSD efficient set.

In other words all the investments included in the SSD efficient set are also included in the FSD efficient set. But the reverse does not hold true; not all the options which are FSD efficient need be SSD efficient. As a result the SSD efficient set cannot be larger (and is usually much smaller) than the FSD efficient set.

To prove the above proposition it is sufficient to show that if $F$ dominates $G$ by FSD, $F$ also dominates $G$ by SSD. Thus if an option $G$ is eliminated by FSD, it cannot be included in the SSD efficient set. A simple and straightforward proof can be given with the aid of Figure 6.10. For any option $F$ to be preferred over another option $G$ by FSD the two cumulative probability distributions must not intersect, and $F$ must lie to the right of $G$. But as the diagram clearly shows, if this is true then SSD, which is defined in terms of the first difference between $G$ and $F$, must also hold.[15] Since there

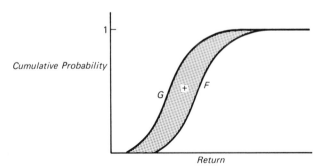

**Figure 6.10**

[15] If $F$ dominates $G$ by FSD then, for all values of $R$, $F(R) \leqslant G(R)$ or $G(R) - F(R) \geqslant 0$. Since this expression cannot be negative it follows that for all values of $R$ the following must also hold:

$$\int_{-\infty}^{R} |G(t) - F(t)| \, dt \geqslant 0$$

that is, $F$ dominates $G$ also by SSD.

may exist other options which are *not* eliminated by FSD (for example, those which intersect option *F*) but which may be eliminated by SSD, the SSD criterion generates the smaller efficient set of the two.

### 6.3.2   The Intuitive Interpretation of the SSD Criterion

While the intuitive explanation of the FSD rule is quite obvious, the intuitive interpretation of the SSD rule is less transparent. Probably the best way to explain the economic rationale of the SSD criterion is by a numerical example. Let *F* and *G* be two options given by the following table:

|     | Option G | | Option F | |
| --- | --- | --- | --- | --- |
| | *Probability* | *Return* | *Probability* | *Return* |
| | $\frac{1}{2}$ | 2 | 1 | 3 |
| | $\frac{1}{2}$ | 4 | | |

The cumulative probability distributions of these two options are given in Figure 6.11, a glance at which suffices to reveal that neither *F* nor *G* dominates the other by FSD, since the two distributions, *F* and *G*, intersect. However, *F* dominates *G* by SSD since $\int_{-\infty}^{R} |G(t) - F(t)| \, dt \geqslant 0$ for all values *R*: indeed, the "+" area in Figure 6.11 is equal to the "−" area, so that the integral vanishes only for $R = 4$ and is positive for all $2 \leqslant R < 4$. The two distributions have the same mean return, since

$$E_G(R) = \tfrac{1}{2} \cdot 2 + \tfrac{1}{2} \cdot 4 = 3$$

$$E_F(R) = 1 \cdot 3 = 3$$

A risk-neutral investor thus would be indifferent between *F* and *G*, since their means are equal. However, for a risk averter, the marginal utility $U'$ declines, and the "−" area

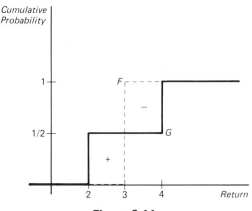

**Figure 6.11**

located at higher values of $R$ (for $3 < R < 4$) is worth less in terms of utility than the "+" area located at lower values of $R$ (for $2 < R < 3$). Hence $F$ is preferred over $G$ by all risk averters.

To show it even more clearly, suppose that a risk averter holds option $F$ which yields $3 with certainty. We offer him to give up option $F$ and to accept option $G$ in return, with no other changes. Would a risk averter accept this offer? In order to answer this question, consider the *marginal* change in his cash flow. Option $F$ can be rewritten in a different form so that the new offer is summarized as follows:

| Option F | | Option G | | Marginal Change | |
|---|---|---|---|---|---|
| *Probability* | *Return* | *Probability* | *Return* | *Probability* | *Return* |
| $\frac{1}{2}$ | 3 | $\frac{1}{2}$ | 2 | $\frac{1}{2}$ | $-1$ |
| $\frac{1}{2}$ | 3 | $\frac{1}{2}$ | 4 | $\frac{1}{2}$ | $+1$ |

Thus shifting from $F$ to $G$ in effect involves a fair game with outcomes of $-1$ and $+1$ with equal probabilities. A risk neutral individual would be indifferent to such a game. A risk averter, on the other hand, would reject this game since his marginal utility declines and the increase in his utility as a result of receiving one unit at high income is less than the damage caused by losing one unit at low income. In other words the change in the investor's expected utility $\Delta U$ on shifting from $F$ to $G$ can be written as

$$\Delta U = \tfrac{1}{2}[U(2) - U(3)] + \tfrac{1}{2}[U(4) - U(3)]$$

Since $U'$ is declining, the utility loss $U(2) - U(3)$ is greater in absolute value than the utility gain $U(4) - U(3)$, and so risk averters would prefer $F$ over $G$.

Figure 6.12 summarizes this case for a risk averter. The utility loss $U(2) - U(3)$ in absolute terms is greater than the gain $U(4) - U(3)$ whenever the marginal utility declines. Again, the monetary loss $(2 - 3)$ times the probability $\frac{1}{2}$ is equal (in absolute value) to the monetary gain $(4 - 3)$ times the probability $\frac{1}{2}$. However, in terms of utility the damage from the loss is larger than the added benefit from the gain. Graphically,

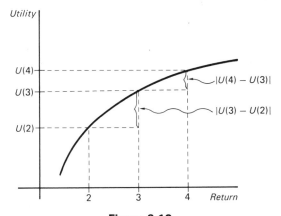

**Figure 6.12**

this means that the "−" area of Figure 6.11 is equal to the "+" area in magnitude but the utility value of the "+" area is greater.

In the above example we assume that the "+" area is equal to the "−" area. This is not necessary. When $F$ dominates $G$ by SSD, the "+" area may be larger than the "−" area, which only enhances the superiority of $F$ over $G$ for all risk averters. Finally, if there are several intersections of the cumulative distributions, the SSD criterion requires that each "−" area should be preceded by a "+" area of larger or equal size. Since $U'$ is declining, each successive "−" area is then worth less in utility terms than the preceding "+" area, and this guarantees dominance by SSD.

## 6.4    Third Degree Stochastic Dominance (TSD)

The FSD rule is derived under the single assumption of nondecreasing utility, $U' \geqslant 0$. When we add the assumption that $U'' \leqslant 0$ (risk aversion), the SSD rule is obtained. If we also add the third assumption $U''' \geqslant 0$ (which is always true once we accept the notion of decreasing absolute risk aversion—see Section 5.4), we obtain a stronger rule called Third Degree Stochastic Dominance (TSD).

The FSD rule requires that $F(R) \leqslant G(R)$ for all $R$. In order to introduce the TSD rule in a simple manner we define

$$F_1(R) = \int_{-\infty}^{R} F(t)\,\mathrm{d}t \quad \text{and} \quad G_1(R) = \int_{-\infty}^{R} G(t)\,\mathrm{d}t$$

and similarly

$$F_2(R) = \int_{-\infty}^{R} F_1(t)\,\mathrm{d}t \quad \text{and} \quad G_2(R) = \int_{-\infty}^{R} G_1(t)\,\mathrm{d}t$$

The SSD rule, which we discussed in the previous section, can be rewritten in this new notation simply as

$$F_1(R) \leqslant G_1(R) \quad \text{for all } R$$

In a similar way we define the TSD rule as follows:

**TSD Rule:** Given two distinct options $F$ and $G$, $F$ is preferred over $G$ by TSD for all risk averters with decreasing absolute risk aversion if and only if $F_2(R) \leqslant G_2(R)$ for all values of $R$ (with a strict inequality holding for at least one $R$) and in addition $E_F(R) \geqslant E_G(R)$.

Since TSD is a little more advanced than FSD and SSD, we will not discuss it in detail in this chapter. A computer program and an algorithm that construct the TSD

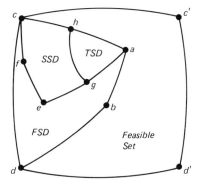

**Figure 6.13**

efficient set are given in Appendix 6.3. Recall that the more information we have, the more effective is the decision rule based on this information. For FSD, the only assumption that we make is $U' \geqslant 0$. When applying the SSD rule, we assume in addition to $U' \geqslant 0$ also $U'' \leqslant 0$. Thus, we expect to find cases where the FSD rule does not distinguish between two options, while the stronger SSD rule makes it possible to prefer one of these two options over the other. By the same token, when applying the TSD rule, we assume, in addition to $U' \geqslant 0$ and $U'' \leqslant 0$, also that $U''' \geqslant 0$. Hence the TSD efficient set must be smaller than the SSD efficient set. Figure 6.13 illustrates hypothetical efficient sets derived by FSD, SSD and TSD criteria.

The square $c'cdd'$ presents graphically the entire population of all possible options and hence is called the feasible set. The area $abdc$ represents the FSD efficient set, which is of course a subset of the feasible set. The area $aefc$ represents the SSD efficient set and the area $agh$ represents the TSD efficient set. Clearly the TSD efficient set is a subset of the SSD efficient set, which in turn is a subset of the FSD efficient set.

Thus, it is possible to find a case where $F$ does not dominate $G$ by SSD but such dominance exists by TSD. Such a case is left to be shown as an end-of-chapter exercise.

The relationship between the three Stochastic Dominance rules can be summarized by the following implication diagram

$$\text{FSD} \Rightarrow \text{SSD} \Rightarrow \text{TSD}$$

which means that dominance by FSD implies dominance by SSD and dominance by SSD in turn implies dominance by TSD.

## 6.5　Efficiency Criteria and Diversification

So far our illustrations of the efficiency analysis of choice under conditions of uncertainty have been based on the assumption that the investor must select one of several alternative investments. These alternatives, in turn, have been referred to as investments, options, securities, or portfolios. In practice the investor is usually faced with the problem of building an investment *portfolio* out of all the potential available securities. Of course, he may decide to put all of his eggs in one basket, that is, to buy a single security, or he may diversify his investment by purchasing a portfolio composed of several securities. The essence of the problem can best be seen by considering the simplified example set out in Table 6.11, which assumes that an individual is confronted with the alternative of investing either in security $A$, or in security $B$, or in a portfolio $C$ made up of equal proportions of $A$ and $B$.

Let us assume that our potential investor has $100 at his disposal. If he chooses to invest the entire $100 in security $A$, he will have an equal probability of earning a net return of either $3 or $4. If he places all of his money in security $B$ he will be faced with an equal probability of earning either $1 or $6. Let us see what happens should he choose to diversify his investment by building a portfolio $C$ comprised of equal amounts of $A$ and $B$. In this case the investor receives the return on $50 invested in $A$ plus the return on $50 invested in $B$. Depending on which alternative return is realized on each of the two securities, the possible returns on the portfolio are $2, $2.50, $4.50 or $5.00.

What are the chances of earning each alternative return? The answer depends on the statistical relationship between the two distributions of $A$ and $B$. Solely for the sake of convenience, let us assume in this instance that the return distribution of security $A$ is statistically *independent* of the distribution of security $B$. In that case the probability of realizing each of the four possible returns on the portfolio is calculated by multiplying the individual probabilities for each component return. Thus the probability of realizing the combination of $3 on $A$ and $1 on $B$ is given by

$$1/2 \cdot 1/2 = 1/4$$

Similarly, the probability of realizing each of the other three possible combinations is also 1/4 (see Table 6.11).

Can we apply our efficiency criteria to these three alternatives, even though one of them is a portfolio? Since a portfolio of securities, like a single security, is also

**Table 6.11**
**Percentage Returns on Three Alternative Options***

| Security A | | | Security B | | | Portfolio C | | |
|---|---|---|---|---|---|---|---|---|
| Prob- ability | Cumu- lative Prob- ability | Return | Prob- ability | Cumu- lative Prob- ability | Return | Prob- ability | Cumu- lative Prob- ability | Return |
| 1/2 | 1/2 | 3.0 | 1/2 | 1/2 | 1.0 | 1/4 | 1/4 | 2.0 |
| | | | | | | 1/4 | 1/2 | 2.5 |
| 1/2 | 1 | 4.0 | 1/2 | 1 | 6.0 | 1/4 | 3/4 | 4.5 |
| | | | | | | 1/4 | 1 | 5.0 |

* The return of portfolio $C$ = 1/2 the return on $A$ plus 1/2 the return on $B$.

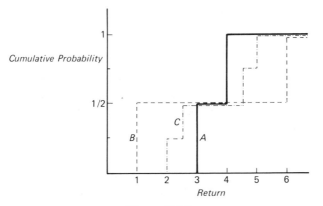

**Figure 6.14**

characterized by a probability distribution of possible returns, the efficiency analysis we presented above is perfectly general and can be applied with equal validity to single investment options or to portfolios comprising two or more securities.

The cumulative probability functions of our three alternatives, security $A$, security $B$, and portfolio $C$, are set out in Figure 6.14. From the diagram it is clear that the cumulative distributions of securities $A$ and $B$ intersect, so that neither fulfills the FSD rule, and a clear-cut preference order cannot be established. Since distribution $C$, representing the composite portfolio, also intersects both distributions $A$ and $B$, all three alternatives, $A$, $B$, and $C$, are included in the FSD efficient set. Thus it cannot be stipulated that all investors, independent of their attitudes toward risk, will tend to diversify their securities investment: the FSD efficient set includes both single security investments as well as the portfolio.

Let us now see whether the additional information that investors are risk averters can help us to establish a clear-cut preference for a mixed portfolio. To do this we calculate the cumulative areas under each of the three distributions (Table 6.12) and apply SSD. Comparing the portfolio $C$ with security $B$ we find that $C$ dominates $B$ so

**Table 6.12**

| Return | Cumulative Area under A | Cumulative Area under B | Cumulative Area under C | B Minus A | B Minus C | C Minus A |
|--------|-------------------------|-------------------------|-------------------------|-----------|-----------|-----------|
| 1.0    | 0       | 0       | 0       | 0     | 0     | 0     |
| 2.0    | 0       | 1/2     | 0       | 1/2   | 1/2   | 0     |
| 2.5    | 0       | 3/4     | 1/8     | 3/4   | 5/8   | 1/8   |
| 3.0    | 0       | 1       | 3/8     | 1     | 5/8   | 3/8   |
| 4.0    | 1/2     | 1 1/2   | 7/8     | 1     | 5/8   | 3/8   |
| 4.5    | 1       | 1 3/4   | 1 1/8   | 3/4   | 5/8   | 1/8   |
| 5.0    | 1 1/2   | 2       | 1 1/2   | 1/2   | 1/2   | 0     |
| 6.0    | 2 1/2   | 2 1/2   | 2 1/2   | 0     | 0     | 0     |

that alternative $B$ can be eliminated. But going on to a comparison of $C$ with security $A$, we find that $A$ dominates $C$, and that portfolio $C$ is eliminated leaving $A$ as the only efficient investment for all risk averters.

Since the single security $A$ dominates portfolio $C$, it might seem to follow that risk averters generally will not diversify their investments. But this is not true. If we vary the investment proportions of the portfolio we can always find at least one mixed portfolio which is SSD efficient. As both securities have the same expected return (3.5%), combining the two securities in the portfolio in varying proportions will not change the portfolio's expected return, which remains invariant at 3.5%. However, it does change the variance. If we choose the proportions of $A$ and $B$ which *minimize* the portfolio variance, 25/26 of $A$ and 1/26 of $B$, the probability distribution of the new portfolio $C'$ changes (see Table 6.13). The reader can verify that security $A$ does not dominate the portfolio $C'$ so that both $A$ and $C'$ are included in the SSD efficient set.

If we compare the results of applying the SSD rule with the previous results of applying the FSD rule to the same three alternatives the following conclusions can be reached:

(a) Applying the SSD rule reduces the FSD efficient set. In our last example, all three alternatives are FSD efficient but only two options, $A$ and $C'$, are SSD efficient, while in the previous example of equal proportions only one option ($A$) was SSD efficient.

(b) The assumption of risk aversion ($U''(R) \leqslant 0$) is *not* sufficient to ensure that all diversified investments will invariably dominate a single asset option. In our example, the single security $A$ is preferable to the two security (equal proportions) portfolio $C$ for all risk averters. The reason for this is not difficult to find. The expected returns on each security and on the portfolio are the same—3.5% in all three cases. And although the portfolio decreases the dispersion of returns relative to security $B$, the portfolio dispersion still *exceeds* that of security $A$, which accounts for $A$'s dominance.

(c) Changing the investment proportions (25/26 of $A$ and 1/26 of $B$), we found that both option $A$ and the portfolio $C'$ are included in the SSD efficient set. Thus some risk averters can be expected to choose the portfolio, but there

**Table 6.13**
**Portfolio $C'$**

| Probability | Cumulative Probability | Return* |
|:-----------:|:----------------------:|:-------:|
| 1/4 | 1/4 | 76/26 |
| 1/4 | 1/2 | 81/26 |
| 1/4 | 3/4 | 101/26 |
| 1/4 | 1 | 106/26 |

* The return of portfolio $C' = 25/26 \times$ the return on $A$ plus 1/26 $\times$ the return on $B$.

can be no guarantee that others will not prefer the single security option to the mixed portfolio.

Let us consider a different example.

EXAMPLE
Assume that an investor is confronted with two *identical* securities, $A$ and $B$, and a portfolio, $C$, comprised of equal proportions of $A$ and $B$. Can an investor be expected to diversify his investments in this case, that is, will he prefer the portfolio? Table 6.14 sets out the relevant data for these three options on the assumption that the returns on the securities are statistically independent. The resulting cumulative probability distributions are drawn in Figure 6.15. Note that since $A$ and $B$ are identical, their cumulative distributions are also identical and the investor is indifferent between them.

A glance at the data of Table 6.14 is sufficient to show that the portfolio has the same expected return as the individual securities, while the dispersion about the mean has been reduced. But since distribution $C$ intersects both $A$ and $B$, all three alternatives—the two identical securities and the composite portfolio—are included in the FSD efficient set. Once again we can conclude that diversification will not necessarily be preferred by all investors, independent of their attitudes toward risk. Now let us apply SSD. Figure 6.15 shows that the area under the cumulative distributions of $A$ or $B$ always exceeds the area under the distribution of the portfolio $C$. Therefore, in this case, *all* risk averters will prefer the portfolio to an investment in *either* of the (identical) securities.

**Table 6.14**

| Security A | | Security B | | Portfolio C | |
|---|---|---|---|---|---|
| Probability | Return | Probability | Return | Probability | Return |
| 1/2 | 2 | 1/2 | 2 | 1/4 | 2 |
| 1/2 | 4 | 1/2 | 4 | 1/2 | 3 |
| | | | | 1/4 | 4 |

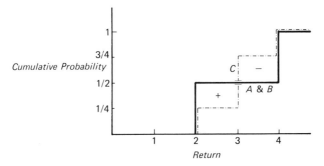

**Figure 6.15**

In both of the preceding examples we assumed that the returns on investments $A$ and $B$ were statistically independent. Let us now take an extreme example where two distributions are assumed to have perfect *negative* statistical interdependence (see Table 6.15) so that by diversifying into a portfolio of two securities, the variance of returns can be reduced to zero and a perfectly certain return assured. Given the *negative* interdependence, a portfolio comprised of 50% of $A$ and 50% of $B$ offers a perfectly certain return of 3. If security $B$ yields a return of 2 the portfolio return equals $1/2 \cdot 2 + 1/2 \cdot 4 = 3$; if the return on $B$ should be 4 the portfolio return is again 3, since

$$1/2 \cdot 4 + 1/2 \cdot 2 = 3$$

Figure 6.16 presents the cumulative distributions of securities $A$ and $B$ and portfolio $C$. (Note that as before, $A$ and $B$ have identical cumulative probability distributions.) Once again the distributions intersect so that by FSD, the portfolio with a perfectly certain return of 3 does *not* dominate the two securities, each of which has a risky expected return also equal to 3. The explanation is not difficult to find. Since FSD is appropriate for risk lovers as well as risk averters, the reduction in variance, inherent in the portfolio, is not a desirable characteristic for the former class of investors.

If we apply the SSD rule to the same sample, it is clear from Figure 6.16 that the areas under each of the identical securities $A$ and $B$ exactly equal the area under the

**Table 6.15**

| | Security B | | Security A | |
| | | | | Conditional |
| Returns | Probability | Returns | Probability |
| --- | --- | --- | --- |
| 2 | 1/2 | 2 | 0 |
| | | 4 | 1 |
| 4 | 1/2 | 2 | 1 |
| | | 4 | 0 |

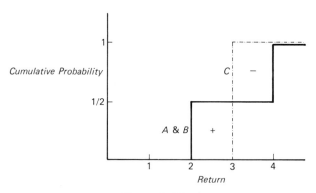

**Figure 6.16**

portfolio distribution $C$. But since the distributions of $A$ and $B$ intersect distribution $C$ from the left, the SSD criterion is fulfilled: the cumulative area under $A$ (or $B$) is always greater than, or equal to, the cumulative area under $C$ over the entire domain of returns. Thus $C$ dominates $A$ and $C$ dominates $B$ for this extreme case of negative inter-dependence, and *all* risk averters will prefer the portfolio with the stabilized return. In sum, while the assumption of negative interdependence does not change our conclusions regarding FSD, it does strengthen the tendency of risk averters to diversify their investments.[16]

## 6.6    The Effectiveness of Stochastic Dominance Criteria

Given a set of mutually exclusive portfolios, and a set of assumptions regarding investor preferences, one can divide all the portfolios into two sets, the efficient set and the inefficient set. Clearly the smaller the efficient set, the more effective is the decision rule. The effectiveness of a decision rule is an important property that should not be over-looked. For example the FSD is the optimal rule for all rational investors (nondecreas-ing utility function, $U' > 0$) and in this respect it is superior to SSD, which is limited to risk averters (concave nondecreasing utility functions, $U' > 0$ and $U'' < 0$). However, the FSD is so unselective that the FSD efficient set may turn out to include, say, 95% of all feasible portfolios. In such a case, in spite of the theoretical superiority of FSD over all other decision rules, we say that FSD is *not effective*. It is inapplicable in practice since it actually fails to establish dominance.

The effectiveness of the various decision rules is an empirical question. However, the results presented below are quite typical and virtually the same results appear in all empirical tests which employ Stochastic Dominance rules.

In order to test the effectiveness of SD rules, we used as a proxy to mutually exclu-sive portfolios all US mutual funds with an unbroken record of annual rates of return for the 22-year period 1959–1980.[17] The record reveals that there are 100 mutual funds in this category. Using the historical distribution of returns, with equal probabilities attached to each of the 22 years, we constructed 100 distributions of 22 observations each. Then Stochastic Dominance rules were applied to these 100 distributions, yielding the FSD, SSD and TSD efficient sets.[18]

Table 6.16 identifies those of the 100 mutual funds which appear in the FSD, SSD and TSD efficient sets. From this table we can draw the following conclusions:

(1) FSD, with all its generality (very weak assumptions on the investors' pref-erences) proved to be quite ineffective: 61 out of the 100 mutual funds entered the FSD efficient set. Though the elimination of 39 funds relegated to the inefficient set is far

---

[16] A much stronger case for diversification can be made when the number of securities is increased. See Chapter 8.

[17] The source for the data are various annual editions of Arthur Wiesenberger, *Investment Companies*.

[18] The efficient sets were constructed using the general SD computer program presented in full in Appendix 6.3.

**Table 6.16**
**Efficient Mutual Funds: 1959–1980 Data**
**(Efficient Funds Marked by +, Inefficient Funds by −)**

| Name | FSD | SSD | TSD |
|------|-----|-----|-----|
| 1. LEXINGTON RESEARCH INVESTING CORP. | + | − | − |
| 2. PENN SQUARE MUTUAL FUND | + | − | − |
| 3. TWENTIETH CENTURY-GROWTH INVESTORS | + | + | + |
| 4. AMERICAN NATIONAL GROWTH FUND | + | − | − |
| 5. COLONIAL GROWTH FUND | + | − | − |
| 6. DE VGGH MUTUAL FUND | + | − | − |
| 7. ENERGY FUND | + | − | − |
| 8. FRANKLIN CUSTODIAN COMMON STOCK | + | − | − |
| 9. KEYSTONE (S–3) GROWTH COMMON | + | − | − |
| 10. MAIRS & POWER GROWTH FUND | + | − | − |
| 11. PHILADELPHIA | + | − | − |
| 12. PUTNAM INVESTORS FUND | + | − | − |
| 13. VALUE LINE FUND | + | − | − |
| 14. WINDSOR FUND | + | − | − |
| 15. BULLOCK FUND | + | − | − |
| 16. AMERICAN INVESTORS FUND | + | − | − |
| 17. DELAWARE FUND | + | − | − |
| 18. DREYFUS FUND | + | − | − |
| 19. KEYSTONE (K–2) GROWTH FUND | + | − | − |
| 20. KEYSTONE (S–4) LOWER-PRICED COMMON | + | − | − |
| 21. NATIONAL INVESTORS CORP. | + | − | − |
| 22. PUTNAM GROWTH FUND | + | − | − |
| 23. TECHNOLOGY FUND | + | − | − |
| 24. VALUE LINE SPECIAL SITUATION | + | − | − |
| 25. AMERICAN NATIONAL GROWTH FUND | + | − | − |
| 26. AXE-HOUGHTON STOCK FUND | + | − | − |
| 27. FUND OF AMERICA | + | − | − |
| 28. FIDELITY FUND | + | − | − |
| 29. INVESTMENT COMPANY OF AMERICA | + | − | − |
| 30. ONE WILLIAM STREET FUND | + | − | − |
| 31. PIONEER FUND | + | − | − |
| 32. STATE STREE INVESTMENT CORP. | + | − | − |
| 33. WASHINGTON MUTUAL INVESTORS FUND | + | − | − |
| 34. AFFILIATED FUND | + | − | − |
| 35. AMERICAN MUTUAL FUND | + | − | − |
| 36. GUARDIAN MUTUAL FUND | + | − | − |
| 37. ISTEL FUND | + | + | + |
| 38. PINE STREE FUND | + | + | − |
| 39. SOUTHWESTERN INVESTORS | + | − | − |
| 40. WALL STREET INVESTING CORP. | + | − | − |
| 41. AXE-HOUGHTON FUND A | + | − | − |
| 42. AXE-HOUGHTON FUND B | + | − | − |
| 43. COMPOSITE BOND & STOCK FUND | + | − | − |
| 44. DODGE & COX BALANCED FUND | + | − | − |
| 45. EATON & HOWARD BALANCED FUND | + | − | − |
| 46. LOOMIS–SAYLES MUTUAL FUND | + | − | − |
| 47. MUTUAL SHARES | + | + | + |
| 48. NATION-WIDE SECURITIES-BALANCED SERIES | + | + | + |

**Table 6.16 continued**

| Name | FSD | SSD | TSD |
|------|-----|-----|-----|
| 49. GEORGE PUTNAM FUND OF BOSTON | + | − | − |
| 50. STEIN ROE & PRANHAM BALANCED FUND | + | − | − |
| 51. WELLINGTON FUND | + | − | − |
| 52. DECATUR INCOM FUND | + | − | − |
| 53. EATON & HOWARD INCOME FUND | + | + | + |
| 54. FRANKLIN CUSTODIAN-INCOMSERIES' | + | + | − |
| 55. KEYSTONE (K–1) INCOME FUND | + | + | + |
| 56. NATIONAL SECURITIES-INCOME SERIES | + | + | + |
| 57. NORTHEAST INVESTORS TRUST | + | + | + |
| 58. PUTNAM INCOME FUND | + | − | − |
| 59. LIFE INSURANCE INVESTORS | + | − | − |
| 60. CANADIAN FUND | + | − | − |
| 61. TEMPLETON GROWTH FUND | + | + | + |

from being a negligible contribution to the decision-making process, yet the investor is still faced with 61 funds from which to choose the optimum portfolio, and a sharper decision rule is clearly desirable.

(2) Assuming risk aversion drastically reduces the size of the efficient set. The SSD efficient set includes only 11 out of the 100 mutual funds. Thus, the SSD rule is quite effective.[19]

(3) Adding the assumption of decreasing absolute risk aversion reduces the TSD efficient set from 11 to 9 mutual funds.

Obviously, the TSD efficient set is a subset of the SSD efficient set and the SSD efficient set is a subset of the FSD efficient set (see Table 6.16).

Thus, to sum up, SSD and TSD are proved to be effective rules that manage to screen about 90% of all portfolios to the inefficient set.


## Summary

The choice among risky investment options by the individual may be regarded as a two-step procedure: first, the investor chooses the efficient set, independent of his tastes or preferences; second, he chooses the optimal portfolio from the efficient set. In the first stage, on the basis of highly general information on a given group of investors, all potential investment options are divided into two groups: an efficient set and an inefficient set. The partition is effected by applying an efficiency criterion which is appropriate for a given class of investors. Using such a decision rule, we can be certain that all individuals belonging to the class in question will make their final choice out of the efficient group. In the second stage, the investor, in accordance with his tastes, chooses the optimal

[19] It is interesting to note that SSD in this case is even more effective than the Mean–Variance rule (see Chapter 7). The MV efficient set includes 17 funds, 50% more than the SSD efficient set.

option out of the efficient set, namely, that alternative which maximizes his expected utility.

Three efficiency criteria, FSD, SSD, and TSD, are defined in this chapter. The FSD rule places no restrictions on the form of the utility function beyond the usual

---

### Summary Table

1. **First Degree Stochastic Dominance (FSD)**

   *Assumptions:* $U'(R) \geqslant 0$

   *Rule:* $F$ dominates $G$ if and only if:

   $F(R) \leqslant G(R)$ for all values of $R$ (with strict inequality for at least one $R_0$),

   where $F$ and $G$ are the cumulative distributions of the two options.

2. **Second Degree Stochastic Dominance (SSD)**

   *Assumptions:* $U'(R) \geqslant 0$, $U''(R) \leqslant 0$

   *Rule:* $F$ dominates $G$ if and only if:

   $F_1(R) \leqslant G_1(R)$ for all values of $R$ (with strict inequality for at least one $R_0$),

   where $F_1(R) = \int_{-\infty}^{R} F(t)\,dt$ and $G_1(R) = \int_{-\infty}^{R} G(t)\,dt$.

3. **Third Degree Stochastic Dominance (TSD)**

   *Assumptions:* $U'(R) \geqslant 0$, $U''(R) \leqslant 0$, $U'''(R) \geqslant 0$

   *Rule:* $F$ dominates $G$ if and only if:

   $F_2(R) \leqslant G_2(R)$ for all values of $R$ (with strict inequality for at least one $R_0$) and

   $E_F(R) \geqslant E_G(R)$, where $F_2(R) = \int_{-\infty}^{R} F_1(t)\,dt$ and $G_2(R) = \int_{-\infty}^{R} G_1(t)\,dt$.

4. **Relationship Between the Three Stochastic Dominance Rules:**

   $$\text{FSD} \Rightarrow \text{SSD} \Rightarrow \text{TSD}$$

   Namely, the TSD efficient set is a subset of the SSD efficient set and the latter is a subset of the FSD efficient set.

5. $E_F(R) \geqslant E_G(R)$ is a necessary condition for dominance of $F$ over $G$ for all three rules. However, $\sigma_F(R) < \sigma_G(R)$ is *not* a necessary condition for dominance of $F$ over $G$.

6. **Information on Preferences and the Implied Decision Criteria**

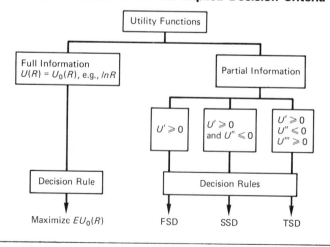

requirement that it be nondecreasing. Thus this criterion is appropriate for risk averters and risk lovers alike since the utility function may contain concave as well as convex segments. Owing to its generality, the FSD permits a preliminary screening of investment options eliminating those options which no rational investor (independent of his attitude toward risk) will ever choose.

The SSD is the appropriate efficiency criterion for all risk averters. Here we assume the utility function to be concave. This criterion is based on stronger assumptions, and therefore it permits a more sensitive selection of investments. On the other hand, the SSD is applicable to a smaller group of investors. The SSD efficient set is of necessity a subset of the FSD efficient set; this means that all the options included in the SSD efficient set are also included in the FSD efficient set, but not necessarily vice versa.

The TSD rule is appropriate for a still smaller group of investors. In addition to the risk-aversion assumption of SSD, the TSD also assumes decreasing absolute risk aversion. The population of risk averters with decreasing absolute risk aversion is clearly a subset of all risk averters, and the TSD efficient set is correspondingly a subset of the SSD efficient set: all TSD efficient portfolios are SSD efficient, but not vice versa.

The three stochastic dominance criteria, FSD, SSD, and TSD, are optimal in the sense that given the assumptions regarding the investors' preferences (utility functions), the application of the corresponding criterion ensures a *minimal* efficient set.

In terms of the structure of the investors' utility functions, the relevant domains of the three stochastic dominance criteria can be defined as follows:

(1)   FSD is optimal for all investors with $U' \geqslant 0$.
(2)   SSD is optimal for all investors with $U' \geqslant 0$, $U'' \leqslant 0$.
(3)   TSD is optimal for all investors with $U' \geqslant 0$, $U'' \leqslant 0$, $U''' \geqslant 0$.

An analysis of the three criteria shows that an investment option's expected return plays a crucial role in determining the preference ordering, while the variance of returns only plays a very limited role.

# APPENDIX 6.1
## Proof of FSD and SSD Criteria

We prove in this Appendix FSD and SSD rules and leave the proof of the TSD rule as an end-of-chapter exercise.

Assume that the returns are bounded between finite $a$ and $b$, thus $a \leqslant R \leqslant b$. Then the expected utilities of options $F$ and $G$ are given by

$$E_F U(R) = \int_a^b U(R) f(R) \, dR \quad \text{and} \quad E_G U(R) = \int_a^b U(R) g(R) \, dR,$$

where $f$ and $g$ are the (probability) density functions of $F$ and $G$ respectively and $U$ is a utility function.

The difference in expected utility, which we denote by $\Delta$, is given by

$$\Delta \equiv E_F U(R) - E_G U(R) = \int_a^b [f(R) - g(R)] U(R) \, dR \qquad (6.1.1)$$

Employing integration by parts, $\Delta$ can be rewritten as

$$\Delta = U(R) \cdot [F(R) - G(R)] \Big|_a^b + \int_a^b [G(R) - F(R)] U'(R) \, dR \qquad (6.1.2)$$

Since $F(b) - G(b) = 1 - 1 = 0$ and $F(a) = G(a) = 0$ we have

$$\Delta = \int_a^b [G(R) - F(R)] U'(R) \, dR \qquad (6.1.3)$$

The same result can be proved over the entire real axis, when $a = -\infty$ and $b = +\infty$. We shall use (6.1.3) to prove FSD.

FSD RULE:
$F$ dominates $G$ by FSD if and only if $F(R) \leqslant G(R)$ for all values $R$, with a strict inequality holding for some value $R_0$.

    The proof is immediate from (6.1.3). If $F(R) \leqslant G(R)$ for all $R$, $[G(R) - F(R)] U'(R) > 0$, and since an integral of a positive number is positive, this implies that $\Delta \geqslant 0$ or $E_F U(R) \geqslant E_G U(R)$ for all $U$ with $U' \geqslant 0$.

    The proof of necessity is left as an exercise.

SSD RULE:
$F$ dominates $G$ by SSD if and only if

$$\int_a^R [G(t) - F(t)] \, dt \geqslant 0 \quad \text{for all } R$$

with strict inequality holding at least for some $R$.

    To prove this claim, integrate by parts the right-hand side of (6.1.3) to obtain:

$$\Delta = \int_a^b [G(R) - F(R)] U'(R) \, dR$$

$$= U'(R) \int_a^R [G(t) - F(t)] \, dt \Big|_a^b + \int_a^b \left( -U''(R) \int_a^R [G(t) - F(t)] \, dt \right) dR$$

or

$$\Delta = U'(b) \int_a^b [G(t) - F(t)] \, dt + \int_a^b \left( -U''(R) \int_a^R [G(t) - F(t)] \, dt \right) dR \qquad (6.1.4)$$

Now if SSD holds, the first term on the right is positive (or, to be more precise, non-negative). The second term is also non-negative, since $-U''(R) \geqslant 0$ and the integral in parentheses is positive by SSD. Hence $\Delta \geqslant 0$ or $E_F U(R) \geqslant E_G U(R)$ for all $U$ with $U' \geqslant 0$ and $U'' \leqslant 0$.

The proof of necessity is left as an exercise.

## APPENDIX 6.2
### Proof of the SSD Criterion When the Cumulative Distributions Intersect Only Once

Let $F$, $G$ be two distributions with mean value $\mu_F$, $\mu_G$ respectively, such that for some $R_0 < \infty$, $F \leqslant G$ for $R \leqslant R_0$ (and $F < G$ for some $R_1 < R_0$) and $F \geqslant G$ for some $R \geqslant R_0$, then $F$ dominates $G$ (for concave utility functions) if and only if $\mu_F \geqslant \mu_G$.

**Proof:**[20]    (a) If $\mu_F \geqslant \mu_G$ we have, by applying equation (6.1.3) of Appendix 6.1 with infinite integration bounds to the case of linear utility, $U(R) = R$, when $E_F U(R) = \mu_F$ and $E_G U(R) = \mu_G$

$$\mu_F - \mu_G = \int_{-\infty}^{\infty} (G - F) \, dt = \int_{-\infty}^{R_0} (G - F) \, dt - \int_{R_0}^{\infty} |G - F| \, dt \geqslant 0$$

Therefore $\int_{-\infty}^{R} (G - F) \, dt \geqslant 0$ for all $R$, and so $F$ dominates $G$ by SSD.

(b) If $\mu_F < \mu_G$

$$\mu_F - \mu_G = \int_{-\infty}^{R_0} (G - F) \, dt - \int_{R_0}^{\infty} |G - F| \, dt < 0$$

Hence, for some $R_2 > R_0$,

$$\int_{-\infty}^{R_2} (G - F) \, dt = \int_{-\infty}^{R_0} (G - F) \, dt - \int_{R_0}^{R_2} |G - F| \, dt < 0$$

whereas for $R_0$ we have $\int_{-\infty}^{R_0} (G - F) \, dt > 0$ and the SSD condition does not hold for all $R$. That is, neither $F$ nor $G$ dominates the other for all concave utilities.    Q.E.D.

## APPENDIX 6.3
### The Stochastic Dominance Algorithms and Program

Most of the Stochastic Dominance tests in practice are carried out using time series of historical rates of returns, such that each of the $n$ observations is assigned an equal

---

[20] This proof appeared originally in G. Hanoch and H. Levy, "The Efficiency Analysis of Choices Involving Risk", *Review of Economic Studies* (July 1969), p. 371.

probability of $1/n$. The empirical cumulative distribution curves are represented by step functions with constant height steps (each step is of height $1/n$). For such cases, there are attractively simple algorithms based on the raw observation matrix that enable us to find the FSD, SSD, and TSD efficient sets by simple arithmetic operations and pairwise comparisons. We briefly present here the three FSD, SSD and TSD algorithms and reproduce in full a simple computer code (written in FORTRAN77) that realizes these algorithms. The algorithms, of course, can be conveniently used also for *manual* performance of SD tests when the data are time series of returns with the same number of equal-probability observations.

### 6.3.1 The SD Algorithms[21]

In what follows we assume that the historical rates of return are arranged in a matrix $x$ of $n$ rows (observation periods) and $m$ columns (risky assets, stocks, securities, etc.). Each column is sorted in ascending order, from the lowest observed rate of return to the highest observation: this is what we usually do in order to draw the cumulative distribution curves. The sorted observations are called *quantiles*, and by $x_{t,i}$ we denote the quantile $t$ of asset $i$ in the matrix.

FSD ALGORITHM

(a) *Construct the matrix of quantiles*
The input matrix of raw observations is sorted column by column in ascending order to form the quantile matrix $x$ for the FSD test.

(b) *Comparison of quantiles*
Asset $i$ dominates asset $j$ if and only if:

$$x_{t,i} \geqslant x_{t,j} \quad \text{for all } t \ (t = 1, \ldots, n)$$

SSD ALGORITHM

(a) *Construct the matrix of SSD sums*
Using the matrix of quantiles from the FSD test, form a new matrix $x'$ such that for each asset (column) $i$:

$$x'_{1,i} = x_{1,i}$$

$$x'_{2,i} = x_{1,i} + x_{2,i}$$

$$x'_{3,i} = x_{1,i} + x_{2,i} + x_{3,i}$$

$$\cdot$$
$$\cdot$$
$$\cdot$$

$$x'_{n,i} = x_{1,i} + x_{2,i} + \cdots + x_{n,i}$$

---

[21] The algorithm is based on Levy, H. and Kroll, Y., "Efficiency Analysis with Borrowing and Lending: Criteria and Their Effectiveness", *Review of Economics and Statistics* (February 1979).

In words, row $k$ in the SSD sums matrix is equal to the sum of the first $k$ rows from the FSD quantile matrix. The last row in the SSD sums matrix clearly contains the means of the $m$ assets, each multiplied by the number of observations $n$.

(b) *Comparison of SSD quantile sums*
Asset $i$ dominates asset $j$ by SSD if and only if:

$$x'_{t,i} \geqslant x'_{t,j} \quad \text{for all } t \ (t = 1, \ldots, n)$$

TSD ALGORITHM

(a) *Construct the matrix of TSD sums*
Using the matrix of SSD sums $x'$, form a new matrix $x''$ such that for each asset (column) $i$:

$$x''_{1,i} = x'_{1,i}/2$$
$$x''_{2,i} = x'_{1,i} + x'_{2,i}/2$$
$$x''_{3,i} = x'_{1,i} + x'_{2,i} + x'_{3,i}/2$$

$$\cdot$$
$$\cdot$$
$$\cdot$$

$$x''_{n,i} = x'_{1,i} + x'_{2,i} + \cdots + x'_{n-1,i} + x'_{n,i}/2$$

In words, row $k$ in the TSD sums matrix is equal to the sum of the first $k-1$ rows from the SSD sums matrix plus *half* the row $k$ in the SSD matrix.

(b) *Comparison of TSD sums*
Asset $i$ dominates asset $j$ by TSD if and only if:

$$x''_{t,i} \geqslant x''_{t,j} \quad \text{for all } t \ (t = 1, \ldots, n)$$

and also in the last row of the SSD sums matrix

$$x'_{n,i} \geqslant x'_{n,j}$$

To reduce the number of comparisons in all the tests, the comparisons should be performed in the order of decreasing asset means, as a necessary condition for dominance of asset $i$ over asset $j$ by any of the SD tests is that the mean return of asset $i$ is no less than the mean return of asset $j$.

Moreover, since FSD implies SSD and SSD implies TSD, each successive test is conducted on the efficient set from the previous test. Thus, SSD tests are performed only on the assets remaining in the FSD efficient set, and the TSD tests are performed only on the SSD efficient assets.

### 6.3.2   The SD Program

The program consists of several blocks and subroutines that realize the three SD algorithms described above. A brief description of the program follows.

The program has four input parameters:

MAXST—maximum admissible number of risky assets, needed to dimension the arrays;

MAXPE—maximum admissible number of observation periods, also needed for dimensioning;

NSTK   —the actual number of risky assets to be read from input file (TAPE1);

NPER   —the number of observation periods in the input data.

These parameters as specified in the program fit the Data Set of mutual funds at the end of the book. They can be easily adjusted to read any given input file on TAPE1.

All the SD tests are performed by SUBROUTINE SDTEST which is called with appropriate parameters identifying FSD, SSD, and TSD test, as needed. All the output data are printed by SUBROUTINE EFFPRNT, also with appropriate parameters identifying the particular test results.

The program executes in the following major steps:

1. Input of raw observations: the raw data are read from TAPE1 into the array X(NPER, NSTK). The input format 101 in the program fits the Data Set at the end of the book and can be easily adapted to other input files.
2. The means are calculated and sorted, to allow performing the comparisons in the order of decreasing means.
3. Each column of the raw data matrix X(NPER, NSTK) is sorted in descending order, from largest to lowest quantile (the SD tests are therefore conducted starting with the bottom row of the matrix, where the lowest quantile is contained).
4. The FSD test is performed by SUBROUTINE SDTEST with appropriate parameters.
5. The SSD sums are formed by SUBROUTINE SSDSUMS and the SSD test is performed by SUBROUTINE SDTEST with appropriate parameters.
6. The TSD sums are formed by SUBROUTINE TSDSUMS and the TSD test is performed by SUBROUTINE SDTEST with appropriate parameters.
7. The results as printed out by SUBROUTINE EFFPRNT list the assets included in each efficient set, identified by serial number and by name. SUBROUTINE SDTEST in the course of execution prints out a record of assets excluded from the corresponding efficient set, identifying the dominant asset by which each inefficient asset was excluded.

The full code is given below. It can be easily run on any installation supporting standard FORTRAN77.

```
 1          PROGRAM STOCH(TAPE1,OUTPUT)
 2   C-
 3   C===================================================================
 4   C-
 5          PARAMETER(MAXST=140,MAXPE=15,NSTK=125, NPER=10 )
 6   C-
 7   C===================================================================
 8   C-
 9          COMMON X(MAXPE,MAXST),XMEAN(MAXST),SD(MAXST),
10        2  INDEX(MAXST),INDEX1(MAXST),XMEAN1(MAXST),SD1(MAXST),XM(MAXST),
11        3  NAME(MAXST),NAME1(MAXST)
12          INTEGER FSDEFF(MAXST),SSDEFF(MAXST),TSDEFF(MAXST)
13   C-
14   C- ******* FORMATS AND INITIALIZATIONS ********
15   101    FORMAT(A10,20X,10F5.1)
16   11     FORMAT(I10,2X,A10,2F10.4)
17          FSDEFF(NSTK+1)=≠FSD≠
18          SSDEFF(NSTK+1)=≠SSD≠
19          TSDEFF(NSTK+1)=≠TSD≠
20          DO 7 I=1,NSTK
21          INDEX(I)=INDEX1(I)=I
22          XMEAN(I)=0
23          XM(I)=0
24   7      CONTINUE
25   C-
26   C-
27   C- ******** READ RAW DATA INPUT FILE ********
28   C-
29   C-
30   C- ******** CALCULATE MEANS AND STANDARD DEVIATIONS **********
31   C-
32   C-
33          DO 1 J=1,NSTK
34          READ [1,101,END=1) NAME (J),(X(I,J), I=1,NPER)
35          SQ=0
36          DO 3 I=1,NPER
37          XMEAN(J)=XMEAN(J)+X(I,J)
38          SQ=SQ+X(I,J)*X(I,J)
39   3      CONTINUE
40          SD(J)=SQRT((SQ-XMEAN(J)*XMEAN(J)/NPER)/(NPER-1))
41          XMEAN(J)=XMEAN(J)/NPER
42          PRINT 11, INDEX(J),NAME(J),XMEAN(J),SD(J)
43   C-****** PRESERVE ORIGINAL MEANS *********
44          NAME1(J)=NAME(J)
45          XMEAN1(J)=XMEAN(J)
46          SD1(J)=SD(J)
47   1      CONTINUE
48   C- **** DESCENDING BUBBLE SORT ON NPER * NSTK MATRIX X(I,J)
49   C-
50          DO 8 J=1,NSTK
51          K=1
52          N=2
53          IF(X(K+1,J).GT.X(K,J)) THEN
54            A=X(K+1,J)
55            X(K+1,J)=X(K,J)
56            X(K,J)=A
57          ENDIF
```

```
58    80    K=N
59    81    IF(K.EQ.NPER) GO TO 8
60          IF(X(K+1,J).GT.X(K,J)) THEN
61            N=K+1
62            A=X(K+1,J)
63            X(K+1,J)=X(K,J)
64            X(K,J)=A
65    82      IF(X(K,J).GT.X(K-1,J)) THEN
66              A=X(K-1,J)
67              X(K-1,J)=X(K,J)
68              X(K,J)=A
69              K=K-1
70              IF(K.EQ.1) GO TO 80
71              GO TO 82
72            ELSE
73              GO TO 80
74            ENDIF
75          ELSE
76            K=K+1
77            GO TO 81
78          ENDIF
79    8     CONTINUE
80    C-
81    C- ******** FIRST DEGREE STOCHASTIC DOMINANCE *********
82          DO 9 J=1,NSTK
83          FSDEFF(J)=1
84    9     CONTINUE
85          CALL SDTEST(FSDEFF,1)
86          CALL EFFPRNT(FSDEFF)
87    C- ******** SECOND DEGREE STOCHASTIC DOMINANCE *******
88          CALL SSDSUMS
89          DO 1990 J=1,NSTK
90          SSDEFF(J)=FSDEFF(J)
91    1990  CONTINUE
92          CALL SDTEST(SSDEFF,2)
93          CALL EFFPRNT(SSDEFF)
94    C-
95    C- ************ THIRD DEGREE STOCHASTIC DOMINANCE *********
96          CALL TSDSUMS
97          DO 1890 J=1,NSTK
98          TSDEFF(J)=SSDEFF(J)
99    1890  CONTINUE
100         CALL SDTEST(TSDEFF,3)
101         CALL EFFPRNT(TSDEFF)
102   C-
103         STOP
104         END

1           SUBROUTINE SSDSUMS
2     C-
3     C-
4     C- ***** SUBROUTINE SSDSUMS FORMS SSD SUMS MATRIX ******
5     C-
6     C-
7     C====================================================================
8           PARAMETER(MAXST=140,MAXPE=15,NSTK=125, NPER=10 )
9     C====================================================================
10          COMMON X(MAXPE,MAXST),XMEAN(MAXST),SD(MAXST),
11        2  INDEX(MAXST),INDEX1(MAXST),XMEAN1(MAXST),SD1(MAXST),XM(MAXST),
12        3  NAME(MAXST),NAME1(MAXST)
```

```
13          DO 19 J=1,NSTK
14          DO 19 I=1,NPER-1
15          X(NPER-I,J)=X(NPER-I,J)+X(NPER-I+1,J)
16   19     CONTINUE
17          RETURN
18          END




 1          SUBROUTINE TSDSUMS
 2   C-
 3   C-
 4   C- ****** SUBROUTINE TSDSUMS FORMS TSD SUMS MATRIX *********
 5   C-
 6   C-
 7   C=======================================================================
 8          PARAMETER(MAXST=140,MAXPE=15,NSTK=125, NPER=10 )
 9   C=======================================================================
10          COMMON X(MAXPE,MAXST),XMEAN(MAXST),SD(MAXST),
11        2  INDEX(MAXST),INDEX1(MAXST),XMEAN1(MAXST),SD1(MAXST),XM(MAXST),
12        3  NAME(MAXST),NAME1(MAXST)
13          DO 18 J=1,NSTK
14          X(NPER,J)=T1=X(NPER,J)/2
15          XM(J)=X(1,J)
16          DO 18 I=1,NPER-1
17          T2=X(NPER-I,J)/2
18          X(NPER-I,J)=X(NPER-I+1,J)+T1+T2
19          T1=T2
20   18     CONTINUE




 1          SUBROUTINE SDTEST(SDEFF,NTEST)
 2   C-
 3   C-
 4   C- ******* SUBROUTINE SDTEST PERFORMS FSD, SSD, OR TSD TESTS **********
 5   C- ******* DEPENDING ON INPUT PARAMETERS SUPPLIED ON CALL *************
 6   C-
 7   C-
 8   C=======================================================================
 9          PARAMETER(MAXST=140,MAXPE=15,NSTK=125, NPER=10)
10   C=======================================================================
11          COMMON X(MAXPE,MAXST),XMEAN(MAXST),SD(MAXST),
12        2 INDEX(MAXST),INDEX1(MAXST),XMEAN1(MAXST),SD1(MAXST),XM(MAXST),
13        3 NAME(MAXST),NAME1(MAXST)
14          INTEGER SDEFF(MAXST)
15   921    FORMAT(' SECURITY ',I3,' EXCLUDED BY ',I3)
16   11     FORMAT(2X,20('*')/2X,'STARTING ',A5/2X,20('*'))
17          PRINT 11,SDEFF(NSTK+1)
18          DO 90 I=1,NSTK
19          K=INDEX(I)
20          IF(SDEFF(K).EQ.0) GO TO 90
21          DO 91 J=1,NSTK
22          IF(K.EQ.J) GO TO 91
23          IF(SDEFF(J).EQ.0) GO TO 91
24          IF(XMEAN1(K).LT.XMEAN1(J)) GO TO 91
25          IF(NTEST.EQ.3.AND.XM(K).LT.XM(J)) GO TO 91
26          DO 92 L=1,NPER
27          IF(X(NPER-L+1,K).LT.X(NPER-L+1,J)) GO TO 91
```

```
28    92    CONTINUE
29          SDEFF(J)=0
30          PRINT 921,J,K
31    91    CONTINUE
32    90    CONTINUE
33          RETURN
34          END


1           SUBROUTINE EFFPRNT(SDEFF)
2     C-
3     C-
4     C- ****** SUBROUTINE EFFPRNT PRINTS OUT EFFICIENT SETS *********
5     C-
6     C-
7     C=================================================================
8           PARAMETER(MAXST=140,MAXPE=15,NSTK=125,NPER=10)
9     C=================================================================
10          COMMON X(MAXPE,MAXST),XMEAN(MAXST),SD(MAXST),
11        2   INDEX(MAXST),INDEX1(MAXST),XMEAN1(MAXST),SD1(MAXST),XM(MAXST),
12        3   NAME(MAXST),NAME1(MAXST)
13          INTEGER SDEFF(MAXST)
14    922   FORMAT(1X,127I1)
15    12    FORMAT(2I4,2X,A10,2F10.4)
16    10    FORMAT(2X,A5,'EFFICIENT SET'/2X,20('='))
17    C- ******** PRINT EFFICIENT SET AFTER TEST **********
18          PRINT 10,SDEFF(NSTK+1)
19          PRINT 922,(SDEFF(J),J=1,NSTK)
20          NUMB=0
21          DO 93 I=1,NSTK
22          IF(SDEFF(I).EQ.0) GO TO 93
23          NUMB=NUMB+1
24          PRINT 12, NUMB,INDEX1(I),NAME1(I),XMEAN1(I),SD1(I)
25    93    CONTINUE
26          RETURN
27          END
```

## Questions and Problems

6.1   Define the following concepts:
      (a) efficiency criterion;
      (b) First Degree Stochastic Dominance (FSD) rule;
      (c) Second Degree Stochastic Dominance (SSD) rule;
      (d) Third Degree Stochastic Dominance (TSD) rule;
      (e) efficient set.

6.2   Distinguish between the concepts of an optimal investment option and an optimal
      efficiency criterion.

6.3   "The FSD rule and the SSD rule are *mutually exclusive* methods for screening investment
      options." Appraise this statement.

6.4    What is the relationship (if any) of the FSD, SSD and TSD rules to investment's expected
       return? What is their relationship to the variance of the distribution of returns?

6.5    What is the relationship between the FSD and SSD *inefficient* sets?

6.6    It is often said that "diversification always pays". Do you agree?

6.7    In what sense can investment decisions be thought of as comprising a "two-step" proce-
       dure?

6.8    Consider the following five investment options:

| A | | B | | C | | D | | E | |
| Prob-<br>ability | Return* | Prob-<br>ability | Return* | Prob-<br>ability | Return* | Prob-<br>ability | Return* | Prob-<br>ability | Return* |
|---|---|---|---|---|---|---|---|---|---|
| 1/4 | 20 | 1/2 | 5  | 1/4 | 15 | 3/4 | 15 | 1/4 | 10 |
| 3/4 | 30 | 1/2 | 40 | 3/4 | 40 | 1/4 | 25 | 1/4 | 15 |
|     |    |     |    |     |    |     |    | 1/4 | 20 |
|     |    |     |    |     |    |     |    | 1/4 | 30 |

\* All the returns are given per $100 investment.

(a) Which of these options will be included in the FSD efficient set?
(b) Demonstrate your answer graphically.

6.9    Consider the following five investment options:

| A | | B | | C | | D | | E | |
| Prob-<br>ability | Return* | Prob-<br>ability | Return* | Prob-<br>ability | Return* | Prob-<br>ability | Return* | Prob-<br>ability | Return* |
|---|---|---|---|---|---|---|---|---|---|
| 1/2 | 10 | 1/3 | 10 | 1/2 | 5 | 1/2 | 12 | 1/4 | 6  |
| 1/2 | 20 | 1/3 | 15 | 1/4 | 6 | 1/2 | 20 | 3/4 | 40 |
|     |    | 1/3 | 30 | 1/4 | 8 |     |    |     |    |

\* All returns per $100 investment.

(a) Which options comprise the FSD efficient set?
(b) Which options are included in the SSD efficient set?
(c) Prove your answers to parts (a) and (b) graphically.

6.10   Distinguish between an option's probability (density) distribution and its *cumulative*
       probability distribution. Use a uniform distribution to demonstrate your answer.

6.11   "If $F$ dominates $G$ by FSD then necessarily $F$ dominates $G$ by SSD." Prove this state-
       ment.

6.12   "The FSD rule is the best of all the efficiency criteria since it does not require strong
       assumptions regarding investors' preferences." Appraise.

6.13   Prove that the FSD rule always results in a *smaller* efficient set than does the following criterion:

F dominates G if for every R, $F(R) + \delta \leqslant G(R)$ (where $\delta > 0$) in a given range $N < R < M$ and $F(R) \leqslant G(R)$ for all other values R.

(*Hint:* Use numerical examples to prove your answer.)

6.14   Consider the following efficiency criterion:

F dominates G if $F(R - 5) \leqslant G(R)$ for every R with strict inequality for at least one R.

Apply this criterion to the following pairs of options:

(a)

| Option A | | Option B | |
|---|---|---|---|
| *Probability* | *Return* | *Probability* | *Return* |
| 1.00 | 4 | 0.50 | 1 |
| | | 0.50 | 7 |

(b)

| Option C | | Option D | |
|---|---|---|---|
| *Probability* | *Return* | *Probability* | *Return* |
| 1.00 | 7 | 0.50 | 1 |
| | | 0.50 | 7 |

(c)

| Option E | | Option H | |
|---|---|---|---|
| *Probability* | *Return* | *Probability* | *Return* |
| 1.00 | 7 | 0.50 | 3 |
| | | 0.50 | 6 |

Options A, C, E should be regarded as G, and options B, D, H as F. What is the efficient set and what is the inefficient set for each of the three cases using the above criterion? How does the efficient set compare to the FSD efficient set? How would you characterize the proposed efficiency criterion (sufficient, necessary, optimal)?
(*Hint:* To construct the distribution $F(R - 5)$, use the value of the original distribution at the point $R - 5$ as the value of $F(R - 5)$ at the point R.)

6.15   (a)  "It is impossible that option A dominates option B by FSD and also that option B dominates option A by FSD."
        (b)  Suppose that we apply the following "shifted criterion" with $\delta > 0$:
            (i)  A dominates B if $F_A(R - \delta) \leqslant F_B(R)$
            (ii)  B dominates A if $F_B(R - \delta) \leqslant F_A(R)$
            "It is impossible that option B dominates A by the shifted criterion and also B dominates A".

Appraise the assertions in (a) and (b) above. Give an example to illustrate your answer to (b).

6.16 Below are given partial data on the distribution of returns of two investment portfolios.

| Portfolio F | | Portfolio G | |
|---|---|---|---|
| Return (%) | Probability | Return (%) | Probability |
| −20 | 1/100 | −19.5 | 50/100 |
| 10 | 5/100 | 10 | 25/100 |
| . | . | . | . |
| . | . | . | . |
| . | . | . | . |

(a) Is it possible for $F$ to dominate $G$ by FSD, or vice versa?
(b) Is it possible for $F$ to dominate $G$ by SSD, or vice versa?
(c) Answer parts (a) and (b) assuming that the expected return of $G$ is 10% and that the expected return of $F$ is 15%.

6.17 A lottery ticket whose price is $X$ has the following distribution of prizes:

| Probability | Prize |
|---|---|
| 25/32 | 0 |
| 4/32 | 4 |
| 2/32 | 8 |
| 1/32 | 64 |

(a) What is the maximum value that $X$ can take in order to make the above lottery worthwhile for some risk averter? (Apply the SSD rule.)
(b) Answer part (a) assuming that the individual may be either a risk lover or a risk averter.

6.18* An investor faces the following two risky portfolios:

| Portfolio F | | Portfolio G | |
|---|---|---|---|
| Return | Probability | Return | Probability |
| 1.49 | 1/2 | 1 | 1/4 |
| 3.51 | 1/2 | 2 | 1/4 |
| | | 3 | 1/4 |
| | | 4 | 1/4 |

Show that $F$ dominates $G$ by TSD but not by FSD or SSD. Carry out all the relevant calculations in detail and demonstrate your answer graphically.
*Hint:* The SSD criterion is the integral over the difference of the cumulative distributions $(G - F)$ and the TSD criterion is the integral over the SSD criterion. Start by drawing a graph of $G - F$ and evaluating the SSD integral as the area under this curve. Then draw a graph of the SSD integral and again evaluate the TSD integral as the area under the new curve.

**6.19\*** Prove necessity of the FSD criterion for all investors with $U' \geqslant 0$.

**6.20\*** Prove necessity of the SSD criterion for all investors with $U' \geqslant 0$, $U'' \leqslant 0$.

**6.21\*** *TSD criterion:* Prove that if $G_2(R) \leqslant F_2(R)$ for all $R$ and $E_F(R) \geqslant E_G(R)$, then every investor with preferences which have the properties $U' \geqslant 0$, $U'' \leqslant 0$ and $U''' \geqslant 0$ will prefer $F$ over $G$ ($F_2$ and $G_2$ are defined as in the text).

**6.22\*** *Financial leverage and valuation:* Consider two corporations $L$ and $U$ identical in all respects, except for their financial structures. While firm $L$ has debt in its capital structure, firm $U$ finances all its operations only with equity. The earnings before interest and tax of each firm (EBIT) is a random variable denoted by $X$. The following data describe the two firms and the random variable $X$:

|  | Firm L | Firm U |
|---|---|---|
| Number of shares of common stock ($N$) | 1,000,000 | 2,000,000 |
| Long-term debt ($D_L$) | \$10,000,000 | — |

Distribution of EBIT for the two firms:

| $X$ | Probability |
|---|---|
| \$2,000,000 | 0.50 |
| \$1,200,000 | 0.25 |
| \$ −500,000 | 0.25 |

The market value of the stock of firm $U$ is \$20,000,000, and the interest rate that firm $L$ pays on its debt is 7%.

Modigliani and Miller have shown that in the absence of corporate taxes the two firms must have the same share price $P$ regardless of capital structure, i.e., $P_L = P_U$. Denote by $Y_U$ the earnings per share of firm $U$ (a random variable) and by $Y_L$ the earnings per share of firm $L$ (also a random variable).

Show that if $P_L > P_U$, arbitrage possibilities exist such that the investor can switch from firm $L$ to firm $U$ while receiving income which dominates the previous income $Y_L$ by FSD.

**6.23** The following table lists the annual returns on four stocks between 1977 and 1981. Assuming that each return is equally probable, determine the efficient set of investments by
(a) first degree stochastic dominance;
(b) second degree stochastic dominance;
(c) (optional) third degree stochastic dominance.

| | | Return on Stock (%) | | |
|---|---|---|---|---|
| Year | Allied Corp. | American Cyanamid | Celanese Corp. | Chrysler Corp. |
| 1977 | 15.31 | 1.51 | −8.63 | −34.40 |
| 1978 | −32.56 | 0.28 | 1.97 | −26.37 |
| 1979 | 83.98 | 42.03 | 26.64 | −19.97 |
| 1980 | 13.33 | 0.94 | 24.57 | −27.78 |
| 1981 | −14.10 | −5.97 | 8.03 | −30.77 |

*Source:* CRSP monthly returns data tape.

6.24  The following table lists annual returns for Celanese Corp. and McGraw Edison Company for 1980 and 1981. The portfolio with minimum variance consists of 86% of Celanese Corp. and 14% of McGraw Edison Co. Would an investor following (1) the FSD rule and (2) the SSD rule diversify by investing in the minimum variance portfolio of the two stocks? Assume each outcome has a probability of $\frac{1}{2}$.

|  | Returns (%) | |
|---|---|---|
| Year | Celanese Corp. | McGraw Edison Co. |
| 1980 | 24.57 | 46.22 |
| 1981 | 8.03 | 4.52 |

*Source:* CRSP monthly returns tape.

6.25*  The inflationary era produced a new investment instrument known as the variable interest bond, periodically adjusting the coupon to prevailing interest rates in order to provide the investor with some protection from the eroding effects of inflation. Perfect protection is provided by the so-called *indexed bonds*, where the principal and the interest are linked to the rate of inflation (usually through the Consumer Price Index or some other index). The nominal (gross) return $1 + R$ on a $1 investment in indexed bonds is represented by $1 + R = (1 + r)(1 + h)$, where $r$ is the stated interest rate on the bond and $h$ is the rate of inflation. Full indexation, however, is a two-edged sword: the return increases at high inflation rates and falls at low inflation rates. An indexed bond with minimum guaranteed interest links the investor to the high tail of the inflation distribution: the nominal return is linked as $1 + R = (1 + r)(1 + h)$ only as long as it exceeds a certain minimum guaranteed return $1 + r_{min}$. Otherwise, the investor gets $1 + R = 1 + r_{min}$.

(a)  A risk-averse investor considers investing $100 in either of the following variable-interest bonds for one year:

(i)  a fully index government bond with 6% interest ($r = 6\%$);

(ii)  an indexed government bond with 5% linked interest ($r = 5\%$) and 10% minimum guaranteed interest ($r_{min} = 10\%$).

Which of the two bonds is preferred in each of the following four alternative states of nature characterized by different distribution of inflation rates:

|  | A | B | C | D |
|---|---|---|---|---|
| Probability of Inflation $p(h)$ | Inflation Rate, h% | Inflation Rate, h% | Inflation Rate, h% | Inflation Rate, h% |
| 1/3 | −3 | −2 | 3 | 6 |
| 1/3 | 0 | 2 | 7 | 11 |
| 1/3 | 3 | 6 | 11 | 16 |

Conduct the analysis in both nominal and real (constant-purchasing-power terms). Prove your results numerically and graphically.

(b)  Draw the schematic cumulative distribution curves of the returns on the two bonds as a function of the inflation random variable. Distinguish between three cases:

(i)  the inflation rate never exceeds 3.77%;

(ii)  the inflation rate is always greater than 3.77%;

(iii) the inflation rate may take any value.

Which of the two bonds is preferred in each of these cases for all risk averters? Conduct the analysis in both nominal and real terms.

## Data Set Problems

1. Assigning a probability of 1/10 to each observation, construct the FSD and the SSD efficient sets for a population consisting of the first four funds (Nos. 1 through 4) in the Data Set. Draw the cumulative distributions of the four funds on one diagram.

2. Use the computer program in Appendix 6.3 to construct the FSD, SSD, and TSD efficient sets from a feasible set that includes all the mutual funds in the Data Set.

3. Repeat the construction of Problem 2 for the case when the feasible set includes also the market portfolio (the Fisher Index $R_m$ at the end of the Data Set). Compare and contrast the results of Problems 2 and 3.

4. Which mutual fund out of all the mutual funds in the Data Set is optimal for an investor with the utility function:

$$U(R) = \log \left( 1 + \frac{R}{100} \right)$$

where $R$ is the rate of return (in percent).

In your answer, relate specifically to the results of Problem 2 above.

5. Suppose that the SSD efficient set constructed in Problem 2 above consists of $k$ mutual funds. Construct a portfolio such that $1/k$ of the total investment is invested in each of the $k$ SSD efficient funds. Is this diversified portfolio SSD efficient? Prove your answer.

## Selected References

Aharony, J., and Loeb, M., "Mean-Variance vs. Stochastic Dominance: Some Empirical Findings on Efficient Sets", *Journal of Banking and Finance*, Vol. 1, pp. 95–102 (1977).

Ali, M. M., "Stochastic Dominance and Portfolio Analysis", *Journal of Financial Economics*, Vol. 2, pp. 205–29 (1975).

Alias, P. M., "Le Comportement de L'Homme Rationnel devant le Risque: Critique des Postulats et Axiomes de l'Ecole Américaine", *Econometrica*, Vol. 21, pp. 503–46 (1953).

Arditti, F. D., and Peles, Y., "Leverage, Bankruptcy, and the Cost of Capital", in *Natural Resources, Uncertainty and General Equilibrium Systems: Essays in Memory of Rafael Lusky*, edited by A. S. Blinder and P. Friedman, New York: Academic Press (1977).

Atkinson, A. B., "On the Measurement of Inequality", *Journal of Economic Theory*, Vol. 2, pp. 244–63 (1970).

Baron, D. P., "Firm Valuation, Corporate Taxes, and Default Risk", *Journal of Finance*, Vol. 30, pp. 1251–64 (1975).

Bawa, V. S., "Optimal Rules for Ordering Uncertain Prospects", *Journal of Financial Economics*, Vol. 2, pp. 95–121 (1975).

Bawa, V. S., "Safety-First, Stochastic Dominance and Optimal Portfolio Choice", *Journal of Financial and Quantitative Analysis*, Vol. 13, pp. 255–71 (1978).

Bawa, V. S., and Lindenberg, E. B., *Capital Market Equilibrium in a Mean, Lower Partial Moment Framework*, Economic Discussion Paper No. 84, Bell Laboratories (1977).

Brumelle, S. L., "When Does Diversification Between Two Investments Pay?" *Journal of Financial and Quantitative Analysis*, Vol. 9, pp. 473–82 (1974).

Diamond, P. A., and Stiglitz, J. E., "Increases in Risk and in Risk Aversion", *Journal of Economic Theory*, Vol. 8, pp. 337–60 (1974).

Dickinson, J. P., "The Reliability of Estimation Procedures in Portfolio Analysis", *Journal of Financial and Quantitative Analysis*, Vol. 9, pp. 447–62 (1974).

Fishburn, P. S., *Decision and Value Theory*, New York: Wiley (1964).

Fishburn, P. C., and Porter, R. B., "Optimal Portfolios with One Safe and One Risky Asset: Effects of Changes in Rates of Return and Risk", *Management Science*, Vol. 22, pp. 1064–73 (1976).

Frankfurter, G. M., and Phillips, H. E., "Efficient Algorithms for Conducting Stochastic Dominance Tests on Large Numbers of Portfolios, A Comment", *Journal of Financial and Quantitative Analysis*, Vol. 10, pp. 177–79 (1975).

Gavish, B., "A Relaxation Algorithm for Building Undominated Portfolios", *Journal of Banking and Finance*, Vol. 1, pp. 143–50 (1977).

Gould, J. P., "Risk, Stochastic Preferences and the Value of Information", *Journal of Economic Theory*, Vol. 8, pp. 64–84 (1974).

Hadar, J., and Russell, W. R., "Rules for Ordering Uncertain Prospects", *American Economic Review*, Vol. 59, pp. 25–34 (1969).

Hadar, J., and Russell, W. R., "Stochastic Dominance and Diversification", *Journal of Economic Theory*, Vol. 3, pp. 288–305 (1971).

Hadar, J., and Russell, W. R., "Diversification of Interdependent Prospects", *Journal of Economic Theory*, Vol. 7, pp. 231–40 (1974).

Hadar, J., Russell, W. R., and Seo, K., "Gain from Diversification", *Review of Economic Studies*, Vol. 44, pp. 363–68 (1977).

Hadar, J., and Seo, K., "Stochastic Dominance and the Case for Diversification", *Research in Finance*, Vol. 2 (1980).

Hakansson, N. H., "Multi-Period Mean-Variance Analysis: Toward A General Theory of Portfolio Choice", *Journal of Finance*, Vol. 26, pp. 857–84 (1971).

Hammond, J. S., "Simplifying the Choice Between Uncertain Prospects where Preference is Non-Linear", *Management Science*, Vol. 20, pp. 1047–72 (1974).

Hang, C. C., Vertinsky, I., and Zimba, W. T., "On Multiperiod Stochastic Dominance", *Journal of Financial and Quantitative Analysis*, Vol. 13, pp. 1–13 (1978).

Hanoch, G., and Levy, H., "The Efficiency Analysis of Choices Involving Risk", *Review of Economic Studies*, Vol. 36, pp. 335–46 (1969).

Hogan, W. W., and Warren, J. M., "Computation of the Efficient Boundary in the E–S Portfolio Selection Model", *Journal of Financial and Quantitative Analysis*, Vol. 7, pp. 1881–96 (1972).

Jean, W. H., "The Geometric Mean and Stochastic Dominance", *Journal of Finance* (March 1980).

Johnson, K. H., and Burgess, R. C., "The Effects of Sample Sizes on the Accuracy of EV and SSD Efficiency Criteria", *Journal of Financial and Quantitative Analysis* (December 1975).

Joy, O. M., and Porter, R. B., "Stochastic Dominance and Mutual Fund Performance", *Journal of Financial and Quantitative Analysis*, Vol. 9, pp. 25–31 (1974).

Kearns, R. B., and Burgess, R. C., "An Effective Algorithm for Estimating Stochastic Dominance Efficient Sets", *Journal of Financial and Quantitative Analysis* (September 1979).

Kroll, Y., and Levy, H., "Stochastic Dominance with a Riskless Asset: An Imperfect Market", *Journal of Financial and Quantitative Analysis* (June 1979).

Kroll, Y., and Levy, H., "Stochastic Dominance: A Review and Some New Evidence", *Research in Finance*, Vol. 2 (1980).

Laffont, J. J., "Risk, Stochastic Preferences and Value of Information: A Comment", *Journal of Economic Theory*, Vol. 12, pp. 483–87 (1976).

Latané, H. A., "Criteria for Choice among Risky Ventures", *Journal of Political Economy*, Vol. 67, pp. 144–55 (1959).

Levhari, D., Paroush, J., and Peleg, B., "Efficiency Analysis of Multivariate Distributions", *Review of Economic Studies*, Vol. 42, pp. 87–91 (1975).

Levy, H., "Stochastic Dominance among Log-Normal Prospects", *International Economic Review*, Vol. 14, pp. 601–14 (1973).

Levy, H., "Stochastic Dominance Efficiency Criteria, and Efficient Portfolios: The Multi-Period Case", *American Economic Review*, Vol. 63, pp. 986–94 (1973).

Levy, H., "Multi-Period Consumption Decision Under Conditions of Uncertainty", *Management Science*, Vol. 22, pp. 1258–67 (1976).

Levy, H., "The Definition of Risk: An Extension", *Journal of Economic Theory*, Vol. 14, pp. 232–34 (1977).

Levy, H., "Multi-Period Stochastic Dominance with One-Period Parameters, Liquidity Preference and Equilibrium in the Log-Normal Case", in *Natural Resources, Uncertainty and General Equilibrium Systems, Essays in Memory of Rafael Lusky*, edited by A. S. Blinder and P. Friedman, New York: Academic Press (1977).

Levy, H., and Hanoch, G., "Relative Effectiveness of Efficiency Criteria for Portfolio Selection", *Journal of Financial and Quantitative Analysis*, Vol. 5, pp. 63–76 (1970).

Levy, H., and Kroll, Y., "Stochastic Dominance with Riskless Assets", *Journal of Financial and Quantitative Analysis*, Vol. 11, pp. 743–73 (1976).

Levy, H., and Kroll, Y., "Ordering Uncertain Options with Borrowing and Lending", *Journal of Finance*, Vol. 33, pp. 553–73 (1978).

Levy, H., and Kroll, Y., "Investment Decision Rules, Diversification and Investor's Initial Wealth", *Econometrica*, Vol. 41, pp. 125–30 (1978).

Levy, H., and Kroll, Y., "Efficiency Analysis with Borrowing and Lending: Criteria and their Effectiveness", *Review of Economics and Statistics* (February 1979).

Levy, H., and Kroll, Y., "Sampling Errors and Portfolio Efficiency Analysis", *Journal of Financial and Quantitative Analysis* (1979).

Levy, H., and Levy, A., "Stochastic Dominance and the Investment Horizon with Riskless Assets", *Review of Economic Studies* (1982).

Levy, H., and Levy, A., "Multivariate Decision Making", *Journal of Economic Theory* (December 1983).

Levy, H., and Paroush, J., "Toward Multivariate Efficiency Criteria", *Journal of Economic Theory*, Vol. 7, pp. 129–42 (1974).

Levy, H., and Paroush, J., "Multiperiod Stochastic Dominance", *Management Science*, Vol. 21, pp. 428–35 (1974).

Levy, H., and Sarnat, M., "Alternative Efficiency Criteria: An Empirical Analysis", *Journal of Finance*, Vol. 25, pp. 1153–58 (1970).

Levy, H., and Sarnat, M., *Investment and Portfolio Analysis*, New York: Wiley (1972).

Markowitz, H. M., "Investment for the Long Run: New Evidence for an Old Rule", *Journal of Finance*, Vol. 31, pp. 1273–86 (1976).

Markowitz, H. M., "An Algorithm for Finding Undominated Portfolios", in *Financial Decision Making Under Uncertainty*, pp. 3–10, edited by H. Levy and M. Sarnat, New York: Academic Press (1977).

Masse, P., *Optimal Investment Decision Rules for Action and Criteria for Choice*, Englewood Cliffs, N.J.: Prentice-Hall (1962).

Mayer, J., "Increasing Risk", *Journal of Economic Theory*, Vol. 11, pp. 119–32 (1975).

Mayer, J., "Choice among Distributions", *Journal of Economic Theory*, Vol. 14, pp. 326–36 (1977).

Merton, R. C., and Samuelson, P. A., "Fallacy of the Lognormal Approximation to Optimal Portfolio Decision Making over Many Periods", *Journal of Financial Economics* (May 1974).

Perrakis, S., and Zerbinis, J., "Identifying the SSD Portion of the EV Frontier: A Note", *Journal of Financial and Quantitative Analysis* (March 1978).

Philippatos, G. C., and Gressis, N., "Conditions of Equivalence Among E–V, SSD, and E–H Portfolio Selection Criteria—the Case for Uniform Normal and Lognormal Distributions", *Management Science* Application (February 1957).

Porter, R. B., "An Empirical Comparison of Stochastic Dominance and Mean-Variance Choice Criteria", *Journal of Financial and Quantitative Analysis*, Vol. 8, pp. 587–608 (1973).

Porter, R. B., "Semi-variance and Stochastic Dominance: A Comparison", *American Economic Review*, Vol. 64, pp. 200–204 (1974).

Porter, R. B., and Bey, R. P., "An Evaluation of the Empirical Significance of Optimal Seeking Algorithms in Portfolio Selection", *Journal of Finance* (December 1974).

Porter, R. B., and Gaumnitz, J. E., "Stochastic Dominance vs. Mean-Variance Portfolio Analysis: An Empirical Evaluation", *American Economic Review*, Vol. 62, pp. 438–46 (1972).

Porter, R. B., and Pfaffenberger, R. C., "Efficient Algorithms for Conducting Stochastic Dominance Tests on Large Numbers of Portfolios: Reply", *Journal of Financial and Quantitative Analysis*, Vol. 10, pp. 181–85 (1975).

Porter, R. B., Wart, J. R., and Ferguson, D. L., "Efficient Algorithms for Conducting Stochastic Dominance Tests on Large Numbers of Portfolios", *Journal of Financial and Quantitative Analysis*, Vol. 8, pp. 71–82 (1973).

Quirk, J. P., and Saposnik, R., "Admissibility and Measurable Utility Functions", *Review of Economic Studies*, Vol. 29, pp. 140–46 (1962).

Rentz, W. F., and Westin, R. B., "A Note on First-Degree Stochastic Dominance and Portfolio Composition", *Management Science* (December 1975).

Robison, L. J., and Barry, P. J., "Risk Efficiency Using Stochastic Dominance and Expected Gain-Confidence Limits", *Journal of Finance* (September 1978).

Rothschild, M., and Stiglitz, J. E., "Increasing Risk: I. A Definition", *Journal of Economic Theory*, Vol. 2, pp. 225–43 (1970).

Rothschild, M., and Stiglitz, J. E., "Increasing Risk: II. Its Economic Consequences", *Journal of Economic Theory*, Vol. 3, pp. 66–84 (1971).

Rothschild, M., and Stiglitz, J. E., "Some Further Results on the Measurement of Inequality", *Journal of Economic Theory*, Vol. 6, pp. 188–204 (1973).

Russell, R. W., and Smith, P. E., "Taxation, Risk-Taking, and Stochastic Dominance", *Southern Economic Journal*, Vol. 36, pp. 423–33 (1970).

Saunders, A., Ward, C., and Woodward, R., "Stochastic Dominance and the Performance of UK Unit Trusts", *Journal of Financial and Quantitative Analysis* (June 1980).

Scott, R. C., and Horvath, P. A., "On the Direction of Preference for Moments of Higher Order than the Variance", *Journal of Finance* (September 1980).

Tehranian, H., "Empirical Studies in Portfolio Performance Using Higher Degrees of Stochastic Dominance", *Journal of Finance* (March 1980).

Tesfatsion, L., "Stochastic Dominance and the Maximization of Expected Utility", *Review of Economic Studies*, Vol. 43, pp. 301–15 (1976).

Vickson, R. G., "Stochastic Dominance Tests for Decreasing Absolute Risk Aversion II: General Random Variables", *Management Science*, Vol. 23, pp. 478–89 (1977).

Vickson, R. G., and Altman, M., "On the Relative Effectiveness of Stochastic Dominance Rules: Extension to Decreasingly Risk-Averse Utility Functions", *Journal of Financial and Quantitative Analysis*, Vol. 12, pp. 73–84 (1977).

Whitmore, G. A., "Third Degree Stochastic Dominance", *American Economic Review*, Vol. 60, pp. 457–59 (1970).

# PART III
# Portfolio Selection:
# The Mean—Variance Approach

# 7

# The Mean–Variance Criterion

As far back as the eighteenth century Bernoulli and Cramer reached the conclusion that decisions under conditions of uncertainty could not be made solely on the basis of expected (mean) returns.[1] Subsequently, various economists have tried to evaluate investments with the aid of two (or more) indicators based on the distribution of returns. Generally one index reflects the profitability of the investment while the other is based on the dispersion of the distribution of returns and reflects the investment's risk. The most common profitability index used is the expected return, that is, the mean of the probability distribution of returns; the risk index is usually based on the variance of the distribution, its range,[2] and so on.

Markowitz[3] and Tobin[4] base their theory of investment choice under conditions of uncertainty on the mean and the variance of the distributions of returns, and Markowitz has developed a mean–variance model for the selection of portfolios. According to this approach investors desire high returns but are averse to a high variance, which is taken as the indicator of an investment's risk. The Markowitz–Tobin analysis remains the cornerstone of much of the work in the field of investment analysis. It also has provided the basis for several extensions to other problems which involve risky decisions.[5]

## 7.1    The Nature of Investment Risk

Before turning to a detailed description of the mean–variance portfolio selection model we shall present a brief review of the literature on the nature of investment risk.

[1] See Chapter 4, Section 4.2.
[2] The range is defined as the difference between the highest and lowest values of the random variable. See P. G. Hoel, *Introduction to Mathematical Statistics*, New York, Wiley, 1966, p. 78.
[3] H. M. Markowitz, "Portfolio Selection", *Journal of Finance* 6 (March 1952); and *Portfolio Selection*, New York, Wiley, 1959.
[4] J. Tobin, "Liquidity Preference as Behavior Towards Risk", *Review of Economic Studies* 26, (February 1958); and "The Theory of Portfolio Selection" in F. H. Hahn and F. P. R. Brechling, eds. *Theory of Interest Rates*, New York, Macmillan, 1965.
[5] For example, the mean–variance model has been successfully applied to the problem of determining equilibrium prices in the securities market. See Chapter 11.

Numerous economists have identified investment risk with the dispersion of returns. Keynes, for example, identifies the risk involved in an investment with the possible deviations from the average return. According to Keynes, an individual who invests in an asset whose returns have a widely dispersed distribution must be given a premium to compensate him for the risk taken.[6]

Like Keynes, Hicks[7] also identifies the variance of returns with risk. Hicks emphasizes the fact that the greater the dispersion of returns (for a given level of expectation), the less attractive is the investment. Nevertheless, Hicks also emphasizes that when returns are uncertain the third moment of the distributions, the index of asymmetry or the skewness, may also be a significant factor affecting investors' decisions.

Although Marschak[8] maintains that decision making under conditions of risk should reflect *all* the moments of the distribution, he also notes that in many cases two moments, "the mathematical expectation and the coefficient of variation", will suffice. In other words, Marschak, too, identifies (in some cases) investment risk with the variance, or rather the coefficient of variation.[9]

Domar and Musgrave, on the other hand, identify the risk involved in making an investment under conditions of uncertainty with the possibility of sustaining a loss, and therefore suggest that investors should measure risk solely on the basis of that possibility:

> Of all possible questions which the investor may ask, the most important one, it appears to us, is concerned with the probability of actual yield being less than zero, that is, with the probability of loss. This is the essence of risk.[10]

These two authors developed a quantitative index of risk affected both by the probability of getting a result less than zero, and by the size of the possible loss. Thus they emphasize the negative segment of the probability distribution, and according to their model, a larger dispersion *per se* does not necessarily involve a greater risk.

Baumol[11] is another author who argues that variance *per se* does not indicate risk. According to Baumol, risk mainly reflects the possibility that the random variable may take on extremely low values. If the expected return $ER$ from an investment is high relative to its standard deviation, Baumol suggests that the spread between the expected return and $k$ times the standard deviation ($ER - k\sigma$) be taken as the risk index, since the probability that a random variable will have a value lower by $k$ standard deviations than its mean is bounded (by Chebyshev's Inequality) by $1/k^2$.[12]

Even from this brief survey we can see that while there is no unanimity of opinion

---

[6] See J. M. Keynes, *The General Theory of Employment Interest and Money*, London, Macmillan, 1937.

[7] J. R. Hicks, *Value and Capital*, 2nd ed., Oxford: Oxford University Press, 1946.

[8] J. Marschak, "Money and the Theory of Assets", *Econometrica* 6 (October 1938).

[9] The coefficient of variation is defined as the standard deviation divided by the mean.

[10] E. Domar and R. A. Musgrave, "Proportional Income Taxation and Risk Taking", *Quarterly Journal of Economics* LVII (May 1944).

[11] W. J. Baumol, "An Expected Gain–Confidence Limit Criterion for Portfolio Selection", *Management Science* 10 (October 1963).

[12] See P. G. Hoel, *op. cit.*

regarding risk, it is often identified with one of the measures of dispersion of the distribution of returns. In what follows we shall see whether it is possible to find a universally applicable quantitative risk index by invoking the expected utility hypothesis. Such an approach implies that the choice among risky alternatives is a function of investment options' expected utility.

Let us assume that an individual is faced with the distribution of a random variable (return) $R$ which can take on only two values, $R_1$ and $R_2$ with the probabilities $p_1$ and $p_2$ ($p_2 = 1 - p_1$), respectively. The expected value of this distribution is given by

$$ER = p_1 R_1 + p_2 R_2$$

The expected utility is

$$EU(R) = p_1 U(R_1) + (1 - p_1) U(R_2)$$

This distribution is plotted in Figure 7.1.

Let us further assume that the individual is a risk averter[13] and can sell this distribution, thereby converting it into a perfectly certain income (for example, by purchasing an insurance policy). How much will the individual be ready to pay to transform the random variable $R$ into a riskless alternative? Since he reaches his decision according to the principles of expected utility, he will be ready to pay as a premium any sum equal to or smaller than $\pi$ in Figure 7.1. $\pi$ represents the maximum premium because such a premium does not change the individual's expected utility.[14] Thus one way to measure the magnitude of risk inherent in a particular distribution of returns is to estimate the size of the premium that an individual is prepared to pay in order to shift this risk to someone else. The higher the maximum risk premium he is willing to pay, the greater is the risk.

Let us now assume that there is another investment option (distribution) $R'$, with a different expected return, as well as a different dispersion, from that of $R$. We proceed in the same manner and ask how much the individual will be ready to pay in order to

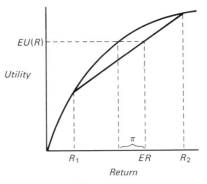

**Figure 7.1**

[13] Therefore the utility function in Figure 7.1 is drawn concave downward.
[14] See Chapter 4, Section 4.5.

burden someone else with the risk. If the risk premium that he is willing to pay is higher than that for $R$, we can conclude that the risk of $R'$ is greater than the risk of $R$. (The reader should note that this does not mean that $R$ is preferable to $R'$ or vice versa; here we have isolated the risk aspect, while other important factors that affect the final decision are ignored.) As far as any *individual* investor is concerned, we can, in principle, array the risks in descending order by attaching to each random variable a quantitative index that reflects the risk to which it exposes the investor. But can the above analysis be generalized for all investors? Since there is every reason to believe that individuals have widely differing tastes, this quantitative index cannot be generalized, even for the subclass of risk averters. This will become apparent when we consider the following example. Suppose that two risk-averse investors face the same choice between two random variables, $R$ and $R'$; their utility functions are drawn in Figure 7.2 and are marked $U_1$ and $U_2$, respectively.

How will these two investors evaluate the risks involved in each of the investments? The investor whose utility function is given by $U_1$ is ready to pay a premium of $a$ in order to shift the risk of $R$ to someone else, but he is not willing to pay anything for shifting the risk of $R'$ (the utility function is linear in the relevant range). For this investor, therefore, the risk involved in $R$ is greater than the risk involved in $R'$. On the other hand, the investor whose utility function is marked $U_2$ is ready to pay a premium of $b$ to avoid the risk of $R$, but an even higher premium, $c$, to avoid the risk of $R'$. Thus to the second investor $R'$ is the riskier alternative.

From this example we can conclude that, in general, there is no universally applicable *quantitative* risk index. While individuals may impute a quantitative measure of risk to each investment alternative, these measures typically will differ from individual to individual. When isolating efficient options, we are interested in selecting a set of efficient investments which is appropriate for a given class of investors. But as we have

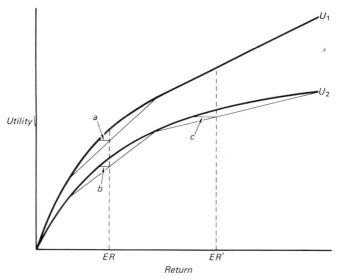

**Figure 7.2**

seen in the above example, even where two investors are known to be risk averters a unique quantitative index cannot be found to reflect the riskiness of investments for all investors of this class.

Despite these conceptual difficulties, attempts have been made to identify risk with a particular measure of dispersion. In the following section we shall consider what is undoubtedly the best known attempt to solve this problem—the identification of risk with the *variance* of the distribution of returns. We shall then go on to determine the exact conditions under which the use of the variance as a risk index and the use of the mean–variance criterion as an investment decision rule are justified.

**7.2    The Mean–Variance Criterion (MVC)**

The efficiency analysis presented in the previous chapter, using the FSD criterion and the SSD criterion, requires, as we have seen, full knowledge of the distribution of returns for each investment option (portfolio) being considered. A striking advantage of the mean–variance model is that the investment analyst can confine himself to the first two distribution moments—the expected (mean) return and the variance (or standard deviation)—of each option being considered.[15] This constitutes a significant advantage and perhaps accounts for the fact that the Mean–Variance Criterion (hereafter referred to as MVC) is by far the most widely known efficiency criterion for investment analysis.

The MVC can be defined as follows: An option $F$ dominates (is preferred to) an option $G$ by the MVC if and only if

$$E_F R \geqslant E_G R$$

$$Var_F(R) \leqslant Var_G(R)$$

on the condition that at least one strong inequality holds.[16] This means that an option $F$ dominates an option $G$ if its expected return is greater than (or equal to) that of $G$, while its variance is smaller than (or equal to) the variance of $G$. The expected return is taken as an indicator of the investment's profitability; the variance serves as an indicator of its risk.

The MVC can also be defined in two other equivalent (and perhaps more familiar) forms

$$E_F R \geqslant E_G R, \quad Var_F(R) < Var_G(R)$$

or

$$E_F R > E_G R, \quad Var_F(R) \leqslant Var_G(R)$$

---

[15] The use of the Mean–Variance Criterion for portfolio selection is analyzed in detail in Chapter 8.

[16] The variance of $R$ under the distribution $F$ is usually denoted by $Var_F(R)$, but for the sake of brevity, the accepted mathematical notation $\sigma_F^2$ will also be used.

This alternative notation clearly shows that $E_F R \geqslant E_G R$ constitutes a *necessary* condition for option $F$ to dominate option $G$. This is the same necessary condition which we found in the FSD and the SSD. Here, however, there also exists a clear-cut requirement regarding the variance; for $F$ to dominate $G$, by the MVC, it is also necessary that $Var_F(R) \leqslant Var_G(R)$. According to the FSD and the SSD, as we have seen in Chapter 6, $F$ can dominate $G$ even though the variance of $F$ is greater than that of $G$.[17]

EXAMPLE 1

To illustrate the application of the MVC, let us calculate the mean and the variance of two mutual funds (denoted by $F$ and $G$) for the ten years 1971–1980. The rates of return (in percent) are taken from Arthur Wiesenberger's *Investment Companies*. We assume that each year out of ten has an equal probability of $\frac{1}{10}$. For simplicity we consider these ten-year figures as representing the entire population rather than a sample, so that no sampling errors are involved. Table 7.1 lists the returns $R_{Ft}$ and $R_{Gt}$ on each of the two fund portfolios for the years 1971–1980 ($t$ is the year index, $t = 1, 2, \ldots, 10$). We also added columns with the squared returns ($R_{Ft}^2$ and $R_{Gt}^2$) and the square sums which one needs in calculating the mean and the variance.

In order to check whether one fund dominates the other by MVC, we calculate the mean and the variance of returns, which are given by the following relations:

$$\text{Means:} \quad E_F R = \frac{1}{n} \sum_{t=1}^{n} R_{Ft}, \quad E_G R = \frac{1}{n} \sum_{t=1}^{n} R_{Gt}$$

$$\text{Variances:} \quad Var_F(R) = \frac{1}{n} \sum_{t=1}^{n} (R_{Ft} - E_F R)^2, \quad Var_G(R) = \frac{1}{n} \sum_{t=1}^{n} (R_{Gt} - E_G R)^2$$

**Table 7.1**
**Rates of Return on Investment in Two Mutual Funds, 1971–1980**

| American Investors Fund (F) | | | Value Line Special Situation (G) | | |
|---|---|---|---|---|---|
| Year | Return $R_F$ (percent) | $R_F^2$ | Year | Return $R_G$ (percent) | $R_G^2$ |
| 1971 | 5.6 | 31.36 | 1971 | 17.6 | 309.76 |
| 1972 | 10.8 | 116.64 | 1972 | −11.0 | 121.00 |
| 1973 | −15.3 | 234.09 | 1973 | −45.7 | 2,088.49 |
| 1974 | −29.7 | 882.09 | 1974 | −29.2 | 852.64 |
| 1975 | 17.9 | 320.41 | 1975 | 47.0 | 2,209.00 |
| 1976 | 34.8 | 1,211.04 | 1976 | 52.7 | 2,777.29 |
| 1977 | 5.1 | 26.01 | 1977 | 12.3 | 151.29 |
| 1978 | 1.6 | 2.56 | 1978 | 21.2 | 449.44 |
| 1979 | 63.4 | 4,019.56 | 1979 | 43.5 | 1,892.25 |
| 1980 | 47.4 | 2,246.76 | 1980 | 54.4 | 2,959.36 |
| Sum Over the 10 Years | 141.60 | 9,090.52 | | 162.80 | 13,810.52 |

---

[17] See Chapter 6, Sections 6.3 and 6.3.1.

A shortcut working formula for the variances is

$$\sigma_F^2 = \frac{1}{n}\left[\sum_{t=1}^{n} R_{Ft}^2 - \frac{1}{n}\left(\sum_{t=1}^{n} R_{Ft}\right)^2\right], \quad \sigma_G^2 = \frac{1}{n}\left[\sum_{t=1}^{n} R_{Gt}^2 - \frac{1}{n}\left(\sum_{t=1}^{n} R_{Gt}\right)^2\right]$$

Using the sums from the bottom line of Table 7.1 we obtain the following results:

*American Investors Fund (F):*

$$\text{Mean} \quad \frac{1}{10}\sum_{t=1}^{10} R_{Ft} = \frac{141.60}{10} = 14.16\%$$

$$\text{Variance} \quad \frac{1}{10}\left[\sum_{t=1}^{10} R_{Ft}^2 - \frac{1}{10}\left(\sum_{t=1}^{10} R_{Ft}\right)^2\right] = \frac{1}{10}\left[9,090.52 - \frac{(141.60)^2}{10}\right] =$$

$$= \frac{7,085.46}{10} = 708.55$$

*Value Line Special Situation (G):*

$$\text{Mean} \quad \frac{1}{10}\sum_{t=1}^{10} R_{Gt} = \frac{162.80}{10} = 16.28\%$$

$$\text{Variance} \quad \frac{1}{10}\left[\sum_{t=1}^{10} R_{Gt}^2 - \frac{1}{10}\left(\sum_{t=1}^{10} R_{Gt}\right)^2\right] = \frac{1}{10}\left[13,810.52 - \frac{(162.80)^2}{10}\right] =$$

$$= \frac{1}{10}[13,810.52 - 2,650.38] = \frac{11,160.14}{10} = 1,116.01$$

Thus,

$$E_G R > E_F R$$

and

$$Var_G(R) > Var_F(R)$$

and neither fund dominates the other by the MVC.

In this example, we calculated the variance as a population parameter. If, however, the data are treated as a sample of $n$ observations, the common practice is to calculate the *unbiased estimate* of the variance, defined as

$$S^2 = \sum_{t=1}^{n} (R_t - \bar{R})^2/(n-1)$$

since the true variance of the population is unknown. For our purposes, dividing by $n$ (as in the calculation of the population parameter) or by $(n-1)$ (as in the calculation of the unbiased estimate of variance) does not affect the final outcome of the analysis, since $S_F^2 > S_G^2$ if and only if $Var_F(R) > Var_G(R)$ and vice versa (so long as the number of observations $n$ is the same for both options).

EXAMPLE 2

To illustrate further the use of MVC in efficiency analysis, let us consider the following five investment options.

| Option | A | B | C | D | E |
|---|---|---|---|---|---|
| Expected Return $ER$ | 10 | 8 | 9 | 11 | 12 |
| Variance $Var(R)$ | 10 | 11 | 10 | 12 | 11 |

We begin the analysis by comparing option $A$ with option $B$ as follows

$$E_A R = 10 > 8 = E_B R$$

$$Var_A(R) = 10 < 11 = Var_B(R)$$

The MVC is satisfied, and therefore $A$ dominates $B$. Accordingly, $B$ is relegated to the inefficient set. Comparing options $A$ and $C$ we find that

$$E_A R > E_C R$$

$$Var_A(R) = Var_C(R)$$

Again $A$ is dominant, and $C$ can also be eliminated from the efficient set. We go on to compare $A$ and $D$ and find that

$$E_A R = 10 < 11 = E_D R$$

$$Var_A(R) = 10 < 12 = Var_D(R)$$

This means that while the expected return of $D$ is greater than that of $A$, which is considered to be to the investor's advantage, the variance of returns of option $D$ exceeds that of option $A$, which is considered to be to the investor's disadvantage. Thus we are unable to say whether $A$ is preferable to $D$, and both investments must, for the time being at least, be retained in the efficient set. Similarly, a comparison of options $A$ and $E$ fails to establish a clear-cut preference between them, so that $E$ is also retained, for the time being, in the efficient set.

Since options $B$ and $C$ have already been eliminated, we go on to compare $D$ and $E$

and find

$$E_E R = 12 > 11 = E_D R$$

$$Var_E(R) = 11 < 12 = Var_D(R)$$

Here again the MVC is satisfied so that investment $E$ dominates investment $D$. As we have already seen, $A$ does *not* dominate $D$, but since another option can be found in the efficient group ($E$) which is preferable to investment $D$, the efficient group is further reduced by the elimination of $D$. There are thus only two investments left in the efficient set: options $A$ and $E$. This set cannot be further reduced since, by the MVC, $A$ does not dominate $E$, nor does $E$ dominate $A$. The inefficient group includes three investments: $B$, $C$, and $D$.

A look at the relevant data shows that option $C$ is preferable to investment option $B$, since

$$E_C R = 9 > 8 = E_B R$$

$$Var_C(R) = 10 < 11 = Var_B(R)$$

Does this really matter? Hardly. Any analysis of priorities *within* the inefficient group is a barren exercise, for the partition into two subsets, an efficient and an inefficient one, means that every investor who acts in accordance with the MVC will make his final selection from the efficient group. Since it is clear that he will never willingly choose any of the options included in the inefficient group, the order of priorities within that group is of no consequence, and can safely be ignored.

Before we examine the utility assumptions which underly the MVC, the reader should note that this criterion can be formulated in terms of either the variance or the standard deviation without affecting the results, because if the variance of option $F$ is greater (less) than the variance of option $G$ this also implies that the standard deviation of $F$ is greater (less) than the standard deviation of $G$, and vice versa. The use of the variance, rather than the standard deviation, has no significance beyond the mathematical convenience of being able to dispense with the use of somewhat awkward square roots.

Appendix 7.1 presents a simple computer program that constructs the set of mean–standard deviation efficient investments from any number of feasible investments.

## 7.3    The Utility Foundations of the MVC

Efficiency criteria are generally based on certain underlying assumptions regarding investors' tastes. In constructing the FSD, we made only one assumption: that every investor always prefers more to less wealth ($U'(R) \geqslant 0$). In the SSD it was further assumed that the marginal utility of money declines ($U''(R) \leqslant 0$). In addition to these two assumptions, the MVC places further restrictions on the shape of investors' utility functions and/or the shape of the distribution of returns. These additional assumptions make a more effective criterion which tends to reduce the size of the efficient set, but they also mean that the criterion is appropriate for a smaller class of investors, or for a restricted class of options.

The MVC provides a relevant decision rule in two cases: (a) when the investor's utility function is quadratic and (b) when the returns are normally distributed. These two cases are discussed in some detail in the following two subsections.

### 7.3.1   Quadratic Utility Functions

In this case the investors are assumed to be risk averters, and in addition their utility function is confined to the following specific form:

$$U(R) = a + bR + cR^2$$

where $a$ can take any value, while $b > 0$ and $c < 0$. Indeed, by the monotonicity axiom we should have $U' > 0$ which implies that

$$U'(R) = b + 2cR > 0$$

and by the risk aversion assumption $U'' < 0$,

$$U''(R) = 2c < 0$$

Hence $c < 0$ and therefore $b > 0$.

The expected utility of $R$ is given by

$$EU(R) = a + bER + cER^2$$

However, since by definition of variance, $\sigma_R^2 = ER^2 - (ER)^2$ the expected utility can be rewritten as

$$EU(R) = a + bER + c(ER)^2 + c\sigma_R^2$$

Thus the expected utility in the quadratic case can be expressed explicitly as a function of the mean portfolio return, $ER$, and the variance $\sigma_R^2$ of the portfolio returns. Moreover we can also draw the following conclusions:

AS VARIANCE GOES UP
UTILITY GOES DOWN

$$\text{(a)} \quad \frac{\partial EU(R)}{\partial \sigma_R^2} = c < 0$$

This follows from the property of the quadratic utility function ($c < 0$), and so when we increase the variance without changing the expected return the investor is worse off, since his expected utility decreases.

$$\text{(b)} \quad \frac{\partial EU(R)}{\partial ER} = b + 2cER > 0$$

This follows from the fact that $U'(R) = b + 2cR > 0$ and hence the expected value (or the mean) of positive numbers must be also positive: $E(b + 2cR) = b + 2cER > 0$. Namely, when the expected return increases (without changing the variance) the investor is better off, since his expected utility increases.

From this analysis we also see why it is important to assume that $b > 0$. If the parameter $b$ were negative, we could have $b + 2cER < 0$ (since $c < 0$), which would imply that investors dislike expected profit. This of course an unacceptable assumption.

EXAMPLE

Suppose that an investor has a quadratic utility function with the following parameters: $a = 1$, $b = 10$, $c = -1$. The investor is required to select one of the two portfolios $A$ and $B$ with the following means and variances:

|          | Portfolio A | Portfolio B |
|----------|-------------|-------------|
| Mean     | 1           | 2           |
| Variance | 2           | 1           |

By the MVC, $B$ dominates $A$ since $E_B R > E_A R$ and $Var_B(R) < Var_A(R)$. Let us check if indeed the expected utility of $B$ is greater than the expected utility of $A$ by calculating directly the expected utility of the two portfolios from the investor's quadratic utility function:

$$E_A U(R) = a + b(E_A R) + c(E_A R)^2 + c\sigma_A^2 = 1 + 10 \times 1 - 1 \times 1^2 - 1 \times 2 = 8$$

$$E_B U(R) = a + b(E_B R) + c(E_B R)^2 + c\sigma_B^2 = 1 + 10 \times 2 - 1 \times 2^2 - 1 \times 1 = 16$$

Thus, as expected $E_B U(R) > E_A U(R)$, which confirms that the MVC is appropriate when a quadratic utility function is assumed.

The quadratic utility function is simple to understand and to employ, hence it is widely used. Nevertheless the restrictions on the form of the utility function in this case are too severe and risk averters with other reasonable utility functions, e.g., $U(R) = \log R$ or $U(R) = \sqrt{R}$, cannot be rigorously analyzed in this framework.[18]

---

[18] Nevertheless, the mean–variance analysis can be applied as an *approximation* for many concave utility functions, such as $U(R) = \log R$, with a negligible error, as long as the range of returns is not too widely spread. For more details, see H. Levy and H. Markowitz, "Approximating Expected Utility by a Function of Mean and Variance", *American Economic Review* (June 1979).

Even a more serious drawback of the quadratic utility function is that it is not defined over the whole range of possible outcomes. To see this result, the quadratic utility function is written in the form

$$U(R) = R + \beta R^2$$

which is obtained simply by subtracting $a$ and dividing by $b > 0$ the previous quadratic utility function (a positive linear transformation), so that $\beta = c/b < 0$, as required.

The resulting quadratic utility function is drawn in Figure 7.3. The two derivatives of the transformed function are

$$U'(R) = 1 + 2\beta R$$

$$U''(R) = 2\beta$$

Since we have assumed that $\beta < 0$, the second derivative is negative ($U''(R) < 0$), which is equivalent to assuming that the marginal utility for money declines; as can be recalled from the discussion in Chapter 4, the graph of such a function is concave. However, only part of the curve of Figure 7.3 is relevant; the declining part of the function which is shown by the dotted line must be ignored in decision making problems since it does not fulfill the basic nonnegativity constraint on the first derivative. (Beyond the point of maximum, the first derivative is negative.) The relevant range of the quadratic function (with $\beta < 0$) must be restricted, therefore, to the values of $R$ such that $U'(R) = 1 + 2\beta R \geqslant 0$, or

$$R \leqslant \frac{1}{-2\beta} \equiv K$$

Since $\beta$ is negative, $1/(-2\beta)$ must be positive. For the sake of convenience, we denote $1/(-2\beta)$ by $K$; the quadratic utility function is appropriate only over the domain $R \leqslant K$ (where $K > 0$). Other values of $K$ are not economically relevant, since in this range additional money increments decrease utility, and this contradicts the basic assumption that an investor is rational and, therefore, prefers more money to less. Thus, use of the

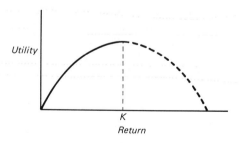

**Figure 7.3**

quadratic utility function is restricted to a limited range of values, which greatly detracts from its usefulness.

The quadratic utility function is appropriate only for relatively low returns (those below $K$), which precludes its use for many types of investments, especially those which like lotteries have some very high values of $R$, albeit with low probabilities of occurrence. This is a very serious drawback since we do not have the option of assuming that some decisions will be reached using a quadratic function while others (those where $R > K$) will be governed by some other function.

Of course it might be argued that since higher values of $K$ shift the point of maximum to the right, the value of $K$ can always be set sufficiently high as to permit the analysis of all possible returns. However, since we have defined $K \equiv 1/(-2\beta)$, raising $K$ is tantamount to lowering $\beta$. Therefore as $K$ grows very large (approaches infinity) $\beta$ becomes very small (approaches zero); at the limit, the quadratic function reduces to the linear function $U(R) = R$, since $\beta R^2$ vanishes. This, of course, may not be acceptable since the linear function represents an investor who is neutral, rather than averse, to risk. Nor is this the only shortcoming of the quadratic utility function: Pratt and Arrow have shown that a quadratic utility function implies increasing absolute risk aversion, which contradicts common experience (see Section 5.4).

Because of these restrictions, one is usually forced to search for a different framework which justifies using the MVC, without all the limitations imposed by the quadratic utility assumption. Such an alternative framework is based on the assumption of normal distribution of returns discussed in the next subsection.

### 7.3.2  *Normal Distributions and Risk Aversion*

Instead of restricting the utility function to an unreasonable form (quadratic) we can justify the MVC for a wide class of utility functions, but at the cost of imposing some restrictions on the distribution of the random variable, namely, assuming normal distributions. Here we provide a graphical proof for the MVC in this case while a more rigorous proof is given in Appendix 7.2.

The MVC is an optimal decision rule if the investors are risk-averse and the rates of return are normally distributed.

In the statistical supplement the normal distribution is analyzed in detail. However, it is well known that the normal distribution has only two parameters, the mean $\mu$ and the variance $\sigma^2$, and that the *cumulative* distributions of two normally distributed variables intersect at most once. To prove the validity of the MVC in the normal case, let us consider various scenarios regarding the parameters of the two portfolios under consideration, which we denote $F$ and $G$.

In Figure 7.4 we show two normal density functions $f(R)$ and $g(R)$ and the corresponding cumulative distribution functions $F(R)$ and $G(R)$. In panel (a) we have no dominance by the MVC since $\mu_F > \mu_G$ and also $\sigma_F^2 > \sigma_G^2$. Indeed as can be seen from the cumulative distributions there is no dominance by SSD either: $F$ cannot dominate $G$ by SSD since

$$\int_{-\infty}^{R_0} [G(t) - F(t)]\, dt < 0$$

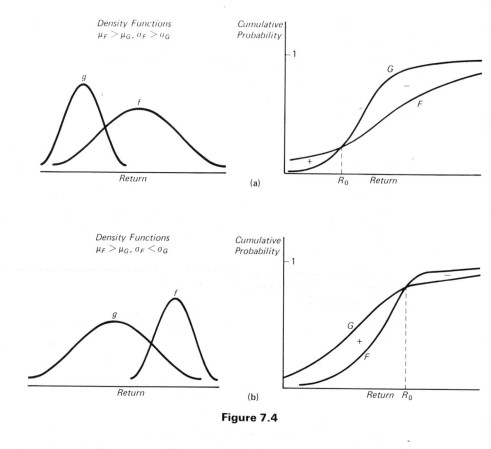

**Figure 7.4**

and $G$ does not dominate $F$ since

$$\int_{-\infty}^{+\infty} [F(t) - G(t)] \, dt < 0,$$

namely the negative area between the two distributions is greater than the positive area.[19] Thus, with normal distributions, when there is no dominance by MVC there is no dominance by SSD either.

In panel (b) we illustrate a case where $F$ dominates $G$ by MVC, since $\mu_F > \mu_G$ and

---

[19] It is shown in Appendix 7.2 that

$$\mu_F - \mu_G = \int_{-\infty}^{\infty} [G(t) - F(t)] \, dt \quad \text{or} \quad \mu_G - \mu_F = \int_{-\infty}^{\infty} [F(t) - G(t)] \, dt$$

But since $\mu_G < \mu_F$ the last integral must be negative. In general the total area between two cumulative distributions measures the mean difference of the two random variables.

$\sigma_F < \sigma_G$. Such dominance exists also by SSD, since clearly

$$\int_{-\infty}^{R} |G(t) - F(t)|\, dt > 0 \quad \text{for all } R \leqslant R_0$$

(see panel (b)) and also

$$\int_{-\infty}^{R} |G(t) - F(t)|\, dt > 0 \quad \text{for all } R > R_0.$$

Indeed, the largest negative area is obtained for $R = +\infty$, so that the integral takes its lowest value for $R = +\infty$. Yet even then it is positive (since for $R = +\infty$ it is equal to $\mu_F - \mu_G$, which is positive because $\mu_F > \mu_G$ — see Appendix 7.2), so it is *a fortiori* positive for all $R < +\infty$, when the negative area is smaller.

Thus, in these two cases the MVC and the SSD rule produce the same decision: both lead to the same dominance relationship. Since SSD is the optimal decision rule for all risk averters, we conclude that MVC is also an optimal decision rule *when normal distributions are assumed*.

Finally, note that if $\sigma_F^2 = \sigma_G^2$ and $\mu_F > \mu_G$, $F$ dominates $G$ by MVC, and such dominance implies dominance by FSD, let alone by SSD.

Two such normal distributions are presented in Figure 7.5: distribution $F$ has a higher mean than distribution $G$, but an identical variance. Does $F$ dominate $G$ for every concave utility function? Clearly $F$ dominates $G$ according to the FSD Criterion since $F$ lies wholly to the right of $G$.[20] This means that $F$ dominates $G$ for any nondecreasing utility function so that it should also be dominant for all concave functions.

Since the MVC depends only on the expected return and the variance of the distribution it appears not implausible that this criterion may be appropriate for all symmetrical distributions since the third moment (skewness), which is usually relevant for decision-making under uncertainty, is zero in such distributions. Table 7.2 and Figure

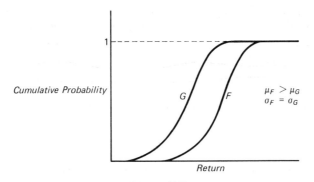

Cumulative Probability

$G$ $F$

$\mu_F > \mu_G$
$\sigma_F = \sigma_G$

Return

**Figure 7.5**

[20] Notice that although $F$ and $G$ do not intersect, the density functions $f$ and $g$ do intersect (see Figure 6 in the Statistical Supplement (page 721).

**Table 7.2**

| | Option F | | Option G | |
|---|---|---|---|---|
| | *Return* | *Probability* | *Return* | *Probability* |
| | −1 | 1/4 | −2 | 0.1 |
| | 0 | 1/2 | 0 | 0.8 |
| | 1 | 1/4 | 2 | 0.1 |
| | $\mu_F = 0$ | | $\mu_G = 0$ | |
| | $\sigma_F^2 = 0.5$ | | $\sigma_G^2 = 0.8$ | |

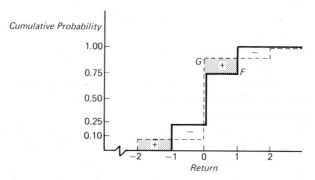

**Figure 7.6**

7.6 present a counter-example which shows that symmetrical distributions of returns, in themselves, do not ensure consistently acceptable results using the MVC.

A glance at Table 7.2 suffices to show that, invoking the MVC, option $F$ dominates option $G$ since their expected values are the same (zero in this case) while $F$ has the lower variance (0.5 as compared with 0.8). However when the cumulative probability distributions of the two options are plotted as in Figure 7.6, we see that $F$ does *not* dominate $G$ by the SSD rule, since the first negative area ($-1 \times 0.15$) is greater than the first positive area ($1 \times 0.10$). Therefore it will not be consistently preferred by all risk-averse investors, the MVC result notwithstanding. Thus the MVC does not ensure an optimal efficient set even if we assume symmetrical distributions of returns.

To sum up, if $F$ dominates $G$ by MVC, such dominance exists also by SSD provided that $F$ and $G$ are normally distributed. If $F$ does not dominate $G$ by MVC, dominance by SSD is impossible for normally distributed options.

**7.4    A Graphical Representation of the Mean–Variance Criterion**

In contrast to the FSD and SSD criteria, the MVC is by its very nature two-dimensional so that the efficiency analysis using this criterion readily lends itself to graphical representation. In Figure 7.7, the vertical axis denotes expected return while the horizontal axis measures the standard deviation (or variance) of the returns. Given its expected return and standard deviation, any investment option can be represented by a point on such a plane and the set of all potential options can be enclosed by an envelope curve such as the one shown in Figure 7.7. The MVC rule can now be applied to this set of potential options to isolate the set of efficient investments. Using the MVC, only the options comprising the northwest segment $AB$ of the envelope curve are efficient; the remaining portion of the envelope curve and all of the options in the interior are inefficient by the MVC. The locus of efficient points $AB$ will also be referred to as the efficiency frontier.

To prove this, consider an interior and therefore inefficient point such as $Z$ in Figure 7.7. From point $Z$ draw a horizontal line to an efficient point $Z'$ on the efficiency frontier. Clearly point $Z'$ is preferable to point $Z$ since for the same expected return it has a lower standard deviation (variance). Similarly, we can draw a vertical line from an inefficient point such as $Y$ to the point $Y'$ on the efficiency locus. Once again the point of the efficiency locus $Y'$ clearly dominates the interior point $Y$ since the former represents a higher expected return for a given standard deviation (variance). If this experiment is repeated for all possible points, the efficiency locus $AB$ will be generated.

To complete the graphical representation of investment choice we must introduce the indifference curves. Note that while in Chapter 3 we introduced the indifference curves between consumption in two periods, here the investor is indifferent between average return and risk. We know that an investor who uses the MVC increases his utility when expected return is increased or when variance is decreased. For example, whenever an option such as $M$ in Figure 7.8 is replaced by an alternative located in the direction of the arrow marked $a$ the investor's utility is increased, since every movement along the line $Ma$ raises the expected return without altering the variance. Similarly, any movement in the direction of arrow $b$ reduces the investor's utility, since the variance of the investment is thereby increased without any change in the expected return, which is clearly to the investor's disadvantage. Since any movement in the direction of arrow $b$ reduces the investor's utility while any movement in the direction of arrow $a$ increases his utility, a point can be found between $a$ and $b$ (say, $K$) at which the investor's utility is neither increased nor decreased. If we substitute option $K$

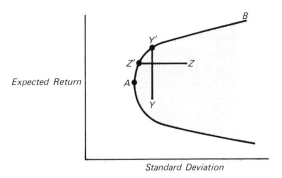

*Expected Return*

*Standard Deviation*

**Figure 7.7**

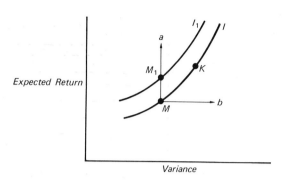

**Figure 7.8**

for option $M$ both the mean and the variance are increased, but since by assumption the investor's utility remains unchanged, the increased mean is exactly offset by the increased variance, so that the investor is indifferent to the choice between these two investments. Other combinations of expected return and variance can also be found which leave the investor indifferent, that is, with the same utility which he derived from option $M$.[21] In principle all such combinations can be plotted along an "indifference curve" such as $MI$ in Figure 7.8. If we start with a point such as $M_1$, we can repeat the process and generate still another indifference curve $M_1 I_1$, and so on until an entire indifference map is constructed which represents the investor's tastes.

The indifference curves in Figure 7.8 rise from left to right which indicates that the risk-averse investor must be compensated with a higher expected return as the variance increases. The curves are drawn convex downward on the assumption that additional increments of variance require increasingly larger increments of expected return to compensate the individual. Another property of the indifference map is that the indifference curves *cannot* intersect (compare Chapter 3).

An investor's final choice out of the efficient set depends on his tastes. In accordance with the expected utility hypothesis he will choose that option which allows him to reach the highest indifference curve, for the higher the curve, the higher his utility. Figure 7.9 superimposes the individual's indifference map on the opportunity set of investments. The investor would prefer an option which would allow him to reach indifference curve $I_5$, but no attainable investment option of this kind exists (indifference curve $I_5$ does not intersect or touch the opportunity set). The best that he can do, given the potential options, is to choose option $a$ out of the efficiency set $AB$, that is, the option which is tangent to indifference curve $I_3$. Since no other choice will permit him to reach a higher level of utility, option $a$ is the investor's *optimal* choice, the one which maximizes his utility. Should he choose another alternative out of the efficient set, say

---

[21] The investor's indifference curve is a continuous curve and is constructed independently of the actual investment projects available to the investor. Clearly, there may be no potential options having the variances and means represented by points such as $K$ and $M$, but from the fact that both these points lie on the same indifference curve we can deduce that had such investments been available, the investor would have been indifferent to the choice between them.

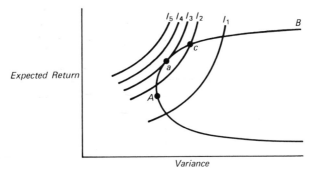

**Figure 7.9**

point *c*, his utility will fall since this option permits him to reach indifference curve $I_2$, which represents a lower level of utility (see Figure 7.9).

Can we infer from this analysis that no investor will ever prefer option *c* or that option *a* represents the optimal choice for all risk-averse investors? Since the shape of the indifference curves varies from one investor to the next it is quite conceivable that a second investor may have indifference curves, representing his individual preferences, which are tangent to the efficient set at point *c* rather than at point *a*. In fact, depending on the slope of the curves, any investment option on the efficient locus *AB* may be the optimal investment for a particular investor. This is illustrated in Figure 7.10, which sets out the indifference curves of two different individuals.[22] It should be noted that while both the investor whose optimal portfolio is represented by point *a* and the one whose optimal portfolio is represented by *c* regard a higher variance of the returns as a disadvantage, they do *not* attach the same weight to this factor. The indifference curve of the investor who selects option *a* ($I_1$) is steeper than that of the investor who prefers investment *c* ($I_2$). This means that when the variance is increased by one unit, the former investor ($I_1$) requires a greater increase in expected return to offset the increased

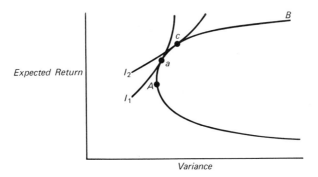

**Figure 7.10**

[22] The intersection of the indifference curves of two *different* individuals does *not* contradict the assertion that the indifference curves of the *same* individual cannot intersect.

variance. For him, a higher variance represents a greater drawback than it does for the investor with the indifference curve $I_2$. The latter individual is more willing to accept a greater variance, and therefore chooses option $c$, which has a higher variance (and a higher return) than point $a$.


## 7.5    Some Empirical Evidence of Normal Distributions of Returns

In this chapter we have shown that the MVC provides a relevant criterion for risk averters (individuals with concave utility functions) if the distribution of returns is normal (and is thus entirely specified by the first two moments, the mean and the variance). This restriction necessarily limits the generality of the MVC when the distributions of returns are known to be of a different form. For example, the criterion cannot be used to explain the behavior of individuals who purchase lottery tickets or take out insurance, since in these cases the higher moments of the distribution are also significant.

There is some indirect evidence, however, which leads us to presume that a significant proportion of investment choices can be explained by the mean–variance model. As we have already noted, risk-averse individuals tend to diversify their holdings; that is, they build portfolios of a number of securities. Mutual funds make relatively large portfolios, of hundreds of individual securities, readily available even to the small investor. To the degree that the returns of the individual securities are independent of one another (or at least are not perfectly correlated), the return on relatively large portfolios should approximate a normal distribution.[23]

Although we do not know whether the returns on individual securities are independent, we can adopt an indirect approach and examine the rate of return to investors in mutual fund shares. In an empirical study we used 22 years of annual rates of return (1959–1980) for a sample of 100 mutual funds.[24] The hypothesis tested is that all these observations constitute a sample drawn from a normal distribution. Before the hypothesis can be tested, however, some standardization is required. Not all the mutual funds follow the same investment strategy. Thus some funds invest most of their assets in growth stocks while others invest their assets in a balanced portfolio of more conservative securities. More speculative stocks usually yield higher returns but they also have higher standard deviations. Accordingly, even if the hypothesis that the rates of return are distributed normally were correct, it still might be rejected, since owing to differences in investment policy, the annual observations are drawn from a number of

---

[23] This follows directly from the Central Limit Theorem:
  Let $f(x)$ denote the density function of a random variable with an expected value equal to $\mu$ and a variance equal to $\sigma^2$ ($\sigma^2 < \infty$). If $\bar{x}_n$ denotes the mean of a sample of size $n$ drawn from this distribution then the random variable $(\bar{x}_n - \mu)/(\sigma/\sqrt{n})$ will approximate a normal distribution with an expected value of zero, and a variance of unity, on the condition that $n$ is sufficiently large. For a more precise formulation of this theorem, see A. M. Mood and F. A. Graybill, *op. cit.*, pp. 149–53.

[24] All data on rates of return were obtained from various annual editions of Arthur Wiesenberger, *Investment Companies*.

normal distributions having different parameters. To bring the distributions to a common basis the annual rates of return of each fund were standardized as follows:

$$z_t = \frac{R_t - \bar{R}}{S}$$

where:

$\bar{R}$ = estimated mean return of a mutual fund over the period studied
$R_t$ = the fund's rate of return in year $t$
$S$ = estimated standard deviation of the distribution[25]
$z_t$ = the standardized rate of return in year $t$

After computing $z_t$ for each one of the funds the histogram describing the distribution of all the values of $z_t$ for the aggregate population of mutual funds was constructed.[26] The histogram is given in Figure 7.11.

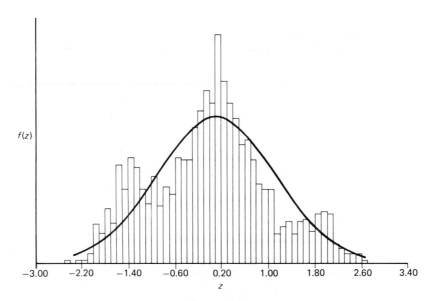

**Figure 7.11**

[25] This was derived by the formula

$$S^2 = \sum_{t=1}^{n} \frac{(R_t - \bar{R})^2}{n-1}$$

[26] Theoretically we should have deducted the actual mean $\mu_i$ for each mutual fund and divided the result by the standard deviation of the population $\sigma_i$; since these data were not available estimates of $\sigma_i$ and $\mu_i$ were used. The error introduced by using estimates rather than the actual parameters becomes smaller, the greater the number of years covered.

On the same diagram we also plotted the standard normal curve. An examination of the diagram shows that the empirical distribution (histogram) approximates a normal distribution. This is also confirmed by a statistical test which shows that the hypothesis that the rates of return are distributed normally cannot be rejected.[27] Thus the distribution of returns to investors in mutual fund shares is approximately normal,[28] and the MVC provides an appropriate criterion for this important segment of the securities market. Moreover, to the extent that mutual funds provide a relevant proxy for investment portfolios in general, the statistical evidence strongly suggests that the MVC can provide an effective decision rule for most risk-averse investors.

## Summary

The popular Mean–Variance Criterion (MVC) is appropriate either when quadratic utility is assumed or when the rates of return are normally distributed and risk aversion is assumed. Since the quadratic utility function is theoretically unacceptable (it has a decreasing section with $U' < 0$ and is characterized by increasing, rather than decreasing, absolute risk aversion), we concentrate in this chapter on the case of normally distributed rates of return.

We assert that investment $F$ dominates investment $G$ by MVC if and only if:

and:

$$E_F R \geqslant E_G R$$

$$\sigma_F^2 \leqslant \sigma_G^2$$

where at least one strong inequality holds. Thus, under the MV rule, expected return is a measure of profitability and the variance of returns serves as the risk index.

We proved that in case of normally distributed returns, if investment $F$ dominates investment $G$ by the MVC, then $F$ also dominates $G$ by SSD and vice versa. Thus, with normally distributed returns, the MVC and the SSD coincide. Since we proved in Chapter 6 that the SSD is the optimal rule when risk aversion is assumed, the MVC is also optimal for risk averters whenever the rates of return are normally distributed.

Finally note that if investors diversify in many risky assets (or buy shares of mutual funds as if "diversifying by proxy"), the distribution of the portfolio rates of return indeed tends to be symmetrical and close to normal. The MVC is thus likely to provide an effective tool for analyzing wide classes of investment decisions.

[27] For this purpose the Kolmogorov–Smirnov test was used. The precise hypotheses tested were $H_0$: the adjusted return distribution is a standard normal distribution; $H_1$: the adjusted return distribution is not a standard normal distribution.

[28] That the distributions are not perfectly normal is already clear from the statistical tests carried out on the same data in Chapter 5, which showed the third moment to be significant in most cases.

These results do *not* rule out the possibility that the underlying distributions belong to a more general class of so-called stable distributions which includes the normal as a special case. See, for example, Eugene F. Fama, "The Behavior of Stock-Market Prices", *Journal of Business* (January 1965), pp. 34–105, and the references cited.

## Summary Table

### (a) Mean–Variance Criterion (MVC)

    (i) Option $F$ dominates option $G$ by MVC if and only if:

    (1) $\qquad\qquad E_F R \geqslant E_G R$   (the condition on means)

    and:

    (2) $\qquad\quad Var_F(R) \leqslant Var_G(R)$   (the condition on variances)

    or alternatively:

    (2') $\qquad\quad \sigma_F \leqslant \sigma_G$   (the condition on standard deviations)

    with at least one strong inequality holding in (1) and (2) or in (1) and (2').

    (ii) For series of $n$ observations assigned equal probabilities of $1/n$ (such as time series of returns) the mean return $ER$ is defined by

$$ER = \bar{R} = \frac{1}{n} \sum_{t=1}^{n} R_t$$

The variance can be calculated either as the population parameter

$$Var(R) = \frac{1}{n} \sum_{t=1}^{n} [R_t - E\,R\,]^2$$

or as its unbiased estimate in the sample:

$$\hat{\sigma}_R^2 = \frac{1}{n-1} \sum_{t=1}^{n} (R_t - \bar{R})^2$$

The standard deviation in either case is the square root of the variance.

### (b) Applicability of the MVC

    (i) MV is an optimal criterion for all risk averters when the returns are normally distributed. In this case the MVC conditions

$$E_F R \geqslant E_G R \quad \text{and} \quad Var_F(R) \leqslant Var_G(G)$$

imply the SSD condition:

$$\int_{-\infty}^{R} [G(t) - F(t)]\,\mathrm{d}t \geqslant 0 \quad \text{for all } R$$

and vice versa, so that MVC and SSD coincide.

    (ii) MVC is an appropriate criterion for individuals with quadratic utility function, $U(R) = a + bR + cR^2$, where $b > 0$ and $c < 0$.

    (iii) MVC *in practice* provides an accurate approximation for various concave utility functions (such as logarithmic utility), when the returns are not too widely spread.

    (iv) Empirical evidence of highly diversified portfolios (as represented by mutual funds) suggests that their returns are close to normally distributed, as required by (i) above.

With this in mind, we now turn our attention in the next chapter to the application of the mean–variance analysis to portfolio selection.

## APPENDIX 7.1
### Computer Program to Construct the Mean–Variance Efficient Set

We reproduce here in full the computer code written in FORTRAN77 that will construct the mean–variance efficient set from a given feasible set consisting of any number of investment options.

The program reads in the raw observations of rates of return for the different options, calculates the means and the variances on the basis of these observations, sorts the options by decreasing mean return, and then applies the MVC to the sorted data to select the MV efficient options. The efficient set is printed on OUTPUT, giving the efficient options' names, mean returns, and standard deviations.

The input format (format 101 in the program) corresponds to the format of the mutual fund data in the Data Set at the end of the book. It can be changed to fit any specific data file.

The program uses four parameters that have to be adjusted in accordance with the specific user requirements:

MAXST = the maximum conceivable number of investment options that you may want to screen, needed to dimension the various arrays in the program.

MAXPE = the maximum conceivable number of rate of return observations for each option, also needed for dimensioning.

NSTK = the actual number of options to be read from input file (TAPE1).

NPER = the actual number of rate of return observations for each option.

Note that the parameters as given in the program code also correspond to the Data Set specifications.

```
 1           PROGRAM MVSET(TAPE1,OUTPUT)
 2      C-
 3      C=====================================================================
 4      C-
 5           PARAMETER(MAXST=140,MAXPE=15,NSTK=126, NPER=10 )
 6      C-
 7      C=====================================================================
 8      C-
 9           COMMON X(MAXPE,MAXST),XMEAN(MAXST),SD(MAXST),MVEFF(MAXST),
10          2 INDEX(MAXST),NAME(MAXST)
11     101   FORMAT(A10,20X,10F5.1)
12     922   FORMAT(1X,127I1)
13      12   FORMAT(2I4,2X,A10,2F10.4)
14      11   FORMAT(I10,2X,A10,2F10.4)
15           DO 7 I=1,NSTK
```

```
16              INDEX(I)=I
17              XMEAN(I)=0
18       7      CONTINUE
19       C- ***** READ RAW DATA INPUT FILE ***********
20       C- ***** CALCULATE MEANS AND STANDARD DEVIATIONS **********
21              DO 1 J=1,NSTK
22              READ(1,101,END=1) NAME(J),(X(I,J), I=1,NPER)
23              SQ=0
24              DO 3 I=1,NPER
25              XMEAN(J)=XMEAN(J)+X(I,J)
26              SQ=SQ+X(I,J)*X(I,J)
27       3      CONTINUE
28              SD(J)=SQRT((SQ-XMEAN(J)*XMEAN(J)/NPER)/(NPER-1))
29              XMEAN(J)=XMEAN(J)/NPER
30              PRINT 11, INDEX(J),NAME(J),XMEAN(J),SD(J)
31       1      CONTINUE
32       C- ****** SORT STOCKS BY MEANS **********
33              K=1
34              N=2
35              IF(XMEAN(K+1).GT.XMEAN(K)) THEN
36                A=XMEAN(K+1)
37                XMEAN(K+1)=XMEAN(K)
38                XMEAN(K)=A
39                A=SD(K+1)
40                SD(K+1)=SD(K)
41                SD(K)=A
42                IA=INDEX(K+1)
43                INDEX(K+1)=INDEX(K)
44                INDEX(K)=IA
45                IA=NAME(K+1)
46                NAME(K+1)=NAME(K)
47                NAME(K)=IA
48              ENDIF
49       40     K=N
50       41     IF(K.EQ.NSTK)  GO TO 48
51              IF(XMEAN(K+1).GT.XMEAN(K)) THEN
52                N=K+1
53                A=XMEAN(K+1)
54                XMEAN(K+1)=XMEAN(K)
55                XMEAN(K)=A
56                A=SD(K+1)
57                SD(K+1)=SD(K)
58                SD(K)=A
59                IA=INDEX(K+1)
60                INDEX(K+1)=INDEX(K)
61                INDEX(K)=IA
62                IA=NAME(K+1)
63                NAME(K+1)=NAME(K)
64                NAME(K)=IA
65       42       IF(XMEAN(K).GT.XMEAN(K-1)) THEN
66                  A=XMEAN(K-1)
67                  XMEAN(K-1)=XMEAN(K)
68                  XMEAN(K)=A
69                  A=SD(K-1)
70                  SD(K-1)=SD(K)
71                  SD(K)=A
72                  IA=INDEX(K-1)
73                  INDEX(K-1)=INDEX(K)
74                  INDEX(K)=IA
75                  IA=NAME(K-1)
```

```
76                    NAME(K-1)=NAME(K)
77                    NAME(K)=IA
78                    K=K-1
79                    IF(K.EQ.1) GO TO 40
80                    GO TO 42
81                  ELSE
82                    GO TO 40
83                  ENDIF
84                ELSE
85                  K=K+1
86                  GO TO 41
87                ENDIF
88      48        CONTINUE
89      C-
90      C- ********MV EFFICIENT SET *************
91      C-
92                DO 700 J=1,NSTK
93                MVEFF(J)=1
94      700       CONTINUE
95                DO 701 J=1,NSTK-1
96                  IF(MVEFF(J).EQ.0) GO TO 701
97                  DO 702 K=J,NSTK-1
98                    IF(MVEFF(K+1).EQ.0) GO TO 702
99                    IF(SD(K+1).GE.SD(J)) MVEFF(K+1)=0
100     702         CONTINUE
101     701       CONTINUE
102               PRINT *,    M-V EFFICIENT SET
103               PRINT *,    =================
104               PRINT 922,(MVEFF(J),J=1,NSTK)
105               NUMB=0
106               DO 703 J=1,NSTK
107                 IF(MVEFF(J).EQ.0) GO TO 703
108                 NUMB=NUMB+1
109                 PRINT 12,NUMB,INDEX(J),NAME(J),XMEAN(J),SD(J)
110     703       CONTINUE
111               STOP
112               END
```

## APPENDIX 7.2
### Proof of the Optimality of the Mean–Variance Criterion: Normal Distributions in Face of Risk Aversion[29]

First note that the difference $E_F R - E_G R$ of the expected returns on the two investment options is actually equal to the accumulated area between the cumulative distribution curves of $F$ and $G$. To see this, recall that for every utility function $U$ we have (see Appendix 6.1):

$$E_F U(R) - E_G U(R) = \int_{-\infty}^{\infty} [G(R) - F(R)] U'(R) \, dR$$

This holds for any utility function $U$ and for any pair of distributions $F$ and G. In particular, it holds for a linear utility function $U(R) = R$, in which case we get (recall

---

[29] For more details of this proof, see G. Hanoch and H. Levy, "The Efficiency Analysis of Choices Involving Risk", *Review of Economic Studies* (July 1969).

that $U'(R) = 1$ for this function):

$$E_F R - E_G R = \int_{-\infty}^{\infty} |G(R) - F(R)| \, dR$$

The integral on the right is the total area accumulated between the cumulative distribution curves $G$ and $F$, and it is thus equal to the difference of the expected returns under the two distributions. We shall use this property in what follows.

Now let us turn to the specific case when $F$ and $G$ are normally distributed, while the investors are assumed to be risk-averse. The two normal distributions are characterized by the following parameters:

$$\text{Option } F: \quad R \sim N(\mu_1, \sigma_1), \quad \text{hence } z_F = \frac{R - \mu_1}{\sigma_1} \sim N(0, 1)$$

$$\text{Option } G: \quad R \sim N(\mu_2, \sigma_2), \quad \text{hence } z_G = \frac{R - \mu_2}{\sigma_2} \sim N(0, 1)$$

Obviously, the greater the standard normal deviate $z$, the greater the area accumulated under the corresponding distribution up to the point $z$.

*Case 1:* Let $\sigma_1 = \sigma_2 = \sigma$ and $\mu_1 > \mu_2$. Thus for every $R$ we have $(R - \mu_1)/\sigma < (R - \mu_2)/\sigma$, so that $F(R) \leqslant G(R)$ for all $R$. In this case, $F$ dominates $G$ by MVC and also by FSD, let alone by SSD (which follows from FSD).

*Case 2:* Let $\sigma_1 > \sigma_2$ and also $\mu_1 \geqslant \mu_2$. In this case the cumulative distributions $F$ and $G$ intersect at the unique point $R_0$ given by the equality:

$$(R_0 - \mu_1)/\sigma_1 = (R_0 - \mu_2)/\sigma_2 \quad \text{or} \quad R_0 = (\mu_2\sigma_1 - \mu_1\sigma_2)/(\sigma_1 - \sigma_2)$$

For $R < R_0$, we have $(R - \mu_1)/\sigma_1 > (R - \mu_2)/\sigma_2$ and so $F(R) \geqslant G(R)$. Hence the left tail of $F$ lies above the left tail of $G$, which implies that $F$ cannot dominate $G$ by SSD. Conversely, since $\mu_1 > \mu_2$, $G$ cannot dominate $F$ by SSD. Thus, in this case also the MVC and the SSD coincide.

*Case 3:* Now let $\sigma_1 < \sigma_2$ and $\mu_1 \geqslant \mu_2$. Then for all $R < R_0$ we have $(R - \mu_1)/\sigma_1 < (R - \mu_2)/\sigma_2$ and so $F(R) < G(R)$, while for all $R > R_0$ we have $(R - \mu_1)/\sigma_1 > (R - \mu_2)/\sigma_2$ and so $F(R) > G(R)$. Thus $F$ intersects $G$ *from below* at the single intersection point $R_0$ of the two cumulative distributions.

Since $\mu_1 - \mu_2 \geqslant 0$, we have:

$$E_F R - E_G R \equiv \mu_1 - \mu_2 = \int_{-\infty}^{\infty} |G(R) - F(R)| \, dR \geqslant 0$$

(see above). However, this implies that also

$$\int_{-\infty}^{R} |G(t) - F(t)| \, dt > 0 \quad \text{for all } R$$

since by integrating up to some point $R < +\infty$ we actually accumulate a smaller negative part of the integral (recall that for $R > R_0$, $F > G$) and the value of the integral increases.

Hence dominance by MVC in this case implies dominance by SSD, and the two rules again coincide.

To sum up, with normal distributions of returns in face of risk aversion, MVC and SSD provide identical decisions and hence generate identical efficient sets, with the exception that in the case $\sigma_1 = \sigma_2$ the MVC rule even coincides with FSD.

## Questions and Problems

7.1 The "risk premium", that is, the maximum amount that an individual is prepared to pay to convert a random distribution into a perfectly certain income, measures the degree of risk associated with such a distribution for all risk averters. Moreover, two risk averters would rank any pair of options by their risk in the same order.
(a) Is this statement correct?
(b) Prove your answer graphically using a hypothetical numerical example.

7.2 Define the Mean-Variance Criterion (MVC). How do you account for its popularity?

7.3 What are the exact conditions for which the MVC provides an optimal efficiency criterion for all risk averters?

7.4 Assume that a risk averter's attitude towards risk can be characterized by a quadratic utility function:

$$U(R) = R + \beta R^2$$

where $R$ is the return (a random variable).
(a) What restrictions must be placed on the parameter $\beta$ of the utility function and on the range of the distribution of the returns $R$?
(b) What are the shortcomings of the quadratic utility function?
*Hint:* Investigate the behavior of the quadratic function and of the risk premium for a risk averter.
(c*) Assume that the investor is confronted with two investment options, $F$ and $G$, with expected returns $E_F R$, $E_G R$ and variances $\sigma_F^2$, $\sigma_G^2$, respectively.
Prove that option $F$ dominates option $G$, for an investor whose utility function is quadratic, if the following two conditions hold:

$$E_F R \geqslant E_G R$$

$$(E_F R - E_G R)^2 - (\sigma_F^2 - \sigma_G^2) \geqslant 0.$$

The above criterion is called the *Quadratic Utility Criterion* (*QUC*) (see G. Hanoch and H. Levy, "Efficient Portfolio Selection with Quadratic and Cubic Utility", *Journal of Business* (April 1970)).
(d*) Show that the MVC, although being a sufficient criterion, is not optimal with regards to quadratic utility functions. (Use a numerical example.)

7.5     Define and graph the MV "efficiency locus".

7.6     (a) Draw the appropriate indifference curves in the mean–variance plane for the following
        types of individuals:
        (i)   a risk averter;
        (ii)  a risk lover;
        (iii) an investor who will never take a risk;
        (iv)  a risk-neutral investor.
        (b) Can the indifference curves of a risk lover and a risk averter intersect?
        (c) Can the indifference curves of two risk averters intersect?
        (d) Can the indifference curves of the same individual intersect?

7.7     (a) What is the significance for the MVC of the empirical evidence on the form of mutual
        funds distributions?
        (b) Do mutual funds constitute an appropriate subject for such a test?

7.8     Assume four investment options with the following relationships between their expected
        returns $ER_i$ and their standard deviations $\sigma_i$:

$$ER_1 < ER_2 < ER_3 < ER_4 \quad \text{and} \quad \sigma_1 < \sigma_2 < \sigma_3 < \sigma_4$$

        that is, all four options are MV-efficient. It is claimed that all risk-neutral investors will
        choose option 4.
        (a) Is this claim correct?
        (b) If it is, does it contradict the MV rule?
        (c) Does such a result contradict the von Neumann–Morgenstern expected utility
        principle?

7.9     The following table gives the annual return per $100 invested in four mutually exclusive
        investment options during the years 1978–1983:

|      | A  | B  | C  | D  |
|------|----|----|----|----|
| 1978 | 20 | 22 | 6  | 10 |
| 1979 | 40 | 21 | 8  | 12 |
| 1980 | 30 | 18 | 5  | 18 |
| 1981 | 22 | 16 | 4  | 20 |
| 1982 | 36 | 20 | 6  | 15 |
| 1983 | 46 | 22 | 10 | 14 |

        Assuming that these data constitute the entire population for each option,
        (a) calculate the expected returns and standard deviations of each investment;
        (b) determine the MV efficient and inefficient sets.

7.10    For the following data:

| A | | B | | C | | D | |
|---|---|---|---|---|---|---|---|
| Return | Probability | Return | Probability | Return | Probability | Return | Probability |
| 18 | 7/8 | 10 | 1/4 | 16 | 3/4 | 5  | 1/2 |
| 26 | 1/8 | 30 | 3/4 | 24 | 1/4 | 25 | 1/2 |

(a) Plot the cumulative probability distribution of each of the options.
(b) Find the MV efficient set.
(c) Find the SSD (Second-Degree Stochastic Dominance) efficient set. What is the relationship between the two efficient sets?

7.11 (a) In general, is the MV efficient set a subset of the SSD efficient set?
(b) When the distributions of return are normal, is the MV efficient set a subset of the SSD efficient set?

7.12* Taylor series expansion of the expected utility $EU(R)$ gives an expansion which depends on *all* the distribution moments of $R$. Yet we know that for a normally distributed $R$, the MV criterion provides an optimal decision rule whereas it is dependent on the *first two moments only* (the mean and the variance). Can you explain the apparent contradiction? (See S. C. Tsiang, *American Economic Review*, June 1972.)

7.13* Show that for an investor with a quadratic utility function $U(R) = R + \beta R^2$ ($\beta < 0$), the indifference curves in the $\mu$–$\sigma$ plane are upward sloping ($d\mu/d\sigma_R > 0$) and convex ($d^2\mu/(d\sigma_R)^2 > 0$). Draw a map of a family of such curves in the $\mu$–$\sigma$ plane.

7.14 Baumol's Expected Gain–Confidence Limit Criterion (EGC—see Section 7.1) states that option $A$ dominates option $B$ if and only if:

$$E_A R \geqslant E_B R$$

and:

$$E_A R - k\sigma_A \geqslant E_B R - k\sigma_B$$

where $k$ is chosen subjectively according to the investor's preferences.

Construct the EGC efficient sets with $k = 1, 2$, and 10 for the eight risky options given below. Construct the MVC and QUC efficient sets for the same options and compare the results obtained by the different criteria (for a formulation of QUC see Problem 7.4 above).

| | | | | Portfolios | | | | |
|---|---|---|---|---|---|---|---|---|
| | *1* | *2* | *3* | *4* | *5* | *6* | *7* | *8* |
| Expected Return | 8 | 10 | 6 | 12 | 18 | 13 | 10 | 7 |
| Standard Deviation | 2 | 4 | 7 | 5 | 12 | 10 | 10 | 1 |

7.15 The following table gives the annual returns for four mutual funds.

| | | Return on Mutual Fund (%) | | |
|---|---|---|---|---|
| *Year* | *Acorn Fund* | *Mutual Shares Corporation* | *Sequoia Fund* | *Value Line Special Situation* |
| 1977 | 6.4 | 15.6 | 19.9 | 12.3 |
| 1978 | 7.7 | 18.1 | 23.9 | 21.2 |
| 1979 | 79.1 | 42.8 | 12.1 | 43.5 |
| 1980 | 56.7 | 19.3 | 12.7 | 54.4 |
| 1981 | −23.2 | 8.9 | 21.5 | −2.3 |

(a) Calculate the sample variance $S^2$ by employing the two alternative formulae

$$S_1^2 = \sum_{i=1}^{n} (R_i^2 - \bar{R})^2/n \quad \text{and} \quad S_2^2 = \sum_{i=1}^{n} (R_i - \bar{R})^2/(n-1)$$

for each of the funds. Find the efficient set, once using the MV rule based on $\bar{R}$ and $S_1$ and once using the same rule based on $\bar{R}$ and $S_2$. What is the relationship between the two efficient sets?

(b) Assigning a probability of 1/5 to each year, find the SSD efficient set. Compare your results to part (a).

## Data Set Problems

1. (a) Calculate the mean rate of return, the variance, and the standard deviation for the last five funds in the Data Set. Assign equal probabilities to each observation ($1/n = 1/10$).

   (b) Construct the MV efficient set from the five funds from part (a) above.

2. (a) Use the computer program from Appendix 7.1 to construct the MV efficient set assuming that the feasible set includes all the mutual funds in the Data Set.

   (b) Which mutual fund constitutes the optimum investment for an investor with the following utility function:

$$EU(R) = a + bER + c(ER)^2 + c\sigma_R^2$$

where $a = 0$, $b = 1$, and $c = -1/1,000$?

## Selected References

See Chapter 8.

# 8

# The Mean–Variance Criterion and Portfolio Selection

Most investors do not fail to heed the warning implicit in the by now rather shopworn adage, "Don't put all your eggs in one basket".[1] As a result, the typical investor tends to diversify his risk by building a portfolio which includes two or more risk assets. The exact composition of the portfolio depends, of course, on the investor's goals (retire at forty, send Junior to college, and so on) and on his attitude toward risk. Applying the Mean–Variance rule, we investigate in this chapter the graphical properties of the efficient set and the composition of diversified portfolios.

## 8.1    The Investment in Liquid Assets

Both individual as well as institutional investors tend to hold a proportion of their assets in cash. The holding of money or "near money" reflects current needs for liquidity and/or anticipated requirements in the near future. However, very often cash assets are held over and beyond the amounts needed to meet those needs; these assets should be considered as an "investment", that is as an integral part of the individual's or firm's investment portfolio.

Given the need to hold cash assets, let us turn our attention to the problem of determining the ratio of actual cash to other liquid assets. For our purpose we define a liquid (or near money) asset as one which can be readily converted to cash without incurring significant losses, for example, a *short-term* government bond, savings account, or the like. Since the return on investments in bonds is positive while investments in idle cash yield no return whatsoever, it seems on the surface rather unreasonable for any firm or individual to hold cash in view of the convenient alternative of

---

[1] The statement in the text is appropriate for risk averters; an appropriate corollary for a risk lover might be, "Put all your eggs in one basket, but keep your eye on the basket".

buying government bonds or some other liquid asset which provides a positive return. However, if we apply the portfolio principle to the problem it can be shown, following Tobin, that the mean–variance (MV) rule implies a liquid portfolio comprising cash as well as bonds.[2]

Consider an individual who wishes to hold one dollar in liquid form and must now decide on the proportions to hold in cash and in government bonds. Although the government regularly meets its obligations to pay interest and/or to pay the principal upon redemption, and the bonds can be readily converted into cash in the market, these assets are not riskless even if we explicitly assume that the government cannot go bankrupt. The reason for this is that in addition to the perfectly certain interest coupon payments, the investor faces the probability of incurring a capital gain or loss as a result of fluctuations in the bond's market price. The price of the bond may fluctuate, independent of any default risk, as a function of changes in the market rate of interest. Take, for example, a government bond which was issued at par (100%) and carries a 5% annual interest coupon. After a while, because of changed market conditions, a new series of 6% bonds (of similar maturity) is issued. Clearly, all rational investors will prefer the 6% to the 5% bond since they are perfect substitutes. Because of the drop in demand, the price of the 5% bond will fall, and will continue to fall until it reaches a level which offers the potential purchaser a 6% yield, that is, the new current market rate.[3] Conversely, should the market rate fall below 5%, a capital gain will be incurred on the old bond. Thus the problem of determining the ratio of bonds (which carry a degree of risk) to riskless cash is analogous to a portfolio problem and can be treated as a special case of risk diversification. To show this let us first define the following symbols:

$$r = \text{the interest paid on bonds, per dollar invested}$$
$$g = \text{the capital gain or loss, per dollar invested}$$
$$R = r + g = \text{the total return on bonds, per dollar invested}$$

We also assume that $g$ is a random variable with a given variance $\sigma_g^2$ and an expected return equal to zero, that is, on the average capital gains are expected to cancel capital losses.

Also, let

$$x_1 = \text{the proportion invested in cash}$$
$$x_2 = \text{the proportion of the liquid reserve invested in bonds (so that by definition } x_1 + x_2 = 1)$$

---

[2] We shall use the term *bonds* throughout as a convenient reference to all interest-bearing liquid assets.

[3] The percentage fall in price required to equate the yields depends on the length of time to maturity. Roughly speaking, the longer the maturity the greater the fall in price; hence the requirement that liquid reserves be held in *short-term* bonds. For a more detailed discussion of the relationship between interest rates and bond prices, see Chapter 2.

$ER =$ the expected return on the combined portfolio of cash and bonds

$\sqrt{Var(R)} \equiv \sigma_R =$ the standard deviation of the portfolio.

Should the individual desire to invest the entire liquid reserve in bonds, his expected return is given by[4]

$$ER = E(r + g) = Er + Eg = r + 0 = r \qquad (8.1)$$

The variance of the returns to an investor who puts all his reserve into bonds is[5]

$$Var(R) = Var(r + g) = Var(r) + Var(g) + 2Cov(r, g) \qquad (8.2)$$

where $2Cov(r, g)$ should be read as twice the covariance between $r$ and $g$. However, since $r$ is constant, $Var(r) = 0$ and therefore, $Cov(r, g) = 0$:[6]

$$Var(R) = Var(g) \qquad (8.3)$$

or, alternatively in terms of the standard deviation:

$$\sigma_R = \sigma_g \qquad (8.3')$$

Thus an individual who invests his entire reserve in bonds obtains an expected return of $r$ with a standard deviation of $\sigma_g$. Should he decide to leave all his reserve in cash, he obtains an expected return of zero and a standard deviation of zero. Now, invoking the MV rule, which of these extremes is preferable? Since both the standard deviation and the expected return of the bond portfolio exceed those of the cash alternative, neither alternative dominates the other by the MV rule. In other words both the 100% cash option and the 100% bond option are MV efficient.

Between these two extremes, there is an infinity of alternative investment options which are all included in the MV efficient set. To demonstrate this let us assume that an individual decides to invest his liquid reserve in the proportions $x_1$ in cash and $x_2$ in

---

[4] Equation (8.1) is based on the well known theorems that
   (a) the expected value of the sum of two random variables is equal to the sum of their individual expected values;
   (b) the expected value of a constant number (a degenerate random variable) equals the number itself.
   See W. Feller, *An Introduction to Probability Theory and its Applications*, 2nd edition, New York, Wiley, 1965, pp. 207–9.

[5] $Var(r + g) = E[(r + g) - E(r + g)]^2$
   $= E[(r - Er) + (g - Eg)]^2$
   $= E[(r - Er)^2 + (g - Eg)^2 + 2(r - Er)(g - Eg)]$
   $= E(r - Er)^2 + E(g - Eg)^2 + 2E(r - Er)(g - Eg)$
   $= Var(r) + Var(g) + 2 \, Cov(r, g)$

[6] For a more detailed discussion of the concepts of variance and covariance see Feller, *op. cit.*, pp. 213–19 and the Statistical Supplement.

bonds. The rate of return on the total portfolio, $R$, can be written as

$$R = x_2(r + g) + x_1 \cdot 0 = x_2(r + g) \tag{8.4}$$

so that the expected return equals[7]

$$ER = E[x_2(r + g)] = x_2 E(r + g) = x_2 r \tag{8.5}$$

and the variance of the portfolio is[8]

$$Var(R) = Var[x_2(r + g)] = x_2^2 \, Var(r + g) = x_2^2 \, Var(g) \tag{8.6}$$

or alternatively in terms of the standard deviation:

$$\sigma_R = x_2 \sigma_g \tag{8.7}$$

This can be rewritten as

$$x_2 = \frac{\sigma_R}{\sigma_g} \tag{8.8}$$

Substituting Equation (8.8) into Equation (8.5) above, the expected return on the portfolio of cash and bonds equals

$$ER = \frac{r}{\sigma_g} \cdot \sigma_R \tag{8.9}$$

This is a linear equation and since $r$ and $\sigma_g$ are constant parameters (that is, exogenous data obtained or estimated by the investor), the straight line represents an infinity of alternative combinations of portfolio expected returns and standard deviations $(ER, \sigma_R)$ which face the investor. Each alternative (portfolio) represents a different proportion

---

[7] In addition to the theorem

$$E(R_1 + R_2) = ER_1 + ER_2$$

we now use the additional theorem

$$E(aR) = aER$$

where $a$ is any constant. *Ibid*, p. 208.

[8] Here we use the rule that

$$Var \, (aR) = a^2 \, Var \, (R)$$

where $a$ is any constant. *Ibid*, p. 214.

($x_2$) invested in bonds.[9] All the possible combinations are set out along the line *ab* in Figure 8.1. Line *ab*, to which we shall refer as the transformation line, has a slope equal to $r/\sigma_g$. At point *a*, the standard deviation (and therefore also the variance) equals zero. This means that the entire liquid reserve has been invested in cash. At point *b*, the expected return and the standard deviation are *r* and $\sigma_g$ respectively, which means that all the liquid assets have been invested in bonds. Each point on the transformation line between *a* and *b* represents a different combination of cash and bonds. Each of these combinations constitutes an efficient portfolio, since there is no other combination on the transformation line that is preferable according to the MV rule. Thus we have an infinity of efficient portfolios.[10]

If we now superimpose the investor's indifference map on Figure 8.1 we see that point *m* represents the optimal combination of cash and bonds, this being the point of tangency between the transformation line and indifference curve $I_2$ which represents the highest attainable level of utility. As the indifference curve generally is tangent to the transformation line at some intermediate point between *a* and *b*, rather than at either corner, it appears that investors typically will hold part of their investment in liquid assets in cash, even though the return on cash holdings is nil.

The intuitive explanation for the willingness to hold cash is that although the return on the investment in cash is zero, the risk involved is also zero. The expected return on a bond, on the other hand, is positive, but an investor who holds a bond for a given period (for example, one year) may incur a capital loss, so that even the "safest" bond carries some degree of risk. Generally investors are not willing to risk all of their liquid reserves, and as a result prefer to hold part of their liquid assets in cash to reduce the overall risk.

EXAMPLE

To clarify our thinking let us consider the hypothetical example of an investor who has a liquid reserve of $1,000 which he wants to hold partly in bonds and partly in cash.

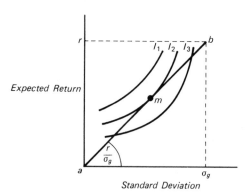

**Figure 8.1**

Let us further assume that bonds yield 10% interest, and that the capital gain on bonds constitutes a random variable ($g$) with a mean of 0 and a standard deviation $\sigma_g = 0.04$ (4%). The investor is assumed to be a risk averter and his subjective preferences (indifference curves) regarding the trade-off between expected returns and the standard deviation (variance) of returns are specified by the following relationship:

$$ER = a + 40\sigma_R^2 \tag{8.10}$$

Now let us find the optimal combination of bonds and cash for our hypothetical investor. We already know that the optimum solution will be given by the point of tangency between one of the investor's indifference curves and the transformation line. Since at the point of tangency the slopes of the two curves are equal, we can solve our problem analytically by equating the first derivatives of the indifference curves and of the transformation line.

Equation (8.10) represents the indifference relationship. Taking its first derivative, we get

$$\frac{\partial ER}{\partial \sigma_R} = 80\sigma_R \tag{8.11}$$

Equation (8.9) specifies the transformation line; differentiating this equation and taking its first derivative, we get

$$\frac{\partial ER}{\partial \sigma_R} = \frac{r}{\sigma_g} \tag{8.12}$$

To find the optimal solution, the point at which the slopes of the two curves are equal, we set their first derivatives equal to one another:

$$80\sigma_R = \frac{r}{\sigma_g} \tag{8.13}$$

Solving this equation explicitly for $\sigma_R$ yields

$$\sigma_R = \frac{r}{80\sigma_g} \tag{8.14}$$

If we substitute the assumed values for $r$ and $\sigma_g$ (0.10 and 0.04 respectively), Equation (8.14) can be solved numerically:

$$\sigma_R = \frac{0.10}{80 \cdot 0.04} = 0.0312$$

From Equation (8.8) we know that

$$x_2 = \frac{\sigma_R}{\sigma_g} = \frac{0.0312}{0.04} = 0.78$$

Thus the optimal portfolio includes $780 in bonds and $220 in cash. And from Equation (8.5) we can find the expected return on this portfolio:

$$ER = x_2 \cdot r = 0.78 \cdot 0.10 = 0.078$$

That is, the expected return is 7.8%.

Now let us see how the proportions of bonds and cash vary as we change the interest rate on bonds. Assume a lower rate of interest, say 9%. From Equation (8.9):

$$ER = \frac{r}{\sigma_g} \cdot \sigma_R = \frac{0.09}{0.04} \sigma_R = 2.25\sigma_R$$

From the tangency condition (8.14) we can solve for $\sigma_R$:

$$\sigma_R = \frac{r}{80\sigma_g} = \frac{0.09}{80 \cdot 0.04} = 0.02812$$

The proportion held in bonds, $x_2$, equals

$$x_2 = \frac{\sigma_R}{\sigma_g} = \frac{0.02812}{0.04} = 0.703$$

In this specific case, the investor reduces the share of assets invested in bonds to $703; the remaining $297 is held in cash.

The same result can be derived graphically. Figure 8.2 reproduces Tobin's expected return–standard deviation diagram.[11] $x_2$ (the proportion invested in bonds) is marked in the negative direction on the vertical axis, the maximum possible value of $x_2$ being 1. Through point $M$ (where $x_2 = 1$) a horizontal line $MN$ is drawn. Point $\sigma_g$ is specified at the appropriate point on the horizontal axis, and through it a vertical line $SN$ is drawn. Point $N$ is then connected to the origin of the axes, whereby line $ON$ is obtained. The transformation line is determined by the relationship

$$ER = \frac{r}{\sigma_g} \cdot \sigma_R$$

[11] See J. Tobin, "Liquidity Preference as Behavior Towards Risk", *Review of Economic Studies* (Feb. 1958).

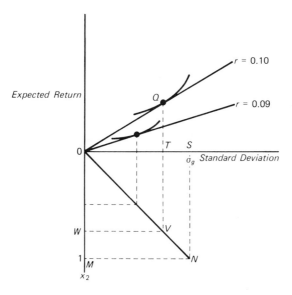

**Figure 8.2**

and is represented diagrammatically by a straight line rising from the origin; the slope of the line increases as $r$ is increased (or $\sigma_g$ is decreased).

The point of tangency between the transformation line and an indifference curve, point $Q$ of Figure 8.2, uniquely determines both the expected return and the standard deviation of the portfolio. Let us now drop a vertical line from point $Q$ which meets line $ON$ at point $V$. Through $V$ pass a horizontal line $VW$ to the vertical axis. The segment $OW$ on the vertical axis measures the optimal proportion of bonds, the optimal proportion of cash being $1 - OW$. With the aid of this diagram we can also determine appropriate values of $ER$, $\sigma_R$, and $x_2$ for various interest rates (and standard deviations) on bonds. The lower the interest rate the smaller the slope of the transformation line; the line for a 9% interest rate lies below the 10% line in Figure 8.2, and therefore is tangent to a lower indifference curve. The corresponding change in $\sigma_R$, $ER$, and $x_2$ can be read off as before. And as we have already noted, in this particular case all three decrease for the lower interest rate.

## 8.2    Portfolios of Two Risky Securities

Let us now assume that the investor is confronted with two risky securities ($A$ and $B$) and that he has the opportunity of investing either in one or in the other, or diversifying his investment by building a portfolio which includes both securities. To analyze the motives underlying the portfolio decision it will be convenient to adopt the following notation: Let

$$R_1 \text{ and } R_2 = \text{random variables denoting the return on one dollar invested in securities } A \text{ and } B \text{ respectively}$$
$$ER_1 \equiv \mu_1 = \text{the expected return on security } A$$
$$ER_2 \equiv \mu_2 = \text{the expected return on security } B$$
$$\sqrt{Var\ (R_1)} \equiv \sigma_1 = \text{the standard deviation of returns for security } A$$
$$\sqrt{Var\ (R_2)} \equiv \sigma_2 = \text{the standard deviation of returns for security } B$$
$$x_1 = \text{the proportion invested in } A$$
$$x_2 = \text{the proportion invested in } B$$
$$Cov\ (R_1,\ R_2) \equiv \sigma_{12} = \text{the covariance of returns on securities } A \text{ and } B$$

Since $x_1 + x_2 = 1$, it is evident that if $x_1 = 1$ (or $x_2 = 1$) the portfolio includes only one security. On the other hand, where $0 < x_1 < 1$, the investor has diversified his portfolio to include both securities. The portfolio return is given by

$$R = x_1 R_1 + x_2 R_2$$

The expected return on the portfolio is

$$ER = x_1 ER_1 + x_2 ER_2$$

or, in abbreviated form,

$$\mu = x_1 \mu_1 + x_2 \mu_2 \tag{8.15}$$

The variance of the portfolio returns is[12]

$$Var\ (R) = x_1^2\ Var\ (R_1) + x_2^2\ Var\ (R_2) + 2x_1 x_2\ Cov\ (R_1,\ R_2)$$

Let us now write the variance of the portfolio in the more usual form:

$$\sigma^2 = x_1^2 \sigma_1^2 + x_2^2 \sigma_2^2 + 2x_1 x_2\ \sigma_{12}$$

The coefficient of correlation between $R_1$ and $R_2$ is defined as follows:

$$\rho_{12} = \frac{Cov\ (R_1, R_2)}{\sigma_1 \sigma_2}$$

Hence $Cov\ (R_1, R_2) = \rho_{12}\sigma_1\sigma_2$ and, alternatively,

$$\sigma^2 = x_1^2 \sigma_1^2 + x_2^2 \sigma_2^2 + 2x_1 x_2 \rho_{12} \sigma_1 \sigma_2$$

---

[12] $Var\ (R) = E(R - ER)^2 = E[(x_1 R_1 + x_2 R_2) - (x_1 \mu_1 + x_2 \mu_2)]^2$
$= E[(x_1 R_1 - x_1 \mu_1) + (x_2 R_2 - x_2 \mu_2)]^2 = E[(x_1 R_1 - x_1 \mu_1)^2$
$+ (x_2 R_2 - x_2 \mu_2)^2 + 2(x_1 R_1 - x_1 \mu_1)(x_2 R_2 - x_2 \mu_2)]$
$= Var\ (x_1 R_1) + Var\ (x_2 R_2) + 2\ Cov\ (x_1 R_1, x_2 R_2)$
$= x_1^2 \sigma_1^2 + x_2^2 \sigma_2^2 + 2x_1 x_2\ Cov\ (R_1, R_2)$

For the time being we shall assume that there is no correlation between the returns to the investor for these two securities, that is, $Cov\,(R_1, R_2) = 0$. (This assumption will be relaxed later in the chapter.) If the returns of the two securities are not correlated then the variance of the portfolio becomes

$$\sigma^2 = x_1^2 \sigma_1^2 + x_2^2 \sigma_2^2 \tag{8.16}$$

As may be seen from Equations (8.15) and (8.16) the investor may choose various combinations of expected returns and variances (standard deviations), depending on the proportions in which he includes the two securities in his portfolio. For instance, if $x_1 = 1$ (and therefore $x_2 = 0$), Equation (8.15) becomes

$$\mu = 1 \cdot \mu_1 + 0 \cdot \mu_2 = \mu_1$$

and Equation (8.16) becomes

$$\sigma^2 = 1^2 \cdot \sigma_1^2 + 0^2 \cdot \sigma_2^2 = \sigma_1^2$$

Thus, when $x_1 = 1$ the entire portfolio is concentrated in security $A$ and the expected return and variance of returns of the portfolio are identical to the expectation and variance of security $A$. Similarly, if $x_2 = 1$ (and therefore $x_1 = 0$) the expected return of the portfolio will be $\mu_2$ and the variance of the returns $\sigma_2^2$. For all other combinations of $x_1$ and $x_2$, however, different values of $\mu$ and $\sigma^2$ will be obtained.

To find how the investor selects his optimal portfolio (the optimal combination of $x_1$ and $x_2$) let us first consider the factors that influence his decision. Since it is assumed that this decision is made according to the MV rule[13] it is clear that his utility level is determined by only two parameters, which are also the sole factors that determine his decision. These parameters are the expected return and the variance of returns of the portfolio. We shall initially analyze the effect of each of these parameters separately and then examine their combined effect.

Let us start with the effect of the expected return, disregarding the variance; that is, we assume that the investor's goal is to select that portfolio which maximizes the expected return. It is clear that if this is the investor's objective he will prefer to put all his money into a single security, the one with the highest return. Thus, if $\mu_1 > \mu_2$ he will choose $x_1 = 1$ and $x_2 = 0$; but if $\mu_2 > \mu_1$ he will choose $x_2 = 1$ and $x_1 = 0$.[14] This result can be illustrated graphically with the aid of a simple device which we will need throughout the remainder of the chapter.

First let us rewrite Equation (8.15) as follows:

$$x_1 = \frac{\mu}{\mu_1} - \frac{\mu_2}{\mu_1} x_2$$

---

[13] The MV rule is optimal when normal distributions and risk aversion are assumed. See Chapter 7.
[14] For the sake of simplicity we have excluded the possibility that $\mu_1 = \mu_2$. In such a case the investor would be indifferent to the choice between securities, since all combinations provide the same return.

This is a linear equation, with $\mu/\mu_1$ as the vertical intercept and with a negative slope equal to $-(\mu_2/\mu_1)$. Since $\mu_1$ and $\mu_2$ are given constants, there are three variables $x_1$, $x_2$, and $\mu$ whose interrelationship we wish to determine. If in the above equation we substitute a particular value, for example 5, for $\mu$, then the linear equation gives us all the combinations of $x_1$ and $x_2$ with an expected return equal to 5. If instead we substitute $\mu = 10$, then we have all the combinations of $x_1$ and $x_2$ which produce portfolios with an expected return of 10. This means that every line consists of the various combinations of $x_1$ and $x_2$ which produce a given expected return. We shall call these lines *iso-return* lines. A family of three such lines is shown in Figure 8.3. The larger the expected return value $E_i$ substituted for $\mu$ in the equation, the higher the iso-return line. From the diagram, it is clear that we assume $E_3 > E_2 > E_1$ since the iso-return line which represents a return of $E_3$ lies above the line which represents $E_2$, and so on.

These lines are parallel since the slope $-(\mu_2/\mu_1)$ is not affected by changes in $\mu$. It is also clear from the diagram that in this case the absolute value of the slope is greater than $45°$, since in this particular example $\mu_2 > \mu_1$. Obviously the investor will desire to reach the highest possible iso-return line, but he cannot invest without limit because of his budget constraint. Such a budget line ($ab$) has been drawn in Figure 8.3. Since we assumed an investment of one dollar and the investor cannot invest more than 100% of his dollar the constraint takes the form $x_1 + x_2 = 1$, which can be rewritten as $x_1 = 1 - x_2$. This is a linear equation with a $45°$ slope. The investor who desires to maximize his expected return will try to reach the highest iso-return line, given the constraint that $x_1 + x_2 = 1$. This means that not all the combinations $x_1$ and $x_2$ on a line are open to the investor; for example, he cannot select a combination located on $E_3$ without violating his budget constraint since on that line $x_1 + x_2 > 1$. Nor will he choose the

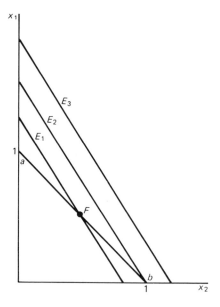

**Figure 8.3**

combination represented by point $F$, whose expected return is $E_1$, since he can increase his return (reach a higher iso-return line) by choosing investment $b$, whose expected return is $E_2$. At point $b$ the expected return is maximized since the budget constraint does not cross or touch a higher iso-return line. As may be seen from Figure 8.3, the portfolio that maximizes the investor's expected return (point $b$) lies on the horizontal axis, which means that $x_1 = 0$ and $x_2 = 1$, so that the investor places all of his funds in security $B$ since it has a higher expected return than security $A$.

Conversely, if we assume $\mu_2 < \mu_1$, then the slope of the iso-return lines will be less than 45°. A family of iso-return lines which reflect this assumption are drawn in Figure 8.4. As could be expected, in this case the introduction of the budget constraint results in a corner solution (point $c$) on the vertical, rather than on the horizontal axis. At this point, $x_1 = 1$ and $x_2 = 0$, which means that the investor maximizes his expected return by placing all of his funds in security $A$ with the higher expected return.

It follows from the graphic analysis that an investor who wants to maximize the expected return of his portfolio, independent of all other factors such as the risk involved, will invariably invest all of his funds in the security that offers the maximum expected return. This conclusion also holds for cases in which he has the opportunity of investing in more than two securities.

Let us now make the alternative extreme assumption that the investor wants to minimize the variance (risk) of the portfolio returns, without regard to the expected return. Here we have the diametrically opposite approach to the one described previously. In the present case all that matters is the risk involved in the investment. In Equation (8.16) we have seen that the variance of the portfolio, assuming zero correlation between the returns from the two securities, is given by

$$\sigma^2 = x_1^2 \sigma_1^2 + x_2^2 \sigma_2^2$$

If we divide both sides of the equation by $\sigma^2$ we obtain

$$1 = x_1^2 \frac{\sigma_1^2}{\sigma^2} + x_2^2 \frac{\sigma_2^2}{\sigma^2} \tag{8.17}$$

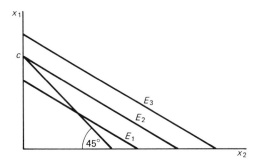

**Figure 8.4**

or

$$1 = \frac{x_1^2}{a_1^2} + \frac{x_2^2}{a_2^2} \tag{8.18}$$

where

$$a_1 = \frac{\sigma}{\sigma_1}; \qquad a_2 = \frac{\sigma}{\sigma_2}$$

Now, (8.18) is the equation of an ellipse having its center at the origin, with the parameters $a_1$ and $a_2$. Since $\sigma_1$ and $\sigma_2$ are given constants, $a_1$ and $a_2$ are determined by $\sigma$. Any increase in $\sigma$ increases both $a_1$ and $a_2$. When we insert a particular value of $\sigma$ in Equation (8.18) $a_1$ and $a_2$ are also determined, so that we can derive all the combinations of $x_1$ and $x_2$ which are located on this ellipse. All the combinations of $x_1$ and $x_2$ located on the same ellipse represent alternative combinations of securities $A$ and $B$ whose variance is constant and equal to the value of $\sigma$ which was inserted in Equation (8.18). Obviously, for each different value of $\sigma$ inserted in Equation (8.18) a different ellipse is derived.

Figure 8.5 presents a family of such ellipses. Since each ellipse represents a constant level of variance we shall call them *iso-variance* curves. A glance at Equation (8.18) will suffice to show that the parameter $a_1$ determines the length of the vertical axis. If we set $x_2 = 0$, Equation (8.18) reduces to $a_1 = \pm x_1$. Similarly if we set $x_1$ equal to zero, this equation reduces to $a_2 = \pm x_2$, that is, the parameter $a_2$ determines the length of the horizontal axis. The greater the distance of the ellipse from the origin, the higher the variance; thus Figure 8.5 has been constructed on the assumption that

$$\sigma_{(3)}^2 > \sigma_{(2)}^2 > \sigma_{(1)}^2$$

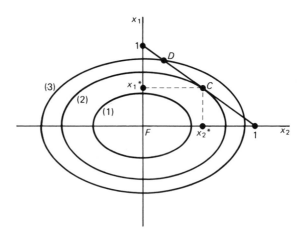

**Figure 8.5**

As was true for the iso-return lines, the iso-variance lines do not intersect since a single point on the diagram cannot represent two different levels of portfolio variance. Again, as in the case of the iso-return lines, not every combination of investments on an ellipse obeys the budget constraint $x_1 + x_2 = 1$. At point $F$, for example, $x_1 = 0$ and $x_2 = 0$; the portfolio variance is also zero at this point. Thus one sure way of minimizing variance is simply to abstain from purchasing securities. As we are interested in the behavior of those individuals who have decided to invest in the securities market, we shall confine ourselves to cases where $x_1 + x_2 = 1$. This constraint indicates that the investor has a fixed sum of money at his disposal, and our problem is to determine the manner in which he allocates the sum between two given (risky) securities. Let us then, on the same diagram, draw the line representing the budget constraint, which as we see is tangent to ellipse (2) at point $C$.[15] Any point of intersection or tangency between an ellipse and the budget line represents an attainable portfolio since the budget constraint is satisfied. Thus point $D$ represents one such portfolio, but as this point is located on ellipse (3) the investor will prefer portfolio $C$ on ellipse (2), as the variance of this portfolio is smaller. The variance can be minimized, given the constraint, by finding that portfolio which is tangent to the budget line, point $C$ in our example. Thus the proportions $x_1$ and $x_2$ at point $C$ represent the *optimal* portfolio for an investor who desires to *minimize* the variance at all costs.[16]

---

[15] Since there exists an infinity of ellipses corresponding to the infinite number of values of σ that can be plugged into Equation (8.18), an ellipse can always be found which is tangent to a straight line.

[16] The optimal proportions $x_1^*$ and $x_2^*$ of the minimum variance portfolio in the case of zero correlation of asset return can be found as follows:
From Equation (8.16) we know that $\sigma^2 = x_1^2\sigma_1^2 + x_2^2\sigma_2^2$. It is further given that $x_1 + x_2 = 1$. Hence

$$\sigma^2 = x_1^2\sigma_1^2 + (1 - x_1)^2\sigma_2^2 = x_1^2\sigma_1^2 + (1 + x_1^2 - 2x_1)\sigma_2^2$$
$$= x_1^2(\sigma_1^2 + \sigma_2^2) - 2x_1\sigma_2^2 + \sigma_2^2$$

Differentiating this equation and setting its first derivative equal to zero, we obtain

$$\frac{\partial\sigma^2}{\partial x_1} = 2x_1(\sigma_1^2 + \sigma_2^2) - 2\sigma_2^2 = 0$$

That is,

$$x_1 = \frac{\sigma_2^2}{\sigma_1^2 + \sigma_2^2}$$

$$x_2 = 1 - x_1 = \frac{\sigma_1^2 + \sigma_2^2 - \sigma_2^2}{\sigma_1^2 + \sigma_2^2} = \frac{\sigma_1^2}{\sigma_1^2 + \sigma_2^2}$$

which means that the optimal investment proportions minimizing the portfolio variance are

$$x_1^* = \frac{\sigma_2^2}{\sigma_1^2 + \sigma_2^2}; \qquad x_2^* = \frac{\sigma_1^2}{\sigma_1^2 + \sigma_2^2}$$

See Figure 8.5. For the case of non-zero correlation, see Problem 8.16 at the end of this chapter.

Unlike the case of the return maximizer, who puts all his money in one security, the risk minimizer diversifies his investment by building a portfolio which includes both securities. This is clear, since at the optimal point $C$, both $x_1^*$ and $x_2^*$ are less than unity. Thus, despite the fact that we have assumed a mean–variance model, diversification can be identified solely with one parameter, the variance associated with the investment.

In both of the above examples we adopted an extreme position of stipulating either an absolute preference for expected return or an absolute preference for stability of returns. On these assumptions we were able to derive the optimal investment proportions without much difficulty. However, if we introduce the more realistic assumption that an investor chooses his portfolio on the basis of both the expected return and the variance of the returns, the optimal investment proportions *cannot* be determined unless further information is available on the investor's tastes. This problem is illustrated in Figure 8.6, which sets out the iso-variance ellipse which is tangent to the budget line $DF$ at the point $C$, and a family of (dashed) iso-return lines. (In this example the iso-return lines have a slope greater than 45° so that $\mu_2 > \mu_1$.) Analysis of Figure 8.6 leads to the following proposition:

> All portfolios which are efficient by the mean–variance rule lie on the segment $CF$ of the budget line.

Since all attainable portfolios (combinations of $x_1$ and $x_2$) must lie on the budget line $DF$, the above proposition states that all attainable portfolios can be divided into two mutually exclusive subsets: an efficient set represented by segment $CF$ and an inefficient set represented by segment $DC$ of Figure 8.6.

To prove this proposition we shall choose an arbitrary point on segment $DC$ and show that it represents a portfolio which is inefficient by the MV rule. Consider, for instance, point $E$ on line $DC$. This point represents an inefficient option since the attainable portfolio represented by point $C$ is preferable to it: point $C$ lies on a higher iso-return line than point $E$ so that $C$ represents a portfolio with a higher profit. Now if we draw an imaginary ellipse through point $E$, it lies outside the ellipse passing through point $C$, so that point $C$ represents a portfolio with both a higher expected value and a lower variance than those of point $E$. Thus portfolio $C$ dominates portfolio $E$ by the MV

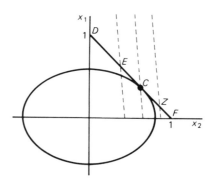

**Figure 8.6**

rule. Similarly it can be shown that all other points on section $DC$ represent inefficient portfolios. The efficient set is represented by section $CF$. As we move from point $C$ to some point on this segment, say point $Z$, both the expected return and the variance increase so that both portfolios are included in the efficient group. Note that point $Z$ represents a higher return and also a higher variance than point $C$. Similarly it may be shown that all other points on segment $CF$ are included in the MV efficient group.[17]

The set of efficient portfolios can also be presented in the perhaps more familiar mean–variance plane. Every point on section $CF$ denotes given proportions $(x_1, x_2)$ of securities $A$ and $B$. Using these proportions the expected return can be computed from Equation (8.15) and the variance can be computed from Equation (8.16) for every point on $CF$ and on $CD$. The resulting combination of expected return and variance can then be plotted on a diagram whose vertical axis measures expected return and whose horizontal axis measures the variance, as has been done in Figure 8.7, which shows the efficient set $CF$ and the inefficient section $CD$, mapped from Figure 8.6.

As we already noted in Figure 8.6, both the expected return and the variance increase as we move from $C$ to $F$; as a result the locus of efficient portfolios in Figure 8.7 rises from left to right. Since point $C$ was on the innermost iso-variance curve, it is located on the extreme left of the efficiency locus of Figure 8.7. Similarly option $F$, which was on the highest iso-return line, lies at the right-hand end of the efficiency locus, and so on for all of the remaining points. Examination of the efficient set shows it to contain numerous mixed portfolios, containing various proportions of both securities $A$ and $B$ as well as one portfolio consisting of security $B$ alone (at point $F$). On the other hand the option of investing solely in security $A$, the security with the lower expected return, is excluded from the efficient set in this case.

The optimal investment can be selected from the efficient set only if we add information regarding the individual investor's preferences. An investor whose preferences are represented by indifference curve $I_1$, for instance, will choose portfolio $Z$, the point of tangency between the efficiency locus $CF$ and the indifference curve $I_1$. Since with

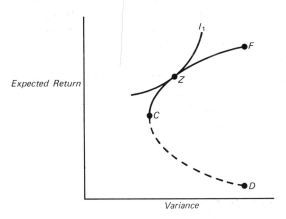

**Figure 8.7**

[17] However, unless all of the requirements regarding the MV rule are met, a preliminary screening using the FSD rule may reduce the efficient set by eliminating some of the points on segment $CF$ (see Chapter 6).

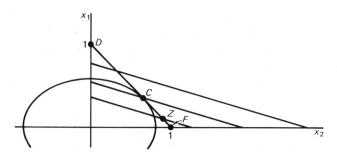

**Figure 8.8**

one exception (point $F$) all the infinity of points on the efficiency curve represent mixed portfolios with varying proportions of both securities, almost every (risk-averse) investor will diversify his investment to include both securities.

To summarize, assuming that investors desire to maximize expected returns, without regard to the variance, they will tend to place all their investment funds in a single security—the one with the highest expected return. On the other hand, if we assume that investors are interested *exclusively* in minimizing the variance of returns, without regard to expected returns, they will diversify their investment by building a portfolio which includes the two securities in fixed proportions, namely, the proportions represented by point $C$ in Figure 8.5. When it is assumed that investors take both the expected return and the variance into account, they are still almost certain to diversify their investments, but in this case the proportions selected by different investors are no longer constant, and depend on the investors' individual preferences.

In Figure 8.6 the iso-return lines are drawn steeper than the slope of the budget line, on the assumption that $\mu_2 > \mu_1$. Accordingly, a portfolio consisting exclusively of security $B$ is included in the efficient group, while the option of investing exclusively in security $A$ is excluded. However, if we assume that $\mu_2 < \mu_1$ these results are reversed: an investment consisting solely of security $A$ is included in the efficient set and that consisting solely of security $B$ is excluded. Similarly, the efficient set is represented by the upper segment $CD$ of the budget line; see Figure 8.8. Point $Z$, for example, now represents an inefficient portfolio since point $C$ has a higher expected return (being located on a higher iso-return line) and a smaller variance (being located on an inner iso-variance curve) and therefore dominates point $Z$. Similarly it can be shown that investment $C$ dominates all other portfolios represented by points on section $CF$, thereby eliminating them from the efficient set.

## 8.3    A Three-Security Portfolio

We shall now extend the analysis to include the possibility of investing in three securities—$A$, $B$, and $C$. For convenience we use the same notation as before except that the subscript 3 will be used, when necessary, to identify the third security. Again we set a limit on the amount invested and require that $x_1 + x_2 + x_3 = 1$; so that the problem is how to allocate a given sum of money among the three securities.

The expected return on a portfolio is given by:

$$\mu = x_1 \mu_1 + x_2 \mu_2 + x_3 \mu_3$$

or, since by the budget constraint $x_3 = 1 - x_1 - x_2$,

$$\mu = x_1 \mu_1 + x_2 \mu_2 + (1 - x_1 - x_2)\mu_3$$

Hence

$$\mu = x_1(\mu_1 - \mu_3) + x_2(\mu_2 - \mu_3) + \mu_3 \qquad (8.19)$$

This equation can also be written in the following form:

$$x_1 = \frac{\mu_3 - \mu}{\mu_3 - \mu_1} + \frac{\mu_2 - \mu_3}{\mu_3 - \mu_1} x_2 \qquad (8.20)$$

This means that in the plane $(x_1, x_2)$ Equation (8.19) and therefore also Equation (8.20) is represented by a straight line having the slope

$$\frac{\mu_2 - \mu_3}{\mu_3 - \mu_1}$$

For example, if $\mu_1 = \$7$, $\mu_2 = \$4$, $\mu_3 = \$6$, then

$$x_1 = \frac{6 - \mu}{6 - 7} + \frac{4 - 6}{6 - 7} \cdot x_2 = \frac{6 - \mu}{-1} + 2x_2$$

The location of the line is determined by the value of $\mu$ and by its slope, which is $+2$ in this case.

A family of such iso-return lines labeled $E_1, E_2$, and so on are shown in Figure 8.9.

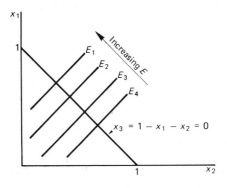

**Figure 8.9**

Obviously an infinity of such lines can be drawn, depending on the assumed level of expected return $\mu$. The higher the expected return, the higher the iso-return line, that is, line $E_1$ represents a higher return than $E_2$ and so on. Moving along an iso-return line in the northeasterly direction, $x_1$ and $x_2$ increase while $x_3$ decreases.

Let us now see how the iso-variance curves can be represented on this plane. First let us find the variance of the returns:[18]

$$Var\ (R) = Var\ (x_1 R_1 + x_2 R_2 + x_3 R_3) = x_1^2 \sigma_1^2 + x_2^2 \sigma_2^2 + x_3^2 \sigma_3^2$$
$$+ 2x_1 x_2 \sigma_1 \sigma_2 \rho_{12} + 2x_1 x_3 \sigma_1 \sigma_3 \rho_{13} + 2x_2 x_3 \sigma_2 \sigma_3 \rho_{23}$$

Let us now substitute $x_3 = 1 - x_1 - x_2$, which yields the following:

$$\sigma^2 = x_1^2 \sigma_1^2 + x_2^2 \sigma_2^2 + (1 - x_1 - x_2)^2 \sigma_3^2 + 2x_1 x_2 \sigma_1 \sigma_2 \rho_{12}$$
$$+ 2x_1(1 - x_1 - x_2)\sigma_1 \sigma_3 \rho_{13} + 2x_2(1 - x_1 - x_2)\sigma_2 \sigma_3 \rho_{23}$$

By opening the brackets and collecting terms we obtain the following equation:

$$\sigma^2 = x_1^2(\sigma_1^2 - 2\sigma_1 \sigma_3 \rho_{13} + \sigma_3^2) + x_2^2(\sigma_2^2 - 2\sigma_2 \sigma_3 \rho_{23} + \sigma_3^2)$$
$$+ 2x_1 x_2(\sigma_1 \sigma_2 \rho_{12} - \sigma_1 \sigma_3 \rho_{13} - \sigma_2 \sigma_3 \rho_{23} + \sigma_3^2)$$
$$+ 2x_1(\sigma_1 \sigma_3 \rho_{13} - \sigma_3^2) + 2x_2(\sigma_2 \sigma_3 \rho_{23} - \sigma_3^2) + \sigma_3^2 \qquad (8.21)$$

This equation generally describes an ellipse in the $(x_1, x_2)$ plane.[19] The greater the diameter of the ellipse, the higher the variance it represents. A family of such iso-variance curves is given in Figure 8.10. The point at the center of the ellipse may or may not represent an attainable portfolio. The set of attainable portfolios is represented by all the points within the triangle formed by the vertical axis, the horizontal axis, and the budget line, $x_3 = 1 - x_1 - x_2 = 0$. For the sake of simplicity we have assumed that the center of the ellipse represents an attainable combination, and therefore it has been drawn within the triangle.

Figure 8.11 sets out the iso-return lines, the iso-variance curves, and the triangle of attainable points. The iso-return line $E_5$ is tangent to the iso-variance curve $V_2$ at point

---

[18] The coefficient of correlation between securities $i$ and $j$ is defined as

$$\rho_{ij} = \frac{Cov\ (R_i, R_j)}{\sigma_i \sigma_j}$$

Hence $Cov\ (R_i, R_j) = \rho_{ij} \sigma_i \sigma_j$. For more details see the Statistical Supplement.

[19] The equation is not an ellipse if and only if one or more of the following conditions hold:
  (a) the variance of the variable $(R_1 - R_3)$ equals 0: $\sigma_1^2 - 2\sigma_1 \sigma_3 \rho_{13} + \sigma_3^2 = 0$
  (b) the variance of the variable $(R_2 - R_3)$ equals 0: $\sigma_2^2 - 2\sigma_2 \sigma_3 \rho_{23} + \sigma_3^2 = 0$
  (c) the random variables $(R_1 - R_3)$ and $(R_2 - R_3)$ have a correlation of $+1$ or $-1$: $\rho_{13} = \pm 1$ or $\rho_{23} = \pm 1$.

The mathematical analysis is the same whether one or more of these conditions are fulfilled. For the sake of convenient graphical representation it was assumed in this chapter that none of the conditions applies.

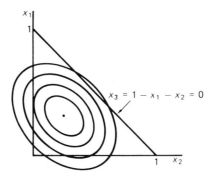

$x_3 = 1 - x_1 - x_2 = 0$

**Figure 8.10**

$K$. Line $E_4$, which represents a higher expected return, is tangent to the iso-variance curve $V_3$ at point $D$, which represents a smaller variance than the ellipse $V_2$. This means that movement from $K$ to $D$ increases the expected return while the variance goes down. If we apply the MV rule, the portfolio represented by point $D$ is preferable to that represented by point $K$. Line $E_3$ passes through point $C$ where the variance of returns is the smallest, and by an analogous argument we can show that the portfolio represented by point $C$ is preferable to that represented by $D$. However, this is not the case for points $C$ and $B$. At point $B$ the expected return is higher than at point $C(E_2 > E_3)$ but the variance is also higher. Thus the portfolios represented by $C$ and $B$ are both MV efficient. Similarly, all of the portfolios (points) along the segments $CG$ and $GH$ are efficient, while all of the other attainable points are inefficient, using the mean–variance rule. For example, at point $F$ the expected return is $E_2$ and the variance is $V_2$. If instead we substitute point $B$, the variance is decreased while the expected return remains constant. Thus point $F$ represents an inefficient option.

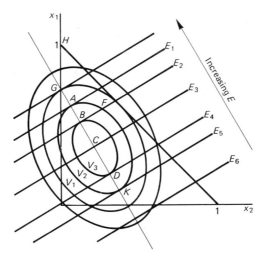

**Figure 8.11**

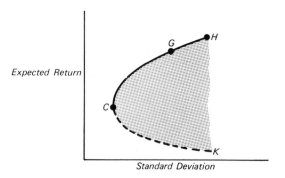

**Figure 8.12**

As in the two security case, the efficiency curve can be plotted in an expected return–standard deviation plane by determining the expected return and the standard deviation for each point on the segments $CG$ and $GH$, and transposing them to a diagram such as Figure 8.12.

### 8.4     The Gains from Diversification: Independent Returns

As we have just seen, the desire to stabilize the income stream is a *sine qua non* for investment diversification. However, some degree of stabilization can be achieved, without impairing the expected return. We can illustrate this proposition by means of a simple example of two securities. Let us assume that we have two identical securities, $A$ and $B$, whose distribution of returns (per $100 invested) is given in Table 8.1. Now consider an investor with $100 at his disposal who must decide whether to buy one (or both) of these securities.

If he invests the entire amount in a single security he has a 50% chance of losing $20 and a 50% chance of gaining $30. His expected gain is $5, with a variance of 625. Now what will he earn should he decide to invest $50 in $A$ and $50 in $B$?

The answer depends on the statistical relationship between the two distributions.

**Table 8.1**

| Security A | | Security B | |
|---|---|---|---|
| *Return* | *Probability* | *Return* | *Probability* |
| −20 | 1/2 | −20 | 1/2 |
| +30 | 1/2 | +30 | 1/2 |
| $ER_A = 5$ | | $ER_B = 5$ | |
| $Var(R_A) = 625$ | | $Var(R_B) = 625$ | |

Let us initially assume that the returns from the two securities are statistically independent of each other.[20] Accordingly, the probability of obtaining any given pair of returns from investments $A$ and $B$ is the product of their individual probabilities. For example, the joint probability that the return on *both* securities will be $-20$ in any given year is $1/2 \cdot 1/2 = 1/4$, so that the investor has a 25% chance of losing $20.

Using this approach we calculate the probability distribution of returns for a mixed portfolio which includes securities $A$ and $B$ in equal proportions (see Table 8.2). The expected return on the portfolio is $5, that is, the same return as that of each of the identical securities, but the variance is considerably reduced. Instead of the two extreme results ($+30$ and $-20$) attainable from the investment in a single security, the portfolio provides an intermediate result ($+5$) as well. Thus the portfolio reduces the dispersion of the distribution of returns, and the chances of suffering a major loss ($-20$) are reduced from a probability of $1/2$ for the single security to a probability of only $1/4$ for the mixed portfolio. However, in all fairness, it should also be noted that the chances of making a big profit ($+30$) are also reduced from $1/2$ to $1/4$. But since the investor who makes his selection using the MV rule is assumed to be a risk averter, his expected utility is increased when the dispersion of returns is reduced, as long as the expected return remains unchanged.

In this example we have demonstrated how the investor can increase his expected utility by diversifying his investments when the returns to the investor from the securities in question are assumed to be statistically independent. In practice, however, the returns on the individual securities are not necessarily statistically independent, but as long as they are not *perfectly* correlated the risk-averse investor can gain from diversification. The size of his gain depends on the degree of the statistical interdependence among the returns on different securities and on the number of securities over which he can spread his risk. The lower the interdependence (or the

#### Table 8.2

| Return | Probability |
|--------|-------------|
| $-20$  | $1/4$       |
| $+5$   | $1/2$*      |
| $+30$  | $1/4$       |

$$ER = +5$$
$$Var\ (R) = 312.5$$

*The probability of earning $5 results from a 1/4 chance that $A$ will lose $20 while $B$ earns $30 or from a 1/4 probability that $A$ will earn $30 while $B$ loses $20. Since the two alternatives are independent events, the probability of earning $5 equals $1/4 + 1/4 = 1/2$.

[20] That is, the correlation between the returns from the two securities is zero.

higher the negative interdependence) among the returns and the greater the number of securities over which he is able to diversify his portfolio, the more he stands to gain from diversification.

## 8.5    The Impact of Interdependence on the Gains from Diversification

To analyze the effect of the various relationships that may exist between the returns of different securities, let us assume that we have two securities, $A$ and $B$, the expected returns and standard deviations of which are ($\mu_1$ and $\sigma_1$) and ($\mu_2$ and $\sigma_2$) respectively. These two points are plotted in Figure 8.13, where $A$ represents ($\mu_1, \sigma_1$) and $B$ represents ($\mu_2, \sigma_2$). Should the individual diversify his investment by purchasing a proportion $x_1$ of security $A$ and a proportion $x_2$ ($x_2 = 1 - x_1$) of security $B$, the expected return on this portfolio is equal to

$$\mu = x_1 \mu_1 + (1 - x_1)\mu_2 \tag{8.22}$$

with a variance of

$$\sigma^2 = x_1^2\sigma_1^2 + (1 - x)^2\sigma_2^2 + 2x_1(1 - x_1)\,\sigma_{12} \tag{8.23}$$

Equation (8.23) can also be written as follows:

$$\sigma^2 = x_1^2\sigma_1^2 + (1 - x_1)^2\sigma_2^2 + 2x_1(1 - x_1)\rho\sigma_1\sigma_2 \tag{8.24}$$

where $\rho$ denotes the coefficient of correlation between the returns of the two securities.
    Let us now examine the effects of combining the two securities in a portfolio, under varying assumptions regarding the coefficient of correlation $\rho$. When $\rho = 0$ the transformation curve, which represents the pairs of expected return and variance which result

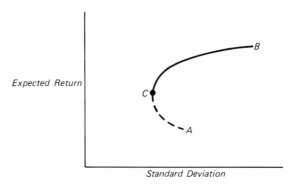

**Figure 8.13**

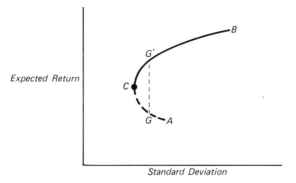

**Figure 8.14**

from combining the two securities in all possible proportions, has the form of the locus $ACB$ of Figure 8.13. This curve has its minimum variance (standard deviation) at point $C$. All the portfolios (points) on curve $ACB$ correspond to the different proportions in which the amount invested is divided between the two securities. The dashed segment $AC$ is irrelevant, since these portfolios are inefficient. The statement can readily be proved by examining the diagram in Figure 8.14. For every point on section $AC$ a corresponding point which is preferable can be found on section $BC$. For example, point $G'$ dominates $G$ since it has a higher mean and an equal variance. Therefore, section $AC$ represents inefficient portfolios which will never be chosen by a rational investor.

The degree to which a two-security portfolio reduces the variance of returns depends on the degree of correlation between the returns of the securities.

EXAMPLE

To quantify this relationship we assume the following expected returns and variances for two securities $A$ and $B$:

$$\mu_1 = 10 \qquad \mu_2 = 20$$
$$\sigma_1^2 = 100 \qquad \sigma_2^2 = 900$$

The expected returns and variances for portfolios of varying proportions and for four alternative assumptions regarding the correlation among returns are given in Table 8.3. The data clearly show that by diversifying his investment an investor can reduce the variance of returns. Moreover, the lower the coefficient of correlation, the greater the reduction in variance.[21] This inverse relationship between the degree of correlation and

---

[21] If we choose the proportions $x_1$ and $x_2$ which minimize the variance, in this case $x_1 = 3/4$ and $x_2 = 1/4$, and assume $\rho = -1$, the portfolio variance is reduced to zero:

$$\sigma^2 = x_1^2 \sigma_1^2 + x_2^2 \sigma_2^2 - 2x_1 x_2 \sigma_1 \sigma_2$$
$$= 9/16 \cdot 100 + 1/16 \cdot 900 - 2 \cdot 3/4 \cdot 1/4 \cdot 10 \cdot 30$$
$$= \frac{900 + 900 - 1800}{16} = 0$$

This portfolio corresponds to the point on the $\rho = -1$ transformation locus which is tangent to the vertical axis in Figure 8.15.

**Table 8.3**

| Proportion of Portfolio Invested in Security A | Expected Return on Portfolio* | Variance of Portfolio Returns for Alternative Coefficients of Correlation† | | | | |
|---|---|---|---|---|---|---|
| | | $\rho = +1$ | $\rho = +1/2$ | $\rho = 0$ | $\rho = -1/2$ | $\rho = -1$ |
| 0 | 20 | 900 | 900 | 900 | 900 | 900 |
| 1/5 | 18 | 676 | 628 | 580 | 532 | 484 |
| 2/5 | 16 | 484 | 412 | 340 | 268 | 196 |
| 3/5 | 14 | 324 | 252 | 180 | 108 | 36 |
| 4/5 | 12 | 196 | 148 | 100 | 52 | 4 |
| 1 | 10 | 100 | 100 | 100 | 100 | 100 |

\* The portfolio mean is independent of $\rho$, and is obtained from the formula

$$\mu = x_1\mu_1 + x_2\mu_2$$

† The formula for the portfolio variance is

$$\sigma^2 = x_1^2\sigma_1^2 + x_2^2\sigma_2^2 + 2x_1x_2\rho\sigma_1\sigma_2$$

the degree of variance reduction can be seen even more clearly in Figure 8.15, which presents a family of transformation curves for varying assumptions regarding the correlation coefficient. Diversification can always reduce variance except in the extreme case where the returns are perfectly correlated ($\rho = +1$). On such an assumption the transformation curve reduces to a straight line joining $AB$.[22] As the correlation coefficient is reduced to $+1/2$, 0, and $-1/2$, the transformation curve bulges out farther and farther to the left, and if we were to superimpose a set of indifference curves on the same plane, we could readily see that the risk-averse investor reaches higher levels of utility for lower coefficients of correlation. And this conclusion holds for all degrees of correlation (positive, negative, or zero) except for the limiting case of perfect positive correlation ($\rho = +1$). It should also be noted that in the case of perfect negative correlation between the returns of the two securities ($\rho = -1$), the transformation curve will at one point be tangent to the vertical axis, which means that there exists a portfolio which completely eliminates the variance. Of course, the final decision to choose the minimum

[22] In the particular case where $\rho = +1$, the variance of the portfolio is given by

$$\sigma^2 = x_1^2\sigma_1^2 + x_2^2\sigma_2^2 + 2x_1x_2\sigma_1\sigma_2 = (x_1\sigma_1 + x_2\sigma_2)^2$$

and hence

$$\sigma = x_1\sigma_1 + x_2\sigma_2$$

The last equation describes a straight line connecting the points $A$ and $B$. In the other extreme case where $\rho = -1$, the portfolio variance is given by

$$\sigma^2 = x_1^2\sigma_1^2 + x_2^2\sigma_2^2 - 2x_1x_2\sigma_1\sigma_2 = (x_1\sigma_1 - x_2\sigma_2)^2.$$

The investment proportions that minimize the variance ($\sigma^2 = 0$) are given by $x_1/x_2 = \sigma_2/\sigma_1$. In this case the variance of the portfolio is zero, and hence curve $AB$ is tangent to the vertical axis.

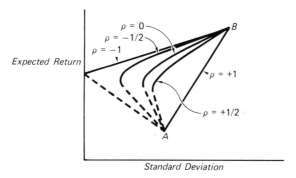

**Figure 8.15**

variance portfolio or some other point on the curve depends on individual preferences (that is, on the slope of the indifference curves).

Figure 8.15 illustrates hypothetical cases with the correlation coefficient ranging from $+1$ to $-1$. While there are many stocks with positively correlated rates of return, and even with correlation coefficients close to $+1$, it is difficult to find two stocks whose rates of return are characterized by perfect negative correlation ($\rho = -1$).

In Figure 8.16 we demonstrate the impact of the correlation coefficient on the curvature (or the "bulging") of the efficient frontier, using the parameters of the actual rates of return of various stocks observed in the period 1971–1980. For each pair of stocks we first estimated the mean rate of return $\bar{R}$, the variance of returns $\sigma^2$, and the correlation coefficient $\rho$. Then using these parameters we constructed the efficient frontiers, as demonstrated above.

Figure 8.16(a) presents the efficient frontier of portfolios consisting of Nabisco and Union Carbide stock. The correlation coefficient for these two stocks is negative, $\rho = -0.14$, and the efficient frontier bulges out far to the left from the straight line connecting the two stocks in the mean–standard deviation plane. Thus, investors can benefit significantly from diversification in Nabisco and Union Carbide. A diversification in IBM and Cleveland Electric Illumination stock is less rewarding, since the rates of return of these two stocks are positively correlated, $\rho = 0.47$ [Figure 8.16(b)]. The gain from diversification in the stock of Republic Steel and Dow Chemicals is minimal: due to the high positive correlation of the rates of return on these two stocks ($\rho = 0.83$) the efficient frontier almost coincides with the straight line connecting the two stocks [Figure 8.16(c)].

Thus the smaller the correlation between two risky assets, the higher the gains from diversification. Investors can stabilize the rate of return, so that the variance decreases without reducing the portfolio expected return.

## 8.6    The Number of Securities and the Gains from Diversification

To see the relationship between the number of securities included in the portfolio and the gain from diversification, let us assume that we now have three securities, $A$, $B$, and

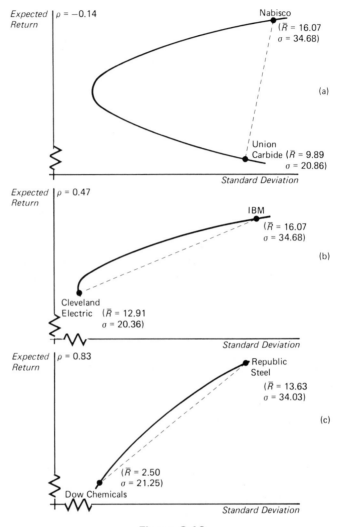

**Figure 8.16**

$C$, each priced at $100. The expected return and variance of each of these securities are given in Table 8.4.

For the sake of convenience we shall assume zero coefficients of correlation between the returns of each pair of securities.

The three-security case is illustrated in Figure 8.17. The investor is confronted with three mutually exclusive alternatives: (a) invest in a portfolio which includes all three securities; (b) confine himself to a two-security portfolio; (c) put all of his money into a single security.

Curve I in Figure 8.17 represents the transformation curve of portfolios comprised of differing proportions of securities $A$ and $B$; curve II and curve III are the relevant

**Table 8.4**

|  | Security | | |
|---|---|---|---|
|  | A | B | C |
| Expected Return | 10 | 20 | 30 |
| Variance of Returns | 100 | 900 | 2,500 |

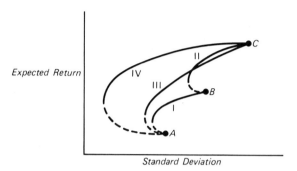

**Figure 8.17**

transformation curves for portfolios which include securities *B* and *C*, and securities *A* and *C*, respectively. Curve IV represents the transformation curve for portfolios which include all possible combinations of all three securities. In that case the investor is offered an additional degree of freedom, and is in a better position to reduce the variance for any given expected return, that is, curve IV lies to the left of the other three curves. This additional possibility for diversifying his investment can only increase, and not decrease, an investor's utility, since he still remains free to put his money into only two of the three securities.

EXAMPLE

Table 8.5 gives numerical examples which show that for a given expected return one can always find a portfolio which includes all three securities that reduces the variance of returns without at the same time reducing the expected return. And although we confine ourselves to only three examples to illustrate the advantages the investor derives from diversification, it should be obvious that an infinity of three-security portfolios can be found which are preferable to a given portfolio consisting of only two securities.

It would seem to follow that investors who select their portfolios according to the MV rule should tend to include a considerable number of securities in their portfolios. In practice, however, the degree of diversification is often limited, for one or more of the following reasons:

(a)  Sometimes an investor has only a relatively small amount of money at his disposal. Diversifying over a large number of stocks would mean investing

**Table 8.5**

| Proportions Invested in Two-Security Portfolios | Expected Return* | Variance of Returns** | Proportions Invested in Three-Security Portfolios | Expected Return* | Variance of Returns** |
|---|---|---|---|---|---|
| $x_1 = 2/5$ $x_2 = 3/5$ $x_3 = 0$ | 16 | 340 | $x_1 = 3/5$ $x_2 = 1/5$ $x_3 = 1/5$ | 16 | 172 |
| $x_1 = 2/5$ $x_2 = 0$ $x_3 = 3/5$ | 22 | 916 | $x_1 = 3/10$ $x_2 = 2/10$ $x_3 = 5/10$ | 22 | 670 |
| $x_1 = 0$ $x_2 = 7/10$ $x_3 = 3/10$ | 23 | 666 | $x_1 = 1/10$ $x_2 = 5/10$ $x_3 = 4/10$ | 23 | 626 |

* The expected return for a three-security portfolio $(x_1 + x_2 + x_3 = 1)$ is calculated from the following formula:

$$\mu = x_1\mu_1 + x_2\mu_2 + x_3\mu_3$$

** The portfolio variance is given by

$$\sigma^2 = x_1^2\sigma_1^2 + x_2^2\sigma_2^2 + x_3^2\sigma_3^2 + 2x_1x_2\rho_{12}\sigma_1\sigma_2 + 2x_1x_3\rho_{13}\sigma_1\sigma_3 + 2x_2x_3\rho_{23}\sigma_2\sigma_3$$

When $\rho_{ij} = 0$ for each pair of securities the last three terms are each equal to zero.

very small amounts in each share, which usually involves excessive brokerage commissions and other costs. Moreover it may sometimes be physically impossible, as it would require buying fractions of shares.

(b)   An individual investor may find it difficult and expensive to keep track of a large number of securities; even a cursory check of the financial statements of a large number of companies is likely to prove a difficult and tedious task for the individual investor.

Thus individual investors often restrict themselves to a relatively small number of individual securities, and seek greater diversification by purchasing shares in mutual funds or investment companies. These institutions pool the funds of many individual investors and thus are able to achieve a high level of diversification. The typical mutual fund often holds the stocks of more than 500 different companies; they are also in a better position to allocate the necessary resources for data collection and financial analysis required to manage such a portfolio.[23]

An individual investor or a mutual fund manager usually diversifies by constructing a portfolio of stocks selected from a given population. The tools that we teach in this textbook are intended to provide optimum decision rules for portfolio construction, but

[23] A more detailed evaluation of mutual fund performance is given in Chapter 15.

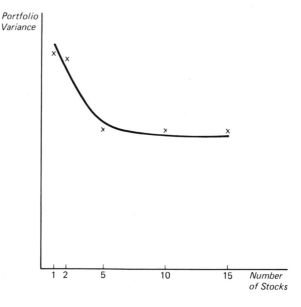

**Figure 8.18**

even the naive strategy that increases the number of stocks in a portfolio by dividing the total investment in equal proportions between the selected stocks attains the goal of return stabilization by reducing the portfolio variance. Figure 8.18 plots the variance of various portfolios as a function of the number of stocks included in the portfolio (in equal proportions). The portfolios were constructed using 1971–1980 rate of return data for a sample of 15 NYSE stocks from a cross-section of industries. The curve starts with a single-stock portfolio (the entire amount invested in the stock with the highest variance, which happened to be IBM stock in the sample), and then the number of stocks is gradually increased to 2, 5, 10, and 15 by diversifying the IBM stocks with other NYSE stocks from the sample. In the two-stock portfolio, 1/2 the total amount is invested in each stock, and in the 15-stock portfolio 1/15 of the total amount is invested in each of the 15 stocks. It is significant that the impact of diversification on portfolio variance rapidly levels off as the number of stocks is increased beyond 5: this may provide a rule-of-thumb justification of the common wisdom that limits the diversification of individual portfolios to few stocks only.

## 8.7    The Efficiency Frontier—The General Case

So far we have illustrated the advantages an investor can derive from diversification by means of examples where the investment is spread over two (or three) securities. In actual fact, thousands of individual securities are traded on the stock exchange and the investor has to decide which of them to include in his portfolio and in what proportions.

To illustrate the general problem of generating the locus of efficient portfolios when the number of securities is very large, let us assume $n$ securities, where $R_i$ is a random variable denoting the return on the $i$th security; $x_i$ denotes the proportion of the portfolio invested in that security; and $\mu_i$ and $\sigma_i$ denote the expected return and the standard deviation of the $i$th security.

Let us now determine the proportions $(x_1, \ldots, x_n)$ which ensure that a portfolio will be efficient. For any proportions $x_1, \ldots, x_n$ that we select, the expected return of the portfolio $\mu_p$ is given by

$$\mu_p = \sum_{i=1}^{n} x_i \mu_i \tag{8.25}$$

while the variance of portfolio returns, $\sigma_p^2$, equals[24]

$$\sigma_p^2 = \sum_{i=1}^{n} x_i^2 \sigma_i^2 + 2 \sum_{i=1}^{n} \sum_{\substack{j=1 \\ j>i}}^{n} x_i x_j \sigma_{ij} \tag{8.26}$$

Since $\sigma_{ij} = \rho_{ij}\sigma_i\sigma_j$ Equation (8.26) can also be written as follows:

$$\sigma_p^2 = \sum_{i=1}^{n} x_i^2 \sigma_i^2 + 2 \sum_{i=1}^{n} \sum_{\substack{j=1 \\ j>i}}^{n} x_i x_j \rho_{ij}\sigma_i\sigma_j \tag{8.27}$$

where $\rho_{ij}$ denotes the coefficient of correlation between the returns of securities $i$ and $j$.

By definition, the portfolio will be efficient if there exists no other having the same expected return and a lower variance of returns.[25] To determine the efficient set we must

---

[24] $\sigma_p^2$ is obtained as follows (by definition):

$$\sigma_p^2 = E\left[\sum_{i=1}^{n} x_i R_i - \sum_{i=1}^{n} x_i \mu_i\right]^2 = E\left[\sum_{i=1}^{n}(x_i R_i - x_i \mu_i)\right]^2$$

$$= E\left[\sum_{i=1}^{n}(x_i R_i - x_i \mu_i)^2 + 2 \sum_{i=1}^{n} \sum_{\substack{j=1 \\ j>i}}^{n}(x_i R_i - x_i \mu_i)(x_j R_j - x_j \mu_j)\right]$$

$$= E\left[\sum_{i=1}^{n} x_i^2(R_i - \mu_i)^2 + 2 \sum_{i=1}^{n} \sum_{\substack{j=1 \\ j>i}}^{n} x_i x_j(R_i - \mu_i)(R_j - \mu_j)\right]$$

$$= \sum_{i=1}^{n} x_i^2 \sigma_i^2 + 2 \sum_{i=1}^{n} \sum_{\substack{j=1 \\ j>i}}^{n} x_i x_j \sigma_{ij}$$

[25] An alternative definition is that a portfolio is regarded as efficient if there is no other portfolio having a higher expected return and the same variance of returns.

accordingly find those investment proportions $(x_1, \ldots, x_n)$ which minimize the variance for a given expected return. The same constraint $\Sigma_{i=1}^{n} x_i = 1$ that applied in the case of a two- or three-security portfolio also applies in the general case.

The optimal proportions are obtained by minimizing the so-called Lagrange function, $C$:

$$C = \sum_{i=1}^{n} x_i^2 \sigma_i^2 + 2 \sum_{i=1}^{n} \sum_{\substack{j=1 \\ j>i}}^{n} x_i x_j \rho_{ij} \sigma_i \sigma_j + \lambda_1 \left( 1 - \sum_{i=1}^{n} x_i \right) + \lambda_2 \left( \mu_p - \sum_{i=1}^{n} x_i \mu_i \right) \quad (8.28)$$

where $\lambda_1$ and $\lambda_2$ are Lagrange multipliers.[26]

Function $C$ has $n + 2$ unknowns: $x_1, \ldots, x_n, \lambda_1, \lambda_2$. If we now differentiate $C$ with respect to $x_i$, $\lambda_1$, and $\lambda_2$, and equate the first derivatives to zero, we derive $n + 2$ equations which provide us with a solution for the $n + 2$ unknowns in the expression for $C$. Using this technique we can determine the minimum variance for any level of expected returns $\mu_p$ which we plug into Equation (8.28), subject to the constraint that $\Sigma_{i=1}^{n} x_i = 1$. The constraint ensures that we deal only with attainable investments, eliminating, for instance, portfolios comprised of securities whose total value exceeds the funds at our disposal.

To determine the set of efficient portfolios in practice, recourse must be had to an electronic computer since the number of calculations rapidly increases as the number of securities increases. The set of equations can be solved with relative ease on existing computers. Different values of $\mu_p$ are inserted in Equation (8.28) and the vector of investment proportions $(x_1, \ldots, x_n)$ which minimize the portfolio variance for any given level of expected return is determined.[27]

In the multi-dimensional case, as in the case of two securities, the efficient set of portfolios can be represented by an envelope curve, such as $ab$ in Figure 8.19. The efficient portfolios lie only on section $ab$, since for every portfolio on section $ac$ another dominant portfolio can be found on section $ab$. All points located to the right of the envelope curve are obviously inefficient, some of these points representing portfolios which include all $n$ securities while others represent partial portfolios or individual securities. The entire envelope curve consisting of both the efficient and the inefficient

---

[26] The Lagrange multipliers guarantee that the relevant constraints are satisfied when the minimum variance portfolio is constructed at each level of expected return. For example, by equating to zero the derivative

$$\partial C / \partial \lambda_1 = 1 - \sum_{i=1}^{n} x_i$$

we find that one of the equations which must be fulfilled at the minimum is

$$\sum_{i=1}^{n} x_i = 1$$

i.e., one of the given constraints. For more detailed explanation of Lagrange multipliers and their use in constrained optimization, see R. Allen, *Mathematical Analysis for Economists*, London: Macmillan, 1950, and the Mathematical Supplement at the end of this book.

[27] The use of this technique is illustrated in Chapter 9.

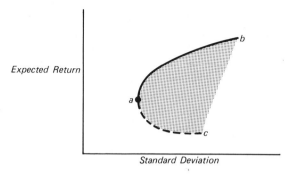

*Expected Return*

*Standard Deviation*

**Figure 8.19**

section is called the *minimum-variance set*, as it is generated by minimizing the portfolio variance at each expected level of portfolio return.

### Summary

Both individual and institutional investors tend to diversify risk by building portfolios which include a number of common stocks as well as cash and bonds. The purpose of this chapter has been to present a graphical analysis of the portfolio selection process based on the Mean–Variance Criterion (MVC).

The first asset combination considered was a portfolio comprising cash and bonds. Despite the fact that cash earns no return, the MVC implies the existence of a mixed portfolio which includes both bonds and cash. This follows from the fact that even a bond without financial risk generates a probability distribution of returns, because of possible fluctuations in the market rate of interest. Should the interest rate rise (fall), the investor in an existing bond will incur a capital loss (gain) in addition to earning the fixed rate of interest. Thus the rate of return (interest plus capital gains or losses) must be treated as a risk asset, which permits an investor to reduce the dispersion of returns by diversifying his liquid assets in a portfolio which includes riskless cash as well as bonds.

The second case discussed is that of an investor who is confronted with two risky securities. Two alternatives are assumed to be open to him: either to invest all of his funds in one of the two securities, or to diversify his investment by building a portfolio which includes both. In effect, the investor may choose various combinations of expected returns and variances, depending on the proportions in which he includes the two securities in his portfolio. An investor who desires to maximize the expected return of his portfolio, independent of all other considerations, will invariably invest all of his funds in the security which offers the maximum return. Investors who wish to minimize risk, independent of all other considerations, always diversify their investments by building a portfolio which includes both securities, in fixed proportions. Thus, in the two-parameter MV model, diversification can be identified solely with one parameter, the

# Summary Table

## 1. A Portfolio of One Risky Asset (Long-Term Bond) and One Riskless Asset (Cash)

The portfolio return $\qquad$ $R = x(r + g)$

The portfolio expected return $\qquad$ $ER = xr$

The portfolio variance $\qquad$ $\sigma_R^2 = x^2 \sigma_g^2$

All combinations $(ER, \sigma_R)$ lie on the straight line $ER = \dfrac{r}{\sigma_g} \sigma_R$

Here $r$ is the riskless interest rate on bonds, $g$ the capital loss or gain on bonds (a random variable), $\sigma_g$ the standard deviation of $g$, $x$ the proportion invested in bonds, and $ER$, $\sigma_R$ stand for the portfolio mean and standard deviation, respectively.

## 2. A Portfolio of Two Risky Assets

The portfolio return $\qquad$ $R = x_1 R_1 + x_2 R_2$

The portfolio expected return $\qquad$ $ER = x_1 \mu_1 + x_2 \mu_2$

The portfolio variance $\qquad$ $\sigma_R^2 = x_1^2 \sigma_1^2 + x_2^2 \sigma_2^2 + 2x_1 x_2 \sigma_{12}$
$$= x_1^2 \sigma_1^2 + x_2^2 \sigma_2^2 + 2x_1 x_2 \rho_{12} \sigma_1 \sigma_2$$

## 3. A Portfolio of $n$ Securities

The portfolio return $\qquad$ $R = \sum_{i=1}^{n} x_i R_i$

The portfolio expected return $\qquad$ $ER = \sum_{i=1}^{n} x_i \mu_i$

The portfolio variance $\qquad$ $\sigma_R^2 = \sum_{i=1}^{n} x_i^2 \sigma_i^2 + 2 \sum_{\substack{i=1 \\ }}^{n} \sum_{\substack{j=1 \\ j>i}}^{n} x_i x_j \, Cov\,(R_i, R_j)$

$$= \sum_{i=1}^{n} \sum_{j=1}^{n} x_i x_j \sigma_{ij}$$

Here $R_i$ is the rate of return on security $i$ (a random variable), $(\mu_i, \sigma_i^2)$ are the mean rate of return and the variance of security $i$, and $Cov\,(R_i, R_j)$ or $\sigma_{ij}$ is the covariance between the returns on securities $i$ and $j$.

## 4. Efficient Set of Portfolios

(a) If the goal is to maximize the portfolio expected return, the security with the highest mean constitutes the optimum portfolio—no diversification takes place.

(b) If the goal is to minimize the portfolio variance, there is one optimum portfolio and, in general, diversification takes place.

(c) If investors consider both expected return and variance in investment decisions, there is a whole set of efficient portfolios, and in general, diversification takes place.

variance of returns. When it is assumed that investors take both the expected return and the variance into account, they are still almost certain to diversify their investments, but the proportions selected by different investors are not constant and depend on their individual preferences. These conclusions hold for the three-security portfolio case as well.

The gains from such diversification were then examined for a risk-averse investor. Such an individual can increase his expected utility by diversifying his investments as long as the returns on the individual securities are not perfectly correlated. The size of the gain depends on the degree of statistical interdependence among the returns and on the number of securities over which he can spread the risks. The lower the positive correlation (or the greater the negative correlation) among the returns, and the larger the number of securities over which he may diversify his portfolio, the greater the gains from diversification. It should also be noted that in the case of perfect negative correlation between the returns of two securities there exists a portfolio which will completely eliminate the variance.

Although the greater the number of securities included in a portfolio, the lower the variance, institutional restrictions and costs limit the size of actual portfolios. For these reasons many small investors seek diversification by means of mutual funds which pool the resources of many individual investors.

### Questions and Problems

8.1  Define and graph the efficiency locus of two-asset portfolios consisting of bonds and cash. Assume that the riskless interest rate on bonds is $r$ and the capital gains (or losses) are represented by a random variable $g$ with zero expected value ($Eg = 0$).

8.2  Why is an individual willing to hold part of his liquid reserve in the form of cash, although cash does not earn any return?

8.3  An investor diversifies his investment between riskless cash and risky bonds which bear an interest rate of 10% and involve a capital gain (or loss) $g$, which is a random variable with zero expected value and a standard deviation of 12%.

(a) For an individual with a quadratic utility function $U(R) = R - bR^2$ ($b > 0$), find the optimal proportions invested in cash and in risky bonds (expressing them in terms of the general coefficient $b$).

(b) Assume that the interest rate rises to 11%, while the distribution of $g$ remains unchanged. How does the proportion invested in bonds change?

(c) Derive the general conditions for the proportion invested in bonds to increase with the increase in the interest rate on the bonds. (*Hint*: Derive a general expression for the proportion invested in bonds for an individual with a quadratic utility function and differentiate the expression with respect to $r$.)

(d) Now assume an individual with indifference curves given by the expression $ER = a + 40\sigma_R^2$ . Answer parts (a) and (b) for this individual. Is the behavior consistent with the result obtained in (c)? If so, will it always remain consistent? If not, why?

8.4    "An investor who ignores risk will not diversify his portfolio; an investor who ignores the
       portfolio's expected return will diversify his portfolio." What is your opinion of these two
       statements? Support your answer by a graphical presentation.

8.5    "Bonds are riskless and should not be included in a risk portfolio." Appraise.

8.6    Consider the following two securities $A$ and $B$:

|            | $A$ | $B$ |
|------------|-----|-----|
| $ER$       | 10  | 20  |
| $Var(R)$   | 5   | 40  |

       (a) Will an individual (using the MV criterion) ever concentrate all of his investment in
           security $A$?
       (b) Will he ever concentrate his entire investment in security $B$?
           Answer under two alternative assumptions:
           (i) The correlation coefficient between $A$ and $B$ is zero.
           (ii) The correlation coefficient between the two securities is $+1$.

8.7    Define the following concepts:

       (a) transformation line
       (b) iso-variance curve
       (c) iso-return line
       (d) variance of a security
       (e) variance of a portfolio.

8.8    What is the connection between gains from diversification and the correlation of the
       returns of securities?

8.9    What is the relationship between the number of available securities and the gains from
       diversification? Does this have any implications for the small investor?

8.10   Assume that an individual is confronted with the following mutually exclusive alter-
       natives:
           (1) Invest $10,000 in security $A$.
           (2) Invest $10,000 in security $B$.
           (3) Invest $10,000 in a portfolio which consists of these two securities in any desired
               proportions.
       The market price of each security is $1.00. The expected return on security $A$ is $0.20 per
       share and on security $B$ $0.40 per share.

       (a) Construct a diagram which shows the proportion invested in each security on the
           assumption that the investor reaches his decision solely on the basis of expected
           return.

(b) Now assume that you are given additional information on security variances and correlation: the variance of returns on security $A$ is 0.1, the variance of returns on security $B$ is 0.3, and the correlation between the returns on security $A$ and security $B$ is zero. What proportion of the $10,000 will the individual invest in each of the securities, assuming that his decision is made solely from considerations of minimum variance, ignoring the expected return?

(c) Answer (b) assuming that the correlation coefficient is $+1$. How do you explain the difference in your answers to (b) and (c)?

(d) Now assume that the investor reaches his investment decision by weighing both the return and the variance.

   (i) Construct the locus of efficient portfolios facing the investor.

   (ii) Identify on the diagram the inefficient alternatives facing the individual. Explain why these alternatives are inefficient.

   (iii) Can you unambiguously determine the proportion invested in each security? If your answer is yes, what are the optimal proportions? If your answer is no, what information do you require in order to determine the optimal proportions?

8.11 Assume that four securities have an *equal probability* of earning the following rates of return:

| A | B | C | D |
|---|---|---|---|
| 40 | −16 | 60 | 5 |
| −10 | 50 | −30 | 5 |
| 20 | −12 | 120 | 5 |
| −6 | 22 | −40 | 5 |

(a) Assuming that the investor is constrained to a single-security portfolio, what are the MV efficient options? Draw the efficient set for this case.

(b) Answer part (a) assuming that the investor also can construct portfolios which include two securities in equal proportions. Assume that the returns on the four securities always occur in combinations as shown in the above table, i.e., a return of 40 on security $A$ is always observed when security $C$ has a return of 60, etc.

(c) Determine the efficient set for the case when the investor is allowed to construct portfolios consisting of three securities in equal proportions.

(d) Draw the three efficient sets from (a), (b), and (c) on one diagram. Explain and analyze your results.

8.12 The following table lists the returns available on four mutual funds between 1977 and 1981.

| | Return on Mutual Fund (%) | | | |
|---|---|---|---|---|
| Year | Amcap Fund | Chemical Fund | Fidelity Trend Fund | Kemper Growth Fund |
| 1977 | 16.4 | − 8.1 | − 3.8 | 2.4 |
| 1978 | 22.4 | 11.9 | 9.7 | 17.8 |
| 1979 | 51.9 | 24.9 | 26.3 | 40.8 |
| 1980 | 27.9 | 30.9 | 25.5 | 44.1 |
| 1981 | 6.2 | − 4.3 | − 5.2 | −11.5 |

*Source*: Wiesenberger, *Investment Companies*.

(a) Assuming that the investor is constrained to a single security portfolio, what are the MV efficient options?

(b) Assuming that the investor can invest in a portfolio composed of equal proportions in two securities, determine the MV efficient options.

(c) Assuming that the investor can invest in a portfolio composed of two securities, with the objective of minimizing the portfolio variance, which pair of mutual funds will he choose from mean–variance considerations? What are the particular investment proportions minimizing the variance? What are the mean return and the variance of the chosen portfolio?

(*Hint*: To solve this part, you will need to calculate the covariances or the correlation coefficients of all the pairs of mutual funds.)

8.13 The following are the expected return, standard deviation of and correlation between returns on Monsanto and Motorola stock.

|                          | Monsanto | Motorola |
|--------------------------|:--------:|:--------:|
| Expected Return          | 11.28%   | 16.35%   |
| Standard Deviation       | 32.19%   | 45.16%   |
| Correlation Coefficient  |   0.40   |          |

*Source*: CRSP monthly returns tape.

(a) Calculate six points on the efficient frontier for $x_1 = 0, 0.1, 0.3, 0.8, 0.9, 1.0$, where $x_1$ is the proportion invested in Monsanto stock. Draw the efficient frontier in the mean–standard deviation plane.

(b) Find the investment proportions which minimize the portfolio variance. What is the variance and the expected return of the minimum–variance portfolio?

(c) How would your answer to (b) change if the correlation coefficient were negative, $-0.40$?

8.14 (a) Derive an expression for the efficient set of two-security portfolios when the correlation coefficient between the constituent securities is $+1$. Draw the efficient set in the mean–standard deviation plane.

(*Hint*: Mathematically, the efficient set is an expression for the portfolio expected return as a function of the portfolio variance.)

(b) Derive an expression for the efficient set of two-security portfolios when the correlation coefficient between the constituent securities is $-1$. Draw the efficient set in the mean–standard deviation plane.

(c) Derive an expression for the efficient set of two-security portfolios for a general correlation coefficient between $-1$ and $+1$ (the two values excluded). Draw the corresponding locus in the mean–standard deviation plane.

8.15 Under what conditions is it possible to construct a portfolio of two risky securities which ensures riskless return? Find the proportions of the two securities in such a portfolio.

8.16 Find a general expression for the proportions of the global minimum variance portfolio of the two-security efficient set. What is the expected return and the standard deviation of such a portfolio? (Assume a general correlation coefficient between $-1$ and $+1$, excluding the two extremes.)

8.17 "A risk-averter guided by the MV criterion will always diversify his investment between two risky securities." Given two risky securities with expected returns $\mu_1$, $\mu_2$ and standard deviations $\sigma_1$, $\sigma_2$, respectively, determine under what conditions on the security parameters risk averters will *not* diversify between the two securities. Perform the analysis in the μ–σ plane without riskless lending and borrowing, examining the following three cases:

(a) Perfect positive correlation of the two assets, $\rho_{12} = +1$.
(b) Perfect negative correlation of the two assets, $\rho_{12} = -1$.
(c) General correlation coefficient $-1 < \rho_{12} < +1$.

In each case consider the implication of short-sale restrictions on diversification.

8.18    What is the relationship between the efficiency frontier of two-security portfolios in the mean–standard deviation plane and in the mean–variance plane in the following two cases:

(a) The correlation coefficient between the two assets is $+1$.
(b) The correlation coefficient between the two assets is 0.

Prove your answer in general mathematical form and illustrate it graphically.
In part (b), determine the global minimum variance portfolio in the two planes.

## Data Set Problems

1. An investor is considering diversifying his portfolio in Affiliated Fund (No. 41) and cash.

   (a) Calculate and draw the line which describes all the possible efficient portfolios in this case.
   (b) Assuming that the investor's utility function is

   $$ER = a + 30\sigma_R^2$$

   find the optimum diversification strategy between cash and Affiliated Fund.
   (c) Summarize your results in a diagram.

2. Use the rates of return on Explorer Fund (No. 8) and Fiduciary Growth Associates (No. 9) and carry out the following calculations:

   (a) Determine the proportions which minimize the variance of the portfolio constructed from the two funds.
   (b) Find ten different points on the MV efficient set of portfolios obtained by combining the two funds. Draw the MV efficient curve in the mean–variance plane and in the mean–standard deviation plane.

3. Calculate the mean rate of return and the variance of the rates of return for each of the first ten funds from the Data Set.
   Calculate the variance of the portfolio which is constructed by combining $i$ funds $(i = 1, 2, \ldots, 10)$ in equal proportions $(1/i$ invested in each fund). You will have to make ten different calculations, one for a portfolio with $i = 1$ fund, another for a portfolio with $i = 2$ funds, and so on, up to the tenth for a portfolio with $i = 10$ funds. Use your results to draw a diagram similar to Figure 8.18 which appears in the body of the chapter.
   Start the calculations with the fund which has the highest variance (thus the portfolio with $i = 1$ consists of the fund with the highest variance; the portfolio with $i=2$ consists of the fund with the highest variance plus another portfolio in equal proportions of $\frac{1}{2}$; the portfolio with $i = 3$ consists of the two securities in the portfolio with $i = 2$ plus a third security in equal proportions of $\frac{1}{3}$, etc.).

## Selected References

Alderfer, C. and Bierman, H., "Choices With Risk: Beyond the Mean and Variance", *Journal of Business* (July 1970).

Ang, J., "A Note on the E, SL Portfolio Selection Model", *Journal of Financial and Quantitative Analysis* (December 1975).

Arditti, F. D., "Risk and the Required Return on Equity", *Journal of Finance* (March 1967).

Arditti, F. D., "Skewness and Investors' Decisions: A Reply", *Journal of Financial and Quantitative Analysis* (March 1975).

Arditti, F. D. and Levy, H., "Distribution Moments and Equilibrium: A Comment", *Journal of Financial and Quantitative Analysis* (January 1972).

Arditti, F. D. and Levy, H., "Portfolio Efficiency Analysis in Three Moments: The Multiperiod Case", *Journal of Finance* (June 1975).

Arrow, K. J., *Aspects of the Theory of Risk Bearing*, Helsinki: Yrjo Jahnssonin Säätiö (1965).

Baumol, W. J., "An Expected Gain-Confidence Limit Criterion for Portfolio Selection", *Management Science* (October 1963).

Bawa, V. S., Elton, E. J., and Gruber, M. J., "Simple Rules for Optimal Portfolio Selection in a Stable Paretian Market", *Journal of Finance* (September 1979).

Borch, K., "A Note on Uncertainty and Indifference Curves", *Review of Economic Studies* (January 1969).

Cheng, P. L., and Deets, M. K., "Test of Portfolio Building Rules: Comment", *Journal of Finance* (September 1971).

Clarkson, G. P., *Portfolio Selection: A Simulation of Trust Investment*, Englewood Cliffs, N.J.: Prentice-Hall (1962).

Cohen, K. J., and Elton, E. J., "Inter-Temporal Portfolio Analysis Based on Simulation of Joint Returns", *Management Science* (September 1967).

Domar, E. and Musgrave, R. A., "Proportional Income Taxation and Risk Taking", *Quarterly Journal of Economics* (May 1944).

Fama, E. F., *Foundations of Finance*, New York: Basic Books (1976).

Fama, E. F. and Miller, M. H. *The Theory of Finance*, New York: Holt Rinehart & Winston (1972).

Farrar, D. E., *The Investment Decision Under Uncertainty*, Englewood Cliffs, N.J.: Prentice-Hall (1962).

Feldstein, M. S., "Mean–Variance Analysis in the Theory of Liquidity Preference and Portfolio Selection", *Review of Economic Studies* (January 1969).

Fishburn, P. C., "Mean–Risk Analysis with Risk Associated with Below-Target Returns", *American Economic Review* (March 1977).

Freimer, M. and Gordon, M. J., "Investment Behavior with Utility a Concave Function of Wealth", in Karl Borch and Jan Mossin, eds., *Risk and Uncertainty*, New York: St. Martin's Press (1968).

Friend, I. and Blume, M. E., "The Demand for Risky Assets", *American Economic Review* (December 1975).

Granito, M. and Walsh, P., "Portfolio Efficiency Analysis in Three Moments—The Multiperiod Case: Comment", *Journal of Finance* (March 1978).

Hakansson, N. H., "Risk Disposition and the Separation Property in Portfolio Selection", *Journal of Financial and Quantitative Analysis* (December 1969).

Hakansson, N. H., "Comment on Merton and Samuelson", *Journal of Financial Economics* (May 1974).

Hakansson, N. H., "Capital Growth and the Mean–Variance Approach to Portfolio Selection", *Journal of Financial and Quantitative Analysis* (January 1971).

Hakansson, N. H., and Miller, B. L., "Compound-Return Mean–Variance Portfolios Never Risk Ruin", *Management Science* (December 1975).

Hanoch, G. and Levy, H., "Efficient Portfolio Selection with Quadratic and Cubic Utility", *Journal of Business* (April 1970).

Hastie, K. L., "The Determination of Optimal Investment Policy", *Management Science* (August 1967).

Hester, D. D. and Tobin, J., *Risk Aversion and Portfolio Choice*, New York: Wiley (1967).

Hicks, J. R., *Value and Capital*, 2nd edition. Oxford: Oxford University Press (1946).

Hogan, W. and Warren, J. M., "Computation of the Efficient Boundary in the E-S Portfolio Selection Model", *Journal of Financial and Quantitative Analysis* (September 1972).

Jahankhani, A., "E-V and E-S Capital Asset Pricing Models: Some Empirical Tests", *Journal of Financial and Quantitative Analysis* (November 1976).

Jean, W. H., "Distribution Moments and Equilibrium: Reply", *Journal of Financial and Quantitative Analysis* (January 1972).

Jean, W. H., "More on Multidimensional Portfolio Analysis", *Journal of Financial and Quantitative Analysis* (June 1973).

Jean, W. H., "A General Class of Three-Parameter Risk Measures: Comment", *Journal of Finance* (March 1975).

Jones, E. I., "Test of Portfolio Building Rules: Comment", *Journal of Finance* (September 1971).

Joyce, J. M. and Vogel, R. C., "The Uncertainty in Risk: Is Variance Unambiguous?" *Journal of Finance* (March 1970).

Keynes, J. M., *The General Theory of Employment, Interest and Money*, London: Macmillan (1937).

Kraus, A. and Litzenberger, R. H., "Skewness Preference and the Valuation of Risk Assets", *Journal of Finance* (September 1976).

Latané, H., "Criteria for Choice Among Risky Ventures", *Journal of Political Economy* (April 1959).

Latané, H., "Investment Criteria—A Three-Asset Portfolio Balance Model", *Review of Economics and Statistics* (November 1963).

Latané, H. A. and Tuttle, D. L., "Criteria for Portfolio Building", *Journal of Finance* (September 1967).

Latané, H. A. and Young, W. E., "Test of Portfolio Building Rules", *Journal of Finance* (September 1969).

Lee, C. F., "Functional Form, Skewness Effect, and the Risk–Return Relationship", *Journal of Financial and Quantitative Analysis* (March 1977).

Lee, S. M. and Lerro, A. J., "Optimizing the Portfolio Selection for Mutual Funds", *Journal of Finance* (December 1973).

Levy, H., "Does Diversification Always Pay?" *TIMS Studies in Management Science*, (1979).

Levy H. and Markowitz, H. M., "Approximating Expected Utility by a Function of Mean and Variance", *American Economic Review* (June 1979).

Mao, J. C. T., "Essentials of Portfolio Diversification Strategy", *Journal of Finance* (December 1970).

Mao, J. C. T. and Helliwell, J. F., "Investment Decisions Under Uncertainty: Theory and Practice", *Journal of Finance* (May 1969).

Markowitz, H. M., "Portfolio Selection", *Journal of Finance* (March 1952).

Markowitz, H. M., *Portfolio Selection*, New York: Wiley (1959).

Markowitz, H. M., "Investment for the Long-Run: New Evidence for an Old Rule", *Journal of Finance* (December 1976).

Marschak, J., "Money and the Theory of Assets", *Econometrica* (October 1938).

McEnally, R. W. and Upton, D. E., "A Re-examination of the Ex Post Risk-Return Tradeoff on Common Stocks", *Journal of Financial and Quantitative Analysis* (June 1979).

Michaelsen, J. B. and Goshay, R. C., "Portfolio Selection in Financial Intermediaries: A New Approach", *Journal of Financial and Quantitative Analysis* (June 1967).

Modigliani, F. and Pogue, G. A., "An Introduction to Risk and Return", *Financial Analysts Journal* (March/April 1974. Part II, May/June 1974).

Ohlson, J. A., "Quadratic Approximations of the Portfolio Selection Problem When the Means and Variances of Returns are Infinite", *Management Science* (February 1977).

Porter, R. B. and Bey, R., "An Evaluation of the Empirical Significance of Optimal Seeking Algorithms in Portfolio Selection", *Journal of Finance* (December 1974).

Pratt, J. W., "Risk Aversion in the Small and in the Large", *Econometrica* (January–April 1964).

Pye, G., "Minimax Portfolio Policies", *Financial Analysts Journal* (March–April 1972).

Pyle, D. H. and Turnovsky, S. J., "Safety-First and Expected Utility Maximization in Mean-Standard Deviation Portfolio Analysis", *Review of Economics and Statistics* (February 1970).

Pyle, D. H. and Turnovsky, S. J., "Risk Aversion in Chance Constrained Portfolio Selection", *Management Science* (November 1971).

Pyle, D. H. and Turnovsky, S. J., "Safety-First and Expected Utility Maximization in Mean-Standard Deviation Portfolio Analysis", *Review of Economics and Statistics* (February 1970).

Renshaw, E. F., "Portfolio Balance Models in Perspective: Some Generalizations that can be Derived from the Two-Asset Case", *Journal of Financial and Quantitative Analysis* (June 1967).

Roy, A. D., "Safety First and the Holding of Assets", *Econometrica* (July 1952).

Rubinstein, M. E. "A Mean-Variance Synthesis of Corporate Financial Theory", *Journal of Finance* (March 1973).

Samuelson, P. A., "The Fundamental Approximation Theorem of Portfolio Analysis in Terms of Means, Variances and Higher Moments", *Review of Economic Studies* (February 1958).

Samuelson, P. A., "General Proof that Diversification Pays", *Journal of Financial and Quantitative Analysis* (March 1967).

Samuelson, P. A., "Efficient Portfolio Selection for Pareto-Levy Investments", *Journal of Financial and Quantitative Analysis* (June 1967).

Scott, R. C. and Horvath, P. A., "On the Direction of Preference for Moments of Higher Order than the Variance", *Journal of Finance* (September 1980).

Sharpe, W. F., "Portfolio Analysis", *Journal of Financial and Quantitative Analysis* (June 1967).

Sharpe, W. F., *Portfolio Theory and Capital Markets*, New York: McGraw-Hill (1970).

Stone, B. K., "A Linear Programming Formulation of the General Portfolio Selection Model", *Journal of Financial and Quantitative Analysis* (September 1973).

Tobin, J., "Liquidity Preference as Behavior Towards Risk", *Review of Economic Studies* (February 1958).

Tobin, J., "The Theory of Portfolio Selection", in F. H. Hahn and F. P. R. Brechling, eds., *Theory of Interest Rates*, New York: Macmillan (1965).

Wachowicz, J. M., Jr. and Shrieves, R. E., "An Argument for 'Generalized' Mean-Coefficient of Variation Analysis", *Financial Management* (Winter 1980).

# 9

# Tracing the Efficient Frontier

In Chapter 7 the mean–variance criterion was introduced and the utility foundations of this rule were stated and analyzed. In Chapter 8 we illustrated the gain from diversification and analyzed the various factors which determine this gain. We also demonstrated the efficient frontier and considered the relationship between the location of the efficient frontier in the mean–standard deviation plane and the number of risky assets from which the frontier is constructed.

In this chapter we demonstrate how to construct the efficient frontier in practice. After a general statement of the problem, we solve in detail the relatively simple case of efficient portfolios consisting of two risky assets only. Once the principles underlying the construction of efficient portfolios are understood, we generalize the analysis to $n$-asset efficient portfolios. In the $n$-asset case hand calculations are too complicated and we demonstrate the $n$-asset efficient frontier by means of a computer output. Moreover, we use the data of a sample of 15 stocks of actual corporations and provide the computer output which presents the means and the variances of the efficient portfolios as well as their actual composition.

## 9.1    Statement of the Problem

Investors in general, and portfolio managers in particular, need a systematic technique that will enable them to choose an efficient investment strategy from among all feasible strategies. Specifically, given $n$ risky assets (such as $n$ different stocks), we seek a diversification strategy which yields a portfolio lying on the efficient frontier.

In order to demonstrate the problem of choice facing the portfolio manager, consider the case of $n$ risky assets with the following parameters (the risky assets are indexed by the subscript $i$ which takes the values $i = 1, 2, \ldots, n$):

$\sigma_i^2$—the variance of the returns on the $i$th risky asset,
$\mu_i$—the expected (or mean) return on the $i$th asset,

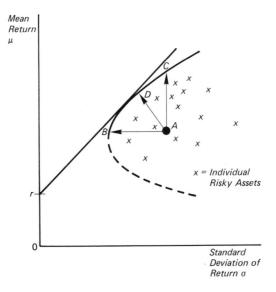

**Figure 9.1**

$\sigma_{ij}$—the covariance of the returns on two different assets $i$ and $j$ ($i \neq j$),

$r$—the risk-free interest rate available to all investors in the money market.

The true parameters are usually unknown, and for practical purposes we can replace them by *ex-post* estimates obtained by statistical processing of past observations of the returns on the $n$ risky assets or even by a set of subjective estimates that the portfolio manager picks for his purpose.

For each risky asset, we thus have a pair of parameters—the mean and the standard deviation ($\mu, \sigma$)—which can be represented by a point plotted in the mean–standard deviation space (M–S space). The $n$ risky assets plot into $n$ points in the M–S space; an additional point represents the riskless asset, whose certain rate of return is $r$ with zero standard deviation (from the definition of certainty). A scattergram of $n$ risky assets plus the riskless asset in the M–S space is shown in Figure 9.1.

Consider an investor with \$1 available for investment (our solution is not affected by the scale of the investment, so we may equally well consider an investor investing \$10, \$100, or even a million dollars). An investment strategy consists of choosing the investment proportions $x_i$ in the $n$ risky assets, while the remainder of funds $1 - \sum_{i=1}^{n} x_i$ is invested in the riskless asset. An investment strategy is thus represented by the $n + 1$ numbers

$$x_1, x_2, \ldots, x_n, 1 - \sum_{i=1}^{n} x_i$$

which all add up to 1 (this is the \$1 initially available for investment). Clearly, if $(1 - \sum_{i=1}^{n} x_i) > 0$, the investor is a lender, lending a certain positive proportion of his funds at the riskless rate $r$ and consequently investing less than his initial \$1 in the $n$ risky assets. If $(1 - \Sigma_{i=1}^{n} x_i) < 0$, the investor is a borrower, he borrows money at the riskless rate $r$ (holds a negative amount of the riskless asset) and uses the proceeds to increase his investment in the $n$ risky assets. Note, however, that for lenders and borrowers alike, the $n + 1$ investment proportions in the risky assets plus the riskless asset must add up to 1.

Suppose that our investor divides his funds in equal proportions between the $n + 1$ assets available to him. He thus invests $1/(n + 1)$ in each asset, so that $x_i = 1/(n + 1)$ for $i = 1, 2, \ldots, n$ (the $n$ risky assets) and also $(1 - \Sigma_{i=1}^{n} x_i) = 1/(n + 1)$ (the same proportion is invested in the riskless asset). Does this naive diversification result in an efficient investment strategy? In other words, is a portfolio with equal proportions invested in all the $n + 1$ assets an efficient portfolio? In general, the equal-proportions strategy is inefficient, resulting in some portfolio like $A$ in Figure 9.1, which is located *inside* the efficient frontier (and not *on* the frontier). By abandoning the naive investment strategy and adjusting the investment proportions in a certain way, the investor can move from the point $A$ toward the efficient frontier (in the direction $AB$, maintaining the same mean portfolio return, or in the direction $AC$, maintaining the same portfolio standard deviation, or even in an arbitrary direction $AD$ with both the mean and the standard deviation of his portfolio changing). In this way, the investor increases his utility compared to the utility from portfolio $A$: in the direction $AB$ he reduces the risk without affecting the mean return, in the direction $AC$ he increases the return without changing the level of risk, whereas in the direction $AD$ he attains higher return at a lower level of risk.

Thus, given the set of parameters of the $n + 1$ assets (or some estimate of these parameters), the investor's objective is to select an investment strategy that results in a portfolio lying on the efficient frontier (such as $B$, or $C$, or $D$ in Figure 9.1). The common solution techniques enable the investor to select the investment proportions which minimize the portfolio variance (or standard deviation) for a given level of expected rate of return (as if by moving along the horizontal line $AB$ in Figure 9.1). As we have seen in Chapter 8, this can be achieved by minimizing the Lagrange function

$$C = \sum_{i=1}^{n} x_i^2 \sigma_i^2 + 2 \sum_{i=1}^{n} \sum_{\substack{j=1 \\ j>i}}^{n} x_i x_j \sigma_{ij} + \lambda_1 \left( 1 - \sum_{i=1}^{n} x_i \right) + \lambda_2 \left( \mu_p - \sum_{i=1}^{n} x_i \mu_i \right) \quad (9.1)$$

where the first two sums on the left represent the variance ($\sigma_p^2$) of the investor's $n$-asset portfolio, the factor following the Lagrange multiplier $\lambda_1$ indicates that the proportions invested in the risky assets add up to 1 (no riskless asset), and the factor following the Lagrange multiplier $\lambda_2$ indicates the desired level of mean portfolio return $\mu_p$.[1]

To minimize the Lagrange function $C$, we differentiate it with respect to the unknown proportions $x_1, x_2, \ldots, x_n$ and the unknown Lagrange multipliers $\lambda_1$ and $\lambda_2$

---

[1] Note that without Lagrange multipliers, the portfolio variance is minimized by the proportions $x_i = 0$ for all $i$ ($i = 1, \ldots, n$). But this implies that we invest nothing at all. Adding the Lagrange multiplier $\lambda_1$, we minimize the variance subject to the constraint that the investment proportions add up to 1, i.e., $\Sigma_{i=1}^{n} x_i = 1$, which means that we decide to invest \$1 and construct a portfolio that minimizes the variance of the return on this investment.

and set the derivatives equal to zero. In this way, we obtain a system of $n + 2$ equations in $n + 2$ unknowns, which in general is solvable.

Note that the partial derivatives of the Lagrange function $C$ with respect to the two Lagrange multipliers $\lambda_1$ and $\lambda_2$ are

$$\frac{\partial C}{\partial \lambda_1} = 1 - \sum_{i=1}^{n} x_i \quad \text{and} \quad \frac{\partial C}{\partial \lambda_2} = \mu_p - \sum_{i=1}^{n} x_i \mu_i$$

Setting these partial derivatives equal to zero (in order to minimize the Lagrange function and thus the portfolio variance), we get

$$1 = \sum_{i=1}^{n} x_i \tag{9.2}$$

from the derivative with respect to the first multiplier, and

$$\mu_p = \sum_{i=1}^{n} x_i \mu_i \tag{9.3}$$

from the derivative with respect to the second multiplier. Equation (9.2) simply indicates that the investment proportions in the $n$ risky assets should add up to 1, so that the Lagrange multiplier $\lambda_1$ in the Lagrange function $C$ guarantees that the total investment is equal to the total funds available ($\$1$). Equation (9.3) sets the desired level of portfolio expected return $\mu_p$, expressed as a sum of the expected returns of the $n$ risky assets multiplied by the respective proportions. The second Lagrange multiplier $\lambda_2$ thus indicates that the portfolio manager should first decide on the desired level of expected return $\mu_p$ on his portfolio and then proceed to derive the investment strategy which minimizes the portfolio risk at this level of portfolio mean return.

The above formulation of the Lagrange function (9.1) does not include investment in the riskless asset: the entire portfolio consists of the $n$ risky assets. If investment in the riskless asset is introduced, the portfolio expected return is given by the return on the $n$ risky assets plus the return on the riskless asset,

$$\mu_p = \sum_{i=1}^{n} x_i \mu_i + \left(1 - \sum_{i=1}^{n} x_i\right) r$$

and the investment proportions in the $n$ risky assets no longer add up to 1 (since the funds are allocated to $n + 1$ assets). The Lagrange function is thus written in the form

$$C = \sum_{i=1}^{n} x_i^2 \sigma_i^2 + 2 \sum_{i=1}^{n} \sum_{\substack{j=1 \\ j>i}}^{n} x_i x_j \sigma_{ij} + \lambda \left[ \mu_p - \sum_{i=1}^{n} x_i \mu_i - \left(1 - \sum_{i=1}^{n} x_i\right) r \right] \tag{9.1'}$$

The portfolio variance in this formulation is identical to that in (9.1), since the riskless

asset (with zero variance) does not contribute to the portfolio risk. Differentiating with
respect to the single Lagrange multiplier $\lambda$, we obtain

$$\frac{\partial C}{\partial \lambda} = \mu_p - \sum_{i=1}^{n} x_i \mu_i - \left(1 - \sum_{i=1}^{n} x_i\right) r$$

and equating this derivative to zero gives

$$\mu_p = \sum_{i=1}^{n} x_i \mu_i + \left(1 - \sum_{i=1}^{n} x_i\right) r$$

The Lagrange multiplier in this case fixes the level of expected return for a portfolio consisting of $n$ risky assets plus 1 riskless asset. The $n + 1$ proportions of course add up to
1, as before: indeed

$$\sum_{i=1}^{n} x_i + \left(1 - \sum_{i=1}^{n} x_i\right) = 1$$

Figures 9.2a and 9.2b demonstrate the difference between the two formulations of
the Lagrange function (9.1) and (9.1'). Suppose that the investor's objective is to
minimize the level of risk for a portfolio with expected return $\mu_p = 10\%$. If the investment is allocated to $n$ risky assets (without the riskless asset), the investor can adjust the
investment proportions so that he moves along the horizontal line $ab$ in Figure 9.2a until
he reaches the efficient portfolio $A$ lying on the efficient frontier. Every investment
strategy producing a portfolio on the line $ab$ satisfies the constraint $\mu_p = 10\%$. But there
is only one portfolio—portfolio $A$—which ensures the desired level of expected return
($\mu_p = 10\%$) and in addition has the minimum variance (or standard deviation) at this
level of expected return. By specifying a different target portfolio mean, say $\mu_p = 11\%$,
we make the investor move along a higher horizontal line which meets the efficient
frontier at point $A'$: this is the minimum standard deviation portfolio at 11% expected
return level. By gradually increasing the target portfolio mean $\mu_p$ in constant steps, we
obtain minimum-variance efficient portfolios corresponding to successive levels of
portfolio expected return. If the steps are sufficiently small, we actually trace the entire
efficient frontier representing the set of all efficient diversification strategies or efficient
portfolios.

Figure 9.2b reveals how the investor can benefit from the addition of the riskless
asset to the $n$ risky assets. For example, for a target portfolio mean $\mu_p = 10\%$, the
investor can attain the point $B$ on the straight line $rr'$ which rises from the point $(r, 0)$
representing the riskless asset in the M–S space and is tangent to the efficient frontier at
the point $m$. Portfolio $B$ has the same expected return as the $n$-asset portfolio $A$, but its
standard deviation is lower. Allowing investment in the riskless asset, we thus enable the
investor to attain a higher level of utility by reducing the minimum risk attainable at the
given expected return. This is made possible by the addition of the riskless asset which
enables the investor to switch from the efficient curve $mA$ (corresponding to Lagrange

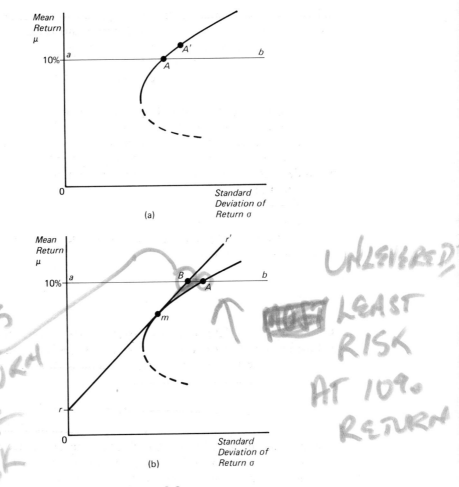

*(handwritten annotations in the margins:)* LEVERED, RISKLESS ASSET ALLOWS SAME RETURN AT LOWER RISK

UNLEVERED LEAST RISK AT 10% RETURN

**Figure 9.2**

function (9.1)) to the straight-line efficient set $rB$ corresponding to Lagrange function (9.1') (see Figure 9.2b).

## 9.2   The Relationship Between the Unlevered and Levered Portfolios

In Figure 9.2b, representing investment opportunities in $n$ risky assets plus the riskless asset, portfolio $m$ is determined by the tangency point between the efficient frontier of $n$-risky-asset portfolios and the straight line $rr'$ rising from the riskless asset. Portfolio $m$ is called the optimum *unlevered* portfolio (corresponding to riskless return rate $r$): this is the optimum portfolio consisting of risky assets only. Portfolio $B$ is a levered portfolio, which is a combination or mixture of the optimum unlevered portfolio $m$ and the riskless asset in certain proportions. In effect, any portfolio on the straight line $rr'$ can be represented schematically as a linear combination

$$B = \alpha m + (1 - \alpha)r$$

where $\alpha$ is the proportion invested in the optimum portfolio of risky assets only and $(1 - \alpha)$ is the residual proportion invested in the riskless asset. The proportion $(1 - \alpha)$ may be either positive or negative: if positive, the investor actually buys bonds for his portfolios. If $(1 - \alpha)$ is negative (and so $\alpha > 1$), this means that the investor borrows at the riskless rate $r$ and uses the loan to purchase more of the risk asset $m$ than his initial funds would allow.

EXAMPLE

Assume three risky assets ($n = 3$) and an optimum unlevered portfolio $m$ given by the following proportions

| $x_1$ | $x_2$ | $x_3$ |
|-------|-------|-------|
| $\frac{1}{4}$ | $\frac{1}{4}$ | $\frac{1}{2}$ |

Thus, one-quarter of the funds is invested in asset 1, one-quarter is invested in asset 2, and the remaining half is invested in asset 3. Portfolio $m$ consists entirely of the three risky assets, and the three proportions add up to 1 as required:

$$\sum_{i=1}^{3} x_i = x_1 + x_2 + x_3 = 1$$

Now suppose that in addition to \$1 of our own funds, we borrow \$1, so that a total of \$2 is now available for investment in the risky portfolio $m$. We have $\alpha = 2$ in our portfolio $B = \alpha m + (1 - \alpha)r$ (instead of $\alpha = 1$ originally), and so doubling our investment in each of the three risky assets (without changing the relative amounts), we obtain a new portfolio with the proportions

| $x_1$ | $x_2$ | $x_3$ |
|-------|-------|-------|
| $\frac{1}{2}$ | $\frac{1}{2}$ | $1$ |

The result is a levered portfolio in which the risky proportions add up to 2 (indeed, $\sum_{i=1}^{n} x_i = 2$) and the proportion invested in the riskless asset is $(1 - \sum_{i=1}^{n} x_i) = -1$ (the minus sign indicates that the levered portfolio has been created by *borrowing*).

Since the ratio of the proportions invested in any pair of risky assets is not changed by leverage when moving from portfolio $m$ to portfolio $B$, we can always find the optimum unlevered portfolio corresponding to the levered portfolio $B$ obtained by minimizing the Lagrange function. Suppose that for $\mu_p = 10\%$ our solution technique has yielded the portfolio $B$ with the proportions $x_1 = \frac{1}{2}$, $x_2 = \frac{1}{2}$, $x_3 = 1$ (see Figure 9.2b). The corresponding unlevered investment strategy represented by point $m$ (the optimum portfolio of risky assets only) is then found by simple standardization; to obtain the proportion $z_i$ invested in the $i$th risky asset in portfolio $m$, divide the proportion $x_i$ in the levered portfolio $B$ by the sum of the proportions of all the $n$ risky assets in portfolio $B$, thus

$$z_i = \frac{x_i}{\sum\limits_{i=1}^{n} x_i}$$

In our example, the proportions of the three risky assets in portfolio $B$ add up to $\sum_{i=1}^{n} x_i = 2$, so that in the optimum unlevered portfolio $m$ consists of the following standardized investment proportions $z_i$:

| $z_1$ | $z_2$ | $z_3$ |
|-------|-------|-------|
| $\frac{1}{2}/2 = \frac{1}{4}$ | $\frac{1}{2}/2 = \frac{1}{4}$ | $1/2 = \frac{1}{2}$ |

Clearly $z_1 + z_2 + z_3 = 1$.

This suggests a technique for tracing the entire efficient frontier by varying the riskless rate of return $r$. Thus, given a certain target portfolio mean $\mu_p$, select a riskless return rate $r$ and find the optimum levered portfolio which lies on the straight line $rr'$ at the specified portfolio mean level $\mu_p$. Then by standardization find the proportions $z_i = x_i/\sum_{i=1}^{n} x_i$ of the risky assets in the corresponding unlevered portfolio. The standardized proportions $z_i$ add up to 1, unlike the original $x_i$. In this way, we have obtained a single point on the efficient frontier of portfolios consisting of risky assets only. Repeating the procedure for a different value of $r$, we obtain another point on the efficient frontier corresponding to new $r$. Changing the value of $r$ in constant steps and repeating the solution procedure, we trace the entire efficient frontier of portfolios consisting of risky assets only (each of these portfolios is the optimum unlevered portfolio for the corresponding value of $r$).

Figure 9.3 summarizes this procedure graphically. For example, let the target portfolio mean be $\mu_p = 8\%$. Take $r = 2\%$ and derive levered portfolio $B_1$ with proportions $x_1, x_2, \ldots, x_n$, $(1 - \sum_{i=1}^{n} x_i)$ by minimizing the Lagrange function. Standardize $z_i = x_i/\sum_{i=1}^{n} x_i$ to obtain the proportions invested in the $n$ risky assets in the optimum all-risk portfolio $m_1$. Increase the riskless return rate to $r = 5\%$, obtain the portfolio $B_2$ and by standardization obtain the optimum all-risk portfolio $m_2$. Repeating this procedure for different values of $r$, we generate the entire segment $ED$ of the efficient frontier. This procedure can be applied technically, regardless of the real nature of the riskless asset. We use $r$ merely as a technical device, which is not necessarily related to the true interest rate or does not necessarily imply that the riskless asset actually exists. For technical reasons, we may have to use a negative value, $r = -10\%$ say, to derive the unlevered efficient portfolio $C$, even though in most cases in reality the riskless interest rate is positive and cannot be $-10\%$.

The reader should bear in mind that in order to find the *optimum* portfolio of risky assets relevant to his situation, it is important to choose that interest rate at which he actually can borrow and lend. However, for the purpose of constructing the entire set of

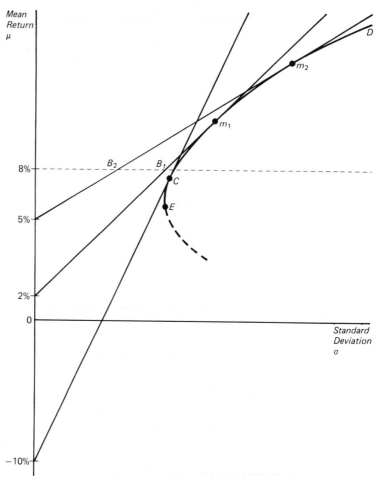

**Figure 9.3**

risky efficient portfolios, all values of $r$ should be used, without regard of the true interest rate. Thus, it is important to distinguish between the *optimum* portfolio of risky assets, which is determined by the tangency point between the efficient frontier and the straight line rising from the *true* interest rate $r$, and an efficient portfolio of risky assets, which corresponds to the tangency point between the efficient frontier and the straight line rising from some (quite arbitrary) interest rate $r$.

This, in principle, summarizes the technique of tracing the efficient frontier. For each value of $r$, solve a system of $n + 1$ simultaneous equations in $n + 1$ unknowns (the investment proportions in $n$ risky assets plus the riskless asset) and by standardization find the corresponding unlevered portfolio, which gives a point on the efficient frontier. In practice, however, the solution is far from simple, and for a large number of risky assets an appropriate computer program is required. We turn now to a detailed solution of the efficient frontier problem for the case of two risky assets and then present the computer output for the case with a larger number of risky assets.

## 9.3    Constructing the Efficient Frontier: The Case of Two Risky Assets

With two risky assets and a riskless asset, the portfolio mean $\mu_p$ is given by

$$\mu_p = x_1\mu_1 + x_2\mu_2 + (1 - x_1 - x_2)r$$

and the portfolio variance $\sigma_p^2$ is given by

$$\sigma_p^2 = x_1^2\sigma_1^2 + x_2^2\sigma_2^2 + 2x_1x_2\sigma_{12}$$

where $\sigma_{12} \equiv Cov(R_1, R_2)$ is the covariance of the returns on the two risky assets. The Lagrange function (9.1′) (with investment in riskless asset) takes the form

$$C = (x_1^2\sigma_1^2 + x_2^2\sigma_2^2 + 2x_1x_2\sigma_{12}) + \lambda[\mu_p - x_1\mu_1 - x_2\mu_2 - (1 - x_1 - x_2)r]$$

Differentiating with respect to the three unknowns $x_1$, $x_2$, and $\lambda$, we obtain

$$\frac{\partial C}{\partial x_1} = 2x_1\sigma_1^2 + 2x_2\sigma_{12} - \lambda(\mu_1 - r)$$

$$\frac{\partial C}{\partial x_2} = 2x_2\sigma_2^2 + 2x_1\sigma_{12} - \lambda(\mu_2 - r)$$

$$\frac{\partial C}{\partial \lambda} = \mu_p - x_1\mu_1 - x_2\mu_2 - (1 - x_1 - x_2)r$$

In order to find the proportions minimizing the portfolio variance $\sigma_p^2$ (or the portfolio standard deviation $\sigma_p$), we equate the three derivatives to zero and obtain a system of three equations in three unknowns,

$$x_1\sigma_1^2 + x_2\sigma_{12} = \frac{\lambda}{2}(\mu_1 - r)$$

$$x_2\sigma_2^2 + x_1\sigma_{12} = \frac{\lambda}{2}(\mu_2 - r) \qquad (9.4)$$

$$\mu_p = x_1\mu_1 + x_2\mu_2 + (1 - x_1 - x_2)r$$

Solving these three equations, we obtain the optimum investment proportions $x_1$, $x_2$, and $x_3 = 1 - x_1 - x_2$. Note that the third equation, as we have seen above, simply guarantees that the investment strategy $x_1$, $x_2$ yields the target portfolio mean $\mu_p$.

EXAMPLE
Suppose that the two risky assets are characterized by the following parameters:

$$\mu_1 = 10\%, \quad \sigma_1^2 = 10$$

$$\mu_2 = 6\%, \quad \sigma_2^2 = 1$$

$$\sigma_{12} = 0$$

The rate of return on the riskless asset is $r = 5\%$.

Let us find the investment proportions which minimize the risk level for a given expected return $\mu_p = 8\%$, say. Plugging these numbers in equations (9.4), we obtain

$$10x_1 + 0 \cdot x_2 = \frac{\lambda}{2}(10 - 5)$$

*[handwritten: $\sigma_1^2 + \sigma_{12}$ ; $10x_1 = \frac{3\lambda}{2}$ ; $2x_1 = \frac{\lambda}{2}$, $x_1 = \frac{\lambda}{4}$]*

$$1 \cdot x_2 + 0 \cdot x_1 = \frac{\lambda}{2}(6 - 5)$$

*[handwritten: $\sigma_2^2 + \sigma_{12}$]*

$$8 = 10x_1 + 6x_2 + (1 - x_1 - x_2) \cdot 5$$

From the first two equations, we express $x_1$ and $x_2$ in terms of the Lagrange multiplier

$$x_1 = \frac{\lambda}{4}$$

*[handwritten: $\{x_2 = \frac{\lambda}{2}(6-5)\} = \{x_2 = \frac{\lambda}{2}\}$]*

$$x_2 = \frac{\lambda}{2}$$

Substituting for $x_1$ and $x_2$ in the third equation their expressions in terms of $\lambda$, we obtain a single equation for $\lambda$,

$$8 = 10 \cdot \frac{\lambda}{4} + 6 \cdot \frac{\lambda}{2} + \left(1 - \frac{\lambda}{4} - \frac{\lambda}{2}\right)5$$

which gives

*[handwritten: $8 = \frac{10\lambda}{4} + \frac{6\lambda}{2} + ($ ]*

$$\lambda = \frac{12}{7}$$

Substituting this result in the above expressions for $x_1$ and $x_2$ in terms of $\lambda$, we get

$$x_1 = \frac{12}{28} = \frac{3}{7}$$

$$x_2 = \frac{12}{14} = \frac{6}{7}$$

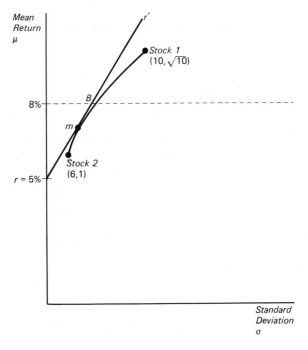

**Figure 9.4**

Figure 9.4 is a graphical illustration of this numerical example. Portfolio $B$ with expected return of 8% lies on the straight line $rr'$. The investment proportions in the risky assets in portfolio $B$ are

$$
\begin{array}{cc}
x_1 & x_2 \\
\frac{3}{7} & \frac{6}{7}
\end{array}
$$

Thus $x_1 + x_2 = \frac{9}{7}$. Since the investor started with only \$1 of his own funds, he by definition had to borrow the amount

$$ 1 - x_1 - x_2 = 1 - \tfrac{9}{7} = -\tfrac{2}{7} $$

The initial \$1 plus the additional loan of \$$\frac{2}{7}$ were used to invest in a levered portfolio of two risky assets. By standardization, we move back to the unlevered portfolio $m$ (see Figure 9.4) with the investment proportions in the two risky assets only,

$$ z_1 = \frac{x_1}{x_1 + x_2} = \frac{\frac{3}{7}}{\frac{9}{7}} = \frac{1}{3}, \quad z_2 = \frac{x_2}{x_1 + x_2} = \frac{\frac{6}{7}}{\frac{9}{7}} = \frac{2}{3} $$

The standardized proportions add up to 1, $z_1 + z_2 = \frac{1}{3} + \frac{2}{3} = 1$.

**9.4**    **Solving for the Investment Proportions: An Alternative Technique**

In the case of two risky assets, we obtain three equations in three unknowns. We have seen how to solve for $x_1$, $x_2$, and $\lambda$ simultaneously. In fact, we do not need to solve for the Lagrange multiplier $\lambda$, and we can only concentrate on the first two equations, solving them for the investment proportions $x_1$ and $x_2$ without explicitly finding the Lagrange multiplier $\lambda$. To fix ideas, we return to our two-asset example. The first two equations in (9.4) are

$$x_1 \sigma_1^2 + x_2 \sigma_{12} = \frac{\lambda}{2}(\mu_1 - r)$$

$$x_2 \sigma_2^2 + x_1 \sigma_{12} = \frac{\lambda}{2}(\mu_2 - r)$$

Dividing both sides by $\lambda/2$, we obtain:

$$\frac{2}{\lambda} x_1 \sigma_1^2 + \frac{2}{\lambda} x_2 \sigma_{12} = \mu_1 - r$$

$$\frac{2}{\lambda} x_2 \sigma_2^2 + \frac{2}{\lambda} x_1 \sigma_{12} = \mu_2 - r$$
(9.5)

Defining new variables

$$y_1 = \frac{2}{\lambda} x_1, \quad y_2 = \frac{2}{\lambda} x_2$$

the two equations (9.5) can be expressed as

$$y_1 \sigma_1^2 + y_2 \sigma_{12} = \mu_1 - r$$

$$y_2 \sigma_2^2 + y_1 \sigma_{12} = \mu_2 - r$$
(9.6)

We thus have *two* equations in *two* unknowns (instead of the previous three equations in three unknowns). We can solve these equations for $y_1$ and $y_2$ and then standardize the solution to obtain the proportions of the unlevered portfolio as follows:

$$z_1 = \frac{y_1}{y_1 + y_2}$$

$$z_2 = \frac{y_2}{y_1 + y_2}$$

The unlevered portfolio proportions $z_1$ and $z_2$ obtained in this way are identical to the proportions derived by standardizing the risky-asset proportions $x_1$ and $x_2$ obtained from the system of three equations in three unknowns. Indeed, recalling the definition of $y_1$ and $y_2$, we have:

$$z_1 = \frac{y_1}{y_1 + y_2} = \frac{\frac{2}{\lambda} x_1}{\frac{2}{\lambda} x_1 + \frac{2}{\lambda} x_2} = \frac{x_1}{x_1 + x_2}$$

$$z_2 = \frac{y_2}{y_1 + y_2} = \frac{\frac{2}{\lambda} x_2}{\frac{2}{\lambda} x_1 + \frac{2}{\lambda} x_2} = \frac{x_2}{x_1 + x_2}$$

These are precisely the same investment proportions which we obtained by employing the previous technique.

Using the specific numerical values of our previous example (namely, $\sigma_1^2 = 10$, $\sigma_2^2 = 1$, $\sigma_{12} = 0$, $\mu_1 = 10$, $\mu_2 = 6$, and $r = 5$), we obtain the following two equations [compare (9.6)]:

$$10 \cdot y_1 + y_2 \cdot 0 = 10 - 5$$

$$1 \cdot y_2 + y_1 \cdot 0 = 6 - 5$$

(9.7)

which can be reduced to:

$$10y_1 = 5$$

$$y_2 = 1$$

Hence $y_1 = \frac{1}{2}$ and $y_2 = 1$. The investment proportions of the optimum unlevered portfolio are obtained by standardization:

$$z_1 = \frac{y_1}{y_1 + y_2} = \frac{\frac{1}{2}}{\frac{3}{2}} = \frac{1}{3}$$

$$z_2 = \frac{y_2}{y_1 + y_2} = \frac{1}{\frac{3}{2}} = \frac{2}{3}$$

The result is of course identical to the previous result obtained for $z_1$ and $z_2$ by solving three equations in three unknowns.

To summarize, since the explicit value of the Lagrange multiplier is not required, we can divide all the equations through by $\lambda/2$ and define new variables $y_i = x_i/(\lambda/2)$. In this way we obtain $n$ equations in $n$ unknowns (instead of the original $n + 1$ equations in $n + 1$ unknowns) and the optimum portfolio proportions can be obtained without solving explicitly for $\lambda$.

**9.5    Deriving All the Efficient Portfolios: The Two-Asset Case**

Using the numerical example of Section 9.4, we obtained the efficient-portfolio equations (9.6) or (9.7)

$$10y_1 = \mu_1 - r = 10 - r$$

$$y_2 = \mu_2 - r = 6 - r$$

with $\mu_1 = 10\%$, $\mu_2 = 6\%$, and $r = 5\%$, where $(y_1, y_2)$ are the optimal investment proportions in the two risky assets for the given riskless rate $r$. We found the optimal investment proportions $y_1$ and $y_2$ for the riskless interest rate $r = 5\%$. By varying the interest rate $r$ and solving the same pair of simultaneous equations, we can derive the entire efficient frontier.

Table 9.1 presents the proportions $y_1$ and $y_2$ and the standardized proportions $z_1$ and $z_2$ for various values of the risk-free interest rate $r$. Note that while $y_1 + y_2 \neq 1$ we always have $z_1 + z_2 = 1$. Figure 9.5 plots in the mean–standard deviation space the two risky assets and the efficient portfolios calculated using the investment proportions of Table 9.1. Given $z_1$ and $z_2$, we calculate the portfolio mean ($\mu_p$) and the portfolio variance ($\sigma_p^2$) by the formulas

$$\mu_p = z_1\mu_1 + z_2\mu_2$$

$$\sigma_p^2 = z_1^2\sigma_1^2 + z_2^2\sigma_2^2 + 2z_1z_2\sigma_{12}$$

**Table 9.1**
**Portfolio Composition for Various Interest Rates**

| Interest Rate | $y_2 = (6 - r)$ | $y_1 = (10 - r)/10$ | $z_2 = y_2/(y_1 + y_2)$ | $z_1 = y_1/(y_1 + y_2)$ |
|---|---|---|---|---|
| 0 | 6 | 1 | 85.7% | 14.3% |
| 1 | 5 | 0.9 | 84.7 | 15.3 |
| 2 | 4 | 0.8 | 83.3 | 16.7 |
| 3 | 3 | 0.7 | 81.1 | 18.9 |
| 4 | 2 | 0.6 | 76.9 | 23.1 |
| 5 | 1 | 0.5 | 66.7 | 33.3 |
| 6 | 0 | 0.4 | 0.0 | 100.0 |
| 7 | −1 | 0.3 | 142.9 | −42.9 |
| 8 | −2 | 0.2 | 111.1 | −11.1 |

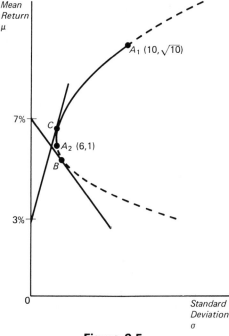

**Figure 9.5**

Since the parameters $\mu_1$, $\mu_2$, $\sigma_1$, $\sigma_2$, $\sigma_{12}$ and the proportions $(z_1, z_2)$ are given, one can easily calculate the mean and the variance of each efficient portfolio plotting the point $(\mu_p, \sigma_p)$ for each $r$ in the mean–standard deviation space.

It is interesting to note that some investment proportions may be negative. For example, for interest rates greater than 6%, $z_2$ appears in positive amount in the efficient portfolio while $z_1$ is negative. We demonstrate the case for $r = 3\%$ and $r = 7\%$ in Figure 9.5. The straight line drawn from $r=7\%$ touches the efficient frontier at its lower part at point $B$. Portfolio $B$ consists of a short position in asset $A_1$ and a long position in asset $A_2$. In general, in the two-asset case, the segment $A_1 A_2$ consists of only long positions in both assets while the dashed segments of the curve above $A_1$ or below $A_2$ include short positions in one of the assets (in $A_1$ or in $A_2$, respectively). Thus the straight line rising from $r = 3\%$ touches the efficient frontier at a higher point $C$ which consists of long positions in the two risky assets.

## 9.6 Constructing the Efficient Frontier: The Case of $n$ Risky Assets

In the previous sections, we have seen how to construct the efficient frontier for the case of two risky assets, $x_1$ and $x_2$. In real life, the investor is faced with more than two risky assets to choose from. Suppose that there are $n$ risky assets and one riskless asset. In this case, the general Lagrange function $C$ (9.1′) has to be differentiated with respect to the $n$ unknowns $x_1, x_2, \ldots, x_n$. Equating these partial derivatives to zero, we obtain a system of $n$ equations in $n + 1$ unknowns $x_1, x_2, \ldots, x_n$ and the Lagrange multiplier $\lambda$:

$$
\left.
\begin{array}{l}
x_1 \sigma_1^2 + x_2 \sigma_{12} + x_3 \sigma_{13} + \cdots + x_n \sigma_{1n} = \dfrac{\lambda}{2}(\mu_1 - r) \\[2em]
x_1 \sigma_{21} + x_2 \sigma_2^2 + x_3 \sigma_{23} + \cdots + x_n \sigma_{2n} = \dfrac{\lambda}{2}(\mu_2 - r) \\[2em]
\cdots \cdots \cdots \cdots \cdots \cdots \cdots \cdots \cdots \cdots \cdots \cdots \\[1em]
x_1 \sigma_{n1} + x_2 \sigma_{n2} + x_3 \sigma_{n3} + \cdots + x_n \sigma_n^2 = \dfrac{\lambda}{2}(\mu_n - r)
\end{array}
\right\} \; n \text{ equations}
$$

Dividing through by $\lambda/2$ and defining new variables $y_i = (2/\lambda)x_i$, as in the case of two risky assets, we obtain a system of $n$ equations in $n$ unknowns $y_1, y_2, \ldots, y_n$:

$$
\left.
\begin{array}{l}
y_1 \sigma_1^2 + y_2 \sigma_{12} + y_3 \sigma_{13} + \cdots + y_n \sigma_{1n} = \mu_1 - r \\[1em]
y_1 \sigma_{21} + y_2 \sigma_2^2 + y_3 \sigma_{23} + \cdots + y_n \sigma_{2n} = \mu_2 - r \\[1em]
\cdots \cdots \cdots \cdots \cdots \cdots \cdots \cdots \cdots \cdots \cdots \\[1em]
y_1 \sigma_{n1} + y_2 \sigma_{n2} + y_3 \sigma_{n3} + \cdots + y_n \sigma_n^2 = \mu_n - r
\end{array}
\right\} \; n \text{ equations} \qquad (9.8)
$$

We solve this system for $y_1, y_2, \ldots, y_n$ by one of the available algebraic techniques (using suitable computer programs) and then perform the standardization

$$
z_i = \frac{y_i}{\displaystyle\sum_{i=1}^{n} y_i} = \frac{\dfrac{2}{\lambda} x_i}{\displaystyle\sum_{i=1}^{n} \dfrac{2}{\lambda} x_i} = \frac{x_i}{\displaystyle\sum_{i=1}^{n} x_i} \qquad (i = 1, 2, \ldots, n)
$$

to obtain the investment proportions in the risky assets in the optimum unlevered portfolio corresponding to the riskless return rate $r$. The standardization ensures that

$$
\sum_{i=1}^{n} z_i = \sum_{i=1}^{n} x_i \Big/ \sum_{i=1}^{n} x_i = 1
$$

By changing the riskless rate $r$, we obtain different unlevered efficient portfolios, one for each value of $r$, and thus trace the entire efficient frontier, as shown in Figure 9.5 for the two-asset case.

APPLICATION

The system of $n$ equations in $n$ unknowns (9.8) is in principle solvable, but in practice its solution is not a simple task when $n$ is large. Computer programs come to our assistance, by solving such linear systems of simultaneous equations easily and quickly, provided of course $n$ is not too large (simple computer programs will readily handle such systems with up to 100 unknowns).[2] As an example, we used a computer program to construct the efficient set of portfolios consisting of 15 risky assets. The risky assets in this case were 15 common stocks traded on the New York Stock Exchange. A historical record of annual rates of return on these stocks for the 25 years 1956–1980 was used to estimate the relevant parameters—the mean return $\mu_i$ and the standard deviation $\sigma_i$ of each stock, and the covariances $\sigma_{ij}$ for all pairs of different stocks $(i, j = 1, 2, \ldots, 15)$. The estimated mean returns and standard deviations of returns are given in Table 9.2, which also lists the stocks by name.

**Table 9.2**
**Rate of Return Parameters of 15 US Stocks: 1956–1980**

| Name | Symbol | Mean $\mu_i$ | Standard Deviation $\sigma_i$ |
|------|--------|--------------|-------------------------------|
| 1  Allied Chemical | ACD | 8.199 | 30.404 |
| 2  Dow Chemical | DOW | 11.366 | 27.592 |
| 3  Union Carbide | UK | 6.298 | 22.139 |
| 4  Cleveland Electric Illumination | CVX | 8.014 | 16.858 |
| 5  Commonwealth Edison | CWE | 7.341 | 17.470 |
| 6  Florida Power and Light | FPL | 10.703 | 24.691 |
| 7  Interlake | IK | 11.465 | 26.329 |
| 8  Republic Steel | RS | 6.780 | 28.009 |
| 9  US Steel | X | 7.858 | 33.018 |
| 10  Burroughs | BGH | 16.526 | 40.805 |
| 11  International Business Machines | IBM | 18.255 | 29.386 |
| 12  NCR | NCR | 15.834 | 42.164 |
| 13  General Foods | GF | 10.148 | 22.841 |
| 14  Nabisco | NAB | 11.906 | 25.058 |
| 15  Quaker Oats | OAT | 15.066 | 33.218 |

Table 9.3 is the variance–covariance matrix of the 15 stocks. Each element in this matrix represents the covariance $\sigma_{ij}$, where $i$ is the row number and $j$ is the column number in the matrix. Thus $\sigma_{13} = 202.22$: this is the covariance of the returns on the Allied Chemicals stock (ACD in row $i = 1$) and the United Carbide stock (UK in column $j = 3$). Similarly $\sigma_{10,14} = -143.56$ is the (negative) covariance on the returns on the Burroughs stock (BGH in row $i = 10$) and the Nabisco stock (NAB in column $j = 14$). Mathematically, the covariance of returns between any given pair of stocks is the same regardless of the order in which the two stocks are taken, so that $\sigma_{ij} = \sigma_{ji}$. For example, taking the UK row $i = 3$ and the ACD column $j = 1$ we have $\sigma_{31} = 202.22$,

---

[2] The computer program is given at Appendix 9.1, at the end of this chapter.

**Table 9.3**
**Variance–Covariance Matrix of 15 US Stocks: 1956–1980**

|  | 1 ACD | 2 DOW | 3 UK | 4 CVX | 5 CWE | 6 FPL | 7 IK | 8 RS | 9 X | 10 BGH | 11 IBM | 12 NCR | 13 GF | 14 NAB | 15 OAT |
|---|---|---|---|---|---|---|---|---|---|---|---|---|---|---|---|
| 1 ACD | 924.41 | 458.52 | 202.22 | 135.62 | 55.59 | 89.90 | 157.61 | 268.84 | 408.08 | 50.31 | 69.63 | 241.89 | 149.24 | 37.16 | 155.05 |
| 2 DOW | 458.52 | 761.29 | 452.99 | 72.25 | 149.14 | 327.08 | 348.09 | 402.77 | 586.42 | 326.01 | 292.44 | 270.87 | 147.78 | 187.31 | 372.36 |
| 3 UK | 202.22 | 452.99 | 490.11 | 109.09 | 141.58 | 306.35 | 419.95 | 378.05 | 508.22 | 27.77 | 171.53 | 118.64 | 168.89 | 217.44 | 302.63 |
| 4 CVX | 135.62 | 72.25 | 109.09 | 284.17 | 222.86 | 222.90 | 194.88 | 230.61 | 254.91 | 39.42 | 171.01 | 137.32 | 204.08 | 234.37 | 220.28 |
| 5 CWE | 55.59 | 149.14 | 141.58 | 222.86 | 305.19 | 332.63 | 139.08 | 194.32 | 288.68 | 24.13 | 258.27 | 231.84 | 308.82 | 340.81 | 334.76 |
| 6 FPL | 89.90 | 327.08 | 306.35 | 222.90 | 332.63 | 609.63 | 166.95 | 338.95 | 488.11 | 124.88 | 495.65 | 515.97 | 431.30 | 469.94 | 603.40 |
| 7 IK | 157.61 | 348.09 | 419.95 | 194.88 | 139.08 | 166.95 | 693.21 | 427.62 | 497.85 | 120.28 | 100.23 | 126.62 | 85.82 | 147.85 | 137.63 |
| 8 RS | 268.84 | 402.77 | 378.05 | 230.61 | 194.32 | 338.95 | 427.62 | 784.50 | 716.80 | 385.32 | 463.39 | 515.92 | 242.44 | 136.68 | 271.03 |
| 9 X | 408.08 | 586.42 | 508.22 | 254.91 | 288.68 | 488.11 | 497.85 | 716.80 | 1090.17 | 197.69 | 483.17 | 491.74 | 331.87 | 321.64 | 417.61 |
| 10 BGH | 50.31 | 326.01 | 27.77 | 39.42 | 24.13 | 124.88 | 120.28 | 385.32 | 197.69 | 1665.02 | 645.36 | 897.40 | -18.37 | -143.56 | 444.72 |
| 11 IBM | 69.63 | 292.44 | 171.53 | 171.01 | 258.27 | 495.65 | 100.23 | 463.39 | 483.17 | 645.36 | 863.53 | 920.95 | 353.28 | 291.09 | 543.81 |
| 12 NCR | 241.89 | 270.87 | 118.64 | 137.32 | 231.84 | 515.97 | 126.62 | 515.92 | 491.74 | 897.40 | 920.95 | 1777.80 | 406.86 | 298.77 | 800.98 |
| 13 GF | 149.24 | 147.78 | 168.89 | 204.08 | 308.82 | 431.30 | 85.82 | 242.44 | 331.87 | -18.37 | 353.28 | 406.86 | 521.70 | 408.43 | 495.04 |
| 14 NAB | 37.16 | 187.31 | 217.44 | 234.37 | 340.81 | 469.94 | 147.85 | 136.68 | 321.64 | -143.56 | 291.09 | 298.77 | 408.43 | 627.91 | 581.17 |
| 15 OAT | 155.05 | 372.36 | 302.63 | 220.28 | 334.76 | 603.40 | 137.63 | 271.03 | 417.61 | 444.72 | 543.81 | 800.98 | 495.04 | 581.17 | 1103.41 |

**Table 9.4**
**Correlation Matrix of 15 US Stocks: 1956–1980**

| | 1 ACD | 2 DOW | 3 UK | 4 CVX | 5 CWE | 6 FPL | 7 IK | 8 RS | 9 X | 10 BGH | 11 IBM | 12 NCR | 13 GF | 14 NAB | 15 OAT |
|---|---|---|---|---|---|---|---|---|---|---|---|---|---|---|---|
| 1 ACD | 1.0000 | .5466 | .3004 | .2646 | .1047 | .1198 | .1969 | .3157 | .4065 | .0406 | .0779 | .1887 | .2149 | .0488 | .1535 |
| 2 DOW | .5466 | 1.0000 | .7416 | .1553 | .3094 | .4801 | .4792 | .5212 | .6437 | .2896 | .3607 | .2328 | .2345 | .2709 | .4063 |
| 3 UK | .3004 | .7416 | 1.0000 | .2923 | .3661 | .5605 | .7205 | .6097 | .6953 | .0307 | .2637 | .1271 | .3340 | .3920 | .4115 |
| 4 CVX | .2646 | .1553 | .2923 | 1.0000 | .7568 | .5355 | .4391 | .4884 | .4580 | .0573 | .3452 | .1932 | .5300 | .5548 | .3934 |
| 5 CWE | .1047 | .3094 | .3661 | .7568 | 1.0000 | .7712 | .3024 | .3971 | .5005 | .0339 | .5031 | .3148 | .7739 | .7785 | .5769 |
| 6 FPL | .1198 | .4801 | .5605 | .5355 | .7712 | 1.0000 | .2568 | .4901 | .5987 | .1240 | .6831 | .4956 | .7648 | .7596 | .7357 |
| 7 IK | .1969 | .4792 | .7205 | .4391 | .3024 | .2568 | 1.0000 | .5799 | .5727 | .1120 | .1295 | .1141 | .1427 | .2241 | .1574 |
| 8 RS | .3157 | .5212 | .6097 | .4884 | .3971 | .4901 | .5799 | 1.0000 | .7751 | .3371 | .5630 | .4369 | .3790 | .1947 | .2913 |
| 9 X | .4065 | .6437 | .6953 | .4580 | .5005 | .5987 | .5727 | .7751 | 1.0000 | .1467 | .4980 | .5216 | .4401 | .3888 | .3808 |
| 10 BGH | .0406 | .2896 | .0307 | .0573 | .0339 | .1240 | .1120 | .3371 | .1467 | 1.0000 | .5382 | .5216 | .5263 | -.1404 | .3281 |
| 11 IBM | .0779 | .3607 | .2637 | .3452 | .5031 | .6831 | .1295 | .5630 | .4980 | .5382 | 1.0000 | .7433 | .5263 | .3953 | .5571 |
| 12 NCR | .1887 | .2328 | .1271 | .1932 | .3148 | .4956 | .1141 | .4369 | .5216 | .5216 | .7433 | 1.0000 | .4225 | .2828 | .5719 |
| 13 GF | .2149 | .2345 | .3340 | .5300 | .7739 | .7648 | .1427 | .3790 | .4401 | .5263 | .5263 | .4225 | 1.0000 | .7136 | .6525 |
| 14 NAB | .0488 | .2709 | .3920 | .5548 | .7785 | .7596 | .2241 | .1947 | .3888 | -.1404 | .3953 | .2828 | .7136 | 1.0000 | .6982 |
| 15 OAT | .1535 | .4063 | .4115 | .3934 | .5769 | .7357 | .1574 | .2913 | .3808 | .3281 | .5571 | .5719 | .6525 | .6982 | 1.0000 |

Table 9.5

**Efficient Frontier (Proceeds of Short Sales Available for Investment)**

| Portfolio No. | 1 | 2 | 3 | 4 | 5 | 6 | 7 | 8 | 9 | 10 |
|---|---|---|---|---|---|---|---|---|---|---|
| Portfolio Mean $\mu_p$ | 15.17 | 16.07 | 17.17 | 18.57 | 20.40 | 22.87 | 25.90 | 31.99 | 41.86 | 64.25 |
| Portfolio Standard Deviation $\sigma_p$ | 14.99 | 15.71 | 16.64 | 17.89 | 19.60 | 22.05 | 25.72 | 31.69 | 42.67 | 68.26 |
| 1 Allied Chemical | 5.78 | 5.95 | 6.16 | 6.42 | 6.76 | 7.23 | 7.90 | 8.94 | 10.79 | 14.99 |
| 2 Dow Chemical | 21.32 | 23.61 | 26.44 | 30.01 | 34.66 | 40.99 | 50.08 | 64.26 | 89.45 | 146.60 |
| 3 Union Carbide | 15.50 | 9.32 | 1.70 | -7.93 | -20.49 | -37.56 | -62.09 | -100.33 | -168.28 | -322.47 |
| 4 Cleveland Electric Illumination | 55.71 | 56.20 | 56.81 | 57.58 | 58.59 | 59.95 | 61.91 | 64.97 | 70.41 | 82.74 |
| 5 Commonwealth Edison | -43.10 | -49.93 | -58.35 | -69.00 | -82.88 | -101.74 | -128.84 | -171.11 | -246.19 | -416.58 |
| 6 Florida Power & Light | -25.37 | -24.81 | -24.12 | -23.25 | -22.11 | -20.57 | -18.35 | -14.88 | -8.73 | 5.23 |
| 7 Interlake | 23.93 | 28.86 | 34.93 | 42.60 | 52.61 | 66.20 | 85.74 | 116.21 | 170.33 | 293.15 |
| 8 Republic Steel | -33.58 | -35.21 | -37.21 | -39.73 | -43.03 | -47.51 | -53.95 | -63.99 | -81.83 | -122.30 |
| 9 US Steel | -19.75 | -20.35 | -21.10 | -22.03 | -23.25 | -24.91 | -27.30 | -31.02 | -37.63 | -52.62 |
| 10 Burroughs | 12.45 | 11.94 | 11.32 | 10.52 | 9.49 | 8.09 | 6.07 | 2.93 | -2.65 | -15.32 |
| 11 International Business Machines | 43.65 | 48.11 | 53.62 | 60.57 | 69.64 | 81.96 | 99.67 | 127.29 | 176.35 | 287.67 |
| 12 NCR | -3.28 | -4.83 | -6.73 | -9.14 | -12.27 | -16.54 | -22.66 | -32.22 | -49.19 | -87.70 |
| 13 General Foods | 37.32 | 39.24 | 41.60 | 44.58 | 48.48 | 53.77 | 61.36 | 73.22 | 94.27 | 142.04 |
| 14 Nabisco | 29.07 | 30.52 | 32.30 | 34.56 | 37.50 | 41.50 | 47.24 | 56.20 | 72.12 | 108.23 |
| 15 Quaker Oats | -19.65 | -18.63 | -17.37 | -15.77 | -13.69 | -10.86 | -6.80 | -.47 | 10.79 | 36.33 |
| **Total** | 100.00 | 100.00 | 100.00 | 100.00 | 100.00 | 100.00 | 100.00 | 100.00 | 100.00 | 100.00 |
| Riskless Rate r | -4.00 | -3.00 | -2.00 | -1.00 | 0.00 | 1.00 | 2.00 | 3.00 | 4.00 | 5.00 |

which is precisely equal to $\sigma_{13}$. This means that the variance–covariance matrix is symmetric, and all the covariances above the diagonal are equal to the corresponding covariance below the diagonal. Along the diagonal we always have $i = j$ (the row number is equal to the column number), so that the diagonal elements are simply the variances of the corresponding stocks $\sigma_{ii} = \sigma_i^2$. Thus the diagonal element at the intersection of row 2 and column 2 is the variance of the returns on the Dow Chemicals stock, $\sigma_2^2 = 761.29$ (the square root of this number $\sigma_2 = 27.59$ is equal to the standard deviation of the same stock listed in Table 9.2).

Table 9.4 shows the correlation matrix derived from the variance–covariance matrix in Table 9.3. Each element in the correlation matrix represents the correlation coefficient $\rho_{ij}$ between the corresponding pair of stocks $i$ and $j$: it is related to the corresponding covariance by the equality $\rho_{ij} = \sigma_{ij}/(\sigma_i \cdot \sigma_j)$. Thus the correlation coefficient of IBM (in row $i = 11$) and General Foods (in column $j = 13$) is $\rho_{11,13} = 0.5263$. It is derivable from the corresponding elements in Table 9.3 and Table 9.2 as follows: $\rho_{11,13} = \sigma_{11,13}/\sigma_{11}\sigma_{13} = 353.28/(29.39 \times 22.84) = 0.5263$. The correlation matrix is also symmetric and its diagonal elements are all equal to 1.0000 (the correlation coefficient of any stock with itself is always 1.00).

The 15-stock efficient frontier generated by the computer program is shown in Table 9.5. The columns in the body of the table give the investment proportions of the 15 stocks in different efficient portfolios, one column to a portfolio. The proportions represent the amounts allocated to different stocks given an initial amount of $100 (rather than $1 as before), and so add up to 100 (rather than 1 as before). Note that about half the proportions are positive, while the remaining half are negative. The proportions in the table can also be interpreted as the investment proportions in percent when the total is 100%. Positive proportions represent stocks held "long", i.e., stocks purchased and included in the portfolio. Negative proportions represent stocks held "short"; these are stocks actually owned by somebody else (usually your broker) that you borrowed and sold, using the proceeds of such short sales to augment your holding of other stocks (the "long" positions). The "shorted" stocks have to be returned to their owner at a pre-agreed date or on demand (for a discussion of short sales, see Chapter 1).

The bottom row of Table 9.5 gives the riskless rate of return $r$ for which the optimal *unlevered* investment proportions were derived by the method outlined in the previous section. Note that the riskless rate of return used in these computations is changed in constant steps of 1% from $-4\%$ to 5% in order to derive different efficient portfolios along the efficient frontier (each column represents a different efficient portfolio). The two top rows in the column are the *unlevered* portfolio mean $\mu_p$ and standard deviation $\sigma_p$. Thus each pair $(\mu_p, \sigma_p)$ plots a point on the curve $AB$ in Figure 9.6. The two numbers are computed using the standardized investment proportions $z_i$ in the corresponding column and the parameters of the 15 constituent stocks from Tables 9.2 and 9.3. The working formulas for computing the portfolio mean and standard deviation are the following:

*Portfolio mean:* $\quad \mu_p = \sum_{i=1}^{15} z_i \mu_i$

$$\text{Portfolio standard deviation:} \quad \sigma_p = \left( \sum_{i=1}^{15} z_i^2 \sigma_i^2 + 2 \sum_{i=1}^{15} \sum_{\substack{j=1 \\ j>i}}^{15} z_i z_j \sigma_{ij} \right)^{1/2}$$

Here, as before, $z_i$ and $z_j$ are the standardized proportions of stocks $i$ and $j$ in the efficient portfolio, $\mu_i$ is the expected return of stock $i$ (taken from Table 9.2), $\sigma_i^2$ is the variance of returns on stock $i$ (the $i$th diagonal element in Table 9.3), $\sigma_{ij}$ is the covariance of returns on stocks $i$ and $j$ (the element at the intersection of row $i$ and column $j$ in Table 9.3).[3]

The mean and standard deviation of the efficient portfolios can be plotted in the mean–standard deviation (M–S) space and then joined by a smooth curve which represents the efficient frontier. The efficient frontier plotted using the efficient portfolios from Table 9.5 is shown in Figure 9.6: geometrically, the efficient frontier in the M–S space is always a hyperbola. In addition to the efficient frontier, Figure 9.6 also plots a scattergram of the 15 individual stocks from Table 9.2: note that the individual stocks all actually lie *inside* the efficient frontier, so that at any given level of expected return or at any given level of risk we can construct an efficient portfolio that will be better (in terms of expected utility) than any individual stock.

The general procedure for tracing the $n$-stock efficient frontier thus can be summarized as follows:

(1)  fix a certain value of riskless rate of return $r$;
(2)  for this riskless return rate $r$, solve the system of $n$ linear equations (9.8), to obtain the portfolio proportions $y_i$ $(i = 1, 2, \ldots, n)$;
(3)  standardize the portfolio proportions $y_i$ to obtain the proportions $z_i$;
(4)  compute the mean and the standard deviation of the efficient *unlevered* portfolio corresponding to these proportions $z_i$;
(5)  increase the riskless rate of return by a certain (constant) amount and repeat the entire procedure from step 2 through 5.

Each repetition of the procedure (for a certain $r$) yields a point on the efficient frontier in the M–S space corresponding to the given value of $r$ (this is the point obtained in step 4). As many points as desired can be computed by choosing a sufficiently small step for changing $r$. The different points are then plotted in the M–S space and joined by a smooth curve to represent the efficient frontier graphically (see curve $AB$ in Figure 9.6).

Before we turn to the next section, two important properties of the efficient frontier should be mentioned.

---

[3] The proportions $z_i$ in each of the columns in Table 9.5 add up to 100 and thus represent actual amounts allocated to each stock $i$ from the initially available $\$100$. Since the stock parameters $\mu_i$, $\sigma_i$, $\sigma_{ij}$ are given in percent and so the portfolio parameters $\mu_p$, $\sigma_p$ are also required in percent, we divide the corresponding $z_i$ and $z_j$ from Table 9.5 by 100 (converting them into proper fractions) in order to calculate the portfolio mean and standard deviation from the two formulas above.

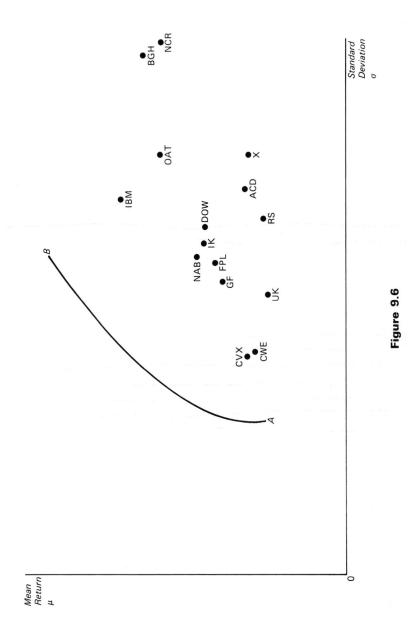

**Figure 9.6**

(a) _The proportion invested in the ith asset changes monotonically along the curve._

First note that the proportion of each asset in the efficient portfolio either decreases or increases monotonically along the efficient frontier. To illustrate this point look at the investment proportion of Nabisco in Table 9.5: it is 29.07% for portfolio 1 with the lowest mean, increases to 30.52 for portfolio 2 with the second lowest mean, and as we move to the right across the table the portfolio mean increases and so the proportion invested in Nabisco increases. It is impossible that the proportion invested in Nabisco will increase, then decrease and then increase again. If it increases in the first step it must continue in the same direction and increase as we move along the efficient frontier in the direction of increasing portfolio means. On the other hand, if the proportion decreases in the first step, it must decrease monotonically as we move to the right to portfolios with higher means. As an example look at the figures for Burroughs: the investment proportion decreases monotonically from 12.45% down to −15.32%. Thus, we cannot have fluctuations in the investment proportion along the efficient frontier. The investment proportion in each asset must either increase or decrease all the way as we move along the efficient frontier.

To illustrate this issue further, Figure 9.7 describes the investment proportions in two assets as a function of the riskless rate $r$. Panel (a) describes the proportions $y_i$ before the standardization, and panel (b) describes the proportion $z_i = y_i/\Sigma y_i$, namely after the standardization as they appear in Table 9.5. While in panel (a) we get straight lines, they are no longer linear after the standardization. In both cases, however, there is a monotonic change in the investment proportion of each asset as we increase the portfolio mean along the efficient frontier.

(b) _All efficient portfolios can be obtained as a linear combination of two efficient portfolios._

Note also that although the computer output yields all the efficient portfolios by solving the system of equations (9.8) for various interest rates $r$, in practice it is sufficient to solve for _only two_ efficient portfolios. All other portfolios can be obtained as a linear combination of these two portfolios.[4] To illustrate this point let $x_{i(1)}$ be the investment proportion in the $i$th asset in portfolio 1 and $x_{i(2)}$ the investment proportion of the same $i$th asset in portfolio 2; the proportion of this asset in all other efficient portfolios can be found by the linear combination:

$$\alpha x_{i(1)} + (1 - \alpha)x_{i(2)}$$

By varying $\alpha$ we get the proportion of the $i$th asset in all efficient portfolios. The important feature of this property is that for a given portfolio (e.g., the one corresponding to $\alpha = \frac{1}{2}$) the same $\alpha$ should be used for all assets ($i = 1, 2, \ldots, n$) in the portfolio.

---

[4] The proof of this statement is a little involved and we choose to illustrate this property with the output of Table 9.5, rather than prove it. Also see Chapter 13, Sec. 13.1.1 and Problem 13.19.

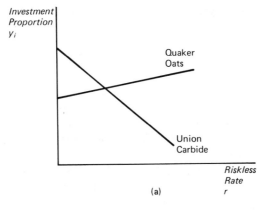

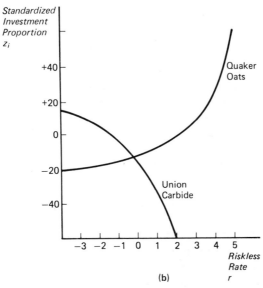

**Figure 9.7**

EXAMPLE

Suppose that we have only two risky assets and that portfolios 1 and 2 (see below) are efficient.

|  | Investment Proportions $(x_i)$ | |
|---|---|---|
|  | In Portfolio 1 | In Portfolio 2 |
| First Asset | −10 | 10 |
| Second Asset | 11 | −9 |
| $\Sigma x_i$ | 1 | 1 |

Then for $\alpha = \frac{1}{2}$ we get a third efficient portfolio with the following investment proportions:

$$x_1 = \tfrac{1}{2}(-10) + \tfrac{1}{2} \cdot 10 = 0$$

$$x_2 = \tfrac{1}{2} \cdot 11 + \tfrac{1}{2}(-9) = 1$$

Thus, the investment proportions in the two assets (0, 1) constitute an efficient portfolio. Repeating the same calculation for various values of $\alpha$ one can obtain as many efficient portfolios as desired.

To confirm that this assertion holds with actual data, let us turn back to Table 9.5 which provides a whole range of efficient portfolios. Take the two extreme portfolios and take the portfolio between them corresponding to the mean $\mu_p = 22.87$. With respect to the first asset ACD, we have

$$\alpha \times 14.99\% + (1 - \alpha) \times 5.78\% = 7.23\%$$

Solving for $\alpha$ we obtain $\alpha = 0.157$.

If our claim is indeed true, the proportions of all $n$ assets in the portfolio with $\mu_p = 22.87$ are linear combinations of the two extreme portfolios, with $\alpha = 0.157$. To demonstrate that the same $\alpha$ serves to calculate all investment proportions of the middle portfolio, take for example the second asset, DOW. For the second asset we obtain,

$$\alpha \times 146.60\% + (1 - \alpha) \times 21.32\% = \text{Investment in DOW}$$

or,

$$0.157 \times 146.60\% + 0.843 \times 21.32\% = 40.99\%$$

Indeed the computer output in Table 9.5 reveals that 40.99% is invested in DOW in the efficient portfolio with mean 22.87%.

Thus, for all practical purposes only the composition of two efficient portfolios should be calculated by solving the $n$ equations with $n$ unknowns. The composition of all other efficient portfolios can be obtained by a simple hand calculation applying the formula

$$\alpha x_{i(1)} + (1 - \alpha)x_{i(2)} = x_i(\alpha)$$

where $x_i(\alpha)$ is the investment proportion in asset $i$ corresponding to the value $\alpha$ that we selected. Carrying out this calculation for all assets $i$, we obtain the composition of an efficient portfolio corresponding to the selected $\alpha$. By varying the value of $\alpha$ we can obtain the composition of all efficient portfolios.

Table 9.5 provides only a few selected efficient portfolios. If an investor wishes to have a portfolio composition which lies on the efficient frontier between any two portfolios given in Table 9.5, simply calculate this portfolio by a linear combination of the two appropriate portfolios. In fact, by varying $\alpha$, one can find an infinite number of portfolios between any two portfolios.

## 9.7    Efficient Frontier with Constraints on the Proceeds of Short Sales

We have so far derived the efficient frontier assuming that the efficient portfolio proportions add up to 1, thus $\Sigma_{i=1}^{n} z_i = 1$. Technically, in the three-asset case for example, solution of the efficient portfolio problem may yield the portfolio proportions $z_1 = 2$, $z_2 = 3$ and $z_3 = -4$: the three proportions add up to 1, $\Sigma_{i=1}^{3} z_i = 2 + 3 - 4 = 1$, but the magnitude of each proportion is greater than 1 (the initial amount available for investment) and some proportions are negative. As we have noted in the previous section, a negative proportion of security 3 indicates that the investor actually sold $4 worth of this security after borrowing it from someone else and then used the proceeds of this short sale to augment his initial funds of $1, investing the full amount of $5 ($1 of his own plus $4 short sale proceeds) in the two other securities 1 and 2 (both held "long"). The $4 obtained by the short sale constitutes a loan and therefore appears with a minus sign. The previous derivation of the efficient frontier thus implicitly assumes that the proceeds of short sales are fully and freely available to the investor for augmenting his initial funds.

In practice, this is not so, however. The $4 cash proceeds from the short sale of security 3 are not available to the short-seller. Since the "shorted" security is "on loan" and has to be returned to the original owner at a preagreed date or on demand, the lender must be protected against the eventuality of the borrower's default. The short-sale proceeds thus serve as collateral and are held on deposit with the lender (usually the broker). In addition to this collateral, the borrower is usually required to maintain a certain cash margin to ensure that the shorted security will be returned even if its market price rises. The exact percentage of the required margin varies depending on the investor.

### Case 1: Interest earned on deposit

Normally, the owner of the shorted security is allowed to use the cash deposit and margin without paying any interest to the short-seller. Dealers and brokers, however, are entitled by special arrangement to a certain interest on the deposited cash and margin held by the original owner (another broker, probably). Thus Lintner assumes that the short sale proceeds plus 100% margin are deposited with the stock owner, who pays interest on the deposited funds.[5] This appears to be a more appropriate assumption for dealers and brokers.

Let us turn back to our example and apply it to Lintner's approach. The short-seller is required to maintain a 100% margin (i.e., the short sale proceeds of $4 plus additional margin of $4, a total of $8, is deposited as collateral with the security owner). On the other hand, we assume that the short-seller is entitled to receive interest at the riskless rate $r$ on the deposited cash (the full $8). Under this dealer–broker scenario, the solution of the efficient portfolio problem yields the same optimum diversification

---

[5] See Lintner, John, "The Valuation of Risk Assets and the Selection of Risky Investments in Stock Portfolios and Capital Budget", *Review of Economics and Statistics* (February 1965).

strategy as in Section 9.6, but with a different standardization. Instead of standardizing the efficient portfolio proportions by $z_i = x_i / \sum_{i=1}^{n} x_i$, as before, we standardize them by a different relation $z_i^* = x_i / \sum_{i=1}^{n} |x_i|$. Here $|x_i|$ is the *magnitude* (or absolute value) of the proportion invested in $i$th asset. In our three-asset example, the negative proportion of the third security ($-4$) is included as the positive number 4 in the standardizing sum, while all the positive "long" proportions are included without change. This type of standardization suggested by Lintner fits the case of short sales with 100% margin and interest payable on the cash deposit. In this case it is not the standardized investment proportions but their magnitudes that add up to one. Indeed, while $\sum_{i=1}^{n} z_i^* = \sum_{i=1}^{n} x_i / \sum_{i=1}^{n} |x_i| \neq 1$, we have $\sum_{i=1}^{n} |z_i^*| = \sum_{i=1}^{n} |x_i| / \sum_{i=1}^{n} |x_i| = 1$.

EXAMPLE

Consider the case of two risky assets and one riskless asset with return rate $r$. Suppose that the solution of the efficient portfolio problem yields an efficient diversification strategy

$$
\begin{array}{cc}
z_1 & z_2 \\
1.5 & -0.5
\end{array}
$$

Here $\sum_{i=1}^{2} z_i = 1.5 - 0.5 = 1$. If the investor is allowed free use of the proceeds from short sales the proportions $z_1$ and $z_2$ can be interpreted as follows. Starting with \$1 of own funds, the investor sells short stock 2 (borrowed from his broker) for \$0.5 and adds the proceeds to his initial \$1. He then invests the resulting \$1.5 in stock 1. If instead of starting with \$1, the investor initially had \$10 available for investment in risky assets, the efficient diversification strategy could be the following:

$$
\begin{array}{cc}
x_1 & x_2 \\
15 & -5
\end{array}
$$

Both proportions add up to the initial funds available, $x_1 + x_2 = 15 - 5 = 10$. Here, the proceeds from the short sale of stock 2 were \$5, so that a total of \$15 were available for investment in stock 1 (the original \$10 plus the \$5 short sale proceeds). Standardizing in the usual way, we would obtain the same proportions as before, $z_1 = x_1 / (x_1 + x_2) = 15/10 = 1.5$ and $z_2 = x_2 / (x_1 + x_2) = -5/10 = -0.5$.

However, if the short-sale proceeds are not available for augmenting the investor's initial funds, we have to use Lintner's standardization with the sum of the *magnitudes* of the corresponding proportions:

$$
\sum_{i=1}^{2} |x_i| = |x_1| + |x_2| = |15| + |-5| = 15 + 5 = 20
$$

Hence the standardized proportions $z_1^*$ and $z_2^*$ in this case are given by

$$
z_1^* = x_1 / \sum_{i=1}^{2} |x_i| = 15/20 = 3/4
$$

$$z_2^* = x_2 / \sum_{i=1}^{2} |x_i| = -5/20 = -1/4$$

The magnitudes of the standardized proportions add up to 1, as required $(|z_1^*| + |z_2^*| = |3/4| + |-1/4| = 3/4 + 1/4 = 1)$.

The ratio between the proportions invested in the risky assets is independent of the particular standardization used. Thus, with normal standardization (no constraints on short-sale proceeds), $z_1/z_2 = 1.5/(-0.5) = -3$, and with Lintner's standardization $z_1^*/z_2^* = (3/4)/(-1/4) = -3$. The only difference is in the scaling factor $\sum_{i=1}^{n} x_i$ or $\sum_{i=1}^{n} |x_i|$. Clearly the sum of the magnitudes $\sum_{i=1}^{n} |x_i|$ in which all the components are positive is greater than the ordinary sum $\sum_{i=1}^{n} x_i$ where some of the components are negative. Therefore, standardizing the proportions by Lintner's factor $\sum_{i=1}^{n} |x_i|$ we effectively reduce the amounts invested in the risky assets. Without constraints on the proceeds of short sales, the investor held $1.5 worth of security 1, whereas standardization by $\sum_{i=1}^{2} |x_i|$ in the case of constraints on short-sale proceeds reduced the amount invested in security 1 to $0.75. The investor's strategy under the two scenarios is summarized by the following table:

| | Short-sale Proceeds Available to Investor (Standardization by $\sum_{i=1}^{n} x_i$) | Short-sale Proceeds plus 100% Margin Held on Interest-bearing Deposit (Standardization by $\sum_{i=1}^{n} |x_i|$) |
|---|---|---|
| Initial funds | $1 | $1 |
| Short | −0.50 | −0.25 |
| Long | 1.50 | 0.75 |
| Invested in riskless asset | 0 | 0.50 |

The table is self-explanatory, except for the last line. With short-sale proceeds available to the investor (standardization by $\sum_{i=1}^{n} x_i$), the investor constructs an unlevered portfolio with $z_1 = 1.50$ and $z_2 = -0.50$, the two proportions adding up to the initial funds of $1. When the short-sale proceeds are held on deposit (standardization by $\sum_{i=1}^{n} |x_i|$), we effectively obtain a portfolio which consists of risky assets and *riskless bonds* bearing interest at rate $r$. The investor sells short one of the risky assets for $0.25. The short-sale proceeds of $0.25 plus the 100% margin (additional $0.25) are deposited with the original owner of the shorted security, and the investor receives interest at the riskless rate $r$ on his total deposit of $0.50 (the "bond" component of the portfolio). Note that under both scenarios *all* the investment proportions add to 1 $(-0.50 + 1.50 = 1$ and also $-0.25 + 0.75 + 0.50 = 1)$, but there is a fundamental difference in what proportions are added up: while in the first case we add up only the proportions invested in the risky assets, in the second case we add up the proportions invested in the risky asset *and* the bond component of the interest-bearing deposit. If

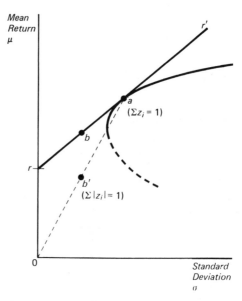

**Figure 9.8**

only the risky proportions are added up, their sum in the second case is no longer 1: instead their *magnitudes* add up to 1, as we have seen above ($|-0.25|+|0.75|=1$).

Figure 9.8 illustrates the relationship between the efficient portfolios obtained under the two different scenarios with two different standardization approaches. Portfolio $a$ is the optimal unlevered portfolio of risky assets corresponding to riskless return rate $r$ and obtained as before by investing all the short-sale proceeds in "long" stocks. Portfolio $b$ is a mix of the all-risk portfolio $a$ and the riskless asset $r$ in certain proportions (compare Sec. 9.2), obtained when the short-sale proceeds are held on interest-bearing deposit. In our example, half the funds is invested in the risky portfolio and half in the riskless asset, so that portfolio $b$ is schematically given by the linear combination

$$b = 0.5a + 0.5r$$

Portfolio $b$ clearly lies on the line $rr'$ rising from the riskless return rate $r$ and tangent to the efficient frontier at point $a$.

An investor forced to hold the mixed portfolio $b$ (because of the constraints on short-sale proceeds) can always borrow additional funds in the money market (at the riskless rate $r$), using the loan to increase his holding of the risky securities until he actually holds portfolio $a$. The loan that he takes is calculated to offset the "bond" component of portfolio $b$ that was forced upon him by the margin arrangements (but it is not equal to the $0.50 that he has on deposit with the owner of the shorted security!). Thus, for a dealer or a broker who is entitled to receive interest on his deposit and margin, the efficient set of all-risk portfolios is the same as in the case when the short-sale proceeds are available for additional investment, regardless of the difference in standardization.

## Case 2: No interest earned on deposit

A private individual who is neither a dealer nor a broker does not enjoy this preferential treatment and usually does not receive any interest on his deposit and margin. In this case, his portfolio consists of \$0.75 invested in security 1 held long and \$0.25 invested in security 2 held short. The "bond" component of the portfolio is like cash, as it does not earn any interest income. As a result the proportions $z_i^{**}$ of the risky assets in this portfolio satisfy the relation $\Sigma_{i=1}^n |z_i^{**}| = 1$, i.e. the *magnitudes* of the investment proportions add up to 1, and not the proportions themselves. The individual's portfolio is represented by point $b'$ in Figure 9.8, which is schematically given by

$$b' = 0.5a$$

(as he only invests half his funds in the risky assets, the other half constituting the deposit and the 100% margin). The mean and the standard deviation of portfolio $b'$ are related to those of portfolio $a$ by the relations

$$\mu_{b'} = 0.5\mu_a$$

$$\sigma_{b'} = 0.5\sigma_a$$

In this case, the individual's efficient frontier changes: his efficient portfolio $b'$ is the midpoint of the straight segment $0a$ joining the origin (the point of zero riskless interest rate) with the all-risk efficient portfolio $a$ corresponding to the case without any constraints on short-sale proceeds. There is no way to move from portfolio $b'$ to portfolio $a$ by borrowing if the investor does not receive any interest income on his deposit and margin.

APPLICATION

Table 9.6 gives the composition of the efficient portfolios in the more realistic case of an individual investor who is not entitled to interest on his deposit and margin (i.e., for the case when $\Sigma_{i=1}^n |z_i^{**}| = 1$). The efficient portfolios were constructed from the same 15 stocks as before (see Table 9.2) and they span the same range of riskless return rates as in Table 9.5 (from $r = -4\%$ to $r = 5\%$). Note that while the underlying assumption in the efficient frontier of Table 9.5 is that the short-sale proceeds are available for investment (or, alternatively, that the investor receives interest at riskless rate $r$ on his deposit and 100% margin), Table 9.6 represents the efficient portfolios for an individual investor not entitled to any interest on his deposit and margin.

There is a straightforward relationship between the investment proportions in the two cases. Denote by $z_i$ the investment proportions in Table 9.5 (i.e., $\Sigma_{i=1}^n z_i = 1$).

Table 9.6
Efficient Frontier (Proceeds of Short Sales plus 100% Margin Held on Interest-free Deposit)

| Portfolio No. | 1 | 2 | 3 | 4 | 5 | 6 | 7 | 8 | 9 | 10 |
|---|---|---|---|---|---|---|---|---|---|---|
| 1 Allied Chemical | 1.48 | 1.46 | 1.43 | 1.36 | 1.26 | 1.17 | 1.07 | .96 | .84 | .70 |
| 2 Dow Chemical | 5.47 | 5.79 | 6.15 | 6.33 | 6.47 | 6.62 | 6.77 | 6.92 | 6.94 | 6.87 |
| 3 Union Carbide | 3.98 | 2.29 | .40 | -1.67 | -3.83 | -6.06 | -8.39 | -10.81 | -13.06 | -15.11 |
| 4 Cleveland Electric Illumination | 14.30 | 13.79 | 13.22 | 12.16 | 10.94 | 9.68 | 8.37 | 7.00 | 5.46 | 3.88 |
| 5 Commonwealth Edison | -11.07 | -12.25 | -13.58 | -14.57 | -15.48 | -16.43 | -17.41 | -18.44 | -19.10 | -19.52 |
| 6 Florida Power and Light | -6.51 | -6.09 | -5.61 | -4.91 | -4.13 | -3.32 | -2.48 | -1.60 | -.68 | .25 |
| 7 Interlake | 6.14 | 7.08 | 8.13 | 8.99 | 9.82 | 10.69 | 11.59 | 12.52 | 13.21 | 13.74 |
| 8 Republic Steel | -8.62 | -8.64 | -8.66 | -8.39 | -8.04 | -7.67 | -7.29 | -6.90 | -6.35 | -5.73 |
| 9 US Steel | -5.07 | -4.99 | -4.91 | -4.65 | -4.34 | -4.02 | -3.69 | -3.34 | -2.92 | -2.47 |
| 10 Burroughs | 3.20 | 2.93 | 2.63 | 2.22 | 1.77 | 1.31 | .82 | .32 | -.21 | -.72 |
| 11 International Business Machines | 11.21 | 11.81 | 12.48 | 12.79 | 13.01 | 13.23 | 13.47 | 13.72 | 13.68 | 13.48 |
| 12 NCR | -.84 | -1.18 | -1.57 | -1.93 | -2.29 | -2.67 | -3.06 | -3.47 | -3.82 | -4.11 |
| 13 General Foods | 9.58 | 9.63 | 9.68 | 9.41 | 9.05 | 8.68 | 8.29 | 7.89 | 7.31 | 6.66 |
| 14 Nabisco | 7.46 | 7.49 | 7.52 | 7.30 | 7.00 | 6.70 | 6.38 | 6.06 | 5.59 | 5.07 |
| 15 Quaker Oats | -5.05 | -4.57 | -4.04 | -3.33 | -2.56 | -1.75 | -.92 | -.05 | .84 | 1.70 |
| *Riskless Rate r* | -4.00 | -3.00 | -2.00 | -1.00 | -0.00 | 1.00 | 2.00 | 3.00 | 4.00 | 5.00 |

Then the investment proportions in Table 9.6 are calculated as $z_i^{**} = z_i / \sum_{i=1}^{n} |z_i|$. Clearly $\sum_{i=1}^{n} |z_i^{**}| = \sum_{i=1}^{n} |z_i| / \sum_{i=1}^{n} |z_i| = 1$, as required.

## 9.8    The Efficient Frontier when Short Sales are not Allowed

The efficient portfolios constructed in the previous sections (with and without constraints on short sale proceeds) included about half the stocks in short positions, and only the remaining 7–8 stocks (out of the total of 15 stocks) were held long. When a stock is held long, the investor may lose at most 100% of his investment in this stock: this dramatic loss is incurred in the event that the stock price drops to zero (the firm goes bankrupt and its stock becomes worthless). Thus, if an individual purchased some stock for $1, he may at most lose the $1 invested in case the issuing corporation defaults. With stocks held in short positions (negative proportions in the efficient portfolio), there is no such lower bound on the potential loss. Suppose that our investor borrows $1 worth of some stock from his broker, undertaking to return the borrowed stock after one month. He "goes short" for $1 in this stock, using the proceeds of the short sale to augment his long positions. If after one month the stock still sells for $1, the investor will be able to buy the stock on the exchange and return it to the original owner without incurring a loss. If the price of the stock drops to 80 cents, he will be able to buy it for less than what he got from the short sale a month earlier so that the overall transaction will end with a profit for the investor. On the other hand, if the stock price rises to $5 a share, the investor will have to pay $5 in order to buy and return the stock which he "sold short" for $1 a month earlier. He thus loses $4, or 400 percent on the transaction!

Recognizing the greater risk involved in short positions, many individuals and especially institutional investors adopt (by choice or by regulation) the policy of holding only stocks in long positions. The efficient frontier of portfolios without short positions (efficient portfolios with all-positive proportions) is much more difficult to construct: the procedure no longer reduces to solving $n$ linear equations in $n$ unknowns, and numerical methods known as *quadratic programming* must be used. Basically, quadratic programming also attempts to minimize the portfolio risk (as measured by variance or standard deviation) at each given return level, but additional *nonnegativity constraints* are imposed which stipulate that no stock can be held in negative proportions. Thus quadratic programming derives efficient portfolios in which some stocks are held long (positive proportions), while all the other stocks are omitted (held in zero proportions): no short stocks are allowed.

The mathematical statement of the problem without short sales is similar to the previous formulation:

Minimize portfolio variance    $\sigma_p^2 = \sum_{i=1}^{n} x_i^2 \sigma_i^2 + 2 \sum_{i=1}^{n} \sum_{\substack{j=1 \\ j>i}}^{n} x_i x_j \sigma_{ij}$

subject to the constraints

(1)  $\mu_p = \sum\limits_{i=1}^{n} x_i \mu_i$                                         (given portfolio mean)

(2)  $\sum\limits_{i=1}^{n} x_i = 1$                                              (all proportions add up to 1)

(3)  $x_i \geqslant 0$   for all $i = 1, 2, \ldots, n$     (nonnegativity constraints)

    Constraints (1) and (2) were previously incorporated in the formulation of the Lagrange function (9.1) or (9.1'). The nonnegativity constraints (3) are new: since these are inequality constraints, it is impossible to construct a Lagrange function for this problem and we have to apply mathematical programming techniques. The function to be minimized (the portfolio variance) is quadratic (of second degree in the unknowns $x_i$) and the constraints 1 and 2 are linear (of first degree in the unknowns $x_i$), so that we can use *quadratic programming* to find the efficient investment strategy $(x_1, x_2, \ldots, x_n)$. The technique involves quite complex mathematics which goes beyond the scope of our book. The interested reader will be able to look it up in any textbook of nonlinear programming. Fortunately, even without looking it up in advanced texts, we have special computer programs capable of solving quadratic programming problems which yield the efficient investment strategy $(x_1, x_2, \ldots, x_n)$ for each portfolio return level $\mu_p$.[6]

    Table 9.7 presents the efficient frontier for the same 15 US stocks as in Tables 9.5 and 9.6, but this time with the additional nonnegativity constraints $x_i \geqslant 0$ for all $i = 1, 2, \ldots, n$. Unlike the portfolios in Tables 9.5 and 9.6, which always include all the 15 stocks in positive or negative proportions, the efficient portfolios without short sales include a relatively small number of stocks in positive proportions, and all the remaining stocks are omitted (their proportions are $x_i = 0$). Moreover, the efficient frontier derived without short sales always includes an efficient portfolio consisting of a single stock, that with the maximum expected return (IBM in our case).

    Figure 9.9 plots the efficient frontiers constructed with and without short sales: the efficient frontier without short sales $NN'$ lies *inside* the efficient frontier with short sales $SS'$, so that an investor choosing a portfolio with nonnegative proportions only will attain a lower level of utility than an investor holding both long and short positions. This

---

[6] The computer program is very long and complicated, and for this reason is not included in the book. Various quadratic programming programs are available in standard computer libraries, such as MPOS or IMSL. These programs, however, generate a single point corresponding to a fixed value of mean return, specified among the input parameters, and in order to generate the full efficient frontier many repeated runs should be made, changing the mean return parameter in each run. A program based on a version of the reduced gradient algorithm, PHIMAQ, developed by Electricité de France and subsequently modified at the Hebrew University of Jerusalem Computation Center generates the entire efficient frontier in one run, as it changes the parameter automatically.

**Table 9.7**
**15 US Stocks 1956–1980: Efficient Frontier Without Short Sales**

| Portfolio No. | 1 | 2 | 3 | 4 | 5 | 6 | 7 | 8 | 9 | 10 | 11 |
|---|---|---|---|---|---|---|---|---|---|---|---|
| Portfolio Mean $\mu_p$ | 11.00 | 11.50 | 12.00 | 13.00 | 14.00 | 15.00 | 16.00 | 17.00 | 18.00 | 18.20 | 18.26 |
| Portfolio Standard Deviation $\sigma_p$ | 14.96 | 15.28 | 15.68 | 16.71 | 18.06 | 19.92 | 22.24 | 25.02 | 28.42 | 29.17 | 29.39 |
| 1 Allied Chemical | 11.58 | 12.04 | 12.14 | 11.92 | 9.38 | 3.57 | — | — | — | — | — |
| 3 Union Carbide | 2.16 | — | — | — | — | — | — | — | — | — | — |
| 4 Cleveland Electric Illumination | 30.09 | 25.57 | 20.28 | 8.20 | — | — | — | — | — | — | — |
| 7 Interlake | 12.74 | 15.23 | 16.71 | 20.07 | 22.50 | 22.94 | 22.01 | 17.01 | 10.36 | 0.29 | — |
| 10 Burroughs | 13.75 | 13.53 | 13.28 | 12.99 | 12.10 | 10.00 | 7.21 | 3.54 | 2.96 | 2.05 | — |
| 11 International Business Machines | 5.56 | 8.89 | 13.13 | 21.16 | 31.21 | 45.13 | 60.76 | 78.24 | 86.67 | 97.66 | 100.00 |
| 13 General Foods | 6.63 | 4.96 | 2.30 | — | — | — | — | — | — | — | — |
| 14 Nabisco | 17.50 | 19.78 | 22.16 | 25.66 | 24.80 | 18.36 | 10.02 | 1.21 | — | — | — |
| 15 Quaker Oats | — | — | — | — | — | — | — | — | — | — | — |
| **Total** | 100.00 | 100.00 | 100.00 | 100.00 | 100.00 | 100.00 | 100.00 | 100.00 | 100.00 | 100.00 | 100.00 |
| Riskless Rate $r$ | — | −9.9 | −5.9 | −1.1 | 3.5 | 5.4 | 7.3 | 8.4 | 10.0 | 10.5 | — |

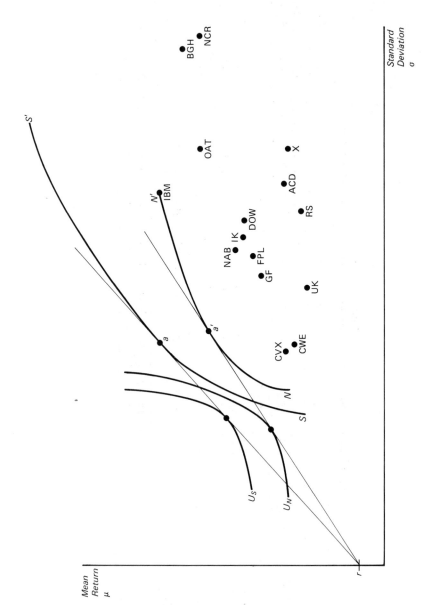

**Figure 9.9**

utility loss is directly attributable to the additional constraints $x_i \geqslant 0$. The loss of utility may be measured by the change in the slope of the straight line rising from the riskless rate $r$ and tangent to the relevant efficient frontier. The straight line $ra$ tangent to the efficient frontier $SS'$ (available when short sales are allowed) is steeper than the straight line $ra'$ tangent to the efficient frontier $NN'$ (when short sales are forbidden) and the change in utility between the two portfolios can be represented in terms of the change in the corresponding slope. Suppose that when short sales are allowed, an institutional investor chooses efficient portfolio $a$ on efficient frontier $SS'$ according to the tangency of the indifference curve $U_S$ with straight line $ra$. If regulatory agencies forbid short sales, the efficient frontier $SS'$ and hence the line $ra$ are no longer available to the institutional investor, and he is forced to invest in portfolio $a'$ located on the efficient frontier $NN'$ without short sales. The nonnegativity constraints $x_i \geqslant 0$ in effect shifted the investor from a portfolio on efficient frontier $SS'$ to a portfolio on efficient frontier $NN'$. As a result of this shift the investor's utility decreased from $U_S$ (tangent to the line $ra$) to $U_N$ (tangent to the less steep line $ra'$).

## Summary

The efficient frontier is traced by minimizing the portfolio variance for a given portfolio expected return and subject to the constraint $\Sigma x_i = 1$ (all investment proportions add to 1 or 100%).

When short sales are allowed, finding each efficient portfolio involves a solution of $n + 1$ equations with $n + 1$ unknowns, where $n$ is the number of risky assets. For each given portfolio expected return, one can solve for the optimum portfolio corresponding to a predetermined interest rate. This is a levered portfolio, a mix of the risky assets and the riskless asset. By an appropriate standardization the optimum unlevered portfolio is found. By gradually changing the riskless rate, one can solve for all efficient unlevered portfolios which constitute the tangency points between the straight line rising from the riskless interest rate point on the vertical axis and the risky assets' efficient frontier.

When the number of assets is small, the efficient frontier can be traced by using a simple hand calculator. However, as $n$ increases (say beyond 5) hand calculations are difficult and a computer program for solution of $n + 1$ equations with $n + 1$ unknowns is available (see Appendix 9.1).

When short sales are not allowed, the constraints $x_i \geqslant 0$ are added, which in turn make the solution more involved. In this case, we have to use quadratic programming, which is very difficult to solve without computer aid.

The computer output includes the optimal investment proportions in an unlevered portfolio at a predetermined riskless interest rate, as well as the mean and the variance of this unlevered efficient portfolio. The number of columns in the output table is equal to the number of riskless interest rates that we plug in as input, since for every riskless interest rate a column of output is generated.

## Summary Table

### 1. Unlevered Efficient Portfolios

The investment proportions in an all-risk efficient portfolio are obtained by minimizing the portfolio variance

$$\sigma_p^2 = \sum_{i=1}^{n} x_i^2 \sigma_i^2 + 2 \sum_{i=1}^{n} \sum_{\substack{j=1 \\ j>i}}^{n} x_i x_j \sigma_{ij}$$

subject to

$$\sum_{i=1}^{n} x_i = 1, \qquad \mu_p = \sum_{i=1}^{n} x_i \mu_i$$

The optimum investment strategy in an unlevered all-risk portfolio is given by $x_1, x_2, \ldots, x_n$, where $x_i$ is the proportion invested in the $i$th risky asset.

### 2. Levered Efficient Portfolios

The investment proportions in an efficient portfolio consisting of $n$ risky assets and the riskless asset with rate of return $r$ are obtained by minimizing the portfolio variance (same as in 1 above)

$$\sigma_p^2 = \sum_{i=1}^{n} x_i \sigma_i^2 + 2 \sum_{i=1}^{n} \sum_{\substack{j=1 \\ j>i}}^{n} x_i x_j \sigma_{ij}$$

subject to

$$\sum_{i=1}^{n} x_i + x_r = 1, \qquad \mu_p = \sum_{i=1}^{n} x_i \mu_i + x_r r$$

The optimum investment strategy in a levered portfolio is given by $x_1, x_2, \ldots, x_n, x_r$, where $x_i$ $(i = 1, 2, \ldots, n)$ are the proportions invested in the $n$ risky assets and $x_r = 1 - \sum_{i=1}^{n} x_i$ is the proportion invested in the riskless asset.

3. The relationship between the unlevered efficient portfolio $m$ and the levered portfolio $B$ is given by

$$B = \alpha m + (1 - \alpha)r$$

where $r$ is the riskless rate of return.

4. If the proportion invested in risky asset $i$ in the levered portfolio is $x_i$, the proportion invested in the same asset $i$ in the corresponding unlevered portfolio is calculated by one of the following standardizations, depending on the assumptions concerning the proceeds of short sales:

   (i) *If the short-sale proceeds are available to the investor,*

$$z_i = \frac{x_i}{\sum\limits_{i=1}^{n} x_i}, \qquad \text{so that } \sum_{i=1}^{n} z_i = 1$$

(ii) *If the short-sale proceeds plus 100% margin are deposited in an interest-bearing account*

$$z_i^* = \frac{x_i}{\sum\limits_{i=1}^{n} |x_i|}, \qquad \text{so that} \quad \sum_{i=1}^{n} |z_i^*| = 1$$

(iii) *If the short-sale proceeds plus 100% margin are deposited in a no-interest account*

$$z_i^{**} = \frac{z_i}{\sum\limits_{i=1}^{n} |z_i|} \qquad \text{so that} \quad \sum_{i=1}^{n} |z_i^{**}| = 1$$

5. In solving for an efficient investment strategy when *short sales are allowed*, we have to solve $n$ equations in $n$ unknowns, where $n$ is the number of risky assets. When the constraint of *no short sales* is imposed, we must use quadratic programming to solve for the efficient investment strategy.

6. Computer programs are available which provide the efficient investment strategies and the mean and standard deviation combinations of all efficient portfolios.

## APPENDIX 9.1
### Computer Program to Calculate the Mean–Variance Efficient Frontier

We give below the full computer code (written in FORTRAN77) that will generate the $n$-asset MV efficient frontier with short sales allowed (without nonnegativity constraints on the investment proportions).[7]

The program reads in raw rates of return on $n$ assets (the parameter NSTK $= n$ specifies the number of assets in the input file TAPE1) with $m$ observations per asset (the parameter NYRS $= m$ specifies the number of observations). It is necessary that NSTK < NYRS, since otherwise the algorithm will fail because of matrix singularity. The input format (13 in line 25) in this version of the program fits the Data Set at the end of the book. The program includes an option of performing the calculations for a subset of the input data. The actual number of stocks to be included in the efficient frontier calculations is specified by the parameter NSTK1 (NSTK1 $\leqslant$ NSTK).

The program starts by computing the vector of $n$ means and the $n \times n$ variance–covariance matrix of the $n$ assets and proceeds to solve the system of equations which yields the $n$ investment proportions in the MV efficient portfolios

---

[7] The algorithm used in this program is based on the efficient frontier mathematics in matrix form as presented, e.g., in the Appendix of R. Roll, "A Critique of the Asset Pricing Theory Tests, I", *Journal of Financial Economics*, 1977.

corresponding to specific values of the riskfree rate RF. To trace the entire efficient frontier, RF is stepped down by DELTA (DELTA = 0.5 in line 89 of the code), starting with the return level RMIN corresponding to the global minimum variance portfolio of the efficient frontier (for the initialization of RF, see line 86 of the code). All the calculations are repeated for each new value of RF, each cycle generating another point (portfolio) on the efficient frontier. The basic repeating calculation cycle extends from label 4 (line 90) to the instruction GO TO 4 (line 116). In this version of the program, the tracing of the efficient frontier is terminated when RF reaches −15% (see line 92).

The program uses three routines from the International Mathematics and Statistics Library (IMSL), which is available in most computer installations. These routines require the two parameters IX and IA, respectively equal to the row dimension of the data matrix X and the inverse variance–covariance matrix AINV. The three IMSL routines are:

BECOVM—calculates the vector of means and the variance–covariance matrix.
LINV1P—inverts the symmetric variance–covariance matrix.
VCVTSF—a matrix manipulation routine which presents the inverse in a full $n \times n$ format as required for further processing.

Therefore, in order to execute the program, appropriate system control instructions should be added, making the IMSL library available to the executing job.

The program output consists of two parts. The first part is a listing of the efficient portfolios, giving a succession of points on the efficient frontier characterized by their mean (MP), standard deviation (SD), and risk-free rate of return (RF). This part also gives the global minimum-variance portfolio identified by its mean RMIN and standard deviation SDMIN. These data are sufficient to trace the entire efficient frontier. The second part consists of tables which give the positive and negative investment proportions for each triple (MP, SD, RF) specifying the composition of an efficient portfolio from the first part. The investment proportions of each portfolio add up to 100%.

```
 1            PROGRAM SHORT(TAPE1,TAPE2,OUTPUT)
 2      C-   ********************************************************
 3      C-   PROGRAM GENERATES EFFICIENT FRONTIER WITH SHORT SALES
 4      C-   INPUT DATA FROM TAPE1 IN FORMAT 13
 5      C-   TAPE2 IS USED AS A SCRATCH TAPE TO EDIT THE OUTPUT TABLES
 6      C-   THE PROGRAM IS DIMENSIONED TO READ UP TO 50 OBSERVATIONS
 7      C-   FOR EACH OF 20 SECURITIES INTO ARRAY X (50,20)
 8      C-   ACTUAL NUMBER OF OBSERVATIONS AND SECURITIES IS SPECIFIED
 9      C-   BY THE FOLLOWING TWO PARAMETERS
10      C-   NSTK=NUMBER OF STOCKS ON DATA FILE
11      C-   NYRS=NUMBER OF OBSERVATIONS ON DATA FILE
12      C-   NSTK1=NUMBER OF STOCKS OUT OF NSTK TO BE INCLUDED IN EFFICIENT SET
13      C-   ********************************************************************
14           DIMENSION X(50,20),XM(20),NBR(6),TEMP(20),VCV(210),
15          2  AINV(20,20),B(20),H(20),TABLE(23,12)
16           REAL MP,MP1,MP2
17           CHARACTER *10 ICOT(3),NAME(20)
```

```
18    C-        ******************** PARAMETER INITIALIZATION *********
19              PARAMETER (NYRS=10,NSTK=8,IA=20,IX=50)
20              NSTK1=NSTK
21    C-        **************************************************************
22    C-        ********************** FORMATS ******************************
23              DATA (ICOT(I),I=1,3)/' MEAN ',' ST. DEV ',' RF '/
24    8         FORMAT(//' NUMBER OF STOCKS =',I5/' BMAX=',F10.3//)
25    13        FORMAT(A10,20X,10F5.1)
26    40        FORMAT (//' EFFICIENT SET WITH RMIN=',2F10.3,
27            2 '  SDMIN=',F10.3/1X,75('='))
28    88        FORMAT(' MP=',F10.3,4X,'SD=',F10.3,4X,'RF=',F10.2)
29    100       FORMAT(///)
30    208       FORMAT(A10,9X,12F9.2)
31    207       FORMAT(1X,A7,4X,F6.2,'I',12F9.2)
32    228       FORMAT(1X,130('*'))
33    230       FORMAT(1X,130('='))
34    C-        ************* INITIALIZATION OF PARAMETERS FOR IMSL SUBPROGRAMS ****
35            NBR(1)=NSTK1
36            NBR(2)=NYRS
37            NBR(3)=NYRS
38             NBR(4)=1
39             NBR(5)=1
40             NBR(6)=0
41    C- ******* READ IN INPUT DATA ******************************
42            REWIND 1
43            REWIND 2
44            PRINT 100
45            DO 11 I=1,NSTK
46            READ(1,13) NAME(I), (X(J,I),J=1,NYRS)
47    11      CONTINUE
48            PRINT 100
49
50
51
52    C- *************************************************************
53    C- COV MATRIX CALCULATE AND INVERT
54    C- *************************************************************
55            CALL BECOVM(X,IX,NBR,TEMP,XM,VCV,IER)
56            DO 5 I=1,NSTK1
57    5       B(I)=XM(I)
58            BMAX=0
59            DO 111 I=1,NSTK1
60            IF(XM(I).GE.BMAX) BMAX=XM(I)
61    111     CONTINUE
62            PRINT 8,NSTK1,BMAX
63            N=NBR(1)
64            CALL LINV1P(VCV,N,AINV,IDGT,D1,D2,IBR)
65            CALL VCVTSF(AINV,N,AINV,IA)
66    C- ******************************
67    C- ANALYTICAL SOLUTION WITH SHORTS
68    C- ******************************
69            A11=A12=A22=0
70            DO 6 I=1,NSTK1
71            DO 6 J=1,NSTK1
72            A11=A11+AINV(I,J)
73            A22=A22+B(I)*B(J)*AINV(I,J)
74            A12=A12+B(I)*AINV(I,J)
75    6       CONTINUE
76            DEL=A11*A22-A12**2
```

```
77              A11=A11/DEL
78              A22=A22/DEL
79              A12=-A12/DEL
80       C- ******* CALCULATE GLOBAL MINIMUM AND FIX RF STEPPING *******
81              SDMIN=SQRT(1./(DEL*A11))
82              RMIN=-A12/A11
83              IRMIN=RMIN*10
84              XRMIN=IRMIN*10.
85              IF(RMIN.GT.XRMIN+.5) XRMIN=XRMIN+.5
86              RF=XRMIN + .5
87              PRINT 40,RMIN,RF,SDMIN
88              ICNT=0
89              DELTA=.5
90       4      RF=RF-DELTA
91              IF(RF.LE.0) DELTA=.5
92              IF(RF.LE.-15.) GO TO 4444
93       C- *******CALCULATE EFFICIENT PORTFOLIO MEAN, ST.DEV. *********
94              MP=(-A12*RF-A22)/(A11*RF+A12)
95              MP1=A11*MP+A12
96              MP2=A22+A12*MP
97              VAR=A11*MP**2 + 2*A12*MP + A22
98              SD=SQRT(VAR)
99              PRINT 88,MP,SD,RF
100      C- ******* CALCULATE EFFICIENT PORTFOLIO PROPORTIONS **********
101             DO 60 I=1,NSTK1
102      60     B(I)=XM(I)*MP1+MP2
103             DO 66 I=1,NSTK1
104             H(I)=0
105                DO 67 J=1,NSTK1
106                H(I)=H(I)+B(J)*AINV(I,J)
107      67        CONTINUE
108             H(I)=H(I)*100
109      66     CONTINUE
110      C- ************************************
111      C- PRINT OUT PORTFOLIO PROPORTIONS
112      C- ************************************
113             WRITE(2,*) MP,SD,RF
114             WRITE(2,*) (H(I),I=1,NSTK1)
115             ICNT=ICNT+1
116             GO TO 4
117      4444 PRINT 40,RMIN,RF,SDMIN
118      C- ************************************
119      C- PRINT OUT EDITED PROPORTIONS
120      C- ************************************
121             REWIND 2
122      44     IF(ICNT.LE.0) GO TO 1111
123             IF(ICNT.LE.12) NN=ICNT
124             IF(ICNT.GT.12) NN=12
125             DO 7 J=1,NN
126             READ(2,*) (TABLE(I,J),I=1,NSTK1+3)
127      7      CONTINUE
128             PRINT 228
129             PRINT 208,ICOT(1),(TABLE(1,J),J=1,NN)
130             PRINT 208,ICOT(2),(TABLE(2,J),J=1,NN)
131             PRINT 228
132             DO 70 I=4,NSTK1+3
133             PRINT 207,NAME(I-3),XM(I-3),(TABLE(I,J),J=1,NN)
134      70     CONTINUE
```

```
135            PRINT 230
136            PRINT 208,ICOT(3),(TABLE(3,J),J=1,NN)
137            PRINT 230
138            PRINT 100
139            ICNT=ICNT-NN
140            GO TO 44
141      1111  STOP
142            END
```

## Questions and Problems

9.1  An investor is faced with the problem of finding the efficient portfolio with an expected return of 8% when the market consists of two risky assets with the following characteristics:

|  | Asset 1 | Asset 2 |
|---|---|---|
| Expected return (%) | 6 | 10 |
| Variance | 2 | 5 |
| Covariance between 2 and 1 | | 3 |

The return available on the riskless asset is $r = 5\%$. Find the corresponding efficient portfolio consisting of the riskless and the risky assets. Does the investor borrow or lend at the riskless rate?

9.2  Investor $A$ invests an equal proportion in each of the three securities—two risky assets and a riskless asset. The two risky assets have mean rates of return of 6% and 9%, respectively. The variances of returns on the two assets are 2 and 5, respectively, and the covariance of the returns on the two risky assets is 3. The riskless asset yields a mean return of 5%. Does $A$'s equal-proportion portfolio lie on the efficient frontier?

9.3  Trace the efficient frontier consisting of portfolios of three risky assets, $i = 1, 2, 3$, and one riskless asset, using the techniques of Section 9.3, and assuming riskless interest rates $r = 2\%, 3\%, \ldots, 10\%$. The following information is given on the three risky assets:

|  | Asset 1 | Asset 2 | Asset 3 |
|---|---|---|---|
| Expected return (%) | 6 | 10 | 8 |
| Variance | 2 | 3 | 4 |
|  | $Cov(R_1, R_2) = 1$ | $Cov(R_1, R_3) = 2$ | $Cov(R_2, R_3) = 3$ |

Assume that the investor requires an expected return of 8% on his portfolio. What level of risk will the investor accept if the riskless rate $r = 2\%$?

Represent the efficient frontier as a linear combination of the riskless asset and the unlevered all-risk portfolio.

9.4  Consider the unlevered all-risk portfolio corresponding to the levered portfolio chosen by the investor in Problem 9.1. Suppose that the proceeds of short sales plus 100% are deposited with the broker in an interest-bearing account. What are the investment proportions of the risky assets in the unlevered portfolio under these conditions?

9.5     Specify the general portfolio selection problem when the investor chooses an optimal portfolio consisting of $n$ risky assets and one riskless asset. Draw a hypothetical efficient set obtained by solving this general problem.

9.6     Consider two investors who diversify between $n$ risky assets and the riskless asset. Show on a diagram that the optimal portfolio of each investor can be represented as a combination of the risk portfolio common to all and the riskless asset. This is known as the *Separation Theorem* of portfolio selection. Does it imply that all investors hold the same optimal portfolio?

9.7     Specify the general portfolio selection problem when the investor chooses a portfolio consisting solely of $n$ risky assets, without riskless asset. Draw the corresponding efficient set and show its relation to the general efficient set of Problem 9.5. Does the Separation Theorem apply in this case also? Explain.

9.8     Suppose that the riskless interest rate increases (from 4% and 6%, say) for all lenders and borrowers, while the risk and return parameters of all the feasible risky assets remain unchanged. Is such a change necessarily beneficial for all investors?

9.9     Define the concepts of optimal unlevered portfolio and optimal levered portfolio. What is the relationship between the two portfolios? Draw a diagram showing such a pair of corresponding portfolios.

9.10    (a) Draw the efficient set in an imperfect market when investors can only *lend* at a riskless interest rate $r_L$, while no borrowing is allowed.
        (b) Draw the efficient set in an imperfect market when the borrowing rate $r_B$ is greater than the lending rate $r_L$.

9.11    The mean annual rates of return and the standard deviations for three groups of risky assets—Common Stocks, Long-Term Government Bonds, and Long-Term Corporate Bonds—were calculated using 1926–1981 historical data. The *ex-post* estimates and the corresponding correlation coefficients are given below.

|  |  | Long-term Bonds | |
| --- | :---: | :---: | :---: |
| | *Common Stocks* | *Government* | *Corporate* |
| $i$ | 1 | 2 | 3 |
| Mean return (%) | 9.1 | 3.0 | 5.7 |
| Standard deviation (%) | 21.9 | 3.6 | 5.6 |

**Sample Correlation Coefficients ($\rho_{ij}$)**

| | *Common Stocks* | *Government Bonds* | *Corporate Bonds* |
| --- | :---: | :---: | :---: |
| $j$ \ $i$ | 1 | 2 | 3 |
| Common Stocks    1 | 1.00 | 0.02 | 0.16 |
| Government Bonds 2 | 0.02 | 1.00 | 0.84 |
| Corporate Bonds    3 | 0.16 | 0.84 | 1.00 |

*Source:* R. G. Ibbotson and R. A. Sinquefield, *Stocks, Bonds, Bills and Inflation*, The Financial Analysts Research Foundation (1982).

The riskless interest rate for the period is estimated at 2%.

Assume that an investor decides to invest in two risky assets out of the three, with or without the riskless asset.

(a) Determine the optimal proportions to be invested for each of the three possible pairs of risky assets. Assume there are no constraints on the investment proportions and that any of the assets may be held short.

(b) Which of the three pairs of assets will the investor choose from mean–variance considerations?

(c) Now assume that no short sales are allowed (so that all the investment proportions are always nonnegative). Answer (b) without making any additional calculations.

9.12 An investor invests \$1 of equity in a portfolio constructed from two risky assets and a riskless asset. The investment proportions are −1 for each of the two risky assets and 3 for the riskless asset. Determine the risk–return characteristics of the portfolio for the following three cases:

(a) The short-sale proceeds are available to the investor at no cost.

(b) The investor deposits the short-sale proceeds plus 100% margin with the broker, and the deposit earns the riskless interest rate.

(c) Same as (b), but the deposit earns no interest.

9.13 An investor may diversify between two risky assets, $A$ and $B$, with the following parameters:

|                     | $A$ | $B$ |
| ------------------- | --- | --- |
| Expected return (%) | 4   | 1   |
| Variance            | 4   | 1   |

The correlation coefficient between the two risky assets is +1.

(a) Determine the efficient frontier when the investor is not allowed to hold any of the assets short.

(b) Determine the efficient frontier when short sales are allowed.

(c) Give an example of a risk averter who may benefit from selling one of the assets short.

9.14 Appraise the following statement: "The exclusion of short sales does not affect risk averters: short sales are such risky investments that no risk averter will contemplate these transactions willingly."

9.15 Consider a market with $n$ risky assets, of which $m$ stocks are industrials, and the remaining $n − m$ stocks represent other branches of business. An investor wishes to construct an optimal portfolio with 10% required portfolio return subject to the constraint that no more than 20% of his funds is invested in industrials. Specify (without solving) the portfolio selection problem appropriate for this specific case.

9.16 The Lagrange function in the portfolio selection problem is usually written for \$1 of investment, so that the proportions $x_i$ represent the percentage of the initial \$1 invested in asset $i$ [or how many cents are invested in asset $i$—see Equation (9.1)]. Write out the Lagrange function when the investor has \$1000 to invest, and not \$1. What is the impact of the change in the scale of the investment on the optimal investment proportions? Assume that investment in the riskless asset is also allowed.

9.17  An investor constructs an optimal portfolio of $n$ risky assets with required portfolio return of 10%. All the $n$ assets have the same mean return (10%), the same variance (10), and all the pairs of assets have zero covariance.

(a) Determine the optimal investment proportions in each asset.
(b) How would the answer to part (a) change if the covariances of all the pairs of assets were equal to 10 (and not zero)? How would the answer change in case of negative covariances equal to $-10$ for all pairs?
(c) How would the answer to part (a) change if the asset mean returns dropped to 5%, while the other parameters remained unchanged?
(d) Answer parts (a) through (c) on the assumption that the investor may also invest in a riskless asset yielding $r = 2\%$.

9.18  Three portfolios which lie on a five-asset MV efficient frontier have the following characteristics:

|                              | Portfolio 1 | Portfolio 2            | Portfolio 3 |
|------------------------------|-------------|-----------------------|-------------|
| Mean return                  | 10%         | Between 10% and 20%   | 20%         |
| Investment proportions (%)   |             |                       |             |
| Stock 1                      | -20         | -25                   | -30         |
| Stock 2                      | 5           | ?                     | 10          |
| Stock 3                      | 15          | ?                     | 20          |
| Stock 4                      | 50          | ?                     | 60          |
| Stock 5                      | 50          | ?                     | 40          |

(a) Find the investment proportions in stocks 2–5 in Portfolio 2.
(b) Calculate the mean return of Portfolio 2.
(c) Is it possible to apply the same technique as in part (a) to determine the investment proportions if the MV efficient frontier were constructed with nonnegativity constraints (no short sales allowed)? Explain.
(*Hint:* See Table 9.7 in the body of the text).

9.19  The following tables list the expected return, variance and covariance of returns of 5 stocks traded on the NYSE.

(a) Use a computer program to solve for the optimal investment proportions for portfolio expected return levels $\mu_p = 1, 2, \ldots, 20\%$ with short sales.
(b) Find the optimum portfolios without short sales for portfolio means $\mu_p = 12, 13, 14\%$.

**Expected Return of Stocks**

| $i$ | Name of Stock                      | Expected Return |
|-----|------------------------------------|-----------------|
| 1   | General Motors Corp.               | 10.35           |
| 2   | Gould, Inc.                        | 14.08           |
| 3   | Grace W.R. & Co.                   | 14.82           |
| 4   | International Business Machines    | 10.26           |
| 5   | McGraw Edison Company              | 14.35           |

## Variance and Covariance of Return

| $i$ | $j = 1$ | $j = 2$ | $j = 3$ | $j = 4$ | $j = 5$ |
|-----|---------|---------|---------|---------|---------|
|     |         | $\sigma_{ij}$ |   |         |         |
| 1 | 987.22 | 182.83 | 303.4 | 141.87 | 616.02 |
| 2 |        | 1664.64 | 861.97 | 382.89 | 615.35 |
| 3 |        |        | 1434.89 | 555.90 | 760.62 |
| 4 |        |        |        | 668.74 | 249.66 |
| 5 |        |        |        |        | 1225.00 |

*Source:* CRSP monthly returns data tape.

## Data Set Problems

1. (a) Calculate the mean rate of return $\mu_i$, the variance $\sigma_i^2$, and the covariance $\sigma_{ij}$ for the first three funds in the Data Set. Write the Lagrange function (9.1) using these numerical values.

   (b) Using the parameters from (a) above, find the optimum investment proportions of a portfolio corresponding to risk-free interest rate $r = 3\%$ and to portfolio mean $\mu_p = 8\%$.

   (c) Find the optimum unlevered portfolio corresponding to the portfolio that you obtained in part (b) above. Calculate the mean and the standard deviation of the unlevered portfolio.

   (d) Repeat the calculations in (b) and (c) above ignoring the empirical covariances $\sigma_{ij}$ and setting $\sigma_{ij} = 0$ for all the pairs $(i, j)$. Analyze your results.

2. Using risk-free interest rates between $r = -0.15$ and $r = 0.05$ in steps of 0.01, construct the MV efficient set of portfolios consisting of the first two mutual funds in the Data Set in varying proportions. What are the proportions of the minimum-variance portfolio? Show graphically the sections of the curve corresponding to short sales of one of the two funds.

3. Use the computer program which appears in Appendix 9.1 to construct the efficient frontier from a feasible set comprising the first mutual fund from each category in the Data Set (in this way, you will construct the MV efficient set of portfolios consisting of eight funds each).

4. Use a quadratic programming package available in your computer installation to construct the MV efficient set of the same seven funds as in Problem 3 above, this time with the non-negativity constraints $x_i \geqslant 0$ for all $i$.

   Compare the results you obtained in Problems 3 and 4, and draw the two efficient frontiers on the same diagram.

5. Referring back to problem 3, find the composition of the efficient portfolio with 30% mean portfolio return, which is not included in the computer output, *without using the computer program.*

   (*Hint:* Use any two efficient portfolios generated by the computer to construct a new efficient portfolio).

## Selected References

See Chapter 10.

# 10

# The Single Index Model

In Chapters 7–9 we established the mathematical properties of the mean–variance efficient frontiers and derived a method of solving for the optimum portfolio at each riskless interest rate. When the number of risky assets is relatively large, however, the exact solution method presented in Chapter 9 becomes very time-consuming and even modern efficient computers may fail us when the number of risky assets is as large as it is on the stock exchange (with 2,000–3,000 securities to choose from). In this chapter an alternative model for constructing the optimum portfolio is discussed. The Single Index Model (SIM) reduces dramatically the amount of work involved in tracing the efficient frontier. Obviously, there is a price to pay for adopting this simple method, as it involves assumptions which do not necessarily conform to actual security price behavior. Yet the SIM assumptions may actually hold *ex-ante*, although due to sampling errors they appear to break down with actual *ex-post* data. In such cases SIM can be safely used, since decisions properly should be made on the basis of *ex-ante* data rather than historical results.

## 10.1    The Input for Constructing the SIM Optimum Portfolio

We have seen in Chapter 9 that an *efficient* diversification strategy is a set of investment proportions $x_1, x_2, \ldots, x_n$ minimizing the portfolio variance $\sigma_p^2$ (or the portfolio standard deviation $\sigma_p$) for a given portfolio expected return $ER_p$. The optimum portfolio, for a given riskless interest rate $r$, is located at the tangency point of the straight line rising from $r$ with the efficient frontier in the mean–standard deviation space. Recall that the expected return of the $n$-asset risk portfolio is given by

$$ER_p = \sum_{i=1}^{n} x_i ER_i$$

and the variance by

$$\sigma_p^2 = \sum_{i=1}^{n} x_i^2 \sigma_i^2 + 2 \sum_{i=1}^{n} \sum_{\substack{j=1 \\ j>i}}^{n} x_i x_j \sigma_{ij}$$

Here $ER_i$ and $\sigma_i^2$ are the expected rate of return and the variance of the $i$th risky asset and $\sigma_{ij}$ (with $i \neq j$) is the covariance of the rates of return on two distinct risky assets $i$ and $j$. Hence, given that there are $n$ risky assets and one riskless asset, in principle we can use the technique discussed in Chapters 7–9 to solve for $x_1, x_2, \ldots, x_n$, which is the optimum investment strategy of the unlevered risk portfolio. However, in employing this technique to find the optimum investment proportions, we face two sets of severe problems:

    (a)   estimation problems
    (b)   technical problems

We now turn to discuss these difficulties in some detail.

### 10.1.1 Estimation Problems

The basic inputs for deriving the optimum portfolio are the following:

$\mu_i$, the expected rate of return of security $i$   for $i = 1, 2, \ldots, n$
$\sigma_i^2$, the variance of rates of return of security $i$   for $i = 1, 2, \ldots, n$
$\sigma_{ij}$, the covariance of rates of return on securities $i$ and $j$   for all pairs $i \neq j$
$r$, the riskless interest rate for the relevant investment period

In practice, all these are unknown parameters and the portfolio managers have to *estimate* their values. One can estimate $r$ quite easily by looking at the interest rate on Treasury Bills or Government Bonds, say, six months from now (if indeed the portfolio manager plans his investment for a period of six months). However, the estimation of $\mu_i$, $\sigma_i^2$ and $\sigma_{ij}$ is more problematic, and the estimation method can range from a simple naïve procedure which looks at *ex-post* (historical) data (substituting the sample values $R_i$, $S_i^2$ and $S_{ij}$ for the true unknown parameters) to sophisticated statistical methods of parameter estimation. No matter which method is employed, the portfolio manager does not face a real difficulty so long as the number of risky assets $n$ is relatively small. However, for large $n$, the number of parameters which have to be estimated increases dramatically.

    For example, in the five-asset case, $n = 5$, we have to estimate five expected returns ($\mu_i$), five variances ($\sigma_i^2$), and 10 covariances $\sigma_{ij}$: there are 10 combinations of different $(i,j)$ pairs for which $\sigma_{ij}$ should be estimated. The formula for the number of all distinct pair combinations from five assets is

$$\binom{5}{2} = \frac{5!}{3!2!} = \frac{5 \times 4}{2} = 10$$

Thus, we have to estimate a total of 21 parameters (including the risk-free interest rate).

If there are $n = 100$ risky assets, we have to estimate the risk-free interest rate $r$, 100 means ($\mu_i$), 100 variances, $\sigma_i$, and 4950 covariances $\sigma_{ij}$:

$$\binom{100}{2} = \frac{100!}{98!2!} = \frac{100 \times 99}{2} = 4950$$

In general, with $n$ risky assets, the number of parameters to be estimated is the following

1 risk-free interest rate

$n$ means $\mu_i$

$n$ variances $\sigma_i$

$$\binom{n}{2} = \frac{n!}{(n-2)!2!} = \frac{n(n-1)}{2} \text{ covariances } \sigma_{ij}$$

Adding up all the parameters that we have to estimate, we get the general formula,

$$\text{Number of estimators needed} = N = (n^2 + 3n + 2)/2$$

Table 10.1 illustrates the magnitude of $N$ for various numbers of risky assets $n$, from 2 to 300.

It is obvious from Table 10.1 that for institutional investors holding even a modest portfolio of 100 risky assets, the portfolio manager's task is far from simple since he has to estimate thousands of parameters which constitute the necessary input for the selection of the optimum portfolio. Clearly it is the estimation of the covariances $\sigma_{ij}$ that mainly accounts for the large value of $N$. For example, for $n = 300$ risky assets, we have to estimate only 300 means $\mu_i$, 300 variances $\sigma_i^2$ and 1 riskless interest rate, compared with 44,850 covariances ($300 \times 299/2 = 44,850$). Indeed, the alternative model which we will discuss in this chapter circumvents the need for estimating all the $\sigma_{ij}$.

Another difficulty with estimation is that the number of historical (*ex-post*) return observations used to estimate the security parameters should exceed the number of

**Table 10.1**

| Number of Risky Assets (n) | Number of estimators needed (N) |
|:---:|:---:|
| 2 | 6 |
| 5 | 21 |
| 10 | 66 |
| 50 | 1,326 |
| 100 | 5,151 |
| 300 | 45,451 |

securities $n$. Otherwise the solution techniques described in Chapter 9 break down for numerical reasons (technically speaking, the determinant of system (9.8) consisting of the variances and covariances of $n$ securities estimated from fewer than $n$ observations vanishes and the system of equations becomes unsolvable). The record of security returns (available on University of Chicago CRSP files) goes back to January 1926, a period of 55–60 years, which automatically limits the application of the technique of Chapter 9 to less than 60 securities with estimators of annual parameters. To work with a larger number of securities, we should use estimators based on quarterly or monthly data, which may extend the allowed range of $n$ to several hundred (assuming that your computer is large and powerful enough to cope with it—see below).

### 10.1.2 Technical Difficulties

Suppose that all the parameters $r$, $\mu_i$, $\sigma_i^2$ and $\sigma_{ij}$ are known and do not need to be estimated. Even in this case (which does not exist outside the realm of textbooks), employing the procedure of Chapter 9 to derive the optimum portfolio is not a simple task. Suppose first that the portfolio manager is willing to consider both long and short positions in each asset, without restrictions. In this case, with say $n = 300$ risky assets, the portfolio manager (or preferably his computer program) has to solve 300 equations in 300 unknowns, clearly a difficult and costly task.

Since most portfolio managers, and in particular, institutional investors, wish (or are restricted) to hold long positions, the portfolio selection problem becomes even more difficult. The program has to employ a quadratic programming technique (with the non-negativity constraints $x_i \geq 0$), which is complex and time-consuming: the computer time to solve a quadratic programming problem increases rapidly with the number of risky assets under consideration.

Both the estimation problems and the technical difficulties are avoided by the Single Index Model which we discuss below.

## 10.2   The Single Index Model (SIM)

The basic idea underlying this model is that stock prices normally go up and down together with some common factor. This factor can be political (war or peace), economical (change in the real interest rate) or even international (oil crisis). Thus the rate of return on stock $i$ is related to some common index $I$ by a linear equation of the form:

$$R_{i_t} = \alpha_i + \beta_i I_t + u_{i_t} \tag{10.1}$$

where

$R_{i_t}$ is the rate of return on stock $i$ in period $t$

$\alpha_i$ is the component of the return of stock $i$ which is independent of the index $I$

$I_t$ is the value of the index for period $t$

$\beta_i$ is a measure of the average change in $R_i$ as a result of a given change in the index $I$

$u_{it}$ is a deviation of the actual observed return from the straight line $\alpha_i + \beta_i I_t$, i.e. it is the error term with variance $\sigma_{u_i}^2$

The parameters $\alpha_i$ and $\beta_i$ are constant, while $u_{it}$ and $I_t$ are random variables. Note that one can choose the index to represent the industrial production, the volume of trade on the NYSE, some index of the unemployment rate, etc. The possible diversity of index choices emphasizes that there is no consistent theoretical set of assumptions from which the SIM is derived. It is only assumed that (10.1) describes the generating process of the stock $i$ returns $R_i$, and based on this assumption (with some additional assumptions) we can derive several pragmatic rules for calculating the optimum portfolio.

The index $I$ generally used for this model is the rate of return on the market portfolio, which we denote by $R_m$. In empirical work, as a proxy for this index we may take the Standard and Poor's (S&P) index, the New York Stock Exchange index, the Fisher arithmetic average index, etc. (see Chapter 1). Ignoring the time subscript $t$ when no confusion can arise and using the return on the market portfolio $R_m$ as the index $I$, we write the rates of return on stocks $i$ and $j$ as:

$$
\begin{aligned}
R_i &= \alpha_i + \beta_i R_m + u_i \quad \text{for stock } i \\
R_j &= \alpha_j + \beta_j R_m + u_j \quad \text{for stock } j
\end{aligned}
\tag{10.2}
$$

The crucial assumption of the SIM is that for every pair of stocks $(i, j)$ the error terms are uncorrelated, i.e., $Cov(u_i, u_j) = 0$. This assumption dramatically reduces the number of parameters that have to be estimated for the portfolio construction problem. Before we turn to demonstrating this property of the SIM, let us summarize the basic assumptions of the model:

(1)  The generating process of returns is described by equation (10.1).

(2)  The error term is on the average zero for every stock $i$, i.e., $Eu_i = 0$.[1] Hence the error variance is simply given by $Eu_i^2 = E(u_i - Eu_i)^2 = \sigma_{u_i}^2$.

(3)  The error term is uncorrelated with the market portfolio,

$$
Cov(u_i, R_m) = E[u_i(R_m - ER_m)] = 0.
$$

(4)  The most crucial assumption of the model is that the error terms of stocks $i$

---

[1] This is not a restrictive assumption, since if the error term is on the average equal to some constant, $Eu_i = a_i$, we can always add $a_i$ to $\alpha_i$ in (10.1) and rewrite the model as:

$$
R_i = (\alpha_i + a_i) + \beta_i R_m + (u_i - a_i)
$$

Here the expected value of $u_i - a_i$ is zero by construction.

and $j$ are uncorrelated, thus

$$Cov\ (u_i,\ u_j) = E[(u_i - Eu_i)(u_j - Eu_j)] = Eu_iu_j = 0$$

(Recall that $Eu_i = Eu_j = 0$ by assumption 2.)

Given these assumptions and the return generating process (10.1) let us turn to calculate all the parameters that are needed in deriving the optimum portfolio.

(a)  *The expected rates of return* $\mu_i$

The expected rate of return $\mu_i$ on the security $i$ is obtained by averaging (10.1), thus

$$\mu_i = ER_i = E(\alpha_i + \beta_i R_m + u_i)$$

Hence (recalling that $Eu_i = 0$ by assumption 2)

$$\mu_i = \alpha_i + \beta_i ER_m \quad \text{for } i = 1, 2, \ldots, n \qquad (10.3)$$

since $\alpha_i$ and $\beta_i$ are constant (for the $i$th stock).

(b)  *The variances* $\sigma_i^2$

For the $i$th stock we have from (10.1) and (10.3)

$$\sigma_i^2 = E(R_i - ER_i)^2 = E(\alpha_i + \beta_i R_m + u_i - (\alpha_i + \beta_i ER_m))^2$$

Collecting and rearranging, we have:

$$\sigma_i^2 = E[\beta_i(R_m - ER_m) + u_i]^2 = \beta_i^2 E(R_m - ER_m)^2 + Eu_i^2$$
$$+ 2\beta_i E[u_i(R_m - ER_m)]$$

Employing assumption 3 and recalling that $Eu_i^2 = \sigma_{ui}^2$ (by definition) we finally have:

$$\sigma_i^2 = \beta_i^2 \sigma_m^2 + \sigma_{ui}^2 \quad \text{for } i = 1, 2, \ldots, n \qquad (10.4)$$

(c)  *The covariances* $\sigma_{ij}$

By definition, for $i \neq j$ we have:

$$\sigma_{ij} = E[(R_i - ER_i)(R_j - ER_j)]$$

Substituting for $R_i$, $R_j$, $ER_i$ and $ER_j$ from (10.2) and (10.3), we obtain,

$$\sigma_{ij} = E[(\alpha_i + \beta_i R_m + u_i - (\alpha_i + \beta_i ER_m))(\alpha_j + \beta_j R_m + u_j$$
$$- (\alpha_j + \beta_j ER_j))]$$

Collecting and rearranging terms we get:

$$\sigma_{ij} = E[(\beta_i(R_m - ER_m) + u_i)(\beta_j(R_m - ER_m) + u_j)]$$

Hence:

$$\sigma_{ij} = \beta_i \beta_j \sigma_m^2 + \beta_j E[u_i(R_m - ER_m)] + \beta_i E[u_j(R_m - ER_m)] + Eu_i u_j$$

The last three terms on the right hand side are zero (by assumptions 3 and 4) and hence for all distinct pairs $(i, j)$ the covariance of returns is given by:

$$\sigma_{ij} = \beta_i \beta_j \sigma_m^2 \quad \text{for all } i \neq j \tag{10.5}$$

Given these properties of the SIM, how many estimators do we need to construct the optimum portfolio? The basic input for constructing the optimum portfolio consists of $\mu_i$, $\sigma_i^2$ and $\sigma_{ij}$. Using (10.3), (10.4), (10.5), we conclude that we have to estimate:

$\alpha_i$ for $i = 1, 2, \ldots, n$, namely, $n$ estimators

$\beta_i$ for $i = 1, 2, \ldots, n$ namely, $n$ estimators

$\sigma_{ui}^2$ for $i = 1, 2, \ldots, n$, namely $n$ estimators

and in addition also the market parameters $ER_m$, $\sigma_m^2$ and the risk-free interest rate $r$. All together the number of estimators required is given by:

$$N = 3n + 3$$

where $n$ is the number of risky assets. Table 10.2 summarizes the required number of estimators for direct application of the mean–variance model and the number of estimators required by the SIM for different values of $n$ (the number of the risky assets). We can see from Table 10.2 that for a case where the total number of risky assets under

**Table 10.2**

| Number of Risky Assets (n) | Number of Estimators Required | |
|---|---|---|
| | Direct Application of MV Model $N = (n^2 + 3n + 2)/2$ | By SIM $N = 3n + 3$ |
| 2 | 6 | 9 |
| 3 | 10 | 12 |
| 4 | 15 | 15 |
| 5 | 21 | 18 |
| 10 | 66 | 33 |
| 50 | 1,326 | 153 |
| 100 | 5,151 | 303 |
| 300 | 45,451 | 903 |

consideration is relatively small (e.g., 4–5 stocks), there is no advantage in using the SIM. Indeed, for very small portfolios (less than 4 stocks), the SIM actually requires more estimators (see the case for $n = 2$ and $n = 3$ in Table 10.2). However, since in real life the number of available risky assets is large, the gain provided by the SIM is tremendous. For example, for $n = 100$ we have to estimate only 303 parameters in comparison with 5151 parameters for direct application of the MV model.

## 10.3    Estimating the Parameters in Practice

The most common way to estimate the various parameters is by using the *ex-post* (historical) rates of return. For example, given the annual rates of return on security $i$ and on the market portfolio (e.g., the Fisher Index) in past years we run the following time series regression:

$$R_{it} = a_i + b_i R_{mt} + e_{it}$$

where

$R_{it}$  is the rate of return on security $i$ in period $t$

$R_{mt}$  is the rate of return on the market portfolio in period $t$

$a_i$  is the vertical intercept of the regression line

$b_i$  is the slope of the regression line

$e_{it}$  is the residual, or the deviation about the regression line (the analog of the error term $u_i$ in (10.1)).

Thus, comparing the regression equation with (10.1), we see that $a_i$ is the estimate of $\alpha_i$, $b_i$ is the estimate of $\beta_i$, the residual variance $\sigma_{e_i}^2$ is the estimate of $\sigma_{u_i}^2$. Also $\bar{R}_m$ and $\sigma_m^2$ calculated from historical data are the estimates of the mean return and the variance of returns on the market portfolio.[2]

EXAMPLE

Using actual data for Union Carbide and IBM stock for the years 1971–1980 we demonstrate with the aid of the simple regression technique how to estimate $\alpha_i$, $\beta_i$, $\sigma_{u_i}^2$. Moreover we also measure the term $\Sigma e_i e_j$ in our sample as an estimate of the covariance of the error terms, which, as the reader will recall, is assumed to be zero by assumption 4 of the SIM. The purpose of this example is to demonstrate numerically and graphically all the concepts which we have so far introduced in this chapter.

Table 10.3 sets out the rates of return on the market portfolio (as represented by

---

[2] Note that in the sample, the ordinary least square regression guarantees that $Cov(e_i, R_m) = 0$ and there is no need to make assumption 3, as required in the population.

## Table 10.3

| | Rates of Return (%) | | | Regression Worksheet | | | | | |
| --- | --- | --- | --- | --- | --- | --- | --- | --- | --- |
| Year, t | Market Index $R_m$ | Union Carbide $R_{UK}$ | IBM $R_{IBM}$ | $R_m^2$ | $R_{UK}^2$ | $R_{IBM}^2$ | $R_{UK}R_m$ | $R_{IBM}R_m$ | $R_{UK}R_{IBM}$ |
| 1971 | 19.48 | 10.80 | 7.64 | 379.47 | 116.64 | 58.37 | 210.38 | 148.83 | 82.51 |
| 1972 | 8.45 | 23.60 | 21.12 | 71.40 | 556.96 | 446.05 | 199.42 | 178.46 | 498.43 |
| 1973 | −29.31 | −28.26 | −22.14 | 859.08 | 798.63 | 490.18 | 828.30 | 648.92 | 625.68 |
| 1974 | −26.53 | 28.07 | −30.01 | 703.84 | 787.92 | 900.60 | −744.70 | 796.17 | −842.38 |
| 1975 | 61.90 | 54.00 | 37.68 | 3,831.61 | 2,916.00 | 1,419.78 | 3,342.60 | 2,332.39 | 2,034.72 |
| 1976 | 45.49 | 5.09 | 28.27 | 2,069.34 | 25.91 | 799.19 | 231.54 | 1,286.00 | 143.89 |
| 1977 | 9.50 | −29.80 | 1.76 | 90.25 | 888.04 | 3.10 | −283.10 | 16.72 | −52.45 |
| 1978 | 14.02 | −10.89 | 13.93 | 196.56 | 118.59 | 194.04 | −152.68 | 195.30 | −151.70 |
| 1979 | 35.31 | 33.14 | −9.50 | 1,246.80 | 1,098.26 | 90.25 | 1,170.17 | −335.45 | −314.83 |
| 1980 | 30.99 | 28.58 | 11.34 | 960.38 | 816.82 | 128.60 | 885.69 | 351.43 | 324.10 |
| Total Σ | 169.30 | 114.33 | 60.09 | 10,408.73 | 8,123.77 | 4,530.17 | 5,687.62 | 5,618.77 | 2,347.97 |
| Average Rate of Return | 16.930 | 11.433 | 6.009 | | | | | | |

the Fisher Index) and on the stock of Union Carbide (UK) and IBM for the 10 years 1971–1980. The worksheet part of the table develops the various squares and cross products that we need for the linear regression model.[3]

The standard expressions for the slope $b_i$ of the regression line of stock $i$ and for the vertical intercept $a_i$ are the following:

$$\textit{Slope:} \quad b_i = \frac{\sum\limits_{t=1}^{n} (R_{it} - \bar{R}_i)(R_{mt} - \bar{R}_m)}{\sum\limits_{t=1}^{n} (R_{mt} - \bar{R}_m)^2} = \frac{\sum\limits_{t=1}^{n} R_{it}R_{mt} - n\bar{R}_i\bar{R}_m}{\sum\limits_{t=1}^{n} R_{mt}^2 - n\bar{R}_m^2}$$

$$\textit{Intercept:} \quad a_i = \bar{R}_i - b_i\bar{R}_m$$

Using the cross sums $\sum_{t=1}^{10} R_{UK_t}R_{mt}$, $\sum_{t=1}^{10} R_{IBM_t}R_{mt}$, the sum of squares $\sum_{t=1}^{10} R_{mt}^2$ and the average rates of return $\bar{R}_{UK}$, $\bar{R}_{IBM}$, $\bar{R}_m$ from Table 10.3, we estimate the slope and the vertical intercept for Union Carbide (UK) and IBM:

*Union Carbide*

$$b_{UK} = \frac{5687.62 - 10 \times 11.433 \times 16.930}{10,408.73 - 10 \times (16.930)^2} = \frac{3752.01}{7542.48} = 0.4975$$

$$a_{UK} = 11.433 - 0.4975 \times 16.930 = 3.010$$

*IBM*

$$b_{IBM} = \frac{5618.77 - 10 \times 6.009 \times 16.930}{10,408.73 - 10 \times (16.930)^2} = \frac{4601.45}{7542.48} = 0.6101$$

$$a_{IBM} = 6.009 - 0.6101 \times 16.930 = -4.320$$

The rate of return on Union Carbide stock is thus related to the rate of return on the market index by the relation:

$$R_{UK} = 3.010 + 0.4975R_m + e_{UK}$$

The corresponding relation for IBM is:

$$R_{IBM} = -4.320 + 0.6101R_m + e_{IBM}$$

Figure 10.1 plots the scattergram of the observed return rates on UK and IBM

---

[3] A simple computer program to run a linear regression estimating the parameters $a_i$ and $b_i$ is given in Appendix 12.1.

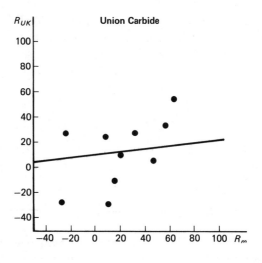

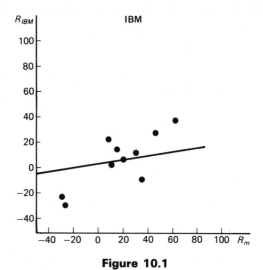

**Figure 10.1**

stock and the corresponding estimated regression lines:

$$\hat{R}_{UK} = 3.010 + 0.4975R_m$$

$$\hat{R}_{IBM} = -4.320 + 0.6101R_m$$

(10.6)

Here $\hat{R}_i$ is a point on the estimated regression line corresponding to a given value of $R_m$.

The observations are scattered around the regression lines and for each point we can calculate the deviations $e_{it}$ as the difference between the observed rate of return $R_{it}$ and the regression estimate $\hat{R}_{it}$:

$$e_{it} = R_{it} - \hat{R}_{it} = R_{it} - (a_i + b_i R_{mt})$$

Table 10.4 lists the return estimates $\hat{R}_{UK}$, $\hat{R}_{IBM}$ from (10.6), the actual observations $R_{UK}$, $R_{IBM}$ from Table 10.3 and the corresponding deviations

$$e_{UK_t} = R_{UK_t} - \hat{R}_{UK_t} \quad \text{and} \quad e_{IBM_t} = R_{IBM_t} - \hat{R}_{IBM_t}$$

The average of these deviation terms is indeed zero, as assumed (this is a property of linear regression). The cross-product column $e_{UK_t} \cdot e_{IBM_t}$ makes it possible to calculate the covariance of the error terms for UK and IBM:

$$Cov\,(e_{UK}, e_{IBM}) = \frac{1}{10} \sum_{t=1}^{10} (e_{UK_t} - \bar{e}_{UK})(e_{IBM_t} - \bar{e}_{IBM})$$

$$= \frac{1}{10} \sum_{t=1}^{10} (e_{UK_t} - 0)(e_{IBM_t} - 0) = \frac{1}{10} \sum_{t=1}^{10} e_{UK_t} e_{IBM_t} = \frac{-628.07}{10} = -62.81$$

This is certainly not zero, so that SIM's most crucial assumption of uncorrelated error terms (assumption 4 above) does not hold—at least not for Union Carbide and IBM stocks when we plug *ex-post* (historical) observations into the model.

Obviously it may be that in the *population* $Cov\,(u_i, u_j) = 0$ as required and the error covariance does not vanish in the *sample* only due to sampling errors. In this case SIM can be safely used even though in the *sample* $Cov\,(e_i, e_j) \neq 0$ for some or all pairs of securities.[4]

Let us now check how the other SIM relations (10.3), (10.4), (10.5) perform compared to standard statistical estimation.

The linear regression properties ensure that the mean rate of return estimated from (10.3) is consistent with ordinary statistical estimation. Indeed, plugging the estimators $a_i$ and $b_i$ for $\alpha_i$ and $\beta_i$ in (10.3) and taking $\bar{R}_m = 16.930$ from Table 10.3 as the estimator of $ER_m$, we obtain:

$$\bar{R}_{UK} = a_{UK} + b_{UK}\bar{R}_m = 3.010 + 0.4975 \times 16.930 = 11.433$$
$$\bar{R}_{IBM} = a_{IBM} + b_{IBM}\bar{R}_m = -4.320 + 0.6101 \times 16.930 = 6.009$$

These results are identical to the average rates of return at the bottom of Table 10.3.

To derive the SIM estimates of the variances $\sigma^2_{UK}$, $\sigma^2_{IBM}$ and the covariance $\sigma_{UK,IBM}$ from (10.4) and (10.5) we need first an estimate of the market portfolio variance:

$$\sigma^2_m = \frac{1}{10} \sum_{i=1}^{10} (R_{m_t} - \bar{R}_m)^2 = \frac{1}{10} \sum_{t=1}^{10} R^2_{m_t} - \bar{R}^2_m$$

Plugging in from Table 10.3, $\sum_{t=1}^{10} R^2_{m_t} = 10,408.73$ and $\bar{R}_m = 16.930$ we obtain:

$$\sigma^2_m = \frac{10,408.73}{10} - (16.930)^2 = 754.25$$

---

[4] Note that if $R_m$ is used as the index and the population consists of *all* the securities included in $R_m$ then by definition $Cov(u_i, u_j) = 0$ cannot hold for *all* pairs $i, j$.

**Table 10.4**

| Year | Union Carbide | | | | IBM | | | | Cross-products |
| t | Observed $R_{UK}$ | Estimated $\hat{R}_{UK}$ | $e_{UK} = R_{UK} - \hat{R}_{UK}$ | $e_{UK}^2$ | Observed $R_{IBM}$ | Estimated $\hat{R}_{IBM}$ | $e_{IBM} = R_{IBM} - \hat{R}_{IBM}$ | $e_{IBM}^2$ | $e_{UK} e_{IBM}$ |
|------|------|------|------|------|------|------|------|------|------|
| 1971 | 10.80 | 12.70 | −1.90 | 3.61 | 7.64 | 7.56 | 0.08 | 0.01 | −0.15 |
| 1972 | 23.60 | 7.21 | 16.39 | 268.63 | 21.12 | 0.84 | 20.28 | 411.28 | 332.39 |
| 1973 | −28.26 | −11.57 | −16.69 | 278.56 | −22.14 | −22.20 | 0.06 | 0.00 | −1.00 |
| 1974 | 28.07 | −10.19 | 38.26 | 1463.83 | −30.01 | −20.50 | −9.51 | 90.44 | −363.85 |
| 1975 | 54.00 | 33.80 | 20.20 | 408.04 | 37.68 | 33.44 | 4.24 | 17.98 | 85.65 |
| 1976 | 5.09 | 25.64 | −20.55 | 422.30 | 28.27 | 23.43 | 4.84 | 23.43 | −99.46 |
| 1977 | −29.80 | 7.74 | −37.54 | 1409.25 | 1.76 | 1.48 | 0.28 | 0.08 | −10.51 |
| 1978 | −10.89 | 9.99 | −20.88 | 435.97 | 13.93 | 4.23 | 9.70 | 94.09 | −202.54 |
| 1979 | 33.14 | 20.58 | 12.56 | 157.75 | −9.50 | 17.22 | −26.72 | 713.96 | −335.60 |
| 1980 | 28.58 | 18.43 | 10.15 | 103.02 | 11.34 | 14.59 | −3.25 | 10.56 | −32.99 |
| **Total** $\Sigma$ | 114.33 | 114.33 | 0.00 | 4950.96 | 60.09 | 60.09 | 0.00 | 1361.83 | −628.07 |

Thus for the covariance from (10.5) we get, using the regression coefficient estimates for the respective betas, $\sigma_{UK,IBM} = b_{UK}b_{IBM}\sigma_m^2 = 0.4975 \times 0.6101 \times 754.25 = 228.93$. An ordinary statistical estimate of the covariance can be obtained using the last column in Table 10.3, which gives the cross-products $R_{UK_t}R_{IBM_t}$. Thus:

$$\sigma_{UK,IBM} = \frac{1}{10}\sum_{t=1}^{10} R_{UK_t}R_{IBM_t} - \bar{R}_{UK}\bar{R}_{IBM}$$

$$= \frac{2347.97}{10} - 11.433 \times 6.009 = 166.10$$

The result is distinctly different from the SIM estimator (which is 228.93) of the covariance: this is not surprising since in the derivation of (10.5) we essentially relied on the assumption of uncorrelated error terms, which as we have seen above does not hold.

To estimate the variances, we use (10.4) and plug in

$$\sigma_{ei}^2 = \frac{1}{10}\sum_{t=1}^{10} e_{i_t}^2$$

for $\sigma_{u_i}^2$ from the corresponding column in Table 10.4. Thus:

$$\sigma_{UK}^2 = b_{UK}^2\sigma_m^2 + \sigma_{e_{UK}}^2 = (0.4975)^2 \times 754.25 + \frac{4950.96}{10} = 681.78$$

$$\sigma_{IBM}^2 = b_{IBM}^2\sigma_m^2 + \sigma_{e_{IBM}}^2 = (0.6101)^2 \times 754.25 + \frac{1361.83}{10} = 416.93$$

Standard estimation using the corresponding sums of squares from Table 10.3 gives:

$$\sigma_{UK}^2 = \frac{1}{10}\sum_{t=1}^{10} (R_{UK_t} - \bar{R}_{UK})^2 = \frac{1}{10}\sum_{t=1}^{10} R_{UK_t}^2 - \bar{R}_{UK}^2 = \frac{8123.77}{10} - (11.433)^2 = 681.66$$

$$\sigma_{IBM}^2 = \frac{1}{10}\sum_{t=1}^{10} (R_{IBM_t} - \bar{R}_{IBM})^2 = \frac{1}{10}\sum_{t=1}^{10} R_{IBM_t}^2 - \bar{R}_{IBM}^2 = \frac{4530.17}{10} - (6.009)^2 = 416.91$$

The results are identical, apart from slight rounding errors. Recall that the SIM formula for the variance (10.4) only uses assumption 3 (the error term is uncorrelated with the market rates of return), which is much more realistic than the assumption of uncorrelated error terms (assumption 4) used to derive the covariance expression (10.5). Moreover, it is true by definition in the sample when linear regression is used.

We thus see that the SIM assumptions have a very significant impact only on the covariance estimates $\sigma_{ij}$: the Single Index Model provides a convenient shortcut for the estimation of the covariances at the cost of making these estimates less accurate.

**10.4     Employing the SIM to Construct the Optimum Portfolio**

As we saw in Chapter 9, there are two main types of efficient frontiers that are considered in portfolio analysis: one is the efficient frontier of portfolios in which both long and short positions are allowed (the proportions $x_i$ may be both positive and negative) while the other consists of efficient portfolios without short positions (derived subject to nonnegativity constraints $x_i \geq 0$ for all $i$). Our analysis of the SIM correspondingly starts with a derivation of the optimum portfolio when short sales are allowed and then continues to the derivation of the optimum portfolio without short sales.

### 10.4.1   Optimum Portfolio with Short Sales

When short sales are allowed, the optimum portfolio with $n$ risky assets is obtained from a system of $n$ equations in $n$ unknowns (see Chapter 9). Although the system is solvable (unless two or more equations are linearly dependent—which usually does not happen as the security returns are never perfectly correlated), hand calculations become very cumbersome even for a relatively small $n$ and we have to resort to the computer.

One of the advantages of the Single Index Model is that the construction of the optimal portfolio requires only simple calculations. It is shown in Appendix 10.1 that under the SIM assumptions the optimal investment proportions $y_1, y_2, \ldots, y_n$ in $n$ risky assets are given by:

$$y_i = \frac{\beta_i}{\sigma_{ei}^2} [(R/V)_i - C^*] \quad (i = 1, 2, \ldots, n) \tag{10.7}$$

where $(R/V)_i = (\mu_i - r)/\beta_i$ is the $i$th security's reward-to-volatility ratio (also see Chapter 15) and:

$$C^* = \sigma_m^2 \sum_{j=1}^{n} \frac{\mu_j - r}{\sigma_{ej}^2} \beta_j \bigg/ \left( 1 + \sigma_m^2 \sum_{j=1}^{n} \frac{\beta_j^2}{\sigma_{ej}^2} \right) \tag{10.8}$$

The standardized optimal proportions $z_i$ are calculated as

$$z_i = y_i \bigg/ \sum_{i=1}^{n} y_i$$

so that they add up to 1 as required:

$$\sum_{i=1}^{n} z_i = \sum_{i=1}^{n} y_i \bigg/ \sum_{i=1}^{n} y_i = 1$$

Let us illustrate the construction of the optimal portfolio by applying the Single Index Model to five stocks traded on the New York Stock Exchange.

EXAMPLE

The left-hand side of Table 10.5 lists the *ex-post* estimates of the parameters of the stock of five large corporations based on historical data for the 25-year period 1956–1980. The beta of each stock (column 2) was determined by regressing the stock returns on the S&P500 Index; $\sigma^2_{ei}$ (column 3) is the residual variance of the observations about the estimated regression line. The second part of the table is a SIM worksheet developing the various quantities needed to calculate the optimum proportions by the Single Index Model. The reward-to-volatility ratio $(R/V)_i = (\mu_i - r)/\beta_i$ (column 4) was calculated for $r = 6\%$ (this figure was selected arbitrarily for purposes of demonstration, ensuring that it was less than the lowest mean rate of return in the sample). The remaining columns list the ratio $\beta_i/\sigma^2_{ei}$ (column 5) which together with $(R/V)_i$ enters formula (10.7) for the optimal investment proportions, as well as the factors $\beta^2_i/\sigma^2_{ei}$ needed to calculate the sums that enter the definition of $C^*$ in (10.8).

Summing columns 6 and 7 in Table 10.5, we calculate $C^*$ as follows:

$$C^* = \frac{\sigma^2_m \times \Sigma\,(\text{column 7})}{1 + \sigma^2_m \times \Sigma\,(\text{column 6})} = \frac{\Sigma\,(\text{column 7})}{1/\sigma^2_m + \Sigma\,(\text{column 6})}$$

The variance of the S&P500 Index used as a market portfolio proxy was $\sigma^2_m = 136.3920$ in the period 1956–1980. We thus have:

$$C^* = \frac{0.015323}{1/136.3920 + 0.003628} = 1.3981$$

The investment proportions are now calculated using formula (10.7) for $y_i$ and standardizing the results to obtain $z_i = y_i/\Sigma^n_{i=1}\,y_i$ that add up to 1. From (10.7) we have:

$$
\begin{aligned}
y_{ACD} &= 0.001211 \times (2.2054 - 1.3981) &&= 0.000978 \\
y_{BGH} &= 0.000603 \times (10.8814 - 1.3981) &&= 0.005718 \\
y_{CWE} &= 0.001435 \times (3.1856 - 1.3981) &&= 0.002565 \\
y_{GF} &= 0.000854 \times (9.3983 - 1.3981) &&= 0.006832 \\
y_{RS} &= 0.001083 \times (0.9875 - 1.3981) &&= -0.000445
\end{aligned}
$$

All the five $y_i$ add up to $\Sigma^5_{i=1}\,y_i = 0.015648$ and we finally get for the optimal investment proportions:

$$
\begin{aligned}
z_{ACD} &= 0.000978/0.015648 = 0.0625 \\
z_{BGH} &= 0.005718/0.015648 = 0.3654 \\
z_{CWE} &= 0.002565/0.015648 = 0.1639 \\
z_{GF} &= 0.006832/0.015648 = 0.4366 \\
z_{RS} &= -0.000445/0.015648 = -0.0284
\end{aligned}
$$

$$\sum_{i=1}^{5} z_i = 1.0000$$

**Table 10.5**

| Stock | | $\mu_i$ (1) | $\beta_i$ (2) | $\sigma_{e_i}^2$ (3) | $(R/V)_i =$ $(\mu_i - 6)/\beta_i$ (4) | $\beta_i/\sigma_{e_i}^2$ (5) | $\beta_i^2/\sigma_{e_i}^2$ (6) | $(\mu_i - 6)\beta_i/\sigma_{e_i}^2$ (7) |
|---|---|---|---|---|---|---|---|---|
| Allied Chemical | ACD | 8.1988 | 0.9970 | 823.1363 | 2.2054 | 0.001211 | 0.001208 | 0.002663 |
| Burroughs Corp. | BGH | 16.5256 | 0.9673 | 1604.2438 | 10.8814 | 0.000603 | 0.000583 | 0.006347 |
| Commonwealth Edison | CWE | 7.3408 | 0.4209 | 293.2536 | 3.1856 | 0.001435 | 0.000604 | 0.001924 |
| General Foods | GF | 10.1484 | 0.4414 | 516.6613 | 9.3983 | 0.000854 | 0.000377 | 0.003544 |
| Republic Steel | RS | 6.7804 | 0.7903 | 729.7117 | 0.9875 | 0.001083 | 0.000856 | 0.000845 |
| **Totals** | | | | | | $\Sigma$ | 0.003628 | 0.015323 |

The results indicate that the optimal portfolio for $r = 6\%$ consists of four stocks held long (ACD, BGH, CWE, GF) and one stock, RS, held short in a proportion of 2.84%. This result is qualitatively obvious from a comparison of the value of $C^*$ with the values of $(R/V)_i$ in column 4 of Table 10.5: $(R/V)_{RS} = 0.9875 < C^* = 1.3987$, while all the other $(R/V)_i$ are greater than $C^*$. By (10.7) this means that RS is the only stock included in a negative proportion in the optimal portfolio: it is held short while all the other stocks with $y_i > 0$ and $z_i > 0$ are held long.

### 10.4.2 The SIM Optimum Portfolio versus the Exact Optimum Portfolio

By employing the SIM, we obtained the optimal investment proportions by very simple and quick calculations. The attractive simplicity of the calculations is attained, however, only if the Single Index Model is assumed to hold. Thus, in effect we assume that $\sigma_{ij} = \beta_i \beta_j \sigma_m^2$ or equivalently that $Cov(e_i, e_j) = 0$, which does not necessarily hold in reality (indeed, we have seen above that for a sample of stocks the covariance of the residual terms is significantly different from zero and the main SIM assumption does not hold). Thus, the proportions obtained by using the SIM technique are only *approximations* to the true optimal proportions, and the quality of the approximation depends on how closely the SIM assumptions approximate to real stock price behavior.

To establish the price that we pay in terms of lost opportunity for the simplicity of the SIM technique, we calculated the optimal investment proportions for a portfolio of 15 NYSE stocks, once assuming that the SIM holds and then again by the exact and lengthy technique of Chapter 9. Table 10.6 lists the SIM parameters of the 15 stocks estimated on the basis of 1956–1980 historical data and develops the worksheet for the calculation of $C^*$ from (10.8) and $y_i$ from (10.7). In these calculations we used $r = 4\%$ as an estimate of the risk-free interest rate and $\sigma_m^2 = 136.3920$ as before. Table 10.7 lists the optimal investment proportions $z_i = y_i / \Sigma_{i=1}^{15} y_i$ for the 15 stocks obtained by the SIM technique and the corresponding proportions of the optimal portfolio for $r = 4\%$ obtained by the exact method of Chapter 9. There is very little in common between the two portfolios: the SIM optimal portfolio for $r = 4\%$ consists of 11 stocks held long and only 4 stocks held short, while the exact optimal portfolio for $r = 4\%$ consists of 8 long positions and 7 short positions. Moreover, not all the stocks shorted in the SIM portfolio are also shorted in the exact portfolio: ACD is sold short in the SIM portfolio ($-3.42\%$) and is held long in the exact portfolio (10.79%).

Another feature of the exact optimal portfolio is that it goes much more heavily into short positions than the SIM portfolio does (thus the exact optimal proportion of Union Carbide stock, UK, is nearly 170% of the originally available funds, whereas the SIM portfolio contains less than 2% of this stock in a short position). As a result, the exact portfolio is much more "aggressively leveraged" by short sales, reaching a mean return $ER_p = 41.86\%$ (with standard deviation $\sigma_p = 42.67\%$) as compared to a mere $ER_p = 13.54\%$ (with standard deviation $\sigma_p = 19.60\%$) for the SIM portfolio. The fact that the SIM portfolio attains a lower mean return at a lower level of risk is not to be construed as indicating that both the exact and the SIM portfolios are MV efficient: efficiency in the portfolio context is measured relative to the MV efficient frontier. The

**Table 10.6**

| Stock | $\mu_i$ (1) | $\beta_i$ (2) | $\sigma^2_{e_i}$ (3) | $(R/V)_i =$ $(\mu_i - 4)/\beta_i$ (4) | $\beta_i/\sigma^2_{e_i}$ (5) | $\beta_i^2/\sigma^2_{e_i}$ (6) | $\dfrac{(\mu_i - 4)\cdot\beta_i}{\sigma^2_{e_i}}$ (7) | $(R/V)_i - C^*$ (8) | $y_i$ (9) |
|---|---|---|---|---|---|---|---|---|---|
| ACD | 8.1988 | 0.9970 | 823.1363 | 4.2114 | 0.001211 | 0.001208 | 0.005086 | -1.4397 | -0.001743 |
| DOW | 11.3664 | 0.9935 | 653.9111 | 7.4146 | 0.001519 | 0.001509 | 0.011192 | 1.7635 | 0.002679 |
| UK | 6.2980 | 0.5194 | 473.0325 | 4.4243 | 0.001098 | 0.000570 | 0.002523 | -1.2268 | -0.001347 |
| CVX | 8.0144 | 0.4106 | 272.5441 | 9.7769 | 0.001507 | 0.000619 | 0.006048 | 4.1258 | 0.006218 |
| CWE | 7.3408 | 0.4209 | 293.2536 | 7.9373 | 0.001435 | 0.000604 | 0.004795 | 2.2862 | 0.003281 |
| FPL | 10.7028 | 0.7457 | 557.0058 | 8.9886 | 0.001339 | 0.000998 | 0.008973 | 3.3375 | 0.004469 |
| IK | 11.4648 | 0.8271 | 626.0060 | 9.0253 | 0.001321 | 0.001093 | 0.009863 | 3.3742 | 0.004457 |
| RS | 6.7804 | 0.7903 | 729.7117 | 3.5182 | 0.001083 | 0.000856 | 0.003011 | -2.1329 | -0.002310 |
| X | 7.8576 | 0.8626 | 1031.6768 | 4.4721 | 0.000836 | 0.000721 | 0.003225 | -1.1790 | -0.000986 |
| BGH | 16.5256 | 0.9673 | 1604.2438 | 12.9490 | 0.000603 | 0.000583 | 0.007552 | 7.2979 | 0.004401 |
| IBM | 18.2552 | 1.1840 | 701.5742 | 12.0399 | 0.001688 | 0.001998 | 0.024058 | 6.3888 | 0.010784 |
| NCR | 15.8340 | 1.6504 | 1467.4181 | 7.1704 | 0.001125 | 0.001856 | 0.013310 | 1.5193 | 0.001709 |
| GF | 10.1484 | 0.4414 | 516.6613 | 13.9293 | 0.000854 | 0.000377 | 0.005253 | 8.2782 | 0.007070 |
| NAB | 11.9056 | 0.7296 | 579.4608 | 10.8355 | 0.001259 | 0.000919 | 0.009954 | 5.1844 | 0.006527 |
| OAT | 15.0660 | 0.9063 | 1034.4764 | 12.2101 | 0.000876 | 0.000794 | 0.009695 | 6.5590 | 0.005746 |
| **Total** | | | | | $\Sigma$ | 0.014705 | 0.124532 | | 0.050955 |

Note:
$$C^* = \frac{\Sigma\,(\text{column }7)}{1/\sigma_m^2 + \Sigma\,(\text{column }6)} = \frac{0.124532}{0.007332 + 0.014705} = 5.6511$$

**Table 10.7**

| Stock | | Optimal Investment Proportions $(z_i)$ for $r = 4\%$ | |
|---|---|---|---|
| | | SIM | Exact Method (Ch. 9) |
| Allied Chemical | ACD | -3.42 | 10.79 |
| Dow Chemical | DOW | 5.26 | 89.45 |
| Union Carbide | UK | -2.64 | -168.28 |
| Cleveland Electric Illum. | CVX | 12.20 | 70.41 |
| Commonwealth Edison | CWE | 6.44 | -246.19 |
| Florida Power & Light | FPL | 8.77 | -8.73 |
| Interlake | IK | 8.75 | 170.33 |
| Republic Steel | RS | -4.53 | -81.83 |
| US Steel | X | -1.94 | -37.63 |
| Burroughs Corp. | BGH | 8.64 | -2.65 |
| IBM | IBM | 21.16 | 176.35 |
| NCR | NCR | 3.35 | -49.19 |
| General Foods | GF | 13.88 | 94.27 |
| Nabisco | NAB | 12.81 | 72.12 |
| Quaker Oats | OAT | 11.28 | 10.79 |
| **Total** | | 100.00 | 100.00 |
| *Portfolio Mean* | | 13.54 | 41.86 |
| *Portfolio Standard Deviation* | | 19.60 | 42.67 |

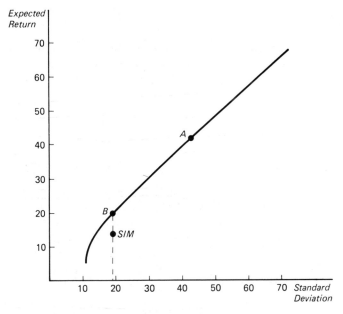

**Figure 10.2**

efficient frontier constructed by the exact method of Chapter 9 is shown in Figure 10.2. Point $A$ is the exact optimal portfolio $ER_p^{(A)} = 41.86\%$, $\sigma_p^{(A)} = 42.67\%$ for $r = 4\%$. SIM is the portfolio obtained by the SIM technique for the same riskless interest rate, $r = 4\%$. It lies *inside* the MV efficient frontier and is not at all efficient! Indeed, portfolio $B$ on the efficient frontier has the same standard deviation as the SIM portfolio and yet its mean return is substantially higher, $ER_p^{(B)} = 20.40\%$. There is thus a definite price to pay for the computational simplicity of the Single Index Model: the quick calculations produce a portfolio that is not necessarily MV efficient and the investor is forced into a suboptimal strategy.

### 10.4.3  Optimum Portfolio without Short Sales

When short sales are not allowed we have to solve the same basic set of $n$ equations with $n$ unknowns but under the additional constraint that the investment proportions are nonnegative. The solution is not trivial and a quadratic programming technique is called for (see Chapter 9). The SIM again greatly simplifies the work involved in tracing the efficient frontier when short sales are not allowed. In principle, we use a similar technique to the one used in the previous case, but a new quantity $C^*$ has to be introduced. We explain and illustrate how to find the optimum portfolio in this framework while the mathematical proof of validity of this procedure is given in Appendix 10.2. The optimum portfolio is constructed by the following sequence of steps:

(a)  Rank the securities in the order of decreasing reward-to-volatility ratios

$$(R/V)_i = \frac{\mu_i - r}{\beta_i}$$

(so that $i = 1$ now corresponds to the stock with the highest $(R/V)$ and $i = n$ to the stock with the lowest $(R/V)$).

(b)  For each security $i$, calculate the value of $C_i$, where $C_i$ is given by:

$$C_i = \frac{\sigma_m^2 \sum\limits_{j=1}^{i} (\mu_j - r)\beta_j/\sigma_{ej}^2}{1 + \sigma_m^2 \sum\limits_{j=1}^{i} (\beta_j^2/\sigma_{ej}^2)} \qquad (10.9)$$

(compare this definition of $C_i$ with the previous $C^*$ in (10.8) above).
  For example for $i = 1$, the calculation of $C_1$ includes only the one stock with the highest $(R/V)$, for $i = 2$ we include the two stocks with the top $(R/V)$s, and for $i = n$ we include all the stock in the calculation of $C_n$.

(c)  Compare the $(R/V)_i$ column with the corresponding $C_i$ column. Find the value $C_i$ such that all securities used to calculate it have $(R/V)_i$ greater than $C_i$ and all securities not used to calculate $C_i$ have $(R/V)_i$ smaller than $C_i$. The value $C_i$ which has this property is then denoted by $C^*$.

(d)   All stocks with $(R/V)_i < C^*$ appear in the given portfolio with zero proportions. All stocks with $(R/V)_i > C^*$ appear in positive proportions.

(e)   The optimum proportion of the $i$th risky asset with $(R/V)_i > C^*$ is given by:

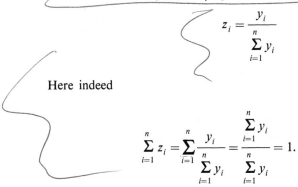

$$y_i = \frac{\beta_i}{\sigma_{ei}^2} \left( \frac{\mu_i - r}{\beta_i} - C^* \right) = \frac{\beta_i}{\sigma_{ei}^2} [(R/V)_i - C^*] \qquad (10.10)$$

(f)   In order to satisfy the constraint $\sum_{i=1}^{n} z_i = 1$, calculate the optimum investment in the $i$th risky asset $z_i$ by the following standardization:

$$z_i = \frac{y_i}{\sum\limits_{i=1}^{n} y_i}$$

Here indeed

$$\sum_{i=1}^{n} z_i = \sum_{i=1}^{n} \frac{y_i}{\sum\limits_{i=1}^{n} y_i} = \frac{\sum\limits_{i=1}^{n} y_i}{\sum\limits_{i=1}^{n} y_i} = 1.$$

This procedure is valid as long as the betas of all risky assets are non-negative.
Since it is exceedingly rare to find a risky asset with a negative beta, the procedure
almost always holds (see Appendix 10.2).

Let us illustrate how to find the optimum portfolio when short sales are not allowed
with the same stocks used above. We also show the optimal quadratic-programming
solution so that one can compare the changes in the investment strategy caused by the
SIM assumption.

EXAMPLE

The basic SIM parameters and the worksheet for 15 NYSE stocks were presented
in Table 10.6, in connection with the construction of the optimal portfolio with short
sales allowed. We now recast in Table 10.8 the data of Table 10.6 in a format that fits
the SIM algorithm for the construction of the optimal portfolio without short sales.

1.  Rank the 15 securities in the order of their decreasing $(R/V)_i$ values (for
$r = 4\%$).
2.  For each $i$, add up all the terms in column 6 and column 7 of Table 10.6 up to
that $i$ (inclusive) to obtain the moving sums

$$\sum_{j=1}^{i} (\beta_j^2 / \sigma_{ej}^2) \quad \text{and} \quad \sum_{j=1}^{i} (\mu_i - r) \beta_j / \sigma_{ej}^2$$

Enter these sums in columns 2 and 3 of Table 10.8.

**Table 10.8**

| $i$ | Stock | $(R/V)_i$ (1) | $\sum_{j=1}^{i} \beta_j^2/\sigma_{ej}^2$ (2) | $\sum_{j=1}^{i} (\mu_j - 4)\dfrac{\beta_j}{\sigma_{ej}^2}$ (3) | $C_i$ (4) | $(R/V)_i - C^*$ (5) | $y_i$ (6) |
|---|---|---|---|---|---|---|---|
| 1 | GF | 13.9293 | 0.000377 | 0.005253 | 0.6814 | 8.0041 | 0.006836 |
| 2 | BGH | 12.9490 | 0.000960 | 0.012805 | 1.5443 | 7.0238 | 0.004235 |
| 3 | OAT | 12.2101 | 0.001754 | 0.022500 | 2.4764 | 6.2849 | 0.005506 |
| 4 | IBM | 12.0399 | 0.003752 | 0.046558 | 4.2005 | 6.1147 | 0.010322 |
| 5 | NAB | 10.8355 | 0.004671 | 0.056512 | 4.7082 | 4.9103 | 0.006182 |
| 6 | CVX | 9.7769 | 0.005290 | 0.062560 | 4.9565 | 3.8517 | 0.005805 |
| 7 | IK | 9.0253 | 0.006383 | 0.072423 | 5.2806 | 3.1001 | 0.004095 |
| 8 | FPL | 8.9886 | 0.007381 | 0.081396 | 5.5323 | 3.0634 | 0.004102 |
| 9 | CWE | 7.9373 | 0.007985 | 0.086191 | 5.6272 | 2.0121 | 0.002887 |
| 10 | DOW | 7.4146 | 0.009494 | 0.097383 | 5.7877 | 1.4894 | 0.002262 |
| 11 | NCR | 7.1704 | 0.011350 | 0.110693 | 5.9252 | 1.2452 | 0.001401 |
| 12 | X | 4.4721 | 0.012071 | 0.113918 | 5.8712 | 0 | 0 |
| 13 | UK | 4.4243 | 0.012641 | 0.116441 | 5.8300 | 0 | 0 |
| 14 | ACD | 4.2114 | 0.013849 | 0.121527 | 5.7376 | 0 | 0 |
| 15 | RS | 3.5182 | 0.014705 | 0.124538 | 5.6514 | 0 | 0 |

$$\sum_{i=1}^{15} y_i = 0.053633$$

3. Calculate the value of $C_i$ from (10.9) using the moving sums from columns 2 and 3 and taking $\sigma_m^2 = 136.3920$, as before. Enter the result in column 4 of Table 10.8.

4. Comparing column 4 with column 1 note that $C_{NCR} = 5.9252$ is the last $C_i$ which does not exceed the corresponding $(R/V)_i$ in column 1. The last four $C_i$s in column 4 are all greater than the corresponding $(R/V)_i$, tending to produce short sales. For a portfolio without short sales thus take $C^* = 5.9252$.

5. Construct the differences $(R/V)_i - C^*$ for the first 11 stocks from GF to NCR (column 5) and calculate $y_i$ from (10.10), using the values of $\beta_i/\sigma_{ei}^2$ from Table 10.6. Enter $y_i$ in column 6.

The optimal investment proportions $z_i$ are calculated by standardizing the corresponding $y_i$ in the usual way,

$$z_i = y_i \Big/ \sum_{i=1}^{15} y_i = y_i/0.053633$$

The corresponding optimal proportions are given in Table 10.9, which also lists for comparison the optimal proportions obtained by the quadratic-programming technique for $r = 4\%$ (see Chapter 9). The two portfolios are represented by points SIM and $A$ in Figure 10.3. Again there are significant differences in the composition of the two

**Table 10.9**

| | SIM portfolio for $r = 4\%$ | | Quadratic programming portfolio for $r = 4\%$ | |
|---|---|---|---|---|
| Stock | Investment proportions $(z_i)$ | | Stock | Investment proportions $(z_i)$ |
| GF | 12.75% | | | |
| BGH | 7.90 | | BGH | 12.10% |
| OAT | 10.27 | | | |
| IBM | 19.25 | | IBM | 31.21 |
| NAB | 11.53 | | NAB | 24.80 |
| CVX | 10.82 | | | |
| IK | 7.64 | | IK | 22.50 |
| FPL | 7.65 | | | |
| CWE | 5.38 | | | |
| DOW | 4.22 | | | |
| NCR | 2.61 | | ACD | 9.38 |
| **Total** | 100.00 | | | 100.00 |
| *Portfolio Mean* | 12.88 | | | 14.00 |
| *Portfolio Standard Deviation* | 18.86 | | | 18.06 |

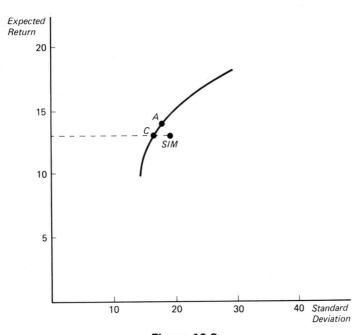

**Figure 10.3**

optimal portfolios, as in the case with short sales. The important point, as before, is that the SIM portfolio without short sales is inefficient: it lies inside the efficient frontier without short sales, shown in Figure 10.3; there is an efficient portfolio $C$ which has the same mean return as the SIM portfolio ($ER_p = 12.88\%$), and yet its standard deviation is only $\sigma_p = 16.47\%$ compared to 18.86% for the SIM portfolio. Thus, the simplicity of SIM calculations in the framework without short sales, as in the case with short sales, is attained at the cost of constructing a suboptimal portfolio which does not lie on the corresponding efficient frontier.

### Summary

Solving for the efficient set of investment portfolios is quite simple as long as the number of securities is not very large. When the number of securities increases, one faces two severe problems: (a) estimation; i.e., it is necessary to estimate hundreds and even thousands of parameters, (b) technical difficulties; i.e., solving a large set of equations, which becomes even more difficult when no short sales are allowed (nonnegativity constraints are imposed).

The Single Index Model (SIM) comes to the rescue. It drastically reduces the number of parameters needed to be estimated and yields the efficient set relatively easily without the technical difficulties characterizing the full-rank solution. If actual data conform to these assumptions, the SIM is clearly superior since it simplifies the calculations without incurring additional cost. However, if the SIM assumptions are in contradiction with the actual data, the simplification of the calculations is achieved at the cost of getting imprecise results.

---

**Summary Table**

1. When the number of risky assets $n$ is large, finding the efficient set of portfolios involves two major difficulties:
   (a) Technical problems (solving many equations with many unknowns)
   (b) The need to compute $N = (n^2 + 3n + 2)/2$ estimators.

2. The Single Index Model intended to overcome these difficulties is given by:

$$R_{it} = \alpha_i + \beta_i I_t + u_{it}$$

   where $R_{it}$ is the return on stock $i$ in period $t$, $I_t$ is the value of the common index in period $t$, $u_{it}$ is the deviation about the regression line with the variance $\sigma_{u_i}^2$.

3. SIM assumptions:
   (a) $Eu_i = 0$
   (b) $Cov(u_i, R_m) = 0$
   (c) $Cov(u_i, u_j) = 0$ for any two distinct stocks $i$ and $j$.

4. Under the SIM we have:

$$ER_i = \alpha_i + \beta_i ER_m$$
$$\sigma_i^2 = \beta_i^2 \sigma_m^2 + \sigma_{ui}^2$$
$$\sigma_{ij} = \beta_i \beta_j \sigma_m^2$$

The number of estimators required is $N = 3n + 3$. If the SIM assumptions are valid, this dramatically reduces the number of required estimators and the optimum investment strategy is obtained relatively simply.

5. The investment proportions under the SIM are given by:

$$y_i = \frac{\beta_i}{\sigma_{ei}^2} [(R/V)_i - C^*]$$

where $(R/V)_i = (\mu_i - r)/\beta_i$ is the reward-to-volatility ratio, $\beta_i$ is the $i$th asset's beta, and in case when short sales are allowed $C^*$ is given by:

$$C^* = \sigma_m^2 \sum_{j=1}^{n} \frac{\mu_j - r}{\sigma_{ej}^2} \beta_j \left/ \left( 1 + \sigma_m^2 \sum_{j=1}^{n} \frac{\beta_j^2}{\sigma_{ej}^2} \right) \right.$$

When short sales are forbidden, the number of assets $n$ in the formula for $C^*$ is replaced with $n_1$, which is the number of assets with $(R/V)_i$ greater than $C^*$.

6. The standardized investment proportions are obtained by:

$$z_i = y_i \left/ \sum_{i=1}^{n} y_i \right.$$

# APPENDIX 10.1
## Derivation of the Optimum Investment Proportions in the Single Index Model

We prove in this Appendix that the optimum investment proportions are given by equation (10.7) in the body of the text. To show this, recall that the optimum investment proportions $y_1, y_2, \ldots, y_n$ in $n$ risky assets are obtained by solving the following $n$ equations (see Chapter 9, equation (9.8)):

$$\mu_i - r = y_i \sigma_i^2 + \sum_{\substack{j=1 \\ j \neq i}}^{n} y_j \sigma_{ij} \quad \text{for } i = 1, 2, \ldots, n \qquad (10.1.1)$$

where:

$$\mu_i = \text{the expected rate of return on the } i\text{th risky asset}$$

$\sigma_i^2 = $ the variance of returns of the $i$th risky asset

$\sigma_{ij} = $ the covariance of returns of risky assets $i$ and $j$ $(i \neq j)$

$r = $ the riskless interest rate

Within the framework of the Single Index Model, we have the following additional information which can be used (see (10.4) and (10.5) in the body of the text):

$$\sigma_i^2 = \beta_i^2 \sigma_m^2 + \sigma_{ei}^2$$

$$\sigma_{ij} = \beta_i \beta_j \sigma_m^2$$

where:

$\sigma_m^2 = $ the variance of returns on the market portfolio

$\sigma_{ei}^2 = $ residual variance used as estimate of the population error variance $\sigma_{ui}^2$

Substituting for $\sigma_i^2$ and $\sigma_{ij}$ in the $i$th equation in (10.1.1), we obtain:

$$\mu_i - r = y_i \beta_i^2 \sigma_m^2 + y_i \sigma_{ei}^2 + \sum_{\substack{j=1 \\ j \neq i}}^{n} y_j \beta_i \beta_j \sigma_m^2$$

which can be rewritten as (verify this by writing out the equations for three risky assets, $i = 1, 2, 3$)

$$\mu_i - r = y_i \sigma_{ei}^2 + \beta_i \sigma_m^2 \sum_{j=1}^{n} y_j \beta_j \quad \text{for } i = 1, 2, \ldots, n$$

Solving for $y_i$:

$$y_i = \frac{\mu_i - r}{\sigma_{ei}^2} - \frac{\beta_i \sigma_m^2}{\sigma_{ei}^2} \sum_{j=1}^{n} y_j \beta_j \quad \text{for } i = 1, 2, \ldots, n \qquad (10.1.2)$$

Since the sum $\sum_{j=1}^{n} y_j \beta_j$ in the right-hand side also includes the unknown $y_i$, we have to get rid of this term. Multiply by $\beta_j$ both sides of the $j$th equation in (10.1.2) and sum over all $j$ to obtain:

$$\sum_{j=1}^{n} y_j \beta_j = \sum_{j=1}^{n} \frac{\mu_j - r}{\sigma_{ej}^2} \beta_j - \sum_{j=1}^{n} \frac{\beta_j^2 \sigma_m^2}{\sigma_{ej}^2} \sum_{j=1}^{n} y_j \beta_j$$

Isolating the term $\sum_{j=1}^{n} y_j \beta_j$, which now appears on both sides, we get:

$$\sum_{j=1}^{n} y_j \beta_j = \sum_{j=1}^{n} \frac{\mu_j - r}{\sigma_{ej}^2} \beta_j \bigg/ \left( 1 + \sigma_m^2 \sum_{j=1}^{n} \frac{\beta_j^2}{\sigma_{ej}^2} \right)$$

Substituting this result for $\Sigma_{j=1}^{n} y_j \beta_j$ in equation (10.1.2) finally yields:

$$y_i = \frac{\beta_i}{\sigma_{ei}^2} \underbrace{\left[ \frac{\mu_i - r}{\beta_i} - \sigma_m^2 \sum_{j=1}^{n} \frac{\mu_j - r}{\sigma_{ej}^2} \beta_j \middle/ \left( 1 + \sigma_m^2 \sum_{j=1}^{n} \frac{\beta_j^2}{\sigma_{ej}^2} \right) \right]}_{C^*} \qquad (10.1.3)$$

Denoting the entire second term on the right-hand side by $C^*$ and noting that $(\mu_i - r)/\beta_i$ is the so-called reward-to-volatility index of the $i$th risky asset $(R/V)_i$ (see Chapter 15), we have:

$$y_i = \frac{\beta_i}{\sigma_{ei}^2} [(R/V)_i - C^*] \qquad (10.1.4)$$

This is in fact equation (10.7) in the body of the text for the optimal investment proportions, and $C^*$ as defined in (10.1.3) coincides with the definition in (10.8) in the body of the chapter.

## APPENDIX 10.2
### Finding the Optimal Portfolio when Short Sales are Not Allowed: The Single Index Model

When short sales are not allowed, in general one needs to employ a quadratic programming technique to obtain the optimum portfolio. With the SIM assumptions, however, one can find the optimal portfolio relatively easily as demonstrated in this Appendix. With the constraints $y_i \geq 0$ (and hence $z_i \geq 0$) for $i = 1, 2, \ldots, n$ the solution should fulfill the following Kuhn–Tucker conditions:

(a)  $\mu_i - r = y_i \sigma_i^2 + \sum_{\substack{j=1 \\ j \neq i}}^{n} y_j \sigma_{ij} - U_i \quad (i = 1, 2, \ldots, n)$

(b)  $y_i U_i = 0 \quad (i = 1, 2, \ldots, n)$ $\qquad\qquad\qquad$ (10.2.1)

(c)  $y_i \geq 0 \quad \text{and} \quad U_i \geq 0 \quad (i = 1, 2, \ldots, n)$

where $U_i$ are artificial variables added to guarantee nonnegativity. By (b), if $y_i > 0$ then we must have $U_i = 0$, which means that $U_i$ drops out from the equality in (a) when there are no short sales of the $i$th asset. However, if $U_i > 0$, then the constraint (b) $y_i U_i = 0$

ensures that $y_i = 0$, and is not negative. Thus, candidates to be sold short will simply appear in zero proportions, rather than negative proportions.

Using the SIM information:

$$\sigma_i^2 = \beta_i^2 \sigma_m^2 + \sigma_{ei}^2 \quad \text{and} \quad \sigma_{ij} = \beta_i \beta_j \sigma_m^2$$

and substituting in (10.2.1) yields:

$$\mu_i - r = y_i \beta_i^2 \sigma_m^2 + y_i \sigma_{ei}^2 + \sum_{\substack{j=1 \\ j \neq i}}^{n} y_j \beta_i \beta_j \sigma_m^2 - U_i \quad (i = 1, 2, \ldots, n)$$

The last equation can be condensed as follows:

$$\mu_i - r = y_i \sigma_{ei}^2 + \beta_i \sigma_m^2 \sum_{j=1}^{n} y_j \beta_j - U_i \quad (i = 1, 2, \ldots, n) \tag{10.2.2}$$

Recall that not all securities are included in the optimal portfolio. Suppose that we reordered the risky assets such that the first $n_1$ securities have $y_i > 0$ and the remaining group of $(n - n_1)$ securities appear in the optimal portfolio with $y_i = 0$. Then, for the first group we know that $U_i = 0$, and for this set of assets equation (10.2.2) can be rewritten as:

$$\mu_i - r = y_i \sigma_{ei}^2 + \beta_i \sigma_m^2 \sum_{j=1}^{n_1} y_j \beta_j \quad (i = 1, 2, \ldots, n_1)$$

The artificial variable $U_i$ has dropped out. Hence, for these $n_1$ assets:

$$y_i = \frac{\beta_i}{\sigma_{ei}^2} \left[ \frac{\mu_i - r}{\beta_i} - \sigma_m^2 \sum_{j=1}^{n_1} y_j \beta_j \right] \quad \text{for } i = 1, 2, \ldots, n_1 \tag{10.2.3}$$

Multiply the $j$th equation in (10.2.3) by $\beta_j$ and sum over all $j = 1, 2, \ldots, n_1$ to eliminate $\sum_{j=1}^{n_1} y_j \beta_j$. Indeed, from (10.2.3):

$$\sum_{j=1}^{n_1} y_j \beta_j = \sum_{j=1}^{n_1} \frac{\mu_j - r}{\sigma_{ej}^2} \beta_j - \sigma_m^2 \sum_{j=1}^{n_1} \frac{\beta_j^2}{\sigma_{ej}^2} \sum_{j=1}^{n_1} y_j \beta_j$$

Hence:

$$\sum_{j=1}^{n_1} y_j \beta_j = \sum_{j=1}^{n_1} \frac{\mu_j - r}{\sigma_{ej}^2} \beta_j \bigg/ \left( 1 + \sigma_m^2 \sum_{j=1}^{n_1} \beta_j^2 / \sigma_{ej}^2 \right) \tag{10.2.4}$$

Plugging this result in equation (10.2.3) we finally get for security $i$:

$$y_i = \frac{\beta_i}{\sigma_{ei}^2} [(R/V)_i - C^*]$$

where

$$(R/V)_i = \frac{\mu_i - r}{\beta_i}$$

is the reward-to-volatility of the $i$th stock and:

$$C^* = \sigma_m^2 \sum_{j=1}^{n_1} y_j \beta_j$$

with $\sum_{j=1}^{n_1} y_j \beta_j$ as given above in (10.2.4).

Since it is very rare to find a stock with a negative $\beta_i$, $y_i$ is positive when $(R/V)_i - C^*$ is positive. Thus, one can rank all the stocks according to their $(R/V)_i$, and calculate for each stock the value $C_i$. The value $C^*$ is equal to that value $C_i$ such that all securities used to calculate $C_i$ have $(R/V)_i$ greater than $C_i$ and all securities that are not used to calculate $C_i$ have $(R/V)_i$ smaller than $C_i$. Also note that if it is known that a given security is included in the portfolio, all securities with higher $(R/V)$ must also be included in positive amounts in the optimum portfolio.

## Questions and Problems

10.1    In deriving the MV efficient set, how many covariances $\sigma_{ij}$ should be estimated for $n$ risky assets, when $n$ takes the following alternative values, $n = 2, 5, 10, 100, 1000$?

10.2    It is given that all the assumptions underlying the SIM hold. The return generating process is:

$$R_i = \alpha_i + \beta_i R_m + u_i$$

Given that $\sigma_i = 10$, $\sigma_m = 10$, $\alpha_i = 1$, $\sigma_{ui} = 5$ and $ER_m = 10$, calculate the $i$th security expected return $\mu_i$ and its beta $\beta_{ei}$.

10.3    "Under the SIM we can safely assert that if $\beta_i = 0$ then necessarily all $\sigma_{ij} = 0$". Appraise this statement.

10.4 The following figure shows the scattergram of the returns of stocks *i* and *j* on a given index *I*. Do the SIM assumptions hold in these two specific examples? Explain.

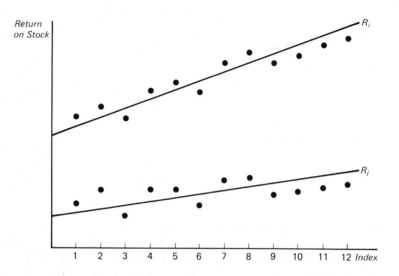

10.5 Using the SIM assumptions, calculate the expected return and the variance of security *A* when the *per capita* GNP is used as the index. Compare the SIM results to the usual statistical estimates of mean and variance.

| Rate of Return on Security A (%) | GNP per Capita (in $) |
|---|---|
| −5 | 4000 |
| +10 | 4100 |
| −20 | 4200 |
| +40 | 5000 |

How will you change your answer if the *per capita* GNP is given in thousands of dollars rather in dollars, namely, 4, 4.1, 4.2, and 5?

10.6 Suppose that there are *n* risky assets all with identical beta and with identical reward-to-volatility ratio $(R/V)_i$. Using the SIM (when short sales are allowed), "we necessarily obtain a portfolio with equal amounts invested in each risky asset $y_i = 1/n$." Appraise this statement.

10.7 What are the difficulties in direct estimation of the optimal investment proportions in a portfolio, and how can these difficulties be resolved by the SIM?

10.8 Hypothetical monthly returns on two stocks ($R_1$ and $R_2$) and on the market portfolio

$(R_m)$ are presented in the following table:

| Month | Monthly Return (%) | | |
|---|---|---|---|
| | $R_1$ | $R_2$ | $R_m$ |
| 1 | 1.99 | −5.13 | 5.50 |
| 2 | 15.89 | 17.46 | 2.67 |
| 3 | 15.03 | 5.57 | 5.49 |
| 4 | 2.16 | 3.79 | −1.02 |
| 5 | 10.33 | 7.22 | 3.36 |
| 6 | 5.25 | −4.04 | 4.89 |
| 7 | 1.34 | −2.43 | 2.23 |
| 8 | 7.71 | −3.51 | 3.13 |

Assuming that these data represent the entire population,
(a) Compute for each of the two stocks the alpha, the beta, and the standard deviation of the residuals of the regression of $R_i$ $(i = 1, 2)$ on $R_m$.
(b) Compute the mean return and the variance of returns of the two stocks using the Single Index Model and by direct estimation.
(c) Compute the covariance between the returns on the two stocks using the Single Index Model and by direct estimation. Explain the results.

10.9 For the two stocks in Problem 10.8 compute the optimal investment proportions in a portfolio composed of the two stocks with short sales allowed, using both the full-rank method (namely, apply the technique of Chapter 9) and the SIM. Assume that the riskless interest rate is $r = 1\%$. Explain the difference in results between the two methods.

10.10 The following table presents data on three stocks. The riskless interest rate is $r = 1\%$ and the variance of the market portfolio is $\sigma_m^2 = 3.70$. It is also given that $Cov(e_i, e_j) = 0$ for all pairs of stocks $i, j$, where $e_i$ is the residual of the $i$th regression.

| Stock | $\mu_i$ | $\beta_i$ | $\sigma_{ei}^2$ |
|---|---|---|---|
| 1 | 2.67 | 1.96 | 9.62 |
| 2 | 1.05 | 1.21 | 3.55 |
| 3 | 1.60 | 0.20 | 17.11 |

(a) Compute the optimal proportions in a risky portfolio composed of the three stocks, *with short sales*, using the full-rank solution technique of Chapter 9.
(b) Answer part (a) by use of the SIM. Compare the solution to that obtained in (a).
(c) Use the SIM technique to compute the optimum proportions in a risky portfolio composed of the above three stocks, when short sales are *not allowed*.

10.11* Prove that the investment proportions found in part (c) of Problem 10.10 are the optimal proportions of the quadratic programming optimization problem (i.e. show that the Kuhn–Tucker conditions hold for the proportions found in part (c) of Problem 10.10).

10.12* Suppose that the true market model is a double index model,

$$R_{it} = \alpha_i + \beta_{i1}I_1 + \beta_{i2}I_2 + e_{it}$$

where $I_1$ and $I_2$ are the two indexes.

Assume that $I_1$ and $I_2$ are uncorrelated. A security analyst decides to use the Single Index Model, and regresses the return of each security on the index $I_1$, while ignoring the index $I_2$. What impact will this estimation procedure have on the estimates of the expected return and the variance of each security and on the covariance between any two securities?

10.13 The annual rates of return on five stocks traded on the NYSE and on the market portfolio are given below.

(a) Estimate the parameters required to calculate the efficient portfolio using the Single Index Model and find the efficient portfolio (with short sales allowed) assuming riskless rate of return $r = 4\%$.

(b)* Use the computer program in Appendix 9.1 to obtain the conventional MV efficient portfolio for $r = 4\%$ and compare the results to those in part (a) above.

| | | | Rate of Return (%) | | | |
|---|---|---|---|---|---|---|
| Year | DuPont | Dow Chemical | Union Carbide | Monsanto | W.R. Grace | Market Portfolio |
| 1972 | 26.33 | 31.19 | 23.60 | 5.04 | −1.95 | 17.77 |
| 1973 | −7.21 | 15.32 | −28.26 | 13.88 | −1.80 | −16.92 |
| 1974 | −39.32 | −2.32 | 28.07 | −22.01 | −4.74 | −26.80 |
| 1975 | 42.21 | 69.55 | 54.00 | 94.95 | 19.84 | 37.77 |
| 1976 | 11.02 | −3.39 | 5.09 | 19.03 | 27.01 | 26.26 |
| 1977 | −6.52 | −36.06 | −29.80 | −31.52 | −1.74 | −4.81 |
| 1978 | 11.33 | −2.14 | −10.89 | −13.14 | 2.78 | 7.39 |
| 1979 | 2.65 | 35.82 | 33.14 | 35.37 | 67.05 | 21.82 |
| 1980 | 11.17 | 5.13 | 28.58 | 22.80 | 53.14 | 32.70 |
| 1981 | −5.60 | −13.19 | 8.55 | 7.50 | −18.37 | −4.22 |

*Source:* CRSP monthly returns data tape.

## Data Set Problems

1. Consider all the funds included in the Senior Securities Policy category in the Data Set.

(a) How many parameters do you have to estimate in order to find the efficient portfolios by the technique of Chapter 9 (this is also known as the "full rank solution")? How many parameters do you have to estimate in order to employ the Single Index Model (SIM)?

(b) For the first two funds, calculate $\sigma_{ij}$ and $\beta_i \beta_j \sigma_m^2$, using the Fisher Index given at the bottom of the Data Set as a proxy to the market portfolio. Compare and analyze your results.

(c) Calculate $Cov(e_1, e_2)$, where $e_1$ and $e_2$ are the regression residuals of Fund 1 and Fund 2, respectively. Is your result consistent with the SIM assumption?

2. (a) Using the first fund from each category in the Data Set, find the optimum investment proportions by the SIM technique of Chapter 10 assuming a risk-free interest rate $r = 2\%$.
   (b) Compare your results to the efficient frontier obtained by the "full rank solution" in Data Set Problem 3 of Chapter 9. How can you account for the differences in the two efficient frontiers?

3. (a) Repeat the SIM calculations of Problem 2 above, with nonnegativity constraints on all the investment proportions (short sales not allowed).
   (b) Compare your results to the efficient frontier obtained by the quadratic programming method with nonnegativity constraints in Data Set Problem 4 of Chapter 9.

## Selected References

Alexander, G. J., "The Derivation of Efficient Sets", *Journal of Financial and Quantitative Analysis* (December 1976).

Alexander, G. J., "Mixed Security Testing of Alternative Portfolio Selection Models", *Journal of Financial and Quantitative Analysis* (December 1977).

Alexander, G. J., "A Re-evaluation of Alternative Portfolio Selection Models Applied to Common Stocks", *Journal of Financial and Quantitative Analysis* (March 1978).

Baron, D. P., "Investment Policy, Optimality, and the Mean–Variance Model: Review Article", *Journal of Finance*, (March 1979).

Barry, C. B. and Radcliffe, R. C., "Bayesian Modeling of Alternative Specifications in Portfolio Analysis", *Journal of Economics and Business* (Spring/Summer 1979).

Barry, C. B. and Winkler, R. L., "Nonstationarity and Portfolio Choice", *Journal of Financial and Quantitative Analysis* (June 1976).

Bawa, V. S., "Admissible Portfolios for All Individuals", *Journal of Finance* (September 1976).

Bawa, V. S., "Mathematical Programming of Admissible Portfolios", *Management Science* (March 1977).

Bawa, V. S., Elton, E. J. and Gruber, M. J., "Simple Rules for Optimal Portfolio Selection in Stable Paretian Markets", *Journal of Finance* (September 1979).

Blume, M. E., "Portfolio Theory. A Step Towards its Practical Application", *Journal of Business* (April 1970).

Bowden, R., "A Dual Concept and Associated Algorithm in Mean–Variance Portfolio Analysis", *Management Science* (December 1976).

Brealey, R. A. and Hodges, S. D., "Playing with Portfolios", *Journal of Finance* (March 1975).

Breen, W. and Jackson, R., "An Efficient Algorithm for Solving Large-Scale Portfolio Problems", *Journal of Financial and Quantitative Analysis* (January 1971).

Brennan, M. J., "The Optimal Number of Securities in a Risky Asset Portfolio Where There are Fixed Costs of Transacting: Theory and Some Empirical Results", *Journal of Financial and Quantitative Analysis* (September 1975).

Burgess, R. C. and O'Dell, B. T., "An Empirical Examination of Index Efficiency: Implication for Index Funds", *Journal of Financial and Quantitative Analysis* (March 1978).

Burnham, J. M., "Conditional Chance Constrained Programming Techniques in Portfolio Selection", *Journal of Finance* (June 1972).

Buser, S. A., "A Simplified Expression for the Efficient Frontier in Mean–Variance Portfolio Analysis", *Management Science* (April 1977).

Buser, S. A., "Mean–Variance Portfolio Selection with Either a Singular or Non-Singular Variance–Covariance Matrix", *Journal of Financial and Quantitative Analysis* (September 1977).

Carpenter, M. D. and Henderson, G. V., Jr., "Estimation Procedures and Stability of the Market Model Parameters", *Review of Business and Economic Research* (Fall 1981).

Chen, A. H., "Portfolio Selection with Stochastic Cash Demand", *Journal of Financial and Quantitative Analysis* (June 1977).

Chen, A. H. Y., Jen, F. C., and Zionts, S., "The Optimal Portfolio Revision Policy", *Journal of Business* (January 1971).

Chen, A. H. Y., Jen, F. C., and Zionts, S., "The Joint Determination of Portfolio and Transaction Demands for Money", *Journal of Finance* (March 1974).

Cohen, K. J. and Pogue, G. A., "An Empirical Evaluation of Alternative Portfolio Selection Models", *Journal of Business* (April 1967).

Connie, T. E., Jr., and Tamarkin, M. J., "On Diversification Given Asymmetry in Returns", *Journal of Finance* (December 1981).

Defaro, C., and Jucker, J. T., "A Simple Algorithm for Stone's Version of the Portfolio Selection Problem", *Journal of Financial and Quantitative Analysis* (December 1975).

Dhingra, H. L., "Effects of Estimation Risk on Efficient Portfolios: A Monte Carlo Simulation Study", *Journal of Finance and Accounting* (Summer 1980).

Dickinson, J. P., "The Reliability of Estimation Procedures in Portfolio Analysis", *Journal of Financial and Quantitative Analysis* (June 1974).

Elgers, P. T. and Murray, D., "Impact of the Choice of Market Index on the Empirical Evaluation of Accounting Risk Measures", *Accounting Review* (April 1982).

Elton, E. J., and Gruber, M. J., "On the Optimality of Some Multiperiod Portfolio Selection Criteria", *The Journal of Business* (April 1974).

Elton, E. J., Gruber, M. J., and Padberg, M. W., "Optimal Portfolios from Simple Ranking Devices", *Journal of Portfolio Management* (Spring 1978).

Elton, E. J., Gruber, M. J., and Padberg, M. W., "Simple Criteria for Optimal Portfolio Selection: Tracing Out the Efficient Frontier", *Journal of Finance* (March 1978).

Elton, E. J., Gruber, M. J., and Padberg, M. W., "Simple Criteria for Optimal Portfolio Selection", *Journal of Finance* (December 1976).

Elton, E. J., Gruber, M. J., and Padberg, M. W., "Simple Rules for Optimal Portfolio Selection: The Multi Group Case", *Journal of Financial and Quantitative Analysis* (September 1977).

Elton, E. J., Gruber, M. J., and Padberg, M. W., "Simple Criteria for Optimal Portfolio Selection with Upper Bounds", *Operation Research* (November–December 1978).

Faaland, B., "An Integer Programming Algorithm for Portfolio Selection", *Management Science* (June 1974).

Fielitz, B. D., "Indirect versus Direct Diversification", *Financial Management* (Winter 1974).

Fishburn, P. C. and Porter, R. B., "Optimal Portfolios with One Safe and One Risky Asset: Effects of Change in Rate of Return and Risk", *Management Science* (June 1976).

Frankfurther, G. M., "Effect of Market Indexes on the *Ex-Post* Performance of the Sharpe Portfolio Selection Model", *Journal of Finance* (June 1976).

Frankfurther, G. M. and Phillips, H. E., "Portfolio Selection: An Analytical Approach for Selecting Securities From a Large Universe", *Journal of Financial and Quantitative Analysis* (June 1980).

Frankfurther, G. M., Phillips, H. E. and Seagle, J. P., "Portfolio Selection: The Effects of Uncertain Means, Variances and Covariances", *Journal of Financial and Quantitative Analysis* (December 1971).

Goldsmith, D., "Transactions Costs and the Theory of Portfolio Selection", *Journal of Finance* (September 1976).

Gonzalez, N., Litzenberger, R. and Rolfo, J., "On Mean Variance Models of Capital Structure and the Absurdity of Their Predictions", *Journal of Financial and Quantitative Analysis* (June 1977).

Gordon, M. J., Paradis, G. E. and Rorke, C. H., "Experimental Evidence on Alternative Portfolio Decision Rules", *American Economic Review* (March 1972).

Grauer, R. R., "Investment Policy Implications of the Capital Asset Pricing Model", *Journal of Finance* (March 1981).

Grauer, R. R. and Hakansson, N. H., "Higher Return, Lower Risk: Historical Returns on Long-run, Actively Managed Portfolios of Stocks, Bonds, and Bills, 1936–1978", *Financial Analysts Journal* (March/April 1982).

Greene, M. T. and Fielitz, B. D., "Long-term Dependence and Least Squares Regression in Investment Analysis", *Management Science* (October 1980).

Hakansson, N. H., "Risk Disposition and the Separation Property in Portfolio Selection", *Journal of Financial and Quantitative Analysis* (December 1969).

Hakansson, N. H. and Liu, T. C., "Optimal Growth Portfolios When Yields are Serially Correlated", *Review of Economics and Statistics* (November 1970).

Ho, P. C. and Paulson, A. S., "Portfolio Selection Via Factor Analysis", *Journal of Portfolio Management* (Spring 1980).

Hodges, S. D., "Problems in the Application of Portfolio Selection Models", *Omega* (1976).

Jacob, N. L., "A Limited Diversification Portfolio Selection Model for the Small Investor", *Journal of Finance* (June 1974).

Jaffe, J. P. and Merville, L. J., "Stock Price Dependencies and the Valuation of Risky Assets with Discontinuous Temporal Returns", *Journal of Finance* (December 1974).

Jobson, J. D., and Korkie, B., "Estimation for Markowitz Efficient Portfolios", *American Statistical Association* (Fall 1980).

Klein, R. W. and Bawa, V. S., "The Effect of Limited Information and Estimation Risk on Optimal Portfolio Diversification", *Journal of Financial and Quantitative Analysis* (November 1977).

Klein, R. W. and Bawa, V. S., "The Effect of Estimation Risk on Optimal Portfolio Choice", *Journal of Financial Economics* (June 1976).

Klemkosky, R. C. and Maness, T. S., "The Predictability of Real Portfolio Risk Levels", *Journal of Finance* (May 1978).

Klemkosky, R. C. and Martin, J. D., "The Effect of Market Risk on Portfolio Diversification", *Journal of Finance* (March 1975).

Kon, S. J. and Lau, W. P., "Specification Tests for Portfolio Regression Parameter Stationarity and the Implications for Empirical Research", *Journal of Finance* (May 1979).

Latané, H. A. and Young, W. E., "Test of Portfolio Building Rules", *Journal of Finance* (September 1969).

Latané, H. A., Tuttle, D., and Young, W. E., "How to Choose a Market Index", *Financial Analysts Journal* (September/October 1971).

Mao, J. C. T., "Essentials of Portfolio Diversification Strategy", *Journal of Finance* (December 1970).

Markowitz, H. M. and Perold, A. F., "Portfolio Analysis with Factors and Scenarios", *Journal of Finance* (September 1981).

Martin, J. D. and Keown, A. J., "Interest Rate Sensitivity and Portfolio Risk", *Journal of Financial and Quantitative Analysis* (June 1977).

Merton, R. C., "An Analytic Derivation of the Efficient Portfolio Frontier", *Journal of Financial and Quantitative Analysis* (September 1972).

Ohlson, J. A., "Complete Ordering of Information Alternatives for a Class of Portfolio-Selection Models", *Journal of Accounting Research* (Autumn 1975).

Ohlson, J. A., "Quadratic Approximations of the Portfolio Selection Problem When the Means and Variances of Returns are Infinite", *Management Science* (1976).

Pang, J., "New and Efficient Algorithm for a Class of Portfolio Selection Problems", *Operation Research* (May/June 1980).

Pang, J., "Parametric Linear Complementarity Technique for Optimal Portfolio Selection with a Risk-free Asset", *Operations Research* (July/August 1980).

Patel, N. R. and Subrahmanyam, M. G., "Simple Algorithm for Optimal Portfolio Selection With Fixed Transaction Costs", *Management Science* (March 1982).

Saniga, E., Gressis, N., and Hayya, J., "The Effects of Sample Size and Correlation on the Accuracy of the EV Efficiency Criterion", *Journal of Financial and Quantitative Analysis* (September 1979).

Sercu, P., "Note on Real and Nominal Efficient Sets", *Journal of Finance* (June 1981).

Sharpe, W. F., "A Simplified Model for Portfolio Analysis", *Management Science* (January 1963).

Sharpe, W. F., *Portfolio Theory and Capital Markets* New York: McGraw Hill Book Co (1970).

Sharpe, W. F., "A Linear Programming Approximation for the General Portfolio Selection Problem", *Journal of Financial and Quantitative Analysis* (December 1971).

Smith, K. V., "Stock Price and Economic Indexes for Generating Efficient Portfolios", *Journal of Business* (July 1969).

Stone, B. K. and Hill, N. C., "Portfolio Management and the Shrinking Knapsnack Algorithm", *Journal of Financial and Quantitative Analysis* (December 1979).

Treynor, J. L. and Black, F., "How to Use Security Analysis to Improve Portfolio Selection", *Journal of Business* (June 1973).

Winkler, R. L. and Barry, C. B., "A Bayesian Model for Portfolio Selection and Revision", *Journal of Finance* (March 1975).

Wallingford, B. A., "A Survey and Comparison of Portfolio Selection Models", *Journal of Financial and Quantitative Analysis* (June 1967).

Williams, J. T., "A Note on Indifference Curves in the Mean–Variance Model", *Journal of Financial and Quantitative Analysis* (March 1977).

Ziemba, W. T., "Solving Nonlinear Programming Problems with Stochastic Objective Functions", *Journal of Financial and Quantitative Analysis* (June 1972).

Ziemba, W. T., Parkan, C. and Brooks-Hill, R., "Calculation of Investment Portfolios with Risk Free Borrowing and Lending", *Management Science Application* (October 1974).

# PART IV
# Equilibrium Models:
# Theory and Empirical Tests

# 11

# The Capital Asset Pricing Model (CAPM): Price Determination in the Stock Market

In the preceding chapters we presented a number of efficiency criteria which can be used to analyze investment decisions under uncertainty and considered the gains from risk diversification. In essence, these chapters spell out a normative theory of investment behavior; for a variety of assumptions regarding investors' utility functions (tastes and preferences), the theory sets out the optimal patterns of investment choice. In this chapter, the *normative* theory will be applied to a *positive* problem: the analysis of the set of relative prices of securities in the stock market, with particular emphasis on the demand and supply of securities and the way in which they interact to determine equilibrium prices.

The model developed in this chapter is applicable to valuation of any risky asset and, in particular, to stocks and risky bonds. Thus, we distinguish between riskless bonds (e.g., Treasury bills or short-term bonds) and risky bonds (e.g., long-term bonds, or bonds with maturities longer than the investment horizon), and the latter are treated as risky securities which are included in the market portfolio.

## 11.1 Some Simplifying Assumptions

A modern securities market is an awesome mechanism incorporating thousands of decision variables, and therefore any attempt to gain insight into the workings of such a market requires a high degree of abstraction. Clearly, no model can be exhaustively descriptive in any meaningful sense. However, granted that simplifying assumptions are required, the choice of a particular set of assumptions regarding investors' behavior is crucial for both the explanatory and predictive powers of the model. The stronger the assumptions governing individuals' investment choices, the sharper the conclusions regarding the market; but the less general the results, and therefore the greater the danger that the model will not accord with the phenomena that it is designed to explain.

In what follows we shall take as our starting point the pioneering model developed by Sharpe and Lintner.[1] The Sharpe–Lintner capital market model represents an extension of the basic Markowitz–Tobin mean–variance portfolio selection analysis in which the variance (or the standard deviation) serves as the risk indicator. As we have seen (in Chapter 7), the use of the mean–variance criterion to characterize investors' behavior implies a set of relatively strong assumptions: investors in securities are risk-averse (have concave utility functions) and the distributions of returns approximate a normal distribution.[2]

Although it is true that with regard to portfolios which include only a small number of different securities the distribution of portfolio returns is likely to deviate significantly from the normal, it can be argued that investors in a competitive capital market tend to include a large number of individual securities in their portfolios, so that the portfolio returns will tend to approximate a normal distribution. The empirical analysis of mutual funds returns lends some support to this contention.[3] Another reason for choosing the mean–variance model is pedagogical: the available alternatives are much more complex and place heavier demands on a student's mathematical abilities.[4] Since mathematical sophistication is not a free good, the trade-off between loss of generality and the simplification of the analysis leads us to prefer the mean–variance model despite its admitted shortcomings.[5]

In addition to the underlying assumption that investors are risk-averse and select their portfolios by the MVC, we shall also assume that the capital market is perfect, which implies the following conditions:[6]

(1)   The market comprises many buyers and sellers of securities, none of whose transactions is large enough to affect the prices in the market, and all of whom have an equal opportunity to invest.

(2)   There are no transaction costs or transfer taxes, nor is there an income or capital gains tax.

(3)   All investors have all relevant information regarding alternative investments, and there are no costs involved in obtaining this information. All investors, therefore, have the same expectations regarding the expected returns and variances of all the alternative investment options.

---

[1] W. F. Sharpe, "Capital Asset Prices: A Theory of Market Equilibrium Under Conditions of Risk", *Journal of Finance* (September 1964), pp. 425–42; and J. Lintner, "Security Prices, Risk and Maximal Gains from Diversification", *Journal of Finance* (December 1965), pp. 587–615.

[2] Because of its logical deficiencies we ignore the alternative of assuming that investors' tastes are characterized by quadratic utility functions.

[3] See Chapter 7.

[4] The distributions could be assumed to be symmetrical and to belong to the class of stable *Paretian* distributions. This is a much broader class which includes the normal distribution as a special case. See E. F. Fama, "Portfolio Analysis in a Stable Paretian Market", *Management Science* (January 1965), pp. 404–19.

[5] It might also be noted that all the market equilibrium models are basically similar so that having mastered one, the reader should be reasonably well prepared to go on to the alternative models.

[6] Some of these assumptions can be relaxed without changing the conclusions of the analysis (see Chapter 13).

(4) All investors can borrow or lend any amount in the relevant range without affecting the interest rate. The borrowing rate equals the lending rate and is the same for all investors both large and small, institutional and individual.

(5) There is a given uniform investment period for all investors; this means that all decisions are taken at a particular point in time, and all investments are held for the same period.

Before turning to the analysis of equilibrium prices in the stock market, one possible objection should be noted explicitly. The very essence of a securities market is that prices fluctuate continuously; in more technical jargon, there is no equilibrium in such a market, or if there is, it is never reached! This would seem to vitiate the use of equilibrium models as a tool for explaining relative prices in such a market. In this context it may be well to recall the famous analogy drawn from dog racing, where the dogs go around the track chasing a mechanical rabbit. Equilibrium is reached should a dog catch the rabbit, but barring failures in the electric power supply, this *never* happens. However, knowledge of the existence of the rabbit is of paramount importance when attempting to explain or predict the otherwise rather peculiar behavior of the dogs.

## 11.2 Single-stock Portfolios with Lending or Borrowing

Let us start the analysis with the most simple case imaginable: investors restrict their portfolios to the shares of one company and to riskless bonds. Thus the individual invests part of his wealth in a common stock and lends the remainder (buys bonds); or he may use all his wealth to buy the common stock and borrow (issue his own bonds) to finance additional stock purchases, that is, he builds a "levered" portfolio. To further simplify matters we shall assume that the rate of return (interest) on bonds and loans is riskless, i.e., *perfectly certain*, while the return on the common stock is uncertain, and therefore constitutes a stochastic variable.

We will use the following notation:

$R$ = a random variable denoting the net return *per dollar* invested in the common stock

$ER$ = the expected return on common stock

$\sigma_R$ = the standard deviation of returns on common stock

$r$ = the *riskless* lending rate (the rate of return on bonds) equal to the borrowing rate

The expected return and standard deviation of return on the common stock can be shown as a point on the familiar mean–standard deviation plane; see point $A$ in Figure 11.1. Similarly, the riskless interest rate $r$ is shown as a point on the vertical axis of the same diagram. (Note that for all points on the vertical axis, $\sigma = 0$.)

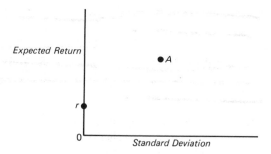

**Figure 11.1**

Consider an investor with an initial wealth of $w$. If he invests all his wealth in (riskless) bonds the expected return and standard deviation of the bond portfolio will be

$$ER_p = wr; \quad \sigma_p = 0$$

where the subscript denotes the portfolio. Alternatively, if he invests all his wealth in the common stock $A$, the return on the portfolio is $R_p = wR$, and the expected return and standard deviation of the all-equity portfolio become

$$ER_p = wER; \quad \sigma_p = w\sigma_R$$

Of course, the investor is also free to choose any combination he desires of bonds (loans) and stock $A$. Thus he may invest any proportion of his wealth $x$ in bonds and the remainder $(1 - x)$ in the stock, on the constraint that $x \leqslant 1$. The return on the portfolio in this general case can be written as follows:

$$R_p = xwr + (1 - x)wR \tag{11.1}$$

Note that we do *not* place a lower bound of $x \geqslant 0$, and, therefore, $x$ can take on negative, as well as positive, values. If $x$ is positive, this means that the individual invests part of his wealth in bonds. Where $x = 1$ all the wealth is invested in bonds and nothing $(1 - x = 1 - 1 = 0)$ is invested in the stock. Where $x = 0$, the opposite holds: nothing is invested in bonds and all the wealth $(1 - x = 1 - 0 = 1)$ is invested in the stock. Negative values of $x$ represent cases in which an individual borrows money (at the interest rate $r$) to invest in stock. For example, an initial wealth of \$100 and $x = 0.25$ denotes the case of a mixed portfolio composed of \$25 in bonds and \$75 in stock; the return on the portfolio is $r \cdot 25 + R \cdot 75$. Now consider a case where for the same initial wealth $x$ is negative, for example, $x = -0.5$. Here the individual borrows \$50 on which he *pays* interest, but the levered stock portfolio now exceeds the investors' initial wealth: $(1 - x)w = [1 - (-0.5)]100 = \$150$.

The expected return and standard deviation of a portfolio which includes any combination of stocks or bonds (loans) are given by the following two equations:

$$ER_p = xwr + (1 - x)wER \tag{11.2}$$

$$\left(w - \frac{\sigma_p}{\sigma_R}\right)r + \left(\frac{\sigma_p}{\sigma_R}\right)ER$$

$$wr - \frac{\sigma_p}{\sigma_r}r +$$

$$\sigma_p = (1 - x)w\sigma_R \tag{11.3}$$

The reader should note that in the equation of the standard deviation the argument $xwr$ vanishes, since it is a perfectly certain sum, and therefore has a zero variance.

The more an investor borrows in order to finance his purchases of common stock, the higher the expected return (the risky expected return $ER$ is, by assumption, higher than the riskless rate of interest $r$), but the greater the risk (standard deviation) as well. This relationship between the expected return and standard deviation can be made explicit by a little algebraic manipulation. Dividing both sides of Equation (11.3) by $\sigma_R$ yields:

$$(1 - x)w = \frac{\sigma_p}{\sigma_R} \tag{11.4}$$

Removing the parentheses and transposing terms:

$$xw = w - \frac{\sigma_p}{\sigma_R} \tag{11.5}$$

Now substituting the right-hand sides of Equations (11.4) and (11.5) into Equation (11.2), we find:[7]

$$ER_p = rw + \frac{ER - r}{\sigma_R}\sigma_p \tag{11.6}$$

Equation (11.6) represents the relationship between expected return and standard deviation for any portfolio, that is, it represents the attainable combination of $ER_p$ and $\sigma_p$ for all possible combinations of stocks and bonds (loans). This equation is linear,[8] so that all the attainable combinations of $ER_p$ and $\sigma_p$ lie along a straight line.

---

[7] Substituting (11.4) and (11.5) into (11.2) yields

$$ER_p = r\left(w - \frac{\sigma_p}{\sigma_R}\right) + ER\frac{\sigma_p}{\sigma_R}$$

Removing the parentheses we have

$$ER_p = rw - r\frac{\sigma_p}{\sigma_R} + ER\frac{\sigma_p}{\sigma_R} = rw + (ER - r)\frac{\sigma_p}{\sigma_R}$$

[8] Of the form $ER_p = a + b\sigma_p$ where

$$a = rw$$

$$b = \frac{ER - r}{\sigma_R}$$

Within the confines of a "one-stock" model it is also easy to determine the "price"
or premium which an investor puts on a unit of risk. When we increase a portfolio'
standard deviation by one unit, the investor requires an addition to his expected return
equal to $(ER - r)/\sigma_R$ to compensate him for the additional risk incurred. Conversely
when he adds bonds to his portfolio, thereby reducing the portfolio's standard deviation
he is willing to forgo $(ER - r)/\sigma_R$ units of expected return per unit of reduction in the
standard deviation.

To facilitate a graphical presentation of this relationship between the expected
return and risk [Equation (11.6)], let us assume an initial wealth of one dollar. The
assumption $w = 1$ is made for convenience, and does not affect the generality of the
analysis.[9] The transformation line *ra* of Figure 11.2 represents all the attainable com
binations of expected return and standard deviation which an investor can secure by
altering the proportions of his portfolio. The intercept on the vertical axis represents
portfolio invested solely in bonds $(ER_p = r; \sigma_p = 0)$; point *A* represents the expected
return and standard deviation for a 100% equity portfolio. All the intermediate point
on the transformation line represent the risk–return characteristics for mixed portfolio
which combine stock *A* and bonds in varying proportions. Since $ER > r$ by assumption
(otherwise no risk averter would be willing to invest in common stock *A*, whose return
are uncertain), the transformation line rises in a northeasterly direction. The slope of
this line $(ER - r)/\sigma_R$ is equal to the difference between the expected return on the stock
of company *A* and the riskless interest rate divided by the risk associated with the
investment in *A*. This is the price or premium which investors place on the risk
associated with investments in this particular company.

All the points along the transformation line represent efficient portfolios, since

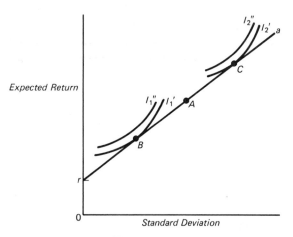

**Figure 11.2**

[9] By setting $w = 1$, we can easily convert the returns which are given in absolute terms in the equa
tions into percentages.

between any two points on the line the following relationships hold:

$$ER_2 > ER_1$$
$$\sigma_2 > \sigma_1$$

Thus the MVC is fulfilled for all points and the MV efficiency locus, in this case, is given by the transformation line itself.

How does the investor choose his portfolio from among the efficient alternatives, that is, how does he allocate his initial wealth between stocks and bonds? As we noted in Chapter 8, the answer to this question depends on the individual's preferences. To illustrate this, the indifference maps of *two different* individuals are drawn in Figure 11.2. (Recall that along each curve in the set expected utility is held constant and that higher curves (in a northwesterly direction) represent higher levels of utility, and therefore more desirable risk–return combinations.) The investor whose preferences are represented by the indifference curves marked $I_1'$, $I_1''$ will choose a portfolio with the risk–return characteristics associated with point $B$ (the point of tangency between the transformation line and his indifference curve). The optimal portfolio for the second investor is given at point $C$ of Figure 11.2.

The optimum portfolio for every investor must satisfy the following (tangency) relationship:

$$\text{Slope of the indifference curve} = \frac{ER - r}{\sigma_R} = \text{Slope of the transformation line}$$

Thus at the optimum the investor's *subjective* trade-off between return and risk must be equal to the *objective* risk–return trade-off provided by the market. The latter is measured by the slope of the transformation line, or "market line" as it is often called.

Since the optimum portfolio depends on individual preferences, its composition can be expected to differ from investor to investor. Thus a point like $B$ on the segment $rA$ of the market line represents an optimal portfolio which includes a proportion of bonds as well as a proportion of the stock. Point $C$, on segment $Aa$, represents the optimal solution for an investor who borrows to build a levered portfolio, that is, who borrows to finance his stock purchases. In the more familiar terms of the market, the points along the segment $Aa$ of the market line represent equity portfolios bought "on margin." The further we move along the segment in a northeasterly direction, the *smaller* the margin provided by the investor's own funds and the larger the proportion of the portfolio which is financed out of loans. Put another way, $x$ is negative along the segment $Aa$ and positive along the segment $rA$. At point $A$, $x = 0$, and the investor who chooses such a portfolio neither borrows nor lends.

## 11.2.1  Choosing among Alternative Single-stock Portfolios

Until now we have limited the investor's choice to a single stock or a combination of that stock with riskless bonds (loans). While retaining the single-stock constraint, let us permit the investor to choose the company in whose stock he wishes to invest. To keep the problem manageable let us further assume that there are five such alternatives, and that their risk–return characteristics are given by the five points $A$, $B$, $C$, $D$, and $E$ of Figure 11.3. (All the returns are given per dollar of investment to facilitate the comparison among the alternatives.) Before deciding on the proportions of his wealth to be invested in stocks or bonds, the investor must first choose the *particular* stock in which to invest. (Remember, we still do not allow him to buy the stock of more than one company.) From the diagram it is clear that he will not choose $D$ or $E$, because $B$, for example, which has a higher expected return and lower risk, dominates both $D$ and $E$. Therefore there are three candidates, $A$, $B$, and $C$, since these three stocks fulfill the MV efficiency conditions:

$$ER_A > ER_B > ER_C$$
$$\sigma_A > \sigma_B > \sigma_C$$

Although the MVC cannot distinguish between these three alternatives, all of which represent efficient options, the possibility of borrowing or lending (buying bonds) allows the investor to make a choice among these alternatives, without recourse to his indifference map. Let us assume a borrowing (or lending) rate equal to $r$. To compare the three alternatives, we have drawn in Figure 11.4 a transformation line from point $r$ on the vertical axis through each of the points $A$, $B$, and $C$. Each of these lines represents all the risk–return combinations which can be obtained from alternative combinations of the stock of a particular company and riskless bonds (loans): the mixed stock–bond portfolios lie on the segments $rA$, $rB$, and $rC$ respectively; the levered portfolios lie along the segments $Ca_1$, $Aa_2$, and $Ba_3$. Since the stock of company $B$ lies on the highest transformation line ($ra_3$) of Figure 11.4 it is clear that an investor who has the opportunity of borrowing or lending at the rate $r$ should choose stock $B$ when making his final portfolio decision, since a mixed (or levered) portfolio which includes $B$

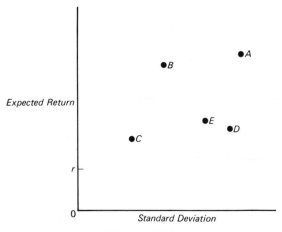

**Figure 11.3**

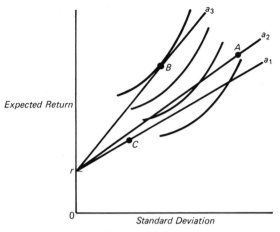

**Figure 11.4**

rather than $A$ or $C$ allows him to reach a higher level of utility. This can be confirmed from Figure 11.4, which superimposes an investor's preference map on the transformation lines and shows that the tangency with the highest indifference curve will be along line $ra_3$, which is the same conclusion we reached by examining the transformation lines themselves *without* recourse to the indifference curves.

As we have seen, it is the option of borrowing or lending which permits us to distinguish among the three alternatives. This result holds even for the investor who chooses not to borrow or lend. In fact, the indifference curves of Figure 11.4 have been drawn so that the optimum portfolio is represented by point $B$. This point represents a portfolio consisting only of stock $B$; the investor neither borrows nor buys bonds. But even in this limiting case we were able to establish the dominance of $B$ over $A$ and $C$ (without recourse to his subjective preferences) simply by assuming that the investor has the *opportunity* of borrowing or lending.

In sum, the investment process has been dichotomized as follows:

(1) Choosing the stock to be included in the portfolio, independent of the investor's subjective tastes.
(2) Choosing the optimal proportion of bonds (loans) and stock, in accordance with the investor's tastes.

The first stage corresponds to finding the stock which lies along the highest transformation (market) line; the second stage corresponds to finding the tangent between the transformation line and the investor's indifference map. It is only at this stage that *subjective* preferences are relevant. Thus, we have a *separation* of the decision into two steps. The first depends only on the objective data while the second is subjective since it depends on the investor's preferences. This separation property is useful in the derivation of the equilibrium prices later in this chapter.

### 11.2.2   Equilibrium in the Stock Market: Single-stock Portfolios and a Unique Interest Rate

It is clear from the previous discussion that the possibility of borrowing or lending allows us to reduce the efficient set of alternative stocks to a single stock. Together with this, a large (strictly speaking infinite) family of efficient portfolios, with alternative proportions of bonds (loans) and stock, is created. Similarly, we can conclude that in the single-stock case, and for a given interest rate, all investors will wish to choose the same stock—in our example that of company $B$. As a result of the increased demand for stock $B$, its price can be expected to rise, thereby lowering the expected return to investors. Conversely, the lack of demand for the shares of the other companies ($A$ and $C$ in our example) will lead to a fall in their prices, thereby raising their expected returns. This process will continue until all the shares lie along the same market line, at which time the investor will be indifferent among them. This is the essence of the market equilibrium process in the single-stock portfolio case.

Let us examine the process more carefully with the aid of some algebra. The following notation will be used:

$R$ = a random variable denoting the net earnings of company $B$
$ER$ = the expected net earnings of company $B$
$S_1$ = the current market value of the company's stock
$ER_1$ = the expected return *per dollar* invested in the company's stock

The return per dollar invested in the company's stock ($R_1$) is clearly obtained by dividing the net income through the market value of the company's stock, $R_1 = R/S_1$, and the expected return per dollar invested is thus:

$$ER_1 = ER/S_1 \tag{11.7}$$

Similarly, since $S_1$ is constant, the standard deviation of the return per dollar invested is:

$$\sigma_1 = \sigma_R/S_1 \tag{11.8}$$

where $\sigma_R$ is the standard deviation of the net earnings $R$.

Now assume that increasing demand for the shares of $B$ raises their price at a rate $g$, so that the new market value of the company's stock is $S_2 = S_1(1 + g)$, where $g > 0$. What will be the new expected return $ER_2$ and standard deviation $\sigma_2$ per dollar invested? Reasoning as before, we have:

$$ER_2 = ER/S_2 = ER/S_1(1 + g) = ER_1/(1 + g) \tag{11.9}$$

and:

$$\sigma_2 = \sigma_R/S_2 = \sigma_R/S_1(1 + g) = \sigma_1/(1 + g) \tag{11.10}$$

We see that both the expected return and the standard deviation *decrease* at the rate $g$ as a result of an increase at the rate $g$ in the price of company's stock.

These results are illustrated graphically in Figure 11.5, which reproduces the market lines of Figure 11.4.[10] The starting point is again point $B$, which represents the initial expected return–standard deviation combination of the shares of company $B$; as we have seen the induced rise in price of $B$ causes both its expected return and standard deviation to fall at the same rate. This is shown in the diagram as a downward movement along the ray $OB$. As $B$ moves toward the origin the slope of the relevant market line also declines. Thus the dashed market line $ra'$ which connects the rate of interest with $B'$ (the new risk–return combination of $B$ after the price rise) has a smaller slope than $ra_3$. The opposite holds true for $A$ and $C$. For example, the fall in the price of $C$ raises its expected return and standard deviation; this is shown as an *upward* movement along the ray $OCC'$, which *raises* the slope of the relevant market line (for stock $C$). This process continues (for $A$ as well) until all three shares ($B'$, $A'$, $C'$) lie along the *same* market line $ra'$ in Figure 11.5. At the new risk–return combinations, $B'$, $A'$, and $C'$, investors are indifferent as to which stock they hold, since all three now lie along the same market line and therefore afford *all* investors with an equal opportunity of maximizing their utilities. Should the price of any of the stocks fall, thereby raising its expected return and standard deviation, it will lie on a new market line with a higher slope. But such an investment will now be so desirable that an increase in demand will be engendered, thereby raising its price until the previous equilibrium is restored.[11] Conversely, a rise in price (fall in return) will make the share an undesirable investment, calling forth a rush of sales and thereby lowering the price (raising the return) until the previous equilibrium price is again restored.

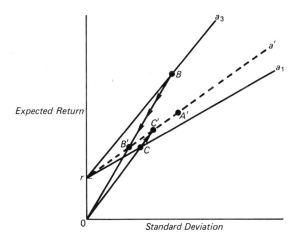

**Figure 11.5**

[10] The market line for $A$ has been omitted to avoid confusion
[11] For the sake of simplicity we ignore any possible effects of the dynamic process on the final equilibrium itself.

## 11.3    Multiple-stock Portfolios

Now let us apply the same type of market equilibrium analysis to the more realistic case where investors can include in their portfolios as many shares of stock as they like, of as many companies as they like. The previous case considered, where investors included the shares of only a single company, is a special case in which the number of companies, $n$, was taken equal to 1. What are the optimal investment proportions in the general unconstrained case? Will the investor include only one company in his optimum portfolio or will he diversify his portfolio to include the shares of many companies?

### 11.3.1    A Graphical Analysis

To answer these questions, we shall approach the problem initially by means of a simplified graphical presentation. Assume a market comprised of the shares of five companies: $A$, $B$, $C$, $D$, and $E$. Figure 11.6 sets out the risk–return characteristics of each of these stocks; the shaded area represents the various combinations of two or more of the shares, in portfolios of differing proportions. Consider an investor who restricts himself to a portfolio which includes only shares of $A$ and $E$: the transformation curve I,[12] connecting points $A$ and $E$, represents all the attainable risk–return combinations from this two-stock portfolio, with each point on the curve representing a different set of investment proportions. Note that only the solid part of the curve represents efficient

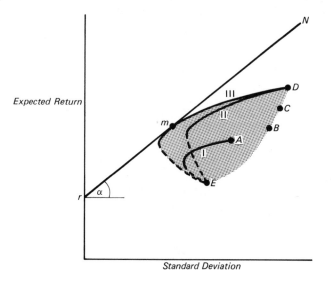

**Figure 11.6**

[12] On the shape of the transformation curve and its relationship to the correlation between the returns of the stocks, see Chapter 8. The curves in Figure 11.6 are drawn for the case without short sales, assuming nonnegative investment proportions (see Chapter 9).

portfolios; the dashed part of the curve represents inefficient combinations. Similarly, transformation curve II is the appropriate curve for portfolios which include various proportions of $D$ and $E$. Clearly, curves could also be generated for other two-stock combinations or for portfolios which include three, four, or more stocks. If we relax all constraints and permit the investor to build his portfolio as he wishes, choosing any proportion of all the five stocks assumed to comprise the market, the envelope curve of the five-stock portfolios will lie to the left of the transformation curves of the constrained portfolios which include the securities of four or fewer companies. The transformation curve for the unconstrained five-stock case is given by curve III of Figure 11.6. This curve sets out all of the combinations of expected return and standard deviation which can be obtained by freely building a pure equity portfolio using all of the available stocks in the market. For graphical convenience only we assume a market which includes the shares of only five companies. The shaded area to the right of the transformation curve III, which includes all of the constrained curves, represents portfolios which are inefficient relative to the portfolios on the solid part of curve III. Here again the lower, dashed, part of the curve is also inefficient since these portfolios are dominated by the upper segment of curve III.

Now let us assume that the investor can borrow or lend (buy bonds) at the rate $r$. Thus in Figure 11.6 the market line which rises from the interest rate $r$ on the vertical axis, and which is tangent to transformation curve III at point $m$, sets out all the alternative combinations of the pure equity portfolio $m$ with the riskless asset (mixed with bonds up to point $m$ on the line $rN$, and levered by loans beyond point $m$). Point $m$ represents the risk–return characteristics of the market portfolio which has *optimal* proportions of the five stocks. This portfolio is optimal, since given the option of borrowing or lending at rate $r$, portfolio $m$ permits the investor to reach the highest market line, thereby permitting him to reach the highest possible indifference curve. Note that the optimal pure equity portfolio, represented by point $m$, has the property of maximizing the angle formed when a straight line is drawn from point $r$ to any point on the transformation curve. Thus the line $rN$ has the highest possible slope of any market line drawn to any point on the transformation curve.

If the indifference curve of an investor is tangent to point $m$, this individual invests all of his wealth in equities.[13] Of course, the indifference curves of many investors will not be tangent to point $m$. Tangency solutions which lie on the segment $rm$ represent mixed stock and riskless bond portfolios; those which occur on the segment $mN$ represent levered portfolios, that is, a pure equity portfolio financed in part by loans. However it must be emphasized that all investors have one important characteristic in common. Whether he chooses a pure equity, mixed, or levered portfolio, an investor who chooses to invest in equities *invariably* builds a portfolio which has the optimal proportions represented by point $m$. Hence the proportions of each stock in the equity portion of the portfolios of *all* investors are the same, independent of their individual

[13] A point of tangency (or corner solution) will always exist since the indifference curves of a risk averter must be concave upward. For proof, see J. Tobin, "Liquidity Preference as Behavior Toward Risk", *Review of Economic Studies*, 1958.

tastes; that is, despite the differences in tastes all individuals will diversify the equity portion of their portfolios in the same proportions among the individual stocks. Differences in individual tastes are operative only in determining the proportion of riskless bonds (loans) which the investor buys (takes). The indifference curves enter the analysis only *after* the optimal proportions of the equity portfolio (represented by point *m*) have been established, and serve to determine the tangency point with the market line *rmN*, but do *not* alter the tangency of the market line with point *m* itself. It is this property of a perfect market (that the equity portfolios of all individuals include the same available risky assets, and in the same proportions) which permits us to aggregate individuals' demands for stocks into a market demand function.

These results are a special case of Tobin's "separation theorem",[14] which dichotomizes the investment process into two separate stages: (1) finding the proportions of the optimal risk portfolio; (2) choosing the mix between the risk assets and riskless bonds (loans).[15]

As we have seen, all investors hold the same proportions of the same stocks in their portfolios. This raises three questions: (a) does the information that all investors hold the same risky portfolio shed light on the risk–return relationship of each individual risky asset? (b) which stocks are held, and (c) in what proportions? The answer to question (b) is straightforward. In a perfect market, in which all lenders and borrowers face the same (riskless) interest rate, the equity portfolios of all investors include the same risky assets, independent of their tastes. Thus if a particular stock is not included in portfolio *m*, no investor holds it. But if no investor desires to hold a stock, its price will fall, thereby raising its return, until it becomes sufficiently attractive to be included in portfolio *m*. It follows that in equilibrium, *all* available risky assets will be included in the risk portfolios of *all* investors. In the rest of this chapter we try to answer the other two questions.

## 11.4  The CAPM: Sharpe's Approach

Suppose that all investors agree with respect to the expected returns, the variance of returns as well as the covariances of returns of all the risky assets. Then by the separation property, all investors hold the same risky portfolio *m*, and they differ only with respect to the mix of this risky portfolio with the riskless asset, whose rate of return is *r*.

In Figure 11.7 the segment *ab* representing the efficient frontier consists of portfolios of all the risky assets and *m* is the efficient portfolio corresponding to the tangency point of line *rr'* with the efficient frontier (the optimal portfolio for riskless rate *r*). Now let us create a portfolio which is a mix of some risky security *i* and the optimal

---

[14] See Tobin (1958), *op. cit.*

[15] In general the risky portfolio (point *m*) also includes risky bonds, since a bond with a positive, standard deviation should be treated as a stock. For simplicity we shall use the terms *equity portfolio, risk portfolio* and *market portfolio* interchangeably, although the reference is to the relevant risky assets.

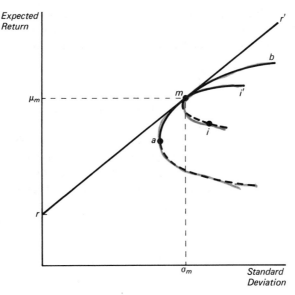

**Figure 11.7**

portfolio $m$. Thus, our new portfolio, with rate of return $R_p$, is given by:

$$R_p = x_i R_i + (1 - x_i)R_m \qquad (11.11)$$

where

$\quad x_i =$ the proportion invested in stock $i$
$1 - x_i =$ the proportion invested in portfolio $m$
$\quad R_i =$ the rate of return on security $i$
$\quad R_m =$ the rate of return on the market portfolio $m$

By changing the proportion $x_i$, we get the curve $ii'$ which describes all portfolios consisting of a mix of these two assets. Note that the segment $mi'$ (see Figure 11.7) corresponds to a strategy of shorting security $i$ and investing more than 100% of the funds in portfolio $m$.

The basic claim which allows us to derive the CAPM is that at point $m$ the curves $ii'$ and $ab$ have the same tangent whose slope is equal to the slope of the straight line $rr'$. This property stems from the fact that the curve $ii'$ touching the point $m$ cannot cross the curve $ab$. If it does, then the curve $ab$ is not the efficient frontier of all the risky assets, as we previously assumed. Thus the slope of the curve $ii'$ at point $m$ is equal to the slope of the straight line $rr'$ and is given by:

$$\frac{\mu_m - r}{\sigma_m} = \text{slope of } ii' \text{ at point } m \qquad (11.12)$$

Here $\mu_m \equiv ER_m$ and $\sigma_m$ are the expected rate of return and the standard deviation of the market portfolio. The expected rate of return and the variance of the portfolio consisting of a mix of security $i$ and market portfolio $m$ are given by:

$$\mu_p = x_i\mu_i + (1 - x_i)\tilde{\mu}_m$$

$$\sigma_p^2 = x_i^2\sigma_i^2 + (1 - x_i)^2\sigma_m^2 + 2x_i(1 - x_i)\sigma_{im} \tag{11.13}$$

where $\mu_p$ and $\sigma_p^2$ are the parameters of any portfolio which lies on the curve $ii'$; $\mu_i$ and $\sigma_i^2$ are the parameters of security $i$, $\mu_m$ and $\sigma_m^2$ are the parameters of the market portfolio and $\sigma_{im}$ is the covariance of return on security $i$ and portfolio $m$. Recall that at point $m$, the curves $ii'$ and $ab$ coincide, hence the proportion $x_i$ invested in security $i$ is zero. Take the derivatives $\partial\mu_p/\partial x_i$ and $\partial\sigma_p/\partial x_i$, and find their value at the point $m$, where $x_i = 0$:

$$\frac{\partial\mu_p}{\partial x_i} = \mu_i - \mu_m \tag{11.14}$$

and

$$\frac{\partial\sigma_p}{\partial x_i} = \frac{1}{2\sigma_p}[2x_i\sigma_i^2 - 2(1 - x_i)\sigma_m^2 + 2\sigma_{im} - 4x_i\sigma_{im}] \tag{11.15}$$

But for $x_i = 0$ (at the point $m$), $\sigma_p = \sigma_m$ and (11.15) reduces to:

$$\frac{\partial\sigma_p}{\partial x_i} = (\sigma_{im} - \sigma_m^2)/\sigma_m \tag{11.16}$$

By the chain rule of differentiation,

$$\frac{\partial\mu_p}{\partial x_i} = \frac{\partial\mu_p}{\partial\sigma_p} \cdot \frac{\partial\sigma_p}{\partial x_i}$$

which can be rewritten as:

$$\frac{\partial\mu_p}{\partial\sigma_p} = \frac{\partial\mu_p}{\partial x_i} \bigg/ \frac{\partial\sigma_p}{\partial x_i} \tag{11.17}$$

The left-hand side of (11.17) is in fact the slope of the curve $ii'$ at point $m$, which is equal to $(\mu_m - r)/\sigma_m$. Thus, using (11.14) and (11.16), we rewrite (11.17) as:

$$\frac{\mu_m - r}{\sigma_m} = \frac{(\mu_i - \mu_m)\sigma_m}{\sigma_{im} - \sigma_m^2}$$

Cross-multiplying, we obtain the CAPM risk–return relationship:

$$\mu_i = r + (\mu_m - r)\sigma_{im}/\sigma_m^2 \qquad (11.18)$$

Since $\sigma_{im} = Cov(R_i, R_m)$ and the regression coefficient of $R_i$ on $R_m$ is given by beta,

$$\beta_i = \sigma_{im}/\sigma_m^2$$

the risk–return relationship can be rewritten in the standard form:

$$\mu_i = r + (\mu_m - r)\beta_i \qquad (11.19)$$

or, using alternative notation for the means

$$ER_i = r + (ER_m - r)\beta_i$$

Here $\beta_i$ measures the risk of security $i$ in the portfolio context. Note that since the same derivation is true for *each* security $i$, the risk–return relationship (11.19) holds for all risky assets.

## 11.5    The CAPM: Lintner's Approach

We turn now to the derivation of the CAPM by Lintner's approach. We first find the optimum investment proportions and then analyze the risk–return relationship.

In order to find the proportions in which the stocks are included in the optimal portfolio $m$, we must analyze the process by which the optimal point $m$ is derived. Let $ER_p$ and $\sigma_p$ denote the expected return and standard deviation per dollar invested of *any* equity portfolio; they are given by the following formulas:

$$ER_p = \sum_{i=1}^{n} x_i ER_i$$

$$\sigma_p = \sqrt{\sum_{i=1}^{n} x_i^2 \sigma_i^2 + 2 \sum_{i=1}^{n} \sum_{\substack{j=1 \\ j>i}}^{n} x_i x_j \sigma_{ij}}$$

where

$x_i$ = the proportion invested in the $i$th security
$n$ = the number of different securities available in the market
$\sigma_i^2$ = the variance of returns (per dollar invested) in the $i$th security
$ER_i$ = the expected return (per dollar invested) in the $i$th security
$\sigma_{ij}$ = the covariance of returns between securities $i$ and $j$

Note that since these formulas hold for any portfolio, the investment proportions $x_i$ need not be optimal. The second term in the formula for the portfolio standard deviation is the (weighted) sum of the covariances between all pairs of stocks; thus it reflects the correlation between the fluctuations in the returns of any two stocks from period to period.

In general $\Sigma^n_{i=1} x_i \neq 1$, that is, the investment proportions in risky assets will not add up to one dollar[16] since the investor may also buy riskless bonds or borrow. When the latter possibilities are taken into account all the investment proportions (including bonds or loans) must add to 1: $\Sigma x_i + x_r = 1$, where $x_r$ denotes the proportion invested in riskless bonds or loans. If the investor borrows, $x_r < 0$ and $\Sigma x_i > 1$; if the investor buys riskless bonds, $x_r > 0$ and $\Sigma x_i < 1$; and if the investor neither borrows nor lends, $x_r = 0$ and $\Sigma x_i = 1$. The latter possibility represents the special case where the indifference curve is tangent to the market line at point $m$ itself.

Recalling our discussion of Figure 11.6, the problem confronting the investor is how to choose a point $(ER_p, \sigma_p)$ on the transformation curve so that the market line connecting it to point $r$ on the vertical axis forms a maximum angle $\alpha$, thereby permitting him to reach the highest possible indifference curve. In analytical terms, the investor must find the vector of investment proportions $x_i$ which maximizes the following expression for the slope tg $\alpha$ of the market line:[17]

$$\text{tg } \alpha_i = \frac{ER_p - r}{\sigma_p} = \frac{\displaystyle\sum_{i=1}^{n} x_i ER_i - r}{\sqrt{\displaystyle\sum_{i=1}^{n} x_i^2 \sigma_i^2 + 2 \sum_{i=1}^{n} \sum_{\substack{j=1 \\ j>i}}^{n} x_i x_j \, \sigma_{ij}^2}} \tag{11.20}$$

Portfolio $m$ represented by the point $(ER_m, \sigma_m)$ in the example given in Figure 11.6 maximizes this expression, and therefore represents the optimum portfolio. The proportions of this portfolio are the optimal investment proportions for all investors.[18]

Note again that in terms of the separation theorem we are discussing stage one in which the optimal *equity* portfolio is determined, that is, we are locating the optimal point on the transformation curve and *not* the tangency point of the transformation curve to an indifference curve.

In order to find the optimum investment proportions $(x_1, x_2, \ldots, x_n)$ and the risk–return relationship we have to take the derivative of (11.20) with respect to the variable proportions $x_i$ $(i = 1, 2, \ldots, n)$. Equating these derivatives to zero yields $n$ equations in $n$ unknowns, which can be solved for $(x_1, x_2, \ldots, x_n)$. These proportions solving the system of $n$ equations maximize the slope of the straight line rising from the riskless asset $r$, namely they maximize tg $\alpha_i$.

---

[16] For mathematical convenience the analysis is carried out in terms of "per dollar invested."

[17] For details of this approach see Lintner (1965), *op. cit.*

[18] Equation (11.20) is formulated in terms of an investor who desires to invest *one dollar* among the various alternative securities. However, it can be shown that these results also hold (that is tg $\alpha_i$ does not change) for the general case in which $Z$ dollars are invested.

Instead of maximizing (11.20), which is quite involved mathematically, we turn to another approach with which, by now, the reader is familiar, and which yields the same results as when maximizing the expression (11.20) suggested by Lintner.

As in (11.20) we seek the investment proportions which maximize the slope of the line $rN$ in Figure 11.6. This line can be found by minimizing the portfolio standard deviation $\sigma_p$ for any given portfolio expected return $ER_p$, where:

$$ER_p = \sum_{i=1}^{n} x_i ER_i + \left( 1 - \sum_{i=1}^{n} x_i \right) r$$

$$\sigma_p = \sqrt{\sum_{i=1}^{n} x_i^2 \sigma_i^2 + 2 \sum_{i=1}^{n} \sum_{\substack{j=1 \\ j>i}}^{n} x_i x_j \, Cov \, (R_i, R_j)}$$

and $x_i$ denotes the proportion of the portfolio invested in the $i$th asset.

Clearly the availability of riskless bonds (or loans) influences, and therefore appears in the formula for, the expected return. However, the inclusion of such bonds (loans) does *not* affect the general form of the expression for the standard deviation of the overall portfolio since the variance of a perfectly certain income (payments) stream $r$ is zero. Hence the covariance of the bonds (loans) with the portfolio's risky assets (e.g. common stock) is also zero.

Now let us define the Lagrange function $C$, as follows:

$$C = \sigma_p + \lambda \left[ ER_p - \sum_{i=1}^{n} x_i ER_i - \left( 1 - \sum_{i=1}^{n} x_i \right) r \right] \qquad (11.21)$$

where $\lambda$ is the Lagrange multiplier (see Chapters 8 and 9 for a discussion of the Lagrange-multiplier technique).

The problem is to determine the vector of investment proportions which *minimizes* the overall portfolio standard deviation for each value of $ER_p$. This is tantamount to finding the market line $rN$ of Figure 11.6, or to maximizing the slope (11.20), since by definition, the market line represents the attainable MV efficient set of alternatives facing the investor. Thus, each point on the line represents the overall portfolio (equities plus bonds or loans) which minimizes the standard deviation, given the portfolio expected return. The market line can be generated analytically by differentiating Equation (11.21) with respect to each $x_i$ and with respect to the Lagrange multiplier $\lambda$, and setting the derivatives equal to zero. This yields the following set of $n + 1$ equations:

$$\frac{\partial C}{\partial x_1} = \frac{1}{2\sigma_p} \left[ 2x_1 \sigma_1^2 + 2 \sum_{j=2}^{n} x_j \, Cov \, (R_1, R_j) \right] - \lambda(ER_1 - r) = 0$$

$$\frac{\partial C}{\partial x_2} = \frac{1}{2\sigma_p} \left[ 2x_2 \sigma_2^2 + 2 \sum_{\substack{j=1 \\ j \neq 2}}^{n} x_j \, Cov \, (R_2, R_j) \right] - \lambda(ER_2 - r) = 0$$

. . . . . . . . . . . . . . . . . . . . . . . . . . . . . . . . . . . . . . . . (11.22)

$$\frac{\partial C}{\partial x_n} = \frac{1}{2\sigma_p} \left[ 2x_n\sigma_n^2 + 2 \sum_{j=1}^{n-1} x_j \, Cov\,(R_n, R_j) \right] - \lambda(ER_n - r) = 0$$

$$\frac{\partial C}{\partial \lambda} = ER_p - \sum_{i=1}^{n} x_i ER_i - \left( 1 - \sum_{i=1}^{n} x_i \right) r = 0$$

These equations hold for all efficient portfolios $p$, and in particular also for portfolio $m$, which is efficient by construction (see Figure 11.6). Reducing by 2 the left-hand side of each equation, multiplying the first equation by $x_1$, the second equation by $x_2$, etc., and summing over all the $n$ first equations yields:[19]

$$\sigma_p = \lambda \left( \sum_{i=1}^{n} x_i ER_i - \sum_{i=1}^{n} x_i r \right)$$

By adding and subtracting $r$ in the right-hand side we obtain:

$$\sigma_p = \lambda \left[ \sum_{i=1}^{n} x_i ER_i + \left( 1 - \sum_{i=1}^{n} x_i \right) r - r \right] = \lambda(ER_p - r)$$

Hence:

$$\frac{1}{\lambda} = \frac{(ER_p - r)}{\sigma_p}$$

where $p$ is a portfolio which lies on the straight line $rN$ in Figure 11.6. Since the slope is the same for all points on the line $rN$, the same relationships can be rewritten in terms of the portfolio $m$:

$$\frac{1}{\lambda} = \frac{(ER_m - r)}{\sigma_m}$$

Here $m$ denotes the market portfolio, which is optimal for all investors (see Figure 11.6).

As we have already noted, the expression $(ER_m - r)/\sigma_m$ defines the slope of the market line ($rN$ of Figure 11.6). The reciprocal of the Lagrange multiplier $(1/\lambda)$ measures the price of a unit of risk, that is the required increase in expected return when one unit of risk (in terms of the standard deviation) is added to the portfolio. The larger the number of different securities available in the market, the greater are the opportunities to reduce risk, therefore the entire efficient set (market line) will rotate to

---

[19] Note that the left-hand side of this summation is simply the portfolio standard deviation $\sigma_p$, since

$$\frac{1}{\sigma_p} \left[ \sum_{i=1}^{n} x_i^2 \sigma_i^2 + 2 \sum_{i=1}^{n} \sum_{\substack{j=1 \\ j>i}}^{n} x_i x_j \, Cov\,(R_i, R_j) \right] = \frac{1}{\sigma_p} \cdot \sigma_p^2 = \sigma_p.$$

the left as the market grows. Thus for a given interest rate, the price of a unit of risk (slope of the market line) will be higher, other things being equal, in larger markets.

Let us now use the above results to determine the equilibrium relationship between an individual asset's expected return and its risk. Since this set of equations, from which we derive the equilibrium conditions for the individual investor, must hold simultaneously for all investors, independent of their tastes, we can also use equations (11.22) to derive the general relationship among the expected returns of all securities and their risk.

In general, the $i$th equation of (11.22) can be rewritten for the efficient portfolio $m$ as:

$$ER_i = r + \frac{1}{\lambda \sigma_m} \left[ x_i \sigma_i^2 + \sum_{\substack{j=1 \\ j \neq i}}^{n} x_j \, Cov \, (R_i, R_j) \right]$$

Recalling the definition of $\lambda$, we obtain:

$$ER_i = r + \frac{ER_m - r}{\sigma_m^2} \left[ x_i \sigma_i^2 + \sum_{\substack{j=1 \\ j \neq i}}^{n} x_j \, Cov \, (R_i, R_j) \right]$$

But since by definition, the return on the market portfolio is given by $R_m = \sum_{i=1}^{n} x_i R_i$ it can be shown[20] that the expected return on any risk asset can be written as:

$$ER_i = r + \frac{ER_m - r}{\sigma_m^2} \, Cov \, (R_i, R_m)$$

or alternatively

$$ER_i = r + (ER_m - r)\beta_i \qquad\qquad (11.23)$$

where

$$\beta_i = \frac{Cov \, (R_i, R_m)}{\sigma_m^2}$$

which is precisely the equilibrium relationship which we obtained earlier by employing Sharpe's approach [compare (11.19)].

---

[20] Since the return on the market portfolio is given by $R_m = x_1 R_1 + x_2 R_2 + \cdots + x_n R_n$, we have

$$Cov \, (R_i, R_m) = Cov \, [R_i, (x_1 R_1 + \cdots + x_n R_n)] = x_i \sigma_i^2 + \sum_{\substack{j=1 \\ j \neq i}}^{n} x_j \, Cov \, (R_i, R_j)$$

It is interesting to note that the $i$th equation in (11.22) can be rewritten as:

$$\frac{1}{\lambda} \frac{\partial \sigma_m}{\partial x_i} = ER_i - r$$

This can be verbalized as follows: The term $\partial \sigma_m / \partial x_i$ is the marginal contribution of asset $i$ to the portfolio total risk at the optimum, namely when the optimal investment proportions are held. This marginal contribution to risk multiplied by the market price of risk $1/\lambda$ must be equal, in equilibrium, to the risk premium $ER_i - r$, required on the $i$th asset. Writing it differently, we obtain:

$$ER_i = r + \frac{1}{\lambda} \frac{\partial \sigma_m}{\partial x_i}$$

which has the following interpretation: the required expected rate of return on the $i$th asset, $ER_i$, is equal to the risk-free interest rate $r$ *plus* the risk premium, which is in fact the marginal contribution of the $i$th asset to the portfolio risk multiplied by the market price of risk. However, by (11.23) we have $ER_i - r = (ER_m - r)\beta_i$ and so:

$$\frac{1}{\lambda} \frac{\partial \sigma_m}{\partial x_i} = (ER_m - r)\beta_i \tag{11.24}$$

The right-hand side of (11.24) measures the risk premium of the market portfolio above the riskless rate $r$, and it is thus seen to be equal to the marginal contribution of asset $i$ to the market portfolio risk times the market price of risk.

### 11.6    Equilibrium in the Stock Market

Using the CAPM equilibrium relationship, we now turn to the problem of deriving the equilibrium conditions for the market as a whole. As a first step let us define some basic aggregate relationships.

Since by the separation theorem every investor holds the same proportions of all available shares in his optimal pure-equity portfolio, the following relationship must hold:

$$Sx_i^* = V_{i0} \tag{11.25}$$

where:

$S =$ total capital invested in the market (equal to the total capital invested in equity securities, since in equilibrium for every borrower there is a lender and the net borrowing or lending is zero)

$x_i^* =$ proportion of stock $i$ in the optimal pure-equity portfolio

$V_{i0} =$ market value of the shares of stock $i$, outstanding in the base period 0

It follows from (11.25) that

$$x_i^* = \frac{V_{i0}}{S} \qquad (11.26)$$

But since the total capital invested by all investors in all shares must equal the total market value of all outstanding shares, we have

$$S = \sum_{i=1}^{n} V_{i0} = T_0 \qquad (11.27)$$

where $T_0$ denotes the market value of all shares, that is, the size of the market.

It follows that if the market is to clear, the relative share of any given security in the optimal portfolio must be proportional to its relative weight in the market

$$x_i^* = \frac{V_{i0}}{S} = \frac{V_{i0}}{T_0} \qquad (11.28)$$

And since we are analyzing the optimal unlevered pure-equity portfolio these proportions must also add to one,

$$\sum_{i=1}^{n} x_i^* = \frac{\sum_{i=1}^{n} V_{i0}}{T_0} = \frac{\sum_{i=1}^{n} V_{i0}}{\sum_{i=1}^{n} V_{i0}} = 1 \qquad (11.29)$$

Since by assumption all investors have the same expectations[21] regarding the returns on the various securities, they also have the same estimate of the market value of each of the shares at the end of the period $V_{i1}$. And as $ER_i$ are determined in equilibrium in accordance with Equation (11.22), the prices of securities will adjust themselves during the investment period changing the current market value $V_{i0}$ so that the following relationship holds for every security:

$$ER_i = \frac{V_{i1} - V_{i0}}{V_{i0}} \qquad (i = 1, 2, \ldots, n) \qquad (11.30)$$

Given the expectations of investors, the value of $V_{i0}$ which fulfills the condition of Equation (11.30) is the aggregate equilibrium value of the $i$ shares outstanding in the base period. But any change in $V_{i0}$ also induces changes in the variance of the shares, and in all the covariances as well. Moreover, although we assume that all investors have the

---

[21] Similar conclusions can be reached if we relax the assumption of full agreement. See Chapter 13.

same expectations regarding $V_{i1}$ these expectations are *not* single-valued. Let us denote the *estimated* variance of the aggregate value of the $i$th security by $\bar{\sigma}_i^2$. The variance and covariance *per dollar* invested can be written as follows:

$$\sigma_i^2 = \frac{\bar{\sigma}_i^2}{V_{i0}^2} \tag{11.31}$$

$$Cov\,(R_i, R_j) = \frac{\bar{\sigma}_{ij}}{V_{i0} \cdot V_{j0}} \tag{11.32}$$

Using these definitions the following relationship can be derived:[22]

$$[V_{i1} - (1 + r)V_{i0}] = \frac{ER_m - r}{\sigma_m^2} \cdot \frac{1}{T_0} \left[ \bar{\sigma}_i^2 + \sum_{\substack{j=1 \\ j \neq i}}^{n} \bar{\sigma}_{ij} \right] \tag{11.33}$$

Equation (11.33) represents the market equilibrium conditions when all investors have the same estimates of $\bar{\sigma}_i^2$, $\bar{\sigma}_{ij}$, and $V_{i1}$ (and therefore of $ER_m$, $\sigma_m$, and $T_0$ as well). Should $V_{i0}$ deviate from its value in (11.33) the prices of securities will adjust until equilibrium is restored. Similar equations can be derived for each of the $n$ securities comprising the market. Solving the set of equations simultaneously and dividing through by the numbers of shares, we derive the set of equilibrium prices for all the securities.[23]

From (11.33) we can also derive the equilibrium market value for the aggregate

---

[22] Let us take one of the CAPM equations out of the set (11.22):

$$\lambda(ER_i - r) = \frac{1}{\sigma_m} \left[ x_i \sigma_i^2 + \sum_{\substack{j=1 \\ j \neq i}}^{n} x_j\, Cov\,(R_i, R_j) \right]$$

Substituting the appropriate expression for $x_i$, $x_j$, $ER_i$, $\sigma_i$, and $Cov\,(R_i, R_j)$ we get:

$$\lambda \left[ \frac{V_{i1} - V_{i0}}{V_{i0}} - r \right] = \frac{1}{\sigma_m} \left[ \frac{V_{i0}}{T_0} \cdot \frac{\bar{\sigma}_i^2}{(V_{i0})^2} + \sum_{\substack{j=1 \\ j \neq i}}^{n} \frac{V_{j0}}{T_0} \cdot \frac{\bar{\sigma}_{ij}}{(V_{i0} \cdot V_{j0})} \right]$$

Multiplying both sides by $V_{i0}$ and cancelling, yields:

$$\lambda[V_{i1} - (1 + r)V_{i0}] = \frac{1}{T_0 \sigma_m} \left[ \bar{\sigma}_i^2 + \sum_{\substack{j=1 \\ j \neq i}}^{n} \bar{\sigma}_{ij} \right]$$

And recalling that the price of unit of risk $1/\lambda = (ER_m - r)/\sigma_m$, this becomes Equation (11.33) of the text.

[23] The equilibrium conditions in terms of individual share prices are given in Appendix 11.1.

shares of any company $i$:

$$V_{i0} = \frac{V_{i1} - \dfrac{ER_m - r}{\sigma_m^2} \dfrac{1}{T_0} \left[ \bar{\sigma}_i^2 + \sum\limits_{\substack{j=1 \\ j \neq i}}^{n} \bar{\sigma}_{ij} \right]}{1 + r} \tag{11.34}$$

If we invest $T_0$ dollars rather than one dollar (that is, the aggregate amount invested in the market in all securities), the optimum portfolio parameters become $T_0 ER_m$ and $T_0^2 \sigma_m^2$. In this case we multiply the numerator and the denominator of the expression $(ER_m - r)/\sigma_m^2$ by $T_0$ (which does not change its value) and rewrite (11.34) as follows:

$$V_{i0} = \frac{V_{i1} - \dfrac{T_0(ER_m - r)}{T_0 \sigma_m^2} \cdot \dfrac{1}{T_0} \left[ \bar{\sigma}_i^2 + \sum\limits_{\substack{j=1 \\ j \neq i}}^{n} \bar{\sigma}_{ij} \right]}{1 + r} \tag{11.35}$$

or:

$$V_{i0} = \frac{V_{i1} - \dfrac{T_0 ER_m - T_0 r}{T_0^2 \sigma_m^2} \left[ \bar{\sigma}_i^2 + \sum\limits_{\substack{j=1 \\ j \neq i}}^{n} \bar{\sigma}_{ij} \right]}{1 + r} \tag{11.36}$$

Here $[T_0 ER_m - T_0 r]/T_0^2 \sigma_m^2$ is the price of risk for investment of $T_0$ dollars, rather than $1, with the risk measured in terms of *variance* (and not standard deviation). Equation (11.36) reduces to

$$V_{i0} = \frac{V_{i1} - \gamma \left[ \bar{\sigma}_i^2 + \sum\limits_{\substack{j=1 \\ j \neq i}}^{n} \bar{\sigma}_{ij} \right]}{1 + r} \tag{11.37}$$

and therefore

$$\frac{V_{i1} - V_{i0}}{V_{i0}} = r + \frac{\gamma \left[ \bar{\sigma}_i^2 + \sum\limits_{\substack{j=1 \\ j \neq i}}^{n} \bar{\sigma}_{ij} \right]}{V_{i0}} \tag{11.38}$$

where $\gamma$ denotes the price of a unit of risk in terms of *variance*[24] when the total amount invested in the market is taken into account. It should also be noted that the present value of a share is equal to its "certainty equivalent" value at the end of the period discounted at the riskless rate of interest [see Equation (11.37)]. Equation (11.38) represents the basic equilibrium conditions of a perfect securities market and can be verbalized as follows: in equilibrium, security prices adjust to the point where the prospective rate of return to investors in every security is just equal to the riskless rate of interest *plus* a risk premium which reflects not only that security's risk but its total contribution to the risk of the optimum portfolio as well.

## Summary

In this chapter the normative theory of investment behavior was applied to the positive problem of explaining equilibrium prices in the securities market. A model, based on the work of Sharpe and Lintner, was developed on the following assumptions:

(a)    investors are risk-averse and choose their portfolios by the Mean–Variance Criterion;
(b)    securities are traded in a perfect market.

The first case considered is an example in which investors are constrained to portfolios which include the shares of one company and/or riskless bonds (or loans). The relationship between the expected return and the standard deviation of such portfolios is linear, with a slope $(ER_p - r)/\sigma_p$. The slope of the linear transformation line measures the "price" of a unit of risk, that is, the number of units of expected return which an investor is willing to forgo per unit reduction in the standard deviation. And the transformation line itself constitutes the MV locus of efficient portfolios. The optimal portfolio is given by the tangency of the transformation line to the investor's indifference curve.

When the investor faces $n$ risky assets and borrowing or lending at a riskless interest rate is allowed, the investment process can be dichotomized as follows:

(1)    Choosing the proportions of the risky securities to be included in the portfolio, independent of the investor's tastes.
(2)    Choosing the optimal proportions of riskless bonds (loans) and of the risky portfolio in accordance with the investor's tastes.

The first stage corresponds to finding the risky portfolio which lies on the highest transformation line; the second stage corresponds to finding the tangency point between the transformation line and the investor's indifference curve.

---

[24] See Lintner, *op. cit.*

The separation of the investment decision into two stages is called the "separation theorem", which implies that all investors independently of their preferences hold the same risky (or unlevered) portfolio. They differ only with respect to the mix of this unlevered portfolio with the riskless asset. Thus, in an unconstrained perfect market, where investors can include in their portfolios as many securities of as many companies as they wish, the proportion of each security in the risky portion of the portfolios of *all* investors is the same, independent of their individual tastes. All investors will diversify the equity portion of their portfolios in the *same* proportions among the individual stocks. It is this property of a perfect market which permits us to aggregate the individuals' demands for securities into a market demand function. Since all investors hold the same proportions of the same stocks in their portfolios, it can also be shown that the optimal portfolio includes *all* available stocks. And since the larger the number of available stocks, the greater are the opportunities to reduce risk, the entire market line rotates to the left, thereby permitting investors to reach higher indifference curves.

---

**Summary Table**

1. **The separation property:** The investment decision is separated into two steps:
    (a) Finding the optimum portfolio consisting of only risky assets
    (b) Finding the optimum mix of the risky portfolio with the riskless asset.
    While step (a) is *objective* and common to all investors, step (b) is *subjective* and depends on the investor's individual preference.

2. The CAPM risk–return relationship,

$$\mu_i = r + (\mu_m - r)\beta_i$$

written also as

$$ER_i = r + (ER_m - r)\beta_i$$

where $\mu_i$ (or $ER_i$) is the expected rate of return on the $i$th asset, $r$ is the risk-free interest rate, $\mu_m$ (or $ER_m$) is the expected rate of return on the market portfolio, $\beta_i$ is the risk measure of the $i$th asset in portfolio context (beta).

3. The $i$th security risk in portfolio context is given by:

$$\beta_i = \frac{Cov(R_i, R_m)}{\sigma_m^2} \quad \text{or} \quad \beta_i = \frac{\sigma_{im}}{\sigma_m^2}$$

4. The equilibrium market value of the $i$th firm, $V_{i0}$, is given by the following certainty equivalence equation:

$$V_{i0} = \frac{V_{i1} - \gamma \left[ \tilde{\sigma}_i^2 + \sum_{\substack{j=1 \\ j \neq i}}^{n} \tilde{\sigma}_{ij} \right]}{1 + r}$$

where

$V_{i1}$ = the expected value of the firm at period 1
$\gamma$ = the market price of risk
$\bar{\sigma}_i^2$ = the variance of the value of firm $i$
$\bar{\sigma}_{ij}$ = the covariance of the value of firm $i$ with the value of firm $j$
$r$ = the riskless interest rate

## APPENDIX 11.1
### Equilibrium Prices in a Perfect Securities Market[25]

In Section 11.6 we analyzed the aggregate equilibrium market value of a company's stock. In this appendix we give the same equilibrium results but in terms of price per share rather than in terms of the aggregate value.

Let us define the following notation:

$N_i$ = the number of shares of firm $i$
$P_{i1}$ = the expected price of the share at the end of the investment period
$P_{i0}$ = the equilibrium price
$\sigma_i$ = the expected variance of the value of the share at the end of the investment period
$\sigma_{ij}$ = the expected covariance of the value of a share of firm $i$ and a share of firm $j$

Hence the aggregate value of the stock is given by:

$$V_{i1} = N_i P_{i1} \tag{11.1.1}$$

$$V_{i0} = N_i P_{i0} \tag{11.1.2}$$

Similarly the variance $(\sigma_i^2)$ and the covariance $(\sigma_{ij})$ in terms of aggregate values are given by:

$$\bar{\sigma}_i^2 = N_i^2 \sigma_i^2 \tag{11.1.3}$$

$$\bar{\sigma}_{ij} = N_i N_j \sigma_{ij} \tag{11.1.4}$$

The equilibrium equation (11.37) is:

$$V_{i0} = \frac{V_{i1} - \gamma \left[ \bar{\sigma}_i^2 + \sum_{\substack{j=1 \\ j \neq i}}^{n} \bar{\sigma}_{ij} \right]}{1 + r} \tag{11.1.5}$$

[25] The proof follows J. Lintner, "Security Prices, Risk and Maximal Gains from Diversification", *Journal of Finance* (1965).

Substituting (11.1.1), (11.1.2), (11.1.3), and (11.1.4) in (11.1.5) we obtain:

$$N_i P_{i0} = \frac{N_i P_{i1} - \gamma \left[ N_i^2 \sigma_i^2 + \sum_{\substack{j=1 \\ j \neq i}}^{n} N_i N_j \sigma_{ij} \right]}{1 + r} \qquad (11.1.6)$$

Reducing by $N_i$, we obtain for the equilibrium share price:

$$P_{i0} = \frac{P_{i1} - \gamma \left[ N_i \sigma_i^2 + \sum_{\substack{i=1 \\ j \neq i}}^{n} N_j \sigma_{ij} \right]}{1 + r} \qquad (11.1.7)$$

Thus the end-of-period variance is weighted by the number of shares outstanding. This weighted average ensures that the aggregate value of a company's stock is independent of stock splits.

## Questions and Problems

 11.1 What are the basic assumptions that characterize the notion of a perfect capital market?

11.2 It has been said that the prices of risky alternatives are determined in a perfect capital market *as if* there was only one investor. Do you agree with this statement? Explain.

11.3 Assume a perfect capital market in which the investors are constrained to holding portfolios that consist of a single stock (a risk asset) and the riskless asset. Two risky securities in this market were observed to have the following parameters *in equilibrium*:

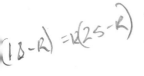

|  | Stock i | Stock j |
|---|---|---|
| Expected return (%) | 18 | 25 |
| Standard deviation (%) | 8 | 12 |

(a) What is the riskless interest rate in this market?
(b) Assume that the investor is confronted with two mutually exclusive alternatives:
    (1) A portfolio of $900 worth of stock *i*;
    (2) A portfolio of $600 worth of stock *j* plus $300 worth of the riskless asset.
Which of the two alternatives is preferable?

11.4 Assume a perfect capital market in which the investors are constrained to holding portfolios that consist of a single stock (a risk asset) and the riskless asset. Two risky securities in this market were observed to have the following parameters *in equilibrium*:

|                         | Stock A | Stock B |
|-------------------------|---------|---------|
| Expected return (%)     | 18      | 22      |
| Standard deviation (%)  | 6       | 8       |

(a) Determine the riskless rate of return in this market.
(b) Find the optimal investment strategy of the two individuals characterized by the following indifference maps:
    (1) $ER = a + 10\sigma^2$
    (2) $ER = a + 25\sigma^2$
    Assume that both are seeking to invest $100 worth in securities. Demonstrate your answer numerically and graphically.
(c) Since the individuals are allowed to hold only one risky asset in their portfolios, enterprising businessmen applied for a government license to set up a mutual fund that will include stock $A$ and stock $B$ in equal proportions. The individual investors will then be allowed to diversify between fund shares and the riskless asset. Find the market line characteristic of the mutual fund and compare it with the market line of the two separate stocks. How would you characterize the gains from diversification in this case? Assume zero correlation coefficient between the two stocks included in the mutual fund.
(d) Estimate the maximum management fee that the fund managers can charge their shareholders. The management fee effectively reduces the mean return that the fund yields to the investors. How will the management fee be affected if the correlation coefficient is negative (say, $-2/3$) rather than zero?

11.5 Consider an imperfect capital market with 8% borrowing rate and 4% lending rate. The two risky securities comprising the stock market are characterized by the following parameters:

|                         | Stock A | Stock B |
|-------------------------|---------|---------|
| Expected return (%)     | 18      | 12      |
| Standard deviation (%)  | 20      | 10      |

An investor seeking to invest $100 in the market is allowed to hold portfolios consisting of a single stock (risk asset) and riskless loans or bonds.
(a) What is the maximum amount that the investor will be willing *to borrow* in order to construct a levered portfolio of stock $B$?
(b) What is the maximum amount that the investor will be willing to lend (invest in riskless bonds) in order to construct a mixed portfolio of bonds and stock $A$?

11.6 Assume that all the individual investors are constrained to holding portfolios that consist of a single stock and riskless loans or bonds. The riskless interest rate in the market is 6% (equal to lenders and borrowers), but the market is temporarily *not* in equilibrium. Three stocks $A$, $B$, and $C$ were observed to have the following parameters at a certain point in time:

|                          | Stock A | Stock B | Stock C |
| ------------------------ | ------- | ------- | ------- |
| Expected return (%)      | 10      | 20      | 30      |
| Standard deviation (%)   | 20      | 60      | 40      |

How will the price of each stock change as the market approaches equilibrium? Demonstrate your answer graphically.

 11.7  Derive the market price of a unit of risk when investors are constrained to holding portfolios that consist of a single stock and riskless bonds (or loans).

11.8   Define the efficient frontier for the case of single-stock and multiple-stock portfolios (a) when the lending and the borrowing rates are equal; and (b) when the borrowing rate is different from the lending rate. Demonstrate your answer graphically.

11.9   "When the borrowing and lending rates are different, the notion of *market price of risk* is meaningless." Appraise this statement.

11.10  "In a perfect capital market, the investment decision is separated into two distinct stages." Explain and discuss.

11.11  What are the theoretical considerations which support the contention that in a perfect market the returns on the optimal portfolio will tend to approximate a normal distribution?

 11.12  What is the general equilibrium relationship between risk (variance) and return which must hold for every risk asset in a perfect market?

11.13  What is the contribution of each risk asset in a perfect market to the variance of the market portfolio?

11.14  "In a perfect market, all stocks have the same risk premium." Do you agree with this statement? Explain.

11.15  Assume a market that consists of two securities such that $\mu_1 > \mu_2$ and $\sigma_1 > \sigma_2$. The correlation coefficient between the two securities is $+1$.
(a) If the market is perfect with riskless interest rate $r = 6\%$, will a risk-averse investor necessarily diversify between the two securities? Find the general conditions that ensure diversification in this case.
(b) Now assume that the market is imperfect, with riskless lending rate $r_L = 6\%$ and riskless borrowing rate $r_B = 8\%$. Under what conditions will the investor diversify between the two stocks? Under what condition will the investor concentrate his risk holdings in one stock only?
(c) Now assume that investors are allowed to diversify between two risky securities and cash. Riskless bonds and loans do not exist. Answer part (b) under these conditions.

11.16  Prove that the covariance of stock $i$ with the market portfolio is equal to the sum of the covariances of stock $i$ with all the stocks included in the market portfolio multiplied by the corresponding proportions, i.e.,

$$Cov(R_i, R_m) = \sum_{j=1}^{n} x_j \, Cov(R_i, R_j)$$

(*Hint:* Express $R_m$ as a linear combination of the constituent stocks.)

11.17   Credit restrictions imposed by the Central Bank in a perfect capital market with equal riskless lending and borrowing rate drive the riskless rate up.
(a) Show diagrammatically in the mean–standard deviation plane the changes that occur in the securities market as a result of the new policy.
(b) Can we state with full certainty whether the investors' welfare will increase or decrease as a result of the new policy? Is it possible that borrowers will become lenders or vice versa as a result of the change in interest rates?
(c) Now assume that only the riskless borrowing rate increased, while the lending rate remained as before. Show diagrammatically the efficient frontier in this case. How did the new policy affect the investors' welfare?

11.18   Consider a market consisting of three risky assets and the riskless asset. The following information is available *in equilibrium*:

$$V_{1,0} = \$100, \quad V_{2,0} = \$200, \quad V_{3,0} = \$300,$$

$$ER_m = 10\%, \quad \sigma_m^2 = 0.07, \quad \sigma_1^2 = 0.1, \quad \sigma_{12} = 0.2, \quad \sigma_{13} = 0, \quad r = 3\%$$

(for notation, see equations (11.31)–(11.34)).
(a) Calculate the expected value of the first firm in period 1 (the future), $V_{1,1}$.
(b) How would your answer to (a) change if the interest rate were $r = 5\%$?
(c) How would your answer to (a) change if it was known that $\sigma_{13} = -0.1$? $\sigma_{13} = +0.1$?

11.19   Suppose that having applied formula (11.1.7) of Appendix 11.1 you find that $P_{i0} = \$100$. Explain in detail how a split of 2-to-1 will affect the various parameters in the formula and the post-split equilibrium price.

## Data Set Problems

1. Assume that every individual investor holds a portfolio consisting of one risky asset and the riskless asset. The entire securities market comprises only the first five mutual funds from the Balanced Funds category.

   Assuming that the *ex-post* parameters (the historical mean rate of return and the historical variance) are good estimates of the *ex-ante* parameters, identify those of the funds that are underpriced and those that are overpriced. Substantiate your conclusions by numerical calculations and with the aid of a diagram. Indicate on the diagram the predicted direction of change in the fund share prices if equilibrium is to be restored.

   In your calculations, assume a riskless interest rate $r = 3\%$.

2. Assume that the entire securities market comprises only the first three funds from the Maximum Gain Funds category. Also assume that the observed rates of return represent population (and not sample) data.

Denote by $V_{i,0}$ the market value of the fund $i$ in period zero ("now") and by $V_{i,1}$ its market value in period 1 ("the future"). It is given for the three funds in the market that:

$$V_{1,0} = \$100, \quad V_{2,0} = \$200, \quad V_{3,0} = \$300$$

(a) On the basis of these market values and the observed mean return of the three funds, calculate the corresponding future market values $V_{i,1}$.
(b) Assuming that the riskless interest rate is $r = 3\%$, establish whether or not the above market values represent an equilibrium.

## Selected References

See Chapter 14.

# 12

# The Risk Index Beta: Measurement and Application

As we have seen in Chapter 11, the risk of each asset is properly measured by its beta, and not by the variance of its returns. In this chapter we explain the meaning of this risk index, show how to measure it and demonstrate its applications.

## 12.1 Calculating Beta in Practice

In order to apply the capital asset pricing model, a method must be found for estimating each firm's *future* beta, i.e. the component of its risk which cannot be eliminated through diversification. Although beta might be estimated solely on the basis of subjective probability beliefs, it is the common practice to use past data to estimate future betas. However, where one expects the historical relationship between the rates of return on a given security and the rates of return on the market portfolio to be materially different in the future, the observed *ex-post* relationship should be modified to reflect such changes.

The method for estimating beta can be illustrated using the hypothetical data of Table 12.1 which sets out the rates of return for an individual security and for the market portfolio during the period 1974–1983. The beta of a security can be estimated on the basis of the historical data using the following regression equation:

$$R_{i_t} = \hat{\alpha}_i + \hat{\beta}_i R_{m_t} + e_{i_t}$$

where:

$R_{i_t}$ = the rate of return on the *i*th security in year *t*

$R_{m_t}$ = the rate of return on the market portfolio in year *t* (portfolio *m* of Figure 11.6)

**Table 12.1**

| Years | Rate of Return on Security $R_i$ (1) | Rate of Return on Market Portfolio $R_m$ (2) | Worksheet $R_m^2$ (2) × (2) | $R_i R_m$ (1) × (2) |
|---|---|---|---|---|
| 1  1974 | 5.2 | 7.4 | 54.8 | 38.5 |
| 2  1975 | 7.3 | 8.2 | 67.2 | 59.9 |
| 3  1976 | 10.1 | 12.3 | 151.3 | 124.2 |
| 4  1977 | 15.4 | 16.9 | 285.6 | 260.3 |
| 5  1978 | 19.8 | 19.1 | 364.8 | 378.2 |
| 6  1979 | 24.9 | 22.5 | 506.3 | 560.3 |
| 7  1980 | 29.7 | 25.1 | 630.0 | 745.5 |
| 8  1981 | 35.2 | 26.4 | 697.0 | 929.3 |
| 9  1982 | 40.1 | 29.8 | 888.0 | 1195.0 |
| 10  1983 | 42.6 | 30.3 | 918.1 | 1290.8 |
| **Total** | 230.3 | 198.0 | 4563.1 | 5582.0 |
| *Annual Average* | 23.0 | 19.8 | | |

$e_{it}$ = the error about the regression line

$\hat{\beta}_i$ = the estimate of the $i$th security's beta

$\hat{\alpha}_i$ = the estimate of the vertical intercept of the security $i$.

The estimate of the risk (denoted by $\hat{\beta}_i$ and also by $b_i$) is given by the standard formula for the regression coefficient (for more details, see the Statistical Supplement at the end of the book),

$$\hat{\beta}_i = \frac{\hat{\sigma}_{im}}{\hat{\sigma}_m^2} = \frac{\sum\limits_{t=1}^{10} (R_{it} - \bar{R}_i)(R_{mt} - \bar{R}_m)}{\sum\limits_{t=1}^{10} (R_{mt} - \bar{R}_m)^2}$$

where $\bar{R}_i$ and $\bar{R}_m$ denote the arithmetic annual average rate of return of the $i$th security and market portfolio respectively and 10 represents the number of years in this specific example (see Table 12.1). "Hats" on variables denote statistical estimates.

Employing some algebraic manipulation this equation can be rewritten as:

$$\hat{\beta}_i = \frac{\sum\limits_{t=1}^{10} R_{it} R_{mt} - 10 \bar{R}_i \bar{R}_m}{\sum\limits_{i=1}^{10} R_{mt}^2 - 10 \bar{R}_m^2}$$

Plugging in the data from Table 12.1, we obtain an estimate of the security's future beta,

$\hat{\beta}_i = 1.6$:

$$\beta_i = \frac{5582.0 - 10 \times 23 \times 19.8}{4563.1 - 10 \times 392.07} = \frac{1028}{643.1} = 1.6$$

In this example we employed hypothetical data to calculate the beta. Let us turn to calculate the risk index for two firms traded on the NYSE using the data for the ten years 1971–1980. We use as a proxy to the market portfolio, $R_m$, the so-called Fisher Index,[1] which provides a measure of the rates of return on a well-diversified portfolio

**Table 12.2**

| | | Rates of Return | | | Worksheet | | |
|---|---|---|---|---|---|---|---|
| Year | Market Portfolio $R_m$ | Quaker Oats $R_1$ | General Foods $R_2$ | $R_m^2$ | $R_1 R_m$ | $R_2 R_m$ |
| 1 1971 | 19.48 | 5.36 | −14.83 | 379.47 | 104.41 | −288.89 |
| 2 1972 | 8.45 | 36.30 | −16.50 | 71.40 | 306.74 | −139.43 |
| 3 1973 | −29.31 | −34.41 | −11.90 | 859.08 | 1,008.56 | 348.79 |
| 4 1974 | −26.53 | −52.93 | −19.72 | 703.84 | 1,404.23 | 523.17 |
| 5 1975 | 61.90 | 110.58 | 63.24 | 3,831.61 | 6,844.90 | 3,914.56 |
| 6 1976 | 45.49 | 3.15 | 15.12 | 2,069.34 | 143.29 | 687.81 |
| 7 1977 | 9.50 | −7.05 | 9.41 | 90.25 | −66.98 | 89.40 |
| 8 1978 | 14.02 | 3.12 | 7.73 | 196.56 | 43.74 | 108.37 |
| 9 1979 | 35.31 | 30.37 | 10.93 | 1,246.80 | 1,072.36 | 385.94 |
| 10 1980 | 30.99 | 13.06 | −3.13 | 960.38 | 404.73 | −97.00 |
| **Total** | 169.30 | 107.55 | 40.35 | 10,408.73 | 11,265.99 | 5,532.72 |
| Average Rate of Return | 16.93 | 10.76 | 4.04 | | | |

*Calculation of Beta*:

**Quaker Oats:** $\hat{\beta}_1 = \dfrac{\sum\limits_{t=1}^{10} R_{1t} R_{mt} - 10 \bar{R}_1 \bar{R}_m}{\sum\limits_{t=1}^{10} R_{mt}^2 - 10 \bar{R}_m^2} = \dfrac{11{,}265.99 - 10 \times 10.76 \times 16.93}{10{,}408.73 - 10 \times (16.93)^2} = \dfrac{9{,}444.43}{7{,}542.48} = 1.2522$

**General Foods:** $\hat{\beta}_2 = \dfrac{\sum\limits_{t=1}^{10} R_{2t} R_{mt} - 10 \bar{R}_2 \bar{R}_m}{\sum\limits_{t=1}^{10} R_{mt}^2 - 10 \bar{R}_m^2} = \dfrac{5{,}532.72 - 10 \times 4.04 \times 16.93}{10{,}408.73 - 10 \times (16.93)^2} = \dfrac{4{,}848.75}{7{,}542.48} = 0.6429$

[1] For more details, see L. Fisher and J. Lorie, "Rates of Return on Investments in Common Stocks", *Journal of Business* (Jan. 1964).

constructed by investing equal amounts in all the stocks listed on NYSE and reinvesting all interim dividend payments. The rates of return on the market index and on the stock of two large corporations in the food industry—Quaker Oats and General Foods—are given in Table 12.2, which also develops a worksheet for the calculation of the betas.

If the historical record is longer than 10 years, manual calculations of beta become too lengthy and tedious. The work is usually entrusted to the computer, using standard package programs to run the basic linear regression of the security rates of return $R_i$ on the market rate of return $R_m$. A sample computer output for the calculation of beta is presented in Appendix 12.1.

## 12.2 The Characteristic Line

The regression line of $R_i$ on $R_m$, or the *characteristic line* as it is usually called, is plotted in Figure 12.1. The reader should note that the characteristic line which is appropriate for the hypothetical example of Table 12.1 has a slope (beta) equal to 1.6. (The ten dots represent the ten annual plots of the relationship between the individual security's rate of return with that of the market portfolio.) The second characteristic line, denoted as beta = 1, has a slope of 45° and is appropriate for any security having the *same* risk as the market portfolio: the return on such security fluctuates, on the average, in the same way as the market as a whole.

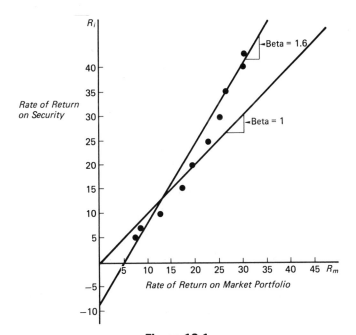

**Figure 12.1**

The concept of a characteristic line also suggests the possibility of classifying companies by their risk. Stocks having a beta greater than one ($\beta > 1$) are classified as *aggressive stocks* since they go up faster than the market in a "bull", i.e. rising market, but fall faster in a "bear", i.e. falling market. Stocks with betas less than one ($\beta < 1$) are *defensive*; their returns fluctuate less than the market as a whole. Finally, the limiting case of stocks with betas equal to unity are *neutral stocks* since they fluctuate, on the average, along with the market.

In selecting risky investments, mutual funds as well as other institutional investors frequently make a preliminary decision regarding the type of securities that they want to include in their portfolio. Some investors concentrate their portfolio in aggressive stocks, which implies that an average high return is earned in a bull market and low return is earned in a bear market. Other investors may be more conservative concentrating on defensive stocks which do not yield an extraordinary return in a bull market but their price falls only moderately in a bear market.

The classification of stocks by their beta is illustrated in Table 12.3. Using the regression technique described above and substituting the observed return on all New York Stock Exchange stocks for the market portfolio, betas were derived using 20 years of historical rates of return for a sample of firms. The betas of the defensive stocks ranged from 0.42 for Abbot Laboratory to 0.92 for Union Carbide. With respect to the aggressive securities, Bethlehem Steel had a beta of 1.37, while the highest beta was 3.44 for Conalco.

The "ideal" stock or portfolio should have the following desirable property: its price should go up faster than the market portfolio in a bull market and go down more slowly than the market portfolio in a bear market. The behavior of such a stock, which combines the most desirable properties of both a defensive and an aggressive stock, is illustrated in Figure 12.2. Unfortunately such stocks (or portfolios) can be only rarely

**Table 12.3**

| *Defensive Stocks* ($\beta < 1$) | |
|---|---|
| | Beta |
| Abbot Laboratory | 0.42 |
| General Telephone | 0.60 |
| Greyhound Corporation | 0.62 |
| RH Macy Corporation | 0.65 |
| Union Carbide Corporation | 0.92 |

| *Aggressive Stocks* ($\beta > 1$) | |
|---|---|
| | Beta |
| Bethlehem Steel | 1.37 |
| Hooper Chemical | 1.43 |
| Cerro Corporation | 1.67 |
| Medusa Portland | 1.86 |
| Conalco Inc. | 3.44 |

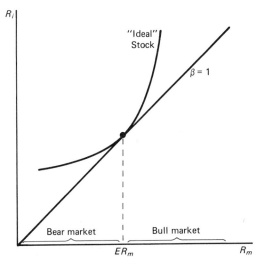

**Figure 12.2**

found in the market, and this ideal investment hardly exists outside the realm of textbooks.

## 12.3    The Security Market Line (SML)

We have seen in Chapter 11 in our discussion of the CAPM that the following risk-return relationship holds in equilibrium for all risky assets:

$$ER_i = r + (ER_m - r)\beta_i \qquad (12.1)$$

Since the term $(ER_m - r)$ is a constant and does not vary from one security to another, the expected return $ER_i$ on security $i$ is given as a linear function of its systematic risk, $\beta_i$, where the slope of this line is $(ER_m - r)$ and its vertical intercept is $r$. Figure 12.3 illustrates this linear relationship, which is known in the financial literature as the *security market line* (SML).

Note that if $\beta_i = 0$, $ER_i = r$, namely, the security has no risk and hence the average return on this security is equal to the risk-free interest rate. If $\beta_i = 1$, the risk of the stock is equal to the risk of the market portfolio, and hence also $ER_i = ER_m$. All stocks with $\beta_i < 1$ are defined as *defensive* stocks and for them $ER_i < ER_m$; all stocks with $\beta_i > 1$ are defined as *aggressive* stocks and for this group $ER_i > ER_m$. Stocks with negative $\beta$, which can be hardly found in the market, yield an expected return smaller than $r$.

Applying the CAPM risk-return relationship to a stock with zero beta, we see that,

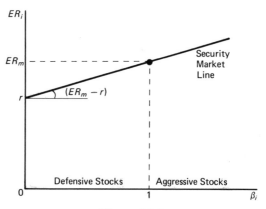

**Figure 12.3**

*on average*, its return is equal to the risk free interest rate $r$. Does it imply that the return on a zero beta security is certain? The answer is, of course, negative. To illustrate this point assume that the market portfolio consists of only two stocks in proportions $x_1$ and $x_2$. Thus,

$$R_m = x_1 R_1 + x_2 R_2$$

and:

$$\beta_1 = \frac{Cov\ (R_1, R_m)}{\sigma_m^2}$$

Since the variance of the market portfolio is always positive, $\sigma_m^2 > 0$, $\beta_1 = 0$ only if:

$$Cov\ (R_1,\ R_m) = Cov\ (R_1,\ x_1 R_1 + x_2 R_2) = x_1 \sigma_1^2 + x_2 \sigma_{12} = 0$$

where $\sigma_1^2$ is the variance of return on security 1 and $\sigma_{12} = Cov\ (R_1, R_2)$ is the covariance of the returns on the two securities. Thus, for some *negative* covariance between the two securities ($\sigma_{12} < 0$), a security may have zero beta ($\beta_1 = 0$) even though its variance is greater than zero ($\sigma_1^2 > 0$), which means that the rates of return on this security are not certain.

EXAMPLE
Take the following numerical example of two securities with negative covariance,

$$x_1 = 0.1 \qquad x_2 = 0.9$$
$$\sigma_1^2 = 10 \qquad \sigma_2^2 = 20$$
$$\sigma_{12} = -10/9$$

Thus, regardless of $\sigma_m^2$,

$$\beta_1 = \frac{0.1 \times 10 - 0.9 \times 10/9}{\sigma_m^2} = 0$$

although the variance of security 1 is positive, $\sigma_1^2 = +10$.

For an investor holding only security 1, it is a risky asset, since its variance is positive. However, in the CAPM framework, investors hold all the risky securities in a portfolio (in our case the two securities), and the risk of the first security is offset by the negative covariance $\sigma_{12}$ with the second security. In other words, although the first security does have a variability and its return is not certain, it has a negative correlation with other assets, so that it contributes to stabilization of the return on the portfolio as a whole, and hence its risk *in a portfolio context* is zero as long as $\beta_1 = 0$. To sum up, though the variance of the return on a given asset may be quite large, its expected return may be equal to the riskless interest rate provided that it has a negative correlation with other assets in the portfolio such that its beta is zero. This leads us to the analysis of the role of the security's variance in determining the asset's risk, an issue which is dealt with in the next section.

## 12.4   Systematic and Non-Systematic Risk

The regression line of the $i$th security return $R_i$ on the market portfolio return $R_m$ (also called the characteristic line) is given by,

$$R_{it} = \alpha_i + \beta_i R_{mt} + e_{it} \tag{12.2}$$

where the subscripts $i$ and $t$ denote the $i$th security examined and the year, respectively;

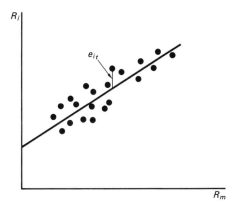

**Figure 12.4**

and $e_{it}$ denotes the deviation of the observed $i$th security return in year $t$ from the regression line. $\beta_i$ is the slope of the line and $\alpha_i$ is the vertical intercept of this line. The hypothetical scatter diagram of such an analysis is set out in Figure 12.4, with each point representing a particular combination of $(R_i, R_m)$ which obtained in a given year. Note that where $R_i$ and $R_m$ are perfectly correlated, $e_{it}$ will be zero in each year, and all the points of Figure 12.4 should lie along the regression line.

We will now use the characteristic line equation (12.2) to derive measures of systematic and non-systematic risk of securities.

### 12.4.1 Decomposition of the Variance

Taking the variance of both sides of Equation (12.2) we obtain[2]

$$\sigma_i^2 = \beta_i^2 \sigma_m^2 + \sigma_e^2 \qquad (12.3)$$

A glance at Equation (12.3) suffices to show that the total risk of a security (portfolio) as measured by its variance can be divided into two components:

(1)  $\beta_i^2 \sigma_m^2$—*systematic* or *nondiversifiable* risk, that is, the risk which is associated with market fluctuations; and

(2)  $\sigma_e^2$—*nonsystematic* or *diversifiable* risk, that is, that portion of the variance which can be eliminated or "washed out" by combining the security in a diversified portfolio. This nonsystematic risk is represented by the variance around the regression line.

Now recall that:

$$\beta_i = \frac{Cov(R_i, R_m)}{\sigma_m^2}$$

Equation (12.3) can be rewritten as:

$$\sigma_i^2 = \frac{[Cov(R_i, R_m)]^2 \sigma_m^2}{\sigma_m^2 \sigma_m^2} + \sigma_e^2$$

Reducing by $\sigma_m^2$ and dividing both sides by $\sigma_i^2$ we get:

$$1 = \frac{[Cov(R_i, R_m)]^2}{\sigma_m^2 \sigma_i^2} + \frac{\sigma_e^2}{\sigma_i^2}$$

---

[2] Equation (12.3) includes the term $Cov(R_m, e_i)$, but its estimate is always equal to zero in the sample; it is also usually assumed in the regression model that the explanatory variable is uncorrelated with the deviation, or disturbance, term $e$. In the rest of the chapter we use the symbol $\beta_i$ for the population parameter and for the sample estimate alike, since most of the discussion holds in both cases. Also $e_i$ stands for deviation from the regression line in the population and sample alike.

By definition:

$$\frac{[Cov\,(R_i, R_m)]^2}{\sigma_m^2 \sigma_i^2} = \rho_{im}^2$$

where $\rho_{im}$ denotes the coefficient of correlation between $R_i$ and $R_m$, and so we write

$$1 = \rho_{im}^2 + \frac{\sigma_e^2}{\sigma_i^2}$$

This gives the following relationship for the nonsystematic risk $\sigma_e^2$:

$$\frac{\sigma_e^2}{\sigma_i^2} = 1 - \rho_{im}^2 \qquad (12.4)$$

When $\rho_{im}^2 = 1$ (i.e., security or portfolio $i$ perfectly correlated with the market $m$), the nonsystematic risk $\sigma_e^2$ is zero and there remains only the systematic or nondiversifiable portion of the variance. We define such a security (portfolio) as being "efficiently diversified" since further diversification will not reduce its risk.[3] The variance about the regression line, $\sigma_e^2$, or the nonsystematic component of total risk, can be eliminated by diversification, so that this component vanishes when the portfolio is efficiently diversified.

The ratio $\sigma_e^2/\sigma_i^2$ [which by (12.4) is bounded between 0 and 1] also serves as an indicator of the desirability of diversification. If this ratio is zero for a given security or portfolio, all diversifiable risk has already been eliminated, so that further diversification cannot reduce risk. On the other hand, when the ratio is positive for a given portfolio, further diversification is desirable to eliminate the remaining nonsystematic risk. The closer the ratio is to unity, the greater the potential gains from diversification. In practice, the gains from risk diversification appear to be substantial; in an empirical study[4] of 63 stocks, Benjamin King found that for the period 1927–1960 only about half of the variance of the returns on these stocks could be attributed to market fluctuations, the remaining 50% representing nonsystematic—that is, diversifiable—risk. For the subperiod 1952–1960, the proportion of the variance which is explained by market factors is only 30%; hence the diversifiable risk component in those years comprised 70% of the total variance, which constitutes a rather strong *prima facie* case for diversification.

Table 12.4 presents the "total" risk $\sigma_i^2$, the systematic risk $\beta_i^2 \sigma_m^2$ and the non-systematic risk $\sigma_e^2$ for 13 US stocks for the years 1971–1980. Also the ratio

[3] Note that even when $\rho_{im}^2 = 1$ the security's (portfolio's) variance can be greater or smaller than the market portfolio's variance. For example, an "aggressive" security (portfolio) may have a beta coefficient greater than 1, while $\rho_{im}^2 = 1$; such a security (portfolio) will be more volatile than the market portfolio [see equation (12.3)].

[4] B. F. King, "Market and Industry Factors in Stock Price Behavior", *Journal of Business* 39 (Jan. 1966).

**Table 12.4**

| Stock | Beta $\beta_i$ | Total Risk $\sigma_i^2$ | Systematic Risk $\beta_i^2 \sigma_m^2$ | Nonsystematic Risk $\sigma_e^2$ | Measure of Diversifiability $\sigma_e^2/\sigma_i^2 = 1 - \rho_{im}^2$ |
|---|---|---|---|---|---|
| Dow Chemical | 0.441 | 1,080.36 | 162.98 | 1,031.74 | 0.95 |
| Union Carbide | 0.497 | 757.41 | 207.01 | 618.77 | 0.82 |
| Cleveland Electric Illumination | 0.479 | 330.19 | 192.28 | 155.43 | 0.47 |
| Commonwealth Edison | 0.484 | 353.27 | 196.32 | 176.38 | 0.50 |
| Florida Power and Light | 0.965 | 1,053.87 | 780.41 | 306.98 | 0.29 |
| Interlake | 0.420 | 755.39 | 147.83 | 683.67 | 0.91 |
| Republic Steel | 0.250 | 415.44 | 52.38 | 408.36 | 0.98 |
| US Steel | 0.436 | 1,222.99 | 159.31 | 1,196.92 | 0.98 |
| IBM | 0.610 | 463.23 | 311.84 | 170.23 | 0.37 |
| NCR | 0.896 | 1,337.38 | 672.80 | 748.19 | 0.56 |
| General Foods | 0.643 | 569.15 | 346.49 | 280.90 | 0.49 |
| Nabisco | 1.111 | 1,295.49 | 1,034.42 | 293.49 | 0.23 |
| Quaker Oats | 1.252 | 1,951.73 | 1,313.65 | 717.21 | 0.37 |

*Note:* Data based on 10-year period 1971–1980. Market variance $\sigma_m^2 = 838.05$.

$\sigma_e^2/\sigma_i^2 = 1 - \rho_{im}^2$ is given, which indicates the potential gain from diversification. In 7 out of 13 cases, this ratio is no less than 0.50, which means that over 50% of the total variance of these stocks is independent of the market fluctuations and can be washed out by diversification.

Thus, only one component of the $i$th security variance ($\beta_i^2\sigma_m^2$) properly determines the risk of the $i$th investment in portfolio context and hence its expected return $ER_i$. Since the market variance $\sigma_m^2$ is common to all risky assets, we can safely assert that the higher the security's beta, the higher is the expected return on the stock.

*A word of caution.* This decomposition of the variance $\sigma_i^2$, however, has one drawback: if we have two stocks, one with $\beta_1 = +\frac{1}{2}$ and another with $\beta_2 = -\frac{1}{2}$, so that $\beta_1^2 = \beta_2^2$ we get that both have the same systematic risk $\beta_i^2\sigma_m^2$, which of course is unreasonable since the stock with $\beta_2 = -\frac{1}{2}$ is much safer, and hence the required rate of return $ER_i$ on this stock must be lower (as a matter of fact, even lower than the risk-free interest rate $r$). Thus, we turn now to another decomposition of the $i$th security total risk which is consistent with the CAPM formula and which also takes into account *the sign* of beta. We also demonstrate the relationship between this decomposition of risk and the expected return on the $i$th asset.

### 12.4.2 Decomposition of the Standard Deviation

In order to identify the two risk components and their impact on a security's risk premium, let us write the two linear equations of the *capital market line* (CML) and of the *security market line* (SML).

The CML is defined as:

$$ER_p = r + \frac{ER_m - r}{\sigma_m}\sigma_p$$

where $p$ denotes an *efficient* portfolio. Thus, this line is drawn in the mean–standard deviation space, and holds only for efficient portfolios. Namely it is the line $rN$ of Figure 11.6 in Chapter 11.

By the SML, however, we have the following equation:

$$ER_i = r + (ER_m - r)\beta_i \tag{12.5}$$

which holds for *all* individual securities and portfolios, whether efficient or not.

Dividing and multiplying the right-hand side of equation (12.5) by $\sigma_m$ we rewrite it as:

$$ER_i = r + \frac{(ER_m - r)}{\sigma_m}(\beta_i\sigma_m)$$

which is analogous to the CML, with the exception that $\beta_i\sigma_m$ is written instead of $\sigma_p$ and hence it is this factor that determines the individual security's risk premium. Thus, the risk component of the individual security which determines the risk premium is the factor $\beta_i \sigma_m$. Each individual stock's standard deviation $\sigma_i$ can be decomposed into two components, the systematic risk $\beta_i \sigma_m$ and the nonsystematic risk $\sigma_i^{NS}$, where:[5]

$$\sigma_i^{NS} = \sigma_i - \beta_i \sigma_m$$

Define the following notations for security $i$:

Diversifiable risk $= \sigma_i^D$,    Nondiversifiable risk $= \sigma_i^{ND}$
Nonsystematic risk $= \sigma_i^{NS}$,        Systematic risk $= \sigma_i^S$

and we have:

$$\sigma_i^{ND} \equiv \sigma_i^S = \beta_i \sigma_m$$

and:

$$\sigma_i^D \equiv \sigma_i^{NS} = \sigma_i - \beta_i \sigma_m$$

The graphical decomposition of a security's standard deviation into the systematic and non-systematic risk is illustrated in Figure 12.5 which depicts the Capital Market Line, the market portfolio $m$, an efficient portfolio $P$ and two securities $i$ and $j$.

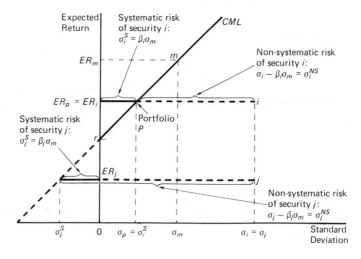

**Figure 12.5**

[5] It is more common in the financial literature to decompose the variance (as in Section 12.4.1 above) rather than the standard deviation. For more details on the difference between the two approaches see M. Ben-Horim and H. Levy, "Total Risk, Diversifiable Risk and Nondiversifiable Risk: A Pedagogic Note", *Journal of Financial and Quantitative Analysis* (June 1980).

Portfolio $P$ and security $i$ both have the same expected rate of return, thus $ER_p = ER_i$. Since for efficient portfolios we have

$$ER_p = r + \frac{ER_m - r}{\sigma_m} \sigma_p$$

where $\sigma_p$ is the risk index of this portfolio, and for the $i$th security we have

$$ER_i = r + \frac{ER_m - r}{\sigma_m} (\beta_i \sigma_m)$$

for the case when $ER_i = ER_p$ we also must have $\beta_i \sigma_m = \sigma_p$, and then $\beta_i \sigma_m = \sigma_i^{ND} = \sigma_i^S$.

Thus the non-diversifiable risk of a security is measured by the horizontal distance of the vertical axis from the CML, at the security's level of expected rate of return. In order to measure the security's risk component which determines the risk premium $ER_i - r$, we draw a line from point $i$ (representing the security's mean and standard deviation) to the CML, parallel to the horizontal axis; at the point of intersection with the CML we reach $\sigma_p$, which is identical to the $i$th security's systematic risk. The non-systematic risk is simply the total risk $\sigma_i$ minus the systematic risk, or:

$$\sigma_i^{NS} = \sigma_i - \beta_i \sigma_m$$

Figure 12.5 shows that the non-diversifiable risk of a security may be negative (see, for example, security $j$) so that its diversifiable risk is greater than the total risk, $\sigma_j$. Adding security $j$ to an efficient portfolio not only does not add to the portfolio's risk, but lends stability to the portfolio. This analysis shows that for all cases where $\beta \geqslant 0$, the terms "diversifiable risk" and "non-diversifiable risk" best convey their own meaning. Some readers, however, may find the terms "nonsystematic risk" and "systematic risk" more appropriate, especially for the cases where $\beta < 0$. A negative systematic risk is best understood, perhaps, as negative systematic co-movement of the rate of return of the security under consideration with that of the market portfolio. Indeed, security $j$ has a negative systematic risk, and as the CAPM formula asserts the expected rate of return on security $j$ must be smaller than the risk-free interest rate $r$ since $ER_j = r + (ER_m - r)\beta_j < r$ where $\beta_j < 0$. This is consistent with our graphical presentation since $ER_j < r$ in Figure 12.5.

The decomposition of standard deviation manages to distinguish between the systematic risk of securities whose betas have different signs. Thus, for two securities with $\beta_1 = +\frac{1}{2}$ and $\beta_2 = -\frac{1}{2}$, the systematic risk respectively is $\beta_1 \sigma_m = +\frac{1}{2}\sigma_m$ and $\beta_2 \sigma_m = -\frac{1}{2}\sigma_m$. This means that security 2 is characterized by a lower systematic risk than security 1 and thus constitutes a desirable and stabilizing addition to the portfolio. We see that the portfolio decision based on the systematic risk of a security as obtained by decomposing its standard deviation is entirely consistent with the decision based on the security's beta. The decomposition of the *standard deviation* is thus free from the

**Table 12.5**
**Security Betas with Performance and Safety Ranks: A Sample Page from The Value Line Investment Survey**

| | Name of Stock | Ticker Symbol | Recent Price | Performance Rank | Rank for Safety | Beta |
|---|---|---|---|---|---|---|
| 1409 | I.T. & T. | ITT | 38 | 3 | 3 | 1.22 |
| 886 | Interpace Corp. | INP | 15 | 3 | 3 | 0.95 |
| 1799 | Interpublic Group | IPG | 18 | 3 | 3 | NMF |
| 1476 | Interstate Brands | IBC | $7\frac{3}{8}$ | 5 | 3 | 0.80 |
| 990 740 | Interstate Power | IPW | 18 | 5 | 1 | 0.58 |
| 1678 | Interstate Stores | ISO | $1\frac{4}{8}$ | 5 | 4 | 1.60 |
| 365 | Interstate United Corp. | IUC | $7\frac{1}{8}$ | 3 | 4 | 1.16 |
| 1984 | Investors Div. Serv. "A" | IDSA | 26 | 4 | 3 | 1.39 |
| 1477 | Iowa Beef Processors | IBP | 23 | 1 | 4 | 1.09 |
| 741 | Iowa Elec. Light & Power | IEL | 18 | 3 | 1 | 0.59 |
| 742 | Iowa Ill. Gas & Elec. | IWG | 18 | 3 | 1 | 0.66 |
| 743 | Iowa Power & Light | IOP | 23 | 3 | 1 | 0.77 |
| 744 | Iowa Public Service | IPS | 20 | 5 | 2 | 0.60 |
| 745 | Iowa So. Utilities | IUTL | 27 | 4 | 2 | 0.77 |
| 533 617 | IPCO Hospital Supply | IHS | 6 | 2 | 4 | 1.34 |
| 1033 | ITE Imperial Corp. | ITE | 23 | 4 | 3 | 1.12 |
| 208 | ITEK Corp. | ITK | 35 | 3 | 4 | 1.47 |
| 233 | ITEL Corp. | I | $5\frac{3}{8}$ | 3 | 5 | 1.68 |
| 470 | IU International Corp. | IU | 27 | 2 | 3 | 1.10 |

| | | | | | | | |
|---|---|---|---|---|---|---|---|
| | 1338 | Jaeger Machine Co. | JAEG | 7 3/8 | 3 | 4 | 1.03 |
| | 1831 | James (Fred S.) & Co. | JMS | 11 | 4 | 3 | 0.78 |
| | 1615 | Jantzen, Inc. | JAN | 17 | 2 | 4 | 1.01 |
| | 1985 | Japan Fund | JPN | 13 | 1 | 4 | 1.03 |
| | 1854 | Jefferson-Pilot Corp. | JP | 39 | 3 | 3 | 0.96 |
| | 1546 | Jewel Companies | JWL | 39 | 3 | 2 | 0.86 |
| | 887 | Jim Walter Corp. | JWC | 21 | 2 | 3 | 1.48 |
| | 1986 | John Hancock Investors | JHI | 24 | 3 | 2 | NMF |
| | 888 | Johns-Manville | JM | 22 | 3 | 3 | 1.04 |
| | 618 | Johnson & Johnson | JNI | 119 | 3 | 2 | 0.92 |
| | 1034 | Johnson Service Co. | JSC | 24 | 4 | 3 | 0.82 |
| | 1616 | Jonathan Logan | JOL | 36 | 4 | 2 | 0.97 |
| | 1240 | Jones & Laughlin | JL | 19 | 3 | 4 | 1.04 |
| | 1241 | Jorgensen (Earle M.) | JOR | 25 | 2 | 2 | 0.89 |
| | 221 | Josiens Inc. | JOS | 21 | 3 | 3 | 1.24 |
| | 1339 | Joy Mfg. | JOY | 39 | 3 | 3 | 1.21 |
| 390 | 1182 | Kaiser Aluminum | KLU | 23 | 3 | 3 | 1.16 |
| | 889 | Kaiser Cement & Gypsum | KCG | 9 | 2 | 3 | 0.89 |
| | 1410 | Kaiser Industries | KI | 7 7/8 | 1 | 3 | 1.47 |
| 296 | 1242 | Kaiser Steel | KASR | 15 | 1 | 4 | 1.02 |
| | 1478 | Kane Miller Corp. | KML | 16 | 1 | 4 | 1.44 |
| | 746 | Kansas City Power & Light | KLT | 29 | 4 | 1 | 0.73 |

weakness that we observed at the end of Sec. 12.4.1 for the decomposition of the *variance*, where the resulting systematic risk failed to distinguish between securities with positive and negative betas.

## 12.5    Beta Services

Since beta is the risk index of each individual security, several institutional investors provide information services which include the beta as an indicator of the security's safety. The main sources which provide the beta information are Merrill Lynch, Pierce, Fenner & Smith, Goldman & Sachs, Wells Fargo Bank, and Value Line. For mutual funds the beta information is reported in Arthur Wiesenberger's *Investment Companies*.

Table 12.5 provides some financial information including the beta as published by Value Line. For each stock, a rank for its past performance and a rank for its safety are given. The safer the stock, the lower its rank. The safety index is based on the standard deviation of the rates of return and on the financial strength of the firm. Although not directly based on beta, there is clearly a very strong positive association between the safety rank and beta. For example, the beta of Kansas City Power is $\beta = 0.73$. This is a defensive stock and its safety rank is 1. Itel Corporation, on the other hand, is aggressive, with $\beta = 1.68$, and its safety rank is 5. All the risk indexes are divided into intervals and for each interval one safety rank is assigned. Thus it is possible to have many stocks (with similar risk indexes and betas) which are assigned the same rank, e.g., Interstate Power, Iowa Power and Light and many other low-beta firms get a safety rank of 1.

Table 12.6 presents the price volatility (another name for beta) of mutual funds. The beta is calculated relative to the NYSE composite index which serves as the market portfolio. Note that the volatility of the market index $R_m$ is always equal to 1 since:

$$\beta_m = \frac{Cov\,(R_m, R_m)}{\sigma_m^2} = \frac{\sigma_m^2}{\sigma_m^2} = 1$$

The beta of various mutual funds is reported for various periods, where there is a distinction between periods of rising prices and declining prices in the stock market. Some betas are stable and do not change much from period to period but most betas are quite unstable, so that historical betas are not very good predictors of future market data. Thus the value of past data for ranking securities according to their safety for future investment decision-making is questionable and a special technique is needed to reconcile between historical estimates and future parameters. It is to this issue of adjustment that we turn next.

**Table 12.6**
**Price Volatility of Mutual Fund Shares: Sample Page from Arthur Wiesenberger's *Investment Companies***

| | Rising Period 8/24/73 to 10/26/73 | Declining Period 10/26/73 to 10/3/74 | Rising Period 10/3/74 to 7/15/75 | Declining Period 7/15/75 to 10/1/75 | Rising Period 10/1/75 to 12/31/76 | Declining Period 12/31/76 to 2/28/78 | Rising Period 2/28/78 to 9/11/78 | Declining Period 9/11/78 to 11/14/78 |
|---|---|---|---|---|---|---|---|---|
| NYSE Common Stock Index (Composite) | 1.00 | 1.00 | 1.00 | 1.00 | 1.00 | 1.00 | 1.00 | 1.00 |
| **III. *Objective: Growth and Current Income* (Cont'd.)** | | | | | | | | |
| One William Street Fund | 1.07 | 0.95 | 0.90 | 0.99 | 0.65 | 0.91 | 1.35 | 1.07 |
| Philadelphia Fund | 1.97 | 0.99 | 1.46 | 1.08 | 0.93 | 0.18 | 1.76 | 1.35 |
| Pine Street Fund | 0.96 | 0.73 | 0.85 | 0.89 | 0.95 | 0.79 | 0.64 | 0.78 |
| Pioneer Fund | 1.26 | 0.74 | 0.95 | 0.75 | 1.20 | 0.39 | 1.17 | 0.93 |
| Pioneer II | 2.45 | 0.86 | 1.19 | 0.96 | 1.95 | CT | 1.19 | 1.05 |
| SAFECO Equity Fund | 1.17 | 0.98 | 1.09 | 0.87 | 1.28 | 0.29 | 1.34 | 1.30 |
| St. Paul Capital Fund | 0.90 | 0.82 | 0.53 | 1.03 | 0.80 | 0.98 | 1.40 | 1.18 |
| Selected American Shares | 1.07 | 1.02 | 0.76 | 0.96 | 0.85 | 0.60 | 0.42 | 0.61 |
| Sentinel Common Stock Fund | 1.33 | 0.70 | 0.76 | 0.70 | 1.02 | 0.82 | 0.61 | 0.86 |
| Shearson Investors Fund | 1.12 | 0.82 | 0.56 | 0.68 | 1.24 | 0.99 | 1.24 | 1.26 |
| Sigma Investment Shares | 1.23 | 0.96 | 1.08 | 0.91 | 1.01 | 0.89 | 0.80 | 0.79 |
| Southwestern Investors | 1.02 | 0.96 | 0.91 | 0.97 | 1.12 | 0.86 | 1.14 | 1.26 |
| Sovereign Investors | 1.19 | 0.89 | 0.92 | 0.87 | 1.06 | 0.91 | 0.87 | 0.98 |
| State Street Investment | 1.05 | 1.02 | 1.00 | 1.01 | 1.08 | 0.60 | 1.29 | 1.10 |
| Steadman Investment Fund | 1.29 | 0.81 | 0.40 | 0.86 | 1.35 | 0.77 | 0.64 | 1.60 |
| Technology Fund | 1.48 | 0.88 | 1.07 | 0.83 | 0.84 | 0.69 | 1.85 | 1.26 |
| Unified Mutual Shares | 1.02 | 1.03 | 1.01 | 1.12 | 1.10 | 0.66 | 0.53 | 0.67 |
| Vance Sanders Investors Fund | 0.95 | 0.76 | 0.63 | 0.68 | 0.91 | 0.64 | 0.89 | 0.79 |
| Varied Industry Plan | 0.46 | 0.91 | 0.78 | 1.09 | 1.01 | 0.52 | 1.37 | 1.12 |
| Wall Street Fund | 0.77 | 1.06 | 0.94 | 0.98 | 0.89 | 0.74 | 0.98 | 0.92 |
| Washington Mutual Investors | 1.41 | 0.72 | 0.90 | 0.65 | 1.16 | 0.96 | 0.96 | 0.98 |
| *Averages* | 1.12 | 0.87 | 0.88 | 0.88 | 0.93 | 0.79 | 1.03 | 1.01 |

### 12.6    The Accuracy and the Adjustment of Beta

In general beta is *estimated* by using a time-series regression of the form:

$$R_{it} = \hat{\alpha}_i + \hat{\beta}_i R_{mt} + e_{it}$$

where $R_{it}$ and $R_{mt}$ are the rates of return on the $i$th security and on the market portfolio in period $t$, $\hat{\beta}_i$ is the estimated slope of the regression line for a sample of $n$ observations given by:

$$\hat{\beta}_i = \frac{\hat{\sigma}_{im}}{\hat{\sigma}_m^2} = \frac{\displaystyle\sum_{t=1}^{n}(R_{it} - \bar{R}_i)(R_{mt} - \bar{R}_m)}{\displaystyle\sum_{t=1}^{n}(R_{mt} - \bar{R}_m)^2} \tag{12.6}$$

$\hat{\alpha}_i$ is the estimate of the intercept of the straight line with the vertical axis, and $e_{it}$ is the vertical distance of each observation point from the regression line.

All these factors are illustrated in Figure 12.6, where the scatter diagram provides the pairs of returns $(R_{it}, R_{mt})$ for time $t$.

The true beta is of course unknown, and one can only estimate it by (12.6). Hence the estimate may change from period to period due to sampling errors, even if the true beta is constant over time. If there is some pattern in the change of beta over time one can use this pattern to adjust the *ex-post* beta in such a way as to ensure better representation of the future beta.

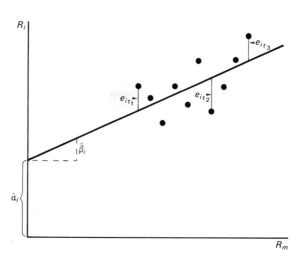

**Figure 12.6**

A glance at Table 12.6 reveals that beta for most funds is quite unstable. In particular, beta varies between periods with "bull" and "bear" markets. But even if we take only periods of say rising prices, beta still varies significantly from period to period. For example the beta coefficient of Pioneer II is 2.45 for the period 8/24/1973–10/26/1973, it drops to 1.19 for the second rising period (1974–1975), then jumps once again to 1.95 in 1975–1976, and falls again to 1.19 in 1978 (see Table 12.6). Although the large changes which characterize the beta of Pioneer II are an exception rather than the rule, still most betas change over time, which makes the calculation with past data almost useless for future investment decision making.

Blume[6] claims that stocks with beta greater than 1 tend to decrease toward 1 over time while securities with beta smaller than 1 tend to increase toward 1. Thus, there is a tendency of all betas to regress toward 1. The economic reasoning for this phenomenon may be that firms with very risky operations, and hence with a high beta, are likely to move back to less risky operations, and hence also their beta decreases over time. Just the opposite holds for stocks with low risk operations.

On statistical grounds one may argue that for high-beta securities the sampling errors may be in the direction which tends to increase the estimated beta. There is only a small probability that errors in the same direction and of the same magnitude will be found in the future, and hence the next period beta will tend to decrease. By the same argument, securities with exceptionally low beta probably involve sampling errors which push the calculated beta downward; in the succeeding period this error will probably not repeat itself and hence the beta will increase.

Whatever the argument, this tendency toward 1 is a solid fact and should be taken into account in estimating the future betas. Table 12.7 shows the beta of six portfolios in two successive periods. The portfolios are ranked from 1 to 6, where 1 stands for the portfolio with the lowest beta and 6 is the portfolio with the highest beta. As can be seen from these figures, the betas of the first three portfolios, which have betas smaller than 1 in the first period, increase in the succeeding period. The beta of the fourth portfolio decreases in spite of having $\beta = 0.987 < 1$ in the first period. Portfolios 5 and 6 with $\beta > 1$ in the first period are characterized by a lower beta in the second period. Thus,

**Table 12.7**
**Betas of Ranked Portfolios for**
**Two Successive Periods**

| Portfolio | 7/54–6/61 | 7/61–6/68 |
|-----------|-----------|-----------|
| 1 | 0.393 | 0.620 |
| 2 | 0.612 | 0.707 |
| 3 | 0.810 | 0.861 |
| 4 | 0.987 | 0.914 |
| 5 | 1.138 | 0.995 |
| 6 | 1.337 | 1.169 |

Source: M. Blume, "On the Assessment of Risk", Journal of Finance (March 1971).

[6] M. E. Blume, "Betas and Their Regression Tendencies", Journal of Finance (June 1975).

apart from portfolio number 4, which has beta close to one, all other portfolios conform with the hypothesis that beta tends to change over time toward one.

Blume[7] calculated the betas of a sample of securities for the period 1947–1954 and the beta coefficients of the same securities for the period 1954–1961. Denoting by $\beta_{i1}$ the beta of the $i$th security in the first period and by $\beta_{i2}$ the beta of the $i$th security in the succeeding period, Blume ran the cross-section regression:

$$\beta_{i2} = a_0 + a_1 \beta_{i1}$$

and obtained that $a_0 = 0.343$, $a_1 = 0.677$. Thus we have the following relationship between past beta ($\beta_{i1}$) and future beta ($\beta_{i2}$):

$$\beta_{i2} = 0.343 + 0.677\beta_{i1} \tag{12.7}$$

If (12.7) indeed characterizes the relationship between past and future betas, it can be used to adjust the *ex-post* estimates of beta. For example suppose that $\beta_{i1} = 0.6$. Then instead of claiming that the future $\beta$ will be 0.6 we can adjust it (or use the knowledge that it will increase in the future) to predict $\beta_{i2}$ as follows:

$$\beta_{i2} = 0.343 + 0.677 \times 0.6 = 0.343 + 0.406 = 0.749$$

Thus the adjusted beta is greater than the past beta. On the other hand, if $\beta_{i1}$ is greater than 1, say $\beta_{i1} = 2$, then the adjusted beta will be:

$$\beta_{i2} = 0.343 + 0.677 \times 2 = 0.343 + 1.354 = 1.697$$

which is of course smaller than 2.

Table 12.8 shows the relationship between the adjusted and unadjusted betas of

**Table 12.8**
**Estimated and Future Beta Values for Portfolios of 100 Securities Each**

| Portfolio | July 1947–June 1954 | | July 1954– June 1961 | July 1961– June 1968 |
| | Unadjusted | Adjusted | | |
|---|---|---|---|---|
| 1 | 0.36 | 0.48 | 0.57 | 0.72 |
| 2 | 0.61 | 0.68 | 0.71 | 0.79 |
| 3 | 0.78 | 0.82 | 0.88 | 0.88 |
| 4 | 0.91 | 0.93 | 0.96 | 0.92 |
| 5 | 1.01 | 1.01 | 1.03 | 1.04 |
| 6 | 1.13 | 1.10 | 1.13 | 1.02 |
| 7 | 1.26 | 1.21 | 1.24 | 1.08 |
| 8 | 1.47 | 1.39 | 1.32 | 1.15 |

*Source:* Marshall E. Blume: "Betas and Their Regression Tendencies", *Journal of Finance* (June 1975).

[7] M. E. Blume, "On the Assessment of Risk", *Journal of Finance* (March 1971).

eight portfolios. The first column simply estimates the actual betas of eight portfolios for the first period (1947–1954). The second column shows the adjusted betas, calculated by the type of regression technique described above.

The third and fourth columns reveal the actual betas estimated for the next two succeeding periods. The common phenomenon of this table is that the actual betas in the succeeding periods change in the predicted direction, and in most cases the shift toward 1 is even faster than the predicted change from formula (12.7).

The systematic pattern of the changes in beta is too important to be ignored by institutional investors. Indeed many of the investment firms adjust the beta in one way or another to take this tendency toward 1 into account.

Table 12.9 illustrates the information provided by Merrill Lynch to their customers regarding the various stocks. The information reported in Table 12.9 is based on the usual monthly regressions of the type:

$$R_{it} = \hat{\alpha}_i + \hat{\beta}_i R_{mt} + e_{it} \quad (t = 1, 2, \ldots, 60)$$

namely we have 60 observations, where $R_{it}$ is the rate of return on the $i$th security in month $t$. After the column with the closing price of the stock, the second and the third columns report on $\hat{\beta}_i$ and $\hat{\alpha}_i$ as estimated by this time series regression. The fourth column provides the coefficient of determination $R^2$ which is a measure of dispersion of the observations about the regression line, while the fifth column yields the standard deviation of the error term $e_t$. Since $\hat{\alpha}_i$ and $\hat{\beta}_i$ are only sample estimates the next two columns provide the standard error of these two estimates. Then comes the adjusted beta which is calculated by a formula of the type suggested by Blume, but with slightly different coefficients. For example, for the first company on this table we have:

$$\beta_2 = 0.34 + 0.66\beta_1 = 0.34 + 0.66 \times 0.85 = 0.34 + 0.56 = 0.90$$

In the same way all the adjusted betas are calculated using the Merrill Lynch formula:

$$\beta_i^{(adj)} = 0.34 + 0.66\hat{\beta}_i$$

### Summary

In a portfolio context, a security may have a very high variance and still may be considered safe as long as it has negative covariances with other securities included in the portfolio. Thus, the beta which appears in the CAPM formula measures the security risk and hence determines its equilibrium expected rate of return.

One can decompose the security variability into two components: the systematic risk (which determines the risk premium) and the non-systematic risk which can be "washed out" by appropriate diversification. One can decompose either the security variance or the security standard deviation into these two components, but only the decomposition of the latter yields results which are consistent with the CAPM, especially in cases of negative beta.

## Table 12.9
### Sample Page from Merrill Lynch, Pierce, Fenner & Smith, Inc., Market Sensitivity Report for November 1979

| Symb | Security Name | 10/79 Close Price | Beta | Alpha | $R^2$ | Residual Standard Deviation | Standard Error of Beta | of Alpha | Adjusted Beta | Number of Observations |
|---|---|---|---|---|---|---|---|---|---|---|
| THRS | Threashold Tecknolog | 9.750 | 0.85 | 1.92 | 0.06 | 12.99 | 0.40 | 1.69 | 0.90 | 60 |
| FXN | Three D Depts | 4.375 | 1.71 | 4.54 | 0.18 | 17.07 | 0.45 | 2.21 | 1.47 | 60 |
| TDMC | Three Dimensional CI | 0.562 | -0.61 | 8.65 | 0.02 | 41.62 | 1.46 | 5.78 | -0.08 | 52 |
| TFTA | Thriftimart Inc. A | 21.375 | 0.80 | 1.21 | 0.13 | 8.49 | 0.26 | 1.11 | 0.87 | 60 |
| THRF | Thriftway Leasing Co. | 0.000 | 1.02 | 3.84 | 0.02 | 26.06 | 0.66 | 3.38 | 1.01 | 60 |
| TFD | Thrifty Corp. | 11.625 | 1.92 | 0.87 | 0.46 | 8.80 | 0.27 | 1.15 | 1.61 | 60 |
| TEXT | Ti-Caro | 20.500 | 0.94 | 1.58 | 0.23 | 7.17 | 0.22 | 0.93 | 0.96 | 60 |
| TIM | Tidewater Inc. | 25.750 | 0.86 | 0.39 | 0.19 | 7.30 | 0.22 | 0.95 | 0.91 | 60 |
| TDW | Tidwell Inds Inc. | 5.750 | 5.11 | 4.85 | 0.17 | 46.73 | 1.42 | 6.10 | 3.73 | 60 |
| FLY | Tiger International Inc. | 19.750 | 1.61 | 1.55 | 0.33 | 9.87 | 0.30 | 1.29 | 1.42 | 60 |
| TI | Time Inc. | 43.250 | 1.24 | 1.39 | 0.36 | 6.87 | 0.21 | 0.90 | 1.16 | 60 |
| TPLX | Timeplex Inc. | 9.125 | 2.38 | 5.23 | 0.11 | 26.83 | 0.82 | 3.50 | 1.91 | 60 |
| PWII | Timberland Industries | 6.250 | 0.78 | 3.18 | 0.06 | 13.68 | 0.35 | 1.77 | 0.85 | 60 |
| TMC | Times Mirror Co. | 32.500 | 1.60 | 1.19 | 0.61 | 5.41 | 0.16 | 0.71 | 1.39 | 60 |
| TKR | Timken Co. | 51.000 | 1.13 | 0.65 | 0.40 | 5.82 | 0.18 | 0.76 | 1.09 | 60 |
| TNSL | Tinsley Labs Inc. | 6.000 | 0.84 | 1.60 | 0.03 | 17.49 | 0.48 | 2.27 | 0.90 | 60 |
| TLK | Tipperary Corp. | 11.250 | 0.95 | 2.12 | 0.08 | 12.86 | 0.39 | 1.68 | 0.97 | 60 |
| TIN | Titan Group | 1.500 | 1.53 | -1.81 | 0.04 | 24.91 | 0.85 | 3.22 | 1.35 | 60 |
| TICT | TLL Industries | 3.000 | 1.61 | -0.23 | 0.12 | 17.29 | 0.53 | 2.26 | 1.40 | 60 |
| AIKZ | Tobias Koizin Co. | 5.000 | 1.18 | 2.44 | 0.07 | 16.98 | 0.52 | 2.22 | 1.12 | 60 |
| TBN | Tobin Packing Inc. | 3.625 | 1.10 | -0.41 | 0.09 | 13.89 | 0.42 | 1.18 | 1.06 | 60 |
| TOCM | Tocom Inc. | 10.500 | 1.72 | 2.98 | 0.19 | 14.69 | 0.45 | 1.92 | 1.48 | 60 |
| TOD | Todd Shipyards Corp. | 23.750 | 0.31 | 3.12 | 0.01 | 16.88 | 0.51 | 2.20 | 0.54 | 60 |
| TOK | Tokheim Corp. | 15.875 | 2.39 | 2.46 | 0.39 | 12.72 | 0.39 | 1.66 | 1.92 | 60 |
| TKM | Tokio Marine Ins. Adr. | 129.500 | 0.32 | 1.43 | 0.01 | 7.57 | 0.23 | 0.99 | 0.55 | 60 |
| TED | Toledo Edison Co. | 18.125 | 0.79 | -0.28 | 0.34 | 4.60 | 0.14 | 0.60 | 0.86 | 60 |
| NOHO | Toledo Trustcorp | 27.500 | 0.35 | 0.91 | 0.09 | 4.35 | 0.13 | 0.57 | 0.57 | 60 |
| TILLY | Tolley Intl. Corp. | 1.000 | 0.21 | -2.34 | 0.01 | 19.46 | 0.59 | 2.54 | 0.48 | 60 |
| TLOC | Tomlinson Oil Inc. | 10.500 | 1.28 | 3.68 | 0.07 | 17.49 | 0.53 | 2.28 | 1.19 | 60 |
| TKA | Tonka Corp. | 10.875 | 1.77 | 0.47 | 0.33 | 10.60 | 0.32 | 1.38 | 1.51 | 60 |

Based on S&P 500 Index Using Straight Regression.

Investors employ betas to rank the safety of the various securities. Since the estimation of beta from past data in general may include a statistical error, one should use the historical beta with great caution. However, a tendency of betas to move toward 1 has been found. Based on this tendency, we can adjust the historical beta for the estimation of future betas. Indeed most investors do not simply rely on historical data, and the adjusted beta is calculated by allowing for the tendency of beta toward 1 over time.

---

### Summary Table

1. The $i$th security systematic risk $\beta_i$ is estimated by the time-series regression

$$R_{it} = \hat{a}_i + \hat{\beta}_i R_{mt} + e_{it}$$

where $R_{it}$, $R_{mt}$ stand for the returns in period $t$ on the $i$th security and the market portfolio, respectively.

2. The estimate of the systematic risk $\hat{\beta}_i$ is given by

$$\beta_i = \frac{\sum\limits_{t=1}^{n} (R_{it} - \bar{R}_i)(R_{mt} - \bar{R}_m)}{\sum\limits_{t=1}^{n} (R_{mt} - \bar{R}_m)^2}$$

3. The regression line given in (1) is called the characteristic line.

4. if $\beta_i > 1$ the stock is classified as aggressive;
   If $\beta_i < 1$ the stock is classified as defensive;
   If $\beta_i = 1$ the stock is classified as neutral.

5. The Security Market Line (SML) is given by $ER_i = r + (ER_m - r)\beta_i$
   It holds for all risky assets $i$.

6. The Capital Market Line (CML) is given by

$$ER_p = r + \frac{ER_m - r}{\sigma_m} \sigma_p$$

   It holds only for efficient portfolios, $p$.

7. Decomposition of the $i$th security variance, $\sigma_i^2$:

$$\sigma_i^2 = \beta_i^2 \sigma_m^2 + \sigma_e^2$$

*Systematic risk* $= \beta_i^2 \sigma_m^2$
*Nonsystematic risk* $= \sigma_e^2$
*In words:*
   Variance = systematic risk + nonsystematic risk

*Alternative definition in words:*
   Variance = nondiversifiable risk + diversifiable risk

8. Decomposition of the standard deviation $\sigma_i$:

*Systematic risk* $= \beta_i \sigma_m$
*Nonsystematic risk* $= \sigma_i - \beta_i \sigma_m$
   Standard deviation = systematic risk + nonsystematic risk

## APPENDIX 12.1
### Linear Regression Program

Linear regression is conveniently run on a computer using one of the many available statistical packages, such as SPSS, BMDP, and others.

The example in this Appendix shows the SPSS linear regression program and a sample output. The program was run to estimate the beta of Dow Chemicals stocks (variable name DOW) against the Fisher Index as market portfolio proxy (variable name RM). Historical rates of return for the period 1956–1980 were used (25 observations or "cases"—too many for manual calculations). The printout includes the SPSS program, a listing of the input data (generated by the LIST CASES instruction in the program), and the regression results. The regression results comprise the following essential information:

(1) Means, standard deviations, and the correlation coefficient of the variables.
(2) The regression $R^2$ (with analysis of variance), as a measure of regression quality. $R^2 = 0.316$ indicates that nearly 32% of the variance of the observations is explained by the calculated regression line.
(3) The two regression coefficients (the coefficient of RM and the constant intercept), $b_i = 0.610$, $a_i = 2.383$.
(4) The significance, the standard errors, the $t$-values and the confidence intervals of the two coefficients.

A glance at the printout shows that the beta estimate of Dow Chemicals stocks, $b_i = 0.610$, has a 95% confidence interval stretching from 0.223 to 0.997. It is thus significantly less than 1 (and significantly greater than 0), so that the Dow Chemicals stock is classifiable as defensive.

The constant intercept, on the other hand, although much greater in magnitude ($a_i = 2.383$), also suffers from much larger estimation errors. Its $t$-value is only 0.440 and the 95% confidence interval is from −8.824 to 13.589, straddling the zero. The constant intercept is thus not significantly different from zero.

### PROGRAM

```
RUN NAME            REGRESSION OF STOCK ON MARKET 1956–80
VARIABLE LIST       DOW,RM
INPUT FORMAT        FREEFIELD
INPUT MEDIUM        DISK
N OF CASES          25
PRINT FORMATS       ALL (2)
LIST CASES          CASES=25/VARIABLES=DOW,RM
REGRESSION          VARIABLES=DOW,RM/
                    REGRESSION=DOW WITH RM/
STATISTICS          ALL
READ INPUT DATA
```

00055200 CM NEEDED FOR REGRESSION

OPTION — 1
IGNORE MISSING VALUE INDICATORS
(NO MISSING VALUES DEFINED...OPTION 1 WAS FORCED)

———————————————————————————————————

**DATA**

REGRESSION OF STOCK ON MARKET 1956—80

FILE    NONAME    (CREATION DATE = 22/03/83 )

| CASE—NO | DOW | RM |
|---|---|---|
| 1 | 15.03 | 6.92 |
| 2 | −17.95 | −14.31 |
| 3 | 47.50 | 59.68 |
| 4 | 33.52 | 15.41 |
| 5 | −21.84 | −1.56 |
| 6 | .28 | 29.45 |
| 7 | −21.84 | −12.75 |
| 8 | 29.83 | 18.69 |
| 9 | 13.62 | 18.13 |
| 10 | 5.31 | 28.61 |
| 11 | −17.52 | −7.06 |
| 12 | 45.26 | 50.38 |
| 13 | −7.75 | 30.55 |
| 14 | −8.75 | −20.30 |
| 15 | 11.42 | −2.90 |
| 16 | 64.94 | 19.47 |
| 17 | 31.19 | 8.45 |
| 18 | 15.32 | −29.31 |
| 19 | −2.32 | −26.53 |
| 20 | 69.55 | 61.90 |
| 21 | −3.39 | 45.49 |
| 22 | −36.06 | 9.50 |
| 23 | −2.14 | 14.02 |
| 24 | 35.82 | 35.31 |
| 25 | 5.13 | 30.99 |

———————————————————————————————————

## VARIABLE PARAMETERS AND CORRELATION COEFFICIENT

REGRESSION OF STOCK ON MARKET 1956–80
FILE   NONAME   (CREATION DATE = 22/03/83 )

* * * * * * * * * * * * * M U L T I P L E   R E G R E S S I O N * * * * * * * * * * * * *

| VARIABLE | MEAN | STANDARD DEV | CASES |
|----------|---------|---------|----|
| DOW | 11.3664 | 27.5917 | 25 |
| RM | 14.7292 | 25.4190 | 25 |

CORRELATION COEFFICIENTS.

A VALUE OF 99.00000 IS PRINTED
IF A COEFFICIENT CANNOT BE COMPUTED.

RM              .56190
                DOW

_____

## R SQUARE AND ANALYSIS OF VARIANCE

REGRESSION OF STOCK ON MARKET 1956–80
FILE   NONAME   (CREATION DATE = 22/03/83 )

* * * * * * * * * * * * * M U L T I P L E   R E G R E S S I O N * * * * * * * * * * * * *

DEPENDENT VARIABLE..   DOW
MEAN RESPONSE        11.36640          STD. DEV.        27.59166
VARIABLE(S) ENTERED ON STEP NUMBER   1..    RM

MULTIPLE R              .56190
R SQUARE                .31573
ADJUSTED R SQUARE    .28598
STD DEVIATION       23.31489

| ANALYSIS OF VARIANCE | DF | SUM OF SQUARES | MEAN SQUARE | F | SIGNIF |
|----------------------|-----|----------------|-------------|----------|--------|
| REGRESSION | 1. | 5768.76298 | 5768.76298 | 10.61246 | .003 |
| RESIDUAL | 23. | 12502.43459 | 543.58411 | | |
| COEFF OF VARIABILITY | 205.1 PCT | | | | |

— — — — — — — — — VARIABLES IN THE EQUATION — — — — — — — — —

| VARIABLE | B | STD ERROR B | F | BETA |
|---|---|---|---|---|
| | | | SIGNIFICANCE | ELASTICITY |
| RM | .60992504 | .18722701 | 10.612457 | .5618985 |
| | | | .003 | .79037 |
| (CONSTANT) | 2.3826922 | 5.4174067 | .19344298 | |
| | | | .664 | |

— — — — — — — — — VARIABLES NOT IN THE EQUATION — — — — — — — — —

| VARIABLE | PARTIAL | TOLERANCE | F |
|---|---|---|---|
| | | | SIGNIFICANCE |

ALL VARIABLES ARE IN THE EQUATION.

**REGRESSION COEFFICIENTS AND CONFIDENCE INTERVALS**

| VARIABLE | B | STD ERROR B | T | 95.0 PCT | CONF INTERVAL |
|---|---|---|---|---|---|
| RM | .60992504 | .18722701 | 3.2576766 | .22261647 , | .99723361 |
| CONSTANT | 2.3826922 | 5.4174067 | .43982154 | −8.8240676 , | 13.589452 |

VARIANCE/COVARIANCE MATRIX OF THE UNNORMALIZED REGRESSION COEFFICIENTS.

RM                        .03505
                RM

## Questions and Problems

12.1    Define the terms *systematic risk* and *nonsystematic risk*.

12.2    "The higher a security's variance, the higher its expected return." Appraise.

12.3    The betas of four stocks in a perfect market are:

$$\beta_A = -1, \quad \beta_B = 0, \quad \beta_C = 1, \quad \beta_D = 2$$

Assume that the market is in equilibrium, the riskless interest rate is $r = 5\%$, and the market portfolio is characterized by 13% expected return and 15% standard deviation. Calculate the expected return on stocks $A$, $B$, $C$, and $D$.

12.4    Give general expressions for the expected returns of a security with zero beta and of another security with negative beta.

Assuming that the riskless interest rate is $r = 5\%$ and that the observed expected return on a security with zero beta is 9%, is the market in equilibrium?

12.5    Assume the following hypothetical rates of return (in percentages) on the market portfolio:

| Year | Rate of Return | Year | Rate of Return |
|------|----------------|------|----------------|
| 1974 | 10 | 1979 | 3 |
| 1975 | 32 | 1980 | 12 |
| 1976 | 20 | 1981 | -5 |
| 1977 | -8 | 1982 | 18 |
| 1978 | 17 | 1983 | 21 |

Set out hypothetical rates of return of an aggressive stock and of a defensive stock. Use your figures to calculate the beta of each stock. Draw the characteristic lines of the two stocks in the same graph.

12.6    The annual rates of return on the market portfolio $R_m$ and the annual rates of return on security $j$, $R_j$, for a period of eight years are given below:

| Year | $R_j$ | $R_m$ |
|------|-------|-------|
| 1 | 0.045 | 0.020 |
| 2 | 0.050 | 0.060 |
| 3 | 0.070 | 0.080 |
| 4 | 0.020 | -0.030 |
| 5 | 0.050 | 0.010 |
| 6 | 0.090 | 0.080 |
| 7 | 0.040 | 0.060 |
| 8 | 0.020 | -0.040 |

Estimate the beta of security $j$, interpret it, and classify the security as aggressive or defensive.

12.7    Assume that the capital market is in equilibrium. The risk-free interest rate is $r = 0.04$ and the market portfolio is characterized by expected return of 0.10 and standard deviation of 0.09.
(a) Write out the equation of the capital market line (CML) and draw it on a graph.
(b) Consider three securities whose returns $R_1$, $R_2$, and $R_3$ have the following covariances with the return on the market portfolio:

$$\text{Cov } (R_1, R_m) = 0.0108, \quad \text{Cov } (R_2, R_m) = -0.0027, \quad \text{Cov } (R_3, R_m) = 0.0054$$

Determine the betas of the three securities.
(c) Write out the equation of the security market line (SML) and determine the expected return on the three securities. Draw the SML on a graph and locate the three securities on the line.
(d) Given that the standard deviations of the three securities are $\sigma_1 = 0.20$, $\sigma_2 = 0.05$, and $\sigma_3 = 0.16$, respectively, what is the *diversifiable* risk of each of these securities? (Decompose the standard deviation, not the variance).

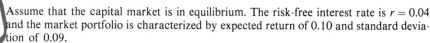

*non –*

12.8  (a) "Efficient diversification reduces the systematic risk of the portfolio to 0." Do you agree? Explain.

(b) "When the security is perfectly correlated with the market, its systematic risk is 0." Appraise.     *non –*

12.9  Security $A$ has a beta of $-1.5$ and security $B$ has a beta of $1.5$. The variance of the market return is $\sigma_m^2 = 4$. Therefore, the systematic risk is $\beta_i^2 \sigma_m^2 = 9$ for both securities. Are both securities equally risky?   *no, B is more, use s.d.*

12.10 Estimate the diversifiable risk and the nondiversifiable risk of the two securities characterized by the following information:

|                    | Security 1 | Security 2 |
|--------------------|------------|------------|
| Standard deviation | 2          | 3          |
| Beta               | 0.5        | -0.5       |

The standard deviation of market returns is $\sigma_m = 1$. Which security would you add to the portfolio in order to increase the stability of the portfolio's returns?

12.11 "The beta of a security estimated from historical returns is equal to the true beta of the security." Appraise.   *false, β chgs. over time*

12.12 What are the difficulties in estimating systematic risk from historical data? Can these difficulties be entirely eliminated?   *est. β, not entirely, moving to 1.*

12.13 Use the data given in Table 12.8 to run a regression of the beta coefficients estimated for the period 1961–1968 on the beta coefficients estimated in the years 1954–1961. Adjust the 1961–1968 beta coefficients with the aid of the estimated regression line.

12.14 The annual rates of return (in percent) of two securities $i$ and $j$ and of the market portfolio for four consecutive years were as follows:

| Year | Security i | Security j | Market Portfolio |
|------|------------|------------|------------------|
| 1    | -20        | +30        | +40              |
| 2    | 0          | +10        | +20              |
| 3    | +20        | -10        | 0                |
| 4    | 0          | +10        | +12              |

Assuming riskless interest rate $r = 5\%$, answer the following questions:

(a) Calculate the means and the standard deviations of returns of securities $i$ and $j$ and the covariances between the returns of each security and the market portfolio.

(b) Calculate the systematic (non-diversifiable) risk $\beta_i \sigma_m$ of the two securities and show graphically the location of the two securities and of the market portfolio in the $ER - \sigma$ plane.

(c) Assume that the market is in equilibrium. What should be the expected rate of return of the two securities in this case? How can you account for the deviation of the above data from the calculated figures?

12.15   The table below provides the annual rates of return on General Motors, American Motor Corporation and the S&P 500 Index (a proxy to the market portfolio).

| Year | GM | AMC | Market Portfolio (S&P 500) |
|------|------|--------|------|
| 1959 | 14.4 | 121.2 | 11.9 |
| 1960 | −22.2 | −33.9 | 0.4 |
| 1961 | 47.5 | 3.7 | 26.9 |
| 1962 | 7.7 | 3.1 | −8.6 |
| 1963 | 42.8 | 17.2 | 22.8 |
| 1964 | 30.7 | −16.9 | 16.5 |
| 1965 | 11.4 | −32.8 | 12.5 |
| 1966 | −32.5 | −30.4 | −10.06 |
| 1967 | 30.5 | 114.0 | 23.9 |
| 1968 | 1.8 | −3.7 | 11.1 |
| 1969 | −6.2 | −33.0 | −8.5 |
| 1970 | 22.3 | −33.2 | 3.9 |
| 1971 | 4.3 | 21.6 | 14.3 |
| 1972 | 6.5 | 17.8 | 19.1 |
| 1973 | −37.8 | 7.5 | −14.7 |
| 1974 | −27.6 | −62.3 | −26.5 |
| 1975 | 97.1 | 65.4 | 37.3 |
| 1976 | 45.85 | −28.02 | 23.8 |
| 1977 | −11.25 | −6.33 | −7.15 |
| 1978 | −4.7 | 26.67 | 12.16 |

Assuming riskless interest rate $r = 3\%$, answer the following questions.

(a) Estimate the systematic risk $\beta_i \sigma_m$, the nonsystematic risk $(\sigma_i - \beta_i \sigma_m)$, and the total risk $\sigma_i$ for each of the two stocks.

(b) Estimate the systematic and the nonsystematic risk using the decomposition $\sigma_i^2 = \beta_i^2 \sigma_m^2 + \sigma_e^2$.

(c) Under what decomposition does the systematic risk constitute a higher percentage of the total risk?

(d) Use the systematic risk to calculate the equilibrium risk premium of GM and AMC.

12.16   The following table lists annual rates of return on the stock of General Motors, Ford Motors, Chrysler and on the market portfolio from 1972–1981. Estimate the risk measure beta of each stock using the market model. Classify the stocks by their risk.

| | *Annual Rate of Return (%)* | | | *Market Portfolio* |
| *Year* | *General Motors* | *Ford Motors* | *Chrysler* | *(Fisher Index)* |
|---|---|---|---|---|
| 1972 | 6.58 | 17.81 | 47.29 | 17.77 |
| 1973 | −37.82 | −46.34 | −59.71 | −16.92 |
| 1974 | −27.64 | −11.07 | −48.17 | −26.80 |
| 1975 | 97.28 | 41.13 | 39.65 | 37.72 |
| 1976 | 47.36 | 46.96 | 104.40 | 26.26 |
| 1977 | −11.36 | −0.54 | −34.40 | −4.81 |
| 1978 | −5.38 | −0.42 | −26.37 | 7.39 |
| 1979 | 2.28 | −16.53 | −19.97 | 21.82 |
| 1980 | −4.40 | −31.51 | −27.78 | 32.70 |
| 1981 | −9.92 | −10.98 | −30.77 | −4.22 |

*Source:* CRSP monthly returns tape.

## Data Set Problems

1. Calculate the beta of the first fund in each category in the Data Set. Note that the Fisher Index listed at the bottom of the Data Set represents a market portfolio proxy. Draw the regression line for Afuture Fund.

2. (a) Use a standard statistical package (such as SPSS or BMDP) to run a regression of each mutual fund in the Data Set on the market portfolio. Prepare a table of all the fund betas. Calculate the average beta for each category of mutual funds. Compare and analyze the average results.
   (b) Classify the funds in each category into aggressive (beta greater than 1), defensive (beta less than 1) and neutral (beta equal to 1). What is the percentage of funds of each kind in each category?
   (c) Now look at the computer output again, find the 95% confidence intervals of the betas and count as aggressive only those funds for which the entire confidence interval falls above 1 (similarly count as defensive only those funds for which the entire confidence interval falls below 1; all the remaining funds are counted as neutral). Recalculate the percentages of the three types in each category taking the confidence intervals into consideration. Compare this frequency count with the results in (b) above.

3. Decompose the total risk of the first four mutual funds from the Balanced Funds category into diversifiable and nondiversifiable risk. Apply both the variance decomposition and the standard deviation decomposition. Analyze your results.

4. Apply Blume's method to adjust the beta of the first two funds from the Maximum Capital Gain category.

## Selected References

See Chapter 14.

# 13

# Extension of the CAPM: Other Risk–Return Models

The Capital Asset Pricing Model (CAPM) has been derived under restrictive assumptions, some of which clearly do not hold in reality. Yet, it is possible that the CAPM in its original form, as given in Chapter 11, is justified on positive grounds if the model actually explains stock price behavior. Nevertheless, some of the restrictions introduced in the model can be relaxed, leading to a theoretical formula which has a similar structure to that of the CAPM and yet is closer to reality in the sense that the underlying assumptions are less restrictive. In this chapter, we first relax some of the assumptions which were employed in the derivation of the CAPM and then analyze other models intended either to extend or to replace the CAPM.

## 13.1  No Riskless Asset: The Zero-Beta Model

In the derivation of the CAPM, it is assumed that investors can borrow and lend any amount of money at the riskless interest rate. In the absence of inflation, the investor can buy Government bonds[1] with maturity identical to the planned investment horizon, so that the exact yield or rate of return on the investment can be calculated in advance. However, while individual investors can *lend* to the government (buy bonds) as much as they want and thus earn the riskless interest rate on their investment, *borrowing* at the same rate is impossible since the borrowing rate, in general, is higher than the lending rate. Moreover, individual investors cannot borrow as much as they want, since lenders usually restrict the volume of loans allowed to a single customer. Finally, in a world of persistent inflation, even if the lending interest rate is known with certainty in nominal

---

[1] Only accrual bonds without interim interest payments, e.g., Treasury Bills, can be properly regarded as a riskless instrument. Interest-paying bonds are risky in the sense that the reinvestment rate of the interim cashflows (interest payments) is not certain, since the future interest rate may change.

terms, the *real* (inflation-adjusted) interest rate is uncertain, since the future inflation is an unknown random variable. Thus, in the inflationary environment characterizing the world since the early 1970s, there is actually no riskless asset, and even borrowing and lending should be considered as uncertain financial transactions in real terms.[2] Thus, the first natural extension of the CAPM is to develop a risk–return relationship without riskless assets. The case of different lending and borrowing rates is treated in Section 13.2.

We continue to assume, as before, that all investors choose portfolios which are mean–variance efficient (see Chapter 11). Since the market portfolio *m* is a weighted average of all the individual investors' portfolios, it must be also MV efficient. Figure 13.1 illustrates the mean–standard deviation efficient frontier and two special portfolios *m* and *Z* that play a central role in the framework without riskless asset. The point *m* on the efficient segment *SS'* of the frontier denotes the market portfolio, while *Z* is some inefficient portfolio whose expected return is $ER_z$. Note that by assumption there is no riskless asset in this framework and hence no risk-free rate is marked on the vertical axis (compare Figure 11.6).

The portfolio *Z* is constructed by drawing a tangent to the efficient frontier at the point *m* and then drawing a horizontal line through the intersection of the tangent with the vertical axis. The point where the horizontal line crosses the MV frontier is the portfolio *Z*.

In order to find an efficient portfolio, the investor first fixes the desired expected

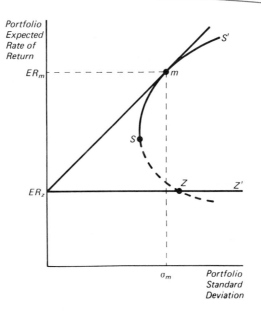

**Figure 13.1**

[2] Bonds indexed to the consumer price index are available in some countries (e.g., Brazil, Finland, Israel). These indexed bonds are of course riskless in real terms (for appropriate maturities).

rate of return on his portfolio and then selects the investment proportions which minimize the portfolio variance at the level of the desired expected rate of return. If the expected market rate of return $ER_m$ is taken as the desired expected rate of return on a portfolio, we have to solve the following problem (see Figure 13.1):

Minimize the portfolio variance:

$$\sigma_p^2 = \sum_{i=1}^n x_i^2 \sigma_i^2 + 2 \sum_{i=1}^n \sum_{\substack{j=1 \\ j>i}}^n x_i x_j \sigma_{ij}$$

subject to the constraints:

$$\sum_{i=1}^n x_i = 1 \quad \text{and} \quad \sum_{i=1}^n x_i ER_i = ER_m$$

Here $\sigma_{ij} = Cov\,(R_i, R_j)$ is the covariance of the rates of return on assets $i$ and $j$. Using the general technique of constrained minimization employed in the previous chapters, we show in Appendix 13.1 that the following linear risk–return relationship holds in the absence of a riskless asset:

$$ER_i = ER_z + (ER_m - ER_z)\beta_i \tag{13.1}$$

This formula is very similar to the traditional CAPM formula with only one distinction: $ER_z$, the expected rate of return on the peculiar inefficient portfolio constructed as shown in Figure 13.1, is substituted for the risk-free interest rate. This portfolio $Z$ is called the *zero-beta portfolio*, for reasons that will become obvious from the next section.

### 13.1.1 Properties of the Zero-Beta Portfolio

We will use the term minimum-variance portfolio to denote a portfolio obtained by minimizing the variance at a given level of expected rate of return. Minimum-variance portfolios on the upward sloping section of the efficient frontier are of course MV efficient. Those on the downward sloping section are MV inefficient, but by derivation they are minimum-variance portfolios for the corresponding expected rate of return level. It can be shown that *any minimum-variance portfolio can be obtained as a linear combination of two other minimum-variance portfolios* (this is left as an end-of-chapter exercise to the reader—see Problem 13.19 and also compare Chapter 9, Sec. 9.6).

Let us now consider some properties of the portfolio $Z$ introduced in the previous section.

(a) *Z is a portfolio with zero beta and it is the minimum-variance portfolio among all the portfolios (or securities) with zero beta.*

To verify this property, consider Figure 13.1.

All the risky assets or risky portfolios on the line $ZZ'$ have one characteristic in common: they all have zero beta. Indeed, in equilibrium we have from (13.1),

$$ER_i = ER_z + (ER_m - ER_z)\beta_i$$

Since all the risky assets which lie on the line $ZZ'$ have the same expected rate of return as portfolio $Z$, $ER_i = ER_z$, while the rate of return on the market portfolio $ER_m$ is different from $ER_z$, then from the above formula $\beta_i$ must be equal to zero. Since portfolio $Z$ by construction has the smallest variance among all risky assets (or portfolios) at the expected rate of return level $ER_i = ER_z$, it is the minimum-variance portfolio among all the zero beta risky assets on this level.

Since by definition $\beta_z = \sigma_{zm}/\sigma_m^2$, the zero-beta property of the portfolio $Z$ implies $\sigma_{zm} = 0$, i.e., it has zero covariance with the market portfolio.

(b) *Portfolio Z is inefficient:*

To see this, recall that portfolio $m$ is efficient, hence the slope $(ER_m - ER_z)/\sigma_m$ (which is equal to $dER_m/d\sigma_m$ at point $m$) is positive. This implies that $ER_m > ER_z$, as plotted in Figure 13.1. Now let us find portfolio $S$ which has the smallest variance of all portfolios, i.e., the portfolio located at the point of global minimum variance of the efficient frontier in Figure 13.1. The rate of return on any minimum-variance portfolio $S$, $R_s$, can be written as a linear combination of the rates of return on two other minimum-variance portfolios (see Problem 13.19), and in particular on portfolios $Z$ and $m$:

$$R_s = x_z R_z + (1 - x_z)R_m$$

where $x_z$ is the proportion invested in portfolio $Z$. The variance of the portfolio $S$ is given by:

$$\sigma_s^2 = x_z^2 \sigma_z^2 + (1 - x_z)^2 \sigma_m^2$$

(recall that $\sigma_{zm} = 0$ since $Z$ is the zero-beta portfolio). To find the portfolio $S$ with the global minimum variance, take the derivative $\partial \sigma_s^2/\partial x_z$ and find the proportion $x_z$ which minimizes the portfolio variance. Thus:

$$\frac{\partial \sigma_s^2}{\partial x_z} = 2x_z \sigma_z^2 - 2(1 - x_z)\sigma_m^2$$

Equating to zero and solving for $x_z$ yields:

$$x_z = \frac{\sigma_m^2}{\sigma_m^2 + \sigma_z^2} \quad \text{and} \quad 1 - x_z = \frac{\sigma_z^2}{\sigma_m^2 + \sigma_z^2}$$

Both proportions are positive. Thus we conclude that in order to obtain portfolio $S$ (see Figure 13.1), investors should invest a positive amount in $Z$ and a positive amount in $m$.

Since we have seen that:

$$ER_m > ER_z$$

a combination of $Z$ and $m$ with positive amount invested in each portfolio must yield:

$$ER_s = x_z ER_z + (1 - x_z) ER_m$$

i.e., $ER_s$ is a weighted average of $ER_z$ and $ER_m$, so that:

$$ER_z < ER_s < ER_m$$

Thus portfolio $S$ has a higher expected rate of return than portfolio $Z$, $ER_s > ER_z$; on the other hand since $S$ is the portfolio with global minimum variance among all portfolios, $\sigma_s^2 < \sigma_z^2$ so that $Z$ must lie on the inefficient section of the MV frontier, as plotted in Figure 13.1. Portfolio $Z$ is thus MV inefficient.

Since there is no riskless asset in this model, the straight line through $m$ in Figure 13.1, unlike that in Figure 11.6 in Chapter 11, *does not* represent the opportunity set available to investors. Investors will choose their portfolio at the tangency point of their indifference map with the MV efficient set. For example, in Figure 13.2, an investor with preferences represented by indifference curve $I_1$ will choose portfolio $m_1$, while an

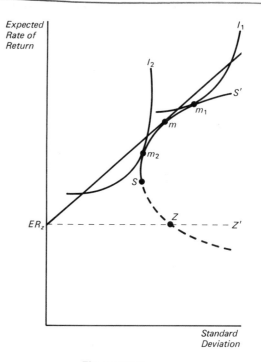

**Figure 13.2**

investor with preferences represented by $I_2$ will choose portfolio $m_2$. However, both can achieve their optimal point simply by finding the appropriate mixes of portfolios $m$ and $Z$. Investor $I_1$ will short portfolio $Z$ and invest his own resources plus the proceeds from the short sale in portfolio $m$, reaching the point $m_1$ by this diversification. Investor $I_2$, on the other hand, will hold long positions in both $Z$ and $m$, and by this diversification he will reach point $m_2$. In this sense, we have two mutual funds $m$ and $Z$ and all investors can reach their respective optimum portfolios simply by mixing these two mutual funds. Thus, a *separation property* applies in this case as in the traditional CAPM with riskless asset. Investors first choose portfolios $m$ and $Z$, then in the second step each investor mixes these two portfolios according to his individual preferences.

However, unlike the traditional CAPM with riskless asset in which the opportunity set is uniquely determined by the pair $(m, r)$, there is more than one possible pair of portfolios $(m, Z)$ by which the risk–return relationship can be derived. This is illustrated in Figure 13.3. The expected rate of return on security $i$ can be written as:

$$ER_i = ER_{z_1} + (ER_{m_1} - ER_{z_1})\beta_{i(1)}$$

or alternatively as:

$$ER_i = ER_{z_2} + (ER_{m_2} - ER_{z_2})\beta_{i(2)}$$

where:

$$\beta_{i(1)} = \sigma_{im_1}/\sigma^2_{m_1} \quad \text{and} \quad \beta_{i(2)} = \sigma_{im_2}/\sigma^2_{m_2}$$

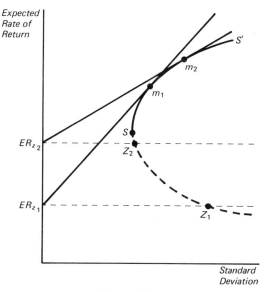

**Figure 13.3**

Thus, for each portfolio on the efficient frontier $SS'$, there is a corresponding zero beta portfolio on the inefficient section. In our case, $Z_1$ is the zero-beta portfolio corresponding to $m_1$, and $Z_2$ is the zero-beta portfolio corresponding to $m_2$. Any point (portfolio) on the efficient frontier can be created as a linear combination of $m_1$ and $Z_1$ or alternatively as a linear combination of $m_2$ and $Z_2$. Thus, unlike the case with riskless asset, in this model the investor's optimum portfolio can be achieved by combining more than one pair of mutual funds. Recall that in Chapter 11, when a riskless asset was assumed to exist, all the investors combined the unique pair of mutual funds $(m, r)$ where $m$ is the unique market portfolio and $r$ is the riskless asset (see Figure 11.6).

### 13.2 Borrowing Rate Higher than Lending Rate

Having derived the risk–return relationship for the case without riskless asset, let us turn to another scenario which may be appropriate in many situations: investors can lend money, receiving the lending interest rate $r_L$, and they can borrow money, paying interest at a certain borrowing interest rate $r_B$. In real life the borrowing rate is higher than the lending rate, $r_B > r_L$, and the gap $r_B - r_L$ is not small and hence cannot be

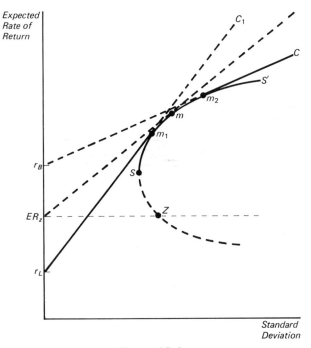

**Figure 13.4**

neglected. For example, in the first half of 1982 we find that the one-year lending rate in the US was about $r_L = 14\%$, while the borrowing rate (for prime borrowers) was $r_B = 19\%$.

Under this realistic scenario, the efficient frontier, which includes risky assets as well as the two riskless assets, is as shown in Figure 13.4. The investor's optimum portfolio may be located at any point along the straight segment $r_L m_1$ (he is then a lender), or at any point along the straight line $m_2 C$ (he is then a borrower), or on the section $m_1 m_2$, a case when he neither borrows nor lends. Note that the dotted segments are not feasible. For example, investors would be glad to lend money at the higher rate $r_B$, but the banks will pay them only the rate $r_L$ on their deposits and hence the segment $r_B m_2$ is not feasible. For the same reason, the segment $m_1 C_1$ is not feasible.

Under this model, as in the case without riskless asset (see Section 13.1), we again lose one of the properties of the classical CAPM, which asserts that *all* investors, independent of their preferences, choose the *same mix of risky assets*. As Figure 13.4 reveals, investors who choose to lend money select the risky portfolio $m_1$, which differs from $m_2$, the optimum mix of risky assets for borrowers. Moreover, there are numerous investors whose indifference maps are tangent to the efficient frontier at some point along the section $m_1 m_2$: each of these investors holds a different mix of risky assets without any borrowing or lending. Without the separation property of the CAPM, the risk–return relationship is less elegant but surely closer to reality, since in real life investors cannot borrow and lend money at the same riskless interest rate.

The market portfolio, which is a weighted average of all MV efficient portfolios, is also MV efficient.[3] Moreover, the market portfolio $m$ lies somewhere between $m_1$ and $m_2$, since it is a weighted average of $m_1$, $m_2$, and of other unlevered efficient portfolios which lie on the section $m_1 m_2$. For the market portfolio $m$ we can construct the zero-beta portfolio $Z$ with expected rate of return $ER_z$ (see Figure 13.4) and then apply the technique of Section 13.1 to derive the linear risk–return relationship for asset $i$,

$$ER_i = ER_z + (ER_m - ER_z)\beta_i$$

[3] To show this, suppose that there are only two investors in the market, investing $T_1$ and $T_2$ dollars, respectively, in the available $n$ assets. Then if the two investors hold proportions $x_{i(1)}$ and $x_{i(2)}$ of security $i$ in their efficient (minimum-variance) portfolios, the total amount $V_i$ invested in security $i$ is clearly given by $T_1 x_{i(1)} + T_2 x_{i(2)} = V_i$. The total amount invested by all investors in the market is $T_1 + T_2 = T_0$, and the proportion of security $i$ in the weighted-average market portfolio, $x_{i(m)}$, is given by $x_{i(m)} = V_i / T_0$ or

$$x_{i(m)} = \frac{T_1}{T_0} x_{i(1)} + \frac{T_2}{T_0} x_{i(2)}$$

The market portfolio $x_m = (x_{1(m)}, x_{2(m)}, \ldots, x_{n(m)})$ is thus a linear combination of the minimum-variance (efficient) portfolios held by investors 1 and 2 (with the weights $T_1/T_0$ and $T_2/T_0$). The market portfolio is therefore also a minimum-variance portfolio (see Problem 13.19 at the end of the chapter; also Chapter 9, Sec. 9.6). To show that it is *efficient*, it suffices to note that its mean is a weighted average of the means of the constituent individual portfolios (with the positive weights $T_1/T_0$ and $T_2/T_0$). Therefore, if the individual portfolios are on the efficient section of the minimum-variance frontier, so is the weighted-average market portfolio.

However, this relationship applies only to risky assets or portfolios without any borrowing or lending. For portfolios with *lending*, we have

$$ER_i = r_L + (ER_{m_1} - r_L)\beta_{i(m_1)}$$

where the security's beta is calculated relative to the lender's optimum unlevered portfolio $m_1$,

$$\beta_{i(m_1)} = Cov\ (R_i,\ R_{m_1})/\sigma_{m_1}^2,$$

For portfolios with *borrowing* we have

$$ER_i = r_B + (ER_{m_2} - r_B)\beta_{i(m_2)}$$

where

$$\beta_{i(m_2)} = Cov\ (R_i,\ R_{m_2})/\sigma_{m_2}^2$$

(calculated relative to the borrower's optimum unlevered portfolio $m_2$).

Thus, even in this more realistic case, with the borrowing rate higher than the lending rate, we get a linear risk–return relationship of the same structure as in the zero-beta model.

## 13.3   Heterogeneous Expectations

So far, we have assumed that all investors have homogeneous expectations regarding the means, the variances, and the covariances of all the securities, and hence all face the same MV efficient frontier. In reality, there is no complete agreement among the investors regarding the future price developments. Hence, each investor faces a different *subjective* efficient frontier. Thus, even if a riskless asset does exist, not all investors will hold the same unlevered portfolio. To see this, suppose that there are only two stocks in the market, IBM and ATT. Let us assume the extreme case when all investors agree with respect to the future risk-free interest rate $r$, the variances $\sigma_{IBM}^2$, $\sigma_{ATT}^2$, the covariance of the two stocks, and also the expected rate of return of ATT. The only disagreement is that one investor believes that the expected rate of return on IBM stock is, say, 10% (see the point IBM$_1$ in Figure 13.5), while the other investor believes that the expected rate of return on IBM stock will be higher, as shown by point IBM$_2$ in Figure 13.5. This disagreement about the expected rate of return on IBM stock is sufficient for the two investors to hold different unlevered optimum portfolios. One holds the unlevered portfolio $m_1$ in Figure 13.5, while the other holds the unlevered portfolio $m_2$, where in general the composition of the two assets is different in $m_1$ and $m_2$.

This simple example is sufficient to illustrate the main impact of disagreement in investor expectations on the CAPM results. First, the separation property of the CAPM

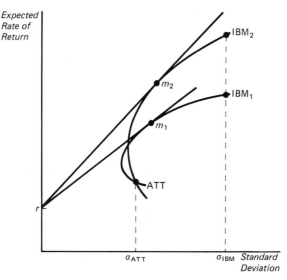

**Figure 13.5**

does not hold with heterogeneous expectations. Moreover, it may be that investors do not hold all the risky assets in their portfolio, or even sell short some assets, quite contrary to the traditional CAPM. Thus, one investor may sell the IBM stock short, since he believes the future price will drop; but this does not imply that *all* investors sell IBM stock short, since other investors may disagree with the first investor and predict that the IBM future stock price will go up. In order to guarantee that the market is cleared, the only requirement is that the aggregate amount of any given security held by all investors is equal to the total amount outstanding of this security, or in other words, for each "sell" there is a "buy" in the market.

The optimal investment of each investor is simply obtained by minimizing the portfolio variance at the desired level of portfolio expected rate of return with *subjective parameters* plugged in for rates of return, variances, and covariances. Each investor is characterized by a system of $n + 2$ equations in $n + 2$ unknowns (see Appendix 13.1), from which the optimum portfolio can be determined. Using this technique for each individual investor and operating across all investors (to ensure that the market clears), Lintner showed that a formula similar to the equilibrium CAPM pricing formula can be derived, in which the future stock price and the rate of return of each share is a weighted average of all the investors' expectations regarding the various parameters. The derivation of Lintner's heterogeneous expectation model is given in Appendix 13.2.

## 13.4   Personal Taxes

Another of the CAPM assumptions is that there are no personal taxes. In reality investors pay income tax on the cash dividend as received, while a lower tax rate is applied to capital gains (when realized).

Since various investors are in different tax brackets, their selection of stocks with different dividend policy is therefore a function of the individual tax rates. Thus, even if all investors have homogeneous expectations and face the same MV efficient frontier in pre-tax terms, each individual faces a different post-tax frontier depending on his personal tax bracket.

Even in such a complicated case, Brennan[4] derived the following risk–return relationship:

$$ER_i = r + (ER_m - r)\beta_i + f(\delta_i, \delta_m, T) \tag{13.2}$$

where the last term on the right is a function of the dividend yield of the $i$th stock $\delta_i$, the dividend yield of the market portfolio $\delta_m$, and $T$, a factor which takes into account the wealth of the various individuals as well as the relevant tax rates. The above equation is similar in structure to the CAPM, but the last term is added to reflect the impact of the dividend policy of different firms and the tax rates on cash dividend and on capital gains.

## 13.5    Equilibrium Under Inflation

The risk-free asset usually exists only in the absence of inflation. However, with random changes in the future price level, even the rate of return on Treasury Bills is risky in *real terms*. In this case, we must shift from the traditional CAPM with borrowing and lending to the zero-beta model without riskless asset. The risky borrowing and lending rates simply become risky rates of return in real terms, after adjustment for inflation. Thus, for each asset (including the nominal riskless asset) we can calculate the real rate of return by adjusting for inflation:

$$R_R = \frac{1 + R_N}{1 + \pi} - 1$$

where

$R_R$ = real rate of return
$R_N$ = nominal rate of return
$\pi$ = the inflation rate (which is a random variable)

Then the zero-beta model can be written using all the parameters in real terms to construct the risk–return relationship.

---

[4] See M. Brennan, "Taxes, Market Valuation and Corporate Financial Policy", *National Tax Journal* (1973). For an after-tax version of the CAPM with progressive (income-related) taxes, see R. Litzenberger and K. Ramaswamy, "The Effect of Personal Taxes and Dividends on Capital Asset Prices", *Journal of Financial Economics* (June 1979).

Friend, Landskroner and Losq[5] showed that even with uncertain inflation the CAPM can be written in nominal terms as follows:

$$ER_i = r + \sigma_{i\pi} + \frac{ER_m - r - \sigma_{m\pi}}{\sigma_m^2 - \dfrac{\sigma_{m\pi}}{\alpha}} \left( \sigma_{im} - \frac{\sigma_{i\pi}}{\alpha} \right)$$                          (13.3)

where

> $\sigma_{i\pi}$ is the covariance of the rate of return on the $i$th asset and the inflation rate $\pi$
> $\sigma_{m\pi}$ is the covariance of the return on the market portfolio and the inflation rate $\pi$
> $\alpha$ is the ratio of nominal risky assets to total nominal value of all assets in the market

If there is no change in the price level, $\sigma_{i\pi} = \sigma_{m\pi} = 0$ and the equation reduces to the standard CAPM risk–return relationship.

## 13.6    Transaction Costs

Empirical evidence reveals that investors hold on average only 3.41 risky assets in their portfolio; actually, some 34% of the investors hold only one stock and 50% hold no more than two stocks. Less than 11% of the investors are found to hold more than 10 stocks in their portfolio.[6] This is in sharp contradiction to the CAPM, which asserts that all investors hold all risky assets in their portfolio.

The CAPM assumes that securities can be bought and sold without paying any commission, and in the absence of transaction costs investors would probably hold a large number of assets in their portfolio. When transaction costs are incorporated, we find that it may be optimal to hold only a *small number* of risky assets, as is actually observed in the market. Moreover, different investors hold a different number of risky assets in their portfolio, so that the separation property breaks down. In this case, the expected rate of return on asset $i$, $\mu_i$, can be written as:[7]

$$\mu_i = r + \frac{\sum\limits_k T_k (\mu_k - r)}{\sum\limits_k T_k} \beta_{ki}$$                          (13.4)

[5] I. Friend, Y. Landskroner, and E. Losq, "The Demand for Risky Assets Under Uncertain Inflation", *Journal of Finance*, Dec. 1976.
[6] For more details see M. Blume, J. Crockett, and I. Friend, "Stock Ownership in the United States: Characteristics and Trends", *Survey of Current Business* (Nov. 1974).
[7] For more details see H. Levy, "Equilibrium in an Imperfect Market: A Constraint on the Number of Securities in the Portfolio", *American Economic Review* (Sept. 1978).

where

$r$ is the risk-free interest rate

$\mu_k$ is the mean rate of return on the portfolio held by investor $k$

$T_k$ is the wealth invested by investor $k$

$\beta_{ki}$ is the beta of asset $i$ with respect to the portfolio held by investor $k$ (which is not necessarily the market portfolio)

Thus, the security's expected rate of return $\mu_i$ is equal to the risk-free rate plus a weighted average of the risk premium required by all investors. If all the investors hold the market portfolio, the risk–return relationship reduces to the classical CAPM. In this case, $\mu_k = \mu_m$ and $\beta_{ki} = \beta_i$, so that:

$$\frac{\sum_k T_k(\mu_m - r)}{\sum_k T_k}\,\beta_{ki} = (\mu_m - r)\beta_i$$

and equation (13.4) reduces to

$$\mu_i = r + (\mu_m - r)\beta_i$$

This is the standard CAPM risk–return relationship as derived in Chapter 11 [see equations (11.19) and (11.23)].

## 13.7 Arbitrage Pricing Theory (APT) Model

There are some other extensions of the CAPM, of which probably the most important is the Arbitrage Pricing Theory (APT) Model developed by Stephen Ross. Unlike the previous models the APT is actually a different model which competes outright with the CAPM, rather than extending it in some direction.

In the derivation of this equilibrium model, Ross[8] does not assume risk aversion, and in particular does not assume that investors make their decisions in the mean–variance framework. Instead, he assumes that the securities' rates of return $R_i$ are generated by the following process:

$$R_i = ER_i + \beta_i(I - EI) + e_i \tag{13.5}$$

[8] See S. Ross, "Mutual Fund Separation in Financial Theory—The Separating Distributions", *Journal of Economic Theory* (Apr. 1978).

Here

$R_i$    is the rate of return on security $i$ ($i = 1, 2, \ldots, n$, when we have $n$ securities), with mean $ER_i$

$I$    is the value of the factor generating the security returns, whose mean is $EI$

$\beta_i$    is a coefficient measuring the effect of changes in the factor $I$ on the rate of return $R_i$

$e_i$    is a random deviation (noise)

Note that $I$ is a *common factor* to all securities $i$: this may be the Gross National Product (GNP), the Dow-Jones Stock Index, or any other factor which one perceives to be appropriate for generation of security rates of return.

The basic idea of the APT Model is that investors can create a zero-beta portfolio with *zero net investment*. If the zero-beta portfolio constructed with zero investment yields nonzero (positive) return, a sure profit can be made by arbitraging. To be more specific, construct a portfolio with proportions $x_i$ such that:

$$\sum_{i=1}^{n} x_i \beta_i = 0$$

$$\sum_{i=1}^{n} x_i = 0$$

The first condition stipulates that this is a zero-beta portfolio, and the second condition indicates that a zero amount is invested in this portfolio. Obviously, such a portfolio can be constructed only when some of the stocks are held short (negative $x_i$) and some are held long (positive $x_i$), and the investors receive the proceeds of the short sales investing them in other securities.

Multiply by $x_i$ the return generating process for security $i$ from (13.5):

$$x_i R_i = x_i ER_i + x_i \beta_i (I - EI) + x_i e_i$$

and sum over all the assets ($i = 1, 2, \ldots, n$) to obtain the portfolio rate of return:

$$\sum_{i=1}^{n} x_i R_i = \sum_{i=1}^{n} x_i ER_i + (I - EI) \sum_{i=1}^{n} x_i \beta_i + \sum_{i=1}^{n} x_i e_i$$

or:

$$R_p = ER_p + (I - EI) \sum_{i=1}^{n} x_i \beta_i + \sum_{i=1}^{n} x_i e_i \qquad (13.6)$$

Here $R_p$ and $ER_p$ stand for the portfolio rate of return and the portfolio mean rate of return, respectively. Since $\sum_{i=1}^{n} x_i \beta_i = 0$ (by construction) and for a very large portfolio the average noise is approximately zero, $\sum x_i e_i \approx 0$, we obtain from (13.6) a constant rate of return $R_p = ER_p$, i.e., a portfolio with zero variability was constructed with zero net investment (recall that $\Sigma_{i=1}^n x_i = 0$). In equilibrium, the mean return on such a portfolio must be zero, $ER_p = 0$. Otherwise, with no risk and no investment, a sure profit can be made by buying (or selling short) such a portfolio. Suppose that this is not so and the mean return is, say, $ER_p = \$3$, and we have from (13.6), $R_p = ER_p = \$3$. With zero investment ($\Sigma_{i=1}^n x_i = 0$), one can earn \$3 with certainty. Investors will continue to buy such a portfolio, its price will go up and the rate of return will go down until $R_p = ER_p = 0$. Thus, in equilibrium, no arbitrage opportunities are available.

To sum up, by construction we have:

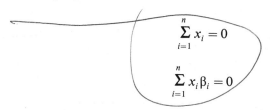

$$\sum_{i=1}^n x_i = 0$$

$$\sum_{i=1}^n x_i \beta_i = 0$$

which implies that

$$ER_p = \sum_{i=1}^n x_i ER_i = 0 \quad \text{and also} \quad R_p = \sum_{i=1}^n x_i R_i = 0$$

since the portfolio has zero variability and the mean return is equal to the return itself.

By a standard theorem of linear algebra, the three equations

$$\sum_{i=1}^n x_i \cdot 1 = 0, \quad \sum_{i=1}^n x_i \beta_i = 0 \quad \text{and} \quad \sum_{i=1}^n x_i ER_i = 0$$

imply that $ER_i$ can be written as a linear combination of 1 and $\beta_i$ as follows (see numerical example below):

$$ER_i = a_0 + a_1 \beta_i \quad (i = 1, 2, \ldots, n) \tag{13.7}$$

where $a_0$ and $a_1$ are the coefficients of the straight line. We now turn to determine the coefficients $a_0$ and $a_1$. First consider a portfolio with zero beta and with $\Sigma_{i=1}^n x_i = 1$. Then, multiplying (13.7) by $x_i$ and summing over all $i$ ($i = 1, 2, \ldots, n$), we obtain:

$$\sum_{i=1}^n x_i ER_i = a_0 \sum_{i=1}^n x_i + a_1 \sum_{i=1}^n x_i \beta_i = a_0 \cdot 1 + a_1 \cdot 0$$

or $ER_p = a_0$. Since by construction $\Sigma_{i=1}^n x_i = 1$ and $\Sigma_{i=1}^n x_i \beta_i = 0$, our portfolio is a zero-beta portfolio $Z$, and so $R_p = R_z$. Thus, $ER_p = ER_z$ and so $ER_z = a_0$. We have determined the intercept $a_0$ to be equal to the zero-beta portfolio mean rate of return.

Now let us look at a portfolio with $\Sigma_{i=1}^n x_i \beta_i = 1$ and $\Sigma_{i=1}^n x_i = 1$. Plugging $ER_z$ for $a_0$ in equation (13.7), we obtain:

$$ER_i = ER_z + a_1 \beta_i$$

Multiply by $x_i$ and sum over all $i$ ($i = 1, 2, \ldots, n$) to obtain:

$$\sum_{i=1}^{n} x_i ER_i = ER_z \sum_{i=1}^{n} x_i + a_1 \sum_{i=1}^{n} x_i \beta_i$$

Since $\sum_{i=1}^{n} x_i = 1$ and $\sum_{i=1}^{n} x_i \beta_i = 1$ we obtain:

$$ER_p = ER_z + a_1$$

Hence $a_1 = ER_p - ER_z$, where $ER_p$ is the mean rate of return on the portfolio with beta equal to 1.

Substituting for $a_0$ and $a_1$ in equation (13.7) we finally get:

$$ER_i = ER_z + (ER_p - ER_z)\beta_i$$

where $ER_p$ is the mean rate of return of a portfolio with beta equal to 1 and $ER_z$ is the mean rate of return on the zero-beta portfolio.

However, by (13.5) the mean rate of return on the portfolio with beta equal to 1 must be equal to the mean of the index $EI$ (expressed in appropriately standardized units), and substituting $EI$ for $ER_p$ we get:

$$ER_i = ER_z + (EI - ER_z)\beta_i \qquad (13.8)$$

Taking the market portfolio with rate of return $R_m$ as the returns generating factor $I$, we obtain the CAPM result without riskless asset:

$$ER_i = ER_z + (ER_m - ER_z)\beta_i \qquad (13.9)$$

Before we turn to a numerical example, let us pinpoint the assumptions of the APT Model. First, a necessary condition for the derivation is that the average portfolio noise is zero ($\sum_{i=1}^{n} x_i e_i \approx 0$). The noise is zero only for a very large portfolio, when the deviations $e_i$ on average cancel out. For a small portfolio, $\sum_{i=1}^{n} x_i e_i \neq 0$. Thus, a basic assumption of the APT Model is that investors hold a very large number of assets in their portfolios.

The second assumption is that short sales are allowed and all the proceeds from the short sales are received by the investor. It should be emphasized that these two assumptions are also characteristic of the classical CAPM.

EXAMPLE

Assume that we have three risky assets with the following parameters:

$$ER_1 = 0.10 \quad ER_2 = 0.40 \quad ER_3 = 0.70$$
$$\beta_1 = 1 \quad\quad \beta_2 = 2 \quad\quad \beta_3 = 3$$

We would like to construct a zero-beta portfolio with zero investment, i.e. $\sum_{i=1}^{3} x_i \beta_i = 0$

and $\Sigma_{i=1}^3 x_i = 0$. These two constraints can be rewritten in expanded form as follows:

$$x_1 + x_2 + x_3 = 0 \quad \text{or} \quad x_3 = -x_1 - x_2$$

and

$$x_1 \beta_1 + x_2 \beta_2 + x_3 \beta_3 = 0 \quad \text{or} \quad x_1 + 2x_2 + 3x_3 = 0$$

Substituting in the last equality $x_3 = -x_1 - x_2$, we obtain:

$$x_1 + 2x_2 + 3(-x_1 - x_2) = 0 \quad \text{or} \quad -2x_1 - x_2 = 0$$

which implies that:

$$x_1 = -\tfrac{1}{2}x_2$$

Take, for instance, $x_2 = 1$, hence $x_1 = -\tfrac{1}{2}$ and $x_3 = -x_1 - x_2 = -1 - (-\tfrac{1}{2}) = -\tfrac{1}{2}$.

For the portfolio $x_1 = -\tfrac{1}{2}$, $x_2 = 1$ and $x_3 = -\tfrac{1}{2}$, we have $\Sigma_{i=1}^3 x_i = 0$ and $\Sigma_{i=1}^3 x_i \beta_i = 0$, as required.

We also claimed that if $\Sigma_{i=1}^n x_i = 0$ and $\Sigma_{i=1}^n x_i \beta_i = 0$, the rates of return on the individual assets must adjust so that in equilibrium $ER_p = \Sigma_{i=1}^n x_i ER_i = 0$. We selected $ER_i$ such that the equilibrium condition holds and no arbitrage profit is available, since:

$$\sum_{i=1}^n x_i ER_i = (-\tfrac{1}{2}) \times 0.10 + 1 \times 0.40 + (-\tfrac{1}{2}) \times 0.70 = 0$$

Also, we indicated that in such a case $ER_i$ can be written as a linear function of the $\beta_i$. First, let us find the slope of the line:

$$ER_i = a_0 + a_1 \beta_i$$

The slope $a_1$ is given by:

$$a_1 = \frac{ER_3 - ER_2}{\beta_3 - \beta_2} = \frac{0.70 - 0.40}{3 - 2} = 0.30$$

Hence, $a_1 = 0.3$. Since $ER_3 = a_0 + 0.3\beta_3$, we have $0.7 = a_0 + 0.3 \cdot 3$, which yields $a_0 = -0.2$.

It is left to show that security 1 indeed lies on the straight line with the coefficients $a_0 = -0.2$, $a_1 = 0.3$ or:

$$ER_i = -0.2 + 0.3\beta_i$$

Since $\beta_1 = 1$ and $ER_1 = 0.1$, it is easy to verify that security 1 indeed lies on the same straight line. Thus, in general, under the conditions of this model $R_i$ is given as a linear function of $\beta_i$.

The main advantage of the APT Model is that we are not confined to the market portfolio and any factor can be included in the return generating process. Actually, more than one factor can be included. In general, the model can be written as:

$$R_i = ER_i + \beta_{i1}(I_1 - EI_1) + \beta_{i2}(I_2 - EI_2) + \cdots + \beta_{in}(I_n - EI_n) + e_i$$

where $I_i$ is the $i$th return generating factor and $\beta_{ik}$ is the security $i$ beta with respect to factor $k$.

## Summary

The classical CAPM risk–return relationship is derived under some assumptions which are clearly inconsistent with the real market conditions. However, some of these assumptions can be relaxed, leading to other risk–return relationships in the spirit of the CAPM, with some adjustments reflecting the relaxation of the appropriate assumptions.

We demonstrated the modification of the CAPM in case of restrictions on riskless borrowing and lending, differential tax rates for cash dividends and capital gains, and adjustment for inflation and transaction costs.

An important risk–return equilibrium model is the APT Model derived by Ross. In the specific case where the return-generating index is taken equal to the market portfolio, the APT Model and the CAPM coincide. However, the APT can include any number of factors relevant to the return generating process.

---

**Summary Table**

1. **Extension of the CAPM**

   (a) *No riskless asset: the zero-beta model*

   $$ER_i = ER_z + (ER_m - ER_z)\beta_i$$

   where

       $R_z$ is the rate of return on the zero-beta portfolio, such that $Cov(R_z, R_m) = 0$

       $R_m$ is the rate of return on a mean–variance efficient portfolio

       $ER_i$ is the mean rate of return on $i$th risky asset

       $\beta_i$ is the beta of the $i$th risky asset (a measure of risk in the portfolio context)

   (b) *Properties of the zero-beta portfolio:*

       (i) $Z$ is a portfolio with zero beta and is the minimum-variance portfolio among all portfolios with zero beta

       (ii) $Z$ is an MV inefficient portfolio

(c) *Borrowing interest rate higher than lending interest rate:*
   (i) For lenders, $ER_i = r_L + (ER_{m_1} - r_L)\beta_{i(m_1)}$
   (ii) For borrowers, $ER_i = r_B + (ER_{m_2} - r_B)\beta_{i(m_2)}$
   (iii) For investors who neither borrow nor lend, $ER_i = ER_z + (ER_m - ER_z)\beta_i$

(d) *Other extensions of the CAPM cover the following cases:*
   (i) Heterogeneous investor expectations
   (ii) Personal taxes
   (iii) Inflation
   (iv) Transaction costs

## 2. The Arbitrage Pricing Theory (APT) Model
(a) *Rates of return generating mechanism:*

$$R_i = ER_i + \beta_i(I - EI) + e_i$$

where *I* is the common factor generating the asset rates of return.

(b) *The equilibrium relationship:*

$$ER_i = ER_z + (EI - ER_z)\beta_i$$

where $ER_z$ is the expected rate of return on the zero-beta portfolio, such that $Cov(I, R_z) = 0$.

## APPENDIX 13.1

### Derivation of the Risk–Return Relationship Without Riskless Asset

As in previous chapters, we form the Lagrange function $C$,

$$C = \sum_{i=1}^{n} x_i^2 \sigma_i^2 + 2 \sum_{i=1}^{n} \sum_{\substack{j=1 \\ j>i}}^{n} x_i x_j \sigma_{ij} + 2\lambda_1 \left[ ER_m - \sum_{i=1}^{n} x_i ER_i \right] + 2\lambda_2 \left[ 1 - \sum_{i=1}^{n} x_i \right]$$

(13.1.1)

[compare equations (8.28) and (9.1)].

Differentiating $C$ with respect to $x_i$ ($i = 1, 2, \ldots, n$), $\lambda_1$, and $\lambda_2$, and setting the derivatives equal to zero, we obtain $n + 2$ equations in $n + 2$ unknowns,

$$\left.\begin{array}{l} 2x_1\sigma_1^2 + 2 \sum_{\substack{j=1 \\ j\neq1}}^{n} x_j\sigma_{1j} - 2\lambda_1 ER_1 - 2\lambda_2 = 0 \\[3ex] 2x_2\sigma_2^2 + 2 \sum_{\substack{j=1 \\ j\neq2}}^{n} x_j\sigma_{2j} - 2\lambda_1 ER_2 - 2\lambda_2 = 0 \\[3ex] \cdots\cdots\cdots\cdots\cdots\cdots\cdots\cdots \\[1ex] 2x_n\sigma_n^2 + 2 \sum_{\substack{j=1 \\ j\neq n}}^{n} x_j\sigma_{nj} - 2\lambda_1 ER_n - 2\lambda_2 = 0 \end{array}\right\} \; n \text{ equations} \quad (13.1.2)$$

$$ER_m = \sum_{i=1}^{n} x_i ER_i$$

$$1 = \sum_{i=1}^{n} x_i$$

2 equations   (13.1.3)

Reducing by 2 and multiplying the $i$th equation of the first $n$ equations (13.1.2) by $x_i$ for $i = 1, 2, \ldots, n$, we sum all the $n$ new equations to obtain:

$$\sum_{i=1}^{n} x_i^2 \sigma_i^2 + 2 \sum_{i=1}^{n} \sum_{\substack{j=1 \\ j>i}}^{n} x_i x_j \sigma_{ij} - \lambda_1 \sum_{i=1}^{n} x_i ER_i = \lambda_2 \sum_{i=1}^{n} x_i$$

By definition, $x_i$ $(i = 1, 2, \ldots, n)$ are the proportions which minimize the portfolio variance for expected rate of return $ER_m$, so that the sum of the first two terms is simply $\sigma_m^2$, the market portfolio variance. Moreover, by equations (13.1.3), $\sum_{i=1}^{n} x_i ER_i = ER_m$ and $\sum_{i=1}^{n} x_i = 1$, and so we obtain:

$$\sigma_m^2 - \lambda_1 ER_m = \lambda_2 \tag{13.1.4}$$

Now, take one equation from (13.1.2), say, the $i$th equation, and substitute for $\lambda_2$ from (13.1.4) to obtain:

$$x_i \sigma_i^2 + \sum_{\substack{j=1 \\ j \neq i}}^{n} x_j \sigma_{ij} - \lambda_1 ER_i = \sigma_m^2 - \lambda_1 ER_m \tag{13.1.5}$$

But since

$$x_i \sigma_i^2 + \sum_{\substack{j=1 \\ j \neq i}}^{n} x_j \sigma_{ij} = \sigma_{im}$$

where $\sigma_{im}$ is the covariance of the $i$th asset with the market portfolio, equation (13.1.5) reduces to:

$$ER_i - ER_m = \frac{1}{\lambda_1} [\sigma_{im} - \sigma_m^2] \tag{13.1.6}$$

In order to complete the risk–return relationship in this model, it remains to eliminate $\lambda_1$ from (13.1.6). Thus, we now turn to analyze the Lagrange multiplier $\lambda_1$. Let us first define the slope at point $m$ by $\delta_m$, where (see Figure 13.1):

$$\delta_m = (ER_m - ER_z)/\sigma_m \tag{13.1.7}$$

The slope of the efficient frontier at point $m$ is also given by $\partial ER_m/\partial \sigma_m$. On the other hand, from the expression for the Lagrange function (13.1.1) we have:[9]

$$\frac{\partial \sigma_m^2}{\partial ER_m} = 2\lambda_1 \tag{13.1.8}$$

Using the chain rule of differentiation, we have:

$$\frac{\partial \sigma_m^2}{\partial ER_m} = \frac{\partial \sigma_m^2}{\partial \sigma_m} \cdot \frac{\partial \sigma_m}{\partial ER_m} \tag{13.1.9}$$

But the second factor in the right-hand side of (13.1.9) is simply the inverse of the slope at point $m$:

$$\frac{\partial \sigma_m}{\partial ER_m} = \frac{1}{\delta_m}$$

[9] By the chain rule of differentiation,

$$\frac{\partial \sigma_m^2}{\partial ER_m} = \sum_{i=1}^{n} \frac{\partial \sigma_m^2}{\partial x_i} \frac{\partial x_i}{\partial ER_m}$$

The first-order conditions (13.1.2) for minimization of the Lagrange function $C$ (13.1.1) may be rewritten as

$$\frac{\partial \sigma_m^2}{\partial x_i} - 2\lambda_1 ER_i - 2\lambda_2 = 0 \quad \text{or} \quad \frac{\partial \sigma_m^2}{\partial x_i} = 2\lambda_1 ER_i + 2\lambda_2$$

Substituting this result for $\partial \sigma_m^2/\partial x_i$ in the above equality, we obtain

$$\frac{\partial \sigma_m^2}{\partial ER_m} = \sum_{i=1}^{n} (2\lambda_1 ER_i + 2\lambda_2) \frac{\partial x_i}{\partial ER_m} = 2\lambda_1 \sum_{i=1}^{n} \frac{\partial x_i}{\partial ER_m} ER_i + 2\lambda_2 \sum_{i=1}^{n} \frac{\partial x_i}{\partial ER_m}$$

But *at the optimum* by (13.1.3) we have $\sum_{i=1}^{n} x_i ER_i = ER_m$ and $\sum_{i=1}^{n} x_i = 1$. Differentiating these two equalities with respect to $ER_m$, we obtain

$$\sum_{i=1}^{n} \frac{\partial x_i}{\partial ER_m} ER_i = 1 \quad \text{and} \quad \sum_{i=1}^{n} \frac{\partial x_i}{\partial ER_m} = 0$$

Collecting the above results, we obtain *at the optimum*

$$\frac{\partial \sigma_m^2}{\partial ER_m} = 2\lambda_1 \cdot 1 + 2\lambda_2 \cdot 0 = 2\lambda_1$$

which is indeed (13.1.8).

and for the first factor we have:

$$\frac{\partial \sigma_m^2}{\partial \sigma_m} = 2\sigma_m$$

Substituting for the left-hand side of (13.1.9) from equation (13.1.8), equation (13.1.9) finally yields:

$$\lambda_1 = \frac{\sigma_m}{\delta_m}$$

Recalling that $\delta_m = (ER_m - ER_z)/\sigma_m$ (see (13.1.7)), we get:

$$\lambda_1 = \sigma_m^2/(ER_m - ER_z) \tag{13.1.10}$$

Now let us turn to equation (13.1.6) and substitute for $\lambda_1$ from (13.1.10). This gives:

$$ER_i - ER_m = \frac{(ER_m - ER_z)}{\sigma_m^2} [\sigma_{im} - \sigma_m^2]$$

Rearranging, we finally write the risk–return relationship without riskless asset in the form:

$$ER_i = ER_z + (ER_m - ER_z)\sigma_{im}/\sigma_m^2$$

But since $\sigma_{im}/\sigma_m^2 = \beta_i$ [see equation (11.19) in Chapter 11], we get the risk–return relationship (13.1) in the body of the text:

$$ER_i = ER_z + (ER_m - ER_z)\beta_i \tag{13.1.11}$$

# APPENDIX 13.2
## The Effects of Investors' Expectations on Equilibrium Prices in the Securities Market [10]

Assuming full agreement among investors about securities' prices in the future, we analyzed in Chapter 11 the forces which determine equilibrium prices. In this Appendix we shall show that similar conclusions can be reached even when we relax the assumption of full agreement. When investors assign different probability distributions to the end-of-period values of the same stock, we say that there is disagreement among

---

[10] The proof follows J. Lintner, "Security Prices, Risk and Maximal Gains from Diversification", *Journal of Finance* (1965).

investors. In this case the equilibrium value of the company's stock is a function of the weighted averages of the various estimates of the end-of-period variances, expected returns, and covariances.

Assuming agreement we find that in equilibrium the price of the $i$th company's stock is given by (see Appendix 11.3):

$$(1 + r)P_{i0} = P_{i1} - \gamma \left[ N_i \sigma_i^2 + \sum_{\substack{j=1 \\ j \neq i}}^{n} N_j \sigma_{ij} \right]$$  (13.2.1)

If investors' judgments differ, the $k$th investor will be in equilibrium if the market price $P_{i0}$ is such that (13.2.1) holds in terms of his individual estimates of $P_{i1}, \sigma_i$, and $\sigma_{ij}$. Hence for the $k$th investor the following equation must hold:

$$P_{i1(k)} - (1 + r)P_{i0} = \gamma_k \left[ N_{i(k)} \sigma_{i(k)}^2 + \sum_{\substack{j=1 \\ j \neq i}}^{n} N_{j(k)} \sigma_{ij(k)} \right] \equiv \gamma_k 0_k$$  (13.2.2)

Here the index $k$ denotes the $k$th investor's estimates and $\gamma_k \equiv A_k / B_k$, where $A_k$ is defined as the aggregate excess dollar return of the investor's portfolio, and $B_k$ is defined as the variance of the end-of-period values of his portfolio. For simplicity we also denote by $0_k$ the entire bracketed term in the right-hand side of (13.2.2).

Using this definition of $\gamma_k$ we get from (13.2.2):

$$B_k [P_{i1(k)} - (1 + r)P_{i0}] = A_k 0_k$$  (13.2.3)

Summing (13.2.3) over all investors in the market, we get:

$$\sum_k B_k P_{i1(k)} - (1 + r)P_{i0} \sum_k B_k = \sum_k A_k 0_k$$  (13.2.4)

Hence:

$$(1 + r)P_{i0} = \frac{\sum\limits_k B_k P_{i1(k)}}{\sum\limits_k B_k} - \frac{\sum\limits_k A_k 0_k}{\sum\limits_k B_k}$$  (13.2.5)

Since:

$$\frac{\sum\limits_k A_k 0_k}{\sum\limits_k B_k} = \frac{\sum\limits_k A_k}{\sum\limits_k B_k} \cdot \frac{\sum\limits_k A_k 0_k}{\sum\limits_k A_k} = \gamma \frac{\sum\limits_k A_k 0_k}{\sum\limits_k A_k}$$

($\gamma$ is the excess dollar return of the total market portfolio divided by its variance, see

Sec. 11.6 in Chapter 11), we obtain from (13.2.5):

$$(1 + r)P_{i0} = \frac{\sum\limits_{k} B_k P_{i1(k)}}{\sum\limits_{k} B_k} - \gamma \frac{\sum\limits_{k} A_k 0_k}{\sum\limits_{k} A_k} \tag{13.2.6}$$

Equation (13.2.6) is very similar to the equilibrium equation when we assume that the investor's judgments of the end-of-period values do not differ [see equation (11.1.7) in Appendix 11.1]. $\gamma$ is identical in both cases and the only difference is that the end-of-period prices as well as the risk of each share in equation (13.2.6) are weighted averages of the various investors' estimates.

### Questions and Problems

13.1 Assume that the securities market consists of two risky assets, stock 1 and stock 2, and there is no riskless asset. The two stocks and the market portfolio, composed solely of these two risky assets, are characterized by the following parameters:

|  | Stock 1 | Stock 2 | Market Portfolio |
|---|---|---|---|
| Expected Return (%) | 5 | 3 | 4 |
| Standard Deviation (%) | 8 | 6 | 5 |

(a) Find the global minimum variance portfolio.
(b) Find the set of all zero-beta portfolios. Which is the minimum variance portfolio among the set of all portfolios with zero beta? Calculate its mean and its variance.
(c) Show that the minimum variance zero-beta portfolio is inefficient.

13.2 Consider a securities market in which investors can hold cash, but there is no interest-bearing riskless asset.
(a) Show graphically the MV efficient frontier assuming zero inflation rate. What is the security market line for investors who diversify between cash and risk portfolios? For investors who do not hold cash?
(b) Answer (a) assuming a positive inflation rate which is known *with certainty*.
(c) Answer (a) assuming the inflation rate is an unknown random variable.

13.3 Suppose the securities' rates of return $(R_i)$ are generated by two underlying factors $(I_1$ and $I_2)$:

$$R_i = \bar{R}_i + \beta_{i1}(I_1 - \bar{I}_1) + \beta_{i2}(I_2 - \bar{I}_2) + e_i$$

where $\bar{R}_i$, $\bar{I}_1$ and $\bar{I}_2$ denote expected values. Assume that $Cov\,(I_1, I_2) = 0$.
(a) What are the properties of a portfolio with zero net investment which has zero betas with respect to each of the two indexes $I_1$ and $I_2$? What is the return on this portfolio? (Assume a very large portfolio.)

(b) Using the portfolio constructed in (a), derive the equilibrium conditions that must hold for each security, according to the Arbitrage Pricing Theory Model. What assumptions are necessary?

(c) Under what conditions is the model derived in part (b) identical to the zero-beta CAPM?

13.4    Suppose that the securities' rates of return $R_i$ are generated by the following process:

$$R_i = \bar{R}_i + \beta_i(R_m - \bar{R}_m) + e_i$$

where $R_m$ is the return on the market portfolio and $\bar{R}_m$ stands for its mean. Prove that for a *large* portfolio with beta equal to 1, the portfolio's mean return is equal to $\bar{R}_m$.

13.5    Suppose that the zero-beta model holds and that the return on a security may be described by:

$$\bar{R}_i = 0.05 + 0.06\beta_i$$

What is the expected return on the zero-beta portfolio and on the market portfolio?

13.6    Assume the following equality holds in equilibrium:

$$\bar{R}_i = 5 + \beta_i$$

where $\bar{R}_i$ is the mean return of security $i$ and $\beta_i$ is its beta. The variance of the market portfolio is $\sigma_m^2 = 4$ and the variance of the corresponding zero-beta portfolio is $\sigma_z^2 = 9$.

(a) Find the mean and the variance of the global minimum variance portfolio assuming the zero-beta model holds.

(b) Draw the MV efficient frontier.

(c) Find the mean and the variance of the market portfolio corresponding to the hypothetical case of a riskless asset with a rate of return of $r = 5.5\%$.

13.7    The expected rate of return of a given security is $ER_i = 10\%$ and its beta is $\beta_i = 2$. The expected rate of return on the market portfolio is $ER_m = 8\%$. What is the expected rate of return on the zero-beta portfolio, $ER_z$?

13.8    The rates of return on the market portfolio $m$ and on portfolio $Z$ are given below:

|  | *Rates of Return* | |
| --- | --- | --- |
| *Probability* | *Market Portfolio m* | *Portfolio Z* |
| 1/3 | 10% | 8% |
| 1/3 | 8% | 0% |
| 1/3 | −5% | −2% |

Is $Z$ the zero-beta portfolio?

13.9    The rates of return on the market portfolio $m$ and on portfolio $Z$ are as follows (in percent):

| Years | Rates of Return | |
| | Portfolio m | Portfolio Z |
| --- | --- | --- |
| 1981 | 10 | 5 |
| 1982 | 20 | 0 |
| 1983 | 15 | 8 |
| 1984 | -10 | x |

Find the value of $x$ which ensures that $Z$ is the zero-beta portfolio.

13.10  Let $m$ and $Z$ be the market portfolio and the zero-beta portfolio, respectively. It is given that:

$$\sigma_m^2 = 10, \quad \sigma_z^2 = 8$$

Can you determine the variance of the global minimum variance portfolio?

13.11  Assume that there are two efficient portfolios $m_1$ and $m_2$ where $ER_{m_2} > ER_{m_1}$. The corresponding zero-beta portfolios are $Z_1$ and $Z_2$. What is the relationship between $ER_{z_1}$ and $ER_{z_2}$? Demonstrate your answer graphically.

13.12  (a) The lending rate $r_L = 5\%$ and the borrowing rate $r_B = 10\%$. Draw the efficient frontier under these conditions. Does the separation property hold in this case?
(b) An investor with initial wealth of $1000 can borrow and lend money. The lending rate is fixed at $r_L = 10\%$ but the borrowing rate $r_B$ changes as follows: $r_B = 15\%$ if the investor borrows $1000, he then has to pay 20% on the additional $1000 borrowed, and so on with the same 5% increment per $1000 additionally borrowed. Construct graphically the MV efficient set of this case.

13.13  Referring to equation (13.3) in the body of the text, assume that $\alpha = 1$ and

$$\sigma_{m\pi} = 10$$
$$\sigma_{i\pi} = 10$$
$$ER_m - r = 20$$
$$\sigma_m^2 = 15$$
$$r = 5\%$$

(a) Find the expected return on the $i$th asset $ER_i$.
(b) Repeat your calculation on the assumption that $\sigma_{i\pi} = -10$, but all the other parameters are unchanged.
(c) Repeat the calculation on the assumption that $\sigma_{i\pi} = \sigma_{m\pi} = 0$.
Compare and analyze your results in (a), (b) and (c) above.

13.14  Suppose that due to imperfections in the stock market, only two investors hold the stock of ABC Corporation. The following information is available regarding these two investors, who are denoted 1 and 2 respectively.
The mean rates of return on the optimal portfolios of investors 1 and 2 are $\mu_1 = 10\%$ and $\mu_2 = 20\%$ respectively. Also, $\beta_{ABC,1} = 1$ and $\beta_{ABC,2} = 2$, where $\beta_{ABC,1}$ is the beta of the return of ABC stock with the portfolio whose mean is $\mu_1$ and $\beta_{ABC,2}$ is similarly defined. The total invested wealth of investors 1 and 2 is $T_1 = \$100$ and $T_2 = \$200$, respectively. The riskless interest rate is $r = 5\%$.
(a) Apply formula (13.4) to calculate the mean rate of return on ABC stock.
(b) How would your results change if $T_2 = \$20,000$ rather than $\$200$? What if $T_1 = 0$ and $T_2 = \$200$? Compare and analyze your results.

13.15 The entire market consists of three securities only, with betas given by $\beta_1 = 1/2$, $\beta_2 = 1$, $\beta_3 = 4$, respectively.
(a) Find the investment proportions $x_1$, $x_2$, $x_3$ of the zero-beta portfolio with zero net investment (i.e. $\Sigma x_i = 0$).
(b) Find the investment proportions $x_1$, $x_2$, $x_3$ fulfilling the constraints

$$\Sigma x_i \beta_i = 1, \quad \Sigma x_i = 0.$$

13.16 The following describes mean return and betas of DuPont, Dow Chemical and Union Carbide.

|  | DuPont | Dow Chemical | Union Carbide |
|---|---|---|---|
| Mean Return (%) | 4.6 | 10 | 11.2 |
| Beta | 0.86 | 0.74 | 0.71 |

Determine the arbitrage portfolio with zero investment at zero beta. Is there room for arbitrage profit?

13.17 What are the effects of:
(1) personal taxes
(2) inflation
(3) transaction costs
on the CAPM?

13.18 What is the effect of introducing heterogenous assumptions in the CAPM?

13.19* Show that any minimum-variance portfolio can be represented as a linear combination of two other minimum-variance portfolios (see Section 13.1.1).

## Data Set Problems

1. Assume that the securities market consists of only two risky assets, Afuture Fund (No. 1) and and American Balanced Fund (No. 61).
(a) Construct the MV efficient frontier of these two funds.
(b) Now assume that the borrowing rate is $r_B = 6\%$ while the lending rate $r_L = 3\%$. Find the optimum unlevered portfolios for borrowers and for lenders. Compare the composition of these two portfolios.

2. (a) Use the same funds from Problem 1 above to find the zero-beta portfolio for two alternative efficient portfolios $m_1$ and $m_2$ such that $ER_{m1} = 10\%$ and $ER_{m2} = 15\%$. Calculate the means and the variances of the zero-beta portfolios. Determine the beta of Afuture Fund against $m_1$ and $m_2$.
(b) Verify that the two portfolios $Z_1$ and $Z_2$ obtained in (a) actually have zero beta. Are they MV efficient?

## Selected References

See Chapter 14.

# 14

# Testing the Equilibrium Models

The theoretical risk–return models are derived under a set of restrictive assumptions, some of which clearly contradict the marketplace conditions. These assumptions are necessary in order to obtain a simple and easily understandable equilibrium risk–return relationship. Whether the assumptions are severe or not should be judged by the explanatory power of the resulting models. If a model explains well the securities' price behavior, we accept the model despite its unrealistic assumptions (unless one can suggest another model with a higher explanatory power).

Testing the CAPM and its modifications is the subject of many empirical studies. In this chapter we mention only some of them and discuss the empirical results. Finally, we discuss Roll's recent criticism of the CAPM empirical tests.

Recently there has been an increasing number of studies attempting to test the Arbitrage Pricing Theory (APT) model (see Chapter 13). A procedure proposed for testing the APT revealed that there are apparently three to five factors in the returns-generating process.[1] The number of factors tends to increase with the universe of securities being investigated, and some very searching questions can be raised concerning the interpretation of the previous empirical findings.[2] The empirical tests of the APT model fall beyond the scope of this book, and the reader will find the relevant references in the readings list at the end of the chapter. Here we focus mainly on tests of the classical CAPM and its modifications.

## 14.1 Variance vs. Beta as the Explanatory Variable

The classical CAPM asserts that the following risk–return relationship holds [see equation (11.23)]:

$$ER_i = r + (ER_m - r)\beta_i \tag{14.1}$$

---

[1] R. Roll and S. Ross, "An Empirical Investigation of the Arbitrage Pricing Theory", *Journal of Finance* (Dec. 1980).

[2] P. Dhrymes, I. Friend, and N. Gultekin, "A Critical Reexamination of the Empirical Evidence on the Arbitrage Pricing Theory", *Working Paper No. 12-82*, University of Pennsylvania, 1982.

Here $ER_i$, $ER_m$ is the expected rate of return on security $i$ and on the market portfolio, respectively, $\beta_i$ is the $i$th security's beta with the market portfolio—its risk index, and $r$ is the risk-free interest rate. But since $\beta_i = Cov(R_i, R_m)/\sigma_m^2$ [see equation (11.18)] and $R_m = \Sigma_{j=1}^n x_j R_j$ by construction (with $x_i$ being the proportion of security $i$ in the market portfolio) the CAPM formula can be rewritten as:

$$ER_i = r + \frac{(ER_m - r)}{\sigma_m^2} Cov\left(R_i, \sum_{j=1}^n x_j R_j\right)$$

This can be developed further and rewritten as:

$$ER_i = r + \frac{ER_m - r}{\sigma_m^2}\left[x_i \sigma_i^2 + \sum_{\substack{j=1 \\ j \neq i}}^n x_j \sigma_{ij}\right]$$

Denoting the constant coefficients $\gamma_0 = r$ and $\gamma_1 = (ER_m - r)$, we obtain the following linear relationship between mean return and risk:

$$ER_i = \gamma_0 + \gamma_1\left[x_i \sigma_i^2 + \sum_{\substack{j=1 \\ j \neq i}}^n x_j \sigma_{ij}\right] / \sigma_m^2 \tag{14.2}$$

Since the market portfolio variance $\sigma_m^2$ is constant for all securities,

$$\left[x_i \sigma_i^2 + \sum_{\substack{j=1 \\ j \neq i}}^n x_j \sigma_{ij}\right]$$

is clearly the risk index of the $i$th security. Thus, the $i$th security's own variance $\sigma_i^2$ as well as all its covariances with all the other securities $j$ in the market enter the risk index. In a very large portfolio, with many securities $j$, the role of the own variance diminishes rapidly, and the risk index is mainly represented by the contribution of the covariances.

To illustrate, assume, for simplicity, that an investor diversifies among $n$ assets by holding $1/n$ of his investment in each asset. Thus $x_i = 1/n$ for $i = 1, 2, \ldots, n$. The risk index thus becomes:

$$\left[\frac{1}{n}\sigma_i^2 + \sum_{\substack{j=1 \\ j \neq i}}^n \frac{1}{n}\sigma_{ij}\right]$$

Since there are $n$ assets in the portfolio, we have $n - 1$ covariances $\sigma_{ij} (j \neq i)$. Denote by $\bar{\sigma}_{ij}$ the arithmetic average of these $n - 1$ covariances,

$$\bar{\sigma}_{ij} = \frac{1}{n-1}\sum_{\substack{j=1 \\ j \neq i}}^n \sigma_{ij},$$

to obtain the following formulation for the risk index:

$$\left[ \frac{1}{n} \sigma_i^2 + \frac{n-1}{n} \bar{\sigma}_{ij} \right]$$

When $n$ is very large, $\sigma_i^2/n$ rapidly approaches zero and what is left in the risk index is $[(n-1)/n]\bar{\sigma}_{ij}$, or the average covariance (note that for very large $n$ we have $(n-1)/n \approx 1$). Since in the CAPM framework each investor holds the entire market portfolio, the number of assets held is large and the $i$th security's own variance plays virtually no role at all in the $i$th security's risk index.

Another way to examine the role of the $i$th security's variance in determining the expected rate of return is to decompose the variance into two components. The rate of return on the $i$th security in period $t$ can be written as a function of the rate of return on the market portfolio in period $t$ as follows (see Chapter 12):

$$R_{it} = \hat{\alpha}_i + \hat{\beta}_i R_{mt} + e_{it}$$

where $\hat{\alpha}_i$ and $\hat{\beta}_i$ respectively are the estimates of the vertical intercept and the regression coefficient and $e_{it}$ is the deviation of observation $t$ from the regression line. Take the variance of both sides to obtain [see equation (12.3)]:

$$\sigma_i^2 = \hat{\beta}_i^2 \sigma_m^2 + \sigma_e^2$$

where $\sigma_e^2$ is the variance of the residuals about the regression line.[3]

Since $\beta_i$ appears as the risk index in the CAPM formula (14.1) and $\sigma_e^2$ does not, it is claimed that the portion $\sigma_e^2$ of the total variance should not affect the expected rate of return. Hence in any cross-section empirical test over all securities with $\sigma_e^2$ included as an explanatory variable, we expect the coefficient of $\sigma_e^2$ to be zero.

The assertion that $\sigma_i^2$ or $\sigma_e^2$ are irrelevant for equilibrium price determination is in sharp contrast to some of the empirical tests, as we shall see below.

## 14.2    The Simple Test of the CAPM

Suppose that there are $n$ securities in our sample and for each security we have a time-series of annual rates of return for $T$ years. Also we have the corresponding rates of return on the market portfolio (as a proxy to the market portfolio we use some index of stock prices, e.g., the rate of return on the NYSE index, rates of return on the Dow—Jones index, the S&P 500 composite index, etc.) Testing the CAPM (or the zero-beta

---

[3] Note that $\hat{\alpha}_i$ and $\hat{\beta}_i$ are constant coefficients and $Cov\,(R_m, e_i)$ is assumed to be zero in the population (it is always zero in the sample, by the properties of linear regression).

model) involves two types of regression:

(a) *First-pass regression (time-series regression).* For each of the $n$ securities in the sample we run the regression over time:

$$R_{it} = \hat{\alpha}_i + \hat{\beta}_i R_{mt} + e_{it}$$

or in an alternative notation

$$R_{it} = a_i + b_i R_{mt} + e_{it}$$

where $R_{it}$ and $R_{mt}$ are the rates of return on the $i$th security and on the market portfolio in year $t$, the estimates of the regression coefficients are denoted by $\hat{\alpha}_i$ or $a_i$ and by $\hat{\beta}_i$ or $b_i$, and $e_{it}$ is the residual term or the deviation of the actual observation in year $t$ about the regression line. We have $n$ first-pass regressions (one regression for each security) by which we estimate the systematic risk $\beta_i$ of all securities in the sample.

(b) *Second-pass regression (cross-section regression).* The second-pass regression is a cross-section regression run over the $n$ securities. It is a simple regression intended to test the CAPM. The second-pass regression is given by:

$$\bar{R}_i = \hat{\gamma}_0 + \hat{\gamma}_1 b_i + u_i$$

where $\bar{R}_i$ is the estimate of the mean rate of return of security $i$ and $b_i$ is the estimate of the $i$th security regression coefficient $\beta_i$ taken from the first-pass regression, $\hat{\gamma}_0$ and $\hat{\gamma}_1$ are the second-pass regression coefficients (to be determined), and $u_i$ is a residual term, or the deviation of the $i$th pair $(\bar{R}_i, b_i)$ from the regression line.

Comparing the second-pass regression

$$\bar{R}_i = \hat{\gamma}_0 + \hat{\gamma}_1 b_i + u_i$$

with the CAPM formula (14.1)

$$ER_i = r + (ER_m - r)\beta_i$$

we see that $\hat{\gamma}_0$ is an estimate of $r$ and $\hat{\gamma}_1$ is an estimate of $ER_m - r$ [as indeed defined above for equation (14.2)] and that in the empirical test the pair $(\bar{R}_i, b_i)$ is used as estimators of the pair $(ER_i, \beta_i)$ which are the unknown true parameters of security $i$. Thus, if the CAPM actually explains the security price determination in the stock market we would expect to find the following for the coefficients of second-pass regression:

$\hat{\gamma}_0$ is not significantly different from $r$

$\hat{\gamma}_1$ is not significantly different from $\bar{R}_m - r$

where $\bar{R}_m - r$ is an estimate of $ER_m - r$. Note that the "hat" on $\hat{\gamma}_0$ and $\hat{\gamma}_1$ indicates that these are the estimates of $\gamma_0$ and $\gamma_1$, the unknown true coefficients. Also if one runs the regression

$$\bar{R}_i = \hat{\gamma}_0 + \hat{\gamma}_1 b_i + \hat{\gamma}_2 \sigma_i^2 + u_i$$

or the regression

$$\bar{R}_i = \hat{\gamma}_0 + \hat{\gamma}_1 b_i + \hat{\gamma}_2 \sigma_{ei}^2 + u_i$$

we expect $\hat{\gamma}_2$ not to be significantly different from zero, since according to the CAPM there is no association between the expected return on the $i$th security and the security's own variance $\sigma_i^2$, or between the expected return and the residual variance $\sigma_{ei}^2$ (see above, Section 14.1).

Finally, the CAPM asserts that there is a *linear* relationship between the mean rate of return and beta. Thus in any regression of the type

$$\bar{R}_i = \hat{\gamma}_0 + \hat{\gamma}_1 b_i + \hat{\gamma}_2 b_i^2 + u_i$$

we expect the coefficient of $b_i^2$ not to be significantly different from zero, as otherwise the relationship is not linear in beta.

## 14.3    The Empirical Results

Since most empirical results are similar and raise the same issues concerning the CAPM, we present below only some of the studies which also highlight the problems surrounding the empirical tests.

Lintner,[4] who examined the CAPM for the years 1954–1963, employed annual rates of return for a sample of 301 stocks. After estimating the betas (which he denotes by $b_i$) and the average returns $\bar{R}_i$ from the 301 time-series regressions, he ran the cross-section regression to test the CAPM. To be more specific he examined the following multiple regression:

$$\bar{R}_i = \hat{\gamma}_0 + \hat{\gamma}_1 b_i + \hat{\gamma}_2 S_{ei}^2 + u_i$$

where $b_i$ is the estimate of $\beta_i$ from first-pass regression, $S_{ei}^2$ is the estimate of the residual variance calculated from the deviations of the actual observations from the first-pass regression line, and $\hat{\gamma}_0$, $\hat{\gamma}_1$, $\hat{\gamma}_2$ are the estimates of the second-pass regression coefficients. If the CAPM holds, we expect to find that $\hat{\gamma}_2$ is not significantly different

---

[4] J. Lintner, "Security Prices and Risk: The Theory of Comparative Analysis of AT&T and Leading Industrials", paper presented at the Conference on the Economics of Regulated Public Utilities, Chicago, June 1965.

from zero. Unfortunately, Lintner obtained the following results:

$$\bar{R}_i = 0.108 + 0.063 b_i + 0.237 S_{ei}^2$$
$$\phantom{\bar{R}_i = 0.108 + } (0.009) \quad (0.035)$$
$$\phantom{\bar{R}_i = 0.108 + } t = 6.9 \quad t = 6.8$$

with the multiple correlation $\rho = 0.541$. In parentheses we give the estimators' standard deviations; the $t$-value is a measure of the coefficient's significance, and is equal to the regression coefficient divided by its standard deviation (e.g., $0.063/0.009 \cong 6.9$). From this result the following conclusions can be drawn:

(1)   As expected (by the CAPM), there is a positive association between $\bar{R}_i$ and $b_i$. However, the value of the coefficient $\hat{\gamma}_1$ (0.063 or 6.3%) is much lower than the *ex-post* average return on the market portfolio in excess of the risk-free interest rate, which in the period considered in this study was $(\bar{R}_m - r) = 16.5\%$.

(2)   $\hat{\gamma}_2$, the coefficient of the residual variance, is positive and significantly different from zero, which contradicts the CAPM.

(3)   The coefficient $\hat{\gamma}_0$ (10.8%) is much higher than the observed average risk-free interest rate.

Thus, the encouraging result of Lintner's study is that indeed there is a significant positive relationship between the mean return and beta. The discouraging result is that the empirical regression line is much flatter than the expected CAPM line, as drawn in Figure 14.1. Also, the residual variance seems to be important in price determination, a phenomenon which repeats itself virtually in all empirical studies.

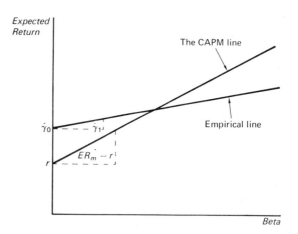

**Figure 14.1**

[5] M. Miller and M. Scholes, "Rate of Return in Relation to Risk: A Reexamination of Some Recent Findings", in Michael C. Jensen, ed., *Studies in the Theory of Capital Markets*, New York: Praeger, 1972.

Miller and Scholes,[5] who analyzed possible biases and measurement errors in the CAPM empirical tests, started their study by replicating Lintner's regression for the same period 1954–1963, but with a larger sample. The first- and second-pass regression results are given in Table 14.1.

Panel (b) of Table 14.1 reveals that Lintner's results are basically unchanged: the residual variance $S_{ei}^2$ is an important factor in price determination. Its coefficient is positive and significantly different from zero. Also the coefficient $\hat{\gamma}_1$ is quite low (7.1%), much less than 16.5%, the observed excess return on the market portfolio during this period. The coefficient of determination ($\rho^2$) is 19% with $b_i$ as the only explanatory variable, 28% with $S_{ei}^2$ as the only explanatory variable, and 33% with both $b_i$ and $S_{ei}^2$ as the explanatory variables. It seems that if one has to choose based on the explanatory power alone, $S_{ei}^2$ performs better than $b_i$, which casts doubt on the validity of the CAPM.

Miller and Scholes tried to incorporate in their study various sources of bias which might have caused this unexpected empirical result. The most promising explanation is that the beta used in the regression is not the true *ex-ante* (expected) beta and the estimate is measured with an error. This error in $b_i$ causes a bias in the estimate $\hat{\gamma}_1$.

**Table 14.1**
**Regressions with Annual Rates of Return, 1954–1963**

(a)  *Sample Values of First-pass Regressions*

|  | $\bar{R}_i$ | $b_i$ | Standard Error of $b_i$ | $S_{ei}^2$ | $\rho^2$ |
|---|---|---|---|---|---|
| Sample average value | 0.193 | 1.00 | 0.320 | 0.076 | 0.515 |
| Cross section standard deviation | 0.089 | 0.548 | 0.182 | 0.119 | 0.218 |

(b)  *Second-pass Regressions*

| $\bar{R}_i =$ | $\hat{\gamma}_0$ | + | $\hat{\gamma}_1 b$ | + | $\hat{\gamma}_2 S_{ei}^2$ | $\rho^2$ |
|---|---|---|---|---|---|---|
|  | 0.122 (0.007) $t = 18.6$ |  | 0.071 (0.006) $t = 12.34$ |  |  | 0.19 |
|  | 0.163 (0.004) $t = 46.1$ |  |  |  | 0.393 (0.025) $t = 15.74$ | 0.28 |
|  | 0.127 (0.006) $t = 21.31$ |  | 0.042 (0.006) $t = 7.40$ |  | 0.310 (0.026) $t = 11.76$ | 0.33 |

*Source:* M. Miller and M. Scholes, "Rates of Return in Relation to Risk: a Reexamination of some Recent Studies", in M. Jensen, ed., *Studies in the Theory of Capital Markets*, New York: Praeger, 1972.

Miller and Scholes found that:

$$\hat{\gamma}_1 = 0.64\gamma_1$$

namely the estimate $\hat{\gamma}_1$ observed in the empirical study is biased downward and it is only 64% of the true parameter $\gamma_1$. Adjusting the estimated coefficient for this bias increases $\hat{\gamma}_1$ to 10.5%, which is still much below the actual observed mean return on the market portfolio (16.5% during the period covered in the study).

Thus, though Miller and Scholes mention some possible biases and errors in measurements, their results are not conclusive. Incorporating some of the possible errors changes Lintner's results in such a way that the empirical findings incline toward the values predicted by the CAPM. However, the discrepancy between the (adjusted) empirical results and the CAPM is still quite large, which casts doubt on the validity of the CAPM.

Black, Jensen, and Scholes[6] tested the CAPM by employing the monthly rates of return for the period 1926–1966. In order to minimize the error in measuring the securities' betas, they grouped all the stocks into ten portfolios, where the portfolios were formed in such a way that 10% of the securities with the largest beta were included in the first portfolio, 10% with the second highest beta were assigned to the second portfolio, and so on. Thus for each of these 10 portfolios one can measure the portfolio's expected return and the portfolio's beta, and then run the second-pass regression:

$$\bar{R}_i - r = \hat{\gamma}_0 + \hat{\gamma}_1 b_i + u_i \quad (i = 1, 2, \ldots, 10)$$

where $\bar{R}_i$ and $b_i$ are the *portfolio* estimators rather than the estimators of the individual stocks. Here $i = 1, 2, \ldots, 10$ since we have ten portfolios.

Unlike Lintner's study, the Black, Jensen and Scholes study employs the excess monthly return $R_{it} - r_t$ in the various regressions rather than the return itself, $R_{it}$. Thus, in this kind of formulation we expect $\hat{\gamma}_0$ to be equal to zero since:

$$ER_i = r + (ER_m - r)\beta_i$$

which implies that in terms of excess return[7]

$$(ER_i - r) = (ER_m - r)\beta_i = \gamma_1 \beta_i$$

In their cross-section regression over the 10 portfolios Black, Jensen and Scholes obtained various estimates for various selected subperiods. However, for the entire

---

[6] F. Black, M. C. Jensen, and M. Scholes, "The Capital Asset Model: Some Empirical Tests", in Michael C. Jensen, ed., *Studies in the Theory of Capital Markets*, New York: Praeger, 1972.
[7] However, if the zero-beta model is substituted for the CAPM we expect to have a positive coefficient $\hat{\gamma}_0$. For more details, see Black, Jensen, and Scholes, *op. cit.*

period studied (1926–1966) they obtained:

$$\hat{\gamma}_0 = 0.00359$$
$$\hat{\gamma}_1 = 0.0108$$

where both $\hat{\gamma}_0$ and $\hat{\gamma}_1$ are significantly different from zero. Also the correlation coefficient is very high, $\rho^2 = 0.98$.

This high correlation seems to support the CAPM or at least the zero-beta model, since we have an almost perfect fit between the average excess return and beta. However, one word of caution: recall that the CAPM is an equilibrium model for price determination of individual assets as well as portfolios. Thus, if empirical results using portfolio rates of return contradict the CAPM, the theoretical model should be rejected. However, if empirical results obtained with portfolios support the model, we cannot assert that the model is valid, since it may not hold for individual stocks. Indeed, the explanatory power as measured by $\rho^2$ is much lower for individual stocks, normally less than 20% (see the results of Miller and Scholes above). Thus, though it is true that the construction of portfolios eliminated some statistical errors, we cannot test the CAPM with portfolios and infer that it holds also for individual risky assets.

Fama and MacBeth[8] tested the validity of the CAPM as well as the role that the residual variance $S_{ei}^2$ plays in price determination. They formed 20 portfolios of stocks and estimated their betas. Using the estimates $b_i$ for these portfolios (from the first-pass regression) they ran the following cross-section regression *for each month*, during the period 1935–1968:

$$\bar{R}_{it} = \hat{\gamma}_{0t} + \hat{\gamma}_{1t}b_i + \hat{\gamma}_{2t}b_i^2 + \hat{\gamma}_{3t}S_{ei} + u_{it}$$

Note that unlike the previous studies, here the subscript $t$ is attached to each of the coefficients $\hat{\gamma}_i$. Obviously, each coefficient may vary from one month to another and we can draw some conclusions regarding the CAPM by examining the average coefficient.

If the theoretical models (CAPM or zero-beta model) hold, we expect the coefficients of $b_i^2$ and $S_{ei}$ not to be significantly different from zero. However, since the coefficients may vary from one month to another, Fama and MacBeth examined the average coefficients across all the months:

$$\bar{\hat{\gamma}}_i = \sum_{t=1}^{T} \frac{\hat{\gamma}_{it}}{T} \qquad (i = 1, 2, 3)$$

where $T$ is the number of months for which the second-pass regression was carried out.

Fama and MacBeth found that the average coefficients $\bar{\hat{\gamma}}_2$ and $\bar{\hat{\gamma}}_3$ indeed were not significantly different from zero. If $E\gamma_2$ is equal to zero, then we can assert that the model is linear in beta, since the coefficient of $b_i^2$ vanishes on the average. $E\gamma_3 = 0$

[8] E. Fama and J. D. MacBeth, "Tests of the Multi-period Two-parameter Model", *Journal of Political Economy* (May 1974).

implies that the standard deviation of the residuals, $S_{ei}$, plays no role in price determination, quite contrary to the results of the previous studies.

The findings of Fama and MacBeth tend to support the theoretical model, since they found that the risk–return relationship is linear in beta and that the residual variance (or standard deviation of the residuals) plays no role in price determination. Since diversification of investments is the very heart of portfolio theory, this last finding is highly important. If the variance (or the residual variance) is a factor which explains price behavior (as Lintner and Miller and Scholes found), then the CAPM and the zero-beta model are refuted.

Thus we have inconclusive results regarding the role of the security's "own" variance (or the residual variance) in stock price determination. Lintner and Miller and Scholes found that the variance plays a central role in price determination, while Fama and MacBeth, who employed a different technique, found that the variance plays no role in stock price determination.

Suppose that indeed the security's "own" variance is found to be important in stock price determination. Does this contradict portfolio theory? Does this contradict the idea that "diversification always pays"? Obviously not: this finding only implies that due to some constraints (e.g. transaction costs) investors do not hold very large portfolios. Indeed if only a small number of assets are held by the typical investor, the $i$th security variance should play an important role in price determination [compare (14.2)]. It does not mean that diversification does not pay. It only asserts that there are also some costs to diversification (transaction costs) which set a practical limit to the gains from diversification.

To illustrate, suppose that the $k$th investor holds a portfolio $k$ whose return is $R_k$. Also assume that this portfolio includes only three risky assets, and for simplicity, assume that $\frac{1}{3}$ of the resources is invested in each asset. In this case the risk–return equilibrium relationship for the first asset, say, is given by:

$$ER_1 = r + \frac{ER_k - r}{\sigma_k^2} Cov(R_1, R_k)$$

But since:

$$R_k = \tfrac{1}{3}R_1 + \tfrac{1}{3}R_2 + \tfrac{1}{3}R_3$$

we obtain:

$$Cov(R_1, R_k) = \tfrac{1}{3}\sigma_1^2 + \tfrac{1}{3}Cov(R_1, R_2) + \tfrac{1}{3}Cov(R_1, R_3)$$

It is obvious that in such a case the variance $\sigma_1^2$ plays a central role in explaining the risk–return relationship. Moreover, one would expect that the individual variance would have an even greater impact on price determination than $\beta_1$, which in our example includes the covariances of asset 1 with all the other securities included in the full market portfolio, most of which are anyhow irrelevant to the investor, simply because these assets are not held in his particular portfolio.

Blume, Crockett and Friend found that, in the tax year 1971, individuals held highly undiversified portfolios. The sample, which included 17,056 individual income tax forms, revealed that 34.1% held only one stock, 50% held no more than two stocks, and only 10.7% of the investors held more than 10 stocks.[9] Another source of data which confirms these findings is the Federal Reserve Board's 1967 survey of the Financial Characteristics of Consumers. According to this survey, which covered all households whether they filed income tax forms or not, the average number of securities in a portfolio was only 3.41.[10]

Thus, if investors hold the market portfolio or a portfolio with a very large number of assets, the security's variance should play no role in price determination and beta is the relevant risk index. At the other extreme, when the investor specializes in only one stock, the stock's own variance is the relevant measure of risk and beta is irrelevant for price determination. The empirical findings reveal that the "truth" lies somewhere between the two extremes. Investors do diversify but probably believe in the dictum that "A little diversification goes a long way."[11]

In order to see which factor $\beta_i$ or $\sigma_i^2$ has more explanatory power, Levy[12] ran several regressions on a sample of 101 stocks for the period 1948–1968. The annual rates of return were employed to calculate the first-pass regression estimates $b_i$ and $S_{ei}^2$. The average return $\bar{R}_i$ and the variance $\sigma_i^2$ were also calculated. Then, various combinations of $\sigma_i^2$, $S_{ei}^2$ and $b_i$ were employed to explain the variation of the mean return $\bar{R}_i$ across securities.

The regression $\bar{R}_i - r = f(b_i)$ (where $f$ stands for the linear function) tests the simple CAPM. The regression $\bar{R}_i - r = f(b_i, S_{ei}^2)$ is similar to the ones formulated by Miller and Scholes and by Lintner. However, as Table 14.2 reveals, a number of additional regressions were tried. The main results are as follows. First, note that the results are very similar to those obtained by Miller and Scholes (who also used annual data) in spite of the fact that a different sample of data is used. We find the $\rho^2$ of the regression $\bar{R}_i - r = f(b_i)$ to be 21% in comparison to 19% in their research; for the regression $\bar{R}_i - r = f(S_{ei}^2)$ we obtain $\rho^2 = 32\%$ in comparison to their 28%; and finally, for the regression $\bar{R}_i - r = f(b_i, S_{ei}^2)$ the $\rho^2$ is equal to 39% in comparison to 33% that they obtain. With annual data, all the regression coefficients are positive and significant in Table 14.2 as well as in Miller and Scholes' research. However, Table 14.2 presents two more regressions which do not appear in Miller and Scholes' paper. These regressions show that: (a) the simple regression $\bar{R}_i - r = f(\sigma_i^2)$ yields $\rho^2$ of 38%. This is only 1% less than with the more complicated regression $\bar{R}_i - r = f(b_i, S_{ei}^2)$ which has been employed in most empirical studies that test the validity of the CAPM. (b) When one runs the regression $\bar{R}_i - r = f(b_i, \sigma_i^2)$ rather than $\bar{R}_i - r = f(b_i, S_{ei}^2)$, one finds that the conventional estimate of the systematic risk $\beta_i$ adds nothing to the explanation of price behavior. The coefficient of the systematic risk is very small and statistically insignificant

[9] For more details, see M. Blume, J. Crockett, and I. Friend, "Stock Ownership in the United States: Characteristics and Trends", *Surv. Curr. Bus.* (Nov. 1974).

[10] M. E. Blume and I. Friend, "The Asset Structure of Individual Portfolios and Some Implications for Utility Functions", *Journal of Finance* (May 1975).

[11] H. Levy and H. Markowitz, "Approximating Expected Utility by a Function of Mean and Variance", *American Economic Review* (June 1979).

[12] See H. Levy, "Equilibrium in an Imperfect Market: A Constraint on the Number of Securities in the Portfolio", *American Economic Review* (Sept. 1978).

**Table 14.2**
**Second-pass Regression with Annual Data, 1948–1968**

| $\bar{R}_i \ =$ | $\hat{\gamma}_0$ | $+$ | $\hat{\gamma}_1 b_i$ | $+$ | $\hat{\gamma}_2 S^2_{ei}$ | $+$ | $\hat{\gamma}_3 \sigma^2_i$ | $\rho^2$ |
|---|---|---|---|---|---|---|---|---|
| | 0.109 (0.009) $t = 12.0$ | | 0.037 (0.008) $t = 5.1$ | | | | | 0.21 |
| | 0.122 (0.005) $t = 22.9$ | | | | | | 0.219 (0.029) $t = 7.7$ | 0.38 |
| | 0.126 (0.005) $t = 23.4$ | | | | 0.248 (0.036) $t = 6.8$ | | | 0.32 |
| | 0.117 (0.008) $t = 14.2$ | | 0.008 (0.009) $t = 0.9$ | | | | 0.197 (0.038) $t = 5.2$ | 0.38 |
| | 0.106 (0.008) $t = 13.2$ | | 0.024 (0.007) $t = 3.3$ | | 0.201 (0.038) $t = 5.3$ | | | 0.39 |

Source: H. Levy, "Equilibrium in an Imperfect Market: a Constraint on the Number of Securities in the Portfolio", *American Economic Review*, Sept. 1978.

($t$ value $= 0.9$). (c) If one had to choose between the traditional CAPM, i.e., $\bar{R}_i - r = f(b_i)$, and the simple model $\bar{R}_i - r = f(\sigma^2_i)$, one would note that the latter performs much better, with $\rho^2 = 38\%$ compared to only $\rho^2 = 21\%$ for the previous model.

To sum up, the assumptions of perfect divisibility of investment and of the absence of transaction costs in the stock market induce a theoretical result which asserts that each investor holds in his portfolio all the securities available in the market. It is obvious that the above assumptions do not conform to reality, since many investors hold stocks of only one company, and most individuals hold stocks of less than four companies.

This survey of findings backed by the empirical second-pass regression casts doubts on the validity of the CAPM. However, it does not imply that portfolio theory is not valid. It only suggests that due to transaction and information costs and other possible imperfections in the market investors do not diversify in all the risky assets, as implied by the CAPM or by the zero-beta model.

## 14.4    Roll's Critique of the Empirical Tests

In a recent breakthrough article, Richard Roll[13] showed that the value of the huge amount of empirical research which had attempted to verify the Sharpe–Lintner Capital

---

[13] See R. Roll, "A Critique of the Assets Pricing Theory's Tests: Part I: On Past and Potential Testability of the Theory", *Journal of Financial Economics*, March 1977, and R. Roll, "Ambiguity when Performance is Measured by the Securities Market Line", *Journal of Finance*, Sept. 1978.

Asset Pricing Model (CAPM) is open to question. Briefly, Roll claimed that if all the empirical investigators were to take a *mean-variance efficient portfolio* as the market portfolio against which they run the regression they would get in *the sample* a perfect linear relationship between average security returns and betas in the second-pass (cross-section) regression. This perfect linear relationship is tautological. It neither proves nor disproves the CAPM theory. It is a technical result, obtainable by straightforward algebra without making any assumption regarding the investors' preference. It is interesting to mention that the equivalence between the linear second-pass regression and the efficiency of the market portfolio was also realized by Fama[14] and Ross.[15] For example Ross asserts that "the efficiency of the market portfolio and the CAPM are equivalent". We turn now to prove Roll's claim.

### 14.4.1 The Exact Linear Relationship between Average Return and Beta in the Sample

Using efficient-set algebra in general matrix notation, Roll proved several theorems which lead to the conclusion that there is an *exact* linear relationship between the betas and the average returns *in the sample* if the betas are calculated against an efficient portfolio. We give here an alternative proof of Roll's corollary which is much simpler and shorter and hence may be easily understood by students. Write the Lagrangian function $C(x_1, \ldots, x_n)$ as follows:

$$C(x_1, \ldots, x_n) = \sum_{i=1}^{n} x_i^2 S_i^2 + 2 \sum_{i=1}^{n} \sum_{\substack{j=1 \\ j>i}}^{n} x_i x_j S_{ij} + 2\lambda \left[ \bar{R} - \sum_{i=1}^{n} x_i \bar{R}_i - \left( 1 - \sum_{i=1}^{n} x_i \right) r \right]$$

where $S_i^2$ and $S_{ij}$ are respectively the *sample* variance of security $i$ and its sample covariance with security $j$, $\bar{R}_i$ is the $i$th security *sample* average return, $\bar{R}$ is the *sample* average return on the portfolio, $r$ is the riskless interest rate, and $x_i$ is the investment proportion in the $i$th security.[16] Differentiating $C(x_1, \ldots, x_n)$ with respect to $x_i$ ($i = 1, 2, \ldots, n$) and setting the derivative equal to zero, one minimizes the portfolio variance for a given portfolio average return $\bar{R}$. The result is by definition an investment strategy $(x_1, \ldots, x_n, x_r)$ which is mean–variance efficient *in the sample*.

To be more specific take the derivative with respect to $x_i$ and equate to zero to obtain (after reducing by 2) the $n$ equations:

$$x_i S_i^2 + \sum_{\substack{j=1 \\ j \neq i}}^{n} x_j S_{ij} = \lambda(\bar{R}_i - r) \qquad (i = 1, 2, \ldots, n)$$

[14] E. Fama, *Foundation of Finance*, New York: Basic Books, 1976.
[15] S. Ross, "The Capital Asset Pricing Model (CAPM), Short-Sales Restriction and Related Issues", *Journal of Finance* (March 1977).
[16] Note that in this formulation of $C$ the investment proportions in the $n$ risky assets plus the proportion $x_r$ invested in the riskless asset with (certain) return $r$ add up to 1.

Multiply the $i$th equation by $x_i$ and sum across all securities $(i = 1, 2, \ldots, n)$ to obtain:

$$\sum_{i=1}^{n} x_i^2 S_i^2 + 2 \sum_{i=1}^{n} \sum_{\substack{j=1 \\ j>i}}^{n} x_i x_j S_{ij} = \lambda \left( \sum_{i=1}^{n} x_i \bar{R}_i - \sum_{i=1}^{n} x_i r \right)$$

(Note that each term of the type $x_i x_j S_{ij}$ appears twice, exactly as in Section 11.5.)

The left-hand side is simply the portfolio sample variance $S_p^2$. The right-hand side can be rewritten as:

$$\lambda \left( \sum_{i=1}^{n} x_i \bar{R}_i - \sum_{i=1}^{n} x_i r \right) = \lambda \left[ \sum_{i=1}^{n} x_i \bar{R}_i + \left( 1 - \sum_{i=1}^{n} x_i \right) r - r \right] = \lambda (\bar{R} - r)$$

where $\bar{R}$ is the sample mean return on the selected portfolio. At the point $\sum_{i=1}^{n} x_i = 1$, $\bar{R}$ is the sample mean return of the optimum unlevered portfolio which we denote by $\bar{R}_p$. Thus:

$$S_p^2 = \lambda(\bar{R}_p - r) \quad \text{or} \quad \lambda = S_p^2/(\bar{R}_p - r)$$

Plugging this result in the $i$th equation yields:

$$x_i S_i^2 + \sum_{\substack{j=1 \\ j\neq i}}^{n} x_j S_{ij} = \frac{S_p^2}{\bar{R}_p - r} (\bar{R}_i - r)$$

But since

$$x_i S_i^2 + \sum_{\substack{j=1 \\ j\neq i}}^{n} x_j S_{ij} = Cov\,(R_i, R_p) = Cov\left( R_i, \sum_{j=1}^{n} x_j R_j \right)$$

where $R_p$ is the return on the optimum unlevered portfolio selected from the sample, and $Cov\,(R_i, R_p)/S_p^2 = b_i$ (the sample beta), we obtain:

$$b_i = \frac{\bar{R}_i - r}{\bar{R}_p - r}$$

which finally can be rewritten as a linear relationship between the sample mean return $\bar{R}_i$ and the sample beta of the $i$th security $b_i$:

$$\bar{R}_i = r + (\bar{R}_p - r)b_i \tag{14.3}$$

This is an exact linear relationship between the sample estimates, without any deviations of the sample observations from the straight line (14.3).

A few comments are called for at this point.

(1)   Note that in this simple proof we use the same technique which originally was used to derive the theoretical relationship of the CAPM (see Chapter 11). We simply replace the population parameters (i.e., $\mu_i$, $\sigma_i$, $\sigma_{ij}$, $\beta_i$) by the corresponding *sample* values. Thus, if $\bar{R}_p$ is the average return of an efficient portfolio, there is an *exact* linear relationship *in the sample* between $\bar{R}_i$ and $b_i$.

(2)   One does not need to hold all the securities traded in the market in order to derive the linear relationship between return and beta. If we take a small sample, say ten stocks, and derive the efficient set for these ten stocks, we still get the linear relationship as long as the betas are calculated against some efficient portfolio taken from the ten-stock efficient set.

   To illustrate this point a sample of 10 stocks listed on the NYSE was taken and the MV efficient frontier was derived for these stocks. In the second step we identified an (arbitrary) efficient portfolio $R_p$ and used this portfolio to run the first-pass regression

$$R_{it} = a_i + b_i R_{pt} + e_{it} \quad (i = 1, 2, \ldots, 10)$$

Having the estimates $b_i$, we conducted the second-pass regression

$$\bar{R}_i = \hat{\gamma}_0 + \hat{\gamma}_1 b_i + u_i$$

As predicted by Roll's analysis, a perfect fit was obtained in the second-pass regression as illustrated in Figure 14.2. Thus, if the (first-pass) regressions are carried out with any efficient portfolio $R_p$, we obtain an exact linear relationship in the second-pass regression.

(3)   The linear relationship (14.3) is obtained as a straightforward technical result only if the efficient set (and hence each efficient portfolio) is derived *without the non-negativity constraints*. In other words, short sales are allowed. Once we impose the constraint that short sales are not allowed (i.e., $x_i \geqslant 0$) the sample linear relationship between $\bar{R}_i$ and $b_i$ does not follow.[17]

Roll's analysis completely changes the interpretation of the empirical studies testing the CAPM. If one obtains less than a perfect fit in the second-pass regression, it only implies that a mean–variance *inefficient* portfolio was employed as a proxy to the market portfolio. On the other hand if one gets an exact linear relationship in the second-pass regression, it only implies that a mean–variance efficient portfolio was used as a proxy to the market portfolio. However, one can use an efficient portfolio of ten stocks or any number that one wishes and get a perfect fit in the second-pass regression, a technical result which by no means proves the CAPM.

Thus, to test the CAPM, one only needs to check that the market portfolio is MV

---

[17] For a formal proof and demonstration of this issue, see H. Levy, "The Capital Asset Pricing Model: Theory and Empiricism", *The Economic Journal* (March 1983).

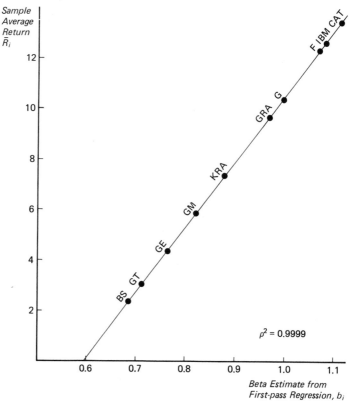

**Figure 14.2**

*Source:* H. Levy, "The Capital Asset Pricing Model: Theory and Empiricism", *The Economic Journal*
(March 1983)

efficient. If it is efficient, the exact linear relationship follows as a technical result. However, it is difficult if not impossible to test the efficiency of the market portfolio. First it includes all the available risky assets. Even if one manages to identify all the risky assets (stocks, real estate, coins, stamps, etc.) it is technically impossible to derive the efficient frontier with so many assets. Thus, testing the efficiency of the market portfolio is almost a hopeless task. Consequently, the empirical tests indeed neither reject nor confirm the theoretical model. All of them, however, displaying less than a perfect fit in the second-pass regression have one common shortcoming: they all employ an inefficient portfolio in estimating the betas. All the other results can be explained from this fact.

**Summary**

Most studies that test the CAPM or the zero-beta model reveal that there are some discrepancies between the empirical results and what one expects to obtain if the theoretical model indeed holds. In particular the following three results are common to most empirical studies.

(a)   The estimator of the return on the risk-free asset $\hat{\gamma}_0$ is much higher than the actual riskless interest rate.

(b)   The estimator of the excess return on the market portfolio $\hat{\gamma}_1$ is much lower than $\bar{R}_m - r$ observed in reality.

(c)   The coefficient of the residual variance $\hat{\gamma}_2$ is significantly different from zero, in contradiction to the CAPM.

In a recent paper Roll questioned the relevance of all the empirical tests. He showed that the only meaningful hypothesis is regarding the efficiency of the market portfolio. If the market portfolio is mean–variance efficient, one gets as a technical result an exact linear relationship between expected return and beta.

Finally, the fact that the expected return is positively associated with the security's variance does not contradict portfolio theory, although it does contradict the CAPM. It only implies that on average investors hold small portfolios and in such a case the variance has a direct impact on the expected return. The reason for holding a small number of assets in the portfolio is the existence of transaction and information costs, which prevent wide diversification.

**Summary Table**

**A Simple Test of the CAPM**

1. Run a first-pass regression for each security to estimate $\beta_i$ by $b_i$:

$$R_{it} = a_i + b_i R_{mt} + e_{it}$$

where $R_{it}$ and $R_{mt}$ are the rates of return in period $t$ on the $i$th security and on the market portfolio, respectively. We have $n$ regressions, one for each security. From these time-series regressions, we estimate the mean return of security $i$ ($\bar{R}_i$) and its systematic risk ($b_i$):

$$\bar{R}_i = \sum_{t=1}^{T} R_{it}/T$$

($T$ is the number of observations, e.g. number of monthly rates of return),

$$b_i = \frac{\displaystyle\sum_{t=1}^{T} (R_{it} - \bar{R}_i)(R_{mt} - \bar{R}_m)}{\displaystyle\sum_{t=1}^{T} (R_{mt} - \bar{R}_m)^2}$$

2. Using the estimates from the first-pass regression ($\bar{R}_i, b_i$), run a second-pass

regression—one regression for all the stocks (a cross-section regression)—of the form:

$$\bar{R}_i = \hat{\gamma}_0 + \hat{\gamma}_1 b_i + u_i$$

Test whether $\hat{\gamma}_0$ is significantly different from $r$ and whether $\hat{\gamma}_1$ is significantly different from $(\bar{R}_m - r)$. Significant differences are incompatible with the CAPM.

3. Grouping stocks by their beta and running the second-pass regression with groups eliminates some statistical errors.

**Roll's Critique of CAPM Empirical Tests:**

If the market portfolio is *ex-post* mean–variance efficient, we necessarily obtain a linear relationship in the second-pass regression. This is a technical result which neither confirms nor rejects the CAPM.

## Questions and Problems

14.1    What are the implications of the Capital Asset Pricing Model (CAPM) concerning the role of a security's own variance in explaining its expected return?

14.2    What is the prediction of the CAPM concerning the effect of the non-systematic risk on the expected return of a risky security?

14.3    What are the two basic stages in the empirical tests of the CAPM?

14.4    Discuss the empirical studies conducted by Lintner and by Miller and Scholes which question the validity of the CAPM.

14.5    Compare the results of the CAPM studies conducted by Lintner and by Miller and Scholes with the results of Black, Jensen and Scholes and of Fama and MacBeth. In particular, focus on the determination coefficient $\rho^2$ of the second-pass regression.

14.6    How does Levy account for the failure of the empirical studies to support the CAPM?

14.7    What is Roll's critique of the empirical studies conducted to verify the validity of the CAPM?

14.8    Suppose that an investor diversifies in equal proportions between $n$ risky assets. It is also given that:

$$\sigma_{ij} = 10 \text{ for all pairs of securities } i \text{ and } j$$
$$\sigma_i^2 = 10 \text{ for security } i$$
$$\sigma_m^2 = 10 \text{ for market portfolio } m$$

Calculate the $i$th security's own variance as a percentage of the $i$th security's beta, taking a market portfolio with $n = 1, 5, 10, 100, 1000$ securities.

14.9 The following hypothetical data relate to security $i$ and to the market portfolio:

| | Rates of Return (%) | |
|---|---|---|
| Year | Security i | Market Portfolio (m) |
| 1980 | 10 | 5 |
| 1981 | 5 | 3 |
| 1982 | −10 | 0 |

Calculate the systematic risk $\beta_i^2 \sigma_m^2$ and the non-systematic risk $\sigma_{ei}^2$ of the security. How do these two components relate to the $i$th security's own variance $\sigma_i^2$?

14.10 Hypothetical rates of return on three securities and on the market portfolio are as follows (in %):

| | Securities | | | |
|---|---|---|---|---|
| Year | 1 | 2 | 3 | Market Portfolio (m) |
| 1980 | 5 | 8 | 10 | 5 |
| 1981 | 10 | 4 | 8 | 10 |
| 1982 | 0 | 3 | −10 | −10 |
| 1983 | 40 | 20 | 20 | 40 |

(a) Estimate the beta of each security by running the appropriate first-pass regressions.
(b) Run the second-pass regressions and test the hypothesis that $\hat{\gamma}_1 = 0$, where $\hat{\gamma}_1$ is the slope in the second-pass regression.

14.11 Use the data of Problem 14.10 to test the hypothesis that the mean rate of return is linearly related to the security's own variance,

$$\bar{R}_i = \hat{\gamma}_0 + \hat{\gamma}_1 \sigma_i^2$$

14.12 The following hypothetical rates of return data (in %) relate to three securities:

| | Securities | | |
|---|---|---|---|
| Year | 1 | 2 | 3 |
| 1977 | 5 | 2 | 5 |
| 1978 | 5 | 3 | 5 |
| 1979 | 9 | 6 | 6 |
| 1980 | 9 | −2 | 6 |
| 1981 | 5 | 1 | 5 |
| 1982 | −7 | 2 | 3 |
| 1983 | 7 | 2 | −3 |
| 1984 | 7 | 2 | −3 |

(a) Construct the mean–variance efficient portfolio with 8% mean rate of return. Assume that this portfolio represents the market portfolio.
(b) Run the second-pass regression with the beta estimated against the market portfolio that you constructed in part (a). Do the results confirm the CAPM? Explain!
(c) How would your answer to (b) change for a mean–variance efficient portfolio with 15% mean rate of return?

14.13   An investor wants to add the stock of Kaiser Aluminum & Chemical to his portfolio. He is worried that the risk of his portfolio might shoot up because the variance of return on Kaiser Aluminum's stock is large, though its covariances with other securities are either small or negative. Should he add the stock to his portfolio? Give a reason for your advice. Demonstrate your answer by assuming equal proportions invested in each asset in the portfolio.

14.14   Is there any evidence that the variance of a security's return plays a more important part than its systematic risk in the return generating process? What does this evidence imply about the assumptions of perfect capital markets made by the CAPM?

## Data Set Problems

1. Use all the funds and the market portfolio in the Data Set to test the CAPM. Analyze the computer output of the first-pass and the second-pass regressions.

2. Repeat Problem 1 by regressing the excess return $R_{it} - r_t$ of security $i$ on the excess return $R_{m_t} - r_t$ of the market portfolio. Here $r_t$ is the risk-free interest rate in period $t$, as it appears at the bottom of the Data Set. Compare your results for Problems 1 and 2.

3. Use the mutual fund returns from the Data Set to test the relationship:

$$\bar{R}_i = \hat{\gamma}_0 + \hat{\gamma}_1 b_i + \hat{\gamma}_2 \sigma_i^2$$

Running a stepwise regression, which explanatory factor is more important in mutual fund price determination? Explain your results.

4. Assume that the first three funds in the Other Funds category comprise the whole market.

(a) Find an efficient portfolio consisting of these three funds (use the computer program from Appendix 9.1).
(b) Calculate the $b_i$ of each fund against the efficient portfolio you obtained in (a) above.
(c) Check Roll's main claim, namely that there is an exact linear relationship between $\bar{R}_i$ and $b_i$ in the sample. (*Hint*: Run a second-pass regression.)

## Selected References

Alexander, G. J., "An Algorithmic Approach to Deriving the Minimum Variance Zero-Beta Portfolio", *Journal of Financial Economics* (March 1977).

Alexander, G. J. and Benson, P. G., "More on Beta as a Random Coefficient", *Journal of Financial and Quantitative Analysis* (March 1982).

Alexander, G. J. and Chervany, N. L., "On the Estimation and Stability of Beta", *Journal of Financial and Quantitative Analysis* (March 1980).

Arzac, E. R. and Bawa, V. S., "Portfolio Choice and Equilibrium in Capital Markets with Safety-First Investors", *Journal of Financial Economics* (May 1977).

Barry, C. B., "Effects of Uncertain and Non-Stationary Parameters Upon Capital Market Equilibrium Conditions", *Journal of Financial and Quantitative Analysis* (September 1978).

Beja, A. and Goldman, B., "On the Dynamic Behavior of Prices in Disequilibrium", *The Journal of Finance* (May 1980).

Ben-Horim, M. and Levy, H., "Total Risk, Diversifiable Risk: A Pedagogic Note", *Journal of Financial and Quantitative Analysis* (June 1980).

Bernstein, P. L., "What Rate of Return Can you 'Reasonably' Expect?" *Journal of Finance* (May 1973).

Bildersee, J. S. and Roberts, G. S., "Beta Instability When Interest Rate Levels Change", *Journal of Financial and Quantitative Analysis* (September 1981).

Black, F., "Capital Market Equilibrium with Restricted Borrowing", *Journal of Business* (1972).

Black, F., Jensen, M. C. and Scholes, M., "The Capital Asset Model: Some Empirical Tests", in Jensen, M. C., ed., *Studies in Theory of Capital Markets*, Praeger, New York (1972).

Blume, M. E., "Betas and Their Regression Tendencies: Some Further Evidence", *Journal of Finance* (March 1979).

Blume, M. E., "On the Assessment of Risk", *Journal of Finance* (March 1971).

Blume, M., Crockett, J. and Friend, I., "Stock Ownership in the United States: Characteristics and Trends", *Survey of Current Business* (Nov. 1974).

Blume, M. and Friend, I., "The Asset Structure of Individual Portfolios and Some Implications for Utility Functions", *Journal of Finance* (May 1975).

Bolton, S. E. and Crockett, J. H., "The Influence of Liquidity Services on Beta", *Review of Business and Economic Research* (Spring 1978).

Bolton, S. E., Kretlow, S. J. and Oakes, J. H., "The Capital Asset Pricing Model Under Certainty", *Review of Business and Economic Research* (Fall 1978).

Bower, D. H. and Bower, R. S., "Test of a Stock Valuation Model", *Journal of Finance* (May 1970).

Boyer, M., Storoy, S. and Sten, T., "Equilibrium in Linear Capital Market Networks", *Journal of Finance* (December 1975).

Breeden, D. T., "An Intertemporal Asset Pricing Model with Stochastic Consumption and Investment Opportunities", *Journal of Financial Economics* (June 1979).

Brennan, M. J., "Taxes, Market Valuation and Corporate Finance Policy", *National Tax Journal* (1973).

Brennan, M. J., "Capital Market Equilibrium with Divergent Borrowing and Lending Rates", *Journal of Financial and Quantitative Analysis* (December 1971).

Brenner, M. and Subrahmanyam, M. G., "Intra-Equilibrium and Inter-Equilibrium Analysis in Capital Market Theory: A Clarification", *Journal of Finance* (September 1977).

Brenner, M. and Smidt, S., "Asset Characteristics and Systematic Risk", *Financial Management* (Winter 1978).

Brito, N. O., "Marketability Restrictions and the Valuation of Capital Assets Under Uncertainty", *Journal of Finance* (September 1977).

Brito, N. O., "Portfolio Selection in an Economy with Marketability and Short Sales Restrictions", *Journal of Finance* (May 1978).

Brown, S. L., "Autocorrelation, Market Imperfections, and the CAPM", *Journal of Financial and Quantitative Analysis* (December 1979).

Carpenter, M. D. and Henderson, J. V., Jr., "Estimation Procedures and Stability of the Market-Model Parameters", *Review of Business and Economic Research* (Fall 1981).

Cass, D. and Stiglitz, J. E., "The Structure of Investor Preferences and Asset Returns, and Separability in Portfolio Allocation: A Contribution to the Pure Theory of Mutual Funds", *Journal of Economic Theory* (June 1970).

Chamberlain, G. and Rothschild, M., "Arbitrage, Factor Structure, and Mean-Variance Analysis on Large Asset Markets". Unpublished Manuscript. University of Wisconsin at Madison (June 1981).

Chen, A. H., Kim, E. H. and Kon, S. J., "Cash Demand, Liquidation Costs and Capital Market Equilibrium Under Uncertainty", *Journal of Financial Economics* (September 1975).

Chen, N.-F., "Some Empirical Tests of the Theory of Arbitrage Pricing", Unpublished Manuscript. University of Chicago, Graduate School of Business (April 1982).

Chen, S., "Beta Nonstationarity, Portfolio Residual Risk and Diversification", *Journal of Financial and Quantitative Analysis* (March 1981).

Chen, S., "An examination of Risk-Return Relationship in Bull and Bear Markets Using Time-Varying Betas", *Journal of Financial and Quantitative Analysis* (June 1982).

Chen, S. and Lee, C. F., "Sampling Relationship Between Sharpe's Performance Measure and its Risk Proxy: Sample Size, Investment Horizon and Market Conditions", *Management Science* (June 1981).

Chen, S. A. and Keoun, A. J., "Risk Decomposition and Portfolio Diversification When Beta is Nonstationary", *Journal of Finance* (September 1981).

Cheng, P. L. and Grauer, R. R., "An Alternative Test of the Capital Asset Pricing Model", *The American Economic Review* (September 1980).

Constanides, G. M., "Intertemporal Asset Pricing with Heterogeneous Consumers and Without Demand Aggregation", *Journal of Business* (April 1982).

Cornell, B. and Dietrich, J. K., "Mean-Absolute-Deviation Versus Least-Squares Regression Estimation of Beta Coefficients", *Journal of Financial and Quantitative Analysis* (March 1978).

Crockett, J. and Friend, I., "Capital Budgeting and Stock Valuation Comment", *American Economic Review* (March 1967).

Diamond, P. A., "The Role of a Stock Market in a General Equilibrium Model with Technological Uncertainty", *American Economic Review* (September 1967).

Dhrymes, P., Friend, I. and Gultekin, N., "A Critical Reexamination of the Empirical Evidence on the Arbitrage Pricing Theory", Working Paper No. 12–82, Univ. of Pennsylvania (1982).

Dybvig, H. and Ingersoll, J. E., Jr., "Mean–Variance Theory in Complete Markets", *Journal of Business* (April 1982).

Eddy, A. R., "Interest Rate Risk and Systematic Risk: An Interpretation", *Journal of Finance* (May 1978).

Elgers, P. T., Haltiner, J. R., and Hawthorne, W. H., "Beta Regression Tendencies: Statistical and Real Causes", *Journal of Finance* (March 1979).

Elton, E. J. and Gruber, M. J., "Taxes and Portfolio Composition", *Journal of Financial Economics* (December 1978).

Elton, E. J. and Gruber, M. J., *Finance as a Dynamic Process*, Englewood Cliffs, N.J.: Prentice-Hall (1975).

Elton, E. J. and Gruber, M. J., "The Multi-Period Consumption Investment Decision and Single Period Analysis", *Oxford Economic Papers* (September 1974).

Epstein, L. G. and Turnbull, S. M., "Capital Asset Prices and the Temporal Resolution of Uncertainty", *The Journal of Finance* (June 1980).

Eubank, A. A. and Zumwalt, J. K., "How to Determine the Stability of Beta Values", *The Journal of Portfolio Management* (Winter 1979).

Everett, J. E. and Schwab, B., "On the Proper Adjustment for Risk Through Discount Rates in a Mean-Variance Framework", *Financial Management* (Summer 1979).

Fabozzi, F. J. and Francis, J. C., "Beta as a Random Coefficient", *Journal of Financial and Quantitative Analysis* (March 1978).

Fabry, J. and van Grembergen, W., "Further Evidence on the Stationarity of Betas and Errors in their Estimates", *Journal of Banking and Finance* (October 1978).

Fama, E. F. *Foundation of Finance*, New York: Basic Books (1976).

Fama, E. F., "The Behavior of Stock Market Prices", *Journal of Business* (January 1965).

Fama, E. F., "Risk, Return and Equilibrium: Some Clarifying Comments", *Journal of Finance* (March 1968).

Fama, E. F., "Portfolio Analysis in a Stable Paretian Market", *Management Science* (Jan. 1965).

Fama, "Multi-Period Consumption-Investment Decision", *American Review* (March 1970).

Fama, E. F., "Risk, Return and Equilibrium", *Journal of Political Economy* (January/February 1971).

Fama, E. F., "A Note on the Market Model and the Two-Parameter Model", *Journal of Finance* (December 1973).

Fama, E., and MacBeth, J., "Tests of Multiperiod Two-Parameter Model", *Journal of Political Economy* (May 1974).

Foster, G., "Asset Pricing Models: Further Tests", *Journal of Financial and Quantitative Analysis* (March 1978).

Frankfurter, G. M., "The Effect of 'Market Indexes' on the *Ex-Post* Performance of the Sharpe Portfolio Selection Model", *Journal of Finance* (June 1976).

Friedman, M., *Essays in Positive Economics*, Chicago: University of Chicago Press (1953).

Friend, I., Landskroner, Y. and Losq, E., "The Demand for Risky Assets and Uncertain Inflation", *Journal of Finance* (December 1976).

Friend, I. and Westerfield, R., "Co-Skewedness and Capital Asset Pricing", *The Journal of Finance* (September 1980).

Friend, I., Westerfield, R. and Granito, M., "New Evidence on the Capital Asset Pricing Model", *Journal of Finance* (June 1978).

Gentry, J. and Pike, J., "An Empirical Study of the Risk-Return Hypothesis Using Common Stock Portfolios of Life Insurance Companies", *Journal of Financial and Quantitative Analysis* (June 1970).

Goldberg, M. A. and Vora, A., "Bivariate Spectra Analysis of the Capital Asset Pricing Model", *Journal of Financial and Quantitative Analysis* (September 1978).

Gonedes, N. J., "Capital Market Equilibrium for a Class of Heterogeneous Expectations in a Two-Parameter World", *Journal of Finance* (March 1976).

Gressis, N., Philippatos, G. C. and Hayya, J., "Multiperiod Portfolio Analysis and the Inefficiency of the Market Portfolio", *Journal of Finance* (September 1976).

Grauer, R. R., "Generalized Two Parameter Asset Pricing Models: Some Empirical Evidence", *Journal of Financial Economics* (March 1978).

Hagerman, R. L. and Kim, E. H., "Capital Asset Pricing with Price Level Changes", *Journal of Financial and Quantitative Analysis* (September 1976).

Hamada, R. S., "Investment Decisions with a General Equilibrium Approach", *Quarterly Journal of Economics* (November 1971).

Harrington, D. R., "Trends in Capital Asset Pricing Model Use", *Public Utilities* (August 1981).

Harris, R. G., "A General Equilibrium Analysis of the Capital Asset Pricing Model", *Journal of Financial and Quantitative Analysis* (March 1980).

Hart, O. D., "On the Existence of Equilibrium in a Securities Model", *Journal of Economic Theory* (November 1974).

Hawawini, G. A. and Vora, A., "Capital Assets Pricing Model and the Investment Horizon", *Review of Economics and Statistics* (November 1981).

Heckerman, D. G., "Portfolio Selection and the Structure of Capital Asset Prices When Relative Prices of Consumption Goods May Change", *Journal of Finance* (March 1972).

Hess, A. C., "The Riskless Rate of Interest and the Market Price of Risk", *Quarterly Journal of Economics* (August 1975).

Hill, N. C. and Stone, B. K., "Accounting Betas, Systematic Operating Risk, and Financial Leverage: A Risk-Composition Approach to the Determinants of Systematic Risk", *Journal of Financial and Quantitative Analysis* (September 1980).

Hogan, W. W., and Warren, J. M., "Toward the Development of an Equilibrium Capital-Market Model Based on Semi-Variance", *Journal of Financial and Quantitative Analysis* (January 1974).

Huberman, G., "A Simple Approach to Arbitrage Pricing Theory", Working Paper No. 44. University of Chicago, Graduate School of Business, 1981 (forthcoming in *Journal of Economic Theory*).

Hughes, P., "A Test of the Arbitrage Pricing Theory", Unpublished Manuscript. University of British Columbia (August 1981).

Ingersoll, J. E. Jr., "Some Results in the Theory of Arbitrage Pricing", Unpublished Manuscript. University of Chicago, Graduate School of Business (May 1981).

Jahankhani, A., "E–V and E–S Capital Asset Pricing Models: Some Empirical Tests", *Journal of Financial and Quantitative Analysis* (September 1976).

James, J. A., "Portfolio Selection with an Imperfectly Competitive Asset Market", *Journal of Financial and Quantitative Analysis* (December 1976).

Jarrow, R., "Heterogeneous Expectations, Restrictions on Short Sales, and Equilibrium Asset Prices", *Journal of Finance* (December 1980).

Jensen, M. C. (ed.), *Studies in the Theory of Capital Markets*, New York: Praeger Publishers (1972).

Jensen, M. C., "Capital Markets: Theory and Evidence", *The Bell Journal of Economics and Management Science* (Autumn 1972).

Jobson, J. D. and Korkie, B. M., "Performance Hypothesis Testing with the Sharpe and Treynor Measures", *Journal of Finance* (September 1981).

Jobson, J. D., "A Multivariate Linear Regression Test for the Arbitrage Pricing Theory", *Journal of Finance* 37 (September 1982), 1037–42.

John, K., "Efficient Funds in a Financial Market with Options: A New Irrelevance Proposition", *Journal of Finance* (June 1981).

Jones-Lee, M. W., "Some Portfolio Adjustment Theorems for the Use of Non-Negativity Constraints on Security Holdings", *Journal of Finance* (June 1971).

Jones-Lee, M. W. and Poskitt, D. S., "An Existence Proof for Equilibrium in a Capital Asset Market", *Journal of Business Finance and Accounting* (Autumn 1975).

Johnson, J. M. and Baesel, J. B., "The Nature and Significance of Trend Betas", *The Journal of Portfolio Management* (Spring 1978).

King, B. F., "Market and Industry Factors in Stock Price Behavior", *Journal of Business* (January 1966).

Klemosky, R. C. and Martin, J. D., "The Adjustment of Beta Forecasts", *Journal of Finance* (September 1975).

Kon, S. L. and Jen, F. C., "Estimation of Time-Varying Systematic Risk and Performance for Mutual Fund Portfolios: An Application of Switching Regression", *Journal of Finance* (May 1978).

Kraus, A. and Litzenberger, R. H., "Market Equilibrium in a Multiperiod State Preference Model with Logarithmic Utility", *Journal of Finance* (December 1975).

Kraus, A. and Litzenberger, R. H., "Skewness Preference and the Valuation of Risk Assets", *Journal of Finance* (September 1976).

Kymn, K. O. and Page, W. P. "A Microeconomic and Geometric Interpretation of Beta in Models of Discrete Adaptive Expectations", *Review of Business and Economic Research* (Spring 1978).

Lakonishok, J., "Stock Market Returns Expectations: Some General Properties", *The Journal of Finance* (September 1980).

Landskroner, Y., "Nonmarketable Assets and the Determinants of the Market Price of Risk", *Review of Economics and Statistics* (November 1977).

Landskroner, Y., "Intertemporal Determination of the Market Price of Risk", *Journal of Finance* (December 1977).

Lee, C. F., "Investment Horizon and the Functional Form of the Capital Asset Pricing Model", *Review of Economics and Statistics* (August 1976).

Lee, C. F., "On the Relationship Between the Systematic Risk and the Investment Horizon", *Journal of Financial and Quantitative Analysis* (December 1976).

Lee, C. F., "Performance Measure, Systematic Risk, and Errors-in-Variables Estimation Method", *Journal of Economics and Business* (Winter 1977).

Lee, C. F., and Jen, F. C., "Effects of Measurement Errors on Systematic Risk and Performance Measure of a Portfolio", *Journal of Financial and Quantitative Analysis* (June 1978).

Levhari, D. and Levy, H., "The Capital Asset Pricing Model and the Investment Horizon", *Review of Economics and Statistics* (February 1977).

Levy, H., "The Capital Asset Pricing Model: Theory and Empiricism", *The Economic Journal* (March 1983).

Levy, H., "The Demand for Assets Under Conditions of Risk", *Journal of Finance* (March 1973).

Levy, H., "Equilibrium in an Imperfect Market. A Constraint on the Number of Securities", *American Economic Review* (September 1978).

Levy, H., "The CAPM and Beta in an Imperfect Market", *The Journal of Portfolio Management* (Winter 1980).

Levy, H. and Markowitz, H., "Approximating Expected Utility by a Function of Mean and Variance", *American Economic Review* (June 1979).

Lewellen, W. G., Lease, R. C. and Schlarbaum, G. G., "Portfolio Design and Portfolio Performance: The Individual Investor", *Journal of Economics and Business* (Spring/Summer 1980).

Leroy, S. F., "Expectations Models of Asset Prices: A Survey of Theory", *Journal of Finance* (March 1982).

Lin, W. T. and Jen, F. C., "Consumption, Investment, Market Price of Risk, and the Risk-Free Rate", *Journal of Financial and Quantitative Analysis* (December 1980).

Lindahl-Stevens, "Some Popular Uses and Abuses of Beta", *The Journal of Portfolio Management* (Winter 1978).

Lindenberg, E., "Capital Market Equilibrium with Price Affecting Institutional Investors", in Elton and Gruber. *Portfolio Theory 25 Years Later*, Amsterdam: North Holland (1979).

Lindenberg, E., "Imperfect Competition Among Investors in Security Markets", Ph.D. Dissertation, New York University (1976).

Lintner, J., "The Valuation of Risk Assets and the Selection of Risky Investments in Stock Portfolios and Capital Budgets", *Review of Economics and Statistics* (February 1965).

Lintner, J., "Security Prices, Risk and Maximal Gains from Diversification", *Journal of Finance* (December 1965).

Lintner, J., "The Aggregation of Investors' Diverse Judgments and Preferences in Purely Competitive Security Markets", *Journal of Financial and Quantitative Analysis* (December 1960).

Lintner, J., "The Market Price of Risk, Size of Market and Investor's Risk Aversion", *Review of Economics and Statistics* (February 1970).

Lintner, J., "Security Prices and Risk: The Theory of Comparative Analysis of AT&T and Leading Industrials", Conf. on Economics of Regulated Utilities, Chicago (June 1965).

Litzenberger, R. H., "Equilibrium in the Equity Market Under Uncertainty", *Journal of Finance* (September 1969).

Litzenberger, R. H. and Budd, A. P., "Corporate Investment Criteria and the Valuation of Risk Assets", *Journal of Financial and Quantitative Analysis* (December 1970).

Litzenberger, R. H. and Joy, O. M., "Target Rates of Return and Corporate Asset and Liability Structure Under Uncertainty", *Journal of Financial and Quantitative Analysis* (March 1971).

Litzenberger, R. H. and Ramaswamy, K., "Dividends, Short Selling Restrictions, Tax-Induced Investor Clienteles and Market Equilibrium", *Journal of Finance* (May 1980).

Livnat, J., "Generalization of the API Methodology as a Way of Measuring the Association Between Income and Stock Price", *Journal of Accounting Research* (Autumn 1981).

Long, J., "Stock Prices, Inflation, and the Term Structure of Interest Rates", *Journal of Financial Economics* (July 1974).

Lorie, J. H., "Some Comments on Recent Quantitative and Formal Research on the Stock Market", *Journal of Business* (January 1966).

Mayers, D., "Nonmarketable Assets, Market Segmentation and the Level of Asset Prices", *Journal of Financial and Quantitative Analysis* (March 1976).

Mayers, D., "Nonmarketable Assets and the Determination of Capital Asset Prices in the Absence of a Riskless Asset", *Journal of Business* (April 1973).

McClay, M., "The Penalties of Incurring Unsystematic Risk", *Journal of Portfolio Management* (Spring 1978).

Mayshar, J., "Transaction Costs and the Pricing of Assets", *Journal of Finance* (June 1981).

Merton, R., "Lifetime Portfolio Selection Under Uncertainty: The Continuous Time Case", *Review of Economics and Statistics* (August 1969).

Merton, R., "Optimum Consumption and Portfolio Rules in a Continuous-Time Model", *Journal of Economic Theory* (December 1971).

Merton, R. C., "Theory of Finance from the Perspective of Continuous Time", *Journal of Financial and Quantitative Analysis* (November 1975).

Miller, M. and Scholes, M., "Rate of Return in Relation to Risk: A Reexamination of Some Recent Findings", in Jensen, M. C., ed., *Studies in the Theory of Finance*, New York (1972).

Milne, F. and Smith, C., Jr., "Capital Asset Pricing with Proportional Transaction Costs", *Journal of Financial and Quantitative Analysis* (June 1980).

Modigliani, F. and Pogue, G. A., "An Introduction to Risk and Return", *Financial Analyst's Journal* (March/April 1974).

Modigliani, F. and Pogue, G. A., "An Introduction to Risk and Return: Part II", *Financial Analyst's Journal* (May/June 1974).

Moore, B. J., "An Introduction to the Theory of Finance: Assetholder Behavior Under Uncertainty", New York: The Free Press (1968).

Mossin, J., "Equilibrium in a Capital Asset Market", *Econometrica* (October 1966).

Mossin, J., "Optimal Multiperiod Portfolio Policies", *Journal of Business* (April 1968).

Mullins, D. W., Jr., "Does the Capital Asset Pricing Model Work?" *Harvard Business Review* (January/February 1982).

Myers, S. C. and Turnbull, S. M., "Capital Budgeting and the Capital Asset Pricing Model: Good News and Bad News", *Journal of Finance* (May 1977).

Nielson, N. C., "The Investment Decision of the Firm Under Uncertainty and the Allocative Efficiency of Capital Markets", *Journal of Finance* (May 1976).

Ohlson, J. A., "Portfolio Selection in a Log-Stable Market", *Journal of Financial and Quantitative Analysis* (June 1975).

Ohlson, J. A., "Equilibrium in Stable Markets", *Journal of Political Economy* (August 1977).

Ohlson, J. A. and Rosenberg, B., "Systematic Risk of the CRSP Equal-Weighted Common Stock Index: A History Estimated by Stochastic-Parameter Regression", *Journal of Business* (January 1982).

Ohlson, J. A. and Ziemba, W. T., "Portfolio Selection in a Lognormal Market When the Investor Has a Power Utility Function", *Journal of Financial and Quantitative Analysis* (March 1976).

Officer, R. R., "Seasonality in Australian Capital Markets: Market Efficiency and Empirical Issues", *Journal of Financial Economics* (March 1975).

Owen, J. and Rabinowitz, R., "The Cost of Information and Equilibrium in the Capital Asset Market", *Journal of Financial and Quantitative Analysis* (September 1980).

Peles, Y., "A Note on Risk and the Theory of Asset Value", *Journal of Financial and Quantitative Analysis* (January 1971).

Perrakis, S., "Capital Budgeting and Timing Uncertainty Within the Capital Asset Pricing Model", *Financial Management* (Autumn 1979).

Pettit, R. R. and Westerfield, R., "A Model of Capital Asset Risk", *Journal of Financial and Quantitative Analysis* (March 1972).

Pogue, G. A., "An Extension of the Markowitz Portfolio Selection Model to Include Variable Transactions' Costs, Short Sales, Leverage Policies and Taxes", *Journal of Finance* (December 1970).

Pye, G., "Portfolio Selection and Security Prices", *Review of Economics and Statistics* (February 1967).

Pye, G., "Lifetime Portfolio Selection in Continuous Time for a Multiplicative Class of Utility Functions", *American Economic Review* (December 1973).

Rabinowitz, R. and Owen, J., "Non-Homogeneous Expectations and Information in the Capital Asset Market", *Journal of Finance* (May 1978).

Rao, R. K. S., "The Impact of Yield Changes on the Systematic Risk of Bonds", *Journal of Financial and Quantitative Analysis* (March 1982).

Reingaum, M. R., "The Arbitrage Pricing Theory: Some Empirical Results", *Journal of Finance* (May 1981).

Reingaum, M. R., "A New Empirical Perspective on the CAPM", *Journal of Financial and Quantitative Analysis* (November 1981).

Renwick, F. B., "Economic Growth and Distributions of Change in Stock Market Prices", *Industrial Management Review* (Spring 1968).

Renwick, F. B., "Theory of Investment Behavior and Empirical Analysis of Stock Market Price Relatives", *Management Science* (September 1968).

Rendleman, R. J., Jr., "Ranking Errors in CAPM Capital Budgeting Applications", *Financial Management* (Winter 1978).

Roberts, G. S., "Endogens Endowments and Capital Asset Prices", *Journal of Finance* (March 1975).

Robichek, A. A. and Cohn, R. A., "The Economic Determinants of Systematic Risk", *Journal of Finance* (May 1974).

Roenfeldt, R. L., Griepentrof, G. L. and Pflaum, C. C., "Further Evidence on the Stationarity of Beta Coefficients", *Journal of Financial and Quantitative Analysis* (March 1978).

Roll, R., "Ambiguity When Performance is Measured by the Securities Market Line", *Journal of Finance* (September 1978).

Roll, R., "A Critique of the Asset Pricing Theory's Tests: Part I: On Past and Potential Testability of the Theory", *Journal of Financial Economics* (March 1977).

Roll, R. and Ross, S. A., "An Empirical Investigation of the Arbitrage Pricing Theory", *Journal of Finance* (December 1980).

Ross, S. A., "The Arbitrage Theory of Capital Asset Pricing", *Econometrica* (1976).

Ross, S. A., "The Capital Asset Pricing Model (CAPM), Short-Sale Restrictions and Related Issues", *Journal of Finance* (March 1977).

Ross, S. A., "The Current Status of the Capital Asset Pricing Model (CAPM)", *Journal of Finance* (June 1978).

Ross, S. A., "A Simple Approach to the Valuation of Risky Streams", *Journal of Business* (July 1978).

Rubinstein, M. E., "An Aggregation Theorem for Securities Market", *Journal of Financial Economics* (September 1974).

Rubinstein, M. E., "A Mean-Variance Synthesis of Corporate Financial Theory", *Journal of Finance* (March 1973).

Rubinstein, M. E., "Mutual Fund Separation in Financial Theory—The Separating Distributions", *Journal of Economic Theory* (April 1978).

Samuelson, P. A. and Merton, R. C., "Generalized Mean–Variance Tradeoffs for Best Perturbation Corrections to Approximate Portfolio Decisions", *Journal of Finance* (March 1974).

Sandmo, A., "Capital Risk, Consumption and Portfolio Choice", *Econometrica* (October 1969).

Scholes, M. and Williams, J., "Estimating Betas from Nonsynchronous Data", *Journal of Financial Economics* (December 1977).

Scott, E. and Brown, S., "Biased Estimators and Unstable Betas", *Journal of Finance* (March 1980).

Sharpe, W. F., "Capital Asset Prices: A Theory of Market Equilibrium", *Journal of Finance* (September 1964).

Sharpe, W. F., "A Simplified Model of Portfolio Analysis", *Management Science* (January 1963).

Sharpe, W. F., *Portfolio Theory and Capital Markets*, New York: McGraw-Hill (1970).

Sharpe, W. F., "Bonds Versus Stocks: Capital Market Theory", *Financial Analyst's Journal* (November/December 1973).

Siegel, J. J. and Warner, J. B., "Indexation, The Risk-Free Asset, and Capital Market Equilibrium", *Journal of Finance* (September 1977).

Smith, K. V., "The Effect of Intervaling on Estimating Parameters of the Capital Asset Pricing Model", *Journal of Financial and Quantitative Analysis* (June 1978).

Stambaugh, R. F., "On the Exclusion of Assets from Tests of the Two-Parameter Model: A Sensitivity Analysis", Unpublished Manuscript, The Wharton School, University of Pennsylvania (1981).

Stapleton, R. C., "Portfolio Analysis, Stock Valuation and Capital Budgeting Decision Rules for Risky Projects", *Journal of Finance* (March 1971).

Stapleton, R. C. and Subrahmanyam, M. G., "Market Imperfections, Capital Market Equilibrium and Corporation Finance", *Journal of Finance* (May 1977).

Stapleton, R. C. and Subrahmanyam, M. G., "Marketability of Assets and the Price of Risk", *Journal of Financial and Quantitative Analysis* (March 1979).

Stone, B. K., "Systematic Interest-Rate Risk in a Two-Index Model of Returns", *Journal of Quantitative Analysis* (November 1974).

Theobald, M., "An Analysis of the Market Model and Beta Factors Using U.K. Equity Share Data", *Journal of Business Finance and Accounting* (Spring 1980).

Theobald, M., "Beta Stationarity and Estimation Period: Some Analytical Results", *Journal of Financial and Quantitative Analysis* (December 1981).

Tobin, J., "Liquidity Preference as Behavior Towards Risk", *Review of Economic Studies* (February 1958).

Trauring, M., "A Capital Asset Pricing Model with Investors' Taxes and Three Categories of Investment Income", *Journal of Financial and Quantitative Analysis* (September 1979).

Treynor, J. L., "Toward a Theory of Market Value of Risky Assets", Unpublished Manuscript.

Trzcinka, C., "On Revising Ex-ante Estimates of Portfolio Risk", *Engineering Economics* (Summer 1981).

Turnbull, S. M., "Value and Systematic Risk", *Journal of Finance* (September 1977).

Umstead, D. A. and Bergstrom, G. L., "Dynamic Estimation of Portfolio Betas", *Journal of Financial and Quantitative Analysis* (September 1979).

Vandell, F. and Stevens, J. L., "Personal Taxes and Equity Security Pricing", *Financial Management* (Spring 1982).

Weston, J. F., "Investment Decisions Using the Capital Asset Pricing Model", *Financial Management* (Spring 1973).

Williams, J. T., "Capital Asset Prices with Heterogeneous Beliefs", *Journal of Financial Economics* (November 1977).

Weinstein, M., "The Systematic Risk of Corporate Bonds", *Journal of Financial and Quantitative Analysis* (September 1981).

# 15

# Performance Measures

If the CAPM actually holds while the market is in equilibrium and is expected to remain permanently in equilibrium, no investor can achieve an abnormal return in the securities market, in excess of the mean return prescribed by the CAPM risk–return relationship. Each stock and each portfolio yields an identical rate of return adjusted for risk. Under such circumstances, there is very little left for the investment analysts to do; they do not possess any special knowledge which may help earn an abnormal return.

This is not the case in real life, however. The stock market is seldom in equilibrium, and once it reaches equilibrium, deviation from equilibrium is likely to occur almost instantaneously. In this realistic situation, some stocks (or some portfolios) may yield an excess return. Hence it is appropriate to employ some indexes which measure the performance of a given stock or a given portfolio relative to the equilibrium risk–return relationship.

In this chapter we compare some performance indexes and illustrate how they are used in practice. We demonstrate in particular the usefulness of such indexes for the evaluation of mutual funds' management. Finally, we examine the prediction power of the performance indexes, projecting from past to future performance.

## 15.1    Mutual Funds' Objectives

Mutual funds, or open-end investment companies as they are often called, pool the resources of many individuals and invest them in a diversified portfolio of securities. Unlike other financial intermediaries such as insurance companies and pension funds, which invest in securities as a means to meet assumed liabilities or risks, investing as such is the primary function of mutual funds. They provide their participating members with an investment experience in the sense that the participant's income is directly determined by the changes in capital values of the portfolio of securities held by the fund.[1]

[1] For an excellent analysis of mutual funds' activities, see Investment Company Institute, *Management of Investment Companies*, Englewood Cliffs, N.J.: Prentice-Hall, 1963. Comprehensive annual surveys are available in Arthur Wiesenberger & Co., *Investment Companies*, annual editions.

Although differences exist among the individual funds, an open-end investment company has two distinguishing characteristics:

(a) Participating shares in the mutual funds are continuously offered to the public at a price which reflects the value of the underlying assets at the time of sale. Hence the term *open-end.*

(b) The fund is obligated to redeem or repurchase all shares presented at a price based on the net asset value per share at the time of redemption.

Mutual funds provide a convenient and very popular investment medium, especially for the small investor. During the past two decades, the rate of growth of US mutual funds' assets outstripped that of insurance companies, saving deposits, and US Government Saving Bonds. There are hundreds of mutual funds, which indicates that investors show a great interest in these investment instruments.

Mutual funds often have varying objectives, and as a result the funds' investment policies also tend to differ. Funds which emphasize capital gains attempt to invest mainly in growth stocks, while funds which emphasize current income tend to build more balanced portfolios. But despite these differences, some investment objectives and policies are common to all (or almost all) the funds. For example, all mutual funds typically attempt:

(a) to increase returns through professional investment analysis, and by taking full advantage of scale economies in the management of the portfolio;

(b) to decrease investment risk by diversifying the portfolio.

When deciding between the alternatives of investing in mutual fund shares or directly in common stocks, investors must first weigh the degree to which the funds have succeeded in achieving these two common objectives against the expenses (usually in the form of a loading charge) incurred in providing the professional management.

Professional investment management, scale economies, and management expenses are all factors which are reflected in the rate of return a fund earns on its investments. If a fund's mean rate of return is higher than the rate of return earned by an investor who randomly diversifies his stock market investments, one might conclude that the mutual fund has succeeded in achieving the first of its main objectives, that is, increasing the average rate of return to investors. But average rate of return is not the sole objective. To see this, consider two funds managed by two distinct professional management teams and our aim is to evaluate the success of the respective fund managements. As a first step, we collect data regarding the rates of return achieved by the two mutual funds (Table 15.1).

During the five-year period studied (1979–1983), which fund management performed better?

One is tempted to measure the performance in terms of the accumulated wealth per $100 initially invested in each mutual fund. In fund $A$, the terminal value of the investment is:

$$\$100(1.15)(1.10)(1.20)(1.15)(1.10) = \$192.027$$

**Table 15.1**
**Annual Rates of Return of Two Funds (in %)**

| Year | Mutual Fund A | Mutual Fund B |
|------|---------------|---------------|
| 1979 | 15 | 20 |
| 1980 | 10 | −30 |
| 1981 | 20 | 90 |
| 1982 | 15 | 40 |
| 1983 | 10 | −10 |
| Mean Return | 14% | 22% |

and in fund $B$:

$$\$100(1.20)(0.70)(1.90)(1.40)(0.90) = \$201.096$$

This implies an annual growth rate of 13.9% for fund $A$ and 15.0% for fund $B$ (calculated as the geometric mean of terminal and initial wealth). Alternatively, we can examine the arithmetic mean annual rate of return of the two funds. It is 22% for fund $B$ and only 14% for fund $A$.

Thus looking either at the arithmetic mean rate of return or at the growth rate it seems that the management of fund $B$ outperformed the management of fund $A$. But this is true only if one considers the whole period 1979–1983 as a single unit, i.e., only if one assumes that the resources were invested for the duration of five whole years. However, suppose that the typical investor invests in a mutual fund for one year only. Can we assert that fund $B$ outperforms fund $A$ in such a case? The answer is not as clear-cut as before. For investors who invested in mutual funds for one-year periods in 1979, 1981, and 1982, fund $B$ actually yielded better results. However, the opposite holds for investors who invested for one-year periods in 1980 and 1983.

The main conclusion which can be drawn from this example is that investment performance should be measured in two dimensions: one for measuring the investment's mean profitability and the other which measures the risk involved. In our specific example, the risk dimension reflects the possible occurrence of "bad" years, like the years 1980 and 1983 for investors in fund $B$.

Thus, the second common objective of mutual funds, decreasing risk, is not reflected in the average rate of return earned by mutual fund investors, but rather in the *variability* of the annual rates of return. Fluctuations of the rate of return can be measured by the standard deviation of the rate of return or by the fund's beta; the smaller the fluctuations, the more stable the series of returns, and consequently the lower the risk associated with such investment. Thus, to evaluate the investment performance of mutual funds, we require two variables: the mean rate of return and the risk index associated with these returns.

To evaluate a particular mutual fund's performance, we shall compare the fund's average rate of return and its risk with the average rate of return and the risk of investments randomly chosen from the stock market, that is, with an *unmanaged* portfolio.

The accepted way to carry out such an evaluation is to compare the mutual fund's average return and risk with the average return and risk of a general index such as Dow-Jones or Standard & Poor's. Using the Standard & Poor's Index of Common Stocks as a proxy for an unmanaged portfolio, we can compute a time series of the annual rates of return (dividends plus the change in the index) for any given period. This series of annual rates of return then can be used to estimate the average rate of return $\bar{R}_m$ and the risk index (standard deviation) $\sigma_m$ for the unmanaged portfolio. These two parameters represent the point S&P in Figure 15.1.

By passing vertical and horizontal dashed lines through point S&P, Figure 15.1 has been divided into four zones marked I, II, III, and IV. Now if we calculate the average rate of return and variability for an individual mutual fund, that fund's performance can be represented by a point in one of these four zones. Should a fund's average return and variability be given by a point in zone I, one can safely conclude that this particular mutual fund outperformed an unmanaged portfolio, since all points in zone I represent higher returns and lower variability than the Standard & Poor's benchmark. On the other hand, if a fund has a combination of mean return and variability represented by a point in zone III, the unmanaged portfolio is clearly superior since point S&P has a higher return and lower risk than all points in zone III. The case is much less clear-cut, however, with respect to funds whose risk–return characteristics place them in either of zones II or IV: a point in zone II represents a higher return, but also a higher risk, than an unmanaged portfolio, while points in zone IV have a lower risk, but also a lower return, than the randomly chosen portfolio.

Unfortunately, most mutual funds have risk–return combinations represented by points in zones II or IV, and consequently the analysis must be further refined if conclusions are to be reached regarding the funds' relative performance. We now turn to an analysis of appropriate fund performance meaures.

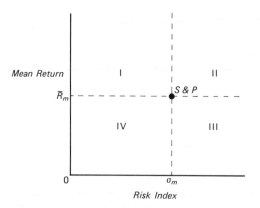

**Figure 15.1**

## 15.2 Alternative Measures of Investment Performance

Basing their research on the Sharpe–Lintner security market model or the CAPM (see Chapter 11), several researchers have suggested alternative measures of portfolio performance. Although these measures differ from one another, they are closely related,[2] and in fact they represent a common attempt to reduce the two-parameter risk–return dimensions of investment performance to a single measure which incorporates considerations of return with an adjustment for risk. While all agree that the profitability should be measured by the average rate of return, there is no complete agreement regarding the risk index.

### 15.2.1 Total Variance vs. Beta as a Risk Index

As we have seen in Chapter 11, the total variance of a security (or its standard deviation) has nothing to do with measuring risk, at least not for a security included in the context of a well-diversified portfolio. The relevant risk in this case is the security's beta, or the slope of the characteristic line of the security under consideration. Suppose that we plan to compare the performance of various mutual funds. Using beta as the risk index, we explicitly or implicitly assume that in addition to the mutual fund under consideration, investors also diversify their holdings in many other securities, so that overall each investor holds the market portfolio. This assumption is true also for any individual stock or security. For example, if beta is used to evaluate the performance of IBM stock, this implies the assumption that, in addition to IBM stock, investors also hold all the other stocks included in the market portfolio. To be more specific, recall that a security's beta is defined as (see Chapter 11),

$$\beta_i = Cov(R_i, R_m)/\sigma_m^2$$

where $R_i$ and $R_m$ are the rates of return on security $i$ and on the market portfolio respectively; $\sigma_m^2$ is the variance of the market portfolio. Since $\sigma_m^2$ is common to all the stocks, the covariance $Cov(R_i, R_m)$ is the only risk factor which distinguishes the riskiness of one security from another. However, $Cov(R_i, R_m)$ measures the comovements of the rates of return of security $i$ with the market portfolio $m$. This comovement constitutes an appropriate risk index only if investors actually hold the market portfolio

---

[2] On the formal relationship of the performance measures formulated by Jensen, Sharpe, and Treynor see Irwin Friend and Marshall Blume, "Measurement of Portfolio Performance Under Uncertainty", *American Economic Review* (Sept. 1970).

All three performance indicators were first applied to the problem of evaluating the investment performance of mutual funds. See W. F. Sharpe, "Mutual Fund Performance", *Journal of Business* (Jan. 1966); J. Treynor, "How to Rate Management Investment Funds", *Harvard Business Review* (Jan.–Feb. 1965); and M. C. Jensen, "The Performance of Mutual Funds in the Period 1945–1964", *Journal of Finance* (May 1968).

$m$. If some investors hold a different portfolio $k$, then for this group of investors the relevant risk index is $Cov(R_i, R_k)/\sigma_k^2$, where $R_k$ and $\sigma_k^2$ are the rates of return and the variance of portfolio $k$ (distinct from the market portfolio $m$).

To sum up, beta is the appropriate risk index of an individual security or of a portfolio (a mutual fund) only within the framework of the Capital Asset Pricing Model, which asserts that *all investors hold the market portfolio m.*

Let us turn now to the other extreme, when *investors hold only one security* in their portfolio. To be more specific, assume that a group of investors hold only AT&T stock. For these investors the beta of AT&T measured against the market portfolio (or against any other portfolio) is completely irrelevant as a risk index, since these investors simply do not hold such a highly diversified portfolio. The appropriate risk measure in this extreme case is the variability of the rates of return on AT&T stock, normally measured by the stock's "own" total risk (variance) or standard deviation.

The security's "own" variability is particularly appropriate as the risk index for mutual funds. The rationale for this assertion is that most investors who buy mutual fund shares simply leave it to the fund's management to select for them the best diversification strategy. Thus, these investors hold only a single security—the mutual fund shares, a case when the variability of rates of return is precisely the appropriate risk index.

Consider now a more realistic case when some investors hold only one stock in their portfolio (say, AT&T), another group of investors hold several securities (a small number) in addition to AT&T stock, and the third group hold the entire market portfolio. In this case, there is no single index which properly measures the risk of AT&T stock for all investors. The proper risk measure is AT&T's variance $\sigma_{ATT}^2$ for the non-diversifiers, $\beta_{ATT}$ for the market-portfolio holders, and some complicated combination of $\sigma_{ATT}^2$ and $\beta_{ATT}$ for the investors holding a diversified portfolio in which the diversification falls short of that required by the CAPM. Thus, the appropriate risk index depends on the assumed degree of diversification. We shall demonstrate in this chapter the performance indexes based on the alternative extreme assumptions that investors hold either a single stock or the entire market portfolio.

Before we turn to the analysis of various mutual funds' performance measures, let us again summarize the aims of this analysis:

(a) Mutual fund managers claim that they have professional knowledge and hence their fund will perform better than a randomly selected "unmanaged" portfolio. If this claim is valid, investors may be willing to allow the fund managers to manage their investments, and will even pay a significant commission for this service. If the claim is false, one would be better off by choosing stocks at random; in this case, even investors who do not possess any knowledge of the stock market should avoid mutual fund shares.

(b) Suppose that mutual funds actually outperform the unmanaged portfolio and it is worthwhile to buy their shares. In this case, we need an index to rank all these funds according to their performance. If past performance indeed predicts future performance, this ranking facilitates the investor's choice among different funds.

(c)   The third aim of performance measurement is for internal needs. To be more specific, suppose that the mutual fund management would like to evaluate the investment performance of their professional teams. Then, every few months or few years, they can analyze their investment results in comparison to other funds as well as in comparison to unmanaged portfolios. This evaluation may be used for fixing compensation and even for such extreme decisions as replacing the professional team should they fail to compete with other teams.

Note that the performance indexes which implicitly assume a single-asset portfolio are appropriate for mutual funds, as investors mostly hold the fund shares without attempting any further diversification on their own. Also most empirical studies use mutual funds data to test if the funds' management is doing better than an unmanaged portfolio.

In what follows we shall focus mainly on three traditional measures of portfolio performance based on the CAPM framework: (a) Sharpe's reward-to-variability ratio, (b) Treynor's reward-to-volatility ratio, and (c) Jensen's performance index. A conceptually different performance measure based on the Stochastic Dominance approach is also considered.

### 15.2.2   Sharpe's Performance Index $(PI_S)$

As we saw in Section 12.4.2, the capital market line is given by

$$ER_p = r + \frac{ER_m - r}{\sigma_m}\sigma_p$$

where

$ER_p$, $\sigma_p$ are respectively the expected rate of return and the standard deviation of the rates of return of an *efficient* portfolio $p$,

$r$ is the risk-free interest rate,

$ER_m$, $\sigma_m$ are the expected rate of return and the standard deviation of the market portfolio $m$.

The capital market line is created by mixing the market portfolio $m$ with the riskless asset $r$. A similar straight line can be created by mixing *any* risky asset (e.g., a mutual fund) with the risk-free asset. Denote by $ER_i$, $\sigma_i$ the expected rate of return and the standard deviation of the rates of return on some mutual fund to obtain [see Chapter 11, equation (11.6)]

$$Ey = r + \frac{ER_i - r}{\sigma_i}\sigma_y$$

where $(Ey, \sigma_y)$ are all the attainable combinations of mean rate of return and standard deviation obtained by various mixes of the riskless asset $r$ and the risky asset $R_i$. Thus, the steeper the slope $(ER_i - r)/\sigma_i$, the higher is the investor's expected utility, since the steeper line will be tangent to a higher indifference curve. The investment performance index suggested by Sharpe ($PI_S$) is correspondingly given by

$$PI_S = \frac{ER_i - r}{\sigma_i}$$

where the subscript $S$ stands for "Sharpe". This performance index measures the risky asset's excess return $ER_i - r$ (in excess of the riskless rate $r$) per unit of risk, as represented by the risky asset's standard deviation.

For empirical work, we plug in the estimates of these parameters: the actual observed average rate of return, the actual interest rate, and the standard deviation of the actual returns. Sharpe called this ratio "reward-to-variability" (R/V) and suggested its use as an indicator of past performance of portfolios in general and of mutual funds in particular.[3] Figure 15.2 illustrates the application of the performance index $PI_S$. An investment in *riskless* bonds is represented by point $r$ in Figure 15.2; a portfolio comprising a cross-section of randomly chosen stocks is again represented by point $S\&P$. The straight line connecting point $r$ and point $S\&P$ represents the set of all attainable combinations of bonds with an unmanaged equity portfolio. For example, point $B$ on this line, which lies halfway between point $r$ and point $S\&P$, represents the risk–return characteristics of a portfolio equally divided between riskless bonds and equities. Points on the continuation of the line from $S\&P$ to $A$ represent levered portfolios, that is, attainable risk–return combinations for the investor in an unmanaged portfolio who borrows money at the riskless rate $r$.

Let us now assume that we wish to compare the performance of mutual funds, or portfolios, represented by points such as $D$ and $E$ in Figure 15.2, with the unmanaged

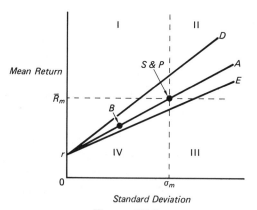

**Figure 15.2**

[3] Arditti, who extends Sharpe's reward-to-variability index, suggests a performance index which also takes into account the portfolio skewness. For more details see F. D. Arditti, "Another Look at Mutual Fund Performance", *Journal of Financial and Quantitative Analysis* (June 1971).

portfolio. Clearly, if the line passing from $r$ through point $D$, which represents all attainable combinations of that mutual fund's shares with riskless bonds, lies *above* the line $rA$, we can conclude that the performance of mutual fund $D$ is superior to that of the unmanaged portfolio, since all points on the line $rD$ represent a higher return for a given risk when compared with the line $rA$. On the other hand, in cases such as $E$, where the line $rE$ lies below $rA$, we can conclude that an investment in the unmanaged portfolio is preferable to an investment in mutual fund $E$. Thus the slope $(ER_i - r)/\sigma_i$ of the line connecting the mutual fund (portfolio) $(ER_i, \sigma_i)$ with the riskless rate $r$, which by definition is the R/V ratio representing $PI_S$, provides a convenient measure of the performance of mutual funds (portfolios). Steeper slopes, that is, higher R/V ratios, indicate better investment performance, since investors can reach higher levels of expected utility as the slope of the transformation line connecting the riskless rate and the point representing the risk–return characteristics of the mutual fund becomes steeper. In a reasonably efficient market, we expect all highly diversified portfolios (and mutual funds comprise an excellent proxy for such portfolios) to cluster in a random fashion along the estimated market line, in our example the line connecting $r$ and the point $S\&P$ in Figure 15.2. A mutual fund, or portfolio, which deviates significantly below the market line indicates a case of inadequate risk–return performance; a rational mean–variance investor will not consciously choose such a fund or portfolio since he can improve his position by investing in a randomly diversified portfolio, such as the one represented by point $S\&P$ of Figure 15.2.

Thus, *ex-post*, the higher the R/V ratio, the more successful the fund's management.

### 15.2.3   Stochastic Dominance (SD) Approach

In constructing Sharpe's performance index, we make the following assumptions:

(a)   investors hold one risky security or one mutual fund;
(b)   investors are risk averters and the rates of return are normally distributed (this is the justification for using the MV framework).

One can relax assumption (b) by extending the analysis to investors who are not necessarily risk averters and allowing any arbitrary distribution of rates of return. In this general case, simply take the annual rates of return on two mutual funds and draw their cumulative distributions, which we denote by $F$ and $G$. If $F(R) \leqslant G(R)$ for all rates of return $R$, i.e., the cumulative distribution of the rates of return on fund $F$ lies entirely to the right of that for fund $G$, we can assert that mutual fund $F$ outperforms mutual fund $G$ regardless of the investor's individual preferences (this follows from the FSD rule—see Section 6.2). If neither $F(R) \leqslant G(R)$ nor $F(R) \geqslant G(R)$ for all values of $R$, i.e., if the two cumulative distributions cross, we can assert that neither fund $F$ outperforms fund $G$ nor fund $G$ outperforms fund $F$ for all investors. In this indecisive case, we may add the assumption of risk aversion (without assuming normal distributions!) and assert (see SSD rule—Section 6.3) that fund $F$ outperforms fund $G$ if and only if [4]

$$\int_{-\infty}^{R} [G(t) - F(t)]\,dt \geqslant 0 \qquad \text{for all values of } R$$

i.e., if the cumulative area between the two distributions remains always positive.

Figure 15.3 illustrates the application of SD rules to evaluate fund performance. In panel (a), the (empirical) cumulative distribution of $F$ is entirely to the right of the

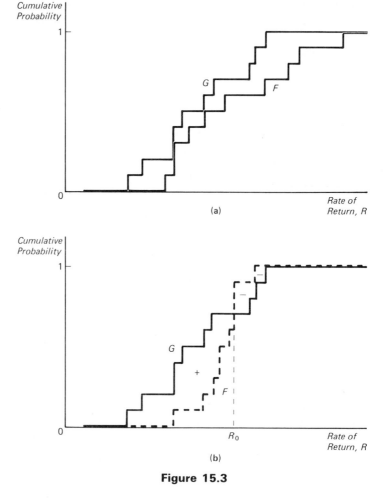

**Figure 15.3**

[4] If no superior performance can be established for one of the funds by SSD, we may also add the assumption of decreasing absolute risk aversion and try to identify the fund with superior performance by the TSD rule (for more details see Chapter 6, Section 6.4).

cumulative distribution of $G$, so that the performance of fund $F$ is superior to that of fund $G$ for *all* investors (both risk averters and risk lovers) by FSD rule. In panel (b), the two empirical cumulative distributions intersect at rate of return $R_0$, so that for lower rates of return $F(R) \leqslant G(R)$, while for higher rates of return the inequality is reversed, $F(R) \geqslant G(R)$. The FSD rule does not apply in this case and no simple judgment can be made for all investors. For *risk averters*, however, fund $F$ outperforms fund $G$, since the cumulative area under the two curves always remains positive for all rates of returns (as we move to the right increasing the value of $R$).

### 15.2.4  Treynor's Performance Index ($PI_T$)

The reward-to-volatility ratio suggested by Treynor as a performance index (which we denote by $PI_T$) is given by:

$$PI_T = \frac{ER_i - r}{\beta_i}$$

This measure is similar to Sharpe's performance index $PI_S$ in the sense that it measures the premium $ER_i - r$ per unit of risk. It differs from Sharpe's index, however, in its choice of the risk index. While Sharpe uses the risky asset's standard deviation $\sigma_i$ as the risk index, Treynor uses its beta, $\beta_i$. Thus, $PI_T$ measures the success of a portfolio (a mutual fund) or a single risky security under the assumption that investors hold many other assets in addition to the asset under consideration. We know that in the context of such a well-diversified portfolio the security's beta is indeed the appropriate risk index (see Section 15.2.1 above).

The derivation of $PI_T$ from the CAPM formula is straightforward. In equilibrium we have the CAPM risk–return relationship:

$$ER_i = r + (ER_m - r)\beta_i$$

where $ER_i$ is the expected rate of return on risky asset (or portfolio) $i$, and $\beta_i$ is its risk measure. Subtracting $r$ from both sides and dividing by $\beta_i$, we obtain:

$$PI_T = \frac{ER_i - r}{\beta_i} = ER_m - r$$

Thus, in equilibrium, we expect the ratio of the excess mean rate of return $ER_i - r$ to the security's risk $\beta_i$ to be constant across all risky assets and equal to the excess mean rate of return on the market portfolio, $ER_m - r$.

With empirical data, deviations from constancy may be observed. Any positive deviation of a mutual fund's average excess rate of return from $ER_m - r$ is considered "success" and any negative deviation from this value is considered "failure". To substantiate this claim, first write the CAPM risk–return relationship substituting the respective estimates for the unknown true parameters. To be more specific, substitute $\bar{R}_i$ for $ER_i$, $\bar{R}_m$ for $ER_m$, and $\hat{\beta}_i$ for $\beta_i$,[5] to obtain,

$$\bar{R}_i = r + (\bar{R}_m - r)\hat{\beta}_i$$

Subtract $r$ from both sides and divide by $\hat{\beta}_i$ to obtain Treynor's performance index,

$$PI_T = \frac{\bar{R}_i - r}{\hat{\beta}_i} = (\bar{R}_m - r)$$

If all risky securities and portfolios have constant reward-to-volatility ratios, equal to $\bar{R}_m - r$, then the risk-adjusted mean rate of return on each portfolio is as predicted by the CAPM. However, since deviations from equilibrium are possible, we may find in the empirical sample the following relationship,

$$PI_T = \frac{\bar{R}_i - r}{\hat{\beta}_i} = (\bar{R}_m - r) + \delta_i$$

where $\delta_i$ is a deviation from the predicted value (which may be either positive or negative). For example, we may find on the basis of empirical data for two mutual funds:

$$\text{fund } A \qquad PI_T^{(A)} = 0.15$$
$$\text{fund } B \qquad PI_T^{(B)} = 0.10$$

while $\bar{R}_m - r = 0.12$. In terms of Treynor's performance index, we can assert that the management of fund $A$ was successful in its investment strategy, while the management of fund $B$ failed. This is evident from the fact that the performance deviation of fund $A$ from the market portfolio, $\delta_A$, is positive (0.03), while the performance deviation of fund $B$, $\delta_B$, is negative (−0.02): fund $A$ outperformed the unmanaged market portfolio, while fund $B$ underperformed.

Since the mean return on the market portfolio (a risky asset) is greater than the riskless rate, the difference $\bar{R}_m - r$ is positive. The above discussion of $PI_T$ implicitly assumes that $\hat{\beta}_i > 0$ (i.e., the security $i$ has a positive risk measure). If $\hat{\beta}_i < 0$ (securities with negative beta estimates are a rarity, but do exist), then for the Treynor index to be meaningful we must have $\bar{R}_i - r < 0$ (the mean rate of return on security $i$ is *less* than the riskless rate—which is consistent with the CAPM prediction for negative beta). If because of temporary market imperfections or sampling errors, we obtain in the sample $\hat{\beta}_i < 0$ and yet $\bar{R}_i - r > 0$ (i.e., the security with negative beta has a *positive* excess return, contrary to the CAPM prediction), the security is obviously highly desirable,

---

[5] The estimate of the security's beta, $\beta_i$, can be denoted either by $\hat{\beta}_i$ or $b_i$. Which of the two symbols is employed is largely a question of accepted usage in different areas of portfolio analysis, and we accordingly use both symbols interchangeably.

and yet the Treynor index meaninglessly takes a negative value, putting it at the bottom of the performance ranking. Extreme caution thus should be exercised when attempting to apply the Treynor performance measure to negative-beta securities.

In order to demonstrate the Treynor measure graphically, we turn back to the definition of the characteristic line, which is the regression line of the time series of rates of return of the $i$th risky asset, $R_{i_t}$, on the market portfolio's rates of return, $R_{m_t}$. The slope of the regression line is the estimate of the $i$th security's beta, $\hat{\beta}_i$, and the vertical intercept is denoted by $\hat{\alpha}_i$,

$$R_{i_t} = \hat{\alpha}_i + \hat{\beta}_i R_{m_t} + e_{i_t}$$

$e_{i_t}$ is the error term or the deviation of the individual observation from the regression line.

Figure 15.4 presents the characteristic line of a hypothetical risky asset. Treynor's performance index is related to the horizontal distance $D$ of the characteristic line from the vertical axis at the riskless rate level $r$. The *smaller* this distance $D$, the *higher* the Treynor performance index $PI_T$. To show this, recall that the regression line passes through the point of the means $(\bar{R}_i, \bar{R}_m)$. Thus, the slope $\hat{\beta}_i$ of the line is given by (see Figure 15.4):

$$\hat{\beta}_i = \frac{\bar{R}_i - r}{\bar{R}_m - D}$$

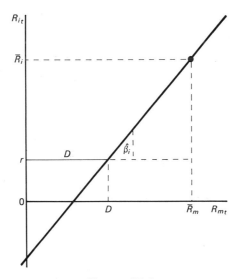

**Figure 15.4**

Multiplying both sides by $\bar{R}_m - D$ and dividing by $\hat{\beta}_i$, we obtain:

$$\frac{\bar{R}_i - r}{\hat{\beta}_i} = \bar{R}_m - D$$

The left-hand side is the Treynor performance index, $PI_T$, and so:

$$PI_T = \bar{R}_m - D$$

Since $\bar{R}_m$ is constant for all assets, it is obvious from this formulation that the smaller the horizontal distance $D$, the larger is the performance index $PI_T$.

In any comparison or ranking of the performance of several mutual funds, we plot the characteristic lines of all the funds, draw the horizontal line at the riskless rate level $r$, and rank all funds by the distance $D$. Figure 15.5 demonstrates the graphical application of Treynor's performance measure with two mutual funds. For $r = 5\%$, fund 2 outperforms fund 1 since at this level its horizontal distance from the vertical axis $D_2$ is smaller. For $r = 2\%$, conversely, fund 1 outperforms fund 2.

The graphical presentation of Treynor's performance index is especially useful for comparing or ranking a large number of funds. The diagrammatic comparison of fund performance is more transparent than the numerical comparison in terms of the ratio $(\bar{R}_i - r)/\hat{\beta}_i$. Moreover, the graphical presentation gives a *range* of interest rates for which one fund outperforms the other.

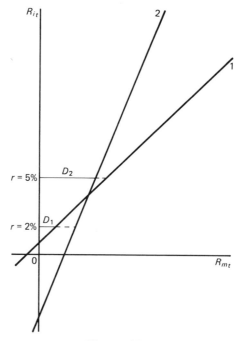

**Figure 15.5**

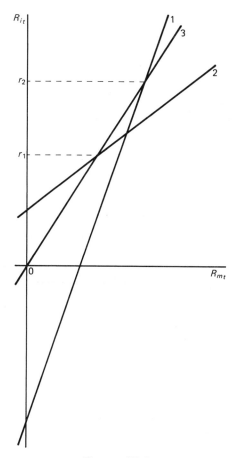

**Figure 15.6**

For example, consider the three funds shown in Figure 15.6. We assume that the parameters will not change in the future, except for the risk-free interest rate which may change. Which of the three funds will show the best results? From Figure 15.6 it is clear that fund 3 outperforms the other two funds for all interest rates $r$ such that $r_1 \leqslant r \leqslant r_2$. For $r < r_1$, fund 2 reveals the best performance, while for $r > r_2$ fund 1 is the best. Thus, the graphical exposition clearly shows the superiority of one fund over the other for whole ranges of possible interest rates.

### 15.2.5  Jensen's Performance Index $(PI_J)$

Jensen's performance index is very similar to Treynor's performance index: both assume that investors hold well-diversified portfolios.

Running a time-series regression of the $i$th security's excess rate of return $(R_{i_t} - r)$

on the market portfolio's excess rate of return $(R_{mt} - r)$, one can estimate the $i$th security's beta (compare Sections 12.1 and 12.4),[6]

$$(R_{i_t} - r) = \hat{\alpha}_i + \hat{\beta}_i(R_{m_t} - r) + e_{i_t}$$

where $\hat{\alpha}_i$, $\hat{\beta}_i$ are the regression coefficients and $e_{i_t}$ is the $i$th security's deviation in period $t$ from this line.

Taking means of both sides, we obtain,

$$\bar{R}_i - r = \hat{\alpha}_i + \hat{\beta}_i(\bar{R}_m - r)$$

The residual term vanishes as in the sample the average deviation, $\bar{e}_i$, is always zero.

Jensen's performance measure $(PI_J)$ is given by the vertical intercept of the regression line, $\hat{\alpha}_i$. If $\hat{\alpha}_i$ is not significantly different from zero $(\hat{\alpha}_i \approx 0)$, we obtain the relationship:

$$\bar{R}_i - r = \hat{\beta}_i(\bar{R}_m - r)$$

This is actually the CAPM risk–return relationship, but with sample estimates substituted for the true parameters $ER_i$, $ER_m$ and $\beta_i$ [see Chapter 11, equation (11.19) and Chapter 12, equation (12.1)]. The mutual fund in this case performs just like the market and its mean rate of return (adjusted for risk) is identical to the market mean rate of return. In Figure 15.7, this fund is represented by the straight line $EF$ through the

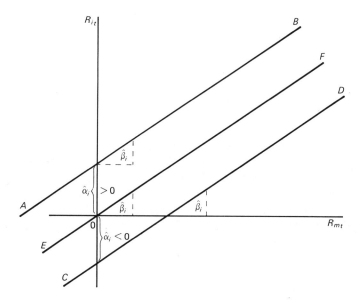

**Figure 15.7**

<hr/>

[6] Here we assume that the riskless interest rate $r$ is constant over time. However, if the interest rate varies over time, simply use $r_t$ for $r$ to obtain the same results.

origin, whose slope is $\hat{\beta}_i$. If $\hat{\alpha}_i$ is significantly different from zero and *positive*, the fund's management is considered to be successful, since the fund's average rate of return (adjusted for risk) is higher than the market rate of return: this situation is represented by the line $AB$ in Figure 15.7 which clearly outperforms the market. On the other hand, if the vertical intercept $\hat{\alpha}_i$ is negative, the fund's investment strategy is a failure as the fund underperforms compared to the market (line $CD$ in Figure 15.7).

According to Jensen's performance measure, the higher the vertical intercept $\hat{\alpha}_i$, the greater is the abnormal rate of return achieved by the fund in excess of the market.

## 15.3 The Relationship between Treynor's and Jensen's Performance Measures

Jensen's performance index, $PI_J$, is given by the vertical intercept $\hat{\alpha}_i$ from the following time-series regression,

$$\bar{R}_i - r = \hat{\alpha}_i + \hat{\beta}_i(\bar{R}_m - r)$$

Dividing through by $\hat{\beta}_i$, we obtain,

$$\frac{\bar{R}_i - r}{\hat{\beta}_i} = \hat{\alpha}_i/\hat{\beta}_i + (\bar{R}_m - r)$$

The left-hand side is Treynor's performance index, $(\bar{R}_i - r)/\hat{\beta}_i = PI_T$, and since "success" by Treynor's measure implies that $PI_T > \bar{R}_m - r$ (see Section 15.2.4), then $\hat{\alpha}_i/\hat{\beta}_i$ must be positive. Since $\hat{\beta}_i > 0$ for virtually all funds, we can safely assert that $\hat{\alpha}_i$ is also positive, $\hat{\alpha}_i > 0$. Thus, as long as $\hat{\beta}_i > 0$, "success" by Treynor's index $PI_T$ implies also "success" by Jensen's index $PI_J$, and vice versa. Similarly, if failure is registered by one of the performance indexes, the other performance index will also signal failure.

The *ranking* of the funds by the two performance indexes, however, is not identical. To illustrate, suppose that we get the following results for the Treynor measure of two funds:

$$\text{fund } A: \quad PI_T = \frac{\bar{R}_A - r}{\hat{\beta}_A} = 0.20$$

$$\text{fund } B: \quad PI_T = \frac{\bar{R}_B - r}{\hat{\beta}_B} = 0.15$$

and $\bar{R}_m - r$ is found to be equal to 0.10. Both funds are successful in their investment strategy by Treynor's index since the performance index $PI_T$ is greater than $\bar{R}_m - r = 0.10$ in both cases. Moreover, in the sense of Treynor's measure, fund $A$ shows better performance than fund $B$ since it has a higher performance index.

In order to determine Jensen's performance index, we introduce the following hypothetical data:

$$\bar{R}_A - r = 0.10, \; \hat{\beta}_A = 0.5 \; [\text{hence } (\bar{R}_A - r)/\hat{\beta}_A = 0.20, \text{ as required}]$$

and

$$\bar{R}_B - r = 0.30, \; \hat{\beta}_B = 2 \quad [\text{hence } (\bar{R}_B - r)/\hat{\beta}_B = 0.15, \text{ as required}]$$

Using for fund $A$ the relationship:

$$\bar{R}_A - r = \hat{\alpha}_A + \hat{\beta}_A(\bar{R}_m - r)$$

and plugging in the numerical data:

$$0.10 = \hat{\alpha}_A + 0.5 \times 0.10$$

we obtain for the vertical intercept $\hat{\alpha}_A = 0.05$.

Similarly for fund $B$ we have:

$$\bar{R}_B - r = \hat{\alpha}_B + \hat{\beta}_B(\bar{R}_m - r)$$

or numerically:

$$0.30 = \hat{\alpha}_B + 2 \times 0.10$$

which gives $\hat{\alpha}_B = 0.10$.

Thus while Treynor's performance index of fund $A$ is higher than that of fund $B$, $PI_T(A) > PI_T(B)$, the opposite holds with Jensen's performance indexes of the two funds, $PI_J(A) < PI_J(B)$. The situation is depicted in Figure 15.8, where clearly the

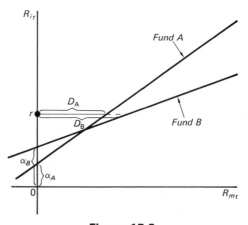

**Figure 15.8**

vertical intercept of fund $B$, representing Jensen's performance index, is greater than that of fund $A$, $\hat{\alpha}_B > \hat{\alpha}_A$, and yet the horizontal distance $D_B$ of the fund $B$ characteristic line from the vertical axis at the level of the riskless interest rate $r$ is also greater than this distance for fund $A$ ($D_B > D_A$, which implies the *inverse* inequality between the Treynor performance indexes of the two funds, see Section 15.2.4). The performance ranking of funds is thus dependent on the particular performance index used.

## 15.4   Performance Measures and Roll's Critique of the CAPM Empirical Studies

Roll's critique of the CAPM empirical tests (see Section 14.4) also has strong implications for the Treynor and Jensen performance measures. We saw in Chapter 14 that if the market portfolio $m$ is mean–variance efficient, as implied by the CAPM, we necessarily obtain in the sample (using *ex-post* observations) an *exact linear relationship* between a security's average rate of return and beta [see equation (14.3)],

$$\bar{R}_i = r + (\bar{R}_m - r)\hat{\beta}_i$$

Thus, if the market portfolio $m$ is indeed *ex-post* efficient we obtain as a pure *technical result*

$$PI_T = \frac{\bar{R}_i - r}{\hat{\beta}_i} = \bar{R}_m - r$$

i.e., the Treynor performance measure is constant across all securities and portfolios (mutual funds)! Similarly, Jensen's index must vanish, since from the above relationship $\hat{\alpha}_i = 0$ for all risky assets.

In reality, however, *ex-post* data reveal that various portfolios have performance indexes which are far from identical (see Section 15.7). According to Roll's interpretation, this means that the "market portfolio" $m$ used in the time-series regression to determine the beta is simply mean–variance inefficient. In other words, the portfolio $m$ actually is not the true market portfolio and hence the estimates obtained by regressing the returns on $m$, which we denote by $\hat{\beta}_i$, are not the true betas. Consequently, the performance indexes calculated using these "market" data do not really evaluate the quality of mutual fund managements.

In spite of this strong criticism, one can justify the use of the performance indexes on the following grounds. We have seen that most investors do not diversify their portfolios among all the risky assets. Nor do they confine their holdings to a single security. Thus, the appropriate risk index is neither the variance $\sigma_i^2$ nor the beta $\beta_i$ (calculated against an efficient portfolio), but some combination of the two. It is not easy to construct such a composite risk index. However, investors may perceive the beta as a proxy to the true risk when the beta is calculated against some portfolio which adequately reflects the market trend, e.g., the S&P index, the Dow-Jones index, or any other acceptable proxy of the market portfolio. Beta is thus a proxy for the true risk index, even though it is calculated against a portfolio which is actually MV inefficient.

## 15.5    Decomposition of Excess Return: Fama's Approach[7]

The whole notion of performance indexes and the rationale for investing in mutual funds are based on the promise of excess return due to the funds' allegedly superior professional management. It is therefore appropriate to consider the meaning of excess return in more detail.

Many investors buy mutual fund shares without further diversifying into other risky assets. In this case, as a result of imperfect diversification, the investors are exposed to both systematic and non-systematic risk (see Section 12.4). The non-systematic risk vanishes only in the following two cases:

(a)   the investor perfectly diversifies his portfolio by mixing the mutual fund shares with many other securities; or

(b)   the rate of return on the mutual fund is perfectly correlated with the market portfolio; in other words, the mutual fund represents a mean–variance efficient portfolio.

In either case, the excess or abnormal return on the mutual fund $i$ should be measured simply by the actual return $\bar{R}_i$ less the expected return $\bar{R}_i^*$, where $\bar{R}_i^*$ is given by the CAPM formula,

$$\bar{R}_i^* = r + (\bar{R}_m - r)\hat{\beta}_i$$

Here

$\bar{R}_m$   is the mean return on the market portfolio
$r$   is the riskless interest rate
$\hat{\beta}_i$   is the systematic risk as represented by the fund's beta

In cases when either the condition of perfect diversification or of portfolio efficiency does not hold, Fama suggested to decompose the mutual fund's excess return so as to make explicit the investor's exposure to non-systematic risk. Figure 15.9 illustrates the suggested decomposition. A mutual fund $i$ is marked by the point $F$ in the mean rate of return vs. beta plane. The actual mean rate of return of fund $i$ is $\bar{R}_i$ and the systematic risk is $\hat{\beta}_i$. The straight line in Figure 15.9 plots the CAPM risk–return relationship, and in equilibrium the fund's rate of return consistent with its risk $\hat{\beta}_i$ should be given by point $E$ on this line, where $\bar{R}_i^* = r + (\bar{R}_m - r)\hat{\beta}_i$. Thus, the vertical difference $\bar{R}_i - \bar{R}_i^*$ is the fund's excess return, equal to:

$$\bar{R}_i - \bar{R}_i^* = \bar{R}_i - [r + (\bar{R}_m - r)\hat{\beta}_i]$$

Recalling the definition of Jensen's performance index $\hat{\alpha}_i$ by $\bar{R}_i - r = \hat{\alpha}_i + \hat{\beta}_i(\bar{R}_m - r)$

[7] E. Fama, "Components of Investment Performance", *Journal of Finance* (June 1972).

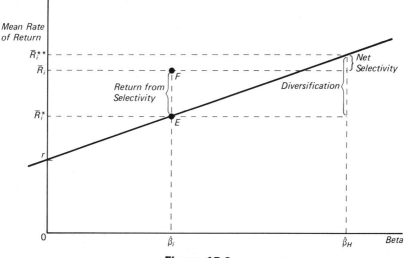

**Figure 15.9**

(see Section 15.2.5), we see that the vertical difference $\bar{R}_i - \bar{R}_i^*$ is simply equal to Jensen's index, $\bar{R}_i - \bar{R}_i^* = (\bar{R}_i - r) - \hat{\beta}_i(\bar{R}_m - r) = \hat{\alpha}_i$.

As a result of imperfect diversification [condition (a) does not hold], the investor holding only the mutual fund share which promises the excess return $\bar{R}_i - \bar{R}_i^*$ is actually exposed to the fund's total risk $\sigma_i^2$ given by

$$\sigma_i^2 = \hat{\beta}_i^2 \sigma_m^2 + \sigma_{ei}^2$$

and not only to the systematic risk $\hat{\beta}_i$. The non-systematic risk $\sigma_{ei}^2$ is not "washed out" in this case, since investors rely on the mutual fund diversification strategy and do not diversify their holdings failing to ensure efficiency of their portfolio [condition (b) does not hold either]. It is thus appropriate to ask if the fund's excess return actually compensates the investors for the additional risk associated with imperfect diversification.

To answer this question, we carry out the following decomposition. First, find the hypothetical mutual fund beta, denoted by $\hat{\beta}_H$, in case of perfect correlation with the market portfolio, i.e., when condition (b) holds and the non-systematic risk vanishes so that the total risk is given by:

$$\sigma_i^2 = \hat{\beta}_H^2 \sigma_m^2$$

Hence for this hypothetical beta we obtain

$$\hat{\beta}_H = \sigma_i / \sigma_m$$

The actual excess return $\bar{R}_i - \bar{R}_i^*$ is defined by Fama as "return from selectivity". However, at the hypothetical risk level $\hat{\beta}_H$, the required rate of return within the CAPM framework is $\bar{R}_i^{**}$ (see Figure 15.9) and the "net" selectivity excess return is thus $\bar{R}_i - \bar{R}_i^{**}$ (which is negative in the specific case shown in Figure 15.9). Thus, we have the following decomposition of the excess return:

$$\underset{\text{(Return from Selectivity)}}{\text{Actual Excess Return}} = \text{Diversification} + \text{Net Selectivity}$$

$$\bar{R}_i - \bar{R}_i^* \quad = \quad (\bar{R}_i^{**} - \bar{R}_i^*) \quad + \quad (\bar{R}_i - \bar{R}_i^{**})$$

Note that the component $(\bar{R}_i^{**} - \bar{R}_i^*)$ is what the investor should get if only the non-diversifiable (systematic) risk is taken into account, namely in the hypothetical case that his portfolio is well-diversified. The component $(\bar{R}_i - \bar{R}_i^{**})$ is the net excess return after the risk is adjusted by moving from $\hat{\beta}_i$ to $\hat{\beta}_H$. The net selectivity is the excess return adjusted for the fact that the mutual fund portfolio may be mean–variance inefficient. It measures the mutual fund's performance adjusted for its imperfect diversification. In our example the net selectivity is negative, indicating that the investor is undercompensated for the extra risk assumed as a result of imperfect diversification. The net selectivity, of course, may also be positive, indicating that the fund actually shows net excess return beyond what could be achieved by wide diversification.

Finally, note that if the mutual fund is *perfectly correlated* with the market portfolio (i.e. the correlation coefficient is $\rho = 1$ and the portfolio is efficient) we have:

$$\hat{\beta}_i = \frac{Cov(R_i, R_m)}{\sigma_m^2} = \frac{Cov(R_i, R_m)}{\sigma_i \sigma_m} \cdot \frac{\sigma_i}{\sigma_m} = \rho \cdot \frac{\sigma_i}{\sigma_m} = 1 \cdot \frac{\sigma_i}{\sigma_m} = \frac{\sigma_i}{\sigma_m} = \hat{\beta}_H$$

The actual beta is equal to the adjusted beta and the return on selectivity is identical to the net selectivity, which in turn is equal to the observed excess return.

EXAMPLE

Consider the performance of the Twentieth Century Growth Investment mutual fund. The estimates of the fund's return parameters, based on *ex-post* data for the 22-year period 1959–1980, were the following:

$$\text{Mean rate of return } \bar{R}_{TC} = 20.664\%$$
$$\text{Standard deviation } \quad \sigma_{TC} = 33.758\%$$
$$\text{Systematic risk } \quad \hat{\beta}_{TC} = 1.098$$

The systematic risk was estimated against an unmanaged market portfolio proxy with the following parameter estimates:

$$\bar{R}_m = 14.360\%$$

$$\sigma_m = 24.473\%$$

The average risk-free interest rate $r$ for the period was around 5%.

Figure 15.10 plots the fund TC at the point $\hat{\beta}_{TC} = 1.098$, $\bar{R}_{TC} = 20.664\%$ and the equilibrium CAPM risk–return relationship:

$$\bar{R}_i^* = r + (\bar{R}_m - r)\hat{\beta}_i = 5 + 9.360\hat{\beta}_i$$

The expected rate of return for $\hat{\beta}_{TC} = 1.098$ is thus:

$$\bar{R}_{TC}^* = 5 + 9.360 \times 1.098 = 15.277$$

and the actual *excess return* is:

$$\bar{R}_{TC} - \bar{R}_{TC}^* = 20.664 - 15.277 = 5.387$$

The fund's total risk is $\sigma_{TC} = 33.758\%$. The hypothetical beta corresponding to the case of perfect diversification with zero non-systematic risk is thus:

$$\hat{\beta}_H = \sigma_{TC}/\sigma_m = \frac{33.758}{24.473} = 1.379$$

The mean rate of return consistent with this risk level in the CAPM framework is calculated from the CAPM relationship above,

$$\bar{R}_{TC}^{**} = 5 + 9.360 \times 1.379 = 17.907$$

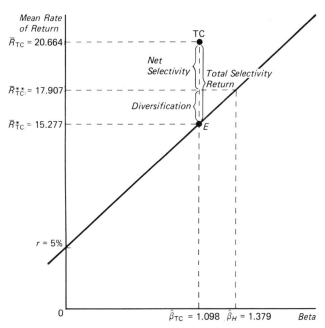

**Figure 15.10**

and the diversification excess return is thus:

$$\bar{R}_{\text{TC}}^{**} - \bar{R}_{\text{TC}}^{*} = 17.907 - 15.277 = 2.630$$

Since the total selectivity excess return is $\bar{R}_i - R_i^* = 5.387$, we have here a *positive* net selectivity effect,

$$\bar{R}_{\text{TC}} - \bar{R}_{\text{TC}}^{**} = (\bar{R}_{\text{TC}} - \bar{R}_{\text{TC}}^{*}) - (\bar{R}_{\text{TC}}^{**} - \bar{R}_{\text{TC}}^{*}) = 5.387 - 2.630 = 2.757$$

so that the fund actually has more than compensated the investors for the additional imperfect diversification risk.

## 15.6    Ex-Post Performance of Bonds and Stocks: Sharpe's Study

The performance measures introduced in the previous section are applicable to portfolios of risky assets. As long-term bonds are properly treated as risky assets, just like common stocks, it is appropriate to consider the performance of portfolios consisting of both stocks and bonds. Sharpe[8] studied the *ex-post* performance of three different portfolios: (a) a portfolio of bonds, (b) a portfolio of stocks, and (c) a portfolio of stocks and bonds mixed in proportion to the total market value of the two investment media. The study covered the period 1938–1971 and separately the post-war period 1946–1971.

The excess quarterly returns were calculated on bonds and on stocks. The excess return is defined as $R_{it} - r_t$, where $R_{it}$ is the return on the risky asset (long-term bonds or common stocks) in quarter $t$ and $r_t$ is the return on 90-days prime banker acceptance (used as a proxy to the risk-free rate for that quarter).

Table 15.2 presents the basic results for the mean average excess return, the standard deviation, and the beta of the three portfolios (here "market" portfolio is the portfolio consisting of a mix of bonds and stocks). As we see from the table, the mean rate of return and the variability of the rate of return on the pure stock portfolio are both much higher than the corresponding quantities for the bond portfolio. The difference in the mean rate of return is particularly pronounced in the post-war period 1946–1971, when the return on bonds was relatively poor. Since the "market" portfolio is a mix of bonds and stocks, its results, as expected, occupy an intermediate position.

The low return on bonds is associated with relatively low variability of returns, namely low risk. The question, of course, is whether the stock portfolio outperformed the bond portfolio and whether (at least *ex-post*) there is justification for including bonds in the investors' portfolios. We now turn to examine this issue in more detail, using two of the performance indexes introduced in the previous sections.

[8] W. Sharpe, "Bonds versus Stocks: Some Lessons from Capital Market Theory", *Financial Analysts Journal* (Nov.–Dec. 1973).

**Table 15.2**
**Performance of Bonds and Stocks**

|  | Period | |
| --- | --- | --- |
| Measure | 1938–71 | 1946–1971 |
| Average quarterly excess return, $\bar{R}_i$ (% per quarter) |  |  |
|    (a)  Bonds | 1.069 | 0.330 |
|    (b)  Stocks | 2.290 | 2.033 |
|    (c)  "Market" Portfolio | 2.132 | 1.788 |
| Standard deviation of quarterly excess returns, $\sigma_i$ (% per quarter) |  |  |
|    (a)  Bonds | 4.069 | 2.703 |
|    (b)  Stocks | 7.745 | 6.491 |
|    (c)  "Market" Portfolio | 6.746 | 5.972 |
| Beta estimated against the 'market' portfolio, $\beta_i$ |  |  |
|    (a)  Bonds | 0.436 | 0.286 |
|    (b)  Stocks | 1.138 | 1.085 |
|    (c)  "Market" Portfolio | 1.000 | 1.000 |

*Source:* W. Sharpe, "Bonds versus Stocks: Some Lessons from Capital Market Theory", *Financial Analysts Journal* (Nov.–Dec. 1973).

### 15.6.1   Sharpe's Performance Index of Bond and Stock Portfolios

Table 15.3 provides the Sharpe performance measure:

$$PI_S = \frac{\bar{R}_i - r}{\sigma_i}$$

for the three portfolios studied (actually, the calculations were made using the *average* risk-free rate $\bar{r}$ for the entire period).

For the entire period 1938–1971, the stock portfolio outperformed the bond portfolio, but the "market" portfolio (a mix of stocks and bonds) outperformed both. This implies that if the investor had the choice to buy a mutual fund specializing only in stocks or a fund specializing only in bonds, the former would be selected (*ex-post*).

**Table 15.3**
**Sharpe's Performance Indexes: Reward-to-Variability Ratios**

| Portfolio | 1938–1971 | 1946–1971 |
| --- | --- | --- |
| Bonds | 0.2627 | 0.1221 |
| Stocks | 0.2957 | 0.3132 |
| "Market" Portfolio | 0.3160 | 0.2994 |

*Source:* Calculated on the basis of data in W. Sharpe, *op cit.*

However, if there were also a "market" fund with both stocks and bonds in the portfolio (in proportion to their market value), it would be superior to the first two options. Thus, for the whole period 1938–1971, bonds would be included with beneficial results in certain proportion in the investor's portfolio. The results for the post-war period 1946–1971, however, are different. We see from Table 15.3 that the pure stock portfolio (with performance index of 0.3132) outperformed the other two portfolios, so that the "market" portfolio including stocks and bonds was inferior to the stock portfolio. Thus, bonds would not be included *ex-post* at all in the investor's portfolio. This is not surprising in view of the very low return on bonds in the post-war period (see Table 15.2).

Figure 15.11 illustrates these results in the mean–standard deviation space. Note that since the returns are defined in excess of the risk-free interest rate, the straight lines all start from the origin (if the investor puts his entire wealth in riskless securities, he earns a return $r$, which in terms of excess return is zero, since $r - r = 0$). In panel (a), the

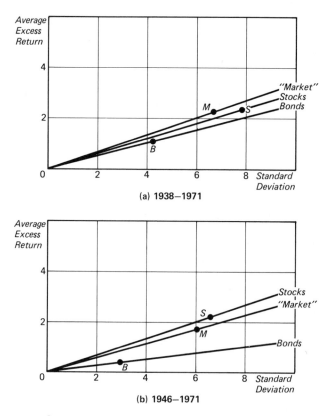

(a) 1938–1971

(b) 1946–1971

Source:   W. Sharpe, "Bonds versus Stocks: Some
Lessons from Capital Market Theory",
*Financial Analysts Journal* (Nov.–Dec. 1973).

**Figure 15.11**

line $OM$ is steeper than the line $OS$, which in turn is steeper than the line $OB$. If an investor had to choose between the three portfolios, he would choose portfolio $M$ which yielded the highest reward to variability. In panel (b)—the post-war period—the line $OS$ is the steepest of the three, which means that the pure stock portfolio outperformed the bond and the stock–bond portfolios.

### 15.6.2   Treynor's Performance Index of Bond and Stock Portfolios

So far, we have assumed that investors buy only the shares of one mutual fund (a stock fund, a bond fund, or a stock–bond "market" fund) plus the riskless asset. Hence the reward-to-variability ratio (Sharpe's index $PI_S$) has been examined, as this is the appropriate performance measure for an investor holding a single asset. We now assume that the investor holds the "market" portfolio, namely a portfolio diversified between bonds and stocks. In this case, the risk index of bonds and of stocks should be measured relative to the variability of the rates of return on the "market" portfolio. In other words, the securities' beta, $\beta_i$, should be substituted for the standard deviation $\sigma_i$ as the measure of risk. This leads to Treynor's performance index

$$PI_T = \frac{\bar{R}_i - r}{\beta_i}$$

which is appropriate in the context of a diversified portfolio.

This index is calculated in a straightforward way from the data of Table 15.2, simply by dividing the excess return of each portfolio by its beta. The results obtained in this way for the Treynor performance index are presented in Table 15.4. We see from Table 15.4 that in a portfolio context (with investors holding the "market" portfolio of both stocks and bonds), bonds outperformed stocks in the 1938–1971 period and, conversely, stocks outperformed bonds in the post-war 1946–1971 period.

To sum up, for the post-war period, the two performance measures (Sharpe's $PI_S$ and Treynor's $PI_T$) show the same performance ranking, with stocks outperforming bonds. For the whole period 1938–1971, however, they differ in their ranking of stock and bond portfolios, which may happen as we saw in Section 15.3.

**Table 15.4**
**Treynor's  Performance  Indexes:  Reward-to-Volatility
Ratios**

| Portfolio | 1938–1971 | 1946–1971 |
|---|---|---|
| Bonds | 2.452 | 1.154 |
| Stocks | 2.012 | 1.873 |
| "Market" Portfolio | 2.132 | 1.788 |

Source:  Calculated on the basis of data in W. Sharpe, op cit.

**15.7    Some Empirical Results of Mutual Fund Performance: Comparison to an Unmanaged Portfolio**

Numerous empirical studies of mutual funds' returns, using the above mentioned performance indicators, were carried out in recent years. Despite the fact that different samples and varying time periods were used, all the researchers concluded that mutual funds' managers are unable to "outguess" the market, and as a result the funds do not outperform the unmanaged portfolio.

Sharpe[9] analyzed the returns of 34 mutual funds for the period 1954–1963 using the reward-to-variability ratio R/V (denoted $PI_S$ in the preceding sections). His results for this ratio varied from 0.78 to 0.43; the relevant ratio for the Dow-Jones Industrial Average (representing an unmanaged portfolio) was 0.63 for the same time period. The average R/V ratio for the funds was considerably lower than that of the Dow-Jones Index, and only 11 funds outperformed the Index, while 23 mutual funds had R/V ratios which were lower than the ratio for the Dow-Jones Index.

These conclusions were also corroborated by Treynor and Mazuy,[10] who used the characteristic line method to study the performance of 57 mutual funds during the years 1953–1962. These authors conclude that with one exception mutual fund managers were not able to predict the major swings in the market. Jensen[11] in a comprehensive study of 115 mutual funds during the period 1945–1964 also concludes that professional investment management was not able to consistently pick out a better cross-section of stocks than could be obtained by mere chance. Thus mutual funds were unable to outperform a simple "buy the market and hold" strategy. This conclusion holds even before management expenses are deducted from the funds' returns.

In a recent comprehensive study, Shawky[12] examined the performance of 255 mutual funds covering the periods 1973–1977. First he showed that, at least for mutual funds, we may use any of the performance measures suggested by Sharpe, Treynor, and Jensen, since in almost all the cases the three performance indexes led to the same ranking. In other words, at least for mutual funds with hundreds of securities in their portfolios, there is a very strong correlation between $\sigma_i$ and $\beta_i$, and hence one gets almost the same ranking by the different performance indexes. For the 255 mutual funds included in the study, an almost perfect correlation was observed between the three performance indexes, as is clear from Table 15.5. Thus one can measure the performance of mutual funds compared to an unmanaged portfolio by any of the three indexes with no essential changes in the results.

According to Shawky's findings, Jensen's performance index $\hat{\alpha}_i$ was significantly different from zero for only 25 out of the 255 mutual funds studied. Out of these 25 funds, 16 had negative $\hat{\alpha}_i$ and 9 positive $\hat{\alpha}_i$. These results indicate some improvement in the performance of mutual funds over the results reported in previous studies, but we can still safely conclude that most funds (230) did not outperform the unmanaged

[9] W. Sharpe, "Mutual Fund Performance", *Journal of Business* (January 1966).
[10] J. L. Treynor and K. K. Mazuy, "Can Mutual Funds Outguess the Market?" *Harvard Business Review* (July–August 1966).
[11] M. C. Jensen, "The Performance of Mutual Funds," *Journal of Finance* (May 1968).
[12] H. Shawky, "An Update on Mutual Funds: Better Grades," *Journal of Portfolio Management* (Winter 1982).

**Table 15.5**
**Correlation Matrix for the Three Performance Indexes**
**(Based on 255 Mutual Funds, 1973–1977)**

|  | Jensen's $PI_J$ | Sharpe $PI_S$ | Treynor $PI_T$ |
|---|---|---|---|
| $PI_J$ | 1.00 | 0.93 | 0.92 |
| $PI_S$ | 0.93 | 1.00 | 0.97 |
| $PI_T$ | 0.92 | 0.97 | 1.00 |

*Source:* H. Shawky, "An Update on Mutual Funds: Better Grades",
*Journal of Portfolio Management* (Winter 1982).

portfolio, 16 were inferior to the unmanaged portfolio (those with negative Jensen's index), and only 9 outperformed the unmanaged portfolio (those with positive Jensen's index). This is clearly a gloomy picture for mutual fund managers.

To check the stability of these findings over time, a study was carried out for a sample of 100 mutual funds over the 22-year period 1959–1980, dividing it into two subperiods 1959–1969 and 1970–1980 of 11 years each. Table 15.6 gives the corresponding results for Sharpe and Treynor performance measures. On the whole, fund performance compared to an unmanaged portfolio was stable over time. With the Treynor performance index, for example, only 30% of the funds outperformed the unmanaged portfolio (as represented by the Fisher Index) over the entire 22-year period, while the corresponding percentages in the two 11-year subperiods were 36% (1959–1969) and 31% (1970–1980).[13] Sharpe's performance index shows that only

**Table 15.6**
**Performance Measures for a Sample of 100 Funds in Different Periods***

|  | 1959–1980 | 1959–1969 | 1970–1980 |
|---|---|---|---|
| *Sharpe's $PI_S$* |  |  |  |
| Unmanaged Portfolio |  |  |  |
| (Fisher Index) | 0.42 | 0.44 | 0.40 |
| Range for Mutual Funds | 0.08–0.69 | 0.17–0.69 | 0.01–0.72 |
| Percent of Funds Outperforming |  |  |  |
| the Unmanaged Portfolio | 14 | 23 | 21 |
| *Treynor's $PI_T$* |  |  |  |
| Unmanaged Portfolio |  |  |  |
| (Fisher Index) | 10.36 | 9.59 | 11.13 |
| Range for Mutual Funds | 2.64–27.80 | 3.89–30.66 | 0.43–29.88 |
| Percent of Funds Outperforming |  |  |  |
| the Unmanaged Portfolio | 30 | 36 | 31 |

* Calculated assuming 4% riskless interest rate ($r = 4\%$).

[13] The Jensen index for the period 1959–1980 shows an even gloomier picture: 15 out of 100 funds had positive values of $PI_J$, but only one of these was significantly different from zero. The remaining 85 funds had negative values of $PI_J$ (none significantly different from zero).

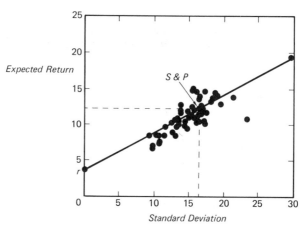

**Figure 15.12**

14% of the funds outperformed the unmanaged portfolio over the entire period, while for the two subperiods the corresponding figures were 23% and 21%.

To add more information, let us look at Figure 15.12, which is a scatter diagram of the average rate of return of the 100 mutual funds against the standard deviation of their returns for the period 1959–1980. The figure also plots the market line for a highly diversified unmanaged portfolio (a proxy to the market portfolio), assuming 4% riskless interest rate. The scatter diagram clearly shows that taken as a group the mutual funds failed to outperform the unmanaged portfolio by Sharpe's performance measure.

To sum up, the empirical evidence strongly suggests that by investing in an unmanaged portfolio, the investors could attain at worst the same financial results as by investing in scientifically managed mutual funds. This failure of mutual funds to outperform the unmanaged portfolio (the S&P Index, the Dow-Jones Index, or the Fisher Index as a proxy to the market portfolio) raises another interesting question. If funds do not succeed in selecting their investment strategy to outperform the market, how can we account for the popularity of this investment medium? We address this question in the next section.

### 15.8    Mutual Fund Performance in an Imperfect Securities Market

As we have just seen, most attempts to evaluate empirically the performance of mutual funds support the contention that the funds, taken as a group, are unable to outguess the market; and as a result, investors would be equally well off to invest their savings in a randomly chosen sample of common stocks. Despite this rather gloomy evaluation, mutual funds, as evidenced by their growth rates, have continued to comprise one of the most popular, if not the most popular, of investment media. The extraordinary growth of mutual funds is, to say the least, hardly accounted for by the empirical evidence on mutual funds' performance.

In view of the above evidence, how can one account for the widespread appeal of mutual funds as an investment medium? This apparent paradox between the performance record and the popularity of mutual funds can be resolved if we recall that securities are traded in a *less than perfect* market. The empirical evaluations invariably compare mutual fund performance with a benchmark provided by some general index of common stocks (Standard & Poor, Dow-Jones, and so on). On reflection, such an alternative is not available to most investors. Unless he has unusual resources at his disposal, an individual cannot invest in the shares of 500 companies, although he can easily purchase the shares of mutual funds whose assets include the shares of 500, or more, corporations. Of course it might be argued that a random sample of shares would suffice to approximate the risk–return characteristics of the index. However, even such an approach implies the purchase of the shares of a dozen or more companies. If we remind ourselves that a portfolio comprising a round lot of AT&T shares and a round lot of IBM shares entails an outlay of several thousand dollars, the number of investors for whom even a two- or three-stock portfolio represents the maximum attainable alternative to mutual fund shares is considerable.

Thus, for many investors the fact that a portfolio comprising a large enough sample of shares will approximate the risk–return characteristics of the Standard & Poor's Index is simply not relevant. It is only under the assumption of a perfect securities market, with infinite divisibility of investments, that the degree of diversification implied by the use of a stock index becomes possible. A more realistic approach is to recognize that because of market imperfections and the indivisibility of investments the relevant alternative confronting most investors in mutual fund shares is to invest directly in a small portfolio of individual shares, rather than in the S&P Index.

To illustrate such an approach the risk–return characteristics of eight mutual funds and of the shares of eight well-known corporations have been set out in Figure 15.13.[14] If an imaginary line is drawn from point $r$ (the riskless interest rate) through the S&P point on the diagram, the eight mutual funds tend to cluster closely along this line. This indicates that the funds' performance approximates, but does not significantly exceed, the performance of the S&P index, which corroborates the much more comprehensive evidence of Sharpe, Treynor and Mazuy, Jensen, and Shawky. But if we recall that the investor cannot "buy the index," more appropriate comparisons can be devised. If imaginary lines are drawn from point $r$ to the 16 points representing the funds and the individual shares, one can readily see that mutual funds almost invariably represent preferable alternatives to the investment in individual shares.

Now let us assume that the investor is prepared to diversify his investment in the shares of two companies. If we choose the example of Colgate and Bethlehem Steel an envelope curve can be constructed which represents the risk–return characteristic for all possible combinations of the two shares into a single portfolio (see Figure 15.13). Since this curve lies *below* the lines which connect point $r$ with each of the mutual funds, every

---

[14] The sample includes two growth funds, two diversified common stock funds, two balanced funds, and two income funds.

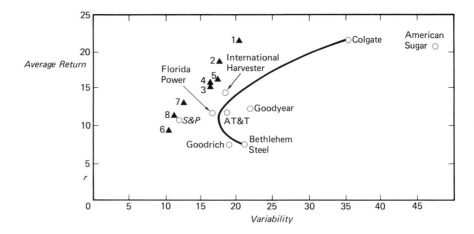

**Figure 15.13**

Key: 1. American Investors Fund. 2. Dreyfus Fund. 3. Fidelity Fund. 4. Washington Mutual Investors Fund. 5. Axe-Houghton Fund A. 6. Investors Mutual. 7. Financial Industrial Income Fund. 8. Northeast Investor Fund.

individual would prefer an investment in one of the mutual funds to an investment in this particular two-share portfolio.

Similar exercises can be carried out to compare mutual fund investments with other two-share combinations, with three-share portfolios, and so on. This constitutes not only a legitimate, but also the only relevant, approach for investors who are constrained to purchase a small number of shares. Because of the indivisibility of investment in an imperfect market, it would be perfectly rational for such investors to buy mutual fund shares even if the funds' performance was significantly inferior to that of the S&P Index. It is this role of providing a "second-best" but attainable alternative which perhaps explains the failure of the negative empirical appraisals to have any perceptible influence on the small investor's penchant for mutual funds, both in the United States and abroad.

In summary, even if we fully accept the view that mutual funds typically show no better results than could be obtained from a randomly chosen unmanaged portfolio, we do not necessarily have to accept the "normative" inferences regarding the desirability of investing in mutual funds shares which are often drawn from the "positive" evidence. A theoretically appropriate case for the investment in mutual funds can still be made once the implicit assumption that securities are traded in a perfect market is relaxed.

## 15.9 Predicting Portfolio Performance

We turn now to explore to what extent *ex-post* or historical data on portfolio efficiency can be used to predict efficiency in the future. For this purpose, we take mutual funds as proxies for portfolios in general and investigate the connection, if any, between the efficient sets of mutual funds in two successive periods.

Table 15.7 sets out the size composition of the efficient sets using the three Stochastic Dominance efficiency criteria (FSD, SSD, and TSD—see Chapter 6) and the Mean–Variance efficiency criterion. The sample for efficiency analysis consists of 100 mutual funds that were in continuous operation over the 22-year period 1959–1980. Using the data on mutual fund returns for the subperiods 1959–1969 and 1970–1980, the efficient sets were calculated for each of the two subperiods (columns 1 and 2 in Table 15.7). The efficient sets in each period were then compared to determine the number of mutual funds common to the efficient sets of *both* periods (column 3 in Table 15.7).

The results of this comparison were then used to construct Table 15.8. Column 1 of this table sets out the probability of picking out an efficient mutual fund when the decision is based on past data. The relevant estimate for each efficiency criterion is derived by dividing column 3 of Table 15.7 by column 1 of the same table. Thus, with respect to the FSD rule, an investor who based his estimates of FSD efficiency for the period 1970–1980 on the *past* performance of the mutual funds during the period 1959–1969 would predict efficiency with probability of 42% ($32/76 = 0.42$); that is, in 32 out of 76

**Table 15.7**

**Number of Mutual Funds Included in Efficient Sets for Selected Efficiency Criteria in the Years 1959–1969 and 1970–1980 (Total Sample Population 100 Funds)**

| Efficiency Criterion | Number of Funds in Efficient Set | | Number of Funds Common to Both Sets (3) |
|---|---|---|---|
| | 1959–1969 (1) | 1970–1980 (2) | |
| FSD | 76 | 41 | 32 |
| SSD | 22 | 9 | 3 |
| TSD | 16 | 7 | 2 |
| MV | 14 | 11 | 2 |

**Table 15.8**

**Probability of Predicting Efficient Mutual Funds in the Period 1970–1980 Based on 1959–1969 Data, for Various Efficiency Criteria (in percent)**

| Efficiency Criterion | Probability Based on Previous Period's Data (1) | Probability of Random Choice (2) |
|---|---|---|
| FSD | 42 | 41 |
| SSD | 13.6 | 9 |
| TSD | 12.5 | 7 |
| MV | 14.3 | 11 |

cases, the funds chosen on the basis of past performance proved to be FSD efficient in the successive period also.

At a first glance, this result is very impressive. However, on reflection it does not necessarily mean that predictions based on past data are superior to simple random choice. This becomes clear when we examine the probability of picking out an efficient fund *at random* out of the 100 funds available—column 2 in Table 15.8. In our example of the FSD rule, there was a probability of 41% ($41/100 = 0.41$) of choosing a FSD efficient fund at random. To determine to what extent past data can be used to *improve* decision making (compared to random choice), we have to compare columns 1 and 2 in Table 15.8. Only in two out of the four cases (SSD and TSD rules) was the probability of choosing an efficient fund increased significantly by the use of past data (from 9% to about 14% in case of SSD and from 7% to 12.5% in case of the stronger TSD). The change for the Mean–Variance criterion and for the FSD rule was relatively slight.

The reasons for this moderately indifferent performance of the efficiency criteria for prediction can be found by reexamining the data of Table 15.7. The composition of the efficient sets over time was not stable enough to derive predictions materially better than simple random choice. In the case of the FSD, moreover, the efficient set was so large that, despite comparatively higher stability of composition between the two periods, random choice alone provided excellent results that could not be materially improved upon.

However, even a moderate degree of success in improving predictions could conceivably translate itself into very significant increases in the return on investment. To this question we now turn in Table 15.9, which sets out the average annual rates of return for the period 1970–1980 for two groups of mutual funds; (a) the group of efficient mutual funds included in the FSD, SSD, TSD, and MV efficient sets constructed on the basis of current (1979–1980) data; (b) the group of mutual funds predicted to be efficient from past (1959–1969) data. Note that in reality the rates of return are never known in advance, so that the results calculated for the "current" efficient set

**Table 15.9**
**Average Annual Rates of Return during 1970–1980 for Mutual Funds Included in Efficient Sets Constructed from Current and Past Data (in percent)**

| Efficiency Criterion | Rates of Return in 1970–1980 for Efficient Mutual Funds Constructed from Current 1970–1980 Data (1) | Rates of Return in 1970–1980 for Mutual Funds Predicted to be Efficient by Past 1959–1969 Data (2) |
|---|---|---|
| FSD | 10.03 | 7.98 |
| SSD | 11.40 | 8.33 |
| TSD | 11.67 | 8.32 |
| MV | 11.54 | 8.82 |
| Total population* | 7.83 | 7.83 |

* Average annual rate of return in 1970–1980 for the 100 mutual funds included in the sample.

(group (a)) are not achievable in practice. Group (b) on the other hand is easily constructed by using predictions based on *ex-post* observable efficient set for the previous period. The table also gives the rate of return during the same period for the 100 mutual funds that comprise our total population. The 11-year average rates of return were computed by taking the geometric means of the annual rates for each individual fund (see Chapter 2). The averages for the various groups were computed by taking the arithmetic average of the mean rates of the funds in the sample.

The average rate of return for 1970–1980 of the entire sample population (100 funds) was 7.83%. Column 1 of Table 15.9 clearly shows that the rate of return would be improved substantially if investors could successfully predict the composition of the efficient sets *in advance*. The average annual rate of return for the funds included in the FSD efficient set was 10.03%, and the relevant figures for the SSD, TSD, and MV efficient sets were even higher (around 11.5%). These results, however, provide little comfort for the investor who is faced with the problem of predicting the efficient set. Column 2 of Table 15.9 lists the average annual rates of return for the efficient sets during 1970–1980, when the composition of the sets is estimated from the *ex-post* data of 1959–1969. All the criteria provide a certain improvement over the rate of return which could be earned by choosing randomly among the funds. Curiously enough, the MV efficient set provides the best results, with average annual rate of return almost 1% higher than the average for randomly chosen funds (8.82% versus 7.83%).

Thus, on the whole, estimating efficient sets using relatively long series of past data appears potentially rewarding, and despite the low predictive power for portfolio composition, investors probably can earn a positive return on the preliminary screening of inefficient portfolios. But we hasten to add that mutual funds may not be representative of portfolios in general, and one 11-year test is certainly not exhaustive. Much work remains to be done. However, by now the reader should be prepared to join in the task and the next step is up to him.

## Summary

*Ex-post* performance of mutual funds provides an indication of the past success of the fund managers in selecting their investment strategy.

The reward-to-variability and stochastic dominance measures of performance assume that the investor holds only a single risky asset. Thus, these measures are particularly suitable for measuring the performance of mutual funds, when it is reasonable to assume that the investors only buy the fund's shares, leaving it to the mutual fund management to take care of diversification.

The reward-to-volatility ratio and Jensen's index measure the *ex-post* performance on the assumption that the investor holds a well-diversified portfolio, specifically the market portfolio. The difficulty with these two measures is that if the market portfolio is indeed MV efficient (as it should be in equilibrium if the CAPM holds), then all the individual stocks and mutual funds alike should have *ex-post* a constant performance index, regardless of the efficiency of the fund managers (this is a corollary of Roll's critique of the CAPM empirical studies). Despite this implication, these two performance measures are widely used in practice, perhaps because the security's beta used in their calculation is a good proxy to the true risk index even in cases when investors are known not to hold the entire market portfolio but only a portfolio with a relatively small number of different securities.

*Ex-post* data reveal that, in general, mutual funds are unable to "outperform" the unmanaged portfolios. However, since many investors simply cannot afford to purchase a sufficiently diversified portfolio, they settle for mutual fund shares as the next best thing to perfect diversification. Recall that the alternative is to diversify in a portfolio which contains only a small number of different stocks, and its performance is definitely inferior to the performance of mutual funds. Thus, in an imperfect market, where real investments are not perfectly divisible (contrary to one of the CAPM assumptions), there is a very good case for buying mutual fund shares, although their performance does not beat an unmanaged but highly diversified random portfolio.

---

### Summary Table

1. **Performance measures appropriate when holding mutual fund shares plus riskless asset**

   (a) *Sharpe's reward-to-variability index*

   $$PI_S = \frac{ER_i - r}{\sigma_i}$$

   where $ER_i$ is the security's expected rate of return and $\sigma_i$ is the security's standard deviation; $r$ is the riskless interest rate.

   In empirical studies of *ex-post* performance, the security parameters are replaced by sample estimates.

   (b) *Stochastic Dominance approach:*
   fund $F$ outperforms fund $G$ if

   a) $F(R) \leqslant G(R)$    for all rates of return $R$    (*FSD Rule*)

   or

   b) $\int_{-\infty}^{R} [G(t) - F(t)]\, dt \geqslant 0$    for all $R$    (*SSD Rule*)

2. **Performance measures appropriate in a portfolio context**

   The investor is assumed to diversify the mutual fund shares with many risky assets and the riskless asset.

   (a) *Treynor's performance index*

   $$PI_T = \frac{ER_i - r}{\beta_i}$$

where the security's beta is given by $\beta_i = Cov\,(R_i, R_m)/\sigma_m^2$. In empirical studies of *ex-post* performance, all parameters are replaced by sample estimates.

(b) *Jensen's performance index*

$$PI_J = \hat{a}_i$$

where $\hat{a}_i$ is the vertical intercept taken from the regression

$$R_{i_t} - r = \hat{a}_i + \hat{\beta}_i(R_{m_t} - r) + e_{i_t}$$

(c) If a fund outperforms the unmanaged portfolio by $PI_T$, then it also outperforms the unmanaged portfolio by $PI_J$, and vice versa, but the ranking of funds by their performance is dependent on the particular index used.

## Questions and Problems

15.1 Hypothetical rates of return on two mutual funds and on the market portfolio are as follows (in %):

| Year | Mutual Fund A | Mutual Fund B | Market Portfolio |
|------|---------------|---------------|------------------|
| 1979 | −10 | +15 | +8 |
| 1980 | +10 | −10 | −5 |
| 1981 | +20 | −10 | 0 |
| 1982 | +30 | +20 | +20 |
| 1983 | −10 | +30 | +20 |

The risk-free interest rate is $r = 5\%$.

(a) Which mutual fund shows a higher performance, given that investors hold only one fund in their portfolio?
(b) Which mutual fund shows a higher performance, given that investors further diversify the mutual fund shares with other assets?

Compare your results in (a) and (b) above.

15.2 Hypothetical rates of return on two mutual funds are as follows (in %):

| Year | Fund A | Fund B |
|------|--------|--------|
| 1979 | −10 | +10 |
| 1980 | −8 | +20 |
| 1981 | +60 | −10 |
| 1982 | +20 | +20 |
| 1983 | −10 | +80 |

(a) Assuming that the risk-free interest rate is $r = 5\%$, which fund performed better by Sharpe's index?

(b) Which fund performed better by Sharpe's index if investors can borrow money at $r_B = 10\%$ and lend at $r_L = 5\%$? Illustrate your answer graphically.

(c) "If fund $A$ dominates fund $B$ by Sharpe's index for both $r_L$ and $r_B$, all investors—borrowers and lenders alike—will choose fund $B$." Appraise this statement, illustrating your answer graphically.

15.3 Hypothetical rates of return on two mutual funds were as follows (in %):

| Year | Fund A | Fund B |
|------|--------|--------|
| 1979 | 10 | 20 |
| 1980 | 5 | 10 |
| 1981 | −1 | 0 |
| 1982 | −5 | −3 |
| 1983 | 20 | 25 |

(a) Which fund performed better by the MV rule?

(b) Which fund performed better by SD rules?
(Assign to each year equal probability of $\frac{1}{5}$.)

Discuss your result.

15.4 The following parameters are available for five mutual funds:

| Fund | 1 | 2 | 3 | 4 | 5 |
|------|-----|-----|-----|-----|-----|
| Expected Return (%) | 5 | 8 | 7 | 6 | 10 |
| Beta | 0.5 | 0.8 | 0.7 | 0.6 | 1.0 |

(a) Calculate Treynor's performance index and rank the funds on the assumption that $r = 5\%$ and alternatively that $r = 1\%$, where $r$ stands for the risk-free interest rate.

(b) What should be the risk-free rate $r$ such that funds 1 and 2 will have the same Treynor's performance index?

15.5 Hypothetical rates of return on two mutual funds and on the market portfolio are as follows (in %):

| Year | Fund A | Fund B | Market Portfolio |
|------|--------|--------|------------------|
| 1979 | 10 | −10 | 5 |
| 1980 | 8 | 9 | 4 |
| 1981 | 20 | 30 | 10 |
| 1982 | 15 | 18 | 9 |
| 1983 | 15 | 20 | 15 |

(a) On the assumption that the risk-free interest rate is $r = 5\%$ rank the two funds by Jensen and Treynor performance indexes.

(b) Now assume that the risk-free interest rate falls between the bounds $2\% < r < 10\%$ but the precise figure is not known. Rank the two funds by their Treynor's performance index. Illustrate your result graphically.

15.6    Give an example such that two mutual funds have different ranking by Jensen's index and by Treynor's index. How do your account for this discrepancy?

15.7    Assume that the entire market consists only of two stocks. The rates of return on these two stocks are as follows (in %):

| Year | Stock A | Stock B |
|------|---------|---------|
| 1980 | +5  | +8  |
| 1981 | +12 | +20 |
| 1982 | +15 | −10 |
| 1983 | −30 | +40 |
| 1984 | +20 | 0   |

The risk-free interest rate is $r = 5\%$

(a) Find the efficient portfolio consisting of risky assets only which corresponds to $r = 5\%$.

(b) Assuming that the portfolio obtained in part (a) is the market portfolio, calculate the betas of the two stocks and rank them by Treynor's performance index.

(c) Calculate Jensen's performance index of the two stocks. Compare and discuss your results.

(d) How would your answer to parts (a), (b) and (c) change if the risk-free interest rate were $r = 1\%$, rather than 5%? Answer (d) without carrying out any calculations.

15.8    Hypothetical rates of return on a mutual fund and on the market portfolio are as follows (in %):

| Year | Mutual Fund | Market Portfolio |
|------|-------------|------------------|
| 1980 | −10 | −8  |
| 1981 | +12 | +7  |
| 1982 | +15 | +10 |
| 1983 | 0   | +20 |
| 1984 | +30 | +10 |

The risk-free interest rate is 5%.

(a) Calculate the fund's excess return.

(b) Use Fama's approach to decompose the excess return into its two components: "Diversification" and "Net Selectivity". Illustrate your answer graphically.

15.9    The rates of return on two mutual funds are as follows (in %):

| Year | Fund A | Fund B |
|------|--------|--------|
| 1979 | −3 | −3 |
| 1980 | 2  | 2  |
| 1981 | 5  | 5  |
| 1982 | 6  | 6  |
| 1983 | 12 | 42 |

The riskless interest rate is $r = 1.5\%$.

(a) Which fund performed better by Sharpe's index?

(b) Which fund performed better by the First Degree Stochastic Dominance criterion?

15.10 "If Jensen's index is zero, then Treynor's index detects no excess return". Appraise the statement.

15.11 (a) Assume that the CAPM holds and the portfolios of any two investors include both risky and riskless assets. How would any two such portfolios be ranked by Sharpe's, Treynor's, and Jensen's indexes?

(*Hint*: In your answer denote by $x_i$ the proportion of risky assets held by the *i*th investor and by $(1 - x_i)$ the proportion invested in the risk-free asset.)

(b) How would any two single securities be ranked by the three indexes?

15.12 Appraise the following statements:

(a) If fund $A$ is mean–variance inefficient in relation to fund $B$, then fund $B$ will always outperform fund $A$ by Sharpe's index.

(b) If two mutual funds, $A$ and $B$, have a mean rate of return which is less than the riskless interest rate, then they have the same rank by Sharpe's performance index.

15.13 Appraise the following statement:

"Even if the CAPM actually holds, the Treynor performance indexes of any two funds are not necessarily equal, since the funds are not *necessarily* mean-variance efficient."

In your answer assume that there exists a mutual fund which is actually MV inefficient.

15.14 The following table gives the rate of return on Delta Trend Fund between 1972 and 1981. The riskless interest rate $r = 5\%$. Calculate Sharpe's performance measure for the mutual fund.

| | *Rate of Return (%)* |
|---|---|
| *Year* | *Delta Trend Fund* |
| 1972 | −7.9 |
| 1973 | −33.8 |
| 1974 | −37.8 |
| 1975 | 37.3 |
| 1976 | 29.5 |
| 1977 | 6.0 |
| 1978 | 2.7 |
| 1979 | 29.3 |
| 1980 | 28.9 |
| 1981 | 21.0 |

*Source:* Wiesenberger Investment Service, *Investment Companies*, 1982.

15.15  The following table lists annual rates of return on two mutual funds. Which fund out-performed the other by the stochastic dominance rules? Assume each return is equally probable.

| | Rate of Return (%) | |
| Year | New York Venture Fund | Oppenheimer Fund |
|---|---|---|
| 1972 | 22.2 | 10.0 |
| 1973 | −24.1 | −24.8 |
| 1974 | −20.1 | −25.9 |
| 1975 | 23.2 | 27.3 |
| 1976 | 20.8 | 15.8 |
| 1977 | 4.5 | −10.4 |
| 1978 | 19.4 | 8.4 |
| 1979 | 38.9 | 38.6 |
| 1980 | 44.0 | 41.9 |
| 1981 | 1.1 | −11.2 |

*Source:* Wiesenberger Investment Service, *Investment Companies*, 1982.

15.16  The following table lists annual rates of return on two mutual funds and on the market portfolio. Calculate Treynor's performance index for the mutual funds. The riskless interest rate $r = 5\%$. Do the funds outperform the market portfolio?

| | Rate of Return (%) | | |
| Year | Pilot Fund | Plitrend Fund | Market Portfolio |
|---|---|---|---|
| 1972 | 4.6 | 13.5 | 17.77 |
| 1973 | −9.5 | −17.2 | −16.92 |
| 1974 | −20.0 | −32.3 | −26.80 |
| 1975 | 23.6 | 36.8 | 37.77 |
| 1976 | 23.8 | 36.3 | 26.26 |
| 1977 | −1.8 | 17.5 | −4.81 |
| 1978 | 4.4 | 23.7 | 7.39 |
| 1979 | 27.5 | 48.1 | 21.82 |
| 1980 | 36.3 | 33.4 | 32.70 |
| 1981 | −8.6 | −0.4 | −4.22 |

*Source:* Wiesenberger Investment Service, *Investment Companies*, 1982 and the CRSP Monthly Returns Data Tape.

15.17  Calculate Jensen's performance index for the two mutual funds in Problem 15.16. Is the ranking of the two mutual funds by Jensen's performance index the same as the ranking of the two mutual funds by Treynor's performance index?

15.18  The following table gives the rates of return on a mutual fund and on the market portfolio. Decompose the excess rate of return on the fund using Fama's method. The risk-free interest rate is 5%.

| Year | Rate of Return (%) | |
| | Evergreen Fund | Market Portfolio |
| --- | --- | --- |
| 1972 | 10.1 | 17.77 |
| 1973 | −26.2 | −16.92 |
| 1974 | −21.4 | −26.80 |
| 1975 | 60.1 | 37.77 |
| 1976 | 48.8 | 26.26 |
| 1977 | 25.4 | −4.81 |
| 1978 | 38.0 | 7.39 |
| 1979 | 46.3 | 21.82 |
| 1980 | 48.1 | 32.70 |
| 1981 | −1.6 | −4.22 |

*Source:* Wiesenberger Investment Service, *Investment Companies*, 1982, and the CRSP Monthly Returns Data Tape.

15.19   What are the implications of Roll's critique of the CAPM empirical studies for the performance measures?

## Data Set Problems

1. Rank the 20 funds in the Maximum Capital Gain category by the following alternative *ex-post* measures:

   (a) by the average return;
   (b) by the geometric mean return;
   (c) by Sharpe's performance index ($PI_S$), assuming riskless interest rate $r = 5\%$.

   Compare and discuss the different rankings.

2. Use the Second Degree Stochastic Dominance (SSD) computer program from Appendix 6.3 to appraise the *ex-post* performance of the 20 mutual funds in the Maximum Capital Gain category:

   (a) Compare the performance of the funds relative to the market portfolio.
   (b) Compare the performance of all pairs of mutual funds (i.e., construct the SSD efficient set).
   Analyze your results.

3. Assuming riskless interest rate $r = 5\%$, rank the 20 mutual funds in the Maximum Capital Gain category:

   (a) by Treynor's performance index;
   (b) by Jensen's performance index. Compare and analyze the results obtained by the two indexes.

(c) Calculate the correlation coefficient between the two ranking measures in (a) and (b) above. Explain your findings.

4. Using the first fund from each category in the Data Set, show on the same diagram the range of riskless interest rates $r$ for which each fund dominates all the other funds included in the comparison. Assume that the interest rate is constant over time.

5. Use Fama's method to decompose the return on the Alpha Fund into the return from selectivity, the diversification effect, and the net selectivity effect. Show your results graphically. Assume $r = 5\%$ for the purpose of this analysis.

## Selected References

Ang, J. S. and Chua, J. H., "Composite Measures for the Evaluation of Investment Performance", *Journal of Financial and Quantitative Analysis* (June 1979).

Arditti, F. D., "Another Look at Mutual Fund Performance", *Journal of Financial and Quantitative Analysis* (June 1971).

Beebower, G. L. and Bergstrom, G. L., "Performance Analysis of Pension and Profit Sharing Portfolios", *Financial Analyst's Journal* (May 1977).

Blume, M. E., "Portfolio Theory: A Step Toward its Practical Application", *Journal of Business* (April 1970).

Bower, R. S., and Wippern, R. F., "Risk–Return Measurement in Portfolio Selection and Performance Appraisal Models: Progress Report", *Journal of Financial and Quantitative Analysis* (December 1969).

Breen, W., and Savage, J., "Portfolio Distribution and Tests of Security Selection Models", *Journal of Finance* (December 1968).

Burns, W. L. and Epley, D. R., "The Performance of Portfolios of REITS + Stocks", *Journal of Portfolio Management* (Spring 1982).

Carlson, S., "Aggregate Performance of Mutual Funds: 1948–1967", *Journal of Financial and Quantitative Analysis* (March 1970).

Chen, S. and Lee, C. F., "The Sampling Relationship Between Sharpe's Performance Measure and Its Risk Proxy: Sample Size, Investment Horizon and Market Conditions", *Management Science* (June 1981).

Cohen, K. J. and Pogue, G. A., "Some Comments Concerning Mutual Fund Versus Random Portfolio Performance", *Journal of Business* (April 1968).

Cranshaw, T. E., "The Evaluation of Investment Performance", *Journal of Business* (October 1977).

Dietz, P. O., "Measurement of Performance of Security Portfolios Components of a Measurement Model, Rate of Return, Risk and Timing", *Journal of Finance* (May 1968).

Evans, J. L., "An Analysis of Portfolio Maintenance Strategies", *Journal of Finance* (June 1970).

Fama, E. F., "Risk and the Evaluation of Pension Fund Performance", in *Measuring the Investment Performance of Pension Funds for the Purpose of Inter-Fund Comparison*. Park Ridge, Ill.: Bank Administration Institute, 1968.

Fama, E. F., "Components of Investment Performance", *Journal of Finance* (June 1972).

Frankfurter, G. M. and Phillips, H. E., "MPT Plus Security Analysis for Better Performance", *Journal of Portfolio Management* (Summer 1982).

Friend, I., and Vickers, D., "Portfolio Selection and Investment Performance", *Journal of Finance* (September 1965).

Friend, I.; Brown, F. E.; Herman, E. S.; and Vickers, D., *A Study of Mutual Funds*. Washington, D.C.: U.S. Government Printing Office, 1962.

Friend, I. and Blume, M., "Measurement of Portfolio Performance Under Uncertainty", *American Economic Review* (September 1970).

Gaumnitz, J. E., "Appraising Performance of Investment Portfolios", *Journal of Finance* (June 1970).

Grant, D., "Portfolio Performance and the Cost of Timing Decisions", *Journal of Finance* (June 1977).

Grauer, R. R., and Hakannson, N. H., "Higher Return, Lower Risk: Historical Returns on Long-Run Actively Managed Portfolios of Stocks, Bonds and Bills, 1936–1978", *Financial Analysts Journal* (March/April 1982).

Grant, D., "Portfolio Performance and the 'Cost' of Timing Decisions", *Journal of Finance* (June 1977).

Gumperz, J. and Page, E. W., "Pension Fund Performance", *Financial Analysts Journal* (May/June 1970).

Henriksson, R. D. and Merton, R. C., "On Market Timing and Investment Performance. II. Statistical Procedures for Evaluating Forecasting Skills", *Journal of Business* (October 1981).

Horowitz, I., "A Model for Mutual Fund Evaluation," *Industrial Management Review* (Spring 1965).

Horowitz, I., "The 'Reward-to-Variability' Ratio and Mutual Fund Performance", *Journal of Business* (October 1966).

Jensen, M. C., "Problems in Selection of Security Portfolios: The Performance of Mutual Funds in the Period 1945–1964", *Journal of Finance* (May 1968).

Jensen, M. C., "Risk, the Pricing of Capital Assets, and the Evaluation of Investment Portfolios", *Journal of Business* (April 1969).

Jobson, J. D. and Korkie, B. M., "Performance Hypothesis Testing with the Sharpe and Treynor Measures", *Journal of Finance* (September 1981).

Joy, M. O. and Porter, R. B., "Stochastic Dominance and Mutual Fund Performance", *Journal of Financial and Quantitative Analysis* (January 1974).

Klemkosky, R. C., "The Bias in Composite Performance Measures", *Journal of Financial and Quantitative Analysis* (June 1973).

Kon, S. J. and Jen, F. C., "Estimation of Time-varying Systematic Risk and Performance for Mutual Fund Portfolios: An Application of Switching Regression", *Journal of Finance* (May 1978).

Kon, S. J. and Jen, F. C., "The Investment Performance of Mutual Funds: An Empirical Investigation of Timing, Selectivity and Market-Efficiency", *Journal of Business* (April 1979).

Lee, C. F. and Jen, F. C., "Effects of Measurement Errors on Systematic Risk and Performance Measure of a Portfolio", *Journal of Financial and Quantitative Analysis* (June 1978).

Levhari, D. and Levy, H., "The Capital Asset Pricing Model and the Investment Horizon", *Review of Economics and Statistics* (February 1977).

Levy, H., "Portfolio Performance and the Investment Horizon", *Management Science* (August 1972).

Malkiel, B. G., "The Valuation of Closed End Investment Company Shares", *Journal of Finance* (June 1977).

Mao, J. C. T., "Essentials of Portfolio Diversification Strategy", *Journal of Finance* (December 1970).

Merton, R. C., "On Market Timing and Investment Performance. I. An Equilibrium Theory of Value for Market Forecasts", *Journal of Business* (July 1981).

Meyer, J., "Further Applications of Stochastic Dominance to Mutual Fund Performance", *Journal of Financial and Quantitative Analysis* (June 1977).

Miles, M. and Esty, A., "How Well do Commingled Real Estate Funds Perform?", *Journal of Portfolio Management* (Winter 1982).

Mills, H. D., "On the Measurement of Fund Performance", *Journal of Finance* (December 1970).

Monroe, R. J. and Trieschmann, J., "Portfolio Performance of Property-Liability Insurance Companies", *Journal of Financial and Quantitative Analysis* (March 1972).

Pohlman, R., Ang, J. and Hollinger, R., "Performance and Timing: A Test of Hedge Funds", *Journal of Portfolio Management* (Spring 1978).

Renwick, F. B., "Asset Management and Investor Portfolio Behavior: Theory and Practice", *Journal of Finance* (May 1969).

Rothstein, M., "On Geometric and Arithmetic Portfolio Performance Indexes", *Journal of Financial and Quantitative Analysis* (September 1972).

Sarnat, M., "A Note on the Prediction of Portfolio Performance from Ex-Post Data", *Journal of Finance* (September 1972).

Schlarbaum, G. G., "The Investment Performance of the Common Stock Portfolios of Property-Liability Insurance Companies", *Journal of Financial and Quantitative Analysis* (January 1974).

Schlarbaum, G. G., Lewellen, W. G. and Lease, R. C., "The Common-Stock Portfolio Performance Record of Individual Investors: 1964–70", *Journal of Finance* (May 1978).

Sharpe, W. F., "Mutual Fund Performance", *Journal of Business* (January 1966).

Sharpe, W. F., *Portfolio Theory and Capital Markets*. New York: McGraw-Hill, 1970.

Sharpe, W., "Bonds versus Stocks: Some Lessons from Capital Market Theory", *Financial Analysts Journal* (November/December 1973).

Shawky, H., "An Update on Mutual Funds: Better Grades", *Journal of Portfolio Management* (Winter 1982).

Shick, R. A. and Trieschmann, J. S., "Some Further Evidence on the Performance of Property-Liability Insurance Companies' Stock Portfolio", *Journal of Financial and Quantitative Analysis* (March 1978).

Simonson, D. G., "The Speculative Behavior of Mutual Funds", *Journal of Finance* (May 1972).

Smith, K. V., "Is Fund Growth Related to Fund Performance?" *Journal of Portfolio Management* (Spring 1978).

Smith, K. V. and Tito, D. A., "Risk-Return Measures of Ex-Post Portfolio Performance", *Journal of Financial and Quantitative Analysis* (December 1969).

Tehranian, H., "Empirical Studies of Portfolio Performance Using Higher Degrees of Stochastic Dominance", *Journal of Finance* (May 1980).

Treynor, J. L., "How to Rate Management Investment Funds", *Harvard Business Review* (Jan.–Feb. 1965).

Treynor, J. L., and Mazuy, K., "Can Mutual Funds Outguess the Market?" *Harvard Business Review* (July–August 1966).

Veit, E. T. and Cheney, J. M., "Are Mutual Funds Market Timers?" *Journal of Portfolio Management* (Winter 1982).

Wallingford, B. A., "A Survey and Comparison of Portfolio Selection Models", *Journal of Financial and Quantitative Analysis* (June 1967).

West, R. R., "Mutual Fund Performance and the Theory of Capital Asset Pricing: Some Comments", *Journal of Business* (April 1968).

Williamson, P. F., "Measuring Mutual Fund Performance", *Financial Analysts Journal* (November/December 1972).

# PART V
# Other Selected Topics

# 16

# Options: Return Profiles

In 1973, the year that the Chicago Board of Options Exchange (CBOE) opened, only eighteen stocks had options listed. Today, alongside the CBOE, several other exchanges (American, Philadelphia and Pacific Exchanges) list options and the number of stocks with options is well over two hundred. The trading volume in options also increased rapidly and it now exceeds the total volume on the American Stock Exchange.

The rising popularity of options trading in the investment community has been accompanied by a rising interest in option valuation among the academic community. Indeed various option valuation models have been developed, some of which are actually used by practitioners to spot mispriced options.

In this chapter we describe various types of options and various investment strategies in options. In the next chapter (Chapter 17), we discuss some valuation models and conclude with some empirical evidence testing the theoretical option valuation formulas.

## 16.1   Types of Options

Options are contracts to buy or sell a particular stock for a fixed price at or before a specified date in the future.

Although there are only two basic option types—a call and a put—the number of possible investment strategies in the options market is quite large and keeps increasing with the introduction of new investment combinations. We describe in this section the main financial instruments available in the options market.

Before starting with option valuation analysis, the basic terminology of the options market has to be introduced:

*Underlying stock* is the stock involved in the option contract.
*Exercise price* (or *striking price*) is the price at which the underlying stock may be bought (for a call option) or sold (for a put option).

**563**

*Expiration date* (or *maturity date*) is the latest date when the option may be exercised.

*European option* is an option that can be exercised only at the maturity date.

*American option* is an option that can be exercised at any time not later than the maturity date.

We now proceed to describe the main types of options available to the investor, which are known as *calls* and *puts*. Although most of the traded options are American options (in the sense of the above definition), the valuation models mostly focus on European options because of their fixed exercise date. Moreover, we show in Section 16.8 below that it does not pay to exercise an American option before maturity, so that in effect American options are generally treated like European options. In some cases, however, the early exercise feature of the American options is valuable, and these cases are also discussed in Section 16.8.

### 16.1.1 Call Options

American calls constitute the most prominent type of options. A *call* option is a right (but not an obligation!) to buy a given number of shares of the underlying stock at a given price (striking price) on or before a specific date (the expiration date).

EXAMPLES

On January 7, 1982, a call on Exxon stock traded for $5\frac{5}{8}$. The expiration date was the last day in April 1982, the striking price was $25, and the market price of the underlying stock on that date was $30\frac{3}{8}$.

Thus the holder of the call option was entitled to buy a share of Exxon stock for $25 at any date before the end of April 1982. The options are traded in the market and in our particular example the price of the call on Exxon stock was $5\frac{5}{8}$. The price of the option plus the striking price was slightly higher than the market price of Exxon stock ($30\frac{5}{8}$ compared to $30\frac{3}{8}$).[1]

On the same day the price of the stock of the Xerox Corporation was $39\frac{5}{8}$. The striking price on an April 1982 call was $60 and the call price was $\frac{1}{16}$. The call price in this case is very close to zero since there is a very small chance that the market price of the call will rise in a relatively short period of less than three months from less than $40 to over $60. Recall that a call option is a *right* to buy the underlying stock, but not an obligation. Thus, if until April 1982 the price of Xerox stock remains below $60, the call value will drop to zero since no rational investor will exercise the option at a striking price of $60 when he can buy the stock in the market for less than $60.

More than one call written on the same stock may be traded in the market. For example on January 7, 1982, 13 different calls on Xerox stock were traded on CBOE as

---

[1] In general call options are protected against splits and stock dividends, but not against cash dividend distribution. Thus, if a stock dividend reduces the stock price, the exercise price of the option is also appropriately adjusted to allow for the stock dividend, while no such adjustment is made following cash dividend distribution.

**Table 16.1**
**Calls on Xerox Corporation Stock**

| Stock Price ($) | Striking Price ($) | Call Price for Various Expiration Dates (in $) | | |
|---|---|---|---|---|
| | | Jan. 1982 | April 1982 | July 1982 |
| $39\frac{5}{8}$ | 35 | $4\frac{3}{4}$ | $5\frac{3}{4}$ | r |
| $39\frac{5}{8}$ | 40 | $\frac{9}{16}$ | $\frac{11}{16}$ | $3\frac{7}{8}$ |
| $39\frac{5}{8}$ | 45 | $\frac{1}{16}$ | $\frac{15}{16}$ | $\frac{13}{16}$ |
| $39\frac{5}{8}$ | 50 | r | $\frac{5}{16}$ | s |
| $39\frac{5}{8}$ | 55 | $\frac{1}{16}$ | $\frac{3}{16}$ | s |
| $39\frac{5}{8}$ | 60 | $\frac{1}{16}$ | $\frac{1}{16}$ | s |

r means "not traded"; s means "no option offered".
Source: Wall Street Journal, January 7, 1982.

shown in Table 16.1. Obviously, the market price of the underlying stock is the same for all calls, $39\frac{5}{8}$. However, the striking price and the expiration date vary from one contract to another. For a given stock price, the lower the striking price, the higher is the chance of making a profit by exercising the option, and hence as expected, the market price of the option increases as the striking price decreases for options with the same expiration date. For example, for options with a January 1982 expiration date, the call price was $4\frac{3}{4}$ for $35 striking price dropping to $\frac{1}{16}$ for $60 striking price (see Table 16.1).

A second interesting phenomenon revealed by the Xerox example is that the option price is higher for later expiration dates. Namely, for two call contracts which are identical in all respects except the maturity date, the call with the longer time to expiration will have the higher market price. Thus in Table 16.1, the call with $35 striking price on Xerox stock expiring at the end of January 1982 (in about three weeks from the date of the market date) trades for $4\frac{3}{4}$, whereas the same call expiring at the end of April 1982 trades for $5\frac{3}{4}$. The reason for this is quite simple: the longer the time remaining until expiration, the greater is the chance that the price of the underlying stock will move up, and this clearly increases the profit potential of the option. This property holds for European as well as American options, yet with American options the intuitive explanation is more transparent: indeed, if investors have a choice of buying an option that can be exercised during the next month or alternatively during the next two months, they will always prefer the latter, since it includes the first month's opportunity to exercise *plus* a right to exercise the option during one additional month. Thus, investors will be willing to pay more for options with longer maturities.

### 16.1.2 Put Options

A *put* is a right (but not an obligation) to sell a given number of shares of the underlying stock at a specified price on or before a specific date.

**Table 16.2**
**Puts on Boeing Stock**

| Stock Price ($) | Striking Price ($) | Put Price for Various Expiration Dates (in $) | | |
|---|---|---|---|---|
| | | Jan. 1982 | April 1982 | July 1982 |
| $22\frac{3}{4}$ | 20 | $\frac{5}{16}$ | $\frac{7}{8}$ | $1\frac{3}{8}$ |
| $22\frac{3}{4}$ | 25 | $2\frac{1}{2}$ | 3 | $3\frac{7}{8}$ |
| $22\frac{3}{4}$ | 30 | $7\frac{1}{2}$ | r | s |
| $22\frac{3}{4}$ | 35 | r | s | s |

r means "not traded"; s means "no option offered".
*Source: Wall Street Journal*, Jan. 7, 1982.

The put option differs from the call option in that the word "buy" is replaced with "sell". For example, on January 7, 1982, the price of the put written on Alcoa stock was $2 for a July 1982 expiration date. The striking price was $25 while the market price of Alcoa stock on that day was $25$\frac{1}{2}$. The put holder has the right to sell one share of Alcoa at $25 at any time before the end of July 1982. As long as the price of Alcoa remains above $25 the put will not be exercised since it is more profitable to sell the stock at the market price, which is higher than $25. Unlike the call options, other things being equal, the *higher* the striking price the *higher* is the put price. To understand this, recall that with put options the investor *sells* the stock at the striking price rather than buys it, so that for a given market price of the underlying stock the profit potential is higher for a higher striking price.

As with the call option, however, the longer the time remaining to expiration, the higher is the put price since the investor is allowed a longer period of time over which to exercise the put.

We demonstrate these two properties of the put options in Table 16.2 using the CBOE data on Boeing puts.

The Boeing put figures reveal the following: (a) for a given maturity, the higher the striking price, the higher is the option market price; (b) for a given striking price, the longer the time remaining until the expiration date, the higher is the put price.

In the next section, we analyze these basic properties of calls and puts in terms of the future price distribution of the underlying stock.

## 16.1.3 Calls and Puts: Graphical Exposition

The put and call prices and their relationship to the price of the underlying stock can be illustrated by graphical means. Suppose that the future price distribution of the underlying stock is as shown in Figure 16.1. For a European call, we define $f(S_t)$ as the probability distribution density of the stock price $S_t$ at some future point of time $t$. For an American call, $f(S_t)$ represents all the possible values which the stock price $S_t$ may take from the present to some future exercise date $t$. $S_0$ denotes the current market price of the stock and $E$ is the exercise price. Assuming that the option is held until the expiration date (see Section 16.8), the holder of the call will make a profit by exercising the call only if the stock price at expiration $S_t$ is higher than $E$ (see Figure 16.1(a)). If the stock price at maturity is less than the striking price, the call is worthless: it is cheaper to buy the stock in the market for $S_t$ than to exercise the call paying $E$ for the same stock. The potential profit of the call holder is thus given by the shaded area in panel (a), which is the right tail of the distribution. Clearly, as the striking price is reduced, the point $E$ shifts to the left and the shaded area (the potential profit) increases. Since the potential profit increases as $E$ decreases, the investor should be willing to pay a higher price for a call with a lower exercise price.

Panel (b) of Figure 16.1 illustrates the case of a put option. The investor has the right to sell the stock at exercise price $E$. If the stock price is greater than $E$ at the expiration date $t$, the value of the put is zero: it is better to sell the stock in the market than to exercise the put. However, if the market price of the underlying stock falls below $E$ on expiration, the put holder can exercise the option and make a profit. Suppose that the stock price falls to $S_1$. In this case the profit is $E - S_1$: even if the investor does not have the stock, he can buy it for $S_1$ and sell it for the higher price $E$, as stated in his contract, thus making the profit $E - S_1$. The potential profit from holding a put option is illustrated by the left tail of the distribution in Figure 16.1(b), the shaded area left to $E$. Obviously, the higher the striking price $E$, the larger is the shaded area and hence the larger is the potential profit from holding a put, so that investors should be willing to pay a higher price for the put as the striking price increases. This is consistent with the data on Boeing put options in Table 16.2.

The prices of various options are published by the financial papers. The full list of traded options is much too long to be included in this chapter. Thus Table 16.3 presents data of a sampling of the options traded on the CBOE for January 6, 1982 to familiarize the reader with the way in which the options' data are published.

Given the stock price distribution (which can be estimated subjectively), the data published in the financial newspapers are sufficient in order to draw the right tail of the price distribution relevant to the holder of a call and the left tail of the stock price

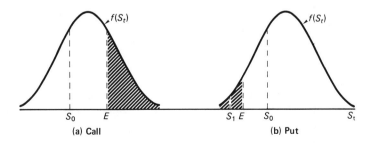

**Figure 16.1**

**Table 16.3**
**Sample Column from *The Wall Street Journal* for January 6, 1982**

# Listed Options Quotations

Wednesday, January 6, 1982
Closing prices of all options. Sales unit usually is 100 shares. Security description includes exercise price. Stock close is New York or American exchange final price.

| Option & NY Close | Strike Price | Calls–Last | | | Puts–Last | | |
|---|---|---|---|---|---|---|---|
| | | Feb | May | Aug | Feb | May | Aug |
| 69⅛ | 80 | 5-16 | 1⅞ | 3⅝ | 10¾ | 10¾ | r |
| 69⅛ | 90 | 1-16 | ½ | s | 21 | 21 | s |
| 69⅛ | 100 | r | ⅛ | s | 31 | 30½ | s |
| Humana | 30 | r | 7¼ | r | ⅜ | 1¼ | r |
| 35¼ | 35 | 2⅛ | 4 | r | 1¾ | 3 | r |
| 35¼ | 40 | ½ | 2⅜ | 3 | 5¼ | 6⅜ | r |
| In Flv | 20 | ⅜ | 1 | 2½ | r | r | r |
| 18⅝ | 25 | r | ⅜ | 11-16 | r | r | r |
| MGIC | 45 | r | r | r | r | 1¼ | r |
| Manvil | 10 | 4⅜ | r | r | r | r | 7-16 |
| 14½ | 15 | 9-16 | 1⅛ | 1⅞ | r | r | 1¾ |
| 14½ | 20 | r | ⅜ | ⅝ | 5½ | r | 5⅝ |
| Mobil | 20 | 4¼ | 5 | 5¼ | r | 5-16 | ½ |
| 24⅛ | 25 | ⅝ | 1 7-16 | 2 5-16 | 1 7-16 | 2 1-16 | 2⅛ |
| 24⅛ | 27½ | 3-16 | s | s | 3⅝ | s | s |
| 24⅛ | 30 | 1-16 | ⅜ | 13-16 | 6 | 6⅛ | r |
| 24⅛ | 32½ | 1-16 | s | s | r | s | s |
| 24⅛ | 35 | 1-16 | 3-16 | s | r | r | s |
| N Semi | 15 | 3¼ | 4½ | 4¾ | 3-16 | ⅝ | 15-16 |
| 18 | 20 | 11-16 | 1 13-16 | 2⅝ | 2⅜ | 2¾ | 3⅛ |
| 18 | 25 | 3-16 | 13-16 | 1 5-16 | 7 | 7¼ | r |
| 18 | 30 | 1-16 | s | s | 11⅞ | s | s |
| 18 | 35 | r | s | s | 16⅞ | s | s |
| Occi | 20 | 4⅛ | 4½ | 4⅞ | 1-16 | ½ | ⅝ |
| 23⅝ | 25 | 9-16 | 1 7-16 | 2⅛ | 1⅝ | 1⅞ | 2¼ |
| 23⅝ | 30 | ⅛ | 5-16 | ¾ | 6½ | 6½ | r |
| 23⅝ | 35 | 1-16 | 3-16 | s | r | r | s |
| Ow Ill | 30 | s | 1 | r | s | r | r |
| Raythn | 30 | 5⅛ | r | s | 1-16 | r | s |
| 35⅜ | 35 | 2 | 3½ | r | 1½ | 2¼ | 2½ |
| 35⅜ | 40 | 9-16 | 1½ | 2¼ | 5 | r | r |
| 35⅜ | 45 | ⅛ | ¾ | 1¼ | 9¾ | 10 | r |
| 35⅜ | 50 | r | ⅜ | s | r | r | s |
| Rynlds | 45 | 2½ | 3½ | r | 1 | r | r |
| 46⅜ | 50 | 7-16 | 1⅝ | 2¼ | 3⅞ | r | r |
| 46⅜ | 55 | 1-16 | ⅝ | r | r | r | r |
| Rockwl | 35 | s | 1 3-16 | r | s | r | r |
| Slumb | 45 | 8 | 9½ | s | ⅜ | 1 | s |
| 51½ | 50 | 3¾ | 6½ | r | 1⅜ | 2¾ | 3 |
| 51½ | 55 | 1½ | 4⅜ | 5½ | 4½ | 5⅛ | 5¼ |
| 51½ | 60 | ½ | 2½ | 3⅞ | 8¾ | 8¾ | r |
| 51½ | 65 | ⅛ | 1⅛ | s | r | 13 | s |
| 51½ | 70 | 1-16 | 9-16 | s | r | r | s |
| Slb o | 60 | ½ | s | s | 8½ | s | s |
| 51½ | 66⅝ | r | s | s | 15 | s | s |
| Skylin | 15 | 11-16 | 1½ | 2¼ | r | 1¾ | r |
| 14⅜ | 20 | 1-16 | ⅜ | r | r | r | r |
| Southn | 10 | 2⅛ | r | 2⅜ | r | r | r |
| 12⅛ | 15 | r | r | ⅛ | r | r | r |
| St Ind | 45 | 4 | 5 | 7 | ⅝ | 1½ | 2¼ |
| 47⅞ | 50 | 1 1-16 | 3⅛ | 4½ | 2¾ | 3⅞ | 4¼ |
| 47⅞ | 55 | ¼ | 1 11-16 | 3 | 6¾ | 8 | 8 |
| 47⅞ | 60 | ⅛ | ¾ | 1½ | 12½ | r | r |
| 47⅞ | 70 | r | ⅛ | s | r | r | s |
| U A L | 15 | 2⅜ | 3⅛ | 3½ | ⅜ | ⅝ | r |
| 16½ | 20 | ¼ | ⅞ | 1¾ | 3½ | 3½ | 4¼ |
| 16½ | 25 | 1-16 | 5-16 | ⅝ | r | r | r |
| UNC Rs | 10 | ⅛ | ½ | r | r | r | r |
| U Tech | 35 | 7⅜ | r | r | ⅛ | r | r |
| 42¾ | 40 | 3⅝ | 4⅞ | r | ⅝ | 1⅝ | r |
| 42¾ | 45 | 13-16 | 2¼ | 3¼ | 3⅜ | 3¾ | r |
| 42¾ | 50 | ⅛ | ¾ | s | r | r | s |
| J Walt | 20 | r | 1¾ | r | r | 1½ | r |
| 20⅛ | 25 | r | 9-16 | 1 | r | r | r |
| WarnCm | 40 | 11¾ | r | s | 1-16 | ⅝ | s |
| 51½ | 45 | 7 | 8½ | s | ½ | 1⅜ | s |
| 51½ | 50 | 3¾ | 6½ | 8 | 1¾ | 3⅜ | 4½ |
| 51½ | 55 | 1½ | 3⅞ | 6 | 4½ | 5⅝ | r |
| 51½ | 60 | ½ | 2¼ | 3¾ | 8⅜ | 9½ | 9⅞ |
| Willms | 20 | 6¼ | 7⅛ | s | r | 7-16 | s |
| 25⅝ | 25 | 2⅛ | 3¾ | 4½ | ⅞ | 1¾ | 2⅝ |
| 25⅝ | 30 | ⅞ | 2 3-16 | 2 13-16 | 4½ | 5 | r |
| 25⅝ | 35 | ⅜ | 1 5-16 | 2 | r | r | r |
| 25⅝ | 40 | 3-16 | 13-16 | s | r | r | s |

*r* denotes *not traded*; *s* denotes *no option offered*.


distribution relevant to the holder of the put. Indeed, the striking price is known for the various options, and if the stock price distribution $f(S_t)$ has been estimated, the tails of the distribution can be drawn. Recall that $f(S_t)$ (and hence the tails) are a function of the time remaining to maturity. Hypothetical stock price distributions relevant for a call option with one day to maturity and a call option with 30 days to maturity are shown in Figure 16.2. The longer the time remaining to maturity, the greater is the uncertainty in future stock prices, so the stock price distribution is more widely spread (has higher variance). Thus, the shaded area right to point $E$ is larger for the 30 days option and hence the price of this call option will be greater. The same argument applies to the left tail determining the put price.

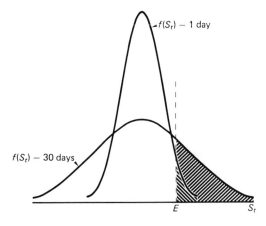

**Figure 16.2**

## 16.2    Option Trading

The transactions in options are not carried out directly between sellers and buyers. All options are bought or written on the exchange through the Option Clearing Corporation. The anonymity of the participants in the transactions creates a current market for options which allows each investor to buy or sell an option in the market at any time.

Normally the option contracts are in units of 100 shares. Thus, if the published quotation of a call is, say, $2 and the exercise price is $30, the holder of the call will have to pay $30 × 100 = $3000 for 100 shares of the underlying stock when the option is exercised and the market price of the call entitling the buyer to this privilege is $2 × 100 = $200.

The transactions are made through a brokerage firm which, of course, charges a commission. The commission is negotiable and hence varies from one broker to another and from one customer to another.

All option trades are taxed as capital gains. Since all listed options have maturities of less than 12 months, the short-term capital gains rules apply.

Finally, unlike with stocks, the purchase of options must be paid for in full and no margin is allowed.

## 16.3    Profit Profiles of Calls and Puts

For each investor buying a call, there must be an investor who sells the call. The latter is known to the financial community as the "writer" (seller) of the call. Since holding a call and writing a call are two opposite transactions, it is clear that whenever one side makes a profit, the other side must lose. Let us describe the payoff matrix of each side (Table 16.4).

**Table 16.4**
**Profit Profiles of a Call**

| Holder of a Call | | Writer of a Call | |
|---|---|---|---|
| $-C$ | if $S_t \leqslant E$ | $C$ | if $S_t \leqslant E$ |
| $(S_t - E) - C$ | if $S_t > E$ | $C - (S_t - E)$ | if $S_t > E$ |

If the stock price on expiration date, $S_t$, is less than the exercise price, i.e., $S_t < E$, the holder of the call will allow it to expire without exercising and his loss is equal to the entire amount $C$ paid when purchasing the call. If conversely $S_t > E$, the holder will exercise the call by paying the striking price $E$ for a share of stock worth $S_t$: his profit will be $S_t - E$ minus his initial investment $C$. Denoting by $y_t$ the call holder's profit (or loss) in the case $S_t > E$, which is equal to $(S_t - E) - C$, we see that $y_t$ is a linear function of the stock price $S_t$ since it can be rewritten as:

$$y_t = -(C + E) + S_t$$

The slope of this line is $+1$ and the vertical intercept is a negative number $-(C + E)$, representing the total "investment" in the stock.

For a call writer we have exactly the opposite cashflows: if $S_t < E$, the call is not exercised and he makes a profit equal to the initial proceeds from writing the call, $C$. If on the other hand $S_t > E$ and the call is exercised, the call writer is obligated to deliver a stock worth $S_t$ for a price $E$. The call writer's profit (or loss) in this case is thus $C - (S_t - E)$, which may be rewritten as:

$$y_t = (C + E) - S_t$$

This is again a straight line as a function of the stock price $S_t$ but with a negative slope of $-1$ and positive vertical intercept $C + E$, representing the total "receipts" from the transaction.

EXAMPLE
Figure 16.3 illustrates the profit profiles of a call writer and a call holder for the following specific numerical example:

| | |
|---|---|
| Call price | $C = \$1$ |
| Exercise price | $E = \$10$ |
| Stock price at expiration date | $S_t =$ an unknown random variable (plotted along the horizontal axis) |

Note that for the call holder [panel (a)], the profit line intersects the horizontal axis at $S_t = \$11$, since for $S_t = \$11$ his profit from exercising the stock $S_t - E = \$11 - \$10 = \$1$ exactly offsets his initial investment $C = \$1$. At the breakeven point we always have $y_t = 0$ or $S_t = E + C$, which in our case gives $S_t = \$10 + \$1 = \$11$. Each dollar of

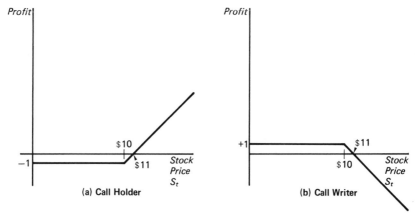

**Figure 16.3**

increase in $S_t$ above \$11 produces a one dollar increase in the profit of the call holder, hence the slope of the profit line is $+1$. A similar argument has been employed to draw the profit profile of a call writer [panel (b)]. His breakeven point is given by $y_t = (C + E) - S_t = 0$ or $S_t = C + E = \$1 + \$10 = \$11$. The call holder and the call writer thus have the same breakeven point, on either side of which their profiles are mirror images of one another.

Let us now turn to describe the cashflow profile of a put (see Table 16.5). The put holder loses the entire investment $P$ if $S_t > E$: it is better to sell in the market than to exercise. Conversely, if $S_t < E$, he makes a profit of $(E - S_t)$, less his initial investment $P$. Thus if the put is exercised, the put holder's profit (or loss) $y_t$ is a straight line as a function of the stock price $S_t$ given by

$$y_t = -P + (E - S_t) = (E - P) - S_t$$

This line has a negative slope of $-1$ and a (positive) vertical intercept $E - P$. The put writer conversely makes a profit of $P$ if $S_t > E$, since the option is not exercised and he gets to keep the cash proceeds $P$ from writing the put. If, however, $S_t < E$, he loses $(E - S_t)$ by selling for $E$ a share of stock worth $S_t$ in the market, and his total cashflow is:

$$y_t = P - (E - S_t) = -(E - P) + S_t$$

**Table 16.5**
**Profit Profiles of a Put**

| Holder of a Put | | Writer of a Put | |
|---|---|---|---|
| $-P$ | if $S_t \geqslant E$ | $P$ | if $S_t \geqslant E$ |
| $(E - S_t) - P$ | if $S_t < E$ | $P - (E - S_t)$ | if $S_t < E$ |

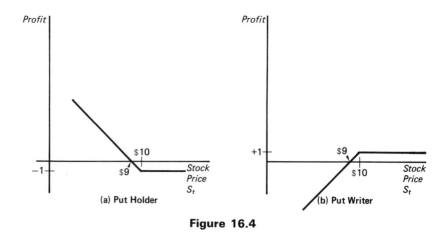

**Figure 16.4**

which is again a linear function of the stock price $S_t$, with a slope of $+1$ and a (negative) vertical intercept $-(E - P)$.

EXAMPLE

Figure 16.4 illustrates the profit profiles of a put holder [panel (a)] and a put writer [panel (b)] for the following specific example: $E = \$10$, $P = \$1$ and $S_t$ is an unknown random variable plotted along the horizontal axis.

Note that if the stock price falls from $10 to $9, both the put holder and the put writer exactly break even, since the cashflow for both sides involved in the transaction vanishes:

$$\text{Put holder:} \quad -P + (E - S_t) = -1 + (10 - 9) = 0$$
$$\text{Put writer:} \quad +P - (E - S_t) = +1 - (10 - 9) = 0$$

## 16.4    Warrants

*Warrants* are similar to call options in the following respect: the holder of a warrant has the right to exercise the warrant on or before the expiration date at some predetermined exercise price. However, unlike call options, warrants are issued by business corporations and thus involve cashflows between corporations and investors, and not between two investors as with call or put contracts. Also warrants can have maturities of several years, unlike options which usually expire in less than 12 months. Thus, the difference between call options and warrants can be summarized as follows:

(1)    The maturity of warrants in general is longer.
(2)    In general, it is the issuing corporation that receives the proceeds from selling the warrants.

(3)    On exercise, the holders of warrants pay the corporation the exercise price
for its stock.

(4)    When a warrant is exercised, the corporation issues stock and the number of
outstanding shares goes up. The corporation gets back the warrant and
hence the number of outstanding warrants decreases, completely vanishing
if all investors exercise their warrants.

Warrants are thus another form of financial instrument for raising money by
corporations. Unlike calls and puts, which are negotiated directly between investors,
warrants have an impact on the corporate cashflows and capital structure. From the
investor's point of view, however, a warrant is an investment with some characteristics
which are similar to the call option, since the warrants will be exercised only if the stock
price is higher than the exercise price.

## 16.5    Combinations

Although it is less common to trade in combinations than in calls and puts, there are
many combinations available in the option market. We will mention only some of them
here.

A combination of a put and a call on the same stock with the same exercise price is
called a *straddle*. For example, assume that the exercise price is $10 and the call and the
put are each priced $1. If the stock price goes up above $10, the investor will exercise
the call (the put is valueless in this case), breaking even at stock price $S_t = \$12$ when his
cashflow from holding a straddle is zero,

$$(S_t - E) - P - C = (12 - 10) - 1 - 1 = 0$$

For $S_t > \$12$, his cashflow will be positive (he will have made a profit).

If the stock price falls below $10, the investor will exercise the put (the call is
valueless in this case) and at $S_t = \$8$ he exactly breaks even since his cashflow from
holding a straddle is zero,

$$(E - S_t) - P - C = (10 - 8) - 1 - 1 = 0$$

For $S_t < \$8$ once again his cashflow will be positive. Obviously, for a writer of a
straddle we have just the opposite cashflow relations, since whenever the straddle holder
makes a profit, the straddle writer loses, and vice versa. Figure 16.5 illustrates the cashflow profiles of a holder and a writer of a straddle [panels (a) and (b), respectively].

Other well-known combinations are *strips* and *straps*. A strip is a combination of
two puts and one call while a strap is a combination of two calls and one put. Indeed,
one can create an infinite number of combinations in the options market, limited only by
the investors' imagination.

Finally, one can combine investments in stocks and in options. These combina-

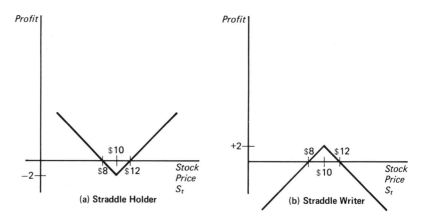

**Figure 16.5**

tions are important because they are employed in deriving the common option pricing formula that we shall discuss in the next chapter. To illustrate, suppose that an investor writes a call on a stock he owns. The cashflow from the resulting combination is as follows:

$$\text{From the call:} \begin{cases} C & \text{if } S_t \leqslant E \\ C - (S_t - E) & \text{if } S_t > E \end{cases}$$

$$\text{From the stock:} \quad S_t$$

Thus the value of his portfolio at the call expiration date will be the sum of the two cashflow components,

$$\text{Value of stock–call portfolio} = \begin{cases} C + S_t & \text{if } S_t \leqslant E \\ C + E & \text{if } S_t > E \end{cases}$$

The value of the portfolio consisting of a stock and a call written on that stock is illustrated in Figure 16.6. Note that the value of the call component is exactly as illustrated before. The value of the stock is described by a straight line with a slope of $+1$, since any increase (or decrease) in the stock price $S_t$ is necessarily followed by the same change in the terminal value of the investment that consists of the stock alone.

However, when the investor who holds the stock also writes a call on that stock, the value of his portfolio is $C + S_t$ for all $S_t \leqslant E$, so that the appropriate profile is achieved by shifting the $S_t$ line upward by the fixed amount $C$. The interesting feature of such a combination is that for $S_t > E$, the investor, by creating the stock–call portfolio, achieves a *certain* income equal to $C + E$. The certain income is achieved despite the possibly high volatility of the stock price. The reason for the stability of income in this

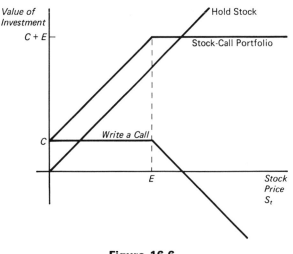

**Figure 16.6**

range is that when $S_t$ rises above $E$, for each \$1 profit on the stock the investor loses \$1 from writing the call (since it is certain to be exercised). Hence the volatility of the stock price has no impact on the value of the portfolio, which remains $C + E$, where $C$ is the proceeds from writing the call and $E$ the proceeds from the exercise of the call.

Creating such *hedged portfolios* that guarantee certain income is the technique used in option valuation models that we will discuss in the next chapter (Chapter 17).

## 16.6    Leverage and Options

Suppose that an investor considers investing a given sum (say \$100) either in a stock or in the corresponding call. If the stock price at the expiration date is below the exercise price, the terminal wealth of the option holder is zero (namely a loss of 100%) and holding the stock rather than the call proves to be a better investment strategy. However, if $S_t > E$ on the expiration date, investment in the option is much more profitable: for each \$1 profit on the stock, we can make \$1 profit by holding the call, but since the call initially costs much less than the stock, the percentage rate of return on the call is much higher. Thus, a relatively small investment in the call guarantees that the investor gets the same absolute profit as the stock holder. This implies that the investment in the option is highly leveraged.

EXAMPLE

Let us demonstrate the leverage component of call options by looking at some data on a stock and the corresponding call price changes recorded on the CBOE.

The quotations for the Exxon call and for the corresponding stock on January 6 and on January 7, 1982, were as follows:

| | *Jan. 6, 1982* | *Jan. 7, 1982* |
|---|---|---|
| Stock price | $\$30\frac{1}{4}$ | $\$30\frac{3}{8}$ |
| Call price | $5 | $\$5\frac{5}{8}$ |

The exercise price was $25 and the option expiration date was the last day in January 1982.

The investor who invested in Exxon stock on January 6, 1982, made $\$\frac{1}{8}$ in one day, which is approximately 0.4%, i.e., less than a half percent on the investment $((\frac{1}{8}:30\frac{1}{4}) \times 100 = 0.41)$. An investor who purchased the call rather than the stock (investing $5 instead of $\$30\frac{1}{4}$) made $\$\frac{5}{8}$, which is 12.5% on the investment. Thus, when the stock price is above the exercise price, any rise in the stock price is followed by a higher percentage rise in the call price. However, as in corporate capital structure, a leverage is a "two-edged sword". When the price of the stock falls, a much sharper percentage loss is incurred by the option holder. For example, the following figures characterize the IBM stock and calls between the same dates:

| | *Jan. 6, 1982* | *Jan. 7, 1982* |
|---|---|---|
| Stock price | $57 | $\$56\frac{5}{8}$ |
| Call price | $7 | $\$6\frac{5}{8}$ |

The striking price was $50 and the expiration date was also the last day in January 1982. It is easy to verify that the loss on the stock in one day was $(\$\frac{3}{8}:\$57) \times 100 = 0.66\%$, while the loss on the call was much greater, $(\$\frac{3}{8}:\$7) \times 100 = 5.3\%$.

Thus, the percentage price movements of the option are much larger than the corresponding percentage price movements of the underlying stock.

## 16.7 Bounds on Option Value

In deriving bounds on option value, we first assume that the option cannot be exercised before expiration date (a European option—see Section 16.8 for more details).

As we shall see, the call price $C$ satisfies the following inequality

$$C \geqslant S_0 - \frac{E}{1 + r}$$

FOR WRITER ≥ S OR ELSE, THE OPTION WOULD NOT BE WRITTEN

$C \geq (0, S_0 - \frac{E}{1+r})$

where

$S_0$ is the current market price of the underlying stock
$E$ is the exercise price
$r$ is the risk-free interest rate (for the period until expiration date)

To derive this lower bound on call price, consider the two alternative investment strategies in Table 16.6, where $S_1$ is the stock price at expiration date. From this table we see that if $S_1 > E$, the two strategies provide the same payoff, $S_1$, and if $S_1 < E$, portfolio $A$ provides a higher payoff, $E$. Thus if the initial investment in the two portfolios is the same, portfolio $A$ will dominate portfolio $B$ and no investor will purchase the stock. Therefore, in reality the initial investment required to build portfolio $A$ must be *larger* than the initial investment in portfolio $B$, otherwise all investors will switch from portfolio $B$ to portfolio $A$ (by a process known as arbitraging). Thus we must have in equilibrium:

$$C + E/(1 + r) \geqslant S_0$$

Hence $C \geqslant S_0 - E/(1 + r)$.

EXAMPLE
On January 7, 1982 we find the following information regarding the Data General stock and call:

| | |
|---|---|
| Stock price | $S_0 = \$52\frac{1}{4}$ |
| Call price | $C = \$10\frac{3}{4}$ |
| Exercise price | $E = \$45$ |
| Expiration date | June 1982 |

Since the interest rate for six months (the period remaining to expiration) was approximately $r = 6\%$ at the beginning of 1982, we find that the call price must be

**Table 16.6**
**Cashflows from Two Alternative Portfolios**

| | Investment | Future Cashflow at Expiration Date | |
|---|---|---|---|
| | | if $S_1 > E$ | if $S_1 \leqslant E$ |
| *Portfolio A* | | | |
| Buy one call | $-C$ | $S_1 - E$ | 0 |
| Buy bonds bearing interest $r$ | $-E/(1 + r)$ | $E$ | $E$ |
| **Total** | $-[C + E/(1 + r)]$ | $S_1$ | $E$ |
| *Portfolio B* | | | |
| Buy one share of the underlying stock | $-S_0$ | $S_1$ | $S_1$ |

greater than \$9.8,

$$C \geqslant 52\tfrac{1}{4} - 45/1.06 = 52.25 - 42.45 = \$9.8$$

The actual market price of the call was $C = \$10\tfrac{3}{4}$, which of course obeys this lower bound condition.

Since in principle the difference $S_0 - E/(1 + r)$ may be negative, while the call price at worst can drop to zero, we conclude that:

$$C \geqslant Max \; [0, \; S_0 - E/(1 + r)]$$

Also since the call is an option to buy the underlying stock, the call price $C$ can never exceed the stock price. Otherwise, investors can buy the stock directly at a cheaper price and no one will purchase the option. So we must have the following upper bound,

$$C \leqslant S_0$$

Collecting these results we have the following upper and lower bounds on the call price

$$S_0 \geqslant C \geqslant Max \; [0, \; S_0 - E/(1 + r)] \qquad (16.1)$$

The option value $C$ can vary in this range. As we have seen, other things being equal, $C$ increases (i.e. moves closer to the upper bound) as the exercise price $E$ decreases and the time to expiration increases.


### 16.7.1   Put–Call Parity

Investors can create two alternative strategies which yield the same income, regardless of the future stock price at expiration $S_1$. These two strategies which we call portfolios $A$ and $B$ are specified in Table 16.7. The following standard notation is used in Table 16.7:

$C$—call price
$P$—put price
$E$—exercise price (the same for the put and the call)
$r$—interest rate (for the period to expiration)
$S_0$—current stock price
$S_1$—stock price at time 1, i.e. at the expiration date
$E/(1 + r)$—the amount borrowed, calculated to ensure repayment of
$(1 + r) \cdot E/(1 + r) = E$ at expiration date.

Since the two portfolios yield the same cashflows irrespective of the future stock price, the initial investment in these two portfolios must also be identical. Otherwise if, say, the investment in portfolio $B$ is higher, an investor who owns a call can sell it, borrow

Table 16.7
**Cashflows from Two Alternative Portfolios**

|  | Investment | Future Cashflow if $S_1 > E$ | Future Cashflow if $S_1 \leqslant E$ |
|---|---|---|---|
| *Portfolio A* |  |  |  |
| Buy stock | $-S_0$ | $S_1$ | $S_1$ |
| Buy put | $-P$ | $0$ | $E - S_1$ |
| Borrow at interest rate $r$ | $+E/(1 + r)$ | $-E$ | $-E$ |
| **Total** | $-S_0 - P + E/(1 + r)$ | $S_1 - E$ | $0$ |
| *Portfolio B* |  |  |  |
| Buy call | $-C$ | $S_1 - E$ | $0$ |

money, buy a put and the underlying stock, and thus create a portfolio with a lower investment and yet with the same future cashflows. If the investment in portfolio $A$ is higher, an investor who holds portfolio $A$ can sell the stock and the put, lend out a corresponding sum (to cancel the borrowing), and buy a portfolio $B$ reducing the investment without any change in the future cashflows. This process is known as arbitraging. Thus, in equilibrium, when no arbitraging opportunities exist, we expect to find the following relationship, which is known as the *put–call parity*,

$$C = S_0 + P - E/(1 + r) \qquad (16.2)$$

Obviously, this relationship is exact in a perfect market with no transaction costs and with the same interest rate for borrowers and for lenders. In real life we do have transaction costs, the borrowing rate is higher than the lending rate, and the switch from one portfolio to another is not costless. Hence we do not find this exact parity between the put and the call prices in reality.

EXAMPLE
Let us look at the put–call relationship of the Union Oil options listed on the Pacific Exchange. On January 7, 1982, we find the following prices:

Stock price $S_0 = \$34$
Call price $C = \$\frac{7}{16}$
Put price $P = \$11\frac{1}{4}$
Striking price $E = \$45$ (the same for the put and the call)

The expiration date is April 1982, so we have approximately $3\frac{1}{2}$ months to expiration.

Since there are many different interest rates (for borrowers, lenders, etc.), we will use the put–call parity equation to solve for $r$, and see if we get a reasonable figure.

Using our specific example, we find,

$$\tfrac{7}{16} = 34 + 11\tfrac{1}{4} - 45/(1 + r)$$

Hence $1 + r = 1.004$ and $r = 0.4\%$.

Is this figure reasonable? Recall that the expiration date is April 1982, so that we have about $3\tfrac{1}{2}$ months to expiration. An interest rate of 0.4% for $3\tfrac{1}{2}$ months implies an annual interest rate of about 1.5%, which is far below the riskless interest rate that prevailed in early 1982 in the USA. The put–call parity is thus not a very realistic feature of the options market. The market is far from perfect and the borrowing interest rate is substantially higher than the lending rate, which may account for the gap. Thus the put–call parity formula should be used with great caution.

### 16.8    European vs. American Calls: Early Exercise Does Not Pay

The difference between European and American calls is that while an American call can be exercised any time before (or at) the expiration date, the European call can be exercised only at the expiration date.

The common option valuation models were developed for European calls. However, the valuation models can be applied also to American calls since in fact it never pays to exercise a call before the expiration date.[2] Thus, if an investor behaves rationally, an American call can be treated exactly as a European call. But what if the call holder needs cash before expiration? We will show that it is always more profitable for the investor to sell the call in the market rather than to exercise it before expiration. To prove this rather surprising claim, first note that other things being equal, the value of the more restrictive European call cannot be greater than the value of an American call, which allows greater freedom of choice. Since we have shown that with respect to the European call [see Equation (16.1) and Table 16.6]:

$$C \geqslant Max\ [0,\ S_0 - E/(1 + r)]$$

and since an American call is worth at least as much as a European call, the above inequality holds also with respect to American calls.

If an American call is exercised at a given date $t$ before expiration, the investor gets $S_t - E$, where $S_t$ is the stock price at date $t$. Since

$$S_t - E < S_t - E/(1 + r)$$

the investor in need of cash is better off by selling the call at the market price, which is

---

[2] This is true only for stocks which do not pay cash dividends. Otherwise it may pay to have an early exercise depending on dividend policy, see below.

never less than $S_t - E/(1 + r)$ ($S_t$ being the current price at that date), rather than exercising the call and selling the stock, which gives him only $S_t - E$ in cash proceeds.

The intuitive explanation for this formal proof is that the market call price has two components:

(a)   the immediate profit in case of exercise, $S_t - E$.
(b)   the additional potential profit if the stock will go up from the present date until the expiration date.

If the option is exercised, the investor gets benefit (a) but gives up benefit (b), which is worth money. Thus, it always pays not to have an early exercise, which accounts for the dictum "a call option is worth more alive than dead".

Early exercise of an American call may be desirable if underlying stock pays cash dividends and the call option is not protected against the decrease in ex-dividend prices. To be more specific, suppose that a holder of an American call expects the price of the stock to be $S_t = \$100$ on December 31, which is the expiration date. Also we know that $E = \$90$, so that the call holder expects a $10 profit on the expiration date. If the corporation does not pay any cash dividends, it pays to hold the call until the very latest moment, i.e., until the expiration date, as we have shown above.

Now suppose that the corporation pays a cash dividend of $20 per share on December 15. The ex-dividend stock price will fall roughly by $20 immediately after the cash dividend is distributed and in all probability it will not exceed the exercise price ($90) on expiration. As a result the call will be worthless on expiration. On the other hand, if the stock price is $S_t = \$98$ on December 14, just before the dividend distribution, the investor can exercise the call and make a profit of $S_t - E = \$98 - \$90 = \$8$. Thus, in reality, with corporations paying cash dividends to their stockholders, an American call with its early exercise option may have a definite advantage over the European call which is not exercisable until the expiration date.

**Summary**

This chapter deals with various contingent claims. Calls, puts, combinations of the two, as well as combinations of options with the underlying stock are discussed. Though warrants are well-established financial instruments, options are relatively new and it is only since the establishment of the Chicago Board of Options Exchange that the interest in options among academics and practitioners has been steadily growing.

Options are written on a given stock, and so there is a certain relationship between the option value and the price of the underlying stock. Although the absolute value of the fluctuations in option price may be close to that of the fluctuations in the price of the underlying stock, the *percentage* fluctuations are much larger because of the lower option price. Hence options are highly leveraged instruments, and as such considered very risky.

We distinguish between American calls and European calls. The difference between the two options is that American calls can be exercised at any time up to the expiration date, while European calls are exercisable only at the expiration date. Surprisingly enough, this flexibility advantage of the American calls has no economic value, since it never pays to exercise an American call before the expiration date. Hence the dictum that options are worth more "alive than dead".

---

**Summary Table**

1. Profit profiles of a call:

$$\text{Call holder:} \quad y_t = -(C + E) + S_t$$
$$\text{Call writer:} \quad y_t = (C + E) - S_t$$

2. Profit profiles of a put:

$$\text{Put holder:} \quad y_t = (E - P) - S_t$$
$$\text{Put writer:} \quad y_t = -(E - P) + S_t$$

3. Bounds on the call price:

$$S_0 \geq C \geq Max\ [0,\ S_0 - E/(1 + r)]$$

4. Put–call parity in a perfect market:

$$C = S_0 + P - E/(1 + r)$$

5. Exercise call only if $S_t > E$,
   Exercise put only if $S_t < E$.

6. European calls can be exercised only at maturity while American calls can be exercised at any date before or on the maturity date. However, it does not pay to exercise calls before the maturity date.

7. Notation:

   $C$ = the call price
   $P$ = the put price
   $y_t$ = the profit (or loss) in dollars
   $E$ = the exercise price (striking price)
   $r$ = the risk-free interest rate (for the period until expiration)
   $S_0$ = the current price of the underlying stock (known)
   $S_t$ = the future price of the underlying stock (a random variable)

---

### Questions and Problems

16.1   On September 1, 1982, two call options on the stock of Delta Airlines with exercise prices of \$30 and \$35 and with maturities of 90 days sold for \$3$\frac{1}{4}$ and \$1, respectively. Can you explain the difference in the prices of the two call options?

16.2  *The Wall Street Journal* records the following information on November 26, 1982, on Bristol Myers stock:

| | |
|---|---|
| Stock price | $65\frac{1}{8}$ |
| Exercise Price | $55 |
| | |
| Price of call option | $11\frac{1}{4}$ (December, 1982 maturity) |
| | $12 (March, 1983 maturity) |

What caused the difference in the two call prices?

16.3  On July 14, 1982, two put options on the stock of Eastman Kodak with exercise prices of $70 and $75 sold for $1\frac{1}{8}$ and $2\frac{9}{16}$, respectively. Explain the difference in the prices of the put options.

16.4  On November 26, 1982, *The Wall Street Journal* lists the price of Dow Chemical stock as $25\frac{3}{4}$. A put option on the stock with exercise price of $25 expiring in December, 1982, had a price of $\frac{5}{8}$, while a similar put option with the same exercise price of $25 expiring in March, 1983, had a price of $1\frac{3}{4}$. How do you account for the difference in prices?

16.5  On July 19, 1982, an investor holds stock of Texas Instruments priced at $86\frac{5}{8}$. He buys a put option and sells a call option on the stock with 90-day maturities at prices of $8 and $4\frac{1}{2}$, respectively. The exercise price of both the put option and the call option is $85. Graph the value of his portfolio as a function of the stock price.

16.6  What are the differences between options and warrants?

16.7  The following table lists the price of IBM stock and of its corresponding call option with a 30-day maturity and with an exercise price of $60, over a 12-day trading period beginning July 1, 1982, and ending July 16, 1982. Would you expect the percentage change in the stock price or in the option price to be greater? Confirm your answer by calculating the mean and the standard deviation of the change in price of the stock and of the option. Draw a frequency histogram of the change in the stock price and in the option price.

| Day | Stock Price ($) | Option Price ($) |
|---|---|---|
| 1 | $60\frac{5}{8}$ | $1\frac{5}{8}$ |
| 2 | $60\frac{5}{8}$ | $1\frac{1}{2}$ |
| 3 | 60 | $1\frac{1}{8}$ |
| 4 | $60\frac{3}{4}$ | $1\frac{3}{8}$ |
| 5 | $60\frac{7}{8}$ | $1\frac{1}{2}$ |
| 6 | $61\frac{5}{8}$ | $1\frac{15}{16}$ |
| 7 | $62\frac{3}{8}$ | $2\frac{1}{2}$ |
| 8 | $63\frac{1}{2}$ | $3\frac{1}{4}$ |
| 9 | $64\frac{5}{8}$ | $4\frac{5}{8}$ |
| 10 | $66\frac{1}{2}$ | $6\frac{5}{8}$ |
| 11 | $66\frac{3}{4}$ | $6\frac{3}{4}$ |
| 12 | $66\frac{1}{2}$ | $6\frac{7}{8}$ |

16.8    Using the following data:

| | |
|---|---:|
| Date of Information | November 30 |
| Stock Price | $50 |
| Call Price | $8 |
| Exercise Price | $45 |
| Expiration Date | December 31 |
| Risk Free Interest Rate (annual) | 5% |

Does the call price lie within its expected lower and upper bounds?

16.9    Assuming that the put–call parity holds, calculate the value of a put option using the information given in Problem 16.8.

16.10   What is the difference between European and American call options?

 16.11 (a) What is the cashflow on a combination of writing a call and buying a put? Assume that the call and the put sell for $5 each and that the exercise price of both options is $50. To what single transaction can this combination be compared? (*Hint:* Assume that one can sell or buy the stock in the futures market, i.e., write a contract to deliver the stock in the future at a predetermined price.)

(b) What is the cashflow on a combination of writing a call, buying a put, and buying the underlying security? What do you expect the equilibrium riskless interest rate to be? Assume that the security sells currently for $40.

16.12   (a) What is the cashflow on a combination of writing a put and buying a call? Assume that the option prices and the exercise prices are the same as in Problem 16.11(a).

(b) What is the cashflow on a combination of writing a put, buying a call, and selling the underlying security short? Assume that the security sells for $60. Is the market in equilibrium?

16.13   (a) Prove that the following inequality holds for a put option:

$$P \geqslant Max \left[ 0, \frac{E}{1+r} - S_0 \right]$$

where $S_0$ is the security's current price, $P$ is the price of the put option, $E$ is the option's exercise price, and $r$ is the riskless interest rate (for the period until maturity).

(b) Can the price of a put option ever exceed the price of the underlying stock?

16.14   (a) Show that a call option, the underlying stock, and riskless bonds can be combined to result in the same payoff as a put option.

(b) Derive the put–call parity from the investment strategy in (a).

16.15   An investor purchased an American call on CBM stock a month ago, and is suddenly in urgent need of cash. Assume that the current price of CBM stock is $S_0 = \$50$, the exercise price is $E = \$40$, and that the stock does not pay cash dividends. The current price of the call is $12.

(a) Should the investor exercise the option? Explain.

(b) The investor received some inside information according to which the CBM corporation has suffered a heavy loss on its overseas operations. He therefore expects the CBM stock price to plunge to $30 a share. He decides to sell the CBM stock short (at the present price of $50 a share). Should the investor keep the call option? Explain.

16.16 Show by an example that if the stock pays cash dividends, early exercise of the option may be profitable.

16.17 Assume that a call option is traded for $C = \$10$. The price of the underlying security is $S_0 = \$120$ and the exercise price is $E = \$110$. The expiration time is one year and the interest rate is 10%.

Do these figures represent an equilibrium in the market? If not, describe the market forces that will change the call price. Using the above figures, demonstrate which transaction should be made in order to exploit the disequilibrium situation.

16.18 A call is traded for $C = \$20$, the price of the underlying stock is $S_0 = \$120$, the call expires in three months, the three-month borrowing rate is 5%, the exercise price $E = \$105$.

Do these figures represent equilibrium prices? If not, what transaction should be made to restore equilibrium?

16.19 Assume that we observe the following market prices and rates. A call which expires in six months is traded for $C = \$10$. The price of the underlying stock is $S_0 = \$109$. The six-month borrowing rate is 8% while the six-month lending rate is 2%. The exercise price is $E = \$102$. Do the above figures represent equilibrium prices? Explain.

16.20 Suppose that a call and a put with six months to expiration are traded with the same exercise price $E$. We observe the following market prices:

| | |
|---|---|
| Call price | $C = \$10$ |
| Put price | $P = \$8$ |
| Stock price | $S_0 = \$100$ |

The interest rate for six months is $r = 5\%$. What should be the exercise price if the put–call parity holds?

16.21 A six-month put and a six-month call are traded on the same stock. The six-month interest rate is $r = 5\%$. We observe the following market prices:

| | |
|---|---|
| Price of call | $C = \$10$ |
| Price of put | $P = \$10$ |
| Price of stock | $S_0 = \$110$ |
| Exercise price | $E = \$105$ |

Are these prices consistent with equilibrium? If not, explain what transaction should be made to exploit the disequilibrium. Describe the transaction exactly and determine what profit is earned in the transaction.

16.22 The stock price is $S_0 = \$100$ and the price of the corresponding call is $C = \$10$. It is given that any change in the future stock price $S_t$ is accompanied by the same absolute change in the future call price $C_t$. Assume that an investor weighs whether to invest $100 in the stock (i.e., buying one share) or to purchase 10 calls.

(a) Write out the relationship between the expected return and the variance of the two alternative strategies.
(b) Draw the cumulative distribution of the return on the two alternative investments. Is either strategy preferred by SSD? Explain your results.

### Data Set Problems

All the Data Set problems for this chapter refer to the data in Table 16.3 in the body of the text.

1. (a) Using the data for all the call options listed in Table 16.3, check whether it is empirically true that "call options are worth more alive than dead".
   (b) Consider all the call options in Table 16.3 which expire in May and for which the underlying stock price is higher than the striking price. Suppose that an investor exercises these calls on Jan. 7, 1982. Calculate the investor's profit from this transaction as percentage of the cashflow corresponding to the sale of the call option in the market.

2. Consider all the corporations in Table 16.3 with both puts and calls expiring in May which have the same striking price. Use the put–call parity theorem to estimate the annual risk free interest rate. Calculate the implied interest rate for each put–call pair and find the average implied interest rate.

3. In this problem use the data for the Mobil option with striking price 25 and May expiration (see Table 16.3).

   Contrast two portfolios: (a) A portfolio comprising one share of the Mobil stock and one put, borrowing $E/(1 + r)$, where $E$ is the exercise price and $r$ the risk-free interest rate (assume that $r = 10\%$ on an annual basis); (b) A portfolio which includes one call.

   Write out the cashflows from these two investments when it is known that at expiration date we may have both $S_1 > E$ and $S_1 < E$.

   Can you draw any conclusion from a comparison of the cashflows on these two portfolios?

4. Repeat Problem 3, taking $r = 100\%$. What conclusion can you draw from a comparison of the two situations?

### Selected References

See Chapter 17.

# 17

# Option Valuation Models: Theory and Empirical Evidence

Along with the growing market for options, there has been a surge of interest in theoretical option valuation models. This chapter presents two call option valuation models and surveys some empirical evidence of their validity.

Option valuation models focus on European calls, i.e., call options that can be exercised on, but not before, expiration date. However, as we have seen in Chapter 16, it does not pay exercising an American call before expiration date, so that these models of valuing European options can apply to the valuation of American calls as well. Before turning to the valuation models, one word of caution: the valuation models presented in this chapter assume that the underlying stock pays no cash dividend before the expiration date.[1] If the underlying stock does pay cash dividends and the call is not protected against the effects of dividend payment on the stock price, it may be worthwhile to have an early exercise before the cash dividend is distributed, since dividend distribution is likely to result in a drop of the stock price and in the value of the call option (see Section 16.8).

We present two basic option valuation models: the *binomial model* and the *Black and Scholes model*. The derivation of these two models is quite difficult and is not presented in the body of the text. In Appendix 17.1 we derive the Black and Scholes formula assuming risk neutrality. The interested reader can find more details on these and other valuation models in the list of references at the end of the chapter. We conclude the chapter with a discussion of some empirical tests of option valuation models.

## 17.1 The Binomial Option Pricing Model

The binomial model for option valuation has two important properties:

(a)   it is attractively simple;

(b)   it provides the starting point for the derivation of other option valuation models· (e.g., the Black and Scholes model and the jump process model).

---

[1] There are some modified valuation models which allow payment of cash dividends, for instance, Geske, R., "The Pricing of Options with Stochastic Dividend Yield", *Journal of Finance* (May 1978).

### 17.1.1 One-period Model

The binomial model assumes only two possible states of nature: during the period from the present (time 0) to expiration (time 1), the stock price can either increase by $x$% or decrease by $y$%, where $x$ and $y$ are specified. Denoting the current stock price by $S_0$ and the end-of-period stock price by $S_1$, we have only the following two possibilities:

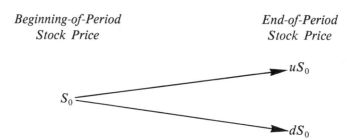

*Beginning-of-Period*
*Stock Price*

*End-of-Period*
*Stock Price*

where $u$ ("up") is 1 plus the percentage change in the stock price if the stock price increases during the period ($u = 1 + x/100$), and $d$ ("down") stands for 1 plus the (negative) percentage change in the stock price if the stock price decreases during the period ($d = 1 + y/100$). Thus while the current stock price $S_0$ is given, the end-of-period stock price $S_1$ may be either $uS_0$ or $dS_0$.

What is the impact of the possible price changes in the stock on the end-of-period call value? The call value at the expiration date (see Equation (6.1)) clearly will be $Max\,(0, uS_0 - E)$ if the stock price increases over the period and $Max\,(0, dS_0 - E)$ if the stock price falls. This can be illustrated graphically as follows:

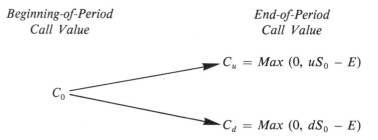

*Beginning-of-Period*
*Call Value*

*End-of-Period*
*Call Value*

where $C_u$ is the call value at expiration date if the end-of-period stock price increases and $C_d$ is its value if the end-of-period stock price falls.

Given these two end-of-period possibilities for the stock price and the option value, we can create a *hedged portfolio* (i.e., a portfolio yielding a *certain* end-of-period cash-flow) from which the current price of the call $C_0$ can be determined. The hedged portfolio consisting of a call and the underlying stock is described in Table 17.1.

Note that the end-of-period income from writing the call is $-C_u$ if the end-of-period stock price goes up and $-C_d$ if it falls. We have a negative sign since we *sell* rather than buy a call and thus forgo the call value at the end of the period. In order to have a hedged portfolio, the end-of-period income must be independent of the stock price

**Table 17.1**
**Creation of a Hedged Portfolio**

| | Cashflows | | |
|---|---|---|---|
| | Beginning | End of Period | |
| Beginning-of-Period Transaction | of Period | $S_1 = uS_0$ | $S_1 = dS_0$ |
| Write One Call | $+C_0$ | $-C_u$ | $-C_d$ |
| Buy α Shares of the Underlying Stock | $-\alpha S_0$ | $\alpha u S_0$ | $\alpha d S_0$ |
| **Total Cashflow** | $C_0 - \alpha S_0$ | $-C_u + \alpha u S_0$ | $-C_d + \alpha d S_0$ |

changes. Thus, if

$$-C_u + \alpha u S_0 = -C_d + \alpha d S_0$$

we have a perfectly hedged portfolio which provides a certain cashflow at the end of the period. The value α which solves this equation, called the hedge ratio, is given by:

$$\alpha = \frac{C_u - C_d}{S_0(u - d)} \tag{17.1}$$

Since the initial investment $(\alpha S_0 - C_0)$ yields a *certain* cashflow $\alpha d S_0 - C_d$ (or $\alpha u S_0 - C_u$: remember that the two cashflows are identical with the hedged portfolio), the rate of return on the investment must be equal in equilibrium to the risk-free interest rate for the period. Denoting $r = 1 +$ the risk-free interest rate for the period, the following relationship must hold under these certainty conditions:

$$(\alpha S_0 - C_0)r = \alpha d S_0 - C_d$$

Hence the current call price $C_0$ must be:

$$C_0 = \frac{\alpha r S_0 + C_d - \alpha d S_0}{r}$$

Substituting for α from equation (17.1) yields,

$$C_0 = \left[ \frac{C_u - C_d}{S_0(u - d)} r S_0 + C_d - \frac{C_u - C_d}{S_0(u - d)} d S_0 \right] \Big/ r$$

Reducing by $S_0$ and bringing to a common denominator $(u - d)$ yields,

$$C_0 = \frac{(C_u - C_d)r + C_d(u - d) - d(C_u - C_d)}{(u - d)} \Big/ r$$

which can be rewritten as,

$$C_0 = \left( C_u \frac{r-d}{u-d} + C_d \frac{u-r}{u-d} \right) \Big/ r \tag{17.2}$$

Denoting

$$p = \frac{r-d}{u-d}, \qquad 1-p = \frac{u-r}{u-d} \tag{17.3}$$

the current value of the option which expires at the end of the period is

$$C_0 = \frac{C_u p + C_d(1-p)}{r} \tag{17.4}$$

This is the basic *binomial call pricing formula*.

Before we turn to a numerical example, a word of caution: $p$ is not a probability. It has nothing to do with the chance of the price going up or down. It is a technical factor which is a function of the interest rate and the anticipated percentage decrease or increase in the stock price ($u$ and $d$), but not a function of the probability of these two events. Also the call price depends on the current stock price $S_0$ and the exercise price $E$, since $C_u$ and $C_d$ are a function of these two values. For example, if the stock goes up and the call has a positive value at expiration, it is equal to $C_u = uS_0 - E$.

EXAMPLE

Assume that the stock currently sells for $S_0 = \$100$ and that $u = 1.5$ and $d = 0.75$. Namely, the stock price at the end of the period will be either $150 (1.5 \times 100)$ or $75 (0.75 \times 100)$. The exercise price is assumed to be $E = \$120$ and the interest rate 10%, so that $r = 1.10$. The end-of-period value of the call is $C_u = uS_0 - E = 1.5 \cdot 100 - 120 = \$30$ if the stock price goes up and $C_d = 0$ if the stock price goes down ($S_1 = \$75$ is less than the exercise price and the call is valueless). The hedge ratio $\alpha$ (17.1) is given by:

$$\alpha = \frac{C_u - C_d}{S_0(u-d)} = \frac{30-0}{100(1.5-0.75)} = \frac{30}{100 \times 0.75} = \frac{30}{75} = \frac{2}{5} = 0.4$$

Thus, in order to create a hedged portfolio, we have to write one call and buy 0.4 shares of the underlying stock. Table 17.2 shows the cashflows associated with this hedged portfolio.

Regardless of the future stock price, the future portfolio cashflow is certain and equal to $30. In equilibrium a certain investment must yield the riskless rate of return, so that we have the following equilibrium relationship,

$$1 + \text{rate of return} = \frac{\text{Cashflow}}{\text{Investment}} = r \qquad \text{or} \qquad \text{Investment} = \frac{\text{Cashflow}}{r}$$

**Table 17.2**
**A Hedged Portfolio: A Numerical Example**

| Beginning-of-Period Transaction | Beginning-of-Period Cashflow | End-of-Period Cashflow | |
|---|---|---|---|
| | | $S_1 = \$150$ | $S_1 = \$75$ |
| Write One Call | $+C$ | $-30$ | 0 |
| Buy 0.4 Shares of Stock | $-0.4 \times 100 = -40$ | $0.4 \times 150 = \$60$ | $0.4 \times 75 = \$30$ |
| **Total Cashflow** | $+C - \$40$ | $\$30$ | $\$30$ |

(where $r$ is 1 plus the riskless interest rate for the period). In our specific case, we pay $40 for the stock and get $C_0$ from writing the call at the beginning of the period, so that our total initial investment is $\$40 - C_0$ and we should have

$$\$40 - C_0 = \frac{30}{1.1} = \$27.27$$

which implies that the call must currently sell for

$$C_0 = \$40 - \$27.27 = \$12.73$$

Let us apply the binomial call pricing formula (17.4) to verify this price. We have

$$C_u = \$30, \quad C_d = 0, \quad u = 1.5, \quad d = 0.75 \quad \text{and} \quad r = 1.1$$

Substituting these figures in (17.3), we obtain:

$$p = \frac{r-d}{u-d} = \frac{1.1-0.75}{1.5-0.75} = \frac{0.35}{0.75} = \frac{7}{15} \quad \text{and} \quad 1-p = \frac{8}{15}$$

and the equilibrium call price by the binomial formula (17.4) is

$$C_0 = \frac{C_u p + C_d(1-p)}{r} = \frac{\$30 \times \frac{7}{15} + 0 \times \frac{8}{15}}{1.1} = \frac{14}{1.1} = \$12.73$$

which is the same as above.

It is interesting to note that while the "magnitudes" of the stock price changes ($u$ and $d$) were taken into consideration in the determination of the call option price, the *probabilities* of price increase or decrease were never even considered in the derivation of the binomial formula. Nevertheless, the probabilities of "up" and "down" price movements affect the current stock price $S_0$ and hence indirectly affect the call value ($S_0$ does enter the binomial model).

### 17.1.2  Call Price and the Arbitrage Process

There is a market mechanism that will make the price of the call option actually equal to $12.73, as calculated above. If the market price of the call differs from the equilibrium price $12.73 investors can go through an arbitrage process which guarantees a sure profit. To see this, take $C_0 = \$10$. Since the call price is less than its equilibrium price ($12.73), we can buy the call and short the stock and thus guarantee a sure profit: the transactions are the reverse of those in Table 17.2. The results will be as follows:

|                                          |                                       | End-of-Period Cashflow |                |
| :--------------------------------------- | :-----------------------------------: | :-----------: | :------------: |
| Beginning-of-Period Transaction          | Beginning-of-Period Cashflow          | $S_1 = \$150$ | $S_1 = \$75$   |
| Buy a Call                               | −10                                   | +30           | 0              |
| Short 0.4 Shares of Stock                | +40                                   | −60           | −30            |
| **Total Cashflow**                       | +30                                   | −30           | −30            |

Note that since we have reversed the transactions of Table 17.2 the cashflows are also reversed.

The investor owes a total of $30 at the end of the period. However he initially had $30 of which he could invest $27.27 elsewhere at 10% return, which would grow to $27.27(1.1) = \$30$ at the end of the period. This amount will cover the $30 that he owes, leaving him a sure end-of-period profit of $30 - \$27.27 = \$2.73$.

This arbitrage process will continue as long as the call price $C_0$ is less than $12.73, the increased demand for calls driving the price up. But the possibility that $C_0 > \$12.73$ is also ruled out. Suppose that $C_0 = \$15$. Then use the following arbitrage transactions:

|                                          |                                       | End-of-Period Cashflow |                |
| :--------------------------------------- | :-----------------------------------: | :-----------: | :------------: |
| Beginning-of-Period Transaction          | Beginning-of-Period Cashflow          | $S_1 = \$150$ | $S_1 = \$75$   |
| Write a Call                             | +15                                   | −30           | 0              |
| Buy 0.4 Shares of Stock                  | −40                                   | +60           | +30            |
| **Total Cashflow**                       | −25                                   | +30           | +30            |

An investment of $25 yields a riskless return at the end of the period. Thus the investor at the beginning of the period can borrow $30/r = 30/1.1 = \$27.27$, and use $25 out of this amount to pay for the initial investment. The investment yields $30 at the end of the period, which is just enough to cover the loan (principal plus interest) $(30/r)r = \$30$. The investor is left holding a sure profit of $27.27 - \$25 = \$2.27$ at the beginning of the period. This arbitrage process will continue, causing the call price to drop until it is exactly equal to $12.73.

### 17.1.3 Two-period Case

So far we have assumed that the option has only one period to expiration. The one-period formula is unrealistic since the stock price, in general, moves many times between a given date and the expiration date. However, the same arbitrage process can be applied also in the multiperiod case. We will demonstrate the two-period case in some detail and explain the binomial formula for the general $n$-period case.

Let the current stock price two periods before the call option expiration be $S_0$. Then after two periods, with the price going either up or down by fixed percentage $u$ or $d$ in each period, we have the following four possible values for the stock price at expiration:

$uuS_0$—the price rises in both periods
$ddS_0$—the price falls in both periods
$udS_0$—the price rises in the first period and falls in the second
$duS_0$—the price falls in the first period and rises in the second.

We can consider one period before expiration as time 1, and the present (two periods before expiration) as time 0. The stock price and the corresponding call option are described in Figure 17.1. Note that in this figure we do not distinguish between the events $udS$ and $duS$ since both these branches lead to the same stock price at the end of two periods and hence to the same option value at the expiration date.

Since at time 1 there is only one period remaining to expiration, we can apply the one-period binomial formula (17.4) to solve for $C_u$ and $C_d$, namely for the call price at time 1 (see Figure 17.1).

Applying the one-period binomial formula (17.4) to end-of-period 2 figures, we obtain for time 1:

$$C_u = \frac{pC_{uu} + (1-p)C_{ud}}{r}$$

$$C_d = \frac{pC_{ud} + (1-p)C_{dd}}{r}$$

when $p$ and $(1-p)$ are as defined before in (17.3). Since $C_{uu}$, $C_{dd}$ and $C_{ud}$ are given (see Figure 17.1), $C_u$ and $C_d$ are also given. However, given $C_u$ and $C_d$ we can apply once again the one-period binomial formula (17.4) to end-of-period 1 figures to solve for the current call price $C_0$,

$$C_0 = \frac{pC_u + (1-p)C_d}{r}$$

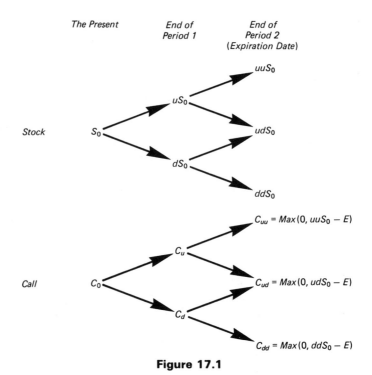

**Figure 17.1**

Substituting $C_u$ and $C_d$ in the last equation yields the *two-period binomial call pricing formula:*

$$C_0 = \frac{p^2 C_{uu} + 2p(1-p)C_{ud} + (1-p)^2 C_{dd}}{r^2} \qquad (17.5)$$

By the same iterative procedure one can apply the binomial model to the *n*-period case, moving one period backward in each step and eventually solving for the equilibrium option price $C_0$.

### 17.1.4  Multi-period Case

When we have $n$ periods to expiration, with the stock moving up or down by a fixed percentage in each period, we can apply the same iterative technique to obtain the *multiperiod binomial valuation formula,*

$$C_0 = \frac{1}{r^n} \sum_{K=0}^{n} \frac{n!}{(n-K)!K!} p^K (1-p)^{n-K} \; Max \, [0, u^K d^{n-K} S_0 - E] \qquad (17.6)$$

The derivation of this formula is tedious and we shall only concentrate on its implications. First note that if $p$ is interpreted as the probability of "success" in a single trial (though in fact $p$ is just a number, $p = (r - d)/(u - d)$, and has nothing to do with the probability of the stock price going up or down), then the term

$$\frac{n!}{(n - K)!K!} p^K (1 - p)^{n-K} \tag{17.7}$$

is the well-known expression for the probability of having $K$ successes and $n - K$ failures in a binomial distribution when $p$ is the probability of a success. If we consider the event $u$ to be a success and $d$ a failure, then with $K$ "successes" and $n - K$ "failures" the stock price at expiration will be $u^K d^{n-K} S_0$. The option value at expiration is

$$Max\,[0,\ u^K d^{n-K} S_0 - E] \tag{17.8}$$

Multiplying the probability (17.7) by the obtained cashflow (17.8), summing over all possible events, and discounting by $1/r^n$ (where $n$ is the number of periods and $r$ the riskless rate for one period), we simply obtain in (17.6) the *expected present value* of the future cashflow to the call holder (a similar approach is used in Appendix 17.1 for the derivation of a different model).

The multiperiod binomial formula (17.6) may include many terms in which the stock price is less than the exercise price, so that in these terms the probabilities are multiplied by zero [the call value at the expiration date (17.8) is zero]. Thus, one can drop all the zero terms and have a more compact form for the multiperiod binomial valuation formula.

Suppose that there is at least one situation when the exercise price is less than the stock price at the expiration date [(17.8) is positive], and at least one situation when the opposite holds [(17.8) is zero]. We identify these extreme situations with the most profitable case, $u^n S_0 > E$ (the price steadily going up during the $n$ periods), and with the least profitable case, $d^n S_0 < E$ (the price steadily going down in each of the $n$ periods).

The lowest price is $d^n S_0$, the next lowest price is $u d^{n-1} S_0$, then $u^2 d^{n-2} S_0$, etc. Thus, there must be some number $m$ of periods with rising price at which the stock price exceeds the exercise price for the first time, so that:

$$u^{m-1} d^{n-(m-1)} S_0 < E < u^m d^{n-m} S_0$$

Thus, we need to sum the binomial terms only for values $K \geqslant m$, since for $K < m$ all the terms are equal to zero. For these $K$, the option value at expiration date is nonzero; thus for $K \geqslant m$ we have,

$$Max\,[0,\ u^K d^{n-K} S_0 - E] = u^K d^{n-K} S_0 - E$$

Deleting terms for which $K < m$ we get

$$C_0 = \frac{1}{r^n} \sum_{K=m}^{n} \frac{n!}{(n - K)!K!} p^K (1 - p)^{n-K} [u^K d^{n-K} S_0 - E] \tag{17.9}$$

Breaking up the bracketed term on the right-hand side into two parts yields

$$C_0 = S_0 \left[ \sum_{K=m}^{n} \frac{n!}{(n-K)!K!} p^K (1-p)^{n-K} \frac{u^K d^{n-K}}{r^n} \right] - \frac{E}{r^n} \sum_{K=m}^{n} \frac{n!}{(n-K)!K!} p^K (1-p)^{n-K}$$

Define

$$p' = \frac{u}{r} p$$

$$1 - p' = 1 - \frac{pu}{r} = 1 - \frac{u}{r} \frac{r-d}{u-d} = 1 - \frac{ur - ud}{ur - dr} = \frac{d}{r} \frac{u-r}{u-d} =$$

$$= \frac{d}{r} \frac{u-d-r+d}{u-d} = \frac{d}{r} \left( 1 - \frac{r-d}{u-d} \right) = \frac{d}{r} (1-p) \tag{17.10}$$

Using these definitions, the multiperiod binomial valuation formula can be rewritten as,

$$C_0 = S_0 \sum_{K=m}^{n} \frac{n!}{(n-K)!K!} p'^K (1-p')^{n-K} - \frac{E}{r^n} \sum_{K=m}^{n} \frac{n!}{(n-K)!K!} p^K (1-p)^{n-K}$$

$$\tag{17.11}$$

where $m$ is the least number of stock price increases after which the stock price at expiration date exceeds the exercise price and $p'$ and $p$ are defined by (17.10) and (17.3) respectively.

This value can be rewritten in terms of a difference of two binomial distributions:

$$C_0 = S_0 B(m, n, p') - Er^{-n} B(m, n, p) \tag{17.12}$$

where $n$ is the number of periods before expiration, and $m$ is the minimum number of upward moves in the stock price for which the stock price at the expiration is greater than the exercise price, so that the call has a positive value at expiration. $B$ is the cumulative probability of getting $m$ "successes" or more out of $n$ trials, with $p'$ and $p$ defined by (17.10) and (17.3) serving as the probabilities of "success" in the first and the second term, respectively. This accounts for the name *binomial model*.[2]

We know from statistical theory that when the number of periods $n$ is very large, the binomial distribution approximates the normal distribution. Thus, if $n$ is large enough one can substitute $N$ for $B$, where $N$ denotes normal distribution. This leads to the next model which yields similar results but with normal rather than binomial distribution in the option valuation formula.

Before we turn to the next theoretical option valuation model, let us demonstrate the application of the multiperiod binomial model to a numerical example.

---

[2] For an extensive discussion of this model and more details, see J. Cox, S. Ross, and M. Rubinstein, "Option Pricing: a Simplified Approach", *Journal of Financial Economics* (Sept. 1979).

EXAMPLE

Consider a three-period case, with $n = 3$. The current stock price is $S_0 = \$100$, the exercise price at the end of period 3 is $E = \$120$. The stock price moves up 25% or down 20% in each period, so that $u = 1.25$ and $d = 0.80$. The riskless interest rate is 10% for each period $(r = 1.1)$.

Figure 17.2 shows the possible evolution of the stock price over the three periods. Thus the following prices are possible at the end of period 3:

| Case No. | Outcome | Future Stock Price $S_3$ | Number of Combinations to Obtain this Outcome |
|----------|---------|--------------------------|-----------------------------------------------|
| 1 | $u^3 S_0$ | $(1.25)^3 \times 100 = \$195.31$ | 1 |
| 2 | $u^2 d S_0$ | $(1.25)^2 \times 0.80 \times 100 = \$125$ | 3 |
| 3 | $u d^2 S_0$ | $1.25 \times (0.80)^2 \times 100 = \$80$ | 3 |
| 4 | $d^3 S_0$ | $(0.80)^3 \times 100 = \$51.20$ | 1 |

The last column gives the number of binomial combinations in which each of the possible outcomes is obtained. These are obtained by simply counting the tree leaves in Figure 17.2, ignoring the sequence of upward and downward price movements (thus $u^2 d S_0$ and $du^2 S_0$ are naturally counted as the same outcome). These numbers are substituted for the coefficients $n!/[(n - K)!K!]$ in the binomial valuation formula. We will show below that one can use either formula (17.6) or formula (17.11) to obtain the equilibrium call value $C_0$.

The future cashflows to a call holder are given by (17.8) as $Max (0, S_3 - E)$, where $S_3$ is the stock price at expiration date (end of period 3). These cashflows are thus equal to $S_3 - E$ whenever $S_3$ is greater than $E$ (cases 1 and 2 above) and to 0 whenever $S_3$ is less than $E$ (cases 3 and 4). In our case $m = 2$, i.e., at least two periods of rising prices are needed to ensure that the stock price at expiration date exceeds the exercise price and the future cashflow does not vanish.

Expressing the current call value $C_0$ as the expected present value of future cashflows, from equation (17.6), we write:

$$C_0 = \frac{1}{(1.1)^3} [1 \cdot (1 - p)^3 \cdot 0 + 3p(1 - p)^2 \cdot 0 + 3p^2(1 - p)(125 - 120)$$

$$+ 1 \cdot p^3(195.31 - 120)]$$

Only the last two terms in this sum do not vanish, since the other two terms (corresponding to cases 3 and 4 above) are characterized by zero future cashflows. The values of $p$ and $1 - p$ are calculated from (17.3),

$$p = \frac{r - d}{u - d} = \frac{1.1 - 0.80}{1.25 - 0.80} = \frac{2}{3}$$

$$1 - p = \frac{1}{3}$$

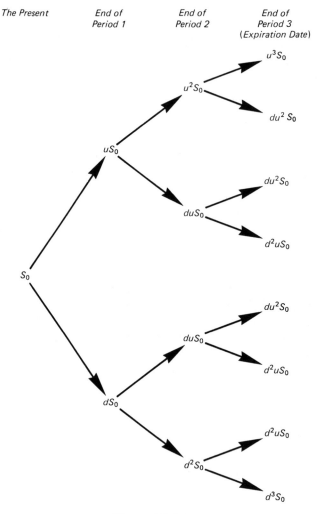

|  The Present | End of<br>Period 1 | End of<br>Period 2 | End of<br>Period 3<br>(Expiration Date) |
|---|---|---|---|

**Figure 17.2**

Substituting in the expression for $C_0$, we get:

$$C_0 = \frac{1}{(1.1)^3} [3 \cdot (\tfrac{2}{3})^2(\tfrac{1}{3}) \cdot 5 + (\tfrac{2}{3})^3 \cdot 75.31] = \$18.43$$

The same result of course can be obtained using formulas (17.11) or (17.12). From (17.11) we have:

$$C_0 = 100 \, [3p'^2(1 - p') + 1 \cdot p'^3] - \frac{120}{(1.1)^3} \, [3p^2(1 - p) + 1 \cdot p^3]$$

From (17.10) we have for $p'$ and $1 - p'$,

$$p' = (u/r)p = (1.25/1.1)(\tfrac{2}{3}) = 0.758$$

$$1 - p' = 0.242$$

and so

$$C_0 = 100\,[3(0.758)^2(0.242) + (0.758)^3] - \frac{120}{(1.1)^3} \cdot [3(\tfrac{2}{3})^2(\tfrac{1}{3}) + (\tfrac{2}{3})^3] =$$

$$= 85.27 - 90.16 \cdot 0.7407 = \$18.49$$

The slight difference in the second decimal place in comparison to the previous calculation is due to rounding errors.

The use of (17.12) requires reference to cumulative binomial distribution tables. There is a practical difficulty, however: the cumulative binomial distribution is usually tabulated in common texts for probability values in steps of 0.05, so that it will be impossible to read from the tables the exact values of $B(2, 3, 0.758)$ and $B(2, 3, 0.667)$ for $p' = 0.758$ and $p = \tfrac{2}{3} = 0.667$, which makes formula (17.12) impracticable for hand calculations. Standard computer programs, however, easily resolve this difficulty.

## 17.2  The Black and Scholes Option Valuation Formula

In the previous section we analyzed the option value when the underlying stock price follows a binomial distribution, with only two outcomes allowed. In this section we discuss the well-known option valuation formula developed by Black and Scholes which is widely used by both academics and practitioners.[3] The derivation of this formula is very complicated and is beyond the scope of this book. However, we explain the underlying principles of the derivation, show how to use this formula, and identify the determinants of the option value.

Let us first introduce the assumptions employed by Black and Scholes in deriving their formula:

1. There are no transaction costs and no taxes.
2. The risk-free interest rate is constant.
3. The market operates continuously.
4. The stock prices are continuous, i.e., there are no jumps in the stock prices: if one plots a graph of the stock price against time, the graph must be smooth.[4]

---

[3] See F. Black and M. Scholes, "The Pricing of Options and Corporate Liabilities", *Journal of Political Economy* (May–June 1973).

[4] To be more specific the stock price follows a so-called Ito process with a constant drift. This implies that for any finite time interval the stock price is lognormally distributed.

5. The stock pays no cash dividends.
6. The option is of European type (exercisable only at expiration).
7. Stock can be sold short without penalty and short sellers receive the full proceeds from the transaction.

   If all these assumptions hold, Black and Scholes proved that the current call price $C_0$ is given by,

$$C_0 = S_0 N(d_1) - E e^{-rt} N(d_2) \qquad (17.13)$$

where

> $S_0$ = the current stock price
> $E$ = the exercise price
> $e$ = the base of natural logarithms = 2.7128
> $r$ = the continuously compounded annual riskless rate of interest (so that the end-of-year value of \$1 invested in the riskless asset is $e^r$, and not $(1 + r)$ as in the discrete-compounding case)
> $t$ = the remaining time to the expiration of the call expressed as a fraction of a year
> $N(d_1)$ and $N(d_2)$ are the values of the cumulative normal distribution at points $d_1$ and $d_2$ respectively, where

$$d_1 = \frac{\ln (S_0/E) + (r + \frac{1}{2}\sigma^2)t}{\sigma\sqrt{t}}$$

$$d_2 = \frac{\ln (S_0/E) + (r - \frac{1}{2}\sigma^2)t}{\sigma\sqrt{t}} = d_1 - \sigma\sqrt{t} \qquad (17.14)$$

$\sigma$ = the standard deviation of the continuously compounded annual rate of return, representing the volatility of the stock price

From this formula we see that the parameters $S_0$, $E$, $r$, $t$ and $\sigma$ determine the option value. Surprisingly enough, the one single parameter which intuitively appears to be most important for valuation—the expected rate of return on the stock $\mu$—does not enter the Black and Scholes formula. The absence of the expected return from the valuation formula can be explained by the fact that in this model, as in the binomial model, the equilibrium value of the option is attained by creating a hedged portfolio (consisting of the option and its underlying stock) that yields a certain income regardless of the future stock price. Whatever the return on the stock, it has no impact on the return of the hedged portfolio which consists of the option and its underlying stock.

   The higher the current stock price $S_0$, and the lower the exercise price $E$, the higher will be the call option value $C_0$. Also the longer the time to expiration $t$, the greater is the chance that a profit will be made on the call and hence the higher is the call value. Though the impact of $r$ and $\sigma^2$ on the call price $C_0$ is not obvious from the Black and Scholes formula, we can determine that the higher $r$ and $\sigma^2$, the higher is the call price $C_0$. A partial intuitive explanation of the relationship between $r$ and $C_0$ is as follows: as the interest rate $r$ increases, the present value of the exercise price $E/r$ becomes smaller and the call price $C_0$ rises. Once again this is not obvious from the Black and Scholes formula but can be illustrated by using the bounds on the call value. We have seen in Chapter 16 [see Section 16.7, formula (16.1)] that:

$$S_0 \geqslant C_0 \geqslant S_0 - E/(1 + r)$$

As $r$ increases, $S_0 - E/(1 + r)$ increases and the lower bound on the call price increases. As $r$ approaches infinity, we get the highest value for the call $C_0 = S_0$.

The interrelationship between $C_0$ and $\sigma$ can also be intuitively (and at least partially) explained: suppose that we have two stocks and two corresponding options. Everything is identical regarding these two pairs apart from the stock variance $\sigma^2$. Figure 17.3 illustrates two density functions of stock price distributions which we denote by $f_1(S_t)$ and $f_2(S_t)$, respectively.

Recall that we have the same exercise price $E$ in both cases. Which call option is worth more, $C_1$ or $C_2$? In risk–return analysis the usual intuitive answer is that $f_1(S_t)$, which has a smaller risk with the same expected return, is preferable and hence the option corresponding to $f_1(S_t)$ is worth more. This is not true here and in fact just the opposite holds: the option on the riskier stock (that with the higher variance) is worth more, $C_2 > C_1$. To explain this assertion, recall that investment in a call option can be represented as an asymmetric game: if the stock deviates to the right (increasing above the exercise price $E$), the profit is $S_t - E$ and it increases with the magnitude of the upward deviation. However, a deviation to the left (below $E$) does not increase our loss, which remains total. Regardless of whether the stock price is $S_1$ or $S_2$ (see Figure 17.3—both below $E$), the call value will be zero, and the loss will be identical for these two events. Thus, a high variability of the stock price provides a possibility of high potential profit without increasing the potential loss! Hence the higher $\sigma$, the higher is the call value (all other parameters being constant).[5]

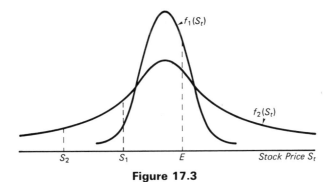

**Figure 17.3**

---

[5] This argument is incomplete. It is conceivable that the potential earnings increase with the variance, but the probability of obtaining this higher profit (i.e., the probability that $S_t > E$) is smaller for high-variance distributions. Thus, in order to complete the argument, we require the derivative $\partial C/\partial \sigma$, which is not easy to find.

These properties of the call price can be summarized as follows:

$$C_0 = f(\overset{+}{S}_0, \overset{-}{E}, \overset{+}{\sigma}{}^2, \overset{+}{t}, \overset{+}{r})$$

where $f$ is the valuation function, "$+$" means that an increase in the appropriate parameter is followed by an increase in the call value, "$-$" implies that an increase in the parameter is followed by a decrease in the call value.

The Black and Scholes formula needs five input parameters. Of these five parameters, four are readily available: $S_0$, $E$, $t$ are parameters of the underlying stock and the corresponding option, published in the financial media. For the interest rate $r$ we can take the yield on Treasury Bills with maturity equal to the expiration of the option under consideration. One parameter, $\sigma^2$, however, has to be estimated. We can take the *ex-post* stock price data and calculate the *ex-post* variance (see Section 17.2.2). However, there is no guarantee that the stock variability will remain constant in the future. Thus option valuation is subject to statistical errors in estimating stock price variability.

### 17.2.1   Derivation of the Black and Scholes Formula for a Linear Utility Function

The Black and Scholes model assumes that investors create a hedged portfolio and in deriving the equilibrium call price no assumption has been made regarding the investors' preferences. The model holds for all types of preferences, risk averters, risk lovers and risk-neutral investors alike. Since the equilibrium call price is independent of the investors' preferences, it may be advisable to determine the call price using a linear utility function, which is of course the most tractable mathematically. Once the call price for such a risk-neutral investor has been obtained, it can be applied to *all* investors, being independent of the particular preference structure.

For risk-neutral investors, the call price is simply the expected future value discounted at the risk-free interest rate $r$. More specifically,

$$C_0 = e^{-rt}E(C^*)$$

where $C^*$ is a random variable which is the terminal value of the call. Since the call has positive terminal value only if $S_t > E$, where $S_t$ is the stock price at expiration date, $C_0$ is given by:

$$C_0 = e^{-rt}\int_E^{\infty}(S_t - E)dF(S_t)$$

where $F(S_t)$ is the (cumulative) stock price distribution. It is shown in Appendix 17.1 that this value is identical to the value derived by the Black and Scholes model.

### 17.2.2 Using the Black and Scholes Formula

Let us examine two numerical examples that demonstrate how the Black and Scholes formula is used in practice.

*Estimating the call price $C_0$*

Suppose that the current stock price is $S_0 = \$100$, the exercise price is $E = \$125$, and the time to expiration is three months, or $t = \frac{1}{4} = 0.25$ if expressed as a fraction of a year. The continuously compounded annual interest rate is taken as $r = 0.12$ (or 12%) from the prevailing yields in the bond market. The Black and Scholes formula (17.13) now takes the form:

$$C_0 = 100 \times N(d_1) - 125e^{-0.12 \times 0.25} N(d_2)$$

where by (17.14)

$$d_1 = \frac{\ln(100/125) + (0.12 + 0.5\sigma^2) \times 0.25}{\sigma\sqrt{0.25}}$$

$$d_2 = \frac{\ln(100/125) + (0.12 - 0.5\sigma^2) \times 0.25}{\sigma\sqrt{0.25}}$$

In order to complete the calculations we need the standard deviation $\sigma$ of the continuously compounded annual rates of return on the stock. This parameter is not known, but it can be estimated from the past record of holding rates of return,

$$R_t = (S_t - S_{t-1})/S_{t-1}$$

calculated for sufficiently short periods (a month or shorter), or alternatively from the past record of stock prices using the formula for the continuously compounded monthly rates of return:[6]

$$R_t = \ln(S_t/S_{t-1})$$

Once a time series of monthly returns has been obtained in this way, its standard deviation can be calculated. The result is standard deviation of *monthly* rates of return, and it should be multiplied by the square root of 12 to obtain the annual estimate of $\sigma$ for the

---

[6] It is easily seen that when the period from $t-1$ to $t$ is short (a month or less), so that the change from $S_{t-1}$ to $S_t$ is small (a few percent at most), the continuously compounded rate of return and the holding rate of return are approximately equal. Indeed for positive $y$ close to 1, $\ln y$ can be expanded in a series as $\ln y = (y-1) + (y-1)^2/2 + \cdots$. Omitting the small terms of second order and higher, we obtain the approximate equality $\ln y \approx y - 1$. In our case, $S_t/S_{t-1}$ is close to 1 (the change in $S_t$ is small over a short period), so that $\ln(S_t/S_{t-1}) \approx (S_t/S_{t-1}) - 1 = (S_t - S_{t-1})/S_{t-1}$, which is equal to the holding rate of return for the same period.

Black and Scholes formula.[7] Table 17.3 lists 13 monthly stock price observations from which 12 monthly rates of return are calculated by the two alternative techniques. The standard deviation of the monthly returns is virtually the same, $\sigma_1 = 0.18$–$0.19$. For the estimate of the corresponding annual parameter in the Black and Scholes formula we thus take $\sigma = 0.18 \times \sqrt{12} = 0.62$: the standard deviation of the continuously compounded annual rates of return is thus estimated at 62%. Plugging this estimate in the

### Table 17.3

| Month | Stock Price $S_t$ | Continuously Compounded Monthly Rate of Return $\ln(S_t/S_{t-1})$ | Holding Period Monthly Rate of Return $(S_t - S_{t-1})/S_{t-1}$ |
|---|---|---|---|
| 1 | $100 | | |
| 2 | 120 | 0.1823 | 0.2000 |
| 3 | 160 | 0.2877 | 0.3333 |
| 4 | 140 | −0.1335 | −0.1250 |
| 5 | 160 | 0.1335 | 0.1429 |
| 6 | 150 | −0.0645 | −0.0625 |
| 7 | 130 | −0.1431 | −0.1333 |
| 8 | 160 | 0.2076 | 0.2308 |
| 9 | 120 | −0.2877 | −0.2500 |
| 10 | 130 | 0.0800 | 0.0833 |
| 11 | 110 | −0.1671 | −0.1538 |
| 12 | 120 | 0.0870 | 0.0909 |
| 13 | 100 | −0.1823 | −0.1667 |
| Standard Deviation of Monthly Rates of Return | | 0.1852 | 0.1879 |

[7] Let $R$ be the continuously compounded rate of return on the stock over one month, i.e., $S_t = S_{t-1}e^R$, where $t$ is the month index. Then $S_t/S_{t-1} = e^R$ and $R = \ln(S_t/S_{t-1})$. Estimating the continuously compounded rate of return $R_t$ for each month $t$, we can calculate the variance of the continuously compounded monthly rates of return $\sigma_1^2 = \Sigma_{i=1}^n (R_i - \bar{R})^2/n$, where $n$ is the number of months used in estimation and the subscript 1 identifies the one-month period. What is the relationship between the monthly variance and the annual variance of continuously compounded rates of return? Denote by $R_a$ the annual rate of return and by $S_{12}$ the price at the end of the year (after 12 months). Then we have:

$$S_{12} = S_0 e^{R_1} e^{R_2} \ldots e^{R_{12}}$$

where $R_1, R_2, \ldots, R_{12}$ are the continuously compounded monthly rates of return for the 12 successive months in the year. Thus $S_{12} = S_0 \exp(R_1 + R_2 + \cdots + R_{12})$ and $\ln(S_{12}/S_0) = R_a = R_1 + R_2 + \cdots + R_{12}$. Assuming independence of the monthly rates of return, we obtain for the variance of the annual rate of return $Var\ R_a = Var \ln(S_{12}/S_0) = Var\ R_1 + Var\ R_2 + \cdots + Var\ R_{12}$. If we further assume that the distribution of the monthly rates of return is stationary over time, so that $Var\ R_1 = Var\ R_2 = \cdots = Var\ R_{12} = \sigma_1^2$, then we obtain:

$$Var\ R_a = 12\sigma_1^2$$

and the standard deviation of the annual rates of return is equal to the standard deviation of the monthly rates of return times the square root of 12, $\sigma = \sigma_1\sqrt{12}$.

expressions for $d_1$, $d_2$ we obtain:

$$d_1 = \frac{\ln(0.80) + [0.12 + 0.5(0.62)^2] \times 0.25}{0.62 \times 0.5} = \frac{-0.2231 + 0.030 + 0.0481}{0.31} =$$

$$= \frac{-0.1450}{0.31} = -0.4677$$

$$d_2 = \frac{-0.2231 + 0.030 - 0.0481}{0.31} = -0.7781$$

The call price is thus given by:

$$C_0 = 100N(-0.47) - 125e^{-0.03}N(-0.78)$$

Here the values of $d_1$ and $d_2$ are rounded to two decimal places because of the restriction imposed by the common normal distribution tables. Taking the corresponding cumulative probabilities from these tables we obtain the final result:

$$C_0 = 100 \times 0.3192 - 125 \times 0.9704 \times 0.2177 = 31.92 - 26.41 = \$5.51$$

If the Black and Scholes formula is valid, the option should trade at $5.51, given the other values and parameters as specified and estimated above.

*Estimating stock volatility*

We saw in the previous example that the major difficulty in practical application of the Black and Scholes formula is estimation of the standard deviation $\sigma$. The Black and Scholes formula can be used "in reverse" to estimate the implied standard deviation if the market call price is known. Suppose that $S_0 = \$100$, $E = \$125$, $r = 0.12$, and $t = 0.25$ (three months) as in the previous example. Also given is the call price $C_0 = \$2.00$. *If the Black and Scholes formula is assumed to be valid*, this $C_0$, given all the other quantities, corresponds to a certain unique $\sigma$. To estimate this implied $\sigma$, we calculate the call price from the Black and Scholes formula for various assumed values of the standard deviation and try to match the market price $C_0 = \$2.00$.

The relevant calculations are summarized in Table 17.4. For different values of $\sigma$ from 0.1 to 0.6, we calculate the corresponding values of $d_1$, $d_2$ using the formula

$$d_{1,2} = \frac{-0.2231 + (0.12 \pm 0.5\sigma^2) \times 0.25}{0.5\sigma} = \frac{-0.1931 \pm 0.125\sigma^2}{0.5\sigma}$$

$N(d_1)$, $N(d_2)$ are then obtained from the normal distribution tables and $C_0$ is calculated from the same formula as in the previous example.

From the last column in Table 17.4 we see that if the Black and Scholes formula is

**Table 17.4**

| $\sigma$ | $d_1$ | $d_2$ | $N(d_1)$ | $N(d_2)$ | $C_0$ |
|------|-------|-------|----------|----------|-------|
| 0.1 | −3.84 | −3.89 | 0.0001 | 0.0001 | 0 |
| 0.2 | −1.88 | −1.98 | 0.0301 | 0.0239 | $0.11 |
| 0.3 | −1.21 | −1.36 | 0.1131 | 0.0869 | $0.77 |
| 0.4 | −0.87 | −1.07 | 0.1922 | 0.1423 | $1.96 |
| 0.5 | −0.65 | −0.90 | 0.2578 | 0.1841 | $3.45 |
| 0.6 | −0.49 | −0.79 | 0.3121 | 0.2148 | $5.15 |

valid, the implied standard deviation of the annual rates of return on the stock is slightly higher than $\sigma = 0.40$ or 40%.

Note that for very small standard deviations (0.1 and 0.2), the call price is virtually zero: given such small standard deviations of annual returns, the chance that the stock price will rise in only three months from $S_0 = \$100$ to more than $125 (the exercise price $E$) is very slight indeed and the option is therefore virtually worthless.

### 17.2.3  Mispriced Options and the Hedge Ratio

Applying the Black and Scholes formula, we can calculate the equilibrium value of an option. If the observed market value differs from the calculated value, we can create a hedged portfolio which yields a sure profit. Thus, the Black and Scholes model can be used to spot mispriced options on which a sure profit can be made. Suppose that an investor believes a certain call option to be overpriced. To be specific, the call price is $C_0 = \$8$, and the investor believes that it should sell for only $7. The natural step for the investor is to write a call for $8, undertaking to deliver the stock in the future for the fixed price $E$. But the investor may prove wrong in his calculations: if the stock price, and with it the option price, rises in the future, the investor will lose. To avoid this risk, the investor may create a portfolio consisting of the option and the underlying stock, characterized by zero variance, and hence zero risk. It thus remains to find the particular "hedge ratio" of options to stocks in the portfolio which completely eliminates risk.[8]

Before we turn to analyze the hedge ratio, let us illustrate the relationship between the changes in the call price $C_0$ and the changes in the stock price $S_0$. Figure 17.4 reveals that the price of the call as determined by the Black and Scholes formula is bounded between two straight lines: on the one hand, it must be greater than $S_0 - Ee^{-rt}$, as we have shown in Chapter 16 [see (16.1)].[9] On the other hand, the price of the call can never exceed the price of the corresponding stock $S_0$. Hence the Black and Scholes

---

[8] However, unlike the arbitrage in the binomial model, hedging in the Black and Scholes model requires not only *finding* the hedge ratio which guarantees a riskless return, but also adjusting the hedge ratio continuously over time, almost every second, since the various parameters that determine the hedge ratio change instantaneously. Thus, complete risk elimination is impracticable.

[9] The only difference is that earlier in (16.1) we used discrete discounting of the exercise price, $E/(1 + r)$, and here we use continuous discounting, $Ee^{-rt}$, in line with Black and Scholes assumptions.

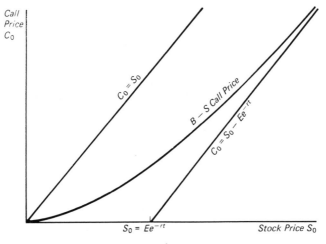

**Figure 17.4**

call price is bounded between the two straight lines $C_0 = S_0$ and $C_0 = S_0 - Ee^{-rt}$. The curved line in Figure 17.4 illustrates the change in the call price resulting from change in the stock price. Note that if $S_0 = 0$ also $C_0 = 0$. When $S_0$ is very large the call value approaches the bound $S_0 - Ee^{-rt}$. This result stems from the fact that for large values of $S_0$, $N(d_1) = N(d_2) = 1$ in (17.13). Thus we have the relationship between the call price and the stock price as described by the curved line in Figure 17.4.

The slope of the line which describes the Black and Scholes call price as a function of the stock price $S_0$ is defined as $\partial C / \partial S$ or the change in the call price resulting from a unit change in the stock price when all the other parameters in the Black and Scholes formula, including the ratio $S_0/E$, remain constant.

From the Black and Scholes formula (17.13), it can be shown[10] that

$$\frac{\partial C}{\partial S} = N(d_1)$$

Namely, the partial derivative $\partial C / \partial S$ is the value $N(d_1)$ of the cumulative normal distribution at some given point $d_1$, as defined by (17.14). Since the total area under the

---

[10] This result is not trivial since both $N(d_1)$ and $N(d_2)$ are functions of the stock price $S$ through $d_1$ and $d_2$, which depend explicitly on $S$ (see (17.14)). Differentiating the Black and Scholes call value (17.13) with respect to the stock price (we use the notation $C$ and $S$ in what follows, to distinguish the variables from the fixed values $C_0$ and $S_0$), we obtain, after applying the chain rule of differentiation,

$$\frac{\partial C}{\partial S} = N(d_1) + S \frac{\partial N(d_1)}{\partial S} - Ee^{-rt} \frac{\partial N(d_2)}{\partial S}$$

$$= N(d_1) + S \frac{\partial N(d_1)}{\partial d_1} \cdot \frac{\partial d_1}{\partial S} - Ee^{-rt} \frac{\partial N(d_2)}{\partial d_2} \cdot \frac{\partial d_2}{\partial S}$$

normal curve is 1, we can determine that $\partial C/\partial S < 1$ and only at very high stock prices ($S_0$ approaches infinity) the slope will asymptotically approach 1.

The analysis of this partial derivative $\partial C/\partial S$ is important since it is one of the main factors which determine the hedged portfolio that the investor should construct if mispriced options are observed in the market. Let us show the relationship between $\partial C/\partial S = N(d_1)$ and the hedge ratio which eliminates any exposure to risk.

A possible hedged portfolio can be constructed as follows:

(a)   Buy a fraction $\partial C/\partial S$ of the underlying stock
(b)   Sell (write) 1 call

Suppose now that there is a *positive* change of $\Delta S$ in the stock price. The profit from the two components in our portfolio is:

| | |
|---|---|
| Gain from the Stock | $(\partial C/\partial S)\Delta S$ |
| Loss from the Call | $(-\partial C/\partial S)\Delta S$ |
| **Total Profit** | 0 |

---

Now since $d_2 = d_1 - \sigma\sqrt{t}$ (see (17.14)) and $\sigma\sqrt{t}$ is constant, we clearly have $\partial d_2/\partial S = \partial(d_1 - \sigma\sqrt{t})/\partial S = \partial d_1/\partial S$. Also $\partial N(d_i)/\partial d_i$ (for $i = 1, 2$) is simply the normal probability *density* at the point $d_i$, namely $\partial N(d_i)/\partial d_i = (1/\sqrt{2\pi})e^{-d_i^2/2}$ $(i = 1, 2)$. Substituting these results in the above expression for the derivative, we obtain

$$\frac{\partial C}{\partial S} = N(d_1) + S\frac{1}{\sqrt{2\pi}}e^{-d_1^2/2}\frac{\partial d_1}{\partial S} - Ee^{-rt}\frac{1}{\sqrt{2\pi}}e^{-d_2^2/2}\frac{\partial d_1}{\partial S}$$

Now, since $d_2 = d_1 - \sigma\sqrt{t}$, we have $d_2^2 = d_1^2 + \sigma^2 t - 2d_1\sigma\sqrt{t}$ and so $e^{-d_2^2/2} = e^{-d_1^2/2} \cdot e^{-\sigma^2 t/2} \cdot e^{d_1\sigma\sqrt{t}}$. Substituting this result for $e^{-d_2^2/2}$ and factoring out the common terms, we obtain

$$\frac{\partial C}{\partial S} = N(d_1) + \frac{1}{\sqrt{2\pi}}e^{-d_1^2/2}\frac{\partial d_1}{\partial S}[S - Ee^{-rt} \cdot e^{-\sigma^2 t/2} \cdot e^{d_1\sigma\sqrt{t}}] \qquad (*)$$

For $d_1\sigma\sqrt{t}$ we have from (17.14)

$$d_1\sigma\sqrt{t} = \ln(S/E) + \ln e^{(r+\sigma^2/2)t} = \ln\left[\frac{S}{E}e^{(r+\sigma^2/2)t}\right]$$

or

$$e^{d_1\sigma\sqrt{t}} = \frac{S}{E}e^{rt}e^{\sigma^2 t/2}$$

Substituting this result in (*) and cancelling, we see that the expression in brackets vanishes

$$\left[S - Ee^{-rt}e^{-\sigma^2 t/2} \cdot \frac{S}{E}e^{rt}e^{\sigma^2 t/2}\right] = S - S = 0$$

and so finally, as required

$$\frac{\partial C}{\partial S} = N(d_1)$$

Note that $\partial C/\partial S$ is the number of shares held and $\Delta S$ is the change in the stock price. Thus, the total change in the value of our stock holding is $(\partial C/\partial S)\Delta S$. The fraction $\partial C/\partial S$ is also the change in the call price resulting from a unit change in $S$ and when the ratio $\partial C/\partial S$ is multiplied by $\Delta S$, the actual change in the stock price, we get the total change in the value of the call. We have a minus sign before $\partial C/\partial S$ since we *write* a call rather than buy it. For example if $\Delta S > 0$, the call writer loses money on the call component. If $\Delta S$ is negative, we still get the zero profit on the portfolio while losing money on the stock and making money on the call.

Another hedged portfolio can be obtained by holding one share of stock long and writing more than one call. To be precise for each share of stock held, write $1/(\partial C/\partial S)$ calls. In this case the total portfolio profit is

| | |
|---|---|
| Profit from Stock | $1 \cdot \Delta S$ |
| Profit from Call | $[-1/(\partial C/\partial S)] \cdot (\partial C/\partial S)\Delta S$ |
| **Total Profit** | $0$ |

The profit on the stock is simply $\Delta S$, since we hold exactly one share of the stock. On the calls the income is $-(\partial C/\partial S)\Delta S$ on each call, as before. But this term should be multiplied by the number of calls, $1/(\partial C/\partial S)$. Also we have a minus sign for the call income since the calls are written, not bought. Once again, if $\Delta S > 0$ we lose on the call, if $\Delta S < 0$, a profit is earned by writing the call.

Thus, $\partial C/\partial S = N(d_1)$ is the hedge ratio. It tells us how many shares of stock to buy per one call that we write in order to create a perfect hedge. Alternatively $1/(\partial C/\partial S)$ tells us how many calls should be written for each share of stocks held long.

The two alternative hedged portfolios and the appropriate cashflow components are summarized in Table 17.5.

Portfolios $A$ and $B$ differ in the magnitude of the two components in the hedged portfolio. Both, however, yield a zero return on the portfolio, independent of the sign and the magnitude of the stock price change $\Delta S$.

EXAMPLE

Suppose we know that $\partial C/\partial S = \frac{1}{2}$ and $\Delta S$ can take the alternative values $-1, 0, +2$ (the stock price goes down one unit, remains unchanged, or goes up two units). Since the hedge ratio is $\frac{1}{2}$, it is required in order to eliminate the risk that $\frac{1}{2}$ a share of the stock must be held long for each call that one writes. The change in the value of the portfolio will be zero no matter which value $\Delta S$ takes:

| | $\Delta S$ | $-1$ | $0$ | $+2$ |
|---|---|---|---|---|
| *Stock Price Change* | | | | |
| Income from $\frac{1}{2} (= \partial C/\partial S)$ a Share | | $-\frac{1}{2}$ | $0$ | $+1$ |
| Income from One Call $[-(\partial C/\partial S)\Delta S = -\frac{1}{2}\Delta S]$ | | $+\frac{1}{2}$ | $0$ | $-1$ |
| **Total Change in the Portfolio Value** | | $0$ | $0$ | $0$ |

**Table 17.5**

| | Investment: Units Held (1) | Change in the Price per Unit Held (2) | Total Change (3) = (1) + (2) |
|---|---|---|---|
| *Portfolio A:* | *Writing One Call and Holding $\partial C/\partial S$ Shares* | | |
| Stock | $\partial C/\partial S$ | $\Delta S$ | $(\partial C/\partial S)\Delta S$ |
| Call | $-1$ | $(\partial C/\partial S)\Delta S$ | $-1 \cdot (\partial C/\partial S)\Delta S$ |
| | | **Net Change** | 0 |
| *Portfolio B:* | *Holding One Share and Writing $1/(\partial C/\partial S)$ Calls* | | |
| Stock | 1 | $\Delta S$ | $\Delta S$ |
| Call | $-1/(\partial C/\partial S)$ | $(\partial C/\partial S)\Delta S$ | $[-1/(\partial C/\partial S)] \cdot (\partial C/\partial S)\Delta S$ |
| | | **Net Change** | 0 |

Thus, the investor is fully protected regardless of future changes in the stock price, since there is no change in the value of his portfolio. Now if the observed market price of the call is say $10 and the investor believes that the option is overpriced and the correct value is only $8, he can write a call and make a sure profit by constructing the corresponding hedged portfolio. However, in reality this is not so simple. The hedge ratio $\partial C/\partial S$, being equal to $N(d_1)$, changes continuously as the stock price and the time to expiration change, since the components of $d_1$ change. Thus in order to create a perfect hedge, the ratio between the stocks and the options in the portfolio should be adjusted continuously until the expiration date, which is quite involved. This is an impractical task when we take into account the transaction costs involved in each transaction which is necessary to restore the hedged portfolio at each step. This implies that investors should make an infinite number of transactions until the expiration date to guarantee a sure profit. However, even if we assume only daily changes in $\partial C/\partial S$, this policy clearly involves heavy transaction costs.

## 17.3 The Relationships Between the Binomial and Black and Scholes Call Valuation Formulas

When the number of periods in the binomial model increases to infinity, the value of the call option given by the binomial formula approaches the call value given by the Black and Scholes formula.[11] It is well known from statistical theory that when the number of periods increases the binomial distribution approaches the normal distribution, yet the proof that the option values under these two models coincide is quite involved.

---

[11] See R. Cox, S. Ross, and M. Rubinstein, "Option Pricing: A Simplified Approach", *Journal of Financial Economics* (Sept. 1979).

Figure 17.5 plots the call value derived by the continuous-time Black and Scholes formula and by the multi-period binomial formula assuming different numbers of periods to maturity. This is done for a hypothetical option expiring in six months. In the figure, if $N = 2$ each period in the binomial formula lasts three $(=\frac{6}{2})$ months, if $N = 6$ each period lasts one month $(=\frac{6}{6})$, etc. This figure reveals that for $N = \infty$ we really have the continuous model and the binomial formula yields exactly the Black and Scholes call value. However, even for $N = 12$, i.e., the six months to expiration are divided into 12 periods, the binomial model yields a value which is very close to the Black and Scholes call value.

Thus, the deviation of the binomial formula from the Black and Scholes formula is a function of $N$, the number of periods used in the binomial model. The greater the number of periods (i.e., the shorter each period), the closer is the binomial formula to the

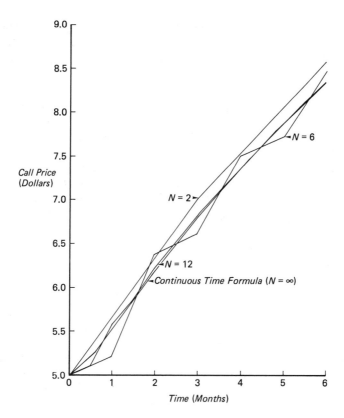

Source:    Richard M. Bookstaber, *Option Pricing and Strategies in Investing*, Reading, Mass.: Addison-Wesley, 1981.

**Figure 17.5**
**The Option Pricing Formula for Various Time Periods (N) in a Six-month Maturity**

Black and Scholes formula, and the call values derived under these two models nearly coincide.

## 17.4 A Critique of the Black and Scholes Formula

The Black and Scholes formula has some attractive features. The most important one is that it does not depend on the investors' expectations of the future stock price changes. However, the formula has some drawbacks, some theoretical and some practical. On theoretical grounds, the formula assumes no taxes and that the stock does not pay cash dividends, assumptions which of course do not hold in reality. However, there are some extensions of the Black and Scholes formula which take into account cash dividends, taxes and even variable interest rates. These extensions weaken the Black and Scholes results to some extent. The assumption regarding the underlying distribution of the stock price also does not hold in reality. We observe stock price distributions with discontinuous "jumps" rather than smooth price changes. Even this assumption can be relaxed and option formulas have been developed for stock prices described by a "jump process".[12]

It seems that the assumption regarding short sales without penalty and the zero transaction costs are the most serious. In practice investors do not get the proceeds from short sales (unless one is a broker or a dealer). Even more severe is the fact that the investor who creates a hedged portfolio must change his portfolio continuously in order to make a sure profit on mispriced options. However, changing the portfolio every minute or even every day involves accumulating transaction costs that even brokers and dealers cannot ignore. The transaction costs are quite high for individual investors, which rules out the possibility of creating a continuously adjusted hedge portfolio. Even dealers and brokers who enjoy the privilege of very low transaction costs are charged about 70 cents per transaction.[13] This is a high cost if we consider the need to make a transaction almost every second. This critique implies the following: if investors face high transaction costs, they will not make a hedge-adjusting transaction every time the observed option price deviates from the value as determined by the Black and Scholes formula and hence there will be no market forces to push the market price instantaneously to the equilibrium value as determined by the Black and Scholes model.

On a practical ground, finding the option value by the Black and Scholes formula involves at least one unknown parameter: the stock price future variance. Any gap between the observed option price and the value as determined by the Black and Scholes formula may indicate either that a potential for sure profit exists, or that our result for the equilibrium call value is incorrect (due to errors in the input parameter—the variance), or else that the particular valuation model used is inapplicable.

[12] For a formula of the jump process, see J. Cox and S. Ross, "The Valuation of Options for Alternative Stochastic Processes", *Journal of Financial Economics* (1976).

[13] See Mihir Bhattacharya, "Empirical Properties of the Black–Scholes Formula under Ideal Conditions", *Journal of Financial and Quantitative Analysis* (Dec. 1980.)

## 17.5    Empirical Tests of the Black and Scholes Model

The Black and Scholes formula can be tested in two ways:

(a)    Calculate the call value using the Black and Scholes formula and compare the result with the observed option price, with the interpretation that the smaller the gap between the two figures the better is the model.

(b)    Create a hedged portfolio revising it according to the hedge ratio, say daily, and check if an excess return has been accumulated at maturity. If no such excess return is obtained, the Black and Scholes formula yields a value which is close to the market value of the option and can be considered a good model.

However, such tests do not yield an unambiguous answer regarding the structure of the Black and Scholes formula. In fact, we are dealing with a "joint hypothesis" which tests three factors combined:

(1)    the mathematical structure of the formula;
(2)    measurements of the formula inputs and outputs;
(3)    the efficiency of the options market.

To demonstrate this point, suppose that the mathematical structure of the formula is precise and the market is efficient. Yet a gap is obtained between the observed option price and the value calculated by the Black and Scholes formula. How did this gap originate if the formula is mathematically correct? One obvious reason is that incorrect inputs were plugged into the formula, e.g., the variance of the rates of return on the underlying stock was incorrectly estimated. It may be estimated from *ex-post* data, but the *ex-post* variance may be entirely different from the *ex-ante* (future) figure, and hence a gap between calculations and market observations will arise.

As an alternative scenario, assume that all the inputs are correct and that the mathematical structure of the formula is valid, and yet a gap (or an excess return) may arise due to market inefficiency. In other words, investors do not possess the information or the knowledge how to take advantage of mispriced options and do not initiate arbitrage transactions that guarantee a sure profit. Thus, any test that is based on measurement of the excess return or the gap between the observed and the calculated option price is indeed a joint test of the above three hypotheses simultaneously.

There is a multitude of empirical studies attempting to test the Black and Scholes model. We will mention here only two.

Galai[14] uses daily returns to measure the excess return on the hedged portfolio by the following quantity $e_k$,

$$e_k = (C_{k+1} - C_k) - h_k(S_{k+1} - S_k) - (C_k - h_k S_k) \, r_k$$

[14] D. Galai, "Tests of Market Efficiency of the CBOE", *Journal of Business* (April 1977).

where

$h_k = N(d_1)$ is the hedge ratio,

$C_{k+1} - C_k$ is the change in the value of the option from day $k$ to day $k + 1$,

$-h_k(S_{k+1} - S_k)$ is the daily change in the stock component of the hedged portfolio (which is sold short),

$(C_k - h_k S_k) r_k$ is the forgone interest income on the initial investment in the hedged portfolio; $r_k$ is the riskless interest rate for the period from $k$ to $k + 1$ (so that in case of monthly observations, say, $r_k$ is the monthly riskless rate).

When investors face 1% transaction costs and revise their portfolio daily according to the changes in the hedge ratio, the accumulated excess return $\Sigma_{k=1}^n e_k$ turns out to be not significantly different from zero. However, this is a test of a joint hypothesis combining simultaneously all the three factors listed above and is not a test of the validity of the Black and Scholes formula.

In an attempt to isolate the hypothesis concerning the Black and Scholes formula, Bhattacharya[15] employs the option values $C$ as derived from the Black and Scholes formula (rather than the observed market prices $C$) to create the hedged portfolio. He also uses the *ex-ante* variance of the stock returns simply by measuring the variance while the option is alive: the variance is measured from each given point in time up to the expiration date.

The main empirical results are that the Black and Scholes model contains some systematic biases. In particular, the excess return is significantly different from zero for short-duration options (five days to expiration or less). However, when transaction costs are taken into account, no significant profit can be made, except on options of one day duration. Thus, although the excess return is significant in many cases, which implies that the Black and Scholes formula is not exact, the excess return in general is "operationally" negligible as it is eliminated by the transactions costs.

When we look at individual options, we find some options which are extensively mispriced. This means that profit can be made on these options even when transaction costs are incorporated. A divergence between the market price and the Black and Scholes value in these cases implies that either investors believe that the formula is correct but they have not yet taken advantage of the gap, or alternatively that investors think the Black and Scholes value is simply incorrect. The possibility that the public will ignore the chance of a sure profit seems to be unlikely, especially when we consider dealers and brokers who have full information on the relevant options and enjoy very low transaction costs. Thus, the sophisticated investors would pounce on the opportunity of making a sure profit if indeed it existed. Another possible explanation of the gap between the market price and the formula value is that investors do not depend

[15] Mihir Bhattacharya, "Empirical Properties of the Black–Scholes Formula under Ideal Conditions", *Journal of Financial and Quantitative Analysis* (Dec. 1980).

entirely on the Black and Scholes formula in their decision-making. They may also take other factors into account, which are not included in the derivation of the pure Black and Scholes formula.

## Summary

Equilibrium models of option valuation are based on the notion of a hedged portfolio. Investors can create combinations of options with their underlying stocks which guarantee a certain return. In equilibrium this certain return must yield the risk-free interest rate, and using this fact we derive the option price. Two models are discussed at some length, the binomial option valuation model and the Black and Scholes model. When the number of periods in the binomial model increases, its results approach those of the Black and Scholes model. When there is a gap between the value produced by the model and the observed market price, the option is considered mispriced and a profit can be made by arbitrage transactions. However, this is true only if the model formula is correct and the stock return variance used to calculate the call value is without error.

The five factors that determine the call price are $S_0$, $E$, $r$, $t$, and $\sigma^2$. The call price increases with every increase in $S_0$, $r$, $t$, $\sigma^2$ and with decrease in $E$. Unlike the value of most financial investments, the call price is independent of the expected return on the underlying stock. Out of these five basic factors, four ($S_0$, $E$, $r$, $t$) are readily available, but $\sigma^2$ has to be estimated. Any error in the estimate of $\sigma^2$ may lead to an error in the derived equilibrium call price $C_0$.

Testing empirically the theoretical valuation model is an involved procedure. The reason is that we are faced with a joint hypothesis simultaneously testing the mathematical structure of the model, the possible errors in the inputs (especially in the estimate of $\sigma^2$), and market efficiency.

---

### Summary Table

#### 1. **The Binomial Option Pricing Model**

(a) *One-period model*

$$C_0 = \frac{C_u p + C_d(1-p)}{r}$$

where

$C_0$ = the equilibrium call price,
$r$ = 1 + the riskless interest rate (for the relevant period),
$p = (r-d)/(u-d)$, with $u$ defined as 1 + the percentage increase in stock price and $d$ as 1 + the percentage decrease in stock price,
$C_u$ = the value of the call if the stock price goes up,
$C_d$ = the value of the call if the stock price goes down.

(b) *Multi-period model*

$$C_0 = S_0 B(m, n, p') - Er^{-n}B(m, n, p)$$

where

$n =$ the number of periods before expiration of the option,
$m =$ the minimum number of upward moves in stock price such that the stock price at expiration date is greater than the exercise price,
$S_0 =$ the current price of the underlying stock,
$E =$ the exercise price,
$r = 1 +$ the riskless interest rate (for the relevant period),
$p = (r - d)/(u - d)$,
$p' = (u/r)p$,
$B$ stands for the cumulative binomial distribution, measuring the probability of getting $m$ or more upward moves of the stock price from $n$ price changes, with $p'$ or $p$ used as the probability of one upward move.

## 2. The Black and Scholes Valuation Model

(a)                    $$C_0 = S_0 N(d_1) - Ee^{-rt}N(d_2)$$

where $N$ stands for the cumulative normal distribution,

$$d_1 = \frac{\ln (S_0/E) + (r + \frac{1}{2}\sigma^2)t}{\sigma\sqrt{t}}$$

$$d_2 = \frac{\ln (S_0/E) + (r - \frac{1}{2}\sigma^2)t}{\sigma\sqrt{t}} = d_1 - \sigma\sqrt{t}$$

$e =$ the base of natural logarithms ($= 2.7128$),
$t =$ time to expirations (in fractions of a year),
$r =$ the continuously compounded annual riskless interest rate,
$\sigma =$ the standard deviation of the continuously compounded annual rates of return on the underlying stock,
$S_0$ and $E$ as defined above.

(b) The effect of the various factors on call option price:

$$C_0 = f(\overset{+}{S}_0, \overset{-}{E}, \overset{+}{\sigma}^2, \overset{+}{t}, \overset{+}{r})$$

(c) Estimating $\sigma$, we can solve the equation for $C_0$ (since all the other parameters are given).
(d) Using the observed call price as $C_0$, we can use the Black and Scholes formula to estimate the stock price variability as represented by $\sigma^2$.

## 3. Hedge Ratios and Relationship between Models

(a) The hedge ratio in the binomial model is

$$\alpha = \frac{C_u - C_d}{S_0(u - d)}$$

(b) The hedge ratio in the Black and Scholes model

$$N(d_1) = \frac{\partial C}{\partial S}$$

(c) If the number of periods $n$ in the binomial model increases indefinitely, the binomial distribution approaches the normal distribution and the two valuation models coincide.

## APPENDIX 17.1
### Derivation of the Option Value

The option value in the Black and Scholes framework is determined independently of investors' preferences. Thus, we can solve for the call price assuming the simplest utility function (linear utility), and the Black and Scholes analysis implies that the resulting value is the equilibrium option price even when the preferences are not linear.

Suppose that there remains a fraction of a year $t$ to expiration. The value of the call at expiration is given by:

$$C = \begin{cases} S_t - E & \text{if} \quad S_t > E \\ 0 & \text{if} \quad S_t \leqslant E \end{cases}$$

Here $S_t$ is the stock price at expiration and $E$ is the exercise price of the call.

Assuming linear utility, the call price $C_0$ is equal to the expected value $E(C)$ of the call at expiration (discounted at the risk-free interest rate $r$ to express it in present value terms). Thus:

$$C_0 = e^{-r} E(C) = e^{-r} \int_{-\infty}^{\infty} C f(C) \, dC$$

$$= e^{-r} \left[ \int_{-\infty}^{E} 0 \cdot f(S_t) \, dS_t + \int_{E}^{\infty} (S_t - E) f(S_t) \, dS_t \right]$$

Here the first integral represents the range of stock prices $S_t$ lower than $E$ (when $C = 0$) and the second integral represents the range of stock prices $S_t$ higher than $E$ (when $C = S_t - E$). Thus finally:

$$C_0 = e^{-r} \int_{E}^{\infty} (S_t - E) f(S_t) \, dS_t \tag{17.1.1}$$

$f(S_t)$, the probability density function of $S_t$, is assumed to be lognormal. The expected option value is discounted by the continuous discounting factor $e^{-r}$, where $r$ is the continuously compounded risk-free interest rate for the entire period $t$ remaining until expiration. $C_0$ is thus the present value of expected future income.

For the purpose of our proof, we define a new variable $S$,

$$e^S = S_t \tag{17.1.2}$$

so that

$$e^S \, dS = dS_t$$

Since $S_t$ is lognormally distributed (by assumption) we have for the expected stock price at expiration:

$$E(S_t) = e^{\mu + \frac{1}{2}\sigma^2} \tag{17.1.3}$$

where $\mu$ and $\sigma^2$ are the distribution mean and variance for the entire period $t$ remaining until expiration.

Again by the assumption of risk neutrality (or linear utility), the current stock price $S_0$ is simply equal to the present value of the expected stock price at expiration, $S_0 = e^{-r}E(S_t)$. We thus have another expression for $E(S_t)$,

$$E(S_t) = S_0 e^r$$

and substituting it in (17.1.3) above, we obtain:

$$e^{\mu + (\sigma^2/2)} = S_0 e^r \tag{17.1.4}$$

Taking the logarithm of both sides yields:

$$\mu + \frac{\sigma^2}{2} = \ln S_0 + r \tag{17.1.5}$$

We shall need (17.1.5) in what follows.

Let us now turn to analyze equation (17.1.1):

$$C_0 = e^{-r} \int_E^\infty S_t f(S_t) dS_t - e^{-r} E \int_E^\infty f(S_t) dS_t \equiv A - B \tag{17.1.1'}$$

We first evaluate $A$ (the first integral) and then $B$.

Using the lognormal density function for $f(S_t)$, we write:

$$A = e^{-r} \frac{1}{\sqrt{2\pi\sigma^2}} \int_E^\infty S_t \frac{1}{S_t} e^{-[\ln S_t - \mu)^2]/2\sigma^2} \, dS_t$$

Reducing by $S_t$ and substituting $e^S$ for $S_t$, $S$ for $\ln S_t$, and $e^S\,dS$ for $dS_t$ [see (17.1.2)] we obtain:

$$A = e^{-r}\,\frac{1}{\sqrt{2\pi\sigma^2}}\int_{\ln E}^{\infty} e^S e^{-[(S-\mu)^2]/2\sigma^2}\,dS = e^{-r}\,\frac{1}{\sqrt{2\pi\sigma^2}}\int_{\ln E}^{\infty} e^{S-[(S-\mu)^2]/2\sigma^2}\,dS$$

(17.1.6)

Note that the new integration variable is $S = \ln S_t$, hence the lower bound of the integral is changed from $E$ to $\ln E$.

The exponent of $e$ in (17.1.6) can be rewritten as:

$$S - \frac{(S-\mu)^2}{2\sigma^2} = \frac{-(S^2 - 2\mu S + \mu^2 - 2\sigma^2 S)}{2\sigma^2} =$$

$$= \frac{-[S^2 - 2S(\mu + \sigma^2) + \mu^2 + 2\mu\sigma^2 + \sigma^4] + 2\mu\sigma^2 + \sigma^4}{2\sigma^2}$$

$$= \frac{-[S - (\mu + \sigma^2)]^2}{2\sigma^2} + \mu + \frac{\sigma^2}{2}$$

Thus the first term $A$ in (17.1.1') can be written as:

$$A = e^{-r}e^{\mu+(\sigma^2/2)}\,\frac{1}{\sqrt{2\pi\sigma^2}}\int_{\ln E}^{\infty} e^{-\{[S-(\mu+\sigma^2)]^2\}/2\sigma^2}\,dS$$

(17.1.7)

Since $e^{\mu+(\sigma^2/2)} = S_0 e^r$ [see (17.1.4)] we get:

$$A = S_0 e^r e^{-r}\,\frac{1}{\sqrt{2\pi\sigma^2}}\int_{\ln E}^{\infty} e^{-\{[S-(\mu+\sigma^2)]^2\}/2\sigma^2}\,dS$$

Seeing that $e^r e^{-r} = 1$ and substituting $[S - (\mu + \sigma^2)]/\sigma = y$ (with $dS = \sigma\,dy$) yields:

$$A = S_0\,\frac{1}{\sqrt{2\pi}}\int_{[\ln E-(\mu+\sigma^2)]/\sigma}^{\infty} e^{-(y^2/2)}\,dy$$

Here again the lower bound is changed to reflect the transformation from $S$ to $y$ as the integration variable.

This is the well-known formula of the standardized normal distribution, representing the cumulative probability from $z = [\ln E - (\mu + \sigma^2)]/\sigma$ to infinity. Thus,

$$A = S_0\Pr\left(z \geqslant \frac{\ln E - (\mu + \sigma^2)}{\sigma}\right) = S_0\Pr\left(z \leqslant -\frac{\ln E - (\mu + \sigma^2)}{\sigma}\right)$$

where $z$ is the normal deviate.

Denoting by $N$ the cumulative normal distribution (i.e., the probability of obtaining $z$-values less than or equal to some $Z_0$), we write:

$$A = S_0 N\left(\frac{\mu + \sigma^2 - \ln E}{\sigma}\right)$$

Since

$$\mu + \sigma^2 = \mu + \frac{\sigma^2}{2} + \frac{\sigma^2}{2} = \ln S_0 + r + \frac{\sigma^2}{2}$$

[see (17.1.5)], we obtain:

$$A = S_0 N\left(\frac{\ln S_0 - \ln E + r + \frac{1}{2}\sigma^2}{\sigma}\right) = S_0 N\left(\frac{\ln(S_0/E) + (r + \frac{1}{2}\sigma^2)}{\sigma}\right) \quad (17.1.8)$$

Now let us turn to evaluate the term $B$ in (17.1.1'):

$$B = e^{-r}E\int_E^\infty f(S_t)dS_t = e^{-r}E\frac{1}{\sqrt{2\pi\sigma^2}}\int_E^\infty \frac{1}{S_t}e^{-[(\ln S_t - \mu)^2]/2\sigma^2}dS_t$$

Substituting $(\ln S_t - \mu)/\sigma = y$ (with $dS_t = S_t\sigma\,dy$) yields:

$$B = e^{-r}E\frac{1}{\sqrt{2\pi}}\int_{(\ln E - \mu)/\sigma}^\infty e^{-(y^2/2)}\,dy = Ee^{-r}\mathrm{Pr}\left(z \geq \frac{\ln E - \mu}{\sigma}\right)$$

or

$$B = e^{-r}E\,\mathrm{Pr}\left(z \leqslant -\frac{\ln E - \mu}{\sigma}\right)$$

However, since $\mu = \ln S_0 + r - (\sigma^2/2)$ [see (17.1.5)] we obtain,

$$B = Ee^{-r}N\left(\frac{\ln S_0 - \ln E + r - \frac{1}{2}\sigma^2}{\sigma}\right) =$$

$$= Ee^{-r}N\left(\frac{\ln(S_0/E) + (r - \frac{1}{2}\sigma^2)}{\sigma}\right) \quad (17.1.9)$$

Substituting in (17.1.1') the results for $A$ and $B$ from (17.1.8) and (17.1.9) we get:

$$C_0 = A - B = S_0 N \left( \frac{\ln (S_0/E) + (r + \frac{1}{2}\sigma^2)}{\sigma} \right) - Ee^{-r} N \left( \frac{\ln (S_0/E) + (r - \frac{1}{2}\sigma^2)}{\sigma} \right)$$

$$(17.1.10)$$

Recall that if the option has half a year to maturity ($t = 0.5$), $r$ and $\sigma$ are the relevant parameters for the six-month period. However, to rewrite the expression in terms of the annual parameters (as Black and Scholes do) simply use the following continuous compounding relationships:

$$r = tr_a \quad \text{and} \quad \sigma = \sigma_a \sqrt{t}$$

where $t$ is a fraction of a year and $r_a$, $\sigma_a$ are the parameters on the annual basis.[16] Plugging these results in (17.1.10) yields the Black and Scholes formula given in the text.

Thus, it is interesting that we obtain exactly the same equilibrium price as Black and Scholes obtained, simply by assuming risk neutrality.

## Questions and Problems

17.1   Suppose that there are only two possible states: in state 1 the stock price rises by 50% and in state 2 it drops by 25%. The current stock price is $S_0 = \$100$, the exercise price of a call option written on this stock is $E = \$105$, and the risk-free interest rate for the period until expiration is $r = 5\%$.

(a) Calculate the hedge ratio $\alpha$ in this specific case.
(b) Use the one-period binomial model to determine the value of the call.

17.2   How would your results for Problem 17.1 change when it is given that $E = \$100$? $E = \$120$? Explain and compare your answers in the different cases.

17.3   (a) Referring to Problem 17.1, assume that we have the additional information that the probability of state 1 occurring is $p = 0.90$ while the probability of state 2 occurring is $p = 0.10$. How does this additional information change your answer to Problem 17.1?
   (b) Alternatively, assume that the probability of state 1 is 1 while the probability of state 2 is zero. What is the call value in this case?

17.4   A stock is currently sold for $S_0 = \$10$. Use the one-period binomial model to evaluate the call written on this stock if the exercise price is $E = \$11$ and the risk-free interest rate for the period until expiration is 10%. Arrange your answer in a table which shows the

---

[16] Recall that $e^r = e^{tr_a}$. Namely, if $r_a = 0.1$ and $t = 0.5$ (of a year) then the interest for half a year (compounded continuously) is 0.05. Also if one divides the year into $n$ intervals then the annual variance is given by $\sigma_a^2 = n\sigma^2$, where $\sigma$ is the variance of each interval. Thus, $\sigma^2 = (1/n)\sigma_a^2$. Since $(1/n) = t$ is given as a fraction of the year we have the relationship $\sigma = \sigma_a \sqrt{t}$.

hedge strategy and the cashflow on each component comprising the portfolio. Assume that the stock price can either go up by 5% or go up by 30%.

17.5    The following data are given regarding a stock and its corresponding call option: current stock price $S_0 = \$100$, current call price $C_0 = \$10$, exercise price $E = \$110$, and the risk-free interest rate for the period until expiration is 10%. Furthermore, it is known that there are only two possible states: in state 1 the stock price rises to $S_1 = \$200$ while in state 2 the stock price drops to $S_1 = \$80$.

Use the one-period binomial model to test if the current call price $(C_0 = \$10)$ is an equilibrium price. If it is not, what transaction would you make to exploit the disequilibrium?

17.6    An investor wants to create a perfectly hedged portfolio by writing a 30-day call option valued at $4 on Delta Air Lines stock, with an exercise price of $30, while the stock price is $34. He has determined that the stock price might either go up to $40 or go down to $28. How many shares of stock should he buy?

17.7    Assume that the binomial pricing model holds and that the share price is $25, $u = 1.2$, $d = 0.8$. The exercise price is $20 and the risk-free interest rate for the period until expiration is 10%. Find the optimal hedge ratio of an investor who wants to create a perfectly hedged portfolio by buying shares of the stock and writing a call option. What do you think the call option should sell for?

17.8    Assume that the binomial pricing model holds, that the share price is $50, the exercise price is $40, $u = 1.2$, $d = 0.9$, the number of periods $n = 3$, and the risk-free interest rate for each period is 10%. What is the value of the call option?

17.9    The current stock price is $S_0 = \$100$. Assume that there are only two equilibrium states in the future: in state 1 the stock price rises to $S_1 = \$115$ while in state 2 it rises to $S_1 = \$200$. The exercise price of a call written on this stock is $E = \$110$ and the risk-free interest rate is 20% (for the period corresponding to the exercise date).

(a) "In this case the equilibrium call price must be at least $4.17." Appraise this assertion.
(b) Use the one-period binomial model to calculate the equilibrium call price. Explain your results in the light of your answer to part (a) above.
(c) What is the hedge ratio in part (b) above? Prove that regardless of the particular figures under consideration, you get the same hedge ratio so long as the stock price in each state is greater than the exercise price.

17.10   Assume a two-period binomial model. The current stock price is $S_0 = \$100$. The stock price may rise in each of the future periods by 50% or drop in each period by 25%. The risk-free interest rate is 10% per period.

(a) Assume that a call is written on this stock with exercise price $E = \$120$. Illustrate graphically the profile of the stock and the call at the end of the first and second periods.
(b) Calculate the equilibrium call price at the end of period 1 on the assumption that in the first period the stock price goes up. Calculate the call price at the end of period 1 on the assumption that in the first period the stock price declines.
(c) Calculate the equilibrium call price $C_0$.

17.11   The current stock price is $S_0 = \$10$. The stock may rise by 20% or decline by 10% in each period. A call is written on this stock, with exercise price $E = \$12$. The riskless interest rate for each period is 5%. Use the binomial model to calculate the equilibrium call price $C_0$ for $n = 10$ periods and for $n = 20$ periods.

Show specifically how you determine the value of $m$, namely the minimum number of upward moves in the stock price for which the stock price on expiration is greater than the exercise price.

17.12  The following data represent a stock and a call option written on that stock. The current stock price is $S_0 = \$100$, the exercise price is $E = \$120$, the annual risk-free interest rate is 10%, and the standard deviation of the continuously compounded annual rate of return is $\sigma = 0.8$. The time remaining to expiration is six months. Use the Black and Scholes formula to calculate the equilibrium call option value.  *17.57*

17.13  Use the data of Problem 17.12 to calculate the call value for the following alternative values of standard deviation: $\sigma = 0.1$, $\sigma = 0.5$, $\sigma = 1$, $\sigma = 2$. Discuss your results.

17.14  Use the data of Problem 17.12 to calculate the value of the call option for alternative values of $t$, $t = 0.25$, $t = 0.75$, $t = 1$. Discuss your results.

17.15  "Other things being equal, a $1 decrease in the exercise price $E$ induces a $1 increase in the equilibrium call value." Appraise the above statement.

17.16  "When the risk-free interest rate approaches infinity, the call price approaches the current stock price." Appraise this statement.

17.17  "In a case where the risk-free interest rate is zero an increase in the current stock price $S_0$ accompanied by an identical increase in the exercise price $E$ will leave the equilibrium call value unchanged." Appraise the above statement.

17.18  What are the assumptions underlying the Black and Scholes option pricing model?

17.19  What effect do the following have on the lower bound of the price of a call option? Explain.

(a) The stock price $S_0$ increases
(b) The exercise price $E$ increases
(c) The risk-free interest rate decreases.

17.20  Given the following information about General Motors stock and its corresponding call option, calculate the call option value using the Black and Scholes option valuation formula.

| | |
|---|---|
| Stock price | $S = \$58\frac{5}{8}$ |
| Exercise price | $E = \$40$ |
| Time to maturity | $t = 3$ months |
| Yield on 90 day Treasury Bill | $r = 7.93\%$ (on annualized basis) |
| Variance of annual rates of return | $\sigma^2 = 0.0987$ |

(calculated from historical data on stock price from the CRSP monthly returns data tapes).

17.21  The Black and Scholes formula applied to a call option states that its value to a risk neutral investor is $4.30. What is its value to
(a) a risk averse investor?
(b) a risk lover?

17.22   *The Wall Street Journal* lists the following information on the stock of National Cash
        Register and its corresponding option on December 13, 1982.

|                              |                          |
|------------------------------|--------------------------|
| Stock price                  | $S = \$86$               |
| Exercise price               | $E = \$55$               |
| Time to maturity             | $t = 3$ months           |
| Call option price            | $C_0 = \$32\frac{3}{8}$  |
| Yield on 90 day Treasury Bill| $r = 7.93\%$ (annualized)|

        Calculate the implied standard deviation of the stock price.

17.23   Have empirical tests of the Black and Scholes formula yielded unambiguous results?
        Why?

17.24   Suppose that the current stock price is $S_0 = \$100$. A call option is written on this stock
        with an exercise price $E = \$110$. The annual interest rate is 20%, and the standard
        deviation of the stock price is $\sigma = 0$. The time to expiration is $t = 0.5$ years. What is the
        equilibrium call value?

17.25   "The value $N(d_1)$ in the Black and Scholes formula is always greater than the value
        $N(d_2)$." Do you agree with this statement? Explain.

17.26   (a) Suppose that a stock price $S_t$ is distributed uniformly

$$S_t \sim U(100, 200)$$

        Namely, the density function is $f(S_t) = \frac{1}{100}$ over the range $(100, 200)$ and zero
        elsewhere.
        The exercise price is $E = \$150$ and the risk-free interest rate is 10% for the year. The
        expiration date is six months hence. Calculate the call value.
        (b) How would you change your answer to part (a) above if $S_t \sim U(200, 300)$, namely,
        $f(t) = \frac{1}{100}$ over the range $(200, 300)$ and zero elsewhere?
        (*Hint:* Assume that a perfect hedge exists, hence investors make decisions "as if"
        they possess a linear utility function.)

17.27   In the following table the *monthly* rates of return on a stock are presented for six con-
        secutive months. It is also known that the current stock price is $100, and the annual risk-
        free interest rate is 5%. A call option is written on this stock with an exercise price $E = \$130$
        and six months to expiration.

| Month             | 1   | 2  | 3  | 4   | 5   | 6   |
|-------------------|-----|----|----|-----|-----|-----|
| Stock price ($)   | 100 | 90 | 80 | 110 | 120 | 100 |

        (a) Estimate the continuously compounded *annual* standard deviation of the stock's
        rate of return.
        (b) Compute the equilibrium price of the call option.

17.28   (a) The current prices of a stock and of its corresponding call option are $S_0 = \$100$,
        $C_0 = \$10$. The exercise price is $E = \$125$ and the annual risk-free interest rate is
        12%. The time to expiration is three months. Use the Black and Scholes formula to
        estimate the stock price variance.
        (b) How would you change your result if the time to expiration is 12 months? Do not go
        through any additional calculations.

17.29   A call option is written on a stock with the parameters given in Problem 17.12. It is also known that the price of the call is $25. Is the call priced correctly? Explain.

17.30   "According to the Black and Scholes model the change in the call price induced by a $1 rise in the stock price $(\partial C/\partial S)$ is equal to $N(d_1)$. Since $N(d_1) \leqslant 1$, the common belief that the call option offers a higher leverage than the stock itself is obviously not true." Appraise this statement.

17.31   Let the probability that $S_t < E$ be zero (where $S_t$ is the price of the stock at the time of expiration and $E$ is the exercise price). What is the equilibrium price of the call? Prove your answer.

17.32   "The assertion that the expected rate of return on the underlying stock is irrelevant for the call price is not true. An increase in the expected rate of return of the underlying stock will raise the equilibrium price of the stock, and as such it will result in an increase in the price of the call option." Comment on this statement.

17.33   The following data from *The Wall Street Journal* of September 15, 1982, correspond to General Motors call options:

$$S_0 = \$49.75; \quad E = \$45; \quad C_0 = \$7.75; \quad t = 0.51.$$

The annual standard deviation of the return on the GM stock is estimated to be 0.3, and the riskless interest rate is approximately 13.5%.

(a) Can you determine whether the GM option is in equilibrium?
(b) If the option is not in equilibrium, how do you account for the difference between the actual and the equilibrium price of the option?

17.34   The following data concern two GM options with different expiration dates:

| $E$ | $C$ | $S$ | *Expiration Date* |
|------|--------|---------|------------------|
| $40 | $9.5 | $49.75 | September 1982 |
| $40 | $10.75 | $49.75 | December 1982 |

*Source: The Wall Street Journal, September 15, 1982.*

Assume that the two options are in equilibrium, in accordance with the Black and Scholes formula, and that the variance and the riskless interest rate are constant for the two time periods. Can you suggest a method for estimating simultaneously the annual standard deviation of GM stock return and the risk-free interest rate? (Do not go through any calculations.)

## Data Set Problems

1. Divide the ten years of data for Afuture Fund into years of positive rate of return (state 1) and years of negative rate of return (state 2). Estimate the value of $u$ (for state 1) and the value of $d$ (for state 2) by the average price change in the two states.

Use the one-period binomial model to calculate the equilibrium call price on the assumption that the call expires in one year and that the annual risk-free interest rate is $r = 10\%$. Assume that the current stock price is $S_0 = \$100$ and the exercise price is $E = \$80$.

2. Repeat the calculations outlined in Problem 1 for Alpha Income Fund. Assume $S_0 = \$100$, $E = \$95$ and the annual risk-free interest rate is 10% as before.

3. Consider a call option written on Ultra Fund share. The call striking price is $E = \$100$ and the current price of the underlying security is $S_0 = \$105$. The call expires in 12 months and the annual risk-free interest rate is $r = 10\%$.

   Use the past record of the fund's rates of return to estimate the variance of the fund share price and then calculate the Black and Scholes equilibrium call price.

4. Use the same parameters as in Problem 3 to determine the equilibrium call price of the United Bond Fund using the Black and Scholes model.

   Compare and analyze the results obtained in Problems 3 and 4. How do you account for the differences in the equilibrium call prices of the two options?

## Selected References

Beckers, S., "Constant Elasticity of Variance Model and Its Implications for Option Pricing", *Journal of Finance* (June 1980).

Bhattacharya, M., "Empirical Properties of the Black–Scholes Formula under Ideal Conditions", *Journal of Financial and Quantitative Analysis* (Dec. 1980).

Bhattacharya, S., "Notes on Multiperiod Valuation and the Pricing of Options", *Journal of Finance* (March 1981).

Black, F., "Fact and Fantasy in the Use of Options", *Financial Analysts Journal* (July/August 1975).

Black, F. and Cox, J. C., "Valuing Corporate Securities: Some Effects of Bond Indenture Provisions", *Journal of Finance* (May 1976).

Black, F. and Scholes, M., "The Pricing of Options and Corporate Liabilities", *Journal of Political Economy* (May/June 1973).

Bookstaber, R. M., "Observed Option Mispricing and the Non-simultaneity of Stock and Option Quotations", *Journal of Business* (January 1981).

Bookstaber, R. M., *Option Pricing and Strategies in Investing*, Reading, Mass.: Addison-Wesley (1981).

Boyle, P., "Options: A Monte Carlo Approach", *Journal of Financial Economics* (May 1977).

Boyle, P. and Ananthanarayanan, A. L., "The Impact of Variance Estimation in Option Valuation Models", *Journal of Financial Economics* (December 1977).

Bracken, J., "Models for Call Option Decisions", *Financial Analysts Journal* (September/October 1968).

Breeden, D. T. and Litzenberger, R. H., "Prices of State-contingent Claims Implicit in Option Prices", *Journal of Business* (October 1978).

Courtadon, G., "The Pricing of Options on Default-free Bonds", *Journal of Financial and Quantitative Analysis* (March 1982).

Cox, J. C. and Ross, S. A., "A Survey of Some New Results in Financial Option Pricing Theory", *Journal of Finance* (May 1976).

Cox, J. C. and Ross, S. A., "The Valuation of Options for Alternative Stochastic Processes", *Journal of Financial Economics* (January/March 1976).

Cox, J., Ross, S. and Rubinstein, M., "Option Pricing: a Simplified Approach", *Journal of Financial Economics* (Sept. 1979).

Dimson, E., "Instant Option Valuation", *Financial Analysts Journal*, (May/June 1977).

Dimson, E., "Option Valuation Nomograms", *Financial Analysts Journal* (November/December 1977).

Farkas, K. L. and Hoskin, R. E., "Testing a Valuation Model for American Puts", *Financial Management* (Autumn 1979).

Fischer, S., "Call Option Pricing When the Exercise Price is Uncertain, and the Valuation of Index Bonds", *Journal of Finance* (March 1978).

Hilliard, J. E. and Leitch, R. A., "Analysis of the Warrant Hedge in a Stable Paretian Market", *Journal of Financial and Quantitative Analysis* (March 1977).

Haugen, R. A. and Senbet, L. W., "Resolving the Agency Problems of External Capital Through Options", *Journal of Finance* (June 1981).

Hausman, W. H. and White, W. L., "Theory of Option Strategy Under Risk Aversion", *Journal of Financial and Quantitative Analysis* (September 1968).

Galai, D., "Tests of Market Efficiency of the Chicago Board Options Exchange", *Journal of Business* (April 1977).

Galai, D., "On the Boness and Black–Scholes Models for Valuation of Call Options", *Journal of Financial and Quantitative Analysis* (March 1978).

Galai, D., "Convexity Tests for Traded Options", *Quarterly Review of Economics and Business* (Summer 1979).

Galai, D. and Maulis, R. W., "The Option Pricing Model and Risk Factor of Stock", *Journal of Financial Economics* (January/March 1976).

Gastineau, G. L., "An Index of Listed Option Premiums", *Financial Analysts Journal* (May/June 1977).

Gastineau, G. L. and Madansky, A., "Why Simulations Are an Unreliable Test of Option Strategies", *Financial Analysts Journal* (September 1979).

Geske, R., "The Pricing of Options with Stochastic Dividend Yield", *Journal of Finance* (May 1978).

Goldman, M. B., Sosin, H. B. and Gatto, M. A., "Path Dependent Options: Buy at the Low, Sell at the High", *Journal of Finance* (December 1979).

Gould, J. P. and Galai, D., "Transactions Costs and the Relationship Between Put and Call Prices", *Journal of Financial Economics* (July 1974).

Gultekin, N. B., "Option Pricing Model Estimates: Some Empirical Results", *Financial Management* (Spring 1982).

Kassouf, S. T., "Warrant Price Behavior—1945 to 1964", *Financial Analysts Journal* (January/February 1968).

Klemkosky, R. C. and Resnick, B. G., "Put–Call Parity and Market Efficiency", *Journal of Finance* (December 1979).

Latané, H. A. and Rendleman, J. R., Jr., "Standard Deviations of Stock Price Ratios Implied on Option Prices", *Journal of Finance* (May 1976).

Leabo, D. A. and Rogalski, R. L., "Warrant Price Movements and the Efficient Market Model", *Journal of Finance* (March 1975).

Leland, H. E., "Who Should Buy Portfolio Insurance?" *Journal of Finance* (May 1980).

Litzenberger, R. H. and Sosin, H. B., "The Theory of Recapitalization and the Evidence of Dual Purpose Funds", *Journal of Finance* (December 1977).

Macbeth, J. D. and Meville, L. J., "Tests of the Black–Scholes and Cox Call Option Valuation Models", *Journal of Finance* (May 1980).

Manaster, S. and Koehler, G., "Calculation of Implied Variances from the Black–Scholes Model", *Journal of Finance* (March 1982).

Manaster, S. and Rendleman, R. J., Jr., "Option Prices as Predictors of Equilibrium Stock Prices", *Journal of Finance* (September 1982).

Margrabe, W., "The Value of an Option to Exchange One Asset for Another", *Journal of Finance* (March 1978).

Marsh, P., "Variation of Underwriting Agreements for UK Rights Issues", *Journal of Finance* (June 1980).

McGuigan, J. and King, W. R., "Security Option Strategy Under Risk Aversion: An Analysis", *Journal of Financial and Quantitative Analysis* (January 1973).

McGuigan, J. and King, W. R., "Evaluating Alternative Stock Option Timing Strategies", *Journal of Financial and Quantitative Analysis* (September 1974).

Merton, R. C., "The Impact on Option Pricing of Specification Error in the Underlying Stock Price Returns", *Journal of Finance* (May 1976).

Merton, R. C., "Option Pricing When Underlying Stock Returns are Discontinuous", *Journal of Financial Economics* (January/March 1976).

Merton, R. C., "The Relationship Between Put and Call Option Prices: Comment", *Journal of Finance* (March 1973).

Merton, R. C., "Theory of Rational Option Pricing", *Bell Journal of Economics and Management Science* (Spring 1973).

Merton, R. C., Scholes, M. S. and Gladstein, M. L., "The Returns and Risk of Alternative Call Option Portfolio Investment Strategies", *Journal of Business* (April 1978).

Merton, R. C., Scholes, M. S. and Gladstein, M. L., "The Returns and Risks of Alternative Put Option Portfolio Investment Strategies", *Journal of Business* (January 1982).

Mueller, P. A., "Covered Options: An Alternative Investment Strategy", *Financial Management* (Autumn 1981).

Officer, D. T. and Trennepohl, G. L., "Prices Behavior of Corporate Securities Near Option Expiration Dates", *Financial Management* (Summer 1981).

Parkinson, M., "Option Pricing: The American Put", *Journal of Business* (January 1977).

Parkinson, M., "Empirical Warrant–Stock Relationship", *Journal of Business* (October 1972).

Parkinson, M., "The Valuation of GNMA Options", *Financial Analysts Journal* (September/October 1982).

Patell, J. M. and Wolfson, M. A., "Ex-Ante and Ex-Post Price Effects of Quarterly Earnings Announcements Reflected in Option and Stock Prices", *Journal of Accounting Research* (Autumn 1981).

Peterson, R., "Investor Preferences for Future Straddles", *Journal of Financial and Quantitative Analysis* (March 1977).

Reback, R., "Risk and Return in CBOE and AMEX Option Trading", *Financial Analysts Journal* (July/August 1975).

Rendleman, R. J., Jr., "Optimum Long-run Option Investment Strategies", *Financial Management* (Spring 1981).

Rendleman, R. J., Jr. and Bartter, B. J., "Two-state Option Pricing", *Journal of Finance* (December 1979).

Rubinstein, M. and Leland, H. E., "Replicating Options with Positions in Stock and Cash", *Financial Analysts Journal* (July/August 1981).

Rudd, A., "Using Options to Increase Reward and Decrease Risk", *Journal of Banking Research* (Autumn 1981).

Schmalensee, R. and Trippi, R. R., "Common Stock Volatility Expectations Implied by Option Premia", *Journal of Finance* (March 1978).

Scholes, M., "Taxes and the Pricing of Options", *Journal of Finance* (May 1976).

Sharpe, W. F., *Investments*, 2nd ed., Englewood Cliffs, NJ: Prentice-Hall (1981).

Slivka, R. T., "Risk and Return for Option Investment Strategies", *Financial Analysts Journal* (September/October 1980).

Smith, C. W., "Option Pricing: A Review", *Journal of Financial Economics* (January/March 1976).

Smith, K. V., "Option Writing", *Financial Analysts Journal* (May/June 1968).

Stoll, H. R., "The Relationship Between Put and Call Option Prices", *Journal of Finance* (December 1969).

# 18

# International Diversification

While traditionally portfolio managers used to diversify the investment portfolio in domestic securities, there has been, in recent years, a strong tendency to go abroad, seeking higher profits and a more stable portfolio which benefits from diversification in various economies. The article "Pension Managers Invest More Overseas, Aware of Risks and Hopeful About Profit" (*The Wall Street Journal*, July 2, 1981) indicates how important may be the benefit from international diversification; even pension funds, which are well known for their conservatism, are ready to invest overseas. The potential benefit is simply too big to be ignored by pension funds, let alone other less conservative and less regulated investors.

However, the recent sharp fluctuations in foreign exchange rates is a "two-edged sword". While investors can exploit the potential gains from international diversification of their portfolios, multinational corporations and exporters and importers suddenly find themselves exposed to a relatively new type of risk, exchange risk. Thus, the analysis of the international capital market and in particular the fluctuations in the exchange rates have implications for two major economic issues:

(a)  Management of internationally diversified portfolios, i.e., exploiting the potential gains from international diversification.

(b)  Managing foreign exchange risk, i.e., we assume that investors and in particular multinational firms are exposed to exchange risk and investigate the means by which this undesirable risk can be eliminated or at least minimized.

We begin the chapter with a survey of the economic background, then explain how to measure the returns and the risk of foreign investments and the potential gains from international diversification. Finally, we consider how corporations and individuals exposed to foreign exchange risk can hedge to protect themselves.

**629**

## 18.1 The Economic Background

In analyzing the exchange rates of various currencies, we distinguish between two major periods, 1944–1971 and 1971 to date.

### (a) The Period 1944–1971

In the negotiations in Bretton Woods, New Hampshire, in 1944, the Allied Powers of World War II agreed to establish the International Monetary Fund (IMF) and the World Bank. Under the 1944 Bretton Woods agreement, all the countries were required to fix their currencies in gold terms (the gold exchange standard), although there was no obligation to exchange the various currencies for gold. The exception was the US dollar, which was convertible to gold at $35 per ounce. It was also agreed that all the currencies will be maintained within 1% of the gold par value by the National Central Banks buying or selling foreign exchange and gold as needed. Devaluation of up to 10% was allowed without IMF approval. A larger devaluation of a weakening currency required prior approval by the IMF.

### (b) The Post-1971 Period

In 1971, the United States showed an alarming deficit in its balance of payments and in August 1971 President R. Nixon suspended the official purchase and sale of gold by the US Treasury. This abolition of the gold standard lessened the confidence in the international monetary system in general and in the US dollar in particular. Toward the end of 1971 most major currencies were allowed to float relative to the US dollar, a move which led to a devaluation of the dollar vis-à-vis the other currencies.

In December 1971, the United States agreed to devalue the dollar to $38 to a gold ounce (this is known as the Smithsonian Agreement). In return, ten leading developed nations agreed to revalue their currencies in relation to the US dollar. The allowed fluctuation band around the par value was raised from 1% to $2\frac{1}{4}$% each way, which meant a maximum fluctuation of $4\frac{1}{2}$% relative to the dollar.

In April–May 1972, members of the European Economic Community (EEC) including some other countries (the United Kingdom) entered into a European Joint Float Agreement, popularly known as "the Snake". Under this agreement, the values of the member country currencies were to be maintained within a $2\frac{1}{4}$% trading band relative to each other. All the currencies were allowed to fluctuate within a $4\frac{1}{2}$% band relative to the US dollar, in accordance with the Smithsonian Agreement. Thus the European currencies were allowed to *float within a float*, an arrangement figuratively described as "the Snake within the tunnel". Since 1972, some new countries joined the Snake and some withdrew, notably the United Kingdom.

The deficit in the US balance of payments persisted, and in August 1972 gold was traded in London for $70 an ounce, as compared with the official rate of $38 an ounce. In early 1973, the US was again forced to devalue the dollar, this time to $42.22 per gold ounce (a 10% devaluation). By February 1973, the fixed exchange rate could no longer withstand the market forces. The major foreign exchange markets were closed for several weeks, and when they reopened on March 1973, most currencies were allowed to float freely to a level determined by supply and demand.

The oil crisis of 1973 was another factor which caused sharp fluctuations in the exchange rates. Starting in October 1973, oil prices began to rise rapidly, and the oil price quadrupled by 1974. Industrial countries with oil reserves (e.g., US and UK) were not hit by the apparent oil shortage as severely as others (e.g., France, Japan). The Snake agreement could not hold under the conditions created by the new redistribution of wealth. France withdrew in 1974, Sweden in 1977, and Norway in 1978.

The oil-producing countries accumulated tremendous wealth in the form of "hot money" which could be shifted freely from one currency into another. This naturally produced very large fluctuations in the exchange rates.

In 1976, the IMF meeting in Jamaica laid down the rules for a new agreement. The main resolution was that floating rates were officially accepted and members no longer were required to maintain fixed bands around the par value.

World events influence the fluctuations in foreign exchange rates. The major events since the 1976 Jamaica agreement were the following:

(a) The dollar crisis in 1977–1978 and the sharp increase in US interest rates by the Carter administration. During this period, the dollar lost about 10% of its value relative to the major European currencies.

(b) The oil crisis of 1979: The OPEC oil-producing countries reacted to the weakness of the dollar by doubling the oil price, which triggered a new worldwide recession.

(c) The Iran–Iraq war in the 1980s affected oil production and led to the freeze on Iranian assets in the USA.

(d) The recession in the West led to a shrinking demand for oil. In March 1983, the OPEC members met again, this time in order to decide on a decrease in the price of oil (from $34 to $29 per barrel) and to stimulate the demand.

Summing this brief survey, we can conclude that while up to 1970 the exchange rates remained fairly fixed, the world scene since 1971 is characterized by wild fluctuations of the exchange rates, which were aggravated in 1973 by the shifting "hot money" of the oil exporting countries.

Figure 18.1 which plots the annual percentage changes in the exchange rates of eight major currencies (UK pounds sterling, Swiss francs, Italian lira, French francs, Japanese yen, German marks, Dutch guilders and Belgian francs) clearly shows the dramatic change in the variability of exchange rates. For example, up to 1967 the exchange rate between the US dollar and the pound sterling was completely stable; however, since November 1967, when the pound sterling was officially devalued, the exchange rate has been fluctuating significantly. Thus if an American firm (or investor) holds pounds, or some other financial asset denominated in pounds, and the exchange rate of the pound rises against the dollar, an *exchange profit* is made. Conversely,

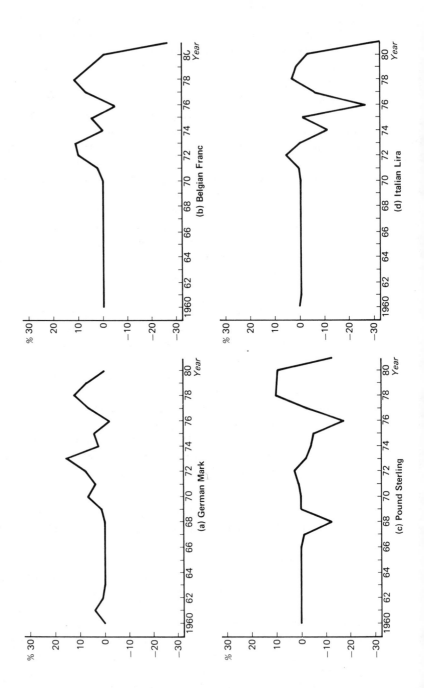

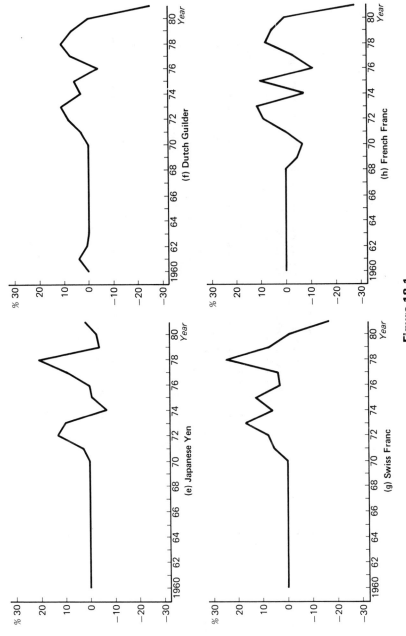

**Figure 18.1**

**Change of the Exchange Rate of Various Currencies Relative to the US Dollar (Yearly Average)**

*Source: International Financial Statistics, various issues.*

**Table 18.1**

**Total Gain or Loss (in %) to a US Investor from the Holding of Non-interest-bearing Foreign Currencies, Selected Periods, 1959–1982**

| Currency | Feb. 1959–Dec. 1961 | Jan. 1966–Dec. 1968 | Jan. 1971–July 1973 | Aug. 1973–Dec. 1973 | Jan. 1971–Dec. 1973 | Jan. 1974–Jan. 1980 | Jan. 1980–Aug. 1981 | Aug. 1981–Jan. 1982 |
|---|---|---|---|---|---|---|---|---|
| Belgian francs | 0.44 | −1.00 | 38.49 | −13.90 | 20.22 | 34.01 | −45.86 | 4.50 |
| French francs | 0.00 | −1.01 | 33.72 | −12.32 | 17.25 | 20.82 | −48.12 | 2.61 |
| German marks | 4.50 | 0.25 | 55.10 | −12.99 | 34.96 | 38.04 | −45.10 | 8.36 |
| Italian lire | 0.13 | 0.19 | 6.50 | −3.78 | 2.48 | −21.83 | −54.57 | 1.36 |
| Japanese yen | −0.50 | 0.89 | 35.76 | −5.91 | 27.73 | 20.41 | 1.79 | 3.89 |
| Dutch guilders | 4.72 | 0.00 | 38.40 | −7.97 | 27.37 | 34.57 | −46.00 | 9.57 |
| Swiss francs | −0.23 | 0.47 | 50.59 | −11.65 | 33.05 | 51.57 | −36.05 | 14.99 |
| UK pounds | 0.00 | −14.29 | 4.98 | −7.55 | −2.95 | −0.57 | −19.65 | 3.72 |

*Source:* Calculated from data in IMF *International Financial Statistics*, various issues.

should the pound fall relative to the dollar, an *exchange loss* will be incurred. Figure 18.1 clearly shows that these potential gains and losses from the holding of foreign currencies can be very large. Note that the charts isolate the gain or loss produced solely by the exchange rate fluctuations; interest, dividends or capital gains on investment are ignored.

The net result of these greatly enhanced exchange rate movements has been to increase both the potential gains and losses to American firms which hold foreign currencies. Exporters, importers, and multinational corporations suddenly found that they were exposed to a new kind of risk—the exchange risk. Table 18.1 quantifies the cumulative profit or loss in the holding of non-interest-bearing foreign currencies for selected subperiods during the years 1959–1982. The two early subperiods 1959–1961 and 1966–1968 illustrate the argument that, prior to the monetary crisis of 1971, there was no motive to include non-interest-bearing foreign currency in a US investor's portfolio. During the two-year period from 1971 to 1973, an American investor could have earned a significant profit by holding all but one of the eight foreign currencies included in our sample. However, in the last five months of 1973, the holding of foreign currencies produced a loss to an American investor in all cases. The fluctuations in foreign exchange rates did not abate after 1973; indeed, the uncertainty regarding both the magnitude and direction of exchange rate fluctuations has continued to be a significant factor in international investment. Thus, Table 18.1 clearly indicates that there is a profit incentive to invest overseas. However we shall show that risk reduction is no less important.

Let us now turn to describe some features of the international investment environment compared to the domestic scene.

## 18.2    Patterns of Domestic and Foreign Stock Prices

The practical as well as theoretical importance of portfolio selection stems from the fact that while the observed security returns for any particular country are positively correlated, they are not perfectly correlated, which implies possible reduction (although not elimination) of risk through diversification.

This can be illustrated by considering the relationships among the prices of common stocks in the United States. Table 18.2 sets out the correlation coefficients between the various stock price indices published by Moody's Investment Services over a 40-year period. Within the economy, a strong tendency usually exists for economic phenomena to move more or less in unison, which gives rise to periods of relatively high or low general economic activity. This is reflected in the prices of individual securities and in industry indexes. For example, during the 40-year period, Moody's price index of industrial common stocks was positively correlated with the indices of railroads, public utilities, New York City banks, and fire insurance companies. The correlation coefficients were 0.82, 0.79, 0.57, and 0.98 respectively. A similar phenomenon is observed for domestic stocks in other countries.

**Table 18.2**
**Correlation Matrix of US Common Stock Price Indices, 1929–69**

|                    | 1       | 2       | 3       | 4       | 5       | 6       |
|--------------------|---------|---------|---------|---------|---------|---------|
| 1. Composite       | 1.00000 | 0.99461 | 0.84277 | 0.81973 | 0.62362 | 0.98430 |
| 2. Industrials     |         | 1.00000 | 0.81697 | 0.79180 | 0.57332 | 0.97810 |
| 3. Railroads       |         |         | 1.00000 | 0.91661 | 0.88329 | 0.79983 |
| 4. Utilities       |         |         |         | 1.00000 | 0.89450 | 0.78741 |
| 5. N.Y.C. Banks    |         |         |         |         | 1.00000 | 0.58572 |
| 6. Fire Insurance  |         |         |         |         |         | 1.00000 |

*Source:* Calculated from data appearing in *Moody's Industrial Manual, 1970*, pp. a24–a25.

The existence of a relatively high degree of positive correlation within an economy suggests the possibility that risk reduction might be facilitated by diversifying securities portfolios internationally. In Figure 18.2 the common stock price indices of the United States, Japan, and West Germany are presented graphically for the period 1960–1980.[1] A glance at Figure 18.2 suffices to show that the correlation among the stock prices of these three countries is much lower than the correlation which we noted among the

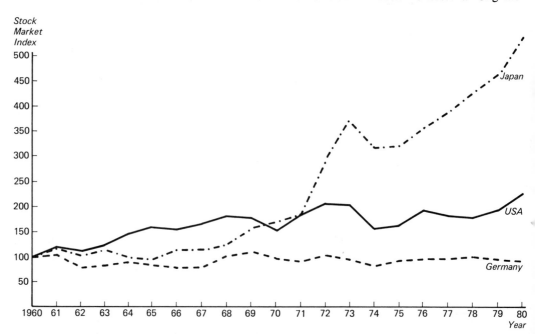

**Figure 18.2**
**Stock Market Indices of the USA, Germany and Japan, 1960–1980**

*Note:* The diagram shows the industrial share prices for the USA and Germany, and the share prices for Japan.
*Source:* IFS.

[1] The data on the indices were obtained from various issues of the International Monetary Fund's *International Financial Statistics*.

common stocks of the United States taken alone. For example, between 1969 and 1970 the American and West German stock prices fell by 14% and 13% respectively while the stock prices in Japan were rising by more than 8%. Between 1979 and 1980 German stock prices fell by 5%, a period in which the American and Japanese stock indices rose by 17% and 5% respectively. These opposite movements definitely reduce the correlation between different international markets.

## 18.3 The Return on Foreign Investments

To estimate the potential gains from international diversification a more refined analysis is required. Data on common stock prices must be adjusted for changes in exchange rates, that is, they must be expressed in some common currency unit such as US dollars or Swiss francs, and the resulting data expressed as rates of return if meaningful comparisons are to be made. Finally, an operational method for applying the portfolio model must be found so that the optimal internationally diversified portfolios can be determined.

This sounds like a tall order, and it is! The first step in the analysis, however, is straightforward and familiar. Taking as our sample 28 countries (see Table 18.3) for which data were available, mean rates of return on the investment in common stocks were calculated for a period of 20 years. The annual dollar rate of return for each country was defined as the percentage change in the *dollar value* of its index of common stocks,[2]

$$R_{i(t)} = \frac{P_{i(t)} - P_{i(t-1)}}{P_{i(t-1)}}$$

where

$P_{i(t)}$ = the value of the $i$th country's common stock index at the end of year $t$, converted to US dollars (and thus adjusted to reflect foreign exchange fluctuations)

$R_{i(t)}$ = the dollar rate of return for the $i$th country in year $t$.[3]

Thus if the index for a particular country expressed in US dollars equalled 120 at the end of year $t - 1$ and rose to 132 at the close of year $t$ the "rate of return" for the year is given by

$$\frac{132 - 120}{120} = 10\%$$

[2] The indices for the 28 countries were obtained from various issues of the *International Financial Statistics*. Notice that we do not measure the maximum potential gain from diversification since we deal with indexes and not individual stock.

[3] Owing to the lack of data for many of the countries dividends are not included; the rates of return, therefore, have a downward bias.

**Table 18.3**
**Mean Rates of Return and Standard Deviations of Common Stocks for 28 Selected Countries: A US Investor's Viewpoint (%)***

| Country | Rate of Return | Standard Deviation | Country | Rate of Return | Standard Deviation |
|---|---|---|---|---|---|
| Australia | 5.0 | 12.0 | Mexico | 1.3 | 17.4 |
| Austria | 14.5 | 26.6 | Netherlands | 9.7 | 19.0 |
| Belgium | 3.6 | 10.2 | New Zealand | 4.9 | 14.7 |
| Canada | 8.4 | 14.3 | Norway | 2.3 | 12.5 |
| Ceylon | −0.2 | 19.7 | Peru | −2.2 | 12.1 |
| Chile | 3.8 | 31.9 | Philippines | 9.2 | 39.4 |
| Denmark | 5.4 | 11.4 | Portugal | 7.2 | 17.7 |
| Finland | 9.5 | 22.4 | South Africa | 8.7 | 19.0 |
| France | 8.6 | 19.8 | Spain | −2.7 | 17.2 |
| Germany | 17.1 | 27.0 | Sweden | 8.5 | 12.8 |
| India | 0.1 | 13.6 | Switzerland | 8.8 | 21.0 |
| Israel | 3.5 | 38.7 | United Kingdom | 6.2 | 15.9 |
| Italy | 10.6 | 21.1 | United States | 11.5 | 11.6 |
| Japan | 17.9 | 29.5 | Venezuela | 4.4 | 15.8 |

* Annual data adjusted for changes in the dollar exchange rate.
*Source:* Calculated from common stock indices and exchange rates appearing in various issues of the International Monetary Fund's *International Financial Statistics*

Table 18.3 provides the mean rate of return and the standard deviation on invest-ment in common stocks of 28 countries from an American investor's point of view. Since we defined the rate of return in terms of dollars, the stock indices, which are originally expressed in domestic currency, must be adjusted to reflect any change in exchange rates during the year.[4]

To clarify the calculation, let us consider a concrete example. In this example we incorporate into the calculation the exchange rates as actually observed in February 1981 and 1982. Let us assume that an American invested $100 in a certain security in the United Kingdom on February 25, 1981, that he held the security for a year and that he earned a 15% nominal rate of return on his investment (in pounds sterling). The exchange rate on February 25, 1981, was £1 = $2.2282. A year later, on February 25, 1982, the dollar appreciated and the exchange rate was £1 = $1.8330. What is the rate of return on the security in terms of dollars? We shall see that while the return was 15% to the British investor, American investors lost money in this case due to fluctuations in the exchange rate.

On February 25, 1981, the US investor acquired £44.88 for $100 at the prevailing exchange rate on that day ($100/2.2282 = £44.88) and invested this sum in the security. After one year he liquidated the investment and received £44.88 × 1.15 = £51.61 (i.e., a 15% rate of return in pounds). However, because of the depreciation of the pound he can now convert the £51.61 only into $94.60 (51.61 × 1.8330 = 94.60),

---

[4] Foreign currency values were converted into dollar values using the exchange rates which prevailed at the end of each year. Data on exchange rates were taken from various issues of *International Financial Statistics*.

and the dollar adjusted rate of return is negative −5.4%! The investment process can be illustrated by the following simple diagram:

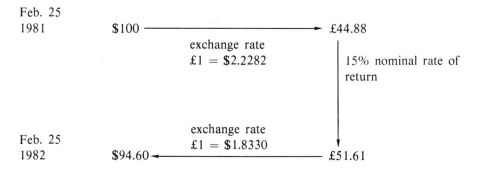

Feb. 25
1981                     $100 ———————————————→ £44.88
                              exchange rate
                              £1 = $2.2282                    15% nominal rate of
                                                             return

                              exchange rate
Feb. 25                       £1 = $1.8330
1982            $94.60 ←——————————————— £51.61

Note that the total rate of return to the American investor is actually the combined return on the British security and the return on holding a foreign currency. To see this, let us separate the two components:

    (a)   the rate of return on the British security ($R_s = 0.15$)
    (b)   the rate of return on holding the sterling ($R_E$)

The second component is calculated as follows. Suppose that the investor buys $100 worth of sterling at the beginning of the period and then converts the sterling back into dollars at the end of the investment period. The investor received at the beginning of the period:

$$100/2.2282 = £44.88$$

which converted back into dollars at the end of the period gives:

$$44.88 \times 1.8330 = \$82.26$$

Thus, the rate of return from holding the pounds is:

$$\frac{\$82.26}{\$100} - 1 = \frac{44.88 \times 1.8330}{44.88 \times 2.2282} - 1 = \frac{1.8330}{2.2282} - 1 = 0.8226 - 1 = -0.1774$$

Namely, by a simple division of the foreign exchange rate at the end of the period by the exchange rate at the beginning of the period we obtain the profit (or loss) from holding foreign currency. (Note that it is customary in certain cases to express the exchange rate in terms of the foreign currency per $1, e.g. $1 = DM 2. In this case, in calculating the rate of return we divide the exchange rate at the beginning of the period by the end of period exchange rate.) The total return to the American investor who invests in the

British security is $R_T$, given by:

$$R_T = (1 + R_s)(1 + R_E) - 1$$

where $R_s$ is the return on the British stock and $R_E$ is the return from holding foreign currency. In our specific example we get:

$$R_T = (1.15)(0.8226) - 1 = 0.946 - 1 = -0.054, \qquad \text{or} \quad -5.4\%$$

as obtained in the previous calculation.

Obviously, a loss to the American investor from holding sterling implies a profit to the British investor who holds American dollars. In our specific example suppose that a British investor invests £100 in an American security. The profit on the American security is assumed to be 15%. Thus, we have the following cashflow from the British investor's point of view. The £100 invested in dollars are equal to $100 \times 2.2282 = \$222.82$. The return in dollars on the American security is: $222.82 \times 1.15 = \$256.24$. The return in pounds (after the conversion into pounds at the end of the period) is: $256.24/1.8330 = £139.79$. Thus, the British investor earned altogether a return of 39.79%. Once again, the return is simply the product of the profit on the security and the profit from holding dollars. To be more specific,

$$R_T = 1.15 \times \frac{2.2282}{1.8330} - 1 = 0.3979, \qquad \text{or} \quad 39.79\%.$$

Note that the total rate of return on the American investor is actually the combined return on the British security and the return on holding a foreign currency. To see this, let us separate the two components:

Let us now generalize the formula so that rates of return can be calculated from each investor's point of view. Denote by $M_{ij,t}$ the exchange rate between currencies $i$ and $j$ at time $t$, expressed in units of currency $j$ per one unit of currency $i$. The first index $i$ designates the investor's country of origin (viewpoint currency) and the second index $j$ designates the foreign currency. Now suppose that investor $i$ decides to hold foreign currency $j$. One unit of currency $i$ will purchase $M_{ij,t}$ units of currency $j$ in period $t$. After one holding period the investor converts back to his domestic currency and receives $M_{ij,t}/M_{ij,t+1}$. Thus the rate of return caused by exchange rate fluctuations is:

$$R_{ij,t}^c = \frac{M_{ij,t}}{M_{ij,t+1}} - 1$$

where the superscript $c$ denotes capital gain (or loss). However, if we further assume that the holding of foreign currency earns interest (or rate of return on a foreign security) at the rate of $r_{j,t}$ the unit of foreign currency holdings increases (in terms of the foreign currency $j$) to $M_{ij,t}(1 + r_{j,t})$ during the period. When this end-of-period amount is converted into domestic currency $i$ at the rate $M_{ij,t+1}$, the investor nets a *total* return of

$$R_{ij,t} = \frac{M_{ij,t}(1 + r_{j,t})}{M_{ij,t+1}} - 1 = \left(\frac{M_{ij,t}}{M_{ij,t+1}} - 1\right)(1 + r_{j,t}) + r_{j,t}$$

$$= R^c_{ij,t} \cdot (1 + r_{j,t}) + r_{j,t} = R^c_{ij,t} + r_{j,t} + R^c_{ij,t}r_{j,t}$$

Thus, the total return is the sum of the exchange rate capital gains return $R^c_{ij,t}$, the interest rate (or rate of return on the foreign security) in currency $j$ for the holding period $r_{j,t}$, and the cross product $R^c_{ij,t}r_{j,t}$ which represents the exchange rate gain (or loss) on interest income.

Let us consider an example which illustrates the components of the total rate of return.

EXAMPLE

Let us assume that at the beginning of the period the exchange rate is $\$1 = DM2$ and that at the end of the period it is $\$1 = DM1.5$. Also, assume that the rate of return on the German security (or on money deposited in German marks) is 10%. Thus, the rate of return for an American investor who buys German marks and invests them in Germany is calculated as follows:

(i)     Invest $\$100$ in Germany, which after being converted to DM200 grow to $200 \times 1.1 = DM220$ due to the investment in the German security.

(ii)    Convert DM220 back into dollars at the end of the period, which yields $220/1.5 = \$146.6$, or a 46.6% profit on this foreign investment.

Let us check our formula,

$$R_{ij,t} = R^c_{ij,t} + r_{j,t} + R^c_{ij,t}r_{j,t}$$

For our specific example,

$$R^c_{ij,t} = \frac{2}{1.5} - 1 = 0.333$$

$$r_{j,t} = 0.10$$

and

$$R^c_{ij,t}r_{jt} = 0.333 \times 0.10 = 0.033$$

Thus the total return is 46.6%, as obtained above.

The calculation for a German who invests in the US reveals different figures:

$$M_{ij,t} = 0.50 \; (DM1 = \$0.5)$$
$$M_{ij,t+1} = 0.667 \; (DM1 = \$0.667)$$

$$R_{ij,t}^{c} = \frac{M_{ij,t}}{M_{ij,t+1}} - 1 = \left(\frac{0.50}{0.67} - 1\right) = 0.75 - 1 = -0.25 \qquad \text{or} \; -25\%$$

Suppose now that the return (interest) on the American security is 10%. Then, the total profit to the German who invests in the US is,

$$R_{ij,t} = R_{ij,t}^{c} + r_{j,t} + R_{ij,t}^{c} r_{j,t} = -0.25 + 0.10 + 0.10 \times (-0.25) = -0.175 \text{ or } -17.5\%$$

Let us check our formula by carrying out the following steps:

(i) Convert DM100 into \$50 at the beginning of the period. Due to the 10% rate of return in the US this amount will grow into \$55 at the end of the period.

(ii) Convert the \$55 into marks at the end of the period, which yields $55 \times 1.5 = DM82.5$. Thus, the total loss on the investment in the US from a German investor's point of view is:

$$\frac{82.5}{100} - 1 = -0.175 \qquad \text{or} \; -17.5\%$$

exactly as obtained by the previous calculation.

Thus, it is clear from this example that the total rate of return from investment in a foreign country depends on the investor's viewpoint. The total rate of return to the American and to the German who invests in, say, Japanese securities, in general, will be different, even if both hold the same Japanese security. The reason is that the exchange rate of the various currencies involved does not remain constant over time.

Table 18.4 presents the rates of return (adjusted for exchange rate fluctuations) earned in 1981 by investors residing in various countries who invested in foreign stock markets. The columns in Table 18.4 represent the various investor's home countries and the rows represent the investment countries. Note that the diagonal of this table does not portray a profit or loss on the holding of foreign currency since it represents the rate of return on investments in the investor's home country. For example, if an American investor (column 19) invests in the S&P 500 (row 19) he loses 10% during 1981. The loss would be −41% if the money was invested in South African securities (row 18 in column 19), −35% if invested in the French stock market (row 6). However, the American investor would be better off should he invest his money in Denmark (+2%) and would make a significant profit should he invest money in Swedish stocks (+15%); he would earn +20% if the money were invested in Singapore.

# Table 18.4
## Currency-adjusted Trends on Major Stock Markets in 1981 (%)

| Investment Country | Index of Stock Market End of Year 1980 | 1981 | Investor's Home Country 1 AUS | 2 B | 3 DK | 4 D | 5 GB | 6 F | 7 HONG | 8 I | 9 JP | 10 CND | 11 NL | 12 N | 13 A | 14 S | 15 CH | 16 SING | 17 E | 18 RSA | 19 US |
|---|---|---|---|---|---|---|---|---|---|---|---|---|---|---|---|---|---|---|---|---|---|
| 1 Australia | 713.60 | 595.50 | **−17** | −3 | −3 | −8 | −1 | 0 | −12 | +3 | −14 | −21 | −8 | −10 | −9 | +1 | −19 | −22 | −2 | +2 | −20 |
| 2 Belgium | 84.19 | 87.24 | −10 | **+4** | +4 | −2 | +6 | +8 | −5 | +11 | −7 | −15 | −1 | −4 | −2 | +8 | −13 | −16 | +5 | +10 | −19 |
| 3 Denmark | 95.61 | 118.77 | +7 | +23 | **+24** | +17 | +27 | +28 | +13 | +32 | +10 | +2 | +18 | +15 | +16 | +29 | +4 | −1 | +25 | +31 | +2 |
| 4 Germany | 222.56 | 221.06 | −10 | +5 | +5 | **−1** | +8 | +9 | −4 | −12 | −6 | −14 | 0 | −3 | −1 | +9 | −12 | −16 | +6 | +11 | −14 |
| 5 United Kingdom | 474.50 | 530.40 | −6 | +9 | +10 | +3 | **+12** | +13 | −1 | +16 | −3 | −10 | +4 | +1 | +2 | +14 | −9 | −12 | +10 | +15 | −10 |
| 6 France | 112.00 | 92.30 | −31 | −21 | −20 | −25 | −18 | **−18** | −28 | −15 | −29 | −35 | −24 | −26 | −25 | −17 | −33 | −36 | −20 | −16 | −35 |
| 7 Hong Kong | 1473.59 | 1405.82 | −10 | +5 | +5 | −1 | +7 | +9 | **−5** | +12 | −7 | −14 | 0 | −3 | −2 | +9 | −12 | −16 | +6 | +11 | −14 |
| 8 Italy | 172.16 | 194.81 | −9 | +6 | +7 | 0 | +9 | +10 | −3 | **+13** | −5 | −13 | +1 | −2 | 0 | +10 | −11 | −15 | +7 | +12 | −13 |
| 9 Japan | 7116.38 | 7681.84 | +4 | +21 | +22 | +15 | +24 | +26 | +10 | +29 | **+8** | −1 | +16 | +12 | +14 | +26 | +1 | −3 | +22 | +28 | 0 |
| 10 Canada | 2278.70 | 1954.24 | −8 | +7 | +7 | +1 | +10 | +11 | −2 | +14 | −4 | **−12** | +2 | −1 | +1 | +11 | −10 | −14 | +8 | +13 | −12 |
| 11 Netherlands | 85.40 | 84.80 | −10 | +4 | +4 | −2 | +7 | +8 | −5 | +11 | −7 | −15 | **−1** | −4 | −2 | +8 | −13 | −16 | +5 | +10 | −14 |
| 12 Norway | 103.24 | 117.31 | +6 | +22 | +23 | +16 | +26 | +27 | +12 | +31 | +9 | +1 | +17 | **+14** | +15 | +28 | +3 | −1 | +24 | +29 | +1 |
| 13 Austria | 66.96 | 57.14 | −22 | −9 | −9 | −14 | −7 | −6 | −17 | −3 | −19 | −25 | −13 | −16 | **−15** | −5 | −24 | −27 | −8 | −4 | −25 |
| 14 Sweden | 422.88 | 612.29 | +20 | +39 | +40 | +32 | +43 | +44 | +27 | +48 | +24 | +14 | +33 | +29 | +31 | **+45** | +16 | +12 | +40 | +47 | +15 |
| 15 Switzerland | 342.20 | 291.00 | −12 | +1 | +2 | −4 | +4 | +5 | −8 | +8 | −10 | −17 | −3 | −6 | −5 | +6 | **−15** | −18 | +2 | +7 | −10 |
| 16 Singapore | 660.82 | 780.78 | +27 | +47 | +48 | +39 | +51 | +52 | +34 | +57 | +31 | +21 | +40 | +36 | +38 | +53 | +23 | **+18** | +48 | +55 | +20 |
| 17 Spain | 100.00 | 124.08 | +6 | +23 | +24 | +16 | +26 | +27 | +12 | +31 | +10 | +1 | +17 | +14 | +16 | +28 | +3 | −1 | **+24** | +30 | +1 |
| 18 South Africa | 408.10 | 308.90 | −38 | −28 | −28 | −32 | −27 | −26 | −35 | −24 | −36 | −41 | −32 | −34 | −33 | −25 | −40 | −42 | −28 | **−24** | −41 |
| 19 United States | 135.76 | 122.55 | −5 | +9 | +10 | +4 | +12 | +14 | 0 | +17 | −2 | −10 | +5 | −2 | +3 | +14 | −8 | −12 | +11 | +16 | **−10** |

*Source:* Swiss Bank Corporation.

So far, we have demonstrated the potential gain (or loss) from holding isolated, single assets denominated in foreign currency. We now turn to consider the broader risk and return profiles of whole portfolios of foreign assets.

We will analyze this basic issue by investigating empirically the *ex-post* returns from internationally diversified portfolios.

## 18.4    The Gains from Currency Diversification: Interest-Bearing Deposits

Table 18.5 sets out the mean monthly rate of return on interest-bearing holdings of foreign currency for the period 1970–1978 from the viewpoints of US and Israeli investors.

The average monthly rate of interest earned on US Treasury bills during the period was 0.48%. It is noteworthy that in all instances the US investor could have increased his mean returns by holding foreign currency deposits—the mean rate of return to a US investor on such deposits, in all but three countries, exceeded the domestic US interest rate. The exceptions were Brazil, Israel and South Africa. However, the increase in return could be obtained only by increasing the risk of exchange rate changes, which of course can be reduced by diversifying over foreign currencies.

**Table 18.5**
**Mean Monthly Rates of Return and Standard Deviations on Interest-bearing Foreign Currency Holdings from US and Israeli Investors' Viewpoints, 1970–1978 (%)**

| Currency | US Viewpoint | | Israeli Viewpoint | |
|---|---|---|---|---|
| | Rate of Return | Standard Deviation | Rate of Return | Standard Deviation |
| Belgian francs | 1.06 | 3.00 | 2.84 | 7.47 |
| French francs | 0.95 | 2.85 | 2.72 | 7.26 |
| German marks | 1.17 | 3.11 | 2.96 | 7.64 |
| Italian lire | 0.54 | 2.31 | 2.32 | 7.22 |
| Japanese yen | 1.24 | 4.65 | 3.03 | 8.40 |
| Dutch guilders | 1.07 | 3.05 | 2.85 | 7.53 |
| Swiss francs | 1.34 | 3.42 | 3.15 | 8.09 |
| UK pounds | 0.49 | 2.39 | 2.25 | 6.99 |
| US dollars | 0.48 | — | 2.25 | 6.68 |
| Australian dollars | 0.66 | 2.71 | 2.43 | 7.26 |
| Brazilian cruzeiros | 0.27 | 5.43 | 2.04 | 8.66 |
| Canadian dollars | 0.43 | 1.11 | 2.20 | 6.80 |
| Israeli shekels | −0.15 | 4.83 | 0.95 | — |
| Norwegian krona | 0.99 | 2.57 | 2.78 | 7.38 |
| South African rands | 0.32 | 2.38 | 2.08 | 6.98 |
| Swedish krona | 0.85 | 2.64 | 3.62 | 7.23 |

*Source:* Calculated from data in the IMF's *International Financial Statistics*, various issues.

The rate of return on foreign investment depends on the investor's viewpoint. For example, American and British investors who purchase the same Japanese security do not face the same return, since the pound sterling and the US dollar follow different fluctuating patterns with respect to the Japanese yen. To illustrate the impact of the exchange rate on the return earned by holders of foreign currencies, let us examine the last two columns of Table 18.5, which set out the mean monthly returns (and standard deviations) on the holdings of interest-bearing foreign currency deposits from the viewpoint of an Israeli investor. Although the domestic interest rates remain the same independent of an investor's country of origin, the return to an Israeli investor was considerably higher than that earned by an American holding the same foreign currency deposit. Thus, an Israeli earned a monthly return from the holding of Swiss franc deposits of over 3% per month (!) during the period 1970–1978 as compared with the 1.34% return enjoyed by American holders of the same deposits of Swiss francs. Clearly the enhanced returns, and the higher standard deviations from the Israeli investor's viewpoint reflect the greater volatility of the Israeli currency.

These viewpoint returns on interest-bearing deposits were used as inputs to generate the mean–variance set of efficient foreign currency portfolios for the investors of various countries. In order to reduce each investor's efficient set to a single optimal portfolio choice, each investor was also given the opportunity to hold a riskless domestic asset (e.g. US Treasury bills for American investors, UK Treasury bills for British investors and so on) in addition to the opportunity of holding risky deposits of foreign currencies. As shown in Chapter 11, the inclusion of riskless lending and borrowing opportunities reduces the efficient locus to a single "optimal" portfolio of risky assets. In our case this yields the optimal composition of the portfolio of foreign currencies from each investor's viewpoint.

Table 18.6 sets out the composition of the optimal portfolios of interest-bearing foreign currency holdings from the viewpoints of the investors of six countries: the USA, Belgium, France, Italy, the Netherlands and the United Kingdom, using the

**Table 18.6**
**Composition of Optimal Foreign Currency Portfolios for Selected Investor Viewpoints (%)***

| Portfolio Components | Investor Viewpoint | | | | | |
|---|---|---|---|---|---|---|
| | USA | Belgium | France | Italy | Netherlands | UK |
| German marks | 11.6 | 49.3 | 19.9 | 11.7 | 49.8 | 28.8 |
| Japanese yen | 20.9 | 4.5 | 7.2 | 11.0 | 3.3 | 12.6 |
| Swiss francs | 67.5 | 46.2 | 72.9 | 77.3 | 46.9 | 58.6 |
| **Total** | 100.0 | 100.0 | 100.0 | 100.0 | 100.0 | 100.0 |
| Portfolio Mean | 1.3 | 0.72 | 1.03 | 1.57 | 0.66 | 1.49 |
| Portfolio Standard Deviation | 3.09 | 1.22 | 2.73 | 2.93 | 1.25 | 2.67 |

* Monthly data.

1970–1978 monthly returns (interest plus exchange rate gains or losses) for our sample of deposits in different countries.

In all instances investors can benefit from inclusion of foreign currency in addition to domestic currency in their portfolios, which illustrates the importance and desirability of international diversification. Although six different viewpoints are considered, the optimal portfolios of all countries are concentrated in three currencies: German marks, Japanese yen and Swiss francs. In most instances the German mark and Swiss franc comprised over 85% of the portfolio with the remainder in Japanese yen. US investors are somewhat of an exception to this pattern: the yen comprised 21% of the optimal portfolio from the viewpoint of American investors.

## 18.5    The Composition of the Optimal Portfolios of Foreign Securities

So far we analyzed only the optimal composition of interest-bearing foreign currencies. Obviously, the investor can also purchase stocks listed on various exchanges rather than simply invest in interest-bearing foreign currencies. Tables 18.7 and 18.8 set out the optimal portfolios of common stock from the viewpoints of US, German, Israeli, Italian, Canadian, French, Belgian, Japanese and English investors for the periods 1960–1969 and 1970–1979. In the earlier period the portfolios are largely comprised of varying proportions of the securities of four countries: Japan, Germany, the United States and Canada. The Japanese and German portfolios do not include US shares while Israel constitutes the major exception; its optimal portfolio is made up solely of Japanese and German shares in roughly equal proportion, 55% and 45%, respectively. In this context it should be recalled that during the 1960s Israel was effectively isolated from the world capital market by an inconvertible currency and stringent exchange controls.

The striking feature of Table 18.8, which sets out the optimal portfolios for the period 1970–1979, is the broad similarity of the composition of the optimal portfolios, independent of the viewpoint adopted. In all cases they are comprised of combinations of Belgian and Japanese shares with Japan accounting for most of the portfolio—the proportion of Japanese shares varying from a low of 63% for US investors to fully 97% in the case of Japanese investors. Table 18.9 provides the input parameters used in calculating the optimal portfolio. Thus, the figures of Table 18.9 give the explanation for the high proportion of the Japanese securities held in the optimal portfolio, from the US viewpoint.

During the period 1960–1969 as well as during the period 1970–1979 the quarterly rate of return on Japanese securities was the highest, 3.1% and 2.8% respectively. While the standard deviation of the Japanese stock index was not the lowest, it is relatively low. Moreover, the correlation of stock returns in Japan with the US was low which increases the tendency to include the Japanese securities in the American optimal portfolio. This is particularly true for the period 1960–1969 when the correlation between the US and Japan was almost zero (0.02—see Table 18.10). In the

**Table 18.7**
**Composition of Optimal Portfolios of Common Stock from Various Investor Viewpoints, 1960–1969 (%)***

| Common Stock of Country | Investor Viewpoint | | | | | | | | |
|---|---|---|---|---|---|---|---|---|---|
| | US | German | Israeli | Italian | Canadian | French | Belgian | Japanese | UK |
| Canada | 6 | 16 | — | 11 | 11 | 2 | 9 | 1 | 20 |
| Germany | 19 | 19 | 45 | 18 | 18 | 18 | 17 | 21 | 15 |
| Japan | 57 | 65 | 55 | 63 | 47 | 59 | 59 | 78 | 60 |
| United States | 18 | — | — | 8 | 24 | 21 | 15 | — | 5 |
| **Total** | 100 | 100 | 100 | 100 | 100 | 100 | 100 | 100 | 100 |
| Portfolio Return | 2.5 | 2.3 | 4.0 | 2.3 | 2.6 | 2.5 | 2.5 | 2.1 | 2.7 |
| Standard Deviation | 5.6 | 5.9 | 11.6 | 6.1 | 4.8 | 6.1 | 5.9 | 6.9 | 6.1 |

* Quarterly data.

**Table 18.8**
**Composition of Optimal Portfolios of Common Stock from Various Investor Viewpoints, 1970–1979 (%)***

| Common Stock of Country | Investor Viewpoint | | | | | | | | |
|---|---|---|---|---|---|---|---|---|---|
| | US | German | Israeli | Italian | Canadian | French | Belgian | Japanese | UK |
| Belgium | 37 | 7 | 18 | 21 | 21 | 18 | 6 | 3 | 7 |
| Japan | 63 | 93 | 82 | 79 | 79 | 82 | 94 | 97 | 93 |
| **Total** | 100 | 100 | 100 | 100 | 100 | 100 | 100 | 100 | 100 |
| Portfolio Return | 2.5 | 1.3 | 2.7 | 2.0 | 2.8 | 1.3 | 1.4 | 2.1 | 1.6 |
| Standard Deviation | 9.0 | 9.3 | 11.2 | 9.9 | 10.0 | 8.6 | 9.9 | 6.9 | 10.6 |

* Quarterly data.

**Table 18.9**
**Mean Rates of Return* and Standard Deviations to US Investors in the Common Stock of Selected Countries (%)**

| Country | 1960–1969 | | 1970–1979 | |
|---|---|---|---|---|
| | Rates of Return | Standard Deviation | Rates of Return | Standard Deviation |
| Belgium | 0.3 | 5.7 | 2.0 | 9.1 |
| Canada | 1.8 | 7.0 | 0.9 | 9.7 |
| Germany | 2.0 | 10.9 | 1.4 | 10.7 |
| France | 0.4 | 8.6 | 1.9 | 13.9 |
| Italy | 0.9 | 10.7 | −2.4 | 13.2 |
| Japan | 3.1 | 8.6 | 2.8 | 10.7 |
| United Kingdom | 1.5 | 7.3 | 2.1 | 19.2 |
| United States | 1.5 | 6.6 | 0.1 | 9.0 |

* Arithmetic mean of inflation-adjusted, real rates of return, quarterly data.
*Source:* Calculated from data in IMF *International Financial Statistics*, various issues.

period 1970–1979 this correlation increased to 0.55 and as a result there was less incentive to hold both US and Japanese securities in the same portfolio. Since Japanese shares showed in this period a much higher performance, US stocks were eliminated from the efficient portfolio. The low correlation up to 1969 and the change in this correlation since 1970 is illustrated by Figure 18.3, which plots the annual rates of return on common stock for the United States and for Japan.

Some additional insight into the portfolio composition can be gained by examining Tables 18.10 and 18.11 which set out the intercountry correlation matrix for the US viewpoint returns in 1960–1969 and 1970–1979 respectively. In the pre-monetary crisis decade of the 1960s the returns to a US investor in Japanese stock had zero correlation with the returns on US stocks, a slightly negative correlation with German shares, and a relatively low positive correlation coefficient with the other countries. The inclusion of high proportions of Japanese and German shares in the optimal portfolio for 1960–1969 is, therefore, readily understandable. Similarly the reduction of the optimal

**Table 18.10**
**Intercountry Correlation Coefficients for the Return on Common Stock* from an American Investor's Viewpoint, 1960–1969 (%)**

| | 1 | 2 | 3 | 4 | 5 | 6 | 7 | 8 |
|---|---|---|---|---|---|---|---|---|
| 1 Belgium | 1.00 | 0.55 | 0.43 | 0.59 | 0.26 | 0.08 | 0.44 | 0.56 |
| 2 Canada | | 1.00 | 0.24 | 0.22 | 0.13 | 0.19 | 0.45 | 0.87 |
| 3 Germany | | | 1.00 | 0.34 | 0.37 | −0.09 | 0.12 | 0.36 |
| 4 France | | | | 1.00 | 0.35 | 0.08 | 0.26 | 0.16 |
| 5 Italy | | | | | 1.00 | 0.29 | 0.14 | 0.01 |
| 6 Japan | | | | | | 1.00 | 0.22 | 0.02 |
| 7 United Kingdom | | | | | | | 1.00 | 0.53 |
| 8 United States | | | | | | | | 1.00 |

* Quarterly data, adjusted for inflation.

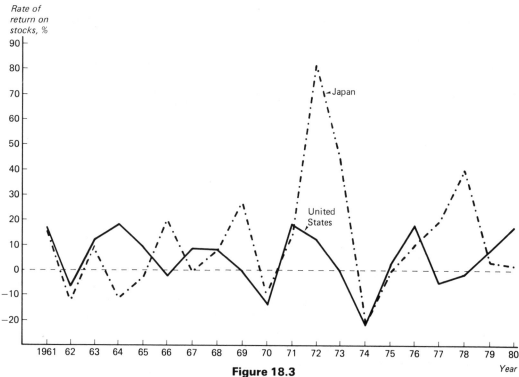

**Figure 18.3**
**Annual Rates of Return on Common Stocks for the USA and Japan, 1961–1980 (%)**

Source: *International Financial Statistics*, various issues.

portfolios to two countries—the shares of Japan and Belgium—reflects the sharp
overall rise in the intercountry correlation coefficients during the 1970s. This, in turn,
suggests that the floating exchange rates of the 1970s have led to a greater degree of
integration among the world's capital markets. Particularly striking is the disappearance
in the 1970s of the very low correlation between Japan and the remaining members of

**Table 18.11**
**Intercountry Correlation Coefficients for the Return on Common Stock\* from an
American Investor's Viewpoint, 1970–1979 (%)**

|  | 1 | 2 | 3 | 4 | 5 | 6 | 7 | 8 |
|---|---|---|---|---|---|---|---|---|
| 1 Belgium | 1.00 | 0.40 | 0.79 | 0.76 | 0.55 | 0.58 | 0.53 | 0.51 |
| 2 Canada |  | 1.00 | 0.31 | 0.37 | 0.28 | 0.40 | 0.46 | 0.75 |
| 3 Germany |  |  | 1.00 | 0.76 | 0.39 | 0.63 | 0.44 | 0.50 |
| 4 France |  |  |  | 1.00 | 0.57 | 0.52 | 0.43 | 0.44 |
| 5 Italy |  |  |  |  | 1.00 | 0.36 | 0.35 | 0.27 |
| 6 Japan |  |  |  |  |  | 1.00 | 0.38 | 0.55 |
| 7 United Kingdom |  |  |  |  |  |  | 1.00 | 0.61 |
| 8 United States |  |  |  |  |  |  |  | 1.00 |

\* Quarterly data, adjusted for inflation.

the set which characterized the earlier period. The rise in the correlation coefficients also suggests the possibility that the degree of benefit from international diversification may have declined somewhat in the latter period.

## 18.6    The Gains from International Diversification: The Efficient Frontier

The gain from international diversification can be analyzed by a comparison of the efficient frontier composed of foreign as well as domestic assets to the efficient frontier composed solely of domestic assets. The gain from international diversification can be measured either by the increase in the average rate of return on the portfolio for a given level of risk or by the portfolio risk reduction for a given mean rate of return.

Table 18.12 sets out two measures of the gains from international diversification from the viewpoint of US investors in the two periods under study. Holding risk constant at the level of domestic investment (standard deviation of 6.62% and 9.05% in 1960–1969 and 1970–1979, respectively) a substantial increase in average return could have been earned on an efficient internationally diversified portfolio without incurring additional risk. The increment in the mean quarterly return for 1960–1969 is 0.36%; the relevant figure for 1970–1979 is 2.38%! The greater increase in the 1970s reflects, of course, the very poor performance of the US stock market during this period. Hence, permitting US investors to diversify their portfolios internationally leads to a very substantial increase in mean returns.

Alternatively, if we hold the level of return constant at the mean return on domestic investment (1.54% per quarter in 1960–1969 and 0.11% per quarter in

**Table 18.12**
**Gains From Efficient International Diversification for US Investors**
**(in percent per quarter)**

|  | 1960–1969 | | 1970–1979 | |
|---|---|---|---|---|
|  | Expected Return | Standard Deviation | Expected Return | Standard Deviation |
| Domestic Investment | 1.54 | 6.62 | 0.11 | 9.05 |
| Constant Risk International Portfolio | 1.90 | 6.62 | 2.49 | 9.05 |
| Constant Return International Portfolio | 1.54 | 4.57 | 0.11 | 7.78 |
| Increase in Return* | +0.36 | | +2.38 | |
| Decrease in Risk† (Standard Deviation) | | −2.05 | | −1.27 |

* Increase in Return = Expected return on constant risk international portfolios less expected return on domestic investment.
† Decrease in Risk = Standard deviation of constant return international portfolio less standard deviation of domestic investment.

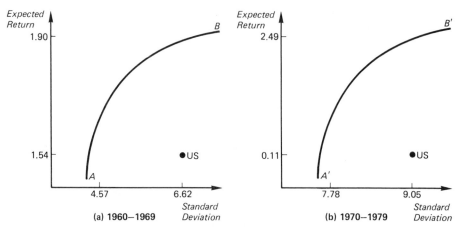

**Figure 18.4**
**Internationally Diversified Efficient Frontier in Two Periods**

1970–1979) we can measure the degree of *risk reduction* from international diversification. Once again, the gain from international diversification, in this instance the reduction of risk (standard deviation), is substantial in both periods. However, as we might have surmised from the correlation matrices, the risk reduction is greater in the earlier period. Efficient international diversification reduces the standard deviation in 1960–1969 by 2.05 percentage points; the relevant figure for 1970–1979 is a reduction of 1.27 percentage points.

Figure 18.4 demonstrates the efficient frontier for a US investor who diversifies internationally.

If the investor buys only US stocks (say the S&P 500 index) his portfolio has a mean and standard deviation denoted by "US". If the investor diversifies internationally he would obtain the efficient frontier *AB* for the period 1960–1969 and *A'B'* for the period 1970–1979. Thus, the fact that the stock indexes in the various countries do not move upwards and downwards simultaneously is a source of risk reduction and hence a source of potential benefit to investors.

## 18.7    International Mutual Funds

The portfolio analysis of international diversification provides some insight into the recent spate of international mutual funds. Independent of tax considerations, these funds, which typically include the securities of a dozen or more countries, reflect the fundamental fact that risk diversification can often be facilitated by including an international cross-section of securities in the portfolio. Perhaps due to the nature of the operations of many of these funds, data are often difficult to obtain, but Table 18.13 sets out the proportion of the portfolios of seven international funds invested in US and Japanese securities. As might have been anticipated from the analysis of the previous

**Table 18.13**
**Share of Japanese and US Securities in the Portfolios of Selected International Mutual Funds, 1969 (%)**

| Name of Fund | Japanese Securities | US Securities | Total |
|---|---|---|---|
| Fonselex | 11 | 29 | 40 |
| ITT | 33 | 39 | 72 |
| Robeco | 8 | 32 | 40 |
| Rolinco | 14 | 24 | 38 |
| Slater Walker | 39 | 4 | 43 |
| Tyndal International | 30 | 17 | 47 |
| Utilco | 10 | 39 | 49 |

section, Japanese and US securities tend to dominate the portfolio, comprising between 38% and 72% of the aggregate investments of the seven funds included in Table 18.13.

## 18.8　The Forward Exchange Rate: Hedging Against Foreign Exchange Risk

So far we have explained how US investors can gain from international diversification. However, the large fluctuations in foreign currencies are also very risky and may cause bankruptcy to firms, even though they may operate quite efficiently. For example, suppose that a US firm exports most of its products to Germany. Assume that the American firm is very efficient in its production. However, it sells its products to Germany on three months' credit. If during this three-month period the exchange rate changes from DM2 to the US dollar to DM3 to the dollar, the American firm will collect for each DM100 of sales to Germany $33.3 (100/3) rather than $50 (100/2) as planned, which may turn a profitable transaction into a disaster, resulting in possible bankruptcy of the American firm.

Fortunately, there are financial instruments which provide a hedge against such foreign exchange risk known as forward transactions. A forward transaction is a contract between two parties to deliver a given amount of foreign currency on a given date in the future at an agreed exchange rate. In this way, the American can sell DM100 forward at the forward exchange rate which is known today with certainty, say 2.1 to the dollar. Clearly, if the American firm expects to receive the marks in three months, it should engage itself in a three-month forward contract.

EXAMPLE

Let us illustrate this with an example of a British firm that exports to the US.

Suppose a British exporter is expecting to receive $100,000 in three months' time from his customers in the US. Although the sum in dollars is certain it is exposed to foreign exchange risk. Suppose the current exchange rate (spot rate) is £1 = $2. Thus, at present the $100,000 are worth £50,000. However, the sum the British exporter will receive in pounds in three months' time will vary in accordance with the unknown dollar/pound exchange rate at that time. In order to hedge against this risk the exporter may engage himself in a *forward contract*: he can sell the $10,000 forward, and assure himself a certain income. Suppose the forward rate is £1 = $2.05. Through the forward contract the exporter will receive £48,780.49 (100,000/2.05) with certainty. Note that the forward contract is between two partners. The other partner may be an American exporter to the UK, so that both partners rid themselves of foreign exchange risk.

## 18.9   Arbitrage Possibilities

The previous section considered only one aspect of the forward foreign exchange market. Other participants in the market are British importers (or American exporters) who supply pounds forward, speculators, and arbitrageurs.[5] Arbitrageurs, in contrast to speculators, are investors who switch from one currency to another, exploiting differences in rates of return, without any foreign exchange risk.

EXAMPLE

Suppose the spot exchange rate is £1 = $2.00, the three-month forward rate is £1 = $2.05 and the three-month *riskless* interest rate on both dollars and pounds is 16% per annum, i.e. about 4% for the three-month period. Any investor can carry out the following arbitrage: borrow, say, $100, convert this sum into pounds, invest the pounds at the 4% riskless interest rate, convert the proceeds back into dollars and come out with a profit. At the end of the period the investor would pay $104.00 (interest plus principal) on the loan while earning

$$\frac{100}{2.00} \cdot (1.04)(2.05) = \$106.60$$

on the investment in pounds. His profit on this transaction would be $2.60. However, if many people are engaged in such transactions we would expect the exchange rates (spot and forward) and/or the interest rates to change, until equilibrium is restored.

More formally, we use the following symbols: $S$—the spot exchange rate (dollars per pound); $F$—the forward exchange rate; $r$—the riskless interest rate on pounds; $r^*$—the riskless interest rate on dollars.

In equilibrium we expect the following equation to hold:[6]

$$\frac{S(1 + r^*)}{F(1 + r)} = 1 \tag{18.1}$$

[5] See Aliber R. Z., "The Interest Rate Parity Theorem: A Reinterpretation," *Journal of Political Economy* (1973), pp. 1451–1459.
[6] Note that we assume a perfect capital market to exist. However equation (18.1) may be generalized to account for transaction costs as well. See J. A. Frenkel and R. M. Levich, "Covered Interest Arbitrage: Unexploited Profits?" *Journal of Political Economy* (1975). Also note that equation (18.1) changes to $S(1 + r)/F(1 + r^*) = 1$ when the exchange rates $S$ and $F$ are quoted in other currency per $1 (and not in dollars per £1 as in the text).

If (18.1) holds, no profit can be made by arbitraging. Indeed, in our example $S = \$2.00$, $F = \$2.05$, and by assumption the interest rate is the same on both currencies, $r = r^* = 0.04$. As a result of this assumption, the equilibrium equation (18.1) does not hold $(2.00 \times 1.04/(2.05 \times 1.04) = 0.9756 \neq 1)$ and investors can profit by arbitraging, as shown. Now suppose that the sterling interest rate is $r = 0.04$, as before, while the dollar interest rate $r^*$ is such that (18.1) is satisfied:

$$1 + r^* = F(1 + r)/S = 2.05 \times 1.04/2.00 = 1.066 \quad \text{or} \quad r^* = 0.066$$

Let us try to arbitrage as before: borrowing $100 at the three-month dollar interest rate of 6.6%, we will have to repay $106.6 at the end of the three months (and not $104.00 as before). But this is precisely the dollar equivalent of our investment in pounds, and the arbitrage profits have been completely wiped out by the adjustment of the interest rates.

## 18.10 Exploring the Arbitrage Possibilities with Actual Data

In the previous section we assumed the existence of a perfect capital market. However, in reality there exist transaction costs, and there is a gap between the buying and selling exchange rate and the lending and borrowing interest rate. In this section we explore the possibility of arbitrage under the existence of transaction costs and using actual data. In Tables 18.14 and 18.15 the various dollar exchange rates and Euro-Currency interest rates are presented. Suppose an investor attempts to perform an act of arbitrage by, say, taking a loan in dollars and investing the sum in German marks (DM). The mark is in premium over the dollar (denoted by *pm.* in Table 18.15), meaning that the forward rate

**Table 18.14**
**Euro-Currency Interest Rates for One Month**
**(in percent per annum), February 24, 1982**

|  | Lending | Borrowing |
|---|---|---|
| Sterling | $14\frac{1}{16}$ | $14\frac{3}{16}$ |
| US Dollar | $14\frac{1}{4}$ | $14\frac{1}{2}$ |
| Canadian Dollar | $14\frac{5}{8}$ | 15 |
| Dutch Guilder | $9\frac{11}{16}$ | $9\frac{13}{16}$ |
| Swiss Franc | $7\frac{3}{8}$ | $7\frac{1}{2}$ |
| West German Mark | 10 | $10\frac{1}{8}$ |
| French Franc | $14\frac{7}{8}$ | 15 |
| Italian Lira | 20 | 21 |
| Belgian Franc | 14 | $15\frac{3}{4}$ |
| Japanese Yen | $6\frac{1}{16}$ | $6\frac{3}{16}$ |

*Source: Financial Times*, February 25, 1982.

**Table 18.15**
**Dollar Spot and Forward Rates, February 24, 1982**

|  | Close | One Month* |
|---|---|---|
| UK† | 1.8295–1.8305 | 0.03–0.13c dis. |
| Ireland† | 1.4920–1.4935 | 0.53–0.43c pm. |
| Canada | 1.2200–1.2205 | 0.01–0.04c dis. |
| Netherlands | 2.5950–2.5980 | 1.20–1.10c pm. |
| Belgium | 43.31–43.33 | par–5c dis. |
| Denmark | 7.9120–7.9150 | 0.20–0.10 ore pm. |
| West Germany | 2.3655–2.3665 | 0.96–0.91 pf pm. |
| Portugal | 69.05–69.25 | 25–80c dis. |
| Spain | 102.70–102.80 | 10–20c dis. |
| Italy | 1,267–1,268 | 6–7 lire dis. |
| Norway | 6.0060–6.0080 | 1.20–1.10 ore pm. |
| France | 6.0275–6.0325 | 0.15–0.30c dis. |
| Sweden | 5.7600–5.7620 | 0.30–0.15 ore pm. |
| Japan | 234.20–234.30 | 1.85–1.70 y pm. |
| Austria | $16.59\frac{3}{4}$–$16.60\frac{3}{4}$ | $9\frac{1}{2}$–$8\frac{1}{4}$ gro pm. |
| Switzerland | 1.8735–1.8745 | 1.21–1.13c pm. |

* dis. – discount of the currency relative to US dollar: spot rate lower than
forward rate (expectation of devaluation); pm. – premium relative to US
dollar: spot rate higher than forward rate (expectation of revaluation).
† UK and Ireland rates are quoted in US currency. Forward premiums and
discounts apply to the US dollar and not to the individual currency.
*Source: Financial Times*, February 25, 1982.

is lower than the spot exchange rate (the mark is expected to strengthen relative to the
US dollar in the future). The spot rate is: 2.3655/2.3665 marks per dollar. (The bank
*sells* one dollar for 2.3665 marks spot and *buys* one dollar for 2.3655 marks spot.) The
premium by Table 18.15 is 0.96–0.91 pfenning, or 0.0096–0.0091 mark, and the
forward rates are thus calculated as follows:

|  | Buying | Selling |
|---|---|---|
| Spot | 2.3655 | 2.3665 |
| Premium | –0.0096 | –0.0091 |
| Forward | 2.3559 | 2.3574 |

The bank *buys* one dollar *forward* for 2.3559 marks and *sells* one dollar *forward* for
2.3574. The interest rates per one month on the dollar and mark are (see Table 18.14):

|  | Dollar | Mark |
|---|---|---|
| % Per Annum | 14.25/14.50 | 10/10.125 |
| For One Month (%) | 1.1875/1.2083 | 0.8333/0.84375 |

The higher rate is the *borrowing* rate and the lower rate the *lending* rate. Note that the one month's interest rate is calculated according to the banker's formula, which is, approximately, the interest rate per annum divided by 12. The exact banker's formula takes into account the exact number of days of investment.

If the arbitrageur borrows one dollar he would have to repay in one month's time 1.012083 dollars for each dollar borrowed. He then exchanges the dollars into marks at the buying exchange rate of 2.3655 marks per dollar. He invests the total sum in marks and receives at the end of one month 1.008333 marks for each mark invested. This total sum can then be converted into dollars at the selling forward rate of 2.3574. If the return on the investment (in dollars) is higher than the cost of borrowing (1.2083%) then the whole transaction is profitable. Let us check this out:

$$\frac{2.3655 \times (1.008333)}{2.3574} - 1.012083 = 1.011798 - 1.012083 = -0.000285 < 0$$

Such a transaction would result in a loss of 0.03 cents for each dollar borrowed and invested, and is found to be unprofitable.[7] Thus, given the actual data, there is no motive to arbitrage.

### Summary

The decade of the 1970s witnessed a remarkable change in the international economic order. The system of fixed exchange rates was replaced by freely or semi-freely fluctuating exchange values. This shift has not only created problems but has also opened new investment opportunities. For example, most international firms which hold large quantities of cash assets tend to use, albeit not always explicitly, the type of portfolio diversification techniques which have been discussed in this chapter. Similarly, investors in risky assets are confronted with the need to diversify their holdings internationally if they are to take maximum advantage of the opportunities afforded by the capital market for risk reduction. In this context, the rise of internationally diversified mutual funds, commodity funds and of course the investment in precious metals all reflect, in part, the quest for risk reduction through diversification in a world characterized by serious inflation.

Finally, one final *caveat* may be appropriate. Throughout the chapter we have used *ex-post* data to demonstrate the gain from international diversification. Clearly, actual decisions should be based on *ex-ante* estimates; however, we feel that the best estimates of the intercountry correlations are likely to be those which are calculated from observed data. Although return estimates may vary widely, the principal motive for diversification will remain, and the techniques outlined in this chapter can be used to derive the optimal portfolio of foreign asset holdings. As is true of *ex-post* data, in employing *ex-ante* data one may expect that the efficient portfolios will generally depend on the "point of view" of investors and that significant benefits from proper diversification among various currencies and securities can be expected.

[7] In some transactions (called swaps) that involve a simultaneous spot and forward deal, the spread between the spot and forward rates is smaller than in the above example. This may change the result of the profitability test.

## Summary Table

1. The rate of return to the American investor who invests in a foreign country, say, the UK, *in terms of pounds sterling* is given by:

$$R_S = \frac{P_t - P_{t-1}}{P_{t-1}}$$

where $P_t$ is the stock price (adjusted for dividends, splits, etc.) in period $t$, given in pounds.

2. The rate of return to the American investor who holds foreign currency (e.g., pounds sterling) is given by

$$R_E = \frac{M_t}{M_{t+1}} - 1$$

where $M_t$ is the number of foreign currency units needed to purchase one dollar in period $t$.

3. The total rate of return, *in dollar terms*, to an American investor who holds foreign securities is:

$$R_T = (1 + R_S)(1 + R_E) - 1$$

4. A profit (loss) to the American investor who holds British pounds implies a loss (profit) to the British investor who holds American dollars.

5. The return on an internationally diversified portfolio is determined by the profit on the securities in the various countries (in the domestic currency) and the fluctuations in the various exchange rates.

6. Arbitrage possibilities guarantee that in equilibrium we have:

$$\frac{S}{F} \frac{(1 + r^*)}{(1 + r)} = 1$$

where

$S =$ the spot exchange rate (dollars per pound)
$F =$ the forward exchange rate (dollars per pound)
$r =$ the riskless interest rate on British pounds
$r^* =$ the riskless interest rate on dollars.

7. If the exchange rate is quoted in foreign currency units per \$1, the spot-forward equilibrium formula becomes

$$\frac{S}{F} \frac{(1 + r)}{(1 + r^*)} = 1$$

## Questions and Problems

18.1    In what way can a US investor profit from international diversification?

18.2    Define the efficient frontier for internationally diversified portfolios.

18.3    "The efficiency curves of an American and a European investor are not necessarily the same even if they are confronted by the same investment opportunities." Appraise.

18.4    "Since US stocks represent high-return, low-risk investments relative to the rest of the world, American investors should *not* include foreign stocks in their portfolios." Appraise.

18.5    How can you account for the fact that, other things being equal, a higher riskless interest rate implies "riskier" investment portfolios?

18.6    Draw the efficiency curves for the following cases:

(a) Investors are constrained to investments in two countries.
(b) Investors are constrained to investments in ten countries.

Which case is more beneficial for the investors?

18.7    On June 1981, a UK industrial share price was £244.3. On June 1982, the price was £266. The exchange rates on June 1981 and June 1982 were as follows:

June 1, 1981,    £1 = $1.9428
June 1, 1982,    £1 = $1.7383

(All data from the International Monetary Fund's *International Financial Statistics*, various issues.)

What is the profit earned by:

(a) A British investor investing in the UK stock market?
(b) An American investing in the UK stock market?

18.8    The exchange rates between US dollars and Swiss francs were as follows:

June 1981    $1 = 2.0298 Swiss francs
June 1982    $1 = 2.1035 Swiss francs

The annual interest rate on Swiss francs on June 1, 1981, was 5.62%.
(All data from the International Monetary Fund's *International Financial Statistics*, various issues.)

Calculate the gain or loss to:

(a) an American investor in Swiss francs
(b) a Swiss investor holding Swiss francs on deposit.

18.9    A German investor is considering investing in a 1-year, 5% riskless bond in Switzerland.

At the beginning of the period the exchange rate is DM1 = SwF 0.9. The exchange rate at the end of the year is a random variable ($x$) having the following probability distribution:

$$x = \begin{cases} \text{SwF } 0.8 \text{ per DM1, with probability } \tfrac{1}{2} \\ \text{SwF } 1.0 \text{ per DM1, with probability } \tfrac{1}{2} \end{cases}$$

(a) What is the total rate of return on the investment in the Swiss bond? Present it as a product of two factors: the certain return on the Swiss bond and the uncertain return from holding an investment in Swiss Francs.

(b) Suppose the investor can receive a 5% *certain* yield on an investment in German marks. Which investment alternative would he prefer, the German or the Swiss? Answer this question using the FSD, SSD, and MV criteria.

(c) Suppose the investor is a risk averter with the following utility function: $U(R) = \ln(1 + R)$, where $R$ is the rate of return on the investment. Which investment alternative would he prefer?

(d) What is the *minimal* rate of return required on the German riskless asset that would cause *every* German risk averter to prefer the investment in Germany over the investment in Switzerland?

(e) Would the investor whose utility function is specified in (c) diversify between the two assets, the German and the Swiss? What would his optimal investment strategy be? (*Hint*: write the expected utility as a function of the proportion invested in the Swiss asset and derive the optimality conditions).

(f) Answer questions (a) to (e) from the point of view of a Swiss investor, considering investment in a 5% riskless German bond. Assume that the interest on the German mark and on the Swiss franc is 5%.

18.10 Suppose that an American investor invests in German marks (as foreign currency). Comment on the following statement: "An increase in the riskless interest rate on an investment in a foreign country may not always be desirable from the point of view of the domestic investor. While it results in an increase in the total expected return it also results in an increase in the total variance of the investment." Do you agree with this opinion?

18.11 Suppose an American exporter is expecting to receive £10,000 in three months' time. The current exchange rate ($S_0$) is £1 = $2. The exchange rate in three months is a random variable $S_3$, with mean $E(S_3) = 2.1$ and standard deviation $\sigma(S_3) = 1.5$. The three months forward exchange rate ($F_3$) is £1 = $1.9. The exporter is a risk averter with the following utility function:

$$U(\mu, \sigma) = \mu^2 - \sigma^2$$

where $\mu$ is the expected value of wealth and $\sigma$ the standard deviation.

(a) Does the utility function specified above seem logical? What restrictions must be placed on the investment alternative for it to have economic sense?

(b) Which of the following two alternatives would the exporter prefer:
   (i) bearing the foreign exchange risk on the entire £10,000;
   (ii) selling the £10,000 forward.

(c) Suppose the exporter may diversify, i.e., sell part of the £10,000 forward while bearing the foreign exchange risk on the rest. What would his optimal strategy be?

(d) Answer (c) under the assumption that the exporter expects to receive £20,000. How does the total wealth affect the optimal strategy?

18.12 Assume that the German Mark spot exchange rate ($S$) is $1 = DM2, the three months forward exchange rate ($F$) is also $1 = DM2, the three months riskless interest rate on marks ($r$) is 2%, and the three months riskless interest rate on dollars ($r^*$) is 4%. Assume, further, that there are no transaction costs.

(a) What arbitrage opportunities exist in this market?

(b) Can these conditions persist for long? If not, which forces will bring about a change, and what are the equilibrium conditions in the market?

18.13 Using the following information on rates of return of US and UK industrial shares and on the exchange rates between US dollars and British pounds, determine the investment proportions in an optimal efficient portfolio of US securities and UK securities from the point of view of a US investor if the investor requires a portfolio with a mean return of 15%.

| | Rates of Return (in percent) | | Exchange Rates per £1 |
|---|---|---|---|
| Year | US | UK | (end of year) |
| 1975 | 3.84 | 25.00 | $2.0235 |
| 1976 | 18.50 | 19.80 | $1.7024 |
| 1977 | −5.23 | 28.21 | $1.9060 |
| 1978 | −2.05 | 12.63 | $2.0345 |
| 1979 | 8.18 | 13.64 | $2.2240 |
| 1980 | 17.14 | 6.87 | $2.3850 |
| 1981 | 7.17 | 12.76 | $1.9080 |

*Source:* The International Monetary Fund's *International Financial Statistics,* various issues.

18.14 The following table shows the average annual nominal rates of return on investments in the stock market in Japan and in the United States, during the period 1970–1980. It also gives the average annual exchange rate of the Japanese yen per $1 from 1969–1980.

| | Stock Market Annual Nominal Rate of Return | | Average Exchange Rate in Yens per $1 |
|---|---|---|---|
| Year | US | Japan | (end of year) |
| 1969 | | | 360.00 |
| 1970 | −14.078 | 8.247 | 360.00 |
| 1971 | 18.710 | 9.714 | 349.83 |
| 1972 | 12.378 | 57.292 | 303.11 |
| 1973 | −1.109 | 28.366 | 271.22 |
| 1974 | −22.837 | −15.219 | 291.51 |
| 1975 | 3.842 | 1.420 | 296.80 |
| 1976 | 18.500 | 11.500 | 296.55 |
| 1977 | −5.232 | 8.430 | 268.51 |
| 1978 | −2.048 | 10.174 | 210.47 |
| 1979 | 8.182 | 8.408 | 219.17 |
| 1980 | 17.143 | 5.332 | 226.75 |

*Source:* International Monetary Fund's *International Financial Statistics,* various issues.

(a) For an American investor who wants to invest in Japan, calculate the rate of return from holding *yens* for each of the years 1970–1980.

(b) For a Japanese investor who wants to invest in US, calculate the rate of return from holding *dollars* for each of the years 1970–1980.

(c) Calculate the *total* rate of return in *dollars* from holding Japanese stocks, from the point of view of an American investor, for the years 1970–1980.

(d) Calculate the *total* rate of return in *yens* from holding US stocks, from the point of view of a Japanese investor, for the years 1970–1980.

(e)* (This part is best solved with the aid of a computer.) Draw the Mean–Variance efficient curve for investments in both the US and Japanese stock markets. Draw two curves, one for a US investor and the other for a Japanese investor. What are the gains from investing abroad for each of these two investors?

## Data Set Problems

1. Test the performance of the three international funds which appear in the Data Set (fund nos. 116, 117, and 118) by the following measures:

   (a) by Jensen's performance index;
   (b) by the reward-to-volatility ratio;
   (c) by Sharpe's performance index.

   In your calculations use the excess return $R_{i_t} - r_t$ on the fund and the excess return on the market portfolio, $R_{m_t} - r_t$, where $r_t$ is the riskless interest rate in year $t$.

2. Calculate the correlation coefficient between each of the three mutual funds nos. 116, 117, 118 and the market portfolio $R_m$. Calculate the correlation coefficient between three other funds in the Other Funds category and the market portfolio $R_m$ (use funds nos. 119, 120, 121). Compare and analyze the correlation coefficients that you obtained for the two groups of funds.

## Selected References

Adler, M., "The Cost of Capital and Valuation of a Two-Country Firm", *Journal of Finance* (March 1974).

Adler, M. and Dumas, B., "Optimal International Acquisitions", *Journal of Finance* (March 1975).

Adler, M., "The Exposure of Long-term Foreign Currency", *Journal of Financial and Quantitative Analysis* (November 1980).

Agmon, T. and Lessard, D. R., "Investor Recognition of Corporate International Diversification", *Journal of Finance* (September 1971).

Aliber, R. Z., "The Interest Rate Parity Theorem: A Reinterpretation", *Journal of Political Economy* (1973).

Beenstock, M., "Arbitrage, Speculation and Official Forward Intervention: The Cases of Sterling and the Canadian Dollar", *Review of Economics and Statistics* (February 1979).

Black, F., "International Capital Market Equilibrium With Investment Barriers", *Journal of Financial Economics* (December 1974).

Bookstaber, R. M., "Corporate Production and Sales Decisions in Achieving International Diversification", *Review of Business and Economic Research* (Winter 1980–1981).

Brillembourg, A., "Purchasing Power Parity and the Balance of Payment: Some Empirical Evidence", *International Monetary Fund Staff Papers* (March 1977).

Brewer, H. L., "Investor Benefits from Corporate International Diversification", *Journal of Financial and Quantitative Analysis* (September 1981).

Callier, P., "One Way Arbitrage, Foreign Exchange and Securities Markets", *Journal of Finance* (December 1981).

Cherneff, R. V., "Policy Conflict and Coordination Under Fixed Exchanges, The Case of an Upward Sloping IS Curve", *Journal of Finance* (September 1976).

Christofides, N., Hewins, R. D. and Salkin, G. R., "Graph Theoretic Approaches to Foreign Exchange Operations", *Journal of Financial and Quantitative Analysis* (September 1979).

Cohn, R. A. and Pringle, J. J., "Imperfections in International Financial Markets: Implications for Risk Premia and the Cost of Capital to Firms", *Journal of Finance* (March 1973).

Cornell, B., "Spot Rates, Forward Rates, and Exchange Market Efficiency", *Journal of Financial Economics* (August 1977).

Cornell, B., "The Denomination of Foreign Trade Contracts Once Again", *Journal of Financial and Quantitative Analysis* (November 1980).

Cornell, W. B. and Dietrich, J. K., "Efficiency of the Market for Foreign Exchange Under Floating Exchange Rates", *Review of Economics and Statistics* (February 1978).

Driskill, R., "Exchange Rate Dynamics, Portfolio Balance and Relative Prices", *American Economic Review* (September 1980).

Dumas, B., "Discussions", *The Journal of Finance* (May 1977).

Eaker, M. R., "Numeraire Problem and Foreign Exchange Risk", *Journal of Finance* (May 1981).

Enrlich, E. E., "International Diversification by United States Pension Funds", *Federal Reserve Bank of New York* (Autumn 1981).

Eitman, D. K. and Stonehill, A. I., *Multinational Business Finance*, 3rd ed., Reading, Mass.: Addison-Wesley, 1982.

Elliott, J. W., "The Expected Return to Equity and International Asset Prices", *Journal of Financial and Quantitative Analysis* (December 1978).

Feige, E. L. and Singleton, K. J., "Multinational Inflation Under Fixed Exchange Rates: Some Empirical Evidence for Latent Variable Models", *Review of Economics and Statistics* (February 1981).

Frenkel, J. A. and Levich, R. M., "Covered Interest Arbitrage: Unexploited Profit?" *Journal of Political Economy* (1975).

Frenkel, J. A. and Mussa, M. L., "Efficiency of Foreign Exchange Markets and Measures of Turbulence", *American Economic Review* (May 1980).

Friedman, A. J. and Sharma, R. M., "Portfolio Risk Reduction Through Foreign Stock", *Pension World* (September 1980).

Grauer, F. L. A., Litzenberger, R. H. and Stehle, R. E., "Sharing Rules and Equilibrium in an International Capital Market Under Uncertainty", *Journal of Financial Economics* (June 1976).

Grubel, H. G., "Internationally Diversified Portfolios: Welfare Gains and Capital Flows", *American Economic Review* (December 1968).

Guy, J. R. F., "Examination of the Effects of International Diversification from the British Viewpoint on Both Hypothetical and Real Portfolios", *Journal of Finance* (December 1978).

Hodgson, J. S. and Phelps, P., "The Distributed Impact of Price-Level Variation on Floating Exchange Rates", *Review of Economics and Statistics* (February 1975).

Ibbotson, R., Carr, R., and Robinson, A., "International Equity and Bond Returns", *Financial Analysts Journal* (July–August 1982).

Kornbluth, J. S. H. and Vinso, J. D., "Capital Structure and the Financing of the Multinational Corporation: A Fractional Multiobjective Approach", *Journal of Financial and Quantitative Analysis* (June 1982).

Lee, C., "A Stock Adjustment Analysis of Capital Movements: The US Canadian Case", *Journal of Political Economy* (July 1969).

Lee, W. Y. and Sachdeva, K. S., "The Role of the Multinational Firm in the Integration of Segmented Capital Markets", *The Journal of Finance* (May 1977).

Lessard, D. R., "International Portfolio Diversification: A Multivariate Analysis for a Group of Latin-American Countries", *Journal of Finance* (June 1973).

Levy, H., "Optimal Portfolios of Foreign Currency with Borrowing and Lending", *Journal of Money, Credit and Banking* (August 1981).

Levy, H., and Sarnat, M., "International Diversification of Investment Portfolios", *American Economic Review* (September 1970).

Levy, H. and Sarnat, M., "Devaluation Risk and the Portfolio Analysis of International Investment", in Elton and Gruber, eds., *International Capital Markets*, Amsterdam: North Holland (1975).

Making, J. H., "Portfolio Theory and the Problems of Foreign Exchange Risk", *Journal of Finance* (May 1978).

Makin, J. H., "Portfolio Theory and the Problem of Foreign Exchange Risk", *Journal of Finance* (June 1981).

Maldonado, R. and Saunders, A., "International Portfolio Diversification and the Inter-temporal Stability of International Stock Market Relationships", *Financial Management* (Autumn 1981).

Mathis, F. J. and Maslin, D. C., "RMA Survey of the Management of International from Portfolio Diversification", *Journal of Commercial Bank Lending* (March 1981).

Mehra, R., "On the Financing and Investment Decisions of Multinational Firms in the Presence of Exchange Risk", *Journal of Financial and Quantitative Analysis* (June 1978).

Obstfeld, M., "Capital Mobility and Devaluation in an Optimizing Model with Rational Expectations", *American Economic Review* (May 1981).

Officer, L. H., "Productivity Bias in Purchasing Power Parity: An Econometric Investigation", *IMF Staff Papers* (November 1976).

Officer, L. H., "Relationship Between Absolute and Relative Purchasing Power Parity", *Review of Economics and Statistics* (November 1978).

Senbet, L. W., "International Capital Market Equilibrium and the Multinational Firm Financing and Investment Policies", *Journal of Financial and Quantitative Analysis* (September 1979).

Solnik, B. H., "An Equilibrium Model of the International Capital Market", Research Paper No. 129, Graduate School of Business, Stanford University (1972).

Solnik, B. H., "International Pricing of Risk: An Empirical Investigation of the World Capital Market Structure", *Journal of Finance* (May 1974).

Solnik, B. H., "An Equilibrium Model of the International Capital Market", *Journal of Economic Theory* (August 1974).

Solnik, B. H., "Testing International Asset Pricing: Some Pessimistic Views", *The Journal of Finance* (May 1977).

Stehle, R. E., "An Empirical Test of the Alternative Hypotheses of National and International Pricing of Risky Assets", *Journal of Finance* (May 1977).

Stein, J. L., "Dynamics of Spot and Forward Prices in an Efficient Foreign Exchange Market with Rational Expectations", *American Economic Review* (September 1980).

Stern, R., "Insurance for Third World Currency Inconvertibility Protection", *Harvard Business Review* (May/June 1982).

Stokes, H. H. and Newburger, H., "Interest Arbitrage, Forward Speculation and the Determination of the forward Exchange Rate", *Columbia Journal of World Business* (Winger 1979).

von Furstenberg, G. M., "Incentives for International Currency Diversification by U.S. Financial Investors", *IMF Staff Papers* (September 1981).

Wallingford, B. A., "International Asset Pricing: A Comment", *Journal of Finance* (May 1974).

Weston, J. F. and Sorge, B. W., *International Managerial Finance*, Homewood, Illinois: Irwin (1972).

Weston, J. F. and Sorge, B. W., *Guide to International Financial Management*, New York: McGraw-Hill (1977).

# 19

# Market Efficiency

Efficiency in the stock market implies that all relevant information regarding a given stock is reflected in its market price. Alternatively, in an efficient market, the best estimate of the true worth of a share is given by its current price.

There are two well-known groups of investment analysts who attempt to evaluate the economic worth of securities. The first group study past price patterns in the hope that past price movements will reveal some information regarding the future price changes. The analysts in this group use charts and graphs of past price data and are correspondingly called *technicians* or *chartists*.

The second group of analysts rely on past balance sheet and income statement data of corporations. These so-called *fundamental analysts* use various sets of publicly available information to detect underpriced stocks.

If the market is efficient, neither the technicians nor the fundamentalists will find "bargains" in the stock market. Their recommendations to "buy" or "sell" have no economic value, since in an efficient market the current share price is the best estimate of the stock's true economic worth. But if there are indeed no bargains in the stock market, what is left to the financial analysts to do? The only task left is to suggest to every investor how to select a portfolio with a risk–return profile that best suits the investor's individual preferences, which is indeed the very heart of this book.

Before we turn to the definitions of market efficiency and to the relevant empirical evidence, we stress that market efficiency is largely a question of the point of view. While most investors may perceive the market to be efficient since all the information available to them (e.g., stock price patterns, income statement data, etc.) is reflected in the stock price, another group of investors (e.g., insiders, corporate managers, etc.) may possess information not yet reflected in the stock price. From the point of view of the latter group, the market is considered to be inefficient.

In general, if one finds an investor who systematically earns an "excess return",[1] then we must conclude that he possesses some information not yet reflected in the stock

---

[1] Throughout this chapter the terms "excess return" and "excess profit" refer to the profit in excess of the reward for risk. Sometimes also the term "abnormal profit" is used. See discussion below.

price. By exploiting this information in his buy or sell orders, he is the first one to drive the stock price up (or down) to its new equilibrium level, reaping an "excess profit" in this transaction.

Essentially all market efficiency tests focus on the speed with which stock prices adjust to new information. Nobody claims that the information itself is worthless. But once it is publicly available, it is already reflected in the stock price and no ordinary investor can profit from it. Who does profit from this new information? Probably the few sophisticated investors who are always ahead of the crowd and maybe also the insiders whose transactions actually create an efficient market for most of us. Thus, we see that the notion of efficiency is not rigorously defined and there are different degrees of market efficiency, which we now proceed to examine.

## 19.1    Alternative Definitions of Market Efficiency

In general, if all the relevant information is reflected in the current stock price, we assert that the market is efficient. The reason is that this information cannot be used to obtain excess return: the information has already been taken into account and absorbed in the prices. In other words, all prices are correctly stated and there are no "bargains" in the stock market.

The alternative definitions of market efficiency relate to the *type of information* that is regarded as relevant.[2]

### Weak-Form Market Efficiency

Suppose that one confines oneself only to past price movements of the relevant security. Then, if all the *information regarding past price movements* is reflected in the current stock price, we assert that we have a weak form of market efficiency. Namely, if the market is weak-form efficient, no amount of charts or analysis based solely on past prices can help to obtain abnormal profit.

### Semi-Strong Form Market Efficiency

The market is semi-strong efficient if all *publicly available information* is reflected in the stock price. Thus, if the market is indeed semi-strong efficient, one cannot make an abnormal profit by looking at any of the publicly available information, such as stock price movements, volume of trade, volume of short sales, the firm's income statements, etc.

### Strong-Form Market Efficiency

The market is said to be strong-form efficient if *all* the information, in particular including the non-public information, is reflected in the stock price. For example, even if

---

[2] These definitions of the three forms of market efficiency are due to Harry Roberts, "Statistical versus Clinical Prediction of the Stock Market", Unpublished Paper, Chicago, 1967.

insiders have access to some private information regarding a given corporation, it is worthless since if the market is indeed strong-form efficient it is already reflected in the stock price.

We repeat and emphasize that market efficiency has to do with the speed with which new information is incorporated into the stock price. If the market is indeed efficient, injection of any new information is instantly incorporated in the stock price, and hence no excess return can be made by those who possess the new information.

In any empirical test of market efficiency, the risk must be held constant. To illustrate, suppose that we observe an investor who consistently makes an average profit higher than the average profit on the S&P index or higher than the average profit other investors are making. Can we assert that this particular investor possesses information not reflected in the stock price? It might be that this investor invests in a highly risky portfolio and hence his return is higher than the average return (see Chapter 11). Thus, in order to test whether the investor actually possesses valuable information, we have to test if he systematically achieves profit in excess of the reward he should get in accordance with the risk characteristic of his portfolio. In this chapter, we denote by "excess return" the return beyond and above what is justified by the portfolio risk.

### 19.2    Weak-Form Efficiency and the Random Walk

In 1953, in a meeting of the Royal Statistical Society in London, a distinguished statistician, Maurice Kendall, presented a paper which dealt with price behavior of stocks and commodities.[3] The purpose of this paper was to analyze price cycles, but surprisingly enough Kendall could not separate out any such cycles.

Each series was just like a set of prices drawn from a table of random numbers, hence the name random walk. It is interesting to note that half a century earlier, Louis Bachelier[4] in his doctoral thesis suggested the same ideas relating to the random walk theory.

Despite being quite old, the random walk concept as applied to stock prices may be considered a new research area still not fully understood by many practitioners. One of the chapters of a recent bestseller written by a very knowledgeable member of the Wall Street community is entitled "What the Hell Is a Random Walk?"[5] The answer is something like this: the random walk approach to security markets asserts that the period-to-period price changes of a security are statistically *independent*, or very nearly so. If this hypothesis holds, the price movements of securities will follow what

---

[3] See M. G. Kendall, "The Analysis of Economic Time Series, Part I, Prices", *Journal of the Royal Statistical Society* (1953).

[4] L. Bachelier, "Théorie de la Spéculation", Paris: Gauthier-Villars, 1900. Reprinted in English in P. H. Cootner (ed.), *The Random Character of Stock Market Prices*, Cambridge, Mass.: MIT Press, 1964.

[5] "Adam Smith", *The Money Game*, Chapter 11. London: Michael Joseph, 1969.

statisticians call a "random walk".[6] The reader may be tempted to ask, "What the hell is all the fuss about?" But to answer this question we must first examine the hypothesis more carefully, and in particular we must derive its implications for investment analysis and portfolio selection.

Random walk theorists usually take as their starting point the model of a perfect securities market in which a relatively large number of investors, traders, and speculators compete in an attempt to predict the course of future prices. Moreover, it is further assumed that current information relevant to the decision-making process is readily available to all at little or no cost. If we "idealize" these conditions and assume that the market is *perfectly* competitive then common stock prices at any given point of time would reflect the market's evaluation of all currently available information. In such ideal markets, prices would change solely as new, hitherto unavailable information becomes known. And unless the new information is distributed over time in a non-random fashion, and we have no reason to presume this, price movements in a perfect market will be statistically independent of one another.

It is an important property of such a market that the analysis of current or past prices can tell us *nothing* about the future, that is, future price changes, which are randomly associated with past and present prices, *cannot* be forecast on the basis of historical time series of price movements. Stock prices "have no memory", so that one might do as well flipping a coin as spending time analyzing past price movements or patterns of past price levels.[7]

Thus, if the random walk hypothesis is empirically confirmed, we may assert that the stock market is weak-form efficient. In this case any work done by chartists based on past price patterns is worthless.

If stock price changes behave like a series of results obtained by flipping a coin, does this mean that on average stock price changes have zero mean? Not necessarily. Since stocks are risky, we actually expect to find a positive *mean* change in stock prices. To see this, suppose that you invest $100 in a stock. Flip a coin; if head comes up you lose 1%, and if tail shows up you make 5%. The value of your investment will be as shown in Figure 19.1.

Suppose that you flip the coin (look up the prices) once a week and it is your decision when to stop gambling (when to sell). If you gamble only once, your average return is:

$$\tfrac{1}{2} \times \$99 + \tfrac{1}{2} \times \$105 = \$102$$

---

[6] The literature on the subject of random walks is voluminous: an excellent non-technical introduction to the subject is provided by Eugene E. Fama, "Random Walks in Stock Market Prices", *Financial Analysts Journal* (Sept.–Oct. 1965). A comprehensive compilation of the pioneering articles on the subject is available in P. H. Cootner (ed.), *The Random Character of Stock Market Prices*, Cambridge, Mass: MIT Press, 1964. Also see an excellent discussion in E. Fama, *Foundation of Finance*, New York: Basic Books, 1975.

[7] P. H. Cootner, "Stock Prices: Random vs. Systematic Changes", *Industrial Management Review* (Spring 1962). Cootner goes on to stress in this article that stock prices do *not* conform to a pure random walk because of the different cost of information available to "professionals" who specialize in the market.

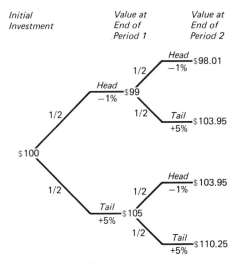

**Figure 19.1**
**Random Walk with Positive Drift (Two-period Case)**

since the probabilities of "head" or "tail" are each equal to $\frac{1}{2}$. The investor may decide to gamble for another week. Then the expected terminal value of his investment will be:

$$\frac{1}{4} \times 98.01 + \frac{1}{4} \times 103.95 + \frac{1}{4} \times 103.95 + \frac{1}{4} \times 110.25 = \$104.04$$

(Recall that each of the four "branches" in Figure 19.1 has a probability of $\frac{1}{2} \times \frac{1}{2} = \frac{1}{4}$.)

Now assume that these means are equal to the value of the given stock at the end of the first week and at the end of the second week. The fact that the stock went up in the first period, to $105 say, does not affect the probability of the price going up 5% or going down 1% in the second period, which remains $\frac{1}{2}$ for each outcome. Thus, stock price changes in each period are independent of the stock price changes in the previous period. In each period we obtain the results which one could obtain by flipping a coin, and it is well known that the next outcome of flipping a coin is independent of the past series of "heads" and "tails".

Note, however, that *on average* we earn 2% if we invest for one week and 4.04% if we invest for two weeks. Thus, the random walk hypothesis does not contradict the theory which asserts that risky assets must yield a positive mean return. We say in such a case that stock price changes can be characterized by a random walk process with a "positive drift". In our specific example the drift is equal to

$$\frac{1}{2} \times 5\% + \frac{1}{2} \times (-1\%) = 2\%$$

which implies that on average the investment terminal value increases every period by 2%.

## 19.3   Weak-Form Efficiency Tests

The weak-form efficiency tests examine whether the time series of past prices can be used to predict the stock future price. If such prediction is possible, one can make an abnormal profit by simply looking at past stock prices. Since an infinite number of trading rules based on past prices can be devised, it is impossible to test them all. However, we present some empirical tests which indicate that no "excess profit" can be made by looking at past series of stock prices.

### 19.3.1   Testing the Random Walk Hypothesis

The random walk hypothesis is usually tested by looking for association between stock price changes on consecutive days. The tests fall into two broad groups: parametric tests (regression analysis) and nonparametric tests (runs test).

*(a) Regression Analysis*

The simplest way to test the random walk theory is by calculating the stock price change $\Delta P_t$ for every day $t$, and then regressing today's price change $\Delta P_t$ on yesterday's price change $\Delta P_{t-1}$:

$$\Delta P_t = a + b\,\Delta P_{t-1}$$

Such regressions may produce one of the three general patterns shown in Figure 19.2 |panels (a), (b) and (c)|. The intercept term $a$ measures the expected price change, unrelated to previous price changes. This is the "positive drift" of the random walk process (see Section 19.2). If all the points tend to cluster around a line with a positive slope |see Figure 19.2, panel (a)|, we conclude that a positive $\Delta P_{t-1}$ tends to produce $\Delta P_t$ which is higher than the expected change in price $a$, or that an observation of a rise in the price on day $t-1$ indicates that there is a high likelihood of the price rising more than the average on the next day $t$. If the price change pattern is as in panel (b) of Figure 19.2, the slope is negative and a negative $\Delta P_{t-1}$ will tend to produce $\Delta P_t$ higher than the expected change; in other words, a price decline in period $t-1$ indicates that there is a high likelihood of the price rising more than the average in the next period $t$. In both cases, investors can use this information to devise trading rules. For example, if the prices rise, $\Delta P_{t-1} > 0$, one should buy the stock when the pattern of panel (a) is the current one (since we expect a positive $\Delta P_t$), and sell the stock when the pattern in panel (b) is the true one (since a negative $\Delta P_t$ is expected). In both cases, we conclude that past price change patterns are important and the trading rules developed by the chartists on the basis of past price data may be of definite economic worth.

However, if panel (c) of Figure 19.2 describes the true price behavior, this confirms the random walk theory as future price changes are independent of past price changes. The knowledge, say, that the price rose yesterday ($\Delta P_{t-1} > 0$) does not give any indication as to whether today's price will change by more or by less than the average, exactly as in the coin-flipping example (see Figure 19.1).

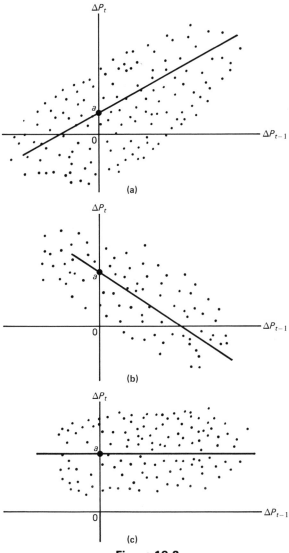

**Figure 19.2**

Most empirical studies indicate that panel (c) actually describes "best stock price behavior". Fama found that the correlation between $\Delta P_t$ and $\Delta P_{t-1}$ is very low and in most cases not significantly different from zero.[8]

Table 19.1 lists Fama's results for the correlation coefficient between price changes in two periods for various stocks. Chartists may claim that even though the consecutive

---

[8] Fama employed log daily price relatives, namely he used the continuously compounded return in periods $t$ and $t-1$. For more details, see E. Fama, "Efficient Capital Market: A Review of Theory and Empirical Work", *Journal of Finance* (March 1970).

**Table 19.1**
**Correlation Coefficients of Daily Price Changes for Various Stocks**

| Stock | Lag, days | | | | |
|---|---|---|---|---|---|
| | 1 | 2 | 3 | 4 | 5 |
| Allied Chemical | .017 | −.042 | .007 | −.001 | .027 |
| Alcoa | .118* | .038 | −.014 | .022 | −.022 |
| American Can | −.087* | −.024 | .034 | −.065* | −0.17 |
| A.T.&T. | −.039 | −.097* | .000 | .026 | .005 |
| American Tobacco | .111* | −.109* | −.060* | −.065* | .007 |
| Anaconda | .067* | −.061* | −.047 | −.002 | .000 |
| Bethlehem Steel | .013 | −.065* | .009 | .021 | −.053 |
| Chrysler | .012 | −.066* | −.016 | −.007 | −.015 |
| Du Pont | .013 | −.033 | .060* | .027 | −.002 |
| Eastman Kodak | .025 | .014 | −.031 | .005 | −.022 |
| General Electric | .011 | −.038 | −.021 | .031 | −.001 |
| General Foods | .061* | −.003 | .045 | .002 | −.015 |
| General Motors | −.004 | −.056* | −.037 | −.008 | −.038 |
| Goodyear | −.123* | .017 | −.044 | .043 | −.002 |
| International Harvester | −.017 | −.029 | −.031 | .037 | −.052 |
| International Nickel | .096* | −.033 | −.019 | .020 | .027 |
| International Paper | .046 | −.011 | −.058* | .053* | .049 |
| Johns Manville | .006 | −.038 | −.027 | −.023 | −.029 |
| Owens Illinois | −.021 | −.084* | −.047 | .068* | .086* |
| Procter & Gamble | .099* | −.009 | −.008 | .009 | −.015 |
| Sears | .097* | .026 | .028 | .025 | .005 |
| Standard Oil (Calif.) | .025 | −.030 | −.051* | −.025 | −.047 |
| Standard Oil (N.J.) | .008 | −.116* | .016 | .014 | −.047 |
| Swift & Co. | −.004 | −.015 | −.010 | .012 | .057* |
| Texaco | .094* | −.049 | −.024 | −.018 | −.017 |
| Union Carbide | .107* | −.012 | .040 | .046 | −.036 |
| United Aircraft | .014 | −.033 | −.022 | −.047 | −.067* |
| U.S. Steel | .040 | −.074* | .014 | .011 | −.012 |
| Westinghouse | −.027 | −.022 | −.036 | −.003 | .000 |
| Woolworth | .028 | −.016 | .015 | .014 | .007 |

* Coefficient is twice its computed standard error.
*Source:* E. Fama, "The Behavior of Stock Market Prices", *Journal of Business* (Jan. 1965).

price changes $\Delta P_{t-1}$ and $\Delta P_t$ are independent (and hence have zero correlation) it may be that $\Delta P_{t-2}$ (the price changes two days earlier) affects the chances of $\Delta P_t$ being positive or negative. Therefore, Fama also examined the association between $\Delta P_t$ and $\Delta P_{t-1}$, $\Delta P_{t-2}$, . . . , $\Delta P_{t-5}$ namely up to a lag of five days.

For the one day lag regression Fama obtains that 22 out of the 30 correlation coefficients are positive, and nine out of the 22 positive numbers are actually significantly different from zero. This seems to support the belief that past price series do contain some information regarding future price behavior. However, from the economic point of view, one should consider also the magnitude of the correlation coefficient; on average, for all 30 stocks, less than 1% of the variation in stock price changes in period $t$ can be explained by stock price changes in period $t - 1$.

This indicates that any trading rules based on past data may be worthless from the economic point of view as even the smallest transaction cost will wipe out the excess profit.

A comparison of various columns in Table 19.1 reveals that the relationship between past price changes and present price changes is weaker for longer lags. The number of significant correlation coefficients is 11 for one-day lag, nine for two-days lag, four for three- and four-days lag, and only three for five-days lag.

### (b) Runs Test

So far, we demonstrated how regression techniques can be used to test the random walk hypothesis. However, the correlation coefficient may be heavily influenced by one pair of extreme observations (so called outliers). In order to correct for this possible bias, we can use the non-parametric *runs test* which takes into account only the *signs* of $\Delta P_{t-1}$ and $\Delta P_t$ and not their magnitude.

Denote a price increase $\Delta P_t > 0$ by "+" and a price decrease by "−". Check the daily price changes and construct a series of "+" and "−" which describes the past price behavior. For example, suppose that one observes the following prices on consecutive days:

| Stock price | $100 | $101 | $95 | $94 | $93 | $120 |
|---|---|---|---|---|---|---|
| Stock price change | | +1 | −6 | −1 | −1 | +27 |

Thus we have the following series of price change signs:

$$+ \quad - \quad - \quad - \quad +$$

Consecutive occurrences of the same sign are called a run. In the above example we have three runs: the first run contains only one element, the second run contains three elements, and the third run again one element. If stock prices are positively associated, we expect to have long runs of "+" sign (consecutive price increases) and long runs of "−" sign (consecutive price declines). Thus, in this case, any series of observations is expected to break into few long runs. If stock price changes are negatively associated, we expect to find a typical behavior of the form $- + - +$, i.e., a price drop followed by a rise and vice versa. Thus we will have many short runs. If stock price changes are independent, neither of the previous extreme cases is observed. In fact if price changes are independent, one can calculate the expected number of runs for any given number of observations from a standard statistical formula.[9]

Table 19.2 lists Fama's findings obtained by applying the runs test to the same sample of stocks as in Table 19.1. This table clearly reveals that the number of actual runs found is very close to the expected number of runs under the random walk hypothesis. For one-day lag, the actual number of runs is slightly less than the expected number, indicating a slight positive association between $\Delta P_t$ and $\Delta P_{t-1}$. For longer lags, the actual number of runs almost coincides with the expected number of runs, strongly supporting the random walk theory.

To sum up, both the linear regression technique and the runs test reveal that there is a very weak association between one-day lagged price changes $\Delta P_t$ and $\Delta P_{t-1}$, and zero association for lags longer than one day. The question is, of course, whether one can exploit this weak positive association to develop a decision rule which yields an abnormal profit. The answer is negative; the reason is that even small transaction costs are sufficient to wipe out any potential profit of this sort.

So far we have tested the relationship between past and future price changes using systematic techniques. We can devise infinite trading rules based on past price series. We turn now to the best known rules of this kind, the so-called *filter rules*.

### 19.3.2  Testing Filter Rules

A popular trading rule based on past prices is the filter rule, which goes as follows: If the price of a security moves up at least $Y\%$, buy the security and hold it until its price moves down at least $Y\%$ from the subsequent high, at which time sell the stock and go short; the short position is maintained until the price rises $Y\%$ above the subsequent low, at which time cover the short position and buy the stock. If the stock price changes by less than $Y\%$ up or down, simply do not make any transaction. Such trading rules are called *Y Percent Filters*. The magnitude of $Y$ is a matter of individual choice, so one can have 1%, 2%, 5%, etc., filter rules, where each filter dictates a different set of

---

[9] The expected number of runs in a random series of observations with $n_1$ plus signs and $n_2$ minus signs is given by

$$\mu_r = \frac{2n_1 n_2}{n_1 + n_2} + 1$$

and the standard deviation of the number of runs is

$$\sigma_r = \sqrt{\frac{2n_1 n_2 (2n_1 n_2 - n_1 - n_2)}{(n_1 + n_2)^2 (n_1 + n_2 - 1)}}$$

For sufficiently large samples with more than 20 plus or minus signs ($n_1 > 20$ or $n_2 > 20$), the ratio

$$Z_r = \frac{r - \mu_r}{\sigma_r}$$

where $r$ is the actual number of runs in the sample, is a standard normal variate with zero mean and unit standard deviation. This fact can be used to check whether the number of runs $r$ in a large sample is significantly different from the expected number of runs $\mu_r$ for a random sample. For small samples (with less than 20 plus and minus signs), special runs test tables are available in order to determine whether or not $r$ is significantly different from the expected number in a random sample. See S. Siegel, *Nonparametric Statistics*, New York: McGraw-Hill, 1956; M. Ben-Horim and H. Levy, *Statistics: Decisions and Applications in Business and Economics*, New York: Random House, 1981.

**Table 19.2**
**Total Actual and Expected Numbers of Runs for One-, Four-, Nine-, and Sixteen-Day Lags**

| Stock | Daily Actual | Daily Expected | Four-Day Actual | Four-Day Expected | Nine-Day Actual | Nine-Day Expected | Sixteen-Day Actual | Sixteen-Day Expected |
|---|---|---|---|---|---|---|---|---|
| Allied Chemical | 683 | 713.4 | 160 | 162.1 | 71 | 71.3 | 39 | 38.6 |
| Alcoa | 601 | 670.7 | 151 | 153.7 | 61 | 66.9 | 41 | 39.0 |
| American Can | 730 | 755.5 | 169 | 172.4 | 71 | 73.2 | 48 | 43.9 |
| A.T.&T. | 657 | 688.4 | 165 | 155.9 | 66 | 70.3 | 34 | 37.1 |
| American Tobacco | 700 | 747.4 | 178 | 172.5 | 69 | 72.9 | 41 | 40.6 |
| Anaconda | 635 | 680.1 | 166 | 160.4 | 68 | 66.0 | 36 | 37.8 |
| Bethlehem Steel | 709 | 719.7 | 163 | 159.3 | 80 | 71.8 | 41 | 42.2 |
| Chrysler | 927 | 932.1 | 223 | 221.6 | 100 | 96.9 | 54 | 53.5 |
| Du Pont | 672 | 694.7 | 160 | 161.9 | 78 | 71.8 | 43 | 39.4 |
| Eastman Kodak | 678 | 679.0 | 154 | 160.1 | 70 | 70.1 | 43 | 40.3 |
| General Electric | 918 | 956.3 | 225 | 224.7 | 101 | 96.9 | 51 | 51.8 |
| General Foods | 799 | 825.1 | 185 | 191.4 | 81 | 75.8 | 43 | 40.5 |
| General Motors | 832 | 868.3 | 202 | 205.2 | 83 | 85.8 | 44 | 46.8 |
| Goodyear | 681 | 672.0 | 151 | 157.6 | 60 | 65.2 | 36 | 36.3 |
| International Harvester | 720 | 713.2 | 159 | 164.2 | 84 | 72.6 | 40 | 37.8 |
| International Nickel | 704 | 712.6 | 163 | 164.0 | 68 | 70.5 | 34 | 37.6 |
| International Paper | 762 | 826.0 | 190 | 193.9 | 80 | 82.8 | 51 | 46.9 |
| Johns Manville | 685 | 699.1 | 173 | 160.0 | 64 | 69.4 | 39 | 40.4 |
| Owens Illinois | 713 | 743.3 | 171 | 168.6 | 69 | 73.3 | 36 | 39.2 |
| Procter & Gamble | 826 | 858.9 | 180 | 190.6 | 66 | 81.2 | 40 | 42.9 |
| Sears | 700 | 748.1 | 167 | 172.8 | 66 | 70.6 | 40 | 34.8 |
| Standard Oil (Calif.) | 972 | 979.0 | 237 | 228.4 | 97 | 98.6 | 59 | 54.3 |
| Standard Oil (N.J.) | 688 | 704.0 | 159 | 159.2 | 69 | 68.7 | 29 | 37.0 |
| Swift & Co. | 878 | 877.6 | 209 | 197.2 | 85 | 83.8 | 50 | 47.8 |
| Texaco | 600 | 654.2 | 143 | 155.2 | 57 | 63.4 | 29 | 35.6 |
| Union Carbide | 595 | 620.9 | 142 | 150.5 | 67 | 66.7 | 36 | 35.1 |
| United Aircraft | 661 | 699.3 | 172 | 161.4 | 77 | 68.2 | 45 | 39.5 |
| U.S. Steel | 651 | 662.0 | 162 | 158.3 | 65 | 70.3 | 37 | 41.2 |
| Westinghouse | 829 | 825.5 | 198 | 193.3 | 87 | 84.4 | 41 | 45.8 |
| Woolworth | 847 | 868.4 | 193 | 198.9 | 78 | 80.9 | 48 | 47.7 |
| Averages | 735.1 | 759.8 | 175.7 | 175.8 | 74.6 | 75.3 | 41.6 | 41.7 |

*Source:* E. Fama, "The Behavior of Stock Market Prices", *Journal of Business* (Jan. 1965).

transactions even though all deal with the same stock and are based on the same set of price changes.

Figure 19.3 provides a graphic description of the 5% filter rule. Suppose that initially the Colleco stock sells for $100. The investor does nothing as long as the stock price moves inside the range $95–$105. But if it goes up 5% relative to our starting level, namely to $105, the 5% filter rule dictates that the stock should be bought (see Figure 19.3). You hold the stock as long as its price continues to go up. Suppose that it reaches a new high of $120, and then it starts declining. You hold the stock even when its price is dropping as long as it is above $114. When it reaches $114 (which is 5% below the high of $120), you sell the stock and go short. The short position is maintained as long as the price continues dropping. Suppose it reaches $80 and starts rising again. When the rising price reaches $84 (which is 5% higher than the last low of $80), it is time to cover the short position and buy the stock.

Does the *Y* percent filter prove itself a good trading rule? In order to answer this question one should compare the investor's terminal wealth under two alternative strategies, say, comparing the *Y* percent filter rule with the naive *buy-and-hold* policy, when the investor buys the stock and does not make any transactions until the end of the period under comparison.

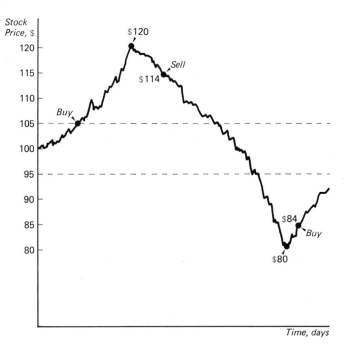

**Figure 19.3**
**Illustrating a 5% Filter Rule**

Comparison of Rates of Return Before Transaction Costs under the Filter Rule (F) and under a Buy-and-Hold Policy (B)

Filter Size

| Security | 0.005 | | 0.010 | | 0.015 | | 0.020 | | 0.025 | | 0.030 | | 0.035 | | 0.040 | |
|---|---|---|---|---|---|---|---|---|---|---|---|---|---|---|---|---|
| | F | B | F | B | F | B | F | B | F | B | F | B | F | B | F | B |
| Allied Chemical | .155 | .068 | .087 | .069 | .042 | .063 | -.030 | .066 | -.105 | .069 | .008 | .066 | -.002 | .064 | -.010 | .051 |
| Alcoa | .401 | .025 | .308 | .023 | .318 | .016 | .330 | .021 | .241 | .022 | .303 | .025 | .270 | .008 | .182 | .006 |
| American Can | .121 | .085 | -.065 | .075 | -.123 | .075 | -.088 | .078 | -.057 | .074 | -.129 | .072 | -.201 | .071 | -.226 | .070 |
| A.T.&T. | .150 | .189 | .146 | .189 | .158 | .189 | .133 | .185 | .135 | .182 | .131 | .180 | .143 | .176 | .076 | .182 |
| American Tobacco | .165 | .170 | .019 | .168 | .018 | .172 | .012 | .168 | -.057 | .170 | -.080 | .168 | .002 | .163 | .048 | .162 |
| Anaconda | .288 | .047 | .101 | .049 | -.012 | .046 | -.048 | .042 | -.038 | .059 | -.005 | .057 | -.030 | .055 | -.019 | .055 |
| Bethlehem Steel | .082 | .032 | .051 | .033 | .030 | .036 | -.004 | .038 | -.038 | .054 | -.128 | .052 | -.250 | .049 | -.169 | .044 |
| Chrysler | .031 | .004 | -.090 | -.002 | -.090 | .002 | -.183 | .016 | -.234 | .015 | -.152 | .015 | -.082 | .012 | .029 | .012 |
| Du Pont | .152 | .107 | .125 | .106 | .087 | .108 | .100 | .105 | .032 | .097 | .054 | .097 | .084 | .098 | .058 | .103 |
| Eastman Kodak | .078 | .194 | .025 | .195 | .005 | .189 | .057 | .185 | .085 | .183 | .009 | .183 | .032 | .178 | .133 | .175 |
| General Electric | .080 | .078 | .046 | .075 | -.015 | .075 | -.016 | .069 | .013 | .069 | -.052 | .069 | .011 | .072 | -.010 | .070 |
| General Foods | .122 | .257 | .122 | .256 | .146 | .257 | .028 | .251 | .084 | .250 | .062 | .246 | .112 | .250 | .080 | .250 |
| General Motors | .107 | .088 | .108 | .091 | .065 | .091 | .048 | .094 | -.063 | .093 | -.101 | .098 | -.151 | .099 | -.171 | .095 |
| Goodyear | -.229 | .086 | -.195 | .083 | -.151 | .085 | -.109 | .076 | -.092 | .070 | .048 | .077 | -.013 | .077 | .076 | .112 |
| International Harvester | -.088 | .180 | -.082 | .177 | -.206 | .176 | -.112 | .174 | -.142 | .170 | -.113 | .178 | -.036 | .175 | -.018 | .178 |
| International Nickel | .218 | .148 | .170 | .136 | .118 | .136 | .077 | .137 | .005 | .155 | .088 | .148 | .105 | .147 | .041 | .160 |
| International Paper | .205 | .010 | .156 | .007 | .095 | .005 | .063 | .003 | .034 | .010 | .026 | .011 | .014 | .011 | -.013 | .015 |
| Johns Manville | .021 | .094 | -.016 | .093 | -.162 | .087 | -.159 | .085 | -.070 | .077 | -.194 | .072 | -.204 | .074 | -.157 | .074 |
| Owens Illinois | .008 | .113 | -.036 | .116 | -.043 | .115 | -.130 | .119 | -.120 | .120 | -.112 | .120 | -.091 | .124 | -.037 | .106 |
| Procter & Gamble | .315 | .210 | .290 | .212 | .221 | .206 | .176 | .208 | .130 | .212 | .066 | .212 | .015 | .219 | .100 | .222 |
| Sears | .337 | .258 | .249 | .256 | .225 | .252 | .167 | .252 | .196 | .251 | .181 | .255 | .238 | .247 | .203 | .241 |
| Standard Oil (Calif.) | .076 | .093 | .052 | .090 | -.079 | .094 | -.106 | .099 | -.124 | .099 | -.123 | .094 | -.117 | .097 | -.158 | .098 |
| Standard Oil (N.J.) | .036 | .077 | -.072 | .067 | -.094 | .067 | -.093 | .070 | -.084 | .068 | -.083 | .064 | -.084 | .057 | -.086 | .056 |
| Swift & Co. | .010 | .047 | .002 | .042 | -.026 | .037 | .016 | .035 | -.044 | .037 | -.115 | .037 | -.052 | .034 | -.060 | .031 |
| Texaco | .172 | .188 | .165 | .192 | .105 | .189 | .095 | .188 | .109 | .186 | .166 | .184 | .144 | .183 | .115 | .178 |
| Union Carbide | .290 | .052 | .124 | .052 | .145 | .049 | .097 | .050 | .067 | .049 | .028 | .047 | .038 | .038 | .089 | .037 |
| United Aircraft | -.025 | .054 | -.020 | .052 | -.023 | .054 | -.110 | .059 | -.134 | .053 | -.189 | .048 | -.025 | .049 | -.026 | .046 |
| U.S. Steel | .101 | .014 | -.039 | .010 | .036 | .014 | .049 | .027 | .077 | .028 | .072 | .035 | .027 | .030 | .032 | .025 |
| Westinghouse | .008 | .038 | -.103 | .040 | -.047 | .038 | -.215 | .054 | -.216 | .048 | -.097 | .049 | -.083 | .051 | -.015 | .047 |
| Woolworth | .068 | .128 | .012 | .132 | .088 | .131 | .029 | .129 | -.058 | .131 | -.076 | .132 | -.052 | .141 | -.061 | .140 |
| **Average** | .115 | .104 | .055 | .103 | .028 | .102 | .002 | .103 | -.016 | .103 | -.017 | .103 | -.008 | .102 | .001 | .101 |

Source: E. Fama and M. Blume, "Filter Rules and Stock Market Trading", *Journal of Business* (January 1966).

Sidney Alexander[10] used daily stock prices to compare the return of the buy-and-hold policy with the returns from various filter rules. He concluded that in order to beat the buy-and-hold policy, we should look for other rules, since the filter rules did not outperform the naive buy-and-hold policy.

Extensive tests of the filter rules were carried out by Fama and Blume,[11] and Table 19.3 presents a summary of their results. They found that small filters (of less than 0.010 or 1%) provide a higher return than the buy-and-hold strategy.[12] However as the filter strategy involves many buy and sell transactions, and the number of transactions is greater for small filters, even a small transaction cost wipes out the excess return. Thus, we may conclude that filter rules do not provide any excess return, which again supports the weak form of market efficiency.

## 19.4  Semi-Strong Form Efficiency Tests

The weak-form efficiency tests focus only on information about the past stock prices. The semi-strong form efficiency tests are concerned with all *publicly available* information, including of course the stock prices. If the market is semi-strong efficient, all public announcements, e.g., changes in the annual earnings, changes in the declared cash dividend, changes in the management of the firm, etc., are fully reflected in the stock price. In other words, suppose that on January 10, 1984, the firm announces an increase in the dividend rate from $0.50 per share to $0.60. Do we rush to buy the stock on the same day? The answer is negative; if indeed the market is semi-strong efficient, then the "good news" is already reflected in the stock price and no excess profit can be made after the information is made public.

Publicly available information is so large and heterogeneous that it is impossible to test for market efficiency relative to all the sources of information. However, one can test several types of information which are conceived to have a major effect on stock prices. We demonstrate the semi-strong form efficiency with some examples of empirical tests.

### 19.4.1  Stock Splits

Many firms split their stock. A stock split of two to one means that each shareholder gets 1 additional share for each share held without paying any extra cash. Thus, instead of one share, the investor now holds two shares. As a result of the split,

---

[10] See S. Alexander, "Price Movements in Speculative Markets: Trends or Random Walk", *Industrial Management Review* (May 1961).

[11] E. Fama and M. Blume, "Filter Rules and the Stock Market Trading", *Journal of Business* (Jan. 1966).

[12] The numbers under  F  in Table 19.3 are on average larger than the numbers under B for the 0.005 filter, where F stands for the filter rule and B for buy-and-hold.

earnings per share, dividends per share, and all other important economic variables per share are cut by two. If the dividend per share was $2 before the split, it is only $1 per share after the split. However, since the investor who held one share before the split holds two shares after the split, the total cash dividend received by him is unchanged. There is a certain disagreement between academics and practitioners about the economic value of splits and their impact on stock prices. Most academics believe that splits have no economic value whatsoever, but even if there is some positive attribute to splits, the question is how fast this attribute is reflected in the stock prices once the split is announced. Fama, Fisher, Jensen and Roll (FFJR)[13] tested the impact of stock splits on the excess return of stocks. For each stock they ran the regression

$$R_{it} = \hat{\alpha}_i + \hat{\beta}_i R_{mt} + e_{it}$$

where

$R_{it}$ = the return on stock $i$ in month $t$

$R_{mt}$ = the return on the market index in month $t$

$\hat{\alpha}_i, \hat{\beta}_i$ = constants (the intercept and the slope of the regression line, respectively)

$e_{it}$ = the deviation from the regression line in month $t$

Fama, Fisher, Jensen and Roll examined the difference between the actual return on the stock in month $t$ and the return predicted by the model (i.e., the deviation term $e_{it}$). This difference is defined as the excess return. Then they calculated the cumulative excess return $\Sigma_{t=-30}^{+30} e_{it}$ over the period from 30 months before the split to 30 months after the split.

Figure 19.4 summarizes the FFJR results. The cumulative average excess return started increasing as early as 30 months before the split, while after the split it leveled off, which implies that no additional excess profit can be made after the split is announced. How can we explain this early market reaction to the split? Thirty months before the split nobody knew about it and probably the firm's management did not even consider the idea of splitting the stock. The answer to this puzzle is as follows. Normally it is the profitable firms who split their stock after it reaches a high price level. Thus, the firm had an exceptional earnings record and the rising stock price 30 months before the split is *a reaction to the increasing earnings*, and not to the forthcoming split.

The split as such has no economic value, but it may serve as a signal of the future earnings. Indeed, when FFJR divided their samples into two groups, one with firms which increased the cash dividend after the split (allegedly as a result of higher earnings) and the other with firms which did not, they found that the cumulative average excess return of those which increased the cash dividend continued increasing (consistently with their higher earnings), while for the other group it declined.

---

[13] E. Fama, L. Fisher, M. Jensen and R. Roll, "The Adjustment of Stock Prices to New Information", *International Economic Review* (Feb. 1969).

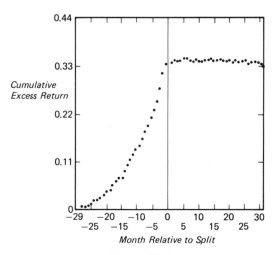

**Figure 19.4**
**Cumulative Excess Return in Months Surrounding Stock Splits**

*Source:* E. Fama, L. Fisher, M. Jensen, and R. Roll, "The Adjustment of Stock Prices to New Information", *International Economic Review* (February 1969).

   To sum up, splits are important from the economic point of view as long as they
convey information about future earnings and future cash dividends. However, it is an
expensive way to provide stockholders with such information, as the firm does not get
any extra cash in the process. The fact that many firms nevertheless split their stock
implies that splits may have other useful functions apart from signaling future earnings.
One of these is related to indivisibility of investments in real life. Suppose that the stock
price is $200 per share. In order to reduce the transaction costs, the investor buys a
"round lot" of 100 shares. Thus, his total cost is $200 × 100 = $20,000. Now, as we
learned in the previous chapters, investors seek to reduce risk by holding a whole
portfolio of securities. Suppose that the typical investor holds four different stocks in his
portfolio. Buying 100 shares of each stock at around $200 price level would cost him
around $20,000 × 4 = $80,000. An investor with only $10,000 to invest in the stock
markets will thus probably diversify in stocks with a much lower market price, and
many small investors simply will not buy the stock of firms trading at high price levels.
This in turn decreases the aggregate demand for the high-priced shares, and in order to
avoid such an undesirable development, firms split their stock. The split automatically
reduces the share price to a fraction of its previous value (a 2-to-1 split will halve the
price from $200 to $100 per share), so that the stock is no longer excluded from small
portfolios simply because of its high absolute market price. This is probably the main
reason for stock splits, while the signaling effect is simply a byproduct of underlying
forces.
   No matter what the purpose of the split is—whether signaling new information or
spurring the demand for the stock by small investors—it is an established fact that the
excess cumulative return is positive over 30 months before the split (see Figure 19.4).

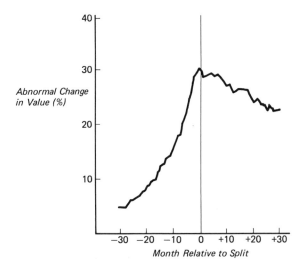

**Figure 19.5**
**Abnormal Changes in Value Before and After Stock Splits**

*Source:* S. Bar-Yosef and L. Brown, "A Reexamination of Stock Splits using Moving Betas", *Journal of Finance* (September 1977).

Since the firms announce the split several months before the split actually takes place, FFJR examined if investors who bought the stock immediately after the split information became available could make an excess return. They found that no such excess return could be made: once the split announcement is made public, it is too late to take advantage of future price changes, as the information is already reflected in the stock price. This finding, of course, supports the semi-strong form of market efficiency.

Another study which covers the period 1945–1965 revealed very similar results. Bar-Yosef and Brown[14] examined 219 stock splits that occurred during the period. The abnormal return on the stock was calculated as the excess return above what is justified by the risk of these stocks. Figure 19.5 reveals that, as in FFJR study, the abnormal cumulative excess return is positive and increasing 30 months before the split. However, this upward trend stops at the split date (denoted by zero on the horizontal axis). Moreover, after this date the abnormal cumulative return actually declines. Does this finding imply that investors who knew in advance about the forthcoming split could exploit this information to obtain excess return? Absolutely not! As explained above, it is probably the other way around: firms with an increasing earnings stream show excess return and when the stock price becomes too high for the average investor, the management decides to split, probably in order to make the stock more tradeable.

The question is of course whether the earnings' announcements 30 months before the split could be used to make an excess return. If this is so, we may say that the

---

[14] S. Bar-Yosef and L. Brown, "A Reexamination of Stock Splits Using Moving Betas", *Journal of Finance* (Sep. 1977).

market is semi-strong inefficient. Most empirical studies reveal, however, that once the information, say, on increasing earnings stream or increasing dividend stream becomes publicly available, it is too late to make an excess return.

### 19.4.2  Brokerage House Recommendations

The performance of institutional brokerage firms also provides valuable evidence on semi-strong form efficiency.

Most large brokers have research departments collecting data on various stocks, and after conducting an economic analysis they prepare a list of recommended stocks to their customers. If their recommendation has some economic value, one expects the profit on the recommended stocks to be higher than the average profit on a random stock portfolio.

In a sample of 99 recommended stocks, Bidwell[15] measured the rate of return on each security. For each recommended stock, he calculated Jensen's excess rate of return $\hat{a}_i$, using the regression:

$$R_{i_t} = \hat{a}_i + \hat{\beta}_i R_{m_t} + e_{i_t}$$

where $R_{m_t}$ is the rate of return on a random (market) portfolio (see Chapter 15). If the average alpha for the 99 recommended stocks is positive, then the brokerage research has economic value, but if the average alpha is not significantly different from zero, we conclude that brokerage firms cannot distinguish between "good" and "bad" stocks. Bidwell found for the average of all the 99 alphas $\bar{a} = \Sigma_{i=1}^{99} \, \hat{a}_i/99 = 2.63\%$ with sample standard deviation $S_a = 43.86$ ($t$-value of 0.06).

The result is thus not significantly different from zero at any reasonable significance level and we can safely conclude that brokerage research does not increase the return on the recommended investments beyond what can be achieved by a random drawing from the list of all stocks registered on the New York Stock Exchange. Assuming the brokerage firms use the available data correctly, this finding confirms the semi-strong form efficiency of the market.

### 19.4.3  Can Joe Granville Time the Market?

Joseph E. Granville is probably the most spectacular market forecaster that has ever aroused the interest of the investment community. For more than three years now he has been forecasting the direction of the stock market with a remarkable success. Just to mention a few of his successes: on Monday, April 21, 1980, he cabled a telegraphic warning to his subscribers informing them that he was changing his earlier recommendations and advising them to hold 100% long, namely to buy stocks. When the market opened, it went up. The influx of buy orders was enormous and the Dow-Jones

---

[15] See C. M. Bidwell III, "How Good is Institutional Brokerage Research?" *Journal of Portfolio Management* (Winter 1977).

Index closed up 30 points. On January 6, 1981, Granville recommended selling all stocks. Indeed, the market opened on a downward gap. There are many other cases which indicate that Granville was successful in his prediction of the market trend.

The popularity of Granville is such that his activities are widely watched by the financial media, e.g., *The Wall Street Journal.*

What is the source of information Granville employs in his predictions? He uses a technical method to beat the market, which includes analyses of several time series, e.g., the ratio of price advances to price declines, the number of daily highs and lows, the 200-day moving averages of the Dow-Jones Index, the price movement of General Motors, etc. Thus, if Granville indeed succeeds in predicting the market trends, we have evidence that the market is semi-strong inefficient.

Baesel, Shows and Thorp[16] tested Granville's predictive ability. For example, in the period from April 12, 1978 to October 15, 1981 there were 719 trading days, which included 372 "up" days and 347 "down" days for the Dow-Jones Index. If we take Granville's recommendations, we find that he forecasted 446 up days out of the total 719 days. Actually, 254 out of these 446 days were up days. Therefore he was 57% successful (see Table 19.4).

Thus, if Granville (or anybody else) picks out one day at random and forecasts an "up" swing, he has a 51.7% chance of proving to be right (372 up days out of 719). In fact, Granville had 57% success, which is higher. A statistical test reveals that the difference between 57% and 51.7% is highly significant,[17] which implies that Granville is indeed successful in his forecasting. This evidence of course is contradictory to the hypothesis that the market is semi-strong form efficient.

Obviously, the market may be semi-strong form inefficient but still *operationally* semi-strong form efficient. For example, it is possible that if one follows Granville's recommendations and allows for transaction costs, his strategy would not beat the "buy-and-hold" strategy.

**Table 19.4**
**Comparison of Granville's Predictive Ability and Random Prediction**

| | Period 4/12/78 through 10/15/81 | | |
|---|---|---|---|
| | Number of Days | Market Up Days | Market Down Days |
| DJI | 719 | 372 (51.7%) | 347 (48.3%) |
| Granville's Up Days | 446 | 254 (57.0%) | 192 (43.0%) |

*Source:* J. Baesel, G. Shows, and E. Thorp, "Can Joe Granville Time the Market?", *Journal of Portfolio Management* (Spring 1982).

[16] See J. Baesel, G. Shows and E. Thorp, "Can Joe Granville Time the Market?", *Journal of Portfolio Management* (Spring 1982).

[17] The statistical test leaves some doubt as to the validity of the conclusions. The authors use the hypergeometric distribution, rather than the more usual binomial, but there is insufficient information to determine the seriousness of the error.

## 19.5   Strong-Form Efficiency Tests

The market is considered to be strong form efficient if all the information, whether public or private, is reflected in the current stock price. Since the weak and the semi-strong form efficiency tests deal with publicly available information, it is natural that testing the strong-form efficiency tests would concentrate on non-public information. However, it is not easy to define such information fully or to identify the investors who have access to such information. Candidates for inclusion in this group are corporate insiders. Insider traders are investors who either hold more than a certain percentage of the outstanding shares of a corporation or are part of the firm's management. By the Securities and Exchange Commission regulations, insiders must announce their purchases and sales to the public. If indeed the insiders have access to non-public information, we expect to observe insiders purchase shares before the stock price increases and sell the stock before the prices decline. Such a policy should provide the insiders with excess return, obtained by exploiting the non-public information to which they have access.

Lorie and Niederhoffer[18] and Jaffe[19] examined the performance of the insider investors. These two studies reveal that insiders indeed possess valuable information, since they actually make excess returns. This clearcut result indicates that the market is strong-form inefficient.

It is possible that these insiders, as well as other sophisticated investors, constitute the main force driving the stock prices up or down once a real economic change occurs in the firm. Thus when the relevant information eventually becomes publicly available, it is worthless since it is already reflected in the stock prices. In other words, investors with access to the non-public information are in fact the main cause for the observed weak and semi-strong form efficiency of the market.

### 19.5.1   Can Investors Mimic Insider Transactions?

We will now discuss a test which constitutes a link between the semi-strong and the strong-form efficiency. The insiders are obliged to file a report of their sales and purchases with the Securities and Exchange Commission, and this information is published in the so-called *Insider Report*. Once this information becomes publicly available, other investors can mimic the insider transactions. If excess return can be made by following this policy, we should conclude that the market is semi-strong form inefficient (recall that the insider information is now publicly available).

Suppose that by looking at the *Insider Report*, we find that a corporate insider buys the firm's stock. Since this may be a sign that he has access to "good" information regarding the firm's profitability, an outsider can mimic the insider's behavior and buy the stock, in the hope that the "good" information will raise the stock price in the near future enabling him to make a quick profit.

---

[18] J. Lorie and V. Niederhoffer, "Predictive and Statistical Properties of Insider Trading", *Journal of Law and Economics* (April 1978).

[19] J. Jaffe, "Special Information and Insider Trading", *Journal of Business* (July 1964).

In order to test if outsiders can profit from the information published in the *Insider Report*, Kerr examined 120 stocks characterized by insider buying in the year 1976.[20]

The rate of return (profit) on a portfolio constructed from the insider buying list and the rate of return on a *random* portfolio (the Standard & Poor's Index in this specific case) were calculated. Kerr tested statistically the hypothesis that the mean rate of return on an insider-based portfolio is greater than the mean return on the random portfolio. Using the *t*-test in order to determine whether the difference in the sample mean returns of the two portfolios is significantly different from zero, he obtained a *t*-value of 0.0484, so that outside investors apparently are unable to earn an excess return by mimicking the corporate insiders. To verify this conclusion, Kerr constructed 12 portfolios taken from the *Insider Report* and compared them to 12 random portfolios. In all cases the *t*-value revealed no significant difference between the return on the insider based portfolio and the random portfolio (see Table 19.5).

Thus, while the insiders do earn excess return (the market is strong-form inefficient), once their transactions are published, it becomes too late for the outsider to earn an excess return, which indicates that the market is semi-strong form efficient.

Finally, the strong-form efficiency is commonly tested by examining the performance of mutual funds. The implicit assumption of these tests is that mutual funds managers have access to some non-public information (e.g., through serving on the Boards of Directors of various corporations), as well as all the publicly available information. If the mutual funds reveal an excess return, one may conclude either that they

**Table 19.5**
**Comparison of Mean Returns on Insider-based Portfolios and Random Portfolios of Same Size**

| Portfolio | Geometric Mean Return | | t Value |
|---|---|---|---|
| | Insider-based | Random | |
| 1 | −0.81 | −0.99 | .0484 |
| 2 | −1.21 | −0.24 | −.2618 |
| 3 | 0.49 | 0.34 | .0372 |
| 4 | 3.26 | 0.75 | .6662 |
| 5 | 2.27 | 0.84 | .0885 |
| 6 | 1.60 | 1.56 | .0104 |
| 7 | 2.61 | 2.38 | .0816 |
| 8 | 1.80 | 1.62 | .0395 |
| 9 | 3.62 | 2.30 | .4762 |
| 10 | 2.83 | 2.39 | .1528 |
| 11 | 3.55 | 2.39 | .3074 |
| 12 | 3.77 | 1.81 | .6924 |

*Source:* H. S. Kerr, "The Battle of Insider Testing vs. Market Efficiency", *Journal of Portfolio Management* (Summer 1980).

[20] See H. S. Kerr, "The Battle of Insider Trading vs. Market Efficiency", *Journal of Portfolio Management* (Summer 1980).

have superior ability to use the publicly available information, or that they possess non-public information. On the other hand, if mutual funds fail to outperform the market, we cannot assert that the market is strong-form efficient, simply because it may be that mutual funds do not have access to any non-public information. The empirical results indicate that mutual funds do not earn any excess return (see Chapter 15) and hence the conclusion is either that the market is strong-form efficient *or* that mutual funds do not have any privileged information. But since we already indicated that insiders do earn an excess return, it is more likely that mutual funds simply do not have access to any privileged information. Testing mutual funds performance is very popular, since the data are readily available. However, this set of data is not the most suitable for testing strong-form market efficiency because of ambiguous implications.

### 19.5.2  P/E Ratio Filters and Market Efficiency

Practitioners usually hold the opinion that stocks with low price/earnings (P/E) ratios yield a higher return than high P/E stocks. P/E-ratio filters thus have been suggested as an investment strategy intended to take advantage of possible market inefficiency. P/E ratios naturally constitute publicly available information and as such they were previously used to test the semi-strong form of market efficiency.[21] A recent study of the information content of P/E ratios establishes yet another link between semi-strong and strong forms of market efficiency.[22]

Since the earnings information becomes publicly available 60 to 90 days from the end of the corporate fiscal year (in March of next year for corporations with fiscal year ending on December 31), the average investor who chooses to follow the recommendation to invest in low P/E stocks generally will not be able to make his investment decision before March of each year. A sophisticated company watcher or an insider, on the other hand, will have access to advance information about corporate earnings, months before it is publicly announced; these investors will make their P/E-based investment decisions much earlier, in January or even before that.

Levy and Lerman examined 424 stocks over the 20-year period 1960–1979, grouping the stocks into portfolios by their P/E ratios (in 10 gradations from low to high P/E ratio). The portfolio return distributions were subjected to Stochastic Dominance tests (see Chapter 6) to check the hypothesis that low P/E stocks indeed performed better. The low P/E portfolio was found to dominate high P/E portfolios and the random buy-and-hold portfolios for all risk-averse investors (by SSD tests—see Chapter 6), provided these investors were able to make their investment decision very early (in January of each year). This conclusion held even with the introduction of fairly

---

[21] S. Basu, "The Investment Performance of Common Stocks in Relation to Their Price-Earnings Ratios: A Test of the Efficient Market Hypothesis", *Journal of Finance* (June 1977).

[22] H. Levy and Z. Lerman, "Testing P/E Ratio Filters by Stochastic Dominance Rules", *Journal of Portfolio Management*, forthcoming.

substantial transaction costs (1% and 2% round-trip commissions), unavoidable in this context since the portfolio must be adjusted to reflect the annual changes in the P/E ratios of the various stocks. However, as the decision date was gradually shifted from January to March, reflecting the public dissemination of the earnings information, the low P/E portfolio lost its clearcut dominance over the other portfolios (even before allowing for transaction costs).

Thus, sophisticated investors and insiders, who have access to earnings information before it is made public, can make excess profit by investing in low P/E stocks. This excess profit is large enough not to be wiped out even by fairly substantial transaction costs. Once the earnings information becomes available to the public, however, it is already worthless: low P/E stocks selected on the basis of the publicly available information will not yield an excess profit.

The implications of this study are consistent with the previous findings on insider trading: they point to strong-form inefficiency of the market and suggest that sophisticated investors and insiders have a definite role in ensuring semi-strong and weak-form efficiency of the market by their advance-knowledge transactions.

## Summary

The market is regarded as *weak-form efficient* if no trading rule based on past price patterns can yield an abnormal return. Evidence indicates that indeed the market is weak-form efficient. This is true in particular when the transaction costs required by the particular trading rule (e.g. a filter rule) are taken into account.

The market is *semi-strong form efficient* if publicly available information cannot be exploited to earn an excess return. Empirical evidence indicates that information on income statements and dividend announcements cannot be used to earn an excess return. Even the brokerage house research departments, which rely on various sources of public information, fail to make an excess return.

The market is *strong-form efficient* if private information cannot be exploited to earn an excess return. Empirical evidence indicates that insiders, who probably do have access to such information, manage to earn excess profit. Thus, the market is strong-form inefficient. In fact, these insiders and sophisticated investors drive the stock price up or down so that once the privileged information becomes available to the public, it is already fully reflected in the stock price. The strong-form inefficiency thus causes the market to be efficient in the weak and semi-strong form.

In view of the above, what is actually the role of the financial analysts? They cannot use income statement analysis or available public data to find bargains in the securities market. Nor can they exploit the insider information, simply because they do not possess it. So, the main task left to the financial analyst and the investment consultant is to construct a portfolio with risk–return profile suitable for the individual customer. And indeed most chapters of this book are devoted to explaining how such portfolios can be constructed.

---

**Summary Table**

1. **Weak-Form Market Efficiency**
   (a) *Definition*: All information regarding past price movements is reflected in the current stock price.
   (b) *Random Walk Theory*: Stock price changes are independent over time. If the random walk theory is confirmed, this supports the weak-form market efficiency.
   (c) Tests of weak-form market efficiency
       (i) *Random Walk Tests*
           (a) $\Delta P_t = a + b\Delta P_{t-1}$ (regression)
           (b) Runs test (non-parametric test)
           These two types of tests confirm the random walk theory and hence support the weak form market efficiency.
       (ii) *Filter Rules*: This strategy does not outperform the "buy and hold" policy, and hence supports the weak form market efficiency.

2. **Semi-Strong Form Market Efficiency**
   (a) *Definition*: All publicly available information is reflected in the stock price.
   (b) Tests of semi-strong form market efficiency
       (i) Stock splits—supports market efficiency
       (ii) Brokerage house recommendations—supports market efficiency
       (iii) Joe Granville's recommendations—does not support market efficiency.

3. **Strong-Form Market Efficiency**
   (a) *Definition*: All information, public and private, is reflected in the stock price.
   (b) Tests of strong form market efficiency
       (i) Performance of insider investors—does not support market efficiency
       (ii) Performance of mutual funds—partial support of market efficiency.
       (iii) Performance of low P/E portfolio—supports market inefficiency.

---

### Questions and Problems

19.1 Define the three forms of market efficiency.

19.2 Assume that you invested in the stock of Burroughs Corporation in Dec. 29, 1982 when the stock price was $41\frac{3}{8}$. On Dec. 30, 1982, the stock price rose to $42\frac{5}{8}$. If the stock price follows a "random walk" can you predict whether the price of Burroughs Corporation's stock will rise or fall on Dec. 31, 1982?

19.3 Can you cite any evidence that stock prices follow a "random walk"?

19.4 If you had a substantial amount of money to invest, do you think you could reap an abnormal return by entrusting your investment to an analyst who based his trading approach on filter rules?

19.5 "The Security and Exchange Commission's rule that trading on inside information is illegal is redundant." Do you agree?

19.6    State the random walk hypothesis. If the market is efficient, what are the implications for:

(a) technical analysis;
(b) security analysis;
(c) portfolio analysis.

19.7    "According to the random walk hypothesis, collecting and analyzing historical security prices is a waste of time and resources, since these prices cannot reveal any indication of future events." Appraise this statement.

19.8    What is the relationship between the random walk hypothesis and the weak form market efficiency?

19.9    The table below presents the monthly rates of return on common stocks and the monthly inflation rate in the period December 1977 to December 1978.

| Month | Total Return on Common Stocks (in Percent) | Rate of Change of Consumer Price Index (in Percent) |
|---|---|---|
| Dec. 1977 | 0.48 | 0.38 |
| Jan. 1978 | −5.96 | 0.54 |
| Feb. 1978 | −1.61 | 0.69 |
| Mar. 1978 | 2.76 | 0.69 |
| Apr. 1978 | 8.70 | 0.90 |
| May 1978 | 1.36 | 0.99 |
| Jun. 1978 | −1.52 | 1.03 |
| Jul. 1978 | 5.60 | 0.72 |
| Aug. 1978 | 3.40 | 0.51 |
| Sep. 1978 | −0.48 | 0.71 |
| Oct. 1978 | −8.91 | 0.80 |
| Nov. 1978 | 2.60 | 0.55 |
| Dec. 1978 | 1.72 | 0.55 |

*Source:* R. Ibbotson and R. Sinquefield, *Stocks, Bonds, Bills and Inflation*, The Financial Analysts Research Foundation, 1982.

(a) Test the random walk hypothesis with regards to the return on common stocks, using the regression method.
(b) Using the regression technique test the random walk hypothesis for the consumer price index.
(c) Compute the *real* rate of return on common stocks, and test the random walk hypothesis for the real return series.

19.10   The following table gives the average quarterly gold price from the first quarter of 1979 to the first quarter of 1982. Test the random walk hypothesis for gold prices, using the nonparametric runs test.

| Quarter | Average Gold Price ($) | Quarter | Average Gold Price ($) |
|---------|------------------------|---------|------------------------|
| 79 $Q_1$ | 237.84 | 80 $Q_4$ | 608.06 |
| 79 $Q_2$ | 258.59 | 81 $Q_1$ | 518.64 |
| 79 $Q_3$ | 316.84 | 81 $Q_2$ | 478.86 |
| 79 $Q_4$ | 412.91 | 81 $Q_3$ | 420.99 |
| 80 $Q_1$ | 631.40 | 81 $Q_4$ | 420.41 |
| 80 $Q_2$ | 543.98 | 82 $Q_1$ | 362.84 |
| 80 $Q_3$ | 648.02 | | |

*Source: International Financial Statistics*, I.M.F., various issues.

(*Hint*: For details of the runs test, see S. Siegel, *Nonparametric Statistics for Behavioral Sciences*, McGraw-Hill, New York, 1956; H. L. Balsley, *Basic Statistics for Business and Economics*, Grid, Columbus, Ohio, 1978; M. Ben-Horim and H. Levy, *Statistics: Decisions and Applications in Business and Economics*, Random House, New York, 1981.)

19.11  An investment analyst claims that he has mastered the art of forecasting the price changes of CBM stock. The following table gives the actual price changes of CBM stock and the analyst's forecasts.

| Month | Actual Price Changes (in Percent) | Forecast (in Percent) |
|-------|-----------------------------------|-----------------------|
| 1 | 7.3313 | 14.981 |
| 2 | −2.1501 | −19.661 |
| 3 | 8.5759 | 7.047 |
| 4 | −1.5554 | −5.267 |
| 5 | 9.1630 | 1.045 |
| 6 | 6.6880 | −0.869 |
| 7 | −4.7732 | −8.361 |
| 8 | −0.7636 | 6.719 |

(a) Test the hypothesis that the expected value of the actual price changes is equal to the expected value of the forecasts. Does this test help us decide whether the analyst's forecasts are better than mere coin tossing?

(b) Apply a regression technique to test whether the analyst's forecast is better than a fair gamble.

(c) Apply the hypergeometric distribution to test (b) above. In this application assume that the investment analyst knows that in 50% of the days we have a "+" sign and he only has to predict on which days the "+" sign occurs.

(d) Apply the binomial distribution to test (b) above, this time when there is no prior knowledge regarding the percentage of the "+" signs.

(e) How can you explain the contradicting results in (b) and (c)–(d) above?

19.12   The following table gives the hypothetical daily prices of a security on 16 consecutive trading days:

| Day | Security Price (in Dollars) | Day | Security Price (in Dollars) |
|-----|------------------|-----|------------------|
| 1 | 100.00 | 9 | 94.64 |
| 2 | 99.20 | 10 | 94.47 |
| 3 | 98.59 | 11 | 94.99 |
| 4 | 97.11 | 12 | 95.43 |
| 5 | 94.33 | 13 | 93.22 |
| 6 | 96.09 | 14 | 92.70 |
| 7 | 95.57 | 15 | 94.70 |
| 8 | 95.59 | 16 | 93.36 |

(a) Compute the return on 100 dollars invested in the security by a 0.3% filter rule (without short sales!) and compare this strategy to a buy and hold policy. Note that investors wait until the price increases by more than 0.3% for the first time.

(b) Do the results in (a) imply that the market is not weak form efficient? Explain.

19.13   The diagram below is a typical plot of the closing prices of the New York Stock Exchange index for the period from July 10 to October 2, 1982.

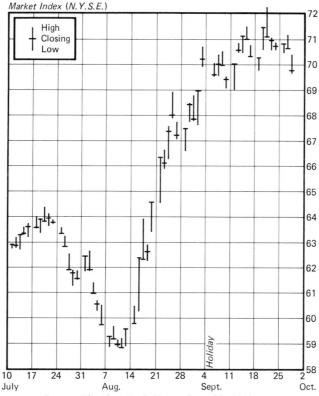

Source: *The New York Times*, Sept. 30, 1982.

Use the runs test to test the random walk hypothesis with this data.

Note that there are five trading days in a week and that in the second trading day of the first week there is actually a decrease in the price indexes which is difficult to see from the diagram itself.

19.14   In the following table the end-of-month exchange rates of the pound sterling are presented. The rate is in US dollars per pound.

| | *1980* | | *1981* | | *1982* |
|---|---|---|---|---|---|
| *Month* | *Price in $ per £1* | *Month* | *Price in $ per £1* | *Month* | *Price in $ per £1* |
| 1 | 2.2675 | 1 | 2.3670 | 1 | 1.8812 |
| 2 | 2.2725 | 2 | 2.2050 | 2 | 1.8205 |
| 3 | 2.1645 | 3 | 2.2440 | 3 | 1.7825 |
| 4 | 2.2577 | 4 | 2.1410 | 4 | 1.7945 |
| 5 | 2.3450 | 5 | 2.0695 | 5 | 1.7917 |
| 6 | 2.3565 | 6 | 1.9287 | 6 | 1.7367 |
| 7 | 2.3427 | 7 | 1.8397 | 7 | 1.7387 |
| 8 | 2.3965 | 8 | 1.8431 | 8 | 1.7192 |
| 9 | 2.3875 | 9 | 1.8015 | 9 | 1.6943 |
| 10 | 2.4365 | 10 | 1.8600 | 10 | 1.6760 |
| 11 | 2.3598 | 11 | 1.9567 | 11 | 1.6310 |
| 12 | 2.3925 | 12 | 1.9135 | | |

(*Source:* Reuters, London.)

(a) Compute the return on $100 invested in pounds by a 3% filter rule, without short sales. Compare this strategy to a buy and hold policy. Assume there are no transaction costs. Note that investors wait until the pound rate increases by more than 3% for the first time. Filter rule decisions are based on cumulative changes of more than 3% (which may occur over more than a single month).

(b) Answer (a), this time with 1% transaction costs. Assume that the transaction costs are paid upon buying and selling the currency.

## Data Set Problems

1. Assume that the share price of every mutual fund listed in the Data Set was $100 in the beginning of 1971.

   (a) Using the rates of return of Affiliated Fund, calculate the share price of this fund at the end of each year for the period 1971–1980 (ignore all distributions, so that the rate of return is fully determined by the change in price).

(b) Using the regression

$$\Delta P_t = a + b\Delta P_{t-1}$$

draw a scatter diagram of the fund prices and test the Random Walk Hypothesis.

2. Repeat the calculations of Problem 1 for a hypothetical fund representing the average of the Growth and Current Income Funds category.

3. Find the share price of AMCAP fund at the end of each year, assuming that the share price at the beginning of 1971 was $100 and there were no distributions to shareholders.

   Determine the number of runs. Can you test the Random Walk Hypothesis by applying the runs test? If not, explain why. What would you suggest to do, in this case, if one wants to test the random walk hypothesis.

   (*Hint*: For details of the runs test see S. Siegel, *Nonparametric Statistics for Behavioral Sciences*, McGraw-Hill, New York 1956; H. L. Balsley, *Basic Statistics for Business and Economics*, Grid, Columbus, Ohio, 1978; M. Ben-Horim and H. Levy, *Statistics: Decisions and Applications in Business and Economics*, Random House, New York, 1981).

4. Assume that the share price of Alpha Income Fund was $100 at the beginning of 1971. Find the share price at the end of each year for the period 1971–1980 (ignoring all distributions).

   (a) Assuming that you hold one share of this fund at the beginning of 1971 and that you follow the 5% filter rule strategy, describe your buy-and-sell policy and plot it in a graph. Calculate your terminal value of the investment at the end of 1980 (you will be able to make buy and sell decisions only at the end of each year, since no other information is available for the fund shares).
   (b) Calculate the terminal value of the investment resulting from a simple "buy-and-hold" strategy. Which strategy provides the higher terminal wealth?

5. Repeat the analysis of Problem 4 using a 1% filter rule strategy.

6. Repeat the calculations of Problems 4 and 5 incorporating a transaction cost of 1% for each sell or buy order that you give. Compare and analyze the results with and without transaction costs. Again, assume that the investor holds one share at the beginning of 1971.

7. Use the regression

$$R_{it} = a_i + b_i R_{mt} + e_{it}$$

to test whether $a_i$ is positive (and significantly different from zero) for the first five funds in the Long Term Growth, Income Secondary category. In running the regression, use for $R_{it}$ the excess return on the $i$th fund in year $t$ (above the riskless interest rate in that year) and for $R_{mt}$ the corresponding excess return on the market portfolio.

## Selected References

Abdel-Khalik, A. R. and McKeown, J. C., "Understanding Accounting Changes In An Efficient Market: Evidence of Differential Reaction", *Accounting Review* (October 1978).

Alexander, S. S., "Price Movement in Speculative Markets: Trends or Random Walk", *Industrial Management Review* (May 1965).

Allvine, F. C. and O'Neill, D. E., "Stock Market Returns and the Presidential Election Cycle: Implications for Market Efficiency", *Financial Analysts Journal* (September/October 1980).

Amihud, Y. and Mendelson, H., "Asset Price Behaviour in a Dealership Market", *Financial Analysts Journal* (May/June 1982).

Bachelier, L., "Théorie de la Speculation", Paris: Gauthier-Villars, 1900. [English translation in Cootner, P., *The Random Character of Stock Prices*, Cambridge, Mass.: MIT Press, 1964.]

Baesel, J., Shows, G. and Thorp, E., "Can Joe Granville Time the Market?" *Journal of Portfolio Management* (Spring 1982).

Baesel, J. B. and Stein, G. R., "The Value of Information: Inferences from the Profitability of Insider Tradings", *Journal of Financial and Quantitative Analysis* (September 1979).

Ball, R., "Risk, Return and Disequilibrium: An Application to Changes in Accounting Techniques", *Journal of Finance* (May 1972).

Baron, D. P., "Information, Investment Behavior, and Efficient Portfolios", *Journal of Financial and Quantitative Analysis* (September 1974).

Bar-Yosef, S. and Brown, L. D., "A Reexamination of Stock Splits Using Moving Betas", *Journal of Finance* (September 1977).

Basu, S., "The Investment Performance of Common Stocks in Relation to Their Price-Earnings Ratios: A Test of the Efficient Market Hypothesis", *Journal of Finance* (June 1977).

Beaver, W. H., "Market Efficiency", *Accounting Review* (January 1981).

Beja, A. and Hakansson, N. H., "Dynamic Market Processes and the Rewards to Up-to-Date Information", *Journal of Finance* (May 1977).

Bernstein, P. L., "Efficiency and Opportunity", *Journal of Portfolio Management* (Fall 1977).

Bidwell, C. M., "A Test of Market Efficiency: SUE/PE", *Journal of Portfolio Management* (Summer 1979).

Bidwell, C. M., "How Good is Institutional Brokerage Research?" *Journal of Portfolio Management* (Winter 1977).

Bishop, E. L., III, and Rollins, J. R., "Lowry's Reports: A Denial of Market Efficiency?" *Journal of Portfolio Management* (Fall 1977).

Black, F., "Random Walk and Portfolio Management", *Financial Analysts Journal* (March/April 1971).

Black, F. and Scholes, M., "The Valuation of Option Contracts and a Test of Market Efficiency", *Journal of Finance* (May 1972).

Brenner, M., "Effect of Model Misspecification on Tests on the Efficient Market Hypotheses", *Journal of Finance* (March 1977).

Carey, K. J., "Non-Random Price Changes in Association with Trading in Large Blocks: Evidence of Market Efficiency in Behavior of Investor Returns", *Journal of Business* (October 1977).

Cheng, P. L. and Deets, M. K., "Portfolio Returns and the Random Walk Theory", *Journal of Finance* (March 1971).

Cootner, P. H., *The Random Character of Stock Prices*. Cambridge: MIT Press, 1964.

Cootner, P. H., "Stock Prices: Random vs. Systematic Changes", *Industrial Management Review* (Spring 1962).

Cowton, C. and Garrod, N., "Clearing the Fog Around the Efficient Capital Market Hypothesis", *Accountancy* (August 1981).

Dann, L. Y., Mayers, D. and Raab, R. J., Jr., "Trading Rules, Large Blocks, and the Speed of Price Adjustment", *Journal of Financial Economics* (January 1977).

Davies, P. L. and Canes, M., "Stock Prices and the Publication of Second-hand Information", *Journal of Business* (January 1978).

DeYoung, H., "Buyers and Sellers Need An Efficient Market Place", *Purchasing* (March 1981).

Dryden, M. M., "A Source of Bias in Filter Tests on Share Prices", *Journal of Business* (July 1969).

Emery, J. T., "The Information Content of Daily Market Indicators", *Journal of Financial and Quantitative Analysis* (March 1973).

Emery, J. T., "Efficient Capital Markets and the Information Content of Accounting Numbers", *Journal of Financial and Quantitative Analysis* (March 1974).

Emmanuel, D. M., "Note on Filter Rules and Stock-market Trading", *Economic Record* (December 1980).

Epps, T. W., "Security Price Changes and Transaction Volumes: Some Additional Evidence", *Journal of Financial and Quantitative Analysis* (March 1977).

Epps, T. W., "Security Price Changes and Transaction Volumes: Theory and Evidence", *American Economic Review* (September 1975).

Eskew, R. K. and Wright, W. F., "An Empirical Analysis of Differential Capital Market Reactions to Extraordinary Accounting Items", *Journal of Finance* (May 1976).

Evans, J. L., "The Random Walk Hypothesis, Portfolio Analysis and the Buy-and-Hold Criterion", *Journal of Financial and Quantitative Analysis* (September 1968).

Fabozzi, F. J., "Quality of Earnings: A Test of Market Efficiency", *Journal of Portfolio Management* (Fall 1978).

Fama, E. F., "The Behavior of Stock Market Prices", *Journal of Business* (January 1965).

Fama, E. F., "Random Walks in Stock Prices", *Financial Analysts Journal* (Sept.–Oct. 1965).

Fama, E. F., "Efficient Capital Markets: A Review of Theory and Empirical Work", *Journal of Finance* (May 1970).

Fama, E. F., *Foundations of Finance*, New York: Basic Books, 1976.

Fama, E. F., Fisher, L, Jensen, M. C. and Roll, R., "The Adjustment of Stock Prices to New Information", *International Economic Review* (February 1969).

Fama, E. F. and Blume, M. E., "Filter Rules and Stock Market Trading", *Journal of Business* (January 1966).

Fama, E. F., and Laffer, A. B., "Information and Capital Markets", *Journal of Business* (July 1971).

Figlewski, S., "Information Diversity and Market Behavior", *Journal of Finance* (March 1982).

Finnerty, J. E., "Insiders' Activity and Inside Information: A Multivariate Analysis", *Journal of Financial and Quantitative Analysis* (June 1976).

Finnerty, J. E., "Insiders and Market Efficiency", *Journal of Finance* (September 1976).

Finnerty, J. E., "The Chicago Board Options Exchange and Market Efficiency", *Journal of Financial and Quantitative Analysis* (March 1978).

Firth, M., "The Information Content of Large Investment Holdings", *Journal of Finance* (December 1975).

Garbisch, M. W. and Alexander, G. J., "Is Standard and Poor's Master List Worthless?" *Journal of Portfolio Management* (Fall 1977).

Geweke, J. and Feige, E., "Some Joint Tests of the Efficiency of Markets for Forward Foreign Exchange", *Review of Economics and Statistics* (August 1979).

Gibbons, M. R. and Hess, P., "Day of the Week Effects and Asset Returns", *Journal of Business* (October 1981).

Gonedes, N. J., "Evidence on the Information Content of Accounting Numbers: Accounting-Based and Market-Based Estimates of Systematic Risk", *Journal of Financial and Quantitative Analysis* (June 1973).

Gonedes, N. J., "The Capital Market, The Market for Information and External Accounting", *Journal of Finance* (May 1976).

Granger, C. W. J., "Some Aspects of the Random Walk Model of Stock Market Prices", *International Economic Review* (June 1968).

Granger, C. W. J., "The Random Walk Misunderstood?" *Financial Analysts Journal* (May–June 1970).

Grier, P. C. and Albin, P. S., "Non-Random Price Changes in Association with Trading in Large Blocks", *Journal of Business* (July 1973).

Grossman, S. J., "On the Efficiency of Competitive Stock Markets Where Trades Have Diverse Information", *Journal of Finance* (May 1976).

Grossman, S. J. and Stiglitz, J. E., "On the Impossibility of Informationally Efficient Markets", *American Economic Review* (June 1980).

Groth, J. C., "Security-Relative Information Market Efficiency: Some Empirical Evidence", *Journal of Financial and Quantitative Analysis* (September 1979).

Grubel, H. G., "Peter Principle and the Efficient Market Hypothesis", *Financial Analysts Journal* (November 1979).

Gupta, S., "Note on the Efficiency of Block Markets in Foreign Currencies", *Journal of Finance* (June 1981).

Hadaway, S. C. and Rochester, D. P., "Seasonality in Individual Common Stocks: Alternative Test Techniques and Implications for Market Efficiency", *Journal of Economics and Business* (Fall 1980).

Ibbotson, R. G. and Jaffe, J. F., "Hot Issue Markets", *Journal of Finance* (September 1975).

Jaffe, J. F., "Special Information and Insider Trading", *Journal of Business* (July 1974).

Jaffe, J. F. and Winkler, R. L., "Optimal Speculation Against an Efficient Market", *Journal of Finance* (March 1976).

Jensen, M. C. and Bennington, G. A., "Random Walks and Technical Theories: Some Additional Evidence", *Journal of Finance* (May 1970).

John, K., "Efficient Funds in a Financial Market with Options: A New Irrelevance Proposition", *Journal of Finance* (June 1981).

Jones, C. P. and Litzenberger, R. H., "Quarterly Earnings Reports and Intermediate Stock Price Trends", *Journal of Finance* (March 1970).

Jordan, R. J., "An Empirical Investigation of the Adjustment of Stock Prices to New Quarterly Earnings Information", *Journal of Financial and Quantitative Analysis* (September 1973).

Kaplan, R. and Roll, R. W., "Accounting Changes and Stock Prices", *Financial Analysts Journal* (January/February 1973).

Katz, S., "The Price Adjustment Process of Bonds to Rating Reclassifications: A Test of Bond Market Efficiency", *Journal of Finance* (May 1974).

Keown, A. J., and Pinkerton, J. M., "Merger Announcements and Insider Trading Activity: An Empirical Investigation", *Journal of Finance* (September 1981).

Kerr, H. S., "The Battle of Insider Trading vs. Market Efficiency", *Journal of Portfolio Management* (Summer 1980).

Klemkosky, R. C. and Resnick, B. G., "Put-Call Parity and Market Efficiency", *Journal of Finance* (December 1979).

Kon, S. J. and Jen, F. C., "Investment Performance of Mutual Funds: An Empirical Investigation of Timing, Selectivity and Market Efficiency", *Journal of Business* (April 1979).

Kraus, A. and Stoll, H., "Price Impacts of Block Trading on the New York Stock Exchange", *Journal of Finance* (June 1972).

Kripke, H., "Inside Information, Market Information and Efficient Markets", *Financial Analysts Journal* (March 1980).

Kwan, C. C. Y., "Efficient Market Tests of the Informational Content of Dividend Announcements: Critique and Extension", *Journal of Financial and Quantitative Analysis* (June 1981).

Laffer, A. B. and Ranson, R. D., "Some Practical Applications of the Efficient Market Concept", *Financial Management* (Summer 1979).

Laub, P. M., "On The Informational Content of Dividends", *Journal of Business* (January 1976).

Lenthold, R. M. and Hartmann, P. A., "Semi-strong Form Evaluation of the Efficiency of the Hog Futures Market", *American Journal of Agricultural Economics* (August 1979).

Levy, H and Lerman, Z., "Testing P/E Ratio Filters by Stochastic Dominance Rules", *Journal of Portfolio Management* (forthcoming).

Levy, R. A., "Relative Strength as a Criterion for Investment Selection", *Journal of Finance* (December 1967).

Litzenberger, R. H., Joy, O. M. and Jones, C. P., "Ordinal Predictions and the Selection of Common Stocks", *Journal of Financial and Quantitative Analysis* (September 1971).

Longworth, D., "Testing the Efficiency of the Canadian–US Exchange Market Under the Assumption of No Risk Premium", *Journal of Finance* (March 1981).

Lorie, J. and Niederhoffer, V., "Predictive and Statistical Properties of Insider Trading", *Journal of Law and Economics* (April 1978).

Losey, R. L. and Talbott, J. C., "Back on the Track With the Efficient Markets Hypothesis", *Journal of Finance* (September 1980).

Madden, G. P., "Potential Corporate Takeovers and Market Efficiency", *Journal of Finance* (December 1981).

Malkiel, B. G. and Finstenberg, P. B., "A Winning Strategy for an Efficient Market", *Journal of Portfolio Management* (Summer 1978).

Mandelbrot, B. B., "When Can Price Be Arbitraged Efficiently? A Limit to the Validity of the Random Walk and Martingale Models", *Review of Economics and Statistics* (August 1971).

Mandelbrot, B., "Forecasts of Future Prices, Unbiased Markets and Martingale Models", *Journal of Business* (January 1966).

Marsh, P., "Equity Rights Issues and the Efficiency of the U.K. Stock Markets", *Journal of Finance* (September 1979).

Niederhoffer, V., "The Predictive Content of First-Quarter Earnings Reports", *Journal of Business* (January 1970).

Niederhoffer, V., "The Analysis of World Events and Stock Prices", *Journal of Business* (April 1971).

Pettit, R. R., "Dividend Announcements, Security Performance, and Capital Market Efficiency", *Journal of Finance* (December 1972).

Pinches, G. E., "The Random Walk Hypothesis and Technical Analysis", *Financial Analysts Journal* (March/April 1970).

Pinches, G. E., and Simon, G. M., "An Analysis of Portfolio Accumulation Strategies Employing Low-Priced Common Stocks", *Journal of Financial and Quantitative Analysis* (June 1972).

Piper, T. R. and Fruhan, W. E., Jr., "Is Your Stock Worth Its Market Price?" *Harvard Business Review* (May/June 1981).

Praetz, P. D., "Rates of Return on Filter Tests", *Journal of Finance* (March 1976).

Praetz, P. D., "Testing for a Flat Spectrum on Efficient Market Price Data", *Journal of Finance* (June 1979).

Praetz, P. D., "A General Test of a Filter Effect", *Journal of Financial and Quantitative Analysis* (June 1979).

Publisi, D. J., "Yield Movements in the Money Market: Evidence and Implications", *Quarterly Review of Economics and Business* (Summer 1978).

Reilly, F. K. and Drzycimski, E. F., "Short-run Profits From Stock Splits", *Financial Management* (Summer 1981).

Rendleman, R. J. and Carabini, C. E., "Efficiency of the Treasury Bill Futures Markets", *Journal of Finance* (September 1979).

Renshaw, E. F., "The Random Walk Hypothesis, Performance Management, and Portfolio Theory", *Financial Analysts Journal* (March/April 1968).

Renshaw, E. F. and Renshaw, V. D., "Test of the Random Walk Hypothesis", *Financial Analysts Journal* (September/October 1970).

Rogalski, R. J., "Trading in Warrants by Mechanical Systems", *Journal of Finance* (March 1977).

Rosenberg, B. and Rudd, A., "Factor-related and Specific Returns of Common Stocks: Serial Correlation and Market Inefficiency", *Journal of Finance* (May 1982).

Roberts, H. V., "Stock Market 'Patterns' and Financial Analysis: Methodological Suggestions", *Journal of Finance* (March 1959).

Samuelson, P. A., "Proof That Properly Anticipated Prices Fluctuate Randomly", *Industrial Management Review* (Spring 1965).

Schulman, E., "Can the Market Forecast Itself?" *Journal of Portfolio Management* (Fall 1971).

Schwartz, R. A. and Whitcomb, D. K., "Evidence on the Presence and Causes of Serial Correlation in Market Model Residuals", *Journal of Financial and Quantitative Analysis* (June 1977).

Schwert, G. W., "Adjustment of Stock Prices to Information About Inflation", *Journal of Finance* (March 1981).

Seelenfreund, A., Parker, G. G. C. and Van Horne, J. C., "Stock Price Behavior and Trading", *Journal of Financial and Quantitative Analysis* (September 1968).

Sharpe, W. F., "Are Gains Likely From Market Timing?" *Financial Analysts Journal* (March/April 1975).

Shannon, D. S., Johnson, K. H. and Neal, G. L., "How to Beat Those Index Funds", *Journal of Portfolio Management* (Fall 1977).

Shiller, R. J., "Effect of Volatility Measures in Assessing Market Efficiency", *Journal of Finance* (May 1981).

Smidt, S., "A New Look at the Random Walk Hypothesis", *Journal of Financial and Quantitative Analysis* (September 1968).

Solt, M. E., and Swanson, P. J., "On the Efficiency of the Markets for Gold and Silver", *Journal of Business* (July 1981).

Stein, J. L., "Dynamics of Spot and Forward Prices in an Efficient Foreign Exchange Market with Rational Expectations", *American Economic Review* (September 1980).

Stevenson, R. A., and Bear, R. M., "Commodity Futures: Trends or Random Walks?" *Journal of Finance* (March 1970).

Stevenson, R. A. and Rozeff, M., "Are the Backwaters of the Market Efficient?" *Journal of Portfolio Management* (Spring 1979).

Taylor, S. J., "Tests of the Random Walk Hypothesis Against a Price-Trend Hypothesis", *Journal of Financial and Quantitative Analysis* (March 1982).

Van Horne, J. C. and Parker, G. C., "Technical Trading Rules", *Financial Analysts Journal* (July/August 1968).

Vasicek, O. A., and McQuown, J. A., "The Efficient Market Model", *Financial Analysts Journal* (September/October 1972).

Verrecchia, R. E., "Proof of the Existence of Concensus Beliefs", *Journal of Finance* (September 1979).

Verrecchia, R. E., "Concensus Beliefs, Information Acquisition and Market Information Efficiency", *American Economic Review* (December 1980).

# Mathematical Supplement

This section is designed for the reader who is unfamiliar with higher mathematics but wants to go beyond the statement that the first derivative measures the rate of change of a function. The presentation is rather intuitive and makes no pretense at being rigorous. Despite this, the supplement should be adequate to familiarize the reader with some of the mathematical techniques mentioned in the text.

## The Derivative

### *Definition*

Given a single-variable function $y = f(x)$ and looking at any point $x_0$, by changing the argument $x$ by the amount of $\Delta x$, the value of the function can be expressed by

$$y + \Delta y = f(x_0 + \Delta x) \tag{1}$$

and since $y = f(x)$, (1) is written as:

$$\Delta y = f(x_0 + \Delta x) - f(x_0) \tag{2}$$

which is the amount of change in $y$ caused by a change of $\Delta x$ in the argument $x$. Furthermore, if we are interested in the relative change caused by $\Delta x$, we have

$$\frac{\Delta y}{\Delta x} = \frac{f(x_0 + \Delta x) - f(x_0)}{\Delta x} \tag{3}$$

This quotient depends on $\Delta x$, because for different $\Delta x$ we get different $\Delta y$. However, as we consider smaller and smaller changes in $\Delta x$, we assume that $\Delta y / \Delta x$ will tend toward a unique number, called the derivative of $f(x)$ at the point $x_0$, which we denote by $f'(x_0)$, or $(dy/dx)_{x_0}$. Thus

$$f'(x_0) = \left[\frac{dy}{dx}\right]_{x_0} = \lim_{\Delta x \to 0} \frac{\Delta y}{\Delta x} = \lim_{\Delta x \to 0} \frac{f(x_0 + \Delta x) - f(x_0)}{\Delta x} \tag{4}$$

### Geometrical Interpretation

Assume we have $y = f(x)$ as represented in Figure 1. It can easily be seen that $[f(x_0 + \Delta x_1) - f(x_0)]/\Delta x_1$ is the slope of the line $AC$. Taking a smaller increment $\Delta x_2$ gives $[f(x_0 + \Delta x_2) - f(x_0)]/\Delta x_2$ which is the slope of the line $AD$. By setting $\Delta x$ smaller and smaller, the expression $[f(x_0 + \Delta x) - f(x_0)]/\Delta x$ will tend to coincide with the slope of the tangent $KL$ to the function $y = f(x)$ at the point $x_0$. Therefore we can say that the derivative of a function $f(x)$ at $x_0$ is exactly the slope of the tangent to the function at this point.

### The Derived Function

Suppose we have a function $f(x)$ whose derivative can be found at each of its points. By finding the value of the derivative of $y = f(x)$ at these points, we define a new function: the *derived function*. This function is denoted by $f'(x)$ or $dy/dx$. Notice that $f'(x_0)$ or $(dy/dx)_{x_0}$ is the value of the derived function at one particular point: $x_0$. Bearing in mind the geometrical interpretation of the derivative, $f'(x)$ is nothing but a function which fits to any point $x$ a value equal to the slope of the tangent to $f(x)$ at $x$ as demonstrated in Figure 2. (Note that when $x = 1$, $f(x)$ reaches its peak and $f'(x) = 0$.)

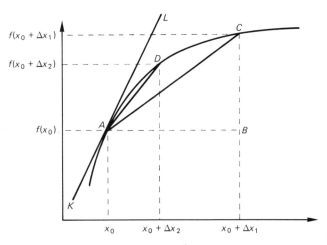

**Figure 1**

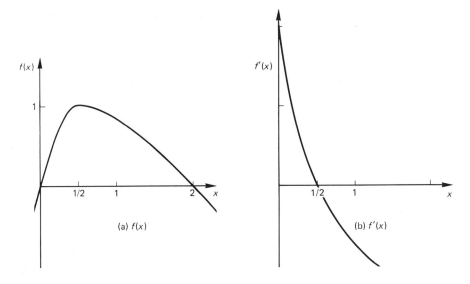

**Figure 2**

### Increasing and Decreasing Functions

A function is said to be an *increasing function*, in some interval, if for each point in this interval higher values of $x$ give higher values of $f(x)$. Adding a positive increment $\Delta x$ results in:

$$f(x + \Delta x) \geqslant f(x) \quad \text{for } \Delta x > 0$$

hence:

$$f(x + \Delta x) - f(x) \geqslant 0$$

and since $\Delta x > 0$

$$[f(x + \Delta x) - f(x)]/\Delta x \geqslant 0$$

This ratio holds for *every* $\Delta x > 0$, and therefore this inequality is also preserved when we let $\Delta x$ go to zero. Therefore, for an increasing function we have:

$$f'(x) = \lim_{\Delta x \to 0} \frac{f(x + \Delta x) - f(x)}{\Delta x} \geqslant 0 \tag{5}$$

A function $f(x)$ is defined as a *decreasing function*, over some interval, if higher values of $x$ result in lower values of $f(x)$. For such functions we have:

$$f(x + \Delta x) - f(x) \leqslant 0 \quad \text{for } \Delta x > 0$$

and in a similar way it can be shown that for a decreasing function and any increment $\Delta x$

$$f'(x) = \lim_{\Delta x \to 0} \frac{f(x + \Delta x) - f(x)}{\Delta x} \leqslant 0 \tag{6}$$

## Rules of Differentiation

The process by which we calculate the derived function is called *differentiation*. Formally this is done by finding the limit which Equation (3) approaches as $\Delta x$ tends to zero. For example, take the function $f(x) = x^2$:

$$\frac{dy}{dx} = \lim_{\Delta x \to 0} \frac{(x + \Delta x)^2 - x^2}{\Delta x}$$

$$= \lim_{\Delta x \to 0} \frac{x^2 + (\Delta x)^2 + 2x\,\Delta x - x^2}{\Delta x} = \lim_{\Delta x \to 0} (\Delta x + 2x) = 2x$$

The derived function or derivative of $y = x^2$ is therefore $f'(x) = 2x$. The above procedure can be carried out for different types of functions.

Following are the differentiation rules for some common classes of functions.[1]

$$f(x) = c, \qquad\qquad f'(x) = 0 \tag{i}$$

where $c$ is a constant;

$$f(x) = x^n, \qquad\qquad f'(x) = nx^{n-1} \tag{ii}$$

$$f(x) = u(x)v(x), \qquad\qquad f'(x) = u'(x)v(x) + v'(x)u(x) \tag{iii}$$

$$f(x) = \frac{u(x)}{v(x)}, \qquad\qquad f'(x) = \frac{u'(x)v(x) - v'(x)u(x)}{[v(x)]^2} \tag{iv}$$

[1] For a more formal discussion of differentiation see Lipman Bers, *Calculus*, Holt, Rinehart and Winston, 1969; or A. C. Chiang, *Fundamental Methods of Mathematical Economics*, McGraw-Hill, 1967.

$$f(x) = \log_a x, \qquad f'(x) = \frac{1}{x} \log_a e \tag{v}$$

where $e = 2.718\ldots$ is the base of the natural logarithm;

$$f(x) = e^{ax}, \qquad f'(x) = ae^{ax} \tag{vi}$$

$$f(x) = u[v(x)], \qquad f'(x) = u'[v(x)]v'(x) \tag{vii}$$

### Higher-Order Derivatives

As we mentioned above the process of differentiation gives us the derived function. This derived function can also be differentiated, thereby yielding a *second order* derived function (whose value at a particular point is called the second derivative). In other words, if $f'(x)$ is the derived function then by differentiating this function at $x_0$ we obtain:

$$\left[\frac{df'(x)}{dx}\right]_{x_0} = \lim_{\Delta x \to 0} \frac{f'(x_0 + \Delta x) - f'(x_0)}{\Delta x} \tag{7}$$

The second derivative of $f(x)$ at $x_0$ is denoted by $f''(x_0)$ or $(d^2 f/dx^2)_{x_0}$. Likewise we can define the $n$th-order derivative by:

$$f^{(n)}(x_0) = \lim_{\Delta x \to 0} \frac{f^{(n-1)}(x_0 + \Delta x) - f^{(n-1)}(x_0)}{\Delta x}$$

EXAMPLE: $f(x) = 2x^2 + 3x + 1$

$$f'(x) = 4x + 3 \qquad \text{is the first derivative}$$
$$f''(x) = 4 \qquad \text{is the second derivative}$$
$$f^{(3)}(x) = 0 \qquad \text{is the third derivative}$$

### Partial Derivatives

Where we have a function of more than one variable, $Z = f(x, y)$, for example $Z = 2xy + x^2$, we can differentiate the function with respect to either one of the variables ($x$ or $y$) while holding the other constant. To distinguish this type of differentiation from the regular one, it is usually denoted by $\partial f(x, y)/\partial x$ when differentiating with respect to $x$ ($y$ held constant) or $\partial f(x, y)/\partial y$ when differentiating with respect to $y$. The partial derivative with respect to $x$ at $(x_0, y_0)$ is defined as:

$$\frac{\partial f(x_0, y_0)}{\partial x} = \lim_{\Delta x \to 0} \frac{f(x_0 + \Delta x, y_0) - f(x_0, y_0)}{\Delta x} \tag{8}$$

We leave it to the reader to work out the definition for $\partial f(x, y)/\partial y$.

## Local Maxima and Minima

Looking at the function $y = f(x)$ in Figure 3, we see that the function has a *local maximum* at points $x_2$ and $x_4$, and a *local minimum* at $x_1$ and $x_3$. A point which is either a local maximum or a local minimum is called an *extremum point*. Formally, what characterizes a local maximum (minimum) at any point $x_0$ is the fact that for any other $x$ in the close neighborhood of $x_0$ the inequality $f(x_0) \geqslant f(x)$ [or $f(x_0) \leqslant f(x)$ for a local minimum] holds.

Figure 4 isolates the interval $(x_1, x_3)$ so as to facilitate an examination of the characteristics of the local maximum at $x_2$. As can readily be seen, in the interval $(x_1, x_2)$, $f(x)$ is an increasing function; while in the interval $(x_2, x_3)$ it is decreasing. Applying our previous discussion of increasing and decreasing functions we know that in the interval $(x_1, x_2)$ we have $f'(x) \geqslant 0$. The closer we approach $x_2$, the smaller is $f'(x)$. Thus we can see that the slope of the tangent at $B$ is smaller than that at $A$. With respect to the interval $(x_2, x_3)$, $f'(x)$ is negative and the closer we come to $x_2$, the less negative the slope of the tangent. At the maximum point itself, $x_2$, the slope (derivative) is exactly zero: the tangent at $E$ is parallel to the horizontal axis. A similar type of argument can be used for the minimum point $x_3$, and the derivative at this point is also zero.

We can summarize by saying that in the neighborhood of a local maximum point, $f'(x)$ is a *decreasing* function with the value zero at the maximum point, and since $f'(x)$

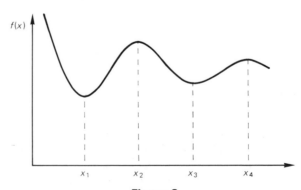

**Figure 3**

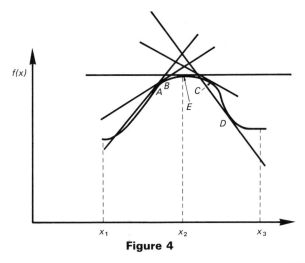

**Figure 4**

is a decreasing function then $f''(x) < 0$, that is, the necessary and sufficient conditions for $f(x)$ to have a local maximum at a point $x_0$ are:

$$\text{(i)} \quad f'(x_0) = 0$$
$$\text{(ii)} \quad f''(x_0) < 0 \tag{9}$$

We leave it to the reader to show that the sufficient and necessary conditions for a function $f(x)$ to have a local minimum at a point $x_0$ are:

$$\text{(i)} \quad f'(x_0) = 0$$
$$\text{(ii)} \quad f''(x_0) > 0 \tag{10}$$

It is worthwhile to mention that Equations (9) and (10) constitute the necessary and sufficient conditions only under the assumption that $f''(x_0) \neq 0$. Where $f''(x_0) = 0$ we require that the third derivative $f'''(x_0)$ will be negative for a local maximum and positive for a local minimum. In general, if the first $n$ derivatives vanish at $x_0$,

$$f'(x_0) = f''(x_0) = f'''(x_0) = \cdots = f^{(n)}(x_0) = 0$$

$x_0$ is a local maximum if the next derivative is negative ($f^{(n+1)}(x_0) < 0$) and it is a local minimum if the next derivative is positive ($f^{(n+1)}(x_0) > 0$).

### Constrained Maxima and Minima

The problem of scarcity of resources, with which every beginning economist has to deal, raises the problem of optimization under certain constraints. For instance: how much of a certain commodity should be consumed under a given budget limitation? How much should be invested in each of the available securities so as to maximize returns from the limited amount of money at our disposal? Let us take a concrete example:

Consider the following function:

$$\sigma^2 = x_1^2\sigma_1^2 + x_2^2\sigma_2^2$$

where:

$x_1, x_2$ = the proportions invested in securities 1 and 2 respectively;
$\sigma_1^2, \sigma_2^2$ = the respective variances[2] of the returns on the two securities;
$\sigma^2$ = the variance of the returns on the portfolio consisting of securities 1 and 2 (assuming independence of security returns).

The portfolio problem is to minimize $\sigma^2$ given the constraint $x_1 + x_2 = 1$. Thus we must invest all of our money (say, \$1), but we cannot invest more than our initial resources. The problem is how to allocate our resources between the two securities. There are two ways to treat this problem.

### The Elimination Method

Eliminate $x_2$ from the constraint:

$$x_2 = 1 - x_1$$

Substitute this expression in $\sigma^2$:

$$\sigma^2 = x_1^2\sigma_1^2 + (1 - x_1)^2\sigma_2^2$$

To find the investment proportions which minimize $\sigma^2$, we have to differentiate this function with respect to $x_1$ and set the derivative equal to zero:

$$\frac{d\sigma^2}{dx_1} = 2x_1\sigma_1^2 - 2(1 - x_1)\sigma_2^2 = 0$$

which gives

$$x_1\sigma_1^2 = (1 - x_1)\sigma_2^2$$

or

$$\frac{x_1}{1 - x_1} = \frac{\sigma_2^2}{\sigma_1^2} \tag{11}$$

Hence:

$$\frac{x_1}{x_2} = \frac{\sigma_2^2}{\sigma_1^2} \tag{12}$$

---

[2] For the definition of the variance of a random variable see the Statistical Supplement.

Thus the variance of the returns subject to the constraint $x_1 + x_2 = 1$ is minimized when the ratio of the proportions invested in the two stocks equals the *inverse* of the ratio of their variances. Note that the unconstrained minimum variance is attained for zero investment proportions $x_1 = x_2 = 0$, when the variance vanishes ($\sigma^2 = 0$).

### Lagrange Multiplier Method

Since $x_1 + x_2 = 1$ we have:

$$1 - (x_1 + x_2) = 0$$

and can form the function:

$$L = x_1^2 \sigma_1^2 + x_2^2 \sigma_2^2 + \lambda[1 - (x_1 + x_2)] \tag{13}$$

which will be called the *Lagrangian function*. Note that as long as $x_1 + x_2 = 1$, the value of this function will be $\sigma^2$. $\lambda$ is called a Lagrange multiplier, and $L$ is a function of the three variables: $x_1, x_2, \lambda$. Looking for a minimum we differentiate with respect to each of these three variables, and set the derivatives equal to zero:

$$\frac{\partial L}{\partial x_1} = 2x_1 \sigma_1^2 - \lambda = 0$$

$$\frac{\partial L}{\partial x_2} = 2x_2 \sigma_2^2 - \lambda = 0 \tag{14}$$

$$\frac{\partial L}{\partial \lambda} = 1 - (x_1 + x_2)$$

By equating $\lambda = 2x_1 \sigma_1^2$ from the first equation and $\lambda = 2x_2 \sigma_2^2$ from the second equation we get $x_1 \sigma_1^2 = x_2 \sigma_2^2$ or:

$$\frac{x_1}{x_2} = \frac{\sigma_2^2}{\sigma_1^2} \tag{15}$$

which provides the same result as the elimination method [Equation (12)]. The proportion $x_1$ can be found using the third equation to substitute $x_2 = 1 - x_1$:

$$\frac{x_1}{1 - x_1} = \frac{\sigma_2^2}{\sigma_1^2}$$

$$x_1 \sigma_1^2 = \sigma_2^2(1 - x_1) = \sigma_2^2 - x_1 \sigma_2^2$$

$$x_1(\sigma_1^2 + \sigma_2^2) = \sigma_2^2$$

so that:

$$x_1 = \frac{\sigma_2^2}{\sigma_1^2 + \sigma_2^2} \tag{16}$$

The same result can be reached without using the Lagrange multiplier method. However, technically this method is much more efficient when the number of the variables and/or the number of constraints are increased. For instance, assuming independence of security returns, we write for the variance of the $n$-asset portfolio:

$$\sigma^2 = \sum_{i=1}^{n} x_i^2 \sigma_i^2$$

In this case we form the function:

$$L = \sum_{i=1}^{n} x_i^2 \sigma_i^2 + \lambda \left( 1 - \sum_{i=1}^{n} x_i \right) \tag{17}$$

Differentiating with respect to $x_1, x_2, \ldots, x_n$ and $\lambda$ we get $n + 1$ equations with $n + 1$ unknowns, whose solution gives the optimal proportions $(x_1, x_2, \ldots, x_n)$.

The Lagrange multiplier method is also very useful in cases where we have more than one constraint; for example, an investor who decides to invest half of his money in stocks 1 to 10 and half of his money in stocks 11 to 30. The first group of stocks might be utilities while the second is made up of industrials. Such a problem has the following form:[3]

$$\text{minimize} \quad \sigma^2 = \sum_{i=1}^{30} x_i^2 \sigma_i^2$$

$$\text{subject to the constraints} \quad \sum_{i=1}^{10} x_i = 0.5$$

$$\sum_{i=11}^{30} x_i = 0.5$$

The Lagrangian function will be of the form:

$$L = \sum_{i=1}^{30} x_i^2 \sigma_i^2 + \lambda_1 \left( 0.5 - \sum_{i=1}^{10} x_i \right) + \lambda_2 \left( 0.5 - \sum_{i=11}^{30} x_i \right)$$

Differentiating $L$ with respect to $x_1, x_2, \ldots, x_n, \lambda_1, \lambda_2$ yields $n + 2$ equations with $n + 2$ unknowns, and hence the system has a solution.

---

[3] We assume independence of security returns. See Statistical Supplement.

From the above discussion it would seem that the Lagrange multipliers have only technical significance; however, in Chapter 11 an economic interpretation is given to $\lambda$ in terms of the price of a unit of risk reduction.

## Integrals

Suppose we have a function $y = f(x)$. The *indefinite integral* of $f(x)$ is a function $F(x)$ (usually denoted by $F(x) = \int f(x)\, dx$) which satisfies:

$$F'(x) = f(x) \tag{18}$$

The *definite integral* is defined as:

$$\int_a^b f(x)\, dx = F(b) - F(a) \tag{19}$$

Notice that the definite integral is a number which gives the value of the difference of the indefinite integral function $\int f(x)\, dx$ at two points: $b$ and $a$. We call $x$ the *integration variable*, while $b$ is the *upper limit of integration* and $a$ is the *lower limit of integration*. $(a, b)$ is the *integration interval* and the function $f(x)$ is the *integrand*.

We shall demonstrate now how the definite integral can be used to measure the area under a curve. Suppose we have a function $y = f(x)$ and we want to find the area under $y = f(x)$ between the points $a$ and $b$ (see Figure 5). Our contention is that this area is given by:

$$S(a, b) = \int_a^b f(x)\, dx \tag{20}$$

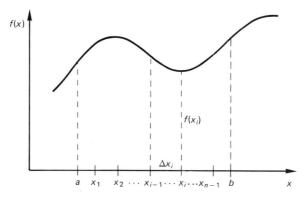

**Figure 5**

where $S(a, b)$ means the area between $a$ and $b$. To show this, divide the interval $(a, b)$ into $n$ subintervals. The area under the curve in each of these intervals is given approximately by the area of the rectangle: $f(x_i) \cdot \Delta x_i$. It is clear that the smaller $\Delta x_i$ (or the larger $n$), the better the approximation, since the deviation of the true area from that of the rectangle will be smaller. Therefore the area from $a$ to $b$ is given by:

$$S(a, b) = \lim_{n \to \infty} \sum_{i=1}^{n} f(x_i) \, \Delta x_i$$

or for any point $x$:

$$S(a, x) = \lim_{n \to \infty} \sum_{i=1}^{n} f(x_i) \, \Delta x_i$$

where the interval $(a, x)$ is divided into $n$ subintervals. Looking now at an interval $\Delta x_i$, its area can be expressed as the difference:

$$S(x_{i-1}, x_i) = S(a, x_i) - S(a, x_{i-1})$$

But this area is approximated by the area of the corresponding rectangle,

$$S(x_{i-1}, x_i) \approx f(x_i) \Delta x_i$$

or:

$$S(a, x_i) - S(a, x_{i-1}) \approx f(x_i) \Delta x_i$$

Hence:

$$f(x_i) \approx \frac{S(a, x_i) - S(a, x_{i-1})}{\Delta x_i}$$

or in the limit:

$$f(x_i) = \lim_{\Delta x_i \to 0} \frac{S(a, x_i) - S(a, x_{i-1})}{\Delta x_i}$$

which by the definition of the derivative yields:

$$f(x_i) = \frac{dS(a, x_i)}{dx_i}$$

or, since it holds for every $x_i$,

$$f(x) = \frac{\mathrm{d}S(a, x)}{\mathrm{d}x} = S'(a, x)$$

Applying now the definition of the definite integral we have:

$$\int_a^b f(x)\,\mathrm{d}x = S(a, b) - S(a, a)$$

But since $S(a, a) = 0$ (the area under the curve from point $a$ to point $a$ is clearly zero) we have:

$$S(a, b) = \int_a^b f(x)\,\mathrm{d}x \qquad (21)$$

which proves our proposition that the definite integral gives the area under $y = f(x)$ between the points $a$ and $b$.

EXAMPLE

Let $y = ax$. The area under $y = ax$ between the points 0 and $b$ is given by:

$$S(0, b) = \int_0^b ax = \left(\frac{ax^2}{2}\right)_0^b = \frac{ab^2}{2}$$

which is the familiar result from high school geometry for the area of a triangle: $S = (ab \cdot b)/2$ (see Figure 6).

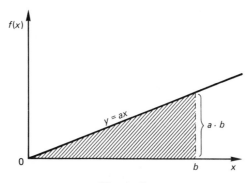

**Figure 6**

### Taylor Series: Power Expansion of Functions

The power expansion of a function is a common technique in economics and in other sciences as well. The main idea is to express a value of any function $f(x)$ in the neighborhood of a point $x_0$ by a polynomial in the powers of the difference $x - x_0$:

$$f(x) = b_0 + b_1(x - x_0) + b_2(x - x_0)^2$$
$$+ b_3(x - x_0)^3 + \cdots + b_n(x - x_0)^n + \cdots \qquad (22)$$

Our task is to find the coefficients of this polynomial. To do this, we first find the value of $f(x)$ at $x_0$ and get:

$$f(x_0) = b_0 + b_1(x_0 - x_0) + b_2(x_0 - x_0)^2 + \cdots + b_n(x_0 - x_0)^n$$

Hence

$$f(x_0) = b_0$$

which gives us the first coefficient $b_0$. We then differentiate $f(x)$ at $x_0$ and find:

$$f'(x_0) = 0 + b_1 + 2b_2(x_0 - x_0) + 3b_3(x_0 - x_0)^2 + \cdots + nb_n(x_0 - x_0)^{n-1}$$

Hence

$$b_1 = f'(x_0)$$

which gives us the second coefficient $b_1$. To find the third coefficient we differentiate again and get:

$$f''(x_0) = 0 + 0 + 2b_2 + 2 \cdot 3b_3(x - x_0) + \cdots + n(n - 1)(x_0 - x_0)^{n-2}$$

or

$$b_2 = f''(x_0)/2$$

The fourth coefficient is determined as follows:

$$f'''(x_0) = 1 \cdot 2 \cdot 3b_3 \quad \text{or} \quad b_3 = \frac{f'''(x_0)}{1 \cdot 2 \cdot 3}$$

and, in general,

$$b_n = \frac{f^{(n)}(x_0)}{1 \cdot 2 \cdot 3 \cdots n} = \frac{f^{(n)}(x_0)}{n!}$$

where $n! = 1 \cdot 2 \cdot 3 \cdots n$ is called $n$ factorial.

Putting all of these terms together we have:

$$f(x) = f(x_0) + f'(x_0)(x - x_0) + \frac{f''(x_0)}{2!}(x - x_0)^2$$

$$+ \frac{f'''(x_0)}{3!}(x - x_0)^3 + \cdots + \frac{f^{(n)}(x_0)}{n!}(x - x_0)^n + \cdots \tag{23}$$

In Chapter 4 this technique is used to show that expected utility, in general, is a function of *all* the distribution moments.

# Statistical Supplement

The purpose of this supplement is to familiarize the reader with those statistical tools which are used in the text. We shall define and explain the concepts of a random variable and of a probability distribution and its characteristics. Since the normal and the uniform (rectangular) distributions are referred to extensively in the text, special attention is devoted to these two distributions.

By nature, portfolio selection deals with combinations of several random variables. The analysis of the relationship between the return and risk of the overall portfolio and the return and risk of the individual securities comprising the portfolio can be facilitated by introducing the statistical concepts of expected return, variance, covariance, and correlation.

### The Random Variable and its Probability Function

A *random variable* is a numerical function defined over the sample space. This variable takes random values with a given probability assigned to each value.

EXAMPLE 1

In tossing a fair coin we have two alternative outcomes: Heads ($H$) and tails ($T$) with equal probabilities 1/2 and 1/2. Hence the result of tossing such a coin constitutes a random variable. A random variable is not necessarily the actual result which occurs but might be defined as any function which assigns numerical values to these two outcomes. For instance, assume that if heads occurs you get a prize of $2 and if tails occurs you get $3. Then the prize that you get is a random variable, that is, $f(H) = 2$, $f(T) = 3$ is the random variable.

EXAMPLE 2

In rolling a fair dice a random variable might be defined as a function which assigns to any outcome the same value $x$: that is, $f(x) = x$. But $f(x) = x^2$ is also a random variable which gives to the player a prize equal to the square of the outcome of the throw.

A *probability function* is a function which assigns to any particular value of the random variable its probability of occurrence. Going back to the fair dice example, and defining the random variable $f(x) = x$, we obtain the following probability function:

$$P(X = x) = \begin{cases} 1/6 & x = 1, 2, 3, 4, 5, 6 \\ 0 & \text{for any other } x \end{cases}$$

Where $P(X = x)$ stands for the probability that the random variable $X$ takes some particular value $x$.[1] Thus there is a probability of 1/6 that the random variable takes one of the values 1, 2, 3, 4, 5, 6 and a probability of zero to get any other value. Notice that $\sum_{x=1}^{6} P(X = x) = 1$ which means that there is a probability of 1 that at least one of the above values will occur.

Similarly, we can write other probability functions; for example, assume a common stock whose price at the end of the year is unknown. However, we do know that the probability that the final price will be \$110 is 1/2, the probability that this price will be \$100 is 1/4, and the same probability is assigned to a final price of \$90. Defining the stock's price as a random variable, we get the probability function

$$P(X = x) = \begin{cases} 1/2 & x = 110 \\ 1/4 & x = 100 \\ 1/4 & x = 90 \\ 0 & \text{otherwise} \end{cases}$$

### The Distribution Function

The probability function provides us with the probability that a random variable $X$ will have a value $x$. We can use this function to define the cumulative distribution function, or in short the *distribution function*, which gives us the probability that a random variable $X$ takes any value smaller or equal to $x$, that is, $P(X \leqslant x)$. A common notation for this function is $F(x) = P(X \leqslant x)$.

EXAMPLE

Assume that the following is a probability function of the price of some stock at the end of the year:

$$P(X = x) = \begin{cases} 1/4 & x = 80 \\ 1/4 & x = 90 \\ 1/4 & x = 110 \\ 1/4 & x = 120 \\ 0 & \text{otherwise} \end{cases}$$

If we want to know what is the probability that the final price will be smaller than or

---

[1] As a general notation we denote the random variable by $X$ while any particular value is denoted by $x$.

equal to any value, we can derive the answer from the following function:

$$F(x) = P(X \leqslant x) = \begin{cases} 0 & x < 80 \\ 1/4 & 80 \leqslant x < 90 \\ 1/2 & 90 \leqslant x < 110 \\ 3/4 & 110 \leqslant x < 120 \\ 1 & x \geqslant 120 \end{cases}$$

If we want to know what is the probability that the price at the end of the year will be smaller than or equal to 112.5, we look at the appropriate interval ($110 \leqslant x < 120$), and find 3/4 as the answer. The graphical representation of this function is given in Figure 1.

To be exact, the probability distribution function is defined on the domain $(-\infty, +\infty)$. Thus, the function enables us to determine the probability of $X$ having a value smaller than or equal to any number between $(-\infty, +\infty)$. However, as by definition $P(X \leqslant -\infty) = 0$ and $P(X \leqslant +\infty) = 1$ for any random variable, it follows that the function $P(X \leqslant x)$ can take any value between 0 and 1. Furthermore, this function is nondecreasing.

### A Continuous Random Variable

So far, we have considered discrete probability functions which are defined only on a finite number of events. What happens when we permit a stock to take on any value between $90 and $100? In this case our random variable is *continuous* rather than discrete. For the continuous case we define a probability *density* function which is the analog of the probability function of the discrete case. The density function $f(x)$ is defined to satisfy:

$$F(x_0) = P(X \leqslant x_0) = \int_{-\infty}^{x_0} f(x) \, dx \qquad (1)$$

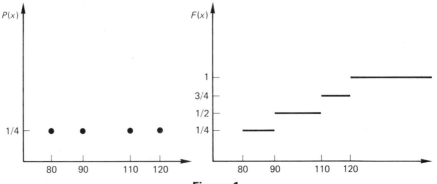

**Figure 1**

That is, $f(x)$ is defined in such a manner that the area under $f(x)$ to some point $x_0$ is exactly the probability that the random variable takes values which are smaller or equal to $x_0$. As an immediate result we have:

$$\int_{-\infty}^{+\infty} f(x)\, dx = 1 \tag{2}$$

because all the probabilities must sum to one.

## Moments

The probability function can be characterized by a series of indices which are called "moments."

### (1) EXPECTED VALUE

The first moment is called the expected value and is defined by:

$$\mu_1 = \sum_{i=-\infty}^{+\infty} x_i P_i(x_i) \quad \text{for the discrete case or} \tag{3}$$

$$\mu_1 = \int_{-\infty}^{+\infty} xf(x)\, dx \quad \text{for the continuous case}$$

This moment is usually called the *expected value* or *mean* of $X$, and will be denoted by $Ex$ or $\mu(x)$. Technically, this moment is the weighted average of all the values of the random variable, where the weight assigned to each value is the probability that this value will occur.

The expected value, or the mean, is a measure of the location of the distribution; the higher the expected value, the more to the right it is located. For example, the two distributions shown in Figure 2 are identical in every respect except for the first moment.

The features of $f(x_1)$ and $f(x_2)$ are identical; the only difference is that $f(x_1)$ is shifted to the left since $\mu(x_1) < \mu(x_2)$, see Figure 2.

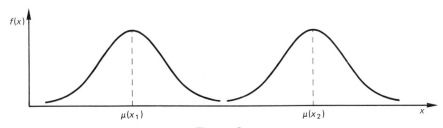

**Figure 2**

(2) THE VARIANCE

The second moment, which is called the variance, is defined by:

$$\mu_2 = E(x - Ex)^2 \tag{4}$$

and is denoted by $\mu_2$ or *Var x* or $\sigma^2(x)$. More explicitly the variance can be written as:

$$Var\ x = E(x - Ex)^2 = \sum_{i=-\infty}^{\infty} (x_i - Ex)^2 P(x_i) \qquad \text{for the discrete case}$$

$$\tag{5}$$

$$Var\ x = E(x - Ex)^2 = \int_{-\infty}^{+\infty} (x - Ex)^2 f(x)\ dx \qquad \text{for the continuous case}$$

The variance is a measure of the dispersion of the random variable around the mean. The larger the variance, the more dispersed is the distribution. As can be seen in Figure 3, though $\mu(x_1) = \mu(x_2)$, $Var\ (x_1) < Var\ (x_2)$. Another measure associated with the second moment is the *standard deviation*, or square root of the variance:

$$\sigma(x) = +\sqrt{Var\ x} = +\sqrt{\sigma^2(x)} \tag{6}$$

where $\sigma(x)$ denotes the standard deviation.

(3) THE SKEWNESS

The third moment, which characterizes the asymmetry of the distribution, is given by:

$$\mu_3 = E(x - Ex)^3 \tag{7}$$

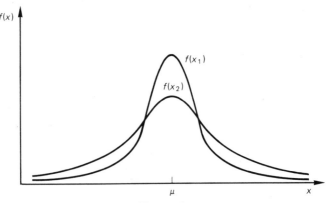

**Figure 3**

or:

$$\mu_3 = \sum_{i=-\infty}^{+\infty} (x_i - Ex)^3 P(x_i) \quad \text{for the discrete case}$$

$$\mu_3 = \int_{-\infty}^{+\infty} (x - Ex)^3 f(x)\, dx \quad \text{for the continuous case}$$

The *skewness* of the distribution is defined in terms of the ratio of the third moment (the asymmetry measure) to the cube of the standard deviation (the dispersion measure):

$$Sk = \frac{\mu_3}{\sigma^3} \tag{8}$$

Looking at Figure 4(a), the expression $(x - Ex)^3$ will be negative to the left of $Ex$ and positive to the right. However, since there are relatively large numbers to the right, $\mu_3$ will be positive. The reason is that we calculate the third power of the deviations from the mean, and even though we have only a small probability of getting such outcomes, these terms will determine the *sign* of $\mu_3$. Therefore skewness to the right is characterized by a positive third moment of the distribution, and the distribution is said to have *positive skewness* ($\mu_3 > 0$). In a similar way we say that a distribution which is skewed to the left [Figure 4(b)] has a negative third moment or *negative skewness* ($\mu_3 < 0$). Notice that in case the distribution is symmetrical, the third moment around the mean is zero.

(4) *n*TH MOMENT

Similarly we can define any moment of order $n$ as:

$$\mu_n(x) = E(x - Ex)^n \tag{9}$$

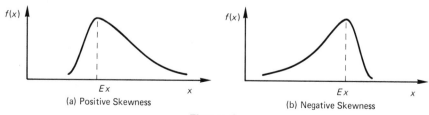

(a) Positive Skewness

(b) Negative Skewness

**Figure 4**

Hence

$$\mu_n(x) = \sum_{i=-\infty}^{+\infty} (x_i - Ex)^n P(x_i) \qquad \text{for the discrete case or}$$

$$\mu_n(x) = \int_{-\infty}^{+\infty} (x - Ex)^n f(x)\, dx \qquad \text{for the continuous case} \tag{10}$$

### The Normal Distribution

The density function of the normal distribution is given by:

$$f(x) = \frac{1}{\sqrt{2\pi}\,\sigma}\, e^{-\frac{1}{2}(x-\mu)^2/\sigma^2} \qquad \text{for} \quad -\infty < x < \infty \tag{11}$$

where $\mu$ is the mean of the distribution and $\sigma$ its standard deviation. $\pi = 3.14\ldots$ is the familiar geometric constant, and $e = 2.71\ldots$ is also a constant, known as the base of natural logarithms. This distribution is very useful both in theory and practice since it represents many random phenomena. Graphically, the normal distribution has the form of a bell, hence the name "bell function" (see Figure 5). It can easily be seen that this distribution is symmetrical around the mean. The "width" of the curve depends on $\sigma$, the standard deviation; the greater the $\sigma$, the wider is the curve, which means that the distribution is more dispersed. Another characteristic of this distribution is that the probability of getting values of $x$ is high in the neighborhood of $\mu$ and diminishes considerably as we move away from the mean. The normal *cumulative* distribution is given by:

$$F(x) = \int_{-\infty}^{x} \frac{1}{\sqrt{2\pi}\,\sigma}\, e^{-\frac{1}{2}(x-\mu)^2/\sigma^2}\, dx \tag{12}$$

which is the area under the bell function to the point $x$. This area gives us the probability that the random variable $X$ will have a value which is smaller than or equal to $x$. To

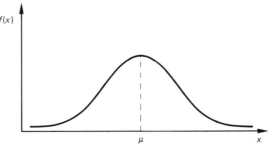

**Figure 5**

calculate this distribution there is no need to compute the integral, since special tables are available which give us the value $F(x)$ for every value $x$.

### The Normal Distribution Parameters

The normal distribution can be fully characterized by two parameters: the mean $\mu$ and the standard deviation $\sigma$.

In Figure 6 we have a case of two distributions which differ only in their means: $\mu(x_1) < \mu(x_2)$; the other parameter $\sigma$, which is a measure of the dispersion or variability, is the same, $\sigma(x_1) = \sigma(x_2)$. Figure 7 gives us the opposite case: two normal distributions with the same mean, $\mu$, but differing in their standard deviation $[\sigma(x_2) > \sigma(x_1)]$.

Normal distribution functions can differ both in their mean and the standard deviations (see Figure 8). However, the area under a normal curve must, by definition, be equal to 1 regardless of $\mu$ or $\sigma$.

The cumulative distribution function of a normal distribution function can be derived by summing up the area under the curve $f(x)$. Figure 9 shows the cumulative distribution functions obtained by summing the areas under the normal density curves $f(x)$ of Figure 8.

In Chapter 6 we use an important characteristic of the normal distribution. Given $X_1$ and $X_2$ such that $\sigma(x_1) \neq \sigma(x_2)$, the two cumulative functions intersect each other once. We shall demonstrate this fact graphically: Assume first that $\mu(x_1) > \mu(x_2)$ but $\sigma(x_1) = \sigma(x_2)$. Then $F(x_1)$ is nothing but a shift to the right of $F(x_2)$ (see Figure 10) and the two curves do not intersect.

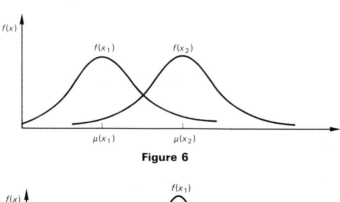

**Figure 6**

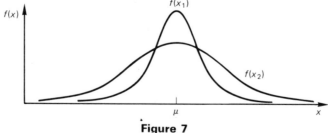

**Figure 7**

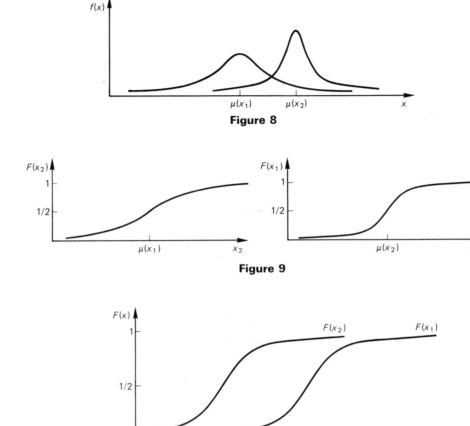

**Figure 8**

**Figure 9**

**Figure 10**

In cases where $\sigma(x_2) > \sigma(x_1)$, and both distributions have the same mean $\mu$, the distribution $F(x_2)$ accumulates, up to any point $a$ $(a < \mu)$, a larger area than $F(x_1)$ does. However, up to the point $\mu$ both of them accumulate the same area, equal by definition to $1/2$ (see Figure 11):

$$\int_{-\infty}^{\mu} f(x_1)\, dx_1 = \int_{-\infty}^{\mu} f(x_2)\, dx_2 = \tfrac{1}{2}$$

The reader should note that the curves intersect at $\mu$. The illustration of the case where $\mu(x_1) \neq \mu(x_2)$ and $\sigma(x_1) \neq \sigma(x_2)$ is given in Figure 12, in which $\mu(x_2) < \mu(x_1)$ but $\sigma(x_1) > \sigma(x_2)$. Another possible combination is when $\mu(x_2) < \mu(x_1)$ and $\sigma(x_2) > \sigma(x_1)$, which is shown in Figure 13. In each of these cases with $\sigma(x_1) \neq \sigma(x_2)$ the two normal distributions intersect ones at a well-defined unique point.

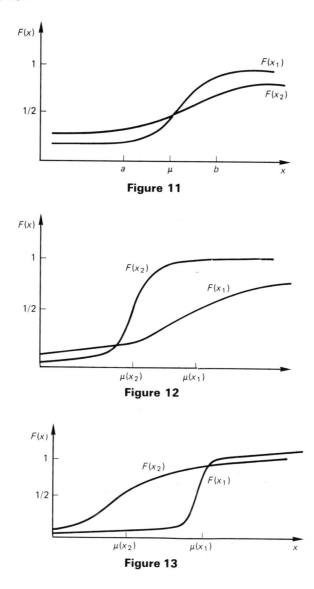

**Figure 11**

**Figure 12**

**Figure 13**

## Covariance and the Correlation Coefficient

So far we have been dealing with a single random variable. But in the more complicated cases we have to explore the relationships among several random variables. Consider an individual who invests part of his money in the construction industry. Since profits in this industry fluctuate strongly, he may be interested in investing part of his money in another industry to stabilize his income. This stabilization can be facilitated by investing part of his money in an industry whose profits fluctuate either independently of or opposite to those of the construction industry. By so doing, the investor can achieve a fairly stable average return; when the return on one type of stock is relatively low, the return from the other stocks will be relatively high, and vice versa. The degree to which diversification stabilizes the return is a function of the association between the two random variables. The two concepts which serve as quantitative measures of the association between the fluctuations of two random variables are the *covariance* and the *correlation coefficient*.

### The Covariance

We define the covariance of two random variables $X$ and $Y$ as:

$$Cov\,(x,\,y) = E[(x - Ex)(y - Ey)] \tag{13}$$

In the discrete case we get:

$$Cov\,(x,\,y) = \sum_{i=1}^{n} (x_i - Ex)(y_i - Ey)P(x_i,\,y_i) \tag{14}$$

where $P(x_i,\,y_i)$ stands for the probability of getting $x_i$ and $y_i$ simultaneously. The above definition of $Cov\,(x,\,y)$ can be rewritten as:

$$Cov\,(x,\,y) = E[(x - Ex)(y - Ey)] = E[xy - yEx - xEy + ExEy]$$
$$= E(xy) - 2ExEy + ExEy = E(xy) - ExEy$$

or:

$$Cov\,(x,\,y) = E(xy) - ExEy \tag{15}$$

where $E(xy)$ is the expected value of the random variable $XY$.

We can explain the intuitive meaning of the covariance as follows. Look at the expression $(x - Ex)(y - Ey)$. Suppose

$$x - Ex > 0 \quad (x \text{ exceeds } Ex)$$

and

$$y - Ey > 0 \quad (y \text{ exceeds } Ey)$$

Then

$$(x - Ex)(y - Ey) > 0$$

We will get a positive value for the product also when both $x$ and $y$ are below their average. However, if:

$$(x - Ex) > 0 \quad \text{and} \quad (y - Ey) < 0$$

or

$$(x - Ex) < 0 \quad \text{and} \quad (y - Ey) > 0$$

which means that one of the variables is above its average and the other is below the average, then:

$$(x - Ex)(y - Ey) < 0$$

Consequently if we get $Cov\,(x, y) = E(x - Ex)(y - Ey) > 0$, we have to conclude that $x$ and $y$ simultaneously tend either to exceed their respective average or to be below it. However, if $Cov\,(x, y) < 0$, we can say that they tend to disperse from their average in opposite directions. That is why our hypothetical investor will try to choose an industry whose returns have a *negative* covariance with the returns in the construction industry.[2]

### Correlation Coefficient

The covariance has been shown to be an indicator of the direction of the dependence between two variables. This indicator, however, changes with any change in the unit of measurement (cents, dimes, or dollars) of the random variables. We need, therefore, an indicator which will be independent of the units used in measuring the outcomes. Furthermore, we desire information concerning *both* the direction and the power of the relationship between the variables. The index which has the required characteristics is called the correlation coefficient and is given by:

$$\rho(x, y) = \frac{Cov\,(x, y)}{\sigma(x)\sigma(y)} \tag{16}$$

---

[2] It is worthwhile to mention that the relationship between $X$ and $Y$ can be written as:

$$y_t = a + bx_t + e_t$$

where $a$, $b$ are constants, $t$ stands for year $t$, and $e_t$ is the deviation of $y_t$ from the straight line. The line which minimizes the sum of squares $\Sigma\,e_t^2$ is called the regression line of $Y$ on $X$. By using this "best" line we find that the slope of the line is:

$$b = \frac{Cov\,(x, y)}{\sigma^2(x)}$$

This coefficient always satisfies:

$$-1 \leqslant \rho(x, y) \leqslant 1 \tag{17}$$

and is independent of the units of measurement.

When $0 < \rho < +1$ the association between the two variables is of a positive nature. The closer we approach to 1, the stronger is the association. When $\rho = 1$ there is a perfect positive correlation. In other words, the relation is linear, which means there are $b$ and $a$ such that $y = a + bx$ where $b > 0$.[3] When $0 \geqslant \rho \geqslant -1$ the association is negative and the smaller $R$, the stronger is the negative association. In the extreme case where $\rho = -1$ we have

$$y = a + bx \quad \text{with } b < 0$$

### The Expected Value and the Variance of the Sum of Random Variables

Suppose $X$ and $Y$ are two random variables. What is the expected value and variance of the sum? Let us start with the expected value of the sum which we denote by $E(x + y)$. From the definition

$$E(x + y) = \sum_{-\infty \leqslant i, j \leqslant +\infty} (x_i + y_j)P(x_i, y_j)$$

where $P(x_i, y_j)$ is the joint probability to get $x_i$ and $y_j$, the expected value can be rewritten as:

$$E(x + y) = \sum_i \sum_j x_i P(x_i, y_j) + \sum_j \sum_i y_j P(x_i, y_j)$$

$$= \sum_i x_i \sum_j P(x_i, y_j) + \sum_j y_j \sum_i P(x_i, y_j) \tag{18}$$

But since $P(x_i, y_j)$ is the probability to get $x_i$ when $y_j$ occurs, we have:

$$\sum_j P(x_i, y_j) = P(x_i)$$

$$\sum_i P(x_i, y_j) = P(y_j)$$

and (18) reduces to

$$E(x + y) = \sum_i x_i P(x_i) + \sum_j y_j P(y_j) = Ex + Ey$$

---

[3] See preceding footnote. This implies that if $\rho = +1$ then $e_t = 0$ and hence $\Sigma e_t^2 = 0$.

Hence:

$$E(x + y) = Ex + Ey$$

and similarly:

$$E(x - y) = Ex - Ey$$

In the case of more than two random variables, multiplied by constant coefficients $a_i$, we can derive:

$$E(a_1 x_1 + a_2 x_2 + \cdots + a_n x_n) = a_1 Ex_1 + a_2 Ex_2 + \cdots + a_n Ex_n$$

or

$$E\left(\sum_{i=1}^{n} a_i x_i\right) = \sum_{i=1}^{n} a_i Ex_i \tag{19}$$

What will be the variance of the sum? We have

$$Var\ (x + y) = E[(x + y) - E(x + y)]^2 = E[(x - Ex) + (y - Ey)]^2$$
$$= E[(x - Ex)^2 + (y - Ey)^2 + 2(x - Ex)(y - Ey)]$$
$$= E(x - Ex)^2 + E(y - Ey)^2 + 2E(x - Ex)(y - Ey)$$
$$= Var\ x + Var\ y + 2\ Cov\ (x, y)$$

or:

$$Var\ (x + y) = Var\ x + Var\ y + 2\ Cov\ (x, y)$$

Similarly: $\tag{20}$

$$Var\ (x - y) = Var\ x + Var\ y - 2\ Cov\ (x, y)$$

Since $\rho(x, y) = Cov\ (x, y)/\sigma(x)\sigma(y)$ implies $Cov\ (x, y) = \rho(x, y)\sigma(x)\sigma(y)$,

$$Var\ (x + y) = Var\ x + Var\ y + 2\rho(x, y)\sigma(x)\sigma(y)$$

Substituting $Var\ x = \sigma^2(x)$, $Var\ y = \sigma^2(y)$, $Var\ (x + y) = \sigma^2(x + y)$, we get:

$$\sigma^2(x \pm y) = \sigma^2(x) + \sigma^2(y) \pm 2\rho(x, y)\sigma(x)\sigma(y) \tag{21}$$

Suppose the above random variables are multiplied by constant factors. What is

$Var(ax + by)$ or generally $Var(\Sigma_{i=1}^{n} a_i x_i)$? From the definition:

$$Var\left(\sum_{i=1}^{n} a_i x_i\right) = E\left(\sum_{i=1}^{n} a_i x_i - \sum a_i E x_i\right)^2 = E\left(\sum_{i=1}^{n} a_i (x_i - E x_i)\right)^2$$

$$= E\left[\sum_{i=1}^{n} a_i^2 (x_i - E x_i)^2 + 2 \sum_{i=1}^{n} \sum_{\substack{j=1 \\ j>i}}^{n} a_i a_j (x_i - E x_i)(x_j - E x_j)\right]$$

$$= \sum_{i=1}^{n} a_i^2 \, Var \, x_i + 2 \sum_{i=1}^{n} \sum_{\substack{j=1 \\ j>i}}^{n} a_i a_j \, Cov\,(x_i, x_j)$$

Thus finally

$$Var\left(\sum_{i=1}^{n} a_i x_i\right) = \sum_{i=1}^{n} a_i^2 \, Var \, x_i + 2 \sum_{i=1}^{n} \sum_{\substack{j=1 \\ j>i}}^{n} a_i a_j \, Cov\,(x_i, x_j) \tag{22}$$

and by substitution in terms of correlation coefficient

$$Var\left(\sum_{i=1}^{n} a_i x_i\right) = \sum_{i=1}^{n} a_i^2 \sigma^2(x_i) + 2 \sum_{i=1}^{n} \sum_{\substack{j=1 \\ j>i}}^{n} a_i a_j \rho(x_i, x_j)\sigma(x_i)\sigma(x_j) \tag{23}$$

and in the special case of independence, when $\rho(x_i, x_j) = 0$,

$$Var\left(\sum_{i=1}^{n} a_i x_i\right) = \sum_{i=1}^{n} a_i^2 \sigma^2(x_i) \tag{24}$$

# Data Set

Annual Rates of Return (in %) of 125 US Mutual Funds
and General Market Characteristics 1971–1980

## Annual Rates of Return (in %) of 125 US Mutual Funds and General Market Characteristics 1971–1980

**MAXIMUM CAPITAL GAIN**

| | | | | | Year | | | | | |
|---|---|---|---|---|---|---|---|---|---|---|
| | 1971 | 1972 | 1973 | 1974 | 1975 | 1976 | 1977 | 1978 | 1979 | 1980 |
| 1 Afuture Fund | 67.5 | 19.2 | −35.2 | −42.0 | 63.7 | 19.3 | 3.6 | 20.0 | 40.3 | 37.5 |
| 2 Alpha Fund | 28.5 | 27.5 | −32.0 | −28.2 | 22.5 | 22.8 | −4.2 | 10.5 | 24.0 | 18.0 |
| 3 American General Comstock Fund | 12.4 | −1.3 | −16.9 | −17.2 | 64.5 | 34.2 | 13.9 | 13.7 | 47.7 | 32.7 |
| 4 Columbia Growth Fund | 36.8 | 5.9 | −25.6 | −22.5 | 42.5 | 31.1 | −0.4 | 8.1 | 40.6 | 39.9 |
| 5 Dreyfus Leverage Fund | 28.8 | 12.6 | −15.5 | −26.3 | 25.9 | 25.2 | 7.5 | 10.8 | 41.2 | 36.6 |
| 6 Eaton & Howard Special Fund | 28.9 | 3.8 | −32.3 | −40.8 | 27.3 | 19.3 | 13.0 | 7.4 | 45.9 | 34.6 |
| 7 Evergreen Fund | 0.0 | 10.1 | −26.2 | −21.4 | 60.1 | 48.8 | 25.4 | 38.0 | 46.3 | 48.1 |
| 8 Explorer Fund | 24.8 | 21.1 | −25.8 | −35.4 | 22.8 | 16.8 | 28.1 | 20.6 | 33.8 | 55.4 |
| 9 Fiduciary Growth Associates | 33.0 | 23.9 | −39.7 | −40.4 | 59.5 | 24.9 | 3.7 | −2.3 | 86.1 | 55.7 |
| 10 44 Wall Street Fund | 71.8 | −5.4 | −46.8 | −52.2 | 184.1 | 46.5 | 16.5 | 32.9 | 73.6 | 36.4 |
| 11 Franklin Dynatech Series | 25.6 | 16.0 | −35.4 | −33.8 | 32.1 | 22.0 | 4.5 | 13.3 | 34.1 | 37.4 |
| 12 Hartwell Growth Fund | 37.7 | −9.5 | −34.7 | −24.7 | 45.8 | 26.9 | 16.8 | 18.9 | 40.6 | 70.0 |
| 13 Ivest Fund | 21.5 | 11.8 | −32.3 | −33.4 | 30.7 | 14.5 | 1.2 | 16.2 | 18.1 | 33.6 |
| 14 Keystone S-4 (Lower Priced) | 35.2 | 13.0 | −40.5 | −44.0 | 36.8 | 32.5 | 8.8 | 19.9 | 47.1 | 60.9 |
| 15 Mathers Fund | 19.8 | 16.1 | −37.2 | −30.6 | 57.1 | 44.4 | 14.2 | 15.1 | 46.6 | 40.3 |
| 16 Oppenheimer A.I.M. Fund | 32.8 | 12.5 | −22.0 | −33.1 | 29.3 | 19.7 | −0.2 | 13.4 | 50.5 | 62.0 |
| 17 Pace Fund | 43.6 | 18.0 | −42.5 | −15.4 | 34.2 | 27.8 | 28.6 | 23.5 | 45.4 | 44.9 |
| 18 Partners Fund | 13.6 | −8.4 | −26.5 | 3.3 | 18.1 | 31.2 | 7.0 | 16.3 | 42.9 | 34.1 |
| 19 Phoenix-Chase Growth Fund Series | 28.8 | −5.6 | −31.4 | −36.6 | 36.4 | 10.6 | −6.0 | 8.0 | 24.7 | 30.3 |
| 20 Security Ultra Fund | 49.5 | 19.2 | −41.7 | −26.4 | 48.4 | 54.9 | 3.0 | 23.7 | 58.9 | 72.3 |
| Average | 32.0 | 10.0 | −32.0 | −30.1 | 47.1 | 28.7 | 9.2 | 16.4 | 44.4 | 44.0 |

## LONG TERM GROWTH; INCOME SECONDARY

| | | | | | Year | | | | | |
|---|---|---|---|---|---|---|---|---|---|---|
| | 1971 | 1972 | 1973 | 1974 | 1975 | 1976 | 1977 | 1978 | 1979 | 1980 |
| 21 AMCAP Fund | 18.9 | 13.3 | -33.4 | -28.5 | 52.1 | 30.4 | 16.4 | 22.4 | 51.9 | 27.9 |
| 22 Anchor Growth Fund | 19.7 | 8.5 | -32.7 | -27.2 | 31.2 | 17.8 | -6.9 | 9.0 | 22.1 | 19.1 |
| 23 Armstrong Associates | 12.5 | 13.2 | -33.7 | -31.6 | 53.2 | 44.4 | -0.7 | 29.2 | 25.3 | 44.8 |
| 24 Beacon Growth Fund | 15.4 | 4.5 | -32.5 | -18.1 | 23.3 | 11.6 | -3.2 | 2.0 | 16.7 | 31.5 |
| 25 Boston Company Capital App. Fund | 26.5 | 25.1 | -21.2 | -31.6 | 31.9 | 16.9 | -5.2 | 8.4 | 20.1 | 28.1 |
| 26 Charter Fund | 36.5 | 36.9 | -13.5 | -27.1 | 32.7 | 41.8 | 5.2 | 32.3 | 44.0 | 33.7 |
| 27 Colonial Growth Shares | 20.9 | 11.6 | -21.6 | -29.6 | 21.6 | 14.3 | -10.2 | 5.8 | 38.6 | 41.4 |
| 28 Country Capital Growth | 26.9 | 11.6 | -20.1 | -23.5 | 27.0 | 14.8 | -5.3 | 2.6 | 20.0 | 30.7 |
| 29 Energy Fund | 8.8 | 11.5 | -6.9 | -18.6 | 33.4 | 32.9 | 2.7 | 5.6 | 49.7 | 41.0 |
| 30 Franklin Growth Series | 23.2 | 20.0 | -16.8 | -30.6 | 24.1 | 11.3 | -4.6 | 15.6 | 8.6 | 14.8 |
| 31 Franklin Option Fund | 17.9 | 21.4 | -33.0 | -26.6 | 41.6 | 22.9 | -8.1 | 10.2 | 27.1 | 40.1 |
| 32 Growth Fund of America | 17.0 | -20.5 | -26.3 | -21.9 | 35.6 | 18.2 | 19.8 | 26.7 | 45.8 | 39.8 |
| 33 John Hancock Growth Fund | 13.5 | 15.0 | -23.9 | -34.9 | 26.3 | 12.5 | -13.6 | 15.8 | 34.0 | 58.3 |
| 34 Investors Research Fund | 24.1 | 20.7 | -14.4 | -12.8 | 22.8 | 11.7 | 5.8 | 14.2 | 18.3 | 73.7 |
| 35 Ivy Fund | 17.9 | 14.2 | -24.2 | -33.0 | 30.0 | 18.2 | -7.3 | 4.9 | 30.9 | 34.7 |
| 36 Kemper Growth Fund | 20.2 | 6.3 | -18.6 | -27.7 | 42.1 | 29.0 | 2.4 | 17.8 | 40.8 | 44.1 |
| 37 Lexington Research Fund | 13.1 | 13.2 | -22.5 | -25.2 | 44.0 | 26.0 | -7.1 | 7.0 | 31.9 | 22.8 |
| 38 Magnacap Fund | 32.2 | 10.0 | -43.2 | -27.7 | 33.6 | 28.2 | -6.3 | 6.0 | 27.5 | 12.3 |
| 39 Newton Growth Fund | 27.7 | 20.2 | -37.5 | -25.4 | 16.2 | 19.4 | 2.1 | 8.4 | 25.0 | 45.3 |
| 40 Sigma Venture Shares | 30.1 | 21.1 | -45.2 | -36.5 | 88.1 | 24.5 | 40.0 | 21.4 | 34.7 | 41.1 |
| Average | 21.1 | 13.9 | -26.1 | -26.9 | 35.5 | 22.3 | 0.8 | 13.3 | 30.6 | 36.3 |

## GROWTH & CURRENT INCOME FUNDS

| | | | | | Year | | | | | |
|---|---|---|---|---|---|---|---|---|---|---|
| | 1971 | 1972 | 1973 | 1974 | 1975 | 1976 | 1977 | 1978 | 1979 | 1980 |
| 41 Affiliated Fund | 8.6 | 12.1 | −5.8 | −16.0 | 39.4 | 34.3 | −6.9 | 3.2 | 28.9 | 24.1 |
| 42 American Mutual Fund | 13.7 | 11.2 | −10.7 | −15.9 | 35.1 | 34.2 | 1.9 | 12.3 | 21.5 | 25.3 |
| 43 Colonial Fund | 12.8 | 10.3 | −8.1 | −19.9 | 23.0 | 16.4 | −5.9 | 5.7 | 17.7 | 24.3 |
| 44 Composite Fund | 10.7 | 4.6 | −26.6 | −10.8 | 29.6 | 17.1 | −4.4 | 5.6 | 30.4 | 26.4 |
| 45 Delaware Fund | 16.4 | 7.6 | −25.3 | −16.2 | 36.5 | 34.1 | −3.1 | 2.3 | 23.9 | 25.9 |
| 46 Dividend Shares | 12.6 | 15.9 | −14.3 | −21.8 | 35.3 | 22.3 | −8.4 | 4.7 | 11.9 | 23.2 |
| 47 Dodge & Cox Stock Fund | 15.6 | −12.5 | −12.5 | −24.6 | 38.9 | 22.2 | −6.1 | 9.6 | 20.8 | 33.2 |
| 48 Eaton & Howard Stock Fund | 13.7 | 14.8 | −17.9 | −33.7 | 21.3 | 15.8 | −7.1 | 6.4 | 17.3 | 24.8 |
| 49 Financial Industrial Fund | 14.1 | 20.2 | −11.9 | −23.6 | 34.5 | 30.1 | 3.6 | 7.6 | 38.2 | 27.8 |
| 50 Fundamental Investors | 17.6 | 7.6 | −21.7 | −22.5 | 36.5 | 19.6 | −5.8 | 6.3 | 15.3 | 21.3 |
| 51 General Securities | −1.0 | −4.2 | −30.0 | −16.1 | 61.8 | 35.9 | −2.9 | 15.2 | 14.3 | 23.9 |
| 52 Investment Trust of Boston | 7.9 | 11.8 | −10.9 | −19.4 | 34.0 | 21.3 | −7.9 | 11.2 | 18.0 | 43.9 |
| 53 Investors Stock Fund | 17.1 | 15.5 | −17.9 | −27.4 | 35.1 | 23.8 | −7.3 | 4.9 | 20.5 | 26.4 |
| 54 Mann (Horace) Fund | 21.1 | 18.4 | −10.9 | −25.0 | 22.7 | 12.6 | −7.7 | 4.0 | 25.1 | 36.3 |
| 55 National Industries Fund | 18.0 | 9.5 | −22.5 | −27.0 | 36.2 | 29.9 | −1.7 | 8.0 | 29.9 | 35.8 |
| 56 National Stock Fund | 9.0 | 8.1 | −16.2 | −14.3 | 38.8 | 33.6 | −3.9 | 4.9 | 25.4 | 32.5 |
| 57 Nel Equity Fund | 17.9 | 7.3 | −0.9 | −29.5 | 29.3 | 29.5 | −2.8 | 8.9 | 25.4 | 20.5 |
| 58 Sovereign Investors | 12.6 | 9.6 | −13.8 | −20.8 | 38.1 | 28.7 | −4.9 | 3.6 | 23.4 | 20.2 |
| 59 Technology Fund | 15.6 | 9.4 | −17.1 | −22.2 | 37.1 | 25.6 | −1.6 | 22.4 | 32.7 | 49.8 |
| 60 Washington Mutual Fund | 12.1 | 8.7 | −9.0 | −17.3 | 44.7 | 31.2 | −4.0 | 7.9 | 14.4 | 24.0 |
| Average | 13.3 | 9.3 | −15.2 | −21.2 | 35.4 | 25.9 | −4.3 | 7.7 | 22.7 | 28.5 |

## BALANCED FUNDS

| | 1971 | 1972 | 1973 | 1974 | 1975 | 1976 | 1977 | 1978 | 1979 | 1980 |
|---|---|---|---|---|---|---|---|---|---|---|
| | | | | | *Year* | | | | | |
| 61 American Balanced Funds | 12.5 | 10.6 | -13.1 | -15.5 | 25.0 | 26.0 | 0.7 | 6.2 | 7.6 | 14.3 |
| 62 Axe-Houghton Fund B | 17.7 | 8.4 | -7.0 | -8.4 | 21.8 | 29.0 | 1.7 | 4.2 | 10.0 | 22.2 |
| 63 Boston Foundation Fund | 13.4 | 9.0 | -15.8 | -20.3 | 26.5 | 22.6 | 1.9 | 1.5 | 14.0 | 14.4 |
| 64 Composite Bond & Stock Fund | 12.3 | 8.3 | -9.0 | -10.4 | 28.4 | 24.5 | -0.9 | 1.8 | 20.1 | 17.3 |
| 65 Convertible Yield Securities | 0.0 | 0.0 | 0.0 | 0.0 | 0.0 | 0.0 | 0.0 | 0.0 | 16.2 | 34.6 |
| 66 Dodge & Cox Balanced Fund | 10.9 | 11.4 | -9.7 | 19.3 | 29.4 | 25.3 | -3.3 | 6.1 | 13.5 | 21.7 |
| 67 Eaton & Howard Balanced Fund | 11.4 | 14.7 | -4.5 | -20.1 | 20.7 | 19.7 | -5.7 | 4.4 | 11.4 | 26.0 |
| 68 John Hancock Balanced Fund | 9.2 | 12.7 | -17.3 | -13.9 | 30.8 | 28.0 | -2.1 | 1.3 | 6.7 | 17.4 |
| 69 Investors Mutual | 14.5 | 13.6 | -13.9 | -17.7 | 24.5 | 22.2 | -1.5 | 3.1 | 11.3 | 18.7 |
| 70 Loomis-Sayles Mutual Fund | 16.7 | 10.9 | -7.5 | -24.9 | 25.6 | 15.9 | -4.0 | 4.9 | 13.7 | 15.0 |
| 71 Massachusetts Fund | 17.1 | 15.8 | -8.6 | -18.1 | 20.1 | 21.5 | -0.8 | 7.1 | 15.0 | 24.9 |
| 72 Nationwide Securities | 12.8 | 11.1 | -9.3 | -14.2 | 30.5 | 25.4 | -2.9 | 1.4 | 9.9 | 13.1 |
| 73 Putnam (George) Fund | 18.1 | 20.1 | -10.9 | -23.6 | 26.1 | 24.1 | -3.5 | 5.7 | 15.5 | 17.0 |
| 74 Sentinel Balanced Fund | 11.3 | 8.3 | -5.0 | -7.3 | 22.0 | 23.9 | 1.4 | -1.7 | 14.1 | 11.3 |
| 75 Signa Trust Shares | 13.2 | 13.0 | -19.0 | -8.6 | 26.7 | 29.7 | 5.6 | 5.5 | 9.5 | 15.6 |
| 76 State Farm Balanced Fund | 9.4 | 9.7 | -16.5 | -13.9 | 27.2 | 24.5 | 3.5 | 9.8 | 26.6 | 18.6 |
| 77 Stein Rue & Farnham Balanced Fund | 22.1 | 18.7 | -14.7 | -26.5 | 28.5 | 14.9 | -5.7 | 6.7 | 17.1 | 26.6 |
| 78 United Continental Income Fund | 16.9 | 6.3 | -17.0 | -20.6 | 27.1 | 25.6 | 1.6 | 1.3 | 11.9 | 20.8 |
| 79 Wellington Fund | 8.9 | 11.0 | -11.8 | -17.7 | 25.2 | 23.4 | -4.3 | 5.3 | 13.5 | 22.5 |
| Average | 13.1 | 11.2 | -11.1 | -13.8 | 24.5 | 22.4 | -1.0 | 3.9 | 13.6 | 19.6 |

## COMMON STOCK POLICY INCOME FUND

| | Year | | | | | | | | | |
|---|---|---|---|---|---|---|---|---|---|---|
| | 1971 | 1972 | 1973 | 1974 | 1975 | 1976 | 1977 | 1978 | 1979 | 1980 |
| 80 American National Income Fund | 14.4 | 7.9 | −12.2 | −4.2 | 33.5 | 34.8 | 7.2 | 8.3 | 25.0 | 18.8 |
| 81 BLC Income Fund | 13.5 | 13.5 | −17.5 | −14.9 | 50.0 | 35.6 | −1.3 | 3.9 | 14.5 | 24.6 |
| 82 Diversified Fund St. Bd. & Mtge. | 9.6 | 10.2 | −14.2 | −22.1 | 39.7 | 30.1 | −0.2 | 3.0 | 18.3 | 27.5 |
| 83 Safeco Income Fund | 13.6 | 15.0 | −15.3 | −15.7 | 38.2 | 34.9 | 2.4 | 1.8 | 21.4 | 22.2 |
| 84 Transamerica Income Fund | 17.0 | 9.0 | −5.1 | −5.0 | 17.5 | 20.7 | −0.5 | 3.5 | 4.5 | 5.2 |
| Average | 13.6 | 11.1 | −12.9 | −12.4 | 35.8 | 31.2 | 1.5 | 4.1 | 16.7 | 19.7 |

## FLEXIBLE POLICY INCOME FUND

| | Year | | | | | | | | | |
|---|---|---|---|---|---|---|---|---|---|---|
| | 1971 | 1972 | 1973 | 1974 | 1975 | 1976 | 1977 | 1978 | 1979 | 1980 |
| 85 Axe-Houghton Income Fund | 16.4 | 7.1 | −15.8 | −4.0 | 17.9 | 22.3 | 4.9 | 0.6 | 1.9 | 7.8 |
| 86 Babson Income Trust | 7.0 | 9.0 | −3.0 | 1.8 | 9.0 | 11.7 | 2.9 | 0.6 | 2.4 | 2.9 |
| 87 CG Income Fund | 9.8 | 6.9 | −9.1 | −7.0 | 21.6 | 18.5 | 5.9 | 0.7 | −0.8 | 3.2 |
| 88 Colonial Income Fund | 15.9 | 9.4 | 0.2 | −9.7 | 15.2 | 19.4 | 6.7 | 1.4 | −1.1 | 0.4 |
| 89 Decatur Income Fund | 16.9 | 6.4 | −14.3 | −11.7 | 34.3 | 37.6 | 2.6 | 2.6 | 25.8 | 24.5 |
| 90 Fidelity Puritan Fund | 13.3 | 11.1 | −7.2 | −12.2 | 32.3 | 30.8 | 0.7 | 4.5 | 14.8 | 20.3 |
| 91 First Investors Nat'l Res. Fund | 8.1 | 12.7 | −21.5 | −22.5 | 26.4 | 31.2 | 0.5 | 0.8 | 5.1 | 11.6 |
| 92 Franklin Income Series | 19.3 | 3.7 | −4.8 | −13.0 | 24.9 | 21.9 | 8.0 | 7.6 | 27.8 | 19.0 |
| 93 Liberty Fund | 23.6 | 7.4 | −28.3 | −29.0 | 29.5 | 26.1 | −5.7 | 2.1 | 11.7 | −0.8 |
| 94 Lord Abbett Income Fund | 11.7 | 13.0 | −15.1 | −12.2 | 34.1 | 32.6 | 2.3 | 0.4 | 3.0 | 2.8 |
| 95 Mass. Income Development Fund | 11.9 | 6.9 | −11.7 | −11.9 | 28.3 | 28.0 | 1.4 | 0.3 | 10.7 | 19.0 |
| 96 MIF Nationwide Fund | 10.2 | 9.7 | −6.7 | −20.3 | 38.6 | 26.7 | −9.1 | 0.8 | 9.8 | 17.9 |
| 97 National Dividend Fund | 15.3 | 5.4 | −16.0 | −13.5 | 28.7 | 39.7 | 3.9 | 4.7 | 24.1 | 31.7 |
| 98 National Income Fund | 17.4 | 6.9 | −13.1 | −10.9 | 27.0 | 36.3 | 5.1 | 5.2 | 13.8 | 16.4 |
| 99 Newton Income Fund | 11.2 | 16.0 | −11.9 | −27.2 | 28.3 | 24.3 | −5.2 | 0.3 | −1.2 | 3.5 |
| 100 Northeast Investors Trust | 14.9 | 9.5 | 0.0 | −7.7 | 17.7 | 22.0 | 6.6 | −0.8 | −1.1 | −0.1 |
| 101 Putnam Income Fund | 13.8 | 10.6 | −2.4 | −7.5 | 17.2 | 20.6 | 5.5 | 0.3 | −1.9 | −0.2 |
| 102 Steadman Associated Fund | 15.7 | 7.4 | −12.3 | −13.2 | 20.1 | 23.7 | 4.6 | −1.4 | 8.8 | 9.5 |
| 103 Value Line Income Fund | 13.5 | 9.1 | −15.9 | −16.1 | 41.7 | 34.5 | 1.8 | 11.1 | 27.6 | 26.8 |
| 104 Wisconsin Income Fund | 14.2 | 8.4 | −20.4 | −26.1 | 34.2 | 22.8 | −5.0 | −2.3 | −2.8 | −2.7 |
| Average | 14.0 | 8.8 | −11.5 | −13.7 | 26.3 | 26.5 | 1.9 | 2.0 | 8.9 | 10.7 |

## SENIOR SECURITIES POLICY

| | Year | | | | | | | | | |
|---|---|---|---|---|---|---|---|---|---|---|
| | 1971 | 1972 | 1973 | 1974 | 1975 | 1976 | 1977 | 1978 | 1979 | 1980 |
| 105 Alpha Income Fund | 12.3 | 15.0 | -15.2 | -17.8 | 15.7 | 17.1 | 5.7 | 2.3 | -3.9 | -2.3 |
| 106 American Gen'l High Yield Inv. | 20.4 | 4.9 | -6.7 | -11.5 | 25.2 | 27.2 | 2.9 | 9.0 | 24.3 | 33.5 |
| 107 Delchester Bond Fund | 12.3 | 7.6 | 0.7 | -8.2 | 16.2 | 22.6 | 6.1 | 2.2 | 1.7 | 0.7 |
| 108 Investors Selective Fund | 13.9 | 8.6 | 2.1 | -2.9 | 14.4 | 20.9 | 2.8 | 2.2 | -0.2 | 1.1 |
| 109 Keystone B-1 (Inv. Bond) | 11.2 | 7.8 | 3.6 | -1.1 | 10.6 | 15.9 | 4.2 | 1.7 | 3.6 | 1.9 |
| 110 Keystone B-2 (Medium Grade Bond) | 18.0 | 9.7 | -1.0 | -7.5 | 19.3 | 22.6 | 7.2 | 2.0 | 5.8 | 6.4 |
| 111 Keystone B-4 (Discount Bond) | 21.5 | 11.9 | -7.3 | -8.2 | 25.1 | 26.9 | 7.6 | 4.5 | 1.9 | 8.6 |
| 112 National Bond Fund | 14.0 | 6.8 | -4.6 | -10.9 | 18.7 | 23.2 | 6.7 | -0.8 | 1.5 | -1.4 |
| 113 Security Bond Fund | 3.0 | 4.9 | 5.1 | 6.5 | 16.0 | 18.3 | 7.6 | 1.9 | 1.2 | 0.3 |
| 114 United Bond Fund | 13.9 | 8.5 | 0.3 | -8.7 | 13.9 | 22.0 | 4.0 | 0.5 | -3.5 | -0.8 |
| Average | 14.0 | 8.6 | -2.3 | -7.0 | 17.5 | 21.7 | 5.5 | 2.5 | 3.2 | 4.8 |

## OTHER FUNDS

| | Year | | | | | | | | | |
|---|---|---|---|---|---|---|---|---|---|---|
| | 1971 | 1972 | 1973 | 1974 | 1975 | 1976 | 1977 | 1978 | 1979 | 1980 |
| 115 Canadian Fund | 10.2 | 24.4 | -1.7 | -21.7 | 10.7 | 4.2 | -1.2 | 12.9 | 30.7 | 20.5 |
| 116 International Investors | -3.7 | 60.3 | 91.9 | 11.0 | -24.1 | -28.5 | 32.8 | 9.5 | 176.7 | 64.6 |
| 117 Putnam International Equities | 33.7 | 21.4 | -25.7 | -20.8 | 35.1 | 24.0 | -1.0 | 22.8 | 19.6 | 25.5 |
| 118 Scudder International Fund | 6.0 | 30.0 | -8.9 | -23.5 | 29.4 | 6.1 | -0.4 | 21.3 | 19.3 | 26.9 |
| 119 Templeton Growth Fund | 21.8 | 68.6 | -9.9 | -12.1 | 37.6 | 46.6 | 20.5 | 19.2 | 26.8 | 25.9 |
| 120 Transatlantic Fund | 17.9 | 28.4 | -3.2 | -12.2 | 32.4 | 1.5 | 5.8 | 25.6 | 15.5 | 49.2 |
| 121 American Insurance & Ind. Fund | 45.7 | 44.8 | -25.4 | -20.7 | 18.1 | 34.1 | 5.1 | 8.2 | 23.3 | 15.1 |
| 122 Century Shares Trust | 30.8 | 20.2 | -13.4 | -32.1 | 14.0 | 36.4 | -2.3 | 9.6 | 21.3 | 6.0 |
| 123 Life Insurance Investors | 29.2 | 33.6 | -26.3 | -32.7 | 10.4 | 43.1 | 14.2 | 14.6 | 28.8 | 2.4 |
| 124 Franklin Utilities Series | -2.7 | 6.7 | -30.0 | -22.0 | 41.0 | 28.9 | 7.7 | -0.4 | -0.9 | 5.6 |
| 125 National Aviation & Tech. Corp. | 29.3 | 0.7 | -38.0 | -18.3 | 50.4 | 34.8 | 3.9 | 34.0 | 18.8 | 29.1 |
| Average | 19.8 | 30.8 | -8.2 | -18.6 | 23.2 | 21.0 | 7.7 | 16.1 | 34.5 | 24.6 |
| Overall Average for all Funds | 18.3 | 12.3 | -16.7 | -19.5 | 31.7 | 24.8 | 2.3 | 8.7 | 23.1 | 25.4 |

## GENERAL MARKET DATA

| | Year | | | | | | | | | |
|---|---|---|---|---|---|---|---|---|---|---|
| | 1971 | 1972 | 1973 | 1974 | 1975 | 1976 | 1977 | 1978 | 1979 | 1980 |
| Fisher Index (market portfolio) | 19.5 | 8.5 | −29.3 | −26.5 | 61.9 | 45.5 | 9.5 | 14.0 | 35.3 | 31.0 |
| Riskless Interest Rate | 4.4 | 3.8 | 6.9 | 8.0 | 5.8 | 5.1 | 5.1 | 7.2 | 10.4 | 11.2 |
| Inflation rate (percentage change of CPI) | 3.4 | 3.4 | 8.8 | 12.2 | 7.0 | 4.8 | 6.8 | 9.0 | 13.3 | 12.4 |

*Source for rates of return of mutual funds:* Wiesenberger Investment Service, *Investment Companies,* 1981 Edition.

# Index

Page numbers with suffix n refer to notes.
Page numbers in bold refer to chapters.